1 MONTH OF
FREE
READING

at

www.ForgottenBooks.com

By purchasing this book you are eligible for one month membership to ForgottenBooks.com, giving you unlimited access to our entire collection of over 1,000,000 titles via our web site and mobile apps.

To claim your free month visit:
www.forgottenbooks.com/free926656

ISBN 978-0-260-08325-8
PIBN 10926656

MINUTES

—— OF THE ——

FIRST SESSION

—— OF THE ——

JOHNSTON COUNTY

BAPTIST ASSOCIATION,

—— HELD WITH ——

Selma Baptist Church, Selma, N. C.,

FRIDAY NIGHT, SATURDAY AND SUNDAY,

November 27, 28 and 29, 1903.

———

Next Session will be held with Clayton Church, beginning Thursday after the first Sunday in November, 1904.

———

NASH BROTHERS,
BOOK AND JOB PRINTERS,
GOLDSBORO, N. C.

6.708

ᵞ MINUTES

—OF THE—

FIRST SESSION

—OF THE—

JOHNSTON COUNTY
BAPTIST ASSOCIATION,

—HELD WITH—

Selma Baptist Church, Selma, N. C.,

FRIDAY NIGHT, SATURDAY AND SUNDAY,

November 27, 28 and 29, 1903.

———

Next Session will be held with Clayton Church, beginning
Thursday after the first Sunday in November, 1904.

———

NASH BROTHERS,
BOOK AND JOB PRINTERS,
GOLDSBORO, N. C.

61708

OFFICERS.

Moderator—R. H. Gower...................Clayton, N. C.
Vice-Moderator—J. P. Canaday...............Benson, N. C.
Clerk—T. J. Lassiter......................Smithfield, N. C.
Treasurer—C. W. Richardson...............Selma, N. C.
Historian—C. W. Blanchard.................Cary, N. C.

EXECUTIVE COMMITTEE.

J. M. Beaty, Chairman.....................Smithfield, N. C.
M. C. Winston, Secretary,.................Selma, N. C.
Joseph F. Pool...........................Auburn, N. C.
J. H. Boon................................Benson, N. C.
J T. Holt.................................Wilson's Mills, N. C.

STANDING COMMITTEES FOR 1904,

STATE MISSIONS—J. M. BEATY.
HOME MISSIONS—C. E. GOWER.
FOREIGN MISSIONS—C. W. BLANCHARD.
ORPHANAGE—C. W. CARTER.
EDUCATION—M. A. ADAMS.
PERIODICALS—J. W. SUTTLE.
TEMPERANCE—M. C. WINSTON.
MINISTERIAL RELIEF—F. P. WOOD.
SUNDAY-SCHOOLS—N. R. POOL.
WOMAN'S WORK—A. A. PIPPIN.

MINISTERIAL REGISTER.

M. A. Adams...............................Auburn, N. C.
C. W. Blanchard...........................Cary, N. C.
Worley Creech.............................Kenly, N. C., R. F. D., No. 2.
N. H. Gibbs...............................Benson, N. C.
J. S. Hagwood.............................Raleigh, N. C.
W. G. Hall................................Benson, N. C.
R. W. Horrell.............................Selma, N. C.
J. W. Nobles..............................Selma, N. C.
A. A. Pippin..............................Wakefield, N. C.
J. W. Smith...............................Clayton, N. C.
J. W. Suttle..............................Smithfield, N. C.
B. Townsend...............................Wake Forest, N. C.

LIST OF MESSENGERS.

Antioch—R. R. Creech, G. R. Whitley and J. W. Corbett.
Baptist Centre—J. C. Hardee.
Bethany—Worley Creech, L. L. Creech, Merritt Pace and David Pace.
Bethesda—J. J. Wallace.
Benson—J. P. Canaday, N. H. Gibbs, M. D. Thomas and J. H. Boon
Blackman's Grove—F. P. Wood, P. L. Hayes and Ernest Grice.
Carter's Chapel—Oscar Mozingo.
Clayton—C. W. Blanchard, C. W. Carter, R. H. Gower and D. H. McCullers.
Clyde's Chapel—J. R. Hood.
Corinth—E. C. Whitley, Oscar O'Neal, A. D. Atkinson and N. G. Williamson.
Four Oaks—J. A. Fort.
Hood's Grove—Represented by J. W. Suttle.
Lee's Chapel—J. B. Bunn.
Live Oak—W. M. Eason.
Mount Moriah—M. T. Wilder and J. F. Pool.
Nobles' Chapel—J. R. Todd and J. B. Mecome.
New Bethel—Represented by J. W. Nobles.
Oliver's Grove—Haywood Johnson and S. Parnell.
Parish Memorial—J. F. Watson, Samuel Parish and Needham Parish.
Pine Level—Alex. Strickland.
Pisgah—J. W. Jones and E. R. Jones.
Princeton—W. R. Pearce.
Sardis—N. B. Stevens.
Shiloh—Represented by W. G. Hall.
Selma—M. C. Winston, C. W. Richardson, H. D. Hood, S. C. Robertson and
　　　　　N. R. Batten.
Smithfield—J. M. Beaty, J. D. Underwood, R. A. Merritt, J. W. Setzer, J. A.
　　　　　Underhill, Jr., H. D. Ellington and T. J. Lassiter
Thanksgiving—W. G. Earp and L. W. Brannan.
Trinity—Arthur Lee.
White Oak—N. E. Jeffreys and R. H. Biggs.
Wilson's Mills—J. T. Holt.

INTRODUCTORY SERMON,

PREACHED AT THE ORGANIZATION OF THE JOHNSTON COUNTY ASSOCIATION, NOVEMBER 27, 1903, BY LIVINGSTON JOHNSON.

Text: Ezekiel 1: 20—"For the spirit of the living creature was in the wheels."

Read the fourth chapter of Revelations and see the very striking similarity between that and this vision of Ezekiel. Whatever one of these visions means the other must mean. The four beasts in Revelations correspond to the four living creatures in Ezekiel; and John's four and twenty elders correspond to Ezekiel's wheels. Trustworthy commentators interpret the vision of John thus: the four beasts represent spiritual beings, and four and twenty elders redeemed human beings, and these unite in worshiping Christ in heaven. If that be a correct interpretation, is it not reasonable to suppose that in Ezekiel's vision the living creatures represent spiritual beings, and the wheels human agencies, and, as in Ezekiel, these are worshipping together in heaven; in John they are working together on earth? Of course, we cannot dogmatize about this. I do not ask you to accept it as a correct interpretation, but if it be reasonable let us draw some helpful lessons from it:

1. In the first place, then, we have the encouraging thought that spiritual beings are down here on earth, helping human beings in the work of the Lord. Verse 19: "And when the living creatures went the wheels went by them." We may not know how much the angels have to do with the affairs of men on earth, more, much more, I some times think, than we are disposed to believe. The angels were the guests of Abraham; they came to deliver Lot from Sodom. An angel announced the birth of John the Baptist, and the same angel came to Mary to tell her that she was to be the mother of the world's Savior. As shepherds kept their watch by night the angels sang that first glad Christmas song: "Glory to God in the highest, and on earth peace, good-will toward men." Through His public ministry the angels came to Christ on many occasions and strengthened Him. Angels stood guard at His tomb and told the women that He had risen from the dead. When "a cloud received Him out of their sight" the angels came to tell His sorrowing disciples that He would come again. If this were all, would it not be enough to lead us to believe that the angels were still interested in the affairs of men? But this is not all. The Psalmist says: "The angel of the Lord encampeth round about them that fear him, and delivereth them." The writer

4

of Hebrews, in speaking of the angels, says: "Are they not all ministering spirits sent forth to minister to them that are the heirs of salvation ?" Brethren, let us try to be more conscious of the presence of these heavenly beings as we toil on here, "till by angel bands attended, we awake among the blest."

2. Another important lesson we learn is that human agencies should work together in harmony. Verse 16: "And their appearance and their work was.as it were a wheel in the middle of a wheel." There are different kinds of wheels in a watch; some large, some small some moving slowly, some swiftly, some going in one direction, others in an opposite direction; but the one object of all is to make the hands indicate the correct time. So in God's machinery there are different wheels. We have our local churches, or associations and conventions, our mission boards and our educational institutions, but the one purpose of it all is to bring a lost world to Christ. "There are diversities of gifts, but one spirit."

3. We should take larger views of the work to be accomplished by these human agencies. Verse 18: "As for their rings (rims) they were so high that they were dreadful." Brethren, we do not attach the importance we should to human agency in the Lord's work. God has taken redeemed humanity into partnership with Himself in the salvation of a lost world. We have been playing at this work of transcendent important. We should project the Lord's work on such a large scale that we would be awed with its very immensity. "Undertake great things for God, and expect great things from God." The only way we can make the wealth of this world abide forever is to invest it in the work of the Lord. Brethren, let us pitch the work of this Association on a high key. "The rims of the wheels were so high that they were dreadful." A church with a hundred, or fifty, or ten, or three, members that reports one dollar for Missions, hasn't gotten the thickness of the tire above the ground! The greater our undertakings for God, the more richly will He bestow His grace upon us, as individuals and as churches.

4. Lastly, we need the spirit in the wheels. All this machinery is necessary, but it is all impotent without the Spirit.

(1) We need the spirit to guide us. In the transaction of our own affairs we often find ourselves in doubt and perplexity as to what is best for us to do; but when it comes to the Lord's work, how much oftener do doubts arise. In such times how much we need the guidance of the Spirit. "And when he, the Spirit of Truth, is come he will guide you into all truth."

(2) We need the Spirit to give us unity. Read Christ's intercessory prayer, as recorded in the seventeenth chapter of John, and see how often and how earnestly Christ prays that His people may be

one. We Baptists have no creed by whose requirements we are held together; therefore, we, of all people, need God's Holy Spirit to make us one.

(3) We need God's Holy Spirit to give us power. Christ said to His disciples: "Tarry ye at Jerusalem till ye be endued with power from on high." Brethren, all our machinery is unavailing, it is abject weakness until the Holy Spirit comes to give it power!

We have met to-night to organize a new Association, to put in place the wheels of this part of God's divine machinery. Now let us pray, and pray earnestly, that the "spirit of the living creature" may come into the wheels!

INTRODUCTORY.

At the ninety-eighth annual session of the Raleigh Baptist Association, held with the Smithfield Baptist Church, Smithfield, N. C., October 29, 30, 31, and November 1, 1903, the following resolutions were passed by a vote of 41 to 31:

Because of the great number of churches now composing the Raleigh Association, and the further difficulty of assembling their representatives for associational purposes on account of the vastness of the territory over which it is now spread; be it

Resolved, 1st. That we advise a division of the present territory and churches with a view to forming a new Association.

Resolved, 2d. That we recommend the lines bounding the territory of Johnston County as the general boundary lines of the proposed new Association.

Resolved, 3d. That we hereby extend to all the churches of the Raleigh Association in or near the territory of Johnston County privilege to elect delegates from their respective bodies to meet at such time and place as may be at this assembly mentioned, to organize themselves into a regular Baptist Association, to form their own plans of operation and co-operation with the State Convention in the missionary work of the denomination.

On motion of Brother A. A. Pippin the vote was made unanimous.

Friday afternoon, October 30, a meeting of those interested in the formation of the new Association was held in the Sunday-school room of the Smithfield Baptist Church. Brother J. W. Suttle presided. On motion a meeting of the representatives from the churches comprising the new body was called to be held with Selma Baptist Church Friday night, Saturday and Sunday, November 27, 28 and 29, 1903, for the purpose of perfecting the organization. Brother Suttle was instructed to issue a letter to all the churches desiring to enter the new organization, asking them to send delegates to Selma at the place and time above mentioned.

PROCEEDINGS.

Pursuant to the call issued by order of the meeting at Smithfield October 30, 1903, representatives from the churches met in Selma Baptist Church Friday night, November 27, 1903, for the purpose of organizing the new Association.

Devotional exercises were conducted by Brother John C. Scarborough, President of Chowan Baptist Female Institute, Murfreesboro, N. C. Sermon by Brother Livingston Johnson, Corresponding Secretary of the Baptist State Convention. Text: "For the spirit of the living creature was in the wheels." Ezekiel 1: 20. Prayer by Brother W. G. Hall.

The meeting was then called to order and Brother J. W. Suttle asked to act as Moderator *pro tem.,* and Brother T. J. Lassiter Clerk *pro tem.*

Brethren C. W. Richardson, of Selma Church, and C. W. Carter, of Clayton Church, were named as tellers, and asked to take the names of delegates and churches represented. It was found that twenty-four churches were represented.

The following Committee on Order of Business was appointed: M. A. Adams, J. M. Beaty and J. P. Canaday.

Brother C. W. Blanchard offered a Constitution for adoption. After some little discussion the Constitution, with some minor changes, was unanimously adopted.

On motion to name the Association the following names were suggested: "Smithfield," "Selma," "Clayton." "Matthew T. Yates," and "Johnston County Baptist Association." After a short, but animated, discussion the Association was named "Johnston County Baptist Association."

The Association then went into the election of permanent officers.

Brother R. H. Gower, of Clayton, was unanimously elected Moderator, and assumed the chair.

On motion the rules were suspended and the following officers were elected by acclamation:

Vice-Moderator—J. P. Canaday, of Benson.
Clerk—T. J. Lassiter, of Smithfield.
Treasurer—C. W. Richardson, of Selma.
Historian—C. W. Blanchard, of Clayton.

The following committee was appointed to recommend an Executive Committee: A. A. Pippin, J. W. Suttle and Worley Creech.

Committee on Order of Business reported as follows for Saturday morning:

9:30 to 10—Devotional exercises by A. A. Pippin.
Ministerial Relief—M. A. Adams.
Education—John C. Scarborough.
State Missions—Livingston Johnson.

Adjourned till Saturday morning 9:30.

SATURDAY MORNING.

The Association met at 9:30. Devotional exercises were conducted by Brother A. A. Pippin.

Minutes of last night's session were read and approved.

The Association recognized the following visiting brethren: J. C. Scarborough, of the West Chowan; J. S. Farmer, of the Central, representative of the Biblical Recorder; Livingston Johnson, Corresponding Secretary of the Baptist State Convention; Brother Broughton, of the Neuse; D. D. Edwards, of the Raleigh; C. E. Gower, of the Raleigh; J. F. Hagwood, of the Tar River.

On motion the Clerk was instructed, in the preparation of the Minutes, to leave off the prefixes of "Rev." and "Prof."

A code of by-laws was offered and unanimously adopted.

The committee to recommend Executive Committee reported the following: J. M. Beaty, M. C. Winston, Joseph F. Pool, J. T. Holt and J. H. Boon. They were unanimously elected.

Representatives from six more churches reported this morning, making thirty in all.

Brother M. A. Adams read the report on

MINISTERIAL RELIEF.

We, your Committee on Ministerial Relief, beg to report as follows: We believe it to be our duty to support the work, both as a duty we owe our brethren and God, and most heartily commend it to the churches.

M. A. ADAMS.

Brother Adams spoke to the report. On motion of Brother Suttle, the churches were asked to increase their pledges 10 per cent. over last year on all objects, except State Missions, and that they be increased 25 per cent.

Pledges were then taken and the report adopted.

Brother John C. Scarborough read the report on

EDUCATION.

In the beginning of the separate life of this new Association it is important to us as a body and to the cause of Christ, for the advancement of which we have organized, that we put proper emphasis on those things which are to have great influence on the progress and final triumph of our Lord's kingdom over "the forces of evil."

Among these influences Christian education occupies one of the chief places of highest importance. Our Baptist fathers saw this and felt the need of our Baptist people for the uplift which Christian education alone can bring and does bring with it. Wake Forest College had its origin in the minds and hearts of its founders because of this sorely-felt need for educated men in the pew, as well as in the pulpit, to hold up the truth as we believe it. A little later on the Baptist people felt the pressing need for women in our homes and churches, educated in Baptist schools and taught the Scriptures as Baptists believe them, that our homes and our churches might have that power which comes from properly-trained womanhood, not with mind training only, which sometimes leads to folly, but with mind and heart training leading to wisdom and to lives of sanctified usefulness. Feeling this need the founders of Chowan Baptist Female Institute set about its building and equipment and did it with a liberality born of a felt necessity for sanctified living in womanhood. Their hope was not disappointed and great have been the blessings to us as a people from its work for our women.

Later on, and in our presence, came the felt need for a woman's school to aid the old mother in her work, and out of this need came, but a few years ago, our Baptist Female University, destined for a high and noble work for us in the centuries which stretch out beyond our ken. All over our State our Baptist people have caught more of the spirit of Christian education and are manifesting more and more the spirit of liberal giving for this great work, and of giving their children opportunities for education.

Our State at large and our Associations as separate bodies are dotting our land with Baptist high schools and academies for the betterment of our Christian and denominational life and for a higher and better citizenship. Ministers and people must have the benefits of Christian education, in order to properly fill our place in this century to be the brightest of all the centuries God has given to our world. Let this new Association, founded near the opening of the century, take hold of its part of the work with a firm grip and meet its obligations to God and humanity by bestowing its gifts with a liberal hand and as God shall prosper us.

The Board of Education at Wake Forest College, having charge of the education of young men called of God and approved by the churches to preach the Gospel, is worthy of our confidence and needs our liberal contributions to meet the expenses of the fifty-two young ministers now at the college and dependent on the Board for support.

JOHN C. SCARBOROUGH,
For Committee.

On motion to adopt, the report was discussed by Brother Scarborough. Pledges were taken and the report was adopted.

Brother Livingston Johnson then read the report on

STATE MISSIONS.

At the very foundation of all our work, lies State Missions. This is our invested capital, our base of supplies. Every mission point which grows into a self-sustaining church, adds to our denominational strength. If all the churches which have been aided by the Board were blotted out to-day, our denomination would be like Samson shorn of his locks.

We have over a hundred Missionaries at work in different parts of the State. They will report a fine year's work. But these hundred men cannot cover the destitution in the State. We must enlarge our work. It has been the policy of our denomination in the past to enlarge its State Mission operations as rapidly as possible. The time is at hand for a march-forward movement. Conditions in the East present an opportunity that we never knew before for preaching the truth as we believe it.

In central North Carolina the industrial awakening calls loudly to our Mission Board. New towns are springing up all through central North Carolina, and we must take them for Christ and the Baptists, or lose our opportunity.

A wave of educational interest is sweeping over the West, the like of which was never known before.

Surely, as we look over the State, "the field is white unto harvest."

Let us thrust in the sickle and gather the golden grain unto the garner of our Lord.   LIVINGSTON JOHNSON,
                                                          For Committee.

On motion to adopt, the report was discussed by Brethren Johnson, J. M. Beaty, M. A. Adams and C. W. Blanchard.

The roll of churches was called and pledges were taken. After the churches had pledged, a number of individual pledges were made. (See table of pledges.)

The following committees were announced:

To Nominate Member of the State Board of Missions—J. W. Suttle, J. W. Jones and R. R. Creech.

On Place and Preachers for next Association—J. T. Holt, F. P. Wood and A. D. Atkinson.

To Represent Woman's Work—C. W. Blanchard.

On Sunday-Schools—J. P. Canaday, J. J. Wallace and J. W. Corbett.

To Nominate Delegates to Baptist State Convention—W. G. Hall N. H. Gibbs and J. C. Hardee.

To Nominate Delegate to Southern Baptist Convention—J. M. Beaty, Arthur Lee and J. B. Mecome.

Committee on Order of Business reported as follows:

12:30—Foreign Missions—A. A. Pippin.
1 to 2—Dinner.
2 to 2:30—Home Missions—C. E. Gower.
2:30 to 3—Woman's Work—C. W. Blanchard.
3 to 3:30—Temperance—Worley Creech.
3:30 to 4—Miscellaneous Business.

NIGHT SESSION.

Orphanage—J. W. Nobles. Address by John C. Scarborough.

SUNDAY MORNING.

9:30—Devotional Exercises.
10—Report on Sunday-Schools—J. P. Canaday. Sunday-School Mass-Meeting.
11—Sermon—A. A. Pippin.
Collection for debt on Thanksgiving Church.

SUNDAY NIGHT.

7:30—Sermon—C. W. Blanchard.

Adjourned at 1 o'clock to meet again at 2:30.
Benediction by Brother J. S. Farmer.

Association met at 2 :45.

In the absence of Brother Farmer, Brother J. W. Suttle read the report on

PERIODICALS.

Realizing the deep need of information among our people, we most cordially commend to them the Biblical Recorder, which stands for the dissemination of the proper information among our people. Every Baptist should keep himself informed regarding the work of his denomination, and to do that he must read the organ of our Convention.

Charity and Children, North Carolina Baptist, Foreign Mission Journal, Home Field and the literature of our Sunday-School Board are worthy and will be found helpful to our people.   J. S. FARMER.

On motion to adopt, the report was discussed by Brother Suttle. Adopted.

Brother N. H. Gibbs announced that he would take subscriptions to *North Carolina Baptist.*

Brother M. A. Adams announced that he was representing the *Biblical Recorder* in the absence of Brother Farmer.

Brother C. E. Gower read the report on

HOME MISSIONS.

Jesus Christ was the great Missionary from Heaven to earth. He says: "As the Father hath sent me, even so send I you." In His great command to "go ye in all the world" and "ye shall be witnesses for me," is included the Home Mission work of the Southern Baptist Convention, in all the five departments of its operations.

God has abundantly blessed this work in the past and it is gratifying to see the Baptists in North Carolina going forward in their contributions to this work. Let this young and vigorous Association keep step with her sisters.   C. E. GOWER,
For Committee.

On motion to adopt, Brother Gower discussed the report. Roll of churches was called and pledges were taken, after which the report was adopted.

Three o'clock Sunday afternoon was the hour appointed for Woman's Meeting to elect a Central Committee, etc. Brother Blanchard was asked to meet with them.

Brother A. A. Pippin read the report on

FOREIGN MISSIONS.

We need to keep on our hearts the souls of men. Our Lord has given the command that we preach the Gospel to all the world. Let us, then, as His servants, feel the great responsibility, and spare no time, means or prayers in the extension of God's kingdom.

We have done well this year in enlarging our contributions and find it stimulating in every way. We can do what we want to do. So let us have large things in our hearts for God and expect great things of Him. If we, this Association, will get in our hearts that China and Africa are at our doors and God expecting us, God's favored people, to rescue these lost souls, we shall be blest in this glorious work.

A. A. PIPPIN,
For Committee.

On motion to adopt, the report was discussed by Brethren Pippin, Blanchard and Scarborough. The roll of churches was called, pledges taken and the report adopted.

MISCELLANEOUS BUSINESS.

Committees reported as follows:

Delegate to Southern Baptist Convention—J. W. Suttle.
Member of State Board of Missions—C. W. Blanchard.

On motion it was ordered that the Clerk be paid $10 for his services, and that 500 copies of the Minutes be printed and distributed to the churches.

On motion Association adjourned to meet at 7:30 p. m.

SATURDAY NIGHT.

Association met at 7:30. Song and prayer service.

The report on Woman's Work was submitted by Brother C. W. Blanchard:

WOMAN'S WORK.

The Baptists of North Carolina owe much of the present prosperity of the various appointments of the denomination to the organized efforts of their consecrated women. The history of almost every prosperous church will trace more or less of its spiritual and temporal prosperity to the efforts of an organized Woman's Mission Society. We therefore recommend that the Woman's Central Committee of the Association strive to enlist in this organized work all the women of all our churches, and that they receive all necessary encouragement from the pastors on the field.

C. W. BLANCHARD,
For Committee.

On motion to adopt, the report was discussed by Brother Blanchard. Adopted.

The report of the Executive Commitee was submitted by Brother M. C. Winston. On motion the Association was asked to raise a sufficient amount to make the pledges for State Missions $700; that the State Mission Board be asked in return $1,000, to be used for supplying destitute sections in this Association; that each church in the Johnston County Baptist Association is hereby requested by the Executive Committee to send in the amounts pledged early in the year, to the end that the expenses be met as accrued. Adopted.

Brother Worley Creech wrote the report on Temperance, which was read by Brother J. T. Holt.

TEMPERANCE.

From our experience in the past, we are encouraged in the fight against intemperance. We have found that by constant endeavor we can slay the lion and the bear in the shape of bar-rooms and dispensaries from strength we have gained by our efforts. We are now willing, and will not be satisfied until we have, by Divine help, slain the great giant of intemperance in every form, and recommend that we not only take a stand against it, but meet the evil and drive it from us.

WORLEY CREECH,
For Committee.

On motion to adopt, the report was discussed by Brother Worley Creech. The report was adopted.

On motion a collection, amounting to $11, was taken for Brother Creech and presented by Brother C. W. Richardson.

Committee on Place and Preachers reported as follows:

Place—Clayton Baptist Church.
Preachers—J. W. Suttle to preach Introductory Sermon and A. A. Pippin as alternate.

Brother J. W. Nobles read the report on

THE ORPHANAGE.

Our Orphanage is a place of which we are proud and for which we are grateful. To administer to the needs of the helpless and dependent fatherless and motherless children, for Christ's sake, is a sweet pleasure.

We have under our care in the Thomasville Orphanage 260 orphans, quite a number of applications on hand, enough to fill every vacant place we have. Indeed, every vacant place in our Orphanage for girls has been filled. The Whitty Building is nearing completion; the walls are up and the roof is being put on. We hope to have the building ready by Christmas— that will give additional room for forty girls. There is being money raised for two other dormitories, but we will not be able to begin work on them before the spring. In addition to that, one of the old buildings will be repaired and enlarged. This will make room for 400 orphans, and this increased capacity requires a corresponding increase in funds.

Our Orphanage has been very fortunate in receiving liberal bequests, but most of it is in the form of endowment, and none of it can be used for curent expenses, and instead of relieving the amount of current funds, it increases it. Our people are called upon throughout the State only to support the orphans, and it ought to be a blessed privilege to feed and clothe them. If God has put it into the hearts of a few well-to-do people to put up the buildings, it is but reasonable and right that the great bulk of the Baptist people in the State should pay their current expenses.

These things ought to be very clearly indicated in our pledges; we ought to advance over our former pledges about 50 per cent. Your committee recommends an increase sufficient for the enlargement. By so doing we will make glad the heart of our noble manager and bring uncounted blessings upon the helpless.   J. W. NOBLES,
                                                          For Committee.

On motion to adopt, the report was discussed by Brother John C. Scarborough, member of the Orphanage Committee. The roll of churches was called, pledges taken and the report was adopted and ordered recorded.

On motion of Brother C. W. Blanchard, the following was adopted:

That the Moderator and Clerk, in co-operation with the Executive Committee, be appointed as a committee to prepare an order of business for the next session and have same published at least one month before Association meets.

The standing committees for 1904 were appointed.

On motion of Brother M. A. Adams, it was ordered that the Union Meetings be left in the hands of the Executive Committee.

' The following resolution was passed:

Resolved, That this Association endorses and commends Brother D. D. Edwards as the colporter of our Association.

On motion of Brother C. W. Blanchard, the Clerk was ordered to furnish and have printed in the Minutes a digest of the church letters.

On motion the Association adjourned to 9:30 Sunday morning.

———

SUNDAY MORNING.

Devotional exercises by Brother C. E. Gower.

Brother J. P. Canaday read the report on

SUNDAY-SCHOOLS.

The Sunday-school is one of the greatest mediums through which moral and religious instructions can be imparted. This is abundantly proven in all churches and communities where Sunday-schools have been conducted—the greatest growth resulting where Sunday-school effort is greatest:

The new Johnston County Baptist Association having been organized and thereby many new churches hitherto remote from each other now brought together, the greatest effort should be made by all our members in co-operating with each other to advance the Sunday-school cause throughout our bounds.

There is much destitute territory in our limits. If possible, Sunday-schools should be conducted in these places. There are many weak churches that may be strengthened by earnest effort in Sunday-school work in these.

To aid the work further, a system of Sunday-school Institutes should be conducted. J. P. CANADAY,
For Committee.

On motion to adopt, the report was discussed by J. P. Canaday and John C. Scarborough. Report was then adopted.

Brother A. A. Pippin offered the following resolution, which was unanimously adopted:

Resolved, That we heartily tender our sincere thanks to our brethren and sisters of Selma Baptist Church, to those of the other denominations, and the people of the community generally for the very generous hospitality and kind care with which this first session of the Johnston County Association has been provided.

Brother A. A. Pippin preached from the following text: "For the righteous Lord loveth righteousness." Psalms 11:7. Subject: The True Use of Life.

At the close of the sermon, Brother M. A. Adams took a collection to pay the indebtedness on Thanksgiving Church. Amount raised, $49.72.

Adjourned with benediction by Brother C. E. Gower.

———

WOMAN'S MEETING.

A Woman's Missionary Society was organized Sunday afternoon at 4 o'clock by Brother C. W. Blanchard, auxiliary to the Johnston County Baptist Association, with Mrs. Ashley Horne, of Clayton, Vice-President, and Mrs. W. M. Pettway, of Smithfield, Secretary.

CHURCH PLEDGES FOR 1904.

CHURCHES.	Ministerial Education.	State Missions.	Ministerial Relief.	Home Missions.	Foreign Missions.	Orphanage.	Totals.
Antioch	$ 1 00	$ 10 00	$ 1 25	$ 1 25	$ 1 00	$ 2 00	$ 16 50
Baptist Centre	1 00	10 00	1 00	2 00	1 00	5 00	20 00
Bethany	1 00	5 00	1 00	1 50	1 00	2 00	11 50
Bethesda	1 00	20 00	1 50	2 50	5 00	12 50	42 50
Benson	2 00	35 00	2 00	5 00	10 00	12 00	66 00
Blackman's Grove	2 50	15 00	1 50	3 00	5 00	15 00	42 00
Carter's Chapel	1 00	5 00	1 00	1 00	1 00	2 00	11 00
Clayton	11 00	100 00	7 50	27 50	100 00	60 00	306 00
Clyde's Chapel	1 00	5 00	1 00	2 50	2 00	3 00	14 50
Corinth	1 00	5 00	1 00	2 50	2 50	3 00	15 00
Four Oaks	1 25	10 00	1 25	3 00	2 50	2 00	20 00
Hood's Grove	1 00	5 00	1 00	1 00	2 00	1 00	11 00
Lee's Chapel	1 00	25 00	2 50	2 50	2 00	1 00	34 00
Live Oak	1 00	2 50	1 00	1 00	1 00	2 00	8 50
Mt. Moriah	5 00	25 00	3 00	10 00	25 00	10 00	78 00
Noble's Chapel	1 00	10 00	1 00	1 00	1 00	1 00	15 00
New Bethel	1 00	15 00	1 00	2 50	1 25	2 50	23 25
Oliver's Grove	* 50	5 00	* 50	1 00	1 00	1 00	9 00
Parish Memorial	1 00	10 00	1 00	1 00	1 00	1 00	15 00
Pine Level	1 00	2 50	50	1 00	1 00	1 00	7 00
Pisgah	1 00	10 00	1 25	1 00	1 00	2 50	16 75
Princeton	1 00	10 00	1 25	2 00	2 50	1 00	17 75
Sardis	1 00	2 50	1 00	1 00	1 00	1 00	7 50
Selma	5 00	50 00	5 00	5 00	10 00	30 00	105 00
Shiloh	2 00	15 00	2 00	2 00	2 50	12 00	35 50
Smithfield	7 50	50 00	11 00	20 00	30 00	30 00	148 50
Thanksgiving	1 00	7 50	1 50	1 50	1 50	2 00	15 00
Trinity	1 00	5 00	1 00	2 50	2 50	2 50	14 50
White Oak	1 00	10 00	1 00	2 00	1 00	1 00	16 00
Wilson's Mills	1 00	5 00	2 00	2 00	10 00	6 00	26 00
Totals	$57 75	$485 00	$58 50	$111 75	$228 25	$227 00	$1168 25

* Paid.

ADDITIONAL STATE MISSION PLEDGES.

J. C. Scarborough, Murfreesboro, N. C., $5; Mrs. J. C. Scarborough, Murfreesboro, N C, $5; Livingston Johnson, Raleigh, N. C., $5; T. J. Lassiter, Smithfield, N. C., $12.50; C. E. Gower, Clayton, N. C., $5; J. M. Beaty, Smithfield, N C, $50; F P Wood Four Oaks N C $10; M A Adams, Auburn, N C., $5; J. W. Nobles, Selma, N. C., $2.50; Mrs. J. W. Suttle, Smithfield, N. C., $10; W. G. Hall, Roxboro, N. C., $5; Biblical Recorder, Raleigh, N C., $5; T. B. Moseley, Raleigh, N. C., $5; J. C. Hardee, Clayton, N. C., $5; A. A. Pippin, Wakefield, N. C., $5; J. T. Holt, Wilson's Mills, N. C., $2.50; Worley Creech, Kenly, N. C., $2.50; D. B. Edwards, Fuquay Springs, N. C., $2.50; Raymond Petway, Smithfield, N. C., $1; Smithfield Junior Union, $2; Selma Sunbeams, $2 50; Baptist Centre Sunday School, $2.50; Benson Sunbeams, $2.50; Clayton Sunday School, $5.

OTHER PLEDGES.

Clayton Sunday School for Orphanage, $60; Clayton Junior Union for Foreign Missions, $25; Four Oaks Sunday School for Orphanage, $5.

CHURCH STATISTICS.

CHURCHES.	PASTORS.	CLERKS AND ADDRESSES.	Preaching Sabbath.	Value of Church Property.	Seating Capacity.	Baptisms.	Received by Letter.	Restored.	Lost by Letter.	Excluded.	Died.	No. Males.	No. Females.	Total Membership.
Antioch	Worley Creech	R. R. Creech, Ennice	2	$500 00	500	3			4	9	4	47	108	155
Baptist Centre	M. A. Adams	A. G. Rogers, Clayton	2	300 00	300		1		7	6	1	35	50	85
Bethany	Worley Creech	Kirkman Creech, Kenly	4	600 00	300	6	3			2	1	27	43	70
Bethesda	J. W. Suttle	J. E. Smith, Clayton	4	600 00	500	5	3		3	2	1	66	104	170
Benson	J. W. Suttle	E. L. Hall, Benson	2	1500 00	400	11			1		1	48	82	130
Blackman's Grove	J. W. Suttle	E. B. Hayes, Four Oaks	3	600 00	300	7			2			19	34	53
Carter's Chapel	J. W. Nobles	w. B. Wall, Micro	1	350 00	500	38						19	28	47
Clayton	C. W. Blanchard	M. G. Gulley, Clayton	1-3	3000 00	900	10	12		10	5	1	97	164	261
Clyde's Chapel	M. A. Adams	C. I. Johnson, Wendell	2	650 00	300	20	4		11	8	2	39	61	100
Corinth	A. A. Pippin	Q. B. Hocutt, Ennice	4	400 00	400	1	2			2		24	37	61
Four Oaks	J. W. Suttle	Miss Willie Creech, Four Oaks	3	600 00	300	12	1			3		5	14	19
Hood's Grove	W. G. Hall	G. w. Naylor, Glenwood	3			5			1			11	12	23
Lee's Chapel	J. W. Nobles	W. I Green, Dry Wells	3	500 00	250		2		5	2	2	100	157	257
Live Oak	Worley Creech	B Broadwell	3			11	1			3		10	21	31
Mt. Moriah	M. A. Adams	J. M. Baucom, Raleigh, r. f. d. 1	1	347 00	500	10	1	1			4	76	93	169
Noble's Chapel	J W. Nobles	J. R. Todd, Taylor	4	750 00	400	2		1	1		1	23	28	51
New Bethel	J. W. Nobles	W. B. Bryan, Garner	1					1	11	5		43	40	83
Oliver's Grove	N. H. Gibbs	H. Johnson, Four Oaks	1	300 00	300	4					1	10	9	19
Parish Memorial	J. W. Nobles	J. D Creech, Pine Level	3	200 00	250	3	3			3	1	6		6
Pine Level	J. S Hagwood	Belva Strickland, Battleboro	1			3					1	8	13	21
Pisgah	J. W. Suttle	A. G. Jones, Smithfield	3			4								50
Princeton	M. A. Adams	J. Ben Howell, Princeton	1	400 00	150						2			58
Sardis	W. G Hall	N. B. Stevens, Smithfield	2-4	2500 00	500	14	5		1	2		3	9	12
Selma	M. A. Adams	S. C. Robertson, Selma	1	800 00	600	7			1	1		47	58	110
Shiloh	W. G. Hall	J. H Holland, Leachburg	1-2	3500 00	700	2			4			33	40	73
Smithfield	J. W. Suttle	J. M. Beaty, Smithfield	1-4	800 00	300		2		2	1		45	56	101
Thanksgiving	M. A. Adams	W. G. Earp, Selma	4				13					14	13	27
Trinity	J. W. Suttle	J. S Lawhon, Benson	2	450 00	450	5			4		2	15	22	37
White Oak	A. A. Pippin	J I Murphrey, Selma	4	700 00	250		9	2		4	3	25	58	88
Wilson's Mills	W. G. Hall	J. T. Holt, Wilson's Mills	4				1					21	26	47

17

SUNDAY SCHOOL STATISTICS.

CHURCHES.	SUPERINTENDENTS AND P. O.	Teachers and Officers	Scholars	Total	Average Attendance	Quarterlies and Papers	Volumes in Library	Months Kept Open	Expenses	No. of Schools	No. of Baptisms from Schools
Antioch	W. M. ...en, Archer	5	40	45	25	45		12	4 50	1	
Baptist Centre	J. C. Hardee, Clayton	5	50	55	35	30	70	12	3 00	1	
Benson	W. D. Boon, Benson	8	133	141		125	60	12	30 00	1	8
Bethany	David Pace and K. ...6th, Micro	8	124	132	65	60		6	6 00	2	7
Bethesda	J. J. Wallace, Clayton	10	60	70	40	60	50	12	6 00	1	2
Blackman's Grove	F. P. Wood, Four Oaks, R. F. D. No 2	5	63	68	40	260		6	2 50	1	5
Carter's Chapel	W. B Wall, Micro	4	48	52	35	35		6		1	
Clayton	R. H. ...er, Clayton	21	200	221	140	303	176	12	36 12		28
...'s Chapel	J R. Hood, ...Will	8	132	140	100	120	50		14 00	2	7
Corinth	J A Estridge, Emit	7	105	112	50	120		9	4 00	1	12
Four Oaks	Mrs. Laura ...6th, Four Oaks	5	32	37	20	40		12	5 00	1	1
Hood's Grove											
Lee's Chapel	W. I. Green, Dry Wells	12	136	148	30	275		12	15 00	2	
Live Oak											
Mt. Moriah	E R. Pool, Clayton	12	126	138	65	130	250	12	30 05	1	9
New Bethel	D. T. Bryan, Garner	6	40	46	25	50	50		7 50	1	
Noble's Chapel											
Oak Grove											
Parish Memorial	J F. Watson, Pine Level	8	44	52	30		36	9	4 00	1	4
Pine Level	Wm Eason, Selma	6	60	66	35				7 50	1	2
Pisgah	W. Jones, Smithfield	5	50	55	40	50		12	3 00		
Princeton	G. F. Woodard, Princeton	5	40	45	25						
Sardis											
Selma	H. E. Craven, Selma	9	131	140	70	154		12	30 00	1	
Shiloh	F. Hardee, Leachburg	5	80	85	60	75		12	8 00	1	
...field	M. Beaty, Smithfield	7	93	100	60	150	200	12	50 00	1	7
Thanksgiving	B O'Neal, Selma	5	70	75	35	60		8	5 00	1	2
Trinity											
White Oak	W. A. Newton, Archer	5	105	110	53	80		12	5 91	1	
Wilson's Mills	J. E. Wall, Wilson's Mills	4	40	44	30	54		12	6 00	1	
Totals		74	2002	2074	1138	2276	942		$283 58	26	94

CONTRIBUTIONS BY CHURCHES, SUNDAY SCHOOLS AND SOCIETIES.

CHURCHES	Number of Members	Pastor's Salary	Building and Repairs	Incidentals	The Poor	State Missions	Home Missions	Foreign Missions	Orphanage	Ministerial Education	Aged Ministers	Other Objects	Total
. . .	155	$22 48	$	$	$8 94	$7 00	$1 00	$60	$2 08	$1 00	$2 00	$72	$46 12
Baptist Centre	85	60 00				3 46		54				6 70	66 59
Benson	130	200 00	75 00	30 00		27 50	2 00	2 50	10 00	1 05	1 00	6 35	363 70
Bethany	70	50 00		2 00		3 50		2 02	1 84		73		81 50
Bethesda	170	110 00	60 00			15 00	1 50	3 77	2 00	2 50	1 00	11 00	214 27
Blackman's Grove	53	40 00		20		10 00	1 50	5 00	1 50	2 00	1 25	13 00	74 25
Carter's Chapel	47	25 00		59 62		6 00	1 00		2 00		1 00		38 20
Clayton	261	500 00	429 53			95 74	49 31	84 52	114 83	10 00	21	304 00	1693 88
Chapel	100	42 25			1 40	1 00	1 00	45	1 00		50		58 70
	61	40 00				5 00	1 00	1 00	1 50	1 00	1 00	5 10	53 40
Four Oaks	19	25 00		5 00		6 00	1 00	1 00	1 00			9 43	51 10
Hood's Grove	23	3 70											13 13
Lee's Chapel	257	100 00				15 00	5 00	1 00	5 00	2 50	1 00	7 60	143 50
Live Oak	31	16 25	31 46			1 32	1 81	85	2 55	1 07	33		22 13
Mt. Moriah	169	120 00				20 00	5 00	5 00	10 00	3 01	4 38	28 80	259 19
New Bethel	83	80 00	313 00		50	22 00		3 00	8 00		5 00	2 50	128 00
Noble's Chapel	51					3 00	50	50	1 00				20 65
Oak Grove						1 00						19 65	40 15
Parish Memorial	21	25 00		6 65		5 00	1 00		1 00	1 00	1 00		7 25
Pine Level	50	8 25				10 00		2 00	1 00				105 00
Pisgah	58	50 00	40 00	3 00		8 00	1 00	2 99	1 00	1 00		15 00	58 99
Princeton	12	25 00	3 00			2 55	2 00	1 00	1 00	1 00			18 55
Sardis	110	15 00				40 0	5 00	25 00	5 00	5 00	3 50		739 56
Selma	73	250 00	27 50			350	15 00	1 94	12 00			176 00	129 94
Shiloh	101	1 00	1007 21	40 00	5 00	2 50		29 07	11 93	6 97	10 00	88 27	1495 95
Smithfield	27	250 00	33 16	1 00		7 50	2 00	2 00	1 00		1 00		32 66
Thanksgiving	37	17 75				2 50	2 00		2 00	2 00			29 25
Trinity	83	30 0		45 00									107 50
White Oak	47	100 00	25 00			10 00		1 00	7 75		1 00		120 75

NOTE.—In the Table of Contributions the Sunday schools and churches should have credit for the following: Clayton Woman's Mission Society—State Missions, $35.23; Home Missions, $35; Foreign Missions, $83.53; Orphanage, $40.29; Ministerial Education, $3.50; Aged Ministers, $4.25. Clayton Sunday School—Building and Repairing, $30.40; Orphanage, $57.22. Clayton Ladies' Aid Society—Building and Repairing—$95.25 Clayton B. Y. P. U—Foreign Missions—$15.36. Clayton church also sent a box valued at $75 to Frontier Missionary Corinth Sunday School—Orphanage, $1. Shiloh Sunday School—Orphanage,

CONSTITUTION OF THE JOHNSTON COUNTY BAPTIST ASSOCIATION.

1. The Association shall be known as the Johnston County Baptist Association.

2. Its object shall be to extend the privileges of the Gospel and liberal culture to all the people within its bounds, and by hearty co-operation with the Baptist State Convention, to help offer these privileges to all mankind in and out of our bounds, by the cordial co-operation of all the churches constituting this body.

3. It shall be composed of the pastors in active service in the Association and such delegates as shall be annually elected by the churches connected with it, each church being entitled to three delegates unless the membership shall exceed fifty, and then an additional delegate for every twenty-five members, provided no church shall have more than eight delegates.

4. The New Hampshire Declaration of Faith shall be the summary of Divine Truth for determining questions of faith and order in this body, and the churches desiring membership in it must commit themselves to the substance of it, together with the covenant therewith submitted, and this Constitution.

5. This Association shall not have power to annul the discipline or exercise authority over any church connected with it, but it may advise with and sever its connection with any church that neglects to preserve Gospel order, or that treats with contempt the objects or advice of the Association.

6. Each church shall send to the annual meetings of the Association a letter (the blanks to be furnished by the Clerk of the Association), carefully filled as per blank suggestions, stating the full work of the church for the year ending with the close of the month previous to the one in which the Association is held.

7. The Association shall foster State Missions, Home Missions, Foreign Missions, Christian Education, the Aged Ministers' Relief Board, the Thomasville Orphanage and the Sunday-School Board, and each church shall be requested to contribute to the support of these objects annually.

8. Missions and education shall have precedence in their claims upon the consideration of this body in its regular sessions.

9. Whenever a church shall fail to be represented by delegates or letter at the annual sessions of the Association or shall fail to contribute to the objects fostered by the Association, inquiry shall be made for the cause, and efforts shall be made to induce such church to do its duty, and the effort shall be continued till the church is recovered or dropped from the roll.

10. The officers of the Association shall be a Moderator, a Vice-Moderator, a Clerk, a Historian and a Treasurer, elected annually by ballot from among its members, to serve until their successors shall have been elected, and to perform the duties usual to such officers, namely, the Moderator in presiding over the meetings, or the Vice-Moderator in his absence; the Clerk in recording and preserving Minutes and other papers belonging to the body; the Treasurer in receiving and disbursing funds belonging to or entrusted to the body according to its will; the Historian in keeping a continuous record of the work and progress of the entire Association and making an annual report of same to each of its sessions.

11. The Association shall appoint annually an Executive Committee of five (5) from its members, who shall be entrusted with the prosecution of Missions in the Association, and any other work for the interest of the Master's kingdom which may be referred to them. This committee shall, as far as possible, co-operate with the State Mission Board in supplying the destitution in our territory, and between the meetings of the Association take such actions as may seem to them advisable for the advancement of its interest. The committee shall present to the Association at its annual meeting a report of its proceedings, with the names of the Missionaries supported

on the field, time of service, and details of their work, together with such recommendations as in the judgment of the committee the Association should follow in planning its subsequent work.

12. The annual sessions of the Association shall begin on Thursday after the first Lord's day in November at such place as may be chosen, and an Introductory Sermon shall be delivered on the first day of the session. Representatives from a majority of the churches constituting the Association shall be a quorum.

13. This Constitution may be amended at any annual session by a two-third's vote of all the members present.

14. Provision shall be made at each annual Association for a session of the Woman's Central Committee and all other necessary encouragement offered for the enlargement of the organized work of the Woman's Missionary Societies in the local churches. The proceedings of the Woman's Central Committee shall be recorded as a part of the Minutes of the Association.

BY-LAWS.

1. The daily sessions of the Association shall be opened and closed with prayer.

2. Delegates shall be recognized by letters from their churches designating them as such.

3. The Moderator shall recognize corresponding messengers or the delegates of newly-received churches by extending to them his right hand.

4. The report of the Executive Board and the Missionary work of the Association shall take precedence of all other business during the morning session of the second day of the annual session.

5. The Clerk shall record and read the proceedings when called for, superintend the publication and distribution of the Minutes, preserve a file of them, and have it present at each annual session, and deliver to his successor all papers belonging to the body.

6. Members desiring to speak shall first rise and address the Moderator; shall use the term "brother" in speaking to each other; shall not speak on the same subject more than twice without permission, and shall observe the courtesy that becomes Christians.

7. Members shall not absent themselves from the session without permission.

8. The roll of members shall be called at least once and absentees marked.

9. Corresponding messengers and visiting brethren shall be invited to seats, with privilege of speaking, but not of voting.

10. A copy of the minutes shall be sent to the Secretary of the State Mission Board; the Secretary of the Southern Baptist Convention; the American Baptist Publication Society, 1420 Chestnut Street, Philadelphia; the Sunday-School Board of the Southern Baptist Convention and the Thomasville Orphanage.

11. All questions of order not herein provided shall be decided by Kerfoot's Parliamentary Law.

MINUTES

OF THE

SECOND SESSION

OF THE

JOHNSTON COUNTY BAPTIST ASSOCIATION,

HELD WITH

THE CLAYTON BAPTIST CHURCH,

CLAYTON, N. C.,

NOVEMBER 10, 11, 12 AND 13, 1904.

———

The Next Session will be held with Benson Church, beginning Thursday after the First Sunday in November, 1905.

———

NASH BROS.
BOOK AND COMMERCIAL PRINTERS,
GOLDSBORO, N. C.

MINUTES

OF THE

SECOND SESSION

OF THE

JOHNSTON COUNTY BAPTIST ASSOCIATION,

HELD WITH

THE CLAYTON BAPTIST CHURCH,

CLAYTON, N. C.,

NOVEMBER 10, 11, 12 AND 13, 1904.

The Next Session will be held with Benson Church, beginning Thursday after the First Sunday in November, 1905.

NASH BROS.
BOOK AND COMMERCIAL PRINTERS,
GOLDSBORO, N. C.

OFFICERS.

Moderator—R. H. GOWER.............................Clayton, N. C.
Vice-Moderator—J. P. CANADAY..........................Benson, N. C.
Clerk—T. J. LASSITER....................................Smithfield, N. C.
Treasurer—C. W. RICHARDSON ....Selma, N. C.
Historian—C. W. BLANCHARD ....Cary, N. C.

EXECUTIVE COMMITTEE.

J. M. Beaty, Chairman...................................Smithfield, N. C.
M. C. Winston, Secretary.............................. Selma, N. C.
Joseph F. Pool..Auburn, N. C.
J. H. Boon...Benson, N. C.
J. T. Holt ....Wilson's Mills, N. C.

STANDING COMMITTEES FOR 1905.

State Missions............................J. M. Beaty.
Home Missions............................J. W. Suttle.
Foreign Missions ....C. W. Blanchard.
Orphanage...............................F. T. Booker.
Education................................J. P. Canaday.
Periodicals..............................A. A. Pippin.
Ministerial Relief.......................R. W. Horrell.
Sunday Schools..........................G. W. Cavenaugh.
Woman's Work...........................B. Townsend.
Temperance..............................C. W. Carter.

MINISTERIAL REGISTER.

S. J. Betts.............................. Raleigh, N. C.
C. W. Blanchard........................Clayton, N. C.
Worley Creech..........................Kenly, N. C., R. F. D. No. 2.
N. H. Gibbs.............................Benson, N. C.
J. D. Bowen .... Four Oaks, N. C.
R. W. Horrell...........................Selma, N. C.
A. A. Pippin .... Wakefield, N. C.
J. W. Smith............................Clayton, N. C.
J. W. Suttle............................Smithfield, N. C.
C. T. Tew..............................Wake Forest, N. C.
B. Townsend ....Broadway, N. C.

ORDER OF BUSINESS
OF THE SECOND ANNUAL SESSION OF THE
JOHNSTON COUNTY BAPTIST ASSOCIATION,
HELD AT CLAYTON, N. C., NOVEMBER 10TH TO 13TH, 1904.

THURSDAY.

11:00 A. M.—Introductory Sermon.
2:00 P. M.—Organization.
    Aged Ministers' Relief.
7:00 P. M.—Home Missions.
    Miscellaneous.

FRIDAY.

9:30 A. M.—Devotional Services.
10:00 A. M.—Report of Executive Committee.
11:00 A. M.—State Missions.
2:00 P M.—Orphanage.
    Woman's Work.
7:00 P. M.—Foreign Missions.
    Miscellaneous.

SATURDAY.

9:30 A. M.—Devotional Services.
    Miscellaneous.
11:00 A. M.—Education—Ministerial and General.
2:00 P. M.—Periodicals.
3:00 P. M.—Sunday Schools.
7:00 P. M.—Temperance.
    Miscellaneous.

SUNDAY.

10:00 A. M.—Sunday School Mass Meeting.
11:00 A. M.—Sermon.
    Farewell.

Meeting of Woman's Central Committee will be arranged for Thursday at 2:00 P.M.

STANDING COMMITTEES FOR 1904.

State Missions.... ....J. M. Beaty.
Home Missions......... .. ..C. E. Gower.
Foreign Missions ....C. W. Blanchard.
Orphanage...... ....C. W. Carter.
Education........... ....J. P. Canaday.
Periodicals............. ... .J. W. Suttle.
Temperance.............................. ....M. C. Winston.
Ministerial Relief................................F. P. Wood.
Sunday Schools.................................N. R. Pool
Woman's Work........................... ....A. A. Pippin.

LIST OF MESSENGERS.

Antioch—R. R. Creech, J. H. Hales, W. H. Maden, Oscar Creech and J. A. Eason.

Baptist Centre—J. C. Hardee and H. A. Jones.

Benson—J. L. Hall, J. H. Boon, Alonzo Parrish and J. P. Canaday

Bethany—E. Creech, C. W. Creech and W. R. Hodge.

Bethel—J. A. Gulley and W. T. Sullivan.

Bethesda—G. A. Smith, Pressie Mathis and M. Johnson.

Blackman's Grove—Ernest Grice, W. B. Creech, Adkin Wood and J. M. Blackman.

Carter's Chapel—H. R. Easom and Theo. Easom.

Clayton—C. W. Carter, M. G. Gulley and Robert Boon.

Clyde's Chapel—W. T. Allen, H. V. Bunch, J. H. Nowell, J. W. Finch and Thad. E. Hinnant

Corinth—J A. Estridge, R. L. Hocutt, A. B. Lowry, A. D. Atkinson and E. C. Whitley.

Four Oaks—J. William Langdon.

Hood's Grove—Joseph W. Wood and Y. L. Blackman.

Lee's Chapel—A. A. Creech and J. M. Driver.

Live Oak—W. M. Eason.

Micro—David Pace, D. C. Smith, L. L. Creech and Charlie Batten.

Mount Moriah—Gaston Jones, J. M. Baucom and J. F. Pool.

New Bethel—J. N. Bryan.

Nobles' Chapel—J. R. Todd and James Mecome.

Oliver's Grove—Not represented.

Parish Memorial—J. F. Watson.

Pauline—W. B. Joyner, D. E. R. Evans and N. W. Smith.

Pine Level—Not represented.

Pisgah—J. W. Jones, Cleveland Johnson and R. H. Higgins.

Princeton—Oscar Mozingo and W. C. Massey.

Sardis—G. M. Phillips.

Selma—C. W. Richardson, N. R. Batten and M. C. Winston.

Shiloh—C. H. Holland, F. T. Booker, D. N. Lee and C. J. Coats.

Smithfield—J. M. Beaty, J. D. Underwood, J. A. Underhill, Jr., and T. J. Lassiter.

Thanksgiving—W. Y. Wood, John Lynch and Marshal Murphrey.

Trinity—Arthur H. Lee and N. L. Morgan.

White Oak—A. L. Batten, J. B. Oneal and R. H. Biggs.

Wilson's Mills—J. T. Holt, Dempsey Vinson, S. D. West and J. A. Wall.

Missionary—R. W. Horrell, Selma, N. C.

PROCEEDINGS.

CLAYTON, N. C., November 10, 1904.

The second annual session of the Johnston County Baptist Association convened with Clayton Baptist Church this morning with devotional services conducted by Bro. A. A. Pippin who read Psalm 19.

The Introductory Sermon was preached by Bro. J. W. Suttle from Jonah 3:1-3. Subject: Personal Responsibility. Prayer by Bro. G. W. Fisher, Pastor Clayton M. E. Church.

The Association was welcomed to Clayton by Pastor Blanchard, after which the body adjourned with benediction by Bro. Suttle.

AFTERNOON SESSION.

The Association opened at 2 o'clock with prayer by Bro. Worley Creech. After the body had been called to order by the Moderator, Bro. R. H. Gower, Bro. C. W. Blanchard made a motion that the reading of the Church letters be dispensed with and that a committee on credentials be appointed for the purpose of enrolling the delegates. The motion prevailed and the Moderator appointed the following brethren: J. L. Hall, of Benson; and J. M. Baucom, of Mount Moriah.

Brethren C. H. Holland, J. T. Holt and Oscar Mozingo were appointed Finance Committee.

The following officers were elected for the ensuing year:

Moderator—R. H. Gower.
Vice-Moderator—J. P. Canaday.
Clerk—T. J. Lassiter.
Treasurer—C. W. Richardson.
Historian—C. W. Blanchard.

Brethren J. W. Suttle, A. A. Pippin and R. W. Horrell were appointed a committee on Petitionary Letters.

The following brethren were recognized and welcomed to the Association: J. S. Farmer, representative of the *Biblical Recorder;* W. G. Hall, of the Beulah Association; G. W. Fisher, pastor of the Clayton M. E. Church; B. W. Spilman, Sunday School Secretary of the Southern Baptist Convention; D. D. Edwards, of the Raleigh Association.

Upon motion of Bro. C. W. Blanchard the subject of Ministerial Education was taken up and discussed. In the absence of a report the subject was discussed by Brethren J. S. Farmer, C. W. Carter and C. W. Blanchard, after which pledges were taken. (See table of pledges for 1905.)

The Committee on Petitionary Letters submitted the following report:

Your committee beg leave to report that Micro, Bethel and Pauline, newly organized Baptist churches, have petitioned for membership with our Association. After having heard from them we are satisfied that they were duly organized into Missionary Baptist Churches. Your committee recommend that they be received.

J. W. SUTTLE,
R. W. HORRELL,
A. A. PIPPIN,
Committee.

Upon motion to adopt, the report was discussed by Brethren J. M. Beaty, C. W. Knight, Worley Creech and R. W. Horrell. The report was adopted and the Moderator welcomed the delegates from the new churches.

The following committee was announced: Home Missions—C. E. Gower, R. W. Horrell and B. W. Spilman.

Adjourned to meet again at 7:30. Benediction by Bro. D. D. Edwards.

NIGHT SESSION.

The Association met at 7:30. Devotional services were conducted by Bro. A. A. Pippin.

The following brethren were recognized and welcomed: S. F. Conrad, Field Editor *North Carolina Baptist;* Archibald Johnson, Editor *Charity and Children,* representing the Thomasville Orphanage; Livingston Johnson, Corresponding Secretary Baptist State Convention; B. Townsend, of the Little River Association; R. T. Vann, President Baptist University for Women.

The regular order was then taken up and Bro. C. E. Gower read the

REPORT ON HOME MISSIONS.

When we come to think, speak or write of the work of Home Missions ot the Southern Baptist Convention we are overwhelmed with the magnitude of the work and the subject. The nation has just passed through a great Presidential election in which no little time, labor and money have been expended "to save our dear country." We do not minimize the value of public office, parties and platforms when we say that we more CONFIDENTLY look to our dear brother, the genial, consecrated B. D. Gray, and the great Baptist hosts with the eternal truth of God as their platform. This kind of work is patriotic, as well as Christian, and ought to appeal to every good citizen.

Some of the Indians are still among us and to them we undoubtedly owe something. The Negroes are very much among us and it is a great problem to decide what to do for them and do it. Foreigners from almost everywhere—nearly one million last year—are coming, bringing all sorts of ideas and religions—coming to be blessed or to be a curse. They must have the civilizing and saving influences of the Gospel. They, with the millions unsaved of our own native population, in the mines, in the mills, in the mountains, on the frontier, in many of our largest cities, in so many places, must be reached, if reached at all, by our Home Mission work.

Last, but not least, Cuba lies down yonder with outstretched wounded arms; with open, bleeding mouth, crying to us for the bread of life. Will we deny her? She has had internal disorders, but they are rapidly healing now, and Bro. Daniel is pleading earnestly for help to secure lots and erect houses of worship while we can. Will we heed the call? The establishment of one Missionary church means not only a benediction to that locality, but its development means held "unto the uttermost part of the earth" in geometrical progression. If the Home field is neglected the Foreign field suffers too. Independent Baptist churches are dependent "to the ends of the earth."

The last report of Treasurer Dunson to the Convention shows $136,540.68 as "total receipts," besides the boxes sent by noble women not a few. If you wish to see the wise expenditure and great profits, refer to the minutes of the Southern Baptist Convention. The work is spreading. Will you enlarge?

CLAUDE E. GOWER,
R. W. HORRELL,
B. W. SPILMAN,
Committee.

After discussion by Brethren Gower and Spilman, pledges were taken and the report was adopted.

The following committees were announced:

State Mission—J. M. Beaty, R. R. Creech and David Pace.
Foreign Missions—C. W. Blanchard, Joseph W. Wood and J. F. Watson
Orphanage—C. W. Carter, J. D. Underwood and J. M. Baucom.
Education—J. P. Canaday, C. W. Richardson and W. B. Creech.
Periodicals—J. W. Suttle, J. C. Hardee and A. A. Creech.
Temperance—M. C. Winston, Worley Creech and D. C. Smith.
Sunday Schools—N. R. Pool, W. B. Joyner and Y. L. Blackman
Woman's Work—A. A. Pippin, E. Creech and W. M. Eason.
Time, Place and Preachers for Next Year—C. W. Carter, M. G. Gulley and W. T. Allen.
Devotional Exercises—Pastor and Deacons of Clayton Church.

On motion of Bro. Blanchard the Moderator was instructed to appoint a committee to digest the church letters.

Adjourned.

FRIDAY MORNING.

The Association met at 9:30. Devotional exercises were conducted by Bro. B. Townsend. Prayer by Bro. S. F. Conrad.

The Association was called to order by Moderator Gower. The minutes of the previous day read, corrected and approved.

The roll was called and new delegates enrolled.

The following committee on Digest of Church Letters was announced: C. W. Blanchard, C. W. Knight and B. Townsend.

The following visiting brethren were recognized and welcomed: John E. Ray, Moderator of the Central Association; S. J. Betts, of the Raleigh Association.

Brother J. M. Beaty, chairman, read the report of the Executive committee.

REPORT OF THE EXECUTIVE COMMITTEE.

We are glad to report a prosperous year of mission work. We engaged with Bro. J. D. Bowen to move to Four Oaks and preach there and at Oliver's Grove, Trinity, Sardis and Pine Level churches. He preached also at three new mission points. At Spilona School House ·and Johnson School House he had good congregations and we believe planted 'seed which will bear good fruit. At Massey's School House he organized a church of twenty-one members. He began March 1st and left us November 1st to attend Louisville Seminary.

Bro. A. A. Pippin served as pastor at White Oak and Corinth churches. Several additions were made to each of these churches and he thinks they will be self-suporting after one more year.

Bro. J. W. Suttle served as pastor at Pisgah, Blackman's Grove and Hood's Grove Churches. Satisfactory progress was made and prospects are bright for the next year's work.

Bro. R. W. Horrell preached at Wilson's Mills, Thanksgiving, Carter's Chapel, Parish Memorial, Micro, Princeton, Woodard School House, Nobles' Chapel and at Mr. J. T. Revel's, a point near Kenly. Good work has been done at all the points, and new churches were organized at the point near Kenly and at Micro.

New places are asking for preaching and owing to the largeness of the work already started we shall be compelled to secure the services of one more man. This calls for increased contributions and we recommend that the Association raise at least nine hundred dollars for the coming year and ask the State Board for three hundred and fifty dollars additional.

J. M. BEATY,
M. C. WINSTON,
J. T. HOLT,
J. H. BOON,
JOSEPH POOL,
Executive Committee.

After discussion by Brethren J. M. Beaty and R. W. Horrell, the report was adopted.

Brother J. M. Beaty read the

REPORT ON STATE MISSIONS.

We greatly rejoice in the fruit our State Mission work has borne. If all our people but knew the wonderful things this work has accomplished, surely they would enthusiastically arise to meet every demand for enlargement which the present situation requires at our hand.

In 1860 there were but five self-supporting churches in the State. At this same date most of the towns along the railroads running through our State were without a single Baptist church and many of them without any Baptist preaching. Now there is scarcely one of these towns without a Baptist church, and in some of them you will find our very strongest and best churches. But this is only a small part of what has been done. The Messenger of the Cross, sustained by our Board of Missions, has pressed his way into the solitary place and destitute field far away from the centers of activity. The fact is State Missions has been, is, and must ever be the base of supply in all our denominational work. Wake Forest College, the Baptist University for Women, the Bapist Orphanage are the legitimate outcome of State Mission work.

Yet we are safe in saying, at least one-third of the adult population of our State are not Christians. The commission of our Lord makes it binding upon us to give these the Gospel. But this is not all. Heretofore the stream of foreign immigration has gone into the States north and west. But now the tide is turning southward. The vast resources of North Carolina and the rapid development of the same means that she will receive her full share of the comers. For the sake of these people themselves, for our own sake, for the sake of Christ, we must give them the Gospel.

Again the Home Mission Board is saying to North Carolina, "Enlarge—give us $12,000." The Foreign Mission Board is saying to North Carolina, "Enlarge—give us $20,000." To do this we must enlarge our State work. Enlargement at home means enlargement all along the line. It is not a question as to whether we ought to enlarge our State Mission work, or as to whether we are able to do it, but a question of willingness on our part. The responsibility is upon us. May God help us to meet it.

J. M. BEATY,
For the Committee.

Upon motion to adopt the subject was discussed by Brethren Livingston Johnson, John E. Ray and J. M. Beaty. Pledges were taken and the report adopted.

Bro. R. T. Vann, President of the Baptist University for Women, was recognized and given fifteen minutes to speak of the College and its work.

Brother J. M. Broughton, Corresponding Messenger from the Raleigh Association being recognized, announced that he brought fraternal greetings from the mother Association.

Brother F. P. Hobgood, President of Oxford Seminary, and J. B. Carlyle, of Wake Forest College, were recognized and made short talks concerning their respective colleges and their work.

On motion of Bro. J. W. Suttle the present Executive Committee was re-elected.

The Association adjourned to meet at 2:30. Benediction by Bro. S. J. Betts.

FRIDAY AFTERNOON.

The Association re-assembled at 2:30. Prayer by Brother D. D. Edwards.

The regular order was taken up and Brother Archibald Johnson read the

REPORT ON THE ORPHANAGE.

What the Orphanage Is.

It is a country home for helpless and homeless children. Its plant is worth $150,000 which includes a bequest of $100,000 from the late Dennis Simmons. It owns a farm of 300 acres and runs a printing office, a wood shop, and a shoe shop. There are eight families and an additional cottage is in process of erection. A good graded school, a live church and Sunday school supply the mental and moral wants of the children. The cost of maintaining a child is $5.00 a month and this covers all the necessary expenses of the institution. At this time there is a distressing scourge of typhoid fever at the Orphanage. There have been upwards of 80 cases but only two have died.

What the Orphanage Does.

It gives our people a larger faith in God. Who can think of its twenty years of marvellous history and not see the hand of a loving Father gently guiding it through all the way?

It calls out our sympathy and tenderness and develops the noblest qualities of our nature.   It has sweetened and toned all our denominational life.

It exhibits the very spirit of Christ and draws us close to Him.

It offers a glorious opportunity to develop our people in the grace of giving.

C. W. CARTER,

A. JOHNSON,

J. M. BAUCOM,

Committee.

After the report had been discussed by Brethren C. W. Carter and Archibald Johnson pledges were taken and report adopted.

On motion of Bro. Blanchard it was ordered that where a church is not represented its pledges for the several objects be put down the same amount as the previous year.

Brother R. W. Horrell in the absence of Brother Pippin read the

REPORT ON WOMAN'S WORK.

Committee on woman's work, desire to submit the following report: The following amounts have been raised for the various objects of the Convention:

State Missions ....$ 93 24

Home Missions 137 54

Foreign Missions 94 00

Total ....$ 324 78

Number of Societies in the Association six. These societies have set the mark for 1905 at $500.

We are glad that the time has come, when the work of our good women is reported in the minutes of our Associations. The Christian women of the early church were very numerous, and the names of a great many of them are honorably mentioned in the New Testament. Some of them are known simply by their heroic deeds of love and fidelity, which entitle them to an everlasting remembrance wherever the gospel is preached. We cannot forget the "Woman of Samaria,' who led the way for "the missionary work among the Samaritans, as the herald of Christ the Messiah; and the woman who touched the hem ot nis garment; and the exemplary Christian giver, the widow of the two mites; the Syrophoenician woman; the lamenting women on their way to Calvary, and the prayerful women of the upper chamber in Jerusalem.   This incomplete list shows that the Christian woman exerted a powerful influence in the Church of the New Testament, and we have no account that she ever betrayed, denied, or doubted her Lord and Savior.

We would recommend that woman develop all her talents and assert her own individuality in her own gentle way. We appreciate the grand work of woman in the Home and Foreign Missions. We rejoice to see her self-sacrificing love and devotion in the various organizations of church services. Her living personality and influence is specially felt in the religious training of the young. Woman is always the queen of the home. In this little kingdom she reigns supreme; and in this sphere she can rule the world through her powerful influence over the children. Here she can by personal contact with them sow the seed of spiritual truths in their young hearts that will spring up into everlasting life; and the children soon respond to the charming influence of Christian women. If all the women of our churches would concentrate their energies, like Hannah, to train the young at home and in the sanctuary, how many more Samuels and less prodigal sons there would be in the world. The Christian women of to-day are specially called of God to sympathize with their less fortunate sisters, to reclaim the fallen, to strengthen and encourage the weak, to nurse the sick, to clothe the naked, and to bring them all into the kingdom. The best qualification for such service is a woman's heart filled with the love of Christ for the dying world. Let our Christian women employ all their talents, use to the full extent all her opportunities, looking always unto Jesus for strength, encouragement, and inspiration, who will reward each one according to her work.

A. A. PIPPIN,
W. M. EASON,
E. CREECH,
Committee.

Talks were made by Brethren R. W. Horrell and J. B. Carlyle and the report adopted.

The brethren from Pauline asked for help in building their new house of worship and a collection amounting to $10.00 was taken.

Brother F. P. Hobgood was given a few minutes to speak of his school.

The following committee to nominate delegates to Southern Baptist Convention and Baptist State Convention was announced: G. A. Smith, J. A. Estridge and J. H. Boon.

Brother J. L. Hall was granted leave of absence.

Adjournment. Benediction by Brother Livingston Johnson.

FRIDAY NIGHT.

Association opened by singing hymn No. 567. Prayer by Bro. B. W. Spilman.

Brother Worley Creech conducted the devotional exercises, reading some verses from the third chapter of Matthew. Prayer by Brethren J. T. Holt and Livingston Johnson.

The regular order was taken up and Brother Livingston Johnson read the

REPORT ON FOREIGN MISSIONS.

Just at this time in our history the subject of Foreign Missions is securing the attention of the world as never before. Several things are conspiring to bring Foreign Missions prominently before the Christian world.

1   God is preparing the world to receive the gospel. The war with Cuba changed the map of the world. While that war was waged primarily to give Cuba its freedom it was very much more far reaching in its results than that. It broke the Iron grasp of Spain, the great standard of Romanism. Whatever may be our opinions about the wisdom of our government's policy in the Philippines, the Christian people must see in it the overruling power of God in opening a door to that dark corner of the earth.

We can but believe that God is guiding affairs in the far East for His glory and the advancement of His kingdom. Should Japan be victorious in the struggle with Russia, it will mean a religious freedom in the Orient never before enjoyed. These things mean the opening of doors of opportunity.

2.   The churches at home are interested in Foreign Missions as perhaps they have never been before. The contributions are being enlarged, and earnest prayers are being offered for world wide evangelization. Young

men and women are asking to be sent as Missionaries. The last session of the Southern Baptist Convention was made notable by the discussion of Foreign Missions. At the close of the discussion scores of young men expressed a desire to go to the foreign field. A resolution was passed instructing the Board to send out fifty new missionaries this year. Twenty-three have already been sent and others have been approved by the Board. The Board expects to send out the full number by the next meeting of the Southern Baptist Convention.

3. The cause is making gratifying progress in foreign lands. Prejudice is giving way, and the Missionary is receiving a welcome never before accorded him. Our missionaries reported a larger number of conversions last year than in any previous year. Surely God is commanding us in thunder tones to go forward.

L. JOHNSON,
For the Committee.

Upon motion to adopt the report was discussed by Brethren L. Johnson and C. W. Blanchard. Pledges were taken and the report adopted.

Brother J. B. Carlyle was given fifteen minutes to tell of the work of Wake Forest College.

Adjourned to meet to-morrow morning at 9:30.

Benediction by Brother S. F. Conrad.

SATURDAY MORNING.

The Association met at 10 o'clock. Devotional exercises were conducted by Brother R. W. Horrell, reading Romans 8. Prayer by Brother Hight C. Moore.

Roll called and new members enrolled.

Minutes of yesterday read and approved.

Brother Hight C. Moore, Field Secretary of Sunday Schools, Baptist State Convention, was recognized and welcomed.

Under the head of Miscellaneous matters remarks were made by Brethren Joseph W. Wood, J. W. Suttle, W. B. Joyner, C. W. Blanchard and R. W. Horrell.

Brother Joseph W. Wood was granted leave of absence.

On motion of Brother J. W. Suttle, Brother C. W. Blanchard was re-elected a member of State Board of Missions.

On motion of C. W. Blanchard the churches of the Johnston county Association were requested to send all their contributions for State Missions, and that object only, to the Treasurer of the Association, C. W. Richardson, Selma, N. C., that they may be at once used in paying local missionaries.

Brother C. T. Tew, of the Eastern Association and E. L. Middleton, Moderator of the Raleigh Association, were recognized and welcomed.

Brother J. P. Canaday read the

REPORT ON EDUCATION.

Civilization is measured by intelligence; progress by improved educational facilities. No man can come into recognition of the possibilities of life who fails to equip himself with the very best mental, moral and physical development. This is an age of progress; it is an age of crises. There are specific demands for the best in man from God, State, and Nation.

Our public school system is a part of our civilization. By means of it only can the whole people be reached and uplifted. We recognize with pride that the recent educational awakening in North Carolina has resulted in a four months term of public school in all the districts, in better school buildings, in increased attendance, in a uniform system of better and cheaper books, and in the establishment of rural libraries. Many country districts have voted special tax to increase the term so that with rural mail deliveries these schools become quite the equal of the city graded schools.

We note with gratitude the growth of the high schools, academies and colleges of the State in all lines of educational life, and especially our denominational schools. The only true education is Christian education. It purifies the social life of the individual and the State. It holds the balances of our fast growing civilization at equipoise by higher spiritual life. With upwards of thirty denominational academies as preparatory and with Wake Forest for the higher training of the young men, and the Female University, and the female colleges, Oxford Female Seminary, Chowan Baptist Female Institute for the higher training of the young women the Baptist cause promises much for the future of North Carolina.

The fifty young men at Wake Forest preparing for the ministry should be supported willingly and promptly by our denomination.

Your committee recommends the establishment of a denominational academy in Johnston county.

Respectfully submitted,
J. P. CANADAY.

The report was discussed by Brethren J. P. Canaday, C. W. Blanchard and E. L. Middleton. Pledges were taken and the report adopted.

Association adjourned. Benediction by Bro. H. C. Moore.

SATURDAY AFTERNOON.

Association re-assembled at the appointed hour. Prayer by Bro. C. T. Tew.

The Committee on delegates to the Southern Baptist Convention and Baptist State Convention reported the following:

Delegate to the Southern Baptist Convention—J. W. Suttle, of Smithfield.

Delegates to Baptist State Convention—R. W. Horrell, Selma; A. A. Pippin, Wakefield, and Hezekiah Pool, Mount Moriah.

Brother J. W. Suttle read the following

REPORT ON PERIODICALS.

At no time in the history of our denomination has the necessity for the better training and greater development of our people been so keenly felt as now. Realizing that the religious press is one of the greatest factors in the accomplishment of this end, we would urge that every Baptist family in the bounds of our Association take and read as much religious literature as possible.

The Biblical Recorder, the organ of our Convention, has stood the test of more than seventy years as the exponent of our Baptist faith and practice in North Carolina. This paper has always been sound as to the distinctive principles of our denomination and as to the best methods of our work. We would urge every family of our Association to take and read the Recorder.

The North Carolina Baptist has, and is doing a great work in our State. We can heartily recommend this paper to all, and urge that all who can, take it. Our people should also take the Foreign Mission Journal and Our Home Field as the organs of our Foreign and Home Mission Boards.

Charity and Children, our great Orphanage paper, ought to be in every home.

As to Sunday School literature we recommend, that our churches use our Convention series, published at Nashville, Tenn.

We desire also to call the attention of the Association to The Church Messenger. We have published this little paper in the interest of the work of our Association, for nearly one year, the paper has not had the support of the churches we had hoped for and expected. Unless more of our people become interested in the paper the publication will have to be discontinued. We recommend that the Association take some action in regard to the paper at this sesion.

J. W. SUTTLE,
For Committee.

On motion to adopt Brethren J. W. Suttle, C. W. Blanchard, C W. Carter, F. T. Booker and T. J. Lassiter took part in the discussion. Report adopted.

Bro. F. T. Booker made a motion that a committee of three be appointed to consider what the Association should do in regard to The Church Messenger. Carried.

The following committee was appointed: F. T. Booker, C. W. Carter and J. H. Boon.

This committee submitted the following report:

We, your Committee, recommend that each Pastor in the Association appoint some live young member, boy or girl in each of his churches to take subscriptions for The Church Messenger, and that they shall call attention to the paper from time to time. Also, we recommend that at the meeting of the Association, any deficit that may appear shall be considered a part of the missionary expense of the Association and treated as such.

F. T. BOOKER,
J. H. BOON,
C. W. CARTER,
Committee.

Report adopted.

Brother C. W. Blanchard submitted a few remarks on the history of the Association .

Brother N. R. Pool read the

SUNDAY SCHOOL REPORT.

The most potent factor in the evangelization of the world to-day, and the best medium through which to impart religious and moral instruction is the Sunday School.

This proposition is abundantly proven and sufficiently demonstrated by the fact that more than seventy-five per cent of the accessions to our churches are directly from the Sunday schools, as a result of the faithful labors of the earnest and consecrated men and women who are striving to ooey the Word. Deut. 31:12, 13. "Gather the peòple together, men and ŵomen, and children, and thy stranger that is within thy gates that they may hear, and that they may learn, and fear the Lord your God and observe to do all the words of this law."

, "And that their children, which have not known anything, may hear, and learn to fear the Lord your God, as long as ye live in the land whither ye go over Jordan to possess it."

We have not possessed the whole land yet, so let us as faithful followers of the Master, not slacken the pace, but redouble our efforts, until there shall be a live, aggressive and enthusiastic Sunday-school in every church in this Association and even reach out into the destitute sections and organize schools convenient for the people, that they may learn the way of life through the study of His Word.

Therefore your committee suggest that you consider the advisability of employing a competent Sunday school missionary within the bounds of your Association. N. R. POOL,
W. B. JOYNER,
Y. L. BLACKMAN.

The report was discussed by Brethren Hight C. Moore and N. R. Pool and then adopted.

The following resolution, offered by Brother C. W. Blanchard, was adopted:

Resolved, That we recommend that each Sunday school in the Johnston County Association, take at least one collection during the year for the support of the Sunday School work in North Carolina, and that the same be forwarded to the Treasurer of the State Convention for such purpose.

Brother J. T. Holt read the Finance Committee's report which was accepted.

Committee on Place, Time and Preachers report as follows:

Place—Benson Baptist Church .
Time—Thursday after the First Sunday in November, 1905.
Preachers—Introductory Sermon, C. W. Blanchard. Alternate, R. W. Horrell.

Adjournment. Benediction by Brother Claude E. Gower.

SATURDAY NIGHT.

The Association met at 7:30. Devotional exercises by Brother C. T. Tew, who read Romans 12. Prayer by Brethren Townsend and Blanchard.

Bro. J. Willis, for the committee, read the

REPORT ON TEMPERANCE.

From our experience in the past, we are encouraged in the fight against intemperance. We have found that by constant endeavor we can slay the lion and the bear in the shape of bar-rooms and dispensaries from strength· we have gained by our efforts. We are now willing, and will not be satisfied until we have, by Divine help, slain the great giant of intemperance in every form, and recommend that we not only take a stand against it, but meet the evil and drive it from us. WORLEY CREECH,
For Committee.

On motion to accept the report was discussed by Brethren Worley Creech and C. W. Carter. Adopted.

Brother C. W. Blanchard offered the following resolution:

Resolved 1st, That we believe the Dispensaries of Johnston County have existed as long as we can expect them to serve us as agents of temperance reform.

2nd, That we believe the time has come when every true citizen of the county should use his strongest influence to rid the county of all legalized manufacture and sale of strong drink in every form.

3rd, That we do herein solemnly memorialize the representatives of this county, to the next General Assembly, with the cry of the consciences of three thousand members of the Baptist churches in said County, to use their best influence in the coming session to give us entire relief from the existence of this needless curse in our county.

The resolution was discussed by Brethren C. W. Blanchard, F. T. Booker and C. W. Carter. It was then unanimously adopted by a rising vote.

Upon motion of Brother C. W. Blanchard the Clerk was instructed to have 1,000 copies of the minutes printed and distributed among the churches as per amount of funds contributed for minutes and Clerk, and that he be allowed ten dollars for his services.

Upon motion of Brother F. T. Booker the thanks of the Association was extended to the members of the Clayton church and the people of Clayton and the community in general for their generous hospitality and kindness.

The following announcement was made for Sunday morning:

Sunday School mass meeting beginning at 9:30.

Ten Minutes Talks led by Brethren B. Townsend, C. T. Tew and Worley Creech and Hight C. Moore.

11:30 A. M. Sermon by Bro. Hight C. Moore.

The regular business of the Association being ended Brother Worley Creech sang two solos, after which the congregation sang, "Praise God From Whom All Blessings Flow." Benediction by Brother Hight C. Moore.

Sunday morning was rainy and disagreeable and no Sunday School Mass Meeting was held. Brother Hight C. Moore preached. Subject "Christ's Crucifixion."

TREASURER'S REPORT.

Receipts.

Minute fund at Selma last year.................................$ 15 35
From Churches prior to meeting of Association..................   273 67
From Individuals 97 50
From Bethany Union Meeting....................................   20 65
From R. W. Horrell..   2 42
From Princeton Church...   3 24
Borrowed from Bank..   500 00
From Finance Committee at Clayton.............................   484 87
From Livingston Johnston, Corresponding Secretary.............   300 00

    Total $1,697 70

Disbursements.

Paid to T. J. Lassiter ....$ 15 35
Paid Interest to Bank...   17 50
Paid R. W. Horrell..   247 24
Paid J. W. Suttle...   15 00
Paid A. A. Pippin...   50 00
Paid J. D. Bowen...   249 00
Paid Bank 500 00

    Total amount paid out....................................$1,094 09
Balance on hand ....$ 603 61

WOMAN'S MEETING.

The Woman's Missionary Societies of the Johnston County Association assembled in the Methodist church at Clayton Thursday afternoon at 2 o'clock, presided over by the Vice-President, Mrs. Ashley Horne. Mrs. Shore, of the Clayton Society, in a few well-chosen words, welcomed the delegates and visitors to the meeting.

Reports were received from five Societies. The financial report shows the amount received for the three objects, State, Home and Foreign Missions, $332.77.

Our aim for next year is five hundred dollars.

We were very much encouraged with the work of the Societies, as this was the first meeting of the new Association.

Miss Heck was with us, and was greeted by a house filled with interested women to hear what this consecrated woman had to say. It was indeed an inspiration to have Miss Heck with us in our meeting.

Altogether we feel hopeful and like pressing forward to more and better work for our Master's cause.

Mrs. W. M. PETTWAY,

Secretary.

CHURCH PLEDGES FOR 1905.

CHURCHES.	State Missions.	Home Missions.	Foreign Missions.	Orph'n'ge	Minister'l Educat'n.	Minister'l Relief.	Total.
Antioch	$15 00	$1 50	$1 50	$2 50	$1 50	$2 00	$24 00
Baptist Centre.....	20 00	3 00	2 50	5 00	1 00	1 50	33 00
Benson....	60 00	7 50	15 00	12 50	5 00	8 00	103 00
Bethany..........	6 00	2 00	1 25	2 25	1 25	1 25	14 00
Bethesda..........	25 00	5 00	6 00	15 00	2 00	3 00	56 00
Bethel	2 00	1 00	50	1 00	1 00	1 00	6 50
Blackman's Grove.	15 00	3 00	5 50	6 00	2 75	2 00	34 25
Carter's Chapel....	10 00	1 50	1 25	2 00	1 00	2 00	17 75
Clayton..........	150 00	40 00	125 00	60 00	25 00	12 50	412 50
Clyde's Chapel.....	6 00	2 50	3 00	3 50	2 00	2 00	19 00
Corinth	7 50	2 50	3 00	3 00	1 00	2 00	19 00
Four Oaks..	10 00	3 00	2 50	2 00	1 25	1 25	20 00
Hood's Grove	7 00	1 25	2 00	1 00	2 00	1 50	14 75
Lee's Chapel......	30 00	5 00	3 00	2 00	1 50	3 00	44 50
Live Oak......... ..	4 00	1 00	1 00	2 00	1 00	2 00	11 00
Micro....	2 00	50	50	1 00	50	1 00	5 50
Mount Moriah.. .	50 00	12 00	100 00	20 00	5 00	4 00	191 00
Nobles' Chapel.....	20 00	2 00	2 00	2 00	2 00	2 00	30 00
New Bethel	15 00	2 50	1 25	2 50	2 50	1 00	24 75
Oliver's Grove.....	6 00	1 00	1 00	1 00	50	50	10 00
Parish Memorial ..	12 50	1 00	1 00	1 00	1 00	2 00	18 50
Pauline	1 00	1 00	1 00	1 00	50	1 00	5 50
Pine Level.......	5 00	1 00	1 00	1 00	1 00	1 00	10 00
Pisgah	12 50	1 00	1 50	2 00	1 00	1 25	19 25
Princeton	15 00	2 00	5 00	2 00	2 00	2 50	28 50
Sardis............	5 00	1 00	1 00	1 00	1 00	1 00	10 00
Selma....	100 00	7 50	30 00	30 00	10 00	10 00	187 50
Shiloh.......	25 00	3 00	2 50	10 00	2 00	2 00	44 50
Smithfield	85 00	25 00	50 00	32 50	10 00	15 00	217 50
Thanksgiving......	15 00	2 00	5 00	3 00	1 00	2 00	28 00
Trinity...........	7 50	2 50	3 25	2 50	1 00	1 00	17 75
White Oak	15 00	3 00	1 00	5 00	1 50	2 00	27 50
Wilson's Mills......	10 00	3 00	5 00	6 00	3 00	4 00	31 00
Total....	769 00	150 75	385 00	243 25	94 75	93 25	1736 00

NOTE.—Clayton Junior Union pledged $25.00 for Foreign Missions; Shiloh Sunday School $2.00 for Orphanage; Corinth Sunday School $1.00 for Orphanage.

CHURCH STATISTICS.

CHURCHES.	PASTORS.	CLERKS AND ADDRESSES.	Preaching Sunday.	Value of Church Property.	Seating Capacity.	Baptisms.	Received by Letter.	Restored.	Lost by Letter.	Excluded.	Died.	Number of Males.	Number of Females.	Total Membership.
...th	Worley Creech	R. R. Creech, Selma, R.F.D.2	2 & 3	$400 00	500	18		4	11	1	3	48	110	158
Baptist Centre	C. W. Blanchard	Allen G. Rogers, Clayton	4	500 00	400		2		4		1	23	44	67
Bethany	Worley Creech	Kirkman Creech, Kenly	4	600 00	600	3	3		8	3		21	40	61
Betheeda	J. W. Suttle	J. E. Smith, Clayton	2	500 00	400	2			6		2	62	104	166
Benson	J. W. Suttle	E. L. Hall, Benson	4	1250 00	300	9	3		3			46	86	132
Bethel	R. W. Herrell	J. A. Gulley, Kenly, R.F.D.3	3			1	4	2		1		6	7	13
Blackman's ...	J. W. Suttle	E. B. Hayes, Four Oaks, R.F.D.2	1 & 3	600 00	300	7	10	4	6	2	2	20	36	56
Carter's Chapel	R. W. Horrell	W. B. Wall, Micro	2	350 00	300	8	1		3	2	1	21	41	62
Clayton	C. W. Blanchard	M. G. Gulley, Clayton	4	5000 00	600	6		10	3			99	160	259
...e's Chapel	A. A. Pippin	C. J. ... Wendell	4	650 00		15	3	1	2			57	65	122
Corinth	A. A. Pippin	Oscar Oneal, Archer	3	400 00	250	10	4		3	3		33	51	84
Four Oaks	J. D. Bowen	J. Wm. Langdon, Four Oaks	4	750 00	200		12					9	19	28
Hood's Grove	J. W. Suttle	Jos. W. Wood, Benson, R.F.D.2	3	400 00	300	4	8	2	2	1		10	17	27
Lee's Chapel	A. A. Pippin	W. I. Green, Wakefield, R.F.D.2	4	500 00	400	22	2	4	10		1	110	154	264
Live Oak	Worley Creech	K. Broadwell, Selma	3	300 00	250		9		7		4	9	18	27
Micro	R. W. Horrell	W. E. Smith, Micro	1	800 00	300	2						72	88	155
Mount Moriah	S. J. Betts	M. T. Wilder, Clayton	4	600 00	300	5	1	2	4	4	3	26	84	60
Nobles Chapel	R. W. Horrell	J. R. ..., Taylor	4	750 00	400	6			1	3	2	43	45	88
New Bethel	C. T. Tew	N. B. Bryan, Garner	1	150 00	400	1	1	1		2		10	8	18
Oliver's Grove	J. D. Bowen	H. Johnson, Four Oaks	4	300 00	250	1		1	2	1	1	17	21	38
Parish Memorial	R. W. Horrell	J. D. Creech, Selma, R.F.D.4	4				1		2	1		7	13	20
Pauline	J. D. Bowen	N. W. Smith, Four Oaks, R.F.D.1	3	200 00	100	2		2	1			7	17	24
Pine ...	J. D. Bowen	Ida Woodard, Pine Level		1000 00	500		4		1			22	25	47
Pisgah	R. W. Horrell	...us Jones, Smithfield, R.F.D.1	3	180 00	800	2		2	1	2	1	23	44	67
Princeton	J. D. Bowen	W. I. Pearce, Princeton	3	300 00	250	6			3		2	4	11	15
Sardis	C. W. Blanchard	N. B. Stevens, Smithfield, R.F.D.2	2 & 4	2000 00	400	5	2				1	53	84	187
Selma	B. Townsend	H. W. Hood, Selma		3500 00	700	12	8		3	2	2	85	88	178
Shiloh	J. W. Suttle	C. H. Holland, Garner, R.F.D	1 & 3	800 00	300	16	8	1				58	64	177
Smithfield	R. W. Horrell	J. M. Beaty, Smithfield	1	800 00				1	3	7	1	25	27	52
Thanksgiving	J. D. Bowen	W. G. Earp, Selma, R.F.D.1	2	300 00	300		6	1	3	3		11	16	27
Trinity	A. A. Pippin	J. S. Lawhon, Benson, R.F.D.2	2	450 00	800	14		2	4	6	2	34	65	89
White Oak	R. W. Horrell	J. I. ..., Selma, R.F.D.1	2	700 00	250	1	6					19	26	45
Wilson's Mills		Miss Arrah Parrish, Wilson's Mills												
Totals				24,450 00		179	100	38	98	45	27	1085	1573	2619

20

SUNDAY SCHOOL STATISTICS.

CHURCHES.	SUPERINTENDENTS AND ADDRESSES.	Officers and Teachers	Scholars	Total	Average Attendance	Qur'rlies and Papers	Volumes in Library	Months kept open	Expenses	No. of Schools	No. Baptisms from School
Antioch	W. H. Maden, Archer, R F D. 1	6	60	66	30	40		12	$5 00	1	
Baptist Centre	J. C. Hardee, Clayton	5	50	55	35	67	50	12	10 00	1	
Benson	G. W. Cavenaugh, Benson	7	123	130		125	100	12	25 00	1	5
Bethel												
Bethany	Kirkman Creech, Kenly	5	61	66	35	50		6	5 00	1	
Bethesda	J. J. Wallace, Wilson's Mills	10	50	60	40	60	50	12	7 00	1	
Blackman's Grove	F. P. Wood, Four Oaks, R.F.D. 2	4	30	34		45		6	50	1	2
Carter's Chapel	J. I Blackman, Micro	7	61	68	42	50		9	4 47	1	6
Clayton	R. H. Gower, Clayton	21	225	246	150	303	176	12	99 27	1	4
Clyde's Chapel	J. W. B. Finch, Wendell	10	125	135	90	110	50		12 00	2	13
Corinth	J. A. Estridge. Archer, R.F.D. 1	6	60	66	30	60		9	4 05	1	6
Four Oaks	Mrs. Laura Creech, Four Oaks	6	46	52	25	48		12	1 60	1	
Hood's Grove												
Lee's Chapel	W. I Green, Wakefield. R.F.D. 2	5	67	72	30	75		9		1	16
Live Oak												
Micro												
Mount Moriah	J. F Pool, Clayton	11	110	121	58	131	275	12	48 14	1	3
New Bethel	James N. Bryan, Garner	6	34	40	35	40	50		5 00	1	2
Nobles' Chapel	J. R. Todd, Taylor	6	80	86	50	60		12		1	
Oliver's Grove												
Parish Memorial	J F Watson, Pine Level	8	40	48	30	120		6	4 00	1	1
Pauline												
Pine Level	William Eason, Pine Level	5	40	45	35	4		12		1	1
Pisgah	R. H. Higgins, Smithfield	6	20	26	18	24		12	12 00	1	
Princeton												
Sardis												
Selma	C. W. Richardson, Selma	7	127	134	90	150		12		1	2
Shiloh	F. T. Booker, Clayton, R.F.D. 1	8	65	73	40	73		12		1	1
Smithfield	J. M. Beaty, Smithfield	8	100	108	55	200	200	12	53 53	1	10
Thanksgiving	G. C. Earp, Selma, R.F.D. 1	6	53	59	45	58		12		1	14
Trinity	A. H. Lee, Benson, R.F.D. 2	4	16	20	10	64			92	1	
White Oak	W. A. Newton, Archer	6	81	87	60	64		12	26 94	1	9
Wilson's Mills	J. T. Holt, Wilson's Mills	5	35	40	30	38		12		1	
Totals		178	1759	1937	1063	1955	951		334 42	26	95

CHURCHES.	Number of Members.	Minutes and Clerk.	Pastor's Salary.	Building and Repairs.	Incid'nt'ls	The Poor.	Sunday School Missions.	State Missions.	Home Missions.	Foreign Missions.	Orph'n'ge.	Ministeri'l Educat'n.	Aged Ministers.	Other Objects.	Total.
...th	153	$0 90	$73 35		$3 50			$10 00	$1 48	$1 00	$2 65	$1 29	$1 25		$96 92
Baptist Centre	67	1 00	60 00		25 00			10 00	2 00	1 00	8 00	1 00	1 00		96 50
Benson	122	4 00	200 00	$40 00				35 00	21 20	10 00	12 00	2 00	2 00	$20 00	393 20
Bethany	71	75	30 00					5 00	1 50	1	3 55	1	1		53 80
Bethel	18							1 50							1 50
Bethesda	166	1 50	110 00		10 00			20 00	2 50	5 00	12 50	1 00	50	20 00	181 00
...s Grove	58	1 00	75 00		8 50			25 00	3 00	5 00	5 00	2 50	1 00		144 00
Carter's Chapel	28	90	28 65	2690 00	95 00	$5 00		9 29	3 00	2 00	2 00	3 50	3 80		58 81
Clayton	29	5 00	500 00					105	33 84	119	78 80	3 50	1 00	193 30	3926 51
...le's Chapel	122	1 00	60 00	2 00	1 79			5 00	2 50	2 00	3 00	1 45	1 00		89 51
Corinth	84	1 00	46 75		4 95			5 00	2 50	2 00	7 00	1 25	1 25		69 40
Four Oaks	25		30 60	275 00				5 00	3 00	2 00	3 00	1 00	1 00		75 90
Hood's Grove	25	75	30 00					25 00	2 50	2 00	8 00	1 00	2 50	12 75	324 25
Lee's Chapel	264	2 00	100 00					2 50	2 00	2 00	2 00	1 00	1 00	7 50	138 00
Live Oak	27	67	19 55				$0 36	70							28 72
M...ro		65									1				1 35
Mount ...h	155	1 50	120 00		18 95	4 09		26 11	10 75	25 84	29 66	7 26	3 00		299 30
New Bethel	83	1 00	75 00					17 50	3 45	1 25	16 60	1 00	1 50		122 30
Nobles' Chapel	63	1 00	40 00	200 00	10 00			1 00	1 00	1 00	1 00	1 00		3 15	265 00
O...s Grove	13	40	6 25					5 00	1 00	1 00	1 00	50	50		18 80
Parish Memorial	33	50	25 00					10 00	1 00	1 50	1 00	1 00	1 00		40 60
Pauline	20	60	13 90												15 90
Pine ...el	2	1 20	11 37					2 50	1 00	1 00	1 00	50			19 57
Pisgah	4	25	50 00	35 00				10 00	2 00	2 00	2 00	1 00	1 25		112 00
Princeton	6	1	21 94		5 00			10 00	2 00	2 00	12 00	1 00	1 00		45 94
Sardis	15	30	18 00					2 50	2 00	1 00	1 00	1 00	5 00		25 80
Selma	15	2 50	500 00		30 52	35 85		57 80	5 00	10 00	30 00	5 00	7 50	210 05	643 02
Shiloh	7	1 00	125 00		46 00	2 80		136 95	2 50	30 00	2 00	11 00	1 50		161 50
Smithfield	11	5 00	250 00	155 75	8 75		6 26	7 50	68 34	1 50	30 00	1 00	5 00		1046 23
Thanksgiving	55	1 70	3 00		8 85			15 00	1 50	2 50	2 00	1 00	1 00		31 20
Trinity	27	60	31 75	27 50				7 00	2 50	2 50	3 51	63	1 00	12 00	78 12
White Oak	95	1 00	26 25		10 00			10 00	2 00	1 00	6 00	6 00	1 00		94 33
Wilson's Mills	45	1 00	35 72					5 00	2 00	10 00			2 00		77 72
Totals	2605	39 68	2667 08	3415 25	27 31	47 74	6 62	596 85	185 06	250 09	268 27	59 88	50 05	478 75	7948 30

DIGEST OF CHURCH LETTERS.

The following amounts were pledged and paid by the churches of the Johnston County Association during the year just ended, November 10, 1904:

CHURCHES.	PLEDGED. 1904	PLEDGED. 1905	Contributed.	Below Pledge.	Above Pledge.	LOSS OR GAIN IN MEMBERSHIP Loss	LOSS OR GAIN IN MEMBERSHIP Gain	PLEDGED IN 1905 ABOVE PLEDGE OF 1904	PLEDGED IN 1905 ABOVE PLEDGE OF Less
Antioch	$16 50	$24 00	$17 02		$0 52		7	$7 50	
Baptist Centre	20 00	33 00	23 00		3 00	3		13 00	
Bethany	11 50	14 00	13 05		1 55	6		2 50	
Benson	66 00	103 00	79 20		13 20		8	36 00	
Bethesda	42 50	56 00	42 50			4		12 50	
*Bethel		6 50	1 50		1 50		13	6 50	
Blackman's Grove	42 00	34 25	47 00		5 00		1		$7 75
Carter's Chapel	11 00	17 75	16 29		5 29		7	6 75	
Clayton	306 00	437 50	512 24		206 24	2		131 50	
Clyde's Chapel	14 50	19 00	14 50				24	4 50	
Corinth	15 00	20 00	15 81		81		20	5 00	
Four Oaks	20 00	20 00	21 50		1 50		5		
Hood's Grove	11 00	14 75	11 00				3	3 75	
Lee's Chapel	34 00	44 50	36 00		2 00		18	10 50	
Live Oak	8 50	11 00	8 50			3		2 50	
*Micro		5 50	70		70		11	5 50	
Mount Moriah	78 00	191 06	106 62		28 62	11		113 00	
Nobles' Chapel	15 00	30 00	15 00				7	15 00	
New Bethel	23 25	24 75	41 80		18 05		4	1 50	
Oliver's Grove	9 00	10 00	9 00			4		1 00	
*Pauline		5 50	1 50		1 50		20	5 50	
Parish Memorial	15 00	18 50	15 00			2		3 50	
Pine Level	7 00	10 00	7 00				3	3 00	
Pisgah	16 75	19 25	15 00	$1 75		1		2 50	
Princeton	17 75	28 50	17 75				7	10 75	
Sardis	7 50	10 00	7 50				5	2 50	
Selma	105 00	187 50	112 80		7 80		3	82 50	
Shiloh	35 50	46 50	33 50	2 00				11 00	
Smithfield	148 50	217 50	308 05		159 55		17	69 00	
Thanksgiving	15 00	28 00	15 00				25	13 00	
Trinity	14 50	17 75	16 50		2 00	10		3 25	
White Oak	16 00	27 50	18 14		2 14		8	11 50	
Wilson's Mills	26 00	31 00	31 00		5 00		1	5 00	
Totals	1168 25	1764 00	1630 47	3 75	464 97	45	217	602 50	7 75

* New churches.

NOTE—Other pledges for State Missions 1903-1904, $158; other pledges for State Missions 1904-1905, $100 50. Two churches fell below their pledges in contributions $3.75. Eleven churches contributed just what they pledged. Twenty churches exceeded their pledges in contributions $164.97 One church pledged $7.75 less than a year ago. One church pledged the same as a year ago. Thirty-one churches advanced on their last year's pledges $602.50. Ten churches reported a loss of 45 members. Twenty-two churches reported a gain of 206 members. Seventeen churches report evergreen Sunday schools. Eight churches report Sunday schools for part of the year. 　　　　　　　C. W. BLANCHARD,
　　　　　　　　　　　　　　　　　　for Committee

Note by Clerk—In table of pledges for 1904, Blackman's Grove church is put down $15.00 for the Orphanage. This was a misprint, and should have been $5.00. Hence this church appears to have pledged less than last year, where it really pledged $2.25 more.

CONTRIBUTIONS FROM SOCIETIES AND INDIVIDUALS.

Churches and Societies.	Orphanage.	Home Missions.	State Missions.	Foregn Missons.	Aged Ministers.	Ministerial Education.	Box to Missionary.	Building and Repairng.	Colleges and Schools.	The Poor.	Total.
Antioch Sunday School	$0 65	$......	$......	$......	$.....	$.....	$.....	$......	$......	$.....	$ 0 65
Benson W. M. Society		13 20									13 20
Clayton W. M. Society	18 80	12 84	37 73	60 83	3 80	3 50	70 00				207 50
Clayton Y. L. M. Society								104 00			104 00
Clayton Ladies' Aid Society								188 80			188 80
Clayton Sunbeams				25 00				15 05			40 05
Clayton Church									98 30		98 30
Four Oaks Sunday School	5 00										5 00
Mt. Moriah Sunday School			4 00								4 00
Selma Sunbeams			2 80								2 80
Smithfield W. M. Society	3 00	12 12	24 70	10 00			36 48		3 00	15 00	104 30
Smithfield Sunday School	4 40	7 04	2 25	3 40		2 21					21 30
Smithfield Junior Union	2 37		2 00								4 87
Smithfield, personal c'ntr'b'n			78 50						25 00		103 50
Smithfield Church									15 00		15 00
Totals	34 22	45 20	171 98	99 23	3 80	5 71	106 48	257 35	161 30	15 00	849 27

ADDITIONAL PLEDGES FOR STATE MISSIONS,

BY SUNDAY SCHOOLS, SOCIETIES AND INDIVIDUALS.

Baptist Centre Sunday School	$2 00	White Oak Sunday School	5 00
Benson Sunday School	5 00	J. M. Beaty, Smithfield	85 00
Clayton Sunday School	5 00	L. Johnson, Raleigh	5 00
Clayton Junior Union	5 00	R. W. Horrell, Selma	5 00
Clayton Y. L. M. Society	5 00	F. P. Wood, Four Oaks	10 00
Clayton Baracca Class	10 00	W. G. Hall, Roxboro	2 50
Clayton Philathea Class	10 00	A. J. Barbour, Clayton	10 00
Clyde's Chapel Sunday School	1 00	Mrs. G. M. Phillips, Smithfield	1 00
Corinth Sunday School	1 00	C. W. Carter, Clayton	5 00
Mount Moriah Sunday School	5 00	A Friend, paid	2 00
Selma Sunday School	5 00	G. H. Broughton, Selma, paid	5 00
Selma Sunbeams	5 00	R R Creech, Selma. R. F. D. 2. paid	5 00
Selma Baracca Class	5 00	T. J. Lassiter, Smithfield, paid	5 00
Selma Philathea Class	5 00	J. W. Jones, Smithfield, paid	5 00
Mrs. R. B. C. Bible Class Selma S. S.	5 00		
Shiloh Sunday School	1 00	Total	245 00
Smithfield W. M. Society	12 00	Amount pledged by churches	769 00
Smithfield B. Y. P. U.	5 00		
Thanksgiving Sunday School	2 50	Total amount	1014 00

CONSTITUTION OF THE JOHNSTON COUNTY BAPTIST ASSOCIATION.

1. The Association shall be known as the Johnston County Baptist Association.

2. Its object shall be to extend the privileges of the Gospel and liberal culture to all the people within its bounds, and by hearty co-operation with the Baptist State Convention, to help offer these privileges to all mankind in and out of our bounds, by the cordial co-operation of all the churches constituting this body.

3. It shall be composed of the pastors in active service in the Association and such delegates as shall be annually elected by the churches connected with it, each church being entitled to three delegates unless the membership shall exceed fifty, and then an additional delegate for every twenty-five members, provided no church shall have more than eight delegates.

4. The New Hampshire Declaration of Faith snail be the summary of Divine Truth for determining questions of faith and order in this body, and the churches desiring membership in it must commit themselves to the substance of it, together with the covenant therewith submitted, and this Constitution.

5. This Associaion shall not have power to annul the discipline or exercise authority over any church connected with it, but it may advise with and sever its connection with any church that neglects to preserve Gospel order, or that treats with contempt the objects or advice of the Association.

6. Each church shall send to the annual meetings of the Association a letter (the blanks to be furnished by the Clerk of the Association), carefully filled as per blank suggestions, stating the full work of the church for the year ending with the close of the month previous to the one in which the Association is held.

7. The Association shall foster State Missions, Home Missions, Foreign Missions, Christian Education, the Aged Ministers' Relief Board, the Thomasville Orphanage and the Sunday-school Board, and each church shall be requested to contribute to the support of these objects annually.

8. Missions and education shall have precedence in their claims upon the consideration of this body in its regular sessions.

9. Whenever a church shall fail to be represented by delegates or letter at the annual sessions of the Association or shall fail to contribute to the objects fostered by the Association, inquiry shall be made for the cause, and efforts shall be made to induce such church to do its duty, and the effort shall be continued till the church is recovered or dropped from the roll.

10. The officers of the Association shall be a Moderator, a Vice-Moderator, a Clerk, a Historian and a Treasurer, elected annually by ballot from among its members, to serve until their successors shall have been elected, and to perform the duties usual to such officers, namely, the Moderator in presiding over the meetings, or the Vice-Moderator in his absence; the Clerk in recording and preserving minutes and other papers belonging to the body; the Treasurer in receiving and disbursing funds belonging to or entrusted to the body according to its will; the Historian in keeping a continuous record of the work and progress of the entire Association and making an annual report of same to each of its sessions.

11. The Association shall appoint annually an Executive Committee of five (5) from its members, who shall be entrusted with the prosecution of Missions in the Association, and any other work for the interest of the Master's kingdom which may be referred to them. This committee shall, as far as possible, co-operate with the State Mission Board in supplying the destitution in our territory, and between the meetings of the Association take such actions as may seem to them advisable for the advancement of its interest. The committee shall present to the Association at its annual meeting a report of its proceedings, with the names of the Missionaries supported on the field, time of service, and details of their work, together with such

recommendations as in the judgment of the committee the Association should follow in planning its subsequent work.

12. The annual sessions of the Association shall begin on Thursday after the first Lord's day in November at such place as may be chosen, and an Introductory Sermon shall be delivered on the first day of the session. Representatives from a majority of the churches constituting the Association shall be a quorum.

13. This Constitution may be amended at any annual session by a two-third's vote of all the members present.

14. Provision shall be made at each annual Association for a session of the Woman's Central Committee and all other necessary encouragement offered for the enlargement of the organized work of the Woman's Missionary Societies in the local churches. The proceedings of the Woman's Central Committee shall be recorded as a part of the Minutes of the Association.

BY-LAWS.

1. The daily sessions of the Association shall be opened and closed with prayer.

2. Delegates shall be recognized by letters from their churches designating them as such.

3. The Moderator shall recognize corresponding messengers or the delegates of newly-received churches by extending to them his right hand.

4. The report of the Executive Board and the Missionary work of the Association shall take precedence of all other business during the morning session of the second day of the annual session.

5. The Clerk shall record and read the proceedings when called for, superintend the publication and distribution of the Minutes, preserve a file of them, and have it present at each annual session, and deliver to his successor all papers belonging to the body.

6. Members desiring to speak shall first rise and address the Moderator; shall use the term "brother" in speaking to each other; shall not speak on the same subject more than twice without permission, and shall observe the courtesy that becomes Christians.

7. Members shall not absent themselves from the session without permission.

8. The roll of members shall be called at least once and absentees marked.

9. Corresponding messengers and visiting brethren shall be invited to seats, with privilege of speaking, but not of voting.

10. A copy of the minutes shall be sent to the Secretary of the State Mission Board; the Secretary of the Southern Baptist Convention; the American Baptist Publication Society, 1420 Chestnut Street, Philadelphia; the Sunday-School Board of the Southern Baptist Convention and the Thomasville Orphanage.

11. All questions of order not herein provided shall be decided by Kerfoot's Parliamentary Law.

MINUTES

of the

THIRD SESSION

of the

JOHNSTON COUNTY

BAPTIST ASSOCIATION

held with the

BENSON BAPTIST CHURCH,

BENSON, N. C.,

November 9, 10, 11 and 12, 1905.

The next Session will be held with Clyde's Chapel Baptist Church, beginning Thursday after the first Sunday in November, 1906.

To Preach Introductory Sermon, ... D. F. PUTNAM.
Alternate, ... R. W. HORRELL.

GOLDSBORO:
NASH BROS., PRINTERS AND BINDERS,
1905.

MINUTES

of the

THIRD SESSION

of the

JOHNSTON COUNTY

BAPTIST ASSOCIATION

held with the

BENSON BAPTIST CHURCH,

BENSON, N. C.,

November 9, 10, 11 and 12, 1905.

The next Session will be held with Clyde's Chapel Baptist Church, beginning Thursday after the first Sunday in November, 1906.

To Preach Introductory Sermon, ... D. F. PUTNAM.
Alternate, ... R. W. HORRELL.

GOLDSBORO:
NASH BROS., PRINTERS AND BINDERS,
1905.

OFFICERS.

Moderator—R. H. Gower....................................Clayton, N.
Vice-Moderator—J. P. Canaday............................Benson, N.
Clerk—T. J. Lassiter.....................................Smithfield, N.
Treasurer—C. W. Richardson............................Selma, N. C.
Auditor—J. D. Underwood.............................Smithfield, N. C.

EXECUTIVE COMMITTEE.

J. M. Beaty, Chairman..................................Smithfield, N. C.
M. C. Winston, Secretary..................................Selma, N. C.
Joseph F. Pool,...Auburn, N. C.
J. H. Boon...Benson, N. C.
J. T. Holt...Wilson's Mills, N. C.

STANDING COMMITTEES FOR 1905.

State Missions.........................C. W. Blanchard.
Home Missions.........................D. F. Putnam.
Foreign Missions............................J. W. Suttle.
Orphanage...................................B. G. Early.
Education.................................R. A. Merritt.
Periodicals.............................T. J. Lassiter.
Ministerial Relief.........................A. A. Pippin.
Sunday Schools..........................R. W. Horrell.
Woman's Work.............................E. L. Hall.
Temperance...........................Worley Creech.

MINISTERIAL REGISTER.

C. W. Blanchard...Clayton, N. C.
Worley Creech...........................R. F. D. No. 2, Kenly, N. C.
B. G. Early...Smithfield, N. C.
N. H. Gibbs...Benson, N. C.
R. W. Horrell..Selma, N. C
A. A. Pippin...Wakefield, N. C.
D. F. Putnam...Benson, N. C.
J. W. Smith..Clayton, N. C.
J. W. Suttle..Smithfield, N. C.
B. Townsend..Broadway, N. C.

LIST OF MESSENGERS.

Antioch—R. R. Creech and G. R. Whitley.

Baptist Centre—Clifford Austin, J. R. Barbour and J. C. Hardee.

Benson—B. D. Creech, J. L. Hall, D. F. Putnam, J. D. Parrish and U. F. Wallace.

Bethany—Kirkman Creech and Worley Creech.

Bethesda—D. L. Jones, M. Johnson, H. A. Jones and W. B. Wallace.

Bethel—J. H. Bell and W. T. Sullivan.

Blackman's Grove—J. M. Blackman, Ernest Grice and E. B. Hayes.

Carter's Chapel—J. I. Blackman, Theo. Easom and W. B. Wall.

Clayton—C. W. Blanchard, Lonnie Duncan, J. W. Smith and D. J. Yelvington.

Calvary—M. L. Barefoot, James M. Johnson and C. F. Wagstaff.

Clyde's Chapel—H. V. Bunch and William Martin.

Corinth—By Letter.

Four Oaks—O. D. Stanley.

Hood's Grove—L. Eldridge, J. A. Lee and D. J. Wood.

Lee's Chapel—By Letter.

Live Oak—Thomas Batten and C. T. Eason.

Micro—C. L. Batten, L. L. Creech, David Pace and D. C. Smith.

Mount Moriah—W. H. Kelly, J. F. Pool and N. R. Pool.

Nobles' Chapel—C. O. Boykin, W. M. Boykin and J. B. Mecome.

New Bethel—Andrew J. Bryan.

Oliver's Grove—By Letter.

Parrish Memorial—J. D. Creech, G. W. Parrish and J. F. Watson.

Pauline—W. B. Joyner and N. W. Smith.

Pine Level—J. M. Underhill.

Pisgah—R. H. Higgins and J. L. Jones.

Princeton—J. B. Howell and L. H. Taylor.

Sardis—N. B. Stevens.

Selma—J. W. Liles, J. M. Oneal, C. W. Richardson, R. W. Horrell, Edward Tuck and M. C. Winston.

Shiloh—C. H. Holland.

Smithfield—D. E. Easom, B. G. Early, E. O. Edgerton, W. B. Guill, R. I. Lassiter, R. A. Merritt, J. M. Beaty and J. W. Suttle.

Thanksgiving—Wade Brannan and John Lynch.

Trinity—J. S. Lawhon and Arthur Lee.

White Oak—By Letter.

Wilson's Mills—J. T. Holt and S. D. West.

PROCEEDINGS.

BENSON, N. C., November 9th, 1905.

The third annual session of the Johnston County Baptist Association convened this morning at eleven o'clock with Benson Baptist church.

The services opened with the singing of "All Hail the Power of Jesus' Name." Prayer by Bro. A. A. Pippin. Hymn "Close to Thee." Prayer by Bro. B. G. Early. Hymn "Revive Us Again."

The Introductory Sermon was preached by Bro. C. W. Blanchard. Text: Luke 24:48. Subject: "The Church of Christ with Power."

In a few words the Association was welcomed to Benson by the pastor, Bro. J. W. Suttle. Announcements were made and the benediction was pronounced by Bro. S. F. Conrad.

AFTERNOON SESSION.

The Association was opened with prayer by Bro. A. A. Pippin.

The body was called to order by the Moderator, Bro. R. H. Gower.

Upon motion the following Committee on Credentials and Enrollment was appointed: Brethren N. W. Smith, C. W. Blanchard and C. H. Holland.

Upon motion, the rules were suspended and the following officers re-elected for the ensuing year, by acclamation:

Moderator—R. H. Gower.
Vice-Moderator—J. P. Canaday.
Clerk—T. J. Lassiter.

The election of Treasurer was postponed for the present.

Upon motion, section 10 of the Constitution was amended by striking out the words "a Historian" in second line, and all the words in the last clause of the same section.

The Moderator appointed the following committees at the afternoon session:

Petitionary Letters—J. W. Suttle, D. F. Putnam and N. H. Gibbs.
Finance—J. L. Hall, U. F. Wallace and R. R. Creech.
Periodicals—A. A. Pippin, J. F. Pool and S. D. West.
Aged Ministers' Relief—R. W. Horrell, E. B. Hayes and W. H. Kelly.
The Church Messenger—D. F. Putnam, J. F. Pool and C. W. Richardson.
Woman's Work—B. G. Early, J. C. Hardee and W. B. Joyner.
Home Missions—J. W. Suttle, J. M. Johnson and J. D. Creech.

The following visitors were recognized: Bro. J. S. Farmer, representative of the *Biblical Recorder;* Bro. S. F. Conrad, Field Editor of the *North Carolina Baptist;* Bro. F. R. Hall, of the Neuse Association; Bro. G. H. Broughton, of the Central Association, and Bro. M. L. Kesler, general manager of the Thomasville Orphanage.

The Committee on Petitionary Letters reported that Calvary Baptist church asked for admission into the Association and presented the following letter:

The South River Baptist Association sends greetings to the Johnston County Baptist Association:

The Calvary Baptist Church in Johnston County is hereby dismissed, to unite with you. It is our wish that this new union may be productive of good to both the Church and the Association.

Done by order of the Association, October 19, 1905.

JOHN A. OATES, Clerk.

Upon motion, the report was adopted and the Moderator welcomed Bro. J. M. Johnson as a delegate from Calvary.

Upon motion, the order of business was changed so that Periodicals should take the place of Woman's Work on the program for the afternoon session.

Bro. R. W. Horrell read the

REPORT ON AGED MINISTERS' RELIEF.

When Christ called the Apostles to preach the Gospel He called them from their boats and nets—their only means of obtaining a temporal support. He sent them out without purse or scrip, saying to them: The laborer is worthy of his hire. Paul tells us that they who preach the Gospel should live of the Gospel. By the teaching of many scriptures God makes it the duty of the people to support the gospel preacher. But what of the men who have worn themselves out in the ministry and are unable to render further services? We can't fatten and beef them as we would 'an ox. Should we treat them as the negro does his mule when his strength has failed, the winds cold and the grass dry and tough, turn him out to graze for his living or starve and die? No, we can not and will not fail to care for the men who have given their lives for our good and God's glory.

Twenty-four of our aged preachers or their widows are now being helped. They receive from twenty-four to sixty-five dollars per year, according to their needs. We raised last year for this object a little over two thousand dollars. We ask that the churches enlarge their pledges to this object, as the demand grows greater each year. R. W. HORRELL,

For the Committee.

Upon motion to adopt, the report was discussed by Brethren Horrell, Blanchard and Suttle. Pledges were then taken and the report adopted.

Bro. A. A. Pippin read the

REPORT ON PERIODICALS.

In this busy age, when the growth of knowledge is so wonderful, when the people are reading so much news, and when the power of the press is so great, a religious paper is almost indispensable. It is difficult to estimate the value of so good a Christian and denominational paper as the Biblical

Recorder. It is a weekly visitor which we soon learn to love and welcome into our homes. It tells us what God is doing in the world. It teaches us to look at passing events from a Christian standpoint. It is filled with news from our churches. It brings greetings and tidings from our missionaries beyond the sea. It keeps us informed concerning the progress of the Kingdom of Christ. It brings us into closer sympathy with every good work. It is a great help to the preacher in his labors. It is a very kind and effective advocate of our denominational principles. We therefore recommend the Biblical Recorder, the recognized organ of North Carolina Baptists, to the brethren, and request them to aid in widening its circulation and enlarging its usefulness.

We also recommend the North Carolina Baptist, which is doing a great work along its line. We most heartily recommend Charity and Children, the representative of our Orphanage, to all the friends of benevolence. We also recommend that we support the Foreign Mission Journal and the Home Field. They are good journals and worthily represent the objects for which they stand.

We also want our churches to see to it that our Church Messenger be most earnestly supported by all the churches in the Association.

We, above all, recommend that our brethren do not allow their families to read the cheap, trashy literature that is sent all over the country to support advertising interests. It does much harm and no good.

A. A. PIPPIN,
J. F. POOL,
S. D. WEST,
Committee.

A motion was made to adopt the report, and the following brethren took part in the discussion: A. A. Pippin, S. F. Conrad, R. W. Horrel and M. L. Kesler, after which the motion prevailed.

Upon motion, the report on the Orphanage was set for to-morrow at 10 o'clock.

Bro. D. F. Putnam was appointed to conduct the devotional exercises to-night, and the Association adjourned with benediction by Bro. Conrad.

THURSDAY—NIGHT SESSION.

The session was opened with devotional exercises conducted by Bro. D. F. Putnam. Prayer by Bro. Worley Creech.

The regular order was taken up and Bro. J. W. Suttle read the

REPORT ON HOME MISSIONS.

The field of the Home Mission Board is divided into a number of distinct departments, and its work is largely co-operative. Nearly all the States find that the resources of the State Mission Boards are insufficient to adequately supply the destitution within their own borders, and so the Home Board supplements the work done by the State Boards.

Among the special departments: Cities, The Negro, Mountain Missions and Schools, Cuba and Frontier Missions.

This has been a year of enlargement with the Home Mission Board. "Enlargement" has been the keynote of the year's work. Every department has been vibrant with the expanding idea. At Nashville, in 1904, the Convention said to the Home Board: "Through you and by the help of God, we shall take this Southland, for the Baptists go forward." It was enough. At once the Board increased its appropriations fifty per cent. over any previous year.

God's favor in a very marked degree has been upon the working forces in the fields. Many have been led to Christ and a deepening spirit of consecration to our Lord has been reported from many directions.

In Cuba baptisms have been frequent. In the territories there have been many notable revivals. Baltimore, Memphis and New Orleans have been greatly stirred by the generous help of the Home Board, to say nothing of St. Louis, Kansas City, Galveston and other cities.

We quote a few figures from the report of 1905: Missionaries, 718; Baptisms, 10,551; additions by letter, 10,019; total additions, 20,570. Increase: Missionaries, 102; baptisms, 3,025; by letter, 749; total, 3,773.

The receipts of the Home Board were $145,705.31, an increase of $12,147.31.

Church Building Loan Fund—Church buildings are an essential force to successful work. Our Secretary, Dr. Gray, says the Home Board needs a great loan fund of not less than $500,000. He further says that in many districts—especially in Texas, Arkansas, Oklahoma, Louisiana and Indian Territory—our cause is well-nigh paralyzed for lack of suitable houses.

Work Among the Negroes—Dr. A. J. Barton is Field Secretary and Superintendent of Negro Work. The wisdom of Dr. Barton's appointment has been abundantly justified by the zeal and tact with which he has labored, both in connection with the negro work and advancing the general interests of the Board.

Rev. M. P. Hunt, who was Field Secretary for the Western territory, says: "The rapid growth along material lines in Oklahoma and Indian Territory calls for hard work to keep the destitution from growing. For every new town we enter two more spring up, calling loudly for help.

Mountain Missions and Schools—Rev. A. E. Brown, the splendid superintendent of this department, says that he finds the mountain people awakening to their conditions and ready to co-operate in efforts to help them. Eighteen schools in North Carolina, Tennessee and Kentucky are now directly connected with the Home Board, having an enrollment of about 4,000 pupils and employing 75 teachers. Two schools in Georgia and one in Alabama are being assisted, and South Carolina has asked the Board to take charge of its mountain school work.

Immigration—A great many influences are now on foot to turn the stream of immigrants southward. One of the highest tests ever put upon Southern Baptists will come with the tide of immigration. We must meet them with the Gospel of Christ.

Cuba—The Home Board has work at eleven places in Cuba, but Havana is the stronghold. Havana contains one-sixth of the population of the whole island, and everything unites to encourage more aggressive work on the part of our people.

New Fields—Isle of Pines and Panama. The former is to become another link in the chain of our missions, extending from Tampa, Key West and Havana on to Panama, and from it adjacent islands may be reached.

Your committee begs leave to recommend that we increase our pledges at least fifteen per cent. over what we gave this year.

We also recommend that all our pastors be asked to urge their members to subscribe for and read Our Home Field.   Respectfully submitted,
J. W. SUTTLE, for Committee.

The report was discussed by Brethren Suttle, Conrad and Kesler, pledges taken and the report adopted.

Bro. B. G. Early then read the

REPORT ON WOMAN'S WORK.

The power of woman holds an undisputable place in almost every phase of life. Her tender touch and wise counsel are to be sought on every hand—

in the home life, in the civic life, in the literary world, in the social life, and last, but not least, in the religious world. I say last, because it is of recent date that she has fully developed in this most important field of her usefulness. It is strange that for so long a time she occupied the small place she did in this great work, for which she is so divinely fitted.

To woman God made the first promise of the coming of a Redeemer to a sin-cursed world. "And I will put enmity between thee and the woman, and between thy seed and her seed; it shall bruise thy head and thou shalt bruise his heel." When the promised Redeemer had suffered and died for a lost world, and was buried, it was a woman that was honored with the privilege to be the first to herald the glad news of His resurrection. Thus we see that God has always honored her and used her for His glory. And we rejoice to see Him giving her such wonderful success in this field of great usefulness.

We are glad to give to the good women of our Association and State our sympathy and co-operation in the noble cause they have so nobly espoused. We recommend their efforts and ask for them your earnest prayers and encouragement.

May God's richest blessings attend their efforts to advance the Master's kingdom. Respectfully submitted,
B. G. EARLY, for the Committee.

Upon motion to adopt, the report was discussed by Brethren Early, Farmer, Conrad and Blanchard. Report adopted.

The following committees were announced :

Orphanage—F. T. Booker, M. L. Kesler and J. S. Lawhon.

State Missions—J. M. Beaty, G. W. Parrish and Ernest Grice.

To Nominate Delegates to the Southern Baptist Convention and the State Convention—C. W. Richardson, G. W. Parrish and C. T. Eason.

Place and Preachers for Next Year—Worley Creech, G. R. Whitley and H. V. Bunch.

To Nominate Member State Mission Board—J. T. Holt, Lonnie Duncan and J. M. Oneal.

To Nominate Executive Committee—J. W. Suttle, W. T. Sullivan and J. D. Parrish.

On motion, Bro. C. W. Blanchard was appointed to prepare the Digest of Church Letters after adjournment of Association and send to the Clerk.

The body adjourned to meet to-morrow morning at 9:30. Benediction by Bro. B. G. Early.

FRIDAY—MORNING SESSION.

Association met according to adjournment. The devotional exercises were conducted by Bro. B. G. Early.

Roll of delegates was called. Upon motion the reading of the journal was dispensed with.

Bro. W. M. Page, of the South River Association, was recognized.

After the enrollment of several new delegates the regular program was taken up.

Bro. M. L. Kesler, of the Thomasville Orphanage, read the

REPORT ON ORPHANAGE.

As a denomination we have had twenty years' experience in Orphanage work. Our Orphanage at Thomasville during this time has cared for 890 helpless children. From nothing the work has grown until we now have near 400 acres of land, nine dormitories for the children, an infirmary for the sick, a central school building, a central dining hall (known also as the Faircloth Building), printing office, workshops, homes for the general manager and treasurer. The force of the Orphanage is composed of about twenty-five people. These and the children share in the work. One-half the Orphanage goes to school in the morning, the other half in the afternoon. Feeding and clothing the children is a very important part of the work; but the training of the children we regard as the main work of the institution. The task of the Orphanage is to take children deprived of their natural protectors, lift them from their helpless and hopeless condition and put them on their feet, so that they may take their proper stand among men. We have 280 now and will soon have over 300. The expense grows heavier every year as the number of children increases. The large debt upon the institution was brought about mainly through the water works and sewerage systems, which are now in full operation.

That the increased daily expenses may be met and this debt be paid your committee recommends that a Thanksgiving or Orphanage service be held in every church, and that the churches, if possible, double their pledges and contributions for the next year.　　　　　　　M. L. KESLER,
For the Committee.

Upon motion to adopt the report was discussed by Bro. Kesler. Pledges were taken and the report adopted.

A cash collection of $13.77 was taken for the Orphanage.

Special order for the hour was then taken up and Bro. J. M. Beaty, chairman of the committee, read the

REPORT OF EXECUTIVE COMMITTEE.

The Lord has greatly blessed us this year, and we report the most prosperous year in the history of our work. There have been 164 additions to the mission churches.

Bro. A. A. Pippin has served White Oak and Corinth. At White Oak there have been twenty-one additions, and at Corinth ten. White Oak has become self-sustaining and the work is prospering at each of these churches.

Bro. D. F. Putnam has preached at Pisgah, Johnson's School House, Hood's Grove, Pauline, Blackman's Grove, Trinity and Four Oaks. Fifty additions have been made to the churches on his field. Blackman's Grove will no longer ask the Association for help. Repairs have been made at Trinity Church; a good house of worship has been built at Hood's Grove, and a building is in course of construction at Pauline.

Bro. R. W. Horrell has been preaching at Parrish Memorial, Carter's Chapel, Micro, Kenly, Princeton, Woodard School House, Nobles' Chapel and Bethel. There have been fifty-seven additions on this field. Parrish Memorial church has been enlarged. At Carter's Chapel the house has been plastered and otherwise improved. Princeton church has been remodeled and greatly improved. Micro Church is in course of construction and most of the lumber has been hauled for Bethel Church.

Bro. B. G. Early has for the past few months had charge of Live Oak, Oliver's Grove, Pine Level, Sardis and a school house near Sardis. Bro. J. W. Smith supplied a part of this field and did good work before Bro. Early came and took charge. At Live Oak there have been six additions and at Pine Level twenty have been added. We need more money and at least one more preacher to do the work as it should be done.

J. M. BEATY,
J. F. POOL,
J. T. HOLT,
J. H. BOON,
Executive Committee.

A motion was made to adopt the report and brethren J. M. Beaty, J. W. Suttle, A. A. Pippin, and C. W. Blanchard took part in the discussion. Pledges were taken for State Missions and further consideration of the subject was postponed till the night session.

The reports on Temperance and *The Church Messenger* were set for the afternoon session.

The Moderator announced the following committee :

Temperance—D. F. Putnam, Worley Creech and William Martin.

The body adjourned with benediction by Bro. M. L. Kesler.

FRIDAY—AFTERNOON SESSION.

Devotional exercises by Bro. Worley Creech. Prayer by Bro. W. M. Page, of the South River Association.

Miscellaneous Business was taken up and disposed of.

Committee on Place and Preachers reported as follows :

Place for Next Session—Clyde's Chapel.
Introductory Sermon—D. F. Putnam; alternate, R. W. Horrell.

Committee on Executive Committee recommend that present committee be re-elected. Adopted.

Upon motion of Bro. J. W. Suttle Bro. C. W. Richardson was re-elected Treasurer by acclamation.

The Committee recommended that Bro. C. W. Blanchard be re-elected Member of State Board of Missions. Adopted.

The following committees were announced :

Foreign Missions—C. W. Blanchard, J. W. Watson and W. B. Wallace.
Education—J. P. Canaday, Andrew Bryan and Arthur Lee.
Sunday Schools—R. A. Merritt, L. Eldridge and B. W. Allen.

The report on *The Church Messenger* was read by Bro. D. F. Putnam.

REPORT ON THE CHURCH MESSENGER.

We, your Committee on The Church Messenger, ask leave to report as follows: We find by consulting the business manager that the paper is not as yet on a paying basis and that there is a debt, which the report of the business manager will show, which report we recommend to be read before the Association. Your committee realizes the need of some medium of communication, and believe it will be unwise to discontinue the paper, as it promises soon to be self-supporting. After consulting some of the leading brethren, we most earnestly recommend that a joint stock company be formed, or that individuals become responsible for the financial support of the paper, and that the Mission Board be relieved of the present responsibility.

D. F. PUTNAM,
C. W. RICHARDSON,
J. F. POOL,
Committee.

The Business Manager's report showed that *The Messenger* had 326 bona fide subscribers. The indebtedness was shown to be about $80.00, with subscriptions due to the amount of about $27.75.

Upon motion to adopt, the reports were discussed by Brethren D. F. Putnam, C. W. Richardson, T. J. Lassiter, J. W. Suttle and C. W. Blanchard. After being fully discussed the reports were unanimously adopted and *The Church Messenger* was made the official organ of the Association.

The election of Editors and Business Manager was then taken up and resulted as follows :

Editor—J. W. Suttle.
Assistant Editors—All the pastors in the Association.
Business Manager—T. J. Lassiter.

Several subscribed to the stock company recommended in the report.

Bro. D. F. Putnam read the

REPORT ON TEMPERANCE.

It has been very popular to pass resolutions and to memorialize legislative bodies against the accursed liquor traffic in our beloved State. Our resolutions and memorials have been enacted into law and we stand to-day on trial. Yes, prohibition will stand or fall according to our faithfulness in executing the temperance laws upon our statute books.

Those who have wrought in the battle of putting Johnston county in the prohibition column deserve great honor. We all have great reason to rejoice, but we must not slacken our pace. The liquor dealers are organized and are fighting most bitterly our every progress. The day of resolutions is passed. We must execute.

We most urgently insist that the time has come for all church members to desist from the use of alcoholic drinks as a beverage, and thereby lending their influence to this, the greatest enemy of the home, church, State and industry.

D. F. PUTNAM,
WORLEY CREECH,
WM. MARTIN,
Committee.

Bro. C. W. Blanchard offered the following resolutions :

"Resolved, That we, the delegates and members of the Johnston County Baptist Association, do hereby express our universal condemnation of the liquor traffic and desire that our next Legislature assembled submit to the qualified voters of the State an amendment to our State Constitution totally abolishing the manufacture and sale of liquor from the State.

"Resolved, second, That we demand of Congress the passage of the bill known as the Hepburn-Dolliver Bill, prohibiting the nullification of the laws of one State by the brewers and distillers of another by the shipment from those outside States of liquors intended for sale in violation of local or the State laws of another. And that until such time as the entire internal revenue system of partnership with the traffic has been abolished we favor the passage of the International Reform Bureau's measure, known as the Humphreys Bill, to prohibit the issuing of Federal liquor tax receipt in no-license territory."

After being discussed by Brethren D. F. Putnam and C. W. Blanchard, the report, together with the resolution, was unanimously adopted.

Adjournment. Benediction by Bro. Livingston Johnson.

FRIDAY—NIGHT SESSION.

Session was opened with devotional exercises by Bro. A. A. Pippin. Prayer by Bro. W. C. Tyree.

The following visitors were recognized: Bro. Livingston Johnson, Corresponding Secretary Baptist State Convention; Bro. W. C. Tyree, of the Central Association, and Vice-President for North Carolina of the Foreign Mission Board; Bro. Hight C. Moore, Field Secretary of the Sunday School Board.

Several new delegates were enrolled.

Bro. Livingston Johnson, for the Committee, read the

REPORT ON STATE MISSIONS.

The State Mission Board began its work seventy-five years ago. The results amply justify the wisdom of our fathers in this great undertaking. Accurate statistics were not given by the missionaries until 1882, just twenty-two years ago. From these statistics were gathered the following interesting figures:

Number baptized by our missionaries, 27,605.

Churches organized on mission fields, 754.

Houses of worship built on mission fields, 746.

Amount paid for building houses of worship, $114,061.74.

Number of Sunday schools organized by the missionaries, 742.

There are in the State 1,792 Missionary Baptist churches. Seven hundred and fifty-four—nearly three-sevenths of these—were organized by the missionaries of the Board within the last twenty-two years. It would be safe to say that at least half the churches in North Carolina were organized by the missionaries of the Board. It is no exaggeration to claim that three out of every four dollars which go into the Lord's treasury for carrying on His work are contributed by churches that were organized by beneficiaries of our Board.

As much as has been done, much still remains to be done. A large area of rich, virgin soil remains untouched. There are five counties in the State with only one preacher to the county, and that one would not be there were he not supported in large part by the Board. There are four county-seats in no one of which there is a Baptist church or a Baptist preacher. Many new towns are yet unoccupied, and are making urgent appeals to the Board for help. Many of the towns which the Board aided in establishing the first church are now asking for help for one or more mission points. This is due to the rapid growth of many of our towns. "Let us go up and possess the land, for we are abundantly able to take it."

J. M. BEATY.
ERNEST GRICE.
G. W. PARRISH.

The report was discussed by Brethren Johnson and Blanchard. Special Pledges were then taken for the State Mission work and the report, with the report of the Executive Committee, was adopted. (See special State Mission pledges.)

Foreign Missions was next taken up and the report read by Bro. C. W. Blanchard.

REPORT ON FOREIGN MISSIONS.

We are commanded by the Saviour to "Go into all the world and preach the Gospel to every creature." The gift of the promised Comforter was to be especially for our preparation for this very service. Christ said, "Ye shall receive power after that the Holy Ghost is come upon you: and ye shall be witnesses unto me, both in Jerusalem and in all Judea, and in Samaria, and unto the uttermost parts of the earth." God unalterably associates the gift of the Holy Spirit with the spirit of the world-wide missions and makes the existence of the one in the human heart the prime evidence of the existence of the other. To be a spirit-filled disciple of the Christ is to be a vessel ladened with His Gospel for the "Uttermost ends of the earth." This idea is the conclusion of the unfailing Word of life, and the history of Christianity in all ages. The church with a world-wide mission spirit is and has ever been full of evangelical power at home and abroad. Every church in all ages has died with the waning of this spirit.

We must enlarge the borders of our tents and heed the Macedonian cry for help from afar if we would be able to subdue with spiritual power the foe that lies next to our own doors.

The fields are white unto harvest. Everywhere in pagan and papal lands the doors are wide open to us, and the cry for help is urgent. The labors of our missionaries are abundantly blessed. Hundreds and thousands are hearing the gospel and heeding its call to repentence for sins and faith in Jesus Christ. Evidenced from the urgent calls of the hour from all the fields for laborers, and the signal blesssing attendant upon the service of our missionaries, this is indeed God's set time to bless the nations of the earth. Surely this is the day of our great opportunity to answer the call of duty. Shall we of the Johnston County Baptist Association not rise up in this God's day of willingness and do valiant service for the triumph of the truth everywhere? Let us here and now answer this call by enlarged liberality to the Foreign Mission Board for the prosecution of its work. Let us study the Word and the work until we have a quickened intelligence of better demands upon us Let us pray for the success of the workers on the field and make hearty offering of some of our own sons and daughters to go far hence to tell the sweet story of the Christ we love.

C. W. BLANCHARD,
For the Committee.

The report was discussed by Bro. W. C. Tyree, pledges taken, and adopted.

The Association adjourned until to-morrow morning 9:30. The benediction was pronounced by Bro. Livingston Johnson.

SATURDAY—MORNING SESSION.

Session opened with devotional exercises conducted by Bro. R. W. Horrell. Prayer by Bro. B. G. Early.

Bro. J. W. Smith, for the Committee, made the following report:

Delegate to Southern Baptist Convention—C. W. Blanchard.
Delegates to Baptist State Convention—B. G. Early, D. F. Putnam and R. W. Horrell.

Report adopted.

Bro. R. A. Merritt read the

REPORT ON SUNDAY SCHOOLS.

The condition of the Sunday school work in our Association is very encouraging. From the letters sent up to this Association we find that there are 26 Sunday schools in our bounds, with a total enrollment of 2,340, a gain of 581 over last report, or a gain of 33 per cent. in enrollment. All the churches in the Association have Sunday schools except nine.

The contributions for Sunday school work show a gratifying increase over last year—an increase of 32 per cent.

We recommend that during the coming year each church make a determined effort to organize a Sunday school; that all strive to incease the attendance; that the work be made more efficient on the part of the superintendents and teachers, and thus more useful to the community.

As churches, God calls upon us and expects us to do our duty in this respect. The duty of teaching, and especially teaching the young, stands out distinctly in the original constitution of the Church of God. Moses, acting under divine sanction, rehearsed the laws of Sinai, and with equal authority he said: "These words which I command you this day shall be in thine heart and thou shall teach them diligently to thy children."

Your committee desires to express its gratification in the splendid work being done by our State Sunday School Secretary, Bro. Hight C. Moore, and through the Association to invite him to come into our midst as often as may be consistent with his duty to other sections, and to assure him of our readiness to co-operate most heartily with him.

R. A. MERRITT,
B. W. ALLEN,
Committee.

The report was discussed by Brethren R. A. Merritt, B. W. Allen, Hight C. Moore and C. W. Blanchard, and adopted.

The following resolution was offered by Bro. T. J. Lassiter and adopted:

Resolved, That each church and each Sunday school in this Association be asked to take one collection during the year for the support of the Sunday school work of the State, and that the Moderator be instructed to set apart

some certain Sunday or some certain month for this collection, and notify
the pastors and Sunday school superintendents of the same.

Bro. B. Townsend, of the Little River Association, was recognized.

Bro. Townsend was appointed to preach to-night and Bro. Blanchard to-morrow morning at eleven o'clock.

Adjournment. Benediction by Bro. B. Townsend.

SATURDAY—AFTERNOON SESSION.

Devotional exercises by Bro. Hight C. Moore. Prayer by Bro.
Putnam.

Upon motion of Bro. J. W. Suttle, the Treasurer of the Association was directed to acknowledge all moneys received by him each
month through the columns of *The Church Messenger.*

Bro. J. P. Canaday read the

REPORT ON EDUCATION.

The success of a free government rests upon the intelligence of the people, hence the subject of education is always paramount. It is declared in
our State Constitution that, "Religion, morality and knowledge, being necessary to good government, schools and the means of education shall forever
be encouraged."

"To live completely" is doubtless the object of man's creation, and the true
mission of life, the performance of duty to self, to fellow-man and to God.
Therefore, the highest conception of the parent and the State is to give
every boy and girl a liberal Christian education. To accomplish the
great purposes of the State, power to control environments must be given
the individual man and woman.

We recognize with pride that our public schools have been greatly improved. The funds for the four-months term given by the State and counties in many places have been supplemented by special taxes. The result is
more beautiful and comfortable school buildings have been erected; longer
school terms and a higher grade of teachers have inaugurated a higher
grade of public education. With the advent of these high grade public
schools, rural libraries and rural mail deliveries, brighter days will soon
dawn in our State.

To aid the public schools in universal education, Christian schools in
the State are flourishing as never before. It is the pride of the Baptists
that more than thirty denominational academies and high schools serve to
feed the Baptist male and female colleges. Wake Forest has become one of
the greatest powers in North-Carolina, not only in the educational and religious life, but in the political, scientific and social life. Each year this
great institution grows stronger and its Christian influences more strengthened upon the Commonwealth. Especially the young men who are there
preparing for the ministry should be liberally aided by all Baptists.

The female colleges are more largely attended than ever before. The
Baptist University for Women has surpassed the expectations of its founders, and the Chowan Baptist Female Institute at Murfreesboro and the
Female Seminary at Oxford are the pride of North Carolina Baptists. They
should have the patronage of the denomination.

Your committee again recommends the establishment of a Baptist denomi-

national preparatory school in the bounds of the Johnston County Baptist Association as early as practicable. J. P. CANADAY,
For the Committee.

Upon motion to adopt, the report was discussed by Brethren Canaday and Blanchard. After pledges were taken the report was adopted.

The following resolution, offered by Bro. Blanchard who stated that it was suggested by Bro. M. C. Winston, was unanimously adopted:

Whereas, a good house of worship is necessarily essential to the proper development of any church, and it is so often a long and tedious struggle for our weak mission churches to build suitable houses for themselves and maintain public worship; and,

Whereas, without some organized plan for raising the funds it has been a difficult task for the missionary on the field to prosecute his evangelistic duties and at the same time raise building funds; be it,

Resolved, That we hereby recommend the formation of a church building association within our territory, whose executive committee shall be the Executive Committee of the Association, and whose members shall be those persons or churches who shall agree to forward to the call of the Executive Committee the sum of one dollar each at any and all times when in the judgment of said committee such help is needed in the continuation of or to finish church houses in destitute places on our territory.

Upon motion, the Clerk was instructed to have one thousand copies of the Minutes printed and distributed as per the amounts sent up for this purpose by the several churches, and that he be allowed ten dollars for his services.

The Association then adjourned till 7 o'clock. Benediction by Bro. Townsend.

SATURDAY—NIGHT SESSION.

Session opened with prayer by Bro. H. L. Hall.

Bro. B. Townsend preached from text, Hebrews 2:3. Subject: "A Great Salvation"

The report of the Finance Committee was read and accepted.

Fearing that there was not a sufficient amount sent up for Minutes and Clerk a collection of $3.26 was taken to supplement this fund.

Upon motion of Bro. C. W. Blanchard, the Treasurer's report was referred to the Executive Committee, with the request that they go over the Treasurer's books with him and that they have report printed in the Minutes.

Upon motion, the Constitution was amended by adding the word

"Auditor" after the word "Treasurer" in line 2, section 10, and further amended same section by defining his duty.

A committee, consisting of Brethren C. W. Blanchard, J. W. Suttle and D. F. Putnam was appointed to nominate an Auditor and report his name to the Association immediately. The Committee retired and soon reported the name of 'Bro. J. D. Underwood, who was unanimously elected.

Upon motion of Bro. Blanchard, a resolution of thanks to the Benson Baptist church and the people of the entire town and community for their generous hospitality and splendid entertainment of the Association, was unanimously adopted.

The following announcement was made:

Sunday School Mass Meeting to morrow morning at ten o'clock led by Bro. R. H. Gower.

Sermon at eleven o'clock by Bro. C. W. Blanchard.

The business of the session ended, motion to adjourn was passed.

The congregation then joined in singing "Blest be the Tie that Binds," and the benediction was pronounced by Bro. J. W. Suttle.

SUNDAY MORNING.

The Sunday School Mass Meeting was opened with prayer by Bro. N. H. Gibbs. The meeting was conducted by the Moderator, Bro. R. H. Gower, who made a short talk on Sunday School work. He was followed by Brethren M. H. Jones, J. W. Suttle and J. P. Canaday, who made short talks on the different phases of the Sunday School work.

At eleven o'clock Bro. C. W. Blanchard preached a very able sermon, using as a subject, "Daniel, the Hero of Babylon." There was an overflow meeting and Bro. D. F. Putnam preached to a good congregation at the Methodist church. A collection of $10.19 was taken for State Missions.

Woman's Missionary Union.

The Woman's Missionary Union of the Johnston County Baptist Association met in the Methodist church at Benson, Friday afternoon, November 11, 1905, and was presided over by the Vice-President, Mrs. Ashley Horne.

Upon invitation Pastor C. W. Blanchard met with us, read the 54th Psalm and made a talk on Woman's Work.

The reports from the different Societies were read. These reports show that the following amounts were contributed during the year:

Clayton W. M. Society—Home Missions, $43.38; State Missions, $61.87; Foreign Missions, $35.55; Box to Missionary, $80.

Clayton Y. L. M. Society—State Missions, $10; Foreign Missions, $5.50.

Clayton Junior Union—State Missions, $25.

Smithfield W. M. Society—Home Missions, $12.50; State Missions, $15; Foreign Missions, $12.50.

Smithfield Sunbeams—Foreign Missions, $8.

Mount Moriah W. M. Society—Home Missions, $1.50; State Missions, $5; Foreign Missions, $2.70.

Benson W. M. Society—Home Missions, $2.30; State Missions, $4; Foreign Missions, $2.35.

Clyde's Chapel W. M. Society—$5.32 for all three objects.

Lee's Chapel W. M. Society—$10 for all three objects.

Total amount contributed, $381.52.

A Sunbeam Society was organized at Wilson's Mills just before the meeting of the Association.

The Union was organized two years ago with three societies—Clayton, Smithfield and Selma. Last year four others were added to our list, and this year we had reports from twelve societies.

Most all the societies took higher aims for the coming year and the outlook is very hopeful.   MRS. W. M. PETTWAY,
                                                            Secretary.

REPORT OF FINANCE COMMITTEE.

We have received and turned over to the clerk, T. J. Lassiter, the following amounts.

CHURCHES.	Minutes and Clerk	State Missions.	Home Missions.	Foreign Missions.	Orphanage.	Ministerial Education.	Aged Ministers' Relief.	Totals.
Antioch	60	15 00	1 50	1 50	2 50	1 50	2 00	24 60
Baptist Centre	2 00	22 00	3 00	2 50	13 08	1 00	1 50	45 08
Benson	3 00	26 00	5 20	15 65	.....	5 00	3 00	57 85
Bethany	1 00	6 10	2 00	1 25	2 90	1 25	1 50	16 00
Bethesda	2 00	.....	5 00	6 00	15 00	2 00	3 00	33 00
Bethel	50	2 00	1 00	50	1 50	1 00	1 00	7 50
Blackman's Grove	1 00	10 00	2 00	3 75	4 50	1 00	1 00	23 25
Carter's Chapel	1 00	6 00	1 50	1 25	2 00	1 00	2 00	14 75
Clayton	5 00	.....	.....	.....	.....	.....	.....	5 00
Clyde's Chapel	1 50	4 54	59	1 30	.....	2 00	2 00	11 93
Corinth	1 00	1 60	1 83	3 00	1 78	1 00	2 00	12 21
Four Oaks	1 00	11 00	3 00	2 50	2 00	1 25	1 25	22 00
Hood's Grove	70	.....	.....	.....	.....	.....	.....	70
Live Oak	1 00	4 50	1 00	1 00	4 12	1 00	2 00	14 62
Micro	40	.....	50	50	2 54	50	1 00	5 44
Mount Moriah	1 00	30 01	3 61	40 20	20 00	5 00	4 00	103 82
Nobles' Chapel	1 00	13 67	2 00	2 00	2 00	2 00	2 00	24 67
New Bethel	1 10	.....	.....	.....	.....	.....	.....	1 10
Oliver's Grove	50	2 50	.....	1 00	50	.....	50	5 00
Parrish Memorial	1 00	7 37	1 00	1 00	1 00	1 00	2 00	14 37
Pauline	55	.....	.....	.....	.....	.....	.....	55
Pine Level	1 30	.....	1 00	1 00	1 00	1 00	1 00	6 30
Pisgah	40	.....	.....	.....	.....	.....	.....	40
Princeton	1 00	8 47	2 00	5 00	2 00	2 00	2 50	22 97
Sardis	50	5 00	1 00	1 00	1 00	1 00	1 00	10 50
Selma	3 00	.....	.....	.....	.....	.....	.....	3 00
Shiloh	1 00	11 76	2 00	3 00	2 05	2 00	.....	26 81
Smithfield	5 00	.....	.....	.....	.....	.....	.....	5 00
Thanksgiving	42	4 00	.....	.....	1 75	.....	.....	6 17
Trinity	1 00	7 50	2 50	3 25	3 00	1 00	1 00	19 25
White Oak	2 00	11 45	3 00	1 00	80	1 50	2 00	21 75
Wilson's Mills	1 00	.....	3 00	5 00	6 00	3 00	4 00	22 00
I. D. Manning	.....	.....	.....	.....	5 00	.....	.....	5 00
General Collection	.....	.....	.....	.....	13 77	.....	.....	13 77
Totals	43 47	210 47	49 23	104 15	116 79	39 00	43 25	606 36

J. L. HALL,

For the Committee.

CHURCH PLEDGES FOR 1906.

CHURCHES.	State Missions.	Home Missions.	Foreign Missions.	Orphanage.	Ministerial Education.	Ministerial Relief.	Totals.
Antioch.	$15 00	$ 1 50	$ 1 50	$ 2 50	$ 1 50	$ 2 00	$ 24 00
Baptist Centre.	22 00	3 00	2 00	10 00	2 00	2 00	41 00
Benson	70 00	10 00	15 00	20 00	5 00	4 00	124 00
Bethany	6 50	2 50	2 00	3 00	1 25	1 25	16 50
Bethesda	25 00	5 00	2 00	15 00	2 00	3 00	52 00
Bethel	4 00	1 00	1 00	2 00	1 00	1 00	10 00
Blackman's Grove	15 00	3 00	5 50	6 00	2 75	2 00	34 25
Carter's Chapel	12 00	2 00	1 50	5 00	1 00	2 00	23 50
Clayton	175 00	40 00	125 00	120 00	25 00	12 50	497 50
Clydes Chapel	7 00	3 00	3 50	5 00	2 00	2 00	22 50
Corinth	7 50	2 50	3 50	5 00	1 00	2 00	21 50
Calvary	3 00	1 50	1 00	2 00	1 00	1 00	9 50
Four Oaks	10 00	3 00	3 00	3 00	1 50	2 50	23 00
Hood's Grove	10 00	2 00	3 00	2 00	2 00	1 50	20 50
Lee's Chapel	35 00	5 00	5 00	5 00	1 50	3 00	54 50
Live Oak	4 00	1 00	1 00	3 00	1 00	2 00	12 00
Micro	5 00	50	1 00	2 00	1 00	1 00	10 50
Mount Moriah	50 00	15 00	50 00	25 00	5 00	5 00	150 00
Nobles' Chapel	17 00	2 50	2 00	4 00	2 00	2 00	29 50
New Bethel	15 00	3 00	2 00	3 00	2 00	1 00	26 00
Oliver's Grove.	6 00	1 00	1 00	1 00	50	50	10 00
Parrish Memorial	15 00	1 00	1 00	2 00	1 00	2 00	22 00
Pauline	2 00	1 50	1 50	1 50	50	1 00	8 00
Pine Level	6 00	1 25	1 50	2 00	1 25	1 50	13 50
Pisgah	12 50	1 00	2 00	2 00	1 00	1 25	19 75
Princeton.	17 00	4 00	5 00	4 00	2 00	2 50	34 50
Sardis.	5 00	1 00	1 00	1 00	1 50	1 00	10 50
Selma.	125 00	10 00	30 00	30 00	11 50	10 00	216 50
Shiloh	25 00	3 25	3 00	12 00	2 00	2 50	47 75
Smithfield	200 00	37 50	50 00	40 00	12 00	16 00	355 50
Thanksgiving	15 00	2 00	5 00	4 00	1 00	2 00	29 00
Trinity	8 00	4 00	3 50	3 00	1 00	1 00	20 50
White Oak	15 00	4 00	2 50	5 00	1 50	2 00	30 00
Wilson's Mills	15 00	5 00	5 00	10 00	3 00	4 00	42 00
Totals.	974 50	183 50	342 50	360 50	100 75	100 00	2061 75

SPECIAL PLEDGES FOR STATE MISSIONS, 1906.

Personal Pledges.

J. M. Beaty	$ 50.00	B. W. Allen	5.00
J. M. Underhill	5.00	D. F. Putnam	10.00
B. G. Early	10.00	J. W. Smith	5.00
J. S. Farmer	5.00	Alonzo Parrish and wife	10.00
A. A. Pippin	10.00	J. H. Boon and wife	10.00
J. T. Holt	5.00	R. A. Merritt	5.00
Mrs. Ashley Horne	10.00	J. W. Whittenton and wife	10.00
T. J. Lassiter	25.00	S. D. West	3.00
H. V. Bunch, paid	2.00	Mrs. Bettie Driver, paid	2.00
F. P. Wood	10.00	John L. Jones	5.00
J. C. Hardee	5.00	G. C. Bryan and wife	10.00
J. S. Lawhon	5.00	W. B. Wall	2.00
E. L. Hall and wife	10.00	J. E. Wall	5.00
Mrs. H. D. Hood	1.00	Wm. Martin, paid	8.00
N. W. Smith	5.00	J. F. Pool	5.00
J. F. Watson	5.00	E. L. Hall & Bro	10.00
G. H. Broughton	5.00	H. L. Hall and wife	5.00
J. W. Holmes	3.00	Richard Barbour	1.00
J. C. Hardee and family	6.00		
R. W. Horrell	10.00	Total personal pledges	$298.00

Sunday School and Society Pledges.

Blackman's Grove S. S.	$ 2.00	Selma Sunbeams	5.00
Benson S. S.	5.00	W. M. Society, Selma	25.00
Mount Moriah S. S.	5.00	Y. L. M. Society, Clayton	5.00
Clyde's Chapel S. S.	1.00	Childs' Mission Band, Benson	4.00
Antioch S. S.	5.00	Clayton Baraca Class	1.00
White Oak S. S.	5.00	Clayton Philathea Class	5.00
Corinth S. S.	1.00	Selma Baraca Class	5.00
Pisgah S. S.	2.00	Selma Philathea Class	5.00
Carter's Chapel S. S.	2.00	Smithfield Baraca Class	5.00
Shiloh S. S.	2.00	Smithfield Philathea Class	5.00
Wilson's Mills S. S.	1.00	Pine Level Baraca Class	2.50
J. L. Hall's S. S. Class	5.00	Antioch Philathea Class	5.00
B. W. Allen's S. S. Class	5.00	Antioch Baraca Class	5.00
Clyde's Chapel Baraca Class.	1.00		

Total Sunday School and Society Pledges $119.00

Total Personal Pledges 298.00

Totals $417.00

CHURCHES	PASTORS	CLERKS AND ADDRESSES	Sunday Preaching	Value Ch. Property	Seating Capacity	Baptisms	Received by Letter	Restored	Lost by L.	Dismissed	Died	Number Males	Number Females	Total Members
Antioch	Worley 6th	R. R. Creech, Selma, r f d 2	2	$400	500	13	1	..	3	1	..	53	114	167
Baptist Centre	C. W Blanchard	G. C. Bryan, Clayton, r. f. d. 1	1-3	500	400	18	1	6	8	1	2	30	48	78
Benson	J. W. Suttle	E. L. Hall, Benson	2	1250	300	14	11	..	4	3	1	50	99	149
Bethany	Worley 6th	Kirkman Creech, Kenly, r f f d 2	4	600	300	9	4	1	..	2	..	29	45	74
Bethesda	J. W. Suttle	J. E Smith, Wilson's Mills	4	500	400	8	1	1	7	1	1	67	102	169
Bethel	R. W Horrell	John Gulley, Kenly	4	..	..	..	2	..	..	..	..	6	8	14
Blackman's Grove	D. F. Putnam	E. B. Hayes, Four Oaks, r. f. d. 2	3	600	300	5	5	..	1	..	1	25	35	60
Carter's Chapel	R. W. Horrell	W. B. Wall, Mro	1	700	350	6	3	9	1	..	..	23	46	69
Clayton	C. W.	M. G. Gulley, Clayton	1-3	5000	600	24	7	..	13	1	5	128	140	268
Clyde's Chapel	A. A. Pippin	C. I. Wendell	2	650	300	16	..	9	3	1	2	67	85	152
Corinth	A. A. Pippin	Oneal, Archer	4	500	400	10	..	1	2	1	..	39	56	95
Calvary	N. H. Gibbs	T. J. Lee, Dunn	4	500	200	7	..	..	1	..	..	13	25	38
Four Oaks	D. F. Putnam	J. Wm. Langdon, Four Oaks	4	700	200	2	6	..	2	..	1	8	23	31
Hd's Grove	D. F. Putnam	Jos. W. Wood, Benson, r. f. d. 2	2	500	400	7	..	..	..	..	..	13	19	32
Live Oak	B. G. Early	K. Broadwell, Selma	1	400	300	6	..	5	..	2	2	11	23	34
Lee's Chapel	A. A. Pippin	W. I Green, Selma, r. f. d	4	600	500	26	6	..	3	..	..	123	175	298
Micro	R. W. Horrell	W. E. Smith, Micro	2	..	..	..	..	..	..	..	..	5	4	9
Mount Moriah	S. J. Betts	M. T. Wilder, Clayton, r. f. d	4	800	300	6	3	..	7	2	..	67	86	153
Nobles' Chapel	R. W. Horrell	N. L. Stott, Taylor	4	700	300	1	..	..	..	2	2	36	42	78
New Bethel		N. B. Bryan, Garner	4	800	400	3	6	..	1	..	1	40	42	82
Oak		H. Four Oaks	2	300	400	..	2	..	..	..	1	7	10	17
Parrish Memorial	B. G. Early	J. D. Selma r, f. d. 4	1	500	400	18	..	1	..	..	1	24	26	50
Pauline	R. W. Horrell	N. W. Smith, Four Oaks, r. f. d. 1	2	..	..	10	4	4	2	..	2	16	19	35
Pine del	B. G. Early	Mrs. Ida Davis, Pine Level	3	200	225	11	1	1	1	..	..	13	25	38
Pisgah	D. F. Putnam	Arelius G. Jones, Smithfield	3	1000	500	3	2	2	..	..	..	23	29	52
Princeton	R. W. Horrell	W. I Pearce, Princeton	3	300	300	18	3	3	1	..	..	34	57	91
Sardis	B. G. Early	N. B. Stevens, Smithfield	4	300	200	..	..	..	..	..	..	4	11	15
Selma	C. W. Blanchard	J. W. Liles, Selma	2-4	1500	400	2	8	1	8	2	2	51	65	116
Shiloh	B. Townsend	C. H. Holland, Garner, r. f. d	2	800	400	2	1	1	2	1	1	31	38	59
Smithfield	J. W. Suttle	T. J. Lassiter, Smithfield	1-3	4500	700	23	25	1	12	2	3	70	77	147
Thanksgiving		W. G. Earp, Selma, r. f. d. 1	3	900	300	..	..	2	1	..	..	25	27	52
Trinity	D. F. Putnam	J. S Lawhon, Benson, r. f. d. 2	3	300	200	7	..	1	2	..	1	11	24	35
White Oak	A. A. Pippin	J. I Murphrey, Selma, r. f. d. 1	2	350	400	21	8	1	2	..	..	42	77	119
Wilson's Mills	J. W. Suttle	R. L. Oey, Wilson's Mills	4	700	300	..	6	..	1	1	..	19	30	49
Totals						296	116	32	86	23	27	1193	1732	2925

SUNDAY SCHOOL STATISTICS.

CHURCHES.	SUPERINTENDENTS AND P. O.	Officers and Teachers	Scholars.	Total.	Average Attendance.	Schools.	Volumes in Library.	Quarterli's and papers taken.	Months kept open.	Baptisms from S. S.	Expenses.
Antioch	W. H. Maden, Archer, r. f. d. 1	7	150	157	73	1		120	12	11	$16 00
Baptist Centre	J. C. Hardee, Clayton, r. f. d. 1	5	50	55	25	1		60	12	7	6 00
Benson	J. E. Wall, Benson	9	162	171	140	2	100	175	12	12	50 00
Bethany	Kirkman Creech, Kenly, r. f. d. 2	6	45	51	25	1		45	6	5	5 15
Bethesda	J. J. Wallace, Wilson's Mills	7	55	62	40	1	40	50	12	2	8 00
Bethel											
Blackman's Grove	F. P. Wood, Four Oaks, r. f. d. 2	5	40	45	30	1		42	12	4	1 71
Carter's Chapel	J. I. Blackman, Micro	6	62	68	40	1			12	6	5 53
Clayton	R. H. Gower, Clayton	20	235	255	145	1	176	388	12	14	63 87
Clyde's Chapel	Luther Bunch, Clayton, r. f. d. 2	12	140	152	80	2	100	100	12	15	9 44
Corinth	J. A. Estridge, Archer, r. f. d. 1	5	68	73	35	1		40	9	7	4 00
Calvary											
Four Oaks	O. D. Stanley, Four Oaks	6	50	56	30	1		50	12		14 19
Hood's Grove											
Lee's Chapel	W. I. Green, Selma, r. f. d. 3	9	128	137	75	2		144	12	18	9 12
Live Oak											
Micro	David Pace, Micro	5	80	85	40	1		65	12		6 00
Mount Moriah	J. F. Pool, Clayton	11	125	136	70	1	350	131	12	5	32 73
Nobles' Chapel	J. R. Todd, Taylor	5	70	75	48	1		40	12	1	
New Bethel	D. T. Bryan, Garner	5	45	50		1	100	50	12		5 00
Oliver's Grove											
P rrish Memorial	J. F. Watson, Pine Level	6	36	36	20	1		72	6	8	2 50
Pauline											
Pine Level	W. M. Eason, Selma, r. f. d. 4	7	46	53	40	1		50	12	7	5 00
Pisgah	R. H. Higgins, Smithfield, r. f. d. 1	5	30	35	20	1		38	12	2	5 38
Princeton	Charlie Holt, Princeton	5	85	90	50	1		96	9	13	36 00
Sardis											
Selma	C. W. Richardson, Selma	10	268	278	125	1		350	12	1	120 00
Shiloh	D. H. Holland, Garner, r. f. d.	8	60	68	30	1		25	12		6 00
Smithfield	J. M. Beatty, Smithfield	17	225	242	160	2	200	350	12	21	71 77
Thanksgiving											
Trinity											
White Oak	V. R. Turley, Clayton, r. f. d. 2	8	78	96	50	1		85	12	15	9 13
Wilson's Mills	J. T. Holt, Wilson's Mills	7	41	48	36	1		61	12		6 00
Totals		196	2368	2564	1427	29	1066	2 627		174	469 52

CHURCHES.	Number of Members	Pastors Salary	Building and repairing	Incidentals	The Poor	State Missions	Home Missions	Foreign Missions	Sunday School Missions	Orphanage	Ministerial Education	Aged Ministers Relief	Other Objects	Minutes and Clerk	Total
Antioch	167	$137 15			$8 82	$15 00	$1 50	$1 50	$	$3 46	50	2 00	$16 00	60	$186 83
Baptist Centre	78	100 00	$80			22 00	3 00	2 50		13 08	1 00	1 00	6 00	2 00	151 88
Benson	149	250 00	23 00	$20 00		66 00	7 00	18 00		16 00		3 00	71 26	3 00	478 76
Bethany	74	30 00				6 00	2 00	1 00		2 90	5 00	1 50	5 15	1 00	51 15
Bethesda	169	150 00		2 00		25 00	5 00	6 00		15 00	1 25	3 00	18 00	2 50	228 00
Bethel	14	12 00				2 00		50	5 00	1 00		1 00			19 00
Blackman's Grove	60	89 76		45		25 00	3 00	5 50		6 00	2 00	2 00	17 71	1 00	153 12
Carter's Chapel	69	32 50	75 00			11 35	1 50	1 25		2 00	75	1 00	17 33	1 00	134 13
Clayton	268	500 00	318 26	47 03		183 13	134 45	125 00		128 38	1 00	12 50	58 50	5 00	1607 02
Clyde's Chapel	152	75 00	40 00			6 00	2 50	3 00		4 00	30 90	2 00	9 69	1 50	145 79
Corinth	95	39 68	75 00			7 50	2 50	3 00		4 00	2 00	2 00	4 00	1 00	139 68
Calvary	38														
Four Oaks	31	33 75	100 00	4 10		11 00	3 00	2 30		7 00	1 25	1 25	14 19	1 00	79 04
Hood's Grove	32	41 75	85 00			7 00	1 00	2 00		1 00		50		70	158 20
Lee's Chapel	298	125 00		3 00		30 00	5 00	3 00		4 33	2 00	3 00	9 12	1 00	266 72
Live Oak	34	20 30				4 00	1 50	1 00		4 12	1 00	2 00	3 85	1 00	41 71
Micro	9	11 65	122 66	40 41				50	5 00	2 54	50	1 00	6 00	90	148 25
Mount Moriah	153	130 20	1 20			50 00	12 00	100 00		20 00	5 00	4 00	32 73	1 00	401 54
Nobles' Chapel	78	33 75	50 00			20 00	2 00	2 00		2 00	2 00	2 00		1 00	
New Bethel	82	100 00	75 00	5 00		20 00	3 00	5 00		12 00	5 00	5 00	5 00	1 10	236 60
Oliver's Grove	17					2 50							50	50	5 50
Parrish Memorial	50	25 00	200 00		50 00	12 50	1 00	1 00		1 00	1 00	2 00	2 50	1 00	245 50
Pauline	35	18 65				1 50	1 00	1 00		50	50	1 00		55	25 20
Pine Level	38			5 80		5 00	1 00	1 50		1 00	1 00	1 00	15 47	1 30	33 57
Pisgah	52	60 00	13 50	5 00		12 50	2 00	5 00		1 00	1 00	1 25	5 88	40	98 03
Princeton	91	21 75	100 00	5 00	50 00	15 00	1 50			2 00	2 00	2 50	36 00	1 00	192 25
Sardis	15	17 00					7 50	32 80		1 00	1 00	1 00	50	1 00	28 00
Selma	116	500 00		50 00		125 00	2 00	3 00		30 00	10 00	10 00	120 00	3 00	938 30
Shiloh	59	125 00		5 00		20 41	25 00	68 50	6 50	32 74	3 00	2 00	6 00	1 00	177 41
Smithfield	147	350 00	300 00	60 00		196 50			2 43	1 75	10 00	15 00	196 77	5 00	1291 74
Thanksgiving	52	3 00				4 50	2 00	3 00	1 00	3 00			9 13	42	9 17
Trinity	35	30 00				7 50	3 00	1 00		5 00	1 00	2 00		1 00	49 25
White Oak	119	76 00		5 00		22 78	3 00	5 00		6 00	3 00	4 00	9 00	1 00	124 84
Wilson's Mills	49	100 00				10 00							49 50	1 00	187 50
Totals	2925	3238 89	1478 42	232 79	108 82	953 27	243 70	408 55	14 93	345 80	102 15	95 50	718 75	45 07	7985 64

CONTRIBUTIONS FROM SUNDAY-SCHOOLS AND SOCIETIES, 1905.

(Included in table of contributions.)

Sunday Schools and Societies.	Building and Repairs	State Missions.	Home Missions.	Foreign Missions	Orphanage.	Ministerial Education.	Aged Ministers Relief.	Total.
Antioch S. School					96			96
Baptist Centre S. S.		2 00						2 00
Benson S. S.		5 00						5 00
Benson Y. L. M. S.		4 00	2 30	2 35				8 65
Benson Sunbeams				3 00				3 00
Clayton L. A. S.	186 25							186 25
Clayton Junior Union	9 91	5 00		25 00				39 91
Clayton W. M. S.		61 87	123 38	36 55		4 40	2 48	228 68
Clayton S. S.		10 00			67 38			77 38
Clayton Y. L. M. S.		10 00		5 40				15 40
Clayton Baracca Class		10 00						10 00
Clayton Philathea Class		10 00						10 00
Clyde's Chapel		1 46	1 91	1 70	4 00			9 07
Carter's Chapel					1 00			1 00
Four Oaks		1 00			5 00			6 00
Lee's Chapel		2 60	1 71	1 38	4 33			10 02
Selma W. M S		15 85	4 80	3 45		1 45	1 80	27 35
Selma S. S. Classes		20 00						20 00
Selma B. Y. P. U		5 00		2 80				7 80
Smithfield W. M. S		15 00	12 50	12 50				40 00
Smithfield S. S		14 24	6 60	5 97		4 30	2 60	33 71
Smithfield B. Y. P. U		5 00						5 00
Smithfield Sunbeams				8 00				8 00
White Oak Sunday School		5 00						5 00
	196 16	198 02	153 20	108 10	86 97	8 45	4 28	760 18

CHURCHES.	Baptisms 1904.	Baptisms 1905.	Pledged.		Contributed.	Above Pledge.	Below Pledge.	Loss or gain in Membership.		Pledged above or below 1905.	
			1905	1906				Gain.	Loss.	Above.	Below.
.ntioch.........	18	13	$ 24 00	$ 24 00	$ 24 00	$....	$. ..	10	...	$....	$....
aptist Centre..	....	15	33 00	41 00	41 58	8 58	......	11	......	8 00	.....
.enson....	9	14	103 00	124 00	114 50	11 50	......	17	......	21 00	.....
ethany........	3	9	14 00	16 50	15 00	1 00	......	8	......	2 50	......
ethesda.......	2	8	56 00	52 00	56 00	......	......	4	... ..	......	4 00
ethel.	1	...	6 50	10 00	6 50	......	......	......	......	3 50	.....
lackman's Grve	7	5	34 25	34 25	34 25	......	......	5	......	......	.....
arter's Chapel..	8	6	17 75	23 50	19 10	1 35	......	9	.....	5 75	.....
layton.........	6	24	412 50	497 50	614 36	101 86	......	9	.....	85 00	......
lyde's Chapel..	15	16	19 00	22 50	19 50	......	......	27	....	3 50	......
orinth....	10	10	19 00	21 50	20 00	1 00	... ..	8	.....	2 50	.....
alvary *	....	7	......	9 50	......	......	......	6	......	9 50	.....
our Oaks......	....	2	20 00	23 00	25 00	5 00	......	5	.....	3 00	......
ood's Grove...	4	7	14 75	ʿ0 50	14 75	......	......	6	.....	5 75	......
ee's Chapel ...	22	26	44 50	54 50	44 50	......	......	30	.....	10 00	.....
ive Oak.......	..	6	11 00	12 00	13 62	2 62	......	6	.....	1 00	.....
[icro.	2	6	5 50	10 50	7 04	1 54	......	......	2	5 00	.....
[ount Moriah...	....	....	191 00	150 00	196 00	5 00	......	.....	2	......	41 00
oble's Chapel..	5	1	30 00	29 50	30 00	......	......	7	......	......	50
ew Bethel.....	5	3	24 75	26 00	50 50	25 75	......	3	......	1 25	.....
liver's Grove..	1	....	10 00	10 00	4 50	......	5 50	.....	1	......	.....
arrish Memorial	1	18	18 50	22 00	18 50	......	......	13	....	3 50	.....
auline	....	10	5 50	8 00	6 00	......	50	15	.....	2 50	.....
ine Level.....:	2	11	10 00	13 50	10 00	.. ..	......	14	......	3 50	.....
isgah.........	....	3	19 25	19 75	19 25	......	......	4	.....	50	.....
rinceton.......	2	18	28 50	34 50	28 50	......	......	22	.....	6 00	.....
ardis.........	6	....	10 00	10 50	10 50	......	......	......	......	50	.....
elma.........	5	2	187 50	216 50	215 30	27 80	.. ..	1	....	29 00	.....
hiloh.........	2	2	44 50	47 75	39 41	......	5 09	.....	2	3 25	.....
mithfield.....	12	23	217 50	355 50	347 74	128 24	......	32	......	138 00	....
hanksgiving...	16	...	28 00	29 00	5 75	......	22 25	......	......	1 00	.....
rinity........	..	7	17 75	20 50	18 25	50	....	8	....	2 75	.....
hite Oak.. ...	14	21	27 50	30 00	35 28	7 78	......	27	......	2 50	.....
ilson's Mills ..	1	1	31 00	42 00	32 00	1 00	....	6	......	11 00	.....
Totals........	179	296	1736 00	5061 75	2027 18	431 02	32 84	308	7	371 25	45 50

* Received at this session.

Note.—Other Pledges for State Missions 1904–'05, $100.50. Other Pledges for State Missions)05–'06, $417. Three churches fell below their Pledges in contributions $32.84. Thirteen .urches contributed just what they pledged. Seventeen churches exceeded their Pledges in)ntributions $431.02. Three churches pledged $45.30 less than a year ago. Twenty-eight .urches pledged $371.25 more than a year ago. Four churches report a loss in membership of ,ven. Twenty-seven churches report a gain of 308 members. Twenty-nine churches report)6 baptisms last year. Twenty-six churches reported 179 baptisms.

T. J. LASSITER, for Committee.

CONSTITUTION

OF THE

JOHNSTON COUNTY BAPTIST ASSOCIATION.

1. The Association shall be known as the Johnston County Baptist Asso-ciation.

2. Its object shall be to extend the privileges of the Gospel and liberal culture to all the people within its bounds, and by hearty co-operation with the Baptist State Convention to help offer these privileges to all mankind in and out of its bounds, by the cordial co-operation of all the churches con-stituting this body.

3. It shall be composed of the pastors in active service in the Association and such delegates as shall be annually elected by the churches connected with it, each church being entitled to three delegates, unless the membership shall exceed fifty, and then an additional delegate for every twenty-five members, provided no church shall have more than eight delegates.

4. The New Hampshire Declaration of Faith shall be the summary of Divine Truth for determining questions of faith and order in this body, and the churches desiring membership in it must commit themselves to the sub-stance of it, together with the covenant therewith submitted, and this Con-stitution.

5. This Association shall not have power to annul the discipline or exercise authority over any church connected with it, but it may advise with and sever its connection with any church that neglects to preserve Gospel order, or that treats with contempt the objects or advice of the Asociation.

6. Each church shall send to the annual meetings of the Association a letter (the blanks to be furnished by the clerk of the Association), carefully filled as per blank suggestions, stating the full work of the church for the year ending with the close of the month previous to the one in which the Association is held.

7. The Association shall foster State Missions, Home Missions, Foreign Missions, Christian Education, the Aged Ministers' Relief Board, the Thomas-ville Orphanage and the Sunday School Board, and each church shall be re-quested to contribute to the support of these objects annually.

8. Missions and education shall have precedence in their claims upon the consideration of this body in its regular sessions.

9 Whenever a church shall fail to be represented by delegates or letter at the annual sessions of the Association inquiry shall be made for the cause and efforts shall be made to induce such church to do its duty, and the effort shall be continued till the church is recovered or dropped from the roll.

10. The officers of the Association shall be a Moderator, a Vice-Moderator, a Clerk, a Treasurer and an Auditor, elected annually by ballot from among its members, to serve until their successors shall have been elected, and to perform the duties usual to such officers, namely, the Moderator, in presid-ing over the meetings, or the Vice-Moderator in his absence; the Clerk in recording and preserving minutes and other papers belonging to the body; the Treasurer in receiving and disbursing funds belonging to or entrusted to the body according to its will; the Auditor to examine the Treasurer's books at each meeting of the Association and report the same before adjournment.

11. The Association shall appoint annually an Executive Committee of five (5) from its members, who shall be entrusted with the prosecution of Missions in the Association and any other work for the interest of the Master's Kingdom which may be referred to them. This committee shall, as far as possible, co-operate with the State Mission Board in supplying the destitution in our territory, and between the meetings of the Association

take such actions as may seem to them advisable for the advancement of its interest. The committee shall present to the Association at its annual meeting a report of its proceedings, with the names of the missionaries supported on the field, time of service and details of their work, together with such recommendations as in the judgment of the committee the Association should follow in planning its subsequent work.

12. The annual sessions of the Association shall begin on Thursday after the first Lord's Day in November at such place as may be chosen, and an introductory sermon shall be delivered on the first day of the session. Representatives from a majority of the churches constituting the Association shall be a quorum.

13. This Constitution may be amended at any annual session by a two-thirds vote of all the members present.

14. Provision shall be made at each annual Association for a session of the Woman's Central Committee, and all other necessary encouragement offered for the enlargement of the organized work of the Woman's Missionary Societies in the local churches. The proceedings of the Woman's Central Committee shall be recorded as a part of the Minutes of the Association.

BY-LAWS.

1. The daily sessions of the Association shall be opened and closed with prayer.

2. Delegates shall be recognized by letters from their churhces designating them as such.

3. The Moderator shall recognize corresponding messengers or the delegates of newly-received churches by extending to them his right hand.

4. The report of the Executive Board and the Missionary Work of the Association shall take precedence of all other business during the morning session of the second day of the annual session.

5. The Clerk shall record and read the proceedings when called for, superintend the publication and distribution of the Minutes, preserve a file of them, and have it present at each annual session, and deliver to his successor all papers belonging to the body.

6. Members desiring to speak shall first rise and address the Moderator; shall use the term "brother" in speaking to each other; shall not speak on the same subject more than twice without permission, and shall observe the courtesy that becomes Christians.

7. Members shall not absent themselves from the session without permission.

8. The roll of members shall be called at least once and absentees marked.

9. Corresponding messengers and visiting brethren shall be invited to seats, with privilege of speaking, but not of voting.

10. A copy of the Minutes shall be sent to the Secretary of the State Mission Board, the Secretary of the Southern Baptist Convention, the American Baptist Publication Society, 1420 Chestnut street, Philadelphia; the Sunday School Board of the Southern Baptist Convention and the Thomasville Orphanage.

11. All questions of order not herein provided shall be decided by Kerfoot's Parliamentary Law.

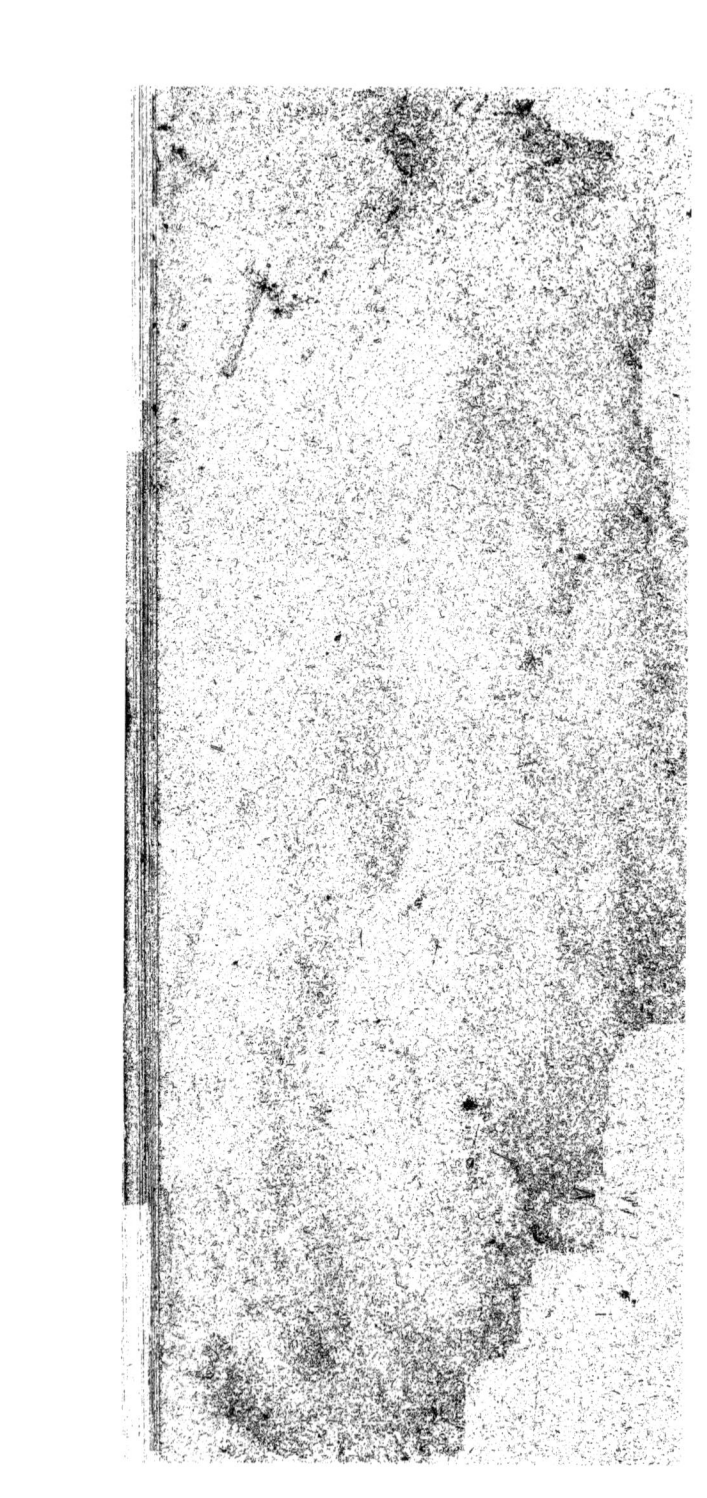

MINUTES

OF THE

FOURTH SESSION

OF THE

JOHNSTON COUNTY

Baptist Association,

HELD WITH

Clyde's Chapel Baptist Church,

NOVEMBER 8, 9, 10 AND 11, 1906.

The next session will be held with Pisgah Baptist Church, beginning Thursday after the first Sunday in November, 1907.

To Preach Introductory Sermon—D. P. Bridges.

GOLDSBORO, N. C.
NASH BROS., PRINTERS AND BINDERS,
1906.

MINUTES

OF THE

FOURTH SESSION

OF THE

JOHNSTON COUNTY

𝕭𝖆𝖕𝖙𝖎𝖘𝖙 𝕬𝖘𝖘𝖔𝖈𝖎𝖆𝖙𝖎𝖔𝖓,

HELD WITH

Clyde's Chapel Baptist Church,

NOVEMBER 8, 9, 10 AND 11, 1906.

———————

The next session will be held with Pisgah Baptist Church, beginning Thursday after the first Sunday in November, 1907

To Preach Introductory Sermon—D. P. Bridges.

———————

GOLDSBORO, N. C.
NASH BROS., PRINTERS AND BINDERS,
1906.

OFFICIAL REGISTER 1906-1907.

Moderator—R. H. Gower.....................................Clayton, N. C.
Vice-Moderator—C. W. Carter..............................Clayton, N. C.
Clerk—T. J. Lassiter......................................Smithfield, N. C.
Treasurer—Will H. Lassiter.............................Smithfield, N. C.
Auditor—J. D. Underwood...............................Smithfield, N. C.

EXECUTIVE COMMITTEE.

J. M. Beaty, Chairman....................................Smithfield, N. C.
J. H. Boon..Benson, N. C.
C. W. Carter...Clayton, N. C.
F. P. Wood.............................R. F. D. No. 2, Four Oaks, N. C.
Alonzo Parrish ....Benson, N. C.

STANDING COMMITTEES.

State Missions ....R. H. Gower.
Home Missions ....D. P. Bridges.
Foreign Missions ....C. W. Blanchard.
Orphanage ....J. M. Hilliard.
Education ....D. F. Putnam.
Periodicals ....J. P. Canaday.
Temperance ....J. M. Beaty.
Ministerial Relief ....A. A. Pippin.
Sunday Schools ....N. R. Pool.
Woman's Work ....C. W. Carter.

Member State Board of Missions.........................C. W. Blanchard.
Delegate to Southern Baptist Convention................D. F. Putnam.
Delegates to Baptist State Convention..................Alonzo Parrish,
                                                       R. H. Gower,
                                                       J. R. Hood.

MINISTERIAL REGISTER.

C. W. Blanchard...Clayton, N. C.
Worley Creech...........................R. F. D. No. 2, Kenly, N. C.
D. P. Bridges..Smithfield, N. C.
N. H. Gibbs..Benson, N. C.
R. W. Horrell..Selma, N. C.
A. A. Pippin...Wakefield, N. C.
D. F. Putnam...Benson, N. C.
J. M. Hilliard......................................R. F. D., Raleigh, N. C.
L. L. Hudson..Wake Forest, N. C.
Jesse Weatherspoon..................................Wake Forest, N. C.

LIST OF MESSENGERS.

Antioch—J. H. Hales and Walter Godwin.

Baptist Center—By letter.

Benson—U. F. Wallace, J. H. Boon, D. F. Putnam, A. Parrish and J. W. Holmes.

Bethany—Moses Creech.

Bethesda—L. B. Smith, W. B. Wallace, T. C. Ellis, D. L. Jones and J. F. Hall.

Bethel—J. H. Bell and W. T. Sullivan.

Blackman's Grove—F. P. Wood, J. M. Blackman and J. L. Smith.

Calvary—J. K. Hudson and J. M. Johnson.

Carter's Chapel—W. B. Wall and H. R. Easom.

Clayton—R. H. Gower, C. W. Carter, C. W. Blanchard, J. H. Johnson and A. Creech.

Clyde's Chapel—J. H. Johnson, H. V. Bunch, J. W. B. Finch and Luther Bunch.

Corinth—N. G. Williamson, J. S. Williamson and J. A. Estridge.

Four Oaks—W. A. Massengill.

Hood's Grove—P. T. George.

Kenly—Represented by R. W. Horrell.

Lee's Chapel—H. W. Wilder and G. T. Allen.

Live Oak—K. Broadwell.

Micro—L. L. Creech.

Mount Moriah—Hezekiah Pool, A. D. Honeycutt and J. M. Baucom.

New Bethel—Andrew Bryan.

Nobles' Chapel—By letter.

Oliver's Grove—By letter.

Parrish Memorial—Not represented.

Pauline—Preston Marler and N. W. Smith.

Pine Level—By letter.

Pisgah—M. Johnson and W. J. Alford.

Princeton—A. J. Mitchell and H. A. Raiford.

Sardis—By letter.

Selma—R. E. Richardson.

Shiloh—D. M. Lee.

Smithfield—J. M. Beaty and T. J. Lassiter.

Thanksgiving—By letter.

Trinity—A. H. Lee.

White Oak—Mallie Green, W. B. Barnes, A. L. Batten and J. W. Barnes.

Wilson's Mills—S. D. West.

Wendell—C. Z. Todd, R. W. Eddins and L. Knott.

PROCEEDINGS.

CLYDE'S CHAPEL, N. C., November 8, 1906.

The fourth annual session of the Johnston County Baptist Association convened this morning at eleven o'clock with Clyde's Chapel Church. The introductory sermon was preached by Brother D. F. Putnam, of Benson, N. C., from Matthew 6:33. "But seek ye first the kingdom of God and His righteousness and all these things shall be added unto you." Subject: "The importance of seeking the kingdom."

In behalf of the church and the community Brother A. A. Pippin, the pastor, welcomed the Association to Clyde's Chapel in a few appropriate sentences.

Before adjournment for dinner the Moderator appointed Brethren U. F. Wallace and Hezekiah Pool as a Committee on Credentials and Enrollment.

AFTERNOON SESSION.

The Association convened at two o'clock. Bro. J. M. Hilliard led the song service and Bro. Hight C. Moore offered prayer.

The body was then called to order by the Moderator, Bro. R. H. Gower. The Committee on Credentials reported, and on motion, the election of officers for the ensuing year was entered into. The rules were suspended and the following officers were elected by acclamation:

Moderator—R. H. Gower.
Vice-Moderator—C. W. Carter.
Clerk—T. J. Lassiter.

The election of Treasurer and Auditor was postponed for the present.

The following visiting brethren were recognized: S. F. Conrad, Field Editor North Carolina Baptist; J. S. Farmer, representative of the Biblical Recorder; G. P. Harrill, representing the Thomasville Orphanage and Charity and Children; Hight C. Moore, Field Secretary of the Sunday School Board; J. M. Hilliard, of the Raleigh Association; D. D. Edwards, of the Raleigh Association; L. L. Hudson, of Wake Forest.

The following committees were announced:

Petitionary Letters—A. A. Pippin, C. W. Blanchard and R. W. Horrell.
Finance—U. F. Wallace, W. A. Massengill and J. W. Barnes.
Program—A. A. Pippin and J. M. Beaty.
Orphanage—F. P. Wood and N. G. Williamson.
Sunday Schools—R. W. Horrell, C. Z. Todd and W. T. Sullivan.

Committee on Petitionary Letters reported that Wendell Church applied for admission and recommended that it be received. Committee's report unanimously adopted and the Moderator welcomed the delegates from Wendell.

On motion it was decided to hold no night sessions.

While waiting for the report of program committee, the report on Temperance was called for which was read by Brother Worley Creech:

REPORT ON TEMPERANCE.

It is known by all thinking men and women that strong drink causes more trouble and sorrow and sin than any one thing in the world; therefore, it becomes us as Christians not to drink it ourselves, and try to get everybody else to quit it if we can.

WORLEY CREECH,
For Committee.

On motion to adopt, the report was discussed by Brethren Worley Creech, S. F. Conrad and J. M. Hilliard. The report then was unanimously adopted.

After the report of the Program Committee was approved the Report on Orphanage, in the absence of Brother B. G. Early, was read by the Clerk.

REPORT ON ORPHANAGE.

The Orphanage holds a large place in the hearts of our people and who can wonder at this, when we think of the great work it is doing? But we have not fully awakened to our responsibility in the care of those left without home and loved ones to care for them. There is but one other class of people that is so much to be pitied as the orphan; that is the insane, and for this class the State makes provision. But the orphans are very largely dependent upon the voluntary contributions of the people for their care.

God has laid the care of a large number of these helpless creatures upon the Baptist brotherhood of North Carolina. We are proud of the records our denomination and State have made in their effort to make provisions for them.

In the Orphanage at Thomasville we have all that can be asked, with few exceptions, to make an ideal home for our orphan children, and these exceptions will be removed as soon as it is possible for those in charge to do so.

The management is superb, the teaching is Christian and up-to-date; the training in the different departments is all that can be looked for to prepare the children for useful citizenship. We appeal to this body for a deeper interest in this institution and ask you to continue to increase your contributions for its support until it shall be able to accommodate every one seeking its help.

We recommend that every church make a special Thanksgiving offering to liquidate the debt of $3,000 that is preventing those in charge, from further increasing its usefulness; that each church increase its pledge at least 25 per cent, the ensuing year; that each Sunday school take a number of Charity and Children.

B. G. EARLY,
For Committee.

After the report was spoken to by Bro. G. P. Harrill, and pledges taken, the same was adopted.

A cash collection of $6.42 was taken for the Orphanage and turned over to Brother Harrill.

Brother R. W. Horrell read the report on Sunday Schools.

REPORT ON SUNDAY SCHOOLS.

Next to the regular preaching service the Sunday School is the most important work in the operation of the church. The Sunday School is even the more important where the church has preaching only once in the month. This is true, because much of the training of the church members for Christian service, and the unsaved to know Christ, must be done by the Sunday School. No church can fill its God-given mission in the world unless it engages in the Sunday School work. The one great mission of the church is to teach the gospel to all people, at home and abroad. The Sunday School affords the best opportunity of presenting the Gospel directly to the individual mind. Every church should have a Sunday-school running fifty-two weeks in the year. It is to be regretted that many of our churches allow their schools to close during the winter season. We very much need more efficiency in our Sunday School work. To have this we must have better prepared officers and teachers than many of our schools now have.

R. W. HORRELL,
For Committee.

Upon motion to adopt the report was discussed by Bro. H. C. Moore. Bro. C. W. Blanchard made a motion to take pledges for Sunday School Missions. Motion carried, and report laid over till to-morrow on account of the lateness of the hour.

Brother L. L. Hudson was appointed to conduct devotional exercises to-morrow. The body then adjourned to meet to-morrow at 9:30. Benediction by Bro. R. W. Horrell.

FRIDAY MORNING.

The Association met this morning according to adjournment. The devotional exercises were conducted by Brother L. L. Hudson, who read a portion of Christ's Sermon on the Mount.

The roll of delegates was called and the Minutes of yesterday's proceedings read and approved.

The moderator announced the following Committee:

Periodicals—T. J. Lassiter, L. L. Hudson and W. J. Alford.
State Missions—C. W. Blanchard, J. H. Hales and D. M. Lee.
Education—C. W. Carter, J. M. Baucom and Moses Creech.
Woman's Work—J. S. Farmer, Mallie Green and J. A. Estridge.
Foreign Missions—Livingston Johnson, L. L. Creech and W. B. Wallace.
Place and Preachers for next meeting—Marion Johnson, H. A. Raiford and S. D. West.
To nominate Executive Committee—C. W. Blanchard, L. B. Smith and N. W. Smith.
To nominate member of State Mission Board—R. W. Horrell, K. Broadwell and A. H. Lee.
To nominate Delegate to Southern Baptist Convention—Alonzo Parrish, R. W. Eddins and A. L. Batten.
To nominate Delegates to Baptist State Convention—R. E. Richardson, Andrew Bryan and N. R. Pool.

The hour for the report of the Executive Committee having arrived, upon motion, the report was postponed for the present and the Report on Periodicals was called for. The report was read by the Clerk.

REPORT ON PERIODICALS.

The Baptist denomination in North Carolina has made rapid strides during the past few years. In a large measure much of our success has been the result of the work of our Baptist papers. They have kept our people in touch with the work, so that the people in our section might know what the people of other sections were doing. This, in many instances, has been a stimulus to the workers to increase their zeal and energy. Without our denominational papers our work in this State would lack one of its most potent factors.

First in importance among our State periodicals we would place the Biblical Recorder, the organ of the Baptist State Convention. This paper was never better than to-day. It is giving to its readers week by week accounts of what our people are doing along all lines. It stands for the advancement of every phase of our denominational life. The good it is doing cannot be measured. Therefore, we most heartily recommend that our pastors urge our people everywhere to subscribe for the Recorder and read it regularly. It would help our churches and stimulate the membership to greater activity in the Master's cause.

We also commend the North Carolina Baptist to the favorable consideration of our people. This paper has been a great agency in the temperance work in this State and is standing, as it has always stood for the principles and doctrines of our denomination.

Charity and Children, the Orphanage paper, is one of the best edited papers in the State, and has no superior in its class anywhere. We comment it to our people.

We also endorse the periodicals and Sunday school literature published by the Baptist Sunday-school Board at Nashville, Tenn., and urge all the Sunday-schools in the Association to use these publications.

The Foreign Mission Journal and our Home Field keeps our people informed of what our Foreign Mission and Home Mission Boards are doing. We commend both these publications to our people, and would urge our pastors to encourage the people to take and read them.

The Church Messenger, the organ of our Association, should have the hearty support of all our people. It can be made a great power for good, and we would like to see it placed in the home of every Baptist within the bounds of the Association.

Let us strive to keep only good periodical literature in the hands of our people, ever encouraging what is good and condemning what is bad.

T. J. LASSITER,
For the Committee.

Upon motion to adopt, the report was discussed by Brethren J. F. Farmer, S. F. Conrad, R. W. Horrell, J. M. Hilliard and C. W. Blanchard. Report adopted.

The Church Messenger was made special order for this afternoon at 2 o'clock.

The report of the Executive Committee was called for and read by Brother J. M. Beaty.

REPORT OF EXECUTIVE COMMITTEE.

We have aided twenty-five churches and Mission points. Bro. A. A. Pippin has served Wendell and Corinth. Six were added at Corinth during the year. A church of twenty-eight members was organized at Wendell.

Bro. R. W. Horrell has preached at Parrish Memorial, Carter's Chapel, Micro, Kenly, Princeton, Woodard School-house, Noble's Chapel and Bethel. Twenty-seven additions have been made to the churches of this field. Micro and Bethel have built houses of worship and are using them. A church of seven members has been organized at Kenly.

Bro. L. L. Hudson has preached at a point in Pleasant Grove township where the prospects for work in the future are encouraging.

Bro. B. G. Early has served Oliver's Grove, Barbour School-house, Thanksgiving, Live Oak, Sardis, Pine Level and Calvary. There were twenty-one additions on this field.

Bro. D. F. Putnam has served Pisgah, Johnson's School-house, Hood's Grove, Pauline, Blackman's Grove, Trinity and Four Oaks. There have been twenty-one additions on this field.

While we have found it hard to make rapid progress in Mission work, we are able to say that the prospects are brighter for the future so far as the work is concerned, but there are two difficulties before us in carrying forward the work. The small amounts raised by some of the churches on pastors salary and the large number of places to be helped, make it very hard for us to keep the finances so as to meet obligations.

J. M. BEATY,
M. C. WINSTON,
J. H. BOON,
J. T. HOLT,
J. F. POOL,
Committee

Upon motion to adopt, the report was discussed by Brother J. M. Beaty, and Brother R. W. Horrell. Report adopted.

Brother Livingston Johnson, Corresponding Secretary of the Baptist State Convention, was recognized.

Brother C. W. Blanchard read the report on State Missions.

REPORT ON STATE MISSIONS.

There is nothing in State Missions to appeal to sentiment but there is very much in it to appeal to reason. Seventy-five years ago the Baptist State Convention was organized. The primary purpose in its organization was to evangelize the State. The brethren were not unmindful of the importance of world-wide evangelization, but wisely concluded that a base of supplies was necessary if we would go to the ends of the earth. During these seventy-five years the Board has had its Missionaries at work in the State. One half of the churches have been organized by Missionaries of the Board and two-thirds of all the money contributed to carry on the Lord's work come from churches that were established and aided by the State Mission Board. If all the churches established by the Board were wiped from the map, our denomination in this State would be a feeble band and could do but little toward advancing the Lord's kingdom. As it is, we are a mighty host and are enlarging our contributions year by year.

While very much has been done, much remains to be done. Our State is rapidly filling up. We may expect thousands of foreigners to come into our borders in the very near future. The country sections are taking on new life and new towns are springing up all over the State. An opportunity now presents itself in the work of State Missions that we have never before known. To neglect this opportunity is to curtail our ability through all the years to come. Every dollar given to State Missions helps every department of our work; for a glance at the Board's report will show that the Missions points are contributing to all the objects of our Convention. As these Mission points grow into self-sustaining churches, they will be able to do more. Thus, by contributing to State Missions we are adding to our invested capital and enlarging the base of supplies.

The State Mission Board has been very liberal to the Johnston Association. It is putting this year more money within our bounds than any other Association save the Tar River. Let us enlarge our contributions to State Missions and begin to look to the day when, instead of receiving from the Board, we will be putting our money into the Treasury to send Missionaries into other sections of the State where there is greater destitution than exists within our own bounds.

C. W. BLANCHARD,
For Committee.

The report was discussed by Brother Livingston Johnson. Pledges were taken and the report unanimously adopted.

At this hour a collection of $14.17 was taken for the benefit of Bethel Church. The sum was turned over to the delegates from that church.

The following additional committees were announced:

Home Missions—D. F. Putnam, P. T. George and G. W. Green.
Ministerial Relief—A. A. Pippin, J. M. Johnson and J. M. Blackman.

The Committee on Petitionary Letters recommended that Kenly church be received into the Association. The Committee's recommendation was unanimously adopted and Kenly Church was welcomed into the body. The body then adjourned for dinner with benediction by Brother J. M. Hilliard.

AFTERNOON SESSION.

The session was opened with prayer by brother C. W. Blanchard. The Church Messenger was taken up and discussed at length, the following brethren taking part in the discussion: T. J. Lassiter, C. W. Blanchard, C. W. Carter, A. H. Lee, R. W. Horrell, C. W. Richardson, J. M. Hilliard, R. H. Gower, and J. M. Beaty.

Brother Beaty suggested that the different churches subscribe for a certain number of The Church Messenger to be furnished at 20 cents per copy per year. This suggestion was received with favor, and 18 of the churches pledged to take several copies each. At this point the disposition of the question was postponed until to-morrow.

Brother C. W. Carter read the

REPORT ON EDUCATION.

Knowledge is power, therefore, it behooves us as Baptists to keep in the forefront of the educational move which seems to pervade our State. Most of the children of our Association are dependent on our public schools for at least a part of their education, therefore we should see to it that they attend these as regularly as possible. We commend our Baptist Institutions to our brethren, especially Wake Forest for all our boys, the Baptist University for Women for all our girls and the Seminary at Louisville for our preachers.

The general educational advancement of our people and the many increasing difficulties arising in ministerial work because of the general growth of isms and schisms as well as the enlargement of the work, make it doubly necessary for our ministry to be educated. The wise management of our Board of Education at Wake Forest College in the past and the outcome of its work, justfy us in giving it henceforth our most ardent support. We urge our young men called of God to preach the gospel to avail themselves of the present open privilege of a liberal education.

C. W. CARTER,
For the Committee.

This report was discussed by Brethren C. W. Carter and C. W. Blanchard. Pledges were taken and the report adopted.

The report on Foreign Missions was next called for.

REPORT ON FOREIGN MISSIONS.

There is no department of our Lord's work that calls for such unselfish effort as Foreign Missions. State pride may lead us to contribute for State Missions, self protection may call for our support to Home Missions, and the Orphanage appeals to our sympathy because it is an Institution to care for the children of our friends and brethren; but when we give to Foreign Missions we are contributing for the good of a people whom we never expect to see in this world and whose religious condition may not affect us as a nation. Nothing but the constraining love of God can impel us to make sacrifices for Foreign Missions. And yet, he who is a friend and supporter of this important object is manifesting the spirit of Christ who came "to seek and to save that which was lost." The interest a church takes in Foreign Missions is a fairly accurate test of its spiritual life. Judged by this standard we are encouraged to believe that our denomination is enjoying some degree of spiritual power.

We have increased more rapidly in our contributions to Foreign Missions than to any other object. Last year the Treasurer's report showed that we had given to Foreign Missions from North Carolina $23,000.00. This year the indications are that we will reach $30,000.00. Throughout the whole South land there is an awakening of interest to Foreign Missions which speaks much for the progress of our Southern Zion. Let us see to it that the Johnston Association takes its place in this mighty forward movement.

LIVINGSTON JOHNSON,
For Committee.

The subject was discussed by Brethren Livingston Johnson and R. W. Horrell. After pledges were taken the report was adopted.

The committee to select an Executive Committee reported as follows: J. M. Beaty, Chairman, J. H. Boon, M. C. Winston, C. W. Carter and F. P. Wood.

The report of the committee was received and the above named were chosen as an Executive Committee for the ensuing year.

Brother M. Johnson, for the Committee on Place and Preachers for next year, recommended that the Association be held with Pisgah Church, four miles west of Smithfield, and that Brother D. P. Bridges preach the Introductory Sermon. The report was adopted.

Other committees reported as follows:

Delegates to Baptist State Convention—A. Parrish, J. R. Hood and R. H. Gower.

Member of State Board of Missions—C. W. Blanchard.

These reports were adopted.

Brother Worley Creech was appointed to conduct the devotional exercises to-morrow morning.

The body then adjourned with benediction by Brother J. S. Farmer.

SATURDAY MORNING.

Association met at 9:30. The devotional exercises were conducted by Bro. Worley Creech.

Reading of Minutes of yesterday's session was dispensed with.

In the absence of Bro. J. S. Farmer, who wrote the report on Woman's Work, the report was read by the clerk.

REPORT ON WOMAN'S WORK.

The inspiration of our Missionary endeavor is the work of women. Year after year they have come to the Convention with words of hope and good cheer. There are now six hundred and sixty-five societies in the State. There were one hundred and seventy-four societies organized last year. This is by far the best year in the history of this work. The contributions last year amounted to $17,158.49, and we can never know the real value of this department of our work. These women are organized into world-wide Mission classes. The contributions to Foreign Missions last year amounted to $5,587.87, to Home Missions $8,311.90, to State Missions $3,092.61 and to expense $167.01.

The Sunbeams contributed $1,102.54 of the above amounts.

Tracts on Missions can be had from the State, Home and Foreign Boards for the asking. Just send a postal card to the Foreign Mission Board, Richmond, Va., and ask for the number of tracts desired; to the Home Mission Board, Atlanta, Ga., for tracts on Home Missions; and for other tracts and information address Miss Fannie E. S. Heck, Raleigh, N. C. Let's enlarge the work.

J. S. FARMER,
For the Committee.

After being discussed by Bro. R. W. Horrell the report was adopted.

The report on Home Missions was called for, and read by Bro. D. F. Putnam.

REPORT ON HOME MISSIONS.

The Home Mission Board is located in Atlanta, Ga., and is composed of a President, VicePresident, Corresponding Secretary, Assistant Corresponding Secretary, Recording Secretary, Treasurer, Auditor and fifteen other managers who reside in Atlanta, with a Vice-President in each State, composing the Convention. W. W. Hamilton, of Atlanta, is General Evangelist, and A. E. Brown, of Asheville, is Superintendent of Mountain Schools.

The field of the Home Board is of vast dimensions, embracing the destitution all over the Southern States, Cuba, Panama and Isle of Pines. In the States the Board work is co-operative as it works in conjunction with the State Boards, where a State is not able to support its own work. The work done in our bounds is designated as frontier work, work in large cities, mountain schools, among the foreign population, and the negroes. The South has twenty-five million population. Eleven million are white natives, nine millions are negroes, and five million are foreigners. The South has become rich and prosperous. The Lord has presented us a great opportunity, and placed upon us a great responsibility, and given us the means to meet the same; shall we not acquit ourselves like men and as soldiers of the cross? Has not God brought Southern Baptists to the kingdom for such a time as this? Think of our own blood and kin, many of whom are not Christians, and the negroes, of whom the gospel is the only hope, with the five million foreigners at present, with more than two millions coming to our shores annually, many of whom will become citizens of the South. We must evangelize them for our own safety. If we fail now, skepticism, infidelity, Romanism, indifference and the licensed saloon will be the dominant forces in the not distant future.

This is already true in New Orleans, Baltimore and St. Louis, which combined have nearly a million and a half of people, with only thirty-six Baptist churches, twenty of which are self-supporting, leaving sixteen that could not exist but for the assistance of the Home Board. The Southwest, where until recently there were no cities and the population very scant, is rapidly building great cities and is becoming very populous.

Many of these people settling in this section are Baptists, and unless the Baptists use the present opportunities they will fail and be great losers; for this section of our country has a great future before it. We have all classes of foreigners right at our door; we must evangelize them or they will paganize us.

In the Appalachian Mountains are two million white people, mostly

Baptists, whose greatest need is education of the right kind. We must educate them or other denominations will do so, and lead them away from us. The Baptists have twenty-two schools that are being helped by the Board. Brother Brown's report shows great progress in this department of the Board's work.

Cuba, which lies so near us, has fallen into the hands of the Southern Baptists for evangelization. The Board has more than twenty missionaries and workers on the island, has much valuable church property, and is building chapels and has recently opened a college in Havana. Many baptisms are reported. Panama has attracted the eyes of the whole world since the United States has acquired possession and undertaken to make the canal. We who live so near should push the work to be done there.

What Has and Is Being Done.

Last year eight hundred and thirty-eight missionaries were employed, doing twenty-two thousand eight hundred and sixty-one weeks' labor, supplying 2,617 churches or stations, preached 102,338 sermons, held 12,772 prayer meetings, made 224,013 religious visits, baptized 12,630, received by letter 12,178, constituted 302 churches, built and repaired 201 houses of worship, organized 541 Sunday schools, distributed 24,798 Bibles and Testaments and 2,217,246 pages of tracts. Total amount raised and expended in this work, $176,411.76. So we see much has been done, but the needs are immeasurable.

The Convention at Chattanooga last May instructed the Board to increase the appropriation and enlarge the work. The Convention also instructed the Board to undertake to raise twenty-five thousand dollars additional for evangelistic work. This is the paramount work it seems to us—the sane evangelization of our Southern States—for, in so doing, we are reaching to a certain extent all nations. Paul's word to Timothy, "Do the work of an evangelist," should receive new emphasis. A converted and well-trained membership will be necessary to meet the demands of our Association, and we urge our members to subscribe for and read Our Home Field.

D. F. PUTNAM,
P. T. GEORGE,
Committee.

Upon motion to adopt the report was discussed by Brethren D. F. Putnam, R. W. Horrell and A. A. Pippin. Pledges were then taken and the report adopted.

Bro. A. N. Cullom, of the Tar River Association, was recognized.

Bro. T. J. Lassiter announced that he would continue the publication of The Church Messenger at his own expense, and thus relieve the Association of any further responsibility. This announcement was received with satisfaction, and the churches were urged to help increase the circulation of the little paper.

A communication was received from Bro. C. W. Richardson resigning as Treasurer of the Association. The resignation was accepted and Bro. Will H. Lassiter, of Smithfield, was unanimously elected Treasurer.

Brother J. D. Underwood was unanimously elected Auditor.

A message was received from Brother M. C. Winston stating that he could not serve as member of Executive Committee. Bro. Alonzo Parrish, of Benson, was elected in his stead.

A resolution was passed instructing all the churches, Sunday Schools and Societies to send all State Mission funds to the Association's Treasurer, Bro. Will H. Lassiter, at Smithfield, N. C., and that the treasurer report promptly all funds received by him in The Church Messenger.

The report on Aged Ministers' Relief was read by Bro. A. A. Pippin.

REPORT ON MINISTERS' RELIEF.

We should feel as a denomination the great responsibility that rests upon us in caring for the good old men, who have worn out their lives going up and down our State teaching the lost how to be saved and establishing churches in destitute places. We should show them our love and appreciation, by supporting them and their families. Every church in our Association should see to it that at least one collection should go to their support. We are very glad to notice that most of our churches in this Association have done something for this noble and very worthy object during the past year.

A. A. PIPPIN,
J. M. JOHNSON,
J. M. BLACKMAN,
Committee.

Upon motion to adopt the report was discussed by Brethren A. A. Pippin and D. F. Putnam. Pledges were taken and report adopted.

The Sunday School report was again taken up. Pledges for the work were taken and the report adopted.

Finance Committee's report was read and received. (See report on another page).

The Executive Committee was instructed to examine the Treasurer's books, make report and have same printed in the Minutes. (Report not received in time for insertion in the Minutes.)

Committee on Delegate to Southern Baptist Convention reported that Bro. D. F. Putnam had been chosen. Report adopted.

A resolution was passed instructing the clerk to have printed 1,000 copies of the Minutes and distribute the same, and that he be allowed $10 for his services.

Upon motion a rising vote of thanks was tendered the people of the community for the hospitable manner in which they entertained the Association.

Bro. Hight C. Moore was appointed to lead in the Sunday School Mass Meeting to-morrow morning at 10:00 o'clock. Bro. C. W. Blanchard was appointed to preach at 11:00 o'clock.

Bro. D. F. Putnam was appointed to preach this afternoon.

The congregation then joined in singing "My Faith Looks up to Thee," after which the body adjourned with benediction by Bro. Worley Creech.

SUNDAY MORNING.

Song service was led by Bro. A. N. Cullom, of Wilson, N. C. According to appointment at 10 o'clock Bro. Hight C. Moore made a strong address on the Sunday School work. At eleven o'clock Bro. C. W. Blanchard preached to a packed house from Isaiah 52:1. After the sermon a collection was taken for the Thomasville Orphanage.

WOMAN'S MISSIONARY UNION.

The Woman's Missionary Union of the Johnston County Association held its Third Annual Meeting with Clyde's Chapel Church, Friday afternoon, November 9th, 1906.

The Association occupying the church, the near-by home of Mrs. Mitchell was kindly-offered to the women, which was accepted.

The meeting was presided over by our Vice-President, Mrs. Ashley Horne, who·read for our scriptural lesson the 103rd Psalm;· Mrs. Bunch, of Clyde's Chapel Society in a short, but sincere and cordial address welcomed delegates and visitors, to ·which Mrs. Carter responded. We then had the pleasure of listening to Bro. L. Johnson, who brought us a beautiful, and we trust an abiding lesson, on faith and duty, using as his subject the widow of Serepta and the prophet Elijah. The first order of business was the election of a Secretary, this vacancy being caused by the removal of our former Secretary, Mrs. Petway, into the Neuse Association. We then heard the reading of reports from fifteen Societies. Enlarged efforts for another year,. seemed to be the spirit of the entire body.

Clayton W. M. S. apportioned aim.................................$ 203.00
Clayton Y. L. S. apportioned aim................................. 35.00
Clayton Junior Union apportioned aim........................... 15.00
Clyde's Chapel 15.00
Mount Moriah 30.00
    Other societies not yet heard from.

MRS. C. W. CARTER,
Secretary.

FINANCIAL REPORT.

SOCIETIES.	State.	Home.	Foreign.	Total.
Clayton W. M. Society.................	$ 72.01	$ 42.68	$ 35.31	$ 150.00
Smithfield W. M. Society...............	21.11	16.37	19.02	56.50
Selma W. M. Society...................	25.00	15.00	10.00	50.00
Benson W. M. Society..................	22.80	12.30	12.30	48.50
Mount Moriah W. M. Society...........	80	16.06	4.31	21.17
Clyde's Chapel W. M. Society..........	2.68	3.35	3.18	9.68
Baptist Center W. M. Society..........	1.20	1.20	1.30	3.70
Four Oaks W. M. Society...............	....	....	....	3.90
Micro W. M. Society...................	24	35	1.00	1.59
Pisgah W. M. Society..................	50	50	78	1.78
Clayton Junior Union Society..........	....	....	25.00	25.00
Selma Sunbeams Society...............	5.00	....	....	5.00
Benson Sunbeams Society..............	4.00	....	....	4.00
Smithfield Sunbeams Society...........	....	....	....	1.65
Micro Sunbeams Society...............	19	19	75	1.13
Clayton Y. L. Society.·................	15.67	5.00	10.00	30.67
				$ 414.27

FINANCE COMMITTEE'S REPORT.

CHURCHES.	Minutes and Clerk.	State Missions.	Home Missions.	Foreign Missions.	Orphanage.	Ministerial Education.	Aged Ministers' Relief.	Sunday School Missions.	Totals.
Antioch									
Baptist Centre	$ 2.00								$ 2.00
Benson	3.00								3.00
Bethany	.75	6.50	2.50	2.00	$ 3.00	$ 1.25	$ 1.25		17.25
Bethesda	1.50	5.14	5.00	2.00	15.00	2.00	3.00		33.64
Bethel	.60	4.00	1.00	1.00		1.00	1.00		8.60
Blackman's Grove	1.00	15.00	3.00		3.20	2.75	2.00	2.00	28.95
Calvary	1.07				2.00	1.00	1.00		5.07
Carter's Chapel	.50	5.95	2.00	1.50	2.80	1.00	1.00		18.05
Clayton	5.00								5.00
Clyde's Chapel	1.60	9.65	1.00	1.00	2.80	1.00	1.00		18.85
Corinth	1.00	4.03	2.17	2.12	3.72	1.00	2.00		16.04
Four Oaks	1.00	11.00	3.00	3.00	3.00	1.50	2.50		25.00
Hood's Grove	.95								.95
Live Oak	1.00								1.00
Lee's Chapel	1.40	32.00	5.00	3.58	2.00	1.50	3.00		48.48
Mount Moriah	1.50	47.47	11.46	44.59	21.66	5.00	2.84	5.00	139.52
Micro	.40	5.00	.50	1.00	2.00	1.00	1.00	2.73	13.63
New Bethel	1.00								1.00
Nobles' Chapel	1.15								1.15
Oliver's Grove	.25	2.00	.50	.50	.75	.50	.50		5.00
Parrish Memorial									
Pauline	.50	2.00	1.50	1.50	1.50	.50	1.00		8.50
Pine Level	1.00				2.00		1.50	2.50	7.00
Pisgah	.55								.55
Princeton	1.20	15.20	4.00	5.00	4.00	2.50	2.00		33.90
Sardis	.25	5.00	1.00	1.00	.25	1.00	1.00		9.50
Selma	3.00								3.00
Shiloh		11.00	1.00	2.50	7.80	1.00	1.00		24.30
Smithfield	5.00								5.00
Thanksgiving	.90	4.20	1.00	2.20	3.00				11.30
Trinity	.60	8.00	4.00		3.00	1.00	1.00		17.60
White Oak	2.00	11.46	4.00	2.50	1.81	1.50	2.00	1.24	26.51
Wilson's Mills		10.85	5.00	5.00	10.00	4.00	3.00	1.00	38.85
Wendell	1.00	1.00	1.00	1.00	1.00				5.00
General Collection					6.42				
Special Collection	4.28								
Total	$46.95	$216.45	$59.63	$82.99	$106.91	$32.00	$35.59	$14.47	$594.99

CHURCH PLEDGES EOR 1907.

CHURCHES.	State Missions.	Home Missions.	Foreign Missions.	Sunday School Missions.	Orphanage.	Ministerial Education.	Ministerial Relief.	Totals.
Antioch	$ 25.00	$ 1.50	$ 1.50	$ 1.00	$ 2.50	$ 1.50	$ 2.00	$ 35.00
Baptist Centre	22.00	3.00	2.00	1.00	10.00	2.00	2.00	42.00
Benson	86.50	13.50	19.00	2.00	20.00	5.00	4.00	150.00
Bethany	6.50	2.50	2.00	1.00	3.00	1.25	1.25	17.50
Bethesda	25.00	5.00	2.00	1.00	15.00	2.00	3.00	53.00
Bethel	4.00	1.50	1.50	.50	2.00	1.00	1.00	11.50
Blackman's Grove	16.00	4.00	6.00	2.00	7.00	3.00	2.50	40.50
Carter's Chapel	10.00	2.50	1.50	1.00	5.00	1.50	2.00	23.50
Clayton	200.00	50.00	125.00	10.00	135.00	25.00	12.50	557.50
Clyde's Chapel	10.00	4.00	4.00	1.50	5.00	2.00	2.50	29.00
Corinth	6.00	1.50	2.00	.50	4.00	1.00	2.00	17.00
Calvary	3.00	1.50	1.00	.50	2.00	1.00	1.25	10.25
Four Oaks	10.00	3.00	3.00	1.00	3.00	1.50	2.50	24.00
Hood's Grove	10.00	2.00	3.00	1.00	2.00	2.00	1.50	21.50
Kenly	3.00	1.00	1.00	.50	2.00	1.00	1.00	9.50
Lee's Chapel	35.00	5.00	5.00	1.00	5.00	2.00	3.00	56.00
Live Oak	5.00	1.00	1.00	.50	4.00	1.00	2.00	14.50
Micro	5.00	1.25	1.25	.50	2.25	1.00	1.00	12.25
Mount Moriah	50.00	20.00	50.00	5.00	30.00	5.00	5.00	165.00
Nobles' Chapel	17.00	3.00	2.00	1.00	4.00	2.00	2.00	31.00
New Bethel	15.00	3.00	2.00	1.00	3.00	2.00	1.00	27.00
Oliver's Grove	6.00	1.00	1.00	.50	1.00	.50	.50	10.50
Parrish Memorial	15.00	1.50	1.50	.50	2.00	1.00	2.00	23.50
Pauline	4.00	1.50	1.50	.50	1.50	1.00	1.00	11.00
Pine Level	6.00	1.25	1.50	.50	2.00	1.25	1.50	14.00
Pisgah	12.50	2.00	2.50	2.00	2.00	1.00	1.50	23.50
Princeton	18.00	4.00	5.00	1.00	4.00	2.00	2.50	36.50
Sardis	5.00	1.00	1.00	.50	1.50	1.00	1.00	11.00
Selma	125.00	10.00	30.00	4.00	30.00	11.50	10.00	220.50
Shiloh	10.00	3.25	2.00	1.00	5.00	2.00	2.50	25.75
Smithfield	225.00	40.00	50.00	10.00	40.00	12.00	16.00	393.00
Thanksgiving	15.00	2.00	5.00	.50	4.00	1.00	2.00	29.50
Trinity	5.00	4.00	3.50	.50	3.00	1.00	1.00	18.00
White Oak	15.00	4.50	2.50	1.00	5.00	1.50	2.00	31.50
Wilson's Mills	15.00	5.50	5.00	1.00	10.00	4.00	3.00	43.50
Wendell	3.00	1.00	2.00	1.00	3.00	1.00	1.00	11.50
Total	$1043.50	$212.25	$349.75	$ 58.50	$378.75	$105.50	$102.50	$2250.75

Additional Pledges for State Missions—F. P. Wood, $10.00; Mount Moriah W. M. Society, $3.00; Blackman's Grove Sunday School, $2.00; Pauline Sunday School, $2.00; A. H. Lee, $2.00.

CHURCH STATISTICS.

CHURCHES.	PASTORS.	Clerks and Addresses.	Preaching Sunday.	Value of Ch. Property.	Seating Capacity.	Baptisms.	Received by Letter.	Restored.	Lost by Letter.	Dismissed.	Died.	Males.	Females.	Total Membership.
Bath	Worley Creech	R. R. ...th, Selma, r. f. d. 2	2½	500	400	6	3	1	1	3	3	52	114	166
Baptist Centre	C. W. Blanchard	G. C. Bryan, ...h, r. f. d. 1	1-3	550	400		1		1			30	47	77
Benson	D. F. Putnam	E. L. Hall, Benson	2-4	1250	400	3	1		6	2		49	96	145
Bethany	W. ...h	Kirkman ...h, Kenly	4	600	300	3	1		1		1	30	47	77
Bethesda	D. P. Bridges	J. E. Smith, Wilson's Mills	4	600	400	24	6	1	5	2		73	119	192
Bethel	R. W. Horrell	John ...y, Kenly, r. f. d. 3	4	400	200	6	1					9	13	22
Blackman's Grove	D. F. Putnam	E. B. Hayes, Four Oaks	3	500	300	4	4	1			1	23	38	61
Carter's Chapel	R. W. Horrell	W. B. Wall, Micro		700	350	4	4	1	4	3	1	23	48	71
Clayton	C. W. Blanchard	R. R. Gulley, ...ton	1-3	5500	600	4	5	1	13	1	2	113	157	270
Clyde's Chapel	A. A. Pippin	C. L. ...n, Wendell		450	400	8	5		1	3	2	64	93	157
Corinth	A. A. Pippin	E. C. ...ley, ...er, r. f. d. 1	4	450	400	5	1		3		1	38	57	95
Calvary	B. G. Early	T. J. Lee, Dunn	4	500	200				1			12	24	36
Four Oaks	D. F. Putnam	J. W. Langdon, Four Oaks	3	700	500	5	5		2			10	27	37
Hood's Grove	D. F. Putnam	Jos. W. ...d, ...n, r. f. d. 2	2	400	350							12	19	31
* Kenly	R. W. Horrell											7		7
Live Oak	B. G. Early	K. Broadwell, Selma	2	300	250	2		1		1		11	23	34
Lee's Chapel	A. A. Pippin	W. I. Green, Selma, r. f. d. 3	4	300	700		2		2	2	2			294
Mt Moriah	R. W. Horrell	W. E. Smith, Selma	2	500	500					3		4	3	7
Nobles' Chapel	J. M. Hilliard	M. T. Wilder, Clayton	4	800	300	6	4		5		1	66	82	148
New Bethel	R. W. Horrell	N. L. Stott, Taylor	4	700	300		6		5		1	28	39	67
Oliver's Grove	Jesse Weatherspoon	N. B. Bryan, Garner	4	800	400	2	2					40	45	85
**Parrish Memorial	B. G. Early	H. Johnson, Four Oaks	1	200	300							7	11	18
Pauline	R. W. Horrell	N. W. Smith, Four Oaks, r. f. d. 1	2	300	300	7	2			2		19	23	50
Pine Level	D. F. Putnam	F. C. Price, Pine Level	3	300	225	8		1	1		3	17	30	47
Pisgah	B. G. Early	A. G. Jones, Smithfield	1	1000	500		2		1		1	22	29	51
Princeton	R. W. Horrell	W. I. Pearce, Princeton	3	800	300	5	5		3	2	1	33	62	95
Sardis	B. G. Early	N. B. Stevens, Smithfield	3	300	200	4	1					7	13	20
Selma	C. W. Blanchard	J. W. ...ds, Selma	2-4	1500	350		2		5	5	1	52	59	111
Shiloh	L. L. Hudson	J. F. Hardee, ...s, r. f. d. 1	3	500	200	14	4	2		2	3	30	40	70
Smithfield	D. P. Bridges	T. J. ...r, Smithfield	1-3	1500	700				15		1	73	75	148
Thanksgiving	B. G. Early	W. G. Earp, Selma	2	800	300	4					1	27	30	57
Trinity	D. F. ...n	J. S. ...n, ...m, r. f. d. 2	3	300	200	3	1	1	2	2		27	30	57
White Oak	A. A. Pippin	J. I. Murphrey, Selma, r. f. d. 1	2	300	400	2	1		2	2		12	28	40
Wilson's Mills	D. P. Bridges	J. T. Holt, Wilson's Mills	4	400	300		7		5	3		39	78	117
												14	27	41

CHURCHES	Superintendents and Addresses	Officers and Teachers	Scholars	Total	Average Attendance	Schools	Volumes in Library	Qu'lies and Papers taken	Months kept open	Baptisms from School	Expenses
...	W. H. Maden, Selma, R. F. D. No. 2	6	150	156	45	1	...	80	12	6	$ 12.00
Baptist Centre	J. C. Hardee, Clayton	5	60	65	30	1	150	55	12	3	3.60
Benson	A. Parrish, Benson	10	181	191	110	2	100	200	12	2	32.65
Bethany	David Pace, ...	8	100	108	50	1	...	100	9	3	5.00
Bethesda	J. J. Wallace, Wilson's Mills	7	53	60	40	1	50	60	12	10	20.00
Blackman's Grove	F. P. Wood, Four Oaks	3	40	43	24	1	...	108	12	2	2.26
Carter's Chapel	J. W. McCall, Selma, R. F. D. No. 4	6	78	84	40	1	176	205	12	2	10.00
Clayton	R. H. Gower, Clayton	17	240	257	144	1	50	325	12	1	59.75
Clyde's Chapel	Luther Bunch, ..., R. F. D. No. 2	6	60	66	40	1	...	75	12	7	6.00
...	J. A. Estridge, Archer, R. F. D. No. 1	7	63	70	40	1	...	65	9	5	10.12
Calvary	M. L. Barefoot, Dunn, R. F. D. No. 2	5	27	32	20	1	...	32	9	...	...
Four Oaks	O. D. Stanley, Four Oaks	4	30	34	25	1	...	35	12	3	27.50
Hood's Grove	J. F. Jernigan, Beasley, R. F. D. No. 2	4	22	26	20	1	...	25	9	...	3.00
...	W. I. Green, Selma, R. F. D. No. 3	5	60	65	30	2	...	75	8	...	10.00
Mt. Moriah	L. L. ..., ...	6	100	106	50	1	360	100	12	6	6.50
Nobles' ...	J. F. Pool, Clayton	11	123	134	70	1	...	146	12	...	20.00
Pauline	J. H. Flowers, Taylor	5	65	70	35	1	...	48	12	2	...
Pine Level	N. W. Smith, Four Oaks, R. F. D. No. 1	7	57	64	30	1	...	30	12	...	...
Pisgah	W. M. Eason, Selma, R. F. D.	4	32	36	26	1	...	60	12	8	6.00
Princeton	R. H. Higgins, Smithfield	7	25	32	...	1	...	35	12	...	...
Selma	... H. Holt, Princeton	10	137	147	75	1	...	132	12	4	12.00
Shiloh	J. R. Hood, Selma	9	194	203	100	1	200	315	12	4	50.00
Smithfield	C. H. Bunday, Garner, R. F. D. No. 1	6	25	31	20	1	...	31	12	4	...
Trinity	J. M. Beaty, Smithfield	17	200	217	115	2	200	250	12	5	101.42
... Oak	J. S. ..., Benson, R. F. D. No. 2	4	16	20	10	1	...	...	6	...	...
Wilson's Mills	V. R. Turley, ..., R. F. D. No. 2	6	75	81	40	1	...	70	12	1	30.00
Wendell	J. T. Holt, Wilson's Mills	6	50	56	40	1	...	75	12	...	...
	C. Z. Todd, ...	8	90	98	65	1	...	80	12	...	12.00
Total		199	2353	2552	1334	31	1086	2752	...	74	$339.80

Note—Bethel, Kelly, Live Oak, New Bethel, Oliver's Grove, Parrish Memorial, Sardis and Thanksgiving report no Sunday Schools.

CHURCHES	No. of Members	Pastor's Salary	Building and repairing	Inci-dentals	The Poor	State Missions	Home Missions	Foreign Missions	Orphanage	Ministerial Education	Aged Ministers' Relief	S. S. Missions	Other Objects	Sunday School Expenses	Totals
Antioch	166	$ 70.25	$ 75.00	30	$ 2.56	$ 25.00	$ 1.50	$ 1.50	$ 2.50	$ 1.50	$ 2.00	$ 2.00	$	$ 12.00	$ 118.81
Baptist Centre	77	100.00		60.00		22.00	3.00	2.00	10.00	2.00	4.00			3.60	219.90
Benson	145	250.00	4.00			82.80	22.30	27.30	45.00	5.00	4.00		91.75	32.65	624.90
Bethany	77	25.00		1.25		.6.50	2.50	2.00	3.00	1.25	1.25			5.00	50.50
Bethesda	192	150.00	150.00			25.00	5.00	2.00	15.00	2.00	3.00		100.00	20.00	323.25
Bethel	22					4.00	1.00	1.00		1.00	1.00				8.00
Blackman's Grove	61	100.00	150.00	40		15.00	3.00	5.50	6.00	2.75	2.00	2.00	25.85	2.26	314.76
Carter's Chapel	71	36.85				12.00	2.00	1.50	7.00	1.00	2.00			10.00	72.35
Clayton	270	500.00	755.00	100.00		180.00	42.08	150.00	120.00	27.00	12.50	6.39		59.75	1079.46
Clyde's Chapel	157	100.00	150.00		3.12	9.65	6.94	4.98	8.12	3.15	1.52		26.14	6.00	284.34
Corinth	95	75.00	1.00		4.45	7.50	2.50	3.50	5.00	1.00	2.00			10.12	112.07
?	36	40.00	20.00			3.00	1.50	1.00	2.00	1.00	1.00				69.50
Four Oaks	37	63.70				10.00	3.00	3.00	8.00	1.50	2.50		32.27	27.50	151.47
Hood's Grove	31	39.55	40.00	25.00		10.00	2.00	3.00	2.00	2.00	1.50			3.00	128.05
*Kenly	7														
Lee's Chapel	204	125.00	200.00			35.00	5.00	5.00	4.00	1.50	3.00			10.00	388.50
Live Oak	34	21.50	25.00	7.00		4.00	1.00	1.00	4.15	1.00	2.00	70			67.35
Mero	7	11.48	225.00	33.05		5.00	50	1.00	2.00	1.00	1.00			6.50	253.44
Mt Moriah	148	150.00	6.31			50.00	15.00	55.00	52.06	5.00	5.00	5.00		20.00	421.09
Nobles' Chapel	67	31.00				17.00	2.50	2.00	4.00	2.00	2.00				60.50
New Bethel	85	100.00	10.00			27.00	5.00	5.00	15.20	2.50	2.50				167.20
Oliver's Grove	18					2.00	50	50	75	50	50				5.00
*Parrish Memorial	50														
Pauline	42	16.55				2.00	1.50	1.50	1.50	50	1.00	50			25.05
Pine Level	47	1.20	55.00			7.00	1.25	1.50	2.75	1.50	1.50	3.00			74.70
Pisgah	51	64.00	15.00	1.00		13.25	1.75	2.75	2.00	1.00	1.25	2.00		6.00	110.00
Princeton	95	30.00	192.17	1.50		17.00	4.00	5.00	4.00	2.00	2.50		1.20	12.00	271.37
Sardis	20	18.00				5.00	1.00	1.00	1.50	1.00	1.00				28.50
Selma	111	500.00		55.00		129.00	10.00	30.00	30.00	11.50	10.00			50.00	825.25
Shiloh	70	128.50				11.00	1.00	2.50	7.80	1.00	1.00				152.80
Smithfield	148	440.00	159.96			286.08	37.50	50.00	40.00	12.00	16.00	6.65	155.46	171.42	1275.07
Thanksgiving	57	19.35	76.17	1.00		8.00	1.00	2.20	3.00	45	50		90	8.00	129.07
Trinity	40				10.25	15.00	4.00	3.50	3.00	1.00	1.00				81.50
White Oak						15.00	4.00	2.50	5.00	1.50	2.00		21.00	30.00	194.25
Wilson's Mills			2.00			15.00	5.00	5.00	10.00	3.00	4.00		21.00	12.00	174.00
Wendell					6.00	1.00	1.00	1.00	1.00						81.00

DIGEST OF CHURCH LETTERS.

CHURCHES.	Baptisms 1905.	Baptisms 1906.	Pledged.		Contributed.	Above Pledge.	Below Pledge.	Loss or gain in Membership.		Pledg'd Above or Below 1906.	
			1906.	1907.				Gain.	Loss.	Above.	Below.
.ntioch	13	6	$ 24.00	$ 35.00	$ 34.00	$ 10.00	$	3	....	$ 11.00	$
:aptist Centre	15	...	41.00	42.00	41.00					1.00	.....
:enson	14	3	124.00	150.00	186.40	62.40		....	4	26.00	.....
:ethany	9	3	16.50	17.50	16.50			3	...	1.00	....
:ethesda	8	24	52.00	53.00	52.00			23	...	1.00	.....
:ethel	...	6	10.00	11.50	8.00		2.00	7	...	1.50	....
:lackman's Grove	5	4	34.25	40.50	34.25			2	....	6.25	.....
'arter's Chapel	6	4	23.50	23.50	25.50	2.00		2	....		.....
'layton	24	1	497.50	557.50	532.18	34.68		....	9	60.00	.....
'lyde's Chapel	16	8	22.50	29.00	34.34	11.84		5	...	6.50	.....
'orinth	10	5	21.50	17.00	21.50			....	....		4.50
'alvary	7	...	9.50	10.25	9.50			....	....	75	.....
'our Oaks	2	5	23.00	24.00	28.00	5.00		9	...	1.00	.....
lood's Grove	7	...	20.50	21.50	20.50			....	2	1.00	.....
Kenly	...	...	....	9.50				7	...	9.50	.....
.ee's Chapel	26	...	54.50	56.00	53.50			....	....	1.50	.....
ive Oak	6	2	12.00	14.50	13.15	1.15		....	....	2.50	.....
1cro	...	...	10.50	12.25	10.50			....	2	1.75	.....
ount Moriah	6	6	150.00	165.00	182.06	32.06		....	1	15.00	.....
obles' Chapel	1	...	29.50	31.00	29.50			....	....	1.50	.....
ew Bethel	3	2	26.00	27.00	57.20	31.20		3	...	1.00	.....
liver's Grove	...	...	10.00	10.50	4.75		5.25	....	....	50	....
arrish Memorial	18	...	22.00	23.50				....	....	1.50	.....
auline	10	7	8.00	11.00	8.00			7	...	3.00	.....
ine Level	11	8	13.50	14.00	15.50			8	...	50	.....
isgah	3	...	19.75	23.50	22.00	2.25		1	...	3.75	.....
rinceton	18	5	34.50	36.50	34.50			5	...	2.00	.....
ardis	...	4	10.50	11.00	10.50			5	...	50	.....
elma	2	...	216.50	220.50	220.50	4.50		....	3	4.00	.....
iloh	2	8	47.75	25.75	24.30		23.45	7	....		22.00
1ithfield	23	14	355.50	393.00	441.58	86.08		....	2	37.50	.....
1anksgiving	...	4	29.00	29.50	13.40		15.60	3	...	50	.....
1inity	7	3	20.50	18.00	20.50			4	....		2.50
hite Oak	21	2	30.00	31.50	30.00			....	2	1.50	.....
ilson's Mills	1	...	42.00	43.50	42.00			....	1	1.50	.....
endell				11.50	4.00			24	....	11.50	.....
					283.16	$46.30		128	26	$ 208.00	$29.00

CONTRIBUTIONS FROM SUNDAY SCHOOLS AND SOCIETIES.
(Included in Table of Contributions.)

Sunday Schools and Societies.	Building and Repairing.	State Missions.	Home Missions.	Foreign Missions.	S. S. Missions.	Orphanage.	Ministerial Education.	Ministerial Relief.	Other Objects.	Total.
Antioch S. S.....	$	$ 10.00	$	$	$	$	$	$	$	$ 10.00
Baptist Centre W. M. Society..		1.20	1.20	1.30						3.70
Benson W. M..S..		12.80	12.30	12.30					6.75	44.15
Benson S. S.....						15.00				15.00
Carter's C. S. S.						2.00				2.00
Clayton W. M. S.		72.01	42.68	35.31			4.70	3.65		158.85
Clayton S. S.....	235.00	5.00		10.00		60.00	2.00			212.00
Clayton L. A. S.	320.00								26.14	346.14
Clayton Jun. Un.				25.00						25.00
Clyde's Chapel W. M. Society..		2.65	3.94	3.18						9.77
Four Oaks S. S...						5.00				5.00
Mt. Moriah S. S.				5.00	5.00	15.00				25.00
Mt. M. Sunbeams									2.00	2.00
Mt. M. W. M. S.									22.67	22.67
Pine Level S. S.					50	75				1.25
Pisgah W. M. S.		75	75	75						2.25
Pisgah S. S.....						2.00				2.00
Selma W. M. S...		37.48	2.50				10.00	5.35		55.33
Smithf'ld W.M.S.		21.11	19.02	16.37					16.00	72.50
Smithfield S. S...		12.88	2.26	3.82	1.64	10.30	2.14			33.04
Smithfield Sunbeams.....				3.00						3.00
Total.	$ 555.00	$ 175.88	$84.65	$ 116.03	$ 9.14	$ 108.05	$18.84	$ 9.00	$73.56	$1050.15

CONSTITUTION OF THE JOHNSTON COUNTY BAPTIST ASSOCIATION.

1. The Association shall be known as the Johnston County Baptist Association.

2. Its object shall be to extend the privileges of the Gospel and liberal culture to all the people within its bounds, and by hearty co-operation with the Baptist State Convention to help offer these privileges to all mankind in and out of its bounds, by the cordial co-operation of all the churches constituting this body.

3. It shall be composed of the pastors in active service in the Association and such delegates as shall be annually elected by the churches connected with it, each church being entitled to three delegates, unless the membership shall exceed fifty, and then an additional delegate for every twenty-five members, provided no church shall have more than eight delegates.

4. The New Hampshire Declaration of Faith shall be the summary of Divine Truth for determining questions of faith and order in this body, and the churches desiring membership in it must commit themselves to the substance of it, together with the covenant therewith submitted, and this Constitution.

5. This Association shall not have power to annul the discipline or exercise authority over any church connected with it, but it may advise with and sever its connection with any church that neglects to preserve Gospel order, or that treats with contempt the objects or advice of the Association.

6. Each church shall send to the annual meetings of the Association a letter (the blanks to be furnished by the clerk of the Association), carefully filled as per blank suggestions, stating the full work of the church for the year ending with the close of the month previous to the one in which the Association is held.

7. The Association shall foster State Missions, Home Missions, Foreign Missions, Christian Education, the Aged Ministers' Relief Board, the Thomasville Orphanage and the Sunday School Board, and each church shall be requested to contribute to the support of these objects annually.

8. Missions and education shall have precedence in their claims upon the consideration of this body in its regular sessions.

9. Whenever a church shall fail to be represented by delegates or letter at the annual sessions of the Association inquiry shall be made for the cause and efforts shall be made to induce such church to do its duty, and the effort shall be continued till the church is recovered or dropped from the roll.

10. The officers of the Association shall be a Moderator, a Vice-Moderator, a Clerk, a Treasurer and an Auditor, elected annually by ballot from among its members, to serve until their successors shall have been elected, and to perform the duties usual to such officers, namely, the Moderator, in presiding over the meetings, or the Vice-Moderator in his absence; the Clerk in recording and preserving minutes and other papers belonging to the body; the Treasurer in receiving and disbursing funds belonging to or entrusted to the body according to its will; the Auditor to examine the Treasurer's books at each meeting of the Association and report the same before adjournment.

11. The Association shall appoint annually an Executive Committee of five (5) from its members, who shall be entrusted with the prosecution of Missions in the Association and any other work for the interest of the Master's Kingdom which may be referred to them. This committee shall, as far as possible, co-operate with the State Mission Board in supplying the destitution in our territory, and between the meetings of the Association take such actions as may seem to them advisable for the advancement of its interest. The committee shall present to the Association at its annual meeting a report of its proceedings, with the names of the missionaries supported

on the field, time of service and details of their work, together with such recommendations as in the judgment of the committee the Association should follow in planning its subsequent work.

12. The annual sessions of the Association shall begin on Thursday after the first Lord's Day in November at such place as may be chosen, and an Introductory sermon shall be delivered on the first day of the session. Representatives from a majority of the churches constituting the Association shall be a quorum.

13. This Constitution may be amended at any annual session by a two-thirds vote of all the members present.

14. Provision shall be made at each annual Association for a session of the Woman's Central Committee, and all other necessary encouragement offered for the enlargement of the organized work of the Woman's Missionary Societies in the local churches. The proceedings of the Woman's Central Committee shall be recorded as a part of the Minutes of the Association.

BY-LAWS.

1. The daily sessions of the Association shall be opened and closed with prayer.

2. Delegates shall be recognized by letters from their churches designating them as such.

3. The Moderator shall recognize corresponding messengers or the delegates of newly-received churches by extending to them his right hand.

4. The report of the Executive Board and the Missionary Work of the Association shall take precedence of all other business during the morning session of the second day of the annual session.

5. The Clerk shall record and read the proceedings when called for, superintend the publication and distribution of the Minutes, preserve a file of them, and have it present at each annual session, and deliver to his successor all papers belonging to the body.

6. Members desiring to speak shall first rise and address the Moderator; shall use the term "brother" in speaking to each other; shall not speak on the same subject more than twice without permission, and shall observe the courtesy that becomes Christians.

7. Members shall not absent themselves from the session without permission.

8. The roll of members shall be called at least once and absentees marked.

9. Corresponding messengers and visiting brethren shall be invited to seats, with privilege of speaking, but not of voting.

10. A copy of the Minutes shall be sent to the Secretary of the State Mission Board, the Secretary of the Southern Baptist Convention, the American Baptist Publication Society, 1420 Chestnut Street, Philadelphia; the Sunday School Board of the Southern Baptist Convention and the Thomasville Orphanage.

11. All question of order not herein provided shall be decided by Kerfoot's Parliamentary Law.

Minutes

Fifth Session

OF THE

JOHNSTON COUNTY

Baptist Association,

HELD WITH

PISGAH BAPTIST CHURCH,

°NOVEMBER 7, 8, 9 AND 10, 1907.

The next session will be held with Selma Baptist Church, beginning Thursday after the first Sunday in November, 1907.

To Preach Introductory Sermon—T. H. Thornton. Alternate—D. F. Putnam.

NASH BROS., PRINTERS AND BINDERS,
1907.

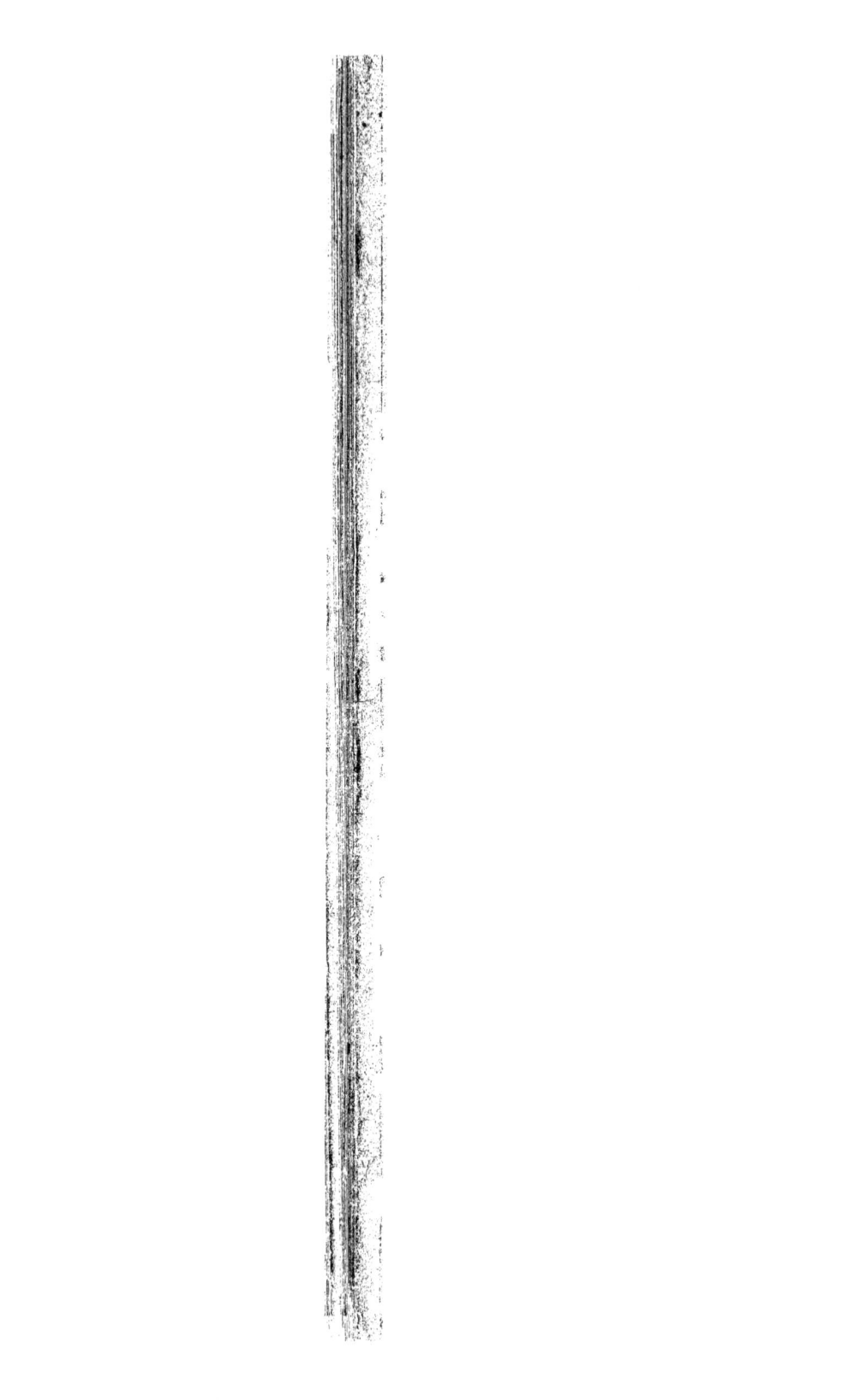

Minutes

OF THE

Fifth Session

OF THE

JOHNSTON COUNTY

Baptist Association,

HELD WITH

PISGAH BAPTIST CHURCH,

NOVEMBER 7, 8, 9 AND 10, 1907.

The' next session will be held with Selma Baptist Church, **beginning** Thursday after the first Sunday in November, 1907.

To Preach Introductory Sermon—T. H. Thornton. Alternate—D. F. Putnam.

GOLDSBORO, N. C.
NASH BROS., PRINTERS AND BINDERS,
1907.

Moderator—R. H. GOWER..................................Clayton, N. C.
Vice-Moderator—C. W. CARTER.............................Clayton, N, C.
Clerk—T. J. LASSITER....................................Smithfield, N. C.
Treasurer—WILL H. LASSITER.............................Smithfield, N. C.
Auditor—J. D. UNDERWOOD................................Smithfield, N. C.

EXECUTIVE COMMITTEE.

J. M. BEATY, Chairman..................................Smithfield, N. C.
J. H. BOON..Benson, N. C.
C. W. CARTER..Clayton, N. C.
ALONZO PARRISH..Benson, N. C.
GEO. L. JONES...Smithfield, N. C.

STANDING COMMITTEES.

State Missions.......................................D. P. Bridges.
Home Missions..D. F. Putnam.
Foreign Missions.....................................T. H. Thornton.
Orphanage..C. W. Carter.
Education..J. P. Canaday.
Periodicals..R. W. Horrell.
Temperance...A. A. Pippin.
Ministerial Relief...................................F. M. Ferrell.
Sunday Schools.......................................J. W. Nobles.
Woman's Work...O. R. Mangum.

MINISTERIAL REGISTER.

D. P. BRIDGES..Smithfield, N. C.
WORLEY CREECH..R. F. D., 2, Kenly, N. C.
D. D. EDWARDS..Cary, N. C.
N. H. GIBBS..Benson, N. C.
J. M. HILLIARD.......................................R. F. D., Raleigh, N. C.
R. W. HORRELL..Selma, N. C.
L. L. HUDSON...Wake Forest, N. C.
O. R. MANGUM...Selma, N. C.
J. W. NOBLES...Kenly, N. C.
A. A. PIPPIN...Wakefield, N. C.
D. F. PUTNAM...Benson, N. C.
T. Y. ODYMORD..Wake Forest, N. C.
T. H. THORNTON.......................................Clayton, N. C.
Member State Board of Missions.......................J. M. Beaty.
Delegate to Southern Baptist Convention..............T. H. Thornton.
Delegates to Baptist State Convention....Alonzo Parrish, T. J. Lassiter,
O. R. Mangum.

Antioch—Jesse B. Creech.

Baptist Center—H. A. Jones.

Benson—E. L. Hall, M. D. Thomas, Alonzo Parrish, J. H. Boon and J. W. Whittenton.

Bethany—Kirkman Creech.

Bethesda—S. V. Smith, J. J. Wallace, W. E. Godwin, L. B. Smith and T. C. Ellis.

Bethel—W. T. Sullivant and C. W. Knight.

Blackman's Grove—J. L. Smith and J. R. Marler.

Carter's Chapel—H. R. Easom and Preston Mozingo.

Clayton—M. M. Gulley, C. L. Barnes, C. W. Carter and R. H. Gower.

Clyde's Chapel—By letter.

Corinth—E. C. Whitley and H. B. Andrews.

Calvary—J. M. Johnson.

Four Oaks—W. A. Massengill, O. D. Stanley and C. H. Grady.

Hood's Grove—P. L. Hayes and J. W. Wood.

Kenly—By letter.

Lee's Chapel—W. E. Estridge and W. Alford.

Live Oak—J. M. Richardson.

Micro—L. L. Creech.

Mount Moriah—F. K. Pool, N. R. Pool, I. C. Pool and Troy Smith.

Noble's Chapel—C. O. Boykin, J. H. Flowers and William Boykin.

New Bethel—By letter.

Oliver's Grove—By letter.

Parrish Memorial—Michael Parrish and Fred Batten.

Pauline—W. B. Joyner and W. D. Strickland.

Pine Level—W. M. Eason.

Pisgah—Robert Higgins, W. J. Alford, J. W. Jones and M. Johnson.

Princeton—L. H. Taylor.

Sardis—N. B. Stevens.

Selma—J. M. Oneal.

Shiloh—J. F. Hardee.

Smithfield—Geo. L. Jones, J. W. Stephenson, E. B. Johnson, J. D. Underwood, B. F. Johnson and Will H. Lassiter.

Thanksgiving—By letter.

Trinity—A. H. Lee.

White Oak—J. B. Oneal, J. H. Eason and V. R. Turley.

Wilson's Mills—S. D. West, G. G. Beaty, Ralph Talton and J. T. Holt.

Wendell—F. M. Ferrell, Amos Dean, Robert Nowell, W. V. Ferrell and J. A. Cooke.

Pastors present—D. P. Bridges, Worley Creech, D. D. Edwards, N. H. Gibbs, R. W. Horrell, O. R. Mangum, A. A. Pippin, D. F. Putnam, T. H. Thornton and J. W. Watson.

PROCEEDINGS.

PISGAH, N. C., November 7, 1907.

The fifth annual session of the Johnston County Baptist Association convened this morning at 11 o'clock with Pisgah church. The session was opened by singing "I Love to Tell the Story" and "My Faith Looks up to Thee," followed with a prayer by Brother A. A. Pippin. After reading the second chapter of the Gospel of Luke, the introductory sermon was preached by Brother D. P. Bridges from the text: "The beginning of the gospel of Jesus Christ, the Son of God." Mark 1:1. The subject chosen for the discourse was "Good News." At the conclusion of the sermon prayer was offered by Brother J. S. Farmer. Adjournment was then taken for dinner.

AFTERNOON SESSION.

The Association opened at 2 o'clock with the song service led by Brother D. F. Putnam and prayer by Brother J. W. Watson.

Brother R. H. Gower, the Moderator, called the body to order and appointed Brethren E. L. Hall and J. T. Holt a committee on Credentials and Enrollment, who reported a majority of the churches of the Association represented. The election of officers for the ensuing year was then taken up and upon motion of Brother R. W. Horrell, Brother D. F. Putnam was instructed to cast the vote of the body for Brother R. H. Gower for Moderator. The motion was carried unanimously and Brother Gower was declared elected. On motion of Brother D. F. Putnam the rules were suspended and the following officers were re-elected by acclamation:

Vice-Moderator—C. W. Carter.
Clerk—T. J. Lassiter.
Treasurer—Will H. Lassiter.
Auditor—J. D. Underwood.

The organization was then declared complete and the body was ready for business.

The Moderator then recognized the following visiting brethren: S. F. Conrad, Field Editor of the *North Carolina Baptist;* J. S. Farmer, Representative of the *Biblical Recorder;* G. P. Harrill, representing the Thomasville Orphanage and *Charity and Children.*

The following pastors who have begun work in this Association since our last meeting were then recognized: Brethren D. P. Bridges, T. H. Thornton, D. D. Edwards, J. W. Watson, O. R. Mangum and N. H. Gibbs.

The following committees were then announced:

Woman's Work—C. W. Carter, Frank Pool and S. D. West.
Temperance—O. R. Mangum, W. B. Joyner and Worley Creech.
Finance—Geo. L. Jones, W. A. Massengill and Amos Dean.

Brother G. P. Harrill being present, the Association voted to hear him present the Orphanage work with the understanding that the matter was to be called up again Saturday morning when the regular report is to be presented and pledges taken. Brother Harrill told of the great work being done at the Orphanage and the need at the present time for more funds to feed and clothe the 360 children who are now being cared for through the generosity of the Baptist people of the State.

The Committee on Woman's Work not being ready to report, the Committee on Temperance, through its Chairman, O. R. Mangum, made its report:

REPORT ON TEMPERANCE.

As the temperance wave sweeps over the South it becomes more apparent that the crimes of violence, crimes of debauchery, political corruption, the waste of wages, the ruin of families, all have their home and origin in the saloon. Civilization will not be a success until the saloon is but a memory of what man once endured. In the South to-day the path to temperance is being followed with more determination than ever in the history of our country. "In more territory is the saloon made illegal, and in a greater part of this territory public opinion is sufficiently strong to make prohibition a success. When it is a success, life will be brighter for the wives and children of hundreds of thousands of fathers and husbands."

In this great movement we are glad to report that North Carolina has a part. Many towns, cities and counties have adopted prohibition laws since last this Association met, the most notable being the county of Anson, and the city of Asheville.

But in Johnston County the cause of temperance seems to have gone backward, largely, we believe, because of the "cider and wine agreement" at Smithfield the summer of 1906. However, we must not let this discourage us, but fight on for the utter destruction of this evil.

To gain what the temperance forces wish, the Christian people of North Carolina must do three things, (1) we must be absolutely temperate ourselves, (2) we must support all the temperance laws we have and see that they are rigidly enforced, (3) we must seek, in all practicable ways, to improve and strengthen our laws regarding this evil, until this curse shall no longer blight our land.

Brethren, let us earnestly pray that the next Legislature will adopt State prohibition and thus rid our State forever of its arch enemy, the saloon.

O. R. MANGUM,
W. B. JOYNER,
WORLEY CREECH,
Committee.

Upon motion to adopt the report was discussed by Brethren O. R. Mangum, Worley Creech, S. F. Conrad, R. W. Horrell, J. S. Farmer, R. H. Gower, J. M. Beaty and W. B. Joyner. The report was then adopted.

On motion Brethren D. P. Bridges and D. F. Putnam were appointed a committee on rearranging the program.

The following committees were then announced :.

State Missions—R. W. Horrell, F. M. Ferrell and W. T. Sullivant.
Foreign Missions—O. R. Mangum, T. H. Thornton and J. M. Johnson.

Brother T. H. Thornton was appointed to conduct the devotional exercises to-morrow morning. The Association then adjourned to meet at 9:30 to-morrow. Benediction by Brother N. H. Gibbs.

SECOND DAY.

FRIDAY MORNING, Nov. 8, 1907.

The devotional exercises were conducted by Brother T. H. Thornton, after which the Committee on Ministerial Relief made its report through Brother A. A. Pippin.

REPORT ON MINISTERIAL RELIEF.

Our aged and infirm ministers who have given their lives to preaching the Gospel and spreading the doctrine so dear to Baptists, richly deserve our sympathy and liberal financial support. A great deal of our wonderful growth as a great denomination is due to their zeal and faithful labors during many years. The Relief Board, located in Durham, N. C., is composed of judicious members who are doing a blessed work in caring for, from twenty to twenty-five of our aged fathers in Israel, or their families, who have been left destitute of support. Your committee is glad to note that the churches of our Association have done well for this object during the past year, and we would respectfully urge each of our churches to take at least one collection for this work during the year to come.

Respectfully submitted,

A. A. PIPPIN,

For Committee.

Pending a motion to adopt, the report was discussed by Brother A. A. Pippin. Pledges were then taken and the report was adopted.

The Moderator then recognized the following visitors:

Livingston Johnson, Corresponding Secretary of the Baptist State Convention, and C. J. Thompson, Vice-President for North Carolina of the Home Mission Board.

The following committees were then announced:

Place and Preachers for next meeting—C. W. Knight, W. E. Estridge, and J. R. Marler.
Education—D. F. Putnam, L. L. Creech and H. R. Easom.
Home Missions—D. P. Bridges, J. M. Hales and J. D. Oneal.

The report of the Executive Committee was then read by Brother J. M. Beaty.

REPORT OF EXECUTIVE COMMITTEE.

Your Committee regards the work of supplying the Gospel to Mission points and Mission churches as the greatest work committed to the churches of this Association, owing to the destitution within our bounds. Some of the churches have about become self-supporting, and there are several new points which demand our attention and help. We cannot supply preaching to all these places unless the churches give liberal support.

We have several places in the Association where our work is suffering for want of houses of worship and it is impossible to get all the money needed at these places with which to build. We are greatly in need of some church extension funds, and will ask you to arrange, if possible, for this help.

Brother D. F. Putnam has served as pastor at Pisgah, Blackman's Grove and Four Oaks. At Parrish Memorial, Pine Level, Kenly, Princeton, Noble's Chapel and Bethel, Brother R. W. Horrell has had charge. He has preached also at Niagara school-house once a month. Brother N. H. Gibbs has preached at Oliver's Grove and Barbour's school-house. At Barbour's school-house a small church has been organized. Brother B. G. Early has preached at Sardis and Woodard school-house. Brother J. W. Watson has served Calvary, Trinity, Hood's Grove and Pauline churches. Brother A. A. Pippin has been pastor at Corinth and Wendell. Brother L. L. Hudson has preached once a month at Pleasant Grove church. We are glad to report general progress in all this work.

Baptisms on the fields of the Missionaries, 108.

J. M. BEATY,
J. H. BOON,
ALONZO PARRISH,
C. W. CARTER,
Executive Committee.

After a short discussion by Brethren J. M. Beaty and Livingston Johnson, the report on State Missions was called for and read by Bro. R. W. Horrell.

REPORT ON STATE MISSIONS.

The Baptist State Convention was organized primarily to give the Gospel to the destitute in our own State. The wisdom of the fathers has ever been obvious.

Their work has grown till to-day we have one hundred and fifty-two Missionaries, and are trying to raise for this object $40,000.00 this year. The unparalleled development of North Carolina along all lines call upon the Baptists of the State, in no uncertain sound, to arise to greater endeavor. The great destitution in all the East and South Eastern sections of our State call for larger things. Twenty more preachers are much needed.

The springing up of new towns in the Piedmont section makes it most urgent that we occupy many places unthought of only a few years ago. The need of strong, wise, well equipped men in the West calls loudly for men. We have no more glorious work to do, so let us look well to the work in our own Association and State. Let us go forward in this work.

R. W. HORRELL,
F. M. FERRELL,
W. T. SULLIVANT,
Committee.

Upon motion to adopt Brother Livingston Johnson suggested that the Missionaries of the Association be called on to tell of their work, and Brethren R. W. Horrell, D. F. Putnam, N. H. Gibbs, J. W. Watson and D. P. Bridges were then heard from. Brother Livingston Johnson then made a strong speech on State Missions, after which pledges were taken and both reports adopted.

After the usual announcements, adjournment was taken for dinner, with benediction by Brother O. R. Mangum.

AFTERNOON SESSION.

The body was called together at two o'clock and prayer was offered by Brother J. W. Watson.

The report on Home Missions was read by Brother D. P. Bridges.

REPORT ON HOME MISSIONS.

The Home Mission Board is composed of twenty-one of our wisest and best brethren from the States composing the Southern Baptist Convention, having its headquarters located at Atlanta, Georgia. These brethren are elected annually by the Southern Baptist Convention.

The field in which the Board does its work lies in the territory of the Southern Baptist Convention, including our native population in our great cities and villages and rural districts, especially in the great South West; the Indians; the foreign population that is flowing into our country by the thousands; the Negro population of our Southland and Cuba, the Isle of Pines and Panama. In these respective fields our Missionaries are going and preaching the Gospel, and here our money is put in order that these faithful, self-denying men and women may have bread and meat for the body while they are carrying that bread of life to the dying souls of the people of these regions.

The Board had last year 865 workers. They supplied 3,128 churches and stations. They baptized into the churches 18,798 converts; an average of 50 per day for the entire year, and received 14,207 into the churches by letter. They organized 271 churches and 703 Sunday schools, and built and improved 309 houses of worship.

The Home Board's evangelists held 14 meetings during the year in which 699 candidates were received for baptism and 349 by letter; also a course of lectures was delivered at our Seminary under the auspices of the Board. All of these departments of the Board are flourishing and growing. They are calling for more workers every year and larger means with which to meet the urgent demands of the work. All these departments of the work are exceedingly important and the needs of the fields are urgent, but we want to lay special emphasis on the work in the great cities of the South and South West, like Memphis, New Orleans and others. Our frontier work which is developing so marvelously and the work among the foreign population which is filling up our country so rapidly. It is a startling fact that for every one converted on the foreign fields last year through the agency of the Southern Baptist Convention, 500 foreigners who need the Gospel, came to our country. You see that if all our energies on the foreign fields had been exerted among these foreigners coming to our shores we would have saved only one in 500 who came.

The saving of the world lies largely on the shoulders of Christians in America. Then if this be true, (and I suppose none will dispute it) we must save America in order that America may save the world. The Home Board is laying out its work this year on a basis of $500,000. We raised last year $231,000 all told. You see that it will take a little more than twice as much to meet the demands of the work this year as the churches raised altogether last year. A half million dollars are the figures set by the Convention for this year. The applications coming in from all parts of the great field indicate that every dollar of this amount will be badly needed. Heroic giving will be needed. All former records must be broken. The number of givers must be doubled and former gifts increased a hundred per cent if we meet these imperative needs. All our forcs must be marshaled, our pastors, laymen, women, and young pople must fall in line and do their best if we gain the victory. If we can elicit, combine and direct all these forces the victory is ours.

> "Not gold, but only men, can make
> A people great and strong:
> Men who, for truth and honor's sake,
> Stand fast and suffer long,
> Brave men who work while others sleep,
> Who dare while others fly— ￼
> They build a Nation's pillars deep
> And lift them to the sky."

What shall we in the Johnston do? Let us rise in our might and do our best. Brethren, God expects every one of us to do our best in this great struggle for the salvation of our people.

Submitted by the Committee.

D. P. BRIDGES,
J. B. ONEAL.

Upon motion to adopt the report was discussed by Brethren D. P. Bridges and C. J. Thompson. Pledges for the work were then taken and the report adopted.

The report on Woman's Work was read by Brother C. W. Carter.

REPORT ON WOMAN'S WORK.

One of the most marked favors of God's blessings upon the work of Baptists in recent years in North Carolina has been the forward movement of our women along Missionary lines. New societies and the increased membership of those already organized, and the increase in their gifts for the various objects of the Convention, prove beyond cavil that God is behind the movement. It is with profound gratitude to God and with sincere interest in our consecrated women, filled with zeal and love for God and souls, that we mark the growing intent and enlargement of this department of the work. The women and children of our State gave, for all objects last year, $20,840.89. The motto for this year, "Large Things," points to increased gifts and membership. God grant that it may be so. Possibly, the greatest blessing arising from this work, is not the money raised, but the Christ-like missionary spirit instilled into the hearts of those not members of the societies. This phase of the work will prove an untold blessing to our State and the Kingdom of our Master in years to come. We commend these noble, consecrated, Christian women, with their work, to our Association, and urge our pastors to use every effort to have a society in every church and every sister in every church a member of the society.

C. W. CARTER,
For Committee.

Upon motion to adopt Brother C. W. Carter submitted a few remarks. Adopted.

The committee on Place and Preachers for Next Meeting reported as follows:

Your Committee on Place and Preachers for next meeting of the Association deem it wise to meet with Selma as they will be in their new church by that time to welcome us, and it is their wish to have a Memorial window to the organization of the Johnston Association, at that place, presented at this time.

To preach introductory sermon, Brother T. H. Thornton. Alternate, Brother D. F. Putnam.

C. W. KNIGHT, Ch'mn.
W. E. ESTRIDGE,
Committee.

After a few remarks on the report and pledges amounting to about $50 for Memorial window were taken, the report was adopted.

CHURCH BUILDING COMMITTEE.

The following resolutions were offered by Brother T. J. Lassiter:

"Resolved, That a committee of five be appointed, to be known as a Church Building Committee, whose duty shall be as follows:

"First, to consider all points at which houses of worship are needed, and select the one, which in their judgment, is in most need of a house of worship.

"Second, to consult with the brethren at which place a church is to be built, as to location, plan and cost of house. This committee will, of course, have nothing to do with churches that do not ask the Association to aid them in building.

"Resolved further, That each church be asked to take at least one collection a year to aid the church or churches that the Building Committee may endorse."

The resolutions were unanimously adopted.

Upon motion the Association took up the election of the following committees, etc.

Executive Committee—J. M. Beaty, J. H. Boon, C. W. Carter, Alonzo Parrish and Geo. L. Jones.

Delegates to Baptist State Convention—Alonzo Parrish, T. J. Lassiter and O. R. Mangum.

Delegate to Southern Baptist Convention—T. H. Thornton.

Member of State Board of Missions—J. M. Beaty.

Brother A. A. Pippin was appointed to conduct the devotional exercises to-morrow morning. The Association then adjourned with benediction by Brother Worley Creech.

SATURDAY MORNING.

The Association met at 9:30. The devotional services were conducted by Brother A. A. Pippin.

The following committees were announced:

Periodicals—J. P. Canaday, R. H. Higgins and I. C. Pool.
Petitionary Letters—A. A. Pippin, O. R. Mangum and D. F. Putnam.
Sunday Schools—N. R. Pool, N. B. Stevens and G. G. Beaty.
Orphanage—D. P. Bridges, M. D. Thomas and V. R. Turley.

The report on periodicals was next called for and read by Brother J. P. Canaday.

REPORT ON PERIODICALS.

Too much importance cannot be attached to the literature people read. This is most emphatically true with respect to salvation. In this onrushing civilization there is great danger of perverting the truth. No power in the State and nation for championing and protecting the truth can be greater than the able and faithful editor of religious papers. Thousands read them that do not read the Bible. Thousands are brought to Christ through them.

It is not known what power for good the Biblical Recorder has been. Growing up with our denomination and the commonwealth as the organ of our Convention, it stands all important to our cause. Its circulation should reach every home in order that every one may see the needs in the Convention, and that every one may get an inspiration from our growth and development.

The North Carolina Baptist occupies a unique position among religious papers. It has always stood boldy for the truth. Its distinctive influence in the temperance cause should forever commend it to the patronage of Baptist people.

The strategic point in the Christian work is upon the young. Therefore, Charity and Children is the greatest power among children. Its great field is being well filled and endeavor should be made to get every child to read it.

The Foreign Mission Journal and Our Home Field, as the organs of our Foreign and Home Boards should be read by all our Baptist people, for thus we are enabled to see the needs abroad and to share in the joy of the spread of the Gospel. Your committee recommends the use in our Sunday schools of literature printed at Nashville, Tennessee, by our Sunday school Board which publishes our Convention series.

It is to be regretted that The Church Messenger, as organ of the Johnston County Baptist Association, has suspended. It is hoped that financial aid may restore the publication of The Messenger. In this connection the thanks of the Association are due Brother T. J. Lassiter for the able, but unrewarded, efforts he put forth in that paper.

Respectfully submitted,
J. P. CANADAY,
For Committee.

Upon motion to adopt the report was discussed by Brother J. P. Canaday, after which it was unanimously adopted.

Brother O. R. Mangum read the report on Foreign Missions:

⸗REPORT ON FOREIGN MISSIONS.

We are standing in the morning light of a new year in Foreign Mission work. Never before was there an era so bright, so fraught with wonderful achievements. And when we remember that our organized Foreign Mission endeavor is less than a century old, and think how the word has been touched and moved by the power of the Gospel, preached by men of God during that time, we are amazed at the magnitude of the results. But why should we be? "O ye of little faith." "Greater things than these shall ye do." What we have seen is only a beginning. The best is yet to be. We have been sent forth with "the promise of the Father" upon us, and not even the gates of hell shall prevail against this all-compelling power. Light is dawning and darkness is fleeing before the coming Christ, and the coming Kingdom; and God is beginning to reign in hearts and nations that never before acknowledged His lordship. He who taught us to pray "Thy Kingdom come" has heard our prayer. In the light of this, let us ponder well the following inspiring facts:

Last year there were 2239 converts baptized on the Foreign Fields and the indications are that a much larger number will be reported this year. During the year 21 new missionaries were sent out to the "far flung battle lines" where "the battle is not with men, but a foe of mightier hand." A number of other missionaries are under appointment to go to their aid soon. There are now 500 workers on the field—203 missionaries and 297 native helpers. There is a wide spread missionary enthusiasm sweeping over our colleges and churches, and many young men and women are offering themselves to this grand work. But even if our missionary force could be doubled during the coming year we could not meet the imperative needs of the situation. "Southern Baptists ought to have ten thousand soldiers in the war of conquest to take the world for Christ."

We have now 233 organized churches and 412 out-stations, with 13,437 members, and only 134 houses of worship. These churches with their missionaries, contributed last year $29,201— a fine lesson of consecration and Christian giving for our home churches.

Last year the Baptists of North Carolina contributed about $30,000 that those in the darkness might see the great light. This year we are trying to raise $35,000—a sum far too meager and mite-like for the God-blessed 200,000 white Baptists of this Commonwealth.

God is certainly calling loudly to Southern Baptists to enlarge, to go forward. He has signally blessed the South, and unless we heed this call and keep our spiritual life at even pace with this mighty tide of prosperity, we shall retrograde, and lose what our fathers died to gain.

God has laid this blessed work upon our shoulders—a work angels would be glad to do—and in the name of Christ, the Coming King, let each of us do his best. "For sooner or later in life we all find out that the one supreme movement in this world, underlying and controlling all the currents in history, is the coming of the Kingdom of God, and that no man's life amounts to much which is not actively and potently consecrated to the hastening thereof."

Brethren, the prayer for the hour ought to be for the coming of God's Spirit in our churches, revealing to us the grand privilege, the glorious opportunity, and the awful responsibility now upon us. Through this conquering Spirit we shall go forward and win, for the "promise of the Father" is still upon us.

OSCAR R. MANGUM,
For Committee.

Pending a motion to adopt, Brother O. R. Mangum spoke to the report, after which pledges were taken and report adopted.

The report on Education was read by Brother D. F. Putnam:

REPORT ON EDUCATION.

A prominent Baptist writer and Educator recently said in an article: "Self activity is the fundamental law. The mind is not a box into which you put all kinds of coins for safe keeping. It is a living, growing thing, education is not information, it is self realization." Plato said that education means to give to the mind all the beauty and perfection it is capable of attaining.

Accepting these definitions of education in which we would combine both the mental and spiritual natures of man we note with pleasure the provision made for the education of our children. The growing efficiency of our public school system for the education of all the children of our country is very commendable. Our Baptist High Schools for higher instruction than is offered in the public schools are a source of pride to the denomination and should have the loyal support and patronage of our Baptist people. Wake Forest College is pre-eminently the place for educating our Baptist boys. We rejoice in its past and present success. Its future will be what we make it by endowment and patronage. The Baptist University for Women at Raleigh is to our girls, as Wake Forest is to our boys It is a source of gratitude that our girls now have an equal chance with their brothers to obtain a college education under distinctive Christian influences.

We recommend our Seminary at Louisville for our young preachers and the Seminary Training School for young women.

D. F. PUTNAM,
L. L. CREECH,
H. R. EASOM,
Committee.

Upon motion to adopt the report was discussed by Brethren D. F. Putnam, D. P. Bridges and A. A. Pippin.

Before a vote was taken on the report, a cash collection of $21.30 was taken for Brother W. C. Royal, a Ministerial student at Wake Forest College. Pledges for education were then taken and the report adopted.

Adjournment was then taken for dinner, the benediction being pronounced by Brother D. P. Bridges.

AFTERNOON SESSION.

The Association opened with prayer by Brother Worley Creech.

The report on Orphanage was then called for and presented by Brother D. P. Bridges.

REPORT ON ORPHANAGE.

We have at our Orphanage at Thomasville about three hundred and sixty children. These children are there because they have no fathers and mothers to care for them. We have adopted them as our children and we stand in stead of father and mother to them. We must see to it that they do not want for something to eat and wear. We urge every Sunday School and every church to take regular collections for this object. "He that giveth to the poor, lendeth to the Lord."

D. P. BRIDGES,

For Committee.

Since the Orphanage work was discussed by Brother Harrill Thursday afternoon, further discussion was omitted, pledges taken and report adopted.

In the absence of the chairman of the committee, the report on Sunday Schools was read by Brother T. J. Lassiter.

REPORT ON SUNDAY SCHOOLS.

Since it is the great mission, and prime mission of the church to teach the gospel to the people, we believe the best, the most effectual and successful way of doing this is in the Sunday schools' work. We believe it to be the duty of every church to see that there is a Sunday School kept open in church the whole year where the fundamental principles and doctrines of the Gospel may be instilled into the hearts and minds of the children as commanded from Sinai, and obeyed by Moses, Joshua and other faithful followers of the commands of the Lord and Savior.

In order that we may do this important work and that there may follow the best results, we need more faithful, consecrated and thoroughly trained teachers in all of our schools.

N. R. POOL,

N. B. STEVENS,

G. G. BEATY,

Committee.

Upon motion the discussion on Sunday School work was postponed until Sunday Morning at 10 o'clock. Pledges were then taken and report adopted.

The report of the Finance Committee was then read by Brother

G. L. Jones. In the absence of the Treasurer, his report was read by the Clerk and both reports adopted.

Upon motion the Clerk was instructed to have 1,000 minutes printed and distributed, and that he be allowed $10.00 for his services. A cash collection of $2.67 was then taken to supplement the Minute fund.

The Moderator then announced the Church Building Committee as follows: J. M. Beaty, J. H. Boon, C. W. Carter, Alonzo Parrish and Geo. L. Jones.

A Sunday School mass meeting was arranged for Sunday morning at 10 o'clock to be led by Brother R. H. Gower. Brother O. R. Mangum was appointed to preach at 11 o'clock.

Upon motion of Brother D. P. Bridges the following resolution of thanks was unanimously adopted by a rising vote.

"Resolved, That a vote of thanks from this body, be, and is hereby tendered to this church and community for the royal manner in which they have entertained the Association."

The Association then joined in singing "God Be With You Till We Meet Again," after which the body adjourned with benediction by Brother A. A. Pippin.

SUNDAY MORNING.

Sunday School Mass Meeting was opened with prayer by Brother Worley Creech. Talks were then made on the Sunday school work in its various phases by Brethren J. P. Canaday, T. J. Lassiter, O. R. Mangum and R. H. Gower.

At 11 o'clock after the reading of first John, second chapter, Brother O. R. Mangum preached the Missionary sermon, using as a text: "Be thou strong therefore, and show thyself a man." I Kings 2:2. At the close of the sermon pledges were taken for the memorial window in the Selma church, amounting to about $85.00. Adding this to the amount raised Friday afternoon, the total in cash and pledges amounted to about $135.00.

The congregation then joined in singing "Praise God from Whom all Blessings Flow," after which the benediction was pronounced by Brother O. R. Mangum.

SPECIAL NOTE TO CHURCH TREASURERS.

It is earnestly desired by the Association that all Church Treasurers send all funds raised for the various objects of the Convention to Treasurer Will H. Lassiter, Smithfield, N. C. Heretofore some of the churches have sent only their State Mission funds to the Associational Treasurer. To avoid mistakes and to keep better up with what the churches are doing, it is deemed wise that all funds be sent to our Associational Treasurer.

WOMAN'S MISSIONARY UNION.

The Woman's Missionary Union of the Johnston County Association held its fourth annual meeting with Pisgah Church, Friday afternoon, November 8th, 1907.

A house at a short distance from the church was kindly tendered for the use of the ladies, but time being so limited, and the day so balmy and ideal, we decided to hold our meeting in the grove surrounding the church.

The meeting was presided over by the Vice-President, Mrs. Ashley Horne. After devotional exercises, opening the meeting, Mrs. Horne said a few words about the new objects that the W. M. U. has assumed, the Margaret Home last year, and this year the permanent maintenance of the Woman's Training School at Louisville, Ky., as well as the raising of a $20,000.00 endowment fund for the same. The next subject brought up was the consideration of having our Annual Meeting at a different time and place from the regular Association. After discussion it was unanimously decided to have our meeting at a separate time and place. Clayton and Smithfield both invited the meeting, but it was decided in favor of Clayton. The exact date of the meeting was left open for future decision.

The next order of business was hearing the reports of the Societies. Fourteen Societies reported. There were no pledges made for another year, but we trust every delegate from every Society went away determined to do more for the Master's cause in the coming year than they had in the past.

Mrs. C. W. Carter, Secretary.

Mrs. E. H. McCullers, Acting Secretary.

FINANCIAL REPORT.

Societies.	Total.
Clayton W. M. Society	$205.10
Smithfield W. M. S.	50.25
Benson W. M. S.	33.85
Clyde's Chapel W. M. S.	4.55
Mt. Moriah W. M. S.	22.42
Four Oaks W. M. S.	9.45
Baptist Center W. M. S.	5.55
Pisgah W. M. S.	1.00
Clayton Junior Union Society	23.26
Clyde's Chapel Sunbeam Society	1.01
Mt. Moriah Sunbeam Society	5.00
Four Oaks Sunbeam Society	2.41
Smithfield Sunbeam Society	1.00
Clayton Y. L. A.	50.00
	$414.85

The above totals include contributions to State, Home and Foreign Missions.

TABLE I.—FINANCE COMMITTEE'S REPORT.

Churches.	State Missions.	Home Missions.	Foreign Missions.	Sunday School Missions.	Orphanage.	Ministerial	Ministerial Relief.	Seminary.	Mtes and Clerk.	Total.
Antioch ...	$ 15.00	$1.50	$1.50	$1.00	$2.50	$1.50	$2.00	$....	$ 90	$ 25.90
Baptist Cen	....	....	.....	.....	.....	.....	.....	.....	1.00	1.00
Benson ...	....	....	.....	.....	.....	.....	.....	.....	2.50	2.50
Bethany ..	6.50	2.50	2.00	1.00	3.00	1.25	1.25	.....	60	18.10
Bethesda ..	19.71	71	12	.....	15.00	1.58	95	.....	1.00	39.07
Bethel	4.00	1.00	1.00	50	1.35	50	50	.....	1.40	10.25
Black'n's G	....	....	.....	.....	.....	.....	.....	.....	1.50	1.50
Carter's C..	10.00	2.50	1.50	1.00	5.00	1.50	2.00	.....	50	24.00
Clayton ...	....	....	.....	:....	.....	.....	.....	10.00	5.00	15.00
Clyde's Ch.	10.00	....	.....	:....	.....	2.00	1.38	.....	1.00	14.38
Corinth ...	6.00	1.50	2.00	50	4.00	1.00	2.00	.....	1.00	18.00
Calvary ...	2.16	....	.....	50	3.00	1.00	1.25	.....	92	8.83
Four Oaks.	....	....	.....	.....	.....	.....	.....	.....	1.00	1.00
Hood's Gro.	10.00	2.00	3.00	1.00	2.00	2.00	1.50	.....	50	22.00
Kenly	....	....	.....	.....	.....	.....	.....	.....	1.00	1.00
Live Oak.	....	....	.....	.....	.....	.....	.....	.....	45	45
Micro	5.00	1.25	1.25	50	2.00	1.00	1.00	.....	50	12.50
Mt. Moriah	33.35	3.04	30.44	5.00	12.25	5.00	5.00	.....	1.50	95.58
Nobles' Ch.	4.35	3.00	2.00	1.00	4.00	2.00	2.00	.....	1.00	19.35
New Bethel	....	....	.....	.....	.....	.....	.....	.....	1.00	1.00
Oliver's G..	1.10	....	.....	.....	.....	.....	.....	.....	50	1.60
Parrish Me	4.40	1.50	1.50	50	2.00	1.05	2.00	.....	1.00	13.95
Pauline ...	4.00	1.50	•1.50	50	1.50	1.00	1.00	.....	35	11.35
Pine Level.	....	....	.....	.....	.....	.....	.....	.....	1.00	1.00
Pisgah	....	....	.....	.....	.....	.....	.....	.....	1.00	1.00
Princeton .	11.00	4.00	.....	1.00	4.00	2.00	2.50	.....	50	25.00
Sardis	5.00	....	.....	1.00	1.50	1.00	1.00	.....	25	9.75
Selma	....	....	.....	.....	.....	.....	.....	.....	3.00	3.00
Shiloh ...	10.00	3.25	2.00	1.00	.....	2.00	2.50	.....	30	21.05
Thanksgiv.	73	....	.....	.....	1.00	.....	.....	.....	1.00	2.73
Trinity	5.00	2.00	3.00	50	3.00	50	80	.....	1.00	15.80
White Oak.	9.12	4.50	2.50	1.00	1.44	1.02	.....	.....	1.50	21.08
Wilson's M.	9.46	3.18	3.76	1.00	1.53	4.00	3.00	.:...	50	26.43
Wendell ..	4.92	1.00	2.00	1.50	2.00	1.00	4.17	.....	1.75	18.34
Collection .	....	.....	...	...	.....	.....	.....	.....	2.67	2.67
Totals ..	190.80	39.93	61.07	20.00	72.07	33.90	37.80	10.00	40.59	506.10

We have turned over to Treasurer, Will H. Lassiter, the above and hold his receipts for same.

GEO. L. JONES,
T. J. LASSITER,
For Committee.

TABLE II—TREASURER'S REPORT.

To the Johnston County Baptist Association:

I submit herewith a report of all money received and paid out from the time I became Treasurer to November 15, 1907.

Churches.	State Missions.	Evangelistic Missions.	Home Missions.	Foreign Missions.	Sunday Sch Missions.	Orphanage.	Ministerial Education.	Ministerial Relief.	Colleges and Schools.	Minutes and Clerk.	Total.
Benson ..	$ 88.30	$30.00	$.....	$......	$.....	$.....	$.....	$.....	$.....	$.....	$ 118.30
Bethesda	7.86	......	1.88	1.85	......	......	......	......	......	......	11.59
Blackn's G	26.00	......	......	......	......	......	......	......	......	......	26.00
Bethel ..	2.01	......	......	......	......	......	......	......	......	......	2.01
Calvary ..	1.52	......	......	......	......	......	......	......	......	......	1.52
Clayton ..	346.07	......	......	......	......	......	......	......	5.75	......	351.82
Four Oaks	11.10	......	......	......	......	......	......	......	......	......	11.10
Live Oak.	5.00	......	1.05	36	......	1.20	......	......	......	......	7.61
Nobles' Ch	7.94	......	3.00	......	......	......	......	......	1.60	......	12.54
Parrish Me	10.60	80	......	......	......	......	......	......	......	......	11.40
Pine Level	5.79	2.36	1.25	1.59	......	1.17	2.03	1.50	......	......	15.69
Pisgah ...	11.43	......	......	......	......	......	......	......	......	......	11.43
Sardis ...	......	1.71	2.00	2.50	......	......	......	......	......	......	6.21
Smithfield	207.59	......	28.25	37.00	10.00	10.41	8.76	16.00	......	5.00	323.00
Smithf'd C	......	4.25	......	......	......	......	......	......	......	......	4.25
Thanksg'g	3.26	......	......	......	......	......	......	......	......	......	3.26
White Oak	1.35	......	......	......	......	......	......	......	......	......	1.35
Wilson's M	5.55	......	......	1.24	......	3.47	......	......	......	......	10.26
F. C. 1907	190.80	......	39.93	61.07	20.00	72.07	33.90	37.80	10.00	40.59	506.16
A. H. Lee	2.50	......	......	......	......	......	......	......	......	......	2.50
T J L,1906	......	......	......	......	......	......	......	......	......	46.95	46.95
T J L,1906	11.62	......	......	......	......	......	......	......	......	......	11.62
Total R..	$ 946.28	$39.12	$77.36	$105.61	$30.00	$88.32	$44.69	$55.30	$17.35	$92.54	$1496.57

Borrowed from Bank of Smithfield for different objects ....$ 500.00

Total receipts $1996.57

DISBURSEMENTS.

Jan'y	12, 1907.	Paid T. J. Lassiter, Clerk and postage.................$	15.93
Jan'y	12, 1907.	Paid Nash Bros., Printing Minutes....................	30.00
April	30, 1907.	Paid Rev. J. W. Watson, Missionary...................	10.50
April	30, 1907.	Paid S. H. Ayeritt, Orphanage........................	114.06
April	30, 1907.	Paid Walters Durham	227.98
May	1, 1907.	Paid Interest	15.00
May	4, 1907.	Paid J. M. Beaty, money advanced to Missionaries....	145.77
Sept'r	23, 1907.	Paid Rev. B. Townsend..............................	25.00
Sept'r	23, 1907.	Paid Rev. O. W. Henderson..........................	10.00
Sept'r	23, 1907.	Paid Rev. O. R. Mangum.............................	20.00
Sept'r	23, 1907.	Paid Rev. W. C. Royal..............................	7.50
Octo.	24, 1907.	Paid Rev. W. C. Royal.............................	10.00
Novr.	14, 1907.	Paid Bank of Smithfield (note).......................	500.00
Novr.	14, 1907.	Paid Interest	1.25

Total Disbursements $1132.99

Nov. 15, 1907. Balance on hand ....$ 863.58

$1996.57—$1996.57

Respectfully submitted,

WILL H. LASSITER, Treasurer.

Approved: J. D. UNDERWOOD, Auditor.

TABLE III—CHURCH PLEDGES FOR 1908.

CHURCHES.	State Missions.	Home Missions.	Foreign Missions.	Sunday School Missions.	Orphanage.	Ministerial Education.	Ministerial Relief.	Totals.
Antioch	$ 15.00	$ 1.50	$ 1.50	$ 2.00	$ 2.50	$ 1.50	$ 2.00	$ 26.00
Baptist Centre	10.00	2.00	1.50	......	10.00	......	1.50	25.00
Benson	100.00	20.00	20.00	2.00	20.00	5.00	4.00	171.00
Bethany	6.50	2.50	2.00	1.00	3.00	1.25	1.25	17.50
Bethesda	25.00	5.00	2.00	1.00	15.00	2.00	3.00	53.00
Bethel	4.00	1.50	1.50	50	1.00	1.00	1.00	10.50
Blackman's Grove	20.00	5.00	7.00	2.00	8.00	4.00	2.50	48.50
Carter's Chapel	10.00	2.50	1.50	1.00	5.00	1.50	2.00	23.50
Clayton	250.00	75.00	125.00	10.00	135.00	25.00	15.00	635.00
Clyde's Chapel	10.00	4.00	4.00	1.50	5.00	2.00	2.50	29.00
Corinth	8.00	1.50	2.00	1.00	4.00	1.00	2.00	19.50
Calvary	4.00	2.00	1.50	1.00	2.25	1.50	1.50	13.75
Four Oaks	15.00	5.00	5.00	1.00	5.00	1.50	3.00	35.50
Hood's Grove	10.00	2.00	3.00	1.00	2.00	2.00	1.50	21.50
Kenly	3.00	1.00	5.00	1.00	2.00	1.00	1.00	14.00
Lee's Chapel	35.00	5.00	10.00	1.00	5.00	3.00	3.00	62.00
Live Oak	4.00	1.00	1.00	......	1.00	......	......	7.00
Micro	3.00	1.25	1.25	50	2.25	1.00	1.00	10.25
Mount Moriah	50.00	20.00	50.00	5.00	30.00	5.00	5.00	165.00
Nobles' Chapel	17.00	3.00	2.50	1.00	4.00	2.00	2.00	31.50
New Bethel	15.00	3.00	2.00	1.00	3.00	2.00	1.00	27.00
Oliver's Grove	2.00	1.00	1.00	50	1.00	50	50	6.50
Parrish Memorial	15.00	1.75	1.50	50	2.00	1.00	2.00	23.75
Pauline	4.00	1.50	1.50	50	1.50	1.00	1.00	11.00
Pine Level	6.00	1.50	1.50	50	2.00	1.25	1.50	14.25
Pisgah	15.00	3.00	5.00	2.00	2.25	1.00	1.50	29.75
Princeton	18.00	4.00	5.00	1.00	4.00	2.00	2.50	36.50
Sardis	5.00	2.00	2.00	50	1.50	1.00	1.00	13.00
Selma	130.00	10.00	35.00	4.00	50.00	12.00	10.00	251.00
Shiloh	10.00	3.25	3.00	1.00	7.50	2.00	2.50	29.25
Smithfield	225.00	40.00	52.00	10.00	40.00	27.00	16.00	410.00
Thanksgiving	5.00	1.00	1.00	50	1.00	1.00	50	10.00
Trinity	5.00	4.00	3.50	1.00	3.00	1.00	1.00	18.50
White Oak	15.00	5.00	5.00	1.50	7.50	2.00	2.00	38.00
Wilson's Mills	15.00	5.00	5.00	1.00	5.00	2.00	3.00	36.00
Wendell	3.00	2.00	3.00	1.00	2.00	1.00	1.00	13.00
Total	$1087.50	$248.75	$374.25	$60.00	$395.25	$119.00	$101.75	$2387.00

TABLE IV—CHURCH STATISTICS.

CHURCHES.	PASTORS.	CLERKS AND ADDRESSES.	Preaching Sun.	Valu of Property.	Seating Capacity.	Baptisms.	Received by letter.	Restored.	Lost by Letter.	Dismissed.	Died.	Males.	Females.	Total Membership.
...	Worley ...	R. R. Creech, Selma, R. 2	2	$ 500.00	400	6	1	1		1	5	53	115	168
Baptist Centre	O. R. Mangum	Victor ..., Clayton		450.00	250	3			2		2	30	46	76
Benson	D. F. Putnam	E. L. Hall, Benson	2—4	1500.00	400	8	3		3	4	1	51	96	147
Bethany	W. Creech	Kirkman ..., Kenly	4	600.00	300	2			3	3	2	30	45	75
Bethesda	D. P. Bridges	J. E. Smith, Wilson's Mills	4	600.00	400	2		1	12		1	71	110	181
Bethel	R. W. Horrell	Jno. A. ..., Kenly	4	500.00	250	2		1			1	9	12	21
Blackman's Grove	D. F. Putnam	E. B. Hayes, Four Oaks, R. 3	3	500.00	300	10	4		2	1		24	46	70
Carter's Chapel	D. D. Edwards	W. B. ..., Micro	1	500.00	300				3	2		20	46	66
Clayton	D. H. Thornton	R. R. ..., ...	1—	5500.00	700	12	12	7	6	3	2	120	163	283
...le's Chapel	L. L. Hudson	C. I. ..., ...	2	500.00	300	6			6	3	3	62	96	158
Corinth	A. A. Pippin	E. C. Whitley, Archer	4	500.00	400	3			2	2	2	37	53	90
Calvary	J. W. Watson	T. J. Lee, Dunn		500.00	200	3	2			4		11	27	38
Four Oaks	D. F. Putnam	J. Wm. ..., Four Oaks	1—3	600.00	250	2	2			1		12	27	39
Hood's Grove	J. W. Watson	Jos. W. ..., ..., R. 2	3	400.00	350	5	2					12	24	36
Kenly	R. W. Horrell	B. W. Harris, Kenly	2—4				8	2	2		2		7	8	15
Lee's	A. A. Pippin	W. I. Green, Selma, R. 3	2	500.00	700	17			3	4	2	119	168	287
Live Oak	D. P. Bridges	K. Broadwell, Selma, R. 1	2	200.00	250	2	2	2	2	2	2	10	22	32
...	D. D. Edwards	Oscar Mozingo, Selma, R. 4	1	500.00	300	2	5		3			4	6	10
Mt Moriah	J. M. Hilliard	M. T. Wilder, ...	1	800.00	300	11	1		2	6	2	62	81	143
Bees ...	R. W. Horrell	N. L. Stott, Taylor	4	700.00	400	11	1		2		1	33	45	78
New Bethel	T. Y. Seymour	N. B. Bryan, Garner	4	800.00	400	1	1	1	2			48	48	96
Oliver's Grove	N. H. Gibbs	Haywood Johnson, Four Oaks	1	200.00	300	6	5					7	12	19
Parrish Memorial	R. W. Horrell	Joe D. ..., ..., R. 4	1	600.00	400	5	1		1	6		24	33	57
Pauline	J. W. Watson	N. W. Smith, Four Oaks	3	400.00	300	5	1	1	2		2	22	23	45
Pine Level	R. W. Horrell	F. C. ..., Pine Level	1	250.00	225	5				1		18	37	55
Pisgan	D. F. Putnam	A. G. Jones, Smithfield, R. 1	1	700.00	300		3		1	1		18	25	43
Princeton	R. W. Horrell	W. I. Pearce, Princeton	3	800.00	300	7	6			2		33	70	103
Sardis	B. G. Early	N. B. Stevens, Smithfield	3	400.00	200	2						8	14	22
Selma	O. R. ...	J. W. ..., Selma	2-3-4	5000.00	250	35	30				2	72	101	173
Shiloh	L. L. Hudson	J. F. Hardee, ..., R. 1	3	700.00	300	4		1			4	30	43	73
Smithfield	D. P. Bridges	T. J. ..., Smithfield	1—3	4500.00	700	3	9	1	13			71	77	148
Thanksgiving	D. P. Bridges	W. G. Earp, Selma, R. 1		800.00	300	3				2		26	32	58
Trinity	J. W. ...	J. S. ..., ..., Benson, R. 2	4	300.00	200	1		1	1			12	28	40
Wite Oak	A. A. Pippin	J. I. Murphrey, Selma, R. 1	2	500.00	450	28	5	1	4	2	1	53	87	140
Wilson's Mills	D. P. Bridges	J. H. Talton, ... Mills	2	400.00	250	6		1	2			12	28	55
Wendell	A. A. Pippin	C. Z. Todd, Wendell	2	2500.00	400	14	24	3			1	25	37	62

CHURCHES	SUPERINTENDENTS AND ADDRESSES.	Officers and Teachers.	Scholars.	Total.	Average Attendance.	Schools.	Volumes in Library.	Quarterlies and Papers taken.	Months open.	Baptisms from school.	Expenses.
Antioch	W. H. Malen, Selma, R. 2	6	160	166	60	1		200	10	1	$ 10.00
Baptist Centre	J. C. Harcee, Clayton	4	35	39	25	1		40	12	2	4.00
Benson	J. L. Hall, Benson	9	182	191	110	1	100	200	12	7	36.04
Bethany	David Pace, Micro	10	96	106	50	1		100	12	2	10.00
Bethesda	J. J. Wallace, Wilson's Mills	8	60	68	40	1	50	60	12	1	8.00
Bethel											
Blackman's Grove	F. P. Wood, Four Oaks, R. 2	4	50	54	30	1		40	12		9.28
Carter's Chapel	Preston Mozingo, Mro	4	42	46	25	1		40	12	5	
Clon	R. H. ..r, Clayton	15	204	219	142	1	246	415	12		88.67
Clyde's Chapel	W. T. ..h, ..n, R. 2	6	44	50	40	1				5	6.00
Corinth	J. A. Estridge, Archer	6	93	99	75	1		80	9	3	5.00
Calvary	Jas Thornton, Dunn, R. 2	3	20	23							
Four Oaks	O. D. Stanley, Four Oaks	5	45	50	30	1		50	12	1	12.57
Hood's Grove	H. V. Rose, Beasley, R. 2	5	48	53		1			8	3	1.00
Lee's Chapel	Wm Lewis, Selma, R. 3	5	35	40		2		260	12	15	6.00
Mro	L. L. ..h, Micro	6	84	90	40	1	350	60	12	2	12.00
Mt Moriah	J. F. Poo, Clayton	11	121	132	45	1		160	10	2	20.50
Mies bel	J. H. Flowers, Taylor	5	44	49	65	1		40	10	8	
New Bethel	L. C. Yeergan, Garner	7	30	37	25	1	53	40	9	4	
Oliver's Grove	Thomas Tyner, Four Oks	3	50	53	35	1		75	8	1	
Parrish Memorial	A. W. Stickey, Princeton	6	50	56	40	1		102	8	1	2.50
Pauline	N. W. Smith, Four Oaks, R. 1	6	65	71	30	1		30	12	4	
Pine Level	J. W. Lilas, Selma	8	101	109	50	1		70	12	5	10.00
Pisgah	R. H. Higgins, Smithfield	4	46	50	30	1		50	12		7.00
Princeton	Chas. H. Holt, Princeton	5	75	80	35	1		75	12	3	15.00
Selma	J. R. Hood, Selma	11	175	186	130			200	12	20	51.07
Shiloh	Dr. G. A McLemore, Clayton, R. 1	7	64	71	35	1		50	12	3	
Smithfield	M. A. Allen, Smithfield	15	155	170	92	2	200	200	12	2	67.25
White Oak	V. R. ..y, ..n, R. 2	5	75	80	50	1		80	12	16	35.00
Wilson's Mills	J. T. Holt, Wilson's Mills	6	60	66	45	1			12		
Wendell	C. Z. ..d, Wendell	9	192	201	100	1		160	12		26.95
Total		204	2491	2703	1487	30	899	2877		115	$ 443.83

TABLE VI—CONTRIBUTIONS BY CHURCHES, SUNDAY SCHOOLS AND SOCIETIES.

	Number of Members	Pastor's Salary	Building and repairs	Incidentals	The Poor	State Missions	Home Missions	Foreign Missions	Sunday Sch. Missions	Orphanage	Ministerial Education	Ministerial Relief	Colleges and schools	Other Objects	Sunday Sch. Expenses	Minutes and Clerk	Total
...h	168	48.75				15.00	1.50	1.50	1.00	2.50	1.50	2.00	10.00		10.00	90	84.65
Bapt't Centre	76	60.00	80.00			20.00	3.00	2.22	2.00	10.00		4.00			4.00	1.00	180.22
Benson	147	400.00				118.30	17.00	30.86	2.00	23.46	15.00			73.56	38.04	2.50	720.02
Bethany	75	30.00	10.00			6.50	2.50	2.00	1.00	3.00	1.25	1.25			10.00	60	68.10
Bethesda	181	150.00		2.00		25.00	5.00	2.00	2.00	15.00	2.00	3.00		15.00	8.00	1.00	229.00
Bethel	21					4.00	1.50	1.50	.50	2.00	1.00					1.40	12.90
Blackman's G	70	102.00		2.00		26.00	4.00	6.00	4.00	7.00	3.00	2.50		28.85	9.28	1.50	194.13
Carter's Ch.	66					10.00	2.50	1.50	1.00	5.00	1.50	2.00				50	24.00
Clayton	298	330.00	689.84	115.00		252.99	74.40	125.10	16.39	171.00	33.40	15.00	15.35	151.31	88.67	5.00	2083.45
Clyde's Ch.	158	100.00	30.00		.76	10.00	4.00	4.00	1.50	8.44	2.00	2.00			6.00	1.00	176.20
Corinth	90	54.25	4.00			6.00	1.50	2.00	.50	4.00	1.00	2.00			5.00	1.00	76.25
Calvary	38	45.35				4.34	2.15	3.50	.50	3.00	1.00	1.25				92	62.01
Four Oaks.	39	118.00	14.00	6.50	.00	12.10	7.45	8.00	1.00	8.00	1.50	2.50		15.50	12.57	1.00	200.12
Kenly Grove	36	50.00				10.00	2.00	3.00	1.00	2.00	2.00	1.50		20.00	1.00	50	96.00
...s Chapel	15	75.00		3.00	.00	3.00	1.00	1.00	.50	2.00	1.00	1.00		25.00		1.00	118.50
Live Oak	287															45	23.26
...ro	32	15.00					1.05	.38	.50	1.20	.20	1.00			12.00	50	69.80
Mt Moriah	10	25.00	10.00	2.00			3.41	4.75	5.00	2.25	1.00	5.00			20.50	1.50	391.92
...p.	143	150.00	3.40	30.00			25.96	59.56		30.00	5.00	2.00				1.00	97.00
New Bethel.	78	65.00					3.00	2.00		4.00	2.00	5.00				1.00	160.50
Oliver's Gro.	96	100.00	50.00				7.00	5.00		10.00	4.00					1.00	1.60
Parrish M	19	64.00								2.00				6.08	2.50	50	141.00
P...ine	57	16.00					1.50	1.50	.50	1.50	1.00	2.00				1.00	27.35
Pine Level.	45	32.49	1.90				1.50	1.50	.50	2.00	1.00	1.00				35	65.47
Pisgah	55	100.50	15.00				1.25	1.50	.50	2.34	1.25	1.50			10.00	1.00	147.04
Princeton	43	100.00	34.93	9.00			2.00	2.50	2.00	4.00	1.00	1.00			7.00	1.00	195.98
Sardis	103	25.00					4.00	5.00	1.00	1.50	2.00	2.50			15.00	50	39.25
Selma	22	600.00	2500.00	28.75			2.00	30.00	1.00	62.00	1.00	10.00		117.50	51.07	25	3435.32
...field	173	440.00	15.00	75.00			10.00	50.00	4.00	40.00	11.50	16.00	20.00	62.21	67.25	3.00	1142.88
Thanksgiving	148	50.00	10.00	2.00			40.00	3.50	10.00	3.00	12.00	1.00		4.31		5.00	181.71
Trinity							1.00	2.50	1.00	5.00	1.00	2.00				1.00	37.86
White Oak.								5.00	.50	10.00	1.50	3.00		15.00	35.00	1.00	248.00
Wilson's M.								3.00	1.50	5.58	4.00	4.17				1.50	193.50
...ll	14							2.00	1.00	5.00	2.00	2.50			26.95	1.75	1445.57

TABLE VII—CONTRIBUTIONS FROM SUNDAY SCHOOLS AND SOCIETIES ETC. (Included in Table of Contributions.)

CHURCHES.	Building and Repairing.	The Poor.	State Missions.	Home Missions.	Foreign Missions.	Sunday Sch. Missions.	Ministerial Education.	Ministerial Relief.	Orphanage.	Sunday Sch. Expenses.	Other Objects.	Total.
Benson W. M. S.	$	$	$ 14.30	$ 8.05	$ 11.50	$	$	$	$	$	$	$ 33.85
Benson Sunday School										28.24	6.76	35.00
Benson Sunbeams			5.00		1.25							6.25
Benson Baraca			5.00						10.00	5.00	7.52	27.52
Benson Philatheas			4.00	2.00	2.00					2.80		10.80
Blackman's Grove Sunday School						2.00						2.00
Clayton W. M. S.			100.00	50.00	50.00		8.40	2.50			5.10	216.00
Clayton Sunday School	235.00					10.00			60.00	88.67	25.00	418.67
Clayton Y. L. M. S.			12.50	14.80	25.00							52.30
Clayton Sunbeams					17.10						6.66	23.76
Micro Woman's Missionary Society			1.12	1.16	1.50							3.78
Micro B. Y. P. U.			1.77	1.00	2.00							4.77
Mount Moriah W. M. S.			6.00	5.96	9.56							21.52
Pine Level Sunday School									2.00	10.00		12.00
Selma Woman's Missionary Society			5.00	1.00	20.00							26.00
Selma Sunday School									32.00			32.00
Smithfield Woman's Missionary Society	11.50	16.88	20.00	14.80	15.45						1.00	79.63
Smithfield Sunday School			5.33	4.59	3.36	3.65	3.24		8.10	67.25		95.52
Smithfield Sunbeams					1.00							1.00
A. H. Lee			2.50									2.50
Total	$ 246.50	$16.88	$ 182.62	$ 103.36	$ 142.72	$15.65	$11.64	$ 2.50	$ 112.10	$ 201.96	$ 52.04	$1104.87

TABLE VIII—DIGEST OF CHURCH LETTERS.

CHURCHES.	Baptisms 1906.	Baptisms 1907.	Pledged. 1907	Pledged. 1908	Contributed.	Above Pledge.	Below Pledge.	Gain	Loss.	Above.	
Antioch	6	6	$ 35.00	$ 26.00	$ 35.00	$.....	$.....	2	.....	$.....	$
Baptist Centre	...	3	42.00	25.00	35.22	......	6.78	......	1	......	1
Benson	3	8	150.00	171.00	210.42	60.42	......	2	......	21.00	..
Bethany	3	2	17.50	17.50	17.50	.....	......	......	2	......	..
Bethesda	24	2	53.00	53.00	53.00	......	......	......	11	......	..
Bethel	6	2	11.50	10.50	11.50	......	......	......	1	......	..
Blackman's Grove	4	10	40.50	48.50	52.50	12.50	......	9	......	8.00	..
Carter's Chapel	4	...	23.50	23.50	23.50	......	......	......	5	......	..
Clayton	1	12	557.50	635.00	703.63	146.13	......	13	......	77.50	..
Clyde's Chapel	8	6	29.00	29.00	31.94	2.94	......	1	......	......	..
Corinth	5	3	17.00	19.50	17.00	......	......	......	5	2.50	..
Calvary	...	3	10.25	13.75	15.74	5.49	......	2	......	3.50	..
Four Oaks	5	2	24.00	35.50	35.55	11.55	......	2	......	11.50	..
Hood's Grove	...	5	21.50	21.50	21.50	......	......	5	......	......	..
Kenly	...	...	9.50	14.00	9.50	......	......	8	......	4.50	..
Lee's Chapel	26	17	56.00	62.00	69.86	13.86	......	3	......	6.00	..
Live Oak	2	...	14.50	7.00	7.81	......	6.69	......	2	......	
Micro	...	2	12.25	10.25	20.80	8.55	......	3	......	......	
Mount Moriah	6	5	165.00	165.00	186.52	21.52	......	......	5	......	..
Nobles Chapel	...	11	31.00	31.50	31.00	......	......	11	......	50	..
New Bethel	2	11	27.00	27.00	59.50	32.50	......	19	......	......	
Oliver's Grove	...	1	10.50	6.50	1.10	......	9.40	1	......	......	
Parrish Memorial	...	6	23.50	23.75	23.50	......	......	7	......	25	..
Pauline	7	5	11.00	11.00	11.00	......	......	3	......	......	
Pine Level	8	5	14.00	14.25	14.00	......	......	8	......	25	..
Pisgah	...	...	23.50	29.75	23.54	4	......	......	1	6.25	..
Princeton	5	7	36.50	36.50	36.50	......	......	8	......	......	..
Sardis	4	2	11.00	13.00	14.00	3.00	......	2	......	2.00	..
Selma	...	35	220.50	251.00	252.50	32.50	......	62	......	30.50	..
Shiloh	8	4	25.75	29.25	25.75	......	......	3	......	3.50	..
Smithfield	14	3	393.00	410.00	417.25	24.25	......	......	......	17.00	.
Thanksgiving	4	3	29.50	10.00	6.50	......	23.50	1	......	......	
Trinity	3	1	18.00	18.50	18.00	......	......	......	......	50	.
White Oak	2	28	31.50	38.00	31.50	......	......	23	......	6.50	.
Wilson's Mills	...	6	43.00	36.00	43.00	......	......	7	......	......	
Wendell	...	14	11.50	13.00	29.20	18.70	......	38	......	1.50	.
Total	296	230	$2230.75	$2387.00							

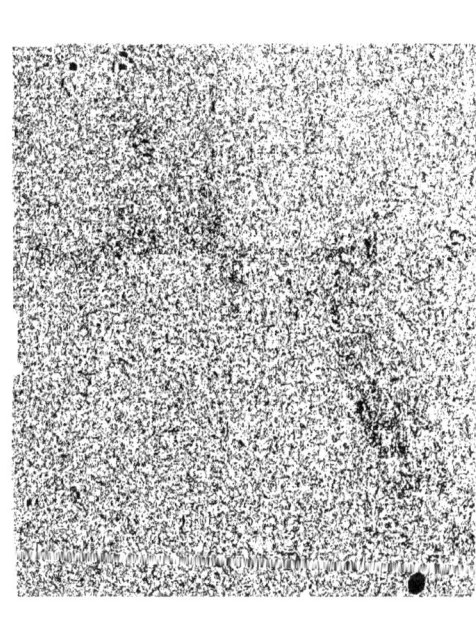

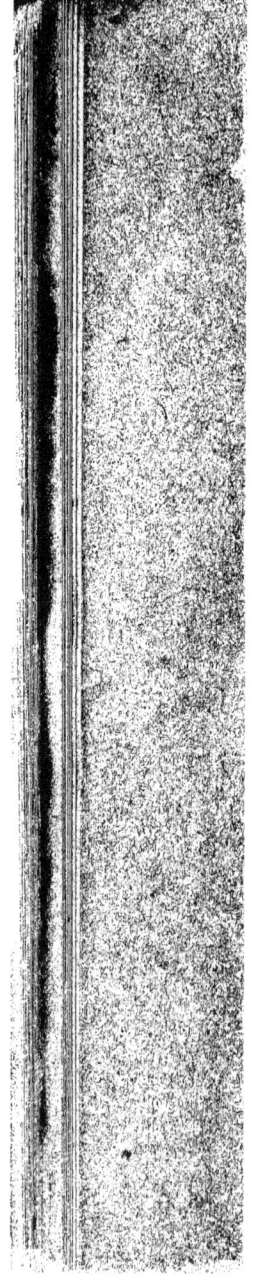

MINUTES

OF THE

SIXTH SESSION

OF THE

JOHNSTON COUNTY

BAPTIST ASSOCIATION,

HELD WITH

SELMA BAPTIST CHURCH, SELMA, N. C.,

NOVEMBER, 5, 6, 7 AND 8, 1908.

The next session will be held with Bethesda Baptist Church, beginning Thursday after the first Sunday in November, 1909.

To preach Introductory Sermon—A. A. Pippin. Alternate—R. W. Horrell.

NASH BROTHERS,
BOOK AND COMMERCIAL PRINTERS,
GOLDSBORO, N. C.

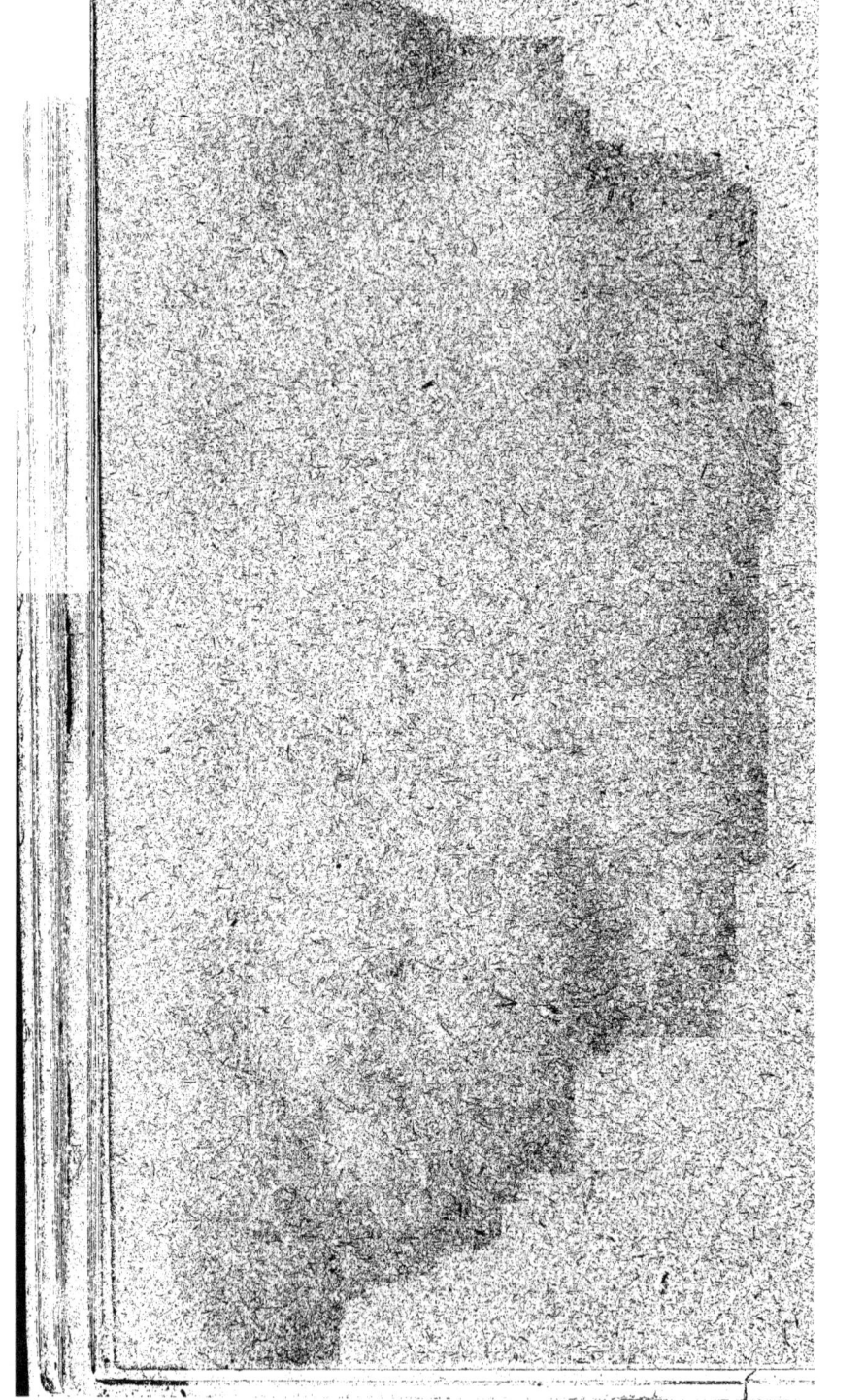

MINUTES

OF THE

SIXTH SESSION

OF THE

JOHNSTON COUNTY

BAPTIST ASSOCIATION,

HELD WITH

SELMA BAPTIST CHURCH, SELMA, N. C.,

NOVEMBER, 5, 6, 7 AND 8, 1908.

The next session will be held with Bethesda Baptist Church, beginning Thursday after the first Sunday in November, 1909.

To preach Introductory Sermon—A. A. Flippin. Alternate—R. W. Horrell.

NASH BROTHERS,
BOOK AND COMMERCIAL PRINTERS,
GOLDSBORO, N. C.

OFFICIAL REGISTER 1908–1909.

Moderator—R. H. Gower.....................................Clayton, N. C.
Vice-Moderator—A. A. Pippin............................Wakefield, N. C.
Clerk—T. J. Lassiter......................................Smithfield, N. C.
Treasurer—Will H. Lassiter............................Smithfield, N. C.
Auditor—J. D. Underwood.............................Smithfield, N. C.

EXECUTIVE COMMITTEE.

J. M. BEATY, Chairman.....................................Smithfield, N. C.
J. H. BOON...Benson, N. C.
J. T. HOLT..Wilson's Mills, N. C.
ALONZO PARRISH...Benson, N. C.
J. F. POOL..Clayton, N. C.

CHAIRMEN STANDING COMMITTEES.

State Missions ....D. F. Putnam.
Home Missions...T. H. Thornton.
Foreign Missions...A. A. Pippin.
Orphanage ....J. M. Hilliard.
Education ....R. W. Horrell.
Periodicals ....W. A. Massengill.
Temperance ....Alonzo Parrish
Ministerial Relief..N. H. Gibbs.
Sunday Schools..C. W. Carter.
Woman's Work...J. W. Nobles.
Member State Board of Missions...........................J. M. Beaty.

MINISTERIAL REGISTER.

D. P. BRIDGES...Smithfield, N. C.
WORLEY CREECH...............................R. F. D. 2, Kenly, N. C.
D. D. EDWARDS...Cary, N. C.
N. H. GIBBS...Benson, N. C.
J. M. HILLIARD.................................R. F. D., Raleigh, N. C.
R. W. HORRELL...Selma, N. C.
L. L. HUDSON.......................................Wake Forest, N. C.
U. R. MANGUM...Selma, N. C.
J. W. NOBLES...Kenly, N. C.
A. A. PIPPIN..Wakefield, N. C.
D. F. PUTNAM..Benson, N. C.
W. C. ROYAL..Benson, N. C.
T. Y. SEYMOUR....................................Wake Forest, N. C.
T. H. THORNTON..Clayton, N. C.

LIST OF DELEGATES TO SESSION OF 1908.

Antioch—J. W. Corbett.

Baptist Centre—J. C. Hardee.

Benson—J. L. Hall, J. E. Wall, J. W. Holmes, Alonzo Parrish and L. T. Royall.

Benson's Grove—J. R. Benson.

Bethany—Kirkman Creech, David Pace and Merritt Pace.

Bethesda—J. J. Wallace and W. B. Wallace.

Bethel—Perry Barnes and W. T. Sullivan.

Blackman's Grove—W. B. Creech and J. L. Smith.

Carter's Chapel—L. T. Wall, Albert McCall and Gray Easom.

Clayton—M. G. Gulley, Jesse W. Hilliard and C. W. Carter.

Clyde's Chapel—William Martin, H. V. Bunch and J. W. B. Finch.

Corinth—J. A. Estridge.

Calvary—J. K. Hudson.

Four Oaks—W. A. Massengill.

Hood's Grove—Not represented.

Kenly—Charles C. Teague.

Lee's Chapel—W. I. Green and J. B. Richardson.

Live Oak—G. W. Chesnut and J. M. Richardson.

Micro—J. W. Mozingo.

Middlesex—G. Lewis.

Mount Moriah—J. F. Pool.

Nobles' Chapel—J. Herbert Liles and J. R. Davis.

New Bethel—A. J. Bryan and D. E. Easom.

Oliver's Grove—Not represented.

Parrish Memorial—G. R. Capps and Joe D. Creech.

Pauline—W. C. Grant and D. B. Joyner.

Pine Level—W. M. Eason and William Crocker.

Pisgah—M. Johnson.

Princeton—W. H. Wells and H. I. Raiford.

Sardis—N. B. Stevens.

Selma—M. C. Winston, R. E. Richardson, J. M. Oneal and C. Richardson.

Shiloh—C. J. Coats.

Smithfield—R. I. Lassiter, J. P. Canaday and J. D. Underwood.

Thanksgiving—E. F. Murphrey and H. E. Earp.

Trinity—Not represented.

White Oak—W. T. Allen, V. R. Turley, J. W. Barnes and A. L. Batton.

Wilson's Mills—G. G. Beaty and J. T. Holt.

Wendell—Not represented.

Pastors Present—D. P. Bridges, Worley Creech, D. D. Edwards, N. H. Gibbs, J. M. Hilliard, R. W. Horrell, O. R. Mangum, A. A. Pippin, J. W. Nobles, W. C. Royal and D. F. Putnam

PROCEEDINGS.

The sixth annual session of the Johnston County Baptist Association met to-day with the Selma Baptist Church. The morning session was called to order by Pastor O. R. Mangum, and was led in prayer by Brother Worley Creech. In the absence of Brother T. H. Thornton, the introductory sermon was preached by Brother D. F. Putnam. His text was: Acts 2:42, 43, and the subject was "The Church Assembled in Worship: Its Power." After several announcements had been made, the session adjourned to meet at 2:15 p. m. in the town hall.

AFTERNOON SESSION.

The afternoon session was opened with singing, and with prayer by Brother N. H. Gibbs. The Moderator, Brother R. H. Gower, then appointed the following as Committee on Credentials and Enrollment: W. C. Royal and J. W. Mozingo.

After the delegates had been enrolled, the body was duly organized. Upon motion of Brother D. F. Putnam, the rules and regulations were suspended and the vote of the Association was cast by Brother Mangum for Brother R. H. Gower to succeed himself as Moderator. The following officers were unanimously elected:

Vice-Moderator—A. A. Pippin.
Clerk—T. J. Lassiter.
Treasurer—Will H. Lassiter.
Auditor—J. D. Underwood.
Historian—R. W. Horrell.

The organization was then declared completed and ready for business. The Moderator then announced the following Committees:

Finance—J. W. Holmes, J. F. Pool and J. T. Holt.
Temperance—A. A. Pippin, Kirkman Creech and M. G. Gulley.
On Re-Arranging Program—J. M. Beaty, D. F. Putnam and O. R. Mangum.
On Religious Services—Pastor and Deacons of Selma Church.
On Home Missions—D. F. Putnam, C. C. Teague and M. Johnson.
On Petitionary Letters—J. M. Hilliard, J. H. Boon and R. W. Horrell.

Upon motion of Brother D. P. Bridges, delegates were elected to the Baptist State Convention and The Southern Baptist Convention:

D. P. Bridges to The Southern Baptist Convention.

V. R. Turley, J. J. Wallace and J. T. Holt to The Baptist State Convention.

Upon motion, Brother J. M. Beaty was elected as member of the State Board of Missions. Brother A. A. Pippin then read the report on Temperance:

REPORT ON TEMPERANCE.

My text for this report is Proverbs 20:1, "Wine is a mocker, strong drink is raging, and whosoever is deceived thereby is not wise."

Intemperance does not pay. It costs time, it costs money, it costs health, character, and happiness. It makes wives wretched, and wrecks homes. It incites to all sorts of sin and misery.

"Wine is a mocker" truthfully declares the proverb. It is an insidious delusion and a snare. It establishes a taste for liquor and, while slower in its deadly work, it is just as hurtful to the physical organism. And it is equally as disgraceful to be drunk on wine or cider as on whiskey. The devil lurks in every wine-glass and he often reaches young men and women through wine and cider where he could not by trying to start them on whiskey.

"And whosoever is deceived thereby is not wise." Yet countless men will dally with the liquor habit, knowing that "at last it biteth like a serpent and stingeth like an adder." The danger lies in man's thinking he will always be master. And what is God's view of such indulgence? The odious sin of drunkenness is condemned through the Scriptures. Nowhere does God's word commend the use of intoxicants as a beverage. No matter where or what our weak spot may be, it will be reflected in what we do. Alexander the Great, conquered all the world except himself and died a drunkard at the age of thirty-three.

We most earnestly recommend the carrying out of the laws passed by the people. Every Christian must stand for sobriety and see to it, that law breakers suffer the penalty of the law.

A. A. PIPPIN,
KIRKMAN CREECH,
M. G. GULLEY,
Committee.

Upon motion to adopt, the report was discussed by Brother J. M. Hilliard and adopted unanimously.

The report of Committee on Re-arranging Program was read by Brother O. R. Mangum, after which it was adopted. There being no further business, a motion to adjourn was made. Brother W. C. Royal was appointed to conduct the devotional exercises to-night. The benediction was then pronounced by Brother Royal.

NIGHT SESSION.

Devotional exercises were conducted by Brother W. C. Royal, after which the Body was called to order by the Moderator. The following committees were announced:

On Place and Preacher for Next Meeting—W. B. Joyner, W. H. Wells and H. V. Bunch.

On Woman's Work—O. R. Mangum, W. T. Sullivan and J. L. Smith.

The Committee on Petitionary Letters made the following report:

Your Committee on the petition from Benson's Grove Church reports favorable and recommends her for membership in the Association.

J. M. HILLIARD,
R. W. HORRELL,
J. F. BOON,
Committee.

Upon motion the report was adopted, and Benson's Grove Church was duly admitted to membership in the Body, and her delegate welcomed to a seat with us.

Brother O. R. Mangum read the report on Woman's Work:

REPORT ON WOMAN'S WORK.

Realizing, as all pastors do, the tremendous importance of woman's work toward the hastening of the Kingdom of Christ, we bespeak for it a larger place in the hearts of our people. It was through woman's potent influence that the human race fell from the height God had planned. And if the lost Eden is ever restored it must be by the combined efforts of our women, whose hearts are aflame with the love of God. This she is grandly endeavoring to do. Daily she is touching the hem of the Master's garment, and thereby she is bringing healing to a wounded race.

The most significant movement of the past hundred years is the emerging of women from centuries of silence, by breaking the supposed Pauline shackles, and then taking her rightful place in the work of the kingdom of God. The intelligent Christian will not ask if they have been successful. Their achievement is a part of history. They have set the idlers to work. They have trained thousands of our young people for service, and have kindled in the heart of the church an ardent desire to see the world brought to the foot of the Cross. But they did not stop at this. They have materially aided in flinging far the battle lines.

Their past achievement is only a prophecy of greater things to come. In the future we may expect them to be the key to the situation in three ways:

1. In raising funds. The success of the societies in this matter is an unanswerable argument for them, and it has demonstrated their right to exist. Last year they raised over $21,000. They have outstripped the men per capita.

2. In awakening an interest in the churches on the subject of missions. It can be safely claimed that their society is the motive of the great Laymen's Movement.

3. In training the coming generation along mission lines. Thus they prepare the way for the coming King.

O. R. MANGUM,
W. T. SULLIVAN,
J. L. SMITH,
Committee.

The report was discussed by Brother Mangum and adopted. The Association then joined in singing hymn No. 567: "Come Ye That Love the Lord." Brother Charles E. Maddrey of The Piedmont Association, and Vice-President of The Home Mission Board for North Carolina, was then recognized. The report on Home Misisons was then called for, and read by Brother D. F. Putnam:

REPORT ON HOME MISSIONS.

The Southern Baptist Convention has committed the evangelization of the Southern States, Panama, Cuba and Isle of Pines to the Home Mission Board.

This territory contains 25,000,000 souls, 9,000,000 of whom are negroes and 5,000,000 foreigners.

In the States the work is classified, as frontier, work in the large cities, the Mission schools in the mountains, co-operation with the negroes, the foreign population and evangelism. Space forbids going into details but it is apparent to the well informed Baptist, that every department of this work should be emphasized. Cuba is a most hopeful field and reports substantial progress.

Panama is a strategic point; the world's eyes are upon it. In the Isle of Pines the work is more settled and hopeful than formerly.

Last year 865 workers were employed, 18,798 baptisms were reported, 14,207 were added to the churches by letter, 271 churches were organized, 309 houses of worship were built or improved, 703 Sunday schools were organized, 112,604 gospel sermons and addresses were delivered by our Missionaries.

These with the influence of the Godly men on the fields were, as indicated above, the beginning of greater things in the future.

Our Association has done well for State Missions and especially for Johnston County. We now believe the time has come, not to do less for State Missions, but more for Home Missions.

D. F. PUTNAM,
M. JOHNSON,
Committee.

Upon motion to adopt, Brother Putnam called for Brother Maddrey to discuss the report. He made a strong address, and was followed by Brother Bridges and Brother Mangum, who made short talks. The roll of the Churches was then called and pledges taken for Home Missions, after which the report was adopted.

The Moderator recognized Brother F. P. Hobgood, President of The Oxford Female Seminary, and Brother J. S. Farmer, of *The Biblical Recorder*. Brother J. T. Holt was appointed to conduct the devotional exercises to-morrow morning. Adjournment was then taken till 9:30 to-morrow morning, with benediction by Brother J. S. Farmer.

SECOND DAY.

FRIDAY MORNING, November 6, 1908.

The Association opened this morning with prayer services led by Brother J. T. Holt. After the enrollment of the new delegates, the following committees were announced:

State Missions—D. P. Bridges, W. T. Allen and J. D. Davis.
Orphanage—C. W. Carter, W. C. Grant and Herbert Liles.
Sunday Schools—J. W. Nobles, Perry Barnes and W. C. Rogers.
Foreign Missions—T. H. Thornton, J. C. Hardee and L. T. Wall.
Education—J. P. Canaday, Albert McCall and William Martin.
On Ministerial Relief—F. M. Ferrell, J. H. Boon and W. M. Eason.
Periodicals—R. W. Horrell, J. M. Richardson and W. A. Massengill.

Brother F. P. Hobgood, of Oxford, was recognized and spoke for a short while in the interest of his school.

Brother J. M. Hilliard for the Committee made the following report on Petitionary Letters:

Your Committee, on petition from Middlesex, recommend the reception of this Church as a member of our body.

J. M. HLLIARD,
R. W. HORRELL,
J. H. BOON,
Committee.

The report was received, and the Church was duly admitted to the Association, and her delegate welcomed.

The Moderator recognized the following visiting Brethren: Archibald Johnson, Editor of *Charity and Children,* representing the Thomasville Orphanage; E. L. Middleton, Sunday School Field Secretary for the State Mission Board; Livingston Johnson, Corresponding Secretary of the Baptist State Convention.

Brother J. M. Beaty, Chairman of the Executive Committee, first read the report of the Building Committee:

REPORT OF BUILDING COMMITTEE.

Since our appointment a year ago we have directed work toward building a church at Benson's Grove. A fine lot and a splendid location was sesured, contracts for the erection of the house and for the lumber were given out and now the weather-boarding is being nailed on. We hope to get the house ready for use by about the middle of December. We have raised only about half enough money to pay for this church but hope to raise the remainder during November and December. We ask every church which has not raised a collection for this building to do so at once. This would enable us to pay up and start to build at another place when the new year opens. Our plans are to help build at least one new church every year.

J. M. BEATY,
ALONZO PARRISH,
J. H. BOON,
GEORGE L. JONES,
C. W. CARTER,
Committee.

After making a few remarks in explanation of the work of the Committee, he read the report of the Executive Committee:

REPORT OF EXECUTIVE COMMITTEE.

We are glad to report a good year's work. While at some places but little has been done, yet at a large number of mission points and mission churches several meetings have been held and satisfactory progress has been made.

Rev. R. W. Horrell has preached at Pine Level, Brown's School House, Pleasant Grove, Benson's Grove, Princeton, Bethel and Moore's School House.

Rev. D. P. Bridges has served Thanksgiving and Live Oak churches.

Rev. J. W. Nobles has preached at Micro, Parrish Memorial, Kenly, Hickory Cross School House, Hood's Grove, Pauline and Noble's Chapel.

Rev. N. H. Gibbs has been pastor at Oliver's Grove and Rev. A. A. Pippin has served Corinth.

Rev. D. F. Putnam has preached at Pisgah, Four Oaks, Blackman's Grove and Pleasant Hill, and Rev. W. C. Royal at Sardis, Woodard School House, Calvary and Trinity.

A house of worship is being built at Benson's Grove.

At Kenly a good house on a fine lot has been erected, but the house needs plastering and doors and windows to make it ready for use. A debt of a little more than three hundred dollars is due on the Kenly church. The work there has had little outside help toward the building. A point has been reached when they must have some help and we urge the other churches of the Association to help before the close of the present year as the cause there is suffering on account of delay in getting into the new church.

We realize more and more that a great work lies ahead of us within the bounds of our Association and ask every member of our churches to help us with their sympathy and prayers and financial support. There are several other points in Johnston County which need to be occupied but cannot be now for want of men and means to support them.

Respectfully submitted,

J. M. BEATY,
ALONZO PARRISH,
J. H. BOON,
GEORGE L. JONES,
C. W. CARTER,
Executive Committee.

Before adopting the above reports, the report on State Missions was called for and read by Brother D. P. Bridges:

REPORT ON STATE MISSIONS.

It is the work of the State Mission Board to make it possible for every man, woman and child in the State of North Carolina to hear the gospel as we hold it. In order that it may be able to do this there are four things laid down in the Scriptures that we must get our people to do. When we have aroused all our Baptist people to these four things we are in a fair way to put our Board in a condition to give the gospel to every community.

1. The first of these is view the field and see the needs. "Lift up your eyes, and look on the fields; for they are white already to harvest." John, 4:35. If we could get our people to study the great needs of our State and know the situation it would go a long ways in solving the problem of our State Boards, and Brother Johnson would not be so distressed about how he would pay the Missionaries. Brethren, look out on the great harvest fields ready for the sickle. In our eastern section there are counties with only one and two Baptist preachers, three or four Baptist churches, and a hand full of struggling Baptists trying to meet the situation with the gospel.

2. Go forth to the work. "Go ye into all the world and preach the gospel to every creature." Mark, 16:15. "Go ye, therefore and teach all nations," Matthew, 28:19. There is a great need for workers to-day, so many are standing idle. Not all can go as preachers in the ordinary sense of the term but nearly all can go as workers. We need more preachers. There are many fields in need of pastors, but one of our greatest needs to-day, is consecrated men and women who are willing to be quiet, but faithful workers standing by our pastors. I suppose that it is the experience of almost every pastor that the one supreme need he feels in his work is really consecrated men and women to stand by him.

3. A recognition of the fact that what we have of earthly goods belongs to God and should be used for the spread of His gospel in the world. "Honor the Lord with thy substance and with the first fruits of all thine increase," Prov. 3:9. "Every man according as he purposeth in his heart, so let him give; not grudgingly, or of necessity; for God loveth a cheerful giver." There are precious few who cannot give something to the work of giving the gospel to our State. The State Convention asked us this year to give on an average to this work a little over twenty cents a piece. It will be a burning shame on our 205,000 members if we fail to give this pitiably small sum. Our Association promised last year in pledges $1,087. This is an average of a little over 33 cents a piece. A very small sum when we consider the great needs in our territory. I hope we can, at least make it 35 cents next year. Let every church and every member in every church do his best.

4. The fourth one of these is something that every member can take part in. Pray for the success of the work. "Pray ye, therefore the Lord

of the harvest, that he would send forth laborers into his harvest." Luke 10:2. "Pray for us that the word of the Lord may have free course and be glorified." 2 Thess. 3:1.

One great need of the Board and the Missionaries in their struggles and hardships is the prayers and sympathy of the brethren. Every one can lift his heart and voice to our Father and invoke His blessings on this work. O brethren and sisters, give us your prayer in the work.

I want us to study the needs in our own bounds. If we get a right conception of these needs surely every one will be aroused to do greater things next year.

There are according to a safe estimate 12,000 white people of accountable age in Johnston county who are members of no church at all. There are only about 6,000 members of all the churches of all the denominations in the county. About half of these are Missionary Baptists. So you see that as much work of evangelizing this 12,000 belongs to us as to all the other denominations in the county.

To do this work we need six other men on the field for all their time. This would, at the very least call for five or six thousand dollars for some years to come to be spent in our bounds. Let us lift up our eyes and look on the field and behold the needs and get down and do our best.

D. P. BRIDGES,
Chairman Committee.

Upon motion to adopt, the report was discussed by Brother Bridges and Brother L. Johnson. Pledges were then taken, and the report adopted:

At this juncture a collection was taken to help in paying for the memorial window in Selma Church. After several miscellaneous announcements, the Body adjourned till 2:30 p. m., with benediction by Brother C. E. Maddrey.

AFTERNOON SESSION.

The Association was called to order at the appointed hour by Vice-Moderator A. A. Pippin. Brother W. H. Puckett, Pastor of The Selma Methodist Church, led in prayer. In the absence of the report on the Orphanage, Brother A. Johnson was called for and made a speech presenting the claims of the Orphanage upon the Churches. Pledges were then taken and the Clerk was instructed to insert the report when received:

REPORT ON ORPHANAGE.

The Orphanage at Thomasville is the property of the Baptists of North Carolina. It was established about 24 years ago. Since that time it has had a warm place in the hearts of North Carolina Baptists

We, as Baptists undertake, not only to feed and clothe these unfortunate ones, but also to educate them and fit them for life's work. We try to fit them for the best Christian citizenship.

The Orphanage now has 385 children, the largest number in its history. The increase in number means increased cost of running expenses, therefore calls for enlargement in our contributions. They need our immediate attention as they are behind in general expenses some $5,000.00.

Let every Sunday School in our Association take one collection each month for our Orphanage, and each church one collection each year. Let us not only provide for our own in the Orphanage, but let us love them, pray for them and visit them when we can. Let us not forget the band of noble men and women in charge of our Orphanage, nor our excellent paper, Charity and Children, which is doing so very much for real charity in our State, through our Bro. Arch. Johnson. This paper now has 11,250 subscribers. Each Sunday school should take a club of this excellent paper.

C. W. CARTER,
For Committee.

The following visiting brethren were recognized by the Moderator: W. P. Campbell, of The Neuse-Atlantic Association, and A. E. Corey, of The Roanoke Association..

The report on Sunday Schools was next called for and presented by Brother J. W. Nobles:

REPORT ON SUNDAY SCHOOLS.

If the Church is of Divine origin and it is admitted by all Christians to be, the Sunday School is likewise of Divine origin.

When the Church comes together on Sunday to study the Scriptures and teach them, that is Sunday School. To learn the Scriptures and teach them to others. is the work of the Church. A Sunday School is the Church coming together on Sunday to study the Scriptures, and teach them to others. The Johnston County Association has about thirty (30) Sunday Schools and thirty-six (36) Churches. Last year, we had a membership of 3,202 with 2,703 in the Sunday School. If half of those in the Sunday School are members of the Church, we have some over 1,200 Church members not in the Sunday School work. Last year the Churches of this Association received by baptism 230. Half of those came through the Sunday School. This ought to inspire our people to greater diligence in the Sunday School work. We recommend, 1st: That each Church have a Sunday School twelve months in the year if possible. 2nd: That Church members take part in the Sunday School work.

J. W. NOBLES,
For Committee.

Upon motion to adopt, the report was discussed by Sunday School Secretary E. L. Middleton. Pledges were' then taken and the report unanimously adopted.

The following were announced as a Committee to recommend an Executive Committee: O. R. Mangum, J. E. Wall and T. J. Lassiter.

Several miscellaneous announcements were made, after which the Body adjourned to meet at 7 o'clock. The benediction was pronounced by Brother D. F. Putnam.

NIGHT SESSION.

The session opened with song and devotional services conducted by Brother Worley Creech.

The report on Periodicals was called for and read by R. W. Horrell:

REPORT ON PERIODICALS.

Since our last Association important changes have taken place in our Baptist paper situation. Mr. J. A. Oates made a proposition to sell the North Carolina Baptist to the Biblical Recorder Company. The proposition was accepted and hence the merging of the papers. Then the Baptist State Convention, complying with a proposition from the stockholders of the

Recorder, appointed a committee of seven non-stockholders to vote equally with the Recorder Directors in electing an editor. Some of the results are: H. C. Moore, as editor; the editorial control of the paper is in the hands of our State Convention, with not one cent of financial responsibility. We have one paper whose influence is second to none in the Southern Baptist Convention. These things being true, the Baptists of North Carolina have the best paper situation in all the land. Then the Convention having control is under obligations to see that the paper reaches the people. We have a good people, the best in the world, but many of them are wanting in information, and hence do little or nothing to help our work or themselves. The few do, (and must) bear the burden until the masses are informed.

The Recorder occupies a place in the scheme of enlightenment among our people which cannot be filled by any other paper. It should therefore reach every Baptist home in North Carolina.

Charity and Children, whose mission it is to represent our Orphanage, should be in every home. The Home Field, representing our Home Mission work, should be widely read by our people. The Foreign Mission Journal, representing our work on the foreign field, should have a place in every home. Through the Church Messenger we are trying to inform our people of Johnston County Association concerning the work done and that to be done to bring the Kingdom of God to pass in our county. We therefore, urge our people to subscribe for and read its pages regularly.

Respectfully submitted,
R. W. HORRELL,
W. A. MASSENGILL,
J. M. RICHARDSON,
Committee.

Upon motion to adopt, the report was spoken to by Brother Horrell and unanimously adopted.

The following visiting Brethren were recognized: N. B. Broughton, of The Raleigh Association, and W. C. Tyree, Vice-President of The Foreign Mission Board for North Carolina. Brother Broughton made a few remarks stating that this was the first time he had had an opportunity to visit the session of the Association since it was organized.

In the absence of the report on Foreign Missions (This report was sent to the Clerk later), it was decided to take up this subject next, and Brother Tyree was called on for a speech. He ably presented the Foreign Mission cause in one of the best addresses heard by the Association. At the conclusion of his address, pledges were taken and the report adopted.

REPORT ON FOREIGN MISSIONS.

As we are passing out of the year 1908, into the year 1909, with the work of our Lord so lovingly entrusted to our hands and keeping, we ought to have high ideals, and press hard to accomplish them. Our watch-word should be, "Forward."

As we review the Lord's work in our hands, we ought to take courage, and press forward as never before.

After the Savior said, "Go," the Disciples grasped slowly the idea contained in the word. They were reluctant to obey, until persecution came upon them. Then they went about preaching the word. Before the death of Paul they had preached the gospel to every creature. Thus teaching us that He meant for each generation to preach to its own people to the end of the ages.

Since the apostolic age, we anxiously trace the work. Here and there we get a glimpse of what has been done. Even through the "dark ages" we get here and there a small glitter of the light, and catch an inspiration. After the Reformation the light grew brighter.

But not until the year 1845 did the thick clouds begin to flee as a shadow. A new era had dawned. The Southern Baptist Convention had been born, and her launching forth was the beginning of greater things, in and for the Master's Kingdom. And during these 63 years the work has shown the approval of the hand of the Almighty. And yet there is room for greater things.

There is a danger, of our organized work defeating in part, the very object of its birth. Depending on organization will never accomplish the work. But an organism such as we have used under the guidance of the Holy Spirit would soon bring on the millenium.

We greatly rejoice in the fact, that during the last Convention year, we had 2,174 baptisms and, under the pressure of one of the most rigid panic in years, our people gave last year $402,328.16. A very good showing when compared with our past. Not, however, what we ought to be doing (only about 20 cents per member). Of this amount our women gave $85,515.15. North Carolina Baptists numbering 202,184, gave only $35,-485.13, or about 17 cents per member. Our women gave of that amount $9,744.70. (The Lord bless our noble band of women.)

We have on our foreign field 139 houses of worship, 229 churches, and 467 out stations, with a membership of 14,179. These churches gave to the work last year $34,825.13, an average of $2.45 per member, (a good average, and a noble example to a great many of our churches). We have 226 Sunday Schools, with 7,526 scholars, 128 day schools, with 3,194 scholars.

With this kind of material as converts from the ranks of heathenism, if we would only consecrate first ourselves, and then the money that the Lord has committed to our keeping to his service so that the Board and our consecrated secretary (Dr. Willingham) could put the men and women whom God has called and placed at our disposal upon the field, we would soon take this world for the Lord,—in other words the knowledge of our Lord would soon cover the earth as the waters do the great deep. And the reflex influence would so overwhelm us that there would not be room enough to receive it.

The world is moving forward commercially speaking, probably as never before, certainly not in the modern times. Expansion is the watch-word of the hour. Our Southland is in a more prosperous condition to-day, than at any time in her history. God is making her the center of attraction for most all the world. All look to her resources, to supply the demands of the hour. The Lord is fast giving her a large hold on the finances of this country.

Then Brethren, as God's Stewards, shall we not use that which He has committed to our trust, as He has said, for the salvation of the world?

How can we make good our watch-word, Forward? 1. By giving our lives unreservedly to His service. Our lives surrendered to His will, will enable Him to accomplish great things through us. 2. By consecrating the money with which He has entrusted us, to Him, to be used as He may direct by His word and the Holy Spirit; and we would very soon under God let this dark world know that there was One and one only who is mighty to save.

Respectfully submitted,
T. H. THORNTON,
Chairman of Committee.

After the miscellaneous business had been disposed of, Brother A. Corey was appointed to conduct the devotional exercises to-morrow morning. The Association then adjourned with benediction.

THIRD DAY.

SATURDAY, November 7, 1908.

The Association met this morning according to adjournment with the devotional exercises conducted by Brother A. Corey. Brother W. R. Cullom, Secretary of the Board of Education of Wake Forest, was recognized.

The regular program was taken up, and Brother Canaday read the report on Education.

REPORT ON EDUCATION.

Ignorance is sin. It was said by one of the inspired writers: "A wise man will hear, and will increase in learning." The truth of this declaration is evident everywhere. The individual, the State, the nation never gets grown. The whole universe of God is a progressive thing.

The march upward to higher planes of thinking and acting leads continually to more power and larger charity. The church enlightening the conscience of the State glorifies, the achievements of science and makes possible human progress. It was laid down by our fathers in the fundamental law that "Religion, morality and knowledge being necessary to good government, schools and the means of education shall forever be encouraged."

The Public Schools.

The State therefore is the foster-mother of the public system. It is unique in power and uniform in purpose. As a free institution it safeguards the inalienable rights of conscience; as a great charitable institution it guarantees the inherent rights to knowledge of the humblest of God's humanity; it breaks down the barrier between the poor and the rich, and on common level offers an intelligent citizenship to all. The State cannot materially advance beyond the efficiency of its public schools.

As the most hopeful sign of the permanent advancement of the State, the public schools continue to be made better. Better school-houses, longer terms maintained by the voluntary tax of the people, call into service abler teachers so that there are brightening hopes for a greater State. Especially is this true when all the colleges are flourishing as never before.

The Denominational Schools.

While rejoicing in the greater success of the public schools for the general enlightenment of the people, we glory in the fact that ours is a Christian civilization. Without Christianity aided by our Christian colleges and schools to purify the social and religious life of the people the natural unchecked depravity of man, the greed for gain, the ambition for power, the base passions and appetites, like the lashing stormwaves, would engulf humanity as in the ancient past in the maelstrom of commercialism, of blighting infidelity, of bloody war, and of moral and spiritual ruin.

Among the Christian schools and colleges of the different religious denominations in this great State, those of the Baptists hold an important place. If reckoned in numbers, in power, in work done, then they are paramount. This prestige is due in very great measure to an able ministry. Therefore, Wake Forest College always has been and always will be very dear to Baptist people. In common they rejoice at its continual growth and endowment. Many young men there whom the Lord has called to preach need the financial support of the denomination. This is a duty laid upon the laity.

Female Education.

To crown its achievements North Carolina is educating its womanhood. The distinguished Dr. McIver said: "The education of woman is the strategic point in our civilization. A man educated only counts one; a woman educated counts a family." It is most gratifying that the Baptist Female Colleges each year are turning out for the State and for God an increased number of cultured women.   Respectfully submitted,

J. P. CANADAY.

Upon motion to adopt, the report was discussed by Brother J. P. Canaday and Brother W. R. Cullom. Pledges were then taken and the report adopted.

Brother W. B. Joyner, for the Committee, reported that they had decided that the next Association be held with Bethesda Church and that Brother A. A. Pippin be appointed to preach the introductory sermon with Brother R. W. Horrell as his alternate. The report of the Committee was adopted.

Brother T. J. Lassiter, for the Committee to name an Executive Committee, reported that they recommend the following Brethren as Executive Committee for the ensuing year: J. M. Beaty, J. H. Boon, Alonzo Parrish, J. T. Holt, and J. F. Pool. The Committee's report was adopted.

The report on ministerial relief was called for and read by Brother J. M. Hilliard:

REPORT ON MINISTERIAL RELIEF.

Our Ministerial Relief Board is located at Durham, N. C. Its efficient Secretary is Brother J. F. McDuffy, who has done a noble work among our old and infirm ministers, with the small amounts received from the churches of our Convention. The object of the Board is to assist our brethren in the ministry who have come to old age without any visible means of support. The Board does not pay them a regular salary, but gives them small amounts each month, so that they may have enough of the good things of this life to keep them from dire want in their old age.

The Board has received from all the churches of the Convention since last December $2,024.00 up to this time, but when we remember that one-third of this amount goes into the permanent fund, we see that our noble Secretary has only had $1,348. With this small amount 31 persons have been helped. Now brethren, this amount is too small, when we think of the number that must be helped. So let those who are younger and have plenty of the goods of this world, see that these noble men of God have not only enough to keep them from suffering, but plenty to make them comfortable in their last days. Let every church in this Association take up at least one collection for this worthy cause.

J. M. HILLIARD,
Chairman Committee

Upon motion to adopt, the report was discussed by Brethren J. M. Hilliard, W. P. Campbell and D. F. Putnam. Pledges were then taken and the report adopted.

After a song, Brother D. P. Bridges made a few remarks giving a special invitation to all to attend the next meeting of the Association at Bethesda. Remarks on various subjects were submitted by Brethren R. H. Gower, D. P. Bridges and others. At this point Brother Beaty took the floor and stated that he wanted the Association to give one collection to help the Kenly Brethren on their new

Church. Brother J. W. Nobles, Pastor of this Church, was called for and made an earnest appeal for help. A collection amounting to about $90.00 was then taken.

A motion was passed asking the Executive Committee to confer with the Pastors of the various Churches and select some member of each Church to represent his Church in the interest of the Building Committee.

The Finance Committee's report was received. This report will be found on another page. Following this the Treasurer made a partial report and was given until the 15th to complete his report and have same inserted in the minutes. (See Table II).

Upon motion, it was ordered that one thousand (1,000) copies of the minutes be printed and distributed, and that the Clerk be allowed Ten Dollars for his services.

Upon motion of Brother J. M. Beaty a rising vote of thanks was extended to the good people of Selma for their royal entertainment and unbounded hospitality during the sessions of the Association.

Services were appointed to be held in the new church to-night and Brother W. P. Campbell, Missionary of the Neuse-Atlantic Association, was selected to preach. It was also arranged to have the Memorial Window presented Sunday morning immediately after the Sunday School Mass Meeting and sermon by Brother D. F. Putnam. The body then adjourned with benediction by Bro. Campbell.

An interesting service was held in the new building at night with sermon by Bro. Campbell, who used as a text: "Enoch walked with God." His subject was "Life's True Greatness."

SUNDAY MORNING.

The new church was crowded to its utmost capacity this morning. A Sunday School meeting was first held, Brethren J. T. Holt, B. F. Hassell and D. P. Bridges taking part in the discussion. Several selections were rendered by the Selma Orchestra.

Bro. D. F. Putnam, who was appointed to preach this morning delivered a splendid discourse from Matthew 26:39, and Luke 22: 41-42. His subject was "Seeing Angels, or Spiritual Visions."

At the close of the sermon a collection was taken to finish paying for the Memorial Window. This collection together with the one taken Friday, amounted to about $143.00.

The Memorial Window was then presented, the presentation speech being made by Moderator R. H. Gower, on behalf of the Association. The speech of acceptance on behalf of Selma church was made by Pastor O. R. Mangum.

The meeting then adjourned.

TABLE I—FINANCE COMMITTEE'S REPORT.

	Minutes and Clerk.	State Missions.	Home Missions.	Foreign Missions.	Sunday School Missions.	Ministerial Education.	Ministerial Relief.	Orphanage.	Associational Missions.	Total.
Antioch	$ 50	$15.00	$ 1.50	$ 1.50	$ 2.00	$ 1.50	$ 2.00	$ 2.50	$.....	$26.50
Baptist Centre	1.60	10.00	2.00	1.50	.....	1.50	.....	10.00	.....	26.60
Benson	5.00	57.00	3.00	3.00	2.00	5.00	4.00	.....	.....	79.00
Benson's Grove	60	.....	.....	.....	.....	.....	.....	.....	.....	60
Bethany	65	6.50	2.50	2.00	1.00	1.25	1.25	3.00	.....	18.15
Bethesda	1.00	17.31	.....	.....	.....	.....	.....	.....	.....	18.31
Bethel	1.00	4.80	.....	.....	.....	.....	.....	.....	.....	5.80
Blackman's Grove	1.00	16.50	.....	.....	1.50	3.00	1.50	6.00	.....	29.50
Carter's Chapel	30	10.00	2.50	1.50	1.00	1.50	2.00	.....	.....	18.80
Clayton	.....	.....	.....	.....	.....	.....	.....	.....	.....	.....
Clyde's Chapel	1.00	9.35	2.82	.....	1.00	2.00	2.00	.....	.....	18.17
Corinth	.....	.....	.....	.....	.....	.....	.....	.....	.....	.....
Calvary	65	3.65	20	1.50	1.00	1.50	1.50	1.00	.....	11.00
Four Oaks	1.00	.....	.....	.....	.....	.....	.....	.....	.....	1.00
Hood's Grove	.....	.....	.....	.....	.....	.....	.....	.....	.....	.....
Kenly	1.00	.....	.....	.....	.....	.....	.....	.....	.....	1.00
Lee's Chapel	1.00	35.00	5.00	5.00	5.00	2.50	2.50	5.00	2.50	63.50
Live Oak (No letter)	35	.....	.....	.....	.....	.....	.....	.....	.....	35
Micro	25	.....	1.25	.....	50	1.00	1.00	2.25	.....	6.25
Mount Moriah	1.50	26.65	10.11	34.93	5.00	5.00	3.40	15.00	.....	101.59
Nobles' Chapel	.....	.....	.....	.....	.....	.....	.....	.....	.....	.....
New Bethel	1.00	13.40	12.25	9.05	.....	5.05	10.70	34.80	.....	86.25
Oliver's Grove (No L.)	20	1.00	.....	.....	.....	.....	.....	.....	.....	1.20
Parrish Memorial	1.03	.....	.....	.....	.....	.....	.....	.....	.....	1.03
Pauline	29	4.00	50	1.00	.....	.....	50	1.50	.....	7.79
Pine Level	1.00	.....	.....	.....	.....	.....	.....	.....	.....	1.00
Pisgah	1.00	12.90	3.18	.....	.....	.....	1.25	.....	.....	18.33
Princeton	.....	15.65	4.00	44	1.00	2.00	2.50	4.00	.....	29.59
Sardis	50	.....	.....	.....	.....	.....	.....	.....	.....	50
Selma	.....	66.24	.....	.....	.....	.....	.....	.....	.....	66.24
Shiloh	1.00	10.00	1.00	2.00	1.00	1.00	1.00	2.60	.....	19.60
Smithfield	5.00	.....	.....	.....	.....	.....	.....	.....	.....	5.00
Thanksgiving	50	.....	.....	.....	.....	.....	.....	.....	.....	50
Trinity	35	.....	1.16	3.50	1.00	1.00	1.00	1.75	.....	9.76
White Oak	.....	10.75	1.17	4.75	1.25	.....	1.70	4.80	.....	24.42
Wilson's Mills	.....	15.00	.....	.....	1.00	.....	2.00	.....	.....	18.00
Wendell	.....	.....	.....	.....	.....	.....	.....	.....	.....	.....
Middlesex	1.50	3.00	1.00	2.00	.....	.....	.....	.....	.....	7.50
Total	31.77	366.20	55.14	73.67	25.25	34.80	41.80	94.20	.....	722.58

Respectfully submitted,
J. W. HOLMES
J. F. POOL,
J. T. HOLT.

TABLE II—TREASURER'S REPORT.

To the Johnston County Baptist Association:
I submit herewith a report of all money received by me and paid out since November 15, 1907, date of last report:

	State Missions.	Home Missions.	Foreign Missions.	Sunday School Missions.	Orphanage.	Ministerial Education.	Ministerial Relief.	Colleges and Schools.	Benson's Grove Church.	W. B. at Orphan'e.	Minute Fund.	Total.
Bethesda ...	$ 6.48	$ 5.00	$ 4.34	$ 1.00	$ 4.27	$ 2.00	$ 2.62	$.....	$16.50	$...	$.....	$ 42.21
Benson	43.00	....	....	....	....	....	....	....	....	...	.....	43.00
Black'n's G..	....	3.50	5.00	....	....	....	.....	....	3.00	...	.....	11.50
Clayton	84.60	....	....	....	....	....	.....	....	7.16	...	.....	91.76
Clyde's Chap	....	....	2.91	....	3.00	....	.....	....	2.50	3.72	.....	12.13
Corinth ...	6.90	2.00	2.65	1.00	4.80	1.25	2.00	....	2.47	...	1.00	23.07
Calvary	36	1.80	....	....	....	....	....	....	....	...	.....	2.16
Four Oaks..	12.00	2.85	2.80	1.00	5.00	1.50	3.00	....	2.50	...	.....	30.65
Kenly	3.00	1.00	5.00	1.00	2.00	1.00	1.00	....	....	...	.....	14.00
Lee's Chapel	35.00	3.29	5.00	....	....	....	....	....	....	...	1.71	45.00
Live Oak...	1.95	1.37	61	....	....	....	1.50	50	....	...	.....	5.93
Mount Mor'h	1.45	....	3.86	....	....	....	....	....	7.31	...	.....	12.62
Micro	3.00	....	1.25	....	....	....	....	....	1.50	...	.....	5.25
Nobles' Chap	16.97	3.00	2.50	1.00	4.00	2.00	2.00	....	3.65	...	.....	35.14
Parrish Me..	15.00	1.75	1.50	50	2.00	1.00	2.00	....	2.80	...	.....	26.55
Princeton ..	2.35	....	4.56	....	....	....	....	....	1.52	...	50	8.89
Pisgah	2.10	2.00	5.34	....	....	....	....	....	2.50	...	.....	11.94
Pine Level..	6.00	1.50	1.50	....	....	....	1.00	1.00	1.45	...	.....	12.45
Sardis	5.50	2.00	2.00	50	2.00	1.00	1.00	....	2.00	...	.....	16.00
Selma	....	10.00	35.00	....	....	....	....	....	....	...	.....	45.00
Trinity	5.51	2.84	....	....	1.25	....	....	....	1.62	...	.....	11.22
Thanksgivi'g	6.07	1.00	53	....	....	....	....	....	1.57	...	.....	9.17
Wilson's M..	1.89	....	10.00	....	19.25	....	....	....	....	...	.....	31.14
White Oak..	1.25	3.33	....	....	1.70	2.30	....	....	3.00	...	.....	11.58
Wendell ...	10.09	....	....	1.00	3.45	1.00	3.54	....	4.79	...	1.00	24.87
Smithfield ..	225.00	40.10	46.25	10.00	43.54	12.00	16.00	....	....	...	.....	392.89
Fin. Com., S	366.20	55.14	73.67	25.25	94.20	34.80	41.80	....	....	...	31.77	722.88
Antoch	....	....	....	....	....	....	....	....	2.00	...	.....	2.00
New Bethel.	....	....	....	....	....	....	....	....	5.00	...	.....	5.00
Oliver's Gr'e	....	....	....	....	....	....	....	....	1.35	...	.....	1.35
WoodardS.H	....	....	....	....	....	....	....	....	50	...	.....	50
Bethany ...	....	....	....	....	....	....	....	....	1.00	...	.....	1.00
Smithfield C. M. Chap.	....	....	....	....	....	....	....	....	3.50	...	.....	3.50
J.P. Canaday	....	....	....	....	....	....	....	....	25.00	...	.....	25.00
Bethel	1.74	....	95	....	....	....	....	....	....	...	.....	2.69
Total Rec.ts	863.43	143.47	217.22	42.25	190.46	62.35	76.46	.....	106.19	3.72	35.98	1741.53
Bal. on hand Nov. 15,1907	423.26	73.13	92.07	30.00	81.17	44.69	55.30	17.35	.....	...	46.61	863.58
Total Am't..	1286.69	216.60	309.29	72.25	271.63	107.04	131.76	17.85	106.19	3.72	82.59	2605.11
Paid as per statement below	581.51	110.61	151.90	30.00	153.54	44.69	55.30	17.85	.....	3.72	43.85	1192.47
Bal. on hand	705.18	105.99	157.39	42.25	118.09	62.35	76.46	.....	106.19	...	38.74	1402.64

DISBURSEMENTS.

Nov.	18, 1907.	Paid Rev. W. C. Royal, Missionary	$	11.00
Nov.	18, 1907.	Paid Rev. D. D. Edwards, Missionary		10.00
Nov.	18, 1907.	Paid Rev. A. A. Pippin, Missionary		100.00
Nov.	25, 1907.	Paid Walters Durham, Various objects		312.54
Nov.	25, 1907.	Paid S. H. Averitt, Orphanage		81.17
Nov.	30, 1907.	Paid Rev. D. F. Putnam, Missionary		24.80
Dec.	13, 1907.	Paid Rev. D. F. Putnam, Missionary		15.00
Dec.	13, 1907.	Paid Rev. B. G. Early, Missionary		10.42
Dec.	13, 1907.	Paid Rev. N. H. Gibbs, Missionary		12.65
Dec.	16, 1907.	Paid Rev. J. W. Nobles, Missionary		11.50
Dec.	21, 1907.	Paid Rev. L. L. Hudson, Missionary		15.00
Dec.	21, 1907.	Paid Rev. R. W. Horrell, Missionary		75.00
Dec.	28, 1907.	Paid Rev. D. P. Bridges, Missionary		31.25
Dec.	28, 1907.	Paid Rev. J. W. Watson, Missionary		50.00
Jan'y	11, 1908.	Paid Nash Brothers, for Minutes		30.00

TABLE II—TREASURER'S REPORT—Continued.

Jan'y	11, 1908.	Paid T. J. Lassiter, Clerk and postage...................................$	13.85
Jan'y	20, 1908.	Paid Rev. W. C. Royal, Missionary.......................................	20.42
Feb'y	17, 1908.	Paid Rev. W. C. Royal, Missionary.......................................	18.77
March	17, 1908.	Paid Rev. W. C. Royal, Missionary.......................................	27.09
March	17, 1908.	Paid Beaty & Lassiter, printing for Association.....................	9.72
April	27, 1908.	Paid Rev. W. C. Royal, Missionary.......................................	18.77
May	1, 1908.	Paid S. H. Averitt...	76.09
May	1, 1908.	Paid Walters Durham	97.31
May	25, 1908.	Paid Rev. . C. Royal, Missionary......................................	18.77
June	29, 1908.	Paid Rev. . C. Royal, Missionary......................................	18.77
July	29, 1908.	Paid Rev. . C. Royal, Missionary......................................	18.77
August	24, 1908.	Paid Rev. . C. Royal, Missionary......................................	18.77
Sept'r	29, 1908.	Paid Rev. w. C. Royal, Missionary....................................	18.77
Oct'r	30, 1908.	Paid Rev. W. C. Royal, Missionary....................................	26.27

$1192.47

Respectfully submitted,
WILL H. LASSITER, Treasurer.

Smithfield, N. C., Nov. 17, 1908.
Approved by J. D. Underwood, Auditor.

TABLE III—CHURCH PLEDGES FOR 1909.

CHURCHES.	State Missions.	Home Missions.	Foreign Missions.	Sunday School Missions.	Orphanage.	Ministerial Education.	Ministerial Relief.	Total.
Antioch	$ 15.00	$ 1.50	$ 1.50	$ 1.50	$ 2.50	$ 1.50	$ 2.00	$ 25.50
Baptist Centre...............	5.00	2.00	2.00	1.00	5.00	1.00	1.50	17.50
Benson	100.00	20.00	20.00	2.00	25.00	5.00	5.00	177.00
Benson's Grove.............	1.00	50	50	50	1.00		50	4.50
Bethany	6.00	2.50	2.00	1.00	3.00	1.00	1.25	16.75
Bethel	4.00	2.00	1.00	50	1.00	1.00	1.00	10.50
Bethesda	25.00	5.00	5.00	1.00	15.00	2.00	3.00	56.00
Blackman's Grove...........	20.00	5.00	7.00	2.00	8.00	4.00	2.50	48.50
Calvary	4.00	2.00	1.50	1.00	2.25	1.50	1.50	13.75
Carter's Chapel.............	10.00	2.50	1.50	1.00	5.00	1.50	2.00	23.50
Clayton	225.00	60.00	100.00	10.00	135.00	20.00	20.00	570.00
Clyde's Chapel..............	10.00	4.00	5.00	1.00	5.00	1.00	3.00	29.00
Corinth	8.00	1.50	2.00	1.00	5.00	1.00	2.00	20.50
Four Oaks...................	15.00	5.00	5.00	1.00	5.00	1.50	3.00	35.50
Hood's Grove................	10.00	2.00	3.00	1.00	2.00	2.00	1.50	21.50
Kenly	5.00	3.00	5.00	1.00	3.00	1.00	1.00	19.00
Lee's Chapel.................	25.00	5.00	10.00	2.00	5.00	2.50	3.00	52.50
Live Oak.....................	4.00		1.25	50	1.50	1.00	1.00	9.25
Micro	3.00	1.25	1.25	50	2.50	1.00	1.00	10.50
Middlesex	10.00		1.00	50	1.00	50	1.00	14.00
Mount Moriah...............	50.00	20.00	50.00	5.00	30.00	5.00	6.00	166.00
New Bethel..................	15.00	3.00	2.00	1.00	10.00	2.00	1.00	34.00
Nobles' Chapel..............	17.00	3.00	2.50	1.00	4.00	2.00	2.00	31.50
Oliver's Grove...............	1.00	50	1.00	50	50	50	50	4.50
Parrish Memorial...........	17.50	1.75	1.50	1.00	2.00	1.00	2.00	26.75
Pauline	4.00	1.50	1.50	50	1.50	1.00	1.00	11.00
Pine Level...................	6.00	2.00	1.50	50	3.00	1.00	1.25	15.75
Pisgah	15.00	3.00	5.00	2.00	2.25	1.00	1.50	27.75
Princeton	20.00	4.25	5.00	1.00	4.00	2.00	2.50	38.75
Sardis	5.50	2.00	2.00	50	3.00	1.00	1.00	15.00
Selma	60.00	10.00	25.00	1.00	25.00	2.00	10.00	133.00
Shiloh	5.00	3.25	3.00	1.00	2.50	2.00	2.50	19.25
Smithfield	150.00	40.00	55.00	10.00	40.00	15.00	20.00	330.00
Thanksgiving	5.00		1.00	50	1.00	1.00	50	9.00
Trinity	5.50	4.00	3.50	1.00	3.00	1.00	1.00	19.00
Wendell	10.00	2.00	3.00	1.00	2.00	1.00	1.00	20.00
White Oak...................	17.50	5.00	5.00	1.50	8.00	2.00	2.00	41.00
Wilson's Mills..............	15.00	5.00	5.00	2.00	10.00	3.00	3.00	43.00
Alonzo Parrish.............							5.00	5.00
Total	914.00	235.00	348.00	61.00	385.00	94.25	120.75	2158.00

Table IV—CHURCH STATISTICS.

CHURCHES.	PASTORS.	CLERKS AND ADDRESSES.	Preaching Sunday.	Value of Property.	Seating Capacity.	Baptisms.	Received by Letter.	Restored.	Lost by Letter.	Dismissed.	Died.	Males.	Females.	Total Membership.
Antioch	Worley Creech	J. B. Creech, Kenly, R. F. D. 2	2 & 3	500.00	400	1	2	1	12	4	2	52	112	164
Baptist Centre	W. C. Royal	W. C. Hardee, Clayton	1	450.00	250		11		8			25	41	66
Benson	D. F. Putnam	E. L. Hall, Benson	2	1250.00	400	9		1		5	2	52	99	151
Benson's Grove	R. W. Horrell	Richard Benson, Benson, R. 1										3	5	8
Bethany	Worley Creech	Kirkman Creech, Kenly	4	550.00	300	7	6		4	2	2	31	47	78
Bethesda	P. P. Bridges	J. E. Smith, Wilson's Mills	4	600.00	400	11		1	5		1	76	113	189
Bethel	R. W. Horrell	Perry Barnes, Kenly	4	400.00	250	14			2	2		16	18	34
Blackman's Grove	L. F. Putnam	E. B. Hayes, Four Oaks, R. 2	3	700.00	400				5	5	6	19	43	62
Carter's Chapel	L. D. Edwards	W. B. Wall, Micro		500.00	300	28	12	1	7	5	2	32	54	86
Clayton	L. H. Thornton	R. R. Gulley, Clayton	1-3	6000.00	700	37	5		3	4		133	183	316
Clyde's Chapel	L. L. Hudson	C. I. Johnson, Archer, R. 2	3	500.00	300						1	62	92	154
Corinth	A. Pippin	E. C. Wey, Archer	3	450.00	400	12	3		2	2		39	59	98
Calvary	W. C. Royal	T. J. Lee, Dunn, R. 2	2	500.00	200			1			1	12	27	39
Four Oaks	D. F. Putnam	J. William Langdon, Four Oaks	1-3	700.00	250	1			1	2	1	12	22	34
Hood's Grove	W. Nobles	Jos. W. Wood, Benson, R. 2	4	400.00	350		2		1	2		13	25	38
Kenly	A. Pippin	B. W. Harris, Kenly	4	1500.00	400		1	2	26		3	8	11	19
Lee's Chapel	D. P. Bridges	W. I. Green, Selma, R. 3	2-4	600.00	600	38			1		3	106	188	294
Live Oak	W. Nobles	K. Broadwell, Selma, R. 1	4	300.00	250	6				1	2	12	24	36
Micro	A. Pippin	Oscar Mozingo, Micro	2	500.00	300		16	3				6	8	14
Mt. Moriah	I. M. Hilliard	W. C. Jackson, Middlesex	4	800.00	300	6			9	3	1	24	32	56
Nobles' Chapel	W. Nobles	J. H. Bryant, Raleigh, R. F. D	4	700.00	400	13	6		2	2		68	82	150
New Bethel	T. Y. Seymour	N. L. Stott, Taylor	1	800.00	400	12	2		1	1	3	37	48	85
Oliver's Grove	N. H. Gibbs	Geo. W. Bryan	4	200.00	300	2		1			1	47	49	96
Parrish Memorial	J. W. Nobles	Haywood Johnson, Four Oaks	1	500.00	350			1	8	8	2	8	12	20
Pauline	J. W. Nobles	Joe D. Joyner, Selma, R. 4	1	400.00	300		7	1				27	24	51
Pine Level	R. W. Horrell	D. B. Joyner, Four Oaks, R. 1	3	250.00	225	17		2	7	1	1	17	17	34
Pisgah	D. F. Putnam	C. I. Godwin, Pine Level	1	1200.00	500	9	3		3	2	1	23	37	60
Princeton	R. W. Horrell	R. H. Higgins, Smithfield	3	1500.00	300	30			2	1		32	22	54
Sardis	W. C. Royal	W. I. Pearce, Princeton	3	400.00	200				5	2	1	53	69	122
Selma	O. R. Mangum	N. B. Stevens, Smithfield, R. 2	1 2 4	12000.00	700	18	14	1	3	1	1	9	17	26
Shiloh	To be supplied	J. M. O'Neal, Selma	2	4500.00	700	16	1		4	1		28	46	197
Smithfield	D. P. Bridges	J. F. Hardee, McCullers, R. 1	1-3	1000.00	350	5	13		5	2	3	71	90	161
Thanksgiving	W. C. Royal	T. J. Lassiter, Smithfield	4	400.00	200	4			1	1		14	30	44
Trinity	D. P. Bridges	J. S. Lawhon, Benson, R. 2	4	800.00	300	7	2	1	2	7		22	27	49
White Oak	A. A. Pippin	W. G. Earp, Selma, R. 1	2	500.00	400	7		2	2			59	93	152
Wilson's Mills	O. R. Mangum	J. I. Murphrey, Selma, R. 1	2	1000.00	300		2		3		1	23	29	52
Wendell	T. H. King	Grover Ellis, Wilson's Mills; C. Z. Todd, Wendell	2	2800.00	400	9	26	1				40	55	95
Total						333	142	26	132	65	33			3447

TABLE V—SUNDAY SCHOOL STATISTICS.

CHURCHES.	SUPERINTENDENTS AND ADDRESSES.	Officers and Teachers.	Scholars.	Total.	Average Attendance.	Schools.	Volumes in Library.	Quarterlies and Papers Taken.	Months Open.	Baptisms from School.	Expenses.
Antioch	J. A. ___, Selma, R. 1	6	120	126	50	1		100	9		$ 6.00
Baptist Centre	J. C. Hardee, Clayton	5	80	85	40	1		60	12		6.00
Benson	W. D. Boon, Benson	10	166	176	85	1		276	12		51.20
Bethany	David Pace, Micro	8	75	80	40	1	40	80	12	4	12.00
Bethesda	J. J. Wallace, Wilson's Mills	8	60	68	40	1		60	12	5	10.00
Bethel	Perry Barnes, Kenly	5	40	45	30	1		27	7	6	9.00
Blackman's Grove	W. B. ___, Four Oaks, R. 2	5	38	41	20	1		45	12	4	4.00
Carter's Chapel	P. Mozingo, Selma, R. 4	3	60	68	40	1		60	12	15	12.00
Clayton	R. H. Gower, Clayton	8	260	274	155	1	246	460	12	26	75.00
___ie's Chapel	W. T. ___, Clayton, R. 2	14	70	76	40	1		64	9	2	8.60
Corinth	J. A. Estridge, Archer	6	85	92	50	1		70	12	9	5.00
Calvary	J. M. Johnson, Dunn, R. 2	7	4	7	3	1					
Four Oaks	W. A. Massengill, Four Oaks	4	60	64	40	1		65	12	1	16.78
Micro	L. L. Creech, Micro	8	42	50	25	1		55	12		11.40
Middlesex	J. W. Strickland, Middlesex	7	161	168	102	1		125	12	6	10.44
Mount Moriah	Frank Pool, Clayton	11	135	146	70	1	375	150	12	13	41.50
Lee's Chapel	J. W. Strickland, Selma, R. 4	7	70	77	50	1		70	12	25	7.00
Live Oak	J. M. Richardson, Selma	3	37	40	30	1		38	9	6	4.00
New Bethel	Andrew Bryan, Garner	6	40	46	30	1	56	30	9		12.50
Parrish Memorial	Joe D. ___, Selma	5	47	52	25	1		128	12		3.00
Pine ___	J. W. Liles, Selma	7	126	133	75	1		300	12	15	10.00
Pisgah	W. J. Alford, Smithfield	4	25	29	15	1		60	12	3	4.39
Princeton	W. H. Wells, Princeton	6	65	71	28	1		125	12	16	10.88
Sardis	William Eason, Smithfield, R. 2	11	25	30	20	1		32	12		3.00
Selma	B. F. Hassel, Selma	15	187	198	110	1	60	200	12	15	27.00
Shiloh	David M. Wood, Garner, R. 1	12	70	75	38	2	200	75	12	5	5.00
Smithfield	M. A. Allen, Smithfield	6	198	210	105	1		325	12	14	63.36
Thanksgiving	W. S. Earp, Archer	4	60	66	40	1		75	6	2	10.00
Trinity	J. M. Lawhon, Benson, R. 2	9	20	24	20	1		24	12		1.65
Wendell	C. Z. Todd, Wendell	7	221	230	110	1		125	12		37.50
White Oak	A. L. Batten, Archer	6	80	87	40	1		90	12	4	30.00
Wilson's Mills	J. T. Holt, Wilson's Mills	8	36	42	35	1		80	12		75.00
___s Grove	Thomas Tyner, Four Oaks		27	30	20	1		30	9		2.50
Total		216	2790	3006	1619	33				193	$ 575.70

CHURCHES.	Number of Members.	Pastor's Salary.	Building and Repairs.	Incidentals.	The Poor.	State Missions.	Home Missions.	Foreign Missions.	Sunday School Missions.	Orphanage.	Ministerial Education.	Ministerial Relief.	Colleges and schools.	Other Objects.	Sunday School Expenses.	Minutes and Clerk.	Total.
Baptist Centre	164	$33.75	$	$ 3.59	$	$ 15.00	$ 1.50	$ 1.50	$ 2.00	$ 2.50	$ 1.50	$ 2.00	$	$	$ 6.00	$ .50	$ 69.84
Benson	66	60.00				10.00	2.00	1.50	2.00	10.00	5.00	1.50			6.00	1.60	92.60
Benson's Grove	151	400.00	1.95			143.10	23.00	26.60	2.00	20.00	5.00	4.00		74.23	51.20	5.00	756.08
Bethany	8	4.00			5.00											.60	4.60
Bethesda	78	25.00	10.00	6.00		6.50	2.50	5.00	1.00	3.00	1.25	1.25			12.00	.60	70.15
Bethel	189	150.00				25.00	5.00	5.00	1.00	31.28	2.00	3.00		31.00	10.00	.65	270.28
Blackman's Grove	34	25.00	40.00			4.00	1.50	7.00	.50	1.00	3.00	1.00			9.00	1.00	185.50
Carter's Chapel	62	100.00	90.00			16.50	2.50	1.50	1.50	6.00	1.50	14.02			4.00	1.00	145.00
Clayton	88	35.00	507.16		6.95	10.00	65.00	123.60	10.00	133.44	13.65	2.50		121.32	12.00	30	160.80
Clyde's Chapel	316	725.00			7.72	250.00	4.00	4.00	1.50	5.00	2.00	2.50	95.00	6.26	75.00		2140.14
Calvary	154	100.00	6.25			10.00	3.80	2.00	1.00	4.00	1.00	2.00		10.00	8.60	1.00	136.26
Four Oaks	98	45.00				8.00	5.00	1.50	1.00	2.25	1.50	1.50			5.00	1.00	65.00
Hood's Grove	39	29.67		11.53		4.35	3.00	5.00	1.00	5.00	1.50	3.00		20.00		.65	62.47
Kenly	34	107.60		10.00		15.00	1.00								16.78	1.00	192.41
Lee's Chapel	38	70.00	923.06	5.00		2.00	5.00	5.00	1.00	2.00	1.00	1.00		1.00	7.00	1.00	83.00
Live Oak	19	89.00				37.50	5.50	5.74	5.00	5.00	2.50	2.50		17.00	4.00	.65	1033.06
Middlesex	294	150.00		6.50		9.05	5.00	1.05		2.25		1.00				.25	237.50
Mount Moriah	36	18.00			8.48	3.00	1.25	15.07	.50	9.19	1.00			11.40	10.44	1.50	35.14
New Bethel	14			16.00		23.35	9.89	9.05		39.00	5.05	1.60		17.16	41.50	1.50	45.70
Noble's Chapel	56	150.00		85.00		13.40	12.25	2.00	1.00	34.80	2.00	10.70			12.50	1.00	35.61
Oliver's Grove	150	185.00				17.00	2.00			4.00							314.07
Parrish Memorial	96	67.00				1.00	1.75	1.50		2.00	1.00	2.00			2.50	.20	318.75
Pauline	85	4.87	3.00			15.00			.50	1.50				1.50	3.00	1.03	88.00
Pine Level	20	50.00	1.00	.50		4.00	1.50	1.50		1.50	1.25	1.50		18.96	10.00	.29	8.57
Princeton	51	2.85	2.00			6.00	1.50	5.00	2.00	2.50	1.00	1.50		2.50	4.39	1.00	77.78
Sardis	34	50.00	3.50	10.00		15.00	3.00	5.00	2.00	4.00	2.00	1.50		15.00	10.88		13.64
Selma	60	100.00	39.75	8.76		38.00	10.00	35.00	1.50	72.55	2.00	1.00		2.00	3.00	.50	86.21
Shiloh	54	100.00		13.86		5.50	3.25	3.00	1.73						27.00		151.34
Smithfield	122	31.50	5573.00	31.50		66.24	2.00		1.00		2.00	2.50			5.00		230.89
Thanksgiving	26	550.00	60.00			1000	10.00	52.00	10.00	43.54	32.00	16.00		240.00	63.38	5.00	62.88
Trinity	194	440.00		30.00		227.30	45.35	1.56	.50	7.50	2.00			16.56	10.00		6367.02
Wendell	73	15.40	10.00			5.00	5.51	3.50	1.00	5.00	1.00			10.00	1.65		99.25
Mite Oak	161	16.40				5.51	4.00	4.60	1.00	3.45	1.00	3.54		1.10	37.50	.50	964.55
Wilson's Mills	49	175.00		149.92		10.09	4.00	4.75	1.25	4.80	1.00	1.70		4.79	30.00	.35	125.62
	44	16.40				10.75	3.00	5.00	1.17	4.80	1.00	2.00			75.00	1.00	38.16
	95	160.00	40.00	5.00		15.00	5.00	5.00	1.00	5.00	3.00	2.00		13.00			405.43
	152	100.00															210.42
	52																369.00
Total	3447	4389.64	7410.67	396.16	28.15	965.14	243.71	349.02	52.48	481.05	93.20	94.31	95.00	618.78	575.70	32.77	15705.78

WOMAN'S MISSIONARY UNION.

The fifth annual meeting of the Woman's Missionary Union of the Johnston County Association convened with the Clayton Baptist Church, October 28th, 1908.

This being our first separate meeting from the regular Association we were filled with hopes and fears, yet we felt it was wise to meet at a different time and place, for then we could have more time to intelligently review and plan our work; a more comfortable meeting place, and a much larger attendance; if this our first meeting be a fore-taste of what is to follow then great blessings await us.

The rain came in torrents most of the day. Many who had planned to be with us were kept at home, however we had a splendid attendance, but the very best part of our meeting was the spiritual part, for which we give thanks. After the Devotional and preliminary exercises of the morning hour were over we entered upon the business of the meeting. The Vice-President reviewed the work of the past year, and talked of future plans, emphasizing each phase of our work urging us to study each department of the work and contribute to each.

We were sorry to note a slight falling off in number of Societies and contributions to Missions, however; by studying the financial report below you will find that the remaining Societies have contributed more money to the different phases of our work than last year. We gave solely to Missions last year $414.85; this year, we contributed to Missions, The Training School Endowment, the current expenses of the Training School, the Expense Fund, The Margaret Home and the Bible Fund, making a total of $477.64.

The Vice-President urges the President of each Society in the Association to report quarterly to her this year. Several Societies last year failed to send in any report of their year's work. Only in this way can the Vice-President know that your society is still alive, then we encourage each other by these reports. So next year let us have more Societies, and each Society doing the best, and each Society sending to the Vice-President of the Association (Mrs. Ashley Horne) a quarterly report.

Our programme was carried out almost to the letter, each sister doing well the part assigned. There was not a dull moment during the day.

This report would be incomplete if I did not add, we all greatly felt the absence of Miss Heck. Hope she may be with us at our next annual meeting in Smithfield. We were delighted to have so many visitors: Mrs. Petway, who talked to us about organizing boys into Mission bands; Mrs. Grant, Vice-President of the Neuse-Atlantic Association brought us words of greeting and encouragement; Miss Briggs talked to us on the "Importance of Children's Work", to the delight and edification of all, while the closing hour of the day was given over to Miss Applewhite, who full of interest and enthusiasm discussed the Y. W. A. work. Did you know we only have one Young Woman's Auxiliary in our bounds? Can this condition of things be true to the young women of your Church?

The delegates I am sure can tell each society of the inspiring meeting we had, but next year let us all go and try to make it our very best meeting. The day closed with sentence prayers from many sisters, thanking God for the great privilege of being "workers-to-gether" with Him, begging to be more used in His service, asking for future help and guidance.

At the evening service Dr. A. B. Dunaway brought us a beautiful and we trust and abiding address on Missions.

We may take courage and press onward.

MRS. C. W. CARTER, Secretary.

FINANCIAL REPORT OF SOCIETIES.

SOCIETIES.	Foreign Missions.	Home Missions.	State Missions.	Exp. Fund.	Marg't Home.	Louisville T. S. Endow.	Exp. of T. S.	S. S. Bible Fund.	Total.
Smithfield M. S....	$13.65	$13.65	$20.00	$...	$...	$ 6.00	$...	$...	$53.30
Selma M. S.......	.....	.....	.....	....	....	.....	....	....	30.00
Benson M. S.......	12.00	10.00	15.30	1.00	....	1.00	1.00	....	40.30
Mt. Moriah M. S....	11.50	9.10	9.80	70	....	2.95	....	....	34.05
Clyde's Chapel M. S	1.92	1.50	2.45	....	....	.....	....	....	5.87
Four Oaks M. S....	1.05	2.00	3.00	....	....	.....	65	....	6.70
Clayton M. S......	40.00	40.00	71.50	3.10	....	65.00	....	....	219.60
Smithfield Sunbeams	.....	5.25	5.75	....	....	.....	....	....	11.00
Clayton Jr. Union..	13.47	7.05	.....	....	1.00	.....	....	....	21.52
Mt. Moriah Sunb'ms	77	3.49	2.80	30	25	1.19	....	6.50	15.30
Clayton Y. W. A....	15.00	10.25	8.65	1.10	....	5.00	....	....	40.00
Total	109.36	102.29	139.25	6.20	1.25	81.14	1.65	6.50	477.64

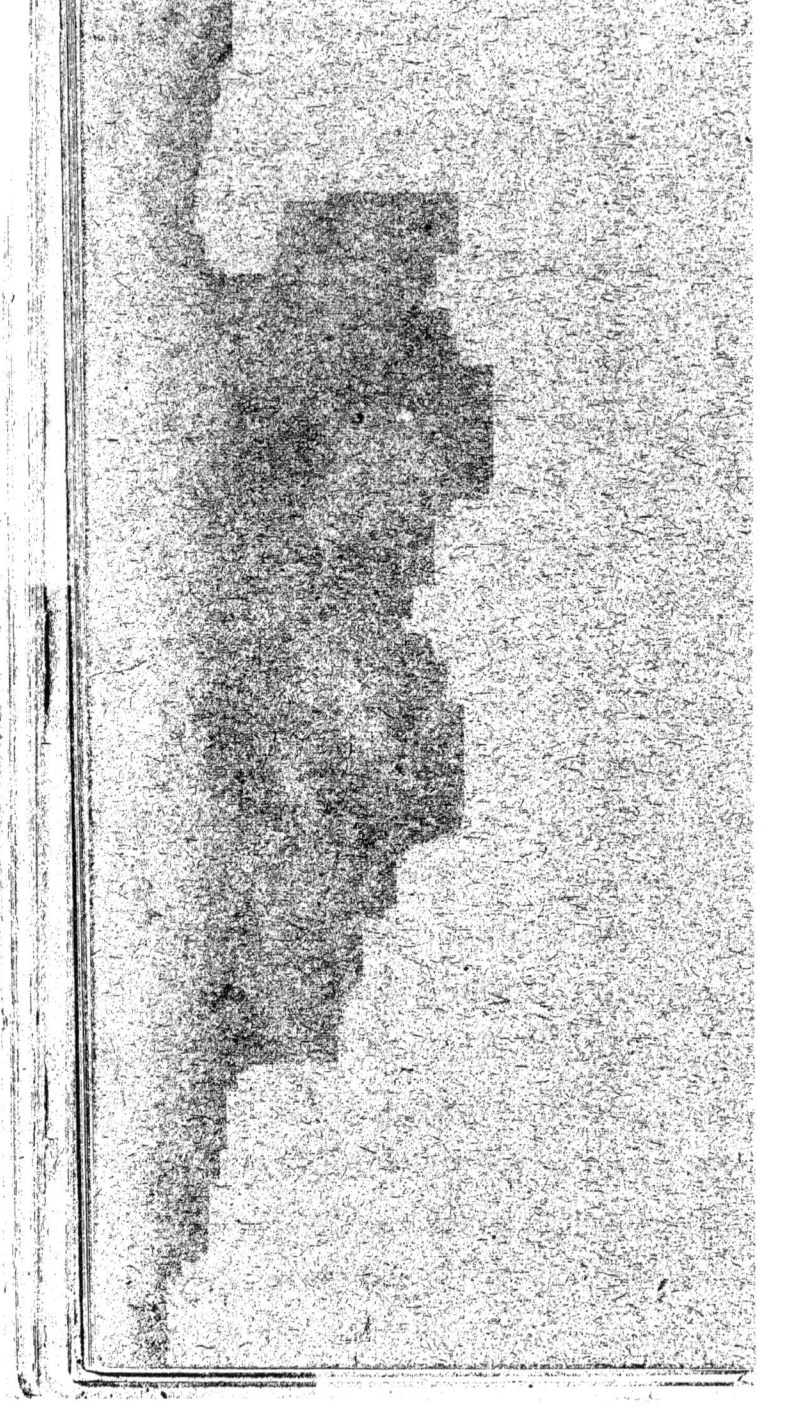

MINUTES

OF THE

SEVENTH SESSION

OF THE

Johnston County

BAPTIST ASSOCIATION,

HELD WITH

Bethesda Baptist Church,

NOVEMBER 11, 12, 13, AND 14, 1909.

The next session will be held with White Oak Baptist Church, at Archer Lodge, beginning Wednesday after the first Sunday in November, 1910.

To preach Introductory Sermon—T. B. Justice.

·OFFICERS.

Moderator—R. H. Gower.................................Clayton, N. C.
Vice-Moderator—A. A. Pippin.......................Wakefield, N. C.
Clerk—T. J. Lassiter....................................Smithfield, N. C.
Treasurer—Will H. Lassiter.........................Four 'Oaks, N. C.
Auditor—J. D. Underwood...........................Smithfield, N. C.
Historian—R. W. Horrell.................................Selma, N. C.

Goldsboro, N. C.
Nash Bros. Book and Commercial Printers,
1909

MINUTES

SEVENTH SESSION

OF THE

Johnston County

BAPTIST ASSOCIATION,

HELD WITH

Bethesda Baptist Church,

NOVEMBER 11, 12, 13, AND 14, 1909.

The next session will be held with White Oak Baptist Church, at Archer Lodge, beginning Wednesday after the first Sunday in No-vember, 1910.

To preach Introductory Sermon—T. B. Justice.

OFFICERS.

Moderator—R. H. Gower................................Clayton, N. C.
Vice-Moderator—A. A. Pippin.........................Wakefield, N. C.
Clerk—T. J. Lassiter..................................Smithfield, N. C.
Treasurer—Will H. Lassiter..........................Four Oaks, N. C.
Auditor—J. D. Underwood.............................Smithfield, N. C.
Historian—R. W. Horrell..............................Selma, N. C.

Nash Bros. Book and Commercial Printers,
1909

EXECUTIVE COMMITTEE.

J. M. Beaty, Chairman.................................Smithfield, N. C.
J. H. Boon.............Benson, N. C.   J. F. Pool..........Clayton, N. C.
J. T. Holt......Wilson's Mills, N. C.   Alonzo Parrish.....Benson, N. C.

LIST OF MINISTERS.

Worley Creech, R. F. D. No. 2, Kenly.   J. E. Hoyle..........Wake Forest.
D. D. Edwards.................Cary.   T. B. Justice.............Benson.
J. B. Eller..............Wake Forest.   J. W. Nobles..............Kenly.
N. H. Gibbs.................Benson.   A. A. Pippin............Wakefield.
J. M. Hilliard............Cary.   W. C. Royal................Micro.
R. W. Horrell................Selma.   T. Y. Seymour.......Wake Forest.
S. C. Hilliard......Wake Forest.   J. W. Smith........Wilson's Mills.

LIST OF DELEGATES.

Antioch—A. J. Lewis, R. L. Hocutt, Jas. R. Hocutt, M. C. Hinton.
Baptist Center—N. L. Austin, J. C. Hardee, J. W. Austin.
Benson—J. H. Boon, E. L. Hall, Alonzo Parrish, U. F. Wallace.
Benson's Grove—J. R. Benson, D. D. Medlin.
Bailey—J. P. Underwood.
Bethany—Merritt Pace, Luther Starling, Moses Creech, Aram Earp.
Bethesda—J. J. Wallace, J. W. Godwin, J. F. Hall.
Bethel—W. T. Sullivant, Perry Barnes, Frank Evans, Luther Stone.
Blackman's Grove—Letter.
Carter's Chapel—Albert McCall, R. M. Cox.
Clayton—M. M. Gulley, M. G. Gulley, C. W. Carter, D. J. Thurston, A. J. Barbour.
Clyde's Chapel—J. W. B. Finch, Luther Bunch.
Corinth—J. A. Estridge, H. B. Andrews, Julius Snipes, E. C. Whitley.
Calvary—J. M. Johnson.
Four Oaks—W. A. Massengill, J. S. Johnson, C. H. Grady.
Hood's Grove—Not represented, but letter sent later.
Kenly—Letter.
Lee's Chapel—J. B. Liles, W. I. Greene, J. L. Driver, J. A. Lewis.
Live Oak—J. M. Richardson.
Micro—Levi Creech, L. L. Creech, Oscar Mozingo.
Middlesex—Gilliam Lewis.
Mount Moriah—N. R. Poole, W. H. Kelley, W. H. Coats, J. F. Poole.
Nobles' Chapel—J. H. Grice, J. H. Flowers, Pharaoh Brewer.
New Bethel—D. T. Bryan, R. I. Smith.
Oliver's Grove—J. A. Tiner, T. B. Tiner, H. Johnson.
Parrish Memorial—Fred Batten, Frank Batten.
Pauline—W. B. Joyner, H. B. Moore.
Pine Level—W. M. Eason.
Pinkney—R. E. Lee, Ida Edgerton.
Pisgah—Robert Johnson, W. D. Johnson.
Pinceton—W. I. Pearce.
Sardis—Letter.
Selma—Paul W. Brown.
Shiloh—Claud Stephenson, F. T. Booker.
Smithfield—J. M. Beaty, Will H. Lassiter, T. J. Lassiter, R. I. Lassiter.
Thanksgiving—J. L. Brannan.
Trinity—A. H. Lee.
White Oak—W. A. Mitchell, W. T. Allen.
Wilson's Mills—C. H. Stevens, G. G. Beaty, W. H. Ellis, J. T. Holt.
Wendell—Letter.

Pastors—W. C. Royal, T. Y. Seymour, R. W. Horrell, T. B. Justice, J. W. Nobles, D. D. Edwards, Worley Creech, N. H. Gibbs, J. E. Hoyle and J. W. Smith.

PROCEEDINGS.

BETHESDA BAPTIST CHURCH,
Thursday, Nov. 11, 1909.

The seventh annual session of the Johnston County Baptist Association convened this morning at 11 o'clock. The services were opened with prayer by Brother J. W. Nobles, of Kenly. Following this, Brother A. A. Pippin, of Wakefield, preached the Introductory sermon. His text was a clause from the third verse of the sixth chapter of Nehemiah, "I am doing a great work," with references to the second and eleventh verses of this chapter. His theme was, "No compromise with Sin." The sermon was a strong and convincing one, and was a fitting beginning to this session of the Association. At the close of the sermon, the usual announcements were made, and the body took recess for dinner.

AFTERNOON SESSION.

The real work of the Association began with the afternoon session, which was opened with a song service and prayer, led by Brother R. W. Horrell. The Moderator, Brother R. H. Gower, appointed Brethren V. R. Turley and Robert Smith as a Committee on Credentials and Enrollment. After delegates had been duly enrolled, the body proceeded to the election of officers for the ensuing year.

Upon motion of Brother Horrell, the rules and regulations were suspended, and Brother R. H. Gower was unanimously re-elected as Moderator. The other officers were elected as follows:

Vice-Moderator—A. A. Pippin.
Clerk—T. J. Lassiter.
Treasurer—Will H. Lassiter.
Auditor—J. D. Underwood.
Historian—R. W. Horrell.

The organization was then declared complete and ready for business, and the Moderator announced the following Committees:

Finance—Oscar Mozingo, D. J. Thurston and J. T. Holt.
Periodicals—C. W. Carter, D. D. Edwards and W. A. Massengill.
Temperance—Alonzo Parrish, T. B. Justice and Worley Creech.
Woman's Work—J. W. Nobles, J. F. Pool and J. S. Farmer.
Petitionary Letters—T. B. Justice, A. A. Pippin and R. W. Horrell.

Brother C. W. Carter then read the report on Periodicals:

REPORT ON PERIODICALS.

That "knowledge is power" is nowhere more clearly demonstrated than it is in regard to reading our religious papers. The dissemination of religious knowledge is exceedingly important. Our people generally are ignorant in great measure as to what the Baptists of our State are doing. They are alarmingly ignorant with reference to the work in our Association. In reference to the foreign fields our knowledge is indeed limited. Especially is this true as to the needs on the various fields. If our people only knew. Religious reading is essential to spiritual growth. The Baptist who reads no religious paper must of necessity be ignorant with reference to the calls from the mission fields and therefore wanting in interest in any sympathy for the kingdom of Christ.

The reading of the Biblical Recorder so ably edited by our Bro. H. C. Moore, is necessary in order that we may keep in touch with the work in our State. Our own Associational paper, The Messenger; is essential if we keep in touch with the work and needs of our own Association. Charity and Children will keep us informed about our children at the Orphanage. Every Baptist home in North Carolina should have a copy once each week. Too few of our sisters read the Foreign Missionary Journal, and far too few of our brethren. This is one of the very best agencies for stimulating mission interest that we have. Will our people not try it for one year?

Home Missions are coming to be in the far front of our mission work. Our people may realize this when it is too late for our Southland. The Home Field will enlighten us on this field.

We commend to all our people the Biblical Recorder, Church Messenger, Charity and Children and Our Home Field. We should support these by subscribing, then we should read them.　　　　C. W. CARTER,
For the Committee.

Upon motion to adopt, the report was discussed by Brethren C. W. Carter, J. S. Farmer and R. W. Horrell. Report was adopted.

The report on Temperance was called for and read by Brother T. B. Justice:

REPORT ON TEMPERANCE.

Of all the evils in the land, the drink evil seems to be the hardest to suppress. We made a hard fight and secured a prohibition law as strong in its provisions as we could ask. The violation of the law is the source of trouble now, and the enforcement of it, is our duty. We can expect nothing of a dealer but that he will evade the law. When a man makes up his mind to engage in a business that destroys life, makes widows and orphans and breeds poverty, disease and depravity, there is no manliness nor mercy left to which we can appeal. The moral support of all Christians and prohibitionists should be given to our sheriffs, constables and policemen, and if necessary such pressure should be brought to bear upon them as will ensure the arrest and punishment of the violators of the law. The jug traffic, fostered by the interstate law is beyond our legal control, but it exposes the drinkers and gives us an opportunity to use our Christian influence to reform the habitual drinkers.

Let us be sure we do not encourage the use of intoxicants, by example, apology or toleration. Our most strenuous efforts are necessary to prevent a reaction of public sentiment. May the Lord pity the man who claims to have a passport to heaven and always has money to order a jug of whiskey and never a dollar to send the gospel to the lost.

W. CREECH,
ALONZO PARRISH,
T. B. JUSTICE,
Committee.

Pending a motion to adopt, the report was discussed by Brethren T. B. Justice and R. H. Gower. Report was adopted.

The following Committee was announced:

On Religious Services—Pastor and Deacons of Bethesda Church.

Brother J. W. Nobles then read the report on Woman's Work:

REPORT ON WOMAN'S WORK.

Our women occupy a very important place in the rank and life of our people in church work. Woman's influence is felt in every department of life's responsibilities. She has her place, and it cannot be filled by another. Her place, influence and power was first seen in the garden of Eden. She demonstrated her influence and power first, in sacred things.

Woman seems to hold man's destiny to a large extent in her hand. She ate first of the forbidden fruit and gave to man and he did eat. Thus condemnation came upon all men.

When God undertook the world's redemption, He sent forth His son born of a woman, made under the law, that he might redeem man from under broken law. Our Saviour was nourished, cherished and trained by a woman, till He went to Jordan unto John to be baptized of him, thus our Saviour and Lord revealed himself and began his public work for man's salvation. Women were closely allied with our Lord in His work. Mary's love and service for Jesus won for woman a memorial in gospel history. "Wheresoever this gospel shall be preached in the whole world, there this, which this woman hath done, shall be spoken of for a memorial of her." Women followed Jesus, and ministered to Him in His public work. Woman was first to place the kiss of honor upon the lovely form of Jesus. First, seemingly, to understand death. Last to leave the cross on which he died. First to the tomb on the third day. First to see the risen Lord crowned with glory. First to receive His blessing and command after His resurrection. First to obey, and herald to the world "he is risen." "Go ye into Galilee there shall ye see Me, lo, I have told you."

Women redeemed by Jesus' blood, understanding as they do, the awful condition of a lost world, worried themselves through organization of societies, to give the world the gospel, that it might be the power of God unto salvation to every one that believes. What our women have accomplished can not be reckoned by dollars and cents. When we stand before our Father's throne, and those with white robes on come up to worship, and we hear redeemed women say Lord, these are mine; then we will understand their importance in the salvation of a lost world.

Our women are rapidly increasing in their gifts to the Lord's work; raising about one fourth of the money for the work of our Convention. Brethren, let us encourage them, consider their plans and help them, that they may more and more help us.

Divided forces means slow progress if any at all. Our women are somewhat in the majority in our numerical strength. If they were all organized into workers bands like some of our ladies missionary societies, the world would soon hear the gospel, and the altars of our Lord set up in most every home and the worship of Jesus upon every high place in the land.

Let us give them our co-operation, and pray "Thy kingdom come, Thy will be done in earth as it is in heaven." Submitted by your committee,

J. W. NOBLES,
JOE F. POOL,
J. S. FARMER,
Committee.

A motion was made to adopt, and the report was discussed by Brethren J. W· Nobles and J. S. Farmer, and unanimously adopted.

The Committee on Religious Services announced that Brother T. B. Justice had been appointed to preach at the evening service.

Brother Worley Creech was appointed to conduct devotional services for to-morrow morning. The body then adjourned, with benediction by Brother W. C. Royal.

FRIDAY MORNING.

The exercises began this morning with a song service conducted by Prof. A. N. Cullom, of Raleigh.

The devotional services were conducted by Brother Worley Creech, after which the Moderator called the body together, and the following visiting Brethren were recognized: Livingston Johnson, Corresponding Secretary of the Baptist State Convention, and T. Y. Seymour, of Wake Forest.

The following Committees were then announced:

State Missions—T. B. Justice, J. C. Hardee and W. H. Kelley.
Place and Preachers—M. G. Gulley, W. B. Joyner and J. M. Johnson.

The hour for the report of the Executive Committee having now arrived, the report was called for, but in the absence of the Chairman of the Committee, the report on State Missions was taken up ·and read by Brother T. B. Justice:

REPORT ON STATE MISSIONS.

There is nothing more explicitly taught in the New Testament than the doctrine of missions. The messages given the apostles clearly set out the minute methods of the work and at the same time impress us with the enormity of its proportions.

Matt. 28 and 19 tells us to "go and teach all nations baptizing them in the name of the Father, Son and Holy Ghost." Luke 24:47 declares that "repentance and remission of sins should be preached in His name among all nations beginning at Jerusalem."

John 12:49-50 tells us that Jesus Christ was the first sent to declare the gospel. "The Father which sent me, he gave me a commandment, what I should say, and what I should speak." John 20:21 startles us with the declaration that "as the Father hath sent me, so send I you."

In the Book of Revelation, chapter 22:17, the whole mission force appears and gets in line of march for the redemption of lost souls and the glory of of others. And lastly, Acts 1:8, we may read: "But ye shall receive power after that the Holy Ghost is come upon you; and ye shall be witnesses unto me, both in Jerusalem and in all Judea and Samaria and unto the uttermost parts of the earth."

Jesus furthermore said: "Lo I am with you always even unto the end of the ages."

Have we done any of this work? Yes, a good deal and we have reason to rejoice in that it has not been in vain.

Jerusalem was home, so North Carolina is home. Being at home not to remain at home, but first to fortify against hurtful influences and then to qualify for the going out.

What do we see at home? 212,879 white Missionary Baptists in North Carolina. What have they done? Been the means of baptizing 12,849 believers last year. That is encouraging. What have they yet to do? About 600,000 adults confront us who have no hope in Christ.

This is more field to cultivate, more harvest to gather for the garner of our Lord. No room for discouragement, only zeal and grace can suffice. The Associations where most of our State Mission work is done, are the Chowan, Neuse-Atlantic, Tar River, Johnston, Raleigh, Mount Zion, Piedmont, Pilot Mountain, South Yadkin, Mecklenburg, and Cabarrus, and South Fork. In this territory there is a lively awakening. In the distinctive mission churches there have been baptized within 10 years 13,844 persons; 169 houses have been built, and $52,756.48 have been paid to the objects of the Convention. Let us look carefully at the field. We need larger contributions— to build some houses and secure more well equipped men to take advantage of this propitious time and condition.

"All power is given unto me." "Lo I am with you" ought to make us enlarge the payments to State Missions this year.

T. B. JUSTICE,
J. C. HARDEE,
W. H. KELLEY,
Committee.

Upon motion to adopt, Brother T. B. Justice spoke to the report.

Just at this juncture, the Chairman of the Executive Committee having arrived, the report was called for and read by Brother J. M. Beaty:

REPORT OF EXECUTIVE COMMITTEE.

During the past year Rev. R. W. Horrell has preached at Pine Level, Parrish Memorial, Bethel, Moore's School-house, Princeton, Brown's School-house, and part of the time at Pinkney, where he organized a new Church. Rev. W. C. Royal has preached at Micro, Thanksgiving, Live Oak, Sardis, Woodard School-house, Calvary and Trinity. Rev. A. A. Pippin, at Corinth and Middlesex. Rev. J. W. Nobles, at Nobles Chapel and part of the time at Bailey, Kenly and Pinkney. At Pauline, Hood's Grove, Blackman's Grove, Oliver's Grove, Benson's Grove, and Pleasant Grove, we have had no regular preachers, but have supplied the work mostly with young men from Wake Forest College. These places need pastors to live among the people and do the pastoral work as well as the preaching. The want of sufficient funds to support the missionaries, and the scarcity of preachers, has been the cause of the conditions which now exist. We are hoping for better conditions next year.

J. M. BEATY,
J. H. BOON,
J. T. HOLT,
ALONZO PARRISH,
J. F. POOL,
Executive Committee.

Upon motion to adopt this report, together with the State Mission report, was discussed by Brethren J. M. Beaty, R. W. Horrell and Livingston Johnson.

Before adopting these reports, the report of the Building Committee was read by Brother J. M. Beaty:

REPORT OF BUILDING COMMITTEE.

The plan of your Committee to build a new Church within the bounds of the Association every year has not been carried out in 1909 for want of funds. We have asked the Churches to send building funds with other money to this Association, and hope to erect a Church building the coming winter. We recommend that the Association ask the Churches to make regular yearly pledges for Church building, as they do other objects.

J. M. BEATY,
J. H. BOON,
J. T. HOLT,
ALONZO PARRISH,
J. F. POOL,
Building Committee.

The pledges for State Missions were taken, and the report on State Missions and report of Executive Committee were adopted unanimously. The report of the Building Committee was also adopted.

The following visiting brethren were recognized:

Rev. T. H. King, of the Neuse-Atlantic Association.

Rev. J. F. Murry, of the Neuse-Atlantic Association.

Rev. I. M. Mercer, D. D., of the Roanoke Association.

Archibald Johnson, Editor of *Charity and Children*.

The Committee on Petitionary Letters made their report, recommending that Pinkney Chapel Baptist Church and Bailey Baptist Church be received into the Association. The report was adopted unanimously, and the Moderator received the delegates from these Churches and gave them a cordial welcome.

The following Committees were announced:

Orphanage—J. T. Holt, J. H. Boon and G. G. Beaty.
Mome Missions: W. C. Royal, W. M. Eason and D. H. Williams.
On Nominations—R. W. Horrell, Claude Stephenson and E. L. Hall.

The Body then adjourned for dinner, with benediction by Dr. Mercer.

AFTERNOON SESSION.

The Body was called to order at 2 o'clock by the Moderator, and Brother C. W. Carter led in prayer.

The unfinished business was taken up and pledges were made for the Church Building Fund.

Brother J. T. Holt was called for and read the report on Orphanage:

REPORT ON ORPHANAGE.

We may consider the Orphanage the child in the family of duties that the church owes the world.

The time was when many looked upon it as Ishmael, and wished to drive it to the wilderness; but by experience we learn that it is the child of promise, and many blessings have come to us through the Orphanage. Through this institution our hopes have revived, our expectations are increased, and as the mother loves her child without command so we should love the Orphanage and through this love feed and clothe, educate and train for life and usefulness.

We would suggest therefore that we spare no pains that shall add to its prosperity and put it on a solid basis for life and for usefulness.

The schooling is all we can ask, with the best of teachers whose influence is silently doing its work. The superintendent is as we believe, one of God's own choosing. Its paper, Charity and Children, is pure in heart and should be a welcome visitor into all our homes. The importance in buildings, and in general appearance, have been beyond our expectation, and as an institution has gained our confidence in its management, and increased our faith in God.

Will suggest therefore that we hear their call, and observe as a custom Thanksgiving day to give expressions of our appreciation for past favors and gifts. That the Sunday schools continue to give their monthly collections and that we ask the Lord's blessings upon it, that no disaster may befall it and that its blessings may increase.

J. T. HOLT,
F. H. BROOKS,
G. G. BEATY,
Committee.

Upon motion to adopt, the report was discussed by Brethren J. T. Holt and Archibald Johnson, after which pledges were taken and the report adopted.

Brother W. C. Royal read the report on Home Missions:

REPORT ON HOME MISSIONS.

For various reasons the fields of the Home Mission Board divide themselves into three, namely: the States east of the Mississippi, the States west of the Mississippi, and Cuba, the Isle of Pines and Panama.

The work in the states is classified as frontier work in the large cities and Mission schools in the mountains. A glance at the situation will show that great throngs of our people are flocking to the cities and a large majority of the foreign population who land never leave the city. Much work is being done by the Home Board in these cities. The need of more missionaries and teachers is pressing. In the mountains of the southern states we have twenty-four schools under the control of the Board. There were enrolled according to the last report 4,316 pupils of whom 78 were ministerial students, and 441 were baptized during the year. Eight of these schools are in North Carolina.

Cuba is an important point. By the aid of our government the country has become an independent nation. This has made the islands of more importance to the world. The construction of the panama canal makes it important as the half-way station between New York and Panama. The coming importance of Cuba in the commercial and political world makes it obligatory upon us to use all energy to firmly plant a pure gospel there.

Another important feature of the Board's work is church building. Important centers of influence frequently demand the erection of suitable houses of worship, but the local churches are weak and totally unable to meet the demands of the times. This Board has frequently made possible that which would otherwise have been impossible along this line.

Summary: The Board employs 1,108 missionaries, a gain of 147 over preceding year. Received from all sources $302,864.74, being an increase over the year before of $37,529.15. Of this amount North Carolina contributed $17,651.76.

Your committee has summarized the workings of the Board and suggest heroic giving for these objects. The same Lord who said, "Go ye into all the world," also said with no less importance, "begin at Jerusalem."

W. C. ROYAL,
D. H. WILLIAMS,
W. M. EASON,
Committee.

Upon motion to adopt Brother Royal spoke to the report, after which the pledges were taken and the report received.

The Committee on Nominations reported as follows:

REPORT ON NOMINATIONS.

We, the Committee appointed to nominate an Executive Board and delegates to the Southern and State Conventions, recommend the following:

Executive Committee—J. M. Beaty, J. H. Boon, J. T. Holt, Alonzo Parrish and J. F. Pool.

Delegates to State Convention—T. B. Justice, C. W. Carter and A. A. Pippin as alternate.

Delegate to Southern Baptist Convention—R. H. Gower.

Member of State Board of Missions—J. M. Beaty.

Respectfully submitted,
R. W. HORRELL,
CLAUDE STEPHENSON,
E. L. HALL,
Committee.

The report of the Committee was received unanimously.

The Committee on Place and Preachers recommended that next session be held with White Oak Church, and that Rev. T. B. Justice preach the Introductory sermon. Report was adopted.

Upon motion of Brother R. W. Horrell, section 12 of the Constitution was amended by substituting the word "Wednesday" for "Thursday", in line one.

Miscellaneous business was taken up, and remarks were submitted by Brethren J. M. Beaty, R. W. Horrell, R. H. Gower and J. W. Nobles.

The following Committees were announced:

Foreign Missions—A. A. Pippin, R. L. Hocutt, W. T. Sullivan.
On Education—R. W. Horrell, D. D. Edwards and W. I. Pearce.
Sunday Schools—T. Y. Seymour, J. W. Godwin and C. H. Grady.
Ministerial Relief—N. H. Gibbs, J. B. Mecome and Moses Creech.

Rev. T. Y. Seymour was appointed to preach to-night. Rev. W. C. Royal was appointed to conduct the devotional exercises to-morrow morning at 9:30, preceded by a song service by Prof. A. N. Cullom. The Body then adjourned, with benediction by Rev. W. C. Royal.

SATURDAY MORNING.

The Body met this morning at the appointed hour with devotional services conducted by Brother W. C. Royal. The Body was called together, and Brother N. H. Gibbs led in prayer.

Brother E. L. Middleton, Sunday-School Field Secretary of the Baptist State Convention, was recognized.

The roll was called, and yesterday's proceedings were read and approved.

The regular order was then taken up, and the report on Foreign Missions was read by Brother A. A. Pippin:

REPORT ON FOREIGN MISSIONS.

The most important question we Baptists have confronting us to-day, is the mission problem. The first and greatest of importance is Foreign Missions. We should be so alert to this important question, that we let not an opportunity pass unimproved.

Oh how we do need men and women to serve our blessed Lord on the foreign field. I tremble to think of the field that God has opened up to us and of our inability to take it! No wonder the Baptists have not won the world to Christ. God opens up the various fields to them; but they refuse, or neglect, to go up and possess the lands. Other denominations, with the exceptions of two or three, cannot send forces, and the Baptists could, but will not. Those other denominations which could send the forces have practically lost their grip, and it is now open to Baptists. We must have workers. Just think of it? Nearly 2,000,000 people in Japan and nearly seventy per cent. of them have never heard of Christ.

Our work in Africa has made great progress since 1891, then our churches numbered 4; now 15. The membership in 1891 was 111; now over 1,000. Native workers were, in 1891, only 9; now 40. Baptisms in 1891 were 31; our last report gave 117. There were in 1891, three schools with twenty-one scholars; we now have twenty-one schools and five hundred and seventy-seven scholars.

I cannot take the time here to outline all the fields, but we must realize the great importance of our work in Brazil, China, India, and Argentina. The future of Argentina especially is great. Her climate is good, her soil is rich. More immigrants come to her than to any other country in the world, except the United States. If Argentina is to take her place in the future among the great nations of the world, she must have the gospel. And when we think of the millions of China and Brazil who have never heard of the blessed Lord, how can we fail to pray and work?

What a disgrace it is, that the Foreign Mission Board is accused of dishonesty. A great many people believe the old falsehood circulated, that the largest part of the mission money is taken up in expenses, regardless of the fact that the Board has frequently published exact statements of the percentage of receipts used in expenses. Eighty-seven and a half cents of every dollar given to foreign missions goes to the misssionaries. It would be larger than that, but the Board borrows money and pays interest on it in order to let the missionaries have their salaries promptly. If money could be had promptly, two and one-half cents would pay all expenses.

Your committee would recommend and encourage Mission Study Classes in our churches, also the reading of our Foreign Mission Journal and Our Home Field.

May we all pray more, work more, and give more to the spread of God's kingdom.

A. A. PIPPIN,
W. T. SULLIVAN,
R. L. HOCUTT,
Committee.

Upon motion to adopt, this report was discussed by Brother Pippin. Pledges were taken and report adopted.

The report on Education was next called for and read by Brother R. W. Horrell:

REPORT ON EDUCATION.

The education of our people is a problem which should claim our most earnest consideration. From the ship of State down to the smallest matters of every day life the safety and prosperity of every enterprise depends upon the efficiency of the people in correct thought and action.

It is highly gratifying to know that our people are more interested in the subject of general education at the present, than ever before. Throughout our State there has been a great awakening along educational lines. And the best work for this cause in all our history is being done at present. In our own county many improvements have been made within the last few years. The small, inconvenient houses have, and are being disposed of, and large and more convenient ones erected. More efficient teachers are employed in our public schools. The lengthening of the school term is another improvement which we note with pleasure. The number of high schools has been so increased that those who desire a higher grade than is taught in our public schools find no difficulty in obtaining it. Our colleges are all at preesnt doing their best work. So we can truly say that the cause of education has never been more prosperous than at the present. But while much has been done for the cause of general education, there is much yet to be done. The great mass of our people are yet uneducated, especially is this true in our own county. There are yet many dark corners. Let us realize and do our duty in spreading the light. In addition to the State schools for the education of the masses, we mention with a legitimate degree of pride, the Baptist high school and colleges for the education of our boys and girls. These should receive our liberal patronage and support. And especially should we not forget Wake Forest College where so many of our best young men are being trained for more efficient service in our Master's kingdom. Many are being aided in their education and our churches should help in this cause.

R. W. MORRELL,
D. D. EDWARDS,
W. I. PEARCE,
Committee.

Upon motion to adopt, the report was discussed by Brethren R. W. Horrell, E. L. Middleton, T. B. Justice, and others. Pledges were taken and report adopted.

Miscellaneous matters were taken up, and a plea was made for help to pay the debt on Middlesex Church. Remarks were made by Brethren A. A. Pippin, J. M. Beaty and E. L. Middleton. A collection was then taken for this Church, and the sum of $202.36 was raised in cash and in pledges, pledges to be paid before January 1st, 1910.

One striking feature of this morning's session was the presentation to the Association of Pleasant Grove Church, with organ, seats, and one acre of ground, by Brother J. M: Beaty. One Brother remarked that this was something that had never occurred in one of our Associations before.

Brother Ray Funderburk, of the Union Association, was recognized and invited to a seat with us. Also Brother J. E. Hoyle, of Wake Forest, was recognized.

At this hour the Body adjourned for dinner.

AFTERNOON SESSION.

The afternoon session was called together after praise and prayer service led by Brother Seymour. The Sunday School report was then called for and read by Brother T. Y. Seymour.

REPORT ON SUNDAY SCHOOLS.

Among the many things which our Lord taught while on earth there are none that received greater emphasis than the work of teaching. To Him the work was so important that He spent much of His time in teaching. We find Him on the mountain side teaching His disciples, by the seaside teaching the multitude, and on the Sabbath we find Him in the Temple teaching the people.

For many years this part of the Christian's work was, for the most part, neglected. About 1780 Robert Raikes saw that many of the poor and degraded children of England were growing up without any religious teaching and set out to remedy the condition, if possible. He soon found in William Fox a faithful co-worker who helped him to carry forward the work. The good accomplished by these great men of God revealed to the Christian world what they were missing by failing to carry out this part of our Master's work. From such a beginning has come our modern Sunday school which is one of our strongest holds for discipling and training our forces for good. Already we have realized glorious results. A large per cent of our church membership is brought into the kingdom through and by the work of the Sunday school.

Since the Sunday school has proven itself to be such a great agency in establishing the kingdom of God in the hearts of men, we believe that no church can do its best work without a Sunday school, and that no church member has done his full duty until he has taken some part in Sunday school work. At present the work suffers because of lack of interest and enthusiasm on the part of church members. Each church member should be aroused to a sense of his duty along this line of work. In order that we may arouse more interest in Sunday school work among our people we recommend the following:

1. That we use one of our Union meetings each year, as a Sunday School Convention.

2. That our pastors and superintendents hold rallies to increase interest and enlarge our membership.

3. That each church give financial support to our State Sunday school work.

T. Y. SEYMOUR,
S. A. GODWIN,
Committee.

Upon motion to adopt, the report was discussed by Brother E. L. Middleton. Pledges were taken, and the report unanimously adopted.

The report on Ministerial Relief was next called for and read by Brother N. H. Gibbs:

REPORT ON MINISTERIAL RELIEF.

The Baptist Minister's Relief Board was established in 1890. It is now located in Durham, and is composed of nine trustees who are elected annually by the Baptist State Convention. The object of this Board is to afford aid and relief to needy Baptist Ministers of North Carolina and their widows. There are four regular meetings of the Board each year—on the fourth Wednesday in February, May, August, and November. It is composed of five preachers, two lawyers and two business men. Rev. J. F. McDuffie is the efficient Secretary. No member of the Board can receive any compensation for services rendered. There are at present thirty-two beneficiaries. Many of these aged Ministers have no visible means of their own, and are dependent on the Board for help. Up to October 9th there had been paid in by the Churches $2,300.00 since last meeting of the Convention. They hope to get $3,000.00 this year by the time the Convention meets in December. One-third of this goes into permanent interest bearing fund. The beneficiaries get the interest on this and the other two-thirds. This is a small amount to be distributed with thirty-two families. Therefore, we, your Committee, urge the Churches of the Johnston County Association to make at least one liberal offering each year as the Lord hath prospered them, for the support of those aged Ministers and their families.

N. H. GIBBS, Chmn. Com.
MOSES CREECH.

The motion to adopt was made, and Brother Gibbs led in the discussion, after which pledges were taken and the report unanimously adopted.

MISCELLANEOUS.

Brother Pippin made a motion to appoint a Sunday School Committee for this Association, and that the Moderator be one of this Committee. The motion prevailed, and upon a vote of the Body, Brother T. B. Justice was named as the other member of the Committee. The Moderator appointed Brother Justice Chairman.

The following Resolution of Thanks to the "Cullom School of Music" was adopted:

"Resolved, That the thanks of this Association and visitors be extended to the 'Cullom School of Music' for the pleasure they gave us in the rendition of many beautiful songs during this session."

Upon motion of Brother E. L. Hall, the following Resolution of Thanks was passed:

"Resolved, That this Association in body assembled, extend to this Church and Community, a rising vote of thanks for its royal entertainment and unbounded hospitality during the session of this body."

The final reports of Finance Committee, Treasurer and Auditor, were deferred and ordered printed complete in the minutes.

Upon motion, the Clerk was ordered to have one thousand copies of the minutes printed and distributed, and that he be allowed $10.00 for his services.

Upon motion of Brother A. A. Pippin, the Churches of this Association were instructed to make up their Church letters each year and forward them to our Church Clerk, Brother T. J. Lassiter, at Smithfield, N. C., by November 1st.

The following appointments were made for services to-morrow: At 10 o'clock, a Sunday School mass meeting, with short talks by several Brethren. At 11 o'clock, a sermon by Brother T. B. Justice.

All the business of the Association having been completed, the Body adjourned at 3:35 p. m., with benediction by Brother A. A. Pippin.

SUNDAY MORNING.

A Sunday-school mass meeting was held this morning beginning at 10 o'clock, with an address on Sunday-school work by Brother J. T. Holt. He was followed by Professor J. P. Canaday, Superintendent of Schools of Johnston County. The next speaker was Professor M. T. Edgerton, of the Fremont Graded Schools. He was followed by Brother E. L. Middleton, our Sunday-school Secretary. After which, Brother T. B. Justice delivered a strong and impressive sermon.

CONSTITUTION OF THE

Johnston County Baptist Association.

1. The Association shall be known as the Johnston County Baptist Association.

2. Its object shall be to extend the privileges of the Gospel and liberal culture to all the people within its bounds, and by hearty co-operation with the Baptist State Convention to help offer these privileges to all mankind in and out of its bounds, by the cordial co-operation of all the churches constituting this body.

3. It shall be composed of the pastors in active service in the Association and such delegates as shall be annually elected by the churches connected with it, each church being entitled to three delegates, unless the membership shall exceed fifty, and then an additional delegate for every twenty-five members, provided no church shall have more than eight delegates.

4. The New Hampshire Declaration of Faith shall be the summary of Divine Truth for determining questions of faith and order in this body, and the churches desiring membership in it must commit themselves to the substance of it, together with the covenant therewith submitted, and this Constitution.

5. This Association shall not have power, to annul the discipline or exercise authority over any church connected with it, but it may advise with and sever its connection with any church that neglects to preserve Gospel order, or that treats with contempt the objects or advice of the Association.

6. Each church shall send to the annual meetings of the Association a letter (the blanks to be furnished by the clerk of the Association), carefully filled as per blank suggestions, stating the full work of the church for the year ending with the close of the month previous to the one in which the Association is held.

7. The Association shall foster State Missions, Home Missions, Foreign Missions, Christian Education, the Aged Ministers' Relief Board, the Thomasville Orphanage and the Sunday School Board, and each church shall be requested to contribute to the support of these objects annually.

8. Missions and education shall have precedence in their claims upon the consideration of this body in its regular sessions.

9. Whenever a church shall fail to be represented by delegates or letter at the annual sessions of the Association inquiry shall be made for the cause and efforts shall be made to induce such church to do its duty, and the effort shall be continued till the church is recovered or dropped from the roll.

10. The officers of the Association shall be a Moderator, a Vice-Moderator, a Clerk, a Treasurer and an Auditor, elected annually by ballot from among its members, to serve until their successors shall have been elected, and to perform the duties usual to such officers, namely, the Moderator, in presiding over the meetings, or the Vice-Moderator in his absence; the Clerk in recording and preserving minutes and other papers belonging to the body; the Treasurer in receiving and disbursing funds belonging to or entrusted to the body according to its will; the Auditor to examine the Treasurer's books at each meeting of the Association and report the same before adjournment.

11. The Association shall appoint annually an Executive Committee of five (5) from its members, who shall be entrusted with the prosecution of Missions in the Association and any other work for the interest of the Master's Kingdom which may be referred to them. This committee shall, as far as possible, co-operate with the State Mission Board in supplying the destitution in our territory, and between the meetings of the Association

take such actions as may seem to them advisable for the advancement of its interest. The committee shall present to the Association at its annual meeting a report of its proceedings, with the names of the missionaries supported on the field, time of service and details of their work, together with such recommendations as in the judgment of the committee the Association should follow in planning its subsequent work.

12. The annual sessions of the Association shall begin on Wednesday after the first Lord's Day in November at such place as may be chosen, and an introductory sermon shall be delivered on the first day of the session. Representatives from a majority of the churches constituting the Association shall be a quorum.

13. This Constitution may be amended at any annual session by a two-thirds vote of all the members present.

14. Provision shall be made at each annual session for a session of the Woman's Central Committee, and all other necessary encouragement offered for the enlargement of the organized work of the Woman's Missionary Societies in the local churches. The proceedings of the Woman's Central Committee shall be recorded as a part of the Minutes of the Association.

BY-LAWS.

1. The daily sessions of the Association shall be opened and closed with prayer.

2. Delegates shall be recognized by letters from their churches designating them as such.

3. The Moderator shall recognize corresponding messengers or the delegates of newly-received churches by extending to them his right hand.

4. The report of the Executive Board and the Missionary Work of the Association shall take precedence of all other business during the morning session of the second day of the annual session.

5. The Clerk shall record and read the proceedings when called for, superintend the publication and distribution of the Minutes, preserve a file of them, and have it present at each annual session, and deliver to his successor all papers belonging to the body.

6. Members desiring to speak shall first rise and address the Moderator; shall use the term "brother" in speaking to each other; shall not speak on the same subject more than twice without permission, and shall observe the courtesy that becomes Christians.

7. Members shall not absent themselves from the session without permission.

8. The roll of members shall be called at least once and absentees marked.

9. Corresponding messengers and visiting brethren shall be invited to seats, with privilege of speaking, but not of voting.

10. A copy of the Minutes shall be sent to the Secretary of the State Mission Board, the Secretary of the Southern Baptist Convention, the American Baptist Publication Society, 1420 Chestnut street, Philadelphia; the Sunday School Board of the Southern Baptist Convention and the Thomasville Orphanage.

11. All questions of order not herein provided shall be decided by Kerfoot's Parliamentary Law.

TABLE I—REPORT OF FINANCE COMMITTEE.

CHURCHES.	Minutes and Clerk.	State Missions.	Home Missions.	Foreign Missions.	Sunday School Missions.	Ministerial Education.	Ministerial Relief.	Orphanage.	Building Fund.	Total.
Antioch	$ 1.00	$15.00	$ 1.50	$ 1.50	$ 1.50	$ 1.50	$ 2.00	$ 2.50	$	$ 26.50
Baptist Centre	1.30	4.37	2.00	1.00	1.00	1.00	1.00			11.67
Benson	3.00	93.25	6.35	15.00	2.00	5.00	5.00			129.60
Benson's Grove	50	1.00	50	50	50	50	50	1.00		5.00
Bethany	85	6.00	2.50	2.00	1.	1.00	1.25	3.15	5.00	22.75
Bethel		1.35								1.35
Bethesda	1.50	25.00	5.00	5.00	1.	2.	63	12.81		52.94
Blackman's Grove	50	13.00	8.00	5.00		2. 0	1.00	7.00		31.50
Calvary	65	2.36		1.20	1.	1. 0	1.50			8.21
Carter's Chapel	80	10.00	2.50	1.50	1.00	1. 0	2.00	5.00	2.27	26.57
Clayton	2.00	136.52			7.00	20.00	20.00			185.52
Clyde's Chapel	1.00									1.00
Corinth	1.50	8.00	1.50	2.00	1.	1.00	2.	5.00	4.00	26.00
Four Oaks	1.00									1.00
Hood's Grove					00		00			
Kenly	75		1.00		1.00	1.00			3.33	7.08
Lee's Chapel	1.50	25.00	5.00	10.00	2.00	2.50	3.00			49.00
Live Oak	35	1.07								1.42
Micro	35	3.00	1.50	1.25	50	1.00	1.00	2.50		11.10
Middlesex	1.50				50	50	1.00	2.00	5.00	10.50
Mount Moriah	2.00	27.97	2.17	29.23		5.00	6.00	22.34		94.71
New Bethel										
Nobles' Chapel		5.43	3.00	2.50	1.00	2.00	2.00	4.00		19.93
Oliver's Grove	1.00	1.00	50	1.00	50	50	50	50	3.00	8.50
Parrish Memorial	1.00	14.05	2.00	2.00	.	2.00	1.00			22.05
Pauline	55	4.00	50	1.00	50	70		1.00	50	8.75
Pinkney	50	1.00	25	25						2.00
Pine Level	1.00									1.00
Pisgah										
Princeton	1.00	14.00	2.25		1.00	2.00	2.50	4.00		26.75
Sardis	50	5.50	2.00	2.00	50	1.00	1.00	2.00		14.50
Selma										
Shiloh	1.26		3.00	2.00	1.00	1.50	1.50	2.50		12.76
Smithfield										
Thanksgiving	50									50
Trinity	50	3.65	4.00	1.20						9.35
Wendell	1.38	3.31			1.00		2.44	7.47		15.60
White Oak	2.00	7.40	2.50	2.50	1.50	2.00	2.00			21.90
Wilson's Mills	50	15.00			2.00	3.00	3.00			23.50
Bailey	50									50
Total	34.24	447.23	54.52	89.63	30.40	61.70	63.82	84.77	23.10	891.01

TABLE II—TREASURER'S REPORT.

To the Johnston County Association:
    I submit herewith a report of all money received by me and paid out since Nov. 17, 1908, date of last report.

Baptist Centre	$ 12.13
Benson	28.40
Clayton	170.95
Clyde's Chapel	25.37
Calvary	3.75
Four Oaks	28.80
Hood's Grove	8.95
Live Oak	8.40
Micro	3.79
Mount Moriah	19.51
New Bethel	2.00
Parrish Memorial	5.85
Pine Level	9.93
Pisgah	32.63
Princeton	13.00
Sardis	2.05
Smithfield	263.96
Thanksgiving	9.15
Trinity	9.65
White Oak	11.40
General Collections at M. and L. Convention	13.00
General Collections at Association	4.25
Finance Committee at Bethesda	891.01
For Benson's Grove	37.61

Total received	$1,615.72
Balance on hand last report	1,412.64
Grand total	$3,028.36

The above amount was received for the following objects:

Error in Finance Committee	$ 1.60
State Missions	874.27
Home Missions	109.47
Foreign Missions	168.94
Sunday School Missions	47.90
Orphanage	131.73
Ministerial Education	87.29
Ministerial Relief	86.47
Colleges and Schools	1.00
Minutes and Clerk	42.74
Building Fund	26.70
Benson's Grove	37.61
Total	$1,615.72

DISBURSEMENTS.

November 21, Walters Durham	$1149.62
November 21, S. H. Averitt	118.09
December 4, R. H. Johnson (Benson's Grove)	105.00
1909.	
January 9, Nash Bros.	30.00
March 2, J. W. Nobles	14.83
April 10, T. J. Lassiter (Clerk)	10.00
November 18, Commercial National Bank, Raleigh (B. G. note)	32.50
November 12, Archibald Johnson, (Orphanage)	84.77
November 24, Walters Durham	1000.51
November 24, S. H. Averitt	46.96
	$2,952.28
Balance on hand	76.08
	$3,028.36

Respectfully submitted,
                            WILL H. LASSITER, Treasurer,
                                    Johnston County Association.
Smithfield, N. C.,
    November 24, 1909.

    Approved.
            J. D. UNDERWOOD, Auditor.

TABLE III—FINANCIAL.

CHURCH.	Pastor's Salary.	Building and Repairs.	Incidentals.	Sunday School Expenses.	The Poor.	State Missions.	Home Missions.	Foreign Missions.	Sunday School Missions.	Orphanage.	Colleges and Schools.	Ministerial Education.	Aged Ministers.	Minutes and Clerk.	Other Objects.	Building Fund.	Totals.
[illegible]	$59.75	$3.00	$	$2.00	$5.00	$15.00	$1.50	$1.50	$1.50	$2.50	$1.50	$1.50	$2.00	$1.00	$	$	$97.75
Baptist Centre	71.85		19.00	7.00		5.00	2.00	2.00	1.00	10.00		1.00	1.50	1.50			102.85
Benson	289.09	102.20	48.50	46.00		100.00	20.00	20.00	2.00	25.00	1.00	5.00	5.00	3.00		5.00	637.29
Benson's Grove	15.00	50.00		5.18	1.00					1.00		1.00	1.00	.50			123.68
Bethany	30.00	120.00	10.00	10.00		1.00	2.00	1.00	1.00	3.15		2.00	1.00	.85		5.00	187.75
Bethel	25.00	150.00		3.00	10.00	4.00	5.00	5.00	1.00	1.00		1.50	3.00	1.00	30.00	2.00	191.50
Bethesda	150.00		10.00	10.00	5.00	25.00	3.00	5.00	1.00	15.00		2.00	1.50	1.00			262.50
Calvary [illegible] grove	31.00				4.00	13.00	54.25	1.50	1.00	7.00		1.50	1.50	.50	7.75		131.50
Carter's Chapel	30.55	7.00		25.00	5.00	1.51	4.25	1.50	1.00	2.25		1.00	2.00	.80	2.27		50.66
Clayton		90.05	112.93	81.87	3.73	10.00	3.00	70.21	10.00	12.00	4.00	20.00	20.00	2.00	145.92		96.12
Clyde's Chapel	612.50		12.00	6.00		208.66	54.25	5.00	1.00	69.19		1.00	3.00	1.00			1504.21
Corinth	100.00	90.00		4.30	5.40	10.00	4.00	5.00	1.00	5.00		1.50	2.00	1.50	1.90	4.00	147.00
Four Oaks	80.00		.75	25.88		15.00	5.00	5.00	.50	5.00		1.50	3.00	1.50			115.45
Hood's Grove	91.33	664.06	1.55			5.45	1.00	2.00		5.00		1.00	3.50	.75	14.00	3.33	247.16
Kenly	18.00		10.00	5.00	15.00	5.00	5.00	2.00	1.00	2.16		2.50	3.00	.50			26.95
Lee's [illegible]	26.25				5.45	25.00		10.25	2.00	1.77		1.00	1.00	.75			724.05
Live Oak	125.00				25.00		5.00	3.09	.50	2.50		1.00	1.00	.35			184.00
[illegible]	9.25	25.25	26.45	5.00	2.35	10.00	3.25	3.00	1.25	24.12		1.50	1.00	.35	35.45	.50	17.97
[illegible]	17.00	576.01	72.50	8.00	5.72	57.46	20.00	50.00	5.00	30.00		.50	8.70	2.00		5.00	94.70
New Bethel	50.00		21.70	10.64	10.00	15.00	12.25	9.05	5.00	34.80	1.00	5.05	2.00	2.00			736.65
Nobles' Chapel	150.00	2.00	8.00	45.00	57.46	15.00	3.00	2.50		4.00		5.05					428.66
Oliver's Grove	125.00	6.15		10.00	15.00	17.00		1.00	.50			.50	.50	1.00		3.10	231.85
Parrish Memorial	70.00		6.00		17.00	17.50	2.00	2.00		4.00		2.50	1.00	1.00	3.00		106.55
Pauline	60.00	20.00			17.50	4.00	2.00	2.00		2.00		2.00	1.00	1.00			8.50
Pinkney					4.00	1.00		1.00	.25	1.00		.70		.30			113.50
Pine Level		.80	.75	4.13	1.00		1.00	.25						.50			8.80
Pisgah					6.00		2.00	1.50					1.50				2.00
Princeton	50.00		10.00	15.41	15.00	6.00	2.00	5.00	.50	3.00		1.25	1.50	1.00	5.75		65.75
Sardis	100.00				20.00	15.00	4.25	5.00	2.00	2.25		2.00	1.50	1.00			138.73
Shiloh	75.37	50.00		5.00	5.50	20.00	3.00	2.00	1.50	4.00		1.00	2.50	1.50	10.00		140.53
Smithfield	42.70		75.00	92.32	7.82	5.50	3.00	2.00		2.50		1.00	2.00	1.26			67.20
Thanksgiving	150.00				150.00	7.82	40.00	55.00	10.00	51.18	6.00	15.00	20.00	5.00	40.00		225.08
Trinity	400.00				4.61			1.70	.50	2.15		.50	.50	1.25			959.50
Wendell	75.00	182.04		110.11	1.35	4.61	2.00	2.30	1.00	3.00		1.00	1.00	1.25	5.25		85.45
White Oak	26.60				9.50	9.50	4.25	18.30	.50	16.20		1.98	2.44	1.38	44.93		42.75
Wilson's Mills	150.00		3.00	1.50	23.43	23.43	2.50	5.44	1.25	5.44		2.00	2.00	2.00	23.12		495.78
Bailey	100.00		22.00	60.00	15.00	15.00	5.00	5.00	2.00	12.00		3.00	3.00	.50	11.00	10.00	218.74
[illegible]																	243.00
[illegible]																	11.52
Total	3856.24	2088.56	460.13	593.84	29.13	746.84	227.09	307.65	56.00	373.26	13.50	92.48	111.89	42.94	374.59	23.93	10283.63

CHURCH	PASTOR AND POSTOFFICE	CLERK AND POSTOFFICE	Time of Preaching	Value of Church Property	Seating Capacity of Church	Baptized	Received by Letter	Restored	Dismissed by Letter	Excluded	Died	Number of Males	Number of Females	Total Membership
Antioch	Worley Creech, Kenly	Jesse B. Creech, Selma	2nd	$ 500.00	200	16		2	4		1	58	66	124
Baptist Center	W. C. Royal, Micro	W. C. Hardee, Clayton	1st	500.00	250	5	1	1	2	2	3	24	40	64
Bailey*	J. W. Nobles, Kenly	R. L. Underwood, Bailey	4th			4	9					7	6	13
Benson	T. B. Justice, Benson	E. L. Hall, Benson	2d-4th	1500.00	400		3		8			51	95	146
Benson's Grove	J. E. Hoyle, Wake Forest	J. R. Benson, Benson	2nd	800.00	250	5	2		4			5	10	15
Bethany	Worley Creech, Kenly	Kirkman Creech, Kenly	4th	700.00	200	9		1		4	1	34	50	84
Bethel	R. W. Horrel, Selma	Perry Barnes, Kenly	4th	500.00	250	6	4	1	3			17	18	35
Bethesda	J. W. Smith, Wilson's Mills	J. E. Smith, Wilson's Mills	4th	500.00	400	6					1	79	112	191
Blackman's Gro.	T. B. Justice, Benson	J. L. Smith, Four Oaks, R. 3	3rd	700.00	200						1	18	18	58
Calvary	W. C. Royal, Micro	T. J. Lee, Dunn, R. 2	4th	500.00	200	21	7		5	2	1	7	18	25
Carter's Chapel	D. D. Edwards, Cary	H. R. Eason, Selma	1st	400.00	300	10			7	4	1	39	61	100
Clayton	Supply	C. I. Johnson, ther, R. 2	1st 3rd	6000.00	700		1	3	5	2	2	145	180	325
Clyde's Chapel	J. W. Bes, Kenly	H. V. Andrews, Archer, Rt. 1	3rd	500.00	300	10	3		7	3	4	60	85	145
Earth	A. A. Pippin, Wakefield	Jos. W. Wood, Benson, R. 2	2nd	450.00	400			2	5	3		37	72	109
Four Oaks	T. B. Justice, Benson	B. W. Harris, Kenly	1st 3rd	800.00	200		1		1	1		13	22	35
Hood's Grove	Supply	W. I. Green, Wakefield, R. 2	3rd	300.00	300							12	26	38
Kenly	Supply	K. Broadwell, Selma, R. 1	2nd	2000.00	350	3			1		2	9	13	22
Lee's Chapel	A. A. Pippin, Wakefield	Oscar Mozingo, Micro	4th	600.00	500	3	1	2			1	106	166	272
Live Oak	W. C. Royal, Micro	W. C. Jackson, Middlesex	2nd	350.00	250	3	3					10	24	34
Micro	W. C. Royal, Micro	J. H. Bryant, Raleigh, R. 2	1st-2nd	550.00	300	4	6	1	1	3	1	12	13	25
Middlesex	A. A. Pippin, Wakefield	G. W. Bryan, Garner	4th			1	6		9	1		22	34	56
Mount Moriah	J. M. Hilliard, Cary	T. B. Tiner, Four Oaks	1st	800.00	300		2		6	1	2	66	77	143
New Bethel	J. W. Seymour, Wake Forest	Joe D. Creech, Selma, R. 4	4th	800.00	400	14		1	2	2		46	49	96*
Nobles' Chapel	Supply	O. N. Hayes, Four Oaks	4th	700.00	350	8					2	41	57	98
Oliver's Grove	R. W. Horrel, Selma	Mrs. Ida Edgerton, Kenly, R.1	3rd	300.00	300	15	5		1	3		12	19	31
Parrish Memor'l	Supply	J. W. Godwin, Pine Level	1st	600.00	400		1		2			32	41	73
Pauline	J. W. Nobles, Kenly	W. H. Higgins, Smithfield, R.1	3rd	400.00	300					23		15	17	32
Pinkney Chapel*	R. W. Horrel, Selma	W. I. Pearce, Princeton	1st		200	3		1				4	8	12
Pine Level	T. B. Justice, Benson	N. B. Sts, Smithfield, R.2	1st	300.00	200	3	3	3	2		2	22	37	59
Pisgah	R. W. Horrel, Selma	N. B. O'Neal, Selma	1st	700.00	300	3				3		22	37	59
Princeton	R. W. Horrel, Selma	John Hardee, McCullers, R. 1	3rd	800.00	400	2			8		2	41	55	96
Sardis	W. C. Royal, Micro	T. J. Lassiter, Smithfield	3rd	400.00	200	2		1				9	19	28
Selma**			2d 4th	12000.00	700									197
Shiloh	R. W. Horrel, Selma	W. G. Earp, Selma	2nd	750.00	350	5	1	3	3		1	31	49	80
Smithfield	Supply	J. S. Lawhon, Benson, R. 2	1st 3d	4500.00	700	4	1		6		1	69	89	158
Thanksgiving	W. C. Royal, Micro	C. Z. Todd, Wendell	2nd	1500.00	600	5		2	2		2	29	29	58
Trinity	W. C. Royal, Micro	J. I. Murphrey, Selma, R. 1	4th	250.00	250				1			13	28	41
Wendell	J. W. Nobles, Kenly	G. H. Ellis, Wilson's Mills	2nd	2000.00	500	12	9				4	47	68	115
Micro	A. A. Pippin, Wakefield		2nd	500.00	400	8	7	3	10	1		63	88	151
Wite Oak	J. B. Eller, Wake Forest		3rd	1000.00	300	2	1		4			24	25	49
Total						192	85	19	97	63	36			3491

* New Churches.
** No report—Same figures in last year's Minutes.

TABLE V—SUNDAY SCHOOL STATISTICS.

CHURCH.	SUPERINTENDENT AND POSTOFFICE.	Officers and Teachers.	Scholars.	Total Enrollment.	No. Schools.	Volumes in Library.	Quarterlies Taken.	No. Officers.	Average Attendance.	No. Baptisms.	Benevolen Contributions.	Sunday School Expenses.	Total Contributions.
Antioch	J. A. Eason, Selma, R. 1	8	95	103	5		200		27	16		$ 2.00	$ 2.00
Baptist Center	J. C. Hardee, Clayton	5	80	85	1		6	12	30	4		7.00	7.00
Benson	J. E. Wall, Benson	9	143	152	1		195	12	62			46.00	46.00
Benson's Grove	J. H. Stephenson, Benson	5	45	50	1		50	9	35	4		5.18	5.18
Bethany	David Pace, Micro	6	75	81	1		50	12	40	6		10.00	10.00
Bethel	Levin Watson, Kenly	5	40	45	1		30	9	30	2		3.00	3.00
Bethesda	J. J. Wallace, Wilson's Mills	9	60	69	1	40	60	12	40	2		10.00	10.00
Blackman's Grove	F. P. Wood, Four Oaks	3	34	37	1			8	20				
Carter's Chapel	Preston Mozingo, Selma	8	58	66	1		94	12	35	15		25.00	25.00
Clayton	R. H. Gower, Clayton	20	218	238	1	246	530	12	125	12	79.19	81.87	151.98
Clyde's Chapel	W. T. Punch, Clayton, R. F. D. 2	7	89	96	1	50	65	9	59	8		6.00	6.00
Corinth	Q. R. Hocutt, Wakefield, R. 1	7	67	74	1		75	9	28	3	1.00	4.30	5.30
Four Oaks	W. A. Massengill, Four Oaks	5	67	72	1		60	12	35	2	1.63	25.88	27.51
Lee's Chapel	Brantley Richardson, Wakefield, R. 2	6	60	66	1		300	9	32			5.00	5.00
Live Oak	J. M. Richardson, Selma	4	45	49	1		75	12	60	3			
Micro	W. C. Jackson, Micro	5	50	55	1		260	12	151	3	16.30	8.00	8.00
Middlesex	J. H. Bryant, Raleigh, R. 2	11	145	152	1	375	215	12	75		5.00	10.64	26.94
Mount Moriah	James Bryan, Mr.	11	125	136	1	55	150	12	75	1		45.00	50.00
New Bethel	J. A. Tyner, Four Oaks	7	35	42	1		40	12	38			10.00	10.00
Oliver's Grove	J. F. Watson, Pine Level	6	66	72	1		60	5	35	5			
Parrish Memorial	R. B. Joyner, Four Oaks	8	30	38	1		108		36				
Pauline	R. H. Higgins, Smithfield	7	97	104	1		35	6	45	1		4.13	4.13
Pisgah	J. W. Liles, Selma	5	35	40	1		50	12	25	2			
Pine Level	W. H. Wells, Princeton	4	75	79	1				45	1		15.41	15.41
Princeton	B. F. Hassell, Selma	6	75	81	1		84	12	40	2			
Selma*	D. M. Lee, Clayton, R. 1	11	187	198	1	200	200	12	40	3		15.41	15.41
Shiloh	T. J. Lassiter, Smithfield	7	48	55	2		60	12	120	3	28.50	5.00	5.00
Smithfield	C. Z. Todd, Wendell	13	200	213	1		375	12	109			92.32	120.82
Wendell	A. L. Batten, Archer, R. 1	10	242	252	1		275	12	40	4		110.00	110.00
White Oak	J. T. Holt, Wilson's Mills	8	94	102	1		60	12	40			3.50	3.50
Wilson's Mills	Parlia Hudson, Beasley, R. 2	4	45	51	1		75	12	85			60.00	60.00
Hood's Grove		4	25	29	1		30	6	20				
Total		261	2745	3006	38					85	151.62	595.23	746.85

* No report—Figures taken from last Minutes.

TABLE VI—CHURCH PLEDGES FOR 1910.

CHURCHES.	State M ss ons.	Home M ss ons.	Fore gn Missions.	Orphanage.	M ti ster al Educat on.	M ti ster al Relief.	Sunday School M ss ons.	Church Bu ld ng Fund.	Total.
Antioch	$15.00	$ 1.50	$ 1.50	$ 2.50	$ 1.50	$ 2.50	$ 1.00	$ 2.00	$ 27.50
Bailey	2.00	50	50	1.00	1.00	1.00	50	1.00	7.50
Baptist Centre	5.00	2.00	2.50	5.00	2.00	1.50	1.50	1.50	21.00
Benson	100.00	20.00	20.00	25.00	5.00	5.00	5.00	10.00	190.00
Benson's Grove	2.00	50	50	2.00	1.00	50	50	1.00	8.00
Bethany	6.00	2.50	2.00	3.00	1.00	1.50	1.00	2.00	19.00
Bethel	5.00	2.00	1.00	1.00	1.00	1.00	50	1.00	12.50
Bethesda	25.00	5.00	5.00	20.00	2.00	3.00	2.00	2.00	64.00
Blackman's Grove	20.00	5.00	5.00	8.00	4.00	2.50	2.00	2.00	48.50
Calvary	4.00	2.00	2.00	2.00	2.00	1.00	1.25	2.00	16.25
Carter's Chapel	10.00	2.50	1.50	10.00	1.50	2.00	1.00	2.50	31.00
Clayton	225.00	60.00	60.00	135.00	20.00	20.00	10.00	25.00	555.00
Clyde's Chapel	10.00	4.00	4.00	5.00	1.00	3.00	1.00	1.50	29.50
Corinth	8.50	1.50	1.50	5.00	1.00	2.00	1.50	1.00	22.00
Four Oaks	15.00	5.00	5.00	5.00	1.50	3.00	1.00	2.50	38.00
Hood's Grove	10.00	2.00	2.00	2.00	2.00	1.50	1.00	1.00	21.50
Kenly	5.00	3.00	3.00	3.00	1.00	1.00	1.00	1.00	18.00
Lee's Chapel	25.00	5.00	10.00	5.00	5.00	3.00	2.50	2.50	57.50
Live Oak	4.00	50	1.25	1.25	1.00	1.00	50	1.00	10.75
Micro	6.00	1.50	1.25	3.00	1.00	1.00	50	1.00	15.25
Middlesex	10.00	1.00	1.00	2.00	1.00	1.00	1.00	1.00	18.00
Mount Moriah	50.00	20.00	50.00	30.00	5.00	6.00	6.00	5.00	170.00
New Bethel	16.00	6.00	5.00	15.00	4.00	2.00	1.00	5.00	54.00
Nobles' Chapel	17.00	3.00	2.50	4.00	2.00	2.00	1.00	5.00	36.50
Oliver's Grove	2.00	50	1.00	2.00	1.00	50	50	2.00	9.50
Parrish Memorial	17.50	2.00	2.00	2.00	2.00	2.00	1.00	1.00	29.50
Pauline	5.00	2.00	1.50	2.00	2.00	1.00	50	2.00	16.00
Pine Level	7.00	2.00	1.50	3.00	1.50	1.50	1.00	1.00	18.50
Pinkney Chapel	5.00	1.00	1.00	2.00	1.00	50	50	4.00	15.00
Pisgah	15.00	3.00	5.00	2.00	2.50	5.00	2.00	4.00	38.50
Princeton	20.00	4.25	5.00	4.00	2.00	2.50	1.00	1.25	40.00
Sardis	5.50	2.00	2.00	2.00	1.00	1.00	50	1.00	15.00
Selma	60.00	10.00	25.00	25.00	4.00	10.00	1.00	10.00	145.00
Shiloh	7.50	2.50	3.00	2.50	3.00	2.50	1.00	1.00	23.00
Smithfield	160.00	42.00	58.00	40.00	20.00	21.00	11.00	25.00	377.00
Thanksgiving	5.00	1.00	1.00	1.00	1.00	1.00	50	1.00	11.50
Trinity	6.00	1.00	3.50	3.00	1.00	50	1.00	1.00	17.00
Wendell	12.00	2.00	3.00	2.00	1.00	1.00	1.00	1.00	23.00
White Oak	20.00	5.00	5.00	8.00	2.00	2.00	1.50	2.00	45.50
Wilson's Mills	15.00	5.00	5.00	10.00	3.00	3.00	2.00	5.00	48.00
Total	958.00	241.25	300.50	405.25	115.50	123.00	70.25	141.75	2363.25
Pledges for 1909	914.00	235.00	348.00	385.00	94.25	120.75	61.00	......	2158.00

N. B. Churches not represented at a Roll-call for Pledges were put down the same amount as last year.

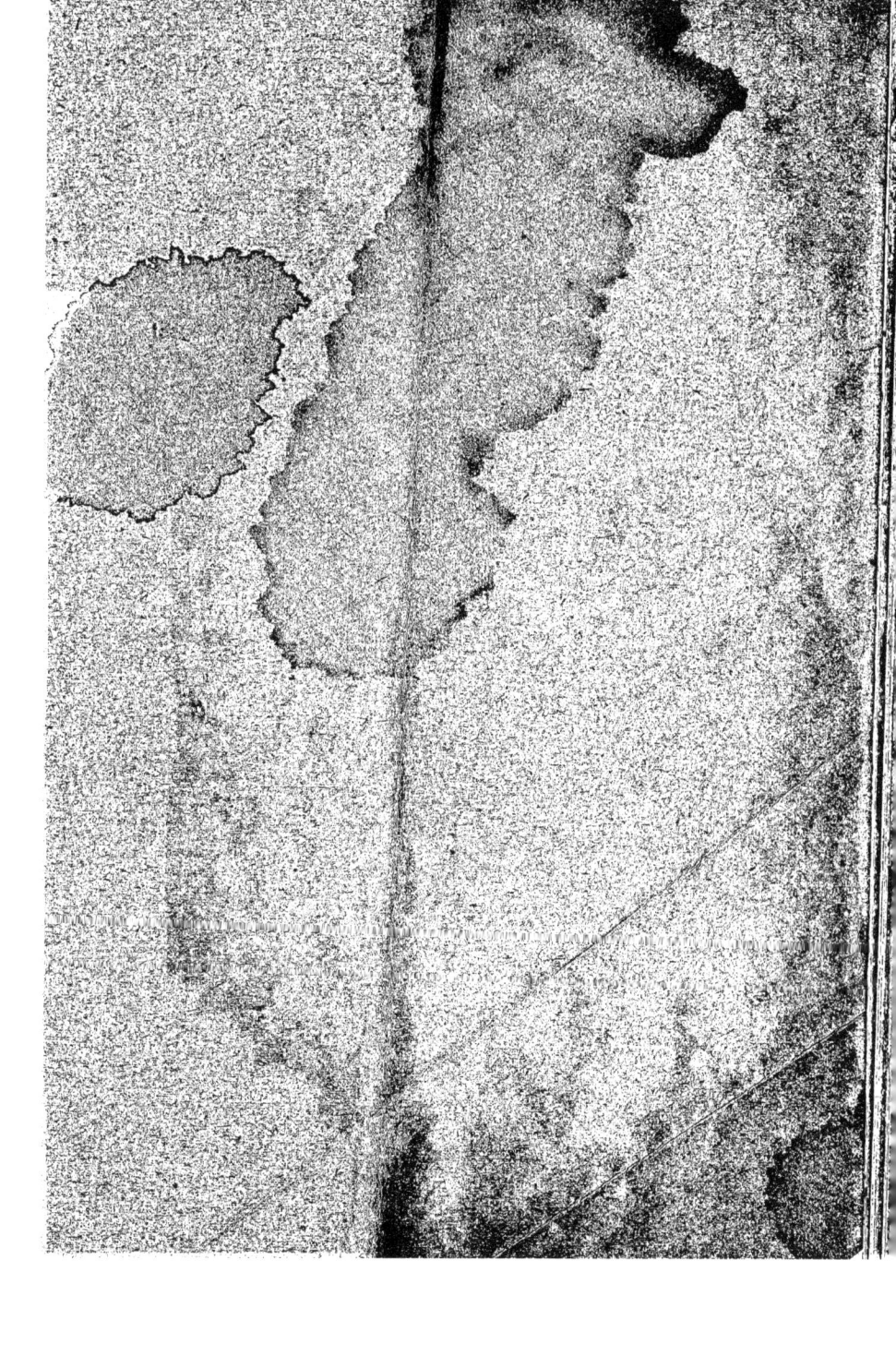

MINUTES

OF THE

EIGHTH SESSION

OF THE

JOHNSTON COUNTY

BAPTIST ASSOCIATION,

HELD WITH

WHITE OAK BAPTIST CHURCH,

NOVEMBER 9th, 10th and 11th, 1910.

The next session will be held with Middlesex Baptist Church, at Middlesex, N. C., beginning Wednesday after the first Sunday in November, 1910.

To preach Introductory Sermon—A. C. Hamby. Alternate—T. H. King.

OFFICERS.

Moderator—R. H. Gower...............................Clayton, N. C.
Vice-Moderator—A. A. Pippin........................Wakefield, N. C.
Clerk—T. J. Lassiter................................Smithfield, N. C.
Treasurer—T. J. Lassiter...........................Smithfield, N. C.
Historian—R. W. Horrell.............................Selma, N. C.

Goldsboro, N. C.
Nash Brothers, Printers and Binders
1 9 1 0

MINUTES

OF THE

EIGHTH SESSION

OF THE

JOHNSTON COUNTY

BAPTIST ASSOCIATION,

HELD WITH

WHITE OAK BAPTIST CHURCH,

NOVEMBER 9th, 10th and 11th, 1910.

The next session will be held with Middlesex Baptist Church, at Middlesex, N. C., beginning Wednesday after the first Sunday in November, 1910.

To preach Introductory Sermon—A. C. Hamby. Alternate—T. H. King.

OFFICERS.

Moderator—R. H. Gower.............................Clayton, N. C.
Vice-Moderator—A. A. Pippin......................Wakefield, N. C.
Clerk—T. J. Lassiter..............................Smithfield, N. C.
Treasurer—T. J. Lassiter..........................Smithfield, N. C.
Historian—R. W. Horrell...........................Selma, N. C.

EXECUTIVE COMMITTEE.

J. M. Beaty, Chairman..................................Smithfield, N C.
J. H. Boon, ...Benson, N. C.   J. F. Pool............Clayton, N. C.
J. T. Holt......Wilson's Mills, N. C.   Alonzo Parrish........Benson, N. C.

Goldsboro, N. C.
Nash Bros, Printers and Binders.
1910

SUNDAY SCHOOL COMMITTEE.

T. J. Lassiter...................... Smithfield, N. C.
B. F. Hassell...................... Selma, N. C.
J. T. Holt........................ Wilson's Mills, N. C.
Mrs. M. D. Thomas................. Clayton, N. C., R. F. D. No. 2.
Miss Christine Gower.............. Clayton, N. C.

CHAIRMEN STANDING COMMITTEES.

State Missions—T. H. King.
Home Missions—R. W. Horrell.
Foreign Missions—T. B. Justice.
Orphanage—J. W. Smith.
Education, Ministerial—A. C. Hamby.

Aged Ministers Relief—J. W. Nobles
Sunday Schools—T. J. Lassiter.
Periodicals—George H. Johnson.
Temperance—T. J. Hood.
Woman's Work—S. C. Hilliard.

LIST OF PASTORS.

D. D. Edwards ....Cary.
R. P. Ellington...........Wake Forest.
J. B. Eller .... Wake Forest.
N. H. Gibbs................ Benson.
R. W. Horrell ....Selma.
S. C. Hilliard ....Wake Forest.
A. C. Hamby.............. Clayton.
T. J. Hood........Goldsboro, r.f.d. 4

W. M. Huggins. .. ..Wilson.
George H. Johnson...... .....Kenly.
T. B. Justice................ Benson.
T. H King ....Smithfield.
J. W. Nobles ..,...... .....Wendell.
A. A. Pippin............... Wakefield.
J. W. Smith .... Wilson's Mills.
B. Townsend .... Broadway.

DELEGATES AND VISITORS ENROLLED.

Antioch—J. W. Corbett, M. C. Hinton, W. H. Maden and G. R. Whitley.
Bailey—James P. Underwood, Jr., and James P. Underwood, Sr.
Baptist Centre—W. H. Hardee.
Beaty Chapel—Neill M. Easom.
Benson—Jesse McLamb, Jr.
Bethesda—D. L. Jones, L. B. Smith, J. E. Smith, J. J. Wallace and W. B.
    Wallace.
Bethel—Perry Barnes, J. H. Bell and W. T. Sullivan.
Bethany—Moses Creech, W. S. Earp and Arthur Price.
Calvary—J. K. Hudson and J. M. Johnson.
Clayton—C. W. Carter, E. L. Hinton, D. J. Thurston, J. M. Turley, M. G.
    Gulley, B. A. Hocutt, Charles Carroll, and D. L. Barbour.
Clyde's Chapel—J. H. Johnson, C. I. Johnson, W. B. Medlin and J. H. Nowell.
Carter's Chapel—Preston Mozingo and Gray Easom.
Corinth—H. V. Andrews, J. B. Woodard and N. G. Williamson.
Four Oaks—R. A. Bain and J. B. Creech.
Kenly—George H. Johnson.
Lee's Chapel—J. L. Driver, G. G. Driver and J. T. Ellis.
Micro—Leonard Pace.
Mount Moriah—C. Taylor Pool, Icana Pool, Carl Barbour, Roy Baucom,
    N. R. Pool and J. F. Pool.
New Bethel—George W. Bryan.
Nobles Chapel—J. H. Flowers.
Pauline—Manly Baker, W. B. Joyner and H. B. Moore.
Pinkney Chapel—Joe Davis, and Neppie Davis.
Pisgah—Marion Johnson, Egbert R. Jones and Effie Jones.
Princeton—W. I. Pearce.
Selma—R. E. Richardson.
Shiloh—J. F. Hardee.
Smithfield—J. M. Beaty, G. L. Jones and T. J. Lassiter.
Thanksgiving— —. —. Murphey.
Wendell—L. M. Knott and E. V. Richardson.
White Oak—Jesse Wall, J. W. Barnes, L. W. Green, J. B. Murphrey, A. L.
    Batton, W. A. Mitchell, J. B. O'Neal and J. M. Eason.
Wilson's Mills—W. H. Ellis and J. T. Holt.
Pastors—A. C. Hamby, Worley Creech, D. D. Edwards, R. W. Horrell, T. H.
    King, T. B. Justice, A. A. Pippin, J. W. Smith, George H. Johnson,
    T. J. Hood.

PROCEEDINGS.

WHITE OAK BAPTIST CHURCH,
Wednesday, November 9, 1910.

· The Association met with the White Oak Baptist church Wednesday, November 9, 1910, at 11 o'clock. The introductory sermon was preached by Rev. T. B. Justice. Text: 2 Kings 4:40.

The Association was called to order by the Moderator, R. H. Gower. The Clerk being absent, T. H. King was asked to act as clerk *pro tem.* The following officers were elected:

Moderator—R. H. Gower.
Vice-Moderator—A. A. Pippin.
Clerk—T. J. Lassiter.
Historian—R. W. Horrell.
Treasurer—T. J. Lassiter.

The following visiting brethren were invited to seats in the body: Revs. J. S. Farmer, J. M. Hilliard and W. D. Poe.

The Moderator appointed the following committees:

Credentials—Roy Baucom and J. M. Green.
Finance—N. R. Pool, Gray Easom and V. R. Turley.
Periodicals—J. T. Holt, J. M. Turley and J. S. Driver.
Temperance—J. M. Beaty, Worley Creech and W. B. Joyner.
Old Ministers' Relief—R. W. Horrell, M. G. Gulley and G. R. Whitley.

On motion, the Association adjourned till 1:30 p. m. Benediction by Rev. D. D. Edwards.

AFTERNOON SESSION.

The Moderator called the Association to order at the appointed hour.

The pastor and deacons of White Oak church were appointed a committee on religious services.

Rev. G. H. Johnsón, a new pastor, was recognized and welcomed.

The report on Periodicals was submitted by Bro. J. T. Holt as follows:

REPORT ON PERIODICALS.

What we know has something to do with what we are; for what we believe is based on knowledge if we believe the truth. As a man thinketh in his heart so is he; because the mind leads the man.

In the wisdom of God nothing is better to lead the mind than the written word, therefore, he gives us the Bible and the periodicals that are men-

tioned in this report, and the rest of the acts of the children of Israel, are
they not written therein?

As long as God works, history continues, and we hear the Macedonian cry
in the Foreign Mission Journal, we have a knowledge of His work in
Jerusalem and in Judea through the Biblical Recorder, and the sweet story
of Moses being found in the bulrushes in different sections of the State
is told in Charity and Children. Our own Church Messenger tells something of our work in this Association.

God's Word tells us how and where, these tell us who and when, and
since what we read has so much to do with what we believe, and what we
believe so much to do with what we are, we beg that you read these things.

J. T. HOLT,
J. M. TURLEY,
Committee.

Pending a motion to adopt, the Moderator recognized Bro. Holt
who spoke to the report. Rev. J. S. Farmer, of the *Biblical Recorder,*
addressed the Association Interesting remarks were made also by
Revs. A. C. Hamby and T. J. Hood. The report was unanimously
adopted.

Bro. G. E. Lineberry, Educational Secretary of the Baptist State
Convention, and Prof. W. J. Ferrell, of Meredith College, were recognized and welcomed.

The report on Temperance was read by Bro. J. M. Beaty.

REPORT ON TEMPERANCE.

We rejoice at the great progress of the cause of temperance in our State.
We re-affirm our devotion to this cause. We enter our protest against the
flagrant violation of the Prohibition Law in our State and call upon our
officials to enforce this law. We call upon all good citizens to do all in
their power to have the law enforced.

We condemn the near-beer saloons about us. They are places of evil
influence. Generally they live in violation of law. All over the State they
have been the centers of crime. The fact that they pay taxes is no excuse
for their existence. We call upon our people to create greater temperance
sentiment. Let us teach it around our firesides and everywhere else we can
teach it. Let us live it. Let us give the cause our moral and financial
support.

J. M. BEATY,
WORLEY CREECH,
W. B. JOYNER,
Committee.

On motion to adopt, remarks were made by J. M. Beaty, J. M.
Hilliard and T. B. Justice. The report was adopted.

Rev. R. W. Horrell read the report on Old Ministers' Relief as
follows:

REPORT ON AGED MINISTERS' RELIEF.

The Ministerial Relief Board located at Durham exists for a most noble
purpose, and is run with the least possible expense. So sacred, so holy is
the work of this Board, that none of its officers feel inclined to accept re-
muneration for any service they render. The orphan child appeals to us
from the point of future possibility, as well as present dependence. The
aged minister appeals from the point of service rendered. They have spent

their days of strength for a bare living, and the shadows find them without support for themselves or loved ones. About thirty-five of these noble soldiers of the cross are now receiving insufficient aid from the Board. For lack of funds the Board can give from forty to one hundred dollars only to each of those now receiving aid, and there are many others who should be helped. Your committee would appeal to all the churches for a more liberal support for this very important object.

Respectfully submitted,

R. W. HORRELL,

G. R. WHITLEY,

M. G. GULLEY,

Committee.

R. W. Horrell and G. E. Lineberry addressed the Association after which pledges were taken and the report adopted.

The following committees were announced:

State Missions—A. C. Hamby, Jas. P. Underwood and J. M. Johnson.

Foreign Missions—T. H. King, N. M. Easom and W. T. Sullivan.

Orphanage—A. A. Pippin, W. S. Earp and M. C. Hinton.

To Nominate an Executive Committee, Delegates to State and Southern Baptist Conventions and Member of State Mission Board—C. W. Carter, Marion Johnson and J. E. Smith.

Petitionary Letters—R. W. Horrell, T. B. Justice and A. C. Hamby.

Place and Preachers—J. J. Wallace, J. B. Oneal and J. F. Hardee.

After announcements, the Association adjourned.

NIGHT SERVICE.

At 7:30 p. m. Rev. T. H. King preached, after which three deacons of White Oak church were ordained.

THURSDAY—Morning Session.

Devotional exercises were conducted by Bro. Geo. H. Johnson.

Bro. Archibald Johnson, editor of *Charity and Children,* was recognized and welcomed.

The report of Building Committee was read by J. M. Beaty.

REPORT OF BUILDING COMMITTEE.

We have been able to do but little in building the past year for want of funds. There has been work done and we have given encouragement and help as far as possible to it. Two hundred dollars was secured through Rev. Livingston Johnson for Middlesex church from the Sunbeam funds of the State. At Bailey the church building has been hulled in and is being used for sevices. Your committee borrowed one hundred dollars to give to this church to do what has been done on the building. At Pinkney the church has secured a lot and the rough lumber for their building. They have asked cs for some help. Pine Level church had a new lot given them and have secured some lumber and raised the sills for a new church. They too are expecting some help from us. Besides the above points, we are asked to help build a new church near Johnson's Cross Roads this winter. We recommend that the churches increase their pledges as much as possible for next year for church building.   Respectfully submitted,

J. M. BEATY,
J. T. HOLT,
J. F. POOL,
J. H. BOON,
ALONZO PARRISH,
Committee.

Pending a motion to adopt, Bro. Beaty spoke of the needs of church building funds in this Association. Remarks were also made by A. A. Pippin, G. H. Johnson and R. W. Horrell. Pledges were taken and the report adopted.

The Moderator recognized and welcomed Bro. Livingston Johnson, Corresponding Secretary of the Baptist State Convention.

The report of the Executive Committee was read by Bro. Beaty.

REPORT OF EXECUTIVE COMMITTEE.

Your committee cannot report a great year's work done yet still some progress has been made. The work at almost all places is developing and at some churches good meetings have been held and good numbers have joined us. Several meetings have been arranged for to be held between now and December 15th. Rev. T. B. Justice has had charge of the work at Pisgah, Four Oaks and Blackman's Grove. Rev. R. W. Horrell has served at Parrish Memorial, Pinkney, Pine Level and Brown School House. Rev. George H. Johnson since last spring has preached at Kenly, Bailey, Bethel and Oliver's Grove. Rev. T. J. Hood has preached at Sardis and Woodard School House, Pauline and for the past few months at Hood's Grove. For several months Rev. J. W. Smith has supplied for us at Micro, Benson's Grove, Pleasant Grove, Trinity and Calvary. Live Oak has been supplied with different preachers and has not had a regular pastor. We have had considerable trouble in securing regular pastors for several of the churches but have done the best we could in arranging for supply work. We recommend that the churches of the Association pledge and raise as much as possible that we may not be so heavy a burden on the State Mission Board.   Respectfully submitted,

J. M. BEATY,
J. T. HOLT,
J. F. POOL,
ALONZO PARRISH,
J. H. BOON,
Committee.

The report on State Missions was read by Bro. A. C. Hamby.

REPORT ON STATE MISSIONS.

The State Mission Board has employed this year on mission fields 148 missionaries. These are to receive for their services $37,000.00. They have collected on their fields $56,000.00. There are 25 houses of worship which have been completed this year, and 68 others under construction. The missionaries report 325 meetings held. They report 2,860 conversions, and 1,951 baptisms. There have been 11 churches organized.

A great portion of North Carolina is mission territory, perhaps sixty per cent. The section covered by the Johnston Association is largely a mission field. The Association is composed of forty churches. These churches with a membership of 3,491 pledged one year ago $914 for State Missions. This is an average of 26.9 cents per member—a very good showing as compared with some other Associations. But we cannot afford to compare ourselves with others. We must think of what the need and the opportunity demand of us and of what God expects of us. We may not give less this coming year than during the past; we cannot afford to pledge "the same as last year"; we must make an advance. Retrenchment is suicidal to the churches and to the Kingdom of God; the "same as last year" is the verge of a retreat. Financial advance in missions is the only road to life, growth and success for the churches and for the Baptist cause. If the ocean should never give back any water to the springs they would soon run dry, the rivers would cease to flow, the ocean itself would become a hollow waste, putrid with the decadence of once living forms. The individual or church that ceases to be missionary in act will soon dry up, in fact, and leave nothing but an unsavory odor to mark a former existence, as witness the non-missionary branch which left us in 1832. A word to the wise is sufficient. Be missionary or give up the hope of our calling.

Respectfully submitted,
A. C. HAMBY,
For Committee.

These reports being considered together, on motion to adopt, the Moderator recognized Bro. Hamby, who presented Bro. Livingston Johnson. Bro. Johnson made a great speech on State Missions. Pledges were then taken and the reports adopted.

After a statement by Bro. Beaty about the needs of the church at Bailey a cash collection of $14.49 cents was taken and turned over to Bro. J. P. Underwood, Sr.

The Committee on Petitionary Letters made the following report:

Your Committee on Petitionary Letters beg leave to report that only one church makes application for membership, to-wit: Beaty Chapel, located in the southern part of Smithfield, and represented by Bro. N. M. Easom. After investigation the committee recommend that said church be received as a member of this Association.

Respectfully submitted,
R. W. HORRELL,
T. B. JUSTICE,
A. C. HAMBY,
Committee.

On motion, the report was adopted and Beaty Chapel was received and the right hand of fellowship extended to Bro. N. M. Easom, delegate from this church.

The following committees were announced:

Education—L. T. Royall, D. J. Thurston and J. W. Smith.
Sunday Schools—Geo. H. Johnson, Geo. W. Bryan and R. E. Richardson.
Home Missions—T. B. Justice, T. J. Hood and H. V. Bunch.
Woman's Work—T. H. King, Carl Barbour and Effie Jones.

The Association adjourned till 1:30. Benediction by Bro. Hamby.

AFTERNOON SESSION.

The body met at 1:30 and was opened with prayer by Bro. R. W. Horrell.

The report on Foreign Missions was called for and read by Bro. T. H. King.

REPORT ON FOREIGN MISSIONS.

"Into all the world" is the motto of Baptists. Until "the knowledge of the Lord shall cover the earth as the waters cover the sea," ours will be an unfinished task. This is a day of great Missionary endeavor. "Hitherto the Lord hath led us." He will be with us to the end of the world. By His providence, age-long barriers have been removed, iniquities and hostile customs, hoary with antiquity are falling to destruction; people who have long sat in darkness are calling for light. As the dissemination of Greek language and culture prepared the way for the coming of Jesus, so the spirit of democracy is making ready the people of the earth for the gospel of Christ. The Foreign Mission Board of the Southern Baptist Convention is doing Mission work in China, Africa, Japan, Italy, Brazil, Mexico and Argentina. In every field the work is prosperous, the workers hopeful and anxious for reinforcements to meet the increasing opportunities.

We have now on the fields 286 Missionaries, more than 700 workers, 300 churches, about 20,000 members, 350 Sunday schools with an enrollment of 2,000. There were 3,223 baptisms on the field last year. We have 128 day schools with 3,300 pupils; nine schools for boys, with 428 pupils; 13 boarding schools for girls, with 600 pupils; two colleges, with 100 students; four women's training schools, with 37 students, and eight theological seminaries, with 176 students, making a total of 164 schools with an attendance of about 55,000. We have four large, well-equipped printing establishments, and among our Missionaries are 13 physicians and a number of hospitals and medical dispensaries. Our contributions last year amounted to $501,-000.00, of which North Carolina Baptists paid $40,000.00 and Johnston county paid $307.65. Ten years ago Southern Baptists paid $140,000.00; this year $501,000.00. Ten years ago we had 1,341 baptisms on the field; this year 3,223. Then 227 workers; now 700. The demands upon us are enormous. At every one of our stations they are calling for more helpers. Thirty-two new missionaries have just been appointed, three of whom are from North Carolina. "It is day-break everywhere." "The harvest truly is great, but the laborers are few." Respectfully submitted,

T. H. KING,
GRAY EASOM,
Committee.

Pending a motion to adopt the report was discussed by T. H. King and R. W. Horrell. Pledges were taken and the report adopted. Following the taking of the pledges, Bro. Hamby submitted a few pointed remarks on the subject of Foreign Missions.

Bro. A. A. Pippin read the report on the Orphanage.

REPORT ON THE ORPHANAGE.

We have long ago realized, we lose nothing by our continual efforts in sustaining our Orphanage at Thomasville. We have gained greatly for our denomination in the saving of the orphan children of our State. And also in the accumulation of property for our Baptist cause. The Orphanage at present, with its Endowment, buildings and equipments, is worth not less than $250,000.00.

It has been crowded to overflow, from its earliest existence. If every Baptist would become a regular contributor, it would soon be able to meet all the demands upon it.

We have now about five hundred Sunday schools that take monthly collections. May the time soon come when there will not be a Baptist Sunday school that does not take regular collections for our Orphanage. Let us all remember that Thanksgiving is Orphanage day. Our churches and schools should plan to make the coming day the most noble in our history.

To the Orphanage we can give our prayers, our hopes and our means. Before it and us lies a greater work. The cry of the homeless still is heard. Young lives growing to man and womanhood is still to be seen. So long as this may be, our duty will not be done.

We also recommend that the Sunday schools take a sufficient number of copies of Charity and Children to place one in each family represented in the school. Respectfully submitted,

A. A. PIPPIN,
W. S. EARP,
Committee.

On motion to adopt, the motion was discussed by Archibald Johnson and J. M. Hilliard. Pledges were taken and the report adopted.

The report on Education was read by Prof. L. T. Royall.

REPORT ON EDUCATION.

The education of our people holds an important place in our church work and should receive our most earnest support. All affairs pertaining to church and State depend upon the ability of the people to think and act correctly. There should be great effort in every church to advance the cause of Christian education.

In our county much has been done for the cause of education. Special tax districts have been formed, thus enabling the communities to erect large convenient buildings and equip them so that efficient work can be done. Our high schools are aiding in the work to a great extent in sending out teachers and preparing boys and girls for college. We heartily commend the movement to endow Meredith College and pledge our support.

Let us as Baptists realize our responsibility and give our liberal support and patronage to our Associational schools and our colleges, Meredith and Wake Forest, so that our best young men and women may be better fitted to render the best service for our Master's Kingdom.

Respectfully submitted,
L. T. ROYALL,
For Committee.

On motion to adopt this report, Prof. Ferrell spoke on Education and Meredith College. Pledges were taken for Ministerial Education and the report was adopted.

The Committee on Place and Preachers reported that the next session would meet at Shiloh, with A. C. Hamby appointed to preach the introductory sermon and T. H. King alternate. The Association then adjourned with prayer by Bro. Justice.

At the night service Bro. R. W. Horrell preached.

FRIDAY—Morning Session.

Devotional exercises were conducted by Bro. J. W. Smith, after which the Association was called to order by the Moderator.

Bro. Pippin made a motion that the report on place for holding the next session be reconsidered. Remarks were made by Brethren Beaty, King, Justice and the Moderator. The motion prevailed. A motion was made by T. H. King to substitute Smithfield in the place of Shiloh as the place of meeting for next session. A motion was also made to amend the report to substitute Middlesex as the place of meeting. After remarks it was decided to hold the next session at Middlesex. A. C. Hamby was appointed to preach the introductory sermon.

The report on Sunday schools was read by Bro. Geo. H. Johnson as follows:

REPORT ON SUNDAY SCHOOLS.

When on earth Jesus was the one most fully conscious of the power of teaching. In His works we read about His sitting in synagogues, in boats, upon mountain tops and in homes teaching His gospel and its power unto salvation. He was also conscious that His gospel must finally triumph through its teachings by His followers. So, when about to leave them He said: "All power is given unto me in heaven and in earth. Go ye therefore, and teach all nations—to observe all things whatsoever I have commanded you."

Teaching Jesus Christ must precede faith in Him. How can they believe on him of whom they know nothing? And not only must faith come to us from learning of Him, but our faith grows stronger and more powerful as our knowledge of Him increases. God's Word is the foundation of our religion, and for its teaching we have become to look to our Sunday schools. We look to them to teach all of God's Word to oll, both young and old, a lamp to their feet, a light to their pathway, and the unconquerable sword of the spirit with which they are to battle against all the temptations of the wicked one.

But the teaching of the Book is not all the good that our Sunday schools are doing. Five hundred of them are making monthly contributions to our Orphaange at Thomasville. So in them our people are not only being taught to be hearers of the Word but doers as well.

Our Sunday school slogan before the world is: all the people in the Sunday school, and before the church all the Sunday school in the church saved and to serve, and all the church working and serving in the Sunday school. Slowly but steadily we are climbing toward the top of the mountain. New schools are being organized and churches are growing out of them. And then here and there a weak church establishes a Sunday school and takes on new life itself.

The field of the Sunday school has grown to be large and white for laborers. The power of its teaching for good to both church and state is incalculable and unlimited. Then let us arise to the fullness of our opportunities in it. Let us pray for it without ceasing. Let us work for its advancement as true, devoted followers of the Master. Let us arise, stretch every nerve and press with vigor on.

Respectfully submitted,
GEO. H. JOHNSON,
GEO. W. BRYAN,
Committee.

Pending the motion to adopt, Bro. E. L. Middleton, Sunday School Secretary, made a very fine address on The Needs of Our Sunday Schools. Pledges were then taken and the report adopted.

On motion of T. J. Lassiter, a Sunday School committee of five was appointed to prepare a program and arrange for a Sunday School Convention to be held sometime during the coming year, and to make efforts to get every Sunday School in the Association to send delegates. The following is the committee: T. J. Lassiter, Smithfield; J. T. Holt, Wilson's Mills; B. F. Hassell, Selma; Mrs. M. D. Thomas, White Oak; Miss Christine Gower, Clayton.

The report on Home Missions was called for and read by Bro. T. B. Justice.

REPORT ON HOME MISSIONS.

As a lawyer becomes identified with the interest of his client, so do we when appointed to write a report on any phase of our Conventional work, find ourselves magnifying that particular branch of our numerous objects. So I find myself reading Acts 1st and 8th "But ye shall be witnesses unto me both in Jerusalem and in all Judea and in Samaria and to the uttermost parts of the earth," and thereby fixing our territory from our doorsteps to the far away fields on distant continents. The divine commission applied to one feature of the work as much as to another. However, that each feature may be under the immediate supervision of zealous and Godly men, we have a State Mission Board to direct and press forward the work which is confined to North Carolina—the Home Mission Board which has a broader scope, and a Foreign Mission Board which supervises the work in foreign countries. My duty is to turn my telescope on the great battlefield where the Home Board is struggling to wrest men and women from the clutches of sin.

In the limits of the Home Board's work is included all the territory in the bounds of the Southern Baptist Convention and also the Island of Cuba and the Panama or Canal Zone.

The character of the work is ten fold, viz.: Aiding weak churches, sustaining mountain mission schools, doing evangelistic work, mission work in cities, church building, looking after foreigners who come to our country, Indians, cooperative work for the benefit of the negroes, preaching the gospel, supporting schools, building churches in Cuba and general missionary work on the Isthmus of Panama.

Weak Churches.

The aiding of weak churches is sometimes done by extending aid direct from the Board, and sometimes joining forces with the State Board in each State, for the most part to help to secure pastors.

Mountain Schools,

There are twenty-seven Baptist Mission schools. All of these have been, and many are still aided wholly or in part, by this Board. They are scattered along the Blue Ridge mountains, from Virginia to Alabama, Virginia has one, North Carolina eight, Kentucky three, Tennessee five, South Carolina two, and Alabama four.

Evangelism.

They have 150 teachers, over 5,000 pupils and own $500,000.00 worth of property. The board now has twelve evangelists preaching in destitute places from thronged cities to brush arbors in the back woods.

There are about one million foreigners who come to make their homes with us in America every year. These are Italians, Poles, Hebrews, Germans, etc. They drift southward more and more every year and unless they be christianized, will become reckless and lawless, anarchistic and a menace to society and good government.

The Indians.

There are somewhere near 300,000 Indians in our territory. 100,000 of whom are in Oklahoma and among these we have 18 working missionaries and churches and in many places parsonages.

- Negroes.

There are about 10,000,000 of negroes in the South and more of them are Baptists than belong to all other denominations. There is a national Baptist Convention and we co-operate with their Board in aiding the negroes who are trying to develop their spiritual lives and christian characters. The work has been satisfactory and will probably continue its present policy.

Cuba.

There are about two million people in Cuba, mainly of Spanish descent and speaking the Spanish language. We began work there in 1886. There are 19 ordained ministers and ten other workers, teachers, etc.

We have 22 organized churches and 25 preaching stations and 1,315 members. The work is promising.

Panama Canal Zone is a ten mile wide strip of land separating the Atlantic and Pacific oceans. It is 47 miles long and the United States has owned it since 1904. The canal is planned to be completed by 1915. Baptists began work there in 1905, one year after the United States flag was unfurled there. Rev. J. L. Wise has two ordained helpers and five native helpers in this work.

There are 50,000 people living there beside a large number working on the canal. We have seven churches and six mission stations and a membership of 519.

Their per capita contributions last year was $7.16. We recommend "The Home Field," by which means we may keep informed as to the work and trust that knowledge of the situation will prompt us to do our full duty.

Respectfully submitted,

T. B. JUSTICE,

For Committee.

Pending a motion to adopt the report was discussed by Bro. Justice. Pledges were taken and the report adopted.

It was decided to go ahead and finish up the work of the Association before adjourning for dinner and the report on Woman's Work was called for and presented by Bro. King as follows:

- REPORT ON WOMAN'S WORK.

"Wheresoever this gospel shall be preached in the whole world, this that this woman hath done shall be told for a memorial of her." The work of the women of North Carolina and our Association should be told for a memorial of them. It is their monument to Christ. The Woman's Missionary Union of North Carolina is a potent factor in all our denominational work. There are societies in all our town and city churches, with very few exceptions, and in almost all of our progressive country churches. The Young Ladies' Auxiliaries, Boys Bands and Sunbeams, all of which are under the auspices of the Woman's Missionary Union, are doing an important work in developing the missionary spirit among the children and young people. The contributions from the Sunbeams have gone to the Church Building Fund for three years. The beautiful Asheboro church, and the church at Swan Quarter, the only Baptist church in Hyde county, were made possible by the Sunbeams. This year all the offering of the Woman's Missionary Union for State Missions are used in the Church Building Fund. In this Association we have only five or six working societies. Our ladies held a very interesting meeting at Benson this year. Their next meeting will be held at Selma. A new society has been organized in Middlesex. The societies of this Association gave last year for missions $290.00.

We recommend that societies be organized in every church and that the brethren lend their encouragement and help. We further recommend that every church, whether it has a society or not, send representatives to the Associational meeting in Selma next year.

Respectfully submitted,
T. H. KING,
For Committee.

The report was adopted after a few remarks by Bro. King.

MISCELLANEOUS BUSINESS.

The following Executive Committee was elected for the ensuing year: J. M. Beaty, J. T. Holt, J. F. Pool, Alonzo Parrish and J. H. Boon.

A resolution of thanks was offered and unanimously adopted by a rising vote as follows:

Resolved, That the delegates and visitors attending this Association congratulate the White Oak church on their beautiful new church building and that we express our great appreciation of the magnificent hospitality and the generous entertainment extended to us, assuring the brethren, sisters and friends that we shall long remember these three days' spent among you.

Bro. V. R. Turley submitted the report of the Finance Committee which will be found on another page. Report received.

Upon motion of Bro. Justice the Clerk's salary was fixed at $15.00.

The Clerk was instructed to have printed and distributed the usual number of minutes among the churches.

At this point a collection of $6.64 was taken to supplement the minute fund.

The following resolution was offered by Bro. Justice which was adopted unanimously:

Whereas, It is rumored that the next legislature will be asked to provide a bond issue of one million dollars for the furnishing and equipment of our State Colleges; therefore, be it

Resolved, That while we welcome every sentiment and would not antagonize any reasonable appropriation to increase advantages of the common and high school; we, the Johnston County Association, declare it to be the sense of this body that the said bond issue would be an injustice to our denominational Colleges, and altogether unwise and inexpedient as a matter of public policy.

Bro. T. H. King was elected as a member of the State Mission Board.

Bro. A. A. Pippin was named as delegate to Southern Baptist Convention.

Brethren T. B. Justice, A. C. Hamby and J: T. Holt were named as delegates to Baptist State Convention.

Upon motion of Bro. King, the churches were instructed to prepare their church letters and send them to the Associational Clerk, T. J. Lassiter, Smithfield, N. C.; by November first in each and every year, so that the Clerk may prepare a digest of the work of the churches for the year and have it ready by the time the Association meets. The motion prevailed.

The business of the body having been completed, a motion to adjourn was carried and the benediction was pronounced by Bro. T. B. Justice.

WOMAN'S MISSION UNION.

The Woman's Missionary Union of the Johnston County Association held its seventh annual and third separate meeting on November 2nd, 1910, with the Society at Benson. The attendance was not so large as the bright balmy day would justify. We found loving hands had preceded us to the church and had it comfortable, bright and cheery, with friends awaiting our arrival. The devotional exercises were conducted by our Vice-President, Mrs. Ashley Horne, reading for our instruction the 8th chapter of Luke. Mrs. Justice, wife of the Benson pastor, extended to all a most cordial welcome. In behalf of the society and visitors the Vice-President responded. One may expect to find the doors at the house wide open in the light of day, but to arrive at midnight, and find the doors thrown open, friends with warm greetings awaiting you, is hospitality, indeed. The first order of business was the roll call. Fourteen of the nineteen societies reported. Two new societies have been organized during the year. We were sorry to note a slight falling off in our financial report. Those of the strongest churches in the Association were pastorless during a part of last year, as a consequence all church work suffered. Now we hope to press forward with redoubled zeal. The total amount reported was $321.14.

The Vice-President's report of the general work in the Association was full of interest. She gave us lofty ideas, and enlarged plans for another year. The open conference which followed was informal and very helpful. Such important subjects as these were discussed:

"How to increase our membership," led by Mrs. Justice. She thinks the key to this is prayer and work.

"Our Gifts," led by Mrs. Beaty, who laid much stress on thought and prayer, then the gift.

"Personal Work," led by Mrs. Nowell, who gave us new and enlarged visions of personal work. We were reminded here of the words of Mrs. Browning: "Count that day lost, whose lowly setting sun, sees from thy hand no good deed done." For "in as much as ye have done it unto one of the least of these my brethren, ye have done it unto me." How many lost days have come into your life and mine?

Miss Bessie Ellis, ever faithful, told us of some personal work she was doing, visiting the sick and holding prayer-meeting. "Go thou and do likewise," is the command of the Savior.

"United prayer," led by Mrs. Moore. She gave us an earnest, thoughtful paper on this subject. All of these questions come home to us, and are worthy of much consideration.

State Missions and the Church Building Fund was emphasized by Mrs. Carter. The Vice-President talked to us of the work and needs of the Training School.

The dinner hour having now arrived, we turned aside for awhile, where we found many good things awaiting us.

The afternoon devotional exercises were conducted by Mrs. Nowell, reading for our lesson the 28th chapter of Matthew.

The Vice-President made Home Missions unusually interesting and instructive by the use of charts. Mrs. Horne also spoke of our Foreign work. The remainder of the afternoon the young ladies held sway. They are due much praise for the progress they have made. We older ones must look out, or we will be left far behind.

Miss Ione Gulley read a splendid paper on the Clayton Y. W. A. work.

Miss Foy Baucom spoke in behalf of the Sunbeam work, telling us of some of her methods of stimulating interest.

Miss Wynona Massey read an excellent paper on "Young Women in Missions."

Miss Lucy Pool stood bravely for the Royal Ambassadors, giving us some splendid ideas and helps for enlisting the boys.

The meeting at Benson was from several view points the best yet; our visions are broadening, our ideas were lofty, the talks and papers were instructive, were helpful. "Our hearts did burn within us as we talked by the way" and felt the presence and blessing of the Holy Spirit.

Our meeting next year will be with Selma.

At the evening service, we heard with pleasure and profit, Mr.

King, pastor of the Smithfield and Selma churches. The subject of his address was "Woman and the Kingdom," dividing it into three parts, Woman without Christ, Woman with Christ, and Woman for Christ. In behalf of the societies we thank Mr. King for his encouragement and promise of hearty co-operation: We also thank the organist, and Miss Jessamine Yelvington for the several solos she rendered.

Now let us turn our faces to the new year, with more hope, more love and more zeal. Mrs. C. W. Carter, Secretary.

FINANCIAL REPORT OF THE WOMAN'S MISSIONARY SOCIETY OF THE JOHNSTON COUNTY ASSOCIATION FOR YEAR ENDING OCTOBER, 1910.

SOCIETIES.	State M ss ons.	Home M ss ons.	Fore gn M ss ons.	Tra n ng Enlargement.	Margaret Home.	Expense Fund.	Tra n ng School Support.	Totals.
Smithfield	$21.95	$12.15	$12.90	$ 2.00	$.....	$ 1.00	$.....	$ 50.00
Benson	16.81	5.50	8.80	.....	.....	40	.....	31.51
Selma	2.75	2.80	3.80	2.25	.....	.....	.....	11.60
Clayton	50.00	30.00	30.00	4.00	.....	1.00	.....	115.00
Mount Moriah	2.00	11.30	16.60	90	.....	1.00	.....	31.80
Clyde's Chapel	55	70	70	.....	.....	19	.....	2.14
Micro	2.30	80	1.90	.....	.....	25	.....	5.25
Bethesda (New)	.....	.....	.....	.....	.....	.....	.....	.....
Wilson's Mills (New)	.....	.....	.....	.....	.....	.....	.....	.....
Clayton—Junior Union	2.35	1.70	5.20	.....	.....	20	.....	9.45
Mount Moriah Sunbeams	5.97	1.38	3.30	.....	.....	25	.....	10.90
Micro Sunbeams	1.30	28	1.28	.....	.....	.....	.....	2.86
Smithfield Sunbeams	4.00	3.55	5.50	.....	1.00	.....	.....	14.05
Clayton Y. W. A.	7.50	4.85	8.81	.....	.....	84	3.00	25.00
Mount Moriah RoyalAmbassadors	4.35	.....	1.23	.....	.....	.....	.....	5.58
Benson Sunbeams	1.00	2.00	3.00	.....	.....	.....	.....	6.00
Total	122.83	77.01	103.02	9.15	1.00	5.13	3.00	321.14

Constitution of the
Johnston County Baptist Association.

1. The Association shall be known as the Johnston County Baptist Association.
2. Its object shall be to extend the privileges of the Gospel and liberal culture to all the people within its bounds, and by hearty co-operation with the Baptist State Convention to help offer these privileges to all mankind in and out of its bounds, by the cordial co-operation of all the churches constituting this body.
3. It shall be composed of the pastors in active service in the Association and such delegates as shall be annually elected by the churches connected with it, each church being entitled to three delegates, unless the membership shall exceed fifty, and then an additional delegate for every twenty-five members, provided no church shall have more than eight delegates.
4. The New Hampshire Declaration of Faith shall be the summary of Divine Truth for determining questions of faith and order in this body, and the churches desiring membership in it must commit themselves to the substance of it, together with the covenant therewith submitted, and this Constitution.
5. This Association shall not have power, to annul the discipline or exercise authority over any church connected with it, but it may advise with and sever its connection with any church that neglects to preserve gospel order, or that treats with contempt the objects or advice of the Association.
6. Each church shall send to the annual meetings of the Association a letter (the blanks to be furnished by the clerk of the Association), carefully filled as per blank suggestions, stating the full work of the church for the year ending with the close of the month previous to the one in which the Association is held.
7. The Association shall foster State Missions, Home Missions, Foreign Missions, Christian Education, the Aged Ministers' Relief Board, the Thomasville Orphanage and the Sunday School Board, and each church shall be requested to contribute to the support of these objects annually.
8. Missions and education shall have precedence in their claims upon the consideration of this body in its regular sessions.
9. Whenever a church shall fail to be represented by delegates or letter at the annual sessions of the Association inquiry shall be made for the cause and efforts shall be made to induce such church to do its duty, and the effort shall be continued till the church is recovered or dropped from the roll.
10. The officers of the Association shall be a Moderator, a Vice-Moderator, a Clerk, a Treasurer and an Auditor, elected annually by ballot from among its members, to serve until their successors shall have been elected, and to perform the duties usual to such officers, namely, the Moderator, in presiding over the meetings, or the Vice-Moderator in his absence; the Clerk in recording and preserving minutes and other papers belonging to the body; the Treasurer in receiving and disbursing funds belonging to or entrusted to the body according to its will; the Auditor to examine the Treasurer's books at each meeting of the Association and report the same before adjournment.
11. The Association shall appoint annually an Executive Committee of five (5) from its members, who shall be entrusted with the prosecution of Missions in the Association and any other work for the interest of the Master's Kingdom which may be referred to them. This committee shall, as far as possible, co-operate with the State Mission Board in supplying the destitution in our territory, and between the meetings of the Association take such actions as may seem to them advisable for the advancement of its

interest. The committee shall present to the Association at its annual meeting a report of its proceedings, with the names of the missionaries supported on the field, time of service and details of their work, together with such recommendations as in the judgment of the committee the Association should follow in planning its subsequent work.

12. The annual sessions of the Association shall begin on Wednesday after the first Lord's Day in November at such place as may be chosen, and an introductory sermon shall be delivered on the first day of the session. Representatives from a majority of the churches constituting the Association shall be a quorum.

13. This Constitution may be amended at any annual session by a two-thirds vote of all the members present.

14. Provision shall be made at each annual session for a session of the Woman's Central Committee, and all other necessary encouragement offered for the enlargement of the organized work of the Woman's Missionary Societies in the local churches. The proceedings of the Woman's Central Committee shall be recorded as a part of the Minutes of the Association.

BY-LAWS.

1. The daily sessions of the Association shall be opened and closed with prayer.

2. Delegates shall be recognized by letters from their churches designating them as such.

3. The Moderator shall recognize corresponding messengers or the delegates of newly received churches by extending to them his right hand. ·

4. The report of the Executive Board and the Missionary work of the Association shall take precedence of all other business during the morning session of the second day of the annual session.

5. The Clerk shall record and read the proceedings when called for, superintend the publication and distribution of the Minutes, preserve a file of them, and have it present at each annual session, and deliver to his successor all papers belonging to the body.

6. Members desiring to speak shall first rise and address the Moderator; shall use the term "brother" in speaking to each other; shall not speak on the same subject more than twice without permission, and shall observe the courtesy that becomes Christians.

7. Members shall not absent themselves from the session without permission.

8. The roll of members shall be called at least once and absentees marked.

9. Corresponding messengers and visiting brethren shall be invited to seats, with privilege of speaking, but not of voting.

10. A copy of the Minutes shall be sent to the Secretary of the State Mission Board, the Secretary of the Southern Baptist Convention, the American Baptist Publication Society, 1420 Chestnut Street, Philadelphia; the Sunday School Board of the Southern Baptist Convention and the Thomasville Orphanage.

11. All questions of order not herein provided shall be decided by Kerfoot's Parliamentary Law.

FINANCE COMMITTEE'S REPORT.

We, the Finance Committee, have received and paid over to T. J. Lassiter, Treasurer, the amounts named in the table below.   Respectfully submitted,

N. R. POOL,
V. R. TURLEY,
GRAY EASOM, Committee.

CHURCHES.	Minutes and Clerk.	State Missions.	Home Missions.	Foreign Missions.	Sunday School Missions.	Ministerial Education.	Ministerial Relief.	Orphanage.	Church Building Fund.	Total.
.och	$1.20	$15.00	$ 1.50	$ 1.50	$ 1.00	$ 1.50	$ 2.50	$ 2.50	$ 2.00	$ 28.70
ey	30	2.00	50	50	50	1.00	1.00	1.00	1.00	7.80
:ist Centre	1.00	3.63	1.00	50	1.50	23	17	1.90	1.50	11.43
iany	1.15	5.00	2.50	2.00	1.00	1.00	1.50	4.30	2.00	21.45
iel	1.00	1.75	.....	1.00		50	.....	1.00	2.00	7.25
iesda	1.50	11.55	.....	.....	2.00	2.00	3.00	20.00	.....	40.05
ary	1.00	4.00	70	50	.....	1.00	.....	1.00	.....	8.20
er's Chapel	25	10.00	2.50	1.50	1.00	1.50	2.00	10.00	2.50	31.25
ton	4.00	114.57	.....	.....	.....	20.00	3.35	90.05	8.60	240.57
e's Chapel	1.00	10.00	4.00	4.00	1.00	1.00	3.00	5.00	1.50	30.50
nth	1.20	8.50	4.00	1.50	1.50	1.00	2.00	5.00	1.00	23.20
· Oaks	1.00	.....	.....	.....	.....	.....	.....	.....	2.50	3.50
ly	50	5.00	3.00	3.00	1.00	1.00	1.00	3.00	1.00	18.50
s Chapel	3.05	25.00	5.00	10.00	2.50	5.00	3.00	5.00	2.50	61.05
nt Moriah	2.00	24.58	97	3.19	6.00	5.00	.....	12.94	5.00	59.63
es' Chapel	1.00	5.00	1.00	1.00	50	1.00	1.00	2.00	1.50	14.00
ine	45	5.00	2.00	1.50	50	2.00	1.00	2.00	2.00	16.45
:ney Chapel	50	.....	1.00	1.00	50	1.00	50	2.00	4.00	10.50
ah	1.00	.....	.....	.....	.....	.....	.....	.....	4.00	5.00
ceton	70	5.20	1.00	.....	1.00	1.00	1.00	5.00	1.00	15.90
)h	50	2.50	1.52	01	1.00	3.00	2.50	2.50	1.00	14.53
iksgiving	1.00	5.00	1.00	1.00	50	1.00	1.00	1.00	1.00	12.50
te Oak	2.00	20.00	5.00	2.75	1.50	2.00	2.00	8.00	2.00	45.25
tal	27.30	284.23	35.69	36.45	24.50	53.23	31.52	184.19	49.60	727.21

I have received and paid out moneys as follows:

CHURCHES.	Minutes and Clerk.	State Missions.	Home Missions.	Foreign Missions.	Sunday School Missions.	Ministerial Education.	Ministerial Relief.	Orphanage.	Other Objects.	Church Building Fund.	Total.
Beaty Chapel......	$1.00	$ 1.00	$ 1.00	$ 1.00	$ 1.00	$ 1.00	$ 1.00	$ 1.00	$.....	$ 1.00	$ 9.00
Benson Grove......	50	......	......	......	50	......	......	......	......	1.00	2.00
Blackman's Grove..	1.00	......	......	......	......	......	......	......	......	......	1.00
Hood's Grove......	50	2.00	......	......	......	......	......	......	......	......	2.50
Live Oak..........	50	1.84	1.00	1.00	50	1.00	1.00	......	......	1.00	7.84
Micro	50	6.00	1.50	1.25	50	1.00	1.00	......	......	1.00	12.75
Middlesex	1.50	......	......	......	......	......	......	......	......	1.00	2.50
New Bethel........	2.25	17.50	......	......	1.00	1.00	2.00	......	......	......	23.75
Oliver's Grove.....	1.00	2.78	50	50	1.00	1.00	50	2.00	......	2.00	11.28
Parrish Memorial..	60	16.85	......	......	1.00	2.00	2.00	2.00	......	1.00	25.45
Pine Level........	1.00	......	......	......	......	......	......	......	......	......	1.00
Sardis	......	5.50	2.00	2.00	50	1.00	1.00	2.00	......	1.00	15.00
Smithfield	5.00	160.00	27.20	41.35	8.00	14.32	17.70	5.43	......	25.00	304.00
Wendell	1.40	12.00	3.77	......	1.00	1.00	2.31	3.03	......	......	24.51
Wilson's Mills......	......	15.00	......	......	2.00	3.00	3.00	......	......	5.00	28.00
Finance Committee (White-Oak) ..	27.30	284.23	35.69	36.45	24.50	53.23	31.52	184.19	......	49.60	727.21
G. W. Chestnut (Live Oak).....	......	5.00	......	......	......	1.00	1.00	2.00	......	1.00	10.00
Collection at Asso.	6.64	......	......	......	......	......	......	......	......	......	6.64
M. & L. Conference at Kenly......	......	6.89	......	......	......	......	......	......	......	......	6.89
Bethel	......	2.05	......	......	......	......	1.00	......	......	......	3.05
Will H. Lassiter Treasurer	1.51	192.21	52.82	73.90	2.40	9.00	10.60	18.29	16.65	38.70	416.0
Total amount rec'd	52.20	730.85	125.48	157.45	43.90	90.55	74.63	219.94	16.65	128.30	1640.4
Paid Walters Durham	......	730.85	125.48	157.45	43.90	90.55	74.63	......	......	......	1222.8
Paid S. H. Averitt	......	......	......	......	......	......	......	217.94	......	......	217.9
Balance on hand from 1910......	52.20	......	......	......	......	......	......	2.00	16.65	128.30	199.6

T. J. LASSITER, Treasurer.

CHURCH.	Pastor's Salary.	Building and Repairs.	Incidentals.	Sunday School Expense.	The Poor.	State Missions.	Home Missions.	Foreign Missions.	Sunday School Missions.	Orphanage.	Ministerial Education.	Ministerial Relief.	Minute Fund.	Church and Building Fund.	Other Objects.	Total.
Antioch	$62.00	$ 3.25	$ 10.00	$ 6.40	$	$15.00	$1.50	$1.50	$1.00	$2.50	$1.50	$2.50	$1.20	$2.00	$	100.35
Bailey	60.00	475.00		8.00		5.00	.50	.50	.50	1.00	1.00	1.00	.30	1.00		492.80
Baptist	50.00	20.00		12.18		5.00	1.00	1.00	1.00	5.00		1.00	1.00	1.50		90.00
Beaty	520.00	160.00	45.00	15.00		100.00	20.00	20.00	.50	25.00	5.00	12.56	1.00	1.00	12.40	91.18
Benson	25.00	75.00	1.00	6.00		6.00	2.50	2.00	1.00	2.00	1.00	1.50	.50	6.00		932.40
Benson's Grove	40.00			10.00	5.00	5.00	2.00		2.00	4.30	2.00	1.00	1.15	2.00		120.76
Bethany	30.00	6.85	6.00	10.00		5.00	5.00	5.00		20.00		3.00	1.00	2.00	5.00	131.45
Bethel	200.00		.30	2.63		25.00	5.00	5.00	2.00	8.00	4.00	2.50	1.00			62.50
Bethesda	100.00					20.00	4.00	5.50	2.00		20.00	20.00		8.60		291.35
Blackman's Grove						4.00			.50							151.43
Calvary																9.20
Clayton	685.48	105.35	121.15	81.44	12.24	225.00	67.17	76.57	14.89	135.00	20.00	10.00	4.00	2.50	130.15	1694.80
Carter's	40.00					10.00	2.50	2.50	1.75	10.00	1.00	3.00	1.00	1.50		83.00
Clyde's	100.00			1.60		10.00	4.00	4.00	1.50	5.00	1.00	3.00	1.00	2.50		131.10
Corinth	54.00	1.07				8.50	1.50	1.50	1.00	5.00	1.50	1.00		1.00		78.27
Four Oaks	100.00	39.35		20.16	20.76	15.00	5.00	5.00	1.00	3.00	1.00	2.00		2.50	4.00	209.24
Hood's Grove																2.50
Kenly	84.00	60.00	10.00	5.00		2.00	3.00	3.00	2.50	3.00	5.00	2.50	3.05	2.00		178.50
Lee's	150.00		10.00	12.00		5.00	1.00	10.00	.50	3.39	1.00	4.00	.50	1.00		245.29
Oak						25.00										18.00
ro	10.00					6.00	2.50	5.00	2.00	27.65	4.00	1.00	.50	5.00		31.39
Mount Moriah	75.00	732.50	30.00	8.00		10.00	19.03	46.81	6.00	17.06	1.00	1.50	1.50	1.50	6.00	917.41
New Bethel	150.00	2.25	8.86	35.61		25.47	1.00	1.00	1.00	2.00	1.00	2.00	2.25	2.00	31.10	372.43
Nobles'	125.00		6.00	48.00		21.00	.50	.50	.50	2.00	2.00	2.00	1.00	1.00	25.00	232.00
Oliver's Grove	53.95			7.50		5.00	2.00	2.00	2.00	2.00	1.50	5.00	.60	1.00		67.00
Parrish Memorial	6.90			4.00		2.78										18.18
Pauline	77.60	100.00		1.64		17.50	2.00	1.50	1.00	3.00	2.50	2.50	1.00	1.00		111.10
Pine Level	9.45					5.00	3.00	1.00	2.00	3.00	1.00	1.00	1.50			127.54
Pinkney Chapel	50.00	150.00				7.00	3.00		1.50	4.00		1.50	.70			69.50
Pisgah	25.00		10.50	7.39		15.00				2.00	2.00	2.50		4.50	2.50	189.50
Princeton	100.00	17.25	10.11	18.73		15.00		8.83		2.50	2.00		1.50	1.00		159.89
Sardis	100.00	41.00				5.50	14.70	23.28			2.00				53.00	183.12
Selma	40.00	32.00	150.00	40.00		23.40	42.00			40.00						149.00
Shiloh	600.00					7.50	1.00	3.00		1.00	20.00	21.00	5.00	25.00		4055.98
Smithfield	150.00	417.26	24.75	99.42	9.20	160.00			11.00	8.29	1.00		1.00	1.00		173.50
Thanksgiving	500.00					5.00	3.77	58.00		40.00					99.20	1526.83
(no report)																12.50
Wendell	250.00	375.50	15.00	72.93		12.00	5.00	19.01	1.00	8.29	1.00	2.31	1.40	2.00	56.52	802.83
White Oak	125.00	1250.00		25.00		20.00	5.00	5.00	1.50	8.00	3.00	2.00	2.00	5.00		1469.50
Wilson's Mills	100.00	5.00			9.00	15.00			2.00	10.00		3.00				153.00
Total	5308.38	7335.56	478.97	878.60	56.26	874.85	246.17	408.73	68.64	414.69	113.00	129.97	45.55	97.60	395.82	16552.73

TABLE II—STATISTICAL.

Church.	Pastor.	Clerk and Postoffice.	Preaching Sundays.	Value of Church Property.	Seating capacity of church.	Baptized.	Received by Letter.	Restored.	Dismissed by Letter.	Excluded.	Died.	Number Males.	Number Females.	Total.
Antioch	Worley Creech	G. R. Ray, Archer	2nd	$ 500.00	700	10		7	1	6	1	60	116	176
Bailey	George H. Johnson	R. L. Underwood, Bailey	First	500.00	250	1	1	1				6	7	13
Baptist Centre	R. P. Ellington	W. C. Hardee, Clayton	First	1000.00	300	15	1	1				25	40	65
Beaty Chapel	R. W. Horrell	N. M. Eason, Smithfield	2nd-3rd	1500.00	400	12	13		12	10	1	10	18	28
Benson	T. B. Justice	E. L. Hall, Benson	2nd-4th	800.00	250		5			1		47	93	140
Benson's Grove	J. W. Smith	J. R. Benson, Benson	Second	800.00	300	2	2		1	1	1	4	12	16
Bethany	Worley Creech	Kirkman Kirch, Kenly	Fourth	600.00	250	13			1			34	50	84
Bethel	Geo. H. Johnson	Perry Barnes, Kenly	Fourth	500.00	400	2	2					19	19	38
Bethesda	R. W. Horrell	J. E. Smith, Wilson's Mills	Fourth	800.00	250	13	3		20	6	1	82	104	186
Min's Grove	T. B. Justice	J. G. Johnson, Four Oaks	Third	600.00	300	1	3					19	40	59
Calvary	J. W. Smith	T. J. Lee, Dunn, R. 2	First	600.00	300		2		2			9	20	29
Carter's	D. D. Edwards	Martin Thorn, Selma, R. 1	First	400.00	300	1	3	1	3	1		41	61	102
Clayton	A. C. Hamby	R. R. Coy, Clayton	Every	6000.00	700	3	4	1	10	6	4	141	180	321
Clyde's	I. W. Nobles	C. L. Johnson, Wendell	Third	500.00	300	3	1	1				56	84	140
Corinth	A. A. Pippin	H. V. Andrews, Archer	Second	400.00	200	5	2	2		2		40	74	114
Four Oaks	T. J. Hood	Preston George, Four Oaks, R.1	1st-3rd	800.00	300							13	22	35
*Hood's Grove		J. Wm. Langdon, Four Oaks, R.1	Third	500.00	300			6				12	26	38
Kenly	G. H. Johnson	Joseph Casper, Kenly	Second	2200.00	350	9	4			2	1	8	12	20
Lee's	A. A. Pippin	W. I. Green, Wakefield, R. 2	Fourth	1500.00	600	9	3			2		113	156	269
*Live Oak	Supply	R. Broadwell, Selma	Third				2		2	2		10	24	34
Micro	J. W. Smith	Oscar Mozingo, Micro	Fourth	600.00	300	9	3	1	5	2	3	10	11	21
Middlesex	A. A. Pippin	W. C. Jackson, Middlesex	Fourth	2250.00	350	3	3		1	1		19	30	49
Mount Moriah	S. C. Hilliard	J. H. Bryan, Raleigh, R. 2	First	800.00	300	9	1	5	1	2	2	74	79	153
New Bethel	J. W. Hall	Geo. W. Bryan, Garner	Fourth	800.00	400	2	1		1	2	1	42	48	90
Sims	W. M. Huggins	N. L. Stott, Sims	Third	700.00	250	17		1		2		43	57	100
Oliver's Grove	G. H. Johnson	T. B. Tiner, Four Oaks	Third	400.00	350	2	2		7	10	1	17	11	28
Parrish	R. W. Horrell	Jos. D. Creech, Selma, R. 3	First	500.00	350	6	3	1		3	1	34	39	73
Pauline	T. J. Hood	A. G. Hayes, Four Oaks, R. 1	First	400.00	300	5		5	14	4		17	23	40
Pine Level	R. W. Horrell	C. I. Godwin, Pine Level	Third	300.00	300	3						23	40	63
Pinkney	R. W. Horrell	Mrs. Ida Edgerton, Kenly, R.1	First			3	2					5	8	13
Pisgah	T. B. Justice	R. H. Higgins, Smithfield	First	1500.00	500	9	2	2	7	8		24	33	57
Princeton	B. Townsend	W. I. Pearce, Princeton	Third	1200.00	400	3	11	2	14	3	1	41	65	106
Sardis	T. J. Hood	Ben C. Powell, Smithfield, R.2	2nd-4th	500.00	200	7	14				1	16	31	47
Selma	T. H. King	R. P. Hardee, Selma	Second	15000.00	700	5	3	3	8	4	4	70	92	162
Shiloh	T. H. Horrell	J. F. Lassiter, Smithfield	1st-3rd	700.00	300	4			3			31	113	144
Smithfield	T. H. King	W. G. Earp, Selma	Second	7500.00	600							34	43	77
*Thanksgiving	Worley Creech	J. S. Lawhon, Benson	Fourth	1500.00	500							29	39	68
*Trinity	J. W. Smith	C. Z. Kidd, Wendell	Second	500.00	250	5	16	1	3	3		13	28	41
Wendell	A. A. Pippin	C. L. Murphy, Zebulon	1st-2d-3d	2000.00	500	5	16		3			54	75	129
White Oak	A. A. Pippin	C. L. Murphy, Zebulon	1st-2d-3d	2000.00	500		9	3			1	75	107	186
Wilson's Mills	J. B. Eller	J. H. Ellis, Wilson's Mills	Third	500.00	250	8		3	1			21	28	49

TABLE III—SUNDAY SCHOOLS.

CHURCH	SUPERINTENDENT AND POSTOFFICE.	Officers and Teachers.	Scholars.	Total Enrollment.	Volumes in Library.	Quarterlies and Papers taken.	Months kept open.	Average Attendance.	Baptisms from school.	Benevolent Contributions.	School Expenses.	Total Contributions.
Antioch	J. A. Bason, Selma	8	94	102		56	12	40	9		$ 6.40	$ 6.40
Baptist Center	J. C. Hardee, Clayton	5	35	40		55	12	25	1		8.00	8.00
Beaty Chapel	W. M. —in, Smithfield	5	45	50		50	12	50			12.18	12.18
Benson	E. L. Hall, Benson	9	142	151	100	150	12		11		15.00	15.00
Benson's Grove	Miss Li y Hamilton, Benson	4	50	54		45	12	35			6.00	6.00
Bethany	David Pace, Selma, R. 3	5	60	65		50	12	40	2		10.00	10.00
Bethel	Levin Watson, Kenly	6	40	46		40	6	20	1		10.00	10.00
Bethesda	J. W. Smith, Wilson's Mills	10	60	70	40	60	12	40	10		10.00	10.00
—s Grove	A. P. —e, Four Oaks, R. 3	4	39	43		38	6	24		2.00	2.63	4.63
Carter's Chapel	Preston Mozingo, Selma, R. 3	7	65	72		70	12	40		6.75	10.00	16.75
Clayton	R. H. —er, Clayton, R. 3	17	220	227	144	375	12	118	3	69.84	81.44	151.28
Clyde's Chapel	W. T. —unch, Clayton, R. 2	7	50	57		75	12	40			1.60	1.60
Four Oaks	W. A. Massengill, Four Oaks	5	50	55		80	12	35			20.16	20.16
Kenly	Not given	6	32	38		38	12	20			5.00	5.00
Lee's Chapel	W. I. Green, Wakefield, R. 2	6	110	116		100	12	80	5		12.00	12.00
Micro	C. C. Latten, Micro	5	40	45		75	12	30			8.00	8.00
Mt. [illegible]		7	142	149	350	174	12	72	8	27.65	35.61	63.26
Mount Moriah	W. C. Jackson, Middlesex	11	91	102		150	12	65	2		48.00	48.00
New Bethel	J. H. Bryant, Raleigh, R. 2	5	38	45	55	50	6	30			7.50	7.50
Oliver's Grove	P. W. Dowd, ——	5	57	62		40	9	20		3.65	5.00	8.65
Parrish ——	J. A. —iner, Four Oaks	6	47	53		40	9	40	6		4.00	4.00
Pauline	Jos. D Creech, Selma, R. 3	5	50	57		60	12	40			1.64	1.64
Pine Level	A. G. Hayes, Four Oaks, R. 1	7	50	57		72	12	50			8.00	8.00
Pisgah	E. B. —— Jones, Smithfield, R. 1	6	50	56		60	12	35	2		7.39	7.39
Princeton	W. H. Wells, Princeton	6	68	74		84	12	40	3		18.73	18.73
Selma	R. P. Noble, Selma	12	200	212	200	250	12	138	9	1.36	40.00	41.36
Shiloh	J. F. Hardee, McCullers, R. 1	10	60	66		60	12	40	4		7.00	7.00
Smithfield	T. J. Lassiter, Smithfield	12	150	160	200	250	12	80	4	2.87	99.42	102.29
Wendell	N. R. Stell, Wendell	12	220	232		125	12	120	1	4.50	72.93	77.43
White Oak	A. L. Batten, Archer	6	75	81		75	12	50			25.00	25.00
Wilson's Mills	J. T. Holt, Wilson's Mills	6	45	51		55	12	33			6.00	6.00
Totals		221	2345	2566					99	118.62	604.63	723.25

Note.—Bailey, Calvary, Corinth, Hood's Grove, Nobles' Chapel, Live Oak, Pinkney Chapel, Sardis, Thanksgiving, and Trinity report no Sunday Schools. Selma reports two schools. If all the churches would report their Sunday Schools on Church Letter, our work would make a better showing.—Clerk.

TABLE IV—PLEDGES FOR 1911.

CHURCHES.	State Missions.	Home Missions.	Foreign Missions.	Sunday School Missions.	Ministerial Education.	Ministerial Relief.	Orphanage	Building Fund.	Total.
Antioch	$15.00	$ 1.50	$ 1.50	$ 1.50	$ 1.50	$ 2.50	$ 2.75	$ 2.25	$ 28.50
Bailey	2.50	.50	1.00	.50	.50	1.00	2.00	2.00	10.00
Baptist Centre..........	5.00	2.00	2.50	1.50	2.00	1.50	5.00	1.50	21.00
*Beaty Chapel...........	2.00	1.00	1.00	.50	1.00	1.00	1.50	1.50	9.50
Benson	100.00	20.00	20.00	5.00	5.00	5.00	25.00	10.00	190.00
Benson's Grove..........	2.00	.50	.50	.50	1.00	.50	3.00	10.00	18.00
Bethany	6.00	3.00	2.00	1.00	1.00	2.00	3.50	2.00	21.50
Bethel	5.00	2.50	1.00	1.00	1.00	1.00	1.50	2.50	15.50
Bethesda	25.00	5.00	5.00	2.00	2.00	3.00	20.00	2.00	64.00
Blackman's Grove.......	20.00	5.00	5.00	2.00	4.00	2.50	8.00	2.00	45.00
Calvary	4.00	2.00	1.00	1.25	2.00	1.00	1.50	2.00	14.75
**Carter's Chapel........	10.00	2.50	1.50	1.00	1.50	2.00	10.00	2.50	31.00
Clayton ....:....	247.50	66.00	66.00	11.00	22.00	22.50	147.50	27.50	610.00
Clyde's Chapel...:......	10.00	5.00	4.00	3.00	1.00	3.00	5.00	1.50	32.50
Corinth	9.00	1.50	2.00	1.50	1.00	2.50	5.00	1.50	24.00
Four Oaks..............	15.00	5.00	5.00	1.00	1.50	3.00	5.00	2.50	38.00
Hood's Grove............	4.00	1.00	1.00	.50	1.00	.50	2.00	2.00	12.00
Kenly	5.75	3.50	4.00	1.25	2.00	2.00	4.00	2.50	24.00
Lee's Chapel............	27.50	5.00	10.00	2.50	5.00	3.55	5.00	5.00	63.50
Live Oak................	4.00	.50	1.25	.50	1.00	1.00	1.25	1.00	10.50
Micro	6.00	2.00	1.25	1.00	1.00	1.00	3.00	2.00	17.25
Middlesex	12.50	1.00	1.00	1.00	1.00	1.00	5.00	2.00	24.50
Mount Moriah...........	50.00	20.00	50.00	6.00	5.00	6.00	30.00	5.00	172.00
New Bethel.............	16.00	6.00	5.00	1.00	5.00	5.00	17.50	5.00	60.50
Nobles' Chapel..........	5.00	3.00	1.00	.50	1.00	2.00	2.00	5.00	19.50
Oliver's Grove...........	2.50	.50	1.50	.50	1.50	1.00	2.00	2.00	11.50
Parrish Memorial........	17.50	2.00	2.00	1.00	2.00	2.00	2.00	2.50	29.50
Pauline	5.00	2.00	1.50	.50	2.00	1.00	3.00	2.50	17.50
Pine Level..............	7.00	2.00	1.50	1.00	1.50	1.50	4.00	2.50	21.00
Pinkney Chapel..........	5.00	1.00	1.00	.50	1.00	1.00	2.00	4.00	15.50
Pisgah	15.00	2.50	5.25	1.00	2.50	4.00	2.25	4.25	36.75
Princeton	20.00	4.25	5.00	1.00	2.00	2.50	4.00	1.25	40.00
Sardis	5.50	2.00	2.00	.50	1.00	1.00	2.00	2.00	16.00
Selma	50.00	10.00	40.00	5.00	4.00	10.00	25.00	10.00	164.00
Shiloh	7.50	2.50	3.00	1.00	3.00	2.50	5.00	2.00	26.50
Smithfield	160.00	40.00	60.00	10.00	20.00	21.00	40.00	25.00	376.00
Thanksgiving	5.00	1.00	1.00	.50	1.00	1.00	1.00	1.00	11.50
Trinity	7.50	1.00	3.50	1.00	1.00	.50	3.00	1.00	18.50
Wendell	12.00	1.00	1.00	1.00	1.00	1.00	2.00	1.00	25.00
White Oak..............	22.50	5.00	5.00	1.50	3.50	5.00	8.00	2.00	52.50
Wilson's Mills.......:...	15.00	5.00	5.00	2.00	3.00	3.00	10.00	5.00	48.00
Total	965.75	247.75	335.75	77.50	120.00	133.00	431.25	180.75	2487.75
Pledges for 1910.	958.00	241.25	300.50	70.25	115.50	123.00	405.25	141.75	2363.25

Note.—Where churches were not represented the pledges were put the same as last year. 10 churches pledged same total as last year. 25 churches increased their pledges while five churches decreased.

* New church. **Baraca Class to pay half of Orphanage pledge.

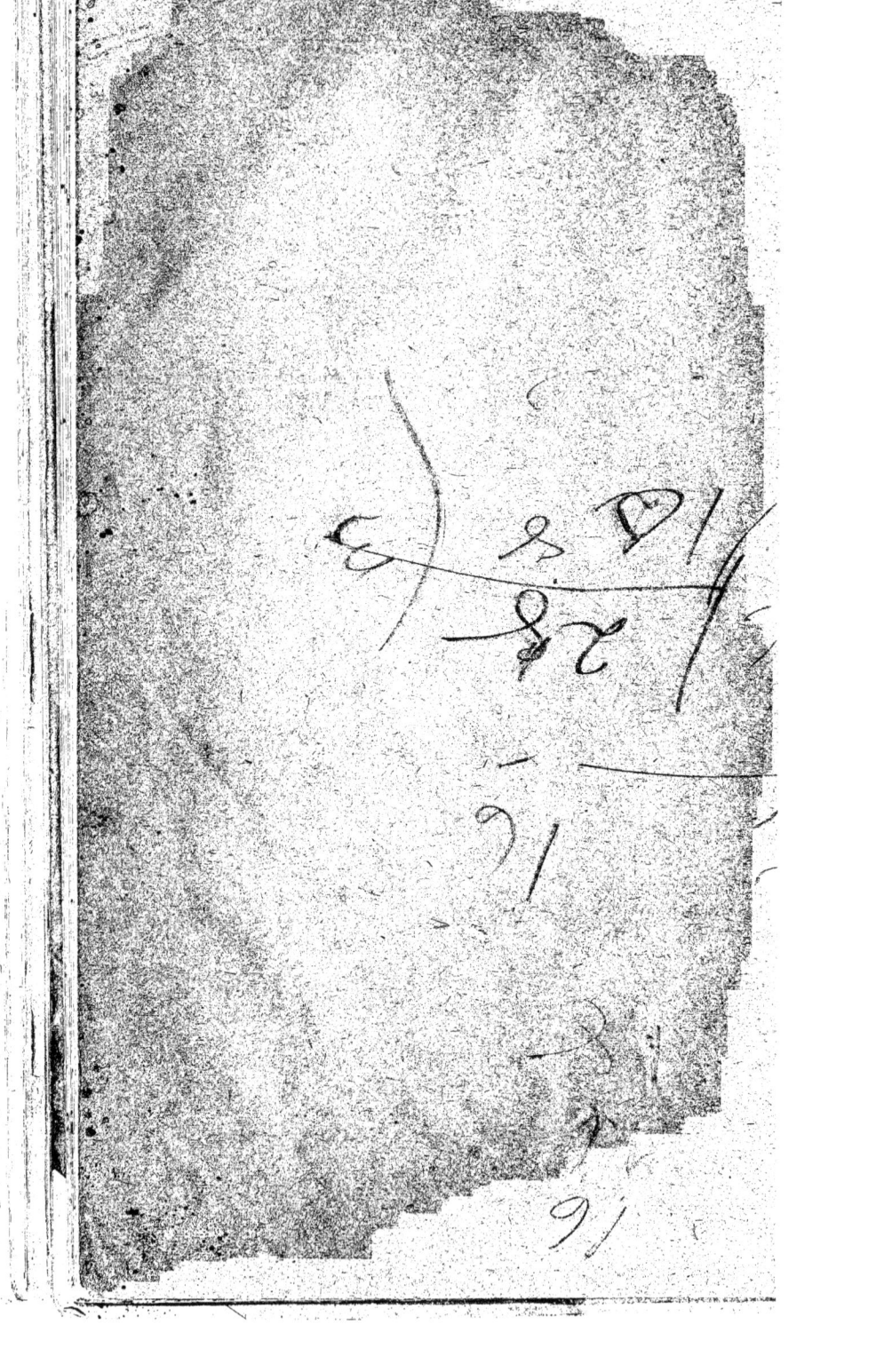

MINUTES

OF THE

NINTH SESSION

OF THE

JOHNSTON COUNTY

BAPTIST ASSOCIATION,

HELD WITH

Middlesex Baptist Church,

NOVEMBER 8th, 9th and 10th, 1911.

The next session will be held with Mount Moriah Baptist Church, near Auburn, N. C., beginning Wednesday after the first Sunday in November, 1912.

To preach Introductory Sermon—A. C. Sherwood.

OFFICERS.

Moderator—R. H. Gower...Clayton, N. C.
Vice-Moderator—A. A. Pippin...................................Wakefield, N. C.
Clerk—T. J. Lassiter..Smithfield, N. C.
Treasurer—T. J. Lassiter..Smithfield, N. C.
Historian—R. W. Horrell...Selma, N. C.

EXECUTIVE COMMITTEE.

J. M. Beaty, Chairman..Smithfield, N. C.
J. T. Holt.....Wilson's Mills, N. C.   J. F. Pool.........Clayton, N. C.
L. T. Royall.....Smithfield, N. C.   Alonzo Parrish......Benson, N. C.

Goldsboro, N. C.
Nash Bros., Printers and Binders.
1912

MINUTES

OF THE

NINTH SESSION

OF THE

JOHNSTON COUNTY

BAPTIST ASSOCIATION,

HELD WITH

Middlesex Baptist Church,

NOVEMBER 8th, 9th and 10th, 1911.

The next session will be held with Mount Moriah Baptist Church, near Auburn, N. C., beginning Wednesday after the first Sunday in November, 1912.

To preach Introductory Sermon—A. C. Sherwood.

OFFICERS.

Moderator—R. H. Gower..............................Clayton, N. C.
Vice-Moderator—A. A. Pippin........................Wakefield, N. C.
Clerk—T. J. Lassiter................................Smithfield, N. C.
Treasurer—T. J. Lassiter...........................Smithfield, N. C.
Historian—R. W. Horrell...............................Selma, N. C.

EXECUTIVE COMMITTEE.

J. M. Beaty, Chairman................................Smithfield, N. C.
J. T. Holt....Wilson's Mills, N. C.   J. F. Pool..........Clayton, N. C
L. T. Royall.....Smithfield, N. C.   Alonzo Parrish......Benson, N. C.

Goldsboro, N. C.
Nash Bros., Printers and Binders.
1912

CHAIRMEN STANDING COMMITTEES, 1912.

State Missions ....R. W. Horrell.
Home Missions ....A. C. Hamby.
Foreign Missions ....A. C. Sherwood.
Orphanage ....J. W. Nobles.
Ministerial Education ....Geo. H. johnson.
Aged Ministers' Relief....................................A. A. Pippin.
Sunday Schools ....E. J. Rodgers.
Periodicals ....W. T. Hurst.
Temperance ....T. J. Hood.
Woman's Work...W. T. Baucom.

SUNDAY SCHOOL COMMITTEE.

T. J. Lassiter...Smithfield, N. C.
F. H. Brooks..Smithfield, N. C.
W. C. Jackson..Middlesex, N. C.

LIST OF PASTORS.

W. R. Beach...Cary, N. C.
W. T. Baucom..Wake Forest, N. C.
A. I. Caudle..Wake Forest, N. C.
D. D. Edwards...R. F. D. 3, Selma, N. C.
R. L. Hocutt...R. F. D. 1, Archer, N. C.
W. T. Hurst..Four Oaks, N. C.
A. C. Hamby...Clayton, N. C.
R. W. Horrell..Selma, N. C.
T. J. Hood...R. F. D. 4, Goldsboro, N. C.
G. H. Johnson...Kenly, N. C.
J. W. Nobles..Wendell, N. C.
A. A. Pippin..Wakefield, N. C.
E. J. Rodgers...Benson, N. C.
J. W. Smith..Smithfield, N. C.
A. C. Sherwood..Zebulon, N. C.
N. H. Shepherd..Stantonsburg, N. C.

THE NINTH ANNUAL SESSION

OF THE

Johnston County Baptist Association,

MET WITH THE

MIDDLESEX BAPTIST CHURCH.

WEDNESDAY, November 8, 1911.

Devotional exercises were conducted by Rev. W. R. Beach.

The Introductory Sermon was preached by Rev. A. C. Hamby from Luke 24:44-49.

A committee on Credentials was appointed consisting of W. T. Hurst and J. P. Underwood.

The following visitors were recognized and welcomed:

Rev. J. M. Hilliard, of the Raleigh Association; R. B. Nichols, of the Raleigh Association; Rev. W. R. Beach, representing the *Biblical Recorder*.

The following delegates were enrolled:

Antioch—J. R. Hocutt, R. B. Creech.
Bailey—R. L. Underwood, J. W. B. Finch.
Baptist Center—
Beaty Chapel—
Benson—E. J. Rogers.
Bethesda—Clarence Medlin, Norman Jones.
Bethel—Perry Barnes.
Bethany—Jesse B. Creech.
Calvary—
Clayton—W. A. Barnes, A. C. Hamby, D. J. Yelvington.
Carter's Chapel—Albert McCall, Preston Mozingo, W. M. Boykins.
Clyde's Chapel—J. M. Todd, W. B. Medlin.
Corinth—J. B. Woodard, J. M. Hocutt.
Four Oaks—W. T. Hurst, J. B. Creech.
Kenly—Mrs. R. T. Renfrow, Mrs. Turner Bailey, Geo. H. Johnson.
Lee's Chapel—W. I. Gavin.
Live Oak—D. D. Edwards.
Micro—L. L. Creech, Minnie Creech.
Middlesex—T. W. Bartholomew, J. W. Strickland.
Mount Moriah—J. F. Pool.
New Bethel—
Nobles Chapel—
Oliver's Grove—J. A. Tiner.
Pauline—
Parrish Memorial—
Pinkney Chapel—Mrs. Rebecca Holland, Mrs. Ida Edgerton.
Pine Level—C. I. Godwin, B. L. Strickland.
Pisgah—
Princeton—
Selma—R. W. Horrell.
Shiloh—

Smithfield—J. M. Beaty, T. H. King.
Thanksgiving—Abram Earp, C. C. Finch.
Wendell—Alex Knott, W. C. Nowell, J. W. Noble, L. M. Knott, N. R. Stell.
White Oak—W. T. Allen.
Wilson's Mills—J. T. Holt.
Officers were elected as follows:
Moderator—R. H. Gower.
Vice-Moderator—A. A. Pippin.
Clerk—T. J. Lassiter.
Treasurer—T. J. Lassiter.
Historian—R. W. Horrell.

The pastor and deacons of this church were appointed a Committee on Religious Exercises.

AFTERNOON SESSION.

The Association was called to order by the Moderator. Prayer by J. W. Smith.

The Report on Home Missions was submitted by R. W. Horrell, as follows:

REPORT ON HOME MISSIONS.

Home Missions is the philosophy of making real a Christian civilization in America. To accomplish its purposes is a matter of surpassing importance in any wisely conceived mission policy.

The Old Testament prophets, whose eyes kindled with a vision of the world turning to God, in furthering this divine purpose gave their whole lives to Home Missions. In the Great Commission our Lord gave commands that extend to the utmost limits of the earth, but for all time they also include for each disciple the limits of his own community. They radiate out from that and take in every place between it and the place furtherest away.

In the prosecution of the purpose of our Lord for the redemption of the world, Peter and Philip and Stephen and James were as truly carrying out the divine plan of missions when they preached to the Jews as Paul was when he carried the glad news to the Gentiles. Foreign Missions succeed only when it settles down and makes itself at home. Home Missions is missions making for itself a real home in the hearts of men, and in the economic, social and civic relationships of our own land. We must insist that the gospel of grace shall rise so high in the hearts of God's people that it shall overflow and enrich the arid fields of greed and injustice and crime and wickedness in our own country. If we do not, we surely can not think that our gospel is strong enough to conquer heathen nations. Moreover, how shall we reply if the heathen nations shall say to us, Physician, heal thyself.

Out of 92,000,000 population in America only about 20,000,000 are members of evangelical denominations. About 12,000,000 belong to the Catholics, but their faith is so foreign to the genius of American institutions and so obscures the teachings of the Savior in its idolatrous dogmas of saint worship and papal infallibility that we must regard this religious body as a spiritual liability rather than an asset.

The present growth of the South in material prosperity is marvelous. Our vast material resources are being developed with an almost greedy haste. The enormous property losses of the Civil War have been retrieved and this section now has more wealth than the entire nation had when the war began.

Shall this material prosperity be a curse or a blessing to the South? The Christian people of the South hold the answer. If our religion is virile enough to consecrate this wealth to spiritual and moral ends, it will be a blessing. But if not—if the prosperity of our people is devoted to selfish luxury and pleasure—it will become a curse to the people and the nation. We stamp the name of God on our minted coin, but only as that name is engraved on the living hearts of men will it avail for the nation, or for a lost soul. The greatest single threat to the power of religion in the South to-day is the Mammon of unconsecrated wealth.

The Home Mission Board conducts many departments of activity for saving the people and preparing them for lives of service. It has about forty-five workers among the foreigners, twenty-eight mountain mission schools with 127 teachers and 4,500 students, eighteen trained evangelists who last year baptized about 3,000 converts, thirty-five Negro missionary evaneglists working effectively among the Southern Negroes, thirty-four missionaries who supply fifty-six churches and mission stations in Cuba, five missionaries and four helpers doing a succesful work in the Canal Zone, a church building department which aided in building 289 churches last year, and twenty missionaries among the Indians in Oklahoma.

Besides the above, the Home Board participates co-operatively (principally with State Mission Boards) in a number of States in maintaining about 1,100 missionary pastors. This co-operative mission work is in line with the Convention's instructions to the Board to form the closest possible relationiship with the existing agencies of the denomination in the various States.

To the end that our Board may enlarge its activities and do for the denomination a work worthy of so great a Christian body and commensurate with the present urgent needs, your Committee pleads for regular and large collections for Home Missions in the churches. Our Board could wisely expend a million dollars a year for it. It ought to do it, if we can only bring our churches to make a liberal response to its needs. Surely Southern Baptists must raise the $400,000 asked, and our own State its apportionment of $————

Your committee recommends:

1. That prayer be made in the churches for Home Missions, that God may open our eyes to see and our purses to use the rich opportunities to establish our country on the everlasting Rock of Ages.

2. That regular collections throughout the year be insisted on, instead of waiting, as so many do, to the end of the year to give to this cause.
our Association is asked to raise.

3. That this body provide for apportioning among the churches the amount

4. That our pastors be requested to make an earnest effort at least once during the year to preach a special sermon on Home Missions, and the magnitude and importance of the problems involved.

5. That a club of subscribers be raised in each church for The Home Field, the unusually attractive and illuminating monthly magazine of the Home Board.

6. That churches and pastors be encouraged to make a large use of the Home Board's informing tracts and sample copies of The Home Field, both of which are free for the asking.

The address of the Home Mission Board in Austell Building, Atlanta, Ga.

D. J. YELVINGTON,
R. W. HORRELL,
L. T. CREECH,
Committee.

Pending a motion to adopt this report, addresses were made by R. W. Horrell and A. C. Hamby.

Pledges for Home Missions were taken and the report adopted. (See table of Pledges.)

The Moderator appointed the following committees:

Place and Preacher: W. A. Barnes, J. W. Smith, J. A. Tiner.
Periodicals: Geo. H. Johnson, J. M. Todd, J. B. Woodard.
Finance: R. R. Creech, J. F. Pool, Norman Jones.

The following Report on Temperance was submitted by Bro. Hood:

REPORT ON TEMPERANCE.

Of all evils in the land the drink evil seems to be the hardest to suppress. We made a hard fight and secured a prohibition law as strong in its provisions as we could ask. The violation of the law is the source of trouble now and enforcement of it is our duty. We can expect nothing of a dealer but that he will evade the law. When a man makes up his mind to engage in a business that destroys life, make widows and orphans and breeds poverty and disease and depravity, there is no manliness nor mercy left to which we can appeal. The moral support of all Christians and prohibitionists should be given to our sheriff, constables and policemen, and if necessary such pressure should be brought to bear upon them as will ensure the arrest and punishment of the violators of the law. The jug traffic fostered by the inter-State law is beyond our legal control, but it exposes the drinkers, gives us an opportunity to use our Christian influence to reform the habitual drinkers. Let us be sure we do not encourage the use of intoxicants by example, apology or toleration. Our most strenuous efforts are necessary to prevent a reaction of public sentiment. May the Lord pity the man who claims to have a passport to heaven and always has money to order a jug of whiskey and never a dollar to send the gospel to the lost.

T. J. HOOD,
W. T. ALLEN,
J. R. HOCUTT,
Committee.

Pending a motion to adopt this report, remarks were made by T. J. Hood and Chas. E. Stevens.

The report was adopted.

W. T. Hurst, Mrs. R. T. Renfrow and Alex Knott were appointed a Committee on Woman's Work, which reported as follows:

REPORT ON WOMAN'S WORK.

We are coming more and more to realize the helping hand of our sister. Her work is becoming to be an important feature both to herself and to our denomination. The work of the woman is giving her a broader view of the Master. As she gathers from time to time in the Missionary Societies she becomes inspired for the advancement of His kingdom. In these meetings she learns to pray in public, to make speeches, and to be useful in many ways for the Master's bidding.

While we do not believe that our women should be engaged in the pulpit and in politics we do believe her influence as a worker in God's kingdom, as a Missionary, either at home or abroad carries with it an untold power.

Our women held their meeting with the Selma Church this year, which was quite a success. Their next meeting will be held with the Clayton church. There are 41 churches in the Association with only 11 Woman's Missionary Societies and a few Young Woman's Auxiliaries, Royal Ambassadors, and Sunbeam Bands.

Our women are to be congratulated on the great work they have already done and should be encouraged by the pastors to do this year a greater work than they have ever done.

We recommend that every Society and every Church that has no Society in the Association send representatives to the Associational meeting in Clayton next year.

W. T. HURST,
MRS. R. T. RENFROW,
ALEX. KNOTT,
Committee.

Bro. Geo. H. Johnson submitted the report on Periodicals, as follows: (This report has not reached the Clerk.)

On motion to adopt this report, Bro. W. R. Beach made an earnest appeal for *The Biblical Recorder.*

Remarks were also made by R. W. Horrell, Dr. Freeman, T. J. Hood, T. H. King.

The report was adopted.

T. H. King, W. C. Jackson and Paul Whitley were appointed a Committee on State Missions.

The Association adjourned. Benediction by J. M. Hilliard.

THURSDAY MORNING.

Religious exercises were conducted by ———.

The Moderator called the Association to order. The proceedings of yesterday were read and adopted.

Visiting brethren were recognized as follows: E. L. Middleton, Sunday School Secretary.

Bro. Middleton brought a message of greeting from Bro. Livingston Johnson and regrets that he could not attend on account of the funeral of Hon. H. C. Dockery.

B. W. Rogers, of Thomasville Orphanage, was recognized, and he also expressed regret that Bro. Kesler could not attend on account of funeral of Hon. H. C. Dockery.

Rev. D. F. Putnam, of Roanoke Association, was recognized and welcomed.

The following committees were appointed to nominate an Executive Committee, a member of the State Mission Board, Delegates to the Baptist State Convention, and Delegate to Southern Baptist Convention: A. C. Hamby, A. A. Pippin, R. W. Horrell, Geo. H. Johnson, J. W. Smith.

The following committee was appointed on the Orphanage: J. W. Smith, W. M. Boykin, W. I. Green.

Bro. J. M. Beaty offered the following report of the Executive Committee:

REPORT OF EXECUTIVE COMMITTEE.

We can report progress at nearly all of the places helped by the Mission Board. The churches aided have done better than usual toward their pastors and toward the objects to which we give but are still behind what they should do. We are trying to get them to do their part. Rev. T. J. Hood has served Pauline and Hood's Grove churches. Rev. W. T. Hurst has been pastor at Four Oaks, Pine Level, Bethel, and part of the year at Blackman's Grove and Oliver's Grove. Live Oak has been served by Rev. D. D. Edwards and Corinth by Rev. A. A. Pippin. Some aid has been given to Middlesex with Rev. A. C. Sherwood as pastor. Rev. R. W. Horrell has had charge of the work at Pisgah, Sardis and Woodard School House. Rev. George H. Johnson has been with Kenly, Bailey, Nobles' Chapel and part of the year with Bethel, Oliver's Grove and Blackman's Grove. Carter's Chapel, Micro, Benson's Grove, Pleasant Grove, Trinity and Calvary have had as pastor Rev. J. W. Smith. Pinkney has been served by Rev. N. H. Shepherd and Princeton by Rev. W. R. Beach. Rev. E. J. Rodgers has served Parrish Memorial. We recommend that the churches increase their pledges for State Missions so that we as an Association shall not have to ask for so much help from other Associations.

J. M. BEATY,
J. F. POOL,
J. T. HOLT,   Committee.

Pending a motion to adopt this report Bro. Beaty told of the work done in the Association this year.

T. H. King offered the report on State Missions:

REPORT ON STATE MISSIONS.

No section of our great republic is making such rapid development now as the South. Among the foremost Southern States is our own North Carolina. While the value of agricultural products in the South has increased in ten years 84 per cent.; in the South it has increased 92 per cent. and in North Carolina, 94 per cent. The value of manufactured products has wonderfully increased and the amount of our bank deposits increased from 1900 to 1910 almost four fold. Our educational progress is very gratifying. A new school building has been erected in the State every day for the past six years. Larger, nicer, more convenient and comfortable houses, better teachers, longer terms and 70 per cent. of our children in school is our present attainment. Good roads and improved farms and homes all over the State indicate the spirit of progress. Religiously, the State is not making the progress we might expect. In the decade just past there was a larger increase in Catholics than in Protestants. North Carolina is the only State in the South which the increase in population was greater than the increase in church membership. Only 38 per cent. of our population is Christian. Of these, about one-half are Baptists. The actual increase of Baptists in this State is greater than the combined increase of all other protestant denominations. Of all the men and women who profess faith in Christ each year, one out of two is baptized into a Baptist Church, and the end is not yet. This is largely due to our aggressive State Mission policy. It is the object of State Missions to establish a flourishing Baptist Church in every community in North Carolina. Last year our missionaries received 3,611 members and collected $11,561 for the benevolent work of our Convention.

There are to-day 128 preachers supported in part or entirely by our State Mission Board. This work is carried on this year on a basis of $48,000. We deplore the fact that two thirds of it must be raised in the three remaining Sundays of the Conventional year.

This Association gave last year to State Missions $875.00, and received from the Board $1,800.00.

We recommend that each church adopt a better financial system and press their benevolence through the entire year; and that our Executive Committee undertake to group our churches in compact fields, so that they may have pastors as well as preachers.　　　　T. H. KING,
.　For Committee.

In the absence of Bro. Johnson, T. H. King, E. L. Middleton, R. W. Horrell and A. C. Hamby spoke on the subject.

A cash collection for State Missions was taken amounting to $42.61.

The reports were adopted.

The Moderator announced the following committees:

Orphanage—J. W. Smith, W. M. Boykin, W. I. Green.
Sunday Schools—T. J. Lassiter, C. W. Knight, B. L. Strickland.
Foreign Missions—E. J. Rogers, C. Z. Todd, J. B. Creech.
Ministerial Relief—J. W. Nobles, C. I. Goodwin, A. J. Broughton.
Ministerial Education—A. C. Hamby, N. R. Stell, C. W. Knight.

THURSDAY—AFTERNOON SESSION.

Prayer by Brother Putman.

The Association was called to order by the Moderator.

T. H. King read the report on Sunday Schools as follows:

REPORT ON SUNDAY SCHOOLS.

The Sunday School is an institution designed for religious instruction and for the worship of God. When either of these is lacking the Sunday School is incomplete. While it is very important that the Sunday School should emphasize the teaching idea, it is no less important that a spirit of worship, and reverence for the home .of God should pervade every meeting.

The teaching of the Scriptures is one of the most important works of the church. In Deuteronomy 6:6 and 7, we read: "And these words, which I command thee this day, shall be in thine heart: And thou shalt teach them diligently unto thy children, and shalt talk of them when thou sittest in thine house, and when thou walkest by the way, and when thou liest down and when thou riseth up." From the days of Samuel, on through the history of the Jews, even in the captivity, the idea of teaching the Scriptures to the people was emphasized. It was Christ's wont to go to the Synagogue on the Sabbath day and read and teach the Scriptures. If Christ himself deemed the teaching of the Scriptures of such importance, how can we of this day, afford to neglect this great work?

In the Sunday School report in the Minutes of the Baptist State Convention for 1910, we find the following:

"If growth and movement are indications of vitality, the Sunday School is assuredly a living institution. It is growing. It is growing in numbers. The world's Sunday School forces reach a total of twenty-eight millions. In the Baptist ranks of our own State we have attained the number of 165,000. While this achievement gives no cause for boasting, for our church membership is 220,223, it presents a condition that is hopeful and even promising.

"The Sunday School is not only growing in numbers, but it is developing in efficiency. It is possessed of movement. Consider the emphasis that has in recent years been placed on the primary department. The work that is being done in the modern city Sunday School, in this department of the work, will bear comparison with similar work done in the day schools by professional teachers.

"Another phase of Sunday School work that is receiving much attention at the present time is the adult department. A persistent effort is being made to interest the grown folks in the Sunday School. It is meeting with gratifying success, largely through the introduction of the "organized class" idea. Enough has been accomplished already to warrant us in continuing the campaign to get the church interested in the Sunday School. Now this adult work is distinctly an American institution, and at the World's Sunday School Convention, held in Washington last May, the parade of adult Sunday School scholars was a revelation to the foreign delegates."

The Minutes of our Association for 1910 show 3,612 church members and 2,566 members of our Sunday Schools. The difference between the two is too great, and we should strive to get a larger per cent. of our church members in the Sunday School than we have at present. In 1910 our Minutes show only 31 Sunday Schools, while we have 41 churches. Some of these churches who had no Sunday Schools last year will report Sunday Schools this year. We are growing along this line, but we should not be content until we have a Sunday School in every church and it kept open twelve months in the year. This is not impossible, and nothing short of this should be our aim.

At our Association last year a committee was appointed and instructed to plan for the holding of a Sunday School Convention sometime this year.

Such a Convention was held with our churches in Selma last June. An interesting and instructive program was planned and carried out. We believe much good was done, but much more might have been accomplished if the attendance had been larger.

Your Committee would recommend that such a Convention should be held each and every year. We must better equip ourselves for our great task of teaching in the Sunday School and one of the best means of doing this is to hold Sunday School Conventions and Institutes. We would urge our people to try to get as many of our teachers and prospective teachers as possible to take the Normal Training Course of our Sunday School Board at Nashville, Tenn.   Respectfully submitted,

T. J. LASSITER,
For Committee.

Pending a motion to adopt this report, the Association was addressed by Bro. E. L. Middleton.

The report on Church Building was read by J. M. Beaty:

REPORT OF BUILDING COMMITTEE.

Your Committee can report a year of progress in Church building but the contributions to this object are small, consequently we have had to borrow some money. We are depending on the churches to increase their contributions to this object to pay this debt. We have aided in the building of churches at Pinkney and Pine Level and helped to repair the church at Pleasant Grove. This being a matter of much interest to our work we recommend that our churches increase their pledges to this object by giving as much to this object as they do to State Missions.

J. M. BEATY,
J. T. HOLT,
J. F. POOL,   Committee.

Bro. Beaty made an earnest plea for the Church Building Fund. Brethren Hamby and Pippin also made remarks.

Pledges were taken for church building.

Bro. Hamby moved that the Moderator appoint a suitable Committee to apportion the amount due on Church Building among the churches, send the pastors of the churches the amounts and request them to raise it. The motion prevailed.

J. W. Smith read the report on the Orphanage:

REPORT ON ORPHANAGE.

The Thomasville Baptist Orphanage is twenty-six years old; more than twelve hundred children have been gathered within its sheltering arms. We have had as many as four hundred at one time, but were over-crowded. Three hundred and eighty to three-hundred and eighty-five is our usual number.

Our effort is to make it an all-round training school and home combined. The foreseeing men who laid its plans purposed that it should be open to dependent orphan children who were capable of education and training. At the end of a quarter of a century we are beginning to see a plant worthy of such an undertaking. We have four hundred and fifty acres of land, one hundred and seventy-five of it in cultivation. There are ten dormitories, central dining hall, central sewing room and central school building where nine grades are taught. Our sanitary arrangements and means for caring for the sick are well up to modern requirement. Within the past year we have gone into the new technical building which turns over the Mills Memorial Building, formely the shop, to Charity and Children. This building was renovated and all given over to the printing office. Valuable equipment has been added leading to its soon becoming an up-to-date job office. The shoe shop was moved to the new building and new machinery added to it also. We hope within a few years to have the entire building equipped for mechanical manual training. Great improvement has been made in the sewing, especially in the training of the girls, since it has been brought under central management. No girl is expected to leave the institution who is not able to make her own clothes, and others' also. Learning to cook is a part of the course. The boys are in the shoe shop, printing office, in the dairy, on the truck farm and all over the farm in general. All these go into our school system. A constant effort is made to surround the life of the place with an atmosphere of culture and refinement, no small part of which is the religious life. We have no complaint to make at the support which the denomination has given us during the past year. We came through practically out of debt. From all sources we received fifty-two thousand dollars. Part of this went into building and repairs. It costs about eighty-five dollars a year to support a child. Our running expenses amount to one hundred dollars a day. We know of no better plan for raising money than the one we have been urging so long—a collection from every Sunday School once a month, and a rousing Thanksgiving Offering in every church on that day; and along with this a club of Charity and Children in every Sunday School—sixty cents a copy in clubs of ten or more. We urge those of larger means to consider whether or not they may not honor God by putting up new buildings We are fearfully crowded. Within the year the West Chowan Association will have a building, the kitchen at the central dining room is to be enlarged and also a new laundry building will be erected. The obligation is upon us, because the opportunity enlarges before us, we need to make haste in measuring up to it.

J. W. SMITH,
W. I. GREEN,
W. M. BOYKIN,
Committee.

Bro. B. W. Rogers spoke on the Orphanage.

On motion of T. H. King, the taking of the pledges was deferred till an opportune time to-morrow. The motion prevailed.

The Committee on Place and Preacher for next session recommended that the next session be held with the church at Mount Moriah; A. C. Sherwood. The recommendation was adopted.

The committee to nominate an Executive Committee and delegates to the Baptist State Convention and Southern Baptist Convention, made the following recommendations:

Executive Committee—J. M. Beaty, Chairman, L. T. Royall, J. T. Holt, J. F. Pool, Alonzo Parrish.

Member State Mission Board: A. C. Hamby.

Delegates to Baptist State Convention—V. R. Turley, C. W. Carter and Alonzo Parrish.

Delegate to Southern Baptist Convention: M. C. Winston, F. H. Brooks, Alternate.

The Moderator appointed A. C. Hamby and the members of the Executive Committee to raise the debt on the Church Building Fund.

The Association then adjourned.

FRIDAY MORNING.

The Association was called to order by the Vice-Moderator.

T. H. King conducted devotional exercises.

On motion, it was agreed that we finish the work of the session before adjournment.

The following report on Foreign Missions was read:

REPORT ON FOREIGN MISSIONS.

Our Lord said "the field is the world" and thereby enjoined upon his followers the obligation to go into all the world even the uttermost parts of the earth.

Our work in Foreign Missions is divided into classes of fields, namely Pagan and Papal. The pagan fields are those in which the people worship idols and sit in heathenish darkness.

The Papal fields are those in which Roman Catholicism prevails and the power of the pope dominates.

The work is encouraging from several view points and doors of the nations are open for the gospel. The number of converts in the Foreign Mission fields is far in excess of the number in our own State in proportion to the number of Christian workers and the amount contributed for this object.

Our Board was instructed by the last meeting of the Southern Baptist Convention to lay out their work on a basis of six hundred thousand ($600,-000) dollars. This and much more could be expended wisely by the board and our Lord would be glorified in it.

Let us hear the great commission of our Lord and in obedience to the Great Head of the Church go by our gifts and prayers carrying the tiding of salvation to a lost world.

On motion to adopt this report the Association was addressed by A. C. Hamby. Pledges were taken for Foreign Missions.

The report was adopted.

Without objection pledges were taken for the Orphaange.

The report on the Orphanage was adopted.

Bro. Horrell read the following tribute to Brother Worley Creech:

BROTHER WORLEY CREECH.

From its organization we have come to these annual meetings with anxious and glad hearts, to meet and greet each other, and together to view and rejoice in the progress of the past, and to plan for the future. It is one of our greatest pleasures as we stand in battle line on the field, to feel the elbow touch of the brother at our side, and in these annual meetings to look into each other's faces. Peculiar is the pleasure that is never marred. It is with sorrow and regret that we report (during the past year) the loss of elbow touch with one of our most Christ-like co-laborers, and call your attention to the absence of one of the most saintly members of our body, Bro. Worley Creech.

Brother Creech had labored long and faithful for his Master. He was one of the pioneer preachers in Johnston county. He gave most of his life to the Lord's work in his own county. He began (according to the divine plan) at home, and though he met with much opposition, he succeeded in planting the seeds of the Kingdom which grew into a number of churches, which stand as so many monuments to his memory, attesting his wisdom and faithfulness. To say that we miss him is to feebly express our feelings.

Whereas, we recognize his great and useful life in our midst; be it

Resolved, by this Association that we by rising vote express our appreciation of his life work and acknowledge our loss in his death.

A rising vote of appreciation was taken.

J. W. Nobles offered the following report on Ministerial Relief:

AGED MINISTERS' RELIEF.

The Board is located at Durham, N. C. It has the least possible expense in the administration of its responsibilities. Its duties are, to care for, support in full or in part as needs may require, on the part of our old ministers who are no longer able to serve our churches as pastors, and have no income to live on. The funds put into the hands of this Board has been wisely managed. However, the Board has not met the demand made upon it for lack of funds to dispense. About thirty-five or more, of our worthy brethren, are receiving inadequate amounts to meet their needs. Many who have asked for nothing, are worthy, and ought to be helped. Our Board is powerless to meet the needs without the funds. Therefore, your committee recommend: 1st. That an earnest effort be made to interest our people as a whole, in the work of our Relief Board.

2nd. That the pastors and delegates of this Association, take up the work of this Board with their churches, and increase our gifts to this work fifty per cent. if possible. Respectfully submitted,

J. W. NOBLES, Committee.

On motion to adopt the report, J. W. Nobles made a plea for Ministerial Relief:

The report was adopted and pledges taken.

The report on Education was submitted by A. C. Hamby:

REPORT ON MINISTERIAL EDUCATION.

There are at this time 63 ministerial students in Wake Forest College receiving aid from the Board of Education. Nine dollars per month is the maximum amount received by any one of them. The cost of living has increased considerably in the last few years, but the amount loaned to each student remains the same. There is a side to this question which is generally overlooked when contributions are made, viz.: That money given to the Board for Ministerial Education is a contribution to each of the benevolent objects which we as a denomination are pledged to promote. These young men come out of College prapared to cope with the ministers of other denominations in the effort to win the world for Christ. They are loyal to every phase of our denominational work and are filling the best pulpits of the State and of the South. Money invested in the education of young preachers is the best possible investment of the Lord's money.

A. C. HAMBY, for Committee.

On motion to adopt the report, Bro. Hamby made a few remarks.

T. H. King introduced Bro. Alex. Knott.

Pledges were taken and report adopted.

A letter was read from Bro. Hobgood relative to the Laymen's Movement.

Bro. Sherwood moved that a Committee be appointed to direct an every member canvass for Missions and visit the churches and hold mission rallies. A. C. Hamby, C. W. Carter and J. M. Beaty were appointed.

A resolution of thanks for the cordial entertainment accorded to the Association. It was adopted by a rising vote.

T. J. Lassiter, F. H. Brooks and W. C. Jackson were appointed a special committee to arrange for and hold a Sunday School Convention in the Association before next session.

On motion, the preachers and churches are earnestly requested to see to it that all the letters are prepared and forwarded to the Clerk at least one week before the Association meets next year; and that all the churches are requested to send up all the money for benevolence to the Treasurer of the Convention except the Building Fund, which the churches will send to T. J. Lassiter, Treasurer; and bring only Minute Fund to the Association.

Association adjourned.

REPORT OF HISTORIAN.

The Johnston County Association was organized in the town of Selma on November the 27th, 1903. The number of churches enrolled were thirty. At present we have forty-one. An increase of eleven. Our membership in 1903 was 2,400. It is now 3,612. The gain is 1,212. Pastors' salary in 1903 was $2,303.93. Last year it was $5,308.38. Showing an advance of $3,004.45.

Ministerial Education in 1903, $57.75; Ministerial Education in 1911, $113; advance, $55.25.

State Missions in 1903, $485.00; State Missions in 1911, $874.85; advance, $389.85.

Foreign Missions in 1903, $228.25; Foreign Missions in 1911, $408.73; advance, $71.47.

Home Missions in 1903, $111.75; Home Missions in 1911, $246.17; advance, $134.42.

Foreign Missions in 1903, $228.25; Foreign Missions in 1911, $408.72; advance, $180.48.

Orphanage in 1903, $227.00; Orphanage in 1911, $414.69; advance, $187.69.

Total advance in all objects $12,797.22.

R. W. HORRELL, Historian.

WOMAN'S MISSIONARY UNION.

The Woman's Missionary Union of the Johnston County Association met with the Selma Baptist Church November 1st, 1911.

Selma is a very easy place to reach and we had hoped to have delegates from every Society in the Association, however the attendance was very creditable. Meeting was one of profit, and spiritual help to every one present.

The Union convened at 10 o'clock. The devotional exercises were conducted by Mrs. W. N. Jones, who presided at this session, of the Union. Here and now in behalf of this body of Christian workers I wish to thank her most sincerely for responding to our Macedonian cry.

Mrs. Jones read for our Scripture lesson a few verses from John 21st chapter. Her heart to heart talk on "The call to service", was searching and beautiful. Interest and responsiveness was written on each face and many hearts determined to render more loving service to our Master. May the vision of God, and the Mission needs of the world be ever before our eyes, while the two great commandments, "Come unto me" and "Go ye into all the world" ring louder and louder in our ears until every woman in Johnston Association shall say, "Here am I, use me." Service the test of love. Do we love much?

Mrs. Carrington brought to us words of welcome from the Selma Society, while Mrs. Spiers of the Methodist, and Mrs. Mitchener of the Presbyterian churches extended words of welcome and Christian greeting to which the Secretary responded in behalf of the Union.

The following Committees were appointed:

Committee on Nomination: Mrs. Carrington, Mrs. Thomas, Mrs. Coats.

Committee on Time and Place—Mrs. Beaty, Mrs. Britton, Mrs. Barnes.

The following committees to report at the next meeting:

Home Missions—Mrs. Hamby, Mrs. N. R. Poole, Mrs. Youngblood.

Foreign Missions—Mrs. King, Mrs. Horrell and Mrs. W. E. Smith.

State Missions—Mrs. Beaty, Mrs. M. G. Gulley and Mrs. Driver.

Training School—Mrs. Hocutt, Miss Boon and Miss Creech.
Margaret Home—Miss Massey, Miss Ellis.

We considered such problems as "Conditions in our Association," Mrs.
J. M. Beaty.

"Problems of Societies in a Country Church," Mrs. N. R. Poole.

A short review of our work since organization in 1903, Mrs. Carter.

Our aims, open discussion. Almost every Society was eager to take
higher aims for the new Association year. The Union adopted the
"Constitution and By-laws" suggested by the Central Committee.

The dinner and social hour was a most enjoyable feature. The ladies
served a tempting lunch in one of the Sunday School rooms of the beautiful new church.

The afternoon devotional exercises were conducted by Mrs. Hurst.
Mrs. Horrell led in prayer.

Home Missions, a paper by Mrs. R. M. Nowell.

Why any church needs a Y. W. A.? Mrs. B. A. Hocutt.

Why the young girls need the Y. W. A., Miss Winona Massey.

The Training School, Mrs. C. W. Carter.

State Missions, Sunbeam Work and the Standard of Excellence were
emphasized by Mrs. W. N. Jones.

The election of officers resulted in the election of Mrs. Carter, President; Mrs. Nowell, Secretary and Treasurer.

The Union desires to express to our retiring President, our grateful
appreciation for her efficient services.

The meeting in Selma goes down in our history as a good and profitable one.

The first Wednesday in November is the time of meeting and the
place Clayton. The closing moments of prayer were impressive and
we felt the blessed presence of the Holy Spirit in our midst. The
people were delighted to hear at the evening service a scholarly sermon
by Rev. A. C. Hamby, of Clayton, on "What Missions meant to Christ."

The evening music was particularly good. The quartette of the Clayton Church lending a helping *"voice."*

FINANCIAL REPORT OF THE WOMAN'S MISSIONARY UNION OF THE JOHNSTON COUNTY ASSOCIATION FOR YEAR ENDING OCTOBER, 1911.

SOCIETIES.	State Missions.	Home Missions.	Foreign Missions.	Training School Support.	Margaret Home.	Expense Fund.	Totals.
Smithfield W. M. S.	$38.87	$19.50	$15.00	$ 5.00	$.....	$ 2.00	$ 80.37
Benson W. M. S.	4.15	.....	.....	.....	.....	.....	4.15
Selma W. M. S.	3.05	8.00	2.65	4.65	.....	1.00	19.35
Mount Moriah W. M. S.	5.05	8.85	15.00	.....	.....	70	29.60
Clyde's Chapel W. M. S.	1.83	1.83	1.84	15	.....	10	5.75
Micro W. M. S.	1.55	45	90	.....	.....	.....	2.90
Bethesda W. M. S.	.....	1.05	1.05	.....	.....	.....	2.10
Wilson's Mills W. M. S.	.....	6.40	.....	.....	.....	.....	6.40
Clayton W. M. S.	70.00	34.00	34.00	.....	.....	1.10	139.10
Four Oaks W. M. S.	8.80	3.65	3.75	.....	.....	1.20	17.40
Wendell W. M. S.	.....	2.00	.....	.....	.....	.....	2.00
Clayton—Junior Union	52	.....	.....	.....	.....	.....	52
Smithfield Sunbeams	8.00	3.65	2.50	.....	1.50	.....	15.65
Micro Sunbeams	93	57	1.60	.....	.....	.....	3.10
Clayton Y. W. A.	17.01	10.00	11.35	5.00	.....	1.70	45.06
Mount Moriah R. A.	2.53	2.65	2.95	.....	.....	.....	8.13
Total	162.29	102.60	92.59	14.80	1.50	7.80	381.58

CONSTITUTION.

1. The Association shall be known as the Johnston County Baptist Association.

2· Its object shall be to extend the privileges of the Gospel and liberal culture to all the people within its bounds, and by hearty co-operation with the Baptist State Convention to help offer these privileges to all mankind in and out of its bounds, by the cordial co-operation of all the churches constituting this body.

3. It shall be composed of the pastors in active service in the Association and such delegates as shall be annually elected by the churches connected with it, each church being entitled to three delegates, unless the membership shall exceed fifty, and then an additional delegate for every twenty-five members, provided no church shall have more than eight delegates.

4. The New Hampshire Declaration of Faith shall be the summary of Divine Truth for determining questions of faith and order in this body, and the churches desiring membership in it must commit themselves to the substance of it, together with the covenant therewith submitted, and this Constitution.

5. This Association shall not have power, to annul the discipline or exercise authority over any church connected with it, but it may advise with and sever its connection with any church that neglects to preserve gospel order, or that treats with contempt the objects or advice of the Association.

6. Each church shall send to the annual meetings of the Association a letter (the blanks to be furnished by the clerk of the Association), carefully filled as per blank suggestions, stating the full work of the church for the year ending with the close of the month previous to the one in which the Association is held.

7. The Association shall foster State Missions, Home Missions, Foreign Missions, Christian Education, the Aged Ministers' Relief Board, the Thomas-

ville Orphanage and the Sunday School Board, and each church shall be requested to contribute to the support of these objects annually.

8. Missions and education shall have precedence in their claims upon the consideration of this body in its regular sessions.

9. Whenever a church shall fail to be represented by delegates or letter at the annual sessions of the Association inquiry shall be made for the cause and efforts shall be made to induce such church to do its duty, and the effort shall be continued till the church is recovered or dropped from the roll.

10. The officers of the Association shall be a Moderator, a Vice-Moderator, a Clerk, a Treasurer and an Auditor, elected annually by ballot from among its members, to serve until their successors shall have been elected, and to perform the duties usual to such officers, namely, the Moderator, in presiding over the meetings, or the Vice-Moderator in his absence; the Clerk in recording and preserving minutes and other papers belonging to the body; the Treasurer in receiving and disbursing funds belonging to or entrusted to the body according to its will; the Auditor to examine the Treasurer's books at each meeting of the Association and report the same before adjournment.

11. The Association shall appoint annually an Executive Committee of five (5) from its members, who shall be entrusted with the prosecution of Missions in the Association and any other work for the interest of the Master's Kingdom which may be referred to them. This committee shall, as far as possible, co-operate with the State Mission Board in supplying the destitution in our territory, and between the meetings of the Association take such actions as may seem to them advisable for the advancement of its interest. The committee shall present to the Association at its annual meeting a report of its proceedings, with the names of the missionaries supported on the field, time of service and details of their work, together with such recommendations as in the judgment of the committee the Association should follow in planning its subsequent work.

12. The annual sessions of the Association shall begin on Wednesday after the first Lord's day in November at such place as may be chosen, and an introductory sermon shall be delivered on the first day of the session. Representatives from a majority of the churches constituting the Association shall be a quorum.

13. This Constitution may be amended at any annual session by a two-thirds vote of all the members present.

14. Provision shall be made at each annual session for a session of the Woman's Central Committee, and all other necessary encouragement offered for the enlargement of the organized work of the Woman's Missionary Societies in the local churches. The proceedings of the Woman's Central Committee shall be recorded as a part of the Minutes of the Association.

BY-LAWS.

1. The daily sessions of the Association shall be opened and closed with prayer.

2. Delegates shall be recognized by letters from their churches designating them as such.

3. The Moderator shall recognize corresponding messengers or the delegates of newly received churches by extending to them his right hand.

4. The report of the Executive Board and the Missionary work of the Association shall take precedence of all other business during the morning session of the second day of the annual session.

5. The Clerk shall record and read the proceedings when called for, super-

intend the publication and distribution of the Minutes, preserve a file of them, and have it present at each annual session, and deliver to his successor all papers belonging to the body.

6. Members desiring to speak shall first rise and address the Moderator; shall use the term "brother" in speaking to each other; shall not speak on the same subject more than twice without permission, and shall observe the courtesy that becomes Christians.

7. Members shall not absent themselves from the session without permission.

8. The roll of members shall be called at least once and absentees marked.

9. Corresponding messengers and visiting brethren shall be invited to seats, with privilege of speaking, but not of voting.

10. A copy of the Minutes shall be sent to the Secretary of the State Mission Board, the Secretary of the Southern Baptist Convention, the American Baptist Publication Society, 1420 Chestnut Street, Philadelphia; the Sunday School Board of the Southern Baptist Convention and the Thomasville Orphanage.

11. All questions of order not herein provided shall be decided by Kerfoot's Parliamentary Law.

REPORT OF FINANCE COMMITTEE.

SOCIETIES.	Minutes and Clerk.	State Missions.	Home Missions.	Foreign Missions.	Sunday School Missions.	Ministerial Relief.	Orphanage.	Church Building Fund.	Ministerial Education.	Total.
Bailey	$.....	$ 2.81	$.....	$.....	$.....	$.....	$.....	$.....	$.....	$ 2.81
Bethany	1.52	6.00	3.00	2.00	1.00	2.00	3.50	2.00	1.00	22.00
Clyde's Chapel*										28.25
Corinth	1.20	9.00	1.56	2.00	1.50	2.50	5.00	1.50	1.00	25.26
Kenly	1.00									1.00
Mount Moriah	2.00	25.12	10.61		5.00	1.42	22.50	5.00	1.12	72.77
Thanksgiving	45	5.00	1.00	1.00	50	1.00	1.00	1.00	1.00	11.95
Wilson's Mills	60	15.00		2.40	2.00	3.00		5.00	3.00	31.00
Middlesex	1.50							2.00		3.50
Benson Grove	50	21			50	50	39	2.00		4.10
Benson	3.00	80.40	15.00	15.00	2.00			10.00		125.40
Special collection**		42.61								42.61
Total	11.75	186.15	31.17	22.40	12.50	10.42	32.39	28.50	7.12	370.65

* Objects not named.
** Of collection Clayton church gave $11.00.

Respectfully submitted,
JOE POOL, for Committee.

TREASURER'S REPORT.

To the Johnston County Association:

I beg to submit the following report showing receipts and disbursements for the year ending November 20, 1911:

Sources of Receipts.	State Missions.	Home Missions.	Foreign Missions.	Sunday School Missions.	Ministerial Education.	Aged Ministers.	Building Fund.	M inute Fund.	Orphanage.	Pastor's Salary.	Total.
On Hand Last Report.	$.....	$.....	$.....	$....	$....	$....	$128.30	$52.20	$ 2.00	$...	$ 182.!
From Churches.......	469.04	81.80	116.71	47.55	81.75	77.42	111.88	40.68	128.00	8.87	1163.'
From J. M. Beaty.....							198.55				198.!
From Will H. Lassiter							14.50				14.!
From Clayton (Middlesex)							50.00				50.(
From Finance Com. 1911.	186.15	31.18	22.40	12.50	7.12	10.42	28.50	11.75	32.39	....	342.·
From last report (Other objects)							16.65				16.(
Borrowed from Bank of Smithfield..							300.00				300.(
Total	655.19	112.98	139.11	60.05	88.87	87.84	848.38	104.63	162.39	8.87	2268.:
Disbursements:											
Paid Walters Durham.	655.19	121.94	139.11	60.05	88.87	87.34					1152.!
Paid S. H. Averitt....									162.39	....	162.:
PaidMrs. Ida Edgerton (For Pinkney)							439.28				439.:
Paid C. I. Godwin (For Pine Level)....							100.00				100.
Paid R. H. Johnston (For Pleasant Grove)							157.85				157.
Paid Nash Bros., (Printing)								30.00			30.
Paid T. J. Lassiter (salary and postage).								18.75			18.
Paid Rev. J. W. Smith (Pastor) ..·.......										8.87	8.
Paid Bank of Smithfield (Interest)							6.75			....	6.
Paid Bank of Smithfield (on note).·.....							100.00				100.
Paid A. A. Pippin for Middlesex							50.00				50.
Total	655.19	121.9									
Amount overpaid	......	8.!									
Balance	......	.....									
Less		8.!									
Balance on hand.......	......	.....									

Respectfully submitted,   T. J. LASSITER,
Treasurer.

I have carefully examined the book and annual report of the Treasurer for the year ending November 20, 1911, and find them to be correct.

Respectfully,   A. C. HAMBY, Auditor.

November 27, 1911.

CHURCH.	Pastor's Salary.	Building and Repairing.	Incidentals.	Sunday School Expenses.	The Poor.	State Missions.	Home Missions.	Foreign Missions.	Sunday School Missions.	Orphanage.	Ministerial Education.	Ministerial Relief.	Minute Fund.	Church Building Fund.	Other Objects.	Total.
Antioch	$19.25	$40.00	$	$	$	$15.00	$1.50	$1.50	$1.50	$2.75	$1.50	$2.50	$.80	$2.25	$	$48.55
Bailey	6.75		68.50			5.31	.50	.50	.50	2.00	.50	1.00	1.00	2.00		60.56
Baptist Center	100.00	70.00	1.75	15.00		5.00	2.00	2.50	2.50	5.00	1.00	1.00	1.00	1.50	63.75	205.50
Beaty Chapel	50.00			6.00		2.00	1.00		.50	1.50	1.00	1.00	1.00	6.50		143.25
Benson	311.19	233.71	20.00			80.40	15.00	15.00		25.00	1.00	5.00	3.50	10.00		
Benson Grove		50.00				2.00			.50					2.00		83.50
Bethany	35.00			3.00		6.00	3.00	2.00	1.00	3.00	1.00	1.00	1.50			
Bethel	20.00		6.00	12.00		5.00	2.50	1.00	1.00	3.50	1.00	1.00	1.00	2.00	2.50	38.00
Bethesda	200.00			6.00	18.00	25.00	3.00	5.00	1.00	20.00	3.00	1.00	.66	2.00	47.00	324.50
Blackman's Grove	50.50					16.00	1.40	1.75	1.00	4.00	1.50	1.50	1.00	1.53		86.16
Calvary	8.50					8.31			.50	1.00	.60	.62	1.00			17.61
Clayton	1200.00	591.01	114.49	90.16		239.90	91.07	85.78	11.00	158.10	14.15	69.47	5.00	27.50	205.99	2903.62
Carter's Chapel	50.00	84.00		10.00		10.00	2.00		3.00	10.00	1.50	2.00	1.50	2.50		191.08
Clyde's Chapel	100.00			6.00		6.00	2.00	4.00	1.00	1.00	1.00	3.00	1.50	1.50		140.00
Corinth	47.00				3.49	9.00	1.00	1.50		10.06	1.50	3.00	1.00	2.50		72.20
Four Oaks	100.00	67.50	2.10	9.14		15.00	7.00	5.75	1.00	5.00	1.00	3.00	.50	2.50	26.20	184.83
Hood's Grove	40.00		23.50	2.50		4.00	1.00	4.00	.50	13.45	2.00		1.50	1.00		54.50
Kenly	84.00		7.50	32.72	1.38	5.75	5.00	4.00	1.25	5.00	5.00	2.00	.75	2.00	2.50	242.17
Lee's Chapel	150.00			10.00		27.50	2.00	4.50	2.50	1.25	1.00	3.00	.80	2.00		235.00
Live Oak	75.00	7.50	7.50			5.00		10.00	.50	3.80	1.00	1.00	.75	1.00		89.75
Micro	25.50	104.12	1.42			6.00	2.00	4.00		29.37	2.00	1.30	1.00	2.00	31.16	151.27
Middlesex	300.00	330.56	42.89	48.40		24.93	9.39	50.12	3.06	7.50	5.00	4.58	2.00	5.00		816.96
Mt Moriah	130.00			30.00		21.00	6.00	6.00	5.00	24.00	6.00	6.00	2.00	5.00	35.00	338.15
New Bethel			10.00			8.43	3.00	1.50		5.00	1.00	1.00		5.00		259.50
Nobles' Chapel	60.00					17.50	3.50		1.50							79.50
Oliver's Grove																19.18
Parrish Memorial			1.00	3.00										1.10		
Pauline	45.00	40.00				5.00	2.00	1.50	.50	3.00	1.25	1.00	1.00	2.50		104.00
Pine Level	50.00	193.58	35.00			6.00	1.00	1.50	.50	3.00	1.50	1.00				65.75
Pinkney Chapel	25.00	5.50		5.77		5.00	2.50	1.00		2.45	2.50	4.00	.50	1.00		263.08
Pisgah	100.00	.65	13.87	16.79		17.52	4.25	5.00	1.00	4.00	2.00	2.50	1.00	4.25		156.74
Princeton	43.00		10.00	24.00		20.00	5.00	5.00		2.00	1.00	1.00	.50	2.00		98.52
Sardis	50.00	30.00	95.00			9.25										110.25
Selma	600.00	55.00					2.50	3.00	1.00	5.00	3.00	2.50	.84	2.00	2.84	
Shiloh	150.00			7.00		8.50	40.00	60.00	10.00	40.43	20.00	21.00	4.50	25.00	50.00	188.18
Smithfield	500.00	400.00		97.71	40.00	160.00	1.00	1.00		3.00		1.00				
Thanksgiving	13.36	5.00		7.20		7.50	1.00	2.50	.50	3.00	1.00	1.50	.50	1.00		37.51
ity							2.50			12.65	2.85					18.00
Wendell	150.30	50.63	50.00	44.73		7.47	8.25	10.15	8.45	3.00	3.50	5.00	2.00	3.00		302.18
White Oak	150.30	45.00	45.00			22.50	5.00	5.00	8.50	8.00	3.00	3.00	2.00	5.00		
Wilson's Mills	100.00	20.00	20.00	30.00		22.75	5.00	5.00	2.00	10.00			.60		20.00	250.00
Total	5459.05	1689.42	820.16	564.10	62.87	891.72	251.95	316.80	71.76	439.31	105.73	170.47	49.43	152.38	478.94	

CHURCH AND PASTOR.	CLERK AND POSTOFFICE.	Preaching Sunday.	Value Church Property.	Seating Capacity.	Baptized.	Received by Letter.	Restored.	Dismissed by Letter.	Excluded.	Died.	Number Males.	Number Females.	Total.
Antioch—R. L. Hocutt	G. R. Whitley, Inter. 1	Second	$1250.00	700	7	2	3	4	3	3	60	123	183
Bailey—Geo. H. Johnson	R. L. Underwood, Bailey	First	2300.00	350	6	12	1	1			14	21	35
Baptist Center—A. I. Caudle	Milton Austin, Clayton	First	1000.00	300	3	4	2		2		26	50	76
Beaty Chapel—R. W. Horrell	W. M. Easom, Smithfield	1-4 S. nl.	700.00	300	3	1		2	6	2	8	16	24
Benson Grove—J. W. Smith	D. D. Medlin, Benson	Second	800.00	200	9	5		6	3		8	17	25
Benson—E. J. Rodgers	S. F. Ivey, Benson	2nd-4th	1500.00	350	9	10	1	5			52	104	156
Bethany—R. L. Hocutt	Kirkman Creech, Kenly	Fourth	600.00	300	3	4					34	50	84
Bethel—Geo. H. Johnson	Jerry Barnes, Kenly	Fourth	600.00	400				4	2	2	9	14	23
Bethesda—R. W. Horrell	J. E. Smith, Wilson's Mills	Fourth	500.00	400	16	5	7		1	2	91	118	209
Blackman's Grove—W. T. Hurst	J. G. Johnson, Four Oaks	Second	500.00	400				2	1		19	39	58
Calvary—J. W. Smith	T. J. Lee, Dunn	Fourth	600.00	400	1	2		3	12	1	8	17	25
Carter's Chapel—J. W. Smith	Martin Thom. Selma	Fourth	400.00	400	34	6	1	5	1		42	54	96
Clayton—A. C. Hamby	R. I. Gulley, Clayton	First	6000.00	500		7	2		3	4	156	176	332
Clyde's Chapel—J. W. Noble	C. L. Johnson, Archer, 2	Third	500.00	300	11		1		1		48	89	137
Corinth—A. A. Pippin	H. V. Andrews, Archer, 1	Second	400.00	400		1		1	2	3	35	70	105
Four Oaks—W. T. Hurst	P. T. George, Four Oaks	Third	800.00	200	7	7					19	31	50
Hood's Grove—T. J. Hood	W. Langdon, Four Oaks	Third	450.00	300		3		2	48	1	13	24	37
Kenly—Geo. H. Johnson	W. C. Casper, Rocky Mount	Second	2500.00	250	9	5	5	3			18	10	28
Lee's Chapel—A. A. Pippin	W. I. Green, Wakefield, 2	Fourth	1000.00	500	35	2			2	7	103	142	245
Live Oak—D. D. Edwards	K. Brodwell, Selma, 3	Second	500.00	300	5	5					13	30	43
Micro—J. W. Smith	Leonard Pace, Selma, 3	Third	700.00	400	2	3	1	2			11	11	22
Middlesex—A. C. Sherwood	W. C. Jackson, Middlesex	2nd-4th	2250.00	300	8	12		3	3		27	38	65
Mount Moriah—W. T.	J. H. Bryant, Raleigh	First	800.00	300	2	6		2		3	73	87	160
New Bethel—J. W. Nobles	Geo. W. Bryan, Garner	Fourth	800.00	400			1			1	39	48	87
Nobles' Chapel—G. H. Johnson	N. L. Stott, Sims	Fourth	700.00	350	3	3			1		37	52	89
Oliver's Grove—W. T. Hurst	T. B. Tyner, Four Oaks	Fourth	400.00	250	5	2		1	6		9	21	30
Parrish Memorial—E. J. Rodgers	Jos. D. Creech, Selma	First	500.00	300			4			1	36	37	73
Pine Level *	C. I. Godwin, Pine Level	Third	300.00	300	13	1		4	1	6	37	36	73
Pauline—T. J. Hood	J. R. Massey, Four Oaks	First	650.00	300		2	2	4	1		23	27	50
Pinkney—N. H. Shepherd	Mrs. Ida Edgerton, Kenly	First	1000.00	400		4			1		21	8	29
Pisgah—R. W. Horrell	R. H. Etins, Smithfield	First	1000.00	250	4	2		3	4		4	8	12
Princeton—W. R. Beach	W. I. Pearce, Princeton	Third	1000.00	400			1	8		1	27	36	63
Sardis—R. W. Horrell	B. C. Powell, Smithfield	2nd-4th	500.00	200	6	3	1	1	1		39	68	107
Selma—R. W. Horrell		Second	15000.00	500	5	4			1		65	92	157
Shiloh—R. W. Horrell	F. D. Holland, McCullers	1st-3rd	700.00	300	13	19		2	1		35	47	82
Smithfield	T. J. Lassiter, Smithfield	First	6000.00	600		4	2	5	1		73	92	165
Thanksgiving—R. L. Hocutt	Aram Earp, Selma, 1	Fourth	1500.00	200	1	3		4	4		31	30	61
Trinity—J. W. Smith	J. M. Lawhon, Benson	Second	250.00	200	2	13			1		14	29	43
Wendell—J. W. Noble	M. C. Todd, Wendell	Second	1000.00	700	21	3		5			45	98	143
White Oak—A. A. Pippin	J. I. Murphy, Zebulon	Second	1500.00	500			2	4			67	111	178
Wilson's Mills—E. J. Rodgers	G. H. Ellis, Wilson's Mills	Third	800.00	250							25	26	51
Total			51550.00		268	150	37	76	130	33			3452

CHURCH.	SUPERINTENDENT AND POSTOFFICE.	Officers and Teachers.	Scholars.	Total Enrollment.	Volumes in Library.	Quarterlies and Papers taken.	Months kept open.	Average Attendance.	Baptisms from School.	Benevolent Contributions.	School Expenses.	Total Contributions.
Antioch	J. R. Hocutt, Selma, 2	12	98	110		54	9	40	3		$15.00	$15.00
Baptist Center	J. C. Hardee, Clayton 1	7	81	88		65	12	45	13			
Beaty Chapel	W. M. Eason, Smithfield	8	80	34			12	65				
Benson	J. E. Wall, Benson	4	130	139		160	12	30	8	$8.43	3.00	3.00
Benson's	Jasper Blackman, Benson	9	53	80		60	12	60	3			
Bethany	David Pace, Selma, 2	5	74	85		70	12	20			12.00	12.00
Bethel	Levin — Kenly	6	30	35		36	6	40				
Bethesda	J. J. Wallace, Wilson's Mills	5	60	70		72	12	20	10		6.00	6.00
Blackman's Grove	T. P. Wood, Four Oaks	10	25	28		150	6	20				
Carter's	Preston Mozingo, Selma	3	68	74	40	320	12	38	1	47.50	10.00	10.00
Clyde's Chapel	R. H. Gower, Clayton	6	309	321	500	200	12	150	29		90.46	169.19
Four Oaks	W. T. Bunch, Clayton 2	12	65	72		105	12	40			6.00	6.00
Kenly	W. A. Massengill, Four Oaks	7	108	114			12	47	8	11.63	9.14	20.77
Lee's Chapel	A. J. Broughton	8	63	71		100	12	19	7		32.72	32.72
Micro	J. W. Strickland, Middlesex	8	100	106		334	12	75	25		10.00	10.00
Middlesex	C. E. Batten, Micro	6	35	41			12	25	2		1.38	1.38
Mount Moriah	W. C. Jackson, Middlesex	6	130	139	350	150	12	85	7	18.93	48.40	77.30
New Bethel	J. H. Bryant, Raleigh	9	93	93			12	67			4.00	4.00
Oliver's Grove	J. A. Tyner, Four Oaks	13	81	85		48	9	50	2			
Pauline	D. E. R. Evans, Four Oaks	4	65	71		12	3	40	8			
Pine Level												
Pisgah	E. R. Jones, Smithfield	10	41	51		216	12	11	1		5.77	5.77
Princeton	W. I. Pearce, Princeton	7	80	87		84	12	44			16.79	16.79
Selma	B. F. Hassell, Selma	11	201	212			12	145	1		24.00	7.00
Shiloh	J. F. Hardee, McCullers	6	54	60		75	12	40	5			
Smithfield	N. R. Stell, Wendell	10	160	170			12	100	7	16.00	97.71	
Wendell	J. A. Batton, Archer, 1	13	261	274		760	12	120	13	5.00	44.73	49.73
White Oak		6	65	71		70	12	40				
Wilson's Mills		6	40	46		75	9	15				
Parrish Memorial	Herbert Pender, Selma, 3	5	30	35		50	12		2		30.00	30.00
Trinity	Jos. E. McLamb, Benson, 2	5	27	30		24	12	25			3.00	3.00
Thanksgiving	Aram Earp, Selma, 1	3	40	45		84	9	35			7.20	7.20
Bailey	J. P. Underwood, Bailey	5	63	68			12	25	1		7.20	
Hood's Grove	P. L. Hayes, Four Oaks	6	34	40			6	25			2.50	
Total		241	2695	2936					162	107.49	584.10	691.59

CHURCHES.	State Missions.	Home Missions.	Foreign Missions.	Sunday School Missions.	Ministerial Education.	Ministerial Relief.	Orphanage.	Fund.	Building.
Antioch	$15.00	$ 1.50	$ 1.50	$ 1.00	$ 1.50	$ 3.00	$ 2.75	$	2.50
Bailey	5.00	1.00	2.00	1.00	50	2.00	5.00		4.00
Baptist Center	5.00	2.00	2.50	1.50	2.00	2.00	5.00		1.50
Beaty Chapel	5.00	1.50	2.00	50	1.50	1.00	2.00		2.50
Benson	75.00	10.00	10.00	.....	.....	5.00	25.00		6.80
Benson's Grove	5.00	1.00	1.00	1.00	1.00	1.00	3.00		2.00
Bethany	6.00	3.00	2.00	1.00	1.00	1.00	3.50		2.00
Bethel	5.00	2.50	1.00	1.00	1.00	1.00	1.50		2.50
Bethesda	25.00	5.00	5.00	2.00	2.00	4.00	20.00		2.00
Blackman's Grove	20.00	5.00	5.00	2.00	4.00	2.00	8.00		2.00
Calvary	8.00	2.00	1.00	1.25	2.00	2.00	1.50		2.00
Carter's Chapel	11.00	2.50	2.50	1.10	2.00	2.00	1.00		2.50
Clayton	272.25	72.50	72.60	3.00	24.20	29.20	162.00		30.00
Clyde's Chapel	10.00	5.50	4.00	12.00	2.00	1.50	5.00		1.50
Corinth	9.50	2.00	2.00	.....	1.00	1.00	5.00		1.50
Four Oaks	15.00	5.00	5.00	15.00	1.50	1.50	5.00		2.50
Hood's Grove	5.00	1.00	1.00	1.00	1.00	1.50	2.00		2.50
Kenly	6.75	3.85	5.00	2.00	2.50	1.00	4.00		2.50
Lee's Chapel	30.00	5.00	10.00	3.00	5.00	5.00	5.00		6.00
Live Oak	7.50	1.00	1.50	50	1.00	1.00	1.25		5.00
Micro	10.00	2.00	1.00	1.00	1.00	1.00	2.00		2.00
Middlesex	15.00	.....	3.00	1.00	1.25	2.00	5.00		2.50
Mount Moriah	55.00	25.00	50.00	6.60	5.50	6.60	30.00		5.50
New Bethel	20.00	6.00	5.00	1.00	5.50	5.00	17.52		5.00
Nobles' Chapel	5.00	1.00	1.00	50	1.00	1.00	2.00		1.50
Oliver's Grove	.....	.....	.....	.....	.....	.....	.....		.....
Parrish Memorial	7.50	1.00	1.00	50	1.60	1.00	1.00		2.00
Pauline	6.50	2.50	1.50	1.00	2.00	2.00	3.00		3.00
Pine Level	7.00	2.50	1.50	.....	1.50	1.50	4.00		4.00
Pinkney Chapel	5.00	1.00	1.00	.....	1.00	1.00	2.00		4.25
Pisgah	17.50	3.00	5.25	.....	2.50	2.50	2.25		.....
Princeton	25.00	4.25	5.00	.....	2.00	2.00	4.00		1.25
Sardis	11.50	2.50	2.00	.....	1.00	1.00	2.00		2.00
Selma	.....	10.00	.....	.....	.....	.....	.....		.....
Shiloh	7.50	2.50	3.00	.....	3.00	3.00	5.00		2.00
Smithfield	180.00	40.00	60.00	10.00	20.00	20.00	40.00		25.00
Thanksgiving	5.00	1.00	1.00	.....	1.00	2.00	2.50		1.00
Trinity	10.00	1.00	3.50	.....	1.00	1.00	8.00		1.00
Wendell	15.00	5.00	10.00	.....	5.00	5.00	25.00		2.00
White Oak	25.00	5.50	5.50	.....	4.00	5.50	9.00		2.00
Wilson's Mills	16.00	5.00	5.00	.....	3.00	3.00	10.00		11.80

MINUTES

OF THE

TENTH SESSION

OF THE

JOHNSTON COUNTY

BAPTIST ASSOCIATION,

MET WITH

MOUNT MORIAH BAPTIST CHURCH,

NOVEMBER 6th, 7th and 8th, 1912.

The next session will be held with Smithfield Church, beginning Wednesday after the first Sunday in November, 1913.

To preach Introductory Sermon—R. W. Horrell.

OFFICERS.

Moderator—R. H. Gower..................................Clayton, N. C.
Vice-Moderator—A. A. Pippin..........................Wakefield, N. C.
Clerk—J. B. Jackson....................................Smithfield, N. C.
Treasurer—T. J. Lassiter...............................Smithfield, N. C.
Historian—R. W. Horrell................................Selma, N. C.

EXECUTIVE COMMITTEE.

J. M. Beaty, Chairman..................................Smithfield, N. C.
J. B. Creech..Four Oaks, N. C.
R. H. Gower...Clayton, N. C.
G. H. Wright..Wendell, N. C.
Claude Stephenson.....................................McCullers, N. C.

GOLDSBORO, N. C.
NASH BROS., PRINTERS AND BINDERS,
1913.

OF THE

TENTH SESSION

OF THE

JOHNSTON COUNTY

BAPTIST ASSOCIATION,

MET WITH

MOUNT MORIAH BAPTIST CHURCH,

NOVEMBER 6th, 7th and 8th, 1912.

The next session will be held with Smithfield Church, beginning Wednesday after the first Sunday in November, 1913.

To preach Introductory Sermon—R. W. Horrell.

OFFICERS.

Moderator—R. H. Gower..................................Clayton, N. C.
Vice-Moderator—A. A. Pippin.........................Wakefield, N. C.
Clerk—J. B. Jackson....................................Smithfield, N. C.
Treasurer—T. J. Lassiter..............................Smithfield, N. C.
Historian—R. W. Horrell................................Selma, N. C.

EXECUTIVE COMMITTEE.

J. M. Beaty, Chairman..................................Smithfield, N. C.
J. B. Creech...Four Oaks, N. C.
R. H. Gower..Clayton, N. C.
G. H. Wright...Wendell, N. C.
Claude Stephenson......................................McCullers, N. C.

GOLDSBORO, N. C.
NASH BROS., PRINTERS AND BINDERS,
1913.

CHAIRMEN STANDING COMMITTEES, 1913.

State Missions ....R. W. HORRELL.
Home Missions ....A. C. HAMBY.
Foreign Missions ....J. B. JACKSON.
Orphanage ....C. W. CARTER.
Aged Ministers' Relief......................................A. A. PIPPIN.
Biblical Recorder ....J. T. HOLT.
Education ....C. A. JENKENS.
Sunday Schools ....J. M. DUNCAN.
Woman's Work...T. J. LASSITER.
Temperance ....T. J. HOOD.

LIST OF PASTORS.

W. T. BAUCUM...Wake Forest.
W. L. BILBRO.. Middlesex.
O. P. CAMPBELL...Wake Forest.
L. CARPENTER ....Wake Forest.
J. M. DUNCAN... .... Benson.
D. D. EDWARDS.......................................R. F. D. 3, Selma.
N. H. GIBBS... Benson.
A. C. HAMBY.. Clayton.
R. L. HOCUTT...Route 1 Archer.
R. W. HORRELL. .... Selma.
T. J. HOOD.....................................R. F. D. 4, Goldsboro.
J. B. JACKSON..Smithfield.
C. A. JENKENS.. Clayton.
W. C. NOWELL...... .... Wendell.
A. A. PIPPIN.. Wakefield.
J. W. SMITH...Wilson's Mills.
C. H. SORRELL .... Wake Forest.

THE TENTH ANNUAL SESSION
—of the—
Johnston County Baptist Association,
—met with the—.
MOUNT MORIAH BAPTIST CHURCH.

Wednesday, November 6, 7 and 8, 1912.

Devotional exercises were conducted by A. C. Hamby.

The Introductory sermon was preached by J. B. Jackson from I Corinthians 1:19, 21.

Adjourned for dinner.

AFTERNOON SESSION.

The Association was organized by electing R. H. Gower, Moderator; A. A. Pippin, Vice-Moderator; N. R. Pool, Clerk; T. J. Lassiter, Treasurer, and R. W. Horrell, Historian.

The following visiting brethren were recognized and welcomed: J. M. Hilliard, of the Piedmont Association; J. S. Hagwood, of the Raleigh Association; C. J. Thompson, of the Foreign Mission Board.

The following Finance Committee was appointed: J. J. Wallace, J. H. Bell and D. J. Yelvington.

The following delegates were enrolled:

Antioch—
Bailey—J. W. B. Finch, J. P. Underwood.
Baptist Center—A. D. Gowen.
Beaty Chapel—
Benson—
Bethesda—D. C. Smith, D. L. Johnson, J. J. Wallace.
Bethel—J. H. Bell.
Bethany—
Calvary—
Clayton—A. C. Hamby, D. J. Yelvington, C. A. Jenkens, C. L. Barnes, and C. W. Carter.
Carter's Chapel—Albert McCall, Martin Thorne.
Clyde's Chapel—J. M. Todd, W. T. Bunch.
Corninth—J. B. Woodard, H. B. Andrews.
Four Oaks—J. S. Thorn, R. A. Bain.
Kenly—
Lee's Chapel—
Live Oak—C. T. Eason, H. L. Broadwell.
Micro—C. L. Batton.
Middlesex—
Mount Moriah—J. M. Baucum, E. P. Powell.
New Bethel—D. E. Hicks.
Nobles' Chapel—J. H. Flowers, Pharoe Bruar.
Oliver's Grove—
Pauline—W. B. Joyner.
Parrish Memorial—J. D. Creech, John Watson and G. V. Parrish.
Pinkey Chapel—
Pine Level—J. F. Watson.

Pisgah—A. G. Thompson.
Princeton—W. W. Wells.
Selma—R. W. Horrell, G. M. Willets, N. G. Wells.
Shiloh—J. T. Williams, D. M. Lee and Claude Stephenson.
Blackman's Grove—W. A. Phelps.
Smithfield—W. R. Smith, J: B. Jackson, J. W. Smith.
Thanksgiving—W. R. Parrish.
Wendell—G. H. Wright.
White Oak—W. T. Allen, L. C. Newton, J. M. Eason.
Wilson's Mills—J. T. Holt, G. G. Beaty.

The report on Foreign Missions was submitted by A. C. Hamby, as follows:

REPORT ON FOREIGN MISSIONS.

A just and comprehensive view of Foreign Mission opportunities at present is the greatest inspiration in the Kingdom of God on earth.

The complete transformation of China within the last few months is one of the greatest events in human history. A radical change of one-fourth of the human race intellectually and politically and the making of them ready for spiritual readjustment, in so short a time, is without parallel in the history of nations.

The Foreign Mission Board located at Richmond, Virginia, is a committee appointed by the Southern Baptist Convention to carry on this, our foreign mission work, by the co-operation of all our churches and in behalf of all our people.

It is our work. One member of the Board lives in each State and is called the State Vice-President. A representative of the Board lives in every association. He is expected to confer with the Board and with the churches in the interest of the work. At the present meeting of the body this association is expected to elect this Representative of the Foreign Mission Board to serve until the next meeting of the association.

Our present fields are Argentina, Brazil, Mexico, Italy, Africa, Japan and China.

The present number of missionaries is 271. The native workers have been increased to 577, making a total force of 848. The 342 native churches are growing in self-support and missionary efforts. The 422 Sunday Schools are doing aggressive work. Nine Women's Training Schools have 312 students, and ten theological schools have 245 students. These with the other 208 schools of all grades have 6,156 pupils. In six hospitals and thirteen dispensaries, thirteen medical missionaries treated 51,796 patients during the year. Four publishing plants are sending out millions of pages of religious literature.

The contributions for 1911-'12 were $580,408, a gain of $70,400 over the previous year. Of this amount 12 per cent. was used for expenses at home as follows: In Richmond, 5 per cent.; W. M. W. 1 per cent.; interest, 2½ per cent.; State expenses, 3½ per cent. This percentage of expenses is larger than the Board wants it to be. Our people can reduce it very much by sending their money all through the year, so as to save the interest account. Let it also be remembered that a large part of the money used at home is expended in efforts to arouse our people and increase contributions.

The work has often been greatly helped by bequests and annuities. More and more our people ought to remember the Board in their wills. Pastors can exert a blessed influence in this direction. A still better way is to give money to the Board on the Annuity Plan whereby the donor receives an income from the gift during his life. Write to the Board for particulars.

The Southern Baptist Convention asked the churches to raise $618,000 for foreign missions this year. Every dollar of it is needed to meet past obligations and maintain the work on a hopeful basis. The Convention apportioned this amount among the various States, and the amount asked of each State is apportioned among the associations. It is very important that this association, either through its executive committee or a special committee, apportion the amount asked of it among the churches.

One hundred years ago Adoniram Judson and Luther Rice went out to India as Congregational Missionaries. By the study of the Bible they became Baptists. This fact aroused the Baptists of America to undertake foreign missions in an organized way.

The most significant advance ever ordered by the Southern Baptist Convention took place when the Oklahoma meeting last May authorized the Foreign Mission Board to raise one million, two hundred and fifty thousand dollars, as an Equipment Fund in honor of the Judson Centennial. One million dollars of this to be used for equipping our schools and publication work. Two hundred and fifty thousand dollars is to be used for building chapels, hospitals, and missionary homes. This is a mighty call, but it is made to a mighty people. This fund is to be raised during the next three years. It is to be entirely separate from the regular foreign mission offerings and the effort will be made to secure it in such a way as not to interfere with any other cause.

- We recommend: 1. That all our people help in foreign mission work by sympathy and prayer; by subscribing and reading the Foreign Mission Journal; by distributing tracts which can be had for the asking; by making our offerings as large as possible; by sending in their gifts now and not waiting for the season of pressure in March and April.

2. That we solemnly pledge ourselves to do our part to raise the amount ($500) which has been asked of our Association this year.

Read by A. C. HAMBY.

Pending a motion to adopt this report, an address was made by C. J. Thompson of the Foreign Mission Board.

The report was adopted.

On motion, J. B. Jackson was elected to represent the Foreign Mission Board in the Johnston County Association.

On motion of R. W. Horrell, the apportionment plan was adopted to take the place of the old pledge system. It was left with the Executive Committee to make the apportionments and notify the churches, and also to explain the system to them.

The report on Ministerial Relief was submitted by A. A. Pippin, as follows:

REPORT ON MINISTERS' RELIEF.

We have a Board in Durham, N. C., organized for the purpose of looking after our aged ministers and their wives who have become helpless and dependent on the charities of the people for support.

- This Board meets four times a year: In February, May, August and November. We have at present thirty-five beneficiaries. There are a few applications each year. This shows there is a gradual increase of those who need, and are asking for help. The Board pays to each of these beneficiaries from forty to two hundred dollars a year. Many of these have no support except the amount they receive from the Board, and this is not enough to make them comfortable. There are at least one-fourth of our Associations of the State that do not give any thing to this work. Some of those that do not help have beneficiaries on the Board. We should contribute more to this work. And all the money for this Board should be sent to the Treasurer of the Convention. If any one desires to know about the work of this Board, write to our Corresponding Secretary, Bro. J. M. Arnette, Durham, N. C., who will be glad to inform you all about the work.

Our Convention requests that each church take a special offering for this work on the Sunday nearest Christmas on which the church may have services. We recommend that each of our churches fall into line and take this special Christmas offering.

Signed for the Committee,

A. A. PIPPIN.

Pending a motion to adopt this report, an address was made by J. M. Arnett, Corresponding Secretary of the Old Ministers Relief Board. The report was adopted.

G. M. Willets, W. B. Joyner and L. C. Newton were appointed a Committee on Time, Place and Preacher for next Association.

The Association adjourned.

Benediction by W. L. Bilbro.

THURSDAY MORNING.

The session was opened with prayer by W. R. Beach.

The Moderator called the session to order, and the proceedings of yesterday were read and approved.

The Moderator recognized and welcomed the following visiting brethren: E. L. Middleton and Livingston Johnson.

The report on Periodicals was read by W. L. Bilbro, as follows:

REPORT ON PERIODICALS.

Your committee on Periodicals take pleasure in commending to the churches of Johnston County Association, The Biblical Recorder, Charity and Children, The Foreign Mission Journal, Our Home Field, and the Sunday School literature, published at Nashville, Tenn.

The Biblical Recorder is the organ of the Baptist State Convention. It is an able exponent of Baptist teaching, and has rendered faithful service to the denomination for nearly four score years.

Charity and Children is among the best papers published in the State. Its office and mission is to keep our churches informed on our Orphanage—its needs and progress.

The Foreign Mission Journal and Our Home Field will keep us in touch with our work in the more distant fields of our efforts to evangelize the world, as well as prove a source of education and inspiration in sending the gospel to all nations.

We would not forget to mention our own Church Messenger, which is published within the bounds of this Association. This journal will keep us informed as to our Associational work.

Inasmuch as there is a great flood of pernicious reading matter, both books and newspapers, on the market and that such publications are seeking a place in our homes, we would warn against all such trash, and would advise our Baptist people to place within the reach of all those entrusted to their care our own literature, which is wholesome and safe.

Respectfully submitted,

COMMITTEE.

Pending a motion to adopt the report, addresses were made by W. L. Bilbro and W. R. Beach. The report was adopted.

The report on State Missions was submitted by R. W. Horrell, as follows:

REPORT ON STATE MISSIONS.

State Missions is simply doing the Lord's business in the order He gave it to us. Our fathers were obeying a divine command, when after they had preached the gospel in their respective communities, they organized the Baptist State Convention to give the gospel to the whole State, and establish a base of supply from which to evangelize the whole world.

The wisdom of their course has been amply evidenced by results. From the beginning, it was the aim of our State Board to evangelize every section of the State, and as far as men and money would admit, this has been done. More than one-half of the churches in the State have been organized by the missionaries of the Board. Our achievements in the past have been great. There is no department of our work which pays a larger dividend on the amount invested than does State Missions. Last year the board employed 152 missionaries who preached at 351 points. They reported 1,921 baptisms, and 1,427 received by letter, making a total of 3,348 additions.

Ten churches were organized, fifty church buildings were in course of erection, and 14 completed. These churches contributed as follows:

To pastor's salary, $25,432.05; to church building, $32,510.51; to the objects of the Convention, $11,021.96; to other objects, $5,011.42, making a grand total of $73,975.74. The mission churches put back into the denominational treasury last year $27,444.93 more than we put into State Missions. Our State Mission work this year is operated on a basis of $50,000.00. Of this amount our Association has pledged $1,394.40. We hope for this and much more to be paid in before the books close. The State Board has employed this year 153 missionaries Several of the mission points that were helped last year came off the Board and new fields have been opened up, and there are still many places of destitution. The State Board could use profitably seventy-five thousand dollars next year. The rapid material development of our State forces upon us the occupation of new fields and necessitates the enlargement of our work each year. Within the bounds of our own Association there are several points which should be taken up at once, while no time should be lost in developing those already occupied. To do this we must enlarge our gifts to State Missions.

Your committee would call attention to the Board's present distressing need, and call upon the pastors in our Association to acquaint their churches with the present situation, and ask them to do their best for State Missions from now until the Convention meets in Goldsboro.

Respectfully submitted,

R. W. HORRELL,

For Committee.

Pending a motion to adopt this report addresses were made by Livingston Johnson and E. L. Middleton. The report was adopted.

S. H. Averitte, of the Orphanage, is recognized and welcomed.

Benediction by W. T. Baucum.

THURSDAY AFTERNOON SESSION.

The Association was called together by the Moderator,

Prayer by J. B. Jackson.

The report on Sunday Schools was read by J. W. Smith, as follows:

REPORT ON SUNDAY SCHOOLS.

We find authority for Sunday Schools in God's word. The fact that a unday School with good organization, equipment and teaching is sure to ecome efficient in winning souls for God and developing them for His use s proof of God's favor.

The Sunday School work of the State is hopeful. There seems to be a steady, healthful growth. Since 1905 we have grown from 1,290 schools to 1,858 in 1911, a gain of 568, or 44 per cent. in six years.

Since March, 1912, about seventy new schools have been organized. It is probable a few of the old ones have been discontinued.

During the same six years, the membership has grown from 104,534 to 174,384, a gain of 69,750, or 67 per cent.

There seems to be now about 125 churches without schools. It seems it is practically impossible to secure schools in some of these.

The Normal Training is exceedingly hopeful. Nearly 2,000 enrolled in North Carolina during the last Southern Baptist Convention year. The special campaign for this work is now on. An effort is being made to enlist at least 1,200 during September and October.

In this Association in 1911 there were 3,626 church members and 3,241 pupils in our Sunday Schools. In the State the ratio of Sunday School pupils to church members is 76 to 100. In our Association it is 89 to 100.

There seems to be no Sunday School at Calvary and Noble's Chapel. We ought to have as many people in our Sunday Schools as in our churches. Over 500 churches in the State did this last year.

As a policy for next year, we would recommend the following:

1. The organization of our Sunday School forces into a convention with needed officers and committees to advance the work. Let the Executive Committee be appointed now to do this work and co-operate with the State Sunday School Committee and Secretary.

2. A vigorous campaign to enlist more of our church members and others not reached for the Sunday School. A religious census will greatly aid in this.

3. Co-operation with other Associations in supporting Sunday School Missions by putting this fund on same basis as other mission and benevolent objects of the Convention. The Sunday School, however, ought to meet this obligation.

4. The organization of Normal classes for the training of our officers and teachers.

5. More definite plans for making our schools evangelistic. These ought to become great soul-saving agencies.

Respectfully,
J. W. SMITH,
Committee.

Pending a motion to adopt this report an interesting and inspiring address was made by E. L. Middleton, Sunday School Secretary, along the line of more thorough organization and better equipment.

The report was adopted.

The report on the Orphanage was read by J. B. Jackson, as follows:

REPORT ON ORPHANAGE.

On November 11, 1885, the first child was received by the Thomasville Orphanage. The last one received this year runs the number which has received the benefits of the institution up to 1,192. There are 390 present now, with 100 others seeking admission, and needy applicants applying almost every day. It costs about $80.00 a year to support an orphan. Children are received between the ages of five and twelve, and dismissed according to preparation rather than age.

The school work is on the graded system and embraces nine grades. The children go to school in the morning and work in the afternoon.

There are twenty-five women and seven men who devote all their time to the institution.

Charity and Children has a circulation of fourteen thousand, and there should be a club of this paper taken by every one of our Sunday Schools.

It costs $1.00 a year, but only 60 cents in clubs of 10 or more. It would greatly help the Orphanage if all our Sunday Schools would make them one contribution a month, and this should be done. But at present only 500 schools out of 1,700 are doing this.

The Technical building is to supply a long felt need by furnishing an opportunity for the boys to learn a trade.

About 800 pairs of shoes are turned out a year, 600 pairs of these being for the children.

One hundred and seventy-five acres of the farm are in cultivation. A large part of this is devoted to trucking and raising feed for the cattle, the herd of cattle consisting of about thirty-five. The boys do most of the work on the farm.

Thanksgiving day for Baptists is Orphanage day. The collection on this day should be a special thank offering and not go to pay pledges.

When the Branch Orphanage on the Kennedy estate is ready to receive orphans, we will be in position to care for more children. But with the increased ability comes renewed obligations.

J. B. JACKSON.

After discussion by S. H. Averitt and J. B. Jackson, the report was adopted.

J. B. Jackson offered the following resolution:

A GOOD RESOLUTION FOR EVERY BAPTIST ASSOCIATION TO PASS THIS YEAR.

Whereas, Baptists are guardians of the spiritual foundations of Democracy, and, whereas, the modern Republic cannot long endure in ignorance of the religious essentials of Democracy, it behooves North Carolina Baptists to make Baptist principles felt in every educational center of our State; therefore, be it

Resolved, 1. That our State Mission Board be encouraged in maintaining an efficient Baptist Sunday School hard by every day school and college in North Carolina, wherever such a course seems expedient; That this Association assert its approval of the State Mission Board's desire to support the strongest possible preacher in every educational center of the State; that this Association go on record as favoring a denominational policy that will ultimately put an adequate house of worship in all our principal educational centers of North Carolina.

2. That it is the sense of this Association that the way should be cleared for working out this policy, by the denomination's coming to the help of the local church at Wake Forest in supplying our own Wake Forest College with a house of worship ample for taking care of all the students that may ever go to Wake Forest to study.

3. That some denominational agency be empowered to push this matter, so that at least every three years a new ample church building shall be erected in one of our educational centers until all of them are supplied with churches.

After discussion by W. T. Bancum and J. B. Jackson, the resolution was adopted.

In the absence of the appointed Finance Committee brethren Columbus Smith and J. T. Holt were asked to act in their places.

The Association adjourned.

Benediction by J. B. Jackson.

THURSDAY MORNING SESSION.

After a devotional exercise, conducted by A. A. Pippin, the Moderator called the Association to order.

R. W. Horrell led in prayer.

R. W. Horrell read the report on State Missions. This question was discussed yesterday in absence of the report.

R. W. Horrell made some remarks on the needs in the Johnston County Association.

A. C. Hamby, J. B. Jackson and John T. Holt were appointed a committee to nominate an Executive Committee, delegates to the Baptist State Convention, delegates to the Southern Baptist Convention, and our Associational member of the State Mission Board.

The report on Woman's Work was called for. J. T. Holt was expected to prepare this report, but having failed to receive the notice he had no report ready. He was requested to prepare the report and send it to the Clerk in time to be printed in the minutes.

REPORT ON WOMAN'S WORK.

The work of the women moves on so quietly and steadily that many of us do not realize how vast and important it has become.

The total number of societies, including Woman's Missionary Societies, Young Woman's Auxiliaries, Sunbeams, and Royal Ambassadors, is about 1,200. If we estimate the average membership to be thirty, which is quite a liberal estimate, the total membership would be 36,000. These 36,000 members of missionary societies gave one-third of all that the white Baptists of North Carolina gave to missions last year.

This is a very striking example of what can be done by systematic and intelligent effort. The members of these societies study missions and inform themselves as to the needs, and they make their contributions regularly through the year. The male members of our churches could learn some valuable lessons from the women as to mission methods.

R. W. Horrell, G. H. Wright and A. C. Hamby made short speeches on Woman's Work.

A. C. Hamby read the report on Home Missions as follows:

HOME MISSION REPORT.

In recent years there has been a great and gratifying advance among Southern Baptists in Home Mission conviction, giving and results.

In 1902 the receipts of our Home Board were $88,874; in 1912 they were $366,050, and the apportionment ordered by the Southern Baptist Convention for the present fiscal year ending May 1, 1913, is $412,000. So great and pressing are the needs that the Board appropriated the whole $412,000, except $97, at its meeting in July.

The results show a corresponding increase during the same period. In 1902 the Board employed 674 missionary workers, who reported 8,150 baptisms and total additions to the churches of 17,201. They reported 231 churches constituted and 674 Sunday Schools organized. In 1912 the Board employed 1,309 missionary workers, who report 26,899 baptisms and total additions to the churches of 47,728. Six hundred and eighty-three churches were constituted and 754 Sunday Schools organized. Many of these workers were maintained wholly by the Home Board, though a still larger number worked in co-operation with other missionary organizations.

It is declared that the meeting of the Home Board last July was the most representative it has ever had. We learn that thirteen of the State Vice-

Presidents were present and participated in making up the budget for the year and planning the work. Evidently the Vice-Presidents contributed much to the occasion and it was the enthusiastic conviction of those present that to supply the urgent demands for help that came up from all over the South the Board could not do less than it was empowered to do, and then put its faith in the brethren everywhere that they will come up to the help of this great cause and raise every dollar of the apportionment, remembering that the work is not the work of the Home Board but of Baptist brethren throughout the South.

The watchword of the Home Board is forward! and it has planned a distinctly aggressive campaign for the present year. Besides the regular work steps forward were taken in two ways.

The first was in conformity to the instructions of the Southern Baptist Convention that the Board at once should take steps to raise a $1,000,000 Church Building Loan Fund. It was decided to complete the raising of this fund within three years and to employ special workers for this purpose at the earliest possible moment. There are 3,000 or more houseless Baptist churches in our territory and in hundreds of these the establishment of strong centers for Christ and his truth only awaits some aid in erecting church houses.

The second large step taken was in response to repeated reports of the Board to the Southern Baptist Convention and repeated committee reports before that body calling for the Home Board to put forth larger efforts to help in training and enlisting backward churches. This note, first sounded in recent years by the lamented Dr. F. H. Kerfoot, has become stronger and stronger until now several of the State Boards have made requests of the Home Board for aid in this work. At its July meeting the Board ordered the establishment of a Department of Enlistment and Co-operation and provided for the election of a special representative to labor in this Department.

We believe that in this movement there are prospective blessings for Southern Baptists and their usefulness that are almost beyond our conception. It looks to "teaching them to observe all things" as well as to saving the lost and baptizing the converted. It will provide for helping to train the churches more fully in all the ways of the Lord as well as enlisting them in larger giving.

Our Board is leading Southern Baptists in a worthy way in the great and fundamental work of saving the South. Your committee warmly commends it and its work to the prayers and enthusiastic and liberal support of the churches in our Association.

We recommend:

1. That clubs of subscribers be raised in every church for the Home Field, the splendid monthly of the Board. Price 35 cents, single copies, or 25 cents in clubs of five or more.

2. That pastors and workers secure and read the Board's instructive new book, "The Home Mission Task." Price, 50 cents in cloth, 10 cents extra for postage; 35 cents in paper, 7 cents extra for postage.

3. That large use be made of the varied and helpful tracts of the Board, which are mailed free on application.

4. That this Association provide for apportioning among its churches the amount we are asked to raise for Home Missions this year.

5. That all of our pastors be requested to preach upon this great cause at least once during the year. The Board will gladly furnish material for special study of pastors on request.

The address of the Home Mission Board is 1002 Third National Bank Building, Atlanta, Ga. Requests for the magazine, tracts, the book, or other printed matter, should be addressed to the Publicity Department.

A. C. HAMBY,
For the Committee.

Pending a motion to adopt this report, it was discussed by A. C. Hamby, W. B. Joyner, W. T. Baucum and R. W. Horrell.

A motion was made, and carried that A. C. Hamby be Home Mission representative for the Johnston County Association.

Benediction by C. A. Jenkens.

FRIDAY AFTERNOON SESSION.

After song service the Association is called to order by the Moderator. W. T. Baucum led in prayer.

After a statement from R. W. Horrell as to deficit in pledge for Students' Aid Fund, a collection was taken amounting to $10.55.

At this point C. A. Jenkens made a very fine address on Foreign Missions. The report on Education was read by A. C. Hamby as follows:

REPORT ON EDUCATION.
By W. L. Poteat, Chairman of Committee.
(Adopted by the Central Association, Sept. 25.)

On the doctrine that everybody ought to have the opportunity of elementary education Baptists and the State are in accord. The Baptist interpretation of Christianity and of man commits us to the policy of universal education. Manhood suffrage in the State and the perpetuity of republican institutions presuppose universal education. It appears, therefore, that the Christian obligation unites with the necessities of the democratic State in the insistent demand for the education of all the people.

The Baptist educational program would seem to include primary schools as well as secondary schools and colleges. But we recognize education as one of the chief functions of the State. For legislation and the administration of justice fall back on the education of the people. The social and political efficiency of the State is an exponent of the education of the people. All the problems of the State are settled in the right education of the people. The State must educate from the primary grades up to the graduate school. We do not antagonize the State system of schools. We support it and pay our proportion of the cost of its maintenance with reasonable cheerfulness. We go farther and adopt a portion of that system as our own in a peculiar sense and so completely that we feel no obligation to provide a duplicate of it under Baptist auspices. The primary public schools of the State cover that period in the school life of our children when they are still under the home roof and their religious training may be still conducted in the family, so that the risk of a wholly secular education for this period is greatly reduced and Baptists may consistently look to the State to make all the needed provision here.

But what is the provision and what by consequence is our educational standing? In 1910 the average rural school term was 92.7 days for white children, the average white teacher's salary was $34.47 a month, and the average appropriation per white child was $2.88. Enrolled in these inadequate schools were 71.6 per cent. of the white school population, and but 45 per cent. were in actual attendance. What wonder that 19.6 per cent. of the native white population ten years of age and upwards are illiterate, and that North Carolina is saved from the shame of being at the bottom of the list of States in illiteracy by New Mexico only? With this disgraceful and alarming situation full in view, the State in the last Legislature made to its three colleges appropriations which were more than five times what they were in 1903, whereas, with the paltry exception of $25,000 in 1909, not one dollar of direct appropriation for the schools of all the people has been added since 1901.

This looks like the perpetuation of the old aristocratic fiction that the masses of the people are accursed and have no rights. On the contrary, the education of the masses in the foundations of character and the first steps of freedom in the intellectual life is more vital to democratic institutions than the elaborate training of a small and elect class of the citizenship, even if we grant what is manifestly not true, that the teachers of the primary schools come out of this class. We insist that the State has gone far enough in expanding the equipment of the institutions which serve less than 5 per cent of the population, quite far enough for the present. If it has extra money to spend, let it go where the need is the greatest and the dishonor the deepest. The stress of the State's educational policy must now be on the foundations of its security and efficiency—the primary education of all its children. It will continue to provide training for its professional men, but its first concern must now be for the rank and file of its citizenship who have no hope except in the common school, and the main current which flows out of the public treasury must henceforth discharge itself in the public schools to extend their term, to enhance their efficiency, and to enforce attendance upon them.

For the high school period we have been unwilling as a people to trust our children to the secular guidance of the State. They are at the age for life decisions, for irrevocable commitment to great ideals and great causes, for the ultimate venture of faith, and the joyous surrender to the friendship of Jesus. And at this responsive, critical time they are not at home. Hence the fourteen Baptist High Schools in North Carolina supported and controlled each by two or more Baptist Associations, with the same courses of study, in close affiliation with our Baptist colleges, and recognizing as primary the Christian obligation as well as the educational. Let their names be known to all our people—Boiling Springs, Dell, Fruitland, Haywood, Liberty-Piedmont, Mars Hill, Mitchell, Murphy, Round Hill, South Fork, Sylva, Wingate, Winterville, Yancey. We do not prize them according to their value and importance. The Christian leaders of the future may get the wider ranges of their training in the colleges but in most cases they get their motive and consecration in these Christian high schools. They are in no peril from the multiplication of the rural high schools of the State, which cannot now approach them in standard and equipment, and can never supply, what is in truth the fundamental need of the high school youth, namely, sympathetic, personal Christian guidance and teaching.

The preparation of high school students to take the college courses shows steady advance, and the high school attendance was never so large. Accordingly, Meredith College and Wake Forest College have both of them unprecedented enrollments. And we must be ready for yet larger numbers in the future. For mere numbers in a catalogue parade we do not care, but we do care for the heavier fertilizing of the field which we cultivate, we do care for a wider service of the Kingdom. And this means larger resources, which Baptists will have to supply. If our colleges are worth maintaining, we must maintain them. Baptists may fill the State treasury, but they will draw not a penny out of it. If we insist upon duplication of the State's provision for college education, we must pay for it. Both our colleges are collecting notes for increased endowments. Wake Forest will begin shortly the erection of a dormitory and a building for the enlarging department of law. What is to be done in the face of the widening opportunity but to walk into it and trust the growing wealth, intelligence, and loyalty of North Carolina Baptists?   J. J. J.

Pending a motion to adopt this report, A. C. Hamby made a few remarks. The report was adopted.

A resolution of thanks for the cordial entertainment accorded the delegates and visitors was presented, and adopted by a rising vote.

It was moved and carried that the Executive Committee furnish their report to the Clerk for publication in the minutes.

REPORT OF EXECUTIVE COMMITTEE.

We have done what we could to advance the work, and feel glad to report that progress has been made. Rev. A. A. Pippin has served Corinth Church, Rev. T. J. Hood has been the pastor at Hood's Grove, Pauline and Pinkney Churches, Rev. J. W. Smith has been in charge of Benson's Grove, Blackman's Grove, Carter's Chapel, Brown's School House and Woodland School House. Rev. R. W. Horrell has served Pisgah, Pleasant Grove, Pine Level, Sardias, and Beaty Chapel. Until he left October first for the Seminary, Rev. George H. Johnson had charge of the work at Kenly, Bethel, Nobles' Chapel and Micro. Rev. W. L. Bilbro is our missionary at Middlesex and Bailey. Rev. D. D. Edwards at Live Oak, while the Princeton Church has been supplied by Rev. C. A. Jenkens and Rev. O. P. Campbell. Parrish Memorial and Four Oaks have been served by Rev. E. J. Rogers. Most of these churches have had conversions and additions to their membership. Conditions are favorable for much better work in 1913.

R. W. Horrell made some remarks on the apportionment plan.

N. R. Pool offered his resignation as Clerk, which was accepted, and J. B. Jackson was elected in his place.

It was moved and carried that $350.00 be apportioned among the churches for Home Missions.

The Clerk was asked to take a message of regret to Bro. J. M. Beaty at his not being able to attend the Association, on the account of sickness, and also to express to him the esteem in which he is held, and confidence placed in him by the Association.

It was moved and carried that the Treasurer's report be put in the minutes.

TREASURER'S REPORT.

By amount from the churches, for State Missions	$ 212.68
By amount from Finance Committee, for State Missions	188.90
By amount from the churches, Home Missions	63.85
By amount from Finance Committee, Home Missions	44.50
By amount from the churches, Foreign Missions	59.26
By amount from Finance Committee, Foreign Missions	46.00
By amount from the churches, Sunday School Missions	24.73
By amount from Finance Committee, Sunday School Missions	15.76
By amount from the churches, Ministerial Education	35.37
By amount from Finance Committee, Ministerial Education	20.10
By amount from the churches, Ministerial Relief	40.01
By amount from the Finance Committee, Ministerial Relief	21.85
By amount from the churches, Orphanage	64.31
By amount from Finance Committee, Orphanage	26.07
Total amount received	$ 863.39

Disbursements.

April 29, Check to Walters Durham	$ 27.65
Nov. 20, Check to Walters Durham	736.40
Nov. 20, Check to S. H. Averitt	90.38
To T. J. L.—Amount overpaid last year	8.96
Total amount paid out	$ 863.39

Church Building Fund.

By amount old debt fund, from the churches......................$ 210.97
By amount regular building fund, from the churches............. 74.90
By amount regular building fund, from Finance Committee........ 45.50
By amount borrowed from the Bank of Smithfield................. 600.00
By amount borrowed from J. M. Beaty........................... 19.62

Total...$ 950.99

Disbursements.

Jan. 1, To amount to T. J. L. (overpaid last year).......$ 5.50
Jan. 2, To check to Bank of Smithfield................... 65.00
Feb. 2, To check to Bank of Smithfield................... 37.80
March 4, To check to Bank of Smithfield................. 69.50
May 14, To check to Bank of Smithfield................. 31.38
Aug. 24, To check to J. M. Beaty....................... 19.62
Aug. 24, To interest to Bank of Smithfield............. 8.10
Sep. 2, To check to J. S. Johnson, lumber for Burnell... 230.00
Sep. 16, To check to Smithfield Hdwe. Co., nails, etc., for
    Burnell.. 13.85
Oct. 10, To check to W. M. Sanders, lime and brick for
    Burnell.. 8.00
Oct. 31, To check to R. H. Johnson, work on Burnell
    Church... 80.00
Nov. 12, To check to J. S. Johnson, lumber, etc., for
    Burnell.. 70.00
Nov. 23, To check to C. M. & W. G. Wilson, doors and
    windows for Burnell.............................. 56.86—$ 695.61

Nov. 23, Balance in hands of Treasurer.................. $ 255.38

Minute Fund.

Nov. 20, 1911, Balance on hand..........................$ 55.88
Paid Nash Bros. for Minutes and express.............$ 30.50
Paid T. J. Lassiter, salary and postage................. 18.85—$ 49.35
Total receipts for 1912................................... 47.08

$ 102.96

Balance in hand of Treasurer...............................$ 53.61

Note.—I have received $9.55 for the Students' Aid Fund at Louisville
Seminary, which I have sent to B. Pressley Smith, Louisville, Ky.

T. J. LASSITER, Treasurer.

Smithfield, N. C., Nov. 23, 1912.

R. W. Horrell was elected to Audit the Treasurer's books.

The following resolution was presented by A. C. Hamby:

Resolved, That we ask the Executive Committee to take into consideration
the employment of a woman missionary, whose duty shall be to organize
Woman's Missionary Societies and train leaders for the work, distribute
literature, secure subscriptions to The Recorder and the Mission Journals,
and to do general Christian work.

After some remarks by R. W. Horrell the resolution was adopted.

The committee on Time, Place and Preacher reported as follows:

Time—Wednesday, Thursday and Friday after the first Sunday in November.

Place—Smithfield.

Preacher—R. W. Horrell.

W. T. ALLEN, for Committee.

The following report was submitted:

Executive Committee—J. M. Beaty, J. B. Creech, R. H. Gower, G. H. Wright, and Claude Stephenson.

The Associational member of the State Board of Missions—A. C. Hamby.

Delegates to the State Convention—C. A. Jenkens, R. A. Bain and G. M. Willets.

Delegate to the Southern Baptist Convention—R. H. Gower.

It was moved and carried that we adjourn.

After song "God be with you till we meet again," the benediction was pronounced by C. A. Jenkens.

REPORT OF BUILDING COMMITTEE.

Since the last session of our Association we have built Burnell Church, near Johnson's Cross Roads, in Elevation township. We are now ready to establish preaching there and hope to organize a church in the near future. We have bought Brown School House in Boon Hill township, where a meeting was held later and nine members received. This church took the name of Hepzibah, and will apply for membership at the next meeting of our Association. To do this work we had to borrow six hundred dollars from the Bank of Smithfield, and must depend on the liberality of churches to pay this money back next year.

REPORT OF FINANCE COMMITTEE.

Bethesda	$ 30.17
Blackman's Grove	32.00
Beaty	4.00
New Bethel	68.00
Carter's Chapel	26.91
Corinth	21.00
Live Oak	17.00
Parrish Memorial	15.60
Pisgah	30.60
Shiloh	12.16
Thanksgiving	13.50
Wilson's Mills	25.50
Mount Moriah	90.85
Pauline	21.50
Total	$408.79
Minute Fund	$ 26.05
Total	$434.84
Extra collection	$ 9.55

J. J. WALLACE,
J. D. YELVINGTON,
D. A. SMITH,
Committee.

Table of Apportionments made by the Executive Committee in accordance with a resolution passed at the last session of the Association.

CHURCH.	State M ss ons.	Home M ss ons.	Fore gn M ss ons.	Sunday School M ss ons.	M n'ts er al Educa on.	Ministerial Relief.	Orphanage.	Building Fund.	Totals.
Antioch	$20.00	$ 5.00	$ 5.00	$ 2.50	$ 2.50	$ 2.50	$ 5.00	$ 7.50	$ 50.00
Bailey	10.00	2.50	5.00	1.00	2.50	2.50	5.00	6.50	35.00
Beaty Chapel	7.50	2.50	2.50	1.00	2.50	1.50	2.50	2.50	22.50
Benson	75.00	10.00	15.00	2.50	5.00	5.00	25.00	12.50	150.00
Benson's Grove	7.50	2.50	2.50	1.00	1.50	1.50	2.50	6.00	25.00
Bethany	10.00	5.00	5.00	1.00	2.50	2.50	4.00	5.00	35.00
Bethel	7.50	2.50	2.50	1.00	2.50	2.00	2.50	5.00	25.50
Bethesda	37.50	5.00	7.50	2.50	5.00	5.00	15.00	12.50	90.00
Blackman's Grove	20.00	5.00	5.00	2.00	4.00	2.00	5.00	7.00	50.00
Calvary	10.00	1.50	2.50	1.00	2.50	1.50	2.50	3.50	25.00
Carter's Chapel	10.00	2.50	5.00	1.00	2.50	2.50	5.00	5.00	35.00
Clayton	275.00	75.00	75.00	5.00	25.00	20.00	100.00	90.00	665.00
Clyde's Chapel	20.00	5.00	7.50	2.50	2.50	3.75	3.75	10.00	55.00
Corinth	10.00	2.50	2.50	1.00	2.50	2.50	5.00	5.00	31.00
Four Oaks	20.00	5.00	5.00	2.50	4.00	4.00	5.00	13.50	60.00
Hood's Grove	7.50	2.50	2.50	1.00	2.50	2.50	2.50	4.00	25.00
Kenly	15.00	2.50	5.00	2.50	2.50	2.50	5.00	5.00	40.00
Lee's Chapel	35.00	10.00	15.00	3.00	5.00	5.00	5.00	12.00	90.00
Live Oak	7.50	1.00	1.50	.50	1.00	1.00	7.50	5.00	20.00
Micro	10.00	2.50	2.50	1.00	1.50	1.50	2.50	5.00	26.50
Middlesex	14.00	5.00	5.00	1.00	2.50	2.50	5.00	5.00	40.00
Mount Moriah	55.00	25.00	40.00	6.60	5.50	6.60	30.00	25.00	193.70
New Bethel	20.00	5.00	7.50	1.00	5.50	5.00	17.50	15.00	66.50
Nobles Chapel	10.00	2.50	5.00	1.00	2.50	2.50	5.00	6.50	35.00
Oliver's Grove	5.00	1.00	1.00	.50	50	1.00	1.00	2.50	12.50
Parrish Memorial	7.50	2.50	2.50	1.00	2.50	2.50	2.50	4.00	25.00
Pauline	7.50	2.50	2.50	1.00	2.50	2.50	2.50	4.00	25.00
Pine Level	10.00	4.00	5.00	1.00	2.50	2.50	5.00	5.00	35.00
Pinkney	6.25	2.50	2.50	1.00	1.50	1.50	2.00	2.75	20.00
Pisgah	17.50	5.00	5.00	1.00	2.50	2.50	3.00	5.00	40.50
Princeton	20.00	5.00	5.00	1.00	2.50	2.50	4. 0	10.00	50.00
Sardis	11.50	2.50	5.00	1.00	2.50	2.50	2. 0	7.50	35.00
Selma	75.00	20.00	30.00	2.50	10.00	10.00	25.	27.50	200.00
Shiloh	15.00	5.00	5.00	1.00	2.50	2.50	5. 0	9.00	45.00
Smithfield	160.00	25.00	40.00	5.00	10.00	10.00	25.00	25.00	300.00
Thanksgiving	7.50	2.50	2.50	1.00	1.00	2.50	2.50	5.50	25.00
Trinity	10.00	2.00	3.00	1.00	1.00	1.00	.00	4.00	25.00
Wendell	30.00	15.00	30.00	5.00	5.00	5.00	25.00	25.00	140.00
White Oak	25.00	7.50	7.50	2.50	5.00	5.00	10.00	12.50	75.00
Wilson's Mill	20.00	2.50	5.00	1.50	2.50	2.50	9.50	12.50	58.00
Baptist Center	15.00	5.00	5.00	1.00	2.50	2.50	5.00	9.00	45.00
Hepzibah	2.50	1.00	1.00	.50	1.00	1.00	1.00	1.00	9.00

CONSTITUTION.

1. The Association shall be known as the Johnston County Baptist Association.

2. Its object shall be to extend the privileges of the Gospel and liberal culture to all the people within its bounds, and by hearty co-operation with the Baptist State Convention to help offer these privileges to all mankind in and out of its bounds, by the cordial co-operation of all the churches constituting this body.

3. It shall be composed of the pastors in active service in the Association and such delegates as shall be annually elected by the churches connected with it, each church being entitled to three delegates, unless the membership

shall exceed fifty, and then an additional delegate for every twenty-five members, provided no church shall have more than eight delegates.

4. The New Hampshire Declaration of Faith shall be the summary of Divine Truth for determining questions of faith and order in this body, and the churches desiring membership in it must commit themselves to the substance of it, together with the covenant therewith submitted, and this Constitution.

5. This Association shall not have power, to annul the discipline or exercise authority over any church connected with it, but it may advise with and sever its connection with any church that neglects to preserve gospel order, or that treats with contempt the objects or advice of the Association.

6. Each church shall send to the annual meetings of the Association a letter (the blanks to be furnished by the clerk of the Association), carefully filled as per blank suggestions, stating the full work of the church for the year ending with the close of the month previous to the one in which the Association is held.

7. The Association shall foster State Missions, Home Missions, Foreign Missions, Christian Education, the Aged Ministers' Relief Board, the Thomasville Orphanage and the Sunday School Board, and each church shall be requested to contribute to the support of these objects annually.

8. Missions and education shall have precedence in their claims upon the consideration of this body in its regular sessions.

9. Whenever a church shall fail to be represented by delegates or letter at the annual sessions of the Association inquiry shall be made for the cause and efforts shall be made to induce such church to do its duty, and the effort shall be continued till the church is recovered or dropped from the roll.

10. The officers of the Association shall be a Moderator, a Vice-Moderator, a Clerk, a Treasurer and an Auditor, elected annually by ballot from among its members, to serve until their successors shall have been elected, and to perform the duties usual to such officers, namely, the Moderator, in presiding over the meetings, or the Vice-Moderator in his absence; the Clerk in recording and preserving minutes and other papers belonging to the body; the Treasurer in receiving and disbursing funds belonging to or entrusted to the body according to its will; the Auditor to examine the Treasurer's books at each meeting of the Association and report the same before adjournment.

11. The Association shall appoint annually an Executive Committee of five (5) from its members, who shall be entrusted with the prosecution of Missions in the Association and any other work for the interest of the Master's Kingdom which may be referred to them. This committee shall, as far as possible, co-operate with the State Mission Board in supplying the destitution in our territory, and between the meetings of the Association take such actions as may seem to them advisable for the advancement of its interest. The committee shall present to the Association at its annual meeting a report of its proceedings, with the names of the missionaries supported on the field, time of service and details of their work, together with such recommendations as in the judgment of the committee the Association should follow in planning its subsequent work.

12. The annual sessions of the Association shall begin on Wednesday after the first Lord's day in November at such place as may be chosen, and an introductory sermon shall be delivered on the first day of the session. Representatives from a majority of the churches constituting the Association shall be a quorum.

13. This Constitution may be amended at any annual session by a two-thirds vote of all the members present.

14. Provision shall be made at each annual session for a session of the Woman's Central Committee, and all other necessary encouragement offered for the enlargement of the organized work of the Woman's Missionary Societies in the local churches. The proceedings of the Woman's Central Committee shall be recorded as a part of the Minutes of the Association.

BY-LAWS.

1. The daily sessions of the Association shall be opened and closed with prayer.

2. Delegates shall be recognized by letters from their churches designating them as such.

3. The Moderator shall recognize corresponding messengers or the delegates of newly received churches by extending to them his right hand.

4. The report of the Executive Board and the Missionary work of the Association shall take precedence of all other business during the morning session of the second day of the annual session.

5. The Clerk shall record and read the proceedings when called for, superintend the publication and distribution of the Minutes, preserve a file of them, and have it present at each annual session, and deliver to his successor all papers belonging to the body.

6. Members desiring to speak shall first rise and address the Moderator, shall use the term "Brother" in speaking to each other; shall not speak on the same subject more than twice without permission, and shall observe the courtesy that becomes Christians.

7. Members shall not absent themselves from the session without permission.

8. The roll of members shall be called at least once and absentees marked.

9. Corresponding messengers and visiting brethren shall be invited to seats, with privilege of speaking, but not voting.

10. A copy of the Minutes shall be sent to the Secretary of the State Mission Board, the Secretary of the Southern Baptist Convention, the American Baptist Publication Society, 1420 Chestnutt Street, Philadelphia; the Sunday School Board of the Southern Baptist Convention and the Thomasville Orphanage.

11. All questions of order not herein provided shall be decided by Kerfoot's Parliamentary Law.

JOHNSTON WOMAN'S MISSIONARY UNION.

The Annual Meeting of the Woman's Missionary Union of Johnston county convened with the Clayton Baptist Church, October 30, 1912.

PROGRAM.

Morning Session—9:30 O'Clock.

Hymn—"Nearer My God to Thee."
Devotional Exercises—Rev. A. C. Hamby.
Address of Welcome—Mrs. Hardee Horne.
Words of Welcome from M. E. Missionary Society—Mrs. C. W. Robinson.
Response—Mrs. R. M. Nowell.
Solo.
Report of Work in Association—Mrs. C. W. Carter.
Enrollment of Delegates.
"Responsibility of Woman's Missionary Societies to Junior Societies"—Miss Blanche Barrus.
"Missionary Literature and Program Making"—Mrs. C. M. Thomas.
Hymn.
"Personal Service"—Mrs. D. J. Thurston.
"Problems of the Country Church"—Mrs. J. W. Sanders.
"The Standard of Excellence—How to Reach It"—Miss Blanche Barrus.
Report on Home Missions—Mrs. A. C. Hamby, for Committee.
Report on Foreign Missions—Mrs. R. W. Horrell, for Committee.
Report on State Missions—Mrs. J. M. Beaty, for Committee.

Afternoon Session—2 O'Clock.

Devotional Exercises.
"Training the Children"—Miss Elizabeth Briggs.
Quartette.
"The Y. W. A.—Past and Future"—Miss Ellen Graham.
Report of the Training School—Mrs. B. A. Hocutt, for Committee.
Report of Margaret Home—Miss Winona Massey, for Committee.
"Tithing"—Mrs. Lacy Nowell.
Hymn.
Open Discussion—"How to Interest the Woman Who Does Not Care for Missions"—Led by Presidents of Societies.
Closing Moments.

Evening Session—7:30 O'Clock.

Sermon—By Dr. T. W. O'Kelly.

The meeting was called to order by A. C. Hamby, after which he conducted the devotional exercises.

The report and plans of our Vice-President (Mrs. C. W. Carter) were encouraging, and showed much thought and faithful work.

The weather was ideal and a large delegation was present. Two members of the Central Committee, Miss Blanche Barrus and Miss Ellen Graham, were with us. They gave us much practical information, and awakened our enthusiasm and caused us to have a larger vision of the work.

The Vice-President made two unusual remarks in stating that each lady who was asked to take part on the program readily consented to do so. Also every active Society in the Union reported regularly each quarter during the past year. The reports bespoke advancement spiritually and financially.

Miss Briggs, we regret so much, was providentially hindered from being present. Upon motion by Mrs. R. M. Nowell, the Union voted to write Miss Briggs a letter of sympathy.

Mrs. Carter suggested that we extend to Mr. J. M. Beaty a rising vote of thanks for his unlimited kindness.

Mrs. R. T. Renfrow was appointed to attend the Whiteville Institute.

Several new Societies were reported, and we hope each will send in their quarterly reports.

The following commitees were appointed, with the addition of two new ones:

Nomination—Mrs. Beaty, Mrs. Lacy Nowell, and Mrs. M. G. Gulley.

Time and Place—Mrs. C. M. Thomas, Mrs. R. T. Renfrow, Mrs. R. H. Gower.

State Missions—Mrs. J. W. Massey, Mrs. W. A. Barnes, Mrs. B. H. Glover.

Home Missions—Mrs. Lacy Nowell, Mrs. Bailey and Mrs. Renfrow.

Foreign Missions—Mrs. Bain, Mrs. L. M. Branch, Mrs. Joe Poole.

Training School—Miss Swannanoa Horne, Mrs. Walter Creech and Miss Mabel Gower.

Margaret Home—Miss Christine Gower, Miss Ruby Ellis, Miss Mary Carter.

Obituaries—Mrs. M. G. Gulley.

Distribution of Literature—Mrs. J. M. Beaty.

The Union felt much encouraged and many expressed themselves as being inspired to try to do more for the cause of Christ than ever before. Our watchword for the ensuing year is "Prayer."

We were glad to have a few encouraging words from Miss White, a good worker of the Presbyterian Church.

The hospitality of the Clayton people was unlimited. Aside from the usual good things, the delegates were given a very enjoyable automobile ride. The sermon by Dr. T. W. O'Kelley was a fitting close for the day.

A very enjoyable feature of the evening service was the well rendered music by the Clayton choir.

Thus closed a very successful meeting. The next session will be held with the Kenly Baptist Church.   MRS. R. M. NOWELL, Secretary.

CONTRIBUTIONS OF THE SOCIETIES.

SOCIETIES.	State Missions.	Home Missions.	Foreign Missions.	Expense Fund.	Training School.	Margaret Home.	Total.
Smithfield W. M. S.	$51.60	$20.00	$25.00	$ 1.40	$ 5.00	$.....	$ 103.00
Benson W. M. S.	2.50	3.00	7.87	......	......	......	13.37
Selma W. M. S.	19.00	8.40	8.00	1.00	4.00	......	40.40
Mount Moriah W. M. S.	6.00	11.25	9.00	80	2.00	......	29.05
Clyde's Chapel W. M. S.	......	......	......	......	......	......	......
Micro W. M. S.	......	......	......	......	......	......	......
Bethesda W. M. S.	......	......	......	......	......	......	......
Wilson's Mills W. M. S.	......	......	......	......	......	......	......
Wendell W. M. S.	3.25	......	7.85	......	5.00	......	16.10
Four Oaks W. M. S.	7.86	5.55	7.90	1.20	2.25	1.40	26.16
Kenly W. M. S. (new)	......	......	......	......	......	......	......
Clayton W. M. S.	65.25	42.50	57.60	1.10	8.25	2.00	176.70
Micro Sunbeams	......	......	......	......	......	......	......
Smithfield Sunbeams	12.50	4.00	8.50	60	......	......	25.60
Kenly Sunbeams	......	......	......	......	......	......	......
Mount Moriah Sunbeams	......	......	......	......	......	......	......
Clyde's Chapel Sunbeams	......	......	......	......	......	......	......
Wendell Sunbeams	......	......	......	......	......	......	......
Clayton Junior Union	2.00	1.00	1.00	......	......	1.00	5.00
Clayton Y. W. A.	29.30	16.20	22.00	60	15.00	......	83.10
Total	199.26	111.90	154.72	6.70	41.50	4.40	518.48

TABLE I—FINANCIAL.

CHURCH.	Pastor's Salary.	Building and Repairs.	Incidentals.	Sunday School Expenses.	The Poor.	Associational Missions.	State Missions.	Home Missions.	Foreign Missions.	Sunday School Missions.	Orphanage.	Colleges and Schools.	Ministerial Education.	Aged Ministers.	Other Objects.	Total.
Antioch	$19.50		$1.20				$15.00	$1.50	$1.50	$1.00	$3.00	$2.75	$2.50		$1.50	$49.31
Bailey	50.00	125.88	1.00	10.00			5.00	1.00	2.00	1.00	5.00		.50	2.00	4.00	206.36
Baptist Center	100.00		1.00	7.00			25.75	1.00	2.50	1.50	2.00		2.00	1.00		141.75
Beaty Chapel	50.00			8.00				1.00	2.50	1.50	25.00		1.50	5.00	2.50	75.50
Benson Grove	500.00	10.00	.68	45.00			75.00	14.92	12.57	1.00	3.00	80.05	7.75	1.00	10.00	775.29
Benson Grove	25.00		1.00				5.00	1.60	2.00	1.00	3.50		1.00	1.00	5.00	55.00
Bethany	40.00			6.00			6.00	2.50	1.00	1.00	1.50		1.00	1.00	2.00	66.50
Bethel	35.00						5.00	3.00	5.00	2.00	20.00		2.00	1.00	3.00	50.50
Bethesda	200.00		6.00	20.00			25.00	5.00	5.00	1.00	8.00		4.00	4.00	44.50	333.50
Blackman's Grove	50.00						20.00	3.00	2.00		1.50		1.00	2.00	2.65	
Calvary	35.00						8.00	2.50	2.50			25.00	2.00	35.60		56.40
Clayton	1200.00	267.35	285.56	89.00	73.10		275.32	138.20	94.65	1.10	110.91		34.20	2.00	99.25	2728.76
Carter's Chapel		7.50		37.77			11.00	2.50	2.50	1.10	15.00		2.00	1.50	2.50	83.87
Clyde's Chapel	100.00			10.00	8.29		19.25	2.50	4.00	3.00	5.00		1.00	1.00	1.50	160.04
Corinth	60.00						9.50	5.00	3.00	1.00	5.00		1.50	1.00	1.50	82.00
Four Oaks	100.00	30.00	11.59	46.48			15.00	18.05	7.90	3.00	2.50		2.00	1.00	24.35	234.73
Hood's Grove	40.00						5.00	1.00	1.00	1.00	10.66			1.00	2.50	85.00
Kenly	152.50	75.00		49.82			6.75	3.85	10.00	3.00	5.00		1.25	5.00	47.27	356.35
Lee's Chapel	150.00	565.81	6.85	19.80			30.00	5.00	1.50		17.00		5.00	2.25	6.00	823.07
Live Oak						7.50	7.50	2.00	1.00	1.00	2.00		1.00		2.00	17.00
Micro	20.00	2.00	.50	19.00			10.00	1.00	8.61		52.01			2.00		57.50
Middlesex	150.00	51.12	69.66	21.30			17.45	38.40	60.70	3.20	30.00			6.60	25.00	412.10
Mount Moriah	150.00	5.50	1.00	49.30			65.74	6.00	5.00	6.00	21.00		1.00	5.00	46.00	465.34
New Bethel	130.00	120.00	34.80	10.00			20.00	5.00	5.00				1.00	1.00	1.50	362.80
Nobles' Chapel	45.00	21.25	1.00				5.00	1.00	1.00	1.50	1.00		1.00	1.00		80.25
Oliver's Grove	30.00															33.00
Parrish Memorial	60.00	40.00	.50	3.00			7.50	1.00	1.60	.50	1.00		1.00	1.00	2.00	118.60
Pauline											1.50		1.50	1.50		
Pine Level	50.00	60.00					8.00	2.50	1.50		2.00		1.50	2.50	4.25	66.15
Pinkney Chapel	25.52		13.70	3.32			5.00	1.00	1.00		2.00		2.50	2.50	12.87	117.79
Pisgah	136.50	.50		4.85			19.50	3.00	5.25		2.25		2.00	1.00	2.25	207.72
Princeton	106.45		5.95	15.60			21.10	2.50	4.00	2.00	4.00		1.00	2.00	2.00	165.85
Sardis	70.00						12.50	23.40	33.00		27.00		3.00	1.00	4.00	93.50
Selma	600.00	316.86	203.12	42.00			60.00	8.00	47.95	2.00	8.00		3.00	3.00	4.00	1311.38
Shiloh	150.00			8.00			7.50	42.98	3.50	12.04	25.40		10.00	10.00	25.00	184.00
Smithfield	500.00			93.60			160.00	1.00	47.95		25.40	90.00	10.00	2.00	1.00	926.97
Thanksgiving	16.05		4.90				5.00		3.50		3.00		3.00	1.00		36.85
Trinity	30.00							26.17	3.50					1.00		
Wendell	434.00	88.21	5.00	75.12	2.15		18.25	6.50	65.75	5.00	44.25		6.50	5.50	36.80	780.47
White Oak	200.00	12.00		15.00			25.00	5.00	5.00	2.00	9.00		4.00	5.50	69.80	349.30
Wilson's Mills	100.00	20.00	20.00	30.00			23.00	5.00	5.00		10.00		3.00	3.00	10.00	209.00

CHURCH	PASTOR AND POSTOFFICE	CLERK AND POSTOFFICE	Time of Preaching	Value of Church Property	Seating Capacity	Baptized	Received by Letter	Restored	Dismissed by Letter	Excluded	Died	Number of Males	Number of Females	Total Membership
Antioch	B. L. Hocutt, Archer, R. 1	J. R. Whitley, Archer, R. 1	Second	$ 1250.00	700	1	11	1	4	3	2	59	109	168
Bailey	A. C. Hamby, Clayton	E. H. Rogers, Clayton	First	1500.00	350						1	17	24	41
Baptist Center	R. W. Horrell, Selma	N. M. Easom, Smithfield	First	1000.00	400	6	2		5	7		24	46	70
Beaty Chapel	J. M. Duncan, Benson	L. Gilbert, Benson	1st–4th	800.00	300	16	4		6		1	13	16	29
Benson	J. W. Smith, Wilson's Mills	Kirkman Creech, Kenly, R. 2	2d–4th	3000.00	200				1			46	103	162
Benson Grove	R. L. Hocutt, Archer, R. 1	Perry Barnes, Kenly	Second	600.00	300	5	1	1	1		1	7	17	24
Bethany	R. W. Horrell, Selma	J. E. Smith, Wilson's Mills	First	500.00	250	1	5	1				32	53	85
Bethel	J. W. Smith, Wilson's Mills	J. G. Johnson, Four Oaks	Fourth	500.00	400	20	3	1	3	1	2	16	17	33
Bethesda	N. H. Gibbs, Benson	T. J. Lee, Dunn	Third	500.00	300	7		1	2	1		103	128	231
Blackman's Grove	A. C. Hamby, Clayton	R. R. Gurley, Clayton	Fourth	500.00	250		6		7			22	48	70
Calvary	J. W. Smith, Wilson's Mills	Martin Thorn, Selma	Every	6000.00	400	26	1	3	1	10	2	9	19	28
Clayton	W. C. Nowell, Wendell	C. I. Johnson, Knightdale, R.	First	700.00	300		10		4	3	4	146	186	348
Carter's Chapel	A. A. Pippin, Wakefield	H. V. Andrews, Wendell, R. 1	Third	500.00	300	3		2	4	8		33	50	83
Corinth	T. J. Hood, Goldsboro, R. 4	J. W. Langdon, Four Oaks	Second	350.00	150	7		1	6	3		50	91	141
Four Oaks		P. T. George, Four Oaks, R. 1	Third	750.00	150	4			3		1	40	71	111
Hood's Grove		R. O. Martin, Kenly	Third	450.00	300	7	1					17	31	48
Kenly	A. A. Pippin, Wakefield	W. L. Green, Wakefield, R. 2	Second	2500.00	330	4	3	1	1	2		16	21	37
Lee's Chapel	D. D. Edwards, Selma	K. Broadwell, Selma, R. 1	Fourth	1500.00	300		3	1	3	1		17	11	28
Live Oak		Lenard Pace, Selma, R. F. D.	Second	1500.00	100		2		2		3	105	150	255
Micro	W. L. Bilbro, Middlesex	W. C. Jackson, Middlesex	Third	2500.00	300		5			3	1	13	29	42
Middlesex	W. T. Baucum, Wake Forest	A. Baucum, Raleigh, R. 2	2d–4th	3300.00	500				1	2	1	9	10	19
Mount Moriah	C. R. Sorrell, Wake Forest	G. W. Bryan, Garner	First	800.00	400						5	26	41	89
New Bethel		N. L. Stott, Sims	Fourth	700.00	350			3		6		38	76	169
Noble's Chapel	N. H. Gibbs, Benson	T. B. Tyner, Four Oaks	Second	300.00	250	2			1	1	3	36	47	85
Oliver's Grove	J. M. Duncan, Benson	Jos. D. Creech, Selma, R. 3	First	500.00	300		5		2	2	1	8	16	24
Parrish Memorial	T. J. Hood, Goldsboro, R. 4	C. F. Godwin, Pine Level	First	300.00	400	5	2	4	2	1		35	38	73
Pauline	T. J. Hood, Goldsboro, R. 4	Mrs. B. R. Edgerton, Kenly, R	First	1000.00	400	10	4	1	4		2	21	29	50
Pine Level	R. W. Horrell, Selma	R. H. Higgins, Smithfield	Third	1000.00		4			1	2		15	13	71
Pinkney Chapel	O. P. Campbell, Wake Forest	W. I. Pearce, Princeton		1200.00	400	6	1		8	1	2	28	39	28
Pisgah	R. W. Horrell, Smithfield	B. C. Powell, Smithfield	2d–4th	500.00	300	19	23		11	2	1	34	64	67
Princeton	J. R. Jackson, Smithfield	B. S. Reynolds, Selma	Second	15000.00	400	7			9	2		20	23	98
Sardis	R. W. Horrell, Selma	F. O. Holland, McCullers	1st–3rd	700.00	300	2	2			1		75	113	43
Selma	J. B. Jackson, Smithfield	T. J. Lassiter, Smithfield	First	6000.00	600	1	5	1	6			39	49	188
Shiloh	R. L. Hocutt, Archer	Aaron Earp, Selma, R. 1	Third	1500.00	200					9		73	88	88
Smithfield	N. H. Gibbs, Benson, R. 1	J. M. Lawton, Benson, R. 2	Third	1000.00	700	2	4		1	3		25	91	164
Thanksgiving	C. A. Pippin, Wakefield	G. H. Wright, Wendell, R. 2	2d–4th	1500.00	500	2	14	1	17	1	1	48	26	51
Trinity	L. Carpenter, Wake Forest	B. Talton, Wilson's Mills	Second	800.00	250	32	11	2	3	1	5	96	28	41
Wendell			Third				2		3			25	76	124
White Oak													118	214
Wilson's Mills													27	52
Total				63,150.00		214	123	21	109	66	41			3858

CHURCH.	SUPERINTENDENT	POSTOFFICE.	Officers and Teachers.	Scholars.	Total Enrollment.	Number of Schools.	Volumes in Library.	Quarterlies Taken.	Months kept open.	Average Attendance.	Number of Baptisms.	Contributions for Missions, Orphanage, Etc.	School Expenses.	Total Contributions.
Antioch	J. R. Hocutt	Selma, Route 2	6	115	121	1		80	12	35			$ 10.00	$
Bailey	J. P. Underwood	Bailey	4	45	49	1		40	12	30			7.00	
Baptist Center	W. C. Hardy	Clayton	6	65	71	1		65	12	40			8.00	
Beaty Chapel	W. M. Easom	Smithfield	4	25	29	1			12				45.00	
Benson	J. L. Hall	Benson	10	130	140	1		190	12	70			2.00	
Benson Grove	L. O. Parrish	Benson	5	50	55	1		50	12	30			6.00	
Bethany	David Pace	Selma	5	60	65	1		50	12	40	10			
Bethel											5			
Bethesda	D. C. Smith	Wilson's Mills	18	100	118	1	40	150	12	80	12		20.00	
Blackman's Grove	F. P. Wood	Four Oaks	5	50	55	1		75	12	30	6		5.00	
Calvary	J. M. Johnson	Dunn	4	60	64	1			12	20				
Clayton	R. R. Gulley	Clayton	14	295	309	1			12	170	24	98.61	89.62	455.58
Carter's Chapel	Gray Easom	Selma	6	70	76	1		95	12	40		5.00	37.77	
Clyde's Chapel	W. T. Bunch	Clayton, R. 2	7	112	119	1		125	12	60	3		10.00	
Corinth	W. A. Mitchell	Wendell, R. 1	6	40	46	1		150	12	30	5			
Four Oaks	W. A. Massengill	Four Oaks, R. 1	6	90	97	1		125	12	50	4	8.00	46.84	46.84
Hood's Grove														
Kenly	A. J. Broughton	Kenly	8	64	72	1		780	12	35	3		49.82	133.48
Lee's Chapel	J. W. Strickland	Middlesex	7	60	67	1			12	50			19.80	
Live Oak														
Micro	C. L. Batten	Micro	4	40	41	1	350	165	12	85		6.60	19.00	68.57
Middlesex	W. C. Jackson	Middlesex	8	140	148	1	55	156	12		2		21.30	55.90
Mount Moriah	N. R. Poole	Clayton	13	118	131	1			12		10		49.30	
New Bethel	Robert Smith	McCullers	8	60	68	1		18	9	40	2		10.00	
Nobles' Chapel	J. H. Grice	Sims	8	50	54	1				30				
Oliver's Grove														
Parrish Memorial	Jos. D. Creech	Selma	6	40	46	1		72	6	15	1		3.00	
Pauline														
Pine Level	B. L. Strickland	Pine Level	7	75	82	1		84	12	50	3			
Pinkney Chapel	W. N. Dixon	Kenly, R. 4	9	56	65	1		72		43			3.32	
Pisgah	J. W. Jones	Smithfield	6	30	36	1			12	20			4.85	
Princeton	W. H. Wells	Princeton	8	70	78	1		96	12	40		1.10	15.60	16.70
Sardis						2								
Selma	B. F. Hassel	Selma	18	300	318	1		400	12	200	16	27.00	42.00	341.00
Shiloh	John F. Hardee	McCullers	7	70	77	1		88	12	50	5		8.00	
Smithfield	T. J. Lassiter	Smithfield	10	160	170	1	100	200	12	88	2	26.03	93.60	119.63
Thanksgiving	Aram Earp	Selma, R. 2	5	50	55	1		226	6	25	1		4.90	
Trinity	J. E. McLamb	Benson, R. 2	5	28	33	1			6					
Wendell	M. C. Todd	Wendell, R. 1	16	217	233	1		420	12	120	2	75.12	17.85	92.97
White Oak	A. L. Batton	Archer, R. 1	6	110	118	1		115	12	60	14		15.00	
Wilson's Mills	J. H. Branch	Wilson's Mills	6	75	81	1		75	12	50			30.00	

MINUTES

OF THE

Eleventh Annual Session

OF THE

JOHNSTON COUNTY

BAPTIST ASSOCIATION,

HELD WITH

SMITHFIELD BAPTIST CHURCH,

SMITHFIELD, N. C.,

October 1913.

The next session will be held with New Bethel Church, near Garner, N. C., beginning Wednesday after the fourth Sunday in October, 1914.

To preach Introductory Sermon—John M. Gibbs.

OFFICERS.

Moderator—R. H. Gower..Clayton, N. C.
Vice-Moderator—A. A. Pippin..................................Wakefield, N. C.
Clerk and Treasurer—T. J. Lassiter........................Smithfield, N. C.
Historian—A. C. Hamby...Clayton, N. C.

Goldsboro, N. C.
Nash Brothers, Printers and Binders
1913

LETTER TO THE CHURCHES

To the Members of

Nobles Chapel ....Baptist Church

DEAR BRETHREN AND SISTERS:

Our Association will meet with New Bethel church on Wednesday, Thursday and Friday, October 28th, 29th and 30th, 1914. We want to have everything in readiness so we can report a good year's work. It is important that every church be represented not only by letter but by delegates also. Send men to represent your church who will come and take interest in all the work of the Association and remain until the Association closes. This is the only way to have a successful meeting. The apportionment for your church for the present year is as follows:

State Missions	$ 10.00
Home Missions	$ 2.00
Foreign Missions	$ 5.00
Sunday School Missions	$ 1.00
Ministerial Education	$ 2.50
Ministerial Relief	$ 2.50
Orphanage	$ 5.00
For Church Building	$ 11.50
Total	$ 40.00

Do not forget to add to the above some money to pay for having the minutes printed. Remember your church will get minutes according to the minute fund paid by them.

We hope these amounts will be raised in full. Please remember in sending the Church Letter to report only what shall actually be paid up to the time the letters are received by the Finance Committee at the Association. The reports are intended to show the money raised and not what is expected to be raised. In other words, our Association year ends with the Association and we cannot count money paid after the Association is over in this year's work. The Lord is blessing our work and we are expecting a great meeting at New Bethel.

New Bethel church is two miles south of Garner, N. C. Persons going by rail will be met there. The church is about seven miles west of Clayton.

Fraternally,
J. M. BEATY,
V. R. TURLEY,
R. H. GOWER,
ALONZO PARRISH,
CLAUDE STEPHENSON,
Executive Committee.

MINUTES

OF THE

Eleventh Annual Session

OF THE

JOHNSTON COUNTY
BAPTIST ASSOCIATION,

HELD WITH

SMITHFIELD BAPTIST CHURCH,

SMITHFIELD, N. C.,

October 1913.

The next session will be held with New Bethel Church, near Garner, N. C., beginning Wednesday after the fourth Sunday in October, 1914.

To preach Introductory Sermon—John M. Gibbs.

OFFICERS.

Moderator—R. H. Gower..................................Clayton, N. C.
Vice-Moderator—A. A. Pippin..............................Wakefield, N. C.
Clerk and Treasurer—T. J. Lassiter......................Smithfield, N. C.
Historian—A. C. Hamby...................................Clayton, N. C.

Goldsboro, N. C.
Nash Brothers, Printers and Binders
1913

EXECUTIVE COMMITTEE.

J. M. Beaty, Chairman..................................Smithfield, N. C.
R. H. Gower...Clayton, N. C.
Claude Stephenson ....Garner, N. C.
V. R. Turley...Clayton, N. C.
Alonzo Parrish ....Benson, N. C.

MISSIONARY COMMITTEE.

A. C. Hamby..Clayton.
John E. Lanier ....Smithfield.
John M. Gibbs...Kenly.
J. J. Lane..Clayton.
J. B. Creech...Four Oaks.

LIST OF MINISTERS.

R. L. BROWN..Wake Forest.
W. L. BILBRO..Middlesex.
J. M. DUNCAN..Benson.
N. H. GIBBS...Benson.
J. M. GIBBS..Kenly.
A. C. HAMBY..Clayton.
R. L. HOCUTT...Route 1 Wendell.
N. J. HOWELL..Beasley.
T. J. HOOD...R. F. D. 4, Goldsboro.
C. A. JENKENS...Clayton.
E. R. NELSON..Selma.
JOHN E. LANIER...Smithfield.
W. C. NOWELL...Wendell.
A. A. PIPPIN...Wakefield.
J. W. SMITH..Wilson's Mills.
W. H. WALL...Four Oaks.
C. G. WELLS...Middlesex.
O. W. YATES..Wake Forest.
J. U. TEAGUE..Wake Forest.

PROCEEDINGS.

Smithfield, N. C., October 29, 1913.

The eleventh annual session of the Johnston County Baptist Association convened with Smithfield Baptist Church this morning at eleven o'clock. Devotional exercises were conducted by Brother A. A. Pippin.

The Introductory sermon was preached by Bro. C. G. Wells, of Middlesex, from the text: "Rise, let us be going"—Matthew 26:46.

Following the sermon the body was called to order by the Moderator, Bro. R. H. Gower, of Clayton.

The following committees were announced:

Credentials and Enrollment—J. T. Holt and F. T. Booker.

Petitionary Letters—J. W. Smith, J. M. Beaty and J. F. Pool.

Delegates were enrolled from a majority of the churches.

Antioch—J. R. Hocutt and W. O. Hocutt.
Bailey—J. W. B. Finch and N. M. Bissett.
Baptist Centre—J. C. Hardee.
Beaty Chapel—W. M. Eason, N. M. Easom and E. F. Anderson.
Benson—Alonzo Parrish, J. W. Whittenton, J. L. Hall, J. M. Duncan and M. T. Britt.
Benson Grove—
Bethany—
Bethel—
Bethesda—W. E. Godwin, W. H. Laughter, Sylvester Smith, H. A. Jones, Marion Johnson and V. S. Smith.
Blackman's Grove—J. R. Holly and F. P. Wood.
Calvary—J. K. Hudson.
Clayton—A. C. Hamby, R. H. Gower, D. J. Yelvington and C. W. Carter.
Carters Chapel—Martin Thorn.
Clydes Chapel—J. M. Todd.
Corinth—H. B. Andrews and J. B. Woodard.
Four Oaks—W. A. Massengil, E. B. Johnson, C. D. Stroup, R. A. Bain, W. H. Wall and J. B. Creech.
Hephzibah—W. G. Creech, C. J. Wiggs, G. W. Pike and Ettie Creech.
Hoods Grove—P. L. Hayes.
Kenly—J. M. Gibbs.
Lee's Chapel—J. L. Driver, G. G. Driver and Aaron Creech.
Live Oak—X. L. Broadwell and J. M. Richardson.
Micro—Stradley Batten and L. L. Creech.
Middlesex—C. G. Wells.
Mount Moriah—J. J. Lane, J. F. Pool, W. H. Coats and R. A. Baucom.
New Bethel—D. T. Bryan.
Nobles Chapel—
Oliver's Grove—
Parrish Memorial—S. P. Parrish and W. J. Parnell.
Pauline—W. B. Joyner, N. J. Howell and D. R. Evans.
Pine Level—Fletcher Thompson and L. Brown.
Pinkney Chapel—Joe Davis, Mrs. Joe Davis and Mrs. B. R. Edgerton.
Pisgah—J. W. Jones and R. H. Higgins.
Princeton—
Sardis—Ben Powell, N. B. Stevens and J. W. Strickland.
Selma—B. S. Reynolds and N. D. Wells.
Shiloh—F. T. Booker and Claude Stephenson.

Smithfield—T. J. Talton, G. L. Jones, H. D. Ellington and F. H. Brooks.
Thanksgiving—G. A. Earp.
Trinity—
Wendell—N. R. Stell and J. W. Davis.
White Oak—N. R. Batten.
Wilson's Mills—M. H. Jones, J. T. Holt and B. A. Turnage.

The election of officers was taken up with the following result.

Moderator—R. H. Gower.
Vice-Moderator—A. A. Pippin.
Clerk and Treasurer—T. J. Lassiter.
Historian—A. C. Hamby.

The Moderator recognized and welcomed Bro. J. A. Campbell, of the Little River Association, and Bro. T. H. Spence, pastor of Smithfield Presbyterian church.

After announcements from the Pastor and Chairman of the Committee on Hospitality, the body took a recess till two o'clock with benediction by Bro. E. R. Nelson.

WEDNESDAY AFTERNOON.

The body opened with song service and prayer by Bro. A. C. Hamby.

Bro. G. A. Martin, pastor at the Thomasville Baptist Orphanage, was recognized and welcomed.

The following committee on Finance was announced: G. L. Jones, E. B. Johnson and B. C. Powell.

Upon motion, Dr. R. T. Vann, President of Meredith College, was given a place on the program for the night session to speak on general education.

In the absence of the report on Biblical Recorder set for this hour, the Orphanage report was called for and read by Bro. E. R. Nelson.

REPORT ON THE ORPHANAGE.

Our Orphanage at Thomasville, with its branch at the Kennedy farm, is enshrined in the hearts of the Baptists of North Carolina, and right worthy is it of our financial support, love and prayers, for it is a mighty factor in the kingdom.

Since its inception in 1885 it has been foster parents to, and provided a home and Christian training for, nearly fifteen hundred homeless and parentless boys and girls. One thousand of these have gone out, equipped for usefulness, to take their places in the world and in the kingdom, while upwards of four hundred are still receiving the care and training of this Christian institution.

Suppose we had had no such charity as this, and those one thousand little orphans had been allowed to drift upon the sea of humanity without teachers, without training in the things that are useful and good, and deprived of most of the necessities of life, what would be their condition to-day? Some of them would not have survived the ordeal; some of them would be criminals; some of them vagabonds, while most of them would be ignorant, untrained in mind and heart, and a drag upon the wheels of Christian progress, if not a real menace to Christian society. In saving these and the four hundred now in its hospitable care this institution is doing a work that can not be estimated in dollars and cents, the dollars and cents enable it to do its work. It is rescuing from ignorance and vice and saving to society many of the bright boys and girls of our Commonwealth who, in the providence of God are left alone and helpless in the world. It trains them in the science of living. It not only provides food and clothing, but instruction and training of the right kind, and is in the business of building character.

This work is done at relatively small cost to our denomination—about $40,000.00, or $100.00 per child per year being the amount expended at present. A good portion of this amount is earned by and through the industries belonging to the institution. The farm of 175 acres; the dairy of 35 head of cows; the printing plant, including Charity and Children, and the shoe shop yield, each of them, a handsome profit, which goes into the current support. This attests wise and economical administration.

But the training that these enterprises supply constitutes their chief value to the inmates. We must not suppose that on account of them the Orphanage needs less our financial support. On the contrary, the cost of living seems to be growing greater all the while; and this, together with the enlargement of the institution by the Kennedy branch, makes increased offerings imperative. Last year our Association contributed $484.85. We can easily make our gifts as much as $600.00 and ought to do so. Our more than forty Sunday schools could raise this at the rate of $14.50 each.

And we urge that every Sunday School within our bounds give to the Orphanage the whole offering of one Sunday in each month. The school that is not doing this is losing a great opportunity to teach in a practical way the young people the blessedness of this Christ-like work. If all the Sunday Schools of our State Convention would do this and the churches make an offering only on Thanksgiving Day an abundant support would be provided. Respectfully submitted, E. R. NELSON.

A motion was made to adopt, and after discussion by Brethren G. A. Martin and E. R. Nelson, report was adopted.

Upon motion, a collection was taken for the Thomasville Orphanage amounting as follows: $7.88. Paid same to Bro. G. A. Martin.

Committee on Petitionary Church Letters made its report as follows:

REPORT ON PETITIONARY CHURCH LETTERS.

We, your committee on Petitionary Church Letters, recommend that Hephzibah Church be received as a member of this body and that the delegates be allowed all its privileges. Respectfully,

J. W. SMITH,
J. F. POOL,
J. M. BEATY,
Committee.

Dr. R. T. Vann, President of Meredith College, and Bro. Hight C. Moore, Editor of the Biblical Recorder, were recognized.

In the absence of the Report on the Recorder, Rev. Hight C. Moore, the editor, was invited to speak, and gave an interesting resume of the paper, what it is and what it stands for.

Upon motion, Bro. Moore was asked to furnish a synopsis of his talk for the minutes, as follows:

REPORT ON BIBLICAL RECORDER.

The following census of contents, appearing editorially in the Recorder's last issue for 1912, shows for one thing that the paper which during that time contained enough matter to make twenty-five volumes of two hundred pages each was certainly worth the subscription price of $1.50 for the year. The editorial was as follows:

As we now close the work of the year, it is rather interesting to look back and see what has appeared in our columns within the twelve month. Our card index of contents is so kept from week to week that we can instantly locate any article or author appearing in the Recorder during the year and a complete summary is but the work of a few minutes.

This summary credits the editor with writing 195 editorials, 628 editorial brevities, 155 Bible studies (for Sunday School, Baptist Young Peope's Union, and Prayer Meeting), 1,827 news notes, 809 items of "News and Views," besides 27 special "Literary Notes" and 16 "Question Drawer" paragraphs. And there is much more in editing a paper than producing "copy".

For example, the enlistment of good correspondents and the handling of great quantities of manuscript without offending writers with rejection and delay, or offending readers with heavy literary "lumber". We think ourselves very happy in having such a fine constituency of correspondents. The contributed articles in our wide columns, numbering 489, have been furnished us by 182 different writers. The showing in our news service from the churches has been even better for we have published 737 letters from 410 correspondents in all parts of the State and in many sections of the world.

The sisters of the Woman's Missionary Union have made good use of their page, having published 257 communications from 130 authors.

Our two pages weekly for the "Young People" and the "Home Circle" have contained some of the best literature of the day, including 90 choice poems and 212 other selections of entertaining stories, household information and the like.

In our obituary columns have appeared 211 memorial tributes to our departed brethren and sisters.

Though not an illustrated paper, the Recorder has contained 104 pictures during the year.

Other features have been the acknowledgments by Treasurer Durham of about $100,000 from about 1,800 of our churches; our Spice Box department with 265 items; about 250 short fillers scattered here and there, most of which are veritable gems for memory.

So, all told, our table of contents has been rather a full one for a State paper, and we think no subscriber can say he has not gotten his money's worth. And now we turn to the future hoping and feeling that a richer menu and better days are ahead.

The following resolution was offered by Bro. A. C. Hamby:

In view of the fact that our Associational program is often changed to suit the convenience of our visiting brethren, and that this change demoralizes the plans of the local constituency, therefore, be it resolved

1st. That hereafter we adhere strictly to the printed program; and

2nd. That the Moderator be requested to have the program printed in the Biblical Recorder at least four weeks before the time of meeting, and that in connection with it the visiting brethren be notified of the nature of this resolution. A. C. HAMBY.

After discussion by Brethren Hamby, Nelson, C. W. Carter, and G. A. Martin, the resolution was adopted.

Moderator announced committee on Home Missions as follows: A. C. Hamby, J. W. Jones and J. J. Lane.

Bro. C. A. Jenkens was appointed to conduct devotional service to-night.

Adjourned with benediction by Bro. J. M. Gibbs.

WEDNESDAY NIGHT.

The body opened with singing "Come Thou Almighty King."

Bro. C. A. Jenkens read 53rd chapter of Isaiah. Prayer by Bro. J. J. Lane, followed by singing "What a Friend we have in Jesus."

The following committees were announced:

State Missions—John M. Gibbs, Sylvester Smith and J. L. Hall.

Place and Preacher—J. F. Pool, W. B. Joyner and J. R. Hocutt.

The committee on Home Missions made the following report, read by Bro. A. C. Hamby:

REPORT ON HOME MISSIONS.

The most conspicuous element in the foundation of our Republic is religion. James Brice, in his great book, "The American Commonwealth," says, "It was religious zeal and religious conscience which led to the founding of New England colonies two centuries ago." The Jamestown Colony was chartered that it "under the providence of God might tend to the glory of the Divine Majesty in propogating the Christian religion." Almost every charter granted in Colonial days had as its chief end and aim the propagation of the gospel, and the history of our country amply justifies those wise provisions. Emerson says, "Our whole history seems like a last effort of Divine Providence in behalf of the human race." These words in view of present facts, appear to have been Divinely given, for the oppressed of every color and clime are looking to America with eager eyes that they may be shown the why and how of better things. The man who reads history cannot help being convinced (unless he read it backwards) that scores of striking events in its discovery and development point unmistakably to a messianic mission for our nation. We have proven, just to the extent of our efforts, that "righteousness exalteth a nation," and have seen also that "sin is a reproach to any people." It is a sad reflection that after all the providential provisions of God fostered by the efforts of our forefathers in seeking to make of this a Christian nation only one-third of our Southern people are members of Protestant churches. There are more lost people in America to-day than there ever were before at one time. The primal task of saving the aborigines and our own people is still far from completion. Added to this is the comparatively new, great and grave task of saving the South's part of the more than million immigrants who land on our shores each year. Our part will be the greater shortly since the Panama Canal is about to be opened.

One of the tasks the Home Board has recently undertaken is the vitalizing of the 11,000 Baptist churches in the South that are virtually dead in missionary spirit. This is a work that ought not to be necessary, and least of all for the Home Board. No one realizes so keenly as the generals commanding our great forces, how grave a matter it is to have in our ranks such a large number of non-contributing churches. This is a sight to sadden the heart of every man who loves the kingdom of our Lord.

The Board has undertaken also to raise a million dollar Church Building Loan Fund with which to help build houses of worship for the 3472 houseless churches in Southern Baptist territory. These churches are weak both in numbers and in finances and cannot build without help. They are located at strategic places and ought to be housed as quickly as possible.

The Home Mission Board apportionment this year for the whole South is $431,750, and for North Carolina $35,000. Of this last amount the Johnston County Association should raise at least $350.00.

We recommend:

1. That this amount be apportioned among the churches.

2. That the church members seek to inform themselves on the great Home

Mission task by taking and reading the Home Field and the tracts which the Board publishes for free distribution.

3. That the churches collect and forward their Home Mission money as early in the year as possible.   A. C. HAMBY,
For the Committee.

Upon motion to adopt, the report was discussed by Bro. A. C. Hamby and adopted.

Dr. R. T. Vann, of Meredith College, delivered an address on General Education.

Bro. J. A. Campbell was called for and spoke briefly on the work of the Buie's Creek Academy.

Bro. C. W. Carter, after speaking on the work of the school offered the following resolution:

Resolved 1st. That this Association endorses the work of Buie's Creek Academy, under the management of Principal J. A. Campbell.

2nd. That we appoint Brethren J. E. Lanier and Alonzo Parrish to represent this body before the "Trustees of Buie's Creek Academy" and to co-operate, if agreeable, with the Little River Association in the ownership and control of the dormitory owned and controlled by said Little River Association.

Benediction by Bro. E. R. Nelson.

THURSDAY MORNING.

Devotional service conducted by Bro. Hight C. Moore who read Matthew 11:20-30, followed by prayer and song "The King's Business."

Body was called to order by Vice-Moderator A. A. Pippin.

Minutes of yesterday read and approved.

New delegates enrolled.

Bro. W. N. Johnson, pastor at Wake Forest, recognized and welcomed.

Report of Executive Committee was read by Bro. J. M. Beaty. Report adopted.

REPORT OF EXECUTIVE COMMITTEE.

We have tried to push the work entrusted to us the past year and are glad to report to you the best year's work done since the organization of the Association. Nearly all of the churches have had conversions and additions to their membership. We employed Rev. C. R. Sorrell to help in meetings from July 15th to October 1st with good results. Our work was crippled at some points because the State Board of Missions did not appropriate enough money for us to carry on the work. We recommend that the churches enlarge their contributions to State Missions in order that we may become as near as possible self-sustaining. Rev. W. L. Bilbro has served Bailey church for us. Rev. Jno. M. Gibbs, located at Kenly, has preached at Kenly, Bethel Mission and Nobles Chapel. Rev. E. R. Nelson at Pine Level and Princeton. Rev. T. J. Hood has served Pinkney, Pauline and Hood's Grove churches. Rev. W. H. Wall has preached at Pisgah, Burnell Pleasant Grove, Sardis, Woodard School house and Beaty Chapel. Rev. J. M. Duncan has served Parrish Memorial, Hephzibah, Benson Grove and Four Oaks churches.   J. M. BEATY,
For Committee.

Bro. John M. Gibbs read the report on State Missions:

REPORT ON STATE MISSIONS.

On the eve of His ascension our Lord announced a comprehensive Missionary program. In this program our Master states things in their natural and logical order. He expressly commended that His disciples should preach first in Jerusalem and Judea—hence our authority for Associational and State Missions. These should receive our first consideration. It is a gospel truth that "Charity should first begin at home." Self preservation is the first law of grace as well as of nature. Self interest demands that we do our best for State Missions at the present time.

Christ commanded the Gadarene Demoniac to go home and tell what the Lord had done for him. Our first duty is to our own kith and kin. Andrew brought his brother Simon Peter to Jesus before he did anything else. This was a matter of prime consideration with him and should be with us. State Missions come first in the plan suggested by our divine Master. If we would evangelize the world we must follow the divine program. One of the chief functions of the State Mission Board is to spend the benevolences entrusted to its hands by the churches, in the development and culture of our people. No more far-reaching work lies before us to-day than the task of developing our undeveloped churches and enlisting them, and all their sacred energies in a combined effort for the bringing in of the reign of Christ. That State Missions does this kind of work is evidenced by the fact that a large number of our leading and strongest churches were started and built up by our State Mission workers, soon becoming self-supporting and enabled to help carry the gospel to others.

By no means has the demand for State Mission work been diminished because of past victories. There is a greater demand to-day for State Mission work than ever before in the history of our denomination.

New doors of opportunity are opening for religious advancement along with the rapid material growth which our State is experiencing. That we may supply their demands it is necessary that our Christian people bend their God-given energies to this work and by the contribution of their prayers and their means with which He has blessed them, surrender themselves as instruments in His hands for the consummation of His plans. We have reached a crisis in our State Mission work. We may make it a crisis of growth or of decadence. We have reached Kadeshbarnea. May the great Head of the church inspire us to put forth our noblest efforts to the end that North Carolina may be taken for our King.

Your committee desires to make the following recommendations:

1. First, that a special effort be made in all of our churches for State Missions between now and the meeting of the Convention in Shelby.

2. That our churches be asked to increase their pledges to State Missions 10 per cent for the coming year.

3. That a mission rally be held within the bounds of the Association at some central point and at some suitable time, for the discussion of all our Convention objects.

4. That some system be inaugurated in our churches.

Respectfully submitted,   JOHN M. GIBBS.

Upon motion, to adopt the report was discussed by Brethren John M. Gibbs, W. N. Johnson, A. C. Hamby, W. H. Wall, Hight C. Moore and others. Adopted.

A collection for State Missions, amounting to $17.90, was taken.

Bro. W. N. Johnson made an earnest appeal to the Association for help on the New Baptist Church at Wake Forest College. Following his address Bro. E. R. Nelson offered the following resolution which was unanimously adopted:

Resolved, That the Johnston County Association is in full sympathy with the situation of the church at Wake Forest, with their effort to supply the need of a house of worship and that we hail with delight the progress already made in building, and that we entrust our Executive Committee to apportion not less than $300.00 among our churches; and that the pastors of the Association endeavor to raise their respective amounts as quickly as possible.

The following committees were announced:

To Nominate Executive Committee, Delegates to State Convention and Southern Baptist Convention—T. J. Lassiter, C. W. Carter and N. D. Wells.
Aged Ministers—W. H. Wall, Alonzo Parrish and G. G. Driver.
Sunday Schools—J. M. Duncan, N. R. Batten and Roy Baucom.

Announcement was made of the critical illness of Dr. Willingham, Secretary of Foreign Mission Board, and prayer was offered in his behalf with Brother Moore leading.

Took recess for dinner.

THURSDAY AFTERNOON.

Opened with singing "God is Able to Deliver Thee." Prayer by Bro. Hobgood.

Bro. N. D. Wells for Committee, reported as follows:

Executive Committee—J. M. Beaty, R. H. Gower, Claude Stephenson, V. R. Turley and Alonzo Parrish.

Bro. R. H. Gower offered resignation as member of Executive Committee, but body refused to accept same.

Delegates to State Convention—V. R. Turley, E. R. Nelson and C. W. Carter.
Delegate to Southern Baptist Convention—J. E. Lanier.
Member of State Mission Board—A. C. Hamby.

Report adopted.

Committee on Place and Preacher reported as follows:

REPORT ON PLACE AND PREACHER.

Place of next meeting of Association: New Bethel.
To preach Introductory sermon: John M. Gibbs.

Report adopted.

The following report on Sunday Schools was submitted by Bro. J. M. Duncan.

REPORT ON SUNDAY SCHOOLS.

We find authority for Sunday Schools in God's word. The fact that a Sunday School with good organization, adequate equipment, and good teaching, is sure to become effective in winning souls for God and in developing them for His use, is proof of God's favor.

The Sunday School work of the State is hopeful. There seems to be a steady, healthful growth. Since 1905 we have grown from 1,290 schools to 1,920 in 1912; a gain of 631 or 49 per cent in seven years. Mere numerical growth, however, is not necessarily indicative of success. We find more general interest in the cause than formerly. Schools are improving their organizations as well as enlarging their membership. Many are training their teachers in the Sunday School Board's training courses. Churches are building class-rooms or using curtains to improve their equipment.

We find the following facts about the work in our own Association: 41 churches, 37 Sunday Schools, 3,800 church members, 3,400 Sunday School members, 281 officers and teachers, one Branch School, gain in enrollment, 159.

As a policy for next year we would recommend the following:

1. The organization of our Sunday School forces into a Convention with needed officers and committees to advance the work. Let the Executive Committee be appointed now to do this work and co-operate with the State Sunday School Committee and Secretary.

2. A vigorous campaign to enlist more of our church members and others not reached for the Sunday School. A religious census followed by grading the school will greatly aid in this.

3. The organization of Teacher Training Classes for officers and teachers. These may pursue the Normal Course or the Reading Course. Free literature will explain both courses.

4. The co-operation with other associations in supporting Sunday School Missions by putting this fund on same basis as the other mision and benevolent objects of the Convention. The Sunday Schools, however, ought to meet this obligation.

5. More definite plans for making our schools evangelistic. These ought to become great soul-saving agencies. Every unsaved member of our classes ought to be brought to a saving knowledge of Jesus.

6. That our officers and teachers secure literature on the various phases of up-to-date Sunday School work. This will be furnished free by our Sunday School Secretary.

7. That we give one week during the early part of next summer for the purpose of discussing Education, Missions and Sunday Schools.

Respectfully submitted,   J. M. DUNCAN.

After discussion by Brethren J. M. Duncan, W. B. Joyner, A. C. Hamby and W. H. Wall the report was adopted.

Moderator recognized and welcomed Bro. Chas. J. Thompson, representative of the Foreign Mission Board, and Bro. F. P. Hobgood, President Oxford College.

Report on Ministerial Relief was read by Bro. W. H. Wall.

REPORT ON MINISTERIAL RELIEF.

Twenty-two years ago the Relief Board was established and the churches were asked to make this one of the objects to which they contribute according to the plans adopted by the Convention.

There are now between 35 and 40 who receive support from this Board who have been left in destitute circumstances. The appropriations made to those worthy brethren range from fifteen to one hundred and five dollars per year. This is a mere pittance, but is the best the Board can do with limited resources. We should greatly increase our contributions to this worthy object. All people who are not able to provide for themselves should be helped by those whom the Lord has more abundantly blessed with the necessaries of life.

It seems that the Lord in his wisdom has left a number of aged ministers in the care of the churches that they may provide for them that "Love may exercise herself."

Of all benevolent objects sure the aged minister who has given his life-service to the cause of our Master should be cared for by the Lord's people. Let us help them so that it may be said "inasmuch as "ye have done it unto one of these my disciples ye have done it unto me." The needs are greater than ever before. We suggest that the pastors preach a sermon on the needs of this Board and that every church take a collection for this object on the Sunday on which they hold services nearest Christmas.

Respectfully submitted,   W. H. WALL.

Report discussed by Bro. W. H. Wall and Bro. F. P. Hobgood and adopted.

On motion of Brother Hamby, Bro. J. E. Lanier, was elected our representative of the Foreign Mission Board for this Association.

On motion of Bro. C. W. Carter, Bro. E. R. Nelson was elected Representative of the Home Mission Board for this Association.

On motion of Bro. Nelson, the body adjourned until seven o'clock for the evening service. Benediction by Bro. T. J. Hood.

THURSDAY NIGHT.

Opened with devotional service by Bro. T. J. Hood who read Psalm 1. Bro. W. L. Bilbro offered prayer.

Bro. Hobgood was recognized and made a statement in regard to Oxford College.

The report on Foreign Missions was called for and read by Brother J. E. Lanier.

REPORT ON FOREIGN MISSIONS.

In this report we do not think it necessary to give scriptural proof that all Christians should support our Foreign Mission work. He, who does not believe in the work, has not fully accepted the message of both the Old and New Testament. The prophets predicted the time when the nations should be brought to God. Jesus sent forth his followers to make the message of salvation known to the world. Not to any special class of people and stop, but to man wherever he might be found.

During the past year there has been made great progress in our Foreign Mission work. The missionaries report more conversions than in previous years. More natives are being trained and sent out into active service than at any previous period in Foreign Missions. This year the Board has sent out thirteen new missionaries to fill the vacancies caused by death and resignation on the field. Three of these have gone from North Carolina. Bro. J. B. Hipps goes to Shanghai, China, and Bro. H. H. McMillan and wife goes to Yang Chow, China. These are three noble and strong Christian workers. This year Southern Baptists have undertaken the greatest missionary campaign in their history. There are many reasons as to why we should be encouraged. Owing, however, to the present financial condition the board is facing practically a crisis.

On October the eighth and ninth a meeting of the board was held and submitted the following facts to Southern Baptists for their consideration:

"1. Your board is finding it difficult to borrow the money needed to meet the drafts from month to month, coming to this office for the support of the missionaries at work upon the field.

"2. The rate of interest upon the sums which have been borrowed has been increased, owing to the same general financial conditions. The total sum paid for interest in past years has mounted into thousands, owing to the fact that the payments by the churches are often delayed until the very close of the Convention year.

"3. You will recall that an indebtedness of $76,000 was left over from last year. If the apportionments accepted by the States are promptly paid the present year, this indebtedness will be wiped out and the work carried forward with added vigor. Unless, however, the full apportionment is raised, you will face at the close of the year on your Foreign Mission work an indebtedness that will prove a handicap to your plans."

To remedy this situation, the Churches are urged to take their collections for Foreign Missions at the earliest possible moment and to make them as large as possible and send them in at once. Every penny given for Foreign Missions in any treasury of a Southern State should be sent to the Foreign Mission Board without fail immediately.

We recommend these suggestions to the Johnston County Association and ask that our people do all in their power to remedy these conditions.

We also recommend that our Association co-operate in raising the Judson Centennial Equipment Fund. This movement works a new epoch in Foreign Mission work by Southern Baptists. If this movement succeed it must enlist all our people.

Let the Johnston County Association do its very best for every phase of our Foreign Mission cause.   Respectfully submitted,

JOHN E. LANIER,
For the Committee.

Report discussed by Brethren J. E. Lanier, Chas. J. Thompson, F. P. Hobgood and E. R. Nelson.

Adjourned with prayer for Dr. Willingham by Bro. C. G. Wells.

FRIDAY MORNING.

The body met in its 3rd day's session. Devotional exercises were conducted by Bro. J. J. Lane, after which the Moderator came to the chair and called the body to order. Bro. Wall led in prayer.

Miscellaneous business was called for. Bro. Beaty presented the matter of Canaan church wishing to become a member of our Association. The church did not present a letter from the South River Association. Bro. J. J. Lane made a motion to instruct our Executive Committee to investigate the matter. Motion was carried.

Bro. Hamby presented the matter of changing the time of the meeting of the Association.

Brother John E. Lanier presented a resolution to change article twelve of our constitution to read: The annual session of the Association shall begin on Wednesday after the fourth Sunday in October. The resolution was unanimously adopted.

On motion of Bro. Beaty, Bro. F. H. Brooks was elected Auditor for the Association.

The following resolution was offered by T. J. Lassiter:

Realizing the great importance of the great missionary enterprise of our denomination, and realizing that the people are not informed on these subjects as they should be, therefore, be it

Resolved, That a Missionary Committee of five be appointed who shall plan and hold, as early as possible in the new year, a series of Missionary Institutes or Rallies, throughout the Association, in order that our people may be informed on these great subjects.

Resolution adopted and Moderator appointed Missionary Committee as follows: A. O. Hamby, J. E. Lanier, John M Gibbs, J. J. Lane and J. B. Creech.

The report of the Committee on Church building was read by T. J. Lassiter. Without discussion the report was adopted.

REPORT OF BUILDING COMMITTEE.

The Building Committee has been unable to build a church the past year for want of funds. As we know of several places where church buildings are needed we urge the churches to enlarge the gifts to this object.

CLAUDE STEPHENSON,
J. B. CREECH,
For the Committee.

The Committee on Woman's Work was not present. Bro. Hamby read a statement from the ladies concerning their work. Brethren Wells and Hamby spoke of the importance of the Woman's Work, and suggested that we give their work an important place on our Associational program. Bro.

E. R. Nelson and Bro. T. J. Hood also made some suggestions on the work.

Report on Ministerial Education was read by Bro. C. G. Wells. On motion to adopt the report, Brethren Wells, Lanier and Nelson discussed the report, the same was adopted.

REPORT ON MINISTERIAL EDUCATION.

(Taken from the report of Rev. W. N. Johnson in last year's Baptist State Convention Annual.)

"Ministerial Education is simply one method of training those to whom God has given the task of preaching His gospel. The preacher is God's man for a specific work. The first thing to be done is to make him the strongest, most intelligent, best-grown man that can be made out of him. The preacher must be a man that knows Jesus Christ. He must know the kingdom of heaven on earth, not as a theory, but as the supreme force in human history and as the mightiest fact of current life. He must know the Book that tells of Jesus Christ and His kingdom; his own life must be an evidence of its inspiration.

"Not only must he know the gospel; he must know the age in which he is preaching this gospel. It is necessary for him to have in view the background of the life of the men and women to whom he is bringing the word of God. He must be in touch with its material advancement, with its educational progress, with its complex organizations for all purposes, with the rise of the common man in the affairs of the world. In all these he must see the coming of the reign of his Lord.

"He is to be made capable of leading the churches of Christ. The churches are in straits these days waiting for leaders that they are willing to follow. Destructive higher criticism, the hostility of labor unions to organized Christianity, the superficial agitation for Christian union, the collapsing of ecclesiasticism hoary with age, have all brought on a confusion in Christendom. This is the hour to sound the Baptist note. Emphasize our difference from all other Christians and our points of contact with them. Democracy taking root all over the world is soon to perish for the want of a religious soil in which to grow if we fail to do our duty in this serious mission. The key to the situation is the local church. If we will only give that its New Testament place, the way is open for Christian unity everywhere. Bishops that can really lead local churches to do God's work, men who out of the immediacy of their experience of God and with developed powers of self-expression can speak with authority are God's only gift that will save the day at this perilous time in church history.

"In a very short time North Carolina Baptists ought to be giving annually to this cause at least ten thousand dollars. It will take that now to carry on all the work that should be done in Wake Forest College, in our secondary schools, and in our Seminary at Louisville, and for our mission volunteers in Meredith and in other female colleges of the State."   C. A. JENKENS.

The session adjourned until one o'clock for the afternoon session.

FRIDAY AFTERNOON.

Opened with prayer by Brother Nelson.

Report on Temperance called for and read by Bro. T. J. Hood.

REPORT ON TEMPERANCE.

We are commanded to be temperate in all things. As we see it, temperance in regard to strong drink is most important. Prohibition was endorsed by 45,000 majority of the voters of North Carolina. What we ask is that the church of God be true to that decision and do away with blind tigers, cider presses and wine shops. The churches of the Johnston Association have the power, if all the members would be true, to do away with these evils.

We also recommend that the churches do all in their power against cigarette smoking among our boys.   T. J. HOOD, for Committee.

Report was discussed by Brother Hood and adopted.

MISCELLANEOUS MATTER.

The following resolution was offered by Bro. E. R. Nelson and unanimously adopted.

Be it resolved, That it is the sense of this Association that we have been most hospitably and graciously entertained during our stay in Smithfield and that we extend a most hearty vote of thanks to this church and to all others who have contributed to our comfort and happiness for their courtesies and kindness.

The following resolution was offered by Bro. A. C. Hamby and unanimously adopted:

Whereas, material prosperity is in large degree conducive to the prosperity of a people, and necessary to the prosecution of the work of the church, and,

Whereas, good roads are one of the prime elements producing prosperity, and facilitating largely the spread of the gospel, therefore, be it resolved:

First. That the Johnston County Association heartily commend Governor Craig's Good Roads Proclamation, and call upon the people to respond loyally.

Second. That the Clerk forward a copy of this resolution to our Governor.

The Clerk of the Association forwarded a copy of the resolutions to Governor Craig and has received the following letter of acknowledgment:

Mr. T. J. Lassiter, Smithfield, N. C.

Dear Sir: Yours of November 1st, enclosing copy of resolutions passed by the Johnston County Baptist Association concerning Good Roads Days received, and I am directed by the Governor to thank you, and through you the Johnston County Baptist Association for the interest they have thus manifested in this great work.   Very truly yours,

JNO. P. KERR, Private Secretary.

Raleigh, N. C., Nov. 3, 1913.

A collection of $25.00 was taken for the Students' Aid Fund at Southern Baptist Theological Seminary. Clerk forwarded same on this day to B. Pressley Smith, Louisville, Ky.

The report of the Finance Committee was read by Bro. G. L. Jones and accepted, as follows:

REPORT OF FINANCE COMMITTEE.

Bailey ....$	7.25
Benson	104.31
Bethesda	63.81
Blackman's Grove	37.45
Corinth	22.35
Clyde's Chapel	25.21
Hood's Grove	25.00
Micro	16.05
Mount Moriah	42.10
Parrish Memorial	22.55
Sardis	4.68
Wilson's Mills	18.00
	$ 388.76

Turned same over to Treasurer, T. J. Lassiter.

G. L. JONES, for Committee.

On motion, the Treasurer's report was ordered to be inserted in the minutes.

On motion, the Clerk was instructed to have the usual number of Minutes printed and distributed and that he be allowed $20 for his services.

After remarks by several brethren the Association adjourned at 2:10 p. m. with benediction by Bro. W. H. Wall.

TREASURER'S REPORT.

By amount from the churches, for State Missions	$ 423.29
By amount from Finance Committee, State Missions	145.01
By amount collected at Association, State Missions	17.90
By amount Bethany, State Missions	7.00
By amount Pauline, State Missions	8.00
By amount from the churches, Home Missions	55.11
By amount from Finance Committee, Home Missions	13.68
By amount from the churches, Foreign Missions	98.28
By amount from the Finance Committee, Foreign Missions	21.54
By amount from the churches, Sunday School Missions	26.50
By amount Finance Committee, Sunday School Missions	11.00
By amount from the churches, Ministerial Education	41.76
By amount Finance Committee, Ministerial Education	19.00
By amount from the Churches, Ministerial Relief	64.46
By amount Finance Committee, Ministerial Relief	6.83
By amount from the Churches, Orphanage	74.14
By amount Finance Committee, Orphanage	39.29

Total		$1072.79
To amount sent Walters Durham	$ 959.36	
To amount sent S. H. Averitt	113.43	—$1072.79

Minute Fund.

Nov. 24, 1912—By Balance		$ 53.61
Jan. 24, 1913—Paid J. B. Jackson, Clerk and postage	$ 16.62	
Jan. 24, 1913—Paid Nash Bros. for minutes	30.00	—$ 46.62
Jan. 24, 1913—By balance		$ 6.99
By amount from the churches		39.55
By amount Finance Committee		14.00
Nov. 15, By balance		$ 60.54

Church Building Fund.

Nov. 24, 1912—By balance		$ 255.38
Dec. 7, 1912—Paid R. H. Johnson, work on Burnell	$ 96.25	
Dec. 7, 1912—Paid J. H. Johnson, lumber for Burnell	15.00	
Dec. 7, 1912—Paid W. M. Sanders, Mdse. for Burnell	63.18	
Feb. 5, 1913—Paid Johnston Lumber Co., for Burnell	43.00	
Feb. 8, 1913—Paid Cotter Hdw. Co., stove for Burnell	8.80	
Apr. 7, 1913—Paid Board of Education for Hephzibah	29.15	—$ 255.38
1913.		
By amount from the churches		$ 181.15
By amount from Finance Committee		94.68
By amount advanced by J. M. Beaty		40.00
Total		$ 315.83
Nov. 1, 1913—To amount paid Bank of Smithfield		300.00
Nov. 15, 1913—By balance on hand		$ 15.83

T. J. LASSITER, Treasurer.

CONSTITUTION.

1. The Association shall be known as the Johnston County Baptist Association.

2. Its object shall be to extend the privileges of the Gospel and liberal culture to all the people within its bounds, and by hearty co-operation with the Baptist State Convention to help offer these privileges to all mankind in and out of its bounds, by the cordial co-operation of all the churches constituting this body.

3. It shall be composed of the pastors in active service in the Association and such delegates as shall be annually elected by the churches connected with it, each church being entitled to three delegates, unless the membership shall exceed fifty, and then an additional delegate for every twenty-five members, provided no church shall have more than eight delegates.

4. The New Hampshire Declaration of Faith shall be the summary of Divine Truth for determining questions of faith and order in this body, and the churches desiring membership in it must commit themselves to the substance of it, together with the covenant therewith submitted, and this Constitution.

5. This Association shall not have power, to annul the discipline or exercise authority over any church connected with it, but it may advise with and sever its connection with any church that neglects to preserve gospel order, or that treats with contempt the objects or advice of the Association.

6. Each church shall send to the annual meetings of the Association a letter (the blanks to be furnished by the Clerk of the Association), carefully filled as per blank suggestions, stating the full work of the church for the year ending with the close of the month previous to the one in which the Association is held.

7. The Association shall foster State Missions, Home Missions, Foreign Missions, Christian Education, the Aged Ministers' Relief Board, the Thomasville Orphanage and the Sunday School Board, and each church shall be requested to contribute to the support of these objects annually.

8. Missions and education shall have precedence in their claims upon the consideration of this body in its regular sessions.

9. Whenever a church shall fail to be represented by delegates or letter at the annual sessions of the Association inquiry shall be made for the cause and efforts shall be made to induce such church to do its duty, and the effort shall be continued till the church is recovered or dropped from the roll.

10. The officers of the Association shall be a Moderator, a Vice-Moderator, a Clerk, a Treasurer and an Auditor, elected annually by ballot from among its members, to serve until their successors shall have been elected, and to perform the duties usual to such officers, namely, the Moderator, in presiding over the meetings, or the Vice-Moderator in his absence; the Clerk in recording and preserving minutes and other papers belonging to the body; the Treasurer in receiving and disbursing funds belonging to or entrusted to the body according to its will; the Auditor to examine the Treasurer's books at each meeting of the Association and report the same before adjournment.

11. The Association shall appoint annually an Executive Committee of five (5) from its members, who shall be entrusted with the prosecution of Missions in the Association and any other work for the interest of the Master's Kingdom which may be referred to them. This committee shall, as far as possible, co-operate with the State Mission Board in supplying the destitution in our territory, and between the meetings of the Association take such actions as may seem to them advisable for the advancement of its interest. The committee shall present to the Association at its annual meeting a report of its proceedings with the names of the missionaries supported on the field, time of service and deaths of their work, together with

such recommendations as in the judgment of the committee the Association should follow in planning its subsequent work.

12. The annual sessions of the Association shall begin on Wednesday after the fourth Lord's day in October as such place as may be chosen, and an introductory sermon shall be delivered on the first day of the session. Representatives from a majority of the churches constituting the Association shall be a quorum.

13. This Constitution may be amended at any annual session by a two-thirds vote of all the members present.

14. Provision shall be made at each annual session for a session of the Woman's Central Committee, and all other necessary encouragement offered for the enlargement of the organized work of the Woman's Missionary Societies in the local churches. The proceedings of the Woman's Central Committee shall be recorded as a part of the Minutes of the Association.

BY-LAWS.

1. The daily sessions of the Association shall be opened and closed with prayer.

2. Delegates shall be recognized by letters from their churches designating them as such.

3. The Moderator shall recognize corresponding messengers or the delegates of newly received churches by extending to them his right hand.

4. The report of the Executive Board and the Missionary work of the Association shall take precedence of all other business during the morning session of the second day of the annual session.

5. The Clerk shall record and read the proceedings when called for, superintend the publication and distribution of the Minutes, preserve a file of them, and have it present at each annual session, and deliver to his successor all papers belonging to the body.

6. Members desiring to speak shall first rise and address the Moderator, shall use the term "Brother" in speaking to each other; shall not speak on the same subject more than twice without permission, and shall observe the courtesy that becomes Christians.

7. Members shall not absent themselves from the session without permission.

8. The roll of members shall be called at least once and absentees marked.

9. Corresponding messengers and visiting brethren shall be invited to seats, with privilege of speaking, but not voting.

10. A copy of the Minutes shall be sent to the Secretary of the State Mission Board, the Secretary of the Southern Baptist Convention, the American Baptist Publication Society, 1420 Chestnutt Street, Philadelphia; the Sunday School Board of the Southern Baptist Convention and the Thomasville Orphanage.

11. All questions of order not herein provided shall be decided by Kerfoot's Parliamentary Law.

WOMAN'S MISSIONARY UNION..

A happy set of women were we as we alighted from the train at Kenly on the morning of October 28, 1913, delegates to the Baptist Woman's Missionary Union, of Johnston County Association. We were taken to our several homes in automobiles and found awaiting us a welcome so warm, and a breakfast so tempting, that women less hungry than we, who had arisen at an early hour and without breakfast, would have enjoyed.

After a brief rest, we betook ourselves to the church where a goodly number had assembled. At the appointed time Miss Blanche Barrus in her easy, persuasive way conducted the devotional exercises. We thank Miss Barrus for her presence on this occasion, and assure her that it lent inspiration to us all. The absence of our beloved Vice-President, Mrs. C. W. Carter, was the only thing that marred our happiness, but we hope that she may be with us at our next and seventh session at Mount Moriah church.

Mrs. B. A. Hocutt, the Vice-President pro tem, then took the chair, and very gracefully presided.

After the addresses of welcome from the Baptist, Methodist and Presbyterian churches, and the response from Clayton Society, the roll was called. Ten Missionary Societies responded, six Sunbeams, one Royal Ambassador, one Y. W. A. and two Junior Y. W. A. The total amount from these Societies was $659.92.

The report on Home Missions by Mrs. Lacy Worrell in which she stated that seven thousand, three hundred and seventy-six churches in Southern Baptist territory were houseless, made us realize more than ever the great importance of Home Missions.

In her report on Foreign Missions, Mrs. Bain urged greater activity in the Master's service and more constant prayer.

From Mrs. Massey's report on State Missions we learn "State Missions is to all our work, what the roots are to the tree. They take hold upon the soil and pass life up into the body of the tree. So as the work of State Missions develops and expands, there is corresponding development along all lines of denominational activity."

A paper on the dangers that threaten our home land by Mrs. A. C. Hamby, showed many causes for greater activity on the part of Christians, the greatest in our opinion being Roman Catholicism. We wish that copies of this might be scattered broadcast over our land.

In closing her paper "What part of our time and possessions belong to God," Mrs. J. W. Sanders says: "God's portion of the mere gold we possess is only a very small part of what really belongs to Him. We must so desire for Him to abide in us that we may become part of Him and He part of us. We must yield our life to the Master's touch."

We were indeed sorry not to have with us our beloved friend and co-worker Mrs. Mark Gulley, who was detained at home on account of illness in her family. She, however, reported the death of Mrs. J. B. Faircloth on April 10th, 1913, a worthy member of the Woman's Missionary Society of Benson.

Mrs. J. M. Beaty realizes that for the women to get much interested in Missions, we should do all we can to get literature distributed and read. She has mailed a considerable quantity of it to ladies in all the churches, urging them to take Mission Journals and organize Societies.

Mrs. Geo. F. Uzzle gave a comprehensive sketch of the Woman's Mission Union, in which she says that "the future of this structure must exceed our greatest hopes."

The morning program completed, we were invited out to the adjoining grounds, where a long table was spread, and fairly groaning with good things. Need we say that we heartily partook, and enjoyed them?

The devotional exercises in the afternoon were conducted by Mrs. Richardson.

A paper on personal service by Mrs. B. A. Hocutt thrilled us, and made us long to do more for our Master's service. We noted especially the telling of a great work that has been started at Liberty Cotton Mills (Clayton) by a member of our own Mission Society. Truly Mrs. Thornton is doing a great work, and great will be her reward.

We tell with sadness the absence of a member of the Y. W. A., Miss Swannanoa Horne, who has recently passed through deep waters. Our hearts go out to her in loving sympathy. May the great Comforter give that peace and resignation which come alone from Him.

Miss Christine Gower in her paper "The Young Woman at Work" says: "Suppose instead of one hundred and thirty-five Y. W. A's we had one thousand, nine hundred and fifty, which is the number of churches in our State what a lot of workers these would be in the vineyard."

Mrs. J. M. Beaty realizes the importance of teaching missions to children. Would that more of our women realized this as does Mrs. Beaty! What a power she is! In truth her's is a life fully given to the Lord!

With a song by the children, and a prayer, thus ended the day service of the sixth session of the Woman's Mission Union of Johnston county.

A fitting climax to the delightful day was a sermon in the evening by Rev. C. A. Jenkens—his theme being "Why I believe in Missions." He is easily one of our State's brainiest men, as those who know him will attest, and that sermon convincing in every argument. We were fortunate to have Dr. Jenkens with us.

Our Vice-President, Mrs. C. W. Carter tendered her resignation for the coming year. The Union, however, did not see fit to accept, and sent notice to that effect.

Mrs. B. A. Hocutt was made Associate Vice-President.

We greatly missed our Secretary, Mrs. R. M. Nowell, who since the death of her husband had not resumed the duties of the Association. The Union by a rising vote sent expressions of sympathy and regret, which were forwarded by the acting Secretary.

Mrs. C. M. Thomas was made Secretary and Treasurer of the Union.

FINANCIAL REPORT OF SOCIETIES.

Smithfield Sunbeams ....$	21.20
Clayton Sunbeams	10.00
Mount Moriah Sunbeams..	4.09
Four Oaks Sunbeams	23.03
Wendell Sunbeams	4.39
Kenly Sunbeams	4.50
Total six societies...............................$	67.21
Mount Moriah Ambassadors....................................$	7.11
Clayton Y. W. A..$	91.00
Wendell Junior Y. W. A...	1.00
Clayton Junior Y. W. A...	8.49
Total two Jr. Y. W. A...	9.49

WOMAN'S MISSIONARY SOCIETIES.

Wendell ....$	45.55
Kenly	19.35
Shiloh	5.70
Clyde's Chapel	17.10
Four Oaks	28.55
Mount Moriah	40.95
Smithfield	110.00
Clayton	176.00
Micro	2.00
Total nine Societies ....$	445.20

TABLE I—FINANCIAL.

CHURCHES.	Minute Fund	Pastor's Salary	Building and Repairs	Incidentals	Sunday School Expenses	The Poor	Building Fund	State Missions	Home Missions	Foreign Missions	Sunday School Missions	Orphanage	Colleges and Schools	Ministerial Education	Aged Ministers	Other Objects	Total
Antioch	.70	33.75	75.00		6.00	1.67	5.25	15.00	3.00	3.00	2.00	3.00		2.00	1.75		152.72
Bailey	.75	75.00			11.00		6.50	20.90	2.00	7.00	1.00	5.00		1.00	2.50	65.22	199.87
Baptist Center	1.00	100.00		6.00	12.00			15.00	2.50	2.00	1.00	5.86		1.00	2.14		142.00
Beaty Chapel	.80			40.00			2.50	7.50	2.50	2.50	2.50	2.50		7.00	5.00	86.26	180.50
Benson	3.00	500.00	75.00	40.00	40.00	5.00	12.00	75.00	12.17	15.00	1.00	25.00		7.00	5.00		819.93
Benson Grove	.85	25.00	25.00		10.00	5.00	6.00	7.50	3.75	2.50	1.00	5.00		1.50	1.50		150.00
Bethany		10.00						7.00	2.50	2.00		5.00		1.00	1.00		86.60
Bethel	2.50			10.00	25.00	10.00	12.50	8.12	2.50	7.50	2.50	15.00		5.00	8.30		23.62
Bethesda	.50	200.00			2.19		7.00	34.20	5.00	5.00	1.00	5.65		4.00	1.35		340.50
Blackman's Grove	.50	56.15						20.00	5.00	2.50	2.00	5.65		1.00	2.50		109.49
Calvary	1.30	50.00					5.00	5.00	1.50	2.50	1.00	10.05		5.00	20.00		55.65
Carter's Chapel	1.50	1200.00	554.66	186.72	12.00	7.34	30.00	275.00	2.50	2.50	1.00	176.69	158.30	25.00	3.75	489.85	102.05
Clayton	5.00	150.00	1000.00		104.15		10.00	20.00	2.50	2.50	28.28	3.75		2.50	7.00	7.00	3390.30
Clyde's Chapel	1.50	150.00		6.00	10.00			20.00	14.04	15.22	2.50	5.00		4.00	26.00		217.61
Corinth	1.50	85.00		4.50	30.85		13.50	23.02	2.50	2.50	1.00	7.40		2.50	4.00	30.00	1145.59
Four Oaks	1.50	100.00			8.00		4.00	2.50	2.20	2.50	2.50	1.00	2.00	1.00	1.00		251.43
Hephzibah	.50							7.50	5.00	2.50	2.50	2.50		2.50	2.50		22.00
Hood's Grove	.30	40.00	9.00		23.36	25.00		20.00	5.00	10.90	2.50	7.00		5.00	5.00		74.00
Kenly	1.00	150.00	275.00	5.00	20.00		5.00	30.00	5.00	10.00	3.00	1.00		5.00	1.50	5.00	531.06
Lee's Chapel	1.50	150.00						1.75				2.50		.25	1.50		234.50
Live Oak								12.00	2.50	2.50	1.00	2.50		1.50	1.50	5.00	5.00
Micro	.35	43.00	349.85	57.98	18.59		2.50	23.22	5.00	10.00	1.00	23.85		2.50	2.50	278.04	92.44
Middlesex	2.10	200.00		39.40	33.40		5.00	75.00	35.00	50.00		35.00		10.00	10.00		999.54
Mount Moriah	2.50	200.00	5.00	48.00	46.61		40.00	10.00	3.50	11.50	1.00	17.50		5.50	2.50		729.74
New Bethel	1.51	226.55	25.00	6.00	16.33		15.00	10.00	3.50	6.23	1.00	2.77		2.50	2.50		336.39
Noble's Chapel					3.50												140.08
Oliver's Grove	1.00	80.00	7.50		5.00		5.00	7.50	2.50	2.50	1.00	2.00		2.50	2.50		119.00
Parrish Memorial	.75						2.50	6.00	1.50	1.50	.50	1.50		1.00	1.00		16.25
Pauline		100.00	48.00	16.00		4.00	2.75	8.00	4.00	5.00	1.00	2.50		1.50	1.50		193.50
Pine Level	1.00	40.00	.25	.65	10.10		2.75	6.25	2.50	5.00	1.00	2.00		2.50	2.50		86.00
Pinkney	1.00	150.00		10.00	8.22	4.00	4.65	17.50	4.00	5.00		3.00		2.50	1.50		210.72
Pisgah	1.00	93.35	40.00	15.96	15.00		4.68	15.00	3.00	5.00	1.00	4.00		2.50	2.00		208.96
Princeton	.89	75.00					5.00	12.58	2.50	5.00	2.00	5.00		2.50	2.65		110.31
Sardis	1.50	800.00	71.33	172.26	81.52	181.78	5.00	30.25	23.25	51.51	1.00	35.93		3.00	2.50	15.00	1446.04
Selma		125.00		7.00			9.00	15.00	9.00	15.00	1.00	5.00		2.50	2.50	22.00	199.00
Shiloh	5.00	1000.00	574.50	117.00	82.62		25.00	160.00	27.77	46.55	5.00	35.93	35.00	13.03	10.00	50.00	2187.40
Smithfield	.50	37.87		15.00	15.00	4.57	4.00	6.00	21.50	1.50	1.00	2.50		2.50	2.50	7.00	99.94
Thanksgiving	.75		5.00								8.48	3.00		1.00	1.50		98.75
Trinity	2.00	37.00		15.00	98.48	10.00	25.00	30.20	29.25	146.08	2.50	83.30		5.00	5.00	64.20	948.91
Wendell	2.00	434.00		55.00	25.00			30.00	7.50	5.00		10.00		5.00	2.50		324.50
White Oak					30.00			20.00	2.00	5.00		9.50		2.50	2.50		282.00

Statistical table of churches (associational minutes).

CHURCH	PASTOR AND POSTOFFICE	CLERK AND POSTOFFICE	Time of Preaching	Value of Church Property	Seating Capacity	Baptized	Received by Letter	Restored	Dismissed by Letter	Excluded	Died	Number of Males	Number of Females	Total Membership
Antioch	R. L. ... Fort, Well...	W. O. Underwood, Selma, R. 2	2nd	$1300	90	8	3		3	4	3	60	114	174
Bailey	W. L. ...	R. L. Underwood, Bailey	1st	1500	350	15	3	3	3	1	1	21	31	52
Baptist Center	Q. W. ...	E. H. Rogers, Clayton	1st	1000	90	9	2	3	1			32	56	88
Beaty	J. M. Wall, Four Oaks	N. M. Eason, Smithfield	4th	1000	90	4	1		2	2		17	23	40
Benson	J. M. Duncan, Benson	L. D. Gilbert, Benson	24th	2000	50	6	5	1	2	3	2	60	102	162
Benson's Grove	J. M. Gibbs, Benson	Perry Barnes, Kenly	2nd	800	90	1						6	16	22
Bethel	J. U. Teague, ... Forest	J. E. Smith, ... Mills	1st	400	90	6		3				19	18	37
Bethesda	J. W. Smith, ... Mills	J. G. Johnson, ...	4th	500	100	30					3	120	140	260
... Grove	N. H. Gibbs, Benson	Kirkman Creech, Kenly, R. 2	3rd	600	90	4			4	4	1	20	42	62
Bethany	N. H. Gibbs, Benson	T. J. Lee, Dunn	4th	600	300	4	3	3	3	4	1	35	53	88
Calvary	J. W. Smith, Wilson's Mills	Martin Thorn, Selma	1st	500	200	2	2	1	4		1	10	17	27
Carter's	A. C. Hamby, Clayton	R. R. Gulley, Clayton	1st	1000	300	4	4		1			33	50	83
Clayton	A. Pippin, ...	C.-I. Johnson, Knightdale, R.2	Every	6000	500	9	8	2	3		1	149	187	336
Clyde's	A. ... Pippin, Weld	H. V. Andrews, ... Four ...	3rd	500	300	7	1	1	3			64	86	150
Four ...		J. Wm. ..., Four ...	2nd	1500	300	13	2		1	3		46	67	113
	T. M. Duncan, Benson		3rd	1000	150	18	2	1	1			25	35	60
...s Grove	T. J. ..., Kenly	P. T. George, Four ... R. 1	3rd	500	300	4		1			1	26	28	54
Kenly	A. L. ..., Weld	R. O. Martin, Kenly	2nd	3000	330	16	15	4	2	3		22	24	46
Lee's Chapel	A. L. ... Fort, Weld	W. I. Green, Zebulon, R. 2	3rd	2000	300	16	3		3		2	57	90	177
...	J. M. Gibbs, Kenly	K. Broadwell, Selma, R. 1	3rd	500	300	6		4				12	25	37
Micro	J. G. Wells, Zebulon	Leonard Pace, Selma, R. 3	2-4	1500	300	11	5				1	9	10	19
Mt Moriah	C. A. Pippin, Weld	J. L. Cornwell, ...	3rd	2500	350	11	3		6		2	29	49	78
New Bethel	J. M. Gibbs, Kenly	R. A. Baucom, Raleigh, R.F.D	1st	3500	500	16	7	4	2	1	1	87	90	177
Noble's		N. L. Satt, Sims	4th	750	350	2						80	86	166
*Oliver's Grove	(No report)											36	50	86
Parrish Memorial	J. M. Duncan, Benson	J. D. ..., Selma, R. 3	1st	750	300	4	6		2				34	24
Pauline	T. J. ..., ...	A. G. ..., ...	3rd	700	300	4	1	1			1	22	38	70
...e Level	E. R. ..., Selma	Clyde Gin, ... Level	1st	1000	400	3	1	2				17		60
Pinkney	W. H. Wall, Four	R. H. ..., Kenly, R. 1	1st	1000	500	6	6		5		1	29	44	72
Pisgah	E. R. Nelson, Selma	W. I. ..., Smithfield	3rd	1200	400	2	2		3			37	37	32
Princeton	W. H. Wall, ...	B. C. Reynolds, Selma	3rd	500	300	5	1					23	62	73
Sardis	W. H. Wall, ...	B. S. Reynolds, Selma	2-4			7	11	2	8		2	24	24	99
Selma		F. D. ...	2nd	700	300			2	1			77	111	47
Shiloh	John E. Lanier, Smithfield	T. J. ...	Every	8000		6	4	2	6		1	70	53	188
Smithfield	J. U. Teague, ... Forest	G. A. ..., Selma	3rd	1500	600	1		1		2	2	85	88	90
Thanksgiving	N. H. Gibbs, Benson	J. M. Lawhon, ... R. 2	3rd	400	200	12	2		3	3	1	30	30	158
Trinity	A. A. Jenkins, Clayton		2-4	1200	400		2	2	2	2		27	27	57
Wendell	A. A. Pippin, Weld	J. I. Murphy, Selma, R. 1	2nd	2500	500	8	9	1	9		1	63	103	40
...	R. L. Brown, ... Forest	J. T. ... Fort, Wilson's Mills	2nd	1000	250	9	1		1		2	93	122	215
Wilson's Mills												26	29	55
Total						253	110	28	85	38	23			3955

*Last year's membership.

TABLE III—SUNDAY SCHOOLS.

CHURCH	SUPERINTENDENT	POST OFFICE	Officers and Teachers	Scholars	Total Enrollment	Number of Schools	Months kept open	Average Attendance	Number of Baptisms	Contributions for Missions Orphanage, etc.	School Expenses
⁂h	J. R. Hocutt	Selma, Route 2	9	68	77	1	12	25	4	$	$ 6.60
Bailey	J. P. ⁂	Bailey	3	60	63	1	12	40		1.00	10.00
⁂t	J. C. ⁂	Clayton	6	119	125	1	12	40	14		12.00
Beaty ⁂el	N. M. Eason	Smithfield	4	30	34	1	12	30		7.50	5.50
⁂n's Grove	J. L. ⁂ll	⁂	8	170	178	1	12	90	4		⁂0
Bethany	Da vi P ce	⁂ Route 3.	5	60	65	1	12	45	3		10.00
Bethel ⁂a	D. C. Smith	Wilson's Mills	12	160	172	1	12	100	15	5.00	20.00
⁂m's Grove	F. P. ⁂d	Four ⁂s	5	31	36	1	6	16			2.19
Calvary ⁂r's Chapel	J. M. ⁂	Selma, ⁂e 3.	4	45	49	1	12	35		8.00	12.00
Clayton	Riley R. Gulley	Clayton, Route 2.	13	275	288	1	12	179	9	455.03	104.15
Clyde's Chapel	W. T. Bunch	Zebulon, R. F. D.	7	60	67	1	12	40	5	.40	10.00
⁂r	Q. B. Hocutt	⁂	6	90	96	1	12	50	5		6.00
⁂s	W. A. ⁂		7	108	115	1	12	60	13	8.80	30.25
⁂n	G. W. Pike	⁂n	5	35	40	1	12	25	3		8.00
Hood's Grove	A. J. Strickland	Kenly	8	83	91	1	12	40	13	52.00	23.36
Kenly	J. W. Strickland	Middlesex	7	70	77	1	12	50			18.00
⁂e's Chapel	No Sunday School										
Live ⁂k	C. L. Bilbro	Micro	6	40	46	1	12	25	10	6.50	12.03
Micro	W. O. Bilbro	Middlesex	9	177	185	1	12	88	1	210.85	39.40
Middlesex ⁂	N. R. ⁂l	Clayton	13	135	148	1	12	83	5	35.79	16.60
New Bethel ⁂l	R. I. ⁂h	McCullers	7	70	77	1	9	25			16.39
⁂s	John ⁂e	Sims	5	60	65	1	6	25			3.50
Oliver's Grove ⁂h	Frank ⁂n	Micro	6	30	36	1	6	15	3		5.00
Pauline ⁂h	J. B. Beasley	Four Oaks	6	64	70	1	6	31			3.62
Pine Level	B. L. Strickland	Pine Level	6	98	104	1	12	42	3		7.50
Pinkney	W. N. Dixon	Kenly R. F. D.	7	71	78	1	12	39	4		10.10
Pisgah ⁂n	Paul E. Whitley	Smithfield	7	75	82	2	12	23	2	.56	8.22
Sardis	W. H. Wells	Princeton	7	88	93	1	12	40	1		15.00
Selma	B. C. Powell	Smithfield	7	53	59	1	12	23			10.00
Shiloh	R. E. Richardson	Selma	12	175	187	1	12	135	7	122.61	81.52
Smithfield	S. B. Hardee	Clayton	6	60	66	1	12	40		160.25	7.00
⁂ng	L. F. Royall	Smithfield	10	210	220	1	12	112	6		82.60
⁂fty	J. A. ⁂	Selma	13	146	159	1	12	75			15.00
Wendell	A. P. Lee	Benson	5	40	45	1	7	20			
⁂e	L. M. ⁂t	Wendell	14	258	272	1	12	123	5	66.78	98.48
⁂n's Mills	A. G. ⁂en	Clayton Route 2	10	115	125	1	12	60	2		25.00
*Burnell	G. G. Beaty	Wilson's Mills	7	76	83	1	6	40		2.00	30.00
	J. S. Johnson	Four Oaks, Route 4			68	1		40			5.05
Total			974	3857	5984O			1961	190	1148.67	812.99

MINUTES

OF THE

JOHNSTON COUNTY

BAPTIST ASSOCIATION,

HELD WITH

New Bethel Baptist Church,

GARNER, N. C.,

October, 1914.

The next session will be held with Clayton Church, Clayton, N. C., beginning Wednesday after the fourth Sunday in October, 1915. To preach Introductory Sermon—John E. Lanier.

OFFICERS.

Moderator—R. H. Gower...............................Clayton, N. C.
Vice-Moderator—J. J. Lane...........................Auburn, N. C.
Clerk—John E. Lanier ....Smithfield, N. C.
Treasurer—T. J. Lassiter............................Smithfield, N. C.
Auditor—Walter Ives ....Smithfield, N. C.

Goldsboro, N. C.
Nash Bros., Printers and Binders,
1914.

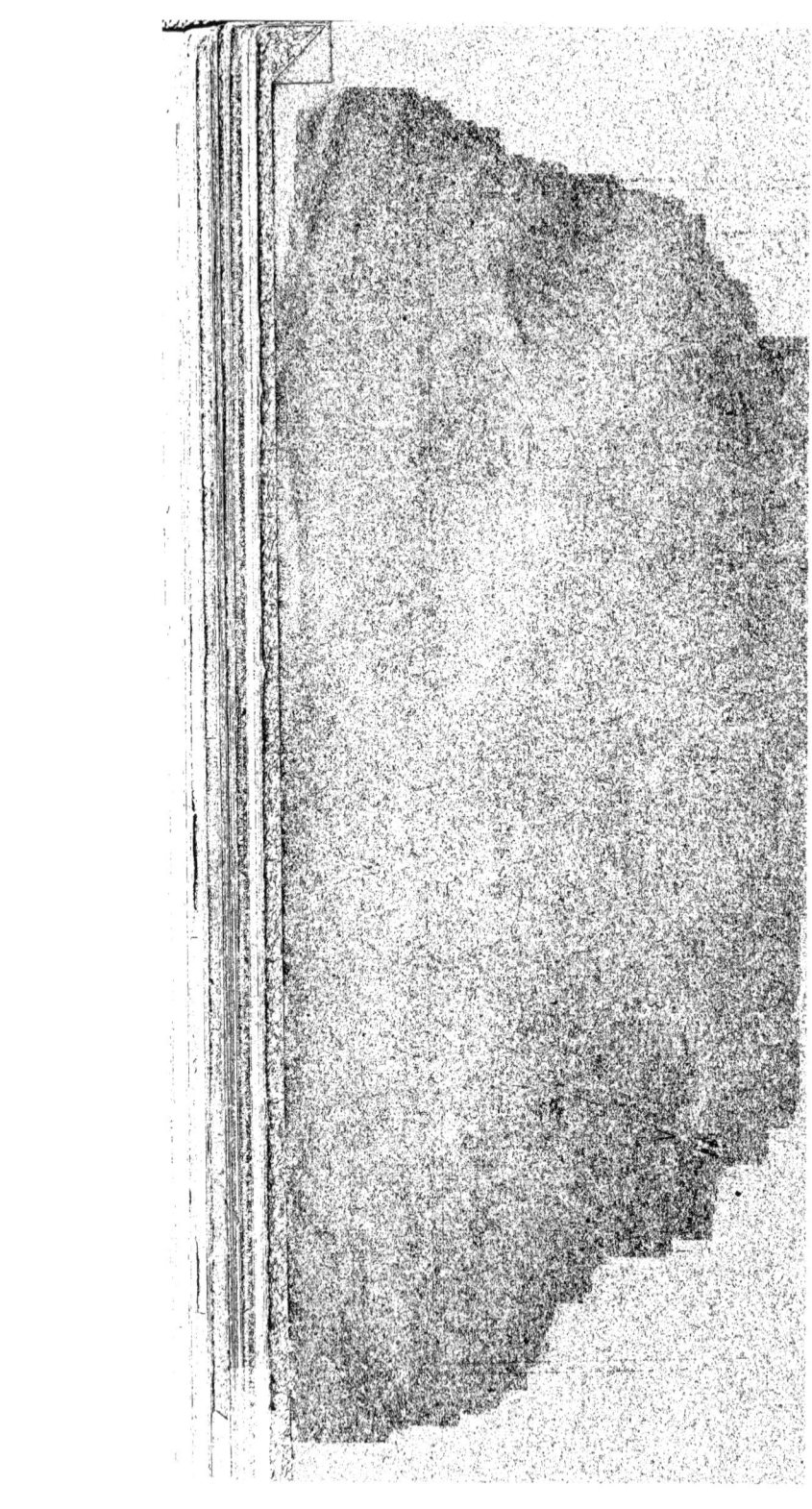

MINUTES

OF THE

JOHNSTON COUNTY

BAPTIST ASSOCIATION,

HELD WITH

New Bethel Baptist Church,

GARNER, N. C.,

October, 1914.

The next session will be held with Clayton Church, Clayton, N. C.,
beginning Wednesday after the fourth Sunday in October, 1915.

To preach Introductory Sermon—John E. Lanier.

OFFICERS.

Moderator—R. H. Gower................................Clayton, N. C.

Vice-Moderator—J. J. Lane............................Auburn, N. C.

Clerk—John E. Lanier ....Smithfield, N. C.

Treasurer—T. J. Lassiter...........................Smithfield, N. C.

Auditor—Walter Ives ....Smithfield, N. C.

Goldsboro, N. C.
Nash Bros., Printers and Binders,
1914.

EXECUTIVE COMMITTEE.

J. M. Beaty, Chairman..Smithfield.
Berry Godwin...Pine Level.
J. J. Lane...Auburn.
J. B. Creech..Four Oaks.
J. T. Holt..Wilson's Mills.

DELEGATES AND BOARD MEMBER.

C. M. Thomas, W. H. Wall, J. J. Lane—Delegates to the Baptist State Convention.

A. C. Hamby, Delegate to Southern Baptist Convention.

John E. Lanier, member of State Board of Missions.

LIST OF MINISTERS.

R. L. BROWN...Wake Forest.
W. L. BILBRO..Middlesex.
I. L. BENNETT...Wake Forest.
J. M. DUNCAN..Benson.
N. H. GIBBS...Benson.
J. M. GIBBS ....Kenly.
T. J. HOOD...Goldsboro.
A. C. HAMBY..Clayton.
R. L. HOCUTT...Route 1, Wendell.
C. A. JENKINS..Clayton.
JOHN E. LANIER..Smithfield.
A. A. PIPPIN...Wakefield.
J. W. SMITH.,..Wilson's Mills.
C. E. STEVENS..Selma.
W. T. TATE...Wake Forest.
J. U. TEAGUE..Wake Forest.
W. H. WALL...Four Oaks.
O. W. YATES..Wake Forest.

PROCEEDINGS.

Garner, N. C., October 28, 1914.

The twelfth annual session of the Johnston County Baptist Association convened with New Bethel Baptist Church this morning at ten-thirty o'clock. Devotional exercises were conducted by Dr. R. T. Vann.

The Introductory Sermon was preached by Dr. C. A. Jenkins, of Clayton, N. C. He used as his topic, "The Believer's Advocate." Text I. John 2:1.

Following the sermon the body was called to order by the Moderator, Bro. R. H. Gower, of Clayton.

The following committee was announced:

Credentials and Enrollment—D. H. Jones and R. I. Smith.

The following delegates and visitors were enrolled:

Antioch—J. R. Hocutt.
Bailey—
Baptist Center—J. Milton Austin and Council Pool.
Beaty Chapel—
Benson—J. M. Duncan and J. L. Hall.
Benson Grove—
Bethany—Kirkman Creech and Norman Jones.
Bethel—
Bethesda—W. T. Tate, J. W. Smith, J. J. Wallace and W. H. Lancaster.
Blackman's Grove—W. A. Phelps and Noah Wood.
Calvary—
Canaan—Mrs. J. T. Hudson.
Carter's Chapel—Martin Thorne.
Clayton—A. C. Hamby, C. W. Carter, Bennett Nooe, Jr., J. D. Smith and A. Creech.
Clyde's Chapel—H. H. Hobbs.
Corinth—S. T. Price, J. B. Woodard and H. B. Andrews.
Four Oaks—W. H. Wall, C. H. Grady and J. W. Sanders.
Hephzibah—W. A. Braswell and C. J. Wiggs.
Hood's Grove—
Kenly—
Lee's Chapel—J. B. Mecome, W. I. Green, G. G. Driver.
Live Oak—
Micro—D. H. Jones, L. L. Creech and D. J. Broadwell.
Middlesex—Mrs. J. L. Cornwell and Mrs. N. B. Lewis.
Mount Moriah—J. M. Baucom, W. H. Kelly, J. J. Lane, J. F. Pool, C. A. Jenkins and H. A. Pool.
New Bethel—D. T. Bryan, Herbert Britt, R. I. Smith and L. J. Weathers.
Noble's Chapel—
Oliver's Grove—
Parrish Memorial—Albert Pincter, N. I. Parrish and J. R. Burgess.
Pauline—H. B. Moore.
Pine Level—B. Godwin and Lawrence Brown.
Pinkney—Henry Gurley.
Pisgah—John W. Jones, W. D. Johnson and R. H. Higgins.
Princeton—N. L. Snipes.
Sardis—John W. Strickland.
Selma—N. D. Wells, C. E. Stevens, Mrs. C. E. Stevens, J. M. O'Neal.
Shiloh—Claude Stephenson, F. O. Holland and J. W. Williams.
Smithfield—J. M. Beaty, J. E. Lanier, Herman Jones, L. T. Royal, T. J. Lassiter and F. H. Brooks.

Thanksgiving—R. E. Earp and Raymond Lynch.
Wendell—N. R. Stell.
White Oak—V. R. Turley and A. L. Batton.
Wilson's Mills—J. T. Holt, W. H. Jones and G. G. Beaty.

The Moderator recognized the following visiting brethren: Dr. R. T. Vann, President of Meredith College; F. B. Hamrick, of the Thomasville Orphanage; Hight C. Moore, Editor of Biblical Recorder; A. B. Smith, of Roan Mountain Association; Brother Tate, of Sandy Run Association.

The Vice-Moderator, Bro. A. A. Pippin, then took the chair and the election of officers was taken up and the following were chosen:

Moderator—R. H. Gower.
Vice-Moderator—J. J. Lane.
Clerk—John E. Lanier.
Treasurer—T. J. Lassiter.
Auditor—Walter Ives.

The Association decided to discontinue the office of historian.

A rising vote of thanks was tendered T. J. Lassiter, who retired as Clerk, after a service of more than ten years.

After several announcements the body adjourned for dinner. Benediction by A. B. Smith.

WEDNESDAY AFTERNOON.

Afternoon session opened with song service and prayer by Hight C. Moore.

The chair announced the following Committee on Finance: Berry Godwin, J. W. Smith, and V. R. Turley.

A motion was made, by A. C. Hamby, to appoint a committee to study the constitution and offer whatever amendments they thought advisable. Brethren A. C. Hamby, A. A. Pippin and C. A. Jenkins were appointed.

Upon motion, Dr. R. T. Vann, President of Meredith College, was granted permission to speak on the work of the College. After the address a voluntary offering was taken to help defray the expense of fitting up the Domestic Science department of the college. The collection was $16.06.

Report on Biblical Recorder was read by J. J. Lane.

REPORT ON BIBLICAL RECORDER.

We, your Committee on the "Biblical Recorder," deem it unnecessary to go into an eulogy of the Recorder or to stress the importance of religious literature. The value of good religious literature in promoting Christ's kingdom on earth is well recognized, and the Biblical Recorder stands as one of the very best of denominational papers. Upon inquiry, however, we find too few copies of the paper in circulation among our members. To remedy this we recommend:

1. That each pastor in our Association be requested to make a personal canvass of his churches and endeavor to place a copy of the Recorder in each family.

2. That each church Clerk be asked to report next year the number of families in his church and the number that take the paper.

J. J. LANE, Committee.

A motion was made to adopt, and after discussion by Brethren J. J. Lane, Hight C. Moore, and A. C. Hamby, report was adopted.

As the chairman of the committee on Woman's Work was absent the question was deferred to some future session.

The Orphanage report was read by J. T. Holt.

REPORT ON THE ORPHANAGE.

The care of the unfortunate is a natural and fundamental expression of Christianity. Jesus was in his ministry what he would have us be. He emphasized things fundamental and cast the programme for all ages. He glorified childhood and so related his gospel to the physical wants of life that we cannot hope to save the soul unless we also provide for the body.

So far Orphanage work has been the principal form of our benevolence, largely because it has been showing the most tangible results. It has been said by some that it is necessary only to let the people know the needs of the Orphanage and they will be supplied. The coming year will show whether this is true or not. With only four hundred and thirty children we have fallen behind.

Children are already being received at the Kennedy Home. We now have 53 children there. The Miles Durham Nursery for very small children, at Thomasville, will be completed before the winter months. If this is filled with children and we provide for those that are being received at the Kennedy Home, the current expenses must be increased $10,000 over last year. It means that we must increase our contributions to this most worthy and needy cause at least 25 per cent. Will this association not go on record favoring this additional increase?

Among North Carolina Baptists nothing has so enlisted men and women in the work of the kingdom as the Orphanage work. It has been the agency for the promotion of harmony, liberality and consecration. Thus in the larger work of the kingdom the little child is the leader.

Since the reception of the first child, Nov. 11, 1885, 1,552 have been enrolled and the present number is 480 (with about 500 by end of the year). Average cost per child, $107.64 a year. The health record of the children for the past year has been remarkable, there being no deaths and few cases of serious illness.

Large and valuable additions are being made to the plant at Thomasville. A modern dairy barn has been completed. This department of our work, along with the various other industrial features is to be emphasized. A splendid auditorium will be completed within a year. The erection of this important and greatly needed building was made possible by the bequest of the late Dr. S. W. Little, of Davie county, whose honored name it will bear. Three new school rooms have been added with improvements on the old school building. A tenth grade has been put in the school course for the purpose of giving those who leave us a better preparation for life's struggles.

We would again urge and recommend: (1) That every Sunday School set aside one Sunday in each month as Orphanage day; (2) a club of Charity and Children in each Sunday School and an individual copy to pastors and all homes that are not represented in the Sunday School; (3) a liberal Thanksgiving offering, emphasizing the importance of "Work Day," giving not less than one day's work to the Orphanage. We would suggest that in many churches it is best to select a Sunday nearest Thanksgiving Day to hold this special service. This can be done to advantage on country fields.

Finally, brethren, let us constantly keep in mind the appeal of the Larger Orphanage and remember as we save the child we not only save the State, but we save ourselves, and in doing this we find our greatest happiness.

J. T. HOLT.

Upon motion to adopt the report it was then opened for discussion. After being discussed by Brethren J. T. Holt and F. B. Hamrick the report was adopted.

After several announcements the body adjourned by prayer by A. C. Hamby.

THURSDAY MORNING.

Second day's session of the body was opened by devotional service led by Rev. W. H. Wall.

Body was called to order by the Moderator. Minutes of Wednesday's sessions were read and approved. Tellers were asked to enroll the delegates who had come in since Wednesday's sessions.

Moderator appointed the following committee to nominate the Executive Board: J. E. Lanier, A. C. Hamby and W. H. Wall.

Committee on Place for the next Association, Claud Stephenson, N. D. Wells and J. T. Holt were appointed.

On petitionary letters Dr. C. A. Jenkins, A. A. Pippin, and W. H. Wall were appointed as committee.

Body was led in prayer by Dr. C. A. Jenkins.

Report of Executive Committee was read by J. M. Beaty.

REPORT OF EXECUTIVE COMMITTEE.

Preaching has been kept up during the year regularly at all the churches and mission points, either by pastors or by supplies. We have found it difficult to get and hold regular pastors for all the places.

Bro. W. L. Bilbro has served the Bailey Church. Noble's Chapel, Kenly, Micro, Carter's Chapel and Princeton were served by Rev. J. M. Gibbs. Pinkney, Hood's Grove and Canaan have had as pastor Rev. T. J. Hood. Pauline, Beaty Chapel, Pisgah, Pleasant Grove, Pine Level and Sardis have had as pastor Rev. W. H. Wall. Rev. J. M. Duncan has served Parrish Memorial, Four Oaks and Benson Grove. Rev. J. U. Teague is preaching at Thanksgiving and Middlesex, and Rev. J. E. Lanier at Hephzibah and Burnell.

On account of conditions on our mission fields and the small support offered the missionaries, we find it hard to get and keep preachers to do the work. However, progress is being made and we hope that within a few years these mission churches will become self-supporting. We are doing all we can to get the churches to feel their responsibility and make advancement in their contributions, as well as in other lines of work.

J. M. BEATY,
CLAUDE STEPHENSON,
V. R. TURLEY,

The report on church building was read by Claude Stephenson.

REPORT OF BUILDING COMMITTEE.

Since our last Association we have paid off nearly half the indebtedness incurred in helping to finish Bailey Church, and in building Burnell Church. We secured three hundred dollars from the State Church Extension Fund and have helped to build Sardis Church, where we now have a good house of worship for our Lord.

J. M. BEATY,
CLAUDE STEPHENSON,
V. R. TURLEY.

Upon motion to adopt the report, it was discussed by Brethren J. M. Beaty, W. H. Wall, A. A. Pippin, J. M. Duncan, C. E. Stevens, J. E. Lanier and adopted.

The committee to nominate the Executive Committee nominated Brethren J. M. Beaty, Chairman, Berry Godwin, J. B. Creech, J. J. Lane and J. T. Holt. These brethren were elected.

The chair recognized Rev. C. J. Thompson representative of our Foreign Board and E. L. Middleton, Secretary of our Sunday School Board.

Report on State Missions was read by Rev. A. C. Hamby.

REPORT ON STATE MISSIONS.

For the first 25 years of the Baptist State Convention, Home and State Mission work were identical in name, but when the Home Board was organized work in the state was called State Missions. The Home Mission Board is located in Atlanta, Ga., and its mission is to aid the States that are not able to meet the needs within their own borders. The work of the State Board is confined to the State. Some sections are strong numerically and able to support their work without aid from the Board. Other sections are weak and cannot maintain regular worship without aid from those that are strong.

No other agency has done so much to strengthen our denomination in numbers, in spirit, in enlightenment and in patriotism as State Missions. Half of our churches have been organized by missionaries employed by the State Board, and these churches brought into existence by State Missions are giving to-day two-thirds of all the money contributed to carry on the work of the Kingdom of God, but their contributions are the least part of the result of State Missions. In 84 years about 70,000 people have been baptized by the State Board missionaries.

Recent Results of State Missions.

Lest some one should think the big results of State Mission work belong to the early part of its history, let us sum up the results of the last dozen years. During this time there have been organized on the mission fields 150 churches. The missionaries of the Board report more than 20,000 baptisms. Two hundred and twenty houses have been built during these years, at a cost of more than $250,000. Out of these 150 churches organized, 100 are now self-sustaining.

But, let us sum up the work of last year under the Board. There were 2,137 baptisms and 1,509 scattered Baptists brought into these mission churches by letter. Forty houses were in course of construction and fifteen were completed. The mission churches and stations contributed to the objects of the Convention $14,000, and a total, including contributions to the missionaries' salaries and to buildings of $105,894.00. That is, the mission fields paid back into the work of the kingdom more than twice as much as the State Board put into them.

The Present Situation.

There are twenty counties in the Eastern part of the State with a white population of at least 190,000, and this number is being added to rapidly as rich farming lands are opened up and drained and railroads threading the timbered sections make it accessible. Of this vast number of people, only one out of each 38 is a Baptist, while to take the whole State, one in every six white people is a Baptist. Then, so far as Baptists are concerned, the East is a field white unto harvest. Does it pay to put our money into mission work in this section? The Board is putting our money there largely. Let us look at the results. The Roanoke Association received more State

Mission money last year than any other Association. Result? It gave more per capita than any other Association in the State. More than those that are strong, well evangelized and well developed. Yes, it pays.

There are in North Carolina about 1,500,000 people who are not members of any church, and about 800,000 that are. That is, about 35 per cent. of the people of the State are professing Christians. There are nearly 400,-000 Baptists in the State. These Baptists, if they do their part, have about 700,000 lost people to win. The task is a large one, but our forces are fully equal to it if each one will do his part. The quickest and most direct way to win the world for Christ is first to win our own country for Him. A contribution to State Missions is an indirect contribution of many dollars to every other phase of our work.   COMMITTEE.

Report was discussed by Brethren A. C. Hamby and C. A. Upchurch and was adopted.

Report on Woman's Work was read by Bennet Nooe, Jr.

REPORT ON WOMAN'S WORK.

It has seemed a long time since I met with this band of Christian workers. I sorely missed you last fall, but I heard many times of the good meeting you had at Kenly. I am glad that you saw fit to give me such a splendid helper in my assistant, and I have called on her several times.

I think it is well at our yearly meeting to take a backward glance, to gather a few facts concerning our work since our organization in 1903. To begin with the least important, we have given over $5,000. Often you have felt your society was doing so little from a financial standpoint, but in union there is strength. If your small, weak society is doing its proportionate part of the work faithfully, then it is doing its duty. We now have 28 societies of all grades.

These 28 societies gave last year almost $800 (I mean from March to March as our State Woman's Missionary Union meets). There has been some noble giving. We have 18 Woman's Missionary Societies, 6 Sunbeams, 1 Y. W. A., 2 Junior Y. W. A., and 1 R. A. We have organized several new societies, and reorganized several; one or two old societies have dropped out, I am sorry to say. Our work is encouraging; we have some workers as loyal and faithful as any in the world, but we need others, who for the sake of their Saviour will be faithful in sunshine and storm, in heat and cold. We still have in our Association 23 churches where we have as yet been unable to find a woman to say, "Here am I; use me."

Most of the societies in the Association have held Jubilate meetings. I hope the others will.

More missionary literature is being taken. Information means interest. The Personal Service phase of our work is speaking, and this is often our best work. It is easier to give money than self.

I have written during the year 120 letters and 75 postals, but am sorry to say I have done very little visiting of societies. I certainly would love to visit every society and know every member in each society. Taking it all together, our work is hopeful, but we need to push forward, "doing our best and leaving the rest." The world is not going to be saved by a half-hearted, lazy service. We work so very hard for other things which perish with the using. When will we awake and learn to put the emphasis of our lives on things eternal? What are life's trifling toys, with which we are allowed to play for a while? Let us talk missions, pray missions and work missions every day in the year. When you have finished your work in life, I am sure you would like to have it said, she was faithful to her friends, faithful to her home, faithful to her community; but you had rather, a thousand times rather, have it said, and be true, she was faithful to her Saviour and His cause! Wouldn't you? So let us work and faint not; the reward is sure if only we are faithful.

Upon motion to adopt, the report was discussed by Brethren Bennet Nooe, Jr., N. R. Stell and C. J. Thompson.

Brother J. M. Beaty made a motion to appoint a committee of five to consider what is the best way to use our fifth Sunday. The following Brethren were appointed: C. E. Stevens, J. W. Smith, F. H. Brooks, Claude Stephenson and N. D. Wells.

Adjourned by prayer by J. M. Duncan.

Afternoon session was opened by song service and prayer by J. F. Pool.

The committee to consider our fifth Sunday meeting submitted the following resolution: That each pastor organize and take charge of a union meeting among his own charge and rotate from church to church during the year.

That where the pastor has only one or two churches in this Association he get two or three near-by churches to help form a circuit of four churches, each church having a union once in each year.

We want to intensify our work in these unions and seek to develop more of our people.

After discussion by Brethren C. J. Thompson, C. A. Upchurch, C. E. Stevens and F. H. Brooks the resolution was adopted.

The committee on place and preacher for the next Association, reported Clayton as the next meeting place and John E. Lanier to preach the sermon. The report was adopted.

Rev. C. E. Stevens presented the following resolution:

Resolved, That early in 1915 we hold a Sunday School Institute for the training of our workers, at some central point, and that we ask our Sunday School Secretary to assist in this meeting.

The resolution was adopted.

The report on Sunday Schools was read by Judge F. H. Brooks.

REPORT ON SUNDAY SCHOOLS.

Sunday Schools are such a fixed part of our religious existence and are institutions of such value in carrying on the Master's work in the world that it is not now necessary to quote scripture in support of the movement. God has greatly blessed the Sunday Schools of our State and Association and increased their usefulness in His great plan of redemption of the world.

Enough has been "reported" and "resoluted" about Sunday Schools to make them even greater institutions and more efficient in their every detail, had the reports and resolutions been put into operation. We have heard the saying that "talk is cheap," but action calls for energy and exertion. As soon as the Association adjourns the delegates return to their respective homes and the matter is forgotten until the meeting of the next Association. We are living in too fast an age; we are too much taken up with the every-day affairs of life to give much attention to God's business.

The policy recommended by the Committee on Sunday Schools at the last meeting of the Association is commended to the Association as a comprehensive program for the Sunday Schools of the Johnston County Baptist

Association; not for "next year," as the report puts it, but for all the years to come, until accomplished in full.

The report of this Association to the last State Convention showed that we had 42 churches with 3,967 members and 40 churches with Sunday Schools with 3,889 scholars enrolled, a gain of 489 in enrollment over the preceding year.

In the State we have 245,000 Baptists in round numbers. There are only 85,000 church members in the Sunday Schools. We have 190,000 Sunday School scholars in round numbers, with only 85,000 members of the churches. We shall not be able to give exact figures for the Johnston County Association, but should say the per centage is near the same.

A great work lies before us. First we should make a strenuous effort to get the 160,000 church members interested in the Sunday School work and enrolled under its banner. Second, we should make a still greater effort to lead the 105,000 non-Christian Sunday School scholars to Christ and into membership of the church.

Your committee recommends: (1) That the pastors of this Association bring before their respective congregations the work of the Sunday Schools as an indispensable part of the church's educational system, and not a separate institution from the church; (2) that the pastors lay before their respective Sunday Schools their privilege and duty of not only teaching the Scriptures, but to become effective institutions for winning souls for God, and developing young converts into workers for His cause.

F. H. BROOKS, for the Committee.

The report was discussed by Judge F. H. Brooks and E. L. Middleton, and adopted.

Foreign Missions report was read by J. E. Lanier.

REPORT ON FOREIGN MISSIONS.

The Foreign Mission Board is located at Richmond, Va., and is composed of nineteen local members and eighteen members at large, representing each State in co-operation with the Southern Baptist Convention. The Board conducts work in Italy, Brazil, Mexico, Argentina, Japan, China and Africa. In these countries we have 380 churches with 833 outstations, 30,000 church members and 542 Sunday Schools with 22,000 scholars enrolled. We have also 9,376 students in mission schools, 420 of whom are in the theological seminaries and training schools seeking specific preparation for Christian work.

The present force of workers embraces just 300, of which number 20 are under appointment, but have not yet sailed for their respective fields of labor. In addition to these home-sent missionaries we have on the combined fields 635 native workers.

The work prospers on nearly all the fields; 5,252 converts were baptized last year, the largest number ever reported for a single year. Conditions at this hour give promise of still more abundant fruits, if we take advantage of the opportunities opening to us everywhere.

But our successes and our opportunities have laid responsibilities upon us and make insistent demands of us which we cannot ignore without turning much of our success into failure, and throwing away our God-given opportunity for still larger achievements. Multitudes have been made ready for the Word of Life; thousands are awaiting training in the Christian life and for Christian service; our schools are overflowing; a score of consecrated young men and women are offering themselves to the Board for the needed work; and untouched fields invite us to harvest. Need and opportunity never combined in such a challenge to Southern Baptists. Nothing less than immediate and immense enlargement can answer this challenge, and set us in a place of great honor, usefulness and advantage for our Gospel.

Shall we prove ourselves worthy of so signal a favor as God is ready to bestow upon us? We are sufficient in numbers, capable in talents and leadership and able in material resources. We can meet the challenge of a great opportunity if we will.

Gifts to the work advanced $44,000 last year over the previous year. But one-half of our people had no part in this advance, and consequently had no part in the blessed results accomplished, and will have no part in the glorious rewards to be bestowed.

Our task for the present year includes: (1) The completion of the Judson Fund; (2) the enlistment of more than one-half of our church members who have not yet given anything for foreign missions; (3) the development of present givers into larger giving; (4) the inauguration in each church of a plan of systematic monthly giving and remitting for this cause, so that the work may be taken care of and debt and interest payments may be avoided. We commend these four objects to the thoughtful consideration of our pastors and churches.

In order to increase intelligence concerning this great work of the denomination, and to enable all our people to work together harmoniously toward the same end, we recommend and urge that the "Foreign Mission Journal" be taken and read by every Baptist family within our bounds; and to secure so desirable an end, we suggest that each pastor in the Association appoint a committee in each church of which he is pastor, to canvass the membership with this object in view. All our people ought to be well informed about a work so great as this of giving the gospel to the lost nations, and the Journal is the publication which the denomination uses to give this information.

J. E. LANIER, for Committee.

After discussion by J. E. Lanier and C. J. Thompson the report was adopted.

REPORT ON PETITIONARY CHURCH LETTERS.

We, your Committee on Petitionary Church Letters, recommend that Canaan Church be received as a member of this body, and that the delegation be allowed all its privileges.

The church was received and Delegate Mrs. J. T. Hudson was extended right hand of welcome by Moderator.

Committee on Constitutional Amendments offered the following amendments:

1. Strike out the word "county" in Article I.
2. In Article X, insert after word "ballot," "or in case when only one brother is put in nomination for an office, then the vote may be by acclamation."
3. In Article XII, for the 4th the 2nd, and for "majority" the word "ten."
4. Retain only last sentence of Article XIV.
5. In By-Laws strike out Article VII.

A motion was made to defer these Amendments until some time Friday.

Body adjourned by prayer by A. A. Pippin.

THURSDAY NIGHT.

At 7:30 the session was opened by a song service. This service was given to a discussion of the state of the churches by several of the delegates. The address of the evening was delivered by C. A. Upchurch. Body adjourned with prayer.

FRIDAY MORNING.

The morning session was opened with song service and devotional exercises. The body was led in prayer by J. T. Holt.

Bro. A. A. Pippin read the report on Ministerial Relief.

REPORT ON MINISTERIAL RELIEF.

The Baptist Ministers' Relief Board was established about 24 years ago. It has done a great deal in helping the old men who gave their lives in the spread of the Gospel. The shadows of death are gathering around most of them, when they apply to the Board for help, and they don't live to enjoy but very little of the amount we give them. We can't always give them what they ask for, because our churches give so little to this object. If we meet the demands upon the Board there must be a larger contribution or the Board must fail to make them comfortable. It should be the earnest desire of every Baptist that not one of these worthy ministers of God's truth suffer for needs of life.

Let each church in this Association take a Christmas offering at their regular services nearest Christmas. "Inasmuch as ye have done it to one of the least of these, my brethren, ye have done it unto me.".

A. A. PIPPIN.

After discussion of the report by Bro. A. A. Pippin it was adopted.

The report on Home Missions was read by Bro. W. H. Wall.

REPORT ON HOME MISSIONS.

That all Christians believe in missions is getting to be more universally understood as we study and better understand God's teaching. Christ was the first great missionary and His programme covers every phase of the work; "Go ye into all the world and preach the Gospel to every creature (Mark 16:15), beginning at Jerusalem (Luke 24:47), and lo, I am with you alway, even unto the end of the age." This mission scheme as outlined by our Saviour took in the entire world, and we should not lose sight of the fact that that includes lost mankind in home lands as well as in foreign fields, or merely in our State.

Peter and John healed the lame man at the temple gates. The lame man of to-day sits at the very gates of our churches. The Jerusalem church was not successful in presenting the Gospel to its own community. Then having power to save those around it, it had the right spirit and that (as before stated), necessarily sends forth streams of saving truth to the dark places beyond, and incidentally to the uttermost parts of the earth.

Our Jerusalem and Judea and Samaria are in the United States. Are we doing our part to take and keep our country for Christ?

Out of 100,000,000 population in the United States, there are only about 22,000,000 members of evangelical denominations. Again, are we not too much neglecting our Jerusalem, Judea and Samaria?

Under our present immigration laws more than a million people flock to our shores yearly, and perhaps two millions of our own people are uprooted from their environments and come together in new towns or communities. In these people-movements it is at once a great problem and an unvoiced cry that ascends up before God for a Gospel that will bring order out of chaos and replace sin with good citizenship and brotherly love. And many of the Christian denominations of America are awakening to the magnitude of these problems. They are turning with an encouraging unanimity to Home Missions as the means whereby such problems must be solved.

We as Southern Baptists must take a large part in saving the lost of America. We hold the gospel in its purity. Since we are able to give to make good Americans, to make Christians, we are under deeper obligations to do large things. Because as a Baptist people we are more numerous than any Christian body in the South, our obligations towards lost humanity are correspondingly greater. We are on the grounds and know the situation, and hence, how can we escape the condemnation if we use not the talents He has entrusted to our care?

Our hearts are made to rejoice as we learn that God has blessed the labors of the missionaries of the Home Board to larger fruitage than that shown by reports of similar boards.

The Board last year reported 30,000 baptisms and 56,000 additions to churches through labors of missionaries supported wholly or in part by it. No mission Board in America, so far as we know, has had results more than one-third as large, though several expended four times as much money in the work.

A notable fact, our people are becoming aroused to the importance of Home Missions, as evidenced by the increase in the receipts from year to year by the Home Board.

This year the Southern Baptist Convention is asking that 436,000 be raised for the work of the Home Board. As Southern Baptists we ought to raise every cent of it and more. We are able. Why not say, by the blessing and help of God, "We will raise it."

Your committtee would recommend:

1. That all pastors be requested to devote some service each year to the Home Mission subject, and the importance of the problems involved, that our people may see more clearly the need of Home Missions and that it is of as much importance, indeed, as State and Foreign Missions.

2. That, so far as possible, every church increase its pledge to this object at least in proportion to the demands of the Board.

3. That the pastors see that clubs of Home Field be raised in every church in the Association, for we need to be informed upon this subject, and until we are informed we can hardly hope for increased gifts.

4. That our pastors and members alike make use of and distribute the Home Board tracts and literature, which is gladly sent free—a better knowledge of our own denominational work being our greatest need to-day.

Respectfully submitted,

W. H. WALL, Committee.

A motion was made to adopt the report and after being discussed by Brethren W. H. Wall and Dr. C. A. Jenkins it was adopted.

The chair appointed the following Brethren: J. T. Pool, J. T. Holt and J. R. Hocutt as a committee to nominate delegates to Baptist State Convention and Southern Baptist Convention, and to name our member of the State Board of Missions.

The next question that was taken up was the proposed Amendments to the Constitution of the Association.

The first proposed amendment was not adopted.

The second proposed amendment was adopted.

The amendment to change the time of meeting was not adopted.

Amendment to insert the word ten for the word majority in article twelve was adopted.

The amendment to strike out section fourteen with the exception of last sentence, was adopted.

The amendment to strike out section seven of By-Laws was adopted.

The report on education was read by Bro. C. E. Stevens.

REPORT ON EDUCATION, MINISTERIAL AND GENERAL.

Baptists have always insisted that religious education must not be neglected, and the day has come when the Baptists of our State have both secondary schools and colleges sufficient to accommodate all who desire to take advantage of them. We feel that the Baptists of North Carolina should patronize our denominational institutions, whose faculties are composed of men and women of the highest Christian character. The moral influence over those entrusted to their care is so wonderful that seldom a student attends one of these schools without becoming a Christian.

We realize more and more that we should not only feel proud of our three great colleges, Wake Forest, Meredith and Chowan; but give praise for our thirteen secondary schools, which are doing a great work in preparing our boys and girls for college.

Oxford College, Buie's Creek Academy, Salemburg and two or three other Baptist schools are owned and controlled by private Baptists, and are doing a wonderful work.

All the institutions mentioned above are worthy of our support and we must rally to their needs. The one phase of Christian education that we now wish to emphasize is ministerial education. Only a few years back we were, with other States and other denominations, praying to the Lord of the harvest to send more laborers into the harvest. Our prayers were abundantly heard, and to-day we have eighty-eight young ministers at Wake Forest, seventy of whom are asking for aid. Dr. Cullom states that it begins to look now as if the Board may be forced to deny others who may come asking assistance. The cry that comes to-day is for means to prepare these laborers for the harvest field. Not that we must stop praying for more laborers, but that the burden of our prayers now be for more money.

In considering the great need of means at Wake Forest we must not forget our obligation in interest of our boys at the Seminary at Louisville. At the opening this fall there were twenty-seven young men from North Carolina present to matriculate, and doubtless many others have entered ere now.

The cause and will of Christ demands that young preachers shall be educated. Therefore, ministerial education is a duty, and that rests not only upon the preachers, but upon every individual Christian.

Whatever pertains to the work of propagating gospel truth and bringing the world to Christ, is of vital concern and binding obligation to every church and child of God.

Respectfully submitted,

C. E. STEVENS.

Upon motion, the report was discussed by Brethren C. E. Stevens and W. H. Wall. Report was adopted.

Bro. J. T. Pool made the following report for his committee.

Delegates to State Convention, C. M. Thomas, W. H. Wall and J. J. Lane.

Delegate to the Southern Baptist Convention Rev. A. C. Hamby.

Member of State Board of Missions, Rev. John E. Lanier.

This report was adopted without discussion.

Report on Temperance was read by J. E. Lanier.

REPORT ON TEMPERANCE.

The Scripture teaches us that wine is a mocker and strong drink is raging, and whosoever is deceived thereby is not wise. This we know to be true. Many men have destroyed their usefulness and ruined their character by forming the habit of indulging in strong drink. So then, seeing the harm that it has done and is doing at present, we urge that all Christian people use their influence against it and do all in their power to see that our prohibition laws are enforced. We thank God for what has been accomplished and go forward to accomplish greater things along this line of reform.

Respectfully submitted,

N. H. GIBBS, for the Committee.

After discussion by J. E. Lanier the report was adopted.

MISCELLANEOUS MATTERS.

The following resolution was offered by Bro. W. H. Wall and unanimously adopted:

Be it Resolved, That it is the sense of this Association that we have been most hospitably and graciously entertained during our stay with the people of New Bethel and that we extend a most hearty vote of thanks to this church and to all others who have contributed to our comfort and happiness for their courtesies and kindness.

Bro. J. J. Lane offered the following resolution:

Resolved, That all moneys contributed to the Convention objects be sent direct to our Convention Treasurer.

A motion was made to discuss this resolution at the two o'clock hour on Thursday at the next meeting of the Association.

Finance Committee submitted the following report:

REPORT OF FINANCE COMMITTEE.

The following amounts were received by the Finance Committee and turned over to the Treasurer:

Minute Fund	$ 19.05
State Missions	182.49
Home Missions	27.31
Foreign Missions	38.04
Sunday School Missions	11.26
Orphanage	91.90
Ministerial Education	32.00
Ministers' Relief	37.30
Building Fund	88.00
Total	$527.35

The Treasurer made the following report:

TREASURER'S REPORT.

	Minute Fund.	State Missions.	Home Missions.	Foreign Missions.	Sunday School Missions.	Orphanage.	Ministerial Education.	Ministerial Relief.	Building Fund.	Wake Forest Church.
Nov. 15, 1913, Bal in Treasury	$60.54	$.....	$.....	$.....	$.....	$.....	$.....	$.....	$15.83	$ .....
Bethesda	.....	10.51	4.33	.....	.....	.....	.....	.....	.....	......
Corinth	1.50	10.00	2.50	2.50	1.00	5.00	2.50	2.50	5.00	......
Micro	.65	8.50	2.50	2.50	1.00	.....	1.00	1.15	5.00	......
Pinkney	.75	3.00	1.00	1.00	1.00	2.00	1.00	1.00	1.00	......
Antioch	1.00	20.00	5.00	.93	2.50	5.00	2.50	2.50	7.50	5.00
Beaty Chapel.......	1.00	4.10	2.50	2.50	1.90	1.55	2.50	1.50	5.00	2.40
White Oak	2.00	25.00	4.53	4.25	2.50	6.26	5.00	5.00	.....	......
Live Oak	.60	3.00	2.00	1.50	.....	4.00	.50	1.00	.....	......
Micro W. M. S....	.....	.....	3.00	4.00	.....	.....	.....	.....	.....	......
Hepzibah	.50	.....	1.00	1.00	.50	1.00	1.00	1.00	1.50	......
Parrish Memorial...	.....	.....	1.28	.....	.....	.....	.....	.....	.....	5.00
Union Meet.—Shiloh	.....	.....	.....	8.54	.....	.....	.....	.....	.....	......
Pisgah	.....	.....	.....	1.10	.....	.....	.....	.....	.....	3.00
Calvary	.....	.....	.....	.....	.....	1.85	.....	.....	.....	5.00
Princeton	.....	.....	.....	.....	.....	.....	.....	.....	1.00	12.00
Shiloh	.....	.....	.....	.....	.....	.....	.....	.....	.....	7.80
Sardis	.....	.....	.....	.....	.....	.....	.....	.....	.....	7.50
Blackman's Grove..	.....	.....	.....	.....	.....	.....	.....	.....	.....	12.00
New Bethel	.....	.....	.....	.....	.....	.....	.....	.....	.....	......
Totals	68.54	84.11	29.64	29.82	10.40	26.66	16.00	15.65	41.83	59.70
Pd. Walters Durham	.....	84.11	29.64	29.82	10.40	.....	16.00	15.65	.....	......
Paid S. H. Averitt	.....	.....	.....	.....	.....	26.66	.....	.....	.....	......
Paid W. N. Johnson	.....	.....	.....	.....	.....	.....	.....	.....	.....	59.7
Pd. printing minutes	35.00	.....	.....	.....	.....	.....	.....	.....	.....	......
Pd. Clerk and post.	24.65	.....	.....	.....	.....	.....	.....	.....	.....	......
Balance on hand...	8.89	.....	.....	.....	.....	.....	.....	.....	41.83	.....

Respectfully submitted,
T. J. LASSITER, Treasurer.

Smithfield, N. C., October 27, 1914.
Audited Nov. 12th, 1914.
W. M. IVES, Auditor.

17

SUPPLEMENTARY REPORT.

Since my report dated October 27, 1914, I have received and paid out the funds as indicated below:

	M inute Fund.	State M ss ons.	Home M ss ons.	Fore gn M ss ons.	Sunday School M ss ons.	Orphanage.	M n ster al Educat on.	M n ster al Relief.	Building Fund.
alance on hand	$ 8.89	$....	$....	$....	$....	$....	$....	$....	$41.83
liver's Grove	.25		1.55						....
ine Level	1.50	10.00	4.00	5.00	1.00	5.00	2.50	2.50	5.00
arter's Chapel	.70	12.00	2.50	2.38	1.00	3.20	2.50	2.50	2.50
ee's Chapel	2.00	25.00	5.00	10.00	2.50	3.00	3.50	3.00	....
anaan	.25	.25							
alvary	.50	2.00			1.00	2.50	1.50	1.00	2.25
ood's Grove	.50	6.00	1.50	1.50	.50	1.00	1.00	1.00	2.00
obles' Chapel	1.00		1.50	1.50			1.50		5.00
ilson's Mills	1.00								5.00
ntioch	.50								
ardis	1.00	11.50	2.50	2.50	1.00		2.50	1.00	3.51
layton	2.50								
inance Committee	19.05	182.49	27.31	38.04	11.26	91.90	32.00	37.30	88.00
Total	39.64	249.24	45.86	60.92	18.26	106.60	47.00	48.30	157.59
ov. 12, 1914, check to Walters Durham		249.24	45.86	60.92	18.26		47.00	48.30	....
ov. 12, 1914, check to S. H. Averitt						106.60			....
heck to First National Bank of Smithfield for borrowed Money									150.00
alance on hand	39.64								7.59

Respectfully submitted,
T. J. LASSITER, Treasurer.

Smithfield, N. C., November 12, 1914.

Audited November 12th, 1914.

W. M. IVES, Auditor.

On motion, the Clerk was instructed to have the usual number of Minutes printed and distributed and that he be allowed twenty dollars ($20.00) for his services.

After song, "Let us Crown Him Lord of All," Bro. A. A. Pippin lead in prayer and the Association adjourned to meet with Clayton Baptist Church for its next session.

CONSTITUTION.

1. The Association shall be known as the Johnston County Baptist Association.

2. Its object shall be to extend the privileges of the Gospel and liberal culture to all the people within its bounds, and by hearty co-operation with the Baptist State Convention to help offer these privileges to all mankind in and out of its bounds, by the cordial co-operation of all the churches constituting this body.

3. It shall be composed of the pastors in active service in the Association and such delegates as shall be annually elected by the churches connected with it, each church being entitled to three delegates, unless the membership shall exceed fifty, and then an additional delegate for every twenty-five members, provided no church shall have more than eight delegates.

4. The New Hampshire Declaration of Faith shall be the summary of Divine Truth for determining questions of faith and order in this body, and the churches desiring' membership in it must commit themselves to the substance of it, together with the covenant therewith submitted, and this Constitution.

5. This Association shall not have power to annul the discipline or exercise authority over any church connected with it, but it may advise with and sever its connection with any church that neglects to preserve gospel order, or that treats with contempt the objects or advice of the Association.

6. Each church shall send to the annual meetings of the Association a letter (the blanks to be furnished by the Clerk of the Association), carefully filled as per blank suggestions, stating the full work of the church for the year ending with the close of the month previous to the one in which the Association is held.

7. The Association shall foster State Missions, Home Missions, Foreign Missions, Christian Education, the Aged Ministers' Relief Board, the Thomasville Orphanage and the Sunday School Board, and each church shall be requested to contribute to the support of these objects annually.

8. Missions and education shall have precedence in their claims upon the consideration of this body in its regular sessions.

9. Whenever a church shall fail to be represented by delegates or letter at the annual sessions of the Association inquiry shall be made for the cause and efforts shall be made to induce such church to do its duty, and the effort shall be continued till the church is recovered or dropped from the roll.

10. The officers of the Association shall be a Moderator, a Vice-Moderator, a Clerk, a Treasurer and an Auditor elected annually by ballot (or in case when only one brother is put in nomination for an office, then the vote may be by acclamation) from among its members, to serve until their successors shall have been elected, and to perform the duties usual to such officers, namely, the Moderator, in presiding over the meetings, or the Vice-Moderator in his absence; the Clerk in recording and preserving minutes and other papers belonging to the body; the Treasurer in receiving and disbursing funds belonging to or entrusted to the body according to its will; the Auditor to examine the Treasurer's books at each meeting of the Association and report the same before adjournment.

11. The Association shall appoint annually an Executive Committee of five (5) from its members, who shall be entrusted with the prosecution of Missions in the Association and any other work for the interest of the Master's Kingdom which may be referred to them. This committee shall, as far as possible, co-operate with the State Mission Board in supplying the destitution in our territory, and between the meetings of the Association take such actions as may seem to them advisable for the advancement of its interest. The committee shall present to the Association at its annual meet-

ing a report of its proceedings, with the names of the missionaries supported on the field, time of service and details of their work, together with such recommendations as in the judgment of the committee the Association should follow in planning its subsequent work.

12.   The annual sessions of the Association shall begin on Wednesday after the fourth Lord's day in October at such place as may be chosen, and an introductory sermon shall be delivered on the first day of the session. Representatives from ten of the churches constituting the Association shall be a quorum.

13.   This Constitution may be amended at any annual session by a two-thirds vote of all the members present.

14.   The proceedings of the Woman's Central Committee shall be recorded as a part of the Minutes of the Association.

BY-LAWS.

1.   The daily sessions of the Association shall be opened and closed with prayer.

2.   Delegates shall be recognized by letters from their churches designating them as such.

3.   The Moderator shall recognize corresponding messengers or the delegates of newly received churches by extending to them his right hand.

4.   The report of the Executive Board and the Missionary work of the Association shall take precedence of all other business during the morning session of the second day of the annual session.

5.   The Clerk shall record and read the proceedings when called for, superintend the publication and distribution of the Minutes, preserve a file of them, and have it present at each annual session, and deliver to his successor all papers belonging to the body.

6.   Members desiring to speak shall first rise and address the Moderator, shall use the term "Brother" in speaking to each other; shall not speak on the same subject more than twice without permission, and shall observe the courtesy that becomes Christians.

7.   The roll of members shall be called at least once and absentees marked.

8.   Corresponding messengers and visiting brethren shall be invited to seats, with privilege of speaking, but not voting.

9.   A copy of the Minutes shall be sent to the Secretary of the State Mission Board, the Secretary of the Southern Baptist Convention, the American Baptist Publication Society, 1420 Chestnut Street, Philadelphia; the Sunday School Board of the Southern Baptist Convention, and the Thomasville Orphanage.

10.   All questions of order not herein provided shall be decided by Kerfoot's Parliamentary Law.

WOMAN'S MISSIONARY UNION.

The large auditorium of Mount Moriah church was well filled with women on the fourteenth day of October, nineteen hundred and fourteen. We do not wonder that these people are proud of their church, as Mrs. Jenkins in her words of welcome that morning said, "Our church is new and a fitting monument to our community." May it be in truth a "temple provided by the Lord," and as a lighthouse set on an hill, whose light cannot be hid! A genuine hand clasp at the door, a smile, a word of greeting and we felt at home at once. And on entering the auditorium beautiful flowers, tastily arranged, met our sight, and in everything there was welcome to the visitor. Mrs. Jenkins concluded her speech of welcome with these words from Dickens "God bless us every one," and so we say, God bless them every one. In words most appropriate Rev. Mr. Jenkins opened the day's session, and then the Vice-President took the chair.

Mrs. Uzzle responded to the words of welcome, in behalf of the Societies.

After a prayer by Miss Briggs, Mrs. Carter gave her report—a part of which we give below. The committee on time and place was next appointed: Mrs. Jenkins, Mrs. Beaty and Mrs. Gower. Also the committee on nomination, Mrs. Saunders and Mrs. Hocutt.

Mrs. Wesley N. Jones, whom we are always so glad to have with us, offered a special prayer for Miss Heck, our beloved President, who lay almost at the point of death in a Richmond hospital. The Union authorized the Secretary to send a night letter to her, which was done that night.

Mrs. B. A. Hocutt made an excellent report on Foreign Missions.

In her report on State Missions Miss Annie Myatt said: "One great need of the Board and of the one hundred and fifty missionaries in their struggle, is the prayers of every Christian. The responsibility is upon us. May God help us to meet it.

Mrs. Wesley Jones in her talk on our obligation and opportunity for service, said "Every door to every foreign land is open. The emergency is greater than ever before. Some time ago it was felt that it was time to go and take Japan for Christ. They were ready, but we were not, so educated Japanese to-day are Atheists, and harder to teach than ever before. The Chinese are clamoring that their girls be sent to foreign schools. If we give them our education without religion, they are worse off than ever before. There is absolute demand that we equip our foreign fields. If we put it off, it is going to be too late. Mary sat at the Master's feet and anointed Him for His burial; she knew that he was going away; she discerned as did not the disciples; she saw and used her opportunity. Shall we not thank God, and seize this great opportunity before it is too late."

After the singing of "Am I a Soldier of the Cross," there was an open Conference in which were discussed many subjects dear to the heart of the true mission woman. Such women as Mrs. Hamby, Mrs. Thurston, Mrs. Hocutt and Mrs. Beaty gave us some of their sincerest thoughts. Mrs.

Nath Pool and Mrs. W. A. Barnes thought that we needed to give more time to the Bible in our meetings.

So short a morning, but dinner was ready, and we spent an hour "refreshing the inner man," and having a social chat.

The children, under Mrs. Daughtery, opened the afternoon session with songs and then remained for a while, until Miss Briggs should talk to them.

After a fervent prayer by Mrs. Weathers, of the Tabernacle, Raleigh, Miss Lanneau of China, took the floor. How our hearts were thrilled as we listened to her, one who in truth is living a life of sacrifice for her Master!

Mrs. Bunn, our new State leader, next spoke in behalf of Young Women's work.

Mrs. Lanier read a comprehensive paper on "Woman's part in missions."

Miss Briggs was then ready to talk to the children, and as she always does, interested them greatly.

Mrs. Mack Gulley, one of our best loved members, reported the death on March the fifteenth, nineteen fourteen, of Mrs. Katie Hardesty who "seemed to think of others more than herself, as she came in and out among us—and for that reason we miss her beautiful Christian spirit in every walk of life."

Mrs. Beaty reported to have sent out two hundred and twenty-nine leaflets and tracts, at times felt a little discouraged that it did not bring forth more fruit, but felt that we should "meet the situation face to face, and with God's help, do our best."

With Mrs. Jones in the chair, Mrs. Carter, our Vice-President, tendered her resignation. She was asked to reconsider for a month. This was left in the hands of the Central Committee, Raleigh. We sincerely hope that Mrs. Carter may decide to continue in this work, as none could do it better than she.

The committee on nomination reported that the same officers be re-elected.

Mrs. Maddry gave helpful suggestions on personal service, one of which was "What of the Negro? Are we responsible for them?"

The committee on time and place reported Benson as the next place of meeting some time during the week following the second Sunday in October, nineteen fifteen.

On "Our Y. W. A." Miss Nellie Pool reported a yearly contribution of five dollars in nineteen hundred and three, and a gradual increase to one hundred dollars for the past year, besides they gave twenty-five dollars to the Judson Centennial fund.

Miss Kelly of the training school said: "Service is the key-note of our work. Service calls for special training. We have heard priests say that they were not afraid of anything but the women who go into the homes, and win the hearts of the people."

We wish that the paper by Mrs. Lane on "Why Give the Gospel to the World?" might be widely read. She said that "Confucianism has been the religion in China for over four thousand years. Think of the opium-dens, the women with bound feet, the natives with bound souls. Think of the child widows in India, where Buddha is worshipped. Toaism is practiced in China, Japan, and other countries. All have failed. Christianity makes men brothers. * * * Is this not a religion which clearly leads to the highest planes? But if there were no other than the fact that Jesus' last command to His disciples to preach the gospel to all nations—that would be a sufficient reason."

Mrs. Thomas resigned as Secretary, Miss Cleve Barnes, of Clayton being elected to that office.

And now before closing, we wish to thank Rev. C. A. Jenkins and the others of the men who so kindly assisted us on this day. We know that it must' have been a little tiresome for them—but we hope that they will in a slight degree feel rewarded, when we say that we just could not have well done without them.

After the singing of "Blest be the Tie," adjournment.

FINANCIAL REPORT OF SOCIETIES.

Smithfield Sunbeams—..$ 15.00
Four Oaks Sunbeams 21.00
Kenly Sunbeams 6.14
Mount Moriah Sunbeams 9.01
Clayton Sunbeams 6.00
    Mount Moriah Royal Ambassadors, just organized.

Report of Woman's Missionary Societies—
    Wilson's Mills ....$ 3.25
    Mount Moriah 50.30
    Four Oaks 27.55
    Middlesex 20.75
    Shiloh 10.00
    Benson 19.55
    Clayton 201.31
    Clyde's Chapel 15.00
    Smithfield 123.45
    Kenly 32.00
Clayton Y. W. A. 100.00
Junior Y. W. A. (Mount Moriah)....................................   2.3
Junior Y. W. A. (Clayton)...   5.8

MRS. C. M. THOMAS, Secretary.

CHURCH.	PASTOR AND POST OFFICE.	CLERK AND POST OFFICE.	Time of Preaching.	Value of Church Property.	Gains. By Baptism.	Gains. By Letter.	Gains. By Restoration.	Losses. By Letter.	Losses. By Exclusion.	Losses. By Death.	Number of Males.	Number of Females.	Total Membership.
Antioch	A. A. Pippin, Wakefield	W. O. Hocutt, Selma, R. 2	Third	$2,000	25	3	2	7	2	1	73	113	186
Bailey	W. L. Bilbro, Middlesex	R. L. Underwood, Bailey	First	1,500		3		7		1	21	33	54
Baptist Center	W. Yates, Wake Forest	E. H. Rogers, Clayton	First	700	23	2	1	1			44	69	113
Beaty Chapel	W. H. Wall, Four Oaks	E. M. Easom, Smithfield	Third	1,000				1	16	1	8	16	24
Benson	J. M. Duncan, Benson	L. Gilbert, Benson	3rd-4th	15,000	1	1		7	4		51	97	148
Benson's Grove	J. M. Duncan, Benson	D. D. Medlin, Benson	2nd-4th	800	6						7	18	25
Bethany	R. L. Hocutt	Kirkman, Kenly, R.	Fourth	800	4	1		1			36	57	93
Bethel	W. T. Tate, Wake Forest	William Johnson, Kenly, R.	First	400	1	6		7			19	18	37
Bethesda	J. M. Smith, Wilson's Mills	J. E. Smith, Wilson's Mills	Fourth	500	1	1	2	1	1	2	121	139	260
Blackman's Grove	N. H. Gibbs, Benson	J. G. Johnson, Four Oaks	Third	500							18	44	62
Calvary	T. J. Hood, Goldsboro	T. J. Lee, Benson	First	500	2	6		1	1		20	10	30
Canaan		Mrs. J. T. Hudson, Bentonville	Third	500	2		2	1			14	30	44
Carter's Chapel		Martin Thorne, Selma	First	1,000	6			2			31	54	85
Clayton	A. C. Hamby, Clayton	W. P. Creech, Clayton	All time	6,000	34	22	2	19	4	1	172	218	390
Clyde's Chapel	L. A. Bennett, Wake Forest	C. I. Johnson, Knightdale	Third	500	25	5	10	2	1	1	83	103	186
Corinth	J. M. Pippin, Wakefield	W. V. Andrews, Wendell	Second	1,600	16	4	3	1			54	82	136
Four Oaks	J. M. Duncan, Benson	J. W. Langdon, Four Oaks	Fourth	1,000	3	1					27	35	62
Hepzibah	John E. Lanier, Smithfield	P. A. Braswell, Princeton	Third	300	7			2			7	11	18
Hood's Grove	T. J. Hood, Goldsboro	P. T. Richardson, Four Oaks	Third	500	3		3			1	27	29	56
Kenly	A. A. Pippin, Wakefield	W. I. Greer, Zebulon, R. 2	Second	2,000		3		5			25	24	49
Lee's Chapel	R. L. Hocutt, Emit	W. I. Greer, Zebulon, R. 2	Third	1,500	15	11	3	8	1	1	112	148	260
Live Oak		D. H. Jones, Micro	1st-3rd	1,000		4	3	6			11	19	30
Middlesex	J. U. Teague, Wake Forest	J. L. Terrell, Middlesex	2nd-4th	2,000	1	1		8	1		15	15	71
Mount	C. A. Jenkins, Clayton	R. A. Baucom, Raleigh, R. 2	First	3,500	17	4	2	3	2	1	27	44	180
New Bethel	A. A. Pippin, Wakefield	Geo. W. Bryan, Garner	Fourth	1,500	1	2	1	1	4		42	98	97
Nobles Chapel		N. L. Stott, Sims	Fourth	700	5			4			31	55	25
Oliver's Grove	J. M. Duncan, Benson	Miss Lena Tyner, Four Oaks	Third	250						1	9	16	67
Parrish Memorial	J. M. Duncan, Benson	J. D., Selma, R. 3	First	500	8			2	1		23	44	60
Pauline	W. D. Harrington	W. B., Four Oaks	Fourth	800	3	4		2	1		23	37	43
Pine Level	W. H. Wall, Four Oaks	Clyde Godwin, Pine Level	Fourth	2,000			1				15	14	29
Pinkney	T. J. Hood, Goldsboro	Mrs. B. R. Edgerton, Kenly, R.	First	1,000	4	2		3	7		29	48	75
Pisgah	W. H. Wall, Four Oaks	W. I. Pearce, Princeton	First	1,200	4	3		2	1	2	36	39	32
Princeton	C. E. Stevens, Selma	W. I. Pearce, Princeton	Third	1,000		6	1	5	1	1	14	18	184
Sardis	C. E. Stevens, Selma	F. C. Powell, Smithfield	1st-2d-4th	2,000			6	11		2	81	103	91
Selma	W. H. Wall, Four Oaks	B. S. Reynolds, Selma	Second	700	25	18	2	5	1	1	37	54	192
Shiloh	John E. Lanier, Smithfield	F. B. Holland, McCullers, R.	Ev. Sun.	7,000	26	2	1	6	2	1	84	108	64
Smithfield	J. U. Teague, Wake Forest	T. J. Lassiter, Smithfield	Third	1,300	6			2			29	35	191
Wendell	C. A. Jenkins, Clayton	Geo. H. Wright, Wendell	2nd-4th	1,500	42	7		14	7	2	74	117	200
White Oak	C. A. Pippin, Wakefield	G. L. Murphrey, Selma, R. 1	Second		2			14	1	1	86	114	55
Wilson's Mills	R. L. Brown, Wake Forest	J. T. Holt, Wilson's Mills	Second	1,300		1			2		28	28	4175
Total					296	114	34	144	60	35	1752	2423	4175

TABLE II—FINANCIAL—FOR THE YEAR 1913-'14.

CHURCH.	Pastor's Salary.	Building and Repairs.	Incidentals.	Sunday School Expenses.	The Poor.	Minute Fund.	Building Fund.	State Missions.	Home Missions.	Foreign Missions.	Sunday School Missions.	Orphanage.	Ministerial Education.	Ministerial Relief.	Colleges and Schools.	Other Objects.	Total.
Antioch	$104.60	$84.00		$14.75	$1.00	$1.50	$7.50	$20.00	$5.00	$5.00	$2.50	$5.00	$2.50	$2.50			$255.85
Bailey	75.00		9.00	12.00		.75	1.55	13.95	2.50	4.00	1.00	5.00	2.00	2.50			110.75
Baptist Center	100.00			15.97	20.00	1.00	5.00	14.00	4.00	4.00	1.00	4.55	1.50	1.50			145.55
Beaty Chapel	50.00		25.00	40.00		1.00		7.50	2.50	2.50		25.23	5.00	5.00		1.00	123.02
Lenson	500.00	12000.00	25.00		5.00		5.00	75.00	10.00	17.13	2.50		5.00	5.00	27.51		12704.89
Benson's Grove	30.00			10.00	5.00	.80	5.00	10.00	5.00	5.00	1.00	4.00	2.50	2.50		75.00	80.80
Bethany			10.00	20.00		2.00		30.00	5.00	5.00		15.00	2.50	5.00		13.00	371.76
Bethel	200.00	7.00		5.00		.60		20.00	5.00	5.00		5.00	4.00	2.00			119.60
Bethesda	50.00					1.00	2.25	2.00	1.15	1.00		2.50			1.00		63.40
Blackman's Grove	50.00					.25		2.85				.55					5.65
Calvary						.70	.50	15.00	2.00	5.00	1.00	14.00	2.50	2.50		1.00	95.70
Canaan	40.00			10.00		2.50	2.50	275.00	54.45	204.50	18.25	100.00	25.00	25.40		427.00	4071.75
Carter's Chapel	1200.00	1371.50	158.66	205.03	4.46		10.00	20.00	7.50	7.50	18.50	3.75	2.50	3.75		80.86	397.23
Clayton	150.00	65.00	35.00	40.00	4.37		5.00	10.00	5.50	5.50	1.00	5.00	2.50	2.50			230.50
Clyde's Chapel	85.00	75.00	33.00		3.00			20.00	15.11	15.00	2.50	3.05	6.75	4.00		37.50	262.70
Corinth	100.00		7.71	40.54			1.50	2.00	1.00	1.50		3.00	1.00	1.00		6.50	47.50
Four Oaks	25.00		2.00	4.00			2.00	2.50	1.00	1.50	.50		1.00	1.00	5.00	10.00	88.50
Hephzibah	40.00			2.50		.50		20.00			.50	6.25					190.43
Hood's Grove	164.50	12.00	11.81	25.92		.50		12.00	5.00	10.00	2.50	3.00	3.00	3.00		146.60	388.78
Kenly	150.00		5.00	33.68			5.00	25.00	2.00	1.50	1.00	4.00	1.50	1.50			96.60
Lee's Chapel	19.00					1.00		13.00	2.50	2.50		2.50	1.50	1.50			167.18
Live Oak	51.05	65.00	110.60	31.98		.65	5.00	20.75	10.00	166.50	10.00	39.12	5.00	6.60		15.24	330.27
Micro	73.50	54.00	16.00	35.56	2.70	.65		55.00	25.00	7.50	1.00	52.00	5.50	5.00	50.00		657.47
Middlesex	200.00		25.00	41.36			15.00	20.00	20.00	1.50	1.00	18.90	1.50			12.00	379.30
Mount Moriah	250.00	3.00		8.00		1.00	5.00	5.00	1.55	1.55		1.82	1.00				112.12
New Bethel	85.80																1.55
Nobles Chapel			2.00	5.00		.75	3.00	11.50	2.50	2.50	1.00	2.50	2.50	2.50	1.00		133.50
Oliver's Grove	71.00	15.00				.40	5.00	7.00	2.50	5.00	1.00	2.50	1.00	2.50			53.40
Parrish Memorial	25.00	4.00	40.00	25.05		1.50	5.00	10.00	4.00	5.00	1.00	5.00	5.00	2.50			329.20
Pauline	100.00	150.00	1.00	9.86		.75	9.50	3.00	1.00	1.00	1.00	2.00	1.00	2.50			47.61
Pine Level	25.00		14.00	6.40		1.00		17.50	7.50	3.54		3.00	2.50	2.50			176.40
Pinkney	110.00	20.00	16.45	15.00	17.85		3.51	11.50	4.00	3.00	2.00	4.00	1.50	1.00		169.99	169.99
Pisgah	90.00					1.00		11.00	2.00	10.00	1.00	3.00	2.00	1.00			1644.51
Princeton	100.00	1500.00	67.44	147.00		1.50	3.51	24.30	6.00	4.50	1.00	11.00	5.00	1.00			1042.74
Sardis	528.65	2.15	7.00	147.00		1.00	10.50	15.65	8.00	88.80	5.00	5.00	10.50	10.37	1.85	276.60	170.50
Selma	125.00		60.00	96.89	40.00	5.00		160.00	67.52			44.85	10.50	10.00	40.00	16.30	2381.26
Shiloh	800.00	676.23	3.95	17.30		2.00	2.00	2.80	3.00			2.50					157.85
Smithfield																	
Thanksgiving																	
Trinity			93.85	52.05	5.11	2.00	2.50	9.30	34.05	49.20	1.00	18.65	2.40	2.50	2.90	14.94	718.24
Wendell	434.00	2.50	4.50	25.00		2.00		25.00	7.50	7.50	2.50	10.00	5.00	5.00			588.11
White Oak	200.00															36.50	
Wilson's Mills	100.00	150.00	25.00	75.00	5.00	1.50	5.00	20.00	2.50	5.00	2.50	10.00	5.00	2.50	5.00		397.50

Church	Superintendent and Postoffice	Secretary and Postoffice	Number of Schools	Officers and Teachers	Pupils	Total Enrollment	Church Members in S.S.	Months Kept Open	Baptisms from School	School Expenses	Missions	Orphanage	Other Objects	Total Contribution
Antioch	W. H. Malden, Selma, R. 2	W. O. Hocutt, Selma, R. 2	1	11	112	123	90	12	13	$ 8.75	$ 2.00		$ 4.00	$ 14.75
aHey	J. P. Underwood, Bailey	J. W. B. Finch, Bailey	1	4	57	61	11	12	15	9.50	1.50			11.00
Baptist Center	J. C. Hardee, Clayton	Newton Branch, Clayton	1	6	50	149	50	12		12.00				12.00
Beaty Chapel	E. F., Smithfield	Buddie Edwards, Smithfield	1	7	50	57	20	12		15.97				15.97
Benson	J. L. Hall, Benson	L. E. Sams, Benson	1	9	240	249	75	12		40.00	6.83	25.00		71.83
Benson's Grove	No school													
Bethany	W. D. Stancil, Kenly	A. R. Creech, Kenly	1	8	90	98	43	12	5	10.00				10.00
Bethel	No school													
Bethesda	D. C. Smith, Wilson's Mills	J. E. ...th, Wilson's Mills	1	10	125	135	75	12	4	20.00				20.00
Blackman's Grove	F. P. Wood, Four Oaks	Nogah Wood, Four Oaks	1	5	37	42		9		7.00				7.00
Calvary	No school													
Canaan	No school													
Carter's Chapel	J. S. Easom, Selma	B. I. Woodruff, Selma	1	6	44	50	35	12		10.00		5.00		15.00
Clayton's Chapel	D. L. Barbour, Clayton	W. F. Weathers, Clayton	1	14	256	270	135	12	30	205.03	113.57	60.00	193.25	571.79
Clyde's Chapel	D. V. ..., Knightdale	L. A. Bunch, Knightdale	2	12	201	213	18	12	20	40.00		31.00	31.00	71.00
Corinth	Q. B. ..., Zebulon	H. B. Andrews, Wendell	1	7	30	37	40	12	8	40.54	2.01	1.05		43.60
Four Oaks	C. D. Stroup, Four Oaks	W. A. Massengill, Four Oaks	1	7	70	77	16		1	4.00				4.00
Hephzibah	W. G. Creech, Princeton	C. J. Wiggs, Princeton	1	6	40	50		12	7	25.92				62.12
Hood's Grove	Parlis Hudson, Bentensville	J. L. ..., Four Oaks	1	9	61	70	25	12		35.68		6.20	30.00	35.68
Kenly	A. J. Broughton, Kenly	C. E. Sampson, Kenly	1	7	60	67		12	12					
Lee's Chapel	Erastus Creech, Miedlesex	Lester Green, Zebulon, R. 2	1	6	45	51	15	12						
Live Oak	No school													
Micro	L. M. Ausley, Micro	D. H. Jones, Micro	1	6	146	135	20	12	1	25.48	10.00	30.02	6.50	31.98
Middlesex	W. D. Bilbro, Middlesex	W. K. Ballentine	1	13	135	148		12	15	35.56	10.00	22.00	2.24	77.82
Mount Moriah	J. J. Lane, Auburn	Hubert Avery, Clayton	1	7	82	89	15	9	15	41.36				73.36
New Bethel	Geo. W. Bryan, Garner	Hubert Britt, Garner	1	7	54	61	35	9	5	12.40				12.40
Nobles Chapel	D. L. Flowers, Sims	Orren Bullock, Sims	1	7	61	36	27	9		5.00			3.00	8.00
Oliver's Grove	No school													
Parrish Memorial	Jasper Parnell, Selma, R. 3	J. D. Creech, Selma, R. 3	1	6	30		20	12	5	5.00				5.00
Pauline		F. C. Price, Pine Level												
Pine Level	B. L. Strickland, Pine Level	R. M. Lee, Kenly, R. 4	1	10	100	110		12	1	25.00				25.00
Pinkney	R. B. Overman, Kenly, R. 1	A. G. Jones, Smithfield	1	7	50	57	15	12	3	9.86				9.86
Pisgah	R. H. Higgins, Smithfield	W. I. Pearce, Princeton	1	7	54	61	18	9	25	6.40				6.40
Princeton	W. H. Wells, Princeton		1	9	35	44		12	6	15.00				15.00
Sardis	No school													
Selma	R. E. Richardson, Selma	Bartha Deans, Selma	1	12	200	212	75	12	3	87.00	14.50	5.00	65.00	157.00
Shiloh	C. J. Coats, Garner, R. 1	Claude Stephenson, Garner, r1	1	7	53	60	30	12	1					7.00
Smithfield	T. S. Ragsdale, Smithfield	John Ives, Smithfield	1	12	189	201	160	12	25	96.89	114.52	19.00	96.29	325.70
Thanksgiving	J. A. Eason, Selma, R. 1	O. J. Braman, Selma	1	18	104	122	43	12	6	17.30		.66	1.50	19.46
Trinity														
Wendell	Geo. H. Wright, Wendell	J. I. Lynch, Wendell	1	14	240	254	75	12	34	52.05	14.50	13.75	9.88	90.18
White Oak	A. L. Batton, Clayton, R. 2	J. M. Green, Clayton, R. 2	1	11	82	93	60	12	1	25.00				25.00
Wilson's Mills	G. G. Beaty, Wilson's Mills	Miss Tyner, Four Oaks	1	10	86	96	20	12	1	75.00	2.00			77.00
Burnell *	J. S. Johnson, Four Oaks, r.f.d		1	16	40	46	12	12		6.00				6.00
Total			36	304	3295	3599	1138		217	1021.69	276.87	187.68	443.66	1937.70

* Branch of Pisgah.

TABLE IV—WOMAN'S MISSIONARY UNION—FOR THE YEAR 1913-1914

CHURCH AND NAME OF ORGANIZATION.	PRESIDENT AND POST OFFICE.	Number of Members.	State Missions.	Home Missions.	Foreign Missions.	Sunday School Board.	Training School.	Other Objects.	Total Contributions.
Bailey—Woman's Missionary Society	Mrs. C. H. Brantley, Bailey	27	$ 3.91	$ 1.15	$ 1.15	$	$	$	$ 6.21
Benson—Woman's Missionary Society	Mrs. W. G. Parrish, Benson			9.25	10.30				19.55
Clayton—Woman's Missionary Society	Mrs. D. Thurston, Clayton	40	95.11	54.95	83.55		47.40	595.80	876.81
Clayton—Young Woman's Auxiliary	Mrs. B. A. Hocutt, Clayton	36	7.70	4.70	.50		1.00	1.10	15.00
Clayton—Sunbeams	Mrs. D. H. McCullers, Clayton	25	14.35	14.10	14.60		3.00	2.50	48.55
Clyde's Chapel—Woman's Missionary Soc.	Helen Bunch, Knightdale, R. 2	20							
Four Oaks—Woman's Missionary Society	Mrs. W. H. Wall, Four Oaks	18	6.75	5.00	8.00				19.75
Four Oaks—Sunbeams	Barham Creech, Four Oaks	35							
Middlesex—Woman's Missionary Society	Mrs. J. B. Outlaw, Middlesex	19							
Mount Moriah—Woman's Missionary Society	Mrs. N. R. Pool, Clayton	14	55.00	25.00	166.50	10.00			256.50
Mount Moriah—Sunbeams	Mrs. W. B. Daughtry, Clayton	30							
Mount Moriah—Royal Ambassadors	Mrs. J. J. Lane, Auburn	12							
Pine Level—Woman's Missionary Society	Mrs. D. B. Oliver, Pine Level	8							
Pine Level—Sunbeams	Mrs. F. C. Price, Pine Level	12							
Selma—Woman's Missionary Society	Mrs. C. E. Stevens, Selma	8	4.00	3.00	3.00				10.00
Selma—Sunbeams	Miss Rubie Richardson, Selma	25							
Shiloh—Woman's Missionary Society	Miss Annie Myatt, Clayton, Route 1	12	.65	3.00	3.50		1.85	1.00	10.00
Smithfield—Woman's Missionary Society	Mrs. J. E. Lanier, Smithfield	25	59.30	31.10	36.30		10.00	3.75	140.45
Smithfield—Girls Auxiliary	Miss Ola Brady, Smithfield	10							
Smithfield—Sunbeams	Mrs. J. M. Beaty, Smithfield	20							
Wendell—Woman's Missionary Society	Mrs. W. G. Pruitt, Wendell	19	3.40	10.50	44.30		2.90	1.35	62.45
Wendell—Sunbeams	Mrs. W. C. Nowell, Wendell	68							
Wilson's Mills—Woman's Missionary Society	Mrs. G. F. Uzzle, Wilson's Mills	7		1.25					1.25
Total			250.17	163.00	369.70	10.00	68.15	605.50	1466.52

CHURCHES.	State Missions.	Home Missions.	Foreign Missions.	S. S. Missions.	Orphanage.	Ministerial Education.	Ministerial Relief.	Building Fund.	Total.
Antioch	$ 20.00	$ 5.00	$ 5.00	$ 2.50	$ 5.00	$ 2.50	$ 2.50	$ 7.50	$ 50.00
Bailey	10.00	2.50	5.00	1.00	5.00	2.50	2.50	6.50	35.00
Baptist Center	15.00	5.00	5.00	1.00	5.00	2.50	2.50	9.00	45.00
Beaty Chapel	10.00	2.50	2.50	1.00	2.50	2.50	1.50	7.50	30.00
Benson	75.00	10.00	15.00	2.50	23.50	5.00	5.00	15.00	150.00
Benson Grove	7.50	2.50	2.50	1.00	2.50	1.50	1.00	6.00	25.00
Bethany	10.00	5.00	5.00	1.00	5.00	2.50	2.50	6.50	37.50
Bethel	7.50	2.50	2.50	1.00	2.50	2.50	2.00	5.00	25.50
Bethesda	37.50	5.00	7.00	2.50	15.00	5.00	5.00	22.50	100.00
Blackman's Grove	20.00	5.00	5.00	2.00	5.00	4.00	2.00	7.00	50.00
Calvary	10.00	1.50	2.50	1.00	2.50	2.50	1.50	3.50	25.00
Canaan	7.50	2.50	2.50	1.00	2.50	2.50	1.50	5.00	25.00
Carter's Chapel	10.00	2.50	5.00	1.00	5.00	2.50	2.50	10.00	40.00
Clayton	275.00	75.00	75.00	5.00	100.00	25.00	20.00	90.00	665.00
Clyde's Chapel	20.00	5.00	7.50	2.50	3.75	2.00	2.50	12.50	57.55
Corinth	13.00	2.50	2.50	1.00	5.00	2.50	2.50	6.00	35.00
Four Oaks	20.00	5.00	5.00	2.50	5.00	4.00	4.00	13.50	60.00
Hephzibah	5.00	1.00	1.00	.50	1.00	1.00	1.00	2.50	13.50
Hood's Grove	10.00	2.50	2.50	1.00	2.50	2.50	2.50	6.50	30.00
Kenly	15.00	5.00	5.00	2.50	7.50	2.50	2.50	10.00	50.00
Lee's Chapel	35.00	10.00	15.00	3.00	5.00	5.00	5.00	12.00	90.00
Live Oak	7.50	1.00	1.50	.50	7.50	1.00	1.00	5.00	20.00
Micro	12.50	2.50	2.50	1.00	2.50	1.50	1.50	6.00	30.00
Middlesex	16.50	5.00	5.00	1.00	5.00	2.50	2.50	12.50	50.00
Mount Moriah	55.00	25.00	40.00	6.60	30.00	5.50	6.60	25.00	193.70
New Bethel	25.00	7.50	8.00	1.00	17.50	5.50	5.50	20.00	90.00
Nobles Chapel	10.00	2.50	5.00	1.00	5.00	2.50	2.50	11.50	40.00
Oliver's Grove	5.00	1.00	1.00	.50	1.00	.50	1.00	2.50	12.50
Parrish Memorial	15.00	5.00	4.00	1.00	2.50	2.50	2.50	10.00	42.50
Pauline	10.00	2.50	2.50	1.00	2.50	2.50	2.50	6.50	30.00
Pine Level	15.00	5.00	5.00	1.00	5.00	2.50	5.00	10.00	48.50
Pinkney	6.50	2.50	2.50	1.00	2.50	1.50	1.50	2.50	20.00
Pisgah	20.00	5.00	5.00	1.00	4.50	2.50	2.00	10.00	50.00
Princeton	20.00	5.00	5.00	1.00	4.00	2.50	2.50	10.00	50.00
Sardis	16.50	5.00	5.00	1.00	2.50	2.50	2.50	10.00	45.00
Selma	75.00	20.00	30.00	2.50	25.00	10.00	10.00	27.50	200.00
Shiloh	20.00	5.00	5.00	1.00	5.00	2.50	2.50	15.00	56.00
Smithfield	100.00	25.00	40.00	5.00	25.00	10.00	10.00	25.00	300.00
Thanksgiving	11.50	2.50	2.50	1.00	1.00	2.50	2.50	7.50	30.00
Trinity	10.00	2.00	3.00	1.00	3.00	1.00	1.00	5.00	26.00
Wendell	40.00	20.00	25.00	5.00	25.00	5.00	5.00	25.00	150.00
White Oak	25.00	7.50	7.50	2.50	10.00	5.00	5.00	22.50	85.00
Wilson's Mills	20.00	2.50	5.00	1.50	9.50	2.50	2.50	12.50	56.00
Total	1177.60	316.85	387.50	69.10	411.75	156.00	149.50	545.50	3264.25

MINUTES

OF THE

THIRTEENTH ANNUAL SESSION

OF THE

Johnston Co. Baptist Association

HELD WITH

CLAYTON BAPTIST CHURCH

CLAYTON, N. C.

OCTOBER 27, 28 and 29, 1915

The next session will be held with Benson Baptist Church, Benson, N. C., beginning Wednesday after the fourth Sunday in October, 1916

To preach introductory sermon—Rev. D. E. Vipperman.

RALEIGH
THE MUTUAL PUBLISHING COMPANY, PRINTERS
1915

MINUTES

OF THE

THIRTEENTH ANNUAL SESSION

OF THE

Johnston Co. Baptist Association

HELD WITH

CLAYTON BAPTIST CHURCH

CLAYTON, N. C.

OCTOBER 27, 28 and 29, 1915

The next session will be held with Benson Baptist Church, Benson,
N. C., beginning Wednesday after the fourth Sunday
in October, 1916

To preach introductory sermon—Rev. D. E. Vipperman.

RALEIGH
THE MUTUAL PUBLISHING COMPANY, PRINTERS
1915

OFFICERS.

Moderator—R. H. Gower....................Clayton, N. C.
Vice-Moderator—J. J. Lane....................Auburn, N. C.
Clerk and Treasurer—John E. Lanier........Smithfield, N. C.
Auditor—Walter Ives......................Smithfield, N. C

EXECUTIVE COMMITTEE.

J. M. Beaty, Chairman.........................Smithfield
Berry Godwin.................................Pine Level
J. J. Lane.......................................Auburn
J. B. Creech..................................Four Oaks
J. T. Holt..................................Wilson's Mills

DELEGATES AND BOARD MEMBER.

Delegates to Baptist State Convention—C. W. Carter, D. E. Vipperman, and J. L. Hall.
Delegate to Southern Baptist Convention—R. H. Gower.
Member of State Board of Missions—John E. Lanier.

LIST OF MINISTERS.

R. L. Brown...............................Wake Forest
J. H. Buck.....................................Micro
I. L. Bennett.............................Wake Forest
J. M. Duncan...................................Benson
A. C. Hamby...................................Clayton
W. D. harrington.............................Four Oaks
C. A. Jenkens ....Clayton
John E. Lanier...............................Smithfield
A. C. McCall.............................Wake Forest
G. T. Mills..............................Wake Forest
A. A. Pippin ....Wakefield
J. W. Smith.............................Wilson's Mills
R. L. Smith..................................Smithfield
C. E. Stevens...................................Selma
C. H. Stevens...........................Wake Forest
W. D. Stancil.................................Kenly
W. T. Tate..............................Wake Forest
J. U. Teague ....Princeton
D. E. Vipperman...............................Kenly
W. H. Wall...................................Middlesex

PROCEEDINGS

Clayton, N. C., October 27, 1915.

The thirteenth annual session of the Johnston County Baptist Association convened with Clayton Baptist Church. The session was opened at ten-thirty o'clock by devotional service conducted by Rev. A. C. Hamby.

The introductory sermon was preached by Rev. John E. Lanier, of Smithfield, N. C. His subject was, "God's Purpose for His People." Text: Jer. 18:4.

Following the sermon the body was called to order by the Moderator, Brother R. H. Gower of Clayton.

The following committee was announced:

Credentials and Enrolllment—C. I. Godwin and Stephen Averitt.

The following delegates and visitors were enrolled:

Antioch—G. R. Whitley, O. A. Whitley, J. H. Hales.

Bailey—J. W. B. Finch, M. N. Bissett.

Baptist Center—W. J. Talton, J. C. Hardy.

Beaty Chapel—R. L. Smith.

Benson—J. E. Wall, Alonzo Parrish.

Benson Grove. _____

Bethany—Mose Creech, Millard Littleton, David Pace.

Bethel _____

Bethesda—J. J. Wallace, W. E. Godwin, J. W. Smith, Marion Jonhson.

Blackman's Grove—Nagah Wood, Ernest Smith, Lewis Johnson.

Canary_____

Canaan_____

Carter's Chapel—Martin Thorn, J. P. Easom.

Clayton—D. J. Thurston, J. M. Turley, J. D. Smith, L. L. Creech.

Clyde's Chapel—William Martin, C. M. Martin, W. A. Adcock, J. M. Todd.

Corinth—W. A. Mitchell, B. B. Hocutt, J. B. Woodard, J. B. O'Neal.

Four Oaks—R. A. Bain, E. B. Johnson, J. B. Creech.

Hephzibah—W. A. Braswell, J. M. Braswell.

Kenly—D. E. Vipperman.

Hood's Grove_____

Lee's Chapel—J. B. Mecome, J. M. Driver.

Live Oak_____

Micro—N. F. Hawkins A. R. Hatcher, J. W. Rose.

Middlesex—N. B. Lewis, G. J. Johnson, W. H. Wall.

Mount Moriah—J. F. Pool, Icana Pool, J. A. Stallings, W. H. Kelley, C. A. Jenkens.

New Bethel—Hubert Britt, Geo. W. Bryan, Miss Mary B. Bryan, D. T. Bryan.

Noble's Chapel—V. B. Boykin, G. T. Manning, O. Bullock.

Oliver's Grove—J. A. Tyner.

Parrish Memorial—J. D. Creech, Ed. Parrish, J. R. Burgess, Troy Pender, Frank Batten.

Pauline—W. B. Joyner.

Pine Level—Floyd Price, Iredell Crocker, Clyde Godwin.

Pinkney—Henry Gurley.

Pisgah—W. D. Johnson, J. B. Parker, J. W. Jones.

Princeton—W. H. Price, W. I, Pearce.

Sardis—J. W. Strickland, J. B. Gardner, B. E. Gardner.

Selma—C. E. Stevens, R. E. Richardson.

ShilohRansom Penny, Stephen Averitt, Claude Stephenson, J. W. Williams.

Smithfield—J. H. Easom, F. H. Brooks, Geo. L. Jones. J. M. Beaty, J. E. Lanier.

Thanksgiving—D. H. Price.

Trinity_____

Wendell—N. R. Stell, Geo. H. Wright.

White Oak—Elbert Green, V. R. Turly.

Wilson's Mills—J. T. Holt.

*Burnell—J. L. Johnson.

The Moderator recognized the following visiting brethren: Rev. A. A. Pippin from the Central Association, Brother Archibald Johnson of Charity and Children, Rev. J. I. Kendrick, representing Wake Forest Church, Rev. O. L. Stringfield, representing our Southern Baptist Assembly work at Ridgecrest, Dr. Hight C. Moore, Editor of the Biblical Recorder, and Brother John E. Ray, President of State Board of Missions.

The Moderator called the Vice-Moderator, J. J. Lane, to the chair and the following officers were elected:

Moderator—R. H. Gower.

Vice-Moderator—J. J. Lane.

Clerk and Treasurer—John E. Lanier.

Auditor—Walter Ives.

The following were appointed as Finance Committee— D. J. Thurston, Stephen Averitt, J. J. Wallace, and D. J. Yelvington. After several announcements the body adjourned for dinner.

WEDNESDAY AFTERNOON.

The afternoon session was opened by song and prayer by Rev. R. L. Smith.

After miscellaneous suggestions the Report on the Orphanage was read by Judge F. H. Brooks.

REPORT ON ORPHANAGE.

One of the sacred duties of the Christian is to look after God's helpless ones and especially care for the orphan children in our community. There is no Christian who would not gladly minister to the Lord Jesus if he were here upon the earth. In reading the New Testament Scriptures as to the treatment that Christ received at the hands of the Jews we hold up our hands in holy horror. We cannot see how they could have treated the Master in such a way. We say in our own hearts that if we had only been there it would have been our delight to have ministered unto the Savior day and night, and that He should not have wanted for anything that our money could buy, or that our hands could do. And yet we same Christians go on our way day after day and year after year without realizing the blessed privileges that are ours daily to minister to the Master, for we read, "In-as-much as ye have done it unto one of the least of these my brethren, ye who have one it unto me." Matt. 25:40.

Thus the Lord Jesus has put His stamp of approval upon this work and we by ministering unto the orphans can minister to Christ.

Some few of the Baptists of the Johnson County Association give liberally to the Orphanage; some few of the Baptist churches in the Association give liberally to the Orphanage, but a great majority of the Baptists of the Association give very sparingly of their means to the support of the Orphanage work in the State, and I doubt whether any of the churches in the Association give as much as they could if the work was properly presented and kept before the people during the entire year. From the reports given it appears that the work is rather spasmodically presented, and certainly the offerings to this cause are not frequently taken in the various churches. A great many of the churches seem to think that if a collection is taken on Thanksgiving for the Orphanage that that should suffice, and frequently no further offering is made for this cause during the year.

According to the report of June 15, 1915, made by Brother M. L. Kesler to the Board of Trustees of the Orphanage, there was at that time 494 children in the Orphanage, receiving 128 during the fiscal year, and making a total of 1,597 that have been cared for at the Orphanage.

With the new buildings recently completed, especially the Miles Durham building, which is equipped for caring for the children under five years of age, the way is opened up for still a greater work, and greatly increased contributions. Will we not measure up to the requirements? The cry of the orphan has never fallen upon deaf ears when made to North Carolina Baptists in the past, and so long as the influence of John Mills and Noah Biggs lives in the hearts of North Carolina Baptists this call will not be in vain. We must rise to the needs of the time. We cannot afford, under God, to let the work suffer for the lack of a few paltry dollars. Let's stress the importance of the work in our local churches during the ensuing year and raise the necessary funds to enable Brother Kesler and his associates to carry on the good work as the needs of the times demand.

In 1913 the Johnston County Association contributed $538.94 to the Orphanage. In 1914 we fell behind a little, giving only $450.65. Our apportionment for 1915 is $545.50, and I trust that we will not only raise that amount, but more.

Your Committee begs leave to stress the "give a day's work to the Orphanage" plan, and suggests that every pastor endeavor to raise a "company" of Orphanage workers in his respective church, in addition to stressing the importance of the work from the pulpit at stated times during the year.

               Respectfully submitted,

                    F. H. BROOKS, for Committee.

Upon motion to adopt, the report was discussed by Judge F. H. Brooks. Brother Archibald Johnson and Brother Stephen Averitt, and adopted.

REPORT ON THE BAPTIST MINISTERS' RELIEF WORK.

The Baptist Ministers' Relief Board was established twenty-three years ago. During that time it has brought relief to one hundred and three needy beneficiaries—ministers and widows of ministers. There are at present thirty-seven on the Board. This is the largest number ever aided at one time. There are several applications pending, showing that the increase of beneficiaries may be expected to continue. The beneficiaries receive from twenty-five to two hundred dollars per year. Many of them need more. Some of them have no other means of support. That the aid extended may be adequate to the needs of the beneficialies, it is frequently necessary to increase the appropriations.

It is the aim of this Board that no one who has been a worthy proclaimer of God's truth shall suffer for the necessities of life. We desire that every Baptist of the State shall share this ambition with us, and contribute towards its accomplishment. Many of our people already give gladly to this work, but nearly three-fifths of the churches of the State contribute nothing. More than one-fourth of the Associations give nothing for this object. From this it may be seen that the work of enlistment is only just begun.

We do, therefore, urge that each church in this Association make regular contributions to this object, just as to State Missions, Orphanage, etc.

In accord with the recommendation of the Baptist State Convention at its meeting in Wilson, we urge, in the second place, that each pastor present the needs and worthiness of this object to his people, and that a special collection for this work be taken on the Sunday nearest to Christmas on which the church may have services. Let it be clearly understood, however, that the Christmas offering is a special offering, not to be used to pay the church's pledge to this object, but separate and distinct from it. A Christmas check is sent to each beneficiary.

Respectfully submitted,

W.H.WALL, Committee.

A motion to adopt was made and report was discussed by Rev. W. H. Wall. Motion was passed.

Rev. J. I. Kendrick was recognized and given time to present the Wake Forest Church situation. After a strong plea for help from our Association, Brother J. J. Lane made a motion that a committee of three be appointed to raise from our churches funds to the amount of around $200.00 for the church fund. The following committee was appointed: J. J. Lane, Alonzo Parrish and J. E. Lanier.

The following committees were appointed:

Committee on Place and Preacher for the next session— J. F. Pool, Ransom Penny and J. W. Jones.

Home Missions—C. E. Stevens, Geo. W. Bryan, and W. H. Kelley.

WEDNESDAY EVENING.

The evening session was opened by devotional service led by Rev. D. E. Vipperman. The body was called to order by the Moderator and introduced Mayor John T. Talton, who, in a very fitting manner, delivered the address of welcome to the Association. He made us all feel that we were welcome to the good town of Clayton.

The chair recognized the following visiting brethren, C. R. Boone, and C. E. Maddry, of Raleigh, C. W. Pender, Superintendent of the K. W. P. Orphanage.

At this time Rev. O. L. Stringfield presented his work, that of establishing a school at Ridgecrest for our ministers to take a summer course in Bible study, who cannot attend our seminaries.

The Report on Home Missions was read by Rev. C. E. Stevens.

REPORT ON HOME MISSIONS.

Denominational work among Baptists can be conducted only by co-operation.

The Home Mission Board co-operates with State bodies, District Associations and churches in raising their funds and in conducting the work itself.

There are many reasons why we should take more interest in Home Missions today than any other time during its history of the past seventy years. More than 3,500 Baptist churches in the South are without houses in which to worship. Southern Baptists have nearly twice as many houseless congregations as the Methodist, Disciples and Presbyterians combined. Baptist lead the South in numbers and in wealth, and are without excuse for the condition mentioned above. Our people have heard the command, "Feed my sheep", but do not seem to realize that it is just as necessary to fold them. A. H. Gordon in "The Home Mission Task", says, "A church is a company of persons gathered in the Lord's name, and a building keeps that name from being crowded from the mind by the urgency of other things. Education, industry, government embody themselves in the school house, the factory, the public building. A church building is the embodiment of the religious idea and keeps the Christian community alive to its higher callng."

We should rally to the call of these homeless churches, for churches helped today means churches helping tomorrow.

Not much less important are our mountain schools, which are doing much by the way of preparing avenues to the reception of the gospel, and not only that but are preparing and sending to our colleges young men and women who are equipping themselves to fill the most responsible places of life.

I will only mention a few of the many other phases of the Home Mission Board which should have our heartfelt interest renewed, in order that this part of our Master's Kingdom may meet its mission.

Evangelism, the Enlistment Department, Indian Missions, aiding the negro and other work of the Home Board should have our prayers and all the financial aid that we can possibly give.

The Home Mission Board must grow in usefulness or languish in accordance with the support and recognition extended to it by the churches.

The pastors of the churches must assume a large share of the responsibility in awakening the people to the importance of action.

There is no other way whereby we can reach the members of the churches, and if there were other ways the Board prefers to work with and through the pastors. They must make the appeal to the congregation, and arouse in the minds and hearts of the members an interest in missions and develop an incentive to contribute to the cause.

Respectfully submitted,

C. E. STEVENS.

Upon a motion to adopt the report was discussed by Rev. C. E. Maddry and adopted. The body then adjourned until Thursday morning at 9:30 o'clock.

THURSDAY MORNING.

At 9:30 o'clock the session was opened with devotional service led by Rev. R. L. Smith, after which the body was called to order by the Moderator, prayer was offered by Rev. A. A. Pippin.

Roll of delegates as enrolled to the present session was called.

The following resolution was offered by J. E. Lanier:

Resolved, That we defer to our Executive Committee, for the ensuing year, the apportionment of the funds to be raised for the various objects of the Convention. And that we ask the churches to instruct their delegates to state in the next annual session of the Association whether they wish the delegates to pledge for the churches or whether they wish to instruct their delegates as to what they shall pledge to the various objects, or whether we should continue the apportionment plan as followed at present.

The Report of the Executive Committee was read by Brother J. M. Beaty.

REPORT OF THE EXECUTIVE COMMITTEE.

We are glad to report that all the mission churches and mission stations heretofore occupied have had preaching the past year.

Rev. J. E. Lanier has preached at Hephzibah and Burwell Churches. Rev. R. L. Smith at Pinkney, Benson Grove, Pleasant Grove, Hood's Grove and Carson Churches. Rev. W. D. Harington at Carter's Chapel, Blackman's Grove, Olive's Grove, Pauline and Stuart School House. Rev. J. U. Teague at Thanksgiving and Live Oak. Rev. J. M. Duncan at Four Oaks and Parrish Memorial. Rev. W. H. Wall at Bailey, Middlesex and Noble's Chapel and at a school house at Sims, N. C. Rev. C. E. Stevens at Sardis Church. Rev. D. E. Vipperman at Pine Level, Princeton, Kenly and Bethel. At all except a few of these places some progress has been made and some of the mission churches have made fine progress. For the better development of the churches we need more money that we may do more intensive work in State Missions.

Our church at Olive's Grove is badly in need of repairs. At Hephzibah we are worshipping in a small school house and a new church is needed there. We know of two other points where new churches should be built as soon as possible. We have done the work the best we could with the means in hand. We ask the churches to continue their gifts to State Mission work and increase them if possible.

J. M. BEATY,

J. B. CREECH,

J. T. HOLT,

J. J. LANE,

Committee.

Report was adopted without discussion.

The Report on State Missions was read by Rev. D. E. Vipperman.

REPORT ON STATE MISSIONS.

State Mission work is set for the betterment of our Jerusalem; it involves the present and future interest of every home and every individual in the State. And the whole world beyond our borders is vitally affected by our faithfulness or unfaithfulness to ourselves. As a State we do not live to ourselves, nor do we die to ourselves. State Missions is to Home and Foreign Missions what the roots are to a tree. There is no way of lengthening our cords without the strengthening of our stakes.

The Present Imperatives of State Missions.

1. The rapid and wide spread growth mangnifies and intensifies our obligation to train and develop for world conquest.

2. The titanic struggle now going on in Europe and the impoverished condition in men and money of our sister nations will bring about a new era in evangelization of the world and they will have to look to the Christians of America for the bread of life for the next generation.

3. Forty per cent of the State are only nominal Christians. There are lost areas in our State where the gospel as we preach it is never heard.

4. The mill people are not permanent fixtures in church activity, yet they are susceptible to religious influences, and are quick to detect any lack of social recognition. No class needs more the saving, uplifting power of the gospel than this one. Here the Board has an opportunity with adequate gospel privileges to save this class of our citizenship, which, if left alone will effect our civilization disastrously.

5. The backward country churches—Here we need a vision —thus our strength would be multiplied an hundredfold. Through

the agencies of our State Mission Board, including our B. Y. P.
U., W. M. U. and the Enlistment Department a better day is
dawning.

6. Atrue evangelistic note must sound out clear and strong
from every pulpit. I do not think a minister will be rewarded
according to the number he has baptized, but according to the
manner in which he has developed those over whom the Holy
Spirit has made him an overseer.

The Appeal of State Missions.

Natural affection for the citizens of our State puts a weight
of obligation upon us to give the gospel to them. Our obligation to the Pagan world is large beyond question, but our
obligation to our home people is far larger and more pressing.
There are wide sections of North Carolina where Baptists are
almost unknown. It may be said that these sections have been
evangelized by other religious bodies. That consideration does
not lessen our obligation to plant churches there. Our interpretation of the New Testament has been of infinte value to us
and our interpretation will be of equal value to others who may
accept it. We owe it to our brethren of other religious bodies to
give them a whole gospel. as much as we owe it to the lost to give
it to them. The simple truth is that Baptists are the only ones
in the world who hold and teach the religion of the New Testament entirely free from all taint of ritualism which has marred
Christianity through the ages more than all other forces put
together.

Christianity does not nor never can conquer by administration. It conquers by growth alone, because it is life. Any
element in any movement that is to be gotten from North Carolina Baptists will come from the growth of the divine life.
The only way to get anything valuable out of a Baptist is to
promote the divine life in him.

If we want our whole home land saved and the whole Pagan
world saved, then save the whole of North Carolina.

The Needs of Our State Mission Board.

1. A more wisely grouping of our fields enabling pastors to
do more effective work and the Board to more wisely expend
its money.

2. To double its effort in making the great body of our
churches and the rank and file of our membership more efficient so that we can meet successfully the on-coming crisis.

3. Earnest prayer to God continually for His blessings upon
our Board, upon our beloved Secretaries and upon the faithful men who labor in the hard places under the direction of
the Board. Our State missionaries may well be named the

patriots of modern Christianity as the pioneers were of ancient time.

Respectfully submitted,

D. E. VIPPERMAN.

.Upon a motion to adopt the report was then discussed by Brethren D. E. Vipperman, R. L. Smith, C. E. Stevens, W. H. Wall, A. C. Hamby and E. L. Middleton. By vote the report was adopted.

Brother J. M. Beaty made a motion that a collection be taken at that time to aid in building a parsonage on the field now served by Rev. W. H. Wall. The collection amounted to $27.25, which was turned over to Brother Wall.

As Brother Hight C. Moore had to leave on the afternoon train he was given time to speak for the Biblical Recorder before the noon hour.

The body adjourned for dinner.

THURSDAY AFTERNOON.

The session opened at 2 o'clock with song and prayer.

The Committee on the Wake Forest Church Fund offered the following report: That we instruct the leading delegate from each church to take up this matter with his church and raise what funds he can for this object, and, if after the first of December, there be any unraised portion of the $200, which we desire to raise, we ask our Executive Committee to apportion this unraised amount to the churches as they may desire to do. Report was adopted.

The Committee on Place and Preacher for the next session of the Association reported Benson as the place and Rev. D. E. Vipperman to preach the introductory sermon. Report was adopted.

The following resolution was introduced by Brother J. J. Lane at the 1914 annual session of the Association:

Resolved, That all moneys contributed to the Convention objects be sent direct to our Convention Treasurer.

On a motion to adopt the resolution it was discussed by several brethren, after which it was adopted with the following amendment: That all Orphanage funds be sent to the Orphanage treasurer.

Brother J. U. Teague of the Tar River Association was recognized by the chair.

Brethren J. W. Smith, J. M. Turley, Claude Stevens, R. E. Richardson, and R. A. Bain were appointed as a committee to nominate delegates to the Baptist State Convention, delegate to Southern Baptist Convention, Member of State Board of Missions, and name the Executive Committee for the Johnston County Association.

The chair called for the Report on Sunday Schools, which was read by Rev. D. E. Vipperman.

REPORT ON SUNDAY SCHOOLS.

A Sunday School, like a church, has perpetuity without record. A divinity as permanent as the plan of God. Some has said it is no accident that history cannot lay its hands on the organization of the first Baptist Church. This is also true of the Sunday School. Through the evolution of the Hebrew Synagogue, family circle, the organic life, the statistical life, and Sunday School literature, the Sunday School has come to a conspicuous and commanding place, and its influence for good girdles the world. It has won its way to triumph as one of the mightiest institutions in the world, as a propaganda of New Testament principles and in the way of saving the young.

A Sunday School, like a church, is local. A local church is the center of its energies even though it has a wider sweep of activity. Like a church, a Sunday School has Christ as its Head, and the New Testament as its authority. It has exalted the efficiency of the church in its mission among men.

A Sunday School, like a church, has laid its foundation and met its problems, not by discussion and debates, but by wonderful development of spiritual forces and the natural adjustment of spiritual agencies. Like a church, a Sunday School has maintained the Bible as its only text-book. Our Sunday Schools have a unique relation to the life of our churches determining the efficiency of our churches and measuring our faithfulness to the great Commission of our Lord to us.

A Sunday School is the home base of four of the greatest movements before the Kingdom today. There is the social movement; the teacher training movement; the adult Bible class movement, and the interdenominational movement. This interdenominational movement started with no creed at all, but has come to be the most intense creed ever before heard of. There is on more reason for unionizing our Sunday Schools with other religious bodies than for unionizing our church organizations with other religious bodies. As well unionize the preaching function of our churches with other religious bodies as the teaching function of our churches with other religious bodies.

Our ideal in Sunday School work is:

1. Baptist classes in Sunday Schools of Baptist churches, and these classes connected with the Southern Baptist Convention in the organized class movement.

2. The Sunday School enrollment, including the whole mem- bership of the church.

3. A Sunday School Institute in connection with every Union Meeting.

4. Certificates of membership, making more significant mem- bership into the Sunday School.

Respectfully submitted,

D. E. VIPPERMAN,
CLYDE GODWIN,
O. BULLOCK,
Committee.

After being discussed by Brethren D. E. Vipperman and E. L. Middleton the report was adopted.

THURSDAY EVENING.

The evening session was opened at 7:30 o'clock by de- votional service led by Brother J. T. Holt. The body was called to order by Moderator Gower and prayer was of- fered by J. E. Lanier.

The Committee to Nominate Delegate to the Baptist State Convention, delegate to Southern Baptist Conven- tion, member of State Board of Missions, and Executive Committee, made the following nominations: Executive Committee, J. M. Beaty, Chairman, Berry Godwin, J. J. Lane, J. B. Creech, and J. T. Holt.

Delegates to Baptist State Convention, C. W. Carter, D. E. Vipperman, and J. L. Hall.

Delegate to Southern Baptist Convention, R. H. Gower.

Member of State Board of Missions, J. E. Lanier.

The nominations were adopted.

The Report on the Biblical Recorder was read by Q. B. Hocutt.

REPORT ON BIBLICAL RECORDER.

The Biblical Recorder is the organ of the North Carolina Bap- tist State Convention. It is the source through which we get our information concerning the churches and their work, not only that but is the means through which we know their needs. Also a messenger of peace in the midst of their prosperity and makes enter into their joy.

It is not God's Word, but it tells us what God's Word is doing through His servants, information that we all need that it may encourage us in the midst of despondency, enlighten us in the midst of prosperity and make us love the brotherhood, because of the information that we get from week to week.

As literature in the home it takes the place of other papers that are calculated to poison the mind of the child and mislead even people of mature age. It is also the hope of the mother and father as they place the Recorder in the hands of their children that it leads them into the church to which they pelong. It makes us rejoice with those that rejoice and weep with those that weep.

We recommend that every family in this Association take the Biblical Recorder as a means of not only strengthening our denomination, but recommend it as good literature in any home.

Respectfully submitted,

Q. B. HOCUTT,
J. T. HOLT,
Committee.

Upon motion to adopt the report was then discussed by Brethren J. B. Hocutt and Stephen H. Averitt. Report was adopted.

The Foreign Mission Report was read by Brother C. A. Jenkens.

REPORT ON FOREIGN MISSIONS.

Our Foreign Mission Board, located at Richmond, Va., is doing work in China, Japan, Africa, Italy, Mexico, Brazil, and Argentina.

The call to believers for enlarged mission work was never more imperative than it is today. Never was it clearer that culture does not save naitons, and that art and science are promoters of unbelief rather than pillars of faith. The state of the world at present emphasizes the fact that all peoples need the simple gospel of Jesus Christ. Without it no high degree of civilization is possible. The New Testament is, under God, the only force that can lift men above Paganism.

Last year the missionaries reported 382 churches with 819 out-stations, 33,584 church members, 442 Sunday Schools with 00,050 scholars, and 0,000 students in mission schools, 084 of whom are in theological seminaries and training schools preparing to preach the gospel to their own people. There are 300 missionaries on the fields, 20 of whom were sent out last year, and a total of 651 native workers. To this force must be added 12 medical missionaries with 8 hospitals and 13 dispensaries, having a total record of patients amounting to 74,829.

During the year there have been advancements made along all lines despite the unsettled state of affairs in Europe and Mexico,

occasioned by bloody wars. The greatest advancement has been
made in China and Brazil. The total number of baptisms on
foreign fields for the year reported by our missionaries amounts
to 5,190. This is a slight decrease from the previous year,
due no doubt to the European war and the chaotic condition in
Mexico.

A recent forecast of foreign missions states that all our mission fields present a most hopeful outlook. Thus, "especially is
this true of China and Brazil. Now is our opportunity in China.
Our civilization appeals to the Chinese mind, and with our civilization it is our great privilege to give them that which has made
our civilization—our Christian religion. Both Brazil and Mexico,
to the south of us, offer us another great opportunity. The
fields in the former are ripe already unto the harvest. In the
latter country the people are groping after political and religious
freedom, and when they get the truth "the truth shall make
them free indeed."

"The trend of thought the world over seems to be toward
pure democracy. While attaining this ideal in government the
nations will break away from ecclesiastical bondage, and in the
entire gospel of Jesus Christ will they find their ideal in religion. It is our privilege, to say nothing of our duty, to have
a part in working out this desired end."

The distressing financial conditions throughout the South
created by the war in Europe, causing a falling off in contributions to Foreign Missions last year. Many of the churches
made heroic and sacrificial efforts, but some of them were not
able to keep up their usual contributions. This will make it
more difficult for us to maintain the work this year unless
God's people meet the situation in a still more heroic spirit.
The Convention in Houston asked for an appropriation of
$624,000 for Foreign Missions this year. Every dollar of it
will be needed to carry on the work successfully. Our supreme
task now should be the raising of the apportionment as a minimum in every Association and every State.

We therefore recommend:

1. That we as an Association undertake to raise for Foreign
Missions our full proportion of the above named sum; that this
amount be divided among the churches on an equitable basis;
that we earnestly urge the churches to contribute the amount
asked of them; that each church inaugurate a plan of systematic weekly or monthly giving to the benevolent objects of
the Convention; and that Foreign Missions be given a prominent place in the schedule of giving; and further, that funds
collected for Foreign Missions be forwarded at once so that the
work make be taken care of and debt and interest payments
may be avoided.

2. That each pastor in the Association appoint a committee
in each church of which he is pastor to canvass the membership with a view to securing a subscription to the Foreign Mis-

sion Journal in every Baptist family in the Association, so that our people may be fully informed as to our world-wide work.

Respectfully submitted,

C. A. JENKENS.

After a discussion of the report by Brother C. A. Jenkens and Brother C. R. Boone it was adopted.

The chair announced the order of business for Friday. Dr. W. L. Poteat was recognized. The body was dismissed by prayer by Rev. J. U. Teague until Friday morning.

FRIDAY MORNING.

The morning session was opened by song and devotional exercise. The Moderator called the body to order and prayer was offered by Rev. W. H. Wall.

The proceedings of the previous sessions of the body were read and approved. The Moderator called for the Report on Woman's Work, which was read by Rev. A. C. Hamby.

REPORT ON WOMAN'S WORK.

It is not the purpose of this report to give counsel to the women of our churches in respect to their work for the Kingdom. On the other hand, we would remind the brethren that they might profit by sitting at the feet of the consecrated and well informed women to be found in all, or nearly all of the churches. Probably the men could thus learn the secret of a wonderful progress and achievement that would furnish inspiration for the doing of larger things for our Lord. If our men had taxed their minds and hearts and resources in trying to answer the requirements of the Lord and the call of the Kingdom of heaven as the women have, we would come together this year to record advancement that, at our present rate of progress, will require yet a dozen years to achieve. And when we shall have reached what ought to be our present status, the women will be still as far ahead of us in devotion to the divine call to evangelize the world as they are now. They are constantly studying the needs and conditions of God's Kingdom at home and on every field where the churches of the Southern Baptist Convention have undertaken to labor. The best informed and most liberal givers—according to their resources— in all of our churches are the women who have banded themselves together for study to get information, interest and inspiration. In doing this they make use of mission literature, study courses and the execution of a well prepared program on some phase of mission work in each of their monthly meetings.

Ignorance is the father of indifference and opposition. Not a few men and women are opposed to Woman's Missionary So-

cieties. When one opposes any good movement he is sure to
lose sight of what those engaged in it are doing. On the other
hand, if they were to take to heart, as seriously as the women
do, the commands of their Lord and the importunate call of
need, they would be anxious for intelligent missionary information, and would set their hearts and brains to the task of helping, rather than hindering, those women that labor in the gospel.

The women in our churches control an infinitely small part
of the money belonging to the membership of the churches, but
in the State of North Carolina they give more than one-third
of all the distinctively mission money sent up by the churches.
In the Johnston County Association they gave last year nearly
sixty-three per cent of the mission money reported as contributed by the churches, and in this year of low prices for cotton
and high cost of living, they have managed to give two-fifths
of the total apportionment for these objects. Facing these facts,
we can do nothing less than honor them and offer them every
encouragement possible.

The men, in too large measure, have left the privilege of mission work to them, and they have seized it with ready, willing
hands. Men need not stand back to give them a chance; they
will find their place of service in the Kingdom of God. They go,
and help others to go, into every place of need. appealing to
the good in men and women in every station and condition in
life. With voice and hand and pen they are doing their part
to purge the atmosphere of moral corruption. They clothe them
selves with good works, a noble adornment, their habit which
gives them likeness to the Savior.

Respectfully sibmitted,

A. C. HAMBY.

Upon a motion to adopt the report was discussed by Rev.
A. C. Hamby, Rev. C. E. Stevens, W. B. Joyner, and adopted.

A motion was made that in the absence of Auditor Walter Ives, the Moderator appoint Brother D. M. Hall to audit
the Report of the Finance Committee. Rev. R. L. Smith
then read the Report on Ministerial Education.

REPORT ON EDUCATION.

The central purpose of the plan of salvation is to win a wandering people back to God. Around this purpose the Bible has
written "come", has been the plea of divinity since man de-
serted God. The tender call of a loving Father, yearning for
His own, is "Come, let us reason together." No higher tribute
has been paid to the intellect of man than that. "Come, learn
of me" is one of the sweetest invitations ever received. Jesus
came that we might be lifted up from darkness into light, and
life.

The world is still far from being won to righteousness; God is still calling "come"; Jesus is still pleading with His people to "go"; and millions of souls are still being lost. If Christians were as interested in religion as in other things it would not be so. That a large majority of church people are not vitally interested in religious work is evidenced by the fact that so few are actively engaged in a determined effort to Christianize the world. Christians are indifferent to religious work because they do not know, do not realize, the necessity of being engaged in it. When our people know what, why, when and how to work for God, they will get busy.

Baptists, as a whole, need to know more about the Lord's work. Therefore, we have a Board of Education, which was elected, as it now exists, at the last Baptist State Convention, and whose work is to look after, and seek to create an interest in, all the educational and social betterment agencies of said Convention.

The number of high schools in our Convention system of schools is at present thirteen; applying to enter, two (in N. C.); Colleges three. The value of these, plants, equipment and endowment, altogether, is $1,498,100. Value of Seminary and Training School, plants, equipments and endowment, $1,670,000.

In institutions fostered by Southern Baptists there were last year 41,000 students in round numbers.

This year there are 466 enrolled in Wake Forest, of whom 83 are ministers. The enrollment at Meredith is 382, five of whom are expected to go to the foreign field. There are about 45 young men from North Carolina at the Seminary.

All of our schools started off well this session, some of them having about all the students they can well accommodate. President Brewer says that another dormitory will be needed before Meredith can take many more. This is very encouraging. It means a greater interest in Christian Education.

One phase of our educational work, which generally receives too little attention in our Associational meetings, is our secondary schools. One of the most valuable objects contributed to by Southern Baptists, is the mountain system of secondary schools—34 in all, in which are 171 teachers and 5,281 students. All of these schools have Young Peoples' Societies and receive instructions from the text-book published by the Sunday School Board; also practically all of the schools have Young Women's Societies. All the schools are located near Baptist churches.

The old Board had for its object the support of young preachers only. The new Board has for its object the promotion of all our educational interests. Therefore it is recommended:

1. 'That the term, "Ministerial Education", be removed from the objects contributed to by the churches and reported for the Association, and that "Christian Education' be substituted in-

stead; the latter term being understood to cover all our educational work, Ministerial Education included.

2. That Christian Education be put in the church budget on a regular footing with other forms of mission work, and that the churches be urged to contribute to this object.

3. That the Association undertake to raise $500 next year. This is less than a fourth of the amount it raised last year for missions, although our Christian schools are at the foundation of all our mission work, since the Boards must depend almost entirely on these schools for their missionaries. The amount asked for can be raised by getting an average of fifteen cents from each Baptist in the Association.

4. TThat, so far as it is at all consistent, our boys and girls be urged to attend our own schools, especialy those fostered by the Convention.

5. That our pastors be asked to secure, and distribute in the churches, all available literature concerning Christian Education.

R. L. SMITH.

After being discussed by Rev. R. L. Smith and Dr. W. L. Poteat, President of Wake Forest College, the Report was adopted.

The body was dismissed by prayer by Rev. W. H. Wall for dinner.

AFTERNOON SESSION.

Session opened with song and prayer by Rev. C. E. Stevens. Brother Wall presented the following resolution, and was adopted:

Be it resolved, That it is the sense of this Association that we have been most hospitably and graciously entertained during our stay with the good people of Clayton; and that we extend a most hearty vote of thanks to the women and the church and to all others who have contributed to our comfort and happiness while here.

Brother Hamby made a motion that the Clerk be allowed twenty dollars ($20) for his services, and that the usual number of copies of the minutes be printed and distributed. As there were not enough funds in hand to do this a collection was taken amounting to $11.09.

The Report on Temperance was read by R. L. Smith.

REPORT ON TEMPERANCE.

One hundred and twenty years ago, Dr. Benjamin Rush published the first treatise on the influence of ardent spirits upon mind and body. Eighty years ago, the first national convention was held and unfurled the salutary principle of total abstinence. So that the reform in its present organized shape, is about eighty years old.

The inherent evil of using all alcoholic beverages and intoxicants is twofold. One reason is that it exposes you and me to danger. The inevitable tendency of alcohol is to strike right to the brain, overturn the throne and through the brain reach the very soul. But that is not the greatest reason. It is because it puts a stumbling-block in the pathway of others, whom you and I, according to the golden rule, are to love as we love ourselves.

Now, listen: a great many drinkers have seen written in invisible letters over the door-ways of many of these splendidly upholstered haunts of temptation, "He that entereth here is not wise: rich men here made poor, thrifty men idle, honest men deceptive and worthless, sound men sick, moral men vicious, parents made childless, children made orphans, wives made widows, and immortal souls by a slow torture put to death that never, never dies."

We, your Committee, do recommend the following resolutions:

Whereas, medical science has demonstrated that alcoholic liquor is a poison and not a food, and has repudiated its use as a medicine, declaring it to be injurious to the user and his posterity; and,

Whereas, investigations show that the liquor traffic injures commerce, increases crime, polutes politics, debauches government, destroys the home and robs the children; and

Whereas more than fifty-five per cent of the people of this nation live in dry territory, and more than six millions have petitioned Congress to submit the amendment for nation-wide prohibition to the States; and

Whereas Congressmen Pou and Small have each stated, in public print, that he stands ready to vote for the Hobson Resolution in the sixty-fourth Congress if assured that a majority of his constituency so desire; therefore, be it resolved—

1. That we, the Association of Johnson County, in meeting assembled, go on record as favoring national constitutional prohibition.

2. That we urge our representatives to vote for the Hobson Resolution, submitting the same to the States.

(Signed) .

A. A. PIPPIN,
R. L. SMITH,
JOS. D. CREECH.

On motion to adopt the report was discussed by Rev. R. L. Davis, Chairman of the Anti-Saloon League. Report was adopted.

Upon motion the Clerk was instructed to send a copy of the resolutions in the Temperance Report to Congressman Pou.

The Finance Committee submitted the following report, which was adopted:

REPORT OF FINANCE COMMITTEE.

The folowing amounts were received by the Finance Committee and turned over to the Treasurer:

Minute Fund	$ 37.45
State Missions	196.96
Home Missions	48.45
Foreign Missions	53.32
Sunday School Missions	19.75
Orphanage	90.85
Ministerial Education	42.25
Ministerial Relief	41.68
Building Fund	148.75
Total	$679.46

Respectfully submitted,

D. J. THURSTON, for Committee.

Audited October 28, 1915.

D. M. HALL,

The Treasurer made the following report:

TREASURER'S REPORT TO THE JOHNSTON COUNTY BAPTIST ASSOCIATION TO THE SESSION AT CLAYTON CHURCH, OCTOBER 27, 28 AND 29, 1915.

Nov. 12, 1914.	MINUTE FUND.	BUILDING FUND.	STATE MISSIONS.	HOME MISSIONS.	FOREIGN MISSIONS.	SUNDAY SCHOOL MISSIONS	MINISTERIAL EDUCATION.	MINISTERIAL RELIEF.	ORPHANAGE.
Bal. on hand	$39 64	$ 7 59	$	$	$	$	$	$	$
Antioch	2 00	7 50	20 00	5 00	5 00	2 50	2 50	2 50	5 00
Baptist Centre		5 00	7 50	2 50	2 50	1 00	2 00	2 00	2 50
Bethesda			3 13						
Burnell			2 05				.65		
Benson Grove		5 00	7 50						2 50
Hephzibah	1 00	2 50	6 20	1 25	1 50	.50	1 55	1 00	1 50
Live Oak			5 00	1 00	1 00		1 00	1 00	5 50
Micro	1 50		10 00	2 50	3 50	1 00	1 50	1 50	
Pisgah	2 10	10 00	11 36	.20	2 00		1 46	2 42	3 00
Princeton Union			8 60						
Olivers Chapel	.50	1 00	5 00	1 00	1 00	.50	1 00	2 00	1 00
Sardis	1 01		12 99			1 00	2 50	2 50	
Smithfield S. S.			6 92	12 65	15 00				
Thanksgiving				1 00		.82			1 00
Parrish Memorial				1 35					
Micro W. M. S.				2 38	2 10				
Carters Chapel				.91					
Car. Chap. Union					3 50				
Corinth								1 06	
Black. Grove									2 40
Smithfield	5 00	25 00							
Four Oaks	2 00	13 50							
Hood's Grove	.50								
Princeton		4 50							
Several Church	7 85								
Selma	3 00	27 50							
Total	$66 10	$109 09	$106 25	$31 74	$37 92	$6 50	$14 16	$15 98	$24 40
Paid to Walters Durham			$106 25	$31 74	$37 92	$6 50	$14 16	$15 98	
Paid to Orphanage Treas.									$24 40
Paid Interest on Note		$ 6 00							
Paid as follows from Minute Fund:									
Pr't'g Minutes	$35 00								
Postage Minutes	$ 3 52								
J. E. Lanier. Sal. Clerk	$ 8 97								
Balance on hand October 26, 1915, Minute Fund	$18 61								
Building Fund		$10 09							
Total balance				121 70					

Respectfully submitted,

JOHN E. LANIER, Treasurer.

Audited—W. M. Ives, Auditor.

Smithfield, N. C., October 26, 1915.

Supplementary Report.

Since the report dated October 26, 1915, I have received the following amounts and paid out as indicated below:

	MINUTE FUND.	STATE MISSIONS.	HOME MISSIONS.	FOREIGN MISSIONS.	SUNDAY SCHOOL MISSIONS.	ORPHANAGE.	CHRISTIAN EDUCATION.	MINISTRIAL RELIEF.	BUILDING FUND	TOTAL.
From T. J. Lasiter, former Tr's-urer	18 61								103 09	123 70
Calvary Lee's		1 00	.50	.50			.45			
Chapel Wilson's	3 00	25 00	10 00	10 00	2 00	5 00	5 00	3 00	5 00	68 00
Mills		20 00	2 50	5 00	1 50	9 50	2 50	2 50	8 35	51 85
Collection from	11 09									
Co'ttee Finance	37|45	196 69	48 45	53 32	19 75	90 85	42 25	41 68	148 75	679 46
Total	70 15	242 96	61 45	68 82	23 25	105 80	49 75	47 18	265 19	923 01
Nov 12, Check to Walters Durham		242 96	61 45	68 82	23 25		49 75	47 19		
Nov. 12 Check to F. B. Hamrick						105 80				
Check to First National Bank of Sm'hfield in payment of note									100 00	
Check to Mrs. L. S. Sta'l'y for note and interest									101 42	
Balance	70 15								63 77	

Respectfully submitted,

JOHN E. LANIER, Treasurer.

Audited—W. M. IVES, Auditor.

Smithfield, N. C., November 12, 1915.

All business having been transacted the thirteenth annual session of the Association adjourned to meet with Benson Baptist Church for the fourteenth annual session.

NOTICE.

By order of the Association all church treasurers are requested to send all moneys collected for State Missions, Home Missions, Foreign Missions, Christian Education, and Ministerial Relief direct to Walters Durham, Raleigh, N. C. Send all money for the Orphanage to the Orphanage Treasurer, F. B. Hamrick, Thomasville, N. C.

Send Minute Fund and Church Building Fund to the Associational Treasurer, John E. Lanier, Smithfield, N. C.

CONSTITUTION.

1. The Association shall be known as the Johnston County Baptist Association.

2. Its object shall be to extend the privileges of the gospel and liberal culture to all the people within its bounds and by hearty co-operation with the Baptist State Convention to help offer these privileges to all mankind in and out of its bounds, by the cordial co-operation of all the churches constituting this body.

3. It shall be composed of the pastors in active service in the Association and such delegates as shall be annually elected by the churches connected with it, each church being entitled to three delegates, unless the membership shall exceed ifty, and then an additional delegate for every twenty-five members, provided no church shall have more than eight delegates.

4. The New Hampshire Declaration of Faith shall be the summary of Divine Truth for determining questions of faith and order in this body, and the churches desiring membership in it must committ themselves to the substance of it, together with the covenant therewith submitted, and this Constitution.

5. This Association shall not have power to annul the discipline or exercise authority over any church connected with it, but it may advise with and sever its connection with any church that neglects to preserve gospel order, or that treats with contempt the objects or advice of the Association,

6. Each church shall send to the annual meetings of the Association a letter (the blanks to be furnished by the Clerk of the Association), carefully filled as per blank suggestions, stating the full work of the church for the year ending with the close of the month previous to the one in which the Association is held.

7. The Association shall foster State Missions, Home Missions, Foreign Missions, Christian Education, the Aged Ministers' Relief Board, the Thomasville Orphanage and the Sunday School Board, and each church shall be requested to contribute to the support of these objects annually.

8. Missions and education shall have precedence in their claims upon the consideration of this body in its regular sessons.

9. Whenever a church shall fail to be represented by delegates or letter at the annual sessions of the Association inquiry shall be made for the cause and efforts shall be made to induce such church to do its duty, and the effort shall be continued till the church is recovered or dropped from the roll.

10. The officers of the Association shall be a Moderator, a Vice-Moderator, a Clerk, a Treasurer and an Auditor elected annually by ballot (or in case when only one brother is put in nomination for an office, then the vote may be by acclamation) from among its members, to serve until their successors shall have been elected, and to perform the duties usual to such officers, namely, the Moderator, in presiding over the meetings, or the Vice-Moderator in his absence; the Clerk in recording and preserving minutes and other papers belonging to the body; the Treasurer in receiving and disbursing funds belonging to or entrusted to the body according to its will; the Auditor to examine the Treasurer's books at each meeting of the Association and report the same before adjournment.

11. The Association shall appoint annually an Executive Committee of five (5) from its members, who shall be entrusted with the prosecution of Missions in the Association and any other work for the interest of the Master's Kingdom which may be referred to them. This committee shall, as far as possible, co-operate with the State Mission Board in supplying the destitution in our territory, and between the meetings of the Association take such actions as may seem to them advisable for the advancement of its interest. The committee shall present to the Association at its annual meeting a report of its proceedings, with the names of the missionaries supported on the field time of service and details of their work, together with such recommendations as in the judgment of the committee the Association should follow in planning its subsequent work.

12. The annual sessions of the Association shall begin on Wednesday after the fourth Lord's day in October at such place as may be chosen, and an introductory sermon shall be delivered on the first day of the session. Representatives from ten of the churches constituting the Association shall be a quorum.

13. This Constitution may be amended at any annual session by a two-thirds vote of all the members present.

14. The proceedings of the Woman's Central Committee shall be recorded as a part of the Minutes of the Association.

BY-LAWS.

1. The daily sessions of the Association shall be opened and closed with prayer.

2. Delegates shall be recognized by letters from their churches designating them as such.

3. The Moderator shall recognize corresponding messengers or the delegates of newly received churches by extending to them his right hand.

4. The report of the Executive Board and the missionary work of the Association shall take precedence of all other business during the morning session of the second day of the annual session.

5. The Clerk shall record and read the proceedings when called for, superintend the publication and distribution of the Minutes, preserve a file of them, and have it present at each annual session, and deliver to his successor all papers belonging to the body.

6. Members desiring to speak shall first rise and address the Moderator, shall use the term "Brother" in speaking to each other; shall not speak on the same subject more than twice without permission, and shall observe the courtesy that becomes Christians.

7. The roll of members shall be called at least once and absentees marked.

8. Corresponding messengers and visiting brethren shall be invited to seats, with privilege of speaking, but not voting.

A copy of the Minutes shall be sent to the Secretary of the State Mission Board, the Secretary of the Southern Baptist Convention, the American Publication Society, 1420 Chestnut Street, Philadelphia; the Sunday School Board of the Southern Baptist Convention and the Thomasville Orphanage.

10. All questions of order not herein provided shall be decided by Kerfoot's Parliamentary Law.

WOMAN'S MISSIONARY UNION.

The Woman's Missionary Union of the Johnston County Baptist Association, held at Benson Baptist Church on October thirteenth, was a great success in every way. It was largely attended and the splendid program, intensely interesting and helpful, was beautifully carried out.

The opening session began at 9:30, devotionals conducted by Mr. Lassiter, Presbyterian pastor at Benson. He used for his lesson the 67th Psalm, after which Mrs. O. A. Barbour gave a hearty welcome from the Woman's Missionary Society to all visitors and the entire Union. All were assured that our town, our churches, our homes and our hearts were thrown wide open to one and all.

Miss Julia Cannady gave such a hearty welcome from the B. Y. P. U's. This is a great work, but the Benson Missionary Society has work before them to enlist these workers in the Y. W. A. work also.

Miss Cannady stated that although the B. Y. P. U. is just emerging from its infancy, its future prospects are in every way bright and hopeful.

Mrs. W. O. Rackley gave a most hearty welcome from the M. E. Church.

Mrs. B. A. Hocutt, Vice-President pro-tem of the Woman's Missionary Union, in the absence of Mrs. Hough, warmly responded, speaking for the entire Union of her sincere appreciation and happiness in being thus welcomed.

The first on the program was Mrs. B. A. Hocutt, who gave us an excellent and instructive talk on "Our Association; Its Relation and Obligation to the W. M. U."

The minutes of the last meeting of the Union, which was held at Mt. Moriah, were read by Miss Cleve Barnes. The report was splendid and the reports from different Societies showed that the work is still moving onward and progressing.

The Committee on Time and Place was next appointed: Mrs. Bailey, Mrs. Duncan and Mrs. J. Coy Pool. Also the Committee on Nomination: Mrs. C. M. Thomas, Mrs. J. J. Lane and Mrs C. E. Stevens. Obituary Committee: Mrs. Mark Gulley.

Mrs. O. E. Bain gave some fine impressions from our State Union, stating "the feeling of nearness to God and that the meetings are ours and the joy in meeting the Central Committee and missionaries." We hear of the missionaries and their work, here we see them face to face and hear them tell of the wonderful work they are doing.

Mrs. Hamby was impressed with the Training School. What a privilege to attend this school whether you are to be a missionary or not, it is a great help in life to have the training one gets at this great and good school.

We were delighted to have with us Miss Blanche Barrus, whose talk on our Missionary Union surely encouraged and inspired each one present to assume a greater responsiblity and with more life and hope take up her work anew.

Mrs. J. J. Taylor, Missionary from Brazil, completely captivated her hearers by a talk on her missionary life in Brazil. She spoke of the immense size of the country of Brazil, stating that it is larger than our own United States with the exception of Alaska, and touched on the religion of the Brazilians, Catholicism, idolatry and superstition, handed down by their forefathers. She spoke of the terrible struggle she and her husband endured in establishing the gospel of Christ amid such surroundings; of the way in which they were jeered, hooted at and utterly despised in the beginning; of their incessant perseverance and untiring years of toil; and, finally, of the wonderful and triumphant victory of the gospel and the marvelous eagerness with which the natives listen to the story of Christ.

Prayer by Mrs. Taylor, after which we adjourned for the very supmtuous dinner which was spread on a large table in the main auditorium, which as yet, is not completed. Such a bountiful and delightful spread is very seldom seen.

Devotional exercises, for the afternoon session, beginning at two o'clock, were conducted by Dr. J. J. Taylor, missionary from Brazil. Hymn—"Work for the Night is Coming," was sung, then prayer by Dr. Taylor. He said we are in danger of two or three things: the proper motive, manner, and measure. The motive of our work should be love toward Christ, personal love to Christ; the manner should be to a view of glorifying His name; the measure of it, "She has done all that she could."

Miss Bessie Lane read a paper on 'Today's Opportunity in Mission Work in Foreign Lands." It showed much study and was an impelling call "to go and send" and take the advantage of the present opportunity.

Mrs. John Saunders brought before us "Today's Opportunity in Mission Work in our Home Land." Never at any time, through the restless march of ages has the importance of mission work been more manifest than now. The people are waking up to the realization that they are their "brothers' keepers."

The Home Mission Board of the Southern Baptist Convention includes in its field the sixteen Southern States, the District of Columbia, part of Illinois, Panama, and more than half of Cuba.

"Today's Opportunity in Mission Work in our State", by Mrs. D. J. Thurston, was a most interesting part of the program. She thrilled every one present with her great enthusiasm and earnestness in pointing out the places needing most our mission work and prayers. She brought clearly and definitely before our minds our great opportunity in our own State.

'Today's Opportunity in Mission Work in our Association". by Mrs. J. M. Beaty, showed us that the opportunities and responsibilities are greater today than they ever were before.

Mrs. J. E. Lanier gave a most impressive talk on "Our Training School at Louisville." The spiritual atmosphere there you do not get anywhere else. We say our Training School because it is the own child of the Missionary Society. Training School girls just long to do something for some one.

Miss Floy Johnson read an excellent paper on "The Importance of Mission Study" and a plan for wider circulation of missionary magazines and for mission study in our Association.

Mrs. C. M. Thomas on "Personal Service in Local Community; Responsibility of Neglect," made each one feel the need of more real personal work. Did not our Savior spend His time in going about doing good? Did he not give Himself yea, His very life, for mankind, and how much less should we give than ourselves to His work?

Miss Blanche Barrus, fired with the intense love she has for working with girls, and young women, talked on the "Pressing Need of Young Woman's Auxiliary Work in our Association," The supreme task is to interest our young girls. Don't neglect the young girl in your church. We should get a vision of our own responsibility. Happiness comes through service.

After the singing of the Woman's Hymn the Committee on Resolutions report was read, composed of Mrs. J. E. Lanier and Mrs. J. M. Turley.

The Union deeply regretted the absence of Mrs. Carter, former Vice-President. In her absence Mrs. C. M. Thomas read her paper on "Training the Children in Mission Thought and Giving; Responsibility of the W. M. U. for the Sunbeam and Junior Leader."

Miss Briggs sends love to each member. She is so in love with her work and so full of sunshine that we always miss her.

The Committee on Nomination reported that Mrs B. A. Hocutt was elected Vice-President of the Union. Miss Cleve Barnes, Secretary, Mrs. J. J. Lane, Superintendent of the Junior Department of the Association.

Committee on Time and Place reported Wendell as the next place of meeting.

As it seemed necessary for a good number of the delegates to return on Wednesday afternoon, the program planned for Thursday morning was completed then. This was only a venture of having two days. It was voted that we have two days at our next meeting.

There was an open conference in which was discussed many subjects dear to the heart of the true mission woman. Such women as Mrs. D. H. McCullers, Mrs. J. M. Beaty and Mrs. J. J. Lane gave us some of their sincerest thoughts.

Mrs. C. E. Stevens read a very instructive paper on the great need of enlisting our young people.

A paper on "Observance of Special Seasons in Country Society", by Mrs. J. J. Lane, was read by Miss Cleve Barnes.

A rising vote of thanks was given Mr. Alonza Parrish for sending to Buie's Creek for Dr. and Mrs. Taylor and to Mr. J. M. Beaty for printing and mailing programs.

In a memorial to Miss Fannie E. S. Heck, Miss Blanche Barrus said that three things about her life impressed her: First, her faithfulness to this task. We can all be faithful. Second, her joy and optimism in her work. She was always so happy in the work. Third, she put things of the Kingdom first.

Mrs. Ed Richardson read Miss Heck's last message to the Union.

Prayer by Mrs. Ed Richardson, special prayer for the meeting at Smithfield requested by Mr. Thiot.

This closed the afternoon session and we were ready for supper, knowing what awaited us in the main auditorium of the new church.

Wednesday evening, beginning at 7:30 with the songs, From Greenland's Icy Mountain and Tell it Out, Tell it Out, Dr. Taylor, with the assistance of Dr. Utley, gave an illustrated lecture on Brazil. This was exceedingly interesting and instructive and enjoyed by all present. Dr. Taylor has the honor of being the first missionary from Brazil who ever spoke to the Union.

After the lecture a collection was taken which amounted to $7.00, all of which was turned over to Dr. Taylor for mission work.

Resolutions were read by Mr. Hall.

Adjournment.

MISS CLEVE BARNES.
Secretary.

TABLE I—STATISTICAL—FOR YEAR 1914-1915.

Church.	Pastor and Postoffice.	Clerk and Postoffice.	Time of Preaching.	Value of Church Property.	Gains By Baptism.	Gains By Letter.	Gains By Restoration.	Losses By Letter.	Losses By Exclusion.	Losses By Death.	Number of Males.	Number of Females.	Total Membership.
Bailey	A. A. Pippin, Wakefield	W. O. Hocutt, Selma, R. 2	3	2,000	7	2	4	8	1	1	76	100	186
Baptist	W. H. Wall, Middlesex	R. L. Underwood, Bailey	1	1,500	17	5	2		1		31	46	77
Beaty	W. T. Tate, Wake Forest	E. H. Rogers, Clayton, R. 1	2	500	4			3	9	1	51	53	104
Benson	R. L. Smith, Smithfield	N. M. Eason, Smithfield	4	1,000		3		3	1		10	20	30
Benson's Grove	J. M. Duncan, Benson	L. Gilbert, Benson	2 & 4	1,500	15		4	1		1	60	105	165
Bethany	R. L. Smith, Smithfield	D. Medlin, Benson	2	800			3	2	3	1	6	18	24
Bethel	W. D. Stancil, Kenly	Kirkman, Kenly	4	800	4	1		1	4		33	59	92
Bethesda	D. E. Vipperman, Kenly	W. N. , Kenly	4	700		4	2	3	15		12	24	36
Blackman's Grove	W. T. Tate, Wake Forest	J. E. Smith, Wilson's Mills	4	4,000	21	1	1	3		2	124	143	267
Calvary	W. D. Harrington, Four Oaks	Joseph Wood, Four Oaks, R. 3	3		7			4		1	21	42	63
Canaan	R. C. McCall, Selma, R.	G. J. , Dunn, R.	3	500					1		10	16	26
Carter's Chapel	R. L. Smith, Smithfield	G. L. Hudson, Bentonsville	3	500	1	4	2	1	1	1	14	30	44
Clayton	W. D. Harrington, Four Oaks	Martin Thorn, Selma, R.	3	1,000	12		1	3	2	1	34	62	96
Clyde's	A. C. Hanby, Clayton	W. P. , Clayton	Fulltim	6,000	97	40	2	14	6	1	211	287	498
Corinth	I. L. Bennett, Wake Forest	C. I. , Knightdale, R. 2	3	500	5	4	1	8	2		79	102	181
Four Oaks	A. A. Pippin, Wakefield	H. V. Andrews, Wendell	3	1,750	15	2		2	6		59	89	148
Hephzibah	J. M. Duncan, Benson	J. W. Langden, Four Oaks	4	700	8	6		4	2		30	40	70
Hood's Grove	J. E. , Smithfield	W. A. Braswell, Princeton	3	400	1				1		7	11	18
Kenly	R. L. Smith, Smithfield	P. T. George, Four Oaks, R. 1	2	500	4	1			1		29	30	59
es	D. E. Vipperman, Kenly	F. C. Richardson, Kenly	2	2,500	4	5	5	5	1	1	17	23	40
Live Oak	W. H. Wall, Middlesex	W. I. , Zebulon, R. 2	3	1,500	47	9		9	1	5	138	162	300
Micro	J. U. , Princeton	K. Broadwell, Selma, R. 1	3	500	2			2	5		10	20	35
Middlesex	W. H. Beck, Micro	D. H. Jones, Micro	2 & 4	2,000	18	17	1	4		2	17	18	86
Mount Moriah	C. A. Jenkins, Clayton	W. H. Ballentine, Middlesex	4	2,500	11	3	1		2	2	33	53	186
New Bethel	A. A. Pippin, Wakefield	Russell Powell,	4	3,500	11	1		1	11		88	98	94
s	W. H. Wall, Middlesex	Geo. W. Bryan, Garner	4	1,500	37	3	6	3			45	49	106
Oliver's Grove	W. D. Harrington, Four Oaks	N. L. Stott, Sims	3	700					1	1	38	68	23
Parrish Memorial	J. M. , Benson	Jas. D. , Selma	1	250	2	4	1	2	5		7	16	71
Pauline	W. D. Harrington, Four Oaks	W. D. Beasley, Four Oaks	4	1,500	7	7			7	1	27	44	63
Pine	D. E. Vipperman, Kenly	Kyle Godwin, Pine Level	1	2,500	3	1		2	4		23	31	54

* Arm of Pisgah.

TABLE II—FINANCIAL—FOR YEAR 1914-1915.

Churches	Pastor's Salary	Building and Repairs	Incidentals	Sunday School Expenses	The Poor	Minute Fund	Building Fund	State Missions	Home Missions	Foreign Missions	S. S. Missions	Orphanage	Ministerial Education	Ministerial Relief	Colleges and Schools	Other Objects	Total
Antioch	$ 97 00	$ 35 00	$	$ 18 00	$50 00	$ 2 00	$ 7 50	20 00	5 00	5 00	2 50	5 00	2 50	2 50	$	20 57	272 57
Bailey	75 00		3 50			1 00	6 50	20 00	2 50	5 00	1 00	5 00	2 00	2 00			113 50
Baptist Center	100 00			10 00			5 00	7 50	2 00	5 00	1 00	2 50	2 00	2 00	1 00		133 00
Beaty Chapel	33 23	17 40	18 70	14 74		50		5 00		2		2 51	75	75		10 83	108 42
Benson	500 00	425 00	40 00	50 00		3 00	15 00	75 00	10 00	15 00		23 50	5 00	5 00		85 00	1,254 00
Benson's Grove	25 00			5 00			2 00	7 50				2 50			25		45 00
Bethany	30 00	15 00	1 50	20 00				10 00	5 00	5 00	1 00	2 00	2 50	2 50		32 90	135 80
Bethel	10 10		15 00		5 00		7 00	2 50	2 35	2 00		45					19 20
Bethesda	200 00	4,000 00		20 00	2 35	90		37 50	5 00	7 00	2 50	15 00	5 00	5 00		11 20	4,328 55
Blackman's Grove	75 00					3 00		20 00	5 00	5	2			4			126 50
Calvary						1 50											2 45
Canaan	30 00					25	25	3 00	1 50		25	1 00	25	3 00			37 00
Carter's Chapel	40 00		263 47				2 00	7 00	5 00	25 00	3 00	11 00	25 00	20 00			76 00
Clayton	1,275 00	2,037 16	158 13	89 71	8 22	5 00	90 00	275 00	322 85	154 20	5 00	100 56	25 00	20 00		96 59	4,767 76
Clyde's Chapel	150 00		40 76	5 00	4 60	2 00	12 50	29 40	8 00	23 25	1 00	3 75	2 50	2 50	25	6 35	253 29
Corinth	100 00	50 00	2 00	31 78		2 00	6 00	13 00	2 50	2 50	2 00	5 00	2 00	2 00			345 13
Four Oaks	110 00			7 85		1 00	13 50	32 20	19 67	2 85	50	75	4 00	4 00		8 86	283 12
Hephzibah	25 00		16 90	25 18	2 50	1 50	2 50	6 00	1 25	1	50	1 00	1 00	1 00		6 65	57 95
Hood's Grove	50 00		12 00	10 60		1 50		2 00	4 13	4 76	1 00	5 00	1 00	1 00		45 00	112 00
Kenly	125 16	49 02		29 34	4 25		5 00	21 43	10 00	1 00	50	5 00	2 50	2 50		5 34	211 15
Lee's Chapel	150 00					1 50		57 00	1 00		2 00	5 00	1 00	1 00			289 62
Live Oak	25 00		54 65	39 37	4 28	2 00	12 50	5 00	2 00	3 00	1 00	5 75	1 00	1 00		5 48	41 90
Micro	36 75	75 00	40 00	48 69	10 50	3 00	25 00	12 50	10 00	14 50	10 00	6 46	2 50	2 50	5 00	200 00	236 25
Middlesex	250 00	150 00	18 35	5 03			20 00	31 02	32 23	8 00	1 00	26 85	10 00	10 00	7 73	50 00	711 00
Mount Moriah	200 00	77 07			1 00	50	1 00	36 05	7 50		1 00	28 55	5 50	5 50		33 90	659 85
New Bethel	250 00			3 00		1 00	3 50	10 00	2 00	1 00		5 00	2 00	2 00			399 00
Noble's Chapel	125 00			5 00				5 00	2 00	1 25	50	1 00	1 00	1 00	1 00		158 50
Oliver's Grove	6 75	1 00	50	4 00				6 00	2 00	2 50		1 25		18			18 75
Parrish Memorial	72 65			12 00		1 00	10 00	20 00	2 50	1 00	1 00	5 00	2 50	5 00			96 15
Pauline	30 71		39 00	13 29		1 80	80	6 50	2 50	1 25	50	2 50	2 50	1 00		11 80	51 89
Pine Level	107 00	66 30	50							2 50	1 00	1 00	2 50	5 00			290 90
Pinkney	25 00	35								5 00	1 00	1 00	2 50	1			53 74

Church	1	2	3	4	5	6	7	8	9	10	11	12	13	14	15	16	Total
Pisgah	150 00	2 70	3 45	11 34	12 00	2 10	10 00	22 25	5 50	5 50	1 00	5 00	2 50	2 42		14 00	249 76
Princeton	40 80	5 00	14 86	12 57		1 50	4 50	24 60		5 00	1 00	3 65	2 50	2 50			108 83
Sardis	100 00		5 00	4 34		1 00	27 50	16 50	5 00	5 00	2 50	25 00	10 00	10 00		263 50	146 99
Selma	80 00	552 00	164 40	53 55		3 00		75 00	20 00	30 00		5 00	2 50	2 50			2,036 45
Shiloh	15 00			15 00	10 00	5 00		20 00	5 00	5 00		39 97	10 00	10 00			205 75
Smithfield	75 00	1 00	136 05	99 19			25 00	125 57	49 55	65 00	1 00	3 50	2 00	2 00	62 85	230 37	1,609 63
Thanksgiving	40 00		8 00	20 00			5 00	11 50	2 50	2 00	1 55	1 48	2 50	2 50		26 33	185 83
Trinity							2 50	5 00	1 00	1 50							13 05
Wendell	434 00	22 39	104 67	49 24	19 29	3 00	25 00	47 97	49 59	59 12	5 00	31 48	5 00	5 34		1 71	847 68
White Oak	150 00		10 00	15 66		2 00		25 00	7 50	5 00	2 50	10 00	5 02	5 00		31 00	290 45
Wilson's Mills	100 00		25 00	85 00		1 50	12 50	20 00	2 50	5 00	1 50	9 50	2 50	2 50			268 00
Burnell*				3 00		1 00	1 00	4 10	1 00	1 00		1 50	1 50	1 00			14 25
Total	7,104 15	7,581 39	1,002 39	807 44	133 9	65 80	373 05	1,206 29	632 62	703 99	73 72	482 84	144 42	140 34	77 83	1,164 48	21,668 61

*Arm of Pisgah.

TABLE III—SUNDAY SCHOOLS—FOR YEAR 1914-1915.

Church.	Superintendent and Postoffice.	Secretary and Postoffice.	Number of Schools.	Officers and Teachers.	Pupils.	Total Enrollment.	Church Members in Sunday School.	Months Kept Open.	Baptisms from School.	School Expenses.	Missions.	Orphanage.	Other Objects.	Total Contributions.
Antioch	W. H. Maiden, Selma, R. 2	W. O. Hocutt, Selma, R. 2	1	11	106	117	75	12	2	18 00		1 26		19 26
Bailey	J. P. Underwood, Bailey	J. W. B. Finch, Bailey	1	5	86	85	25	12	14	15 00				15 00
Baptist Center	A. D. Gower, Clayton, R. 3		1	7	103	110	40	12		10 00			5 24	10 00
Beaty	E. F. Crump, Smithfield	Buddie Edwards, Smithfield	1	6	65	71	9	12		14 74		2 51		22 49
Benson	J. L. Hall, Benson	L. E. Stevens, Benson	1	10	260	270		9		50 00	15 15	11 96		77 11
Benson's Grove	R. A. Holland, Benson	C. P. Stewart, Benson	1	5	50	55		12		5 00				5 00
Bethany	Moses Creech, Kenly	A. R. Creech, Kenly	1	8	138	146	60	12	4	20 00		2 25		22 25
Bethel														
Bethesda	D. C. Smith, Wilson's Mills	J. E. Smith, Wilson's Mills	1	12	100	112	75	12	15	20 00	3 50		6 00	29 50
Blackman's Grove	T. P. Wood, Four Oaks, R. 2	Noga Wood, Four Oaks, R. 2	1	4	31	35	10	8	1	2 73				2 73
Calvary														
Canaan	Carroll Bryant, Newton Grove	Miss P. Bryant, Newton G've	1	4	30	34		8	10	10 30			2 00	12 30
Carter's Chapel	Martin Thorn, Selma	Frank Woodruff, Selma	1	6	100	106	40	12	61	89 71	82 38	60 00	244 97	477 06
Clayton	D. L. Barber, Clayton	Foster Barnes, Clayton	1	14	330	344	250	12	4	5 00	7 75			18 75
... Chapel	L. V. Bunch, Knightdale	Lester Bunch, Knightdale	1	6	88	94	59	12	8	10 50			6 00	10 50
Corinth	W. A. Mitchell, Wendell	Coster Hocutt, Wendell	1	7	76	83		12	3	31 78	14 75			46 53
Four Oaks	R. A. Bain, Four Oaks	J. W. Sanders, Four Oaks	1	7	140	147	50	12	1	5 00	70			5 70
Hephzibah	W. G. Creech, Princeton	W. G. Creech, Princeton	1	3	31	34	10	12						
Hood's Grove														
Kenly	A. J. Broughton, Kenly	Fielden Harris, Kenly	1	6	45	51	20	12	3	24 00	1 18			25 18
Lee's Chapel	G. G. Dyer, Middlesex, R. 1	Lester Green, Zebulon, R. 2	1	7	60	67	45	12	40	10 60				10 60
Live Oak														
Micro	L. M. Ausley, Micro	Miss Louetta Pittman, Micro	1	8	40	48	20	12	2	29 34		1 26	28 73	58 07
Middlesex	W. H. Maiden, Selma, R. 2	W. O. Hocutt, Selma, R. 2	1	11	106	117	75	12	2	18 00	8 70	20 26		19 26
Mt ...	J. J. ..., Arn	Robert Pool, Clayton, R. 3	1	12	148	160	87	12	9	48 69	11 05		5 00	82 65
New Bethel	H. P. Smith, McCullers	Hubert Britt, Garner	1	7	56	64	25	6	13	5 00				16 05
Noble's Chapel	D. L. Flowers, Sims	Oeren Bullock, Sims	1	5	30	58	6	12	2	3 00				3 00
Oliver's Grove	Mrs. Robert Allen, Four Oaks	A. J. Jernigan, Four Oaks	1	5	35	40	12	6	1	5 00	1 00			6 00
Parrish Memorial	Frank Batten, Micro	Minnie Batten, Micro	1	5	35	40		9		5 00				
Pauline	J. B. B. ...ley, Four Oaks	Mrs. W. E. Wallace, F. Oaks	1	5	166	173	55	9	5	4 00				4 00
Pine Level	B. L. Strickland, Pine Level	Miss P. Braxton, Pine Level	1	7	125	134	20	6	3	12 00	5 00	5 00	1 80	23 80
Pinkney	R. E. Lee, Kenly, R. 1	R. M. Lee, Kenly, R. 1	1	9	40	47	11	12	1	13 29	1 31			14 60

TABLE IV—WOMAN'S MISSIONARY UNION—FOR YEAR 1914-1915.

Church.	Name of Organization.	President and Postoffice.	Number of Members.	State Missions.	Home Missions.	Foreign Missions.	Expense Fund Central Committee	Training School	Other Objects.	Total Contribution.
Clayton	Woman's Missionary Society	Mrs. D. I. Thurston, Clayton	75	51 60	42 35	97 08		14 95		206 08
Clayton	Young Woman's Auxiliary	Mrs. B. A. Hocutt, Clayton	35	7 55	16 50	20 85		3 10	2 00	50 00
Clayton	Sunbeams	Mrs. D. H. McCullers, Clayton	75	5 00	10 00	10 00				25 00
Clyde's Chapel	Woman's Missionary Society	Hellen Bunch, Knightdale	31	9 40	3 00	8 00		1 00	35	21 75
Four Oaks	Woman's Missionary Society	Mrs. S. M. Boyett, Four Oaks	18	6 45	7 45	5 20		4 10	1 15	24 35
Four Oaks	Sunbeams	Miss Bertha Langdon, Four Oaks	37	4 73	10 72	2 15		2 91	70	21 21
Kenly	Woman's Missionary Society	Mrs. F. J. Hough, Kenly	11	5 25	4 25	3 60		1 50	16 48	31 08
Middlesex	Woman's Missionary Society	Mrs. S. B. Sengilitary, Middlesex	22	10 00	10 00	12 00		5 00	9 44	46 44
Middlesex	Sunbeams	Miss Ada Whitley, Middlesex	30							
Mount Moriah	Woman's Missionary Society	Mrs. J. W. Johnson, Clayton, R. 3	15	21 05	5 95	5 85		2 90		35 75
Mount Moriah	Young Woman's Auxiliary	Miss Margaret M. Lane, Auburn	15							
Mount Moriah	Sunbeams	Mrs. Della Daughtry, Clayton, R. 3	22		2 40					3 26
Mount Moriah	Royal Ambassador	Mrs. J. J. Lane, Auburn	12	8 74		2 29		3 23		14 26
Mount Moriah	Girls Auxiliary			1 20		1 21				7 50
Pine Level	Woman's Missionary Society	Mrs. Mary Oliver, Pine Level	13	7 30	9 70			50		17 50
Pisgah	Woman's Missionary Society	Mrs. J. A. Smith, Smithfield, R. 1	15	9 20	5 55	1 30		1 20		9 10
Selma	Woman's Missionary Society	Mrs. C. E. Stevens, Selma	25	9 25	1 10	11 60		2 65	1 00	33 15
Shiloh	Woman's Missionary Society	Mrs. Annie Wyatt, Clayton, R.	13	54 51	2 25	2 20		1 50		12 25
Smithfield	Woman's Missionary Society	Mrs. J. E. Lanier, Smithfield	23	54 51	30 80	31 65		13 35	12 50	142 81
Smithfield	Girls Auxiliary	Miss Pearl Stancil, Smithfield	12	4 95		3 62		1 60		10 17
Smithfield	Sunbeams	Miss Lillie Bell Johnson, Smithfield		8 50		5 00		1 50	1 00	15 75
Wendell	Woman's Missionary Society	Mrs. E. V. Richardson, Wendell		3 00	18 20	22 14		4 15		47 49
Wendell	Sunbeams	Mrs. R. R. Smithwick, Wendell		3 32	7 00	2 08			1 71	14 11
Benson	Woman's Missionary Society	Mrs. W. G. Parrish, Benson	22	8 15	7 25	7 56		3 00	1 70	27 66
Total				281 45	194 47	255 43		66 64	47 13	866 67

Churches.	State Missions.	Home Missions.	Foreign Missions.	Sunday School Missions.	Orphanage.	Christian Education.	Ministerial Relief.	Building Fund.	Minute Fund.	Total.
Antioch	$ 22 50	$ 5 00	$ 5 00	$ 2 50	$ 5 00	$ 5 00	$ 2 50	$ 5 00	$ 2 50	$ 55 00
Bailey	12 50	3 50	5 00	1 00	5 00	4 00	2 50	6 50	1 50	41 50
Baptist Center	10 00	5 00	5 00	1 00	5 00	5 00	2 50	5 00	1 50	40 00
Beaty Chapel	7 50	2 50	2 50	1 00	2 50	5 00	1 50	4 00	1 00	27 50
Benson	75 00	10 00	15 00	2 50	20 00	10 00	5 00	15 00	2 50	155 00
Benson's Grove	5 00	2 50	2 50	1 00	2 50	2 00	1 00	4 00	1 00	21 50
Bethany	10 00	5 00	5 00	1 00	4 00	4 00	1 50	5 00	1 00	36 50
Bethel	5 00	2 50	2 50	1 00	2 50	2 50	1 00	2 50	1 00	20 50
Bethesda	45 00	5 00	7 50	2 50	15 00	10 00	5 00	5 00	2 50	97 50
Blackman's Grove	22 50	5 00	5 00	1 50	5 00	7 50	2 00	5 00	1 50	55 00
Calvary	5 00	1 50	1 50	50	1 50	2 50	1 50	2 50	1 00	17 50
Canaan	5 00	1 50	1 50	50	1 50	2 50	1 50	2 50	1 00	17 50
Carter's Chapel	10 00	2 50	2 50	1 00	2 50	5 00	2 00	5 00	1 50	32 00
Clayton	275 00	75 00	75 00	5 00	100 00	65 00	20 00	50 00	5 00	670 00
Clyde's Chapel	20 00	5 00	7 50	2 50	4 00	6 00	2 50	12 50	1 50	61 50
Corinth	13 00	2 50	2 50	1 00	5 00	5 00	2 50	5 00	1 50	38 00
Four Oaks	20 00	5 00	5 00	2 50	5 00	8 50	4 00	10 00	1 50	61 50
Hephzibah	5 50	1 00	1 00	50	1 00	2 50	1 00	2 50	1 00	16 00
Hood's Grove	7 50	2 50	2 50	1 00	2 50	5 00	2 50	5 00	1 00	29 50
Kenly	15 00	5 00	5 00	2 50	5 00	5 00	2 50	5 00	1 50	46 50
Lee's Chapel	25 00	7 50	7 50	3 00	5 00	7 00	5 00	5 00	2 50	67 50
Live Oak	5 00	1 00	1 00	50	2 50	2 50	1 00	2 50	1 00	17 00
Micro	12 50	2 50	2 50	1 00	2 50	5 00	1 50	2 50	1 00	31 00
Middlesex	20 00	5 00	5 00	1 00	5 00	5 00	2 50	12 50	1 50	57 50
Mouht Moriah	66 00	30 00	50 00	7 00	35 00	25 00	10 00	25 00	3 50	251 50
New Bethel	30 00	7 50	7 50	1 00	15 00	10 00	5 50	15 00	2 50	94 00
Noble's Chapel	15 00	2 50	5 00	1 00	5 00	10 00	2 50	5 00	1 50	47 50
Oliver's Grove	5 00	1 00	1 00	50	1 00	2 50	1 00	2 50	1 00	15 50
Parrish Memorial	10 00	2 50	2 50	1 00	2 50	5 00	2 50	5 00	1 00	32 00
Pauline	7 50	2 50	2 50	1 00	2 50	5 00	2 50	5 00	1 00	29 50
Pine Level	20 00	5 00	5 00	1 00	5 00	5 00	5 00	10 00	1 50	52 50
Pinkney	5 00	2 50	2 50	1 00	2 50	2 50	1 50	1 50	1 00	20 00
Pisgah	22 50	5 00	5 00	1 00	5 00	10 00	2 00	10 00	2 00	62 50
Princeton	20 00	2 50	2 50	1 00	2 50	5 00	2 50	5 00	1 50	42 50
Sardis	20 00	5 00	5 00	1 00	2 50	5 00	2 50	5 00	1 50	47 50
Selma	75 00	20 00	30 00	2 50	25 00	25 00	10 00	20 00	3 50	211 00
Shiloh	25 00	5 00	5 00	1 00	5 00	10 00	2 50	5 00	1 50	60 00
Smithfield	160 00	40 00	50 00	5 00	25 00	25 00	10 00	25 00	3 50	343 50
Thanksgiving	15 00	2 50	2 50	1 00	2 50	7 50	2 50	5 00	1 50	40 00
Trinity	7 50	2 00	2 00	1 00	2 00	2 50	1 00	2 50	1 00	21 50
Wendell	40 00	20 00	25 00	5 00	25 00	25 00	5 00	25 00	3 50	173 50
White Oak	25 00	7 50	7 50	2 50	10 00	15 00	5 00	5 00	2 50	80 00
Wilson's Mills	20 00	2 50	5 00	1 00	5 00	5 00	2 50	10 00	1 50	52 50
Burnell*	4 00	1 00	1 00	1 50	1 00	2 00	1 00	3 00	50	15 00
Total	1,254 00	329 50	391 50	80 00	388 50	383 50	151 00	370 00	75 50	3,404 50

*Arm of Pisgah.

M NUTES

OF THE

Fourteenth Annual Session

OF THE

JOHNSTON COUNTY

BAPTIST ASSOCIATION,

HELD WITH

BENSON BAPTIST CHURCH,

OCTOBER 25th, 26th and 27th, 1916.

The next session will be held with Corinth Baptist Church, beginning on Wednesday after the fourth Sunday in October, 1917.
To preach Introductory sermon—R. M. VonMiller; Alternate, A. C. Hamby.

MINUTES

OF THE

Fourteenth Annual Session

OF THE

JOHNSTON COUNTY

BAPTIST ASSOCIATION,

HELD WITH

BENSON BAPTIST CHURCH,

OCTOBER 25th, 26th and 27th, 1916.

The next session will be held with Corinth Baptist Church, beginning on Wednesday after the fourth Sunday in October, 1917.

To preach Introductory sermon—R. M. VonMiller; Alternate, A. C. Hamby.

Goldsboro, N. C.
Nash Bros., Printers and Binders,
1917.

OFFICERS:

Moderator—R. H. Gower..................................Clayton, N. C.
Vice-Moderator—J. J. Lane ....Auburn, N. C.
Clerk and Treasurer—John E. Lanier.................Smithfield, N. C.
Auditor—J. L. Hall....................................Benson, N. C.

EXECUTIVE COMMITTEE.

J. M. Beaty, Chairman................................Smithfield, N. C
J. B. Creech...Four Oaks, N. C.
J. T. Holt..Wilson's Mills, N. C.
J. F. Pool...Clayton, N. C.
C. I. Godwin...Pine Level, N. C.

DELEGATES AND BOARD MEMBERS.

Delegates to Baptist State Convention—C. E. Stevens, R. A. Bain, and J. M. Turley.
Delegate to Southern Baptist Convention—Judge F. H. Brooks.
Member of State Board of Missions—John E. Lanier.

LIST OF MINISTERS.

H. F. Brinson.......................................Smithfield.
J. M. Duncan..Benson.
A. C. Hamby...Clayton.
R. L. Hocutt,.......................................Wendell, R. 1
C. A. Jenkins.......................................Clayton.
John E. Lanier......................................Smithfield.
A. C. McCall..Wake Forest.
G. T. Mills...Apex.
A. A. Pippin..Wakefield.
W. D. Pridgen.......................................Micro.
R. L. Smith...Four Oaks.
J. W. Smith...Wilson's Mills.
C. E. Stevens.......................................Selma.
C. H. Stevens.......................................Wake Forest.
W. D. Stancil.......................................Kenly.
R. M. VonMiller.....................................Four Oaks.
W. H. Wall..Middlesex.

Benson, N. C., October 25, 1916.

The fourteenth annual session of the Johnston County Baptist Association met with the Benson Baptist Church. The session was opened at ten thirty o'clock by devotional service conducted by the Pastor Rev. J. M. Duncan.

Bro. H. F. Brinson, of Smithfield, preached the introductory sermon. He used as his subject: The Brotherhood of Man.

Following the sermon the Moderator Bro. R. H. Gower called the body to order for the purpose of organization and work.

The following committee was announced.

Credentials and Enrollment—Brethren J. F. Pool, B. Godwin and J. M. Duncan.

The following delegates were enrolled.

Antioch—A. J. Batten, Johnnie Brannan, G. R. Whitley, Joseph H. Hales and J. M. Maden.

Bailey—J. P. Underwood and J. W. B. Finch.

Baptist Center—J. C. Hardee, J. L. Talton, D. A. Boone and Clifford Austin.

Beaty Chapel—N. M. Eason.

Benson—S. F. Ivey, J. L. Hall and Alonzo Parrish.

Benson's Grove—R. L. Smith and D. D. Medlin.

Bethany—Moses Creech and Julian Creech.

Bethel—Miss Bessie Bell.

Bethesda—J. W. Smith, G. A. Smith and L. H. Johnson.

Blackman's Grove—F. P. Wood and Nagah Wood.

Calvary—J. K. Hudson.

Canaan—A. W. Bizzell and R. H. Hudson.

Carter's Chapel—Jasper Starling and Martin Thorn.

Clayton—A. C. Hamby, Mrs. G. M. Turley, J. D. Smith and C. W. Carter.

Clyde's Chapel—

Corinth—W. A. Mitchel, H. B. Andrews and S. T. Price.

Four Oaks—R. M. VonMiller, R. A. Bain, W. A. Massengill, and J. B. Creech.

Hephzibah—J. M. Braswell, W. G. Creech, and J. F. Earp.

Hood's Grove—E. T. Lee, Parlie Hudson, L. Eldridge, J. C. Wood.

Kenly—Mrs. J. H. Renfro, Jr., Mrs. C. E. Huff and Mrs. Pittman.

Lee's Chapel—J. B. Mecome, J. C. Overman, A. G. Lewis, and Waylan Estridge.

Live Oak—Thomas Batten.

Micro—W. D. Pridgen, Odessa Batten, J. W. C. L. Batten, and J. F. Batten.

Middlesex—W. H. Wall.

Mount Moriah—J. J. Lane, Icana Pool, and J. F. Pool.

New Bethel—

Noble's Chapel—

Parrish Memorial—J. M. Watson, N. I. Parrish, Frank Batten and Miss Minnie Batten.

Pauline—W. B. Joyner.

Pine Level—C. I. Godwin, J. F. Thompson, W. M. Gurley and Floyd Price.

Pisgah—P. H. Higgins, J. A. Smith, Percy Whitley, and W. D. Johnson.

Princeton—

Sardis—

Selma—C. W. Stallings, L. H. Lewis, Norwood Creech, C. E. Stevens, and Mrs. C. E. Stevens.

Shiloh—Claude Stephenson, S. H. Averitt, and Ottis Coats.

Smithfield—H. F. Brinson, J. M. Beaty, F. H. Brooks.

Thanksgiving—

Trinity—J. L. Johnson, and J. M. Lawhon.

Wendell—George H. Wright, and W. H. Rhodes.

White Oak—Elbert Green.

Wilson's Mills—J. T. Holt.

Burnell—J. S. Johnson.

The following visiting brethren were recognized by the Moderator—J. S. Farmer, Business Manager of the Biblical Recorder; Dr. R. T. Vann, Secretary of Christian Education; W. N. Johnson, Secretary of State Board of Missions; F. B. Hamrick, Orphanage Treasurer; R. L. Gay, representative of the Anti-Saloon League.

The Moderator called the Vice-Moderator J. J. Lane to the Chair for the election of officers for the ensuing year. The following officers were elected: Moderator, R. H. Gower; Vice-Moderator, J. J. Lane; Clerk and Treasurer, J. E. Lanier; Auditor, J. L. Hall.

The new pastors in the Association were recognized by the Moderator and by the body. After which the session adjourned for the noon hour.

Benediction by W. D. Pridgen.

WEDNESDAY AFTERNOON.

The session was opened with song and prayer. The Moderator called the body to order and announced the following committees.

Finance Committee-Chairman J. W. Smith, C. I. Godwin and Parley Hudson.

Committee on Biblical Recorder—J. J. Lane, Berry Godwin and A. L. Batten.

Committee on Sunday Schools—Judge F. H. Brooks, W. A. Mitchel and Mrs. J. H. Renfrow, Jr.

The regular order of business was taken up and J. J. Lane read the report on The Biblical Recorder.

REPORT ON BIBLICAL RECORDER.

The efficiency of a democracy depends upon the intelligence of its units. The Biblical Recorder, the organ of our State Convention, is the chief source of intelligence in our Baptist democracy here in North Carolina. Hence, the importance of its free and wide circulation amongst us. We should all become subscribers to and readers of our denominational paper.

Respectfully submitted,

J. J. LANE,
A. L. BATTON,
B. GODWIN,   Committee.

On motion to adopt, the report was discussed by J. J. Lane and J. S. Farmer, and adopted.

Bro. J. M. Beatty made a motion to take up miscellaneous business for the purpose of deciding what method we, as an Association, shall follow in raising our funds for the various objects of the Convention and Association. After being discussed by a number of the brethren, the apportionment plan was adopted, allowing those churches who had rather pledge for themselves the privilege of handing their pledges to the Executive Committee by December the first.

The report on Sunday Schools was deferred until a later session as Judge Brooks was not present who was to write the report.

By a motion passed the Executive Committee was instructed to assist any delegates having funds that should go to Walters Durham, our Convention Treasurer, and F. B. Hamrick, our Orphanage Treasurer, in sending same to the respective treasurers.

The chair appointed S. H. Averitt, W. D. Pridgen and Moses Creech as Committee on Orphanage.

Committee on Foreign Missions—W. H. Wall, R. M. VonMiller and N. M. Eason.

There being no further business the session adjourned until 7:30 for the evening session.

WEDNESDAY EVENING SESSION.

The session opened with devotional service conducted by Rev. R. L. Smith. After which the body was called to order by Vice-Moderator J. J. Lane. The report on Orphanage was read by S. H. Averitt.

REPORT ON ORPHANAGE.

We consider it a waste of time to try to show to the Baptists of North Carolina, and especially to the Johnston County Association, that the Orphanage is a good institution and worthy of our support, therefore, we will take time and space only to call attention briefly to some of the needs of our great institution. There are at Thomasville 450 children; at the Kennedy Home 50 children. The daily cost for the support of a child is 30 cents, the annual cost $109.09. The daily cost for the support of 500 children is $150 and the yearly cost for the support of 500 children is $54,545.00; so large an amount as this cannot be raised annually by spasmodic giving, hence we urge that every church and Sunday school in this Association make their contributions to the Orphanage once a month and that every Sunday school take a club of Charity and Children (the best Orphanage paper in the South) and furthermore, that on or about Thanksgiving day give the proceeds of one day's work to the Orphanage for without an extra effort on Thanksgiving day (in addition to our monthly contributions) the Orphanage cannot meet its present debt of about $20,000.00. The Orphanage has grown faster than our people (as a whole) are aware, therefore the debt has gradually grown bigger and bigger but we may as well face the facts and figures and put forth heroic effort to wipe out this debt and place the Orphanage on the "Pay as you go" plan and by adopting the suggestion set forth in this report (which is not by any means original with writer) we can keep it there.

Respectfully submitted,

S. H. AVERITT, Committee.

On motion to adopt, the report was discussed by S. H. Averitt and F. B. Hamrick. Report was adopted.

Report on Foreign Missions was presented by W. H. Wall.

REPORT ON FOREIGN MISSIONS.

The Foreign Mission Board of the Southern Baptist Convention, located at Richmond, Virginia, in its last report tells of a year of triumphant success both at home and abroad. The total contributions for the year, including the amount raised on the debt and on the Judson Centennial Fund, was $806,729. The only drawback on the year's work was the fact that the contributions for the current support amounting to $518,323, left a deficit which, combined with the old debt, made a total indebtedness of $180,000. During the meeting of the Convention in Asheville a great movement was started for the purpose of paying off this heavy indebtedness, and many of our brethren and sisters have made beautiful and joyful responses to this appeal.

The campaign to raise the Judson Centennial Fund of $1,250,000 has been successful. There is need that our pastors encourage the prompt collection of the subscriptions to this fund.

During the year there have been 6,471 converts baptized and 77 churches instituted. Our foreign missionaries now number 315, of whom 133 are men and 182 women. The membership of our mission churches is now 42,632 organized into 459 churches, 95 of which are self-supporting. The native Christians contributed $129,561.00 to the work in their midst. We have 462 Sunday schools which report 10,490 scholars. There are 453 mission schools with 13,531 students. Of these mission schools six are Women's Bible Training Schools, with 200 students, and ten are Theological Training Schools, with 191 students. We have now 19 medical missionaries, 9 hospitals, and 10 dispensaries. Our medical missionaries treated 74,866 patients last year.

Attention should be called to the great strides which the native churches are taking toward self-support, self-government and self-propagation. One field will serve to illustrate this. In Brazil the per capita gifts for all objects is $5.72. Our Brazilian Baptists have their own Home and Foreign Mission Boards. Amongst our members in foreign lands there are many tithers. There are indeed churches which make tithing a test of fellowship. Many churches in the foreign fields are building their own houses of worship, paying the salaries of their pastors and contributing to the support of missionary work in their own lands and elsewhere. Native workers are being trained, and as we look into the near and far future the outlook is indeed bright.

Like everything that grows, our Foreign Mission work has increasing necessities. Our success has carried us into a situation from which there is no turning back and which lays new claims upon us. We have tasks which we can neither turn loose nor turn over to others. To turn loose means to ignore opportunities, forsake converts and churches or turn them over to other denominations. We ought not to do either. Perhaps there is nothing connected with Foreign Missions so imperfectly understood by the masses of our people as this of the unescapable necessities of the work. Conditions at home may be pieced out by other means, and in emergencies matters can be deferred for the time being, but such is not the case on the foreign fields where foreign missionary salaries and other items have to be met.

We would urge that our churches make use of the many free tracts which can be secured from the Foreign Mission Board.

The Convention at Asheville ordered the consolidation of the Foreign Mission Journal and the Home Field into one Magazine to be published by the Sunday School Board at Nashville. This consolidated magazine will still be the organ through which the Board and its missionaries will be able to speak most effectively to the churches at home. It is of very great importance that all the churches take steps immediately looking to a large circulation of this magazine.

In addition to the mass of material in tract form, the Educational Department of the Foreign Mission Board calls special attention to the mission study class method. We would urge that a larger number of classes be organized to study the latest Foreign Mission Board report which will be put into text-book form, and can be secured from the Educational Department of the Foreign Mission Board, Richmond, Virginia. This report is a valuable study on our own foreign mission work. We wish that a large number of our men and young people would study the report in mission study classes or discussion groups, and that the women would see to it that special classes are organized for the men and young people, or that these be invited to the sessions of the women's classes.

In view of the imperative need of re-enforcement on all our foreign fields and the very great importance of meeting the current support of this work this year and avoiding another debt, we recommend that this association divide among the churches on an equitable basis the apportionment for this year, and earnestly urge the churches to undertake to raise the amounts asked of them before April 30, 1917. The amount asked of this State is $55,000, of which this Association is asked to give $————

In order to save the large amount of interest paid out on borrowed money, we earnestly suggest that our churches send in their contributions regularly each month through the regular channels. We recommend the Every Member Canvass and Systematic Giving as the Biblical plan for contributing to foreign missions.

In a thousand ways God is calling upon Southern Baptists to make a great advance in Foreign Mission work. We would plead that sacrificial effort and constant prayer for the success of this year be practiced in all the churches.

We would close this report as we began it, by ascribing praise to God who has "crowned the year with His goodness." We should be profoundly grateful for the unity that prevails throughout our ranks. Let us put Christ first in our lives, in our thoughts, in our affections, in our efforts, and make His glory the chief desire of our hearts.

What marvelous opportunities present themselves to us to-day. What a privilege it is to live in this time of the world's history.

We in this highly favored land are enjoying the blessings of peace, while so much of the world is rent and torn by war. With what consuming earnestness we should address our selves to the mighty task of bringing in the reign of the Prince of Peace, of hastening the fulfillment of that glorious prophecy, "That at the name of Jesus every knee should bow, of things in heaven, and things in earth, and things under the earth; and that every tongue should confess that Jesus Christ is Lord, to the glory of God the Father."

Respectfully submitted,

W. H. WALL, Chairman.

On a motion to adopt, the question was discussed by Rev. W. H. Wall, Rev. R. M. VonMiller and Dr. R. T. Vann, and adopted.

The report on Sunday Schools which was deferred at the afternoon session was taken up and report read by Judge F. H. Brooks.

REPORT ON SUNDAY SCHOOLS.

According to reports made to our last Association at Clayton, there were forty Baptist Sunday Schools in the Johnston County Baptist Association, with a total enrollment of 4295, of this number only 2010 are church members. There were five Sunday Schools not reporting number of church members affiliating. I secured information from two, and estimated other three—Benson's Grove at 40, (I have since learned there were only 7 and this Sunday School is now closed) Wendell 200 and Burnell 30. This would leave 2285 Sunday School scholars who are not church members. Total Church membership in Association 4675, according to said report, which shows that there are 2665 church members in our Association who are not enlisted in the great work of the Sunday School.

According to reports to last Association there were Sunday Schools run in connection with all churches except four—Bethel, Calvary, Hood's Grove and Live Oak. All but nine of the Sunday Schools are run twelve months in the year. Twenty-nine gave nothing to orphanage and twenty-two gave nothing to Missions during year 1915-1916, according to said reports.

I thought if not out of place to bring these statistics to attention of the Association in this report in order that we might discuss ways and means to help better conditions in our Sunday Schools. It is true that these statistics can be found in the minutes of our last Association, but I fear but few take time to study the table published and collate the facts and figures. I confess that I was just a little surprised when I began writing this report and found the facts that exist, although I had been studying Sunday School work and going around the county making talks on the subject. This is a matter for serious consideration and strenuous action. May God open our eyes to the situation that exists, and impress upon the brethren and sisters of the churches the great task of interesting the 2665 church members in the Sunday School work, and leading the 2285 Sunday School scholars into the church.

In my travels around the Association, I find that the lack of trained leaders and teachers the greatest draw-back to the accomplishment of the greatest good in the Sunday Schools. There are scores of self-sacrificing, God-fearing humble men and women engaged in the Sunday School work, who are doing the best they know-how, and I wouldn't say a thing to discourage them or discount their work, but if we were all better equipped we could accomplish so much more. If we could induce the officers and teachers to take up the normal training course, it would mean so much for the betterment of our

Sunday School work. Let the pastors of the churches take up this matter and lead in the organization of these study courses and in the work.

We recommend that a Standing Committee be annually named by this Association to be known as "Sunday School Organization and Promotion Committee," whose business it shall be to look after Sunday School work in the Association. F. H. BROOKS, for Committee.

Amendment: That we use one of our fifth Sundays as a Sunday School Convention Rally.

On motion to adopt, the report was discussed by Judge Brooks and adopted.

Having finished all the business of the evening session; adjourned until 9:30 Thursday morning.

THURSDAY MORNING SESSION.

At 9:30 the session was opened with devotional services led by W. D. Pridgen. After which the Vice-Moderator called the body to order, and announced the following committees:

Committee on State Missions.—J. E. Lanier, J. T. Holt and W. D. Johnson.

Permanent Sunday School Committee—Judge F. H. Brooks, J. F. Pool and J. T. Holt.

Committee on place and preacher of our next session—J. F. Pool, W. H. Wall and J. B. Creech.

The report of the Executive Committee was read by J. M. Beaty, and without discussion, on motion it was adopted.

REPORT OF EXECUTIVE COMMITTEE.

Your Executive Committee makes their report as follows: Rev. W. H. Wall has preached at Middlesex, Bailey and Nobles Chapel churches and at Sims depot at a salary from the State Mission Board of $325.00. Rev. R. M. VonMiller has had charge of Kenly, Bethel, Four Oaks, Burnell, Oliver's Grove, Blackman's Grove and Pauline churches and Stewart school house at a salary of $450.00. Rev. W. D. Pridgen has preached at Carter's Chapel, Micro, Pinkney and Beaty Chapel churches at $400.00 salary. Rev. J. V. Teague served Thanksgiving, salary $50.00. Rev. J. M. Duncan preached at Parrish Memorial and Princeton at a salary of $200.00. Rev. R. L. Smith has preached at Benson's Grove, Hood's Grove, Trinity and Calvary churches, salary $350.00. Rev. C. E. Stevens served as pastor at Sardis and Hephzibah churches, salary $150.00. Rev. C. H. Stevens has preached at Canaan, salary $100.00. At most of these churches progress has been made and we hope soon that several other points will become self-sustaining so that you may take up other points which need to be worked. We are glad to report that our churches are showing increased interest in State Missions. We urge our churches to make their contributions to State Missions as large as possible that we may not have to call on the State Board of Missions for so much money.

J. M. BEATY,
J. J. LANE,
J. B. CREECH,
J. T. HOLT, Committee.

REPORT OF BUILDING COMMITTEE.

We are glad to report that the contributions from the churches to the church building fund last year was much larger than ever before. This enabled us to pay off all indebtedness of the committee and to repair Oliver's Grove church. Heretofore it has not been the policy of the committee to repair churches but at Oliver's Grove the house was going to ruin and the local church was not able to make the repairs by themselves. That church is now in first class condition except the painting which will be done in a short time. There are several other places where we should build churches. Our next place to help in building is at Hephzibah in Boon Hill township. This is one of the largest townships in Johnston county and we have only two organized churches in it. The house now used by Hephzibah church is a small school house which was given up by the school committee because it was too small for the school of the neighborhood. We have not enough room there for the preaching services, to say nothing of the Sunday school. We must build there or lose ground. The money contributed this year is expected to go to help build a church at Hephzibah.

> J. M. BEATY,
> J. J. LANE,
> J. B. CREECH,
> J. T. HOLT,
> Building Committee.

Report on State Missions was presented by J. E. Lanier.

REPORT ON STATE MISSIONS.

When our Lord left the world He gave the Church the one great mission that of making the gospel message known to the world. The work here in our Association is our Jerusalem, while our Judea is the State of North Carolina. As other interests are increasing so rapidly we must preserve the spiritual development of our State. Self-preservation is the first law of Grace as well as of nature. The conditions in our State are such as to demand that we do our best for State Missions at the present time.

Because of the past achievements in our State Mission work the question is often asked Why continue this phase of our work? By no means has the demands for State Mission work diminished because of past victories.

The rapid material growth which our State is experiencing opens new doors and furnishes greater opportunities for religious achievements. In order that we may supply their demands it is necessary that our Christian people bend their God-given energies to this work and by the contribution of their prayers and their means with which He has blessed them, and surrender themselves as instruments in His hands for the consummation of His plans. We have reached a crisis in our State Mission work. We may make it a crisis of growth or of decadence. We have reached our Kadeshbarnea. Let us go up and possess the land and not turn back for a forty-years wandering in the wilderness. May the Great Head of the Church inspire us to put forth our noblest efforts to the end that North Carolina may be taken for Christ.

In view of the facts that the needs in all sections of the state are great and that the State Mission Board is putting about two dollars to our one in the work here in our own Associational territory, and also for self-respect and self-preservation, we your committee recommend:

1. That all our churches give their hearty co-operation to the work of our Executive Committee and State Board of Missions.

2. That all our churches increase their offerings to State Missions.

3. That all our mission churches increase their own pastor's support and in this way increase the apportionments from the Board.

4. That the Executive Committee investigate the mission points and if possible launch some of them out as self-supporting churches. And that the committee comply with the plans of work suggested by our Secretary and State Board of Missions.   Respectfully submitted,

> J. E. LANIER,
> J. T. HOLT,
> W. D. JOHNSON,
> Committee.

By a motion to adopt, it was discussed by Dr. W. N. Johnson. The missionaries of the board in our Association gave an account of their work for the year. The report was adopted.

By a special order of business Dr. R. T. Vann discussed Christian Education. He presented the following report, which was adopted.

REPORT ON EDUCATION.

The Board of Education of the Baptist State Convention has for its object not only the maintenance of the young men preparing for the ministry at Wake Forest and the Seminary, but also of young women at our colleges preparing for mission work, and also the promotion of Christian education in general for all our young people.

In our Baptist school system at present there are fourteen high schools, Wake Forest for young men, and Meredith and Chowan Colleges for young women. These institutions represent a money value of a million and a half dollars; they enrolled last year 3,788 students.

The teaching and example of our divine master, the evident plan of God as revealed in nature, the growing demand for trained workers in all secular employment, the examples of other great denominations, the crying needs of our own, all these seriously impress the necessity of religious training for our people, and calls us loudly to lose no time in going about it.

In view of the facts stated, and the other fundamental fact, namely, that consecration and training lie at the basis of every enterprise now engaging the efforts of our denomination, the Board of Education is calling upon the churches to raise this year for Christian Education $20,000.00, or two-fifths as much as they raise for state missions. Since the amount raised for missions is spent in supporting the missionaries, surely it is not unreasonable to spend two-fifths as much in preparing missionaries for their work. And since eighty-three per cent of all our ministers and ninety-one per cent of our missionaries, have been trained in Christian schools, it would seem that if those schools should die every mission board would soon have to go out of business. And let it be widely known and ever remembered that these schools must die unless our people come to their support.

Your committee recommends, therefore, that our association approve the plan of the convention for promoting general education.

Second, that we approve the effort of the Board of Education to raise $20,000.00 this year for education, or two fifths as much as we raise for state missions.

Third, that the Association endeavors to raise among the churches during the year $———, and request each of the churches to assume its proportional part of this amount, and that either by pledges or apportionment arrangements be made to effectuate this plan with the churches.

Fourth, that as long as the work of our schools equals that of the State schools or those of other denominations we earnestly urge our people to patronize their own.

The body then took recess for one hour.

THURSDAY AFTERNOON.

The afternoon session was opened with song and prayer.

After which the Vice-Moderator called the body to order. Miscellaneous business was taken up. The committee on place and preacher for the next session of the Association reported Corinth as the place and Rev. R. M. Von-Miller as preacher, Alternate, Rev. A. C. Hamby.

On motion the report was adopted.

Rev. J. M. Duncan read some resolutions presented by the Anti-Saloon League. By a motion the Association approved the resolutions. Bro. R. L. Gay was granted the privilege to speak to the resolutions.

Bro. A. C. Hamby made a motion that the Clerk have the minutes printed and distributed and that the Clerk be given $20.00 for his services.

The report on Woman's Work was read by Rev. C. E. Stevens. On motion to adopt, the question was debated by C. E. Stevens, R. M. VonMiller. Report was adopted.

REPORT ON WOMAN'S WORK.

The organization of the Woman's Missionary Union in Richmond in 1888 was one of the greatest blessings that has ever come to the Baptist cause of the world. All honor to our Southern women who have long since discovered the manner of living up to the gospel standard, and never forget the one purpose of the Union, or showing the world there is but one thing—the love of Christ. I am glad that we have lived to see the day in which woman is being recognized, and is given the place in life she rightfully owns. The greatest compliment Christ ever paid any one he paid it to woman when he said "She hath done what she could." Why should she not have a part in the evangelization of the world, for she was last at the Cross and first at the Sepulchre? The work that the women have accomplished in those twenty-eight years is marvelous. They have clearly proven to us that "in unity there is strength." We must acknowledge that this is where the secret of their success lies, for the more we study their work we find that they insist in unity in all things. Their thoroughness in organization should be an example to us, and make the brethren ashamed of the careless and indifferent way in which they conduct the Master's business.

The women plan their work and work their plans, they have system in everything. The W. M. U. is the only organization that pays regularly each month for definite features of our denominational work. They are systematic in their study, having well organized mission study classes, and well planned programs for their monthly meetings. They are regular and generous in their gifts, every year they aim high and often go beyond their goal, making an increase up to the present time of more than $1,000 annually in North Carolina, for all objects. Twenty-eight years ago the amount contributed was only $500.80. Last year they gave the enormous amount of $52,959.41. In Johnston County Association the women alone gave last year $866.67.

What the women have done in a financial way is only a secondary matter as compared with the spiritual and the sacred influences which have accompanied their labors. The Training School which is owned entirely by the Union has sent out numbers of fine young women who have accomplished much in the evangelization of our Home and Foreign lands.

Let us heed Paul's admonition and "help these women which labor in the gospel with us." It will be a great day for our Southern Baptist forces when we have a Woman's Missionary Society in every Baptist Church.

Respectfully submitted, C. E. STEVENS.

Brother J. M. Beaty made a motion that Miscellaneous business be taken up. He then presented the Benson church debt for which an offering was made amounting to $83.65.

The committee to name the delegates to the Baptist State Convention, and to the Southern Baptist Convention, and nominate the Executive Committee and members of State Board of Missions made the following report.

Delegates to Baptist State Convention—Brethren C. T. Stevens, R. A. Bain and J. M. Turley.

Delegate to Southern Baptist Convention—F. H. Brooks.

Members of Executive Board—Brethren J. M. Beaty, Chairman, J. T. Holt, J. B. Creech, J. F. Pool and C. I. Godwin.

Member of State Board of Missions—J. E. Lanier.

Bro. A. C. Hamby made a motion that the delegates report the Benson church debt to their churches, and forward such amounts as may be raised to Bro. J. L. Hall, Benson, N. C.

On a motion by Rev. R. M. VonMiller, the Clerk was instructed to purchase a chart for the use of the Association.

The regular order of business was taken up and Rev. R. L. Smith read the report on Ministerial Relief.

REPORT ON MINISTERIAL RELIEF.

Many years ago some of our people learned that our ministers are the poorest paid men that we·have.· Of course Baptist people do not realize that about $25.00 per month is the average salary of a Baptist preacher. He is expected to go whenever needed, whatever the expense (to himself). He must be away from home most of the time in summer, making it almost impossible for him to engage profitably in any money making business. With these conditions he can hardly lay by anything for old age.·

The Ministerial Relief Board is aiding about 37 ministers and widows of ministers. These live with their kindred or friends. The Board receives about $4,000 or $5,000 a year for this work. Half of this goes into a sinking fund, which it is hoped, will soon be large enough that the interest thereon will support those who receive aid.

These noble men and women have put the best of their lives into this work that is as much ours as theirs, and we must not forget these loyal soldiers who carried the banner into the thicket of the fight.

Respectfully submitted,   R. L. SMITH.

On a motion to adopt the report was discussed by R. L. Smith and adopted.

Rev. A. C. Hamby made a motion, which was carried, to amend section six of the Constitution.

The following resolution was presented:

Resolved, That Article six of the Constitution be amended by striking out the words, "with the close of the month previous to the one in which the Association is held." And in their stead insert the words, "with the last Sunday previous to the session of the Association."   R. M. VonMILLER.

Brother VonMiller made a motion that the programme committee be instructed to provide a place on the programme for B. Y. P. U. work. The motion was carried.

The body then adjourned until the evening session.

THURSDAY EVENING SESSION.

Devotional exercises were conducted by Rev. R. M. VonMiller.

Under the head of miscellaneous business a new church "Lizzie Chapel,", asked for membership into the Association by presenting the following letter:

LETTER TO THE ASSOCIATION.

On Monday night, October 23rd, 1916, a meeting was arranged at the Lizzie Chapel, Selma, N. C., for the purpose of organizing a Missionary Baptist church. The Presbytery consisted of Rev. T. J. Hood as Moderator and Rev. C. E. Stevens, Secretary. There were eighteen who presented themselves to become members of the new church.

The body accepted the New Hampshire Declaration of Faith, and the New Testament as their creed. This body petitions the Johnston County Baptist Association for admittance as a church.

REV. T. J. HOOD, Moderator.
REV. C. E. STEVENS, Secretary.

Miss Sarah Creech was elected church clerk.

The following committee was appointed to investigate the organization and doctrines of the church: Brethren H. F. Brinson, W. D. Pridgen and A. C. Hamby.

The chair appointed Brethren C. W. Stallings and Geo. F. Moore as a committee to make a digest of the church letters.

SPECIAL REPRESENTATIVES.

On motion by Rev. H. F. Brinson the following representatives were appointed:

Biblical Recorder—T. J. Lassiter, Smithfield, N. C., and J. B. Creech, Four Oaks, N. C.

B. Y. P. U. Work—C. W. Carter, Clayton, N. C., and E. H. Lyles, Clayton, N. C.

Foreign Missions—J. F. Wall, Benson, N. C., and T. T. Lanier, Benson, N. C.

Home Missions—L. T. Royal, Smithfield, N. C., and C. W. Stallings, Selma N. C.

State Missions—J. M. Beaty, Smithfield, N. C.

Orphanage—S. H. Averitt, Auburn, N. C.

Sunday Schools—F. H. Brooks, Smithfield, N. C.

Christian Education—J. J. Lane, Auburn, N. C.

The report on Home Missions was read by Rev. A. C. Hamby.

REPORT ON HOME MISSIONS.

There is every evidence necessary to the belief that the United States has a Divine mission to the nations of the earth. Its location, resources, institutions, form of government and, chief of all, its tolerance and religious standards and purity of Bible doctrines point that way. Surely God is turning the eyes of the world this way. Our dealings with China, Cuba, Mexico and the Philippine Islands are sufficient evidence that our part among the nations is being carried out in good faith; That we will not exploit them for selfish ends, but seek only to help and bless. Both in Mexico and in Europe, torn by such a conflict as the world has never before known, our nation is seeking to establish that peace and goodwill which Christ brought to earth. Our sense of responsibility is tremendous, for the situation is grave indeed.

There never was a time when the untiring labors of our Home Missionaries counted for so much. Never before have they been able to accomplish so much. And never before was so much expected of them. Our nation needs every ounce of strength and every grain of gospel truth they can give. In this trying hour the nation needs to be strongly gripped by the gospel, and the places of greatest need are the places where these Missionaries of our Home Board are set to work. The immigrant forces in our country are not a negligible quantity. Their influence in government, politics and diplomacy is considerable. The one thing needful is that their influence shall be permeated by the Gospel and their efforts guided by the Spirit of the Lord. When the European war ends there will be such an influx of people from those stricken regions beyond the seas seeking a better country in which to build up their shattered fortunes, that the task of the Home Mission Boards of all denominations will be overwhelmingly great, unless in this period of immigrant cessation the Christian people hasten to prepare against that day.

The Home Mission Board is the agency through which the Baptist hosts of the South, as a body, are laboring to save the lost and to save the nation. The task is enormous. Eighteen million lost souls scattered over 1,000,000 square miles of territory. Last year 1,409 Missionaries labored in this territory under direction of the Board. They reported 43,792 baptisms and 27,-594 unrelated Baptists brought into the churches in the communities in which they lived. Out of the 220,000 baptisms reported by the 25,000 churches in the Convention last year, twenty per cent were by Home Board Missionaries. They were brought in from the mountains and plains, from cities and country districts, from Cuba and the Canal Zone. They were natives white and black, foreigners of many nationalities, Central Americans and Cubans. To do this our Missionaries proclaimed the gospel in more than 5,000 different and distinct communities.

It would require too much space in our minutes to tell adequately of the work being done in Cuba and Panama, in the cities and countryside by direct mission work, and of co-operative Missions, Evangelism, Mountain Schools, Publication and Enlistment, each a great and telling task. The Board publishes and sends free to all who ask for them, an Annual Report of its work and many admirable tracts that tell the whole story. Get them.

Respectfully submitted,　　A. C. HAMBY, Committee.

On motion to adopt it was discussed by Brethren A. C. Hamby, R. M. Von-Miller and H. F. Brinson. The Moderator called on J. E. Lanier to lead the body in a special prayer for the work. The report was adopted.

There being no further business the session adjourned until Friday morning.

FRIDAY MORNING SESSION.

The session opened with devotional service conducted by Rev. R. L. Smith. The journal up to the present session read and approved as read.

The committee on receiving Lizzie Chapel, reported that they had examined the organization and doctrines of Lizzie Chapel and found the chapel to be of the same faith as our body and recommend that it be admitted as a member of this body. The recommendation was accepted and in the absence of the delegates the Moderator extended the right hand of fellowship to the pastor Rev. C. E. Stevens and Brother Taylor who has taken interest in the organization of the church.

Bro. R. M. VonMiller presented the following resolution:

Resolved, That a collection be taken each annual session of the Association to defray the expense of printing the programs and such other stationery as is needed and postage. Brethren who are sending official mail or programs are to present bills of such to the Treasurer of the Association and he is to pay accordingly such bills as are presented.

The Temperance report was read by H. F. Brinson.

REPORT ON TEMPERANCE.

The outlook for temperance was never brighter in the history of the world. With liquor outlawed or under the ban in practically all of Europe we are making rapid strides toward national victory in America. Nineteen states are now under prohibition and six others will vote on it in a few days. There is not a single state that does not have more or less dry territory. There are fewer saloons south of the Mason and Dixon line than in the city of Chicago. In Alaska and Canada the fight is being waged with gratifying results. In 1915 the production of distilled liquor was 42,477,492 gallons less than in 1914.

But these very gratifying results together with the fact that the fight for legal prohibition has passed not only from our own but the adjoining states as well has a tendency to lessen our interest in the cause. But with the decrease already mentioned, we must remember that there were 132,134,152 gallons produced last year. Just how much of that has found and is still finding its way into the territory of the Johnston County Association we do not know. We do know, however, that hundreds of dollars are going every year to fill the coffers of the saloon or to keep the courts, prisons and asylums going to punish or provide for its victims. In the United States 80 per cent of the paupers and 90 per cent of the adult criminals are the product of the saloon. How many of these must we contribute next year to appease the greed of the great octopus which reaches its deadly tentacles into every community in our land? The liquor advocates cry loudly for personal liberty and in the same breath deny us the liberty to protect our homes against its blight. It has drawn upon the manhood of our community in spite of all that we have been able to do to prevent it.

We recognize and commend the aggressive fight our local officers and courts are making on the illicit trade but we would not forget that their success depends largely upon the attitude of the public for which the Christian people are to a great extent responsible. We shall never be free from its iron grasp so long as the mail-order house, blind tiger, winery and cider joint exists and we cannot cease the fight until national prohibition shall stop the first and an effective local government backed by a determined public sentiment the others.   Respectfully submitted,

H. F. BRINSON, for Committee.

On a motion to adopt, the report was discussed by H. F. Brinson, R. L. Gay and R. M. VonMiller. The report was adopted.

Finance Committee made the following report:

REPORT ON FINANCE.

Your finance committee have received the following amounts:

Building Fund ....$ 186.30
Minute Fund 43.50

Total ....$ 229.80

J. W. SMITH,
C. I. GODWIN,
PARLEY HUDSON,

Audited and find correct. Oct. 27, 1916.

J. L. HALL, Auditor.

The committee on a digest of the Church letters made the following report: Increase in membership this year 289.

All the churches seem to have met their apportionments for the year, except Calvary. Total gain in membership during the year 223. Present membership 4,898.

The following churches report no Sunday Schools: Benson's Grove, Bethel, Calvary, Live Oak, Nobles Chapel and Parrish Memorial.

J. E. Lanier presented the following resolution which was adopted. In view of the fact that we have to pay so much a page for the printing of our minutes, be it

Resolved, That the reports on the various subjects which are to be printed in our minutes be limited to not more than five hundred words.

The Treasurer submitted the following report which was adopted:

TREASURER'S REPORT OF THE JOHNSTON COUNTY BAPTIST ASSOCIATION.

I have received and disbursed the amounts as indicated below.

October 25, 1916.	State M ss ons.	Home M ss ons.	Fore gn M ss ons.	Sunday School M ss ons.	Orphanage.	Christian Education.	Ministerial Relief.	Building Fund.	Minute Fund.	Wake Forest Church.
Received during the year	$175.69	$34.95	$58.33	$15.35	$67.61	$64.24	$37.06	$271.74	$101.15	$52.35
Disbursements— Check to Walters Durham	38.98	4.05	28.60	.....	.....	6.66	7.26	.....	.....	52.35
Sent to F. B. Hamrick	.....	.....	.....	.....	17.15	.....	.....	.....	.....	.....
To Woodall & Peterson for work on Officer's Store	.....	.....	.....	.....	.....	.....	.....	157.02	.....	.....
Printing Minutes	.....	.....	.....	.....	.....	.....	.....	.....	35.00	.....
Clerks fee, postage and express	.....	.....	.....	.....	.....	.....	.....	.....	35.40	.....
Balance on hand.	136.71	30.90	29.73	15.35	50.46	57.58	29.80	113.82	30.75	.....

Audited October 25, 1916. W. M. IVES, Auditor.

SUPPLEMENTARY REPORT TO THE REPORT MADE BY TREASURER AT THE ASSOCIATION.

I have received and disbursed the following amounts as indicated below:

	State Missions.	Home Missions.	Foreign Missions.	Orphanage.	Sunday School Missions.	Christian Education.	Ministerial Relief.	Minute Fund.	Building Fund.
Balance on hand at the Association	$136.71	$30.90	$29.73	$50.46	$15.35	$57.58	$29.80	$20.75	$ 113.82
Received from Finance Committee								43.50	186.30
Special collection at the Association								7.50	
From W. H. Wall's field								2.50	
From R. L. Smith's field								1.00	.50
From Corinth Church								1.00	
Disbursements— Check, Walters Durham	136.71	30.90	29.73		15.35	57.58	29.80		
Check to F. B. Hamrick				50.46					
Balance in Treasury								86.25	300.62

Audited November 29th, 1916. J. L. HALL, Auditor.

There being no further business for the fourteenth annual session of the Association it adjourned with prayer led by H. F. Brinson. The body adjourned to meet with Corinth Church in its fifteenth annual session, Wednesday after the fourth Sunday in October, 1917.

NOTICE.

By order of the Association all church treasurers are requested to send all moneys collected for State Missions, Home Missions, Foreign Missions, Christian Education, and Ministerial Relief direct to Walters Durham, Raleigh, N. C. Send all money for the Orphanage to the Orphanage Treasurer, F. B. Hamrick, Thomasville, N. C.

Send Minute Fund and Church Building Fund to the Associational Treasurer, John E. Lanier, Smithfield N. C.

CONSTITUTION.

1. The Association shall be known as the Johnston County Baptist Association.

2. Its object shall be to extend the privileges of the gospel and liberal culture to all the people within its bounds and by hearty co-operation with the Baptist State Convention to help offer these privileges to all mankind in and out of its bounds, by the cordial co-operation of all the churches constituting this body.

3. It shall be composed of the pastors in active service in the Association and such delegates as shall be annually elected by the churches connected with it, each church being entitled to three delegates, unless the membership shall exceed fifty, and then an additional delegate for every twenty-five members, provided no church shall have more than eight delegates.

4. The New Hampshire Declaration of Faith shall be the summary of Divine Truth for determining questions of faith and order in this body, and the churches desiring membership in it must commit themselves to the substance of it, together with the covenant therewith submitted, and this Constitution.

5. This Association shall not have power to annul the discipline or exercise authority over any church connected with it, but it may advise with and

sever its connection with any church that neglects to preserve gospel order, or that treats with contempt the objects or advice of the Association.

6. Each church shall send to the annual meetings of the Association a letter (the blanks to be furnished by the Clerk of the Association), carefully filled as per blank suggestions, stating the full work of the church for the year ending with the Sunday previous to the meeting of the Association.

7. The Association shall foster State Missions, Home Missions, Foreign Missions, Christian Education, the Aged Ministers' Relief Board, the Thomasville Orphanage and the Sunday School Board, and each church shall be requested to contribute to the support of these objects annually.

8. Missions and Education shall have precedence in their claims upon the consideration of this body in its regular sessions.

9. Whenever a church shall fail to be represented by delegates or letter at the annual sessions of the Association inquiry shall be made for the cause and efforts shall be made to induce such church to do its duty, and the effort shall be continued till the church is recovered or dropped from the roll.

10. The officers of the Association shall be a Moderator, a Vice-Moderator, a Clerk, a Treasurer and an Auditor elected annually by ballot (or in case when only one brother is put in nomination for an office, then the vote may be by acclamation) from among its members, to serve until their successors shall have been elected, and to perform the duties of such officers, namely, the Moderator, in presiding over the meetings, or the Vice-Moderator in his absence; the Clerk in recording and preserving minutes and other papers belonging to the body; the Treasurer in receiving and disbursing funds belonging to or entrusted to the body according to its will; the Auditor to examine the Treasurer's books at each meeting of the Association and report the same before adjournment.

11. The Association shall appoint annually an Executive Committee of five (5) from its members, who shall be entrusted with the prosecution of Missions in the Association and any other work for the interest of the Master's Kingdom which may be referred to them. This committee shall, as far as possible, co-operate with the State Mission Board in supplying the destitution in our territory, and between the meetings of the Association take such actions as may seem to them advisable for the advancement of its interest. The committee shall present to the Association at its annual meeting a report of its proceedings, with the names of the missionaries supported on the field, time of service and details of their work, together with such recommendations as in the judgment of the committee the Association should follow in planning its subsequent work.

12. The annual sessions of the Association shall begin on Wednesday after the fourth Lord's day in October at such place as may be chosen, and an introductory sermon shall be delivered on the first day of the session. Representatives from ten of the churches constituting the Association shall be a quorum.

13. This Constitution may be amended at any annual session by a two-thirds vote of all the members present.

14. The proceedings of the Woman's Central Committee shall be recorded as a part of the Minutes of the Association.

BY-LAWS.

1. The daily sessions of the Association shall be opened and closed with prayer.

2. Delegates shall be recognized by letters from their churches designating them as such.

3. The Moderator shall recognize corresponding messengers or the delegates of newly received churches by extending to them his right hand.

4. The report of the Executive Board and the missionary work of the Asso-

ciation shall take precedence of all other business during the morning session of the second day of the annual session.

5. The Clerk shall record and read the proceedings when called for, superintend the publication and distribution of the Minutes, preserve a file of them, and have it present at each annual session, and deliver to his successor all papers belonging to the body.

6. Members desiring to speak shall first rise and address the Moderator, shall use the term "Brother" in speaking to each other; shall not speak on the same subject more than twice without permission, and shall observe the courtesy that becomes Christians.

7. The roll of members shall be called at least once and absentees marked.

8. Corresponding messengers and visiting brethren shall be invited to seats, with privilege of speaking, but not voting.

9. A copy of the Minutes shall be sent to the Secretary of the State Mission Board, the Secretary of the Southern Baptist Convention, the American Publication Society, 1420 Chestnut Street, Philadelphia; the Sunday School Board of the Southern Baptist Convention and the Thomasville Orphanage.

10. All questions of order not herein provided shall be decided by Kerfoot's Parliamentary Law.

WOMAN'S MISSIONARY UNION.

On Wednesday, November 8th, at 3:30 p. m., the Woman's Missionary Union of the Johnston County Baptist Association was called into session by its Superintendent, Mrs. B. A. Hocutt, of Clayton. The Union regretted the absence of our Secretary, Miss Cleve Barnes. Mrs. Walter Creech acted in her absence. Wendell had invited the Union to meet with them, and most graciously did the good people of that bustling little town perform their part. Their hospitality was unlimited, and the attending delegation, the largest in the history of the Union. From year to year enthusiasm grows and interest increases, and the programs are full and very instructive. On account of the death of a relative of Mrs. Hocutt, Mrs. C. W. Carter presided over the meeting on Thursday.

The following programs were carried out, beginning with the opening session at 3:30 Wednesday p. m.

Devotional exercises by Mrs. J. W. Sanders and Mrs. Lanier. Prayer was also offered by Mrs. Richardson. The address of welcome from the Wendell Society was given by Mrs. Wiggins, and was followed by an address of welcome by Mrs. Whitley on behalf of the Christian Church. Mrs. McLean, of the Methodist Church, tendered the use of that church to the Union, which she welcomed to the town. Mrs. Hocutt thanked the Methodists for the use of the church, and Miss Jessamine Poole responded to all of the words of welcome.

Next followed the Organization—enrollment of delegates, reading of the Minutes, etc.

A committee on Time and Place was appointed: Mrs. Johnson, Chairman, Mrs. Bailey, Mrs. J. W. Smith, and then the session was dismissed by Mrs. Stevens.

On Wednesday evening at 7:30 the program was continued by a very able address by Dr. O'Kelly, of Raleigh, and devotional exercises by Mr. M. C. Todd. The exercises by the Sunbeams were beautiful and inspiring.

On Thursday morning at 9:30 the Union again convened, and a very full and interesting program continued through the day.

Devotional exercises were conducted by Mrs. J. W. Smith and prayer offered by Mrs. D. J. Thurston. Enrollment was continued, and a splendid address followed on District Divisions and Quarterly meetings by Mrs. C. E. Stevens. The Chair then announced the following members of the Nominating Committee: Mrs. Ed. Richardson, Chairman, Mrs. C. E. Stevens, Mrs. Walter Creech.

Committee on Resolutions: Mrs. D. J. 'Thurston, Chairman, Mrs. R. H. Gower, Mrs. J. J. Lane.

A very interesting conference on Methods, led by Mrs. C. W. Carter, followed the appointment of committees. The Superintendent's report was also read by Mrs. Carter and was very interesting, but showed that there is still room for much work in the County. Out of the 44 churches in the Association there were reported 40 Societies in all—grouped as follows: 20 W. M. S., 4 R. A.'s, 1 Y. W. A., 5 G. A.'s, 9 Sunbeams. Only 29 Societies sent in an annual report, an average of 20 have sent in quarterly reports, and 15 new Societies have been organized during the year. There are 346 members in the 20 W. M. Societies and 593 members, including the Junior Societies. Of course having no record for 11 Societies. 100 Foreign Mission Journals are subscribed for in the Societies, 67 Recorders, and 76 Royal Service.

Then Mrs. W. N. Jones spoke very earnestly and interestingly on the Observance of the Seasons of Prayer.

Reports from the different Societies were handed to the Secretary, and it is hoped that they will show that we exceeded our aim of $800 for the year. We contributed last year $790.10. Upon estimating report it was found that our contribution for year amounted to $994.98.

The following subjects were then ably presented and discussed: Deepening the Spirituality, Mrs. John E. Lanier; Enlistment of New Members, Mrs. C. M. Thomas; Systematic Giving and the Use of Envelopes, Mrs. J. J. Lane; The Pastor and the Society, Mrs. W. H. Wall; The Duty of the Society to the Community, Mrs. D. J. Thurston.

After a most delightful dinner hour, devotional exercises were led by Mrs. E. V. Richardson, and followed by prayer by Mrs. Hamby.

Then Mrs. J. W. Sanders gave us much information on Installation Service, and Mrs. W. N. Jones spoke briefly on the same topic; Mrs. Jones then spoke on "How to Send in the Mission Funds."

Miss Viola Poole then conducted a devotional exercise for the young people of the Union, which was followed by a Conference on Young People's Work, led by Miss Elizabeth Briggs.

Mrs. Lane spoke ably on "When Boys Outgrow the Sunbeam Band," and Mrs. Hamby on "Keeping the Girls Interested."

Programs Worth While, and Best Time for Meeting were enthusiastically discussed by Miss Briggs, and Ideals for our Association, and our Training School were presented by Mrs. Jones in her own inimicable manner, and with her usual force.

Committee reports were then called for, and the Nominating Committee recommended a re-election of officers for the coming year.

Committee on Resolutions presented their report, and the Committee on Time and Place recommended that the next Union be held at Selma beginning on the second Wednesday of November and continuing through Thursday. All of the reports were adopted.

A motion then prevailed that we send a message of love and sympathy to three of our absentees, Mrs. Bunch, Mrs. Beaty, and Mrs. Hocutt.

After the closing moments by Mrs. Carter, and prayer by Mrs. Jenkins, the Union adjourned to meet in Selma in November of 1917.

MRS. WALTER CREECH,
MRS. D. J. THURSTON,
Secretaries pro tem.

TABLE I—STATISTICAL.

CHURCH	PASTOR AND POSTOFFICE	CLERK AND POSTOFFICE	Time of Preaching	Value of Church Property	By Baptism	By Letter	By Restoration	By Letter	By Exclusion	By Death	Number of Males	Number of Females	Total membership
...	A. A. Pippin, Wakefield	W. O. Hocutt, Selma, R. 2	Third	$2000.00	24	6	2	1	11	4	82	119	201
Bailey	W. H. Wall, ...	J. P. Underwood, Bailey, R. 1	First	1500.00	3	3	1	9		1	33	39	72
Baptist Center	J. E. Lanier, Smithfield	E. H. Rogers, ..., R. 1	Third	600.00	15	3		1			58	71	129
Beaty Chapel	W. D. Pridgen, ...	N. M. ..., Smithfield	Fourth	1000.00	13	11	1	5	3	1	9	21	30
Benson	J. M. Duncan, Benson	..., Benson, R. 1	2nd-4th	20000.00				1			67	106	173
Benson's Grove	R. L. Smith, Four Oaks	Kir... Creech, Kenly	Second	800.00	11	1		1			5	18	23
Bethany	W. D. Stancil, Kenly	Miss Bertha Bell, Kenly	Fourth	800.00				2	2		38	55	93
Bethel	R. M. VonMiller, Four Oaks	J. E. Smith, Wilson's Mills	Second	1000.00	20	12	1	6	6		10	15	25
Bethesda	J. E. Lanier, Smithfield	Joseph Wood, Four Oaks	Fourth	3500.00	7		1		7	5	114	146	200
Blackman's Grove	R. M. VonMiller, Four Oaks	T. J. Lee, Dunn	First	1000.00		3	1		4		24	45	69
Calvary	R. L. Smith, Four Oaks	T. L. Hudson, Bentonsville	First	500.00	3	1		4		1	9	12	21
...	C. H. Stevens, Wake Forest	Martin Thorn, Selma	First	600.00									
Carter's Chapel	W. D. Pridgen, Clayton	W. P. ..., ...	Third	1000.00	3	9		3	1		41	58	99
Clayton	A. C. Hamby, Clayton	C. I. ..., Mill, R. 1	full time	6000.00	5	9	2	15		2	211	283	494
Clyde's Chapel	G. T. Mills, Apex	..., Mell	Third	500.00	2	7		3		2	81	104	185
Corinth	A. A. Pippin, Wakefield	H. B. (...), ...	Third	1800.00	4			4			51	92	143
Four Oaks	R. M. VonMiller, Four Oaks	R. A. Bain, Four Oaks	1st-3rd	1000.00	8	9		4	1	2	31	46	77
Hephzibah	C. E. Stevens, Selma	W. A. Braswell, Princeton	Third	400.00				2			7	11	18
Hood's Grove	R. L. Smith, Four Oaks	P. T. George, Four Oaks, R. 1	Third	650.00	1	1	3	2	2	1	27	32	59
Kenly	R. M. VonMiller, Four Oaks	Mrs. F. C. Richardson, Kenly	Second	2500.00	24	4		1	1		22	30	52
Lee's ...	W. H. Wall, ...	K. L. Green, Zebulon	Third	1500.00		2	4				132	162	324
Live Oak	W. D. Stancil, Kenly	K. L. Broadwell, Selma, R. 1	Third	600.00		1		2	1	1	11	13	24
Micro	W. D. Pridgen, Micro	D. H. Jones, Micro	Third	2000.00	35	9	3	1		2	45	32	77
Middlesex	W. H. Wall, Middlesex	W. K. Ballentine, Middlesex	2nd-4th	2500.00	11	4		8	3		45	56	101
Mount Moriah	C. A. Jenkins, Clayton	Russell Powell, ...	Third	3500.00	2	2		1	1	1	88	99	187
New Bethel	W. H. Wall, Middlesex	Geo. W. B ..., ...	Fourth	1500.00	3	2		2			47	56	103
Nobles ...	R. M. VonMiller, Four Oaks	Miss Lena Tyner, Four Oaks	First	500.00	1	2		2			8	16	24
Oliver's Grove	J. M. Duncan, Benson	J. D. ..., Selma, R. 3	First	500.00	1	2			3		29	40	69
Parrish Memorial	R. M. VonMiller, Four Oaks	Mrs. Annie Hays, Four Oaks	Fourth	800.00	6	4		4			19	40	59
Pauline	C. H. Pridgen, Micro	N. M. Gurley, Pine Level	First	3000.00	7			2	5		29	35	64
Pine Level	W. D. Pridgen, Micro	Mrs. B. R. Edgerton, Kenly	Third	1000.00	8	2	1	6			16	14	30
Pinkney	J. E. Lanier, Smithfield	R. H. Higgins, Smithfield, R. 1	First	1000.00	1	1		1			36	53	89
Pisgah	J. M. Duncan, Benson	W. S. Pearce, Princeton	Third	1500.00	8			4			27	46	73
Sardis	C. E. Stevens, Selma	B. C. Powell, Smithfield	Third	1500.00	1			4			21	22	43
Selma	C. E. Stevens, Selma	B. S. Reynolds, Selma	1-2-4	1700.00	43	10	17		3		108	166	284
Shiloh	J. F. Lanier, Smithfield	J. W. Williams, Garner, R.	Second	800.00	10	9	1	7	6		46	65	111
Smithfield	H. F. Brinson, Smithfield	T. J. Lassiter, Smithfield	full time	6000.00	4	1		8	1	2	92	106	198
Thanksgiving	J. V. Teague, Louisburg	D. H. Price, Selma, R. 1	Second	1000.00	11	4		7	1	3	36	42	78
Trinity	J. M. Smith, Four Oaks	J. M. ..., Benson	Fourth	500.00	23	1		3			35	56	91
Wendell	C. A. Jenkins, Clayton	Geo. H. Wright, Wendell	2nd-4th	1500.00	18	2	1	10	5	3	98	143	241
White Oak	A. A. Pippin, Wakefield	J. I. Murphrey, Selma, R. 1	2nd-4th	2500.00	14	4	1	6		1	96	124	220
Wilson's Mills	J. E. Lanier, Smithfield	J. T. Holt, Wilson's, R. 1	Third	1000.00				2		3	23	21	44

	Pastor's Salary	Buildi and R.	Incide	Sunday Expen	The F	Minute	Buildi Fund	State Mission	Home Mission	Foreig Mission	Sunday Mission	Orphan	Minist Educa	Minist Relief	College and Sc	Other Object	Total
Antioch	$171.25	$85.00	$....	$30.17	$....	$2.50	$5.00	22.50	$5.00	$5.00	2.50	5.00	$5.00	2.50	$....	$38.75	$306.02
Bailey	75.00	....	35.00	20.00	....	2.35	6.50	10.00	2.50	5.00	1.00	5.00	2.50	2.50	....	....	167.35
Baptist Center	125.00	....	2.00	15.00	....	1.5	4.00	10.00	5.00	5.00	1.25	5.00	5.00	1.50	....	8.33	185.58
Beaty Chapel	50.00	....	....	20.58	....	1.5	4.00	7.50	2.50	2.50	1.00	2.50	5.00	1.00	....	6.31	98.08
Benson	350.00	3300.00	353.00	60.00	....	2.50	15.00	75.00	10.00	15.00	1.00	20.00	10.00	5.00	39.15	....	4718.00
Benson's Grove	25.00	25.00	....	....	....	1.0	4.00	5.00	5.00	5.00	....	2.50	2.00	1.00	....	15.00	52.81
Bethany	45.00	....	15.00	15.00	....	1.0	1.00	10.00	.50	1.00	1.00	11.78	4.00	....	....	....	143.28
Bethel	5.00	....	19.50	....	....	.50	1.00	1.00	....	....	....	1.00	.50	....	....	....	10.50
Bethesda	300.00	1400.00	....	20.00	....	2.50	10.00	45.00	5.00	8.60	2.50	15.00	10.00	5.00	....	5.00	1838.60
Blackman's Grove	100.00	3.00	....	7.00	....	1.50	5.00	22.00	1.00	1.80	2.50	5.00	7.00	2.50	....	....	190.00
Calvary	55.00	....	....	....	....	1.00	....	....	1.20	....	.60	....	....	....	....	....	33.35
Cannan	50.00	....	....	....	....	1.00	1.00	4.35	....	4.77	....	1.00	1.00	1.00	....	....	58.60
Carter's Chapel	156.00	5.00	....	....	....	1.50	1.50	15.00	3.42	....	1.00	5.00	5.00	5.00	....	....	288.40
Clayton	1500.00	2459.88	60.00	10.71	....	2.50	50.00	275.00	75.00	205.38	10.75	127.05	65.00	20.00	....	803.92	6074.39
Clyde's Chapel	150.00	33.00	184.56	83.35	72.56	1.5	....	32.15	9.00	12.50	2.50	4.00	6.00	2.50	....	5.21	283.76
Corinth	100.00	45.00	....	12.90	13.05	2.00	6.00	13.00	2.50	2.50	....	2.50	2.50	2.50	....	....	189.65
Four Oaks	266.55	421.89	49.93	70.26	....	1.50	10.00	26.40	17.40	19.27	.71	9.64	8.50	4.00	....	5.00	912.51
Hephzibah	25.00	....	....	....	....	1.00	....	....	....	.71	....	....	....	....	....	....	46.71
Hoil's Grove	50.00	....	....	1.00	....	1.50	5.00	7.50	2.50	2.50	1.00	2.50	5.00	2.50	....	20.00	88.50
Kenly	142.50	29.80	61.15	20.25	....	2.35	5.00	15.00	7.50	6.60	2.50	2.50	5.00	2.50	....	2.25	304.17
Lee's Chapel	150.00	5.00	....	16.20	....	1.00	2.50	25.00	7.50	7.50	3.00	5.00	5.00	5.00	....	2.50	234.20
Live Oak	....	....	....	....	....	1.0	2.50	5.00	1.00	1.00	1.00	1.00	5.00	5.00	....	....	17.00
Mru	100.00	100.00	18.25	11.09	25.00	1.54	2.50	17.50	8.55	14.40	1.00	26.15	....	1.50	....	104.05	436.03
Middlesex	200.00	....	74.51	28.44	16.25	3.3	10.00	23.25	15.78	10.75	1.00	23.48	25.00	2.50	6.00	92.66	684.57
Mount Moriah	200.00	....	53.30	43.86	6.25	2.50	25.00	66.00	30.00	50.00	7.00	35.00	10.00	10.00	18.39	34.59	638.09
New Bethel	250.00	6.00	....	8.07	....	....	15.00	30.00	7.50	7.50	1.00	28.45	....	5.50	....	20.00	396.77
Nobles' Chapel	....	....	....	....	....	.50	....	....	....	1.00	.50	....	....	....	....	....	62.54
Oliver's Grove	18.25	25.50	....	3.31	....	1.00	2.50	5.00	1.00	2.50	1.00	6.00	2.50	1.00	....	....	137.00
Parrish Memorial	100.00	....	3.65	5.00	....	1.00	5.00	10.00	2.50	2.50	1.00	1.00	5.00	2.50	....	....	85.65
Pauline	50.00	....	75.00	25.00	....	1.5	5.00	7.50	2.50	2.50	1.00	5.00	5.00	2.50	....	2.00	772.50
Pine Level	120.00	500.00	3.44	12.87	12.21	1.00	1.50	20.00	2.50	2.50	1.00	5.00	5.00	5.00	....	....	113.58
Pinkney	35.17	37.10	3.50	13.60	....	2.00	....	5.00	16.86	18.05	17.22	2.50	5.00	3.13	....	20.65	324.72
Pisgah	150.00	6.00	10.75	10.00	13.50	1.50	10.00	23.50	3.00	7.50	2.50	17.22	2.50	2.50	....	44.94	218.59
Princeton	104.40	....	....	10.00	....	3.50	5.00	20.00	5.00	5.00	2.50	2.50	25.00	2.50	....	....	141.00
Sardis	100.00	....	207.54	5.00	....	3.50	20.00	20.00	20.90	38.16	25.00	25.00	10.00	10.00	....	14.10	1477.08
Selma	800.00	151.80	14.00	75.91	34.08	3.50	....	83.18	38.16	10.11	9.35	66.92	5.00	....	....	19.55	271.09
Shiloh	150.00	14.00	17.48	17.48	13.50	1.00	25.00	25.00	10.11	78.16	66.92	....	2.50	10.00	19.25	102.35	1910.64
Smithfield	1000.00	75.00	111.83	134.40	....	3.50	25.00	160.00	57.15	....	5.00	113.80	5.00	10.00	....	3.25	153.90
Thanksgiving	74.40	4.00	30.85	8.00	....	1.00	2.82	9.53	3.55	2.00	2.00	2.00	2.50	1.50	....	....	121.75
Trinity	35.00	38.00	19.50	7.75	3.14	3.00	2.00	29.45	21.96	36.94	3.84	113.80	15.00	1.00	2.05	10.50	748.96
Wendell	434.00	....	36.19	32.83	3.56	2.50	11.50	25.00	7.50	7.50	2.50	10.00	8.00	5.00	....	35.00	407.16
White Oak	250.00	....	5.00	33.60	....	1.50	5.00	17.00	5.00	5.00	10.00	1.00	15.00	5.00	....	....	152.82
Wilson's Mills	100.00	35.00	20.00	33.00	....	.50	4.80	1.00	1.00	1.00	1.00	10.00	8.00	5.00	....	....	53.76
Burnell	6.81	....	35.45	3.00	....	....	2.00	....	....	....	....	1.00	1.00	2.50	....	....	
Total	5433.24	9087.99	1493.09	941.55	197.50	69.85	322.62	1205.21	1384.42	628.99	64.44	613.00	359.50	147.23	94.84	1408.91	34734.04

TABLE III—SUNDAY SCHOOLS.

CHURCH.	SUPERINTENDENT AND POSTOFFICE.	SECRETARY AND POSTOFFICE.	Number of Schools.	Officers and Teachers.	Pupils.	Total Enrollment.	Church Members in S. S.	Months kept open.	Baptisms from School.	School Expenses.	Missions.	Orphanage.	Other Objects.	Total Contributions.
Antioch	J. R. Talton, Selma, R. 2	W. O. Hocutt, Selma, R. 2	1	8	95	103	75	12	11	$22.00	$.57	$1.50	$26.00	$40.07
Bailey	J. P. Underwood, Bailey	Rome Finch, Bailey	1	7	84	91	51	12	14	15.00	2.00			17.00
Baptist Center	J. C. Hardee, Clayton, R. 1	Nowel Bryan, Clayton, R. 1	1	9	120	129		12	14	19.36			1.22	20.58
Beaty Chapel	E. F. Crump, Smithfield	Jessie Parrish, Smithfield, R.2	1	9	55	64	125	12	13	60.00	15.00			75.00
Benson	J. L. Hall, Benson	L. E. Stevens, Benson	1	10	525	335		12					15.00	
Benson's Grove	Moses Creech, Kenly	Carmel Creech, Kenly	1	8	119	127	49	12	10	15.00	15.00		15.00	30.00
Bethany														
Bethel	J. W. Smith, Wilson's Mills	J. E. Smith, Wilson's Mills	1	14	75	89	50	12	12	25.00	12.33	2.40	1.53	38.86
Bethesda	Nogah Wood, Four Oaks	Newel Mahler, Four Oaks	1	6	67	79	30	12	2	7.00				9.40
Blackman's Grove														
Calvary														
Canaan	Martin Thorn, Selma, R. 1	B. F. Woodruff, Selma, R. 3	1	7	85	92	50	12	3	10.71	10.78	66.61	18.75	10.71
Carter's	D. L. Barbour, Clayton	Foster Barnes, Clayton	1	14	327	341	280	12	2	83.35				160.74
Clayton	C. M. Martin, Wendell, R. 1	L. A. Bunch, Wendell, R. 1	1	7	89	96	50	12	2	9.00	8.00			12.30
Corinth	Auburn													
Four Oaks	W. G. Sanders, Four Oaks	J. W. Sanders, Four Oaks	1	4	140	149	45	12	3	70.23	12.22		5.00	88.55
Hephzibah	W. G. Creech, Princeton	W. G. Creech, Princeton	1	7	25	29	8	12		5.00	.71			5.71
Hood's Grove	Almon Hood, Bentonsville	Jessie Jernigan, Bentonsville	1	7	40	47								
Kenly	J. A. Broughton, Kenly	J. L. Rackley, Kenly	1	7	77	84	28	12	1	20.35	8.01	5.00	2.50	35.86
Lee's Chapel	Waylan Estridge	Lester Green, Zebulon, R. 1	1	7	65	72	60	12	15	16.20				16.20
Live Oak														
Micro	E. L. M. Ausley, Micro	Ottis Pridgen, Micro	1	9	75	82	40	12	13	11.09	3.00	19.35	18.75	51.72
Middlesex	E. H. Las, Middlesex	M. Ballentine, Middlesex	1	10	107	116	50	12	6	28.44	7.45	23.43	13.86	73.18
Mt Moriah	J. J. Lane, Auburn	Robt. G. Foole, Clayton, R. 5	1	12	114	126	78	12	2	43.86	5.75		25.00	74.61
New Bethel	W. R. Britt, Garner	Hubert Britt, Garner	1	7	110	117	50	9	3	8.07	5.25		6.00	19.32
Nobles' Chapel	Mrs. Emma Allen, Four Oaks	Miss Kate Tyner, Four Oaks	1	5	56	61	10	9		3.31				3.51
Oliver's Grove	Frank Batten, Micro	Flossie Capps, Selma									3.06			
Parrish Memorial	George Massey, Four Oaks	Miss Pearl Creech, Four Oaks	1	6	70	76	12	6	6	3.00	22.50		15.00	6.05
Pauline	N. M. Gurley, Bel Level	Miss Pat. Braxton, Pine Level	1	9	100	109	33	12	7	25.00	1.00			62.50
Pine Level	R. H. Lee, Kenly	Odis Lee, Kenly, R. 4	1	7	78	85	15	12	2	12.87	19.35			13.87
Pinkney	R. H. Higgins, Smithfield, R.1	A. G. Jones, Smithfield	1	6	116	122	29	12	3	13.60				19.85
Pisgah	W. I. Pearce, Princeton	W. I. Pearce, Princeton	1	5	40	45	12	12	4	5.00				7.70
Princeton	C. H. Stevens, Smithfield, R. 2	B. H. Watson, Smithfield	1	5	20	25	15	12	1	5.91	6.30	8.19	2.70	7.70
Sardis	B. H. Watson, Smithfield	R. H. Watson, Smithfield	2	23	278	301	150	12	35	75.91				90.40
Selma	M. G. Futrell, Selma	M. G. Futrell, Selma	1	5	88	94	38	12	2	17.48	6.30	8.19		17.48
Smith	S. H. Richardson, Garner	J. A. Woodcock, Garner	2	12	148	160		12	3	134.40	49.53	32.35	37.85	254.13
Smithfield	T. S. Ragsdale, Smithfield	John Ies, Smithfield	1	12	85	97	36	12	4	8.00	8.50			8.50
Thanks	W. S. Earp, Selma, R. 1	C. Earp, Selma, R. 1												

CHURCHES.	NAME OF ORGANIZATION.	PRESIDENT AND POST-OFFICE.	Number of Members.	State Missions.	Home Missions.	Foreign Missions.	Sunday School Board.	Training School.	Other Objects.	Total Contributions.
Bailey	Woman's Missionary Society	Mrs. C. H. Brantely, Bailey	7			$2.60				$2.60
Baptist Center	Woman's Missionary Society	Mrs. J. E. Lanier, Smithfield	16	$2.90	$2.00	3.00		$3.50		11.40
Baptist Center	Sunbeam	Hugh Hardie, Clayton	20	.45						.45
Benson	Woman's Missionary Society	Mrs. J. L. Hall, Benson	25	5.45	7.90	5.10		1.00	$30.00	49.45
Benson	Sunbeam	Mrs. C. A. Fisher, Smithfield	11	3.90		.50		2.60		7.00
Bethesda	Woman's Missionary Society	Mrs. J. E. Lanier, Smithfield	9	84.60	47.15	52.80		33.10	33.18	250.88
Blackman's Grove	Woman's Missionary Society	Mrs. Nogah Wood, Four Oaks..2	71	10.00						10.00
Clayton	Woman's Missionary Society	Mrs. J. M. Turley, Clayton	18	12.15	4.00	5.00		1.50	36.50	36.50
Clayton	Young Woman's Auxiliary	Melba McCullers, Clayton		10.45	8.65	9.73		5.00	20.00	20.00
Clayton	Sunbeam	Miss Cleve Barnes, Clayton		.30	1.30	2.45				22.15
Clayton	Royal	Mrs. B. A. Hocutt, Clayton								
Clyde's Chapel	Woman's Missionary Society	Alice Phipps, Middlesex	22	2.00	4.83	2.82		1.00	1.00	53.67
Four Oaks	Woman's Missionary Society	Mrs. Lillian Sanders, Four Oaks	9							4.05
Four Oaks	Young Woman's Auxiliary	Mrs. Cora Johnson, Four Oaks	4						23.70	9.65
Four Oaks	Sunbeam	Clyde Sanders, Four Oaks		7.45		6.60		5.00	55.50	69.55
Kenly	Woman's Missionary Society	V. J. Hough, Kenly	13	7.00	13.00	5.00		1.00		34.75
Middlesex	Woman's Missionary Society	Mrs. W. H. Wall, Middlesex	10	1.00				1.00	2.00	2.00
Middlesex	Girls' Auxiliary	E. J. Nobles, Middlesex	8			5.25	2.75			16.13
Mex	Sunbeam	Clyde Whitley, Middlesex	25	8.85	2.78	6.60			2.60	29.70
Mt Moriah	Woman's Missionary Society	Mrs. J. W. Johnson, Clayton R. 3	13	7.05	7.05	1.15		3.50	2.20	5.00
Mount Moriah	Young Woman's Auxiliary	Bessie Lee Poole, Raleigh R. 2	16	4.10	1.00				.85	5.85
Mount Moriah	Sunbeam	Jessamie B. Raleigh, R. 2	16	5.00	3.75	8.00		10.62		23.25
Mount Moriah	Royal Ambassadors	Mrs. J. J. Lane, Auburn	12	9.50	13.50	4.00	4.00	.60		31.02
Pine Level	Woman's Missionary Society	Mrs. D. B. Oliver, Pine Level	12	1.55	.76	5.76			2.50	42.33
Pisgah	Woman's Missionary Society	Mrs. J. E. Lanier, Smithfield							8.52	3.41
Pisgah	Sunbeam	Miss Pearl ... Smithfield		3.55	8.20	11.90		10.10	3.00	35.50
Princeton	Woman's Missionary Society	Miss M. M. Holt, Princeton	10	1.35					1.75	4.25
Selma	Woman's Missionary Society	Mrs. Geo. D. Vick, Selma	32	1.17	3.07	1.28		1.00		7.32
Selma	Young Woman's Auxiliary	Annie May Roberts, Selma	7					2.00		1.00
Selma	Sunbeam	Reta Reynolds, Selma		7.95	6.00	5.00		5.05	13.00	37.00
Selma	Royal Ambassadors	D. Reynolds, Selma		1.00						1.00
Shiloh	Woman's Missionary Society	Miss Annie Myatt, Clayton	16	70.60	33.35	40.00		19.25	2.00	183.50
Shiloh	Woman's Missionary Society	Irene ... Garner	12	1.35						4.75
Smithfield	Girls' Auxiliary	Mrs. Howard Gray, Smithfield		4.27	4.27	3.40				19.77
Smithfield	Sunbeam	Mrs. J. M. Beaty, Smithfield							10.50	22.50
Smithfield	Woman's Missionary Society	Mrs. S. T. Wiggins, Wendell	19	4.15	2.25	5.00		2.05		2.20
Wendell	Sunbeam	Mrs. S. C. Hamrick, Wendell				6.03				
Wilson's Mills	Woman's Missionary Society	Mrs. J. E. Lanier, Smithfield	8	3.85	2.15	1.70		1.85		9.55
Total			464	295.12	83.31	204.11	6.75	121.72	258.80	1057.38

CHURCHES.	State Missions.	Home Missions.	Foreign Missions.	Sunday Schools.	Orphanage.	Min Education.	Ministerial Relief.	Building Fund.	Mte Fund.	Total.
Antioch	$ 25.00	$ 7.50	$ 7.50	$ 2.50	$ 7.50	$ 7.50	$ 5.00	$ 10.00	$ 2.50	$ 75.00
Bailey	12.50	3.50	5.00	1.00	5.00	4.00	2.50	6.50	1.50	41.50
Baptist Center..	15.00	5.00	5.00	2.00	5.00	5.00	2.50	5.00	1.50	46.00
Beaty Chapel...	7.50	2.50	2.50	1.00	2.50	5.00	1.50	4.00	1.00	27.50
Benson	75.00	10.00	15.00	2.50	20.00	10.00	5.00	15.00	2.50	155.00
Benson's Grove.	5.00	2.50	2.50	1.00	2.50	2.00	1.00	4.00	1.00	21.50
Bethany	1.00	5.00	5.00	1.00	6.50	2.50	2.50	2.00	1.00	36.50
Bethel	5.00	2.00	2.00	1.00	2.50	2.50	1.00	2.50	1.00	20.50
Bethesda	45.00	5.00	7.50	2.50	15.00	10.00	5.00	7.50	2.50	100.00
Blackman's Gr'e	25.00	7.50	7.50	1.50	5.00	7.50	2.00	7.50	2.50	66.00
Calvary	5.00	1.50	1.50	.50	1.50	2.50	1.50	2.50	1.00	17.50
Canaan	5.00	1.50	1.50	.50	1.50	2.50	1.50	2.50	1.00	17.50
Carter's Chapel.	12.50	5.00	5.00	1.00	5.00	5.00	2.00	7.50	1.00	44.00
Clayton	275.00	75.00	75.00	5.00	100.00	65.00	20.00	50.00	5.00	670.00
Clyde's Chapel .	25.00	7.50	7.50	2.50	5.00	10.00	2.50	12.50	1.50	75.00
Corinth	15.00	2.50	5.00	1.00	5.00	5.00	2.50	5.00	2.50	43.50
Four Oaks ...	23.50	7.50	7.50	2.50	7.50	10.00	5.00	10.00	1.50	75.00
Hephzibah ...	5.50	1.00	1.00	.50	1.00	2.50	1.00	2.50	1.00	16.00
Hood's Grove. .	7.50	4.00	4.00	1.00	2.50	5.00	2.50	7.50	1.00	35.00
Kenly	15.00	5.00	5.00	2.50	5.00	5.00	2.50	5.00	1.50	46.50
Lee's Chapel...	25.00	10.00	10.00	3.00	5.00	7.00	5.00	7.50	2.50	75.00
Live Oak	5.00	1.00	1.00	.50	2.50	2.50	1.00	2.50	1.00	17.00
Lizzie Mill ...	2.00	1.00	1.00	1.50	1.00	2.00	1.00	1.00	.50	10.00
Micro	14.00	5.00	5.00	1.00	2.50	5.00	1.50	5.00	1.00	40.00
Middlesex	20.00	5.00	5.00	1.00	5.00	5.00	2.50	12.50	1.50	37.50
Mount Moriah .	75.00	30.00	50.00	7.00	35.00	30.00	10.00	36.50	3.50	275.00
New Bethel	35.00	10.00	10.00	2.00	15.00	12.50	7.50	20.00	2.50	115.00
Nobles' Chapel..	15.00	2.50	5.00	1.00	5.00	10.00	2.50	5.00	1.50	47.50
Oliver's Grove..	5.00	1.00	1.00	.50	1.00	2.50	1.00	2.50	1.00	15.50
Parrish Memor'l	10.00	2.50	2.50	1.00	2.50	5.00	2.50	5.00	1.00	32.00
Pauline	7.50	2.50	2.50	1.00	2.50	5.00	2.50	5.00	1.00	29.50
Pine Level.. .	23.00	7.50	7.50	2.50	7.50	7.50	5.00	12.50	2.00	75.00
Pinkney	7.50	2.50	2.50	1.00	2.50	2.50	1.50	4.00	1.00	25.00
Pisgah	25.00	15.00	10.00	1.00	7.50	10.00	3.00	10.00	2.00	83.50
Princeton . .	20.00	2.50	2.50	1.00	2.50	5.00	2.50	5.00	1.50	42.50
Sardis	27.50	5.00	5.00	1.00	2.50	5.00	2.50	5.00	1.50	50.00
Selma	75.00	25.00	30.00	2.50	25.00	31.00	10.00	25.00	3.50	225.00
Shiloh	25.00	7.50	5.00	1.00	10.00	10.00	5.00	2.00	1.50	76.00
Smithfield ...	160.00	50.00	70.00	10.00	50.00	25.00	10.00	25.00	3.50	403.59
Thanksgiving	15.00	2.50	2.50	1.00	2.50	7.50	2.50	5.00	1.50	40.00
Trinity	7.50	2.00	2.00	1.00	2.00	2.50	1.00	2.50	1.00	21.50
Wendell	50.00	25.00	25.00	5.00	26.50	30.00	5.00	30.00	3.50	200.00
White Oak	25.00	7.50	10.00	2.50	15.00	12.50	5.00	5.00	2.50	85.00
Wilson's Mills ..	15.00	2.50	5.00	1.00	5.00	5.00	2.50	5.00	1.50	42.50
Burwell *	2.00	1.00	1.00	.50	1.00	2.00	1.00	1.00	.50	10.00
Total	1078.50	387.50	443.50	85.00	432.00	409.50	142.50	401.50	78.50	3805.50

* Mission Station.

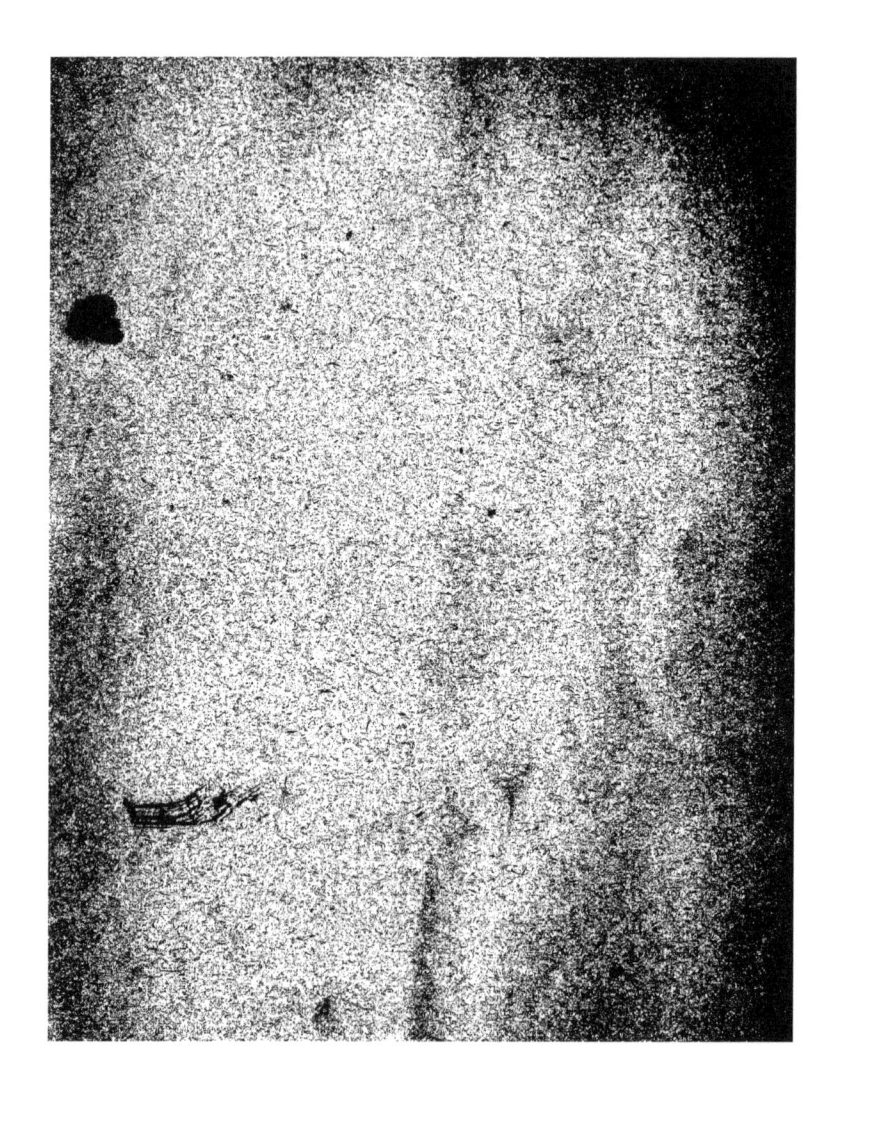

MINUTES

OF THE

Fifteenth Annual Session

OF THE

JOHNSTON COUNTY

BAPTIST ASSOCIATION,

HELD WITH

CORINTH BAPTIST CHURCH,

October 31 and November 1 and 2.

The next session will be held with Bethesda Baptist Church, beginning on Wednesday after the fourth Sunday in October, 1918.

To preach the Introductory sermon—Rev. G. W. Rollins.

Goldsboro, N. C.
Nash Bros., Printers and Binders,
1918

OFFICERS:

Moderator—R. H. Gower..................................Clayton, N. C.
Vice-Moderator—J. J. Lane................................Auburn, N. C.
Clerk and Treasurer—J. E. Lanier.....................Smithfield, N. C.
Auditor—J. L. Hall......................................Benson, N. C.

EXECUTIVE COMMITTEE.

John E. Lanier, Chairman..............................Smithfield, N. C.
J. B. Creech...Four Oaks, N. C.
J. T. Holt...Wilson's Mills, N. C.
J. F. Pool...Clayton, N. C.
J. L. Hall...Benson, N. C.

DELEGATES AND BOARD MEMBERS.

Delegates to Baptist State Convention—J. F. Pool, A. J. Broughton, and M. T. Britt.

Delegate to Southern Baptist Convention—Rev. H. F. Brinson.

Member of State Board of Missions—Judge F. H. Brooks.

COMMITTEE IN CHARGE OF AND TO WRITE THE REPORT ON DIFFERENT OBJECTS FOR THE YEAR 1918.

State Missions—J. T. Holt.
Home Missions—S. H. Averitt.
Foreign Missions—J. J. Lane.
Sunday Schools—Prof. L. T. Royal.
Orphanage—J. F. Pool.
Christian Education—T. J. Lassiter.
Ministerial Relief—Q. B. Hocutt.
Temperance—J. B. Creech.
Woman's Work—C. W. Carter.
B. Y. P. U. Work—Judge F. H. Brooks.

LIST OF MINISTERS.

H. F. Brinson...Smithfield, N. C.
J. M. Duncan..Mount Olive, N. C.
A. C. Hamby...Clayton, N. C.
R. L. Hocutt..Wendell, R. 1, N. C.
C. A. Jenkins...Clayton, N. C.
John E. Lanier..Smithfield, N. C.
A. C. McCall..Selma, N. C.
R. P. Merritt...Pine Level, N. C.
G. T. Mills...Wendell, N. C.
A. A. Pippin..Wakefield, N. C.
G. W. Rollins...Benson, N. C.
C. E. Stevens...Selma, N. C.
W. D. Stancil...Kenly, N. C.
R. M. VonMiller.......................................Four Oaks, N. C.
W. H. Wall..Middlesex, N. C.

PROCEEDINGS.

The fifteenth annual session of the Johnston County Baptist Association convened with Corinth Baptist Church. Devotional services were conducted by Rev. A. C. Hamby. Following which the Introductory sermon was preached by Rév. R. M. VonMiller.

At 12 o'clock noon Moderator R.·H. Gower called the session to order for the purpose of organization. Song, "This is My Story," was sung by the congregation. Prayer was offered by Rev. H. F. Brinson.

The Moderator appointed the following committee on enrollment: T. J. Lassiter, Q. B. Hocutt, and J. L. Hall.

The following delegates were enrolled:

Antioch—A. D. O'Neal, W. O. Hocutt, G. R. Whitley.

Bailey—J. P. Underwood, J. W. B. Finch.

Baptist Center—

Beaty Chapel—

Benson—J. L. Hall, G. W. Rollins.

Benson's Grove—

Bethany—Eula Wood, G. W. Wood, J. C. Wood, David Pace, Jesse B. Creech.

Bethel—

Bethesda—L. Johnson, J. Bunch.

Blackman's Grove—

Calvary—

Canaan—

Carter's Chapel—J. T. Blackman, Clara Richardson, W. M. Boykin, J. P. Easom, Miss May Sellars.

Clayton—D. J. Yelvington, A. C. Hamby, Ralf Allen, Fontane Allen, B. A. Hocutt, Mrs. B. A. Hocutt.

Clyde's Chapel—J. H. Nowell, E. V. Johnson, W. B. Medlin.

Corinth—J. L. Liles, Julius Williamson, H. B. Andrews, W. A. Mitchell, Q. B. Hocutt.

Four Oaks—R. M. VonMiller.

Hephzibah—J. F. Earp, W. G. Creech.

Hood's Grove—

Kenly—

Lee's Chapel—J. A. Lewis, Jr., J. L. Driver, J. A. Lewis, J. S. Atkinson.

Live Oak—J. M. Richardson

Lizzie Mill Chapel—

Micro—S. C. Batten, C. L. Batten, W. H. Green, Jr., Worley Wall, W. I. Green.

Middlesex—D. H. Bunn, Mrs. J. W. Bailey, Mrs. K. W. Ballentine, W. H. Wall.

Mount Moriah—J. F. Pool, J. M. Baucom, R. A. Baucom, C. D. Kelley, J. J. Lane.

New Bethel—W. K. Britt, George W. Bryan.

Noble's Chapel—N. L. Stott.

Oliver's Grove—J. A. Tyner.

Parrish Memorial—J. N. Watson, J. M. Watson, G. W. Parrish, Frank Batten.

Pauline—

Pine Level—Floyd Price, N. M. Gurley, Lorena Godwin, Clyde Godwin, J. F. Watson, Mrs. D. B. Oliver.

Pinkney—R. E. Lee.

Pisgah—Miss Vera Beasley, Mrs. J. E. Lanier, E. W. Massey, J. E. Lanier.

Princeton—

Sardis—

Selma—Theo. Easom, C. E. and Mrs. C. E. Stevens.

Shiloh—

Smithfield—F. H. Brock, T. J. Lassiter, L. T. Royal, H. F. Brinson, Geo. L. Jones.

Thanksgiving—Dally H. Price, Bonnie Phillips, W. S. Earp.

Trinity—J. L. Johnson.

Wendell—Oscar Griswold, W. H. Rhodes, E. V. Richardson.

White Oak—A. L. Batton, W. T. Hinton, A. C. Batton.

Wilson's Mills—J. T. Holt.

Burnell Mission—

The following visiting brethren were recognized: Rev. J. E. Dupree, of the South River Association; Rev. Wallace Hartsell, of the Tar River Association; Rev. W. N. Johnson, Secretary of State Board of Missions; Rev. J. M. Arnett, Secretary of Ministerial Relief Board; Rev. C. J. Thompson, representing Biblical Recorder.

The body then went into the election of officers. The Moderator called J. J. Lane to the chair. The present Moderator was nominated and elected by acclamation; J. J. Lane was elected Vice-Moderator; J. E. Lanier was elected Clerk and Treasurer; J. L. Hall was elected Auditor.

The regular program was taken up, and the report on Christian Education was read by Bro. J. J. Lane. On motion to adopt, the report was discussed by Brother Lane and adopted.

REPORT ON CHRISTIAN EDUCATION.

As good citizens of the State of North Carolina we should cheerfully submit to a tax to support our State schools. As loyal members of our great denomination we should contribute money enough to put our own colleges in a sufficiently strong financial condition to compete with the State schools for patronage. Now as never before in the history of the world, we need to emphasize Christian Education. We should urge our churches as a matter of denominational loyalty to give regularly and liberally to this great cause.

J. J. LANE.

On motion, the body adjourned with prayer by J. F. Pool.

WEDNESDAY AFTERNOON SESSION.

The session was opened with song and prayer by G. W. Rollins. Under the head of miscellaneous business, Brother Gower made mention of Bro. J. M. Beaty, on the account of sickness would not be able to attend the present session of the body. Bro. A. A. Pippin lead the congregation in a special prayer for Brother Beaty.

Bro. R. M. VonMiller made the following motion which was adopted. That the Association give the ladies of our W. M. U. of the Johnston Association an opportunity to hold a session of their own in connection with the report on Woman's Work on Thursday afternoon, if they so desire.

The report on Biblical Recorder was read and, on motion, was discussed by Brother T. J. Lassiter and adopted.

REPORT ON THE BIBLICAL RECORDER.

If the Baptists of the State fully realized the proper relation between the Recorder and the Convention, we feel sure they would give to the Recorder a more generous support.

The impression prevails that the Recorder is on a par with any other business enterprise; that it is owned by stockholders who conduct it for their own profit; and that a subscription to the Recorder is somewhat like purchasing a bill of goods from a merchant. The facts are these: The Recorder is owned by a stock company, but the brethren who purchased the stock did so because they believed the existence of the Recorder was essential to the interests of the Kingdom. The paper was offered to the Convention, but that body refused to assume financial responsibility. A resolution was passed by the Convention requesting the Editor to organize a joint stock company which would own and publish the paper. This was done, and for years the paper was run in this way, the company owning and controlling it. On their own initiative the stockholders presented to the Convention the plan by which the paper is now controlled. They asked that the Convention appoint a committee of seven, who, with the seven Directors, would make a joint committee, which committee should have power to elect the Editor. In this way the stockohlders voluntarily gave practical control of the paper to the Convention without asking the Convention to assume one cent of financial responsibility.

There was considerable complaint because the Recorder carried in its columns patent medicine advertisements. While the stockholders had a perfect right to continue such advertising, which was the most profitable advertising that the Recorder carried, in deference to what they believed to be the wish of the majority of the brethren, patent medicine advertisements were eliminated. This does not include proprietary remedies wihch the doctors do not put in the same class with patent medicines. But even these proprietary medicines arc submitted to reputable physicians before they are admitted to the columns of the Recorder. A few patent medicine advertisements are still carried because the contracts have not expired since the action of the Directors in eliminating this class of advertising. By cutting out patent medicine advertisements, the Recorder suffers a loss of at least $2,500 a year. This, with the advanced price in paper and other materials, has necessitated a loss in conducting the paper for the last two years. Unless the Baptists of the State give to it a more liberal support, the paper cannot be the great power in the denomination which it otherwise might be.

Our people need to learn that the Recorder is not a liability, but an asset. Every department of our denominational work depends largely for its success upon the Recorder. If the paper were to suspend publication, and no other medium of communication established to take its place, the effect upon all our denominational work would be well nigh disastrous. Believing that the Recorder is essential to the best interests of our denomination, we recommend:

First, that all the churches in the Association appoint some Sunday as Recorder Day, and that the pastors be asked to bring the claims of the paper before their people and urge them to subscribe to it.

Second, that a committee on Biblical Recorder be appointed in each church whose business it shall be to solicit subscriptions. just as they would endeavor to secure pledges for any of the objects of the Convention.

Respectfully submitted,

T. J. LASSITER,
J. W. B. FINCH.

Report on Home Missions was read by Prof. L. T. Royal. On motion to adopt it was discussed by Prof. Royal, Rev. H. F. Brinson and adopted.

REPORT ON HOME MISSIONS.

The Home Mission Board is located in Atlanta, Ga., and its field is the States included in the Southern Baptist Convention, Cuba and the Canal Zone.

In the State the work is conducted under the following departments: Church Extension, Evangelism, Mountain Schools, Enlistment and work among the Foreigners, Negroes and Indians.

In the Church Extension work the Board is trying to reach the 8,000 homeless churches in the South and help them to build houses of worship. There is a campaign on now to raise $1,000,000 for this purpose. The women are proposing to give one third of it.

There are twenty-eight evangelists at work under the Board and last year the department of Evangelism reported 20,709 baptisms.

The department of Mountain Schools reports 34 schools with 177 teachers, and 5,319 students. North Carolina has nine of these schools with 55 teachers and 1610 students.

There are 15 Enlistment workers in eight States. Of these North Carolina had two last year. The purpose of this department is to reach the hundreds of churches that are doing comparatively nothing and develop them into active workers.

Work among the Foreigners is done in practically all the cities that have a large foreign population.

Extension mission work is done among the Negroes and Indians.

Cuba has 43 churches and stations with 1,876 members reported last year.

Panama reports nine churches.

One of the most important activities at the present time is the work among the soldiers at the various cantonments. These are our own boys. Every community is represented among them and they are exposed to fearful temptations on every side. The Home Board is making every effort possible to carry the gospel into the ranks.

North Carolina is asked to give to this work this year $37,500 and there is perhaps no place in the kingdom where it will mean more to the future.

Respectfully submitted,   L. T. ROYAL.

The Moderator presented the work of the Food Commission and, on motion, the work was endorsed.

Brother Brinson presented the following resolution which was passed:

RESOLUTION.

On motion by H. F. Brinson, the Moderator was empowered to appoint a committee of laymen to represent the various objects of the State Convention one for each object, requesting these brethren to visit as many of the churches of the Association as possible in the interest of the object which he represents and to write the report on that object at the next meeting of the Association.

Brother T. J. Lassiter presented the resignation of Brother J. M. Beaty as Chairman of the Executive Committee of the Association.

The chair announced the following committee to decide the place and preacher for the next meeting of the Association, J. T. Holt, Geo. W. Bryan and J. P. Underwood.

The body was dismissed with prayer by Rev. J. E. Dupree.

THURSDAY MORNING SESSION.

The morning session was opened with song, "What a Friend we have in Jesus." Devotional service was conducted by Rev. J. E. Lanier.

The Vice-Moderator called the body to order and prayer was made by Rev. R. M. VonMiller. The report of the Executive and Building Committee was called for, but owing to Brother Beaty's absence the reports were not present. Report on State Missions was read by Rev. G. W. Rollins. On motion to adopt the chair recognized Brother Rollins, who yielded his time to our State Secretary, Rev. W. N. Johnson, who discussed State Missions in a very able speech. The following pastors made short reports of their work. Brethren VonMiller, Wall, Pippin, and Rollins. Report was adopted.

REPORT ON STATE MISSIONS.

That branch of our Christian work which we for convenience term State Missions might properly be regarded as the seed bed of our denominational activities in the great enterprise of evangelizing the world.

A survey of our work in the state through the medium of the Annual of the North Carolina Baptist State Convention plainly shows that those churches that have been most diligent in "strengthening their stakes", that is, in supporting State Missions, have been most successful in "lengthening their cords," that is, in witnessing "in the uttermost parts of the earth."

"Wisdom is justified of her children." In the midst of their joyful work of preaching the gospel in their own communities, our fathers foresaw that if Baptists were ever to play any important part on the far flung battle line they must build up the waste places, and enlist and organize the forces, at home. This they began to do through the Baptist State Convention and what is now the Board of State Missions. And how sound their reasoning was may be evidenced by the fact that of the $47,925.56 contributed by the entire state to Foreign Missions last year, six one-time proteges of the State Board gave over $15,000.

There is no department of our work which pays a larger dividend on the amount invested than does State Missions. Last year the missionaries employed by the Board preached 11,568 sermons at 435 points. They held 447 meetings resulting in 3,487 conversions. They also reported 41 church houses in process of construction, 11 buildings finished and 7 churches organized. This year the statistics available show that 150 missionaries are preaching to 276 churches in 45 associations.

Last year 4,834 Baptists in the Johnston County Association contributed $1,205.21 to State Missions, receiving in return $1,500.00 to be used in their own work. The pledges for this year from the churches of the Association amount to $1,078.50 which, it will be observed, is a fraction over 22 cents per Baptist for State Missions. This amount added to an Associational Mission Fund of $500.00 which has been raised and spent in the Association this year, will enable us to just about break even with the Board and sit down just barely outside the pauper class.

Our people have never been so prosperous as now. More automobiles are parked outside the average country church on a preaching Sunday now than could be found ten years ago in the average North Carolina town of 10,000 people. And the man with the automobile spends more for gasoline in an hour than the average Johnston County Baptist spent for State Missions all last year.

Your committee would respectfully recommend that "Evangelization" be indelibly inscribed upon our banner as our watchword; but with the added reminder that since time began no battles have been won with merely listed names: they have all been won by ENLISTED MEN.

Respectfully submitted,   G. W. ROLLINS,
For the Committee.

The chair announced the following committees:

Foreign Missions—H. F. Brinson, C. D. Kelley and E. W. Massey.
Orphanage—W. H. Wall, Clyde Godwin, and J. P. Watson.
Woman's Work—A. C. Hamby, R. A. Baucom and W. T. Hinton.
B. Y. P. U. Work—C. W. Carter, Julius Williamson and J. M. Baucom.
Ministerial Relief—Rev. C. E. Stevens, J. L. Johnson and A. J. Batton.
Temperance—Rev. A. C. McCall, J. F. Pool, and J. A. Finch.

To nominate Executive Committee, member of State Board of Missions, Representative of Foreign Missions, Delegates to Baptist State Convention and delegate to Southern Baptist Convention—J. L. Hall, H. F. Brinson, J. J. Lane, R. M. VonMiller and F. H. Brooks.

After song, "How Firm a Foundation," the report on Foreign Missions was read by Rev. H. F. Brinson. On motion to adopt, the report was discussed by Rev. H. F. Brinson, Rev. R. M. VonMiller and adopted.

REPORT ON FOREIGN MISSIONS.

Under the Foreign Mission Board we have missionaries at work on fourteen fields located in seven countries: In China there are five, in Italy, Brazil and

Mexico there are two each and in Africa, Japan and Argentina there are one each. On these fields there are 459 churches, of which 95 are self-supporting, and 910 out stations. Last year they reported 42,630 members.

The unsettled condition resulting from the present war together with the tremendous increased cost of living makes it exceedingly difficult for the board to maintain its standard of efficiency upon the fields. The missionaries realize the situation and are making untold sacrifices. Only as driven by dire necessity do they ask for an increase of salary. On some fields prices have almost doubled which is equivalent to a reduction of the salary of the missionary to little more than half. To many this means sacrifice that borders on absolute want.

It is an hour that appeals to the heroic at home as well as on the fields. Not only must we maintain our present work but we must be ready for the new opportunities that will be opened up to us at the close of the war. Russia and the Turkish provinces will be opened as never before and the Macedonian call will again be heard from the Balkan peninsular. We must enter these fields or soon the opportunity will pass as it did in Japan.

God is shattering traditionalism as never before, with it He is changing. men's ideas and ideals, He is opening wide new doors and issuing the challenge of the ages to His people to obey the command "Go ye into all the world and preach the gospel to every creature."

Respectfully submitted, H. F. BRINSON,
For Committee.

The report of the Executive Committee having come in was read by Bro. J. T. Holt, and by a motion, which was carried, report was referred back to the committee for some amendments.

Bro. J. F. Pool read the report of the Building Committee, which was adopted.

REPORT OF BUILDING COMMITTEE.

We expected last winter to build a church, to take the place of the little school house in which Hephzibah church was organized. We had in the hands of our treasurer towards this building about two hundred and fifty dollars but could not erect the building with this and what we could raise in the neighborhood. So we applied to the State Board of Missions for some help thinking they would surely grant it as they had not helped us on any building for several years. This help the Board was unable to grant and so we could not go ahead with the work. We have now let a contract for the building of this church and if the church building funds raised this year can be applied to this point the church will soon be built and ready for use.

J. M. BEATY,
J. F. POOL,
J. T. HOLT.

The body adjourned with prayer by Rev. J. M. Arnett.

THURSDAY AFTERNOON SESSION.

After a song the body was called to order by the Moderator and prayer was offered by Rev. W. H. Wall.

Report on Woman's Work was read by Rev. A. C. Hamby. On motion to adopt the report was discussed by Rev. A. C. Hamby, and report was adopted.

REPORT ON WOMAN'S WORK.

Last year the Woman's Missionary Societies, the Girl's Auxiliaries, the Sunbeams, the Royal Ambassadors and the one Y. W. A. society, working under the direction of consecrated women in our churches, reported contributions to missions totaling $994.98, which was considerably beyond the goal they set before them. This year their aim is $1100 and the hope of the President of their Union is that they may go beyond it.

Last year there were 939 members in these societies, or 20 per cent of the total membership of the association. This 20 per cent gave 45 per cent of all the mission money reported. The more one knows about any subject the greater his interest. These 939 women, boys and girls are organized for systematic study of the Bible and missions. As the volume of their information grows the sum of their gifts increases. They gave $1.05 each while the others of us, 3895, gave an average of 31 cents each. They gave three and one-fifth times as much per capita. If the 80 per cent had been engaged in systematic study of the Bible and missions and had given proportionately, we should have reported $4975 for missions instead of $2218. Are the members of these societies doing too much? Are they giving more than they ought to give? Ask them, and you know what the answer will be. The question is, Are we doing what we ought to do?

There is a steady growth each year in the number of societies and in contributions. This year has seen an increase from 39 to 45 societies. The missionary societies are the best assets of the churches, and the church without one or more lacks the leaven that can save its missionary spirit from stagnation. And when the missionary spirit is gone all is gone.

THE COMMITTEE.

The committee on Place and Preacher of next session reported Bethesda as the place and Rev. G. W. Rollins as preacher. The report was adopted.

The report on Sunday Schools was read by Judge F. H. Brooks, and on motion to adopt, it was discussed by Judge Brooks and adopted.

REPORT ON SUNDAY SCHOOLS.

There is no more undisputed fact in the Bible than that God wants his Word taught the people. There are various ways and institutions for the teaching of the Bible, but one of the most universally recognized institutions for this work is the Sabbath School.

In 1916 there were 2,123 Sabbath Schools of the Baptist denomination in North Carolina with a membership of 221,148. Less than twenty years prior thereto, there were only 914 Sabbath Schools of the Baptist Denomination in North Carolina with a membership of 66,046. This increase alone is sufficient to demonstrate that the work has been greatly blessed by God.

Taking a glance at our own Association and running back only a few years, we find that in 1912 there was reported to the Association 35 Sunday Schools with a total enrollment of 3,350 scholars, officers and teachers. Only four years after, or 1916, there was reported to the Association 37 Sunday Schools with a total enrollment of 4,077. There are yet some places in the Johnston Association where no Sunday School is maintained. These are Benson's Grove, Bethel, Calvary, Canaan, Corinth, Live Oak and Noble's Chapel, unless there are Sunday Schools at some of these points that were not reported to the 1916 Association, nor to the Association several years back.

By reference to the report on Sunday Schools made to the Association of 1915, page 7, of the Minutes, it will be seen that there was reported 40 Baptist Sunday Schools in the Johnston County Association with a total enrollment of 4,295. This discrepency between the reports of 1915 and 1916 must be due to the fact that some of the Sunday Schools did not report to the Association of 1916. Possibly the rolls of the various Sunday Schools were revised since that report and this accounts for the lessened number in the Sabbath Schools according to the report of 1916 than the one in 1915. However, this may be, it is a lamentable fact that the interest in Sunday School work has not been maintained to the highest point during the past few years. There are thousands of boys and girls, men and women, who ought to be in the Sunday School. There are thousands of church members who ought to enlist in the Sunday School work. The great task before the Sunday School workers of the State, and this applies to the Johnston Association also, is to enlist the church members into the work of the Sabbath Schools in order to lend dignity to the Sunday Schools as well as wisdom of years and experience.

In the State at large there are 80 members in the Sunday School for every 100 members in the church; but only about 34 per cent of the church members are affiliating with the Sunday School. If we had the other 66 per cent of church members enlisted in the Sunday School work, what a great Sunday School band we hould have.

It is useless to report and resolute on Sunday Schools if the reports and resolutions are to be read in the Association and never acted on in the Sunday Schools and churches. I would suggest that the report on each of the various objects made to this Association, and especially the Sunday School report, be read on a given Sunday in each of the Sunday Schools in the Association. For instance, set apart a day for State Missions in the Sunday Schools and read the report to the Association on this object. Again, have a day on Sunday School Missions, and read the report on the Sunday Schools to this Association. At each of these meetings, some speaker or speakers, ought to speak of these reports and the work being done in the Association and the plans and suggestions made, and in this way the Sunday Schools could be brought in touch with what was done at the Association. I believe if this is put into practice during the coming associational year, the effects of it in contributions and in other ways will be felt at the next Association. This could be done in the churches with profit, also, we think.

In order to reach these aims and to do the best work, the Sunday School Secretary has made five definite suggestions and I include them in this report for the consideration of the Association, to-wit:

1. Definite campaigns for reaching more of our people for our schools. A religious census with a follow-up canvass will help greatly.

2. A lining up of our men and women in the "Convention Adult Bible Class Department" of our Sunday School Board at Nashville.

3. An earnest effort to get our officers and teachers enlisted in the great work of Teacher Training. Our schools can never be what they should be until we have trained workers.

4. A close touch and co-operation with the Sunday School Department of our Mission Board. The Secretary, E. L. Middleton, Raleigh, N. C., will furnish free, valuable tracts and suggestions on every phase of Sunday School work. Let this co-operation include liberal offerings in our schools for the expenses of Sunday School Missions.

5. Finally, a vitalizing of all our schools to make them more effective in evangelism and definite in training every one for personal service.

F. H. BROOKS, for Committee.

Brother J. M. Arnett was given an opportunity to speak on Ministerial Relief.

The Committee to nominate Executive Committee, etc., made the following report:

Executive Committee—T. J. Lassister, Chairman, J. B. Creech, J. T. Holt, J. F. Pool, J. L. Hall and Bro. J. M. Beaty as Honorary member.

Delegates to Baptist State Convention—J. F. Pool, A. J. Broughton, and M. G. Britt.

Delegate to Southern Baptist Convention—Rev. H. F. Brinson.

Member of State Board of Missions—F. H. Brooks.

The report was adopted.

The chair announced the following committees to prepare the reports on the different objects for the next annual session of the Association.

State Missions—J. T. Holt.
Home Missions—S. H. Averette.
Foreign Missions—J. J. Lane.
Sunday Schools—Prof. L. T. Royal.
Orphanage—J. F. Pool.
Christian Education—T. J. Lassister.
Ministerial Relief—J. L. Hall.
Biblical Recorder—Q. B. Hocutt.
Temperance—J. B. Creech.
Woman's Work—C. W. Carter.
B. Y. P. U. Work—Judge F. H. Brooks.

The Clerk was instructed to secure Orphanage report.

REPORT ON ORPHANAGE.

As the years come and go, the Baptist Orphanage at Thomasville, founded by John H. Mills, in the year 1885, grows dearer to the average Baptist in North Carolina. Our orphanage has at present 505 children, 57 of these being in the Kennedy Home near Kinston. The cost of maintenance per capita rises with each year.

The income from the Kennedy Home farm was $14,155.29; the income from the Thomasville farm was $8,671.13. The fine herd of cows turned in $7,595.52 worth of milk, cream and butter. The income to the orphanage for the closing year amounted to $113,324.75 from all sources. The voluntary contributions from the churches and Sunday schools of the State were $64,800.26, which was $10,000.00 above that of the previous year. Editor Johnson, in his report on Charity and Children, states that $10,490.88 has been received in subscriptions, which is a very pleasing record.

There have been no deaths at the Orphanage for the past year, and very little serious illness.

The endowment fund of $11,000.00 is safely invested in real estate mortgages.

The General Manager is planning to make many improvements at Thomasville, but the main enlargement, he thinks, should take place at the Kennedy Home, which will soon become a strong arm. Another arm will be started in Haywood county on a fine tract of land which has been given to the Orphanage by some benevolent women.

We recommend:

1. That the Sunday schools in the Johnston Association and the state increase the number of copies of Charity and Children.

2. That all Sunday schools take monthly offerings.

3. That every man, woman and child give the price of one day's work on each national Thanksgiving Day. Respectfully submitted,

W. H. WALL.

The body granted a request of Brother Pippin, that a collection be taken for Corinth church to finish the house of worship. The offering was $15.23, which was turned over to Brother Pippin.

Brother J. E. Lanier presented to the body a bound copy of the first ten years session of the Association which was furnished by the former clerk Brother T. J. Lassiter.

On motion of Judge F. H. Brooks, a vote of thanks was extended to Brother Lassiter.

The body adjourned until Friday morning with prayer by Rev. C. E. Stevens.

FRIDAY MORNING SESSION.

Bro. J. T. Holt led the devotion exercises. After which the Vice-Moderator J. J. Lane called the session to order and prayer was offered by Rev. C. E. Stevens. The report on Ministerial Relief was read by Rev. C. E. Stevens. After being discussed by Brethren Stevens and Lane the report was adopted.

REPORT ON MINISTERS' RELIEF BOARD.

Every year since the "Ministers' Relief Board" was launched in 1890, the demand for old ministers' aid has increased, and for many reasons we may expect the need to be greater as the years go by. First, because preachers' salaries have not increased in proportion to the high cost of living. Second, because there are larger demands upon the preacher's income than ever before. Third, because more of our ministers than ever before are giving their entire time to preaching the gospel.

Since the preacher dare not become entangled with financial ventures of worldly gain, we may expect the demands upon this Board to increase with the years, and there is a growing sentiment throughout the state, that we ought to begin to plan larger things for the future of this work, either by endowment or otherwise.

It is the purpose of this Board to extend aid to every aged or afflicted minister who is in want, and whose poverty is the result of a life given to the preaching of the gospel. We of the Johnston County Association have a right to feel gratified, that instead of numbering with the dozen associations in the state that pay not one cent to Ministers' Relief Board, have only three churches in our Association which failed to contribute something to this object last year.

It is greatly desired that every church have some part in brightening the last days of those who for many years have proclaimed the "Glad Tidings of Salvation" to men. We also urge that the Christmas offering be a liberal one this year.   Respectfully submitted,   C. E. STEVENS.

Report on Temperance was read by Rev. A. C. McCall, and on motion to adopt it was discussed by Rev. A. C. McCall and Rev. A. A. Pippin and was adopted.

REPORT ON TEMPERANCE.

When we consider in detail the relations of alcoholic indulgence to disease, education, progress, and the uplift of society to say nothing of the misery and sadness it causes mothers and children of our land one can hardly avoid realizing that it stands almost if not altogether in the front rank of enemies to be combatted in the struggle for progress, in the land in which we live and have to do. If disease, education and progress were all that it was hindering we would need to get it out of our land. But alas! it is the beginning of so many things that at last destroys life and causes the soul of man to go down to hell. To deal just right now is of the greatest importance for upon the present generation is laid the responsibility of choosing the part it will play toward prosperity and thereby shaping the character of future generations let us do all we can at home, Sunday school and from the pulpit to instill into the youth of our land, sound knowledge in regard to alcohol and its effects.

When we think of the results of our temperance workers they are gratifying and encouraging. The great task of making our nation a prohibition nation has much more than half been accomplished, so far as the majority of states are concerned, and the prospects for the others becoming such are growing brighter every year, and it will be realized before so long.

The selling of strong drink has been disgraced. Where it was once sold in the public places on front streets it is now sold in secluded corners of the towns and country.

When we think of the food situation we are facing today and realize that in the year ending June, 1916, (the latest statistics we have at hand) that there were used for both brewers and distilleries over six billion pounds of food stuffs, we can think in part how needful it is that both be discontinued. That the food may be used to support those men that go to the front to defend our nation and others also.

Of course we are responsible in part for national prohibition but we are more responsible for North Carolina and Johnston county. We have prohibition laws. We have the Jones-Reed amendment to the postoffice appropriation bill passed by Congress. This means much to North Carolina. But both are as other things without being used they become useless. What we need now is men in offices who will carry them out. Men in the towns who will see that those who refuse to obey the law are reported to such. In communities where alcohol is made and sold men who will stand up for the enforcement of the law. With such we can hope for temperance workers to accomplish the task that lies out before them but without such aid they must fail.   COMMITTEE.

Bro. J. F. Pool made some timely remarks along the line as to what our churches ought to do in giving financial support to our Associational work.

The proceedings of the sessions of the Association were read and approved.

Brother Hamby presented some resolutions to be incorporated in the report on the Biblical Recorder, which were adopted.

As the report on B. Y. P. U. work was not present, on motion the work was discussed by Rev. H. F. Brinson, J. J. Lane and R. A. Baucom. The Clerk was instructed to secure the report for the minutes

Under the head of Miscellaneous business Bro. J. T. Holt re-read the report of the Executive Committee. On motion to adopt it was discussed by Rev. A. C. Hamby, J. E. Lanier, R. H. Gower and J. J. Lane. After making some changes in the phraseology of some parts of the report, it was adopted.

REPORT OF EXECUTIVE COMMITTEE.

This has been by far the hardest year we have ever known. The State Mission Board without warning cut off from the amount we received last year five hundred dollars. For a while it looked as if quite a number of our churches would have to go without preaching. Your committee finally decided on the plan of making a canvass for aid among certain individuals and in this way we have raised the money to keep the work going. This required right much sacrifice on the part of your committee and on others who helped. We have managed in this way to carry on the work and are glad to say that at many points we have had unusual success. In view of the scarcity of money in the treasury of the State Board of Missions and the urgent demands of mission work, we recommend that as early as possible the churches of the Association undertake to raise their own Associational money, and do their own work without asking help from the State Board. Our work at several places has been hard and slow and we regret to note that at this time of greatest opportunity and at a time when other denominations are doing most the State Board of Missions is unable to give us the help and some of our own people are becoming discouraged and are slackening their efforts. Let us pray to God that He may open the eyes of our people to see the great opportunities before us in the vast mission territory within the bounds of our Association.

                              J. M. BEATY,
                              J. F. POOL,
                              J. T. HOLT.

14

The following resolution was presented by J. E. Lanier:

Where, as the apportionment which the State Board of Missions is not sufficient to adequately carry on our mission work in our Association; be it

Resolved: That the Association adopt in its budget Associational Missions, and that the churches be asked to raise $750.00 for this object, to be used by the Executive Committee of the Association to supplement the apportionment granted by the State Board of Missions, and that the Executive Committee be instructed to apportion the amount to be raised by each church in the Association. The resolution was adopted.

Bro. J. F. Pool made a motion that the Clerk be allowed $30.00 for his salary. The motion was adopted.

On motion of Rev. A. A. Pippin, the Clerk was instructed to correspond with the churches not represented at this session of the Association and ascertain why they are not represented and report same to the next session of the Association.

Bro. T. J. Lassister refused to serve as chairman of the Executive Committtee. Bro. J. J. Lane nominated J. E. Lanier to serve as Chairman of the Executive Committee. He was elected for this year.

Bro. George L. Jones presented a resolution to change the time of meeting of the Association. The resolution, by a motion, was referred to the Executive Committee to consider and report on at the next annual session of the Association.

The treasurer made the following report which was adopted:

TREASURER'S REPORT OF THE JOHNSTON COUNTY BAPTIST ASSOCIATION.

I have received and disbursed the following amounts during the year:

October 31, 1917.
Associational Missions—

Received during the year		$ 295.50
Paid to L. L. Johnson, supply work	$ 15.33	
Paid to G. A. Bain for Benson's Grove	66.42	
Paid to C. H. Stevens, Trinity	100.00	
Paid to J. E. Lanier, for Beaty Chapel	58.34	
Nov. 2, Total amount paid out		$ 240.09
Nov. 2, Balance on hand		$ 55.41

Building Fund—

Balance on hand as reported in last Minutes		$ 300.62
Received from Selma Church		20.00
Total		$ 300.62
Paid to Lizzie Mill Chapel		50.00
October 10, 1917, balance on hand		$ 270.62
Received during the year		321.44
Nov. 2, balance on hand		$ 692.06

Minute Fund—

Balance on hand as reported in last Minutes		$ 86.25
Nov. 3, paid Nash Bros., for printing minutes	$ 40.00	
Nov. 14, paid J. E. Lanier, Clerk, salary	20.00	
Nov. 10, paid express and postage	3.90	
October 10, 1917, balance on hand		$ 22.35
Received during the year		73.50
Nov. 2, balance on hand		$ 95.85

Totals—
    Balance on hand as reported in last minutes....................$ 300.62
    Received from Selma Church................................. 20.00

                                                                                  $ 320.62
    Amount paid out..$ 50.00

    Balance on hand..$ 270.62

Audited November 1st, 1917.
                    J. L. HALL, Auditor.

There being no further business for the present session of the Association to transact a motion was made to adjourn. The motion was carried and Rev. H. F. Brinson presented the closing prayer. The Moderator declared the fifteenth annual session of the Johnston County Baptist Association adjourned to meet in its sixteenth annual session with Bethesda Baptist Church Wednesday after the fourth Sunday in October, 1918.

NOTICE.

By order of the Association all church treasurers are requested to send all moneys collected for State Missions, Home Missions, Foreign Missions, Christian Education, and Ministerial Relief direct to Walters Durham, Raleigh, N. C. Send all money for the Orphanage to the Orphanage Treasurer, F. B. Hamrick, Thomasville, N. C.

Send Minute Fund, Church Building Fund and Associational Missions to the Associational Treasurer, John E. Lanier, Smithfield, N. C.

MINUTES OF WOMAN'S MISSIONARY UNION.

On Wednesday, the 14th of November, at three-thirty o'clock at the Baptist Church at Selma, the Woman's Missionary Union of the Johnston County Baptist Association was called into the annual session by its Superintendent Mrs. B. A. Hocutt, of Clayton.

Never has there been greater enthusiasm, better attendance and less confusion than at this meeting. The hospitality of the entire town was unlimited as was so delightfully spoken in the words of welcome from the different societies.

The program for the afternoon session was devotional service by Mrs. E. V. Woodard, followed by words of welcome by Mrs. G. D. Vick from the W. M. S. of the Baptist church, Miss Margaret Etheridge from the Methodist church and Mrs. W. C. P. Bethel from the Presbyterian church. All these ladies assured us a hearty welcome into their own homes and hearts.

Mrs. Charles DeLacy Bass responded in a most charming manner, assuring all that after such warm words of welcome we felt at home.

Next was the organization, enrollment of delegates, reading of minutes, etc. We were delighted with our visitor from the Little River Association, Mrs. S. J. Beeker, of Duke, N. C.

Closing devotional by Mrs. N. G. Rand.

On Wednesday evening, at 7:30, the program was continued by a very able missionary talk by Mr. Odis B. Hinnant, of Wilmington, N. C., and the devotional exercises by Rev. C. K. Proctor, of the M. E. Church, Selma.

The anthem of the choir and a vocal solo by Miss Baum were very much enjoyed.

On Thursday morning at 9:30 the Union again convened and a very full and interesting program continued through the day.

Morning prayer service by Mrs. J. J. Lane, after which Mrs. B. A. Hocutt read her report of year's work in the Association. Mrs. J. W. Sanders gave a most hearty welcome to all new societies.

District Division and quarterly meetings of these societies was splendidly discussed by Mrs. C. E. Stevens. Mrs. D. B. Olive told how to organize and run societies.

Mrs. J. M. Beaty on Correspondence Course for Training Leaders, showed how we all may become better leaders.

Our Home Mission Work, its Opportunities and Possibilities, by Mrs. D. J. Thurston. In her discussion of this subject, she used maps, in this way she gave us a clearer vision of the work.

Mrs. N. E. Ward urged all to take our magazines—Royal Service, Home and Foreign Fields, Biblical Recorder.

In the absence of Mrs. C. W. Carter, Mrs. D. J. Thurston conducted a model Missionary Society.

Mrs. Thurston had a very interesting program.

Mrs. Hardee Horne told of the wonderful "Blue Ridge", closing her remarks with an original poem on Blue Ridge.

The following subjects were then ably discussed.

Missionary Study—Its value, Books for the year, Mrs. Howard Gray.

Traveling Library—Mrs. N. B. Lewis.

Prayer, It's Place and Powers—Mrs. John E. Lanier.

Then Mrs. W. N. Jones talked very earnestly on The Church Building and Loan Fund. Mrs. Jones is always interesting and her talks full of inspiration.

Closing devotional by Mrs. G. C. Youngblood.

After a most delightful dinner served on the church lawn, devotional services were led by Mrs. A. F. Tunnell. Prayer by Mrs. E. V. Richardson.

The program for the afternoon was then taken up and the following subjects most interestingly discussed: The Louisville Training School and North

Carolina's Part in New Building, Mrs. Brinson; The Importance of the Y. W. A., Mrs. S. J. Beeker; Y. W. A.'s and G. A.'s Opportunity in Personal service, Miss Veola Pool; How to Reach the Ministerial Girl and Keep All Girls Interested, Mrs. C. A. Fisher; Sunbeams and R. A.'s Round Table Association, Miss Elizabeth Briggs.

The Missionary Pageant, by four R. A.'s from Clayton, was very much enjoyed. These boys with some others left their homes on the early train so they might be at the meeting and do their "bit". We have no slackers in this work. Just ask the boys and they are ready for service.

The Selma G. A.'s exercises were very unique and gave us an idea of the home life of Mrs. McClure and the girls at our Training School.

Just here we were glad to hear from Floy Johnson who is at the Training school.

The quartette, by Mrs. Chas. DeLacy Bass, Misses Maud Barbour, Douschka Barnes, LaRue Williams was beautiful.

Although our hearts were filled with the missionary spirit, we could not forget our soldier boys. Mrs. J. J. Lane read a tribute to Our Soldier Boys, after which Mrs. Charles Gulley in her charming manner and lovely voice, sang, "Keep the Home Fires Burning." Prayer for our Soldier boys by Mrs. D. J. Thurston.

Committee reports were then called for and the nominating committee recommended a re-election of officers for the coming year.

Committee on Time and Place recommended that the next Union be held at Four Oaks, beginning on the second Wednesday of November and continuing through Thursday. All of the reports were adopted.

A motion then prevailed that we give Mr. J. M. Beaty and Mr. W. S. Penn a vote of thanks for their printing announcements, etc.

After the closing prayer by Mr. D. J. Thurston the Union adjourned to meet in Four Oaks in November, 1918.   CLEVE BARNES, Secretary.

CONSTITUTION.

1. The Association shall be known as the Johnston County Baptist Association.

2. Its object shall be to extend the privileges of the gospel and liberal culture to all the people within its bounds and by hearty co-operation with the Baptist State Convention to help offer these privileges to all mankind in and out of its bounds, by the cordial co-operation of all the churches constituting this body.

3. It shall be composed of the pastors in active service in the Association and such delegates as shall be annually elected by the churches connected with it, each church being entitled to three delegates, unless the membership shall exceed fifty, and then an additional degelate for every twenty-five members, provided no church shall have more than eight delegates.

4. The New Hampshire Declaration of Faith shall be the summary of Divine Truth for determining questions of faith and order in this body, and the churches desiring membership in it must commit themselves to the substance of it, together with the covenant therewith submitted, and this Constitution.

5. This Association shall not have power to annul the discipline or exercise authority over any church connected with it, but it may advise with and sever its connection with any church that neglects to preserve gospel order, or that treats with contempt the objects or advice of the Association.

6. Each church shall send to the annual meetings of the Association a letter (the blanks to be furnished by the Clerk of the Association), carefully filled as per blank suggestions, stating the full work of the church for the year ending with the Sunday previous to the meeting of the Association.

7. The Association shall foster State Misssions, Home Misssions, Foreign Missions, Christian Education, the Aged Ministers' Relief Board, the Thomasville Orphanage and the Sunday School Board, and each church shall be requested to contribute to the support of these objects annually.

8. Missions and Education shall have precedence in their claims upon the consideration of this body in its regular sessions.

9. Whenever a church shall fail to be represented by delegates or letter at the annual sessions of the Association inquiry shall be made for the cause and efforts shall be made to induce such church to do its duty, and the effort shall be continued till the church is recovered or dropped from the roll.

10. The officers of the Association shall be a Moderator, a Vice-Moderator, a Clerk, a Treasurer and an Auditor elected annually by ballot (or in case when only one brother is put in nomination for an office, then the vote may be by acclamation) from among its members, to serve until their successors shall have been elected, and to perform the duties of such officers, namely, the Moderator, in presiding over the meetings, or the Vice-Moderator in his absence; the Clerk in recording and preserving minutes and other papers belonging to the body: The Treasurer in receiving and disbursing funds belonging to or entrusted to the body according to its will; the Auditor to examine the Treasurer's books at each meeting of the Association and report the same before adjournment.

11. The Association shall appoint annually an Executive Committee of five (5) from its members, who shall be entrusted with the prosecution of Missions in the Association and any other work for the interest of the Master's Kingdom which may be referred to them. This committee shall, as far as possible, co-operate with the State Mission Board in supplying the destitution in our territory, and between the meetings of the Association take such actions as may seem to them advisable for the advancement of its interest. The committee shall present to the Association at its annual meeting a report of its proceedings, with the names of the missionaries supported on the field, time of service and details of their work, together with such recommenda-

tions as in the judgment of the committee the Association should follow in planning its subsequent work.

12. The annual sessions of the Association shall begin on Wednesday after the fourth Lord's day in October at such place as may be chosen, and an introductory sermon shall be delivered on the first day of the session. Representatives from ten of the churches constituting the Association shall be a quorum.

13. This Constitution may be amended at any annual session by a two-thirds vote of all the members present.

14. The proceedings of the Woman's Central Committee shall be recorded as a part of the Minutes of the Association.

BY-LAWS.

1. The daily sessions of the Association shall be opened and closed with prayer.

2. Delegates shall be recognized by letters from their churches designating them as such.

3. The Moderator shall recognize corresponding messengers or the delegates of newly received churches by extending to them his right hand.

4. The report of the Executive Board and the missionary work of the Association shall take precedence of all other business during the morning session of the second day of the annual session.

5. The Clerk shall record and read the proceedings when called for, superintend the publication and distribution of the Minutes, preserve a file of them, and have it present at each annual session, and deliver to his successor all papers belonging to the body

6. Members desiring to speak shall first rise and address the Moderator, shall use the term "Brother" in speaking to each other; shall not speak on the same subject more than twice without permission, and shall observe the courtesy that becomes Christians.

7. The roll of members shall be called at least once and absentees marked

8. Corresponding messengers and visiting brethren shall be invited to seats with privilege of speaking, but not voting.

9. A copy of the Minutes shall be sent to the Secretary of the State Mission Board, the Secretary of the Southern Baptist Convention, the American Publication Society, 1420 Chestnut Street, Philadelphia; the Sunday School Board of the Southern Baptist Convention and the Thomasville Orphanage.

10. All questions of order not herein provided shall be decided by Kerfoot's Parliamentary Law.

TABLE I—STATISTICAL.

CHURCH.	PASTOR AND POSTOFFICE	CLERK AND POSTOFFICE	Time of Preaching	Value of Church Property	By Baptism	By Letter	By Restoration	By Letter	By Exclusion	By Death	Number of Males	Number of Females	Total Membership
							Gains		Losses				
Antioch	A. A. Pippin, Wakefield.	W. O. Hocutt, Selma, R. 2	3rd	$ 2,100	16	5	1	6	4	2	94	120	214
Bailey	J. E. Hocutt, Nashville.	J. P. Underwood, Bailey.	1st	1,500	2	2		11	1	1	30	38	68
Baptist Center	J. E. Lanier, Smithfield.	E. H. Rogers, Clayton, R. 1	3rd	600	3			3	1	1	56	66	122
Beaty Chapel	J. E. Lanier, Smithfield.	N. M. Easom, Smithfield.	4, 3 nights	100							8	20	28
Benson	G. W. Rollins, Benson.	G. Gilbert, Benson.	1st, 3d, 4th	20,000	3	3		5		3	68	104	172
Benson's Grove	G. A. Bain, Bule's Creek.	D. D. Medlin, Benson, R. 1	2nd	800	7			2			6	57	123
Bethany	W. D. Stancil, Kenly.	Kirkman Creech, Kenly.	4th	1,000	1	3			6	3	41	57	98
Bethel	R. M. VonMiller, Four Oaks.		4th	1,000	6	1				4	10	13	23
Bethesda	J. E. Lanier, Smithfield.	J. E. Smith, Wilson's Mills	4th	3,500	3			17	6		110	134	244
Blackman's Grove	R. M. VonMiller, Four Oaks.	Joseph Wood, Four Oaks, R. 2	1st	1,000				1	3		27	46	73
Purnell Mission	R. M. VonMiller, Four Oaks.	J. S. Johnson, Four Oaks.	1st	1,200	7	1					1	1	2
Canaan	G. W. Rollins, Benson.	T. J. Lee, Dunn.	1st	500	1			1	2	2	15	24	32
Carter's Chapel	G. W. Rollins, Benson.	Gray Easom, Selma.	1st	500	5			4	1	3	22	29	44
Clayton	A. C. McCall, Selma.	W. P. Creech, C...	1st	1,000		1		15	5	3	22	54	76
Clyde's Chapel	G. T. Hamby, Clayton.	C. I. Johnson, Wendell.	All	6,000	18	8		9	3	2	227	269	496
Corinth	A. A. Pippin, Wakefield.	L. T. Davis, Wendell.	3rd	500		3		7	13	1	80	102	182
Four Oaks	R. M. VonMiller, Four Oaks.	J. W. Langdon, Four Oaks.	1st—3rd	2,500	15	4		6			51	94	145
Hephzibah	J. M. Duncan, Mount Olive.	W. G. Creech, Princeton.	2nd	5,000	3	1		1			30	48	78
Hood's Chapel	G. W. Rollins, Benson.	P. T. George, Four Oaks.	3rd	400				1		1	6	11	17
Kenly	R. M. VonMiller, Four Oaks.	Mrs. F. C. Richardson, Kenly	2nd	500	3			8	1		28	33	61
Lee's Chapel	W. H. Wall, Middlesex.	W. I. Green, Zebulon.	3rd	2,500	5	5		3			22	27	49
Lizzie Mill Chapel	J. M. Duncan, Mt Olive.	J. M. Richardson, Selma.	2nd	1,500	8	1	3			10	126	166	292
Micro	R. P. Merritt, Pine Level.	Miss Sarah ..., Selma.	1st	400				1					25
Middlesex	W. D. Stancil, Kenly.	S. C. Ratten, Micro.	2nd	500		2	3	1	1		6	24	30
Mount Moriah	W. H. Wall, Middlesex.	C. A. Barber, Middlesex.	2nd—4th	1,500		6		6			41	34	75
New Bethel	C. A. Jenkins, Clayton.	Russell Powell, Anburn.	1st	2,500		1		1			45	56	101
Noble's Chapel	A. A. Pippin, Wakefield.	Geo. W. Bryan, Garner.	4th	4,200	11	5		2	3		88	99	187
Oliver's Grove	W. H. Wall.	N. L. Stott, Sims.	4th	1,500		2		2			49	57	106
Parrish Memorial	R. M. VonMiller, Four Oaks.	Miss Lena Tyner, Four Oaks	4th	700	4			3			41	71	112
Pauline	R. M. VonMiller, Four Oaks.	J. D. Creech, Selma.	1st	800	24	2	2		5		7	12	19
Pine Level	C. H. Stevens, Louisville, Ky.	Geo. Massey, Bentonsville.	4th	800	2	2	1	1			35	59	94
Pinkney	A. C. McCall, Selma.	J. F Thompson, Pine Level	1st	1,000	19	12		3	2		18	42	60
Pisgah	J. E. Lanier, Smithfield.	Mrs. B. R. Edgerton, Kenly	3rd	3,000	1				1		37	54	91
Princeton	J. M. Duncan, Mount Olive.	R. H. Higgins, Smithfield.	1st	1,500	2	3					16	15	51
Sardis	C. E. Sims, Selma.	W. I. Pearre, Princeton.	3rd	1,500	5		1	8	2		35	53	88
Selma	J. E. Lanier, Smithfield.	B. C. Powell, Smithfield.	2nd	150				9	2	2	26	45	71
Shiloh	H. F. Brinson, Smithfield.	R. S. Reynolds, Selma.	1st, 2d, 3d	1,500	11	8	1	24	2	1	21	21	43
Smithfield	C. E. Stevens, Selma.	Walter Williams, Garner.	2nd	800	11	1		11	3	2	061	162	268
Thanksgiving	G. T. Mills, Wendell.	T. J. Lassiter, Smithfield.	All	10,000	13	8		4		3	38	62	100
Trinity	A. A. Pippin, Wakefield.	Daily H. Price, Selma.	2nd	1,200	12	4	1	4			95	119	214
Wendell	J. E. ..., Smithfield.	J. M Lawhon, Benson.	3rd	1,200	9	1	1	1			43	52	95
White Oak		Geo. H. Wright, Wendell.	2nd—4th	2,500	4	1		7	2		38	62	100
	A. A. Pippin, Wakefield.	J. I. Murphrey, Selma.	2nd	3,000				2		3	102	147	249
Wilson's Mills	J. E. ..., Smithfield.	J. T. Holt, Wilson's Mills.	2nd—4th	1,000		3		2		1	97	118	217
											24	31	55

CHURCH.	Pastor's Salary.	Building and Repairs.	Incidentals.	Sunday School Expenses.	The Poor.	Minute Fund.	Building Fund.	State Missions.	Home Missions.	Foreign Missions.	Sunday School Missions.	Orphanage.	Min'sterial Education.	Ministerial Relief.	Colleges and Schools.	Oth'r Objects.	Total.
Antioch	$164.00	$285.00	$	$17.52	$	$2.50	$5.00	$25.00	$5.00	$5.00	$2.50	$5.00	$5.00	$2.50	$2.75	$35.00	$496.77
Bailey	175.00		1.00	12.00	4.00	1.50	6.50	12.50	3.50	5.00	2.00	5.00	4.00	2.50			132.50
Baptist Cntr	125.00			20.00	3.00	1.00	5.00	15.00	6.40	5.00	2.00	2.50	5.00	2.70		98.00	293.60
Beaty Chapel	39.56			7.00		2.50	4.00	7.50	6.50	2.50	1.00	2.50	3.00	1.50		21.00	95.06
Benson	554.11	932.11	105.56	39.80		2.50		93.68	23.78	18.30	2.50	179.60	30.00	5.00	4.65	73.50	3980.09
Benson's Grove	30.00		1.00	6.00	5.00	1.00	4.00		5.00	1.00	1.00	2.50	2.50	1.75			84.25
Bethany	66.00			27.00			2.00	11.00	1.00	1.00		6.50	2.50	2.50			34.30
Bethel	32.00										1.00						5.00
Bethesda	300.00	1000.00	12.00	40.00		2.30	7.50	45.00	6.40	7.50	2.50	15.00	10.00	5.00	5.00	121.00	502.40
Blackman's Grove	125.00	30.00	15.00	20.00		2.00	1.50	22.50	8.00	6.00	1.50	8.50	7.50	1.50			224.91
Bail Mission	7.36			8.50				2.60	1.00	1.00		7.41	7.00				20.86
	43.40		.50	4.00		1.00	1.00	2.00	1.50	2.00	1.50	1.50	2.50	.50			85.65
	43.90		2.00	4.75		1.00	1.50	2.50	1.00	1.00	.50	1.00		.50		2.10	51.90
Carter's Chapel	1.27					1.00	.50	12.50	5.00	5.00	1.00	9.00		1.50			177.27
Clyde's Chapel	500.00	789.48	247.95	10.00	7.50	3.00	50.00	275.00	75.00	200.40	5.00	185.94	65.00	2.00	62.41	1053.91	4675.72
Corinth	175.00		25.30	73.13	7.50	2.50	12.50	46.00	16.50	18.50	5.00	15.00	13.00	20.00			322.95
Four Oaks	125.00	360.00	14.72	41.89		1.00	15.00	15.00	2.50	15.00	2.00	15.00	10.00	3.50	41.00	599.69
Hephzibah	324.98	1287.81	61.75	61.75		2.00	10.00	25.70	12.61	14.33	1.00	12.50	12.50	5.00	10.45	5.30	1839.98
Hall's Grove	25.00		1.40	7.00		1.00	2.50	5.00	2.00	3.00	2.50	3.10	2.50	1.50	4.30	54.30
Kenly	150.00		25.00	2.25		1.50	5.00	17.80	3.00	3.00	2.50	2.00	2.50	1.50		202.45
Lee's Chapel	150.00		85.00	23.83		2.50	5.00	15.00	5.00	10.00	2.56	18.61	2.50	5.00		321.47
Live Oak	150.00	30.00	3.00	0.60	10.85	2.50	2.50	25.00	10.00	3.00	2.50	2.00	2.50	1.00		267.50
Lizzie Mill	23.71					1.00	2.50	5.00	1.00	1.15		1.00	2.30	1.00		40.71
Micro	50.00		1.25			.50	1.00	5.00	.30	1.00	1.50	1.00	1.50	1.00	2.10	8.69
	68.00		3.00	6.40		1.50	12.50	14.75	6.45	5.00	1.00	14.38	9.00	2.50		300.00	160.08
Mount Moriah	200.00	3.35	5.29	48.24		3.50	26.34	76.71	33.00	56.34	1.18	29.93	30.00	10.00	242.24	708.98
eW Bethel	200.00	726.50	30.50	23.52		2.30	23.52	33.00	10.00	10.00	1.00	25.00	12.50	7.50	13.06	55.00	1524.24
Noble's Chapel	250.00			0.00		2.30	20.00	15.00	10.00		1.00	15.00	10.00	2.50		35.00	424.50
Oliver's Grove	126.80			3.25		1.00		10.00	2.50	10.00	.50	12.50	7.50	1.00	3.25	180.80
Parrish Memorial	12.50	2.50				1.00	5.00					2.50	2.50	2.00			28.00
Pauline	100.00	37.50	2.60	0.00		2.00		10.00	2.50	2.50	2.00	2.00	5.00	2.00	33.00	212.00
Pine Level	50.00		74.00	7.00		2.00	12.50	7.50	7.50	2.50	.50	2.50	5.00	2.00	1.00	96.50
Pinkney	150.00	50.00	.88	40.00	5.00	2.00		23.00	7.50	7.50	2.00	7.00	7.50	1.50		390.00
Pisgah	170.00	21.55	50.00	2.08		1.00	4.00	7.50	2.60	19.00	1.00	2.50	5.00	1.50		109.57
Princeton	79.33		2.60	23.75	12.00	1.50	10.00	35.46	21.89		1.00	20.00	10.00	2.50	556.00	959.45
Sardis	00.00			16.44	10.25	1.50	5.00	20.00	2.50	2.50	1.00	2.50	2.50	2.00	25.25	198.40
Selma	800.00	6.25	11.04	47.54	5.00	3.50		25.58	25.41	30.04	2.30	4.32	25.00	2.50		150.10
Shiloh	150.00		10.50	10.54		2.00	25.00	94.23	15.85		2.50	37.20	10.00	10.00	232.00	1212.57
Smithfield	1108.56	23.48	104.64		19.40	3.50	25.00	160.60	51.85	70.00	1.00	135.50	25.00	5.00	5.50	69.00	338.55
Thanksgiving	118.30	2.60	10.00	10.00		1.60	5.00	15.00	2.50	2.50	1.44	5.58	7.50	2.50	22.85	573.12	3558.30
	55.00	800.00	5.70	90.78		3.50	25.00	40.00	2.00	2.00	6.06	2.50	16.00	10.00	169.95
Wendell	500.00	1270.20			7.50	.94		7.50	37.13	42.37	6.66	53.78	16.00	7.50	4.10	95.92	2247.54
White Oak	250.00					3.50	25.00	15.00	7.50	2.50	2.50	15.00	12.50	7.50		368.60
Wilson's Mills	100.00	40.00	12.00	40.00	5.00	1.50	5.00	15.00	2.50	2.50	1.50	5.00	5.00	2.50	75.00	314.50
Total	8740.80	9677.61	1255.61	960.27	94.50	78.80	331.94	1361.61	1461.18	675.35	83.38	948.38	400.00	173.40	137.52	3596.92	29773.39

TABLE III.—SUNDAY SCHOOLS.

CHURCH.	SUPERINTENDENT AND POSTOFFICE.	SECRETARY AND POSTOFFICE.	No. Schools.	Officers and Teachers.	Pupils.	Total Enrollment.	Church Members in S. S.	Months kept open.	Baptisms from School.	School Expenses.	Missions.	Orphanage.	Other Objects.	Total Contributions.
Bailey	J. R. Talton, Selma	W. O. Hocutt, Selma	1	8	118	126	90	12	12	$10.00	$2.25	$2.59	$2.75	$17.62
Center	J. P. Underwood, Bailey	J. R. Finch, Bailey	1	5	88	88	21	12	2	12.00	1.65			13.05
Bethel	J. C. Hardee, Clayton	John Ellis, Clayton	1	6	120	126	60	12	2	20.00				20.00
Benson	J. M. Beaty, Smithfield	Jesse Parrish, Smithfield	1	3	35	39	10	12	2	7.00				7.00
Benson's Grove	W. L. Hall, Benson	E. H. Dixon, Benson	1	24	220	244	85	8	6	39.80		35.00	370.50	445.30
Bethany	William Heath, Benson	L. E. Barber, Benson	1	3	50	53	6	8	6	6.00				6.00
Bethel	Moses Creech, Kenly	Carmel Creech, Kenly	1	10	107	117	65	12	6	15.00		7.50	5.00	27.00
Bethesda	Lemon Johnson, Clayton	V. S. Smith, Wilson's Mills	1	10	75	85	50	12	10	12.00				12.00
Blackman's Grove	F. P. Wood, Four Oaks	N. Mahler, Four Oaks	1	6	56	62	35	12	1	8.00	2.00	2.00		12.50
Burnell Mission	J. S. Johnson, Four Oaks	Miss Kate Tyner, Four Oaks	1	4	42	46	3	6	7	5.00				5.00
Calvary	C. F. Wagstaff, Dunn	Miss Lessie Lee, Dunn	1	4	25	29	11	8		4.75				4.75
Canaan														
Carter's Chapel	J. T. Blackman, Micro	B. F. Woodruff, Selma	1	6	104	110	60	12	5	10.05				10.05
Clayton	J. T. Talton, Clayton	L. M. Edgerton, Clayton	1	13	300	313	250	12	10	73.13	143.80	76.38	196.45	489.76
Clyde's Chapel	C. M. Martin, Well	J. E. Johnson, Wendell	1	7	100	107	60	12	1	15.00				15.00
Corinth	J. N. Stipes, Zebulon	T. T. Davis, Wendell	1	5	106	111	6	12	7	6.85	3.54		31.50	41.89
Four Oaks	R. A. Bain, Four Oaks	J. W. Sanders, Four Oaks	1	8	95	103	52	12	3	61.75	24.96	12.35	12.00	111.46
Hephzibah	W. G. ——, Princeton	J. F. Earp, Pine Level	1	5	30	35	10	12		7.00				7.00
Hood's Grove	Carver Wood, Bentonsville	Roland Hayes, Four Oaks	1	7	45	52	40	6		23.83	12.00	18.61		54.44
Kenly	A. J. Broughton, Kenly	C. E. Pittman, Kenly	1	8	70	77	40	12	4			1.25		1.25
Lee's	Malone Eskridge, Middlesex	Earl Lewis, Middlesex	1	8	60	68	40	12	4	7.16				7.16
Live Oak	M. B. Richardson, Selma	W. B. Morris, Selma	1	3	50	53		8		6.49				6.49
Lizzie Mill Chapel	R. P. Merritt, Pine Level	J. M. O'Neal, Selma	1	5	95	100	50	12						
Micro	D. C. A. Barber, Middlesex	Clyde Smith, Micro	1	11	100	111	50	8		40.00	.75	8.38		49.13
Mount Moriah	C. A. Barber, Middlesex	W. K. Ballentine, Middlesex	1	11	105	115	40	12	10	43.15	5.18	79.05	1.05	129.33
New Bethel	Elliott Pool, Clayton	Eugene Britt, Clayton	1	10	114	124	78	9	8	23.02	30.20	81.60	113.26	248.59
Noble's	Ralph Britt, Garner	Robert Britt, Clayton	1	7	80	87	20	12		10.00	1.00			10.00
Oliver's Grove	D. L. Flowers, Sims	O. Bullock, Sims	1	6	80	86	20	12		3.25	1.00			4.25
Parrish Memorial	E. S. Holloman, Selma	Miss M. Holloman, Benson	1	5	50	55	25	10	10	9.50			.50	10.00
Pauline	A. G. Adams, Four Oaks	Miss Pearl Creech, Four Oaks	1	4	50	54	29	6		7.00				7.00
Pine Level	N. M. Gurley, Pine Level	Miss Pat. Braxton, Pine Level	1	9	150	159	100	12	16	19.54	20.80			40.34
Pinkney	R. E. Lee, Kenly, R. 1	Otis Lee, Kenly	1	7	16	16	10	12	16	12.08	2.37		1.00	15.45
Pisgah	F. E. Whitley, Smithfield	A. G. Jones, Smithfield	1	1	75	85	35	12	1	28.75	5.00			33.75
Princeton	J. B. Bridges, Princeton	W. I. Pearce, Princeton	1	5	50	55	20	12	5	16.44				16.44
Sardis														
Selma	B. S. Reynolds, Selma	N. J. Wiggs, Selma	1	17	289	316	150	12	10	47.54	12.75	10.65		70.94
Shiloh	S. H. Averitt, Garner	Ransom Averitt, Garner	1	7	107	114	37	12		10.50				10.50
Smithfield	T. S. Ragsdale, Smithfield	John Ives, Smithfield	1	14	184	198	90	12	11	104.64	106.32	126.66	100.69	445.68
Thanksgiving	W. S. Earp, Selma	Orange Earp, Selma	1	7	101	108	45	12	3	10.00	.75			18.55
Trinity	W. H. Godwin, Benson	Miss Pearl Lawhon, Benson	1	3	35	48	32	12	3	5.00			2.80	5.00
Wendell	W. H. Rhodes, Wendell	W. R. Johnson, Wendell	1	11	290	301	68	12	3	90.75	27.15	40.96	320.55	475.34
White Oak	A. L. Batton, Clayton	J. M. Green, Clayton	1	9	89	92	66	12		33.60	4.00			37.60
Wilson's Mills	J. T. Holt, Wilson's Mills	Jas. Turnage, Wilson's Mills	1	9	65	74	30	12		40.00	4.00			44.00

CHURCHES	NAME OF ORGANIZATION	PRESIDENT AND POSTOFFICE	Number of Members	State Missions	Home Missions	Foreign Missions	Sunday School Board	Training School	Other Objects	Total Contributions
Bailey	Woman's Mary Society	Miss Mary Underwood, Bailey	12	$ 2.50	$ 6.30	$ 5.70		$ 3.25		$ 12.00
Baptist Center	Woman's Society	Mrs. J. C. Hardee, Clayton	10	7.95	11.80		3.00	3.65	10.00	6.30
Benson	Woman's Missionary Society	Mrs. J. L. Hall, Benson	20	3.00	4.50	32.00			5.95	68.40
Benson	Young Woman's Auxiliary	Mrs. C. A. Fisher, Benson	14	4.84	1.75	3.30	2.10	.50	1.00	13.45
Benson	Sunbeam Society	Lillie Canaday, Benson	40	2.89	2.50					13.49
Bethesda	Royal Ambassadors	O'Neal Brady, Benson	9	1.50	1.90			5.00		8.40
Clayton	Woman's Society	Mrs. J. E. Barr, Smithfield	9	91.35	55.15	91.45		43.55	20.50	302.00
Clayton	Woman's Society	Mrs. C. W. Carter, Clayton	60	25.00	10.10	10.10		6.35	80.30	136.75
Clayton	Young Woman's Auxiliary	Mrs. Lois Pass, Clayton		8.60	3.69	1.20		7.50		21.00
Clayton	Sunbeam Society	Mrs. W. J. Payne, Clayton	53	2.50	2.00	.50		.50		10.90
Clayton	Royal Ambassadors	Mrs. D. J. Bam, Clayton		27.72		2.00		4.50	17.50	51.72
Clayton	Girls' Auxiliary	Mrs. B. A. Hocutt, Clayton	20	16.00	4.00	5.00			5.30	25.00
Four Oaks	Woman's Society	Mrs. W. H. Bunch, Bell	23	3.00	5.80	9.00		10.45		35.55
Four Oaks	Woman's Missionary Society	Mrs. J. W. Sanders, Four Oaks	15	2.70		3.03				5.73
Kenly	Sunbeam Band	Mrs. VonMiller, Four Oaks	12	7.00	1.80	1.20		3.50	3.30	16.80
Kenly	Woman's Society	Mrs. H. B. Bain, Kenly	15						1.00	1.00
Lake Mill Chapel	Sunbeam Band	Mrs. E. Bain, Kenly			1.00				2.40	3.40
Micro	Woman's Society	Mrs. C. A. White, Selma	15	7.00	1.45	5.00		5.00		1.45
Middlesex	Woman's Missionary Society	Mrs. H. J. Corbett, Micro	24	5.00	5.00	4.00		2.00	24.83	46.83
Middlesex	Sunbeam Band	Mrs. W. H. Wall, Middlesex	13	3.00	4.00	1.00		2.25	7.55	14.00
Mont Moriah	Woman's Missionary Society	Janice Ballentine, Middlesex		8.00	8.00			1.50	.50	25.80
Mont Moriah	Sunbeam Band	Mrs. C. B. Hinnant, Bain	12					6.25	5.00	12.00
Mount Moriah	Royal Ambassadors	Miss Jessamine Pool, Raleigh	15							19.46
Parrish Memorial	Woman's Missionary	Guy Bancom, Raleigh	10	11.00	5.50	5.00		4.50	2.50	28.50
Pine Level	Woman's Missionary Society	Mrs. Anie Pender, Selma	10	.40	15.30	10.45		15.25	6.75	58.10
Pisgah	Woman's Missionary Society	Mrs. D. B. Oliver, Pine Level	30	10.65	11.05	18.90		7.90	2.75	51.25
Selma	Young Woman's Auxiliary	Mrs. J. E. Lanier, Smithfield	10	1.65	2.00	1.35		3.35		7.75
Selma	Sunbeam Band	Mrs. E. V. Bird, Selma	40	1.52		1.58		1.18		4.28
Shiloh	Woman's Society	Scdice Stallings, Selma	12	5.00	5.50	2.50		5.50	16.00	40.50
Shiloh	Woman's Band	Miss Anie Myatt, Clayton							1.00	1.00
Smithfield	Woman's Missionary Society	Mrs. H. G. Gray, Smithfield		80.00	26.35	30.05		22.85	39.35	208.60
Smithfield	Young Woman's	Miss Ola Brady, Smithfield			1.00	3.00				4.00
Smithfield	Sunbeam Band	Mrs. J. M. Beaty, Smithfield	3	8.50	4.00	5.00				17.50
Thanksgiving	Woman's Missionary Society	Mrs. Alger Wood, Selma	17							
Thanksgiving	Sunbeam Band	Miss Melissia Linch, Selma								
Wendell	Woman's Missionary Society	Mrs. L. S. Wiggins, Wendell		2.35	9.95	2.10		4.10		18.50
Wendell	Sunbeam Band	Mrs. G. T. Pris, Wendell		1.60						1.60
Wells Mills	Woman's Society	Mrs. G. F. Uzzel, Wilson's Mills		2.50	2.50	2.50				5.00
Total				295.42	222.79	155.36	5.10	170.40	252.48	1303.45

PLEDGES FOR 1918.

Churches.	State Missions.	Home Missions.	Foreign Missions.	Sunday School	Orphanage.	Christian Education.	Ministerial Relief.	Association Missions.	Building Fund.	Minute Fund.	Total.
Antioch	$ 25.00	$ 7.50	$ 7.50	$ 2.50	$ 5.00	$ 3.00	$ 5.00	$10.00	$ 5.00	$ 2.50	$ 75
Bailey	12.50	3.50	5.00	1.00	5.00	4.00	2.50	8.50	6.50	1.50	50
Baptist Center.	15.00	5.00	5.00	2.00	5.00	5.00	2.50	10.00	5.00	1.50	56
Bealy Chapel..	7.50	2.50	2.50	1.00	2.50	3.00	1.50	5.00	4.00	1.00	30
Benson	75.00	10.00	15.00	2.50	20.00	10.00	5.00	25.00	15.00	2.50	180
Benson's Grove.	8.50	2.50	2.50	1.00	2.50	2.00	1.00	5.00	4.00	1.00	30
Bethany	10.00	5.00	5.00	1.00	2.50	2.00	2.50	5.00	2.00	1.00	50
Bethel	5.00	2.00	2.00	1.00	2.50	2.50	1.00	2.50	2.50	1.00	23
Bethesda	45.00	5.00	7.50	2.50	15.00	10.00	5.00	25.00	7.50	2.50	125
Blackman's G've	25.00	7.50	7.50	1.50	5.00	7.50	2.00	9.00	7.50	2.50	75
Burnell Mission	5.00	1.00	1.00	.50	1.00	2.00	1.00	2.50	1.00	.50	15
Calvary	7.50	1.50	1.50	.50	1.50	2.50	1.50	5.00	2.50	1.00	25
Canaan	5.00	1.50	1.50	.50	1.50	1.50	1.00	2.50	1.50	1.00	17
Carter's Chapel.	12.50	5.00	5.00	1.00	5.00	5.00	2.00	6.00	7.50	1.50	50
Clayton	275.00	75.00	75.00	5.00	100.00	65.00	20.00	50.00	50.00	5.00	725
Clyde s Chapel.	25.00	7.50	7.50	2.50	5.00	10.00	2.50	25.00	12.50	1.50	100
Corinth	16.00	3.50	6.00	1.00	6.00	6.00	2.50	10.00	5.00	2.50	58
Four Oaks......	23.50	7.50	7.50	2.50	7.50	10.00	5.00	15.00	10.00	1.50	90
Hephzibah	5.50	1.00	1.00	.50	1.00	2.50	1.00	4.00	2.50	1.00	20
Hood's Grove...	10.00	4.00	4.00	1.00	2.50	5.00	2.50	7.50	7.50	1.00	45
Kenly	15.00	5.00	5.00	2.50	5.00	5.00	2.50	13.50	5.00	1.50	50
Lee's Chapel...	25.00	10.00	10.00	3.00	5.00	7.00	5.00	20.00	5.00	2.50	92
Live Oak	5.00	1.00	1.00	.50	2.50	2.50	1.00	3.00	2.50	1.00	20
Lizzie Mill Chap	2.50	1.00	1.00	1.50	1.00	2.00	1.00	2.50	1.00	.50	14
Micro	4.00	5.00	5.00	1.00	2.50	5.00	1.30	12.50	2.50	1.00	50
Middlesex	.00	5.00	5.00	1.00	5.00	5.00	2.50	12.50	12.50	1.50	70
Mount Moriah..	45.00	30.00	50.00	7.00	35.00	30.00	10.00	50.00	36.50	3.50	325
New Bethel.....	35.00	10.00	10.00	2.00	15.00	12.50	7.50	25.00	20.00	2.50	140
Noble's Chapel.	15.00	2.50	5.00	1.00	5.00	10.00	2.50	12.50	5.00	1.50	60
Oliver's Grove .	5.00	1.00	1.00	.50	1.00	2.50	1.00	4.50	2.50	1.00	20
Parrish Memo..	15.00	4.00	4.00	1.00	2.50	5.00	2.50	10.00	5.00	1.00	50
Pauline	7.50	2.50	2.50	1.00	2.50	2.50	1.00	5.50	5.00	1.00	35
Pine Level	25.00	7.50	7.50	2.50	7.50	7.50	5.00	15.00	12.50	2.00	92
Pinkney	10.00	2.50	2.50	1.00	2.50	2.50	1.00	7.50	4.00	1.00	35
Pisgah	30.00	17.50	12.50	2.00	20.00	12.50	4.00	15.00	10.00	2.00	125
Princeton	20.00	2.50	2.50	1.00	2.50	5.00	2.50	7.50	5.00	1.50	50
Sardis	20.00	5.00	5.00	1.00	2.50	5.00	2.50	7.50	5.00	1.50	50
Selma	75.00	25.00	30.00	2.50	25.00	31.00	10.00	25.00	25.00	3.50	250
Shiloh	25.00	7.50	5.00	1.00	13.00	12.50	5.00	15.00	2.00	1.50	88
Smithfield	160.00	50.00	70.00	10.00	50.00	25.00	10.00	25.00	25.00	3.50	428
Thanksgiving ..	15.00	2.50	2.50	1.00	2.50	7.50	2.50	10.00	5.00	1.50	50
Trinity	7.50	2.00	2.00	1.00	2.00	2.50	1.00	6.00	2.50	1.00	27
Wendell	50.00	25.00	25.00	5.00	26.50	30.00	5.00	25.00	30.00	3.50	225
White Oak.....	25.00	7.50	10.00	2.50	15.00	12.50	5.00	15.00	5.00	2.50	100
Wilson's Mills .	15.00	2.50	5.00	1.00	5.00	5.00	2.50	7.50	5.00	1.50	50
Total	1219.00	390.00	446.50	82.50	463.50	410.50	163.50	579.00	399.50	78.00	4416

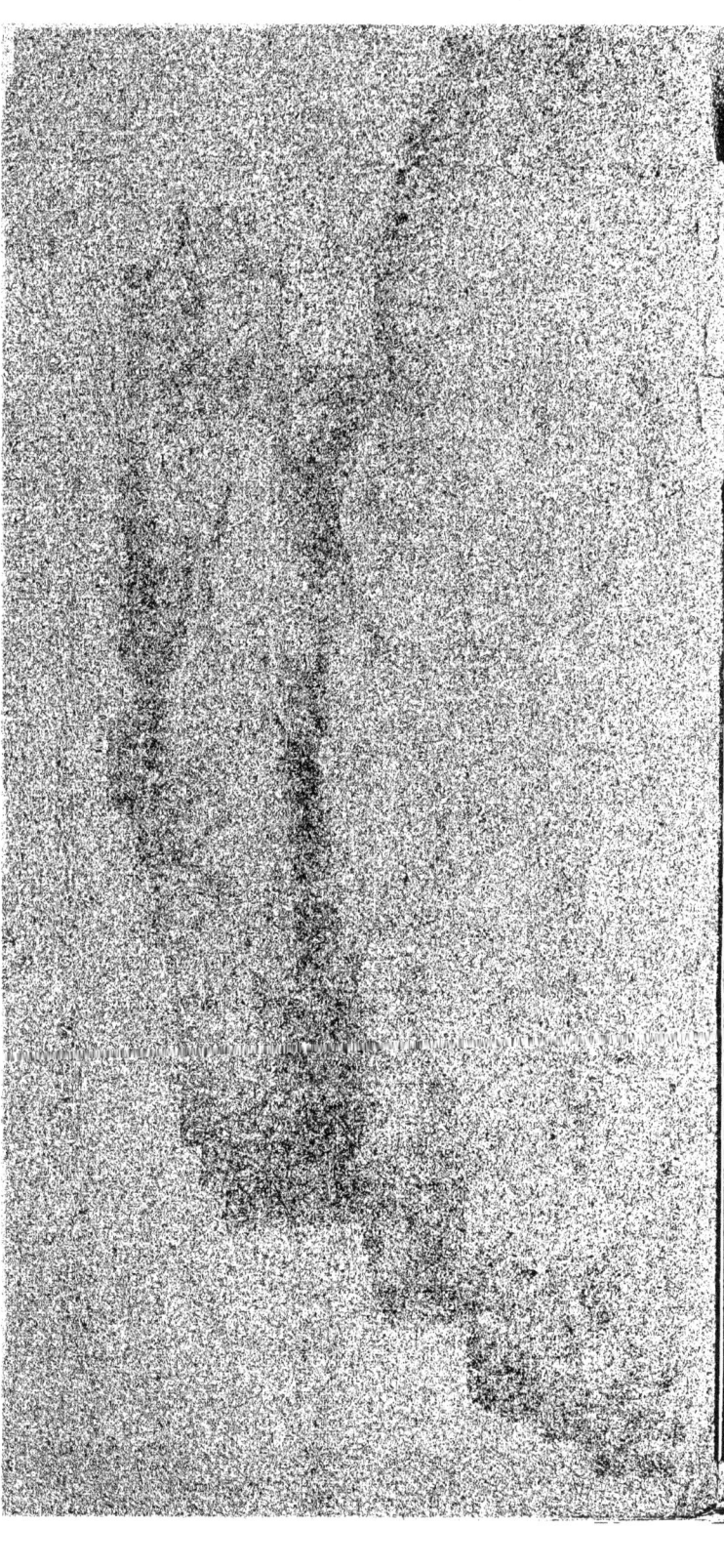

MINUTES

OF THE

SIXTEENTH ANNUAL SESSION

OF THE

Johnston Co. Baptist Association

HELD WITH THE

BETHESDA BAPTIST CHURCH

NOVEMBER 26 and 27, 1918.

The next session will be held with Bailey Baptist Church, October 29, 30 and 31, 1919.

Rev. R. R. Lanier to preach the Introductory Sermon.

RALEIGH
MUTUAL PUBLISHING COMPANY, PRINTERS
1919

MINUTES

OF THE

SIXTEENTH ANNUAL SESSION

OF THE

Johnston Co. Baptist Association

HELD WITH THE

BETHESDA BAPTIST CHURCH

NOVEMBER 26 and 27, 1918

The next session will be held with Bailey Baptist Church, October 29, 30 and 31, 1919.

Rev. R. R. Lanier to preach the Introductory Sermon.

RALEIGH
MUTUAL PUBLISHING COMPANY, PRINTERS
1919

OFFICERS.

Moderator—R. H. Gower...........................Clayton
Vice-Moderator—J. J. Lane........................Auburn
Clerk and Treasurer—J. E. Lanier...............Smithfield
Auditor—J. L. Hall...............................Benson

EXECUTIVE COMMITTEE.

John E. Lanier, Chairman.......................Smithfield
J. B. Creech...................................Four Oaks
J. F. Pool.......................................Clayton
J. L. Hall...Benson
L. H. Johnson..............................Wilson's Mills

DELEGATES AND BOARD MEMBERS.

Delegates to Baptist State Convention—Roy Baucom, G. A.
Smith and Alonzo Parrish.
  Delegate to Southern Baptist Convention—R. H. Gower.
  Member of State Board of Missions—Judge F. H. Brooks.
  Home Missions Representative—A. C. Hamby.
  Foreign Missions Representative—R. M. Von Miller.

COMMITTEE IN CHARGE OF AND TO MAKE REPORTS ON OBJECTS FOR THE YEAR 1919.

  State Missions—J. W. Smith.
  Home Missions—S. H. Averitt.
  Foreign Missions—J. J. Lane.
  Sunday-schools—Prof. L. T. Royal.
  Orphanage—J. F. Pool.
  Christian Education—T. J. Lassiter.
  Ministerial Relief—D. J. Thurston.
  Temperance—J . B. Creech.
  Woman's Work—C. W. Carter.
  B. Y. P. U. Work—Judge F. H. Brooks.
  Biblical Recorder—J. E. Dupree.

LIST OF MINISTERS.

H. F. Brinson..................................Smithfield
A. C. Hamby......................................Clayton
J. E. Dupree.......................................Selma
R. L. Hocutt...............................Wendell, R. 1
R. R. Lanier.......................................Selma
John E. Lanier.................................Smithfield
R. P. Merritt.................................Smithfield
G. T. Mills.......................................Wendell
Wallace Hartsell...............................Middlesex
A. A. Pippin....................................Wakefield
G. W. Rollins......................................Benson
C. E. Stevens...................................Four Oaks
W. D. Stancil......................................Kenly
R. M. Von Miller..................................Wilson

ENROLLED DELEGATES.

Antioch—G. R. Whitley.

Bailey—J. P. Underwood, C. T. Phillips, J. W. B. Finch.

Baptist Center—Herbert Hardee.

Beaty Chapel—W. M. Eason.

Benson—J. L. Hall, G. W. Rollins.

Benson's Grove— ————.

Bethany—W. D. Stancil, Kirkman Creech, Hobson Creech.

Bethel—Mrs. J. R. Burns.

Bethesda—D. L. Jones, A. E. Godwin, J. T. Coats.

Blackman's Grove—C. E. Stevens, Mrs. C. E. Stevens.

Burnell Mission— ————.

Calvary— ————.

Canaan—Mrs. Hudson.

Carter's Chapel—Martin Thorn.

Clayton—C. W. Carter, A. C. Hamby, J. M. Turley, D. J. Yelvington.

Clyde's Chapel—C. I. Johnson.

Corinth—B. B. Hocutt, H. B. Andrews, S. T. Price, J. B. Woodard, Julius Williams.

Four Oaks—R. M. Von Miller, J. B. Creech.

Hale's Chapel—J. P. Price, J. B. Richardson.

Hephzibah—J. F. Earp.

Hood's Grove— ————.

Kenly— ————.

Lee's Chapel—L. M. Price.

Live Oak— ————.

Lizzie Mills—Mrs. R. P. Merritt, R. P. Merritt.

Micro—C. L. Batten, J. H. Broadwell, Belva L. Batten, Mrs. R. L. Batten.

Middlesex—Wallace Hartsell.

Mount Moriah—W. A. Brummitt, J. F. Pool, J. J. Lane, R. A. Baucom.

New Bethel—Mrs. George W. Bryan, Mary Bryan, C. L. Britt.

Noble's Chapel— ————.

Oliver's Grove— ————.

Parrish Memorial—E. S. Holloman, Frank Batten, Z. A. Parrish.

Pauline—W. B. Joyner.

Pine Level—J. E. Dupree, C. I. Godwill, F. C. Price, N. M. Gurley.

Pinkney—W. T. Radford.

Pisgah—P. E. Whitley, Mrs. P. E. Whitley, Florida Bailey, W. D. Johnson.

Princeton— ————.

Sardis—N. B. Stevens.

Selma—R. R. Lanier.

Shiloh—S. H. Averitt, Ottis Coats.

Smithfield—H. F. Brinson, J. M. Beaty, F. H. Brooks.

Thanksgiving—Crange Earp.

Trinity—J. L. Johnson.

Wendell—G. T. Mills.

White Oak—C. C. Liles.

Wilson's Mills—J. T. Holt, G. G. Beaty, J. D. Beasely.

PROCEEDINGS

On account of the epidemic of influenza in our country, the meeting of the Association was postponed until November the 26th and 27th. On the morning of the 26th the body met with Bethesda Church. Devotional exercises were conducted by Rev. J. E. Dupree. The Moderator then called the Sixteenth Annual Session of the Johnston County Association to order.

The following brethren were appointed as the Committee on Credentials and Enrollment: J. L. Hall, J. J. Wallace and J. B. Beasley.

Delegates were enrolled, and sixteen churches were reported.

The Moderator called the Vice-Moderator, J. J. Lane, to the chair, and declared the election of officers in order. The following were elected:

Moderator—R. H. Gower.

Vice-Moderator—J. J. Lane.

Clerk and Treasurer—J. E. Lanier.

Auditor—J. L. Hall.

The organization being perfected, the regular order of business was taken up.

The report on the Biblical Recorder was called for. Rev. Wallace Hartsell, who was to have read the report, was not present. On motion, the report was discussed by Dr. Livingston Johnson.

Rev. A. C. Hamby read the following resolution, which was adopted:

Resolved, (1) That the Johnston Association join heartily with the Board of Missions in the effort to add 12,000 new subscribers to the list of the Biblical Recorder, and that we undertake to secure 250 of these subscribers in this session of the Association; that we apportion to each church of the Association one new subscriber to every twenty of its membership; and that we send statement of its apportionment to each church directly from this Association, with the request that the church pass on this matter at its first conference after the Association, and that the new subscribers be secured and forwarded at once to the Board of Missions.

(2) That in order to reach some of the people in our churches who do not take the Recorder, and as an aid to our churches in keeping the Recorder and other phases of our work before their members, we recommend that the churches of this Association take a club of the Monthly Bulletin printed by the Board of

Missions, each copy enclosing also a great Tract, at the rate of $1.00 per dozen per year.

(3) That this Association co-operate with the Board of Missions in the location and operation of one of the simultaneous and uniform Schools of Pastors and Workers to be held each year within the boundaries of this Association.

The introductory sermon was preached by Rev. G. W. Rollins. Subject: "Individual Christian Conscience," Text, Luke, 16.

Following the sermon, a petitionary letter from Hale's Chapel, a church organized during the year, was read. The letter was turned over to the Committee on Credentials for investigation, which, after investigation, recommended that the church be received into the membership of our Association. On a motion, the body voted unanimously to receive Hale's Chapel into the Association, and the Moderator extended the right hand of fellowship to Brothers J. P. Price and J. B. Richardson, delegates from the new church.

Brother J. F. Pool made a report for the Executive Committee on the resolution presented last year to the Association by Brother George L. Jones, as to changing the time of meeting. He reported unfavorably on the resolution. A motion was made to accept the report of the committee, which was carried

There being no further business, the body was dismissed with prayer by Brother Hamby for recess.

Tuesday Afternoon.

The afternoon session was opened with a song and praise service. After calling for miscellaneous matters, the report of the Executive and Building Committee was read by J. E. Lanier, after which the Moderator asked Brother Von Miller to offer a prayer of thanksgiving to God for His blessing upon us. A motion to adopt the report was discussed by J. E. Lanier, J. E. Dupree, C. E. Stevens and R. M. Von Miller. Brother Von Miller mentioned the debt on the Four Oaks Church and the effort which was being made to raise the indebtedness. An offering was taken up for same, amounting to $78.70.

Report of the Executive Committee.

Your committee is glad to report that this has been a good year for the mission work in our Association. One church has become self-sustaining, and several others reduced their requests for aid from the State Board. We secured regular resident pastors for all our mission churches. From all reports, the pastors have done faithful and efficient work.

The State Board of Missions increased the appropriations to the work in our Association. This increase, with the aid from our Associational Missions, have enabled us to place good men in the fields. Three men have given all their time to mission churches, while four others have given a part of their time. Yet, because of the scarcity of funds, our men have had to serve too many points to do their best work.

The reports that have come from our mission work are very gratifying. Good meetings have been reported, with quite a number of members added to the membership of the churches. In most all the churches there has been an increase in the contributions to the benevolent objects. Most all have made some increase in the pastor's salary.

The policy that your Board has tried to carry out has been developing the work we have started, instead of organizing new points. However, there has been a church organized at Hale's Schoolhouse, in the northern part of our territory. The people in the community bought the school property and called a presbytery to organize a church at the above-named place. Rev. W. G. Hall has served the work as pastor since the organization.

We, your committee, submit the following recommendations:

1. That all our mission churches become self-supporting as soon as possible for them to do so.

2. That the members of these churches take a greater interest in the local work and the cause at large, and take and read our Baptist papers and literature, that they may be informed as to our denominational work.

3. That all our churches make more generous offerings to State and Associational Missions.

Respectfully submitted,

JOHN E. LANIER,
J. B. CREECH,
J. L. HALL,
J. F. POOL,
J. T. HOLT.

Report of Building Committee.

At the meeting of our Association a year ago plans were then made to build a new house of worship at Hephziban. As Brother J. M. Beaty had begun this work, your committee asked him to continue it. But, owing to the conditions of building on account of the war, the work was delayed for some time. Within the last few weeks the material for the house has been placed on the ground. A carpenter has been secured to do the work, and we hope that it will not be long before the house will be in such condition that the congregation can use it for services.

As there was no new point at which the Committee thought it wise to build a house at the present time, and seeing the need

of a new house of worship at Shiloh, and realizing the diffculty
before the Church to build a house sufficient to meet the needs·
of the community, the Committee voted unanimously to donate
this year's Building Fund to aid in the erection of a new house
of worship at Shiloh.

Respectfully submitted,

J. E. LANIER,
J. B. CREECH,
J. L. HALL,
J. F. POOL,
J. T. HOLT.

· The report on State missions was read by Brother J. T.
Holt. A motion to adopt it was discussed by Dr. Livingston Johnson and H. F. Brinson. Report adopted.

State Missions.

State Missions is the task of permeating and transforming the
life of the people of North Carolina with the Gospel of Jesus
Christ.

This work is administered by the Board of Missions, Raleigh,
N. C.

We are seeking to raise for this work this year $50,000. Last
year we gave $45,273.

The following is a tabulation of the work for this year in the
mission field:

Churches served, 283; number of missionaries, 161; conversions, 2,851; baptisms, 1,765; received by letter, 2,215; average
Sunday-school attendance, 17,264; mission study classes, 77; men
in mission study classes, 256; houses of worship building, 37;
houses of worship built, 11; churches organized, 14; number of
delegates attending denominational meetings, 1,208; number of
business meetings this year, 1,720; pastoral conferences, 133;
every-member canvasses, 178; sermons, 11,028; for missions,
undesignated, $2,322.29; for State Missions, $5,812.28; for Foreign Missions, $2,929.77; for Home Missions, $2,542.28; for education, $1,190.94; for Sunday-school Missions, $876.24; for
ministers' relief, $613.82; for Orphanage, $5,995.79; other objects, $19,043.42; amount raised for all church purposes, except
pastors' salaries, $31,477.80; amount paid on pastors' salaries,
$41,828.97.

Our State Mission work is now divided into five regular departments, namely, Evangelization, Church Building, Sunday-
schools, B. Y. P. U., and Woman's Auxiliary Union.

Two new departments have recently been added in the work
of State Missions:

1. The Schools of Pastors and Workers.—We have had nine
of these schools this year. We enrolled in them about 500 students. In these schools pastors and loyal members of churches
met in groups of from 40 to 100, and for four or five days really

studied the Bible and our Baptist work. It is believed that these schools will create a new epoch in our Baptist life. Next year we plan for sixty of these schools, and we expect to enroll 3,000 students in them. The Home Mission Board is going to aid us in the support of them. A five years' course of study is being worked out, and it is hoped that we can co-ordinate the work of these schools with the work of two summer Assemblies—the one at Wrightsville and another in the mountains of our State. There is in mind a plan to use these schools in improving the services our pastors may give to our churches and at the same time to use some volunteer enlistment workers to get the churches to give better support to the pastors who attend these schools regularly. There will be two series of schools this year, the first series occurring in the early spring, ten in number. The second series will occur in the summer, being about fifty in number.

2. Colportage Department.—We are just now getting this work started. There are three lines along which we are going to work:

(1) Selling Good Books.—We do this through Colporters or through mail orders. If you want any book on the market, write the Colportage Department, Board of Missions, Raleigh, N. C.

(2) Distributing Free Tracts and Literature.—It is easy to print free tracts, but the problem is to get them handed out to the readers.

We think we have solved the problem. The Board of Missions prints a Bulletin each month. This is sent to the churches in clubs by parcel post at the rate of only $1 per dozen per year. Each copy of the Bulletin serves as a wrapper for a good free tract each month, and these are to be distributed in the churches.

Let each church in this Association take a club of this Bulletin and Tract Wrapper large enough to supply each family in its membership every month in the year.

(3) Enlarging the Circulation of the Biblical Recorder.—This is at present the most vital thing in our Baptist work in North Carolina. Our Baptist State Convention can never outgrow the circulation of its medium of communication.

The Board of Missions is undertaking to aid the Biblical Recorder in getting 12,000 new subscribers. This Association is asked by the Board to secure 250 of these new subscribers to the Recorder; and to appoint a committee to apportion this number of new subscribers out to the churches and report at this session of the Association, and to aid the Board of Missions throughout this year in securing these new subscribers thus assigned to the churches.

It is further urged that as an aid in increasing the Recorder subscriptions that each church take a club of the Tract Wrapper Bulletin which will carry each month to its membership an appetizing flavor of the Recorder and at least two good tracts each year on the work of the Recorder.

Let's be in earnest about this business. One thousand new paid-up subscribers to the Recorder would perhaps be worth more to the cause in the end than $10,000 given directly to State Missions.

Brother Hamby made a motion that the Moderator appoint a committee of two or three to confer with the State Board of Missions in regard to holding a school for pastors and workers during the coming year in our Association. The motion was approved.

The Moderator announced the following committees:

Place and Preacher for the Next Session of the Association—Q. B. Hocutt, G. G. Beaty and W. B. Joyner.

To Nominate Executive Committee, Member of the State Board of Missions, Home and Foreign Mission Representatives, and Delegates to Baptist State Convention and Southern Baptist Convention—H. F. Brinson, J. J. Lane, C. W. Carter, J. W. Smith and R. R. Lanier.

The report on temperance was read and adopted.

Temperance.

Since our Association met a year ago, the temperance forces in this country have made gratifying progress. The election a few weeks ago has clinched ratification of the Prohibition Amendment. Incidentally, it has added at least four more States to the dry column. As the score now stands, there are twenty-three Prohibition States that have not yet acted on the amendment. Assuming that each one of these will do as well for the nation as they have done for themselves and ratify, these, with the fourteen States that have already ratified, will give the amendment thirty-seven, or one more than the required thirty-six. In addition to these, we have a number of wet States that will unquestionably ratify. Ratification is clinched.

However, our great trouble is in having our prohibition laws enforced. As it stands now, with national prohibition for the period of the war, with ratification of the amendment in sight, it seems that every effort should be put forth to wipe out the greatest enemy of mankind. As churches, we should back this movement with our prayers, but we also should put forward every moral effort to help free the world of this deadly enemy—the drink evil. We should also see to it that men are elected to office who will perform their sworn duty by enforcing the law.

Respectfully submitted,

J. B. CREECH.

There being no further business, the session adjourned with prayer by Dr. Livingston Johnson.

Tuesday Night.

At 7:30 o'clock a song service began. Rev. C. E. Stevens conducted the devotional service, after which the regular program for the evening was taken up.

In the absence of the Moderator and Vice Moderator, the Clerk called the body to order, and Brother J. F. Pool was appointed to act as Moderator pro tem.

The report of Woman's Work was called for, but in the absence of Brother C. W. Carter, who was to have read the report, the reading of it was deferred, and Brother Von Miller, Brother Pippin and Brother Stevens discussed the subject.

Report on Woman's Work.

In this State the societies have 30,000 women enlisted—perhaps the largest organization of women in the State. They have a graded organizaion in 51 of the 65 associations in the State. They have 1,557 societies; this includes the Young Women's Auxiliary, the Girls' Auxiliary, the Sunbeams, and the Royal Ambassadors. Of the 1,557 organizations, 734 are Woman's Missionary Societies. These societies, of all grades, gave last year, in round numbers, $63,000. This year their aim is $65,000.

In our Association there are 51 societies of all grades. There are 2,821 women in our Baptist churches in our Association, and only 600 of these in the Missionary societies. Where are the others? Why can't they be enlisted?

Their apportionment last year was $1,100. They went "over the top" and gave $1,300. Their apportionment this year is $1,200. They are hoping to go beyond this, but are not able to make a report yet, as they have not held their annual meeting.

C. W. CARTER.

The report of Home Missions was postponed to a future session.

Prof. L. T. Royal, who was to prepare the report on Sunday-schools, was not present. On a motion, the subject was discussed by Rev. R. R. Lanier and Dr. Johnson, and the Clerk was instructed to insert the report in the minutes.

There being no further business, the session, with prayer by Brother Pippin, adjourned until Wednesday morning.

Wednesday Morning.

The morning session was opened with devotional service, conducted by Rev. A. A. Pippin.

The Moderator recognized Dr. M. L. Kesler, of the Orphanage.

. Miscellaneous business was taken up.

On motion, the subject of Home Missions was taken up, and Brother Hamby discussed the subject. The Clerk was instructed to insert the report in the files of the minutes.

Home Missions.

The most urgent mission task that confronts us today is the spiritualization of the life of the New South. The astonishing increase of the South's wealth will crush the souls of the people if they are not strong enough to master it for spiritual ends. And only a vital religious life and service can give the strength.

In the South's unmixed native American blood and evangelical faith Southern Christian bodies have had, and still have, their best chance to show what they can do for God, people, and country. It is at once our radiant opportunity and our supreme religious responsibility.

Baptists are now the most numerous evangelical body in America. American Baptists have five-sixths of their members in the South. Here we greatly outnumber any other religious group. Only yesterday we felt burdened beyond our strength in trying to solve the problem of spiritualizing the South's new wealth. And while the battle was still on as to whether we had religion enough to master our wealth we were swept into the whirlpool of the greatest war in history.

No people was ever great enough to overcome the downpull of such overwhelming forces, except as they placed their faith in the strength of God and his Christ. A greatly enlarged program of Home Missions has been our almost instinctive response to such challenges. While our people have humbled themselves to their knees, they have, through the instruction of the Southern Baptist Convention, ordered their Home Board to undertake tasks that formerly we would have considered far beyond us.

In days of trial we instinctively turn to the foundations of things which in prosperity we are likely to forget. The modest home missionary has always wrought among the foundations, near the soil. It is the inspiration of God which in this hour of unusual stress has prompted the Southern Baptists greatly to mutliply the number and increase the efficiency of these modest messengers of God's truth.

The Southern Baptist Convention instructed the Home Board to outline its work for this year on the basis of a million-dollar apportionment. It told this Board to enlarge greatly its efforts to serve. Especially did it declare for large and worthy efforts to help our soldier boys. Not fewer than one in five of the boys in the Army are from Baptist homes and have Baptist preferences. To serve and safeguard the deepest needs of these boys of ours in a time when they will be subjected to severe and unaccustomed stress and trial is the ranking mission task of Southern Baptists at this hour.

The Home Board is momentarily increasing its successful work in the army camps. This calls for greatly enlarged giving by our people. It calls for a doubling, or more, of the contributions of our churches to Home Missions. But our people are well able to do this. Every noble impulse will inspire us to declare that we will do it. For country and human liberty our boys are giving their all. A loyal Baptist cannot afford to do less, and will do no less than his best in helping to guide and stand by these boys in their deepest spiritual longings and needs.

Your Committee recommends:

1. That all our pastors and churches give frequent special seasons of preaching and praying for Home Missions and of giving to the work.

2. That this Association gladly accept and apportion among the churches its increased apportionment for Home Missions.

3. That our pastors and women be requested to arouse an interest in the unusually vital Home Mission Study books issued by the Home Mission Board, and to urge the formation of Mission Study Classes in these books.

4. We urge that our pastors and workers order and make a larger use of the splendid free Home Mission tracts issued by our Board. An order of a "one-each" package will enable each to determine for himself which tracts are suitable for his church. Orders for tracts and books should be addressed to the Publicity Department, Baptist Home Mission Board, Atlanta, Ga.

Respectfully submitted,

S. H. AVERITT.

The report of the Orphanage was read by Brother J. F. Pool. On motion to adopt, the report was discussed by Brother Pool and Dr. M. L. Kesler, with strong appeals for the Orphanage. The report was adopted.

Report on Orphanage.

Since the Baptist Orphanage at Thomasville was founded, thirty-three years ago, the last year's enrollment runs the number up to 1,860. Some months we receive as many as fifty applications, most of them being turned away for lack of room It costs $150 to support one child a year. There are now enrolled 500 children.

The "Charity and Children," as the organ of the institution, is its right arm. The business of the Job Department having considerably increased, twelve boys are employed half time in the department. Only about one-third of our Baptist Sunday-schools take the "Charity and Children." We ought to have a club in every Sunday-school in the State.

We have 2,000 Sunday-schools in the State, and about 40 per cent of the current funds come from about one-third of them.

We earnestly urge that every Sunday-school take the "Charity and Children;" also that they take regular monthly offerings for the Orphanage. We also most earnestly ask that every Baptist in the Association give at least one day's earnings to the Orphanage.

As we return thanks to God for His past blessings, we pray that His guiding hand may still lead and guide us all in the work of caring for the orphans of our State. During the great epidemic that has just swept over our country there are possibly thousands of orphans left. Shall we, as Baptists, do our part in caring for these orphans? No doubt there will be more calls for admittance to the Orphanage in the next two years than ever before. God grant that we, as Christians, may hear their cry and open our hearts and all that we have to them! We should be grateful to God for His blessings on us during the past year. The Orphanage has no debt. The children's health has no doubt ever been better. We should go forth with renewed inspiration to do greater things for the coming of the Kingdom.

                                                    J. F. POOL.

In the absence of Brother T. J. Lassiter, Brother Brinson read the report on Christian Education. On motion to adopt, the report was discussed by Rev. H. F. Brinson, Dr. Livingston Johnson and J. M. Beaty. The report was adopted.

Christian Education.

The importance of Christian Education was never so great as it is today. The world needs trained men and women—men and women who love the Lord and are interested in the growth of His Kingdom. The door of opportunity is open today as never before in the history of Christianity. The great conflict which has swept over the nations of Europe like a mighty hurricane and left it torn and bleeding has brought about new problems and new conditions, not only over there, but also over here. Only the trained worker will be able to meet the demands of the times.

The great war has touched America in a deeper sense than the average person realizes at first glance. It has created new problems for us here at home to solve. These new problems call for brave leaders and workers who shall be big enough and broad enough to meet them as they arise, and go forth to solve them with a courage and a determination that knows no defeat. Only the trained worker with a knowledge and understanding of God's Word and a broad vision of the teachings of Christ can measure up to the opportunities before us. To prepare men and women to meet these new and ever-increasing opportunities is the mission of our Christian colleges and schools.

That was a great day at Durham last December when the

Baptist Convention, with a deep and abiding faith in God and a new and splendid vision of service in its broadest and best sense, launched the Million-Dollar Campaign for the enlargement of the work of our Christian colleges and schools. It meant the dawning of a new day in North Carolina—a day in which the salvation of men will mean more than ever before: salvation for service.

We commend the movement most earnestly to the churches of the Johnston Association. It is the greatest opportunity for service that has ever come to us. The campaign leaders have fixed our part at $23,000, to be paid in four years. We can make no better investment. It will return larger dividends than any stocks or bonds in the enlarged and enriched lives of our people in the years to come.

A campaign for Christian Education was carried on in the Johnston Asosciation the past summer with only partial success. While many hearty responses were received, many people were unreached by the appeals made. We urge that we increase our efforts until this Association has gone "over the top" with a bound and has given to the Million-Dollar Fund even more than is asked of us. This will be no diffcult task if we can but lay the importance of the cause on the minds and hearts of our people. This is the great problem before us.

Respectfully submitted,

T. J. LASSITER,
For the Committee.

The report on Ministerial Relief was read by Brother Q. B. Hocutt. On motion to adopt, it was discussed by Brother Hocutt and J. E. Dupree. The report was adopted.

Report on Ministerial Relief.

There are objects to which we are asked to contribute which demand larger sums but none more worthy than Ministerial Relief. Taken altogether, our pastors are poorly paid, very few receiving more than enough to provide the necessities of life and nothing to lay aside for a "rainy day" or old age. Therefore, many of our pastors, when old age renders them physically unable to perform their former duties; find themselves without means of support There is no class of men which render a greater service to mankind than the preacher of the Gospel of Jesus Christ. Without them the world would drift backward into darkness and sin. The future would hold nothing in store for us but ruin. They teach us the way of truth and righteousness and of life. For truly, "How can they believe in Him of whom they have not heard, and how can they hear without a preacher?" Therefore, it becomes our urgent

duty to provide for those who are not able to provide for themselves after they have toiled so nobly for us.

Respectfully submitted,

              ` Q. B. HOCUTT.

Under the head of miscellaneous business, Brother Hamby
made the following motion:

That, as early as possible, the chairman of our Executive
Committee forward to the secretary of the State Board of Missions the pledges of each church and the treasurer of each
church and address.

The committee on Place and Preacher for the Next Session made the following report:

Place—Bailey. Preacher—Rev. R. R. Lanier.

The report was adopted.

The Committee on Nominations for the Executive Committee, Delegates to the Baptist State Convention and the
Southern Baptist Convention, and Representatives of Home
and Foreign Missions made the following report:

Executive Committee—J. E. Lanier, chairman; J. B.
Creech, J. L. Hall, J. F. Pool and Leman Johnson.

Delegate to State Convention—Ray Baucom.

Delegate to Southern Baptist Convention—R. H. Gower.

Member of the State Board of Missions—Judge F. H.
Brooks.

Representative of Foreign Missions—R. M. Von Miller.

Representative of Home Missions—A. C. Hamby.

There being no further business, the body took recess
for dinner.

Wednesday Afternoon.

The afternoon session was opened with song and praise
service.

The report on B. Y. P. U. Work was read by Judge F. H.
Brooks. On motion to adopt, it was discussed by Judge
Brooks and Rev. Wallace Hartsell. The report was adopted.

B. Y. P. U. Report.

The Baptist Young People's Union should be a live organization in every Baptist church in the Johnston Association. If
such was the case, there would no doubt be a larger and more
lively Association in session here now. The B. Y. P, U. should
be the training school of the church, where the young people—
boys and girls—are taught Baptist doctrines and instructed in
church leadership. The boys and girls of today will be the men

and women of tomorrow, and it will be only a question of time
—possibly short for some—when the leaders in the various
Baptist churches of the Johnston Association will lay their
armor down and answer the call of the Master, and their places
will have to be filled with the boys and girls of today. Will
they be ready to respond when the church calls them? Will
they be prepared to take up the duties and do justice to the
Cause and uphold the Baptist denomination? The Church and
the Kingdom cannot depend altogether on the preachers, but
must look to the lay members for help. In the past—yea, now!
—the Church (I speak of the membership as a whole) has been
and is doing entirely too little work along all lines, and depending entirely too much upon the preacher. In fact, the preacher,
generally speaking, in the vernacular of the day, is "the whole
show"—preaches, leads the prayer meeting, teaches in Sunday-
school, visits his own congregation and the sick of the community, buries the dead, as well as serving on various committees
of the church, and occasionally marrying a couple.

I speak reverently, God Almighty is not satisfied with this
condition of affairs! Professing Christians—men and women,
boys and girls—have got to equip themselves for efficient service for the Lord and place their services at His command through
the agency He has established—the organized church.

The B. Y. P. U. is one of the best organizations among Baptists for the training of young people for this service. The
pastor should assist in the organization of a B. Y. P. U. in each
of his churches and help in getting it started off, but should not
monopolize the meetings. He should help to "harness up" the
boys and girls, and then sit back and watch them "pull" and
give them a "lift" when necessary.

I must apologize to my brethren and sisters of the Association for failing to discharge the duties laid upon me by the last
Association when making me chairman of the B. Y. P. U. Committee. I have been so tied up with war work of various kinds
that I have been unable to visit the church of the Association
during the year in the interest of this cause. I do not mean to
convey the idea that I place war work above or ahead of God's
work; yet there is a limit to human endurance, and by the end
of the week I would be too tired and worn out to do more than
keep up with my own church work.

The war is ended, thank God, and there is no reasonable excuse why we should not turn wholly to God's work and put that
same enthusiasm in His work that we have in war work; and
now that we have whipped the Kaiser and "made the world
safe for democracy," let us whip the devil and make the earth
a "Garden of Eden," a Paradise gained.

All together for the greatest year in the history of the Johnston Association!

Respectfully submitted,

F. H. BROOKS,
Chairman.

Brother J. J. Lane read the report on Foreign Missions. On motion to adopt, Brother Lane was recognized and spoke to the report, after which it was adopted.

Report on Foreign Missions.

The Southern Baptist Convention, in session at Hot Springs in May, decided that in order, to take care of our Foreign Mission work, Southern Baptists should be requested to give one and a half million dollars to this cause before the next meeting of the convention. Compared with Southern Baptist numbers and wealth, and with what they are doing for other objects and what others are doing for Foreign Missions, this amount is small.

The Foreign Mission fields represent a thousand-millions of people, the most destitute and needy of all the inhabitants of the earth. The work conducted includes everything that our people and our churches are doing at home. A million and a half dollars for this work will not equal a tenth of what we are doing on the same lines for the thirty-odd millions who live in the South, to say nothing of the help which other Christians and denominations are giving to provide religious privileges for the people at home. A million and a half dollars is a great advance upon what we have been doing, and we will have to bestir ourselves to realize it, but it does not measure our full duty in this matter.

God's blessings are upon Foreign Missions. Even the war is helping instead of hindering this great enterprise which Southern Baptists are conducting. There were 6,290 baptisms last year. We have now 464 churches on all the fields, of which 141 have assumed self-support. We have a church membership above 53,000, with 715 Sunday-schools, enrolling more than 34,000 scholars. In other schools which we are conducting we have enrolled nearly 9,000 scholars. We are conducting theological schools in Japan, China, Africa, Italy, South America. We have but few doctors under appointment, yet these gave more than 100,000 treatments last year. By His blessing upon the work God is inviting us to enlarge it.

Eighteen new missionaries were appointed in June, and many others are greatly needed. Doors of opportunity are open everywhere.

Every pastor and every church in the Association is admonmonished to lay large plans, organize the forces, and press vigorously the greatest campaign we have ever undertaken for Foreign Missions. Every Christian in this nation is at this time called distinctly to this international Christian service. This Association should undertake to raise a worthy part of the million and a half dollars, and every church should voluntarily increase its contribution proportionately. The amount of increase for the whole South is 75 per cent. We recommend that the churches of the Association attempt the same increase.

"The Home and Foreign Fields," price 50 cents, is recommended to all church members. The Foreign Mission Board, Richmond, Va., furnishes free of charge tracts for distribution. Order this magazine and these tracts; and inform yourself concerning what God is doing through Southern Baptists throughout the world.

Brother Lane introduced the following resolution:

Resolved, That as soon as possible next year the chairman of our Executive Committee be requested to furnish the convention treasurer at Raleigh with the pledges and name of treasurer of each church in our Association, with the request that if there be any churches behind with their pledges on the 15th day of October next, he take the matter up with them by correspondence.

The resolution was adopted.

Brother J. F. Pool submitted the following:

Resolved, That we extend our heartfelt thanks to this church and community for the royal manner in which we have been entertained during the session.

The resolution was unanimously adopted.

The Chair announced the following committee:

Committee to confer with the State Board of Missions in regard to arranging an associational school for pastors and workers during the coming year—H. F. Brinson, A. C. Hamby and R. R. Lanier.

The body voted to double the Clerk's fee, and ordered him to have the usual number of minutes printed and distributed to the churches.

The journal was read and approved.

The Treasurer submitted the following report

Treasurer's Report for the Year 1918.

November 27, 1918.

I have received and paid out all moneys as indicated below:

Associational Missions:

Balance for last year, as shown in minutes.......... $54.41

Received from the churches this year, as finance table of these minutes will show........................ 506.00

Total ....'$560.41

Paid out as follows:

To C. E. Stevens..............................$196.00
To R. M. Von Miller........................... 48.00
To J. E. Dupree............................... 20.00
To W. D. Stancil.............................. 20.00
To G. A. Bain................................. 16.67
To R. M. Childers............................. 10.00
To W. G. Camp................................. 10.00
To J. E. Lanier............................... 16.67

  Total 337.34

  Balance $223.07
Building Fund:
Balance from 1917............................. 592.06
Amount received from churches................. 299.80

  Total $891.86
Paid out as follows:
Check to Gillet, for lumber...................$121.90
Check to Gillet, for lumber................... 130.57
Check to Cotter Hardware Company.............. 191.50
Check to W. S. Ragsdale....................... 100.72
Check to J. M. Beaty.......................... 47.37

  Total amount paid out.....................$592.06

  Balance on hand today.....................$299.80
Minute Fund:
Balance on hand from last year................ $95.85
Received from the churches this year.......... 64.00

  Total $159.85
Paid out:
To Nash Brothers, for printing minutes........ $40.00
For postage and express....................... 4.56
To J. E. Lanier, clerk's fee.................. 30.00

  Total amount paid out..................... 74.56

  Balance on hand today..................... $85.29
  Audited by A. C. Hamby and found correct—November 27,
1918.

There being no further business for this session of the
Association to transact, a motion was made to adjourn,
which was carried.

The adjourning prayer was offered by Rev. H. F. Brinson,
after which the Moderator declared the Sixteenth Annual

Session of the Johnston County Association adjourned, to meet next year with Bailey Baptist Church, beginning on Wednesday after the fourth Sunday in October, 1919.

R. H. GOWER,
Moderator.

J. E. LANIER,
Clerk.

CONSTITUTION.

1. The Association shall be known as the Johnston County Baptist Association.

2. Its object shall be to extend the privileges of the Gospel and liberal culture to all the people within its bounds, and, by hearty co-operation with the Baptist State Convention, to help offer these privileges to all mankind in and out of its bounds by the cordial co-operation of all the churches constituting this body.

3. It shall be composed of the pastors in active service in the Association and such delegates as shall be annually elected by the churches connected with it, each church being entitled to three delegates, unless the membership shall exceed fifty, and then an additional delegate for every twenty-five members, provided no church shall have more than eight delegates.

4. The New Hampshire Declaration of Faith shall be the summary of Divine Truth for determining questions of faith and order in this body, and the churches desiring membership in it must commit themselves to the substance of it, together with the covenant therewith submitted and this Constitution.

5. This Association shall not have power to annul the discipline or exercise authority over any church connected with it, but it may advise with and sever its connection with any church that neglects to preserve Gospel order or that treats with contempt the objects or advice of the Association.

6. Each church shall send to the annual meetings of the Association a letter (the blanks to be furnished by the Clerk of the Association), carefully filled as per blank suggestions, stating the full work of the church for the year ending with the Sunday previous to the meeting of the Association.

7. The Association shall foster State Missions, Home Missions, Foreign Missions, Christian Education, the Aged Ministers' Relief Board, the Thomasville Orphanage, and the Sunday School Board, and each church shall be requested to contribute to the support of these objects annually.

8. Missions and Education shall have precedence in their claims upon the consideration of this body in its regular sessions.

9. Whenever a church shall fail to be represented by delegates or letter at the annual sessions of the Association, inquiry shall be made for the cause , and efforts shall be made to induce

such church to do its duty; and the effort shall be continued till the church is recovered or dropped from the roll.

10. The officers of the Association shall be a Moderator, a Vice Moderator, a Clerk, a Treasurer, and an Auditor, elected annually by ballot (or in case when only one brother is put in nomination for an office, then the vote may be by acclamation) from among the members, to serve until their successors shall have been elected, and to perform the duties of such officers, namely, the Moderator, in presiding over the meetings, or the Vice Moderator, in his absence; the Clerk, in recording and preserving minutes and other papers belonging to the body; the Treasurer, in receiving and disbursing funds belonging to or entrusted to the body, according to its will; the Auditor, to examine the Treasurer's books at each meeting of the Association and report the same, before adjournment.

11. The Association shall appoint annually an Executive Committee of five (5) from its members, who shall be entrusted with the prosecution of Missions in the Association and any other work for the interest of the Master's Kingdom which may be referred to them. This committee shall, as far as possible, co-operate with the State Mission Board in supplying the destitution in our territory, and between the meetings of the Association take such action as may seem to them advisable for the advancement of its interest. The committee shall present to the Association at its annual meeting a report of its proceedings, with the names of the missionaries supported on the field, time of service, and details of their work, together with such recommendations as, in the judgment of the committee, the Association, the Association should follow in planning its subsequent work.

12. The annual sessions of the Association shall begin on Wednesday after the fourth Lord's day in October, at such place as may be chosen, and an introductory sermon shall be delivered on the first day of the session. Representatives from ten of the churches constituting the Association shall be a quorum.

13. This Constitution may be amended at any annual session by a two-thirds vote of all the members present.

14. The proceedings of the Woman's Central Committee shall be recorded as a part of the Minutes of the Association.

BY-LAWS.

1. The daily sessions of the Association shall be opened and closed with prayer.

2. Delegates shall be recognized by letters from their churches designating them as such.

3. The Moderator shall recognize corresponding messengers or the delegates of newly received churches by extending to them his right hand.

4. The report of the Executive Board and the missionary work of the Association shall take precedence of all other business during the morning session of the second day of the annual session.

5. The Clerk shall record and read the proceedings when called for, superintend the publication and distribution of the Minuutes, preserve a file of them and have it present at each annual session, and deliver to his successor all papers belonging to the body.

6. Members desiring to speak shall first rise and address the Moderator, shall use the term "Brother" in speaking to each other, shall not speak on the same subject more than twice without permission, and shall observe the courtesy that becomes Christians.

7. The roll of members shall be called at least once and absentees marked.

8. Corresponding messengers and visiting brethren shall be invited to seats, with privilege of speaking but not voting.

A copy of the Minutes shall be sent to the Secretary of the State Mission Board, the Secretary of the Southern Baptist Convention, the American Publication Society, 1420 Chestnut street, Philadelphia; the Sunday School Board of the Southern Baptist Convention, and the Thomasville Orphanage.

10. All questions of order not herein provided shall be decided by Kerfoot's Parliamentary Law.

TABLE I—STATISTICAL

Church	Pastor and Post-Office	Clerk and Post-Office	Time of Preaching	Value of Church Property	By Baptism	By Letter	By Restor'tion	By Letter	By Exclusion	By Death	No. of Males	No. of Females	Total Membership
Antioch	A. A. Pippin, Wakefield	W. O. Hocutt, Selma, R. 2	3d	$ 2,500	6	1	1	6		2	88	119	207
Bailey	C. E. Stevens, Four Oaks	J. P. Underwood, Bailey	1st	1,500	4			1			31	37	68
Baptist Center	J. E. Lanier, Smithfield	J. H. Canady, Clayton, R. 3	3d	600			1	1		1	54	71	125
Beaty Chapel	J. E. Lanier, Smithfield	Jessie Parrish, Smithfield	1st & 3d	1,800							7	19	26
Benson	G. W. Rollins, Benson	J. L. Hall, Benson	2d & 4th	2,000	7	2		7		2	68	100	168
Benson's Grove	C. E. Stevens, Four Oaks	P. G. Morgan, Four Oaks	3d	1,000	5	1	1			1	30	50	80
Bethany	R. M. Von Miller, Four Oaks	Kirkman Creech, Kenly	4th	1,000		4					44	60	104
Bethel	J. E. Lanier, Smithfield	Mrs. J. B. Atkinson, Kenly	2d	1,000				1		1	4	11	15
Beda	C. E. Stevens, Four Oks	J. E. Smith, Wilson's Mills	4th	5,000	3	3		1		1	110	130	240
Blackman's Grove	C. E. Stevens, Four Oaks	P. G. Morgan, Four Oaks	3d	1,000	7	1	1	7		1	30	50	80
Burnell Mission	G. W. Rollins, Benson	J. S. Johnson, Four Oaks	2d	1,200							1	1	2
Calvary	G. W. Rollins, Benson	T. J. Lee, Dunn	1st								9	16	25
Canaan	R. R. Lanier, Selma	T. L. Hudson, Bentonsville	3d	500				2		1	15	28	43
Carter's Chapel	A. C. Hamby, Clayton	Gray Eason, Selma	1st & 3d	500	9	3		3	2	1	43	56	99
Clayton	G. T. Mills, Wendell	W. P. Creech, Clayton	full time	6,000	5	3		11	3	3	222	270	492
Clyde's Chapel	A. A. Pippin, Wakefield	C. I. Johnson, Wendell, R. 1	3d	600		3		4	1	3	75	98	173
Corinth	R. M. Von Miller, Four Oaks	L. T. Davis, Wendell, R. 1	3d	3,000	8	6		1	2	1	52	103	155
Four Oaks	E. Dupree, Pine Level	L. Wm. Langdon, Four Oaks	1st & 3d	6,000	1	2	1	2	5	2	26	38	64
Hepzibah	G. W. Rollins, Benson	W. G. Creech, Princeton, R.	1st & 3d	400							3	3	6
Hood's Grove	R. M. Von Miller, Four Oaks	Beulah Bailey, Kenly	3d	500		2		4		5	28	31	59
Kenly	R. R. Lanier, Selma	A. E. Allen, Middlesex	2d	2,500				22	2	1	10	15	25
Lee's Chapel	R. P. Merritt, Smithfield	J. M. Richardson, Selma	2d	2,000	11		3	2		2	94	91	185
Live Oak	W. D. Stancil, Kenly	Mrs. R. P. Merrit, Smithfield	3d	500	1			2			11	13	24
Lizzie Mill	Wallace Hartsell	S. C. Batten, Micro	2d & 4th	500				1	14		3	14	17
Micro	W. R. Cu lm, Wake Forest	Manley Liles, Middlesex	2d	1,500		3		2		1	43	29	72
Middlesex	A. A. Pippin, Wakefield	Russell Powell, Auburn	2d & 4th	2,500	12	3		7		3	38	57	93
Mount Moriah	R. M. Von Miller, Four Oaks	George W. Bryan, Garner	1st & 4th	4,200	12	12	1	5	1		91	102	198
New Bethel	W. D. Stancil, Kenly	N. L. Stott, Sims	4th	1,700	10	5		5		1	53	61	114
Noble's Chapel		Lena Tyner, Four Oks	4th		2	2	1	2		1	41	70	111
Oliver's Grove			1st	800									19
Parrish Memorial	J. E. Dupree, Pine Level	J. D. Creech, Selma, R. 3	2d	1,000		1		1	2	1	34	56	90
Pauline	J. E. Dupree, Pine Level	Mrs. A. Allen, Four Oaks, R. 1	4th	1,000	2			6		1	15	35	50

Church	Pastor	Preaching	Value							Members		
Pine Level	J. F. Dupree, Pine Level Oaks.	1st	2,500	1	10				3	41	58	99
Pinkney	R. H. Von Miller, Four Oaks.	1st	1,000	1					1	15	17	32
	J. F. Lanier, Smithfield.	1st	1,800	1	1		1		1	36	51	87
Princeton	W. I. Pearce, Princeton.	3d	1,500	1	1		6	1		24	43	67
Sardis	B. C. Powell, Smithfield, R. 2.	1st & 3d	1,800	3	5		11		6	21	26	47
Selma	B. S. Reynolds, Selma.	2d & 4th	15,000	3	11		26	14		90	146	236
Shiloh	J. W. Williams, Garner, R. 1.	2d	500			1	1			37	62	99
Smithfield	T. J. Lassiter, Smithfield.	full time		3	14	1	7		4	94	121	225
	Dolley H. Price, Selma, R. 1.	1st	1,000	3	6			1		51	56	107
Thanksgiving	W. P. Lee, Benson, R. 2.	4th	1,800	2	1				1	39	62	101
Trinity	R. E. Lanier, Selma.								3	96	137	233
Wendell	George H. Wright, Wendell.	2d & 4th	2,500		8		11			93	126	219
White Oak	C. C. Mills, Clayton.	2d	3,000			2	3	1		93	126	219
Wilson's Mills	A. P. Pippin, Wakefield.	4th & 2d	1,000	14	13		2			38	43	81
Hale's Chapel	W. C. Hall, Zebulon.	3d	300	12	24				1	15	19	34
			111,000	146	148	11	157	62	48	2133	2893	5026

TABLE II—FINANCIAL

Churches	Pastor's Salary	Building and Repairs	Incidentals	Sunday School Expenses	The Poor	Minute Fund	Asso. Missions	State Missions	Home Missions	Foreign Missions	S. S. Missions	Orphanage	Christian Educa.	Ministerial Relief	Other Objects	Building Fund	Total
Antioch	220 50	200 00		10 00		2 50	10 00	25 00	7 50	7 50	2 50	5 00	5 00	5 00	60 00	5 00	565 50
Bailey	150 00	120 00		20 00		1 00	8 00	12 00	5 00	5 00	1 00	5 00	4 00	2 50		6 50	331 77
Bapt. Center	125 00			15 00		1 00	10 00	15 00	7 00	5 00	2 00	5 00	5 00	2 50	35 00	5 00	231 00
Beaty Chapel	50 00	60 00	6 14	10 00		2 50	5 00	7 00	2 50	2 50	1 00	59 33	3 00	1 50		4 00	156 64
Benson	628 94	606 48	826 63	39 80		2 50	25 00	112 95	64 12	76 36	2 50	2 50	10 00	5 00		15 00	2484 61
Benson's Grove	100 00			10 00		1 00	5 00	8 50	2 50	2 50	1 00	2 50	2 00	1 00		4 00	142 00
Bethany	75 00		10 00	15 00	22 75	1 00	5 00	10 00	1 00	1 50	1 00	1 00	2 50	2 00	10 00	2 00	162 75
Bethel	40 00		12 50			1 00	1 00	2 00	1 00	1 00		1 50		1 50	1 00	1 00	60 50
Bethesda	300 00	150 00	12 00	22 50		2 00	25 00	45 00	8 40	7 50	2 50	15 00	10 00	5 12	263 00	7 50	726 02
Blackman's Grove	200 00		5 00	7 00		2 00	9 00	25 00	7 50	7 50	1 00	15 00	7 50	2 00	27 00	7 50	313 50
Burnell Mission	12 00			5 00		1 00	2 00	5 00	1 00	1 00		2 00	2 00	1 1		1 00	36 70
Calvary			4 20				2 50	13 73	6 07	9 00	50		2 50	1 50		2 50	40 80
Canaan	50 00					1 00		6 60	5 00	5 00		2 00		2 00			73 00
Carter's Chapel	250 00		330 33	18 00	6 25	1 50	6 00	15 00	40	41	1 00	7 00	120 00	2 00	82 30	7 50	444 25
Clayton	1500 00	2849 27	16 00	80 85		5 00	50 00	275 00	461 39	208 50	5 00	196 71	165 00	20 00	24 10	50 00	6129 26
Clyde's Chapel	250 00	100 00	50 50	20 00		3 00	25 00	25 00	7 50	7 50	2 50	7 50	10 00	2 50	8 50	12 50	403 00
Corinth	150 00	100 00	94 70	40 39	10 75	2 00	10 00	22 25	5 00	2 50	1 00	12 00	6 00	5 00		10 00	415 30
Four Oaks	350 00	551 29		6 75		1 00	15 00	23 50	7 50	8 00	2 50	9 49	10 00	5 00			1128 87
Hepzibah	30 00	2 00				1 00	4 00	14 55	2 00	62		2 00	2 50	1 50	5 00	7 50	62 75
Hood's	150 00	100 00	3 61	38 59		1 00	7 50	14 50	11 75	17 40	2 00	1 50	5 00	2 50	20 00	5 00	320 00
Kenly	175 20	18 00	12 50	10 00		2 50	13 50	28 97	5 00	16 41	2 50	2 50	5 00	1 00			201 99
Lee's Chapel	28 42	200 00	21 81	3 96		2 50			19 62		1 50	15 20	2 65	5 00	2 00	4 00	472 50
Live Oak	6 25	200 00	75 00	8 97	12 00	2 00	5 00	1 50	1 50	2 00	1 00		5 12	10 00		1 00	243 38
Lizzie Mill Chapel			35 00		3 00	2 50	2 50	14 00	5 00	5 00		1 00	2 50	7 50	2 00	2 50	47 33
Micro	80 00	7 25	36 45	12 50	17 28	3 50	12 50	17 00	29 29	19 00	14 00	146 77	12 00	2 00	57 75		302 27
Middlesex	325 00			76 85		2 00	50 00	80 00	41 86	102 68	2 00	44 64	10 00	1 00	3 8 15	36 50	609 24
Mount Moriah	260 00			54 00		3 00	25 00	35 00	10 00	10 00	2 00	153 00	2 00	5 00		20 00	1193 06
New Bethel	250 00	10 00		10 00		1 00	12 50	15 00	2 50	5 00	1 00	15 00	5 00	2 50		5 00	444 50
Noble's Chapel	166 60	3 00	21 00	10 52		1 00	4 50	15 00	4 00	4 00		15 00	5 00	5 00	9 00	2 00	285 57
Oliver's Grove	25 00			5 00		1 00	10 00	15 00				2 00		2 50		5 00	45 00
Parrish Memorial	125 00			3 31		1 00	5 00	15 00	4 00	4 00	1 00	2 50	2 50	2 50		2 50	180 00
Pauline	64 00	90 00	21 00			1 00	5 00	7 50	2 50	2 50	1 1	2 50	5 00	1 1		5 00	213 31

Pine Level	200 00	105 00	125 00	30 00	20 00	15 00	2 00	25 00	7 50	7 50	2 50	7 50	7 50	5 00		12 00	574 00
Pinkney	88 00		30 95	14 17			1 00	10 00	2 50	2 50	1 00	2 50	2 50	1 00			171 32
Pisgah	282 75		8 50	8 10		15 00	2 00	31 55	20 00	12 50	2 00	28 40	12 50	6 06	3 10	10 00	630 29
Princeton	100 00	25 10		14 82		7 50	2 00	20 00	2 50	2 50	1 00	2 50	2 50	2 50	240 93	5 00	189 92
Sardis	100 00		1 00			7 50	1 50	20 00	5 00	5 00	1 00	2 50	5 00	2 50		5 00	178 00
Selma	600 00	300 00	50 00	45 00		19 50	3 50	65 85	23 45	34 55	2 50	25 39	23 64	10 00	22 00	25 00	1222 68
Shiloh	150 00			15 00	6 40	16 53	3 50	25 03	15 85	11 00	1 00	36 00	12 50	5 00		2 00	417 81
Smithfield	1200 00	900 00	100 00	107 52		25 00	3 50	172 44	84 45	108 55	10 00	98 00	161 50	28 15	120 00	25 00	4016 00
Thanksgiving	200 00			12 00		10 00	1 50	15 00	5 00	5 00	1 00	2 00	7 50	2 50	940 53	5 00	276 00
Trinity	125 00	125 00	2 00	5 00		6 00	1 00	7 50	2 00	2 00		2 00	2 50	1 00	14 00	2 00	282 50
Wendell																	
White Oak	250 00		5 00	25 00	11 75	7 50	3 00	25 00	7 50	10 00	2 50	15 00	12 50	5 00	21 16	5 00	434 71
Wilson's Mills	100 00		175 00	50 00			1 50	15 00	2 50	5 00	3 80	5 00	5 00	2 50	130 00		507 80
Hale's Chapel	51 00	32 00		18 29			1 00	5 00	5 00	1 66		2 00					110 95
Totals	9709 13	6854 89	2060 82	902 39	110 18	494 53	77 20	1340 82	929 50	774 02	83 90	959 78	631 43	171 83	2436 72	380 50	27478 35

TABLE III—SUNDAY SCHOOLS

Church	Superintendent and Post Office	Secretary and Post Office	No. Schools	No. Officers and Teachers	Pupils	Total Enrollment	Church Members in Sunday School	Mos. Kept Open	Baptisms from School	School Expenses	Missions	Orphanage	Other Objects	Total
Antioch	W. H. Maiden, Selma, R. 2	W. D. Hocutt, Selma, R. 2	1	8	110	118	85	12	5	$ 10 00	$ 8 14	$ 7 00	$ 5 00	$ 15 00
Bailey	J. W. B. Finch, Bailey	J. R. Finch, Bailey	1	8	68	76	25	12	2	20 00				35 14
Baptist Center	J. C. Hardee, Clayton	Charley Talton, Clayton	1	6	90	96	35	12		15 00				15 00
Beaty Chapel	W. M. Eason, Smithfield	Jessie Parrish, Smithfield	1	6	25	31	12	12		10 00				10 00
Benson	A. Parrish, Benson	L. E. Stevens, Benson	1	18	200	218	89	12	10	39 50			350 00	389 50
Benson's Grove	R. A. Barbour, Benson	L. E. Barbour, Benson	1	6	45	51	20	12	3	10 00	5 00			10 00
Bethany	Carmel Creech, Kenly		1	6	60	66	40	12	8	15 00		7 00	5 00	32 00
Bethel														
Bethesda	L. H. Johnson, Wilson's Mills	V. S. Smith, Wilson's Mills	1	7	81	88	40	12	1	22 50	3 00	13 50	6 00	42 85
Blackman's Grove	Joseph Wood, Four Oaks	E. Mahler, Four Oaks	1	6	50	56	20	12	4	7 00				10 00
Burnell Mission	J. S. Johnson, Four Oaks	Tida Tyner, Four Oaks	1	5	35	40	2			5 00				5 00
Calvary														
Canaan														
Carter's Chapel	Gray Eason, Selma	B. F. Woodruff, Selma, R. 3	1	6	96	102	50	12	5	15 00			3 00	18 00
Clayton	John T. Talton, Clayton	L. M. Edgerton, Clayton	1	13	301	314	225	12		80 85	246 00	60 00	297 94	684 79
Clyde's Chapel	C. M. Martin, Wendell, R. 1	Elva Phipps, Wendell, R. 1	1	9	95	103	60	12	6	16 00			8 00	24 00
Corinth	Q. B. Hocutt, Wendell, R. 1	L. T. Davis, Wendell	1	8	121	130	80	12		20 00	5 00	5 00		31 00
Four Oaks	R. A. Bain, Four Oaks	J. W. Sanders, Four Oaks	1	5	80	86	45	12	1	40 89	29 44	2 44	6 00	78 27
Hepzibah	W. G. Creech, Princeton	J. F. Earp, Pine Level	1	3	25	28	7			6 75			50	7 25
Hood's Grove														
Kenly	A. J. Broughton, Kenly	Mary Lassiter, Kenly	1	5	35	40	12	12		38 59	4 58	15 00		58 24
Lee's Chapel	W. I. Green, Zebulon, R. 2	L. M. Price, Zebulon, R. 1	1	5	100	105	60	12	11	10 00				10 00
Live Oak														
Lizzie Mill Chapel	R. P. Merritt, Smithfield	Pearl Churchill, Selma	1	3	25	28	10	12		8 97			4 50	13 47
Micro	D. C. Smith, Selma	Clyde Smith, Selma	1	6	35	41	20	12		12 50		131 00	15 50	159 85
Middlesex	W. K. Ballentine, Middlesex	J. M. Davis, Middlesex	1	9	100	109	60	12	11	76 35	7 00	4 44		128 09
Mount Moriah	Elliott S. Pool, Clayton	Robert Pool, Clayton	1	12	146	158	86	12	8	54 09		120 40		174 49
New Bethel	Ralph Britt, Garner	Eugene Britt, Garner	1	10	85	95	69	9		6 00				10 00
Noble's Chapel	D. L. Flowers, Sims, R. 1	Elnior Boykin, Sims	1	6	90	96	60	12	3	6 00	2 52	1 00	1 00	10 52
Oliver's Grove														
Parrish Memorial	R. F. Batten, Micro	Flossie Capps, Selma, R. 3	1	5	20	25	20	6		5 00				5 00
Pauline	G. W. Massey, Bentonsville	Pearl Creech, Four Oaks	1	5	75	25	25	6	2					

Church	Pastor	Clerk											
Pine Level	N. M. Gurley, Pine Level	Pattie Braxton, Pine Level	1	9	98	107	65	12	1	19 00	56 60		1 00	75 00
Pinkney	R. E. Lee, Kenly, R. 4	Otis Lee, Kenly, R. 4	1	6	65	71	15	12	1	14 17	3 34	1 00		19 50
Pisgah	P. E. Whitley, Smithfield	A. G. Jones, Smithfield	1	8	67	75	25	12		8 10	1 54		54 93	64 57
Princeton	W. I. Pierce, Princeton		1	4	30	34	10	12	1	12 79				12 79
Sardis	C. M. Strickland, Pine Level	Miss Rosa Howell, Pine Level	1	6	34	40	16	9	1	9 00				9 00
Selma	B. S. Reynolds, Selma	N. J. Wiggs, Selma	1	17	150	167	75	12	1	45 00	5 00			50 00
Shiloh	Walter Williams, Garner	Sidney Parnell, Garner	1	6	102	108	27	12	2	12 00		8 50		20 50
Smithfield	T. S. Ragsdale, Smithfield	John Ives, Smithfield	1	13	168	181		12	3	107 52	129 10	80 05	367 78	684 45
Thanksgiving	W. S. Earp, Selma, R. 1	Vernon Hinton, Selma, R. 1	1	11	121	131	54	12	3	12 00	1 27		14 00	27 27
Trinity	W. P. Lee, Benson, R. 1	Lillian Marshburn, Benson, R. 2	1	6	35	41	20	12	2	5 00				5 00
Wendell	W. H. Rhodes, Wendell	W. R. Johnson, Wendell												
White Oak	A. L. Batton, Clayton, R. 2	J. M. Green, Clayton, R. 2	1	5	75	80	50	12		25 00	3 00			25 00
Wilson's Mills	J. T. Holt, Wilson's Mills	Walter Boyd, Wilson's Mills	1	10	60	70	50	12	10	50 00			9 00	62 82
Hale's Chapel	A. D. Parrish, Zebulon	L. C. Allen, Zebulon	1	9	59	56	36	12	12					
Totals			40	296	3257	3442	1671		118	1839 85	510 53	367 68	1148 65	3133 56

TABLE IV—WOMAN'S MISSIONARY UNION

Churches	Name of Organization	President and Post-Office	No. Members	State Missions	Home Missions	Foreign Missions	Training School	Other Objects	Total
Bailey	Woman's Missionary Union	Miss Mary Underwood, Bailey		$	$ 3 57	$	$ 2 55	$ 5 65	$ 11 77
Beaty	Man's Missionary Union	Mrs. E. F.		37 95		9 48	3 60	13 48	66 91
Benson	Woman's Missionary Union	Mrs. J. L. Hall, Benson		6 40	6 00		50	5 00	15 85
Blackman's	Woman's Missionary Union	Mrs. Norah Wd, Four Oaks		1 50	85	25			2 00
Burnell Mission	Man's Missionary Union	Mrs. J. S. Johnson, Four Oaks	5	107 00	123 60	135 20	10 00	16 65	492 50
Clayton	Auxiliary	Mrs. C. W. Carter, Clayton	60	11 00	38 35	32 50	2 00	47 40	130 75
Clayton	Sunbeams	Mrs. A. C. Hamby, Clayton	19	7 47	10 70	13 50	1 00	8 50	43 36
Clayton	Royal Ambassadors	Mrs. W. J. Payne, Clayton	60	7	11 70	12 28	9 00	3 50	35 00
Clayton	Girls' Auxiliary	Mrs. D. J. Thurston, Clayton		29	1 70	14 75	1 00	102 80	173 65
Corinth	Woman's Missionary Union	Mrs. B. A. Hocutt, Clayton	24	75	30		1 00	7 00	11 05
	Sunbeams	Mrs. S. T. Bee, Wendell	9	50					11 50
Four Oaks	Sunbeams	Elgie Mott, Wendell	35	50					1 50
Four Oaks	Missionary Union	Mrs. J. W. Sanders, Four Oaks	19	2 00	6 10	7 00	4 30	17 86	37 26
Kenly	Missionary Union	Miss Clyde Sanders, Four Oaks	15	58		1 00	1 29	5 00	4 29
	Woman's Missionary Union	Miss Beulah Bailey, Kenly	10	2 58	2 00	2 00		6 05	11 58
Middlesex	Young Women's Auxiliary	Mrs. W. H. Hartsell, Middlesex		8 00	16 60	12 00	2 00	1 50	44 65
Middlesex	Sunbeams	Mrs. M. L. Phillips, Mex	10	6 00			65		7 15
Mount Moriah	Woman's Missionary Union	Mrs. N. B. Lois,		16 00	7 19	7 00		1 25	20 44
Mount Moriah	Sunbeams	Mrs. Claude Hinnant, Clayton, R. 3	14	16 20	16 20	16 20			49 85
Mount Moriah	Royal Ambassadors	Mrs. Eleanor Lane, Un	38	1 86	1 86	1 86			5 60
Noble's	Missionary Union	Mrs. J. J. Lane, Sims		5 00	10 00	8 20	1 00	22 00	46 20
Pine Level	Missionary Union	Mrs. J. H. Grice, Sims	29	6 00	5 50	8 45	3 50	15 00	21 00
Pine Level	Missionary Union	Mrs. E. E. Dupree, Pine Level	12	12 00	2 50	2 50	6 50	6 50	35 95
Pisgah	Sunbeams	Mrs. R. H. Brown, Pine L	17			14 65		5 00	10 00
Pisgah	Young Women's Auxiliary	Mrs. E. R. Jones, Smithfield		8 80	24 90		3 25	8 25	59 85
Princeton		Miss Pearl Un, Smithfield	7	2 50					2 50
Sardis	Woman's Missionary Union	Mrs. W. M. Joyner, Princeton		7 20					7 20
Shiloh	Missionary Union	Mrs. B. E. Gardner, Pine Level	10	12 00	8 35	6 00	6 00	1 00	33 35
Selma	Missionary Union	Miss Anie Unt, Smithfield							
Selma	Girls' Auxiliary	Mrs. George D. Vick, Selma	8	7 25	1 60	3 30	5 00	90	17 05
Smithfield	Woman's Missionary Union	Mrs. R. R. Lanier, Selma	25	77 50	56 90	74 30	30 00	393 00	631 70
Smithfield	Young Women's Auxiliary	Mrs. Howard Gray, Smithfield	7	2 50	5 00	5 00		3 00	10 50
Smithfield	Sunbeams	Miss Ola Brady, Smithfield	20	5 00	85	8 25			18 25
Wendell	Woman's Missionary Union	Mrs. J. M. Beaty, Smithfield					1 10		1 95
Wendell	Woman's Missionary Union	Miss Mie Lee, Benson							
Benson's Grove	Sunbeams	Mrs. Maurice Richardson, Wendell							
	Woman's Missionary Union	Mrs. les Benson, Benson							
		Totals	453	438 08	387 61	396 27	94 96	692 54	2130 66

Churches	State Missions	Home Missions	Foreign Missions	Sunday-school Missions	Orphanage	Christian Education	Ministerial Relief	Associational Missions	Building Fund	Minute Fund	Total
Antioch	$25 00	$10 00	$10 00	$2 50	7 50	7 50	6 00	12 50	7 50	5 00	93 50
Bailey	15 00	5 00	5 00	1 50	7 00	5 00	5 00	10 00	10 00	3 00	69 50
Baptist Center	15 00	6 00	6 00	2 00	6 00	5 00	2 50	10 00	5 00	3 00	60 50
Beaty Chapel	7 00			1 00			1 50		4 00	1 50	31 00
Benson's Grove	90 00	25 00	25 00	5 00	30 00	15 00	7 50	30 00	15 00	5 00	247 50
Bethany	10 00	5 00	5 00	1 50	5 00	5 00	2 00	5 00	5 00	2 00	46 50
Bethel		5 00	5 00	1 00	5 00	6 00	2 50	7 50	2 50	2 00	46 50
Bethesda	10 00	2 00		1 00		1 00	1 00	2 50	2 00	1 50	18 50
Blackman's Grove	45 00	10 00	10 00	2 50	15 00	10 00	5 00	25 00	7 00	5 00	130 50
Calvary	30 00	7 00	8 00	2 00	8 00	10 00	5 00	10 00	10 00	5 00	100 00
Canaan	10 00	1 50	2 50	1 50	2 50	5 00	2 00	5 00	5 00	2 50	38 50
Carter's Chapel	5 00	1 00		1 00	1 50	1 00	1 00	2 00	1 00	1 00	18 00
Clayton	20 00	7 50	7 50	2 50	7 50		5 00	10 00	10 00	3 00	77 00
Clyde's Chapel	275 00	75 00	75 00	2 50	100 00	65 00	20 00	60 00	50 00	10 00	735 00
Corinth	30 00	10 00	10 00	1 00	10 00	10 00	5 00	25 00	15 00	3 50	118 50
Four Oaks	20 00	10 00	7 50	2 50	10 00	10 00	5 00	15 00	10 00	5 00	79 00
Hale's Chapel	25 00	10 00	10 00	2 00	10 00	10 00	5 00	20 00	10 00	3 00	106 00
Hepzibah	6 00	2 50	2 50	1 00	1 00	2 50	1 00	5 00	2 50	2 00	43 50
Hood's Grove	12 50	5 00	5 00	1 00	5 00	2 00		10 00	2 50	2 50	26 50
Kenly	20 00	5 00	5 00	1 00	7 50	3 00	10 00	15 00	5 00	3 00	56 00
Lee's Chapel	20 00	5 00	10 00	2 00	2 50	5 00	5 00	5 00	5 00	1 00	78 00
Live Oak		5 00	1 50	2 00	5 00	5 00	1 00	5 00	5 00	2 50	70 00
Lizzie Mill	2 00	1 00	5 00	1 00	5 00	2 00	1 50	2 50	2 50	1 00	29 50
Micro	15 00	5 00	7 50	1 00	7 00	2 50	2 50	12 50	15 00	2 50	17 50
Middlesex	25 00	35 00	60 00	7 00	50 00	10 00	10 00	15 00	25 00	7 50	58 50
Mount Moriah	90 00	15 00	15 00	2 00	15 00	20 00	10 00	25 00	10 00	5 00	99 50
New Bethel	40 00	15 00	15 00	1 00	7 50	12 50	3 00	15 00	10 00	5 00	399 50
Noble's Chapel	25 00	5 00	2 50	1 00	2 50	5 00	1 50	10 00	10 00	2 50	172 00
Oliver's Grove	5 00	5 00	5 00	2 50	5 00	2 50	1 50	10 00	5 00	2 50	90 00
Parrish Memorial	20 00	5 00	10 00	1 00	2 50	5 00	2 50	5 00	5 00	2 50	27 00
Pauline	10 00	10 00	15 00	2 00	10 00	10 00	5 00	16 00	15 00	5 00	63 50
Pine Chapel	25 00		15 00	2 00		12 50	1 50	15 00	15 00	5 00	48 50
Pinkney	12 50	18 00		2 50	20 00		5 00	15 00	10 00	4 00	107 50
Pisgah	30 00	6 00	5 00	1 00	5 00	5 00	2 00	7 00	6 00	3 00	47 00
Princeton	20 00	6 00	6 00	2 00	5 00	35 00	10 00	25 00	25 00	3 00	131 50
Selah	20 00	25 00	30 00	2 50	15 00	12 50	10 00	15 00	2 00	7 50	61 00
Selma	75 00	50 00	5 00	10 00	25 00	25 00	10 00	40 00	25 00	3 00	260 00
Shiloh	25 00		70 00	1 00	50 00	10 00	10 00	10 00	2 50	7 50	91 00
Smithfield	160 00	50 00	5 00	1 00	5 00		2 50	10 00	30 00	3 00	447 50
Thanksgiving	20 00	5 00	5 00	5 00	5 00	30 00	5 00	10 00	16 00	2 00	69 50
Trinity	10 00		35 00	1 00	30 00	15 00	3 00	10 00		7 00	48 50
White Oak	50 00	35 00	10 00	1 00	8 00		5 00	25 00	16 00	5 00	252 50
Wills Mills	25 00	10 00	6 00	2 50	8 00	15 00	3 00	16 00	2 00	3 00	107 00
Burnell Mission	15 00	5 00	1 00	1 00	2 50	2 00	1 00	8 00			69 50
	5 00							2 50			19 50
Totals	1431 00	488 00	536 50	92 00	562 00	493 00	208 50	643 00	442 00	172 00	5058 50

MINUTES

OF THE

SEVENTEENTH ANNUAL SESSION

OF THE

JOHNSTON COUNTY

BAPTIST ASSOCIATION

HELD WITH

SMITHFIELD BAPTIST CHURCH

October 29 and 30

1919

The next session will be held with Bailey Baptist Church, beginning on Wednesday after the fourth Sunday in October, 1920.

To preach the Introductory sermon, Rev. L. B. Padgett

P. D. Gold Publishing Co., Wilson, N. C.

MINUTES

OF THE

SEVENTEENTH ANNUAL SESSION

OF THE

JOHNSTON COUNTY

BAPTIST ASSOCIATION

HELD WITH

SMITHFIELD BAPTIST CHURCH

October 29 and 30

1919

———

The next session will be held with Bailey Baptist Church, beginning on Wednesday after the fourth Sunday in October, 1920.

To preach the Introductory sermon, Rev. L. B. Padgett

OFFICERS

Moderator—R. H. Gower _____Clayton
Vice-Moderator—J. J. Lane _____Auburn
Clerk—R. M. Von Miller _____Wilson
Treasurer—J. A. Smith_____Smithfield
Auditor—J. L. Hall_____Benson

EXECUTIVE COMMITTEE

H. W. Baucom, Chairman_____Smithfield
J. F. Pool _____Clayton
J. L. Hall _____Benson
J. A. Smith_____Smithfield
S. H. Averitt _____Clayton

DELEGATES AND BOARD MEMBERS

Member of State Board of Missions—Judge F. H. Brooks.
Delegate to Southern Baptist Convention—R. H. Gower.
Delegates to Baptist State Convenion—R. M. Von Miller.
Geo. H. Wrigh, and N. M. Gurley.

COMMITTEE IN CHARGE OF AND TO MAKE REPORTS ON OBJECTS FOR THE YEAR 1920

State Missions _____H. W. Baucom
Home Missions _____C. E. Stevens
Foreign Missions _____L. B. Padgett
Sunday Schools _____T. S. Guy
Orphanage _____R. L. Gay
Christian Education _____R. M. Von Miller
Ministerial Relief _____J. W. Smith
Temperance _____A. A. Pippin
Woman's Work _____A. O. Moore
B. Y. P. U. Work _____B. Townsend
Biblical Recorder _____J. E. Dupree

LIST OF MINISTERS

H. W. Baucom _____Smithfield
J. E. Dupree _____Kenly
S. A. Edgerton _____Buies Creek
J. R. Everett _____Wake Forest
T. S. Guy _____Zebulon
J. E. Hocutt _____Nashville
R. I. Hocutt _____Wendell, R. 1:
R. P. Merritt _____Smithfield
G. T. Mills _____Buies Creek
A. O. Moore _____Clayton
J. W. Nobles _____Middlesex
L. B. Padgett _____Wendell
A. A. Pippin _____Wakefield
K. F. Pool _____Wake Forest
W. D. Stancil _____Kenly
C. E. Stevens _____Four Oaks
R. M. Von Miller _____Wilson

2

Antioch _____

Bailey—Alvin Underwood, Preston Finch.

Baptist Center—J. C. Horder.

Beaty Chapel—W. M. Eason, J. J. Parrish, Allen Edwards.

Benson—J. Benton, J. L. Hall.

Benson Grove_____

Bethany—Kirkman Creech, Eason M. Smith, Jesse B. Creech.

Bethel_____

Bethesda—W. A. Price, J. B. Coates.

Blackman's Grove—W. M. Lee, J. R. Blackman.

Burness Mission—J. S. Johnson.

Calvary—_____

Canaan—J. T. Hudson, T. J. Hudson.

Carter's Chapel—L. D. Wall, Martin Thorn, Mrs. Viola Thorn, O. Brown, Mrs. Martha McCall, Mrs. Mamie McCall.

Clayton—A. O. Moore, W. A. Barnes, J. W. Smith, J. J. Ellis, W. T. Allen, D. J. Yelverton, V. R. Gurley, R. H. Gower.

Clyde's Chapel—_____

Corinth—L. T. Davis, H. B. Andrews, J. B. O'Neil, I. B. Hocutt, S. T. Price.

Four Oaks—J. B. Creech, R. A. Bain, P. G. Keen, C. E. Stevens, Mrs. C. E. Stevens, Mrs. J. W. Sanders.

Hale's Chapel—T. S. Guy.

Hephzipah—W. A. Braswell, T. F. Earp, W. G. Creech.

Hood's Grove—J. C. Wood, D. J. Wood, Jr., Mrs. J. C. Wood.

Kenly—J. E. Dupree, Mrs. T. W. Bailey, J. B. Johnson.

Lee's Chapel—J. W. Creech, J. J. Kemp.

Live Oak—_____

Lizzie Mills—_____

Micro—J. W. Wall, S. C. Batton, D. C. Smith, J. H. Braswell,

Middlesex—_____

Mount Moriah—Mrs. Jas. J. Lane, Elinor Lane, W. R. Stallings, J. A. Stallings, J. J. Lane, C. V. Kelly, Mrs. J. J. Lane.

New Bethel—W. R. Britt, D. E. Hicks, J. N. Bryan.

Noble's Chapel—Mrs. J. H. Grice, R. M. Von Miller.

Oliver's Grove—J. E. Royals.

Parrish Memorial—J. D. Creech, Mrs. J. D. Creech, R. F. Batton, J. N. Watson.

Pauline—W. B. Joyner.

Pine Level—J. F. Watson, Floyd C. Price,, N. M. Gurley, Mrs. B. L. Strickland.

Pinkney—Leslie Davis, Nathan Davis, Mrs. B. R. Edgerton, Mrs. Rebecca Holland.

Pisgah—J. A. Smith, A. G. Tonilson, S. C. Higgins, A. J.

Whitley, J. E. Lanier.

Princeton—Caspian S. Hall, W. I. Pearce.

Sardis—C. M. Strickland.

Selma—----------------

Smithfield—T. J. Lassiter, E. R. Jones, J. M. Beaty, H. W. Baucom.

Thanksgiving—K. Broadell, L. R. Poole.

Trinity—J. L. Johnson, W. P. Lee, H. C. Lee.

Wendell—W. H. Rhoades, E. C. Carroll, J. W. Wright, L. B. Padgett.

White Oak—A. A. Pippin, J. W. Bunn, A. F. Batton.

Wilson's Mills—G. G. Beaty, J. T. Holt, Geo. W. Boyd.

CONSTITUTION

1. The Association shall be known as the Johnston County Baptist Association.

· 2. Its object shall be to extend the privileges of the Gospel and liberal culture to all the people within its bounds, and, by hearty co-operation with the Baptist State Convention, to help offer these privileges to all mankind in and out of its bounds by the cordial co-operation of all the churches constituting this body.

3. It shall be composed of the pastors in active service in the Association and such delegates as shall be annually elected by the churches connected with it, each church being entitled to three delegates, unless the membrship shall exceed fifty, and then an additional delegate for every twenty-five members, provided no church shall have more than eight delegates.

4. The New Hampshire Declaration of Faith shall be the summary of Divine Truth for determining questions of faith and order in this body, and the churches desiring membership in it must commit themselves to the substance of it, together with the covenant herewih submitted and this Constitution.

5. This Association shall not have power to annul the discipline or exercise authority over any church connected with it, but it may advise with and sever its connection with any church that neglects to preserve Gospel order or that treats with contempt the objects or advice of the Association.

6. Each church shall send to the annual meetings of the Association a letter (the blanks to be furnished by the Clerk of the Association), carefully filled as per blank suggestions, stating the full work of the church for the year ending with the Sunday previous to the meeting of the Association.

7. The Association shall foster State Missions, Home Missions, Foreign Missions, Christian Education, the Aged Ministers' Relief Board, the Thomasville Orphanage, and the Sunday

4

School Board, and each church shall be requested to contribute to the support of these objects annually.

8. Missions and Education shall have precedence in their claims upon the consideration of this body in its regular sessions.

9. Whenever a church shall fail to be represented by delegates or letter at the annual sessions of the Association, inquiry shall be made for the cause, and efforts shall be made to induce such church to do its duty; and the effort shall be continued till the church is recovered or dropped from the roll.

10. The officers of the Association shall be a Moderator, a Vice Moderator, a Clerk, a Treasurer, and an Auditor, elected annually by ballot (or in case when only one brother is put in nomination for an office, then the vote may be by acclamation) from among the members, to serve until their successors shall have been elected, and to perform the duties of such officers, namely, the Moderator, in presiding over the meetings, or the Vice Moderator, in his absence; the Clerk, in recording and preserving minutes and other papers belonging to the body; the Treasurer, in receiving and disbursing funds belonging to or entrusted to the body, according to its will; the Auditor, to examine the Treasurer's books at each meeting of the Association and report the same before adjournment.

11. The Association shall appoint annually an Executive Committee of five (5) from its members, who shall be entrusted with the prosecution of Missions in the Association and any other work for the interest of the Master's Kingdom which may be referred to them. This committee shall, as far as possible, co-operate with the State Mission Board in supplying the destitution in our territory, and between the meetings of the Association take such action as may seem to them advisable for the alvancement of its interest. The committee shall present to the Association at its annual meeting a report of its proceedings, with the names of the missionaries supported on the field, time of service, and details of their work, together with such recommendations as, in the judgment of the committee, the Association, should follow in planning its subsequent work.

12. The annual sessions of the Association shall begin on Wednesday after the fourth Lord's day in October, at such place as may be chosen, and an introductory sermon shall be deliv ered on the first day of the session. Representatives from ten of the churches constituting the Association shall be a quorum.

13. This Constitution may be amended at any annual session by a two-thirds vote of all the members present.

14. The proceedings of the Woman's Central Committee shall be recorded as a part of the Minutes of the Association.

BY-LAWS

1. The daily sessions of the Association shall be opened and closed with prayer.

2. Delegates shall be recognized by letters from their churches designating them as such.

3. The Moderator shall recognize corresponding messengers or the delegates of newly received churches by extending to them his right hand.

4. The report of the Executive Board and the missionary work of the Association shall take precedence of all other business during the morning session of the second day of the annual session.

5. The Clerk shall record and read the proceedings when called for, superintend the publication and distribution of the Minutes, preserve a file of them and have it present at each annual session, and deliver to his successor all papers belonging to the body.

6. Members desiring to speak shall first rise and address the Moderator, shall use the term "Brother" in speaking to each other, shall not speak on the same subject more than twice without permission, and shall observe the courtesy that becomes Christians.

7. The roll of members shall be called at least once and absentees marked.

8. Corresponding messengers and visiting brethren shall be invited to seats, with privilege of speaking but not voting.

A copy of the Minutes shall be sent to the Secretary of the Sate Mission Board, the Secretary of the Southern Baptist Convention, the American Publication Society, 1420 Chestnut street, Philadelphia; the Sunday School Board of the Southern Baptist Convention, and the Thomasville Orphanage.

10. All questions of order not herein provided shall be decided by Kerfoots Parliamentary Law.

PROCEEDINGS

On account of the 75 Million Dollar Campaign, the meeting of the Johnston County Baptist Association was held with the Smithfield Church owing to its central location.

On the morning of the 29th of October the body met with the Smithfield Church. Devotional exercises were conducted by the pastor, Bro. H. W. Baucom. The Moderator then called the Seventeenth Annual Session of the Johnston County Baptist Association to order. Prayer by Bro. W. B. Joyner.

The following brethren were appointed as the Committee on Credentials and Enrollment: J. W. Smith, J. A. Smith and Turlan Allen.

6

· Delegates were enrolled and the Moderator announced a quorum present, and declared the election of officers as next in ordr, asking the Vice Moderator, J. J. Lane, to the chair. The following officers were elected:·

Moderator—R. H. Gower.
Vice Moderator—J. J. Lane.
Clerk—R. M. Von Miller.
Treasurer—J. A. Smith.
Auditor—J. L. Hall.

The organization being perfected, the regular order of business was taken up. After the singing of: "More About Jesus Would I Know," the Moderator recognized and welcomed Brethren, Rev. L. B. Padgett, Rev. H. W. Baucom and Rev. T. S. Guy as new pastors in the Association, also Rev. A. Corey as a visitor.

The first subject on the program for consideration being the Biblical Recorder. In the absence of Rev. J. E. Dupree, who was to present the report, a motion was made and seconded that the subject before the body be discussed without report, the Moderator called on Rev. H. W. Baucom to open the discussion on the Biblical Recorder. Brethren J. F. Pool, S. H. Averitt and J. J. Lane likewise discussed the Biblical Recorder. The motion was adopted. The Moderator appointed Rev. A. A. Pippin to look after subscription for the Biblical Recorder and other denominational periodicals.

REPORT ON BIBLICAL RECORDER

The members of our Baptist Churches who read the Biblical Recorder are the members who are most interested in the kingdom affairs. These, too, are the most liberal in their gifts to the kingdom causes.

It, therefore, should be the purpose and plan of those who do take and read our denominational papers to interest our non-subscribing members in taking, and reading the Biblical Recorder.

The Biblical Recorder surely needs the support of every Baptist in the State. The Baptists of the State most sorely need the inspiration and information to be gotten by regularly reading this valuable paper.

Respectfully submitted,
J. E. DUPREE, Committee.

The report of temperance as next in order was called for, and in the absence of Bro. J. B. Creech, no report being on hand, the Moderator appointed Bro. L. B. Padgett, to write report for insertion into the minutes, who also spoke on the subject.

TEMPERANCE

Since the Association met a year ago, the temperance forces in this country have made phenominal progress. The constitutional amendment ratified by an overwhelming majority, assures national prohibition. The international prohibition movement is gaining momentum, and the largest part of the world is now greatly in sympathy with prohibition.

However, the execution of the prohibition laws is still a problem, which invites the support and the interest of every Christian man and woman. We should also see to it that men are elected, who will perform their sworn duty by enforcing the law.

Respectfully submitted,

L. B. PADGETT.

After the singing of several selections and prayer by Bro. J. J. Lane, Bro. A. O. Moore, Pastor of Clayton, N. C., preached the Annual Introductory sermon from the 14th Chapter of Exodus. Subject: "Speak to my people that they go forward."

Following the sermon the Moderator appointed Brethren D. E. Dupree and A. A. Pippin, to conduct the devotional exercises prior to the afternoon and night session respectively.

There being no further business, the body was dismissed for recess with prayer by Brother A. A. Pippin.

WEDNESDAY AFTERNOON

At 1:30 P. M. Bro. J. E. Dupree conducted the devotional exercises. The Moderator called the meeting to order asking Bro. L. B. Padgett to lead in prayer. The Moderator then appointed the following Committees:

Committee to nominate the Executive Committee: Jno. E. Lanier, F. H. Brooks, J. J. Lane and S. H. Averitt.

Committee on time place and preacher: J. F. Pool, W. B. Joyner and G. G. Beaty.

The report of Woman's Work was called for, in the absence of Bro. C. W. Carter, Bro. J. J. Lane read last year's report. On motion to instruct the clerk to ask Mrs. B. A. Hocutt to furnish copy of her report before the annual W. M. U. meeting at Four Oaks, N. C., for insertion into the minutes, Rev. T. S. Guy, Rev. C. E. Stevens and Bro. S. H. Averitt discussed the Woman's Work. The motion was adopted.

WOMAN'S WORK

The W. M. U. of Johnston County Association was organized in 1903 with three Societies. The report of 1914 shows 4 Societies, these contributed $332.77.

In 1919 we have 46 churches in the Association. During the

8

periods from 1903 to 1919, 55 Societies have been organized. Number of Societies on roll now 46; 34 of them are active, and 12 are semi-active. W. M. S's, 28; Y. W. A's, 2; G. A's,\2; R. A's, 4, and Sunbeams, 4. The average reports sent in each quarter for the year of 1919 has been 24. Twenty-one Societies sent report every quarter. Six new Societies have been organized and one reorganized.

The following statistics are not accurate, since only 19 societies sent in annual report, and this report is made from the 19 reports, and such information as I have been able to obtain from the 27 societies not reporting.

450 members in Societies. Number of subscribers to the different periodicals are as follows: Home and Foreign Field, 98; Biblical Recorder, 130; Royal Service, 90. Fourteen Societies observe State Mission Day; 13 observed week of prayer; 14 made Christmas offering, 12 observed week for interest of Home Mission.

Your Superintendent wrote 509 letters, 100 postal cards, and traveled 140 miles. The aim set by the State W. M. U. for the W. M. U. of Johnston County Association for the year 1919 was $1000.00. The annual report from these 19 societies shows that we have given $1,888.42 this year. The Banner Societies in contributions are: W. M. U., Smithfield; Y. W. A., Clayton; G. A., Clayton; R. A., Mt. Moriah; Sunbeams, Clayton.

Respectfully submitted,
MRS. B. A. HOCUTT, Supt. W. M. U.

REPORT OF EXECUTIVE COMMITTEE

This has been one of the hardest years in our Associational Mission work. Difficult, because we, your Committee, have not been able to secure the services of men that would stay in the work. At the beginning of the year we grouped the most of our Mission points into four fields. While several of our Churches have been served by other pastors than the ones on the four fields mentioned above. We secured the services of two men for these fields, while for the other two we have had to use supplies.

One field two men agreed to accept the work, but each after being on the field for three months, gave up the work, leaving us with no one in view to take the work.

Rev. J. F. Dupree has had charge of Parrish Memorial, Princeton, Pauline, Bethel and Lizzie Mill. Rev. C. E. Stevens has served Four Oaks, Blackman's Grove, Benson's Grove, Trinity, Hood's Grove and Burnell Mission, which is too large for one man to serve. Rev. G. W. Rollins preached at Micro, up to the time of his leaving the Association. Pinkney, Bailey, Noble's Chapel and Simms School house have been served by Rev. R.

9

M. Von Miller.

Rev. T. S. Guy, the pastor of Zebulon has preached at Hale's Chapel. Rev. W. D. Stancil has been pastor of Oliver's Grove. The writer of this report has been pastor of Sardis, Hephzibah and Beaty Chapel.

For two years the Committee has been trying to open up the work at Pleasant Grove. During this year, this work has been opened. A Sunday school was organized, and the outlook is encouraging. The following Churches have been served by various supplies: Canaan, Calvary, Kenly and Live Oak. In view of the needs of the work in our Association, we your committee submit the following recommendations:

1. That the new board continue the work at Pleasant Grove, if it can possibly secure a man for the work.

2. That an effort be made to build parsonages for these Mission fields.

3. That there be a general increase in salaries by the Churches to pastors, in order that the field can give a man a living salary.

4. That all the Churches accept their apportionment in the 75 Million Dollar Campaign, and that each Church co-operate with our Associational director and the plans for the campaign.

Respectfully submitted,

J. E. LANIER, Chairman

J. F. POOL,

J. L. HALL, Committee.

REPORT OF THE BUILDING COMMITTEE

During the year the building that was being built at Hephzibah a year ago, has been completed. The Church has been worshipping in their new building since about May 1st.

Repairs have been made at Beaty Chapel and Live Oak. These houses are now in first class condition. We your Committee, wish to thank Bro. J. M. Beaty for the part he has taken in the work of these places, for it was largely by the efforts he has made and his generous gifts, that Hephzibah was built, and Beaty Chapel and Live Oak have been repaired.

The last year's Building Fund has been paid to aid in the building of a new house of worship at Shiloh. This building will soon be ready for use.

The Committee has designated that $200.00 of this year's Building Fund be used in helping on the house of worship at Trinity.

Respectfully submitted,

J. E. LANIER,

J. F. POOL,

J. T. HOLT, Committee.

10

On motion to adopt, the report was discussed by J. E. Lanier, J. E. Dupree, R. M. Von Miller, Bro. J. M. Beaty, Rev. H. W. Baucom, Rev. A. O. Moore, and Rev. C.E. Stevens. The report was adopted.

The Report on Sunday School was called for next in order. In the absence of Bro. L. T. Royal, it was moved and carried that the Sunday School be discussed and report inserted in the minutes. County Supt. of Public Schools, W. H. Hibbs, and Bro. S. H. Averitt, spoke interestingly on the subject before the body.

REPORT ON SUNDAY SCHOOLS

A study of the Sunday School work in our Association will disclose that some progress has been made, and at the same time, suggests changes perhaps that should be made in the Sunday School program.

It is hardly necessary at this late hour to speak of the importance of Sunday School work. Christians should be impressed with the conception of the Sunday School, with the idea that it is an organization whose purpose is to teach men to know Christ and to live Christ, and they should come to appreciate the fact, as apparently many have not done, that the Sunday School, existing as it does for such lofty purpose and for such worthy end, and being inspired in its efforts by the Commission of Christ and that working in harmony and in co-ordination with all other Christian organization, is entitled to the attendance and the attention and the most intelligent support of every member of the Church.

Your Committee, therefore recommends:

1. That an organized effort be made to enlist every Church member in Sunday School work.

2. That teachers-training classes be organized in every Church where, conditions will permit, and that the Schools be graded and otherwise adequately organized.

3. That the Schools co-operate with the State Sunday School Secretary in the work of improving Sunday School work in the State.

Respectfully submitted,

L. T. ROYAL.

On motion the report was adopted.

No further business on hand the session adjourned with prayer by Rev. A. A. Pippin.

WEDNESDAY NIGHT

Rev. A. A. Pippin conducted the devotional exercises, after which the regular order of the hour was taken up. The report

11

on the Orphanage was called for and the Moderator recognized
Bro. J. F. Poole, who read the report.

REPORT ON THE ORPHANAGE

During the past year there have been many obligations to
meet, but they have now been met, and a good years work has
been done in spite of all the changes thatcame. But our blessings have so out-numbered our reverses, that we come to the
close of the year with a cheerful report in which there is much
room for praise and thanksgiving.

First, we are glad to report no debt. We had a good year
financially. The "One Day's Thanks Offering," went beyond our
expectation, coming as it did in the midst of the great epidemic
which closed the majority of our Churches. We need no further
proof that North Carolina Baptists can take care of a cause
when they unanimously and heartily want to do it.

At the present we have 530 children, 86 of these being at the
Kennedy home. We received during the year 82, average attendance 513, returned to relatives 38.

There is a greater need for more room than ever before. There
is no doubt that there are more Orphans in the State at this
time than any time during the history. The Baptists have never
been so bountifully blessed with wealth as at this time. What
shall we say to the orphans?

Only about 19,000 copies of Charity and Children are going
out weekly. There are 17,000 club subscriptions, there should
not be less than 40,000 going out every week. We urge the
pastors of the Churches to see that the Sunday Schools take
Charity and Children, for it seems that this is the only way to
inform the people about the Orphanage.

We earnestly ask that our people remember the Orphanage
with a liberal Thanksgiving Offering. We also ask the Superintendents of the Sunday Schools to take the collection one
Sunday in each month for the Orphanage.

Our health record has been remarkable. We had 481 cases of
influenza, and not a single death. We had two deaths by accident.

We express the hope that when this 75 Million Dollar Campaign is put over, we may be able to care for the orphans better. May we all do our best.

Respectfully submitted,

J. F. POOL.

On motion to adopt the report was discussed by Bro. J. F.
Pool. The report was adopted. The report on Christian Education was presented by Bro. T. J. Lassiter.

12

The hope of the world in this day of unrest, strife and turmoil lies in the acceptance of the teachings of Jesus. The evangelization of the world depends very largely upon the enlistment of God's people in the work of the kingdom. The enlistment of the forces depends upon enlightenment, the enlightenment that comes through a more perfect conception and understanding of God and His dealings with men. It was for this that our great leaders under the guidance of God's Holy Spirit formulated and put in motion the 75 Million Dollar Campaign.

We rejoice that they gave such an important place to Christian Education, placing it beside Foreign Missions on the program, keeping in mind the Master's Great Commission: "Go ye therefore, and teach all nations, baptizing them in the name of the Father, and of the Son, and of the Holy Ghost; teaching them to observe all things whatsoever I have commanded you; and lo, I am with you alway, even unto the end of the world."

Our Baptist task is the enthronement of Jesus over all the world. Our resources for the accomplishment of this task are evangelical religion, Christian Education, and the gifts which the people of God are willing to make for religion and education. To further Christian educations the Educational Board of the Southern Baptist Convention has been established. The scope of the work to be accomplished by the board is:

To mobilize the Baptists of the South in the interest of education, to awaken in the thinking of Baptist fathers and mothers an appreciation of higher education which shall lead them to make personal sacrifices, to send their children to the High School and the College.

To co-operate with all the existing state agencies of our denomination engaged in the prosecution and support of our Baptist educational institutions.

To participate enthusiastically in the Baptist 75 Million Dollar Campaign for the purpose of uniting the Southern Baptists in one supreme effort by which all Baptist enterprises shall be adequately supported; one definite goal of this effort being to raise $20,000,000 for Christian Education in five years; the inspiration of this endeavor being the acknowledged need of trained Christian leaders and the imperative demand that in the new era upon which we are entering the Baptist interpretation of Christianity shall have a world-wide presentation to a distracted world.

Briefly stated, the work of the Baptist Education Board shall be the promotion of education throughout the South under Baptist auspices, and for distinctively Christian ends.

                            Respectfully submitted,
                                T. J. LASSITER,
                                    For the Committee.

On motion the report was adopted. The Moderator recognized Rev. Q. C. Davis, who addressed the body on the subject relating to the 75 Million Dollar Campaign. A rising vote of thanks was extended to the speaker in appreciation of his splendid address.

After the singing of the Campaign song: "Millions for the Master," the session was closed with prayer by Rev. C. E. Stevens.

THURSDAY MORNING

Rev. R. M. Von Miller conducted the devotional exercises. The Moderator recognized Rev. J. B. Harris of Macon, N. C., who spoke briefly in behalf of the Biblical Recorder. The subject of B. Y. P. U. work being next in order, the Moderator recognized Bro. F. H. Brooks, who read the report.

B. Y. P. U. REPORT

In my report at the last Association, on this subject, I think I made clear my convictions in regard to the value of the B. Y. P. U., but since the reading of the last report, I am sorry to confess, that I have not done anything in the Association towards organizing this work, neither have I heard of any one else making an effort to put forth this work in the Ass.

In discussing this report, I stated on the floor of the Association, that it was useless to "resolut" about the B. Y. P. U. work or any phase of our work in the County, and then to drop it, but suggested that a report on the B.Y. P. U., as well as a report on any of the other various objects of our Association be taken up separately at some meeting of the Church or Sunday school and discussed with a view to establish the work in the various churches wherever it is not established, and improving the work in the other churches, where it was established. In my own church, during the past year there has not been a single report that was made to the Association, read or discussed, and I plead guilty for the Smithfield church, for failing to carry out the very suggestion that I made myself, and which I still consider of vital importance. So far as I know, the Clayton, Mt. Moriah, Four Oaks and Wendell churches are the only ones in the Association which have a B. Y. P. U. organized and working. The Smithfield B. Y. P. U. has not been in operation for a year or more; if there is any other B. Y. P. U. in the Association I do not know of it.

                            14

In my former report I said that "the boys and girls of today will be the men and women of tomorrow, and it will be only a question of time—possibly short for some—when the leaders in the various Baptist Churches of the Johnston County Association will lay their armor down and answer the call of the Master, and their places will have to be filled with the boys and girls of today. Will they be ready to respond when the Church calls them? Will they be prepared to take up the duties and do justice to the cause and uphold the Baptist denomination? This is not a pleasant matter to contemplate, but nevertheless it is a situation that we will have to face some day, and if we as a denomination allow it to go thoughtlessly along in this Association without preparing the young people to take the places of the old, as they fall by the wayside, then the cause of Christ and the Baptist denomination will suffer.

There are two great religious training schools—one of these is the Sunday school and the other is the B. Y. P. U., and if the churches fail to uphold and push forward these two great agencies, then the Churches of the future are bound to be loser, and the kingdom of God will suffer. What training in the religious work that I have had, I got in the Sunday school and the B. Y. P. U., when I was less than 15 years of age, I remember being at work in the B. Y. P. U. in the Williamsburg Baptist Church, and because of the training I got there, I have always felt at ease on my feet when in any church gathering, or called upon to speak. I feel sure that there are a number of laymen, as well as preachers, who got their first experience in church work in the Sunday school and in the B. Y. P. U., and I believe the Association and we, as a denomination cannot too strongly impress upon our young people the value of a well organized working B. Y. P. U. in each church in this Association. I realize that it will be hard to organize a B. Y. P. U. in some country churches, it it could be easily done in town churches and possibly in some country churches, and I think that a Committee of one or more should be appointed to assist each local church in organizing a B. Y. P. U. in the various churches in the Association, where possible. I have no statistics at hand, but I know that there are in the United States a large number of Baptist young people who are engaged in this work, and in a great many of the churches the B. Y. P. U. is the life of the Church, spiritually and socially, and I earnestly hope that before the next meeting of the Association there may be many active, working unions in our Association.

Respectfully submitted,

F. M. BROOKS,
For the Committee

15

On motion to adopt, the report was discussed by Brethren F. H. Brooks, A. O. Moore, R. M. Von Miller and Dr. Chas. E., Brewer. Motion adopted.

Bro. F. H. Brooks made a motion that the organizations and reports of the B. Y. P. U. Societies be tabulated hereafter in our Minutes, the motion was carried. It was also moved and carried that at our next session of the Association, an hour be set aside for a demonstration of the B. Y. P. U. work. In presenting the work of State Mission, the Moderator recognized Rev. J. W. Smith, who read the report.

STATE MISSION

State Mission is the task of permeating and transforming the life of the people of North Carolina with the Gospel of Jesus Christ. This work is administered by the Board of Missions at Raleigh, N. C. There are seven departments of this work, namely Evangelization, Church Building, Sunday Schools, B. Y. P. U., Woman's Missionary Union, the School of pastors and workers, and colportage work. A number of training schools have been held this year with good results. We would insist on a larger attendance in these schools. In order to be efficient, we must be thoroughly trained. We would urge the necessity of putting the best trained men in the destitute fields.

Hence, we would encourage larger salaries for our pastors, and more compact fields. We have learned long ago that the Biblical Recorder is the pastor's true helper, and we rejoice in the large circulation it has reached, but there are a good number of Baptist homes into which the paper does not go. Let us put forth our best effort to put it into every home.

Our State Mission work is undergoing a distinct change in character. It has been our conception that State Missions was almost entirely a question of evangelization. There is need that we do more evangelistic work than ever, but now we confront the necessity of developing the churches brought into existence by our evangelistic efforts. Hence, an increase of emphasis is to be laid upon Church building and development work.

Respectfully submitted,

J. W. SMITH, Chairman.

The report of Home Missions was read by Bro. S. H. Averitt.

HOME MISSION

When our Saviour said to His disciples to begin at Jerusalem, "Go into Judea and into Samaria, and to the uttermost parts of the world," to preach His Gospel to every creature, we do not think that He meant that the lost souls in one locality were of more importance than those of any other, however, he gave us the proper order in which to do the work. The souls of the

people in heathen darkness are as precious as any in our homeland. But we are not prepared to carry the Gospel to others,
until we know the Gospel at home. The more thoroughly we
preach, teach and educate at home, the more anxious will we be
that others shall have the good news of salvation, and the better
will we be prepared to take the news to others, as He said:
"Unto the uttermost parts of the world."

Respectfully submitted,

S.H.AVERITT, Chairman.

The Moderator called on Bro. J. J. Lane, who read the report
on Foreign Missions.

Never in the history of the world has the American Missionary had the opportunity that is his today. In fact the American
soldiers in Europe were in some sense missionaries, as they
represented a government that asked no material gain out of the
war; but we sent them to Europe that right, and justice might
triumph.

The fields are white unto the harvest and laborers are ready
to go forth to the work, and now our leaders are calling upon
us for the means to send them. What shall the answer be?

Respectfully submitted,

J. J. LANE, Chairman.

On motion to adopt, these three reports were adopted as a
whole.

The hour set aside for the interests of the 75 Million Dollar
Campaign having arrived, the Moderator requested Rev. H. W.
Baucom, the Associational Director of the Campaign, to take
charge of this phase of the program. Rev. Baucom spoke briefly
on the enlistment feature of the Campaign, after which Dr. Chas.
E. Brewer, president of Meredith College, Raleigh, N. C., was
introduced. Dr. Brewer delivered a most interesting and illuminating address on the subject of the hour. Rev. H. W. Baucom
then called on the different delegates of the various churches to
express themselves on the progress of the organization of the
Campaign in their respective churches, and their allotment to be
raised. These reports were very encouraging.

Under Miscellaneous business the Moderator called for reports
of Committees. The Committee on nominating the Executive
Committee, member of the State Mission Board, delegates to
State Convention and Southern Baptist Convetnion was presented by Rev. J. E. Lanier as follows:

Executive Committee, Rev. H. W. Baucom, Chairman, Brethren J. F. Pool, J. L. Hall, J. A. Smith and S. H. Averitt. Member of the State Board of Missions, Bro. F. H. Brooks. Delegate
to the Southern Baptist Convention, Bro. R. H. Gower. Dele-

gates to the State Convention, R. M. Von Miller, Geo. H. Wright and N. M. Gurley.

Respectfully submitted,

J. E. LANIER, Chairman
F. H. BROOKS
J. J. LANE
S. H. AVERITT
J. L. HALL, Committee.

The report was adopted.

THURSDAY AFTERNOON

Rev. C. E. Stevens with a number of B. Y. P. U. workers, representing various churches conducted very interesting devotional exercises. A rising vote of thanks was extended to these workers. The Moderator then appointed Rev. J. W. Smith as Auditor pro tem., and asked Bro. J. J. Lane to prepare the report on Ministerial Relief. The report on time, place and preacher was presented by Bro. J. F. Pool and was as follows:

Place, Bailey, N. C.; Rev. B. L. Badgett to preach the introductory sermon. Time, Wednesday after the fourth Sunday in October, 1920.

J. F. POOL, Chairman
W. B. JOYNER,
G. G. BEATY.

On motion the report was adopted.

The Moderator recognized Bro. J. J. Lane, who read the report on Ministerial Relief.

MINISTERIAL RELIEF

We rejoice to know that the 75 Million Dollar Campaign prepares to take care of the aged Ministers Relief Fund. These servants of God who have given their best days for the glory of God and the good of the Churches, for the conversion and saving of sinners, they deserve our best, our love, our sympathy and our support.

Respectfully submitted,

J. J. LANE, For the Committee.

On motion this report was adopted.

According to the program the Moderator called on Rev. H. W. Baucom to take charge of further consideration of the 75 Million Dollar Campaign, a round-table discussion followed, after which the Moderator called the Vice Moderator, Bro. J. J. Lane to the chair and presented the following resolution:

In view of the great need of parsonages in our Mission fields, be it resolved that we instruct our Executive Committee to apportion amounts as they deem best in their judgment, to be raised by the various Churches of our Association. These amounts shall be paid into the treasury of the Association and shall constitute a "Parsonage Building Fund." Said fund shall be appropriated by our Executive Committee from time to time for the erection of parsonages in the Mission fields, as they shall deem it wise and expedient in their judgment.

On motion this resolution was adopted.

The report of the treasurer of the Association was presented by Rev. J. E. Lanier.

Treasurer's Report of the Johnston County Baptist Association. October 29th, 1919.

I have received and disbursed the amounts as indicated below:

ASSOCIATIONAL MISSIONS

Balance on hand from last year _____$168.66
Received from the Churches during this year _____ 264.72
Disbursements:
To C. E. Stevens, for work _____$72.00
To R. M. Von Miller, for work _____ 59.00
To R. P. Merritt, for work _____ 20.00
To Ross Yokley, for supply work _____ 5.50
To J. R. Everitt, for supply work _____ 50.00
To A. L. Brown, for meeting at Pinkney ____ 13.00
To T. S. Guy, for work at Hale's Chapel _____ 50.00
To J. E. Lanier, for work at Pleasant Grove
    and postage _____ 33.00

            Total _____$322.50 $433.38
Balance on hand _____$110.88

                          $433.38 $433.38

BUILDING FUND
Balance on hand from last year _____$312.30
Received from churches this year _____ 136.00

                          Total_____$448.30

Disbursements:
Check to Miss Annie Myatt for building Church at Shiloh 312.30

Balance on hand to date _____$136.00

MINUTE FUND
Balance on hand from last year _____$89.79
Received from Churches _____ 40.50

            Total_____$130.29
19

Disbursements:

For Printing and Mailing Minutes _____$83.00
For Postage _____- 1.75
For Clerk's salary _____ 60.00

Total_____$144.75 $130.29
Amount due J. E. Lanier for money advanced__ 14.46
Respectfully submitted,
J. E. LANIER, Treasurer.

Audited by J. W. Smith, October 29th, 1919 and found correct.

A motion to adopt, the motion was carried.

Upon motion by Rev. R. M. Von Miller that a special collection be taken to supplement our Minute Fund, which was adopted, the Moderator ordered this collection to be taken. The amount of the collection was $41.36.

A motion by Bro. J. F. Pool to pay the Clerk $60.00 for his service was adopted.

Rev. L. B. Badgett offered the following resolution:

Resolved, "That we extend to the Smithfield Baptist Church our sincere appreciation of the splendid fellowship with them, and of their most excellent entertainment of this Association."

On motion the resolution was adopted.

There being no further business for this session of the Association to transact, a motion was made to adjourn by Rev. A. O. Moore, which was carried.

The adjourning prayer was offered by Rev. A. O. Moore, after which the Moderator declared the Seventeenth Annual Session of the Johnston County Baptist Association adjourned, to meet next year with Bailey Baptist Church, beginning on Wednesday after the fourth Sunday in October, 1920.

R. H. GOWER, Moderator.
R. M. VON MILLER, Clerk.

WOMAN'S MISSIONARY UNION

On Wednesday, October 8th, 1919, at 3:30 P. M. at the Baptist Church at Four Oaks, N. C., the Woman's Missionary Union of the Johnston County Baptist Association, was called into the Annual Session by its Superintendent, Mrs. B. A. Hocutt of Clayton, N. C.

The program for the afternoon session was devotional service by Mrs. Creech, prayer by Mrs. Foy Willingham, followed by words of welcome by Mrs. C. E. Stevens from the W. M. U. of the Four Oaks Baptist Church, and Mrs. B. B. Adams from the Four Oaks M. E. Church South. Both these ladies in a most pleasing manner assured us of our welcome to their homes and hearts. Mrs. C. M. Thomas of Clayton, N. C., responded, assuring all that after such a hearty welcome we were made to feel in such a short time, that it is good to be here.

Recognition of Mrs. Foy Willingham, our missionary from Japan, after which she talked to us for a few minutes. In the absence of Miss Myrtie Lee, who was to have conducted the closing devotional, Mrs. B. A. Hocutt called for as many as would, to repeat a verse of Scripture and reminded us of the benefit of learning "a verse a day" in order to keep the tempter away. After singing our Campaign song: "Millions for the Master," we were dismissed with prayer by Miss Viola Pool.

Wednesday night at 8:30 o'clock the service was opened with a song, "Onward Christian Soldiers," Scripture reading by the pastor, Rev. C. E. Stevens, prayer by Rev. H. W. Baucom. A collection was taken, which amounted to $19.50 for the expense of the meeting. This was followed by a solo by Mrs. Lois Massey Bass, "Have Thine Own Way." Rev. J. B. Turner read for his Scripture lesson the 25th Chapter of Matthew, using for his subject: "Stewardship." He preached a wonderful sermon.

Thursday morning at 9:30 o'clock the Union was again called to order by its Superintendent, and a very interesting program followed. Morning prayer service by Viola Pool. The key note of her talk was "To give ourselves." First give yourself to the Master's work. What a great opportunity we have at this time in the 75 Million Campaign to give self for service in this great work. Next on the program was the singing of "Come Women Wide Proclaim." Minutes of Wednesday afternoon read. Roll Call of Societies. Nomination Committee. Mrs. J. M. Beaty, Mrs. E. V. Woodard and Mrs. J. W. Sanders. Resolution Committee, Mrs. D. J. Thurston and Mrs. Geo. Vick. Time and place, Mrs. Oliven and Mrs. Creech.

Mrs. B. A. Hocutt read the annual report of the year's work in the Association. Mrs. C. E. Stevens, on a larger enrollment, brought before us the great need of this work. We were very fortunate to have with us Mrs. Foy Willingham, who in her sweet and beautfiul manner told of her work in Japan and its needs. This was very illuminating and instructive. Solo: "The Prayer Perfect," by Mrs. Bennette Nooe, Jr. Song, "Millions for the Master," and after prayer by Mrs. J. W. Massey we adjourned for dinner. After a most delightful dinner served on the lawn of the Church, the program of the afternoon was again taken up.

Devotional service by Mrs. D. B. Oliven. Committee reports were then called for and the nomination Committee recommended the following officers for the coming year: Mrs. B. A. Hocutt, Supt., Miss Cleve Barnes, Secretary and Treasurer; Mrs.

21

H. W. Baucom, Junior Supt.; District leaders: Mrs. H. W. Baucom, Smithfield, Mrs. J. M. Beaty, Assistant; Mrs. C. W. Carter, Clayton; Mrs. H. E. Earp, Selma, Mrs. J. W. Sanders, Four Oaks, and Mrs. N. B. Lewis, Middlesex.

Committee on time and place recommended that the next Union be held at Middlesex, the first or second week in October, 1920. All the reports were adopted. A motion then prevailed that we give Mrs. J. M. Beaty and Mrs. W. S. Penn a vote of thanks for their printing announcements, etc. The Secretary was asked to write the following ladies, expressing regret of their absence: Mrs. H. W. Baucom, Mrs. H. M. Finch and Mrs. H. P. Johnson. Mrs. C. W. Carter on special prayer seasons and offerings made a splendid and most impressive talk. Mission study and Mission literature by Mrs. Howard Gray showed how important that we study more about Missions, for without knowledge we cannot have interest. After which a beautiful solo was rendered by Mrs. Lois Massey. Bass. Mrs. Thurston on Christian Education showed the importance of this great line of work. The song by the Sunbeams was enjoyed by all. Talk on the Training School by Miss Mattie Bain, gave us all an idea of the home life and work of the girls in this school.

We greatly regretted that Mrs. H. M. Finch of Rocky Mt., could not be with us and tell us more about the Baptist 75 Million Campaign.

Our hearts were made sad at this part of the program, when Mrs. C. W. Carter read the names of Mrs. J. M. Turley, Mrs. M. E. Yelvington, Mrs. R. A. Bain and Mrs. Floy Johnson Mangum, who had slipped away from us since our last meeting to a brighter world above. Here we paused in memory of them and Mrs. Carter led in prayer. After reading of Minutes and closing prayer by Mrs. Floy Willingham, the Union adjourned to meet in Middlesex the first or second week in October, 1920.

Mrs. B. A. HOCUTT, Supt.
Miss CLEVE BARNES, Secretary.

STATISTICAL TABLE OF B. Y. P. U.

Name of Union.	Name of Pres. and Address.	No. of Members
Clayton—Rev. A. O. Moore, Clayton, N. C.		25
Mount Moriah—Miss Veola Pool, Clayton, N. C.		30
Wendell (Jr.)—Miss Thelma Honeycutt, Wendell, N. C.		24
Wilson's Mills—Geo. Boyd, Wilson's Mills, N. C.		60

Apportionment for Associational Building and Minute Funds

Name of Church	Assn. Bld. Fund	Minute Fund
Antioch	$ 25.00	$ 7.50
Bailey	25.00	5.00
Baptist Center	20.00	5.00

22

Beaty Chapel	10.00	5.00
Benson	10.00	5.00
Benson Grove	20.00	5.00
Bethany	20.00	5.00
Bethel	10.00	5.00
Bethesda	50.00	10.00
Blackman's Grove	40.00	10.00
Burnell Mission	10.00	2.50
Calvary	20.00	5.00
Canaan	10.00	5.00
Carter's Chapel	50.00	7.50
Clayton	200.00	15.00
Clyde's Chapel	50.00	10.00
Corinth	25.00	7.50
Four Oaks	25.00	10.00
Hale's Chapel	10.00	5.00
Hephzibah	10.00	5.00
Hood's Grove	25.00	7.50
Kenly	25.00	5.00
Lee's Chapel	40.00	10.00
Live Oak	10.00	2.50
Lizzie Mill	10.00	2.50
Micro	25.00	5.00
Middlesex	25.00	7.50
Mt. Moriah	150.00	15.00
New Bethel	75.00	10.00
Noble's Chapel	40.00	10.00
Oliver's Grove	10.00	2.50
Parrish Memorial	20.00	5.00
Pauline	15.00	5.00
Pine Level	50.00	10.00
Pinkney	20.00	5.00
Pisgah	50.00	7.50
Princeton	25.00	5.00
Sardis	25.00	5.00
Selma	75.00	10.00
Shiloh	25.00	5.00
Smithfield	150.00	15.00
Thanksgiving	25.00	5.00
Trinity	20.00	5.00
Wendell	75.00	10.00
White Oak	25.00	7.50
Wilson's Mills	25.00	5.00

Totals _____$1,745.00 $322.50

TABLE I—STATISTICAL

CHURCH	PASTOR	POST-OFFICE	CLERK	POST-OFFICE	Time of Preaching	Value of Church Property	By Baptism	By Letter	By Restoration	By Letter	By Exclusion	By Death	Number of Males	No of Females	Total Membership
							GAINS			LOSSES					

TABLE II—FIN

CHURCHES	Pastor's Salary	Building and Repairs	Incidentals	S S Expenses	The Poor	Minute Fund	Associational Missions	State Missions
Antioch	200 00	50 00		80		5.00	12.50	25
Bailey	125 00			85	1 00	3.00	10.00	15
		5.00		11 00		3.00	10.00	15
		4.00	140 57			50	5.00	15
Benson's Grove	124 00	19 28	363 77	10 00		5.00	6.00	100
	100 00			10 00		1 00	5.00	10
	60 00		10 00			50	2.50	10
Bethesda	300 00	10 00	3.00	37 30	80	5.00	25.00	45
Blackman's Grove	272 00		10 00	80		1 00	2.50	30
	15 00					1 50	5.00	5
Calvary	75 00	5.00	85			1 50	5.00	10
Canaan						3 00	2.50	10
Carter's Chapel	1,750 00	10,760 72	532 24	80			60.00	30
Clayton	250 00		13 55	60.00		5.00	25.00	50
Eve's Chapel	250 00	171.75	3 02	80		80	20.00	25
Hale's Chapel		1,000.00	62 30	80	70 00	80	3.00	6
Hephzibah	24 95	1,500 00				1 00	10.00	12
Grove	163 70		1 00	25 50		3.00	5.00	10
Kenly	300 00		84 35	20 00		5.00	5.00	20
Lee's	13 00		35 00					
Live ... Mill	5 00		2 00	85	25 00	1 00	2.50	2
Micro		477 00	47 07	80		2 00	12.50	16
Mount Moriah	240 00	0	75 00	80		7.50	50 00	21
New	250 00		12 00	12 00	13 50	5.00	16 50	115
Oliver's Grove	23 10		78 05	85		5.00	12 50	40
Parrish	50 00			80			7 50	25
Pauline	65 00	10 00	89 00	80		2.00	10.00	20
Pine Level			18.00	40 00	10 00	5.00	15 00	10
Pinkney	102 00	4 00	71 40	30 10	80	85	15 00	25
Pisgah	450 00					4 40	15 00	12
Princeton	100 00		3.00			80	15 00	34
Saulls			5 00	80	10 00	3.00	17 50	20
Selma	600 00	10 00	25 00	8.27		80	19 50	65
Shiloh		300 00		45.00		7.50	40 00	23
Smithfield		2,000 00		18. 80	40 00	80	10.00	20
Trinity	179 30		65 85	30.00		80	10.00	20
Wendell	149 00	150 00		80		50	10.00	10
White Oak	585 00	450 00	175.00	50.00		3.00	10.00	50
Wil ...'s Mills	300 00	168. 85	34.50	40.00	15 00	80	8. 00	15
	13. 417,450.33	2,306.40	1,565.47	281 62	281	148.90	617 55	1,642

TABLE III—SUNDAY SCHOOLS

CHURCH	SUPT.	POST-OFFICE	SECT'Y	POST-OFFICE	No of Schools	Officers and Teachers	Pupils	Total Enrollment	Church Membership in S S	Mo Kept Open	Baptisms from School	School Expense	Missions	Orphanage	Other Objects	Total Contribution
Antioch	J D Johnson		W. O. Hocutt	Middlesex, N. C.	1	12	120		90 12			21 00	16 09	28 45		12 00
Bailey	J C Finch	Bailey, N. C.	Alvin Underwood	Bailey, N. C.	1	8	80		20 12			21 50				71 32
Baptist Cen	L C He	Clayton, N. C.	John Ellis	Clayton, N. C.		4	40		25 12							
Beaty Chapel	W M Eason		J. J. Parrish	Smithfield, N. C.	1	4	35		6 12			1 00	8 20			19 20
Benson	J B Benton		Julian Godwin	Benson, N. C.	1	26	260		98 12			174 80				174 80
Bethany	R A Barr		I. E. Barbour	Benson, N. C.	1	3	35		6 12			10 00		5 00	7 50	37 00
Bethel Grove	Cornell Che	Kenly, N. C.	C. S. Creech	Kenly, N. C.	1	5	60		40 12			20 00		7 00		37 00
Bethesda	J B Coats	Wilson's Mills, N. C.	V. S. Smith	Wilson's Mills, N. C.	1	12	100		75 12			19 45	9 75	2 00		37 20
Blackman's Gro	Joseph Wood	Four Oak	Freni Mahler	Four Oaks, N. C.	1	3	37		44 12			13 00	5 00	7 00	6 00	28 00
Barn Mission	J S Johnson	Four Oaks, N. C.	W. L. Massengill	Four Oaks, N. C.	1	4	45		5 8			6 00				6 00
Calvary																
Canaan	Gray Eason	Selma, N. C.	B. F. Woodruff	Selma, N. C.	1	12	109		60 12			16 50				16 50
Clayton Cha	John T Talton	Clayton, N. C.	Chas. G. Gulley	Clayton, N. C.	1	33	3 46		200 12			116 73	329 83	91 53	120 20	655 29
Clyde's Gro	S M Mhr	Wendell,N.C.,R.1	Elva Phipps	Wendell, N. C.	1	4	125		75 12			60 00		25 00		85 00
Corinth	Z B Hocutt	Wendell,N.C.,R.1	L. F. Davis	Wendell, N. C., R. 1	1	12	128		31 12			13 95	5 00	2 21	5 00	26 16
Four Oaks	J W Sanders	Four Oaks, N. C.	W. E. Barbour	Four Oaks, N. C., R. 1	1	12	120		51 12			41 83	16 00	8 25	255 00	324 08
Hale's Chapel	A D Pea	Zebul n, N. C.	W. E. Parrish	Zebulon, N. C.	1	3	130		30 12			14 63				14 63
Hephzibah	W G Creh	Princeton, N. C.	J. F. Earp	Pine Level, N. C.	1	3	5		5 9			5 29				5 29
Hood's Gro																
Kenly	A J Broughton	Kenly, N. C.	Talmage Watson	Kenly, N. C.	1	37	37		23 12			25 50	3 00	5 00		33 50
Lee's Cha	W I Green	Zebulon,N.C.,R.1	V. E. Lewis	Middlesex, N. C.	1	6	104		65 12			20 00				20 00
Live Oak																
Lizzie Mi																
Micro	L M Ansley	Micro, N. C.	D. C. Smith	Micro, N. C.	1	10	105		15 12			33 15		14 18		45 33
Middlesex	W K Ballentine	Middlesex, N. C.	J M Davis	Middlesex, N. C.	1	12	93		40 12			185 00	65 00	260 64	15 75	385 39
Mount Moriah	Elliot S Pol		Bernard Pleasant	Garner, N. C.	1	14	147		50 12			4 60		15 75		185 00
New Bethel	R I Smith		Eugene Britt	Garner, N. C.	1	9	95		35 9			12 00	10 20		10 00	32 20
New Chapel	Albert Nel	Simms, N. C.	Claw Wilson	Simms, N. C.	1	4	44		36 12			7 23	5 33	1 30	5 00	19 56
Oliver's Grove																
Parrish Memorial	J D Che	Selma, N. C.	Herbert Bender	Selma, N. C.	1	4	24		20 12			10 00				10 00
Pauline																
Pine Level	B L Strickland	Pine Level, N. C.	Miss Sadie Britt	Pine Level, N. C.	1	10	105		60 12			40 00	16 00		15 00	71 00
Pisgah	R E Lee		Otis Lee	Kenly, N. C.	1	3	38		15 12			10 64	2 01			14 44
Princeton	Paul Whitley	Princeton, N. C.	G G Jones	Smithfield,	1	7	50		20 12			3 04	4 41	59	4 30	19 81
Sardis	W I Pearce	Princeton, N. C.	Caspin Johs	Princeton,	1	5	52		5 9							
Shiloh	J W Williams	Selma, N. C.	Mrs J B Oir	Pn Level, N. C.	1	8	97		105 12			8 27	72 17			80 44
Smith	T S Smith	McCullers, N. C.	John Ives	Garner, N. C.	1	3	85		35 12			16 06	6 06	30 00		52 12
Thanksgiving	W S Ragsdale	Selma, N. C.	Columbus Wood	Smithfield, N. C.	1	16	196		50 12			158 85	388 65	100 05	562 04	1,209 55
Selma				Bertie Godwin	Selma, N. C.	1	12	125		50 12			12 00			50 00	50 00
Trinity	W P Lee	Fremont, N. C.	Berta Godwin	Benson, N. C., R. 2	1	4	46		15 12			45 00	5 00			17 00
Wendell	R E Richardson	Wendell, N. C.	W. R. Johnson	Wendell, N. C., R. 1	1	6	40		20 12			12 00	18 39	66 75	11 20	300 99
White Oak	A L Batton	Clayton, N. C., R. 2	J. M. Green	Clayton, N. C., R. 2	1	10	124		50 12			50 00	7 50			47 50
White Mills	J F Holt	Wilson's Mills,N.C.	Walter Boyd	Wilson's Mills, N. C.	1	7	71		3 12			40 00				50 00
					38 3 30		3,707	4,037	1,698		167	550 94	1,004 09	618 45	340	7314 275 50

TABLE IV—WOMAN'S MISSIONARY UNION

CHURCH	NAME OF ORGANIZATION	PRESIDENT	POST-OFFICE	No. Members	State Missions	Home Missions	Foreign Missions	S. S. Board	Training School	Other Objects	Total Contributions
Bailey	W. M. Union	Mrs. W. Underwood	Bailey, N. C.	12	$ 1. 45		$ 4. 50	$		$34. 70	$ 40 65
Beaty	W. M. U.	Mrs. E. F.	Smithfield, N. C								12. 31
Benson's	Woman's M'ry Union	Mrs. M. T. Britt	Benson, N. C.	6	5. 71	6. 67					12. 31
Benson's	Woman's M'ry Union	Ms. Chess.	Benson, N. C.	22	6. 40		9. 23		6. 60	21. 00	61. 80
Clayton	W. M'ry Un.	Mrs. J. S.	Four Oaks, N. C.	5	4. 00				18. 50		4. 00
Clayton	W. M'ry Union	Ms. C. W	Four Oaks, N. C.	60	100. 00	9. 00	113. 00		30. 00	11. 20	33. 20
Clayton	W. M. Women's	Ms. C. D. Bass	Clayton, N. C.	15	13. 45	15. 15	10. 35		9. 45	50. 0	48. 40
Clayton	W. M. Women's	Mrs. W. J. Payne	Clayton, N. C.	77	23. 03	10. 49	10. 75		7. 00		81. 27
Clayton	Royal Ambassadors	Mrs.	Clayton, N. C.		8. 00	9. 00	14. 00		15. 00	18. 00	50. 00
Clayton	Girls' Union	Miss G. L. Goby	Clayton, N. C.	24	17. 55	41. 00	19. 65			183. 05	26. 30
	W. M. Missionary Union	Mrs. Anie Ice	Clayton, N. C., R. 1	15	20. 00	3. 00	4. 00	2. 00	2. 00	4. 00	35. 00
	Woman's Missionary Union	Elgie Hocutt	Clayton, N. C., R. 1	5			6. 40				6. 40
Four Oaks	W. M. Union	Mrs. A. H. Phelps	Four Oaks, N. C.	35	10. 20	8. 00	11. 50		2. 90	66. 55	99. 15
	W. M'ry Union	Miss Clyde Sanders	Four Oaks, N. C.	15	1. 05	14. 75			14. 0		29. 80
	W. M'ry Union	Miss Beh.	Selma, N. C.	10							
	Sunbeams	Mrs. N. B.	Selma, N. C.	10	8. 25	8. 90	10. 00		155. 40	7. 70	190. 25
Mt. Moriah	Sunbeams	Mrs. N. B. Lewis	Selma, N. C.	13	13. 00	3. 00	7. 00		2. 00	2. 25	27. 25
Mt. Moriah	Sunbeams	Mrs. C. B.	Selma, N. C.	12	15. 0	15. 00	15. 00				45. 00
Mt. Moriah	W. M.	Rosa Lee	Selma, N. C., R. 3	32	5. 25	6. 25	5. 00	1. 00			17. 50
Noble's Chapel	W. M'ry Union	Mrs. J. J. Lane	Auburn, N. C.	29	9. 00	16. 05	10. 00	5. 00	20. 00	59. 05
Pine Level	W. M. Union	Mrs. Me. Boykin	Simms, N. C., R.	10		1. 25	3. 22			25. 45	29. 92
Pine Level	W. M. Union	Mrs. B. L. Smith	Pine Level, N. C.		20. 00	8. 00	8. 00			7. 55	47. 55
Pisgah	W. M.	Mrs. D. B. Oliver	Pine Level, N. C.	15		15. 60	6. 75		3. 00		36. 55
Pisgah	Young	Mrs. W. D. Johnson	Smithfield, N. C.		6. 20	3. 00	3. 00		4. 00	7. 0	7. 0
Pisgah	W. M.	Miss Pearl	Selma, N. C.	14		3. 00	4. 00			1. 00	8. 00
Princeton	W. M. Missionary Union	Mrs. W. M. Joyner	Selma, N. C.							1. 00	
Sardis	W. M. Missionary Union	Mrs. B. E. Gardner	Selma, N. C.								
Shiloh	W. M. Missionary Union	Mrs. Lee Mt.	Smithfield, N. C.	30	131. 95	8. 00	7. 00		8. 00	1. 00	24. 00
Smithfield	W. M. Missionary Union	Mrs. W. N. Holt	Smithfield, N. C.	2	2.	62. 59	81. 7		39. 25	112. 00	87 52
Selma	Young Sunbeams	Miss I. Me Ennis	Smithfield, N. C.	20	1. 85	9. 00	6. 75		3. 50	1. 11	15. 46
Selma	W. M. Missionary Union	Miss Myrtle Lee	Benson, N. C., R. 2	20	5. 70	11. 48			4. 00		27. 93
Selma	W. M'ry Union	Mrs. H. F.	Selma, N. C.				3. 30	8. 00	5. 00	.90	18. 05
Selma	Sunbeams	Mrs. L. V. T.	Selma, N. C.								
Selma	Girls' Auxiliary	Mrs. I. R. hi	Selma, N. C.	8	7. 25	1. 60					82. 31
				583	434. 29	358. 83	374. 13	8. 00	20. 60	586.	

MINUTES

OF THE

EIGHTEENTH ANNUAL SESSION

OF THE

Johnston Co. Baptist Association

HELD WITH

BAILEY BAPTIST CHURCH

OCTOBER 28 and 29, 1920

The next session will be held with Blackman's Grove Baptist Church, beginning on Wednesday after the fourth Sunday in October, 1921.

To preach the Introductory Sermon, Rev. B. Townsend; Rev. C. C. Wheeler, alternate.

RALEIGH
MUTUAL PUBLISHING COMPANY, PRINTERS
1920

MINUTES

OF THE

EIGHTEENTH ANNUAL SESSION

OF THE

Johnston Co. Baptist Association

HELD WITH

BAILEY BAPTIST CHURCH

OCTOBER 28 and 29, 1920

The next session will be held with Blackman's Grove Baptist Church, beginning on Wednesday after the fourth Sunday in October, 1921.

To preach the Introductory Sermon, Rev. B. Townsend; Rev. C. C. Wheeler, alternate.

RALEIGH
MUTUAL PUBLISHING COMPANY, PRINTERS
1920

OFFICERS.

Moderator—R. H. Gower ....Clayton
Vice-Moderator—S. H. Averitt ....Clayton
Clerk—R. M. Von Miller ....Wilson
Treasurer—J. A. Smith ....Smithfield
Auditor—K. L. Hall ....Benson

EXECUTIVE COMMITTEE.

H. W. Baucom, Chairman ....Smithfield
R. A. Bain ....Four Oaks
J. A. Smith ....Smithfield
J. F. Pool ....Clayton
Alonzo Parrish ....Benson

DELEGATES AND BOARD MEMBERS.

Member of State Board of Missions—R. L. Gay.

Delegate to Southern Baptist Convention—F. H. Brooks.

Delegates to Baptist State Convention—B. Townsend, A. L. Brown and W. H. Hipps.

Committee in charge of and to make reports on Convention objects:

1. *Education.* (a) Colleges. Rev. C. C. Wheeler, Chairman; (b) Preparatory Schools, J. J. Lane; (c) Periodicals, Books and Tracts, Alonzo Parrish.

2. *Social Service.* (a) Orphanage, Rev. R. L. Gay, Chairman; (b) Hospitals, D. L. Barbour; (c) Ministerial Relief, J. F. Pool; (d) Temperance, R. H. Gower.

3. *Teaching and Training.* (a) Sunday-schools, Rev. B. Townsend, Chairman; (b) B. Y. P. U. and B. Y. P. U. Demonstration, Rev. A. O. Moore; (c) Bible Conference, Rev. T. S. Guy.

4. *Missions.* (a) Associational Missions, Rev. H. W. Baucom, Chairman; (b) State Missions, Rev. J. W. Nobles; (c) Home Mission, Rev. A. L. Brown; (d) Foreign Missions, Rev. R. M. Von Miller (e) Women's Work, representative of W. M. U.

5. *Business.* (a) Church Government, Judge F. H. Brooks, Chairman; (b) Church Finance, Rev. A. Corey; (c) Report of Executive Committee, Rev. H. W. Baucom.

LIST OF MINISTERS.

H. W. Baucom ....Smithfield
A. L. Brown ....Fremont
A. Corey ....Jamesville
J. H. Donald ....Raleigh
J. R. Everett ....Wake Forest
B. G. Earley ....Raleigh
R. L. Gay ....Smithfield
T. S. Guy ....Zebulon
J. E. Hocutt ....Nashville
T. S. Hood ....Goldsboro
S. F. Hudson ....Wake Forest
J. C. Martin ....Fuquay Springs
A. O. Moore ....Clayton
G. T. Mills ....Apex
J. W. Nobles ....Middlesex
L. B. Padgett ....Wendell
W. D. Stancil ....Kenly
C. E. Stevens ....Four Oaks
B. Townsend ....Selma
R. M. Von Miller ....Wilson
C. C. Wheeler ....Benson

ENROLLED DELEGATES.

Antioch—A. G. Lewis, Mrs. A. G. Lewis, Mrs. Nancy Hales, Mrs. G.
R. Whitley, Geo. R. Whitley.

Bailey—M. H. Bisett, J. P. Underwood, J. W. B. Finch, Mrs. J. W.
Privett.

Baptist Center—J. C. Hardee, Mrs. J. C. Hardee.

Beaty's Chapel—

Benson—Rev. C. C. Wheeler.

Benson Grove—J. H. Hamilton.

Bethany—L. N. Littleton, Jesse B. Creech.

Bethel—

Bethesda—L. B. Smith, Clarence Medlin, J. J. Wallace, Milton Durham.

Blackman's Grove—Nogah Wood, William Lee, J. P. Morgan.

Burnell Mission—

Calvary—

Canaan—

Carter's Chapel—W. M. Boykin, J. S. Nichols, Ernest Grice, Martin
Thorn, Viola Thorn.

Clayton—D. L. Barbour, W. T. Allen, Mrs. Martha Spencer, Rev. A.
O. Moore, D. J. Yelverton, R. H. Gower.

Clyde's Chapel—D. C. Ponits, N. B. Medlin, C. W. Lewis.

Corinth—C. B. Hocutt, Mrs. J. B. Oneal, Mrs. C. B. Hocutt, J. B.
Oneal.

Four Oaks—W. A. Massongill, W. P. Massongill, R. A. Bain, Rev. C. E. Stevens.

Hale's Chapel—Rev. T. S. Guy, May Bell Price, J. P. Price, Mrs. J. P. Price, B. M. Price, J. B. Richardson.

Hepzipah—

Hood's Grove—Rev. S. F. Hudson.

Kenly—

Lee's Chapel—P. D. Chamble, Mrs. A. A. Morgan. J. M. Dixon.

Live Oak—

Lizzie Mill—

Micro—Walter L. Barton, D. C. Smith, J. H. Broadwell.

Middlesex—Rev. J. W. Nobles, J. T. Moore, L. J. Johnson.

Mount Moriah—J. G. Lane, Mrs. J. G. Lane, Elliot S. Pool, Miss Emily Bryan, J. F. Pool, W. R. Stallings, S. Wilder, Mrs. N. R. Pool, N. R. Pool.

New Bethel—Eugene B. Britt, Wiley P. Dowd, Mary B. Bryan.

Noble's Chapel—Mrs. J. H. Grice, J. H. Grice, T. B. Boykin, Mrs. T. B. Boykin, L. F. Boykin, N. L. Stott, Rev. R. M. Von Miller, E. B. Deans.

Oliver's Grove—

Parrish Memorial—G. W. Parrish, J. N. Watson, Jesse Worley, J. B. Creech, Eddie Parish.

Pauline—

Pine Level—N. M. Turley, B. Golis.

Pinkney—Nathan Davis, Mrs. B. R. Edgerton, Mrs. Rebecca Holland, Leslie Davis, Rev. A. L. Brown.

Pisgah—Rev. R. L. Gay, R. H. Higgins, A. J. Whitley, Jr., N. D. Johnson.

Princeton—Mrs. L. D. Grantham, Lizzie Pearce, J. J. Boyette.

Sardis—C. M. Strickland, N. E. Stevens, J. R. Olive.

Selma—Rev. B. Townsend, Theo. Eason, J. A. Eason, J. M. Oneal.

Shiloh—S. H. Averitt.

Smithfield—Rev. H. W. Baucom, T. J. Talton, R. R. Talton, L. Brown, F. H. Brooks.

Thanksgiving—W. C. Whitley.

Trinity—

Wendell—Rev. L. B. Padgett, J. T. Allen, E. C. Carroll, Mrs. T. J. Hester, Mrs. W. C. Privett, Mrs. Ed. V. Richardson, Amos Dean.

White Oak—

Wilson's Mills—

PROCEEDINGS.

The Johnston County Baptist Asscoiation met in its eighteenth session, with the Bailey Baptist Church, October 27
and 28, 1920.

The body was called to order by the Moderator, Bro. R. H.
Gower, on Wednesday, 10 a. m. According to the program,
he called on Rev. T. S. Guy to conduct the devotional exer-
cises, after which the Moderator appointed Brethren J. B.
Underwood, D. J. Yelverton, and A. B. Wilder to serve as a
Committee on Credentials and Enrollment.

A quorum being present, the Moderator declared that the
next item of business was the election of officers, calling
Rev. A. A. Pippin to the chair. The following officers were
re-elected:

Moderator—R. H. Gower.

Vice-Moderator—S. H. Averitt.

Clerk—R. M. Von Miller.

Treasurer—J. A. Smith.

Auditor—J. L. Hall.

The Moderator appointed Rev. H. W. Baucom, Rev. A. L.
Brown, and Rev. A. A. Pippin to serve as Committee on
Order of Business.

The Moderator then called on Rev. J. W. Nobles to lead
in prayer.

The next item in order was the report on Temperance.
This report was presented by Rev. A. A. Pippin:

REPORT ON TEMPERANCE.

No more brewing of spirituous liquors; let us gather inspiration
and courage when we think of those who have pledged their loyal
support in "holding the fort" against John Barleycorn. For we
know that ever since the Eighteenth Amendment became effective
the booze profiteers have been struggling to find some way to break
our victory. This has been a great year in our history, but it will
be a year also of remorse if we sleep on our obligations and our
opportunities and allow the enemy to steal our justly-earned victories.

For twenty-five years the Anti-Saloon League has been under
heavy fire against all liquor forces, so we from the pulpit and the

platform and the press, by personal work and literature must impress the unknowing and unthinking with the fact that the Eighteenth Amendment was adopted in a loyal way and is what the majority of the people of America want.

The penalties for various violations are as follows:

Failure to register still $500 penalty, fine of between $100 and $1,000 and imprisonment of between one month and two years; for making liquor in a community where it is prohibited by local or State law, tax of $1,000; for violation of war-time prohibition, $1,000 fine or one year imprisonment or both; for making whiskey or beer, fine of between $500 and $5,000, and imprisonment of between six months and three years.

Beer making comes within the same prohibition.

Respectfully submitted,

A. A. PIPPIN, *Committee.*

On motion to adopt, the following brethren spoke on the report: Rev. A. A. Pippin, Rev. R. L. Gay, Judge F. H. Brooks, S. H. Averitt. The report was adopted.

The Moderator then recognized Rev. A. L. Brown, who presented the report on Periodicals:

PERIODICALS.

It is essential in a democracy that all of the people be enlightened. The Baptists being the purest democracy in the world, it is essential that they be enlightened Baptists or the work will not go forward. Therefore, every Baptist should be a reader of the denominational papers that he may be able to participate in the work intelligently. There should not be a Baptist home where the Biblical Recorder, the Home and Foreign Fields and other Baptist papers and magazines are not read. We therefore urge that every effort possible be put forward to place one or more of these periodicals in every Baptist home in this Association.

Respectfully submitted,

A. L. BROWN, *Committee.*

On motion to adopt, the report was discussed by Rev. A. L. Brown, Judge F. H. Brooks, and Editor Archibald Johnson. The report was adopted.

After song and prayer, the annual introductory sermon was preached by Rev. L. B. Padgett; subject, "The Master's Conception of Life and Service"; text, John 9:4.

Following the sermon, the Moderator appointed the fol

lowing Committee on Place and Preacher for the next meeting: F. H. Brooks, J. F. Pool, and Q. B. Hocutt.

The body then adjourned for dinner, with prayer by Rev. A. O. Moore.

Wednesday Afternoon.

Devotional service conducted by Rev. B. Townsend.

The Moderator, in calling the meeting to order, raised the question as to the advisability of adding two brethren to Committee on Reports. It was moved and carried to omit this.

The Moderator then recognized Rev. A. O. Moore, who presented the report on Woman's Work:

WOMAN'S WORK.

The W. M. U. of Johnston County Baptist Association organized in 1903, with three societies. In 1904 they reported five societies with $332.77 contributed.

There are at present 46 churches in the Association with 48 societies, 28 W. M. U., 12 Y. W. A. and G. A.'s, six Sunbeams and two R. A.'s. Of these 23 sent annual reports. Sixteen societies sent reports every quarter. Four new societies were organized, and six were reorganized this year. Twenty-three societies reported in their annual reports 717 members, 123 Home and Foreign Fields, 135 Biblical Recorders, 139 Royal Services, 13 societies observed State Mission Day, and 15 Home Mission Day; 16 societies reported observance of week of prayer, nine Mission Study Classes; 13 societies are doing personal work. Superintendent reported having written 50 postal cards and travelled 175 miles and wrote 300 letters. They raised last year $1,888.22 and this year $5,442.72. There were 45 delegates present at the annual meeting at Middlesex.

Respectfully submitted,

A. O. Moore, Committee.

On motion to adopt, the Moderator recognized Rev. A. O. Moore, who spoke on the report. The report was adopted.

Rev. R. M. Von Miller made a motion that the Superintendent of the W. M. U. be asked to appoint a member of their Union to present a report at our next meeting, and also discuss same. The motion was carried and the Clerk instructed to convey this request to Mrs. A. B. Hocutt, the Superintendent of the W. M. U. of our Association.

The Moderator then recognized Rev. R. M. Von Miller, who presented the report on Christian Education:

CHRISTIAN EDUCATION.

The creation of a Board of Education six years ago by the Baptists of North Carolina was in our judgment divinely guided, for the service of this board has been marked by special evidences of Divine favor, for which we should thank God and take courage. Conditions have been unsettled, and apparently unpropitious in civic, economical, social and religious life. Repeated efforts have been made by men of high places to undermine evangelical faith and obliterate denominational lines. Nevertheless, "the foundation of God standeth sure" and His people have reunited steadfast and have abounded in the work of the Lord.

The hope of this distracted world in this day of unrest, turmoil and strife lies in the acceptance of the teaching, of Jesus: "Teaching them to observe all things, whatsoever I have commanded you," is a part of the divine commission.

The evangelization of the world depends largely upon the enlistment of God's people in the work of the kingdom. The enlistment of forces depends upon enlightenment, the enlightenment that comes through a more perfect understanding of God's will in His dealings with men.

We rejoice therefore that the Southern Baptists gave such an important place to Christian Education, placing it beside Foreign Missions, which is in accordance with the Commission of Christ.

Perhaps at no time in the history of mankind was there ever such a great opportunity for the enthronement of Jesus Christ over all the world as today. Our resources for the accomplishment of this great task are evangelical religion, Christian Education, and the gifts which the people of God are willing to make for the Kingdom.

To further Christian Education, the Educational Board of the Southern Baptist Convention has been established. The scope of the work to be accomplished by this Board is:

(1) To mobilize the Baptists of the South in the interest of Christian Education, to awaken in the thinking of Baptist fathers and mothers an appreciation of higher education, which shall lead them to make personal sacrifices to send their children to Christian high schools and colleges.

(2) To participate enthusiastically in the pledging and collecting of our Baptist 75 Million Dollar Campaign for the purpose of unifing the Southern Baptists in one supreme effort by which all Baptist enterprises shall be adequately supported; one definite goal of

this effort being to raise $20,000,000 for Christian Education in five years; the inspiration of this endeavor being the acknowledged need of trained leaders and the imperative demand that in the new era upon which we are entering, the Baptist interpretation of Christianity shall have a world-wide presentation to a distracted world.

(3) To co-operate with all the existing State agencies of our denomination engaged in the prosecution and support of our Baptist educational institutions.

Briefly stated, the work of the Baptist Educational Board shall be the promotion of Christian Education throughout the South under Baptist auspices, and for distinctively Christian ends.

To commit ourselves to this noble task, we solicit the co-operation of every church within the bounds of our Association.

Respectfully submitted,

R. M. Von Miller, *Committee.*

On motion to adopt, Rev. R. M. Von Miller spoke on the report. The report was adopted.

The Moderator called on Rev. H. W. Baucom to discuss the report on Church Finance, in place of Bro. J. J. Lane, who was absent. An open discussion followed, in which Brethren A. O. Moore, R. M. Von Miller, S. F. Hudson, and T. S. Guy participated.

On motion of Rev. A. O. Moore, the following resolution was adopted:

"Resolved, That the Association in its 18th session earnestly urge that the churches adopt a budget system of finance, and that they endeavor to enlist the membership to bring their offerings at each regular service."

The Moderator then recognized Rev. T. S. Guy, who presented the report on Sunday-School Work:

SUNDAY-SCHOOL WORK.

There was never a time when we needed to emphasize the work of every religious agency so much as now. Our Sunday-school work has such large possibilities in winning the lost to Christ and training the saved for efficient service, that we cannot afford to treat it lightly.

Southern Baptists have undertaken a great Sunday-school program. As one of the features of the 75 Million Campaign, our Sunday-school Board, with the campaign workers, have outlined for us a great challenging task. Therefore, we in our Association commit ourselves to the following policies for next year and the years following:

1. *Enlargement.* There are at least 500,000 people in North Carolina unreached by any Sunday-school, for whom white Baptists are responsible, if we do our proportionate part of reaching the unreached. We commend the religious census as the best way of performing this task effectively.

2. *Adequate Organization and Equipment.* These are necessary if we are going to properly take care of these people and those already enrolled. This means that our workers must learn how to group, or grade, our pupils into the right kind of classes and departments. Then again, we must not forget the $_{phy}sica_l$ equipment that will at least meet minimum educational standards. We must provide class rooms, suitable seats, maps, black boards, etc.

3. *Teacher Training.* This is a basal necessity in such an hour as this. Our Sunday-school Board is urging our people to so press this work that by 1924 we shall have 150,000 people holding the Normal Diploma. This means a great forward movement in our work. We urge the heartiest co-operation on the part of our pastors, officers and teachers.

4. *Organized Classes* are the most effective organization for reaching, training and using the men and women of our churches and congregations. No other plan has succeeded so we_{ll} as this. We commend the "Organized Class Magazine" as the best periodical available for the officers of these classes.

5. *Evangelism* should be the main objective in the work of every Sunday-school. Every year in our Baptist constituency at least 20,-000 children reach the year of accountability. This does not include thousands and tens of thousands of larger boys and girls and men and women who are not saved and yet who must be reached by us if they are ever reached for the Kingdom. We commend the study of the book, "Winning To Christ," by all of our Sunday-school workers.

6. *Co-operation With the Sunday-school Department* of the Mission Board is our duty. This department stands ready at all times to send helpful tracts on practically every phase of Sunday-school work. These are absolutely free and can be secured from Secretary E. L. Middleton, Raleigh, N. C. He will also aid in every possible way in providing training schools and institutes for groups or churches in cities, towns or country. We urge inquiry from everyone who has an unsolved Sunday-school problem.

Respectfully submitted,

T. SLOANE GUY.

On motion to adopt, Rev. T. S. Guy spoke on the report. Report was adopted.

Rev. R. L. Gay was recognized, who presented the report on Orphanage:

ORPHANAGE.

The Orphanage manifests the response of the best impulse of the human heart to God's high call for service. And its support in sympathy prayers, and money furnishes a splendid agency for the enlistment and development of one of the purest traits of Christian character. Every child at the Orphanage is one of God's appeals to the sympathy, prayers and Christian charity of every Baptist in North Carolina. The Orphanage, therefore, apart from the inestimable benefit to the child is one of the richest assets of the denomination in the State. The strongest arguments for the Orphanage is the orphan and its strongest appeal is the need of the helpless child. The Old Testament law abounds in provisions for the care of the fatherless and the widows, and James summarizes the content of undefiled religion in that pregnant passage, "Pure religion and undefiled before God and the Father is this, to visit the fatherless and the widows in their affliction and to keep himself unspotted from the world." On the other hand, the blessings received by the orphans and imparted by them to others can be computed only in eternity. Of the nearly two thousand received at our Orphanage since 1885, many have filled with usefulness their places in the various walks of life; some have risen to places of prominence, and some have gone to their reward. The Orphanage is better equipped for service now than ever before and is growing daily in the affections of the people. But still its needs are far greater than its capacity.

The following facts are gathered from the last annual report to the Board of Trustees:

Certain buildings and repairs are absolutely necessary notwithstanding soaring prices and, indeed all other operations had to be carried on under the abnormal high prices that have prevailed for several years. The general manager calls attention to the necessity for the performance of another function of "pure and undefiled religion: viz., that of caring for the needy widows in their homes.

It will also be noted that of the 667 applicants for admission last year, only 69 were received. The fact that 598 applicants had to be rejected in a year would indicate an urgent necessity for greatly enlarged capacity and therefore for greatly enlarged gifts.

It is a source of gratification that an increasingly large number of organized classes in our Sunday-schools are undertaking to support a child. There are other classes and, indeed, entire schools which make no monthly offering. These ought to be enlisted and others which are already contributing might greatly enlarge their gifts. The thank offering last year was the largest ever made. We should see to it that, under the declining prices of farm products, there is no falling off in this much-needed source of revenue.

With thanksgiving for and pride in this splendid institution, it should be our earnest prayer and constant effort that its sources of power be greatly increased and its capacity greatly enlarged as the Orphanage so richly deserves and the cause it represents so deeply needs.

Orphanage Information.

Number of children at Thomasville 440; at Kennedy Home 87	527
Children received since November 15, 1885	1,970
†Daily cost for the support of each child	55c
Monthly cost per child	16.43
Monthly cost per child six years ago	$8.35
Annual cost per child	197.14
Daily cost for the support of 527 children	$289.85
Farm products made and consumed	$9,457.95
Dairy products made and consumed	$21,565.59
Milk 47,532 gallons at 40c.	$19,012.80
Number applications for year	667
Number received	69
Profit Kennedy Home farm	$5,065.63
Profit Charity and Children	$7,910.01

†This includes: three meals, clothing, shoes, house furnishing, school supplies, lights, power, fuel, insurance, medicine, medical attention, laundry, etc.

Respectfully submitted,

R. L. GAY, *Committee.*

On motion to adopt, Bro. Archibald Johnson, editor of "Charity and Children," very ably spoke on the cause of Thomasville Orphanage. The report was adopted.

The Moderator appointed Rev. C. C. Wheeler to conduct the devotional exercises at the night session.

Judge F. H. Brooks introduced the following resolution:

"Be it resolved, that this body employ a stenographer at its next and subsequent sessions, to take addresses by speakers, to be specially printed for benefit for churches." The resolution was referred to a committee appointed by the chair, consisting of Brethren S. H. Averitt, C. E. Stevens and D. C. Smith, with instructions to report on the resolution before the close of the present session.

No other business on hand, the body adjourned for recess, with prayer by Rev. R. M. Von Miller.

Wednesday Night.

Rev. C. C. Wheeler conducted the devotional exercises, after which the Moderator announced the session open for business.

The Moderator recognized Rev. Charles E. Brewer, Ph.D., President of Meredith College, welcoming him to a seat on behalf of the body.

Rev. H. W. Baucom then presented the report on State Missions:

STATE MISSIONS.

At the very foundations of all our work lies State Missions. This is our home base .Every mission point which grows into a self-sustaining church adds to our strength.

Many of our strongest churches were for some time aided by State Missions, and never could have become what they are without this help.

The State Mission Board is aiding this year 51 full-time churches 59 half-time churches and 169 quarter-time churches. About $5,000 per month is being paid out on the salaries of missionaries and colporteurs. More than $3,000 is being spent in our Association this year.

Truly "the harvest is white," and our State Mission Board is doing a great deal toward helping to provide laborers for our needy fields, obeying the command of our Saviour, when He said: "Go ye into all the world—beginning at Jerusalem."

Surely State Missions should receive our hearty support.

Respectfully submitted,

H. W. BAUCOM. *Committee.*

On motion to adopt, the Moderator recognized Rev. H. W. Baucom, who stated that Dr. Charles E. Brewer would speak later on this subject. The report was adopted.

The Moderator recognized Rev. C. E. Stevens, who presented the report on Home Missions:

HOME MISSIONS.

Our very civilization is on trial. The foundations of government are threatened; commercialism, anarchy and Bolshevism, which aided German militarism to bring ruin and chaos in Europe, have been and still are a great menace. They will be the downfall of our civilization unless they are counteracted by adequate constructive forces.

To meet the needs of the perilous days, the Home Mission Board has sent forth the gospel of salvation, which is the gospel that assures public uprightness and clean citizenship.

Dr. B. D. Gray gives the following figures for the past year's record: Under the direction of the Home Board labored 1,541 missionaries, who have leavened with the gospel thousands of communities. They have baptized 33,576 converts, added 57,000 members to the churches, preached more than 150,000 sermons, kept open 61 mission schools in which 12,000 youths were taught and hundreds of preachers prepared.

They have led 2,336 persons to offer themselves for the ministry and missionary service, brought 661 foreigners and 464 Indians into the churches, built or improved 429 church houses and organized 196 churches and 655 Sunday-schools. The financial record has been great. The increase has been 34.6 per cent. This increase proves at least two things: Our people believe in their souls that great issues hang on Home Missions, and they propose to enable their Board to move forward worthily and greatly in a day that calls for power to comprehend and purpose to take hold and to do in a measure far beyond the standards of the past.

Respectfully submitted,

C. E. STEVENS, *Committee.*

On motion to adopt, Rev. C. E. Stevens spoke on the report. The report was adopted.

The Moderator then recognized Dr. Charles E. Brewer, who addressed the body on the subject of "Missions, Education, and Social Service."

After the singing of a song, and prayer by Rev. A. A. Pippin, the meeting adjourned.

Thursday Morning.

Rev. J. W. Nobles conducted the devotional exercises, after which the Moderator called the session to order, asking Bro. J. F. Pool to lead in prayer.

The Clerk was then requested to read the journal of the proceedings. The minutes were adopted as read.

The next item on the program was the report of the Executive Committee.. The Moderator recognized Rev. H. W. Baucom.

REPORT OF THE EXECUTIVE COMMITTEE.

, During the past year the following brethren have served churches aided by the Board of Missions:

Rev. A. L. Brown, at Bailey, Micro, Pinkney, Beaty's Chapel, and at Bethel a part of the year.

Rev. C. E. Stevens, at Blackman's Grove and Kenly.

Rev. J. R. Everett, at Princeton, Hepzipah, Benson Grove and Burnell.   ..

Rev. R. M. Von Miller, at Noble's Chapel.

Rev. S. F. Hudson, at Trinity, Pauline, Hood's Grove, Calvary and Canaan.

Rev. B. Townsend, at Live Oak and Lizzie Mill.

Rev. J. G. Dowell, at Parrish Memorial.

Rev. T. S. Guy, at Hale's Chapel.

The writer has held services at Pleasant Grove since February, and expects to organize a church there in the near future.

We are greatly encouraged with the work on most of these fields. Your committee is trying to assist the churches in the arrangement of fields so the pastor can live among his people. One of the great drawbacks still to our work is the lack of houses for them. We have secured a lot at Peacocks Cross Roads, where we feel that there is a great need for a pastor's home.

If there is a church in the Association that has ignored the action of the Association last year, and has failed to send an offering to our treasurer for this work, we hope it will do so at the earliest possible moment.

Feeling that the need for more parsonages is imperative, we recommend that each church be asked for a liberal donation next year.

                    Respectfully submitted,

                         H. W. BAUCOM, *Chairman.*

On motion to adopt, Rev. H. W. Baucom spoke on the report and called on the following brethren — Rev. A. L. Brown, Rev. C. E. Stevens, Rev. R. M. Von Miller, and Rev. S. F. Hudson—who gave a verbal report of their respective fields. The report was adopted.

The hour for the missionary sermon having arrived, the pastor of the local church conducted a short song service, after which Rev. C. C. Wheeler preached the annual missionary sermon, choosing for his subject "Life's Greatest

Misfortune to the Redeemed Soul"; text, Matthew 21:19.
This able and impressive sermon was greatly enjoyed by
those present.

After the sermon, the Moderator appointed Bro. D. L.
Barbour as Auditor pro tem., to serve in the absence of Bro.
J. L. Hall.

Thursday Afternoon.

Bro. A. B. Wilder conducted the devotional exercises,
after which the Moderator called the meeting to order.

Under miscellaneous items, the Committee on Place and
Preacher reported as follows:

"We, your committee, beg leave to recommend Blackman's Grove
as the place for our next meeting, and Rev. B. Townsend, with
Rev. C. C. Wheeler as alternate, to preach the introductory sermon."

Respectfully submitted,

J. F. Pool, *Chairman.*

The report was adopted.

The Committee on recommendation for members of the
Executive Committee made the following report:

"We, your committee, beg leave to recommend the following
brethren to serve as Executive Committee of the Association for the
ensuing year: Rev. H. W. Baucom, Chairman; R. A. Bain, J. A.
Smith, J. F. Pool, Alonzo Parrish.

Member to the Mission Board, Rev. R. L. Gay.

Delegate to the Southern Baptist Convention, Judge F. H. Brooks.

Delegates to the State Convention, Rev. B. Townsend, Rev. A. L.
Brown and W. H. Hipps.

On motion, the report was adopted.

The Moderator recognized Bro. J. A. Smith, Treasurer of
the Association, who presented the Treasurer's Report of
the Johnston County Baptist Association:

TREASURER'S REPORT OF THE JOHNSTON COUNTY BAPTIST ASSOCIATION OCTOBER 27TH 1920.

I have received and disbursed the amounts as indicated below:

Associational Missions.

Received from former treasurer, J. E. Lanier $110.88
Received from churches during this year 291.72

Disbursementss

To R. P. Merritt, for supply work ....$ 20.00
To C. E. Stevens, for supply work 24.00
To W. D. Stancil, for supply work 27.50
To R. M. Von Miller, for work at Simm's School.. 12.00
To H. W. Baucom, supply work at Benson Grove.... 100.00

Total $183.50
Balance on hand $219.10 $402.60

Building Fund.

Received from former treasurer, J. E. Lanier $136.00
Received from churches this year 215.00

Total $351.00

Disbursements.

To C. E. Stevens, for building church at Trinity....$200.00
Paid for land for building lot at Peacock's X·Rd... 400.00

Total $600.00
Balance due treasurer, J. A. Smith $249.00

Minute Fund.

Received from churches $101.90
Received from special collection at the Association..$ 41.86

Total $143.76

Disbursements.

To former treasurer, J. E. Lanier ....$ 14.46
To Beaty & Lassiter, for printing programs 2.50
To R. M. Von Miller, for salary as clerk 60.00
To R. M. Von Miller, for postage 6.56
To R. M. Von Miller, for printing minutes 90.00

Total $173.52
Balance due J. A. Smith, treasurer ....$ 29.76

This is to certify that I have carefully audited the books of Bro. J. A. Smith, treasurer of the Johnson County Baptist Association for year ending October 28th, 1920, and find them to be correct and in good shape.

D. L. BARBOUR, *Auditor, pro tem.*

Upon motion, this report was adopted as read.

Bro. S. H. Averitt presented the following resolution:

Resolved: That this Association extend hearty thanks to the members of the Bailey Baptist Church and citizens of the community for their kind hospitality and splendid entertainment during this present session.

This resolution was adopted by a rising vote.

The Moderator then called on Rev. A. O. Moore to take the chair and preside during the hour of presentation of B. Y. P. U. Work.

In the absence of Rev. B. Townsend, Rev. H. W. Baucom presented the report on B. Y. P. U. Work:

B. Y. P. U. WORK.

Knowing the need of reaching and training our young people for the work of the Kingdom and for our church activities, we want to encourage the B. Y. P. U. in every way possible. Let it be our aim for every church in the Association that has not now a B. Y. P. U. to look forward to such an organization in their church and if possible for this Association to organize a Johnston County B. Y. P. U. Union, convention or some such name as may be agreed upon, the purpose of which would be to organize new Unions and encourage the work in those already organized.

Respectfully submitted,

B. TOWNSEND, *Committee.*

Upon motion to adopt, the chair recognized Bro. Perry Morgan, State Secretary of B. Y. P. U. Work, who addressed the Association very ably on the subject before the body. The report was adopted.

Rev. C. C. Wheeler presented the following resolution:

Resolved: "Be it resolved, that Bro. A. O. Moore be appointed Associational Director of our B. Y. P. U. Work.

This resolution was unanimously adopted.

MINISTERIAL RELIEF.

In the absence of a report the following brethren spoke very helpfully on this phase of our work, Rev. C. C. Wheeler and Rev. L. B. Padgett.

Rev. L. B. Padgett presented the following resolution:

Resolved, That we adopt the following plan for the presentation and discussion of the various reports of the work in the Association:

1. That we group all our reports under five general heads as follows:

1. *Education.* (a) Colleges, (b) Preparatory Schools, (c) Periodicals, Books and Tracts.

2. *Social Service.* (a) Orphanage, (b) Hospitals, (c) Ministerial Relief, (d) Temperance.

3. *Teaching and Training.* (a) Sunday-schools, (b) B. Y. P. U. and B. Y. P. U. demonstration, (c) Bible Conference.

4. *Missions.* (a) Associational Missions, (b) State Missions, (c) Home Missions, (d) Foreign Missions, (e) Women's Work.

5. *Business.* (a) Church Government, (b) Church Finance, (c) Report of the Executive Committee.

2. That five reports be presented to cover objects considered under these five general heads.

3. That five committees be appointed to prepare these reports.

4. That as many members be appointed on each committee as there are objects to be considered under each general head.

Respectfully submitted,

L. B. PADGETT.

This resolution was adopted.

Rev. L. B. Padgett, as pastor and in behalf of the Wendell Baptist Church, asked for a letter from this Association, in order that this church may join the Raleigh Association.

On motion of Rev. A. O. Moore, this request was granted and the Clerk was instructed to send a letter of dismsisal to the Raleigh Association.

There being no further business to transact, a motion to adjourn was made by Rev. A. O. Moore, which was carried.

The adjourning prayer was offered by Rev. B. G. Early, after which the Moderator declared the eighteenth annual session of the Johnston County Baptist Association adjourned, to meet again next year with Blackman's Grove Baptist Church, beginning on Wednesday after the fourth Sunday in October, 1921.

R. H. GOWER, Moderator.

R. M. VON MILLER, Clerk.

MINUTES OF THE WOMAN'S MISSIONARY UNION

The Woman's Missionary Union of the Johnston County Baptist Association held its annual session with the W. M. U. at Middlesex, N. C., October 25-26th, 1920. Opening session was Monday night at 7 p. m. The Union was called to order by its superintendent, Mrs. B. A. Hocutt, of Clayton, N. C. Devotional exercise by Mrs. E. V. Richardson, who read the fifth chapter of Mark, after the opening song, "Love Lifted Me." Prayer was offered by Mrs. H. M. Finch.

We are always happy to have the Sunbeams. On this occasion the demonstration of their work was a beautiful and helpful part of the program.

How important to train the children, for they are our future leaders.

Mrs. Lois M. Bass in her own sweet way sang: "In the secret of His presence."

The Union was fortunate in having such a wonderful worker as Mrs. H. M. Finch, of Rocky Mount, present. Her subject, "God, the world and you," was most interesting. How great is the love of God, the greatest privilege we have is to serve Him. Are you doing your best for Him, are you using your best time for God?

Tuesday Morning.

The Union opened its session at 9:30 a. m., with singing, "Jesus shall reign." Prayer by Mrs. D. J. Thurston, and Scripture reading Matthew chapter 25, by Mrs. N. B. Lewis. After singing again, "Jesus calls us," the business of the Union was then taken up. The Minutes of the last meeting were read and approved. In the absence of Mrs. Ballentine, Mrs. Moore gave us a warm welcome from the local Baptist church, and Mrs. S. V. Lewis, of the local Methodist Church, assured us of their welcome to their hearts and homes. Mrs. J. Dwight Barbour being absent, Mrs. W. J. Payne in a most beautiful way responded to these words of welcome. The Union was happy to have for its visitors Mrs. W. H. Reddish, of Raleigh, and Mrs. H. M. Finch, of Rocky Mount, N. C.

Report of district leaders—Mrs. J. M. Beaty of No. 2 reported three new societies organized. District leaders from Nos. one, two and three being absent, so there was no report. Mrs. N. B. Lewis of No. 5 gave a good report.

Roll call of societies—18 present. Report of the superintendent for year's work. The report showed the great work she has been doing and she urged us to put first things first.

Mrs. H. W. Baucom gave a most hearty welcome to all the new

societies, after which Mrs. Lois M. Bass sang, "In the Garden."

The secretary was asked to write Mrs. J. L. Hall regrets at her absence. Mrs. C. E. Stevens on reaching the uninterested churches, said she thought the best way is to keep everlastingly at it. "Be thou faithful unto death and I will give thee a crown of life."

Meeting the needs of our communities, by Mrs. Thomas, who urged us to go, give ourselves and do more personal work. The world is hungry for the personal touch of love.

Mrs. D. J. Thurston, always interesting, seemed even more so, as she brought before us the great subject of "the lost idea." If the Christians neglect their duty what may we expect?

Quartette "I will be true to thee," by Mesdames C. M. Thomas, Bennetti Nooe, Jr., Lois Bass and Miss Telza Barnes.

The Union was grieved at the absence of Mrs. W. N. Jones, State leader, who is in a hospital at Richmond, Va. The secretary sent a telegram of sympathy and love from the Union to Mrs. Jones.

We were indeed fortunate in having with us Mrs. W. H. Reddish, of Raleigh, who gave us a most instructive talk. After prayer by Mrs. Finch, we adjourned for dinner, which was served on the church lawn.

Afternoon Session, at 1:30 P. M.

With Mrs. H. W. Baucom, Junior Superintendent, presiding. Devotional exercises by Mrs. M. L. Philips, of Middlesex; prayer by Mrs. Finch.

Mrs. Baucom's report showed much work has been done and a great improvement in all the departments. Next on the program was a quartette, "All for Jesus," by Smithfield Y. W. A.'s. How beautiful it is to use our voices in praise to Him. Miss Ruth Brown showed the importance of well-prepared programs. What a wonderful service we can render if we prepare our part on any program.

Dorothy Gower on personal service showed what a power this service is, and how sweet to work for the Master in this personal way.

Geraldine Parrish told of her own personal service. How she nursed the sick and cared for the feeble grandfather, and carried waiters to friends.

How happy this child is in doing this work, for she is only a little school girl.

Mrs. Joseph Turley told us how to attain the standard of excellence.

Duet, by Mrs. Bennetti Nooe, Jr. and Miss Telza Barnes, "I come to thee."

Mrs. Lois Bass gave a report of the Mission Rally at Smithfield. It was decided at this meeting to have a rally at Clayton in the summer of 1921.

Mrs. Baucom read some most interesting letters from China. These letters will be in the Recorder at an early date.

The Committee on Time and Place reported that the Union will meet with the society at Clayton, N. C., October, 1921. The day of the month to be named later.

The following officers were nominated and elected:

Mrs. B. A. Hocutt, Superintendent.

Mrs. H. W. Baucom, Junior Superintendent.

Miss Cleve Barnes, Secretary.

District Leader No. 1, Mrs. J. W. Sanders.

District Leader No. 2, Mrs. J. M. Beaty.

District Leader No. 3 Mrs. C. W. Carter.

District Leader No. 4, Mrs. Aaron Earp.

District Leader No. 5, Mrs. N. B. Lewis.

A rising vote of thanks was given Mr. J. M. Beaty and Mr. Penn for printing and mailing programs. We could not adjourn without offering to the Middlesex Woman's Missionary Society our sincere appreciation, for the splendid fellowship, and their most excellent entertainment of the Union.

After prayer by Mrs. D. J. Thurston, the Union adjourned to meet at Clayton, N. C., October, 1921.

Mrs. B. A. Hocutt, *Superintendent,*

Miss Cleve Barnes, *Secretary.*

STATISTICAL TABLE OF B. Y. P. U. SOCIETIES.

Name of Church and Union.	Name of President and Address.	No. of Members
Benson	L. M. Cavenaugh, Benson, N. C.	29
Clayton	Mrs. C. D. Bass, Clayton N. C.	30
Mount Moriah	Avera Wilder Raleigh, N. C., R. 2	30
Selma	Miss Iva Young, Selma, N. C.	20
Smithfield	H. P. Johnson, Smithfield, N. C.	30
Wendell	J. V. Richardson, Wendell, N. C.	29

APPORTIONMENTS FOR ASSOCIATIONAL BUILDING AND MINUTE FUNDS.

Name of Church.	Ass. Bldg. Fund.	Minute Fund.
Antioch	$ 25.00	$ 7.50
Bailey	25.00	5.00
Baptist Center	20.00	5.00
Beaty's Chapel	10.00	5.00
Benson	50.00	10.00
Benson Grove	20.00	5.00
Bethany	20.00	5.00

Bethel	10.00	5.00
Bethesda	50.00	10.00
Blackman's Grove	40.00	10.00
Burnell Mission	10.00	2.50
Calvary	20.00	5.00
Canaan	10.00	5.00
Carter's Chapel	50.00	7.50
Clayton	200.00	15.00
Clyde's Chapel	50.00	10.00
Corinth	25.00	7.50
Four Oaks	25.00	10.00
Hale's Chapel	10.00	5.00
Hepzipah	10.00	5.00
Hood's Grove	25.00	7.50
Kenly	25.00	5.00
Lee's Chapel	40.00	10.00
Live Oak	10.00	2.50
Lizzie Mills	10.00	2.50
Micro	25.00	5.00
Middlesex	25.00	7.50
Mount Moriah	150.00	15.00
New Bethel	75.00	10.00
Noble's Chapel	40.00	10.00
Oliver's Grove	10.00	2.50
Parrish Memorial	20.00	5.00
Pauline	15.00	5.00
Pine Level	50.00	10.00
Pinkney	20.00	5.00
Pisgah	50.00	7.50
Princeton	25.00	5.00
Sardis	25.00	5.00
Selma	75.00	10.00
Shiloh	25.00	5.00
Smithfield	50.00	15.00
Thanksgiving	25.00	5.00
Trinity	20.00	5.00
Wendell	75.00	10.00
White Oak	25.00	7.50
Wilson's Mills	25.00	5.00
Total	$1,785.00	$327.50

TABLE I—STATISTICAL

Church	Pastor and Post-Office	Clerk and Post-Office	Time of Preaching	Value of Church Property	By Baptism	By Letter	By Restoration	By Letter	By Exclusion	By Death	No. of Males	No. of Females	Total Membership
Antioch	R. M. Von Miller, Wilson	W. O. Hocutt, Middlesex, R. 1	2nd	$3000	5			6	1	6	84	110	194
Bailey	A. L. Brown, Fremont	J. P. Underwood, Bailey	1st	4000	8			1			31	40	71
Baptist Center	R. L. Gay, Smithfield	J. C. Hardee, Clayton	3rd	600				3			56	76	132
Beaty Chapel	A. L. Brown, Fremont	J. J. Parrish, Smithfield	4th	2000	2					1	5	16	21
Benson	C. C. [Mr], Benson	Julian [Von], Benson	F. T.	25000	5	17		10		1	75	117	192
Benson Grove	J. R. Everett, Wake Forest	D. D. Medlin, Benson	2nd	800	3	3				3	21	24	45
Bethany	W. D. Stancil, Kenly	Kirkman Creech, Kenly	4th	2000	13	1	1	1			49	71	120
Bethel	A. L. Brown, Freemont	Luther Stone, Kenly	4th	1000			2		3		5	9	14
Bethesda	R. L. Gay, Smithfield	J. E. Smith, Wilson's Mills	4th	3500		6		12	1	3	102	120	222
Blackman's Grove	C. E. [Sims], Four Oaks	P. J. Morgan, Four Oaks	2nd	1500	14	4	1	1	2		23	61	84
Burnell Mission	J. R. Everett, Wake Forest	J. S. Johnson, Four Oaks		1200	5	3					5	8	13
Calvary	S. F. Hudson, Dunn	T. J. Lee, Dunn	1st	1500		3					10	14	24
Canaan	S. F. Hudson, Dunn	T. L. Hudson, Bentonsville	3rd	800			2	2	5		17	27	44
Carter's Chapel	J. L. Martin, Fuquay Springs	Gray Eason, Selma	1st	16| 1500		3		9	1		51	64	115
Clayton	A. O. Moore, Clayton	W. P. [6th], Clayton	1st	80000	42	30	2	4	1	3	244	308	552
Corinth	C. H. Cashwell, Wake Forest	L. T. [aDis], Wendell, R. 1	4th	3000	15		3	10	1	3	59	112	171
Clyde's Chapel	G. T. [Mls], Apex, R. 1	C. I. Johnson, Wendell, R. 1	1st, 3rd	800	10	6	1	6	3	1	90	124	214
Four Oaks	C. E. Stevens, Four Oaks	W. J. [Wis], Four Oaks	1st, 3rd	30000	19	8		2	2		28	58	86
Hale's Chapel	T. S. [G], Zebulon	A. D. Parrish, [Kan], R. 2	4th	2000							19	28	47
Hepzibah	J. R. Everett, Wake Forest	W. A. Braswell, Princeton	1st	2000	2						4	10	14
Hood's Grove	C. E. Stevens, Four Oaks	Beulah Bailey, Kenly	4th, 5th	2500	4	10	2	1		1	16	21	37
Kenly	J. E. Hocutt, Nashville	W. I. Green, Zebulon, R. 2	3rd	2500	20	4		1	1	1	100	108	208
Lee's Chapel	B. Townsend, Selma		3rd	1000							4	4	6
Live Oak	B. Townsend, Selma												
Lizzie Mills	A. L. Brown, Fremont	S. C. Batton, Micro	3rd	2500	4	4		3	1	1	26	29	55
Micro	J. W. Nobles, Middlesex	Mrs. J. T. Moore, Middlesex	1, 2, 4	5000	2	5		5		1	36	55	91
Middlesex		Russell Powell, Auburn	1st	4200	5			5		2	95	101	196
Mount Moriah	B. G. Early, Raleigh	George W. Bryan, Garner	4th	2000	1			11		1	49	63	112
New Bethel	R. M. Von Miller, Wilson	N. L. Stott, Simms	4th	2000	5					2	51	70	121
Noble's Chapel	W. D. Stancil, Kenly	Miss Lena Tyner, Four Oaks	2nd	800	1	1		2	3	1	5	12	17
Oliver's Grove													

Church	Pastor											
Parrish Memorial	George J. Dowell, Raleigh		3000				1			37	56	93
Pauline	H. E. Hudson, Dunn	1st	700	9	2				1	33	53	86
Pine Level	T. J. Head, Goldsboro	2nd	5000	3				3		14	31	45
Pine Level	F. A. Price, Pine Level	1st	1500	2				3	1	18	17	35
Pinkney	Mrs. B. R. Edgerton, Kenly	3rd	3000	4	6		1	4		34	49	83
Pisgah	R. L. Gay, Smithfield	1st, 4th	2000					5	1	25	37	62
Princeton	W. I. Pearce, Princeton to	1st, 3rd	1500					6		26	23	40
Sardis	B. Townsend, Wake	1st	15000	21	52		12	12	3	101	130	291
Selma	R. C. Powell, Clayton	P. T.	3000	3		2		3	3	41	56	97
Shiloh	B. Townsend, Selma	2nd	20000	23	44		35	15	2	126	142	268
Smithfield	H. W. Benson, Smithfield	P. T.								57	45	102
Thanksgiving	R. L. Gay, Smithfield	2nd	2500	4	3		3	1	1	42	64	106
Trinity	H. W. Townsend, Selma	4th	6000	10	12		3	12	1	129	177	98
Wendell	S. P. Hudson, Dunn	P. T.	3000	3				5	1	93	110	203
White Oak	L. R. Puckett, Wendell	2nd, 4th										
Wilsons Mills	C. T. Mill., Apex, R. 1											
			257700	264	232	24	170	34	52	2196	2848	5044

TABLE II—FINANCIAL

Churches	Pastor's Salary	Building and Repairs	Incidentals	Sunday School Expenses	The Poor	Minute Fund	Other Objects	75 Million (Undesignated)	State and Associational Missions	Home Missions	Foreign Missions	S. S. Missions	Orphanage	Christian Educa.	Ministerial Relief	Total
Antioch	$452 71	$40 00	$33 00	$13 17	—	$7 50	$25 00	$236 75	$3 20	—	—	$3 42	$1 51	—	—	$810 18
Bailey	300 00	—	78 99	30 00	—	5 00	155 77	218 50	15 47	—	—	3 50	15 83	—	—	810 71
Beaty	54 79	—	—	15 00	—	1 50	30 00	18 00	—	—	—	—	10 00	—	—	148 76
Baptist Center	300 00	15 00	15 00	—	—	—	—	150 00	—	—	—	—	—	—	—	465 00
Benson	1756 83	315 00	1034 33	380 52	—	5 00	558 00	2586 00	—	50 00	—	—	—	1 00	—	6,635 68
Benson Grove	125 00	100 00	20 00	15 00	24 00	5 00	—	100 00	—	—	—	—	—	—	—	295 00
Bethany	100 00	1 40	10 50	25 00	10 00	2 00	27 00	121 50	—	—	—	—	—	—	—	392 50
Bethel	36 76	—	25 00	—	—	—	—	4 01	—	—	—	—	—	—	—	53 17
Bethesda	500 00	300 00	3 25	46 15	10 00	10 00	136 05	777 41	1 00	1 00	1 00	1 00	—	1 00	1 00	1,695 56
Blackman's Grove	300 00	166 00	1 00	29 27	20 40	10 00	11 00	217 30	—	—	—	—	—	—	—	882 27
Burnell Mission	25 00	—	—	8 00	—	2 50	—	25 00	—	—	—	—	—	—	—	91 50
Calvary	75 00	—	65 57	5 34	—	2 00	502 00	112 75	—	—	—	—	35 00	—	—	762 66
Canaan	30-06	—	—	—	—	—	—	78 70	—	—	—	—	—	—	—	108 76
Carter's	110 00	—	—	—	—	1 25	—	272 25	5 00	—	—	—	—	—	—	463 50
Clyde's	500 00	—	50 00	30 00	—	4 00	36 00	460 55	—	18 50	20 00	—	—	5 00	—	1,119 84
Corinth	334 82	700 00	13 12	20 00	—	10 00	63 00	202 00	60 79	54 95	61 63	—	—	—	—	642 14
Four Oaks	800 00	1468 37	59 58	25 35	—	3 00	225 36	314 00	82 28	—	—	—	—	—	—	3,538 59
Hale's	200 00	—	—	190 79	—	2 00	10 00	50 50	—	—	—	—	—	—	—	1,731 87
Hepzibah	36 00	—	70 77	—	—	—	5 00	87 60	—	—	—	—	—	—	—	1,201 37
Hood's Grove	—	—	—	—	—	—	—	—	—	—	—	—	—	—	—	
Kenly	190 00	97 50	19 05	35 00	—	3 00	65 00	91 00	25 00	10 00	10 00	—	60 00	50 00	10 00	610 55
Lee's	300 00	181 18	—	18 00	35 00	5 00	5 00	114 00	11 00	—	—	—	9 37	10 00	1 00	732 55
Live Oak	—	—	—	—	—	—	—	—	—	—	—	—	2 00	—	—	74 00
Clayton	2475 00	43831 61	681 36	195 34	23 00	15 00	664 35	5798 43	—	—	—	—	316 83	—	—	53,982 92
Lizzie Mills	—	—	—	—	—	—	—	—	—	—	—	—	—	—	—	
Micro	220 00	18 00	115 90	25 00	—	5 00	80 63	334 50	26 00	28 45	38 10	—	134 00	12 00	—	942 03
Middlesex	562 50	2 00	75 00	76 30	—	15 00	130 26	54 00	—	—	—	—	94 85	—	—	1,099 46
Mount Moriah	300 00	—	41 50	100 00	146 00	10 00	246 50	1941 36	—	—	—	—	381 90	—	—	3,172 26
New Bethel	300 00	80 00	90 00	55 00	—	7 50	21 25	642 50	—	—	—	—	—	—	—	1,198 75
Noble's Chapel	300 00	—	72 14	19 56	—	1 00	30 00	348 47	5 00	1 00	50	—	1 00	—	—	777 67
Oliver's Grove	28 75	2 00	—	10 00	—	—	1 00	10 00	—	—	—	—	—	—	—	60 25

	150 00	53702 41	200 0*	10 00	761 40	2 00	15 00	839 78	20 00	5 00	5 00	1 00	5 00	5 00	5 00	
Parrish Memorial	150 00	---	---	5 00	---	---	---	---	---	---	---	---	---	---	---	423 00
Pauline	47 25	---	---	5 00	---	---	---	50 70	---	---	---	---	---	---	---	102 95
Pine Level	300 00	85 00	25 0C	30 00	---	10 00	50 00	400 00	---	---	---	---	---	---	---	900 00
Pinkney	122 88	13 10	62 35	17 08	---	7 50	7 85	154 12	---	---	---	---	16 15	---	---	398 53
Pisgah	500 00	241 85	124 40	30 79	---	7 50	---	350 00	---	---	---	---	78 65	159 54	33 90	1,526 63
Princeton	63 62	---	31 95	47 02	---	2 00	5 00	61 00	5 00	5 00	---	---	10 00	---	5 00	240 59
Sardis	150 00	3500 00	200 0C	85 00	25 00	5 00	747 62	233 00	15 25	26 80	23 25	---	22 89	40 35	---	283 00
Selma	2100 00	---	---	15 00	---	5 00	---	412 45	---	---	---	---	---	---	---	7,203 61
Shiloh	175 00	1395 50	743 53	218 00	476 00	15 00	476 79	238 45	---	---	---	---	947 00	---	---	433 45
Smithfield	2100 00	---	41 88	55 00	---	5 00	10 49	6123 38	---	---	---	---	---	---	---	12,495 20
Thanksgiving	155 65	10 00	2 0C	49 40	---	5 00	---	161 45	---	---	---	---	---	---	---	429 47
Trinity	116 75	---	---	386 88	476 00	---	---	102 20	---	---	---	---	222 76	---	---	237 35
Wendell	2000 00	13 90	699 02	30 00	2 00	10 00	75 00	1084 60	---	---	---	---	---	---	---	4,492 16
Wite Oak	750 00	125 00	200 00	30 00	---	7 50	9 10	900 00	---	---	---	---	---	---	---	2,021 60
Wilsons Mills	---	---	---	---	---	---	---	---	---	---	---	---	---	---	---	---
	19494 37	53702 41	4890 19	2347 50	761 40	214 75	4425	839 78	271 99	200 70	158 48	8 92	2373 74	282 89	55 90	114.82ª 14

TABLE III—SUNDAY SCHOOLS

Church	Superintendent and Post Office	Secretary and Post Office	No. Schools	No. Off. & Teach.	Pupils	Total Enrollment	Church Mem,rs in Sunday School	Mos. Kept Open	Bap. from School	School Expenses	Missions	Orphanage	Other Objects	$
Antioch	A. D. Oneal, Middlesex, R. 3	W. O. Hocutt, ?ex, R. 3	1	6	85	91	24	12	6	13 71	1 51	15 83	44 00	1
Bailey	J. W. B. ?th, Bailey	Relmon Warren, Bailey	1	7	55	63	20	12		30 00	11 62			
Baptist Center	John C. Hardie, Clayton	John Ellis, Clayton	1	5	40	45	6	12	2					3
Beaty Chapel	R. O. Minton, Smithfield	Estella Moye, Smithfield	1	6	45	49		12		15 00	4 47			
Benson	J. B. Benton, Benson	Julian Godwin, Benson	1	27	216	243	135	12		380 52			25 00	4
Benson Grove	L. E. Barbour, Benson, R. 1	L. E. Barbour, Jr., Benson, R. 1	1	3	51	54				15 00				
Bethany	B. B. Batten, Kenly	C. S. ?th, Kenly	1	5	50	55	40	12	13	55 00			12 00	
Bethel			1											
Bethesda	J. B. ?ts, Wilson's Mills	V. S. Smith, Wilson's Mills	1	12	100	112	60	12	6	26 04	8 11	115 26		
Blackman's Grove	J. S. Blackburn, Four Oaks	P. J. Morgan, Four Oaks	1	10	40	50	30	12	5	29 37	10 00			
Burnell Mission	J. S. ?in, Four Oaks, R. 4	Miss M. Massengill, Four Oaks, R. 4	1	7	40	47	13	9		8 00				
Calvary			1											
Canaan			1											
Carter's	C. P. Rose, Selma	B. F. Woodruff, Sel ?a	1	43	101	107	40	12	8	30 00	18 46		73 46	4
Clayton	W. P. ?th, Clayton	Charles G. ?ay, Clayton	1	8	300	343	200	12	37	195 34			30 00	
Clyde's Chapel	J. B. Boyette, Clayton	Miss Elva Phipps, ?ndell, R. 1	1	8	135	143	80	12		20 00				
Corinth	L. T. Davis, Wendell, R. 1	H. V. Andrews, Wendell, R. 1	1	12	166	174	65	12		25 35			4 00	
Four Oaks	J. W. Sanders, Four Oaks	W. J. Lewis, Four Oaks	1	8	118	130	50	12	10	56 64	7 00	15 00	112 15	1
Hale's Chapel	A. D. Parrish, Zebulon	C. E. Parrish, ?bon	1	8	96	104	43	12		17 50				
Hepzibah			1											
Hood's Grove			1											
Kenly	A. J. Broughton, Kenly	M. C. Bridgers, Kenly	1	6	54	60	35	12	4	35 00		60 00	105 00	2
Lee's Chapel			1											
Live Oak			1											
Lizzie Mills			1											
Micro	L. M. Ausley, Micro	D. C. Smith, ?o	1	7	50	57	25	12	1	25 00	00			
Middlesex	W. K. Ballentine, Middlesex	J. M. Davis, Middlesex	1	11	112	123	34	12	1	76 30		94 85		
New Bethel	R. I. Smith, McCullers	Eugene Britt, ?er	1	7	150	157	40	12	2	55 00	7 00		2 00	1
Noble's Chapel	L. F. Boykin, Simms, R. 1	O. Bullock, Simms, R. 1	1	6	75	81	38	12	1	19 56	7 66	6 81		
Oliver's Grove	J. A. Tyner, Four Oaks	Miss Kate Tyner, Four Oaks	1	5	50	55	15	9		10 00				
Parrish Memorial	J. D. ?th, Selma, R. 3	Q. J. Collins, Selma, R. 3	1	5	25	30	15	12		10 00	1 00			1

TABLE III—SUNDAY SCHOOLS

Church	Superintendent and Post Office	Secretary and Post Office	No. Schools	No. Off. & Teach.	Pupils	Total Enrollment	Church Members in Sunday School	Mos. Kept Open	Bap. from School	School Expenses	Missions	Orphanage	Other Objects	
Antioch	A. D. Oneal, Middlesex, R. 3	W. O. Hocutt, Middlesex, R. 3	1	6	85	91	43	12	3	13 71	1 51	15 83	44 00	$ 1
Bailey	J. W. B. Finch	Reimon Warren, Bailey	1	7	55	63	24	12	6	30 00	11 62			3
Baptist Center	John C. Hardie, Clayton	John Ellis, Clayton	1	5	40	45	20	12						
Beaty Chapel	R. O. Hardie, Smithfield	Estella Moye, Smithfield	1	4	45	49	6	12	2	15 00	4 47		25 00	
Benson	J. B. Benton, Benson	Julian Godwin, Benson	1	27	216	243	135	12		380 52				4
Benson	L. E. Barbour, Benson, R. 1	L. E. Barbour, Jr., Benson, R. 1	1	5	51	54	40	12	13	15 00				1
Bethany	B. B. Batten, Kenly	C. S. Creech, Kenly	1	5	50	55	40	12		55 00				
Bethel	J. B. —, Wilson's Mills	V. S. Smith, Wilson's Mills	1	12	100	112	60	12	6	26 04	8 11		12 00	2
Bethesda	J. B. Blackburn, Four Oaks	P. J. Morgan, Four Oaks	1	10	40	50	30	12	5	29 37	10 00			
Blackman's Grove	J. S. —, Four Oaks, R. 4	Miss M. Massengill, Four Oaks, R. 4	1	7	40	47	13	9		8 00				
Burnell Mission			1											
Canaan			1											
Carter's	C. P. Rose, Selma	B. F. Woodruff, Selma	1	6	101	107	40	12		30 00	18 46	115 26	73 46	
Clayton	W. P. Creech, Clayton	Charles G. Gulley, Clayton	1	43	300	343	200	12	8	195 34		4	30 00	
Clyde's Chapel	J. B. Boyette, Clayton	Miss Elva Phipps, Wendell, R. 1	1	8	135	143	80	12	37	20 00			4 00	
Corinth	J. T. Davis, Wendell, R. 1	H. V. Andrews, Wendell, R. 1	1	8	166	174	65	12	9	25 35	7 00	15 00	112 15	
Four Oaks	J. W. Sanders, Four Oaks	W. J. Lewis, Four Oaks	1	12	118	130	50	12	1	56 64				
Hale's	A. D. Parrish, Zebulon	C. E. Parrish, Zebulon	1	8	96	104	43	12	10	17 50				
Hephzibah														
Hood's														
Kenly	A. J. Broughton, Kenly	M. O. Bridgers, Kenly	1	6	54	60	35	12	4	35 00		60 00	105 00	
Lee's														
Live Oak														
Pine Mills														
Micro	L. M. Ausley, Micro	D. C. Smith, Micro	1	7	50	57	25	12	1	25 00				
New Bethel	W. K. Ballentine, Middlesex	J. M. Davis, Middlesex	1	11	112	123	34	12	1	76 30		94 85	2 00	
Noble's Chapel	R. I. Smith, McCullers	Eugene Britt, Garner	1	6	150	157	40	12	2	55 00		6 81		
Oliver's	L. F. Boykin, Simms, R. 1	O. Bullock, Simms, R. 1	1	6	75	81	38	9	1	19 56	7 66			
	J. A. Tyner, Four Oaks	Miss Kate Tyner, Four Oaks	1	5	50	55	15	9		10 00	1 00			
Parrish Memorial	J. D. Creech, Selma, R. 3	Q. J. Collins, Selma, R. 3	1	5	25	30	15	12		10 00				1

TABLE IV—WOMEN'S MISSIONARY UNION

Churches	Name of Organization	President and Post-Office	No. Members	75 Million (Un-designated)	Missions	Christian Education	Orphanage	Training School	Other Objects	Total
Bailey	Woman's Union	Miss Ruth Bragg, Bailey	16	60 05	2 60				12 85	75 50
Beaty Chapel	Woman's Union		32	877 06						877 06
Benson	Woman's Union	Mrs. J. L. Hall, Benson	25	41 05				10 00	2 00	53 05
Blackman's Grove	Woman's Union	Miss Cora Lee, Four Oaks	61	1323 86		40 00			6 74	1,370 60
Burnell Mission	Woman's Union		80	102 48					6 06	108 54
Clayton	Young Woman's	Mrs. C. W. Carter, Clayton	20		99 29				6 00	105 29
Clayton	Sunbeams	Mrs. B. A. Hocutt, Clayton								
Clayton	Royal Ambassadors	Mrs. W. J. Payne, Clayton								
Clayton	Girls' Auxiliary	Mrs. D. J. Thurston, Clayton								
Clyde's Chapel	Woman's Union									
Corinth	Woman's Union	Mrs. Mamie Batton, Clayton								
Corinth	Sunbeams									
Four Oaks	Woman's Union	Mrs. Alton Massongill, Four Oaks	31		155 55	5 00		24 40	11 00	195 95
Four Oaks	Sunbeams	Willie Massongill, Four Oaks	6		32 18				72	32 90
Kenly	Woman's Union	Mrs. Andrew Balance, Kenly	21			5 50			105 00	155 00
Middlesex	Woman's Union	Mrs. J. T. Moore, Middlesex	24		54 70	11 50		10 00	3 00	79 20
Middlesex	Woman's Union	Mrs. N. B. Lewis, Middlesex	15		34 85				6 00	40 85
Mt Moriah	Woman's Union									
Mt Moriah	Royal Ambassadors	Mrs. Jim Lane, Auburn	25						14 40	14 40
Mt Moriah	Sunbeams									
Noble's Chapel	Woman's Union	Mrs. Minnie Boykin, Simms, R. 1	11	167 00					10 08	177 08
Pine Level	Woman's Union	Ms. B. L. Strickland, Pine Level	20	13 00	40 00	17 00	20 00	10 00	19 00	119 00
Pine Level	Young Woman's	Mrs. D. B. Oliver, Pine Level	15		1 75			1 00	1 40	4 15
Pisgah	Woman's Union									
Pisgah	Young Women's	Mrs. W. D. Johnson, Smithfield								
Princeton	Woman's Union	Mrs. L. M. Edgerton, Princeton	12						150 00	150 00
Sardis	Woman's Union									
Smithfield	Woman's Missionary Union	Miss Annie Myatt, Smithfield	30	1257 35	100 00			65 00	89 11	1,511 46
Smithfield	Young Woman's	Ms. W. N. Holt, Smithfield	20	70 04				10 00		80 04
Smithfield	Young Woman's	Miss Ruth Brown, Smithfield	20	85 00						85 00
Smithfield	Girls' Auxiliary	Mrs. H. H. Radford, Smithfield	16						6 00	6 00
Smithfield	Sunbeams	Miss Thelma Medlin, Smithfield								
Wendell	Woman's Union	Mrs. Paul C. Brantley, Wendell								
Wendell	Sunbeams									
Selma	Woman's Missionary Union	Mrs. George D. Vick, Selma	26		70 95			11 35	459 20	541 50
Selma	Young Women's	Mrs. B. L. Talton, Selma	15				2 89		2 00	4 89
Selma	Sunbeams	Mrs. G. M. Willets, Selma	30	3 00	5 68	4 00			2 00	14 68
Benson	Sunbeams	Pearl Raynor, Benson	48	5 15						5 15

MINUTES

OF THE

NINETEENTH ANNUAL SESSION

OF THE

Johnston County Baptist Association

HELD WITH

BLACKMAN'S GROVE BAPTIST CHURCH

OCTOBER 26 and 27, 1921

The next session will be held with Noble's Chapel Baptist
Church, beginning on Wednesday after the Fourth
Sunday in October, 1922.

To Preach Introductory Sermon, Rev. A. O. Moore,
Rev. M. P. Davis, alternate.

MINUTES

OF THE

NINETEENTH ANNUAL SESSION

OF THE

Johnston County Baptist Association

HELD WITH

BLACKMAN'S GROVE BAPTIST CHURCH

OCTOBER 26 and 27, 1921

The next session will be held with Noble's Chapel Baptist
Church, beginning on Wednesday after the Fourth
Sunday in October, 1922.

To Preach Introductory Sermon, Rev. A. O. Moore;
Rev. M. P. Davis, alternate.

BARRETT'S PRINTING HOUSE
Wilson, N. C.

OFFICERS

Moderator, R. H. Gower.. Clayton
Vice-Moderator, Rev. M. P. Davis................................... Four Oak
Clerk, Rev. R. M. Von Miller... Wilson
Treasurer, J. A. Smith.. Smithfield
Auditor, J. L. Hall.. Benson

EXECUTIVE COMMITTEE

J. M. Beaty, Chairman.. Smithfield
J. A. Smith .... Smithfield
J. F. Pool... Clayton
H. P. Johnson... Smithfield
N. M. Gurley.. Pine Level

DELEGATES AND BOARD MEMBERS

Member of State Board of Missions........................... Rev. R. L. Gay
Delegate to Southern Baptist Convention................. Rev. A. O. Moore
Delegates to Baptist State Convention .... Rev. B. Townsend, Rev.
R. M. Von Miller and J. J. Lane

Committee in charge of and to make reports on Convention objects.

1. *Missions*—Associational, State, Home, Foreign, and Womans Work. Rev. A. O. Moore.

2. *Social Service:*—Orphanage, Ministerial Relief, Temperance; Hospitals, Judge F. H. Brooks.

3. *Church Business:*—Church Government, Church Finance, Rev. R. M. Von. Miller.

4. *Teaching and Training:*—Sunday Schools, B. Y. P. U. and demonstration, Rev. R. L. Gay.

5. *Christian Education:*—Colleges, Preparatory Schools, Periodicals, Books and Tracts, Rev. B. Townsend.

LIST OF MINISTERS

N. D. Blackman ....Goldsboro
C. H. Cashwell ....Wake Forest
M. P. Davis ....Four Oaks
S. A. Edgerton ....Buies Creek
R. L. Gay ....Smithfield
A. L. Goodrich ....Wake Forest
J. E. Hocutt ....Nashville
A. O. Moore ....Clayton
J. W. Nobles ....Middlesex
I. L. Powers ....Bentonsville
B. M. Shacklett ....Angier
W. D. Stancil ....Kenly
B. Townsend ....Selma
D. E. Vipperman ....Elm City
B. M. Von Miller ....Wilson
E. P. West ....Warsaw
C. C. Wheeler ....Benson

ENROLLED DELEGATES

Antioch—Albert Whitley, Geo. R. Whitley.
Bailey—J. W. B. Finch, Mrs. J. W. Privett, Hazel Finch, S. H. Underwood, J. P. Underwood.
Baptist Center—Milton Austin. J. C. Hardee.
Beaty's Chapel.
Benson—J. L. Hall, Mrs. J. J. Hall, Mrs. M. A. Peacock.
Benson Grove.
Bethany—W. T. Durham, A. R. Creech, D. C. Smith.
Bethel,
Bethesda—W. N. Parrish, Mrs. N. Jones, J. B. Coates, Miss Mamie Jones.
Blackman's Grove—Conley Lee, P. J. Morgan, W. M. Lee.
Burnell—J. S. Johnson, Mrs. J. S. Johnson, W. L. Massengill.
Calvary—M. L. Barefoot.
Cannan.
Carter's Chapel—W. M. Boykin, Martin Thorn.
Clayton—H. Pool, W. T. Allen, F. E. Allen. D. J. Yelverton, Rev. A. O. Moore.
Clyde's Chapel.
Corinth—S. T. Price, Mrs. S. T. Price, H. B. Andrews, J. B. Woodard, Mrs. J. B. Woodard, Julius Williamson, Sudie Williamson.
Four Oaks—W. A. Massengill, Mrs. W. A. Massengill, C. H; Grady, Rev. M. P. Davis.
Hale's Chapel.
Hepzipah—W. A. Brasswell, J. F. Earp.
Hood's Grove—N. L. Blackman, P. L. Hayes.

Kenly.

Lee's Chapel—J, W. Strickland, H. W. Wilder, A. G. Lewis, Rev.
J. E. Hocutt.

Live Oak—L. B. Batton.

Micro—B. L. Batton, Fred Batton. S. C. Batton, F. T. Batton, James
C. Batton.

Middlesex—Rev. J. W. Nobles.

Mount Moriah—S. Wilder, Robert Pool, W. R. Stallings. W. A.
Brummitt, J. J. Lane.

New Bethel—Z. D. Britt, Eugene B. Britt, Mary B. Bryan.

Noble's Chapel—Miss Pearl Liles, Miss Bruce Grice. Vernon Boykin

Oliver's Grove—Miss Kate Tyner.

Parrish Memorial—Frank Batton, J. W. Watson-

Pauline—J. Joyner, W. B. Joyner.

Pine Level—N. M. Gurley, B. Godwin.

Pinkney—John H. Davis, Leslie Davis.

Pisgah—J. A. Smith, R. H. Higgins, Rev. R. L. Gay.

Pleasant Grove—Claude Stephenson, J. E. Gilbert.

Princeton—C. S. Holt, Alberta Boyette, J. J. Boyette.

Sardis—Mrs. L. H. Wester, J. B. Gardner, N. S. Stevens, Mrs. J.
B. Gardner, Mrs. F. G. Strickland, F. G. Strickland.

Selma—J. M. Oneal, J. N. Wiggs, Rev. B. Townsend.

Shiloh—Richard Stephenson.

Smithfield—F. H. Brooks, J. M. Beaty, Mrs. J. M. Beaty

Thanksgiving—D. H. Price.

Trinity—H. C. Lee, W. P, Lee, W. M. Morgan. N. F. Cox, Mrs H.
C. Lee, R. M. Barefoot.

White Oak—N. H. Green, M. Price.

Wilson's Mills—Gilbert Beaty, J. T. Holt,

CONSTITUTION

1. The Association shall be known as the Johnston County
Baptist Association.

2. Its object shall be to extend the privileges of the Gospel and
liberal culture to all the people within its bounds, and by hearty co-
operation with the Baptist State Convention, to help offer these
privileges to all mankind in and out of its bounds by the cordial co-
operation of all the churches constituting this body.

3. It shall be composed of the pastors in active service in the
Association and such delegates as shall be annually elected by the
churches connected with it, each church being entitled to three delegates, unless the membership shall exceed fifty, and then an additional delegate for every twenty-five members, provided no church
shall have more than eight delegates.

4. The New Hampshire Declaration of Faith shall be the summary of Divine Truth for determining questions of faith and order

in this body, and the churches desiring membership in it must commit themselves to the substance of it, together with the covenant herewith submitted and this Constitution.

5. This Association shall not have power to annul the discipline or exercise authority over any church connected with it, but it may advise with and sever its connection with any church that neglects to preserve Gospel order or that treats with contempt the objects or advice of the Association.

6. Each church shall send to the annual meetings of the Association a letter (the blanks to be furnished by the Clerk of the Association), carefully filled as per blank suggestions, stating the full work of the church for the year ending with the Sunday previous to the meeting of the Assiociation.

7. The Association shall foster State Missions, Home Missions, Foreign Missions, Christian Education, the Aged Ministers' Relief Board, the Thomasville Orphanage and the Sunday School Board, and each church shall be requested to contribute to the support of these objects annually,

8. Missions and Education shall have precedence in their claims upon the consideration of this body in its regular sessions.

9. Whenever a church shall fail to be represented by delegates or letter at the annual sessions of the Association, inquiry shall be made for the cause, and efforts shall be made to induce such church to do its duty; and the effort shall be continued till the church is recovered or dropped from the roll.

10. The officers of the Association shall be a Moderator, a Vice Moderator, a Clerk, a Treasurer and an Auditor, elected annually by ballot (or in case when only one brother is put in nomination for an office, then the vote may be by acclamation) from among the members, to serve until their successors shall have been elected, and to perform the duties of such officers, namely, the Moderator, in presiding over the meetings, or the Vice-Moderator, in his absence; the clerk, in recording and preserving minutes and other papers belonging to the body; the Treasurer, in receiving and disbursing funds belonging to or entrusted to the body, according to its will; the Auditor to examine the Treasurer's books at each meeting of the Association and report the same before adjournment.

11. The Association shall appoint annually an Executive Committee of five (5) from its members, who shall be entrusted with the prosecution of Missions in the Association and any other work for the interest of the Master's Kingdom which may be referred to them. This committee shall, as far as possible co-operate with the State Mission Board in supplying the destitution in our territory, and between the meetings of the Association take such action as may seem to them advisable for the advancement of its interest. The committee shall present to the Association at its annual meeting a report of its Proceedings, with the names of the missionaries supported on the

field, time of service and details of their work, together with such recommendations as, in the judgment of the committee. the Association, should follow in planning its subsequent work.

12. The annual sessions of the Association shall begin on Wednesday after the fourth Lord's day in October, at such place as may be chosen, and an introductory sermon shall be delivered on the first day of the session. Representatives from ten of the churches constituting the Association shall be a quorum.

13. This Constitution may be amended at any annual session by a two-thirds vote of all the members present.

14. The proceedings of the Woman's Central Committee shall be recorded as a part of the Minutes of the Association.

BY-LAWS

1. The daily sessions of the Association shall be opened and closed with prayer.

2. Delegates shall be recognized by letters from their churches designating them as such.

3. The Moderator shall recognize corresponding messengers or the delegates of newly received churches by extending to them his right hand.

4. The report of the Executive Board and the Missionary work of the Association shall take precedence of all other business during the morning session of the second day of the annual session.

5. The Clerk shall record and read the proceedings when called for, superintend the publication and distribution of the Minutes, preserve a file of them and have it present at each annual session, and deliver to his successor all papers belonging to the body.

6. Members desiring to speak shall first rise and address the Moderator, shall use the term "Brother" in speaking to each other, shall not speak on the same subject more than twice without permission, and shall observe the courtesy that becomes christians.

7 The roll of members shall be called at least once and absentees marked.

8. Corresponding messengers and visiting brethren shall be invited to seats, with privilege of speaking but not voting.

A copy of the Minutes shall be sent to the Secretary of the State Mission Board, the Secretary of the Southern Baptist Convention, the American Publication Society. 1420 Chestnut St., Philadelphia: the Sunday School Board of the Southern Baptist Convention, and the Thomasville Orphanage.

10. All questions of order not herein provided shall be decided by Kerfoots Preliamentary Law.

PROCEEDINGS

The Johnston Baptist Association met in its nineteenth session, with the Blackman's Grove Baptist Church, Oct. 26 and 27th, 1921.

The body was called to order by Rev. A. O. Moore, who acted as Moderator pro tem, in the absence of Bro. R. H. Gower the regular Moderator.

According to program he called on Rev. R. L. Gay at 10:15 A. M. to conduct the devotional exercises, after which the Moderator appointed Rev. R. L. Gay and Bro. J. F. Pool to act as enrollment and credentials Committee.

The clerk then called the roll of the churches. A quorum being present, the body preceeded to the next item on the program which was the election of officers. The following officers were elected:

Moderator—R. H. Gower.

Vice-Moderator—Rev. M. P. Davis.

Clerk—Rev. R. M. Von Miller.

Treasurer—J. A. Smith.

Auditor—J. H. Hall.

Communications from Pleasant Grove and Burnell Churches were presented. These churches asked for reception into the fellowship of the Association. The Moderator appointed Rev. A. O. Moore, Rev. B. Townsend and Bro. J. P. Underwood to act as a committee on reception of new churches.

The Moderator then recognized Rev. M. I. Kessler, D. D., General Manager of the Thomasville Baptist Orphanage, and Prof. Dr. J. H. Gorrell of Wake Forest College. Bro. M. P. Davis was recognized as a new pastor in the Association.

Under miscellaneous business the body unanimously aggreed to give Dr. Chas. E. Maddry an opportunity to speak on State Missions at the close of the afternoon program.

The next item in order was Education. The Moderator called on Rev. A. O. Moore to act as Moderator, while he presented the report on Colleges.

REPORT ON COLLEGES

Education is often misunderstood because of the fools who have attended College, some of whom hold a diploma. They try to impress themselves upon people by the use of "pig" words and the proclamation of new ideas and doctrines, things they know the hearers know nothing about as things that are contradictory to former teachings. A realy educated man can and does make any subject that is under consideration so plain that the average man can see their view point. Education is the art of instruction, that brings us nurture, enlarges the view, trains in order to see all angles of view of a subject, and to weigh each argument, and to come to a sane conclusion.

Education gives the possessors power over things and men. College training does not necessarily give this power; but it points the way, if he will only perserve, to attain heights without a limit.

Man in the full sense of the word. is threefold, body, mind and soul. Failure to train all these three, the man falls short of what God intended him to be. To train and develop the body and mind without a cultivated soul. is to create a Goliath, to defy the best in life, God's kingdom. The state cannot directly develop the soul, hence the necessity of christian education. The christian home, the Sunday School, and the christian school and college, are absolutely necessary to train the whole man to attain unto the height that his creator put within his his reach.

The christian home and the Sunday School begin the good work, and the christian school and college continue it until the student is safely anchored.

Enviroment is the greatest moulder of the human soul. Let the child grow up in the enviroment of impurity nearly all will be impure. Let the inviroment be anti-religious and we will have an enemy of religion—nine cases out of ten. Let the enviroment be irreligious and we will have irreligious citizens. Let the enviroment be thoroughly christian and but few will go to the bad. Let the enviroment be baptist and Baptists will be the product.

Our schools and colleges should be thoroughly christian and Baptist and the product will be active christian workers in our Baptist Churches, extending the kingdom with their enlarged powers and influences to the ends of the earth.

North Carolina Baptists have three colleges and thirteen High Schools. The Colleges are Wake Forest for men and Meredith and Chowan for women. In our schools we have 189 teachers and 4411 students. When boys and girls are sent from their homes to school, they aught to be sent where the highest part of man, the soul, could be trained along with the body and mind, Hence it is desirable that our Baptist parents send their children to our own christian schools.

8

We especially recommend to our High School boys and girls Buies Creek. Buies Creek is recognized by our State Department of Education as a standard High School; Graduates of Buies Creek can enter any college in North Carolina without an entrance examination,

The Christian spirit of Buies Creek cannot be surpassed. The atmosphere is such that the best in the student will come to the front.

M. P. DAVIS, Committee

On motion to adopt the Moderator recognized Professor J. H. Gorrell of Wake Forest, who spoke on Wake Forest College. In the absence of reports on Periodicals, Books and Tracts, also on preparatory schools, both items on the program were omitted.

After singing "All Hail the Power of Jesus Name", and prayer by Rev. M. P. Davis, Rev. B. Townsend delivered the introductory sermon, using for his subject, "They first giving self unto the Lord", and selected 2 Cor. 8;5 and 2 Chron. 17.16 for his texts. At the close of the sermon Rev. R. M. Von Miller led in prayer. After several announcements, the body adjourned with prayer by Professor Gorrell for dinner.

WEDNESDAY AFTERNOON

The afternoon session opened with the usual devotional exercises, after which the Committee on place and preacher made the following report:

We your Committee beg to make the following report: We recommend Noble's Chapel as the place of our next meeting, and Rev. A. O. Moore as preacher with Rev. M. P. Davis as alternate.

W. R. STALLINGS
ROBERT POOL
H. D. PRICE, Committees

A motion by Rev. R. M. Von Miller, that hereafter the name of the Brother, who shall preach the Missionary sermon be inserted in the Minutes, was carried.

The Committee on the reception of new churches, made the following report:

"We your Committee recommend the reception of Pleasant Grove, and Burnell Churches into the fellowship of our Association"

A. O. MOORE.
B, TOWNSEND
P. UNDERWOOD, Comm.

This report was adopted and the Moderator called on the delegates present from these churches to come forward, and on behalf of the Association gave the right hand of fellowship to the representatives of these Churches. The order of business of the hour being Social Service, the Moderator recognized Rev. R. L. Gay, who presented the report on the

ORPHANAGE

The Orphanage needs neither eulogy nor commendation. The cause it represents, together with the wisdom of the management and the wonderful prosperity, has long since secured for it a large place in the hearts of North Carolina Baptists. We have sufficient confidence in the liberality of the Churches and in their love for the Orphanage to believe that a statement of its urgent needs will secure the means to supply these needs.

It is deemed necessary. in this report, to call attention to some of the special features of the work.

During the past year an entirely new feature has been introduced which is best described in the language of the Gen. Supt.

"A year ago you granted me the privilege of trying out a few cases in which mothers should be aided with their children in their own home. We are now aiding five families under our care. The plan is to do this work in conjunction with the local church, the church appointing a committee to look after the case receiving the money and helping the mother in handling her affairs. The chairman of this committee is to take monthly report to the church and the Orphanage, And to look after the material and spiritual welfare of the child. It is the duty of this committee to help the mother and her children as rapidly as possible to become independent and self-supporting. The amount required per month must be settled by the local committee and is passed on by the Orphanage. In some cases the church assumes a portion of this amount needed. So far it is working well. The cost is about half of that at the Orphanage. While I have no question as to the soundness of this principle, yet I am well aware of the difficulties which beset the work, and am prepared to accept modifications of plans as experience may dictate. If the number greatly increases a regular system of visitation will have to be employed."

This commends itself as harmonizing a little more closely with the Scripture injunction to provide for the "widow" as well as the "orphan". It also seems to provide an economical way of aiding a number of children, who would not otherwise, receive the benefit of the orphanage work.

Moreover, it recognizes the wisdom of God's arrangement for

caring for children in the home—an arrangement which should not be violated except when really necessary.

Attention should also be called to some losses sustained by the Orphanage during the year. First, the temporary loss of twenty-nine thousand dollars, due to the failure of the bank at Thomasville. This could not have been foreseen, and no blame whatever attaches to the management of the Orphanage. Churches should endeavor to remove any embarrassment caused by this loss.

Another heavy loss was the burning of the Simmons Nursery from which of course nothing was saved, and nothing could be reclaimed except $2,680.00 insurance on the building. This calls for greater liberality, to rebuild this building,

We earnestly insist that all our Churches hold Thanksgiving services, either on the day appointed by the President or our Governor, or if thought best, on the regular preaching day nearest to that day, Pastors should advertise that day and the object, and we should endeavor to express our thanksgiving to God by the largest possible offering for the "little ones". The once a month offering should never be forgotten.

Respectfully submitted,
R. L. Gay, Committee

The chair then recognized Bro. J. F. Pool, who presented the report on Ministerial Relief:

MINISTERIAL RELIEF

The Ministers Relief Board has been combined with the General Relief Board of the Southern Baptist Convention. All the States except one entered into this great work.

The Annuity plan seems to be the newest in giving aid to the aged Ministers. The Southern Baptist Convention has charge of all this work, and through this in cooperation with the State Relief Boards aid is given to these aged ministers their widows and orphans. During the last few months Mr. John D. Rockefellow has donated $300,000 in interest bearing securities to the Board, all of which has gone to increase one endowment fund, the money having been given with the express understanding that only the income on the principal was to be used from year to year.

$100,000 was given by the Sunday School Board. This annuity fund has been operated only about two years. At the beginning there were only 400 beneficiaries, but now there are over 700, and they will increase as the years go by. So we must meet our obligations to the 75 Million Campaign so that we shall be able to care for our aged ministers. The board reports no debt. What we are doing however is so small, when one considers the needs of these old people and the smallness of their income.

There are hundreds of our old ministers who are very. very poor, who never know anything of the luxuries of life while others are still worse off and are marching down to the grave like the inmates of the poorhouse. They need our love, sympathy and support, this will be most pleasing to our father in heaven.

J. F. POOL, Committee

Upon motion both reports were adopted. The Moderator recognized Rev. R. L. Gay, who gladly gave his time to Rev. L. M. Kessler, D. D., who spoke very interestingly on the Orphanage. The Moderator also recognized Bro. J. F. Pool, who spoke on Ministerial Relief.

Both Rev. J. M. Kessler and Rev. R. E. Ingram spoke briefly on Hospitals. The Moderator appointed the following Committees:

Periodicals, Books and Tracts—Rev. J. E. Powers.

Temperance—Rev. A. O. Moore.

Hospitals—Rev. A. L. Goodrich.

The afternoon program being finished, the Moderator recognized Rev. Chas. E. Maddry, D. D., our Cor. Sec. ot the Board of Missions, who addressed the Association on State Missions. By unanimous consent the session for the night according to program was eliminated. A motion to adjourn was carried. Rev. R. L. Gay led in the closing prayer.

THURSDAY MORNING

Rev. A. L. Goodrich led the devotional exercises. After which the Moderator called the body to order and asked the clerk to read the Journal of the previous sessions of the preceding day. The minutes were approved as read. Taking up the order of the hour, the Moderator called on Rev. A. O. Moore to present the report on Hospitals.

In the absence of a report, the item was omitted. The Moderator recognized Judge F. H. Brooks.

Judge F. H. Brooks reported on Temperance as follows:

TEMPERANCE

Since the meeting of the Johnston County Baptist Association a year ago, the cause of Temperance has been greatly advanced in Johnston County, and the prohibition laws are being more strenuosly enforced.

On June 24th, 1921, while the writer of this report was lying in bed nursing a sprained ankle, he wrote on article to the Editor of the Smithfield Herald, expressing his thoughts and sentiments on the whiskey question, in which he stated that he had decided that the only solution to the whiskey question was to love the men into abandoning this unlawful business, by holding up God's Love and teaching in Jesus Christ's name to forsake this awful business and prepare for eternity, and called on the good people of the County to get together and have a season of prayer and plead to God for the abolishment of the whiskey Traffic in the County. Several meetings were held, and the Christian people of all denominations met in Smithfield and discussed the matter, and prayed over it. In an appeal all christian people both white and black were asked to pray about this matter every day at sunset. A great many people joined in this sunset prayer and God answered this petition, possible not in a way expected. But at the August term of Court, Hon. E. H. Cramer a conscientious, christian judge was sent to hold the criminal term of the Johnston Superior court. He sentenced the violators of the whiskey traffic to terms upon the county road. Six white and four negro men were sent for an aggregated term of ten years and four months. This news caused consternation among the whiskey stillers and sellers in the county,

Since August term of court, as Judge of the recorders court, I have sentenced 14 white men and 2 negroes for making and selling whiskey, for an aggregated term of 5 years and 10 months. Instead taking an appeal as heretofore, they now come in a pleading manner, begging mercy and pleding to abandon the unlawful traffic.

In addition to this the writer felt compelled by the Spirit of God to try to convert these men to Christ, and send them back to their dark places in the county and let them be missionaries to those still violating the law. The writer has made therefore weekly visits, every Sunday afternoon, to the Convict Camp, Sometimes taking preachers with him, distributing religious literature and Bibles among these unfortunate men.

In a recent meeting of this kind at which time Rev, Neil McInnins preached a powerful sermon, at the conclusion the writer appealed to the convicts, asking how many of them would accept Christ for their Saviour, and abonding the whiskey and liquor traffic and go back and act as missionaries in their comunities to those who still live in darkness to stand up. Every man, white and black stood up.

Rev. McInnis was doubtful feeling they had misunderstood. So on the next occasion, when Rev. Mr. Sherwood preached a sermon on the "Prodigal Son", the writer explained that Rev. McInnius thought they had misunderstood, and asked them again to accept Christ as

13

their Saviour and if they were willing to forsake their life of sin and go back as missionaries to their respective comunities and try to influence others to live lawabiding and give up the liquor traffic, if so to come forward and give him their hand, every white man came forward. And an appeal was then made to the colored men, saying that we were not ashamed to shake hands with them if they desired to live better lives, every one came forward. There were about 40 men, and most of these are under sentence for violating the liquor traffic.

With these men converted and going back to their comunities when released, as missionaries, we believe that the cause of Temperance in Johnston Connty will receive a great impetus, and that there will be even a more glorious report, when this Association meets again.

R spectfully submitted,
F. H. BROOKS, Committee

On motion to adopt Judge F. H. Brooks spoke to the re-report. The report was adopted, and the body unanimously asked Judge F. H. Brooks to write an article in the Biblical Recorder on the work of Temperance in Johnston County.

Rev. J, W. Nobles who was to read the report on State Missions being indisposed, begged to be excused. In view of the splendid address by Dr. Chas. E. Maddry, on State Missions, further discussions were omitted.

The Moderator then recognized Rev. R. L. Gay who read the following report on:

HOME MISSIONS

Resolved, That we regret the absence of a report on Home Missions, and that we declare our unbounded confidence in the Home Mission Board and its work as an essential part of the great work of world wide evangelization.

Resolved, That we recognize the necessity for every phase of its work—in evangelism, in education and in church building. We also endorse its work=in every field it occupies—among the native whites, among the negroes, the Indians. the foreigners along our coasts, in Cuba and in the Canal Zone.

Resolved, That we commend the Board to our churches as worthy of and entitled to their sympathy, their prayers and their liberal support.

R. L. GAY, Committee

On motion to adopt, Rev. R. L, Gay spoke briefly to the

14

resolutions. The resolutions were adopted. Rev. R. M. Von Miller presented the following report on Foreign Missions.

FOREIGN MISSIONS

The year has been an eventful one, and, in many things, a truly significant period in the history of Southern Baptist Foreign Missions. Long-cherished hopes have been fulfilled, achievements have crowned long and faithful efforts in some of the older missions, and doors of opportunity have opened to new and inviting fields. Southern Baptists have begun a new career in missionary service.

It is well for us to reflect upon the magnitude to which we have expanded our foreign Mission operation during recent months. For years Southern Baptists have prosecuted mission work in China,—North. Central, Interior and South China—in Japan. Africa, Mexico, Brazil, Argentina, Chile and Italy. We have now added Palestine. Syria, Siberia, and of European territory assigned by the London conference, Spain, Jugo-Slavia, Hungaria and Roumania, and part of Russia known as the Ukraine with the territory east thereof.

The task is worthy of Southern Baptists and is characterized by thrilling prospects. We have undertaken on our foreign fields, new and old to give the gospel of Jesus to approximately 200,000.000 black people. 475,000.000 yellow people and 4,000.000 brown people, and to a white population of 225,000.000.

In the vast expance of our enlarged work and the various aspects of it, Southern Baptists have in truth undertaken a world ministry. We have a program which brings us into relation with well-nigh all geographical, ethnological, linguistic and religious conditions. We have the coveted privilege of demonstrating that the gospel held forth in original and primitive simplicity can win anywhere, and that our principles and practices as a Christian people are applicable and acceptable everywhere. Henceforth, we may labor under the inspiration, that we are literally advancing under the Great Commission into all the world and in quest of every Creature.

Therefore your committee recommends that we as pastor's and Christian workers and leaders keep the claims of a lost world upon the minds, hearts and conscience of our people, and that within the bounds of our Association, we foster an undivided interest in foreign Missions, and continue faithful in prayer and loyal financial support for the spread of the glorious Gospel unto the uttermost parts of the earth.

Below are some of the fruits of Foreign Missions:

6,698 Baptisms. The greatest number ever reported.

We have 611 churches, of which 187 (almost one third) are self supporting. Their contributions last year amounted to about $5.00

15

per member.

347, or a few more than half, own their own houses of worship.
41,727 scholars were instructed in 907 Sunday Schools.

405 foreign missionaries are now under appointment. 72 having been sent out during the year.

The Board owns 94 residences, to be used by these missionaries. This is about one-half the number needed for the present force.

978 native workers are employed.

Our 632 schools are crowded with 22,866 students. Of these, 284 are theological students.. This represents an increase over last year of 63 schools and 4.352 students. These schools throb with life and possibilities.

We have now 21 foreign physicians and 8 foreign mission nurses, who gave last year 154.070 treatments.

Respectfully submitted,

R. M. VON MILLER, Committee

On motion to adopt Rev. R. M. Von Miller spoke to the report, the report was adopted.

In absence of Mrs. D. J. Thurston, Mrs. H. A. Hocutt, Supt. of the W. M. U. of the Johnston County Baptist Association, presented the following report:

REPORT ON WOMANS WORK

There are 46 churches in the Association and 48 Societies to whom I send quarterly letters. There are 26 W. M. S., 11 Y. W. M. A. and G. A., 9 Sunbeam S, and 2 R. A.

Of these 48 only about 30 are really active. 19 sent in an annual report. Have arranged getting quarterly reports from 22 Societies. New Societies for the year: Sunbeam, Bailey; Sunbeam, Trinity; Sunbeam, Kenly; W. M. S., Kenly.

650 members reported in 19 reports. 46 Home & Foreign Fields taken, 122 Biblical Recorders and 66 Royal Services taken. 10 Stewardship cards signed. Three Mission study classes reported. 7 observed week of prayer for world wide Missions. 13 observed week of prayer for Home Missions. 11 observed week of prayer for State Missions. 11 have done organized personal service. 100 postals and 300 letters written by Supt. 75 letters written by Jr Supt. Supt. traveled 100 miles. 22 financial reports sent or handed in. Amount raised or reported this year $5,637.43.

At the Womans meeting which met with Clayton Baptist Church October 11th and 12th, 1921. 11 churches were represented. 11 W. M. S, 4 Y. W. A., 3 G. A., 1 R. A.. and 8 Sunbeam Soc. were represented. Making a total of 27 Societies represented. 65 members from these societies present, also 20 guests from other churches.

Total present 87. Churches represented: Smithfield, Selma, Pine Level, Middlesex, Kenly, Four Oaks, Bethesda, Mt. Moriah, Corinth, Clayton, Clyde's Chapel. The W. M. U. of Johnston County Baptist Association was organized in 1903 with 3 Societies. In 1904 5 Societies who reported with a contribution of $332.77.

As Supt. of the Association, I beg the cooperation and prayers of every pastor, and every woman in the Association for the advancement of the work,

MRS. B. A. HOCUTT, Supt.

On motion to adopt Mrs. B, A. Hocutt spoke to the report. The entire report on missions were adopted. A motion to postpone report on Associational Missions for the afternoon was carried.

The Moderator recognized Rev. A. L. Goodrich, who spoke on Bible Conference and recommended that Rev. A. O. Moore be instructed to arrange for a Bible Conference within the bounds of our Association. This recommendation was adopted.

The hour for the Missionary sermon having arrived, the assembly joined in singing, "At the Cross", and prayer led by Rev. J. W. Nobles. Rev. M. P. Davis delivered the Missionary sermon, using for his subject, "The Christian Work" and selecting for his text John 17;18.

After the sermon Rev. J. S, Farmer, General Manager of the Biblical Recorder, spoke briefly on the Biblical Recorder.

After prayer by Rev. A. L. Goodrich, the body adjourned for dinner and recess.

THURSDAY AFTERNOON

Bro. J. F. Pool led the devotional exercises. After which the Moderator recognized Bro. J. M. Beaty, acting Chairman of the Executive Committee, who presented the following report:

REPORT OF THE EXECUTIVE COMMITTEE

Your Executive Committee begs to report one of the best years from the standpoint of church growth in the life of the Association. Revival meetings have been held at all the Mission Churches and in most cases they resulted in a number of additions to the Churches. Two new churches, Pleasant Grove and Burnell, have joined the Association during this session. Rev. B. Townsend has been pastor at Sardis Church. Rev. E. P. West at Parrish Memorial, Rev. J. L. Powers at Calvary, Trinity, Pauline, Hood's Grove and Canaan

17

Churches. Rev. J. S. Johnson at Micro, Pinkney, Bethel, Kenly and Bailey Churches. Rev. M. P. Davis at Blackman's Grove, Burnell and Pleasant Grove Churches. Rev. Sloan Guy at Hale's Chapel. Rev. H. W. Baucom at Beaty's Chapel. Rev. A. L. Goodrich at Princeton. Rev. C. C. Wheeler at Benson Grove. Rev. N. D. Blackman at Hepzipah. Your Committee finds its way much blocked on account of not having parsonages in which the preachers could live, if called to our work. We urge the churches to furnish money with which to build parsonages on all the fields.

Respectfully submitted,

J. M. BEATY,
J. F. POOL,
J, A. SMITH,
R. A. BAIN,
ALNZO PARRISH, Com.

Upon motion to adopt Bro. J. M. Beaty spoke to the report. The report was adopted. As Wendell Church has joined the Raleigh Association, and Lizzie Mills having been absorbed by the Selma Church, a motion by Rev. B. Townsend to drop these Churches from the roll was carried.

Rev. A. O. Moore was recognized, who presented a verbal report on B. Y. P. U. work. This report was adopted. The Treasurer, Bro. J. A. Smith then presented his annual report.

REPORT OF TREASURER

Associational Missions:
Balance in Treasury .... $ 219.10

Disbursements:
Dec. 24th 1920. To Miss Warrington, for work at
     Beaty's Chapel ....$ 20.00
Dec. 29th. Loaned to the Building Fund ....$199.10 $ 219.10

Building Fund:
Received from Churches...$810.38
Borrowed from Citizens National Bank $400.00
Borrowed from Associational Missions.............., ...$199.10 $1409.48

Disbursements:
Oct. 30th, 1920. Paid to J. A. Smith, due 1920.. ....$249.00
Nov. 11th, 1920. Paid to S. Guy for Hale's Chapel..$150.00
Dec. 28th, 1920. Paid to J. M. Beaty, for house
    and lot at Kenly $1000.00
Dec. 28th. 1920. Paid to Citizens National Bank
    for interest ....$ 20.68 $1419.68
Balance due to Treasurer J. A. Smith .... $ 10.20

Minute Fund:
Received from Churches......... ....$202.75 $ 202.75
Disbursements 1920:
Oct. 30th. To J. A. Smith balance due for 1919 ....$ 29.76
Oct. 30th. To R M. Von Miller, postage .... $ 1.50
Nov. 11th. To R. M. Von Miller, for salary as
     Clerk ... .$ 60.00
1921
Jan. 4th. To R. M. Von Miller, for printing of
     minutes and postage ....$128.60 $ 219.86
Balance due Treasurer J. A. Smith............ .... $ 17.11

This is to certify that I have carefully audited the books of Bro. J. A. Smith, Treasurer of the Johnston County Baptist Association for year ending October 27th, 1091, and find them correct and in good shape. J. L. Hall, Auditor.

Respectfully submitted,

J. A. SMITH, Treasurer

On motion this report was adopted. On motion by Rev. R. M. Von Miller a collection was taken for Minute Fund. The collection amounted to $8.83.

Upon motion by Bro. J. M. Beaty the clerk was instructed to have 1000 copies of the Minutes printed for the ensuing year.

The Moderator then recognized Judge F. H. Brooks, who presented the report on "Church Government".

REPORT ON CHURCH GOVERNMENT

The Baptist have adopted the Congregational form of government. We do believe that this is the scriptural mode of government. We do believe in the proper and legitimate application of New Testament principles and apply same to the work we do.

The evidence for congregational form of government and its authority is as follows: (1) Christ's own words as to his discipline, Matt. 18.17, and this as confirmed by Paul in 1 Cor. 5:5;2; 2 Cor. 2:4,5, where he appeals to the church, not to its officials or to a court. (2) The election of Mathias to the apostleship was by congregational vote (Acts 1;15-26), as was also the case with the first seven deacons (Acts 6:1-6) and the selection of men to go with Paul (1 Cor. 16;18.) It is also probable (3) that when Paul and Barnabas "ordained elders in every place" that in the original word it implies they "caused to be chosen or elected." The meeting between Paul and the church at Jerusalem (Acts 15) was also a church meeting in which the judgment was rendered by all. Over against this is the fact that there is no reference whatever in the Scriptures to any

19

control beyond the local congregation.

Such a system of church government pre-supposes vital religion and unselfish devotion to Christ's cause, but without these any other system also becomes a menace to true religion. With us the absence of these things leaves our organization useless and weak, and this is a constant reminder to us all that our polity and practices are based upon this doctrine of a membership having spiritual religion.

Respectfully submitted.
F. H BROOKS, Com.

On motion to adopt, Judge F. H. Brooks spoke to the report. The report was adopted. The Moderator recognized Bro. J. J. Lane who presented the report on Church Finance.

REPORT ON CHURCH FINANCE

Resolved: That we reaffirm our faith in the principles of the 75 Million Campaign, which means that we shall endeavor:

First, to obtain a definite pledge from each member of our churches for all objects of our convention work

Second, that we try to get these pledges paid weekly or monthly.

Third, that we try to have all funds to pass through the hands of the church treasurer.

Respectfully submitted,
J. J. LANE, Com.

Upon motion to adopt, Bro. J. J. Lane spoke to these resolutions. Resolutions were adopted. Upon motion the Moderator was instructed to appoint five Chairman who shall bring report to the next Association each on his complete group of objects of our work.

The Committee on suggesting Executive Committee made the following report:

We your Committee, submit the following names: For Executive Committee, J. M. Beaty, Chairman. J, A. Smith, H. P. Johnson. J. F. Pool, N. M. Gurley.

Delegate to Southern Baptist Convention, Rev. A. O. Moore.

Delegates to Baptist State Convention, Rev. B. Townsend, Rev. R. M. Von Miller and Bro. J. J. Lane.

R. L. GAY, For Com.

On motion of Rev. A. L. Goodrich, a rising vote of thanks was extended to the members of Blackman's Grove Baptist Church, for the most gracious and bountiful hospitality in entertaining the Association.

No other business on hand, a motion to adjourn by Rev. A. O. Moore was carried. The Moderator then declared the nineteenth session of the Johnston County Association adjourned, to meet again with the Noble's Chapel Baptist Church, Wednesday after the fourth Sunday in October 1922, Rev. A. O. Moore led in the closing prayer.

Rev. M. P. Davis, Vice Moderator
Rev. R. M. Von Miller, Clerk

MINUTES OF THE WOMAN'S MISSIONARY UNION

The Woman's Missionary Union of the Johnston County Baptist Association held its annual session with the W. M. S. at Clayton, N. C. October 11-12, 1921.

Rev. A. O Moore pastor of the church gave a hearty welcome to the young people in opening the meeting Tuesday night at 7:30 o'clock. Then followed the processional of the Y. W. A's and junior societies of the Association. Miss Pridgett Williams of Smithfield conducted the devotional exercises. Miss Sulon McCullers of Clayton Y. W. A., gave a most cordial welcome.

Mrs. H. W. Baucom, junior Supt. presided over the meeting and asked for a roll call of the Junior Societies with response of the reports for the year. The G. A. Society of Clayton led in gifts with $280.90.

Special music by the Junior Choir was enjoyed by all. Mrs. Baucom told a beautiful illustrative story, "Is it worth while", to the young people. This story was written by Mrs. S. J. Becker of the Pilot Mt. Association. Mrs. J. D. Herring of Smithfield Y. W. A , gave a splendid talk on the importance of Mission Study. Ruth Thurston of Clayton G. A. Society, read an interesting paper on "Personal Service," The night session closed with a most impressive pageant, "The Open Door", by the Clayton Y. W. A., R. A. and G. A. Societies.

The morning session of Oct. 12th opened with a large crowd of out of town delegates present and the W. M. S. of Clayton well represented.

At 9:45 Mrs. C. A. Jenkins led the devotional exercises, who took for her subject "Love". A cordial address of welcome by Mrs. A. O. Moore followed and the Senior Societies responded through Mrs. D. H. Creech. Mrs. B. A. Hocutt, Supt. of the Union presided over the meeting. Roll call of senior societies, each responding as

21

to standing of Society in regard to payment of Campaign pledge. These reports were very encouraging, and Mrs. Hocutt's report showed increase in gifts and a broadening of the work in the county. The amount reported being $5,637.43. We are always glad to hear Mrs. Lois Massey Bass, here she sang in her own beautiful way, "This is my Task".

The following ladies made interesting talks on the following subjects; Mrs. H. G. Gray, Home and State; Mrs. C. W. Carter, Orphanage and Hospitals.

Mrs. Carter reported 21 Baptist Orphanages and 27 Hospitals in the South. Miss Viola Pool spoke earnestly on "Prayer and Bible Study". A male quartet from the church choir, Messrs Carter, Barbour, Hall and Adams rendered a beautiful selection.

The morning session was made more interesting with a demonstration, "When the Standard Convinced," by the G. A's of Clayton.

Mrs. W. N. Jones of Raleigh, made a most instructive address on "The All-Sufficient One", and a new vision came to us. Mrs. Jone's addresses are always full of interest and information and especially was it helpful on this occasion, for it showed our women how they can emerge from this business panic to a great missionary victory. Committees were appointed as follows: Obituary, Mrs. D. J. Thurston; Nominating, Mrs. Holt and Mrs. Sanders, Time and place, Mrs. Woodard, Miss Batten and Mrs. Oliver. The session adjourned for dinner which was served in the church in cafeteria style. This delightful lunch was served under the supervision of a committee of ladies.

At 2:00 o'clock the afternoon session opened by singing; "Jesus Calls Us". The big feature of the afternoon was the address by Mrs. Bostic from China. As this consecrated woman presented the needs of China, we women of the homeland realized how meager have been our gifts where the needs are so great. For 17 years Mrs. Bostic has lived in a mud hut, in order to tell the Chinese of Jesus Christ, and yet she cheerfully looks forward to going back to this noble sacrifice.

Mrs. Weston Bruner of Raleigh spoke very interestingly on the Baptist W. M. U. Training School. North Carolina has 20 young Baptist women now training for christian work. Miss Campbell of Meredith College told of the devotional services of the college. Twenty of the girls have given themselves for definite service in the home land, and twenty five for foreign work.

Miss Elizabeth Briggs gave a fine report on the Sunbeam work; reporting that the children have more than met their 75 Million pledge.

Mrs. Oliver of Pine Level spoke on Evangelism. The Sunbeam song, "Jesus Bids us Shine" brought joy and sunshine to the many

22

listeners, as the children each sang with a lighted candle. Mrs.
Beaty of Smithfield presented "Enlistment and Stewardship".

The Time and Place Committee reported an invitation for next
year to meet with the women of Smithfield on Oct. 13th and 14th.

The Nominating Committee recommended the re-election of all
officers with the exception of Mrs. W. H. Baucom, who has moved
to Winston-Salem, to be succeeded by Mrs. H. G. Gray of Smithfield
who with Mrs. Lois Massey Bass as Junior Secretary. Just at this
time of the afternoon we paused in memory of those four who have
passed from earth to heaven. Mrs. Honeycutt, Mrs. Moneyham,
Mrs. Jesse Mitchell, Mrs. S. T. Coates. Sarah Parrish and Majorie
Williams have enlisted for training for definite service from the
Clayton G. A. Society.

The closing music was a beautiful duet by Mrs. Bennett Noe and
Miss Kittie Pool. After a most pleasant and beneficial meeting we
adjourned to meet with Smithfield W. M. S. Oct, 13-14, 1922.

MRS. B. A. HOCUTT, Supt.

MISS CLEVE BARNES, Sec,

STATISTICAL TABLE OF B. Y. P. U. SOCIETIES

Name of Church and Union	Name of Pres. and address	No. Members
Benson	William Woodall, Benson, N. C.	38
Blackman's Grove	J. R. Blackman, Four Oaks, N. C.	24
Clayton	Mrs. J. B. Turley, Clayton, N. C.	50
Mount Moriah	Miss Maud Stallings, Raleigh, R. 2	30
Pisgah	R. H. Higgins, Smithfield, N. C.	25
Selma	C. B. Earp, Selma, N. C.	30
Smithfield	Maurice Biggs, Smithfield, N C.	00
Wilson's Mills	Lillian Youngblood, Wilson's Mills	20

APPORTIONMENTS FOR ASSOCIATIONAL BUILDING AND MINUTE FUNDS

	Ass. Bldg Fd.	Minute Fd.
Antioch	$ 15.00	$ 5.00
Bailey	15.00	5.00
Baptist Center	10.00	5.00
Beaty's Chapel	5.00	2.50
Benson	50.00	10.00
Bethel	5.00	2.50
Bethesda	25.00	7.50
Blackman's Grove	25.00	7 50
Burnell	5.00	2.50
Calvary	10.00	5.00
Canaan	5.00	2.50
Carter's Chapel	25.00	7.50
Clayton	100.00	15.00
Clyde's Chapel	25.00	7.50
Corinth	25.00	7.50
Four Oaks	25.00	7.50
Hale's Chapel	10.00	5.00
Hepzipah	10.00	5 00
Hood's Grove	15 00	5.00
Kenly	15 00	5.00
Lee's Chapel	25.00	10.00
Live Oak	5.00	2.50
Micro	12.50	2.50
Middlesex	10.00	5.00
Mount Moriah	150.00	15.00
New Bethel	50.00	10.00
Noble's Chapel	25.00	7 50
Parrish Memorial	20.00	5.00
Pauline	10.00	2.50
Pine Level	50.00	10.00
Pinkney	10.00	5.00
Pisgah	25.00	7.50
Pleasant Grove	5.00	2.50
Princeton	25 00	5.00
Sardis	25.00	5.00
Selma	5.00	10.00
Shiloh	12.50	5.00
Smithfield	50.00	15.00
Thanksgiving	25.00	5.00
Trinity	10.00	5.00
White Oak	15.00	7.50
Wilson's Mills	15.00	5.00
TOTAL	$895.00	$267.30

STATISTICAL TABLES

TABLE I—STATISTICAL

CHURCH	Pastor and Postoffice	Clerk and Post Office	Time of Preaching	Value of Church Property	Gains			Losses			Number of Males	No. of Females	Total Membership
					By Baptism	By Letter	By Restor'tion	By Letter	By Exclusion	By Death			
Antioch	R. M. Von Miller, Wilson, N. C.	W. O. Hocutt, Middlesex, R 3	2nd	3000	24	4	2	1	1	3	88	123	2
Bailey	R. L. Gay, Smithfield	J. P. Underwood, Bailey	1st	4000	16	1		2			37	49	
Baptist Center		Milton Austin, Clayton	3rd and 4th	3000	15	1				1	60	96	1
Beaty's Chapel	C. C. Wheeler, Benson	J. J. Parish, Micro	3rd	1000				3			4	8	1
Benson	Julian Goodwin, Benson	F. T.	1st and 2nd	2500	12	9	1	4		2	76	120	2
Benson Grove	C. C. Wheeler, Benson	D. D. Medlin, Benson, R 1	4th	800	8	2	1	2		1	32	29	
Bethany	W. D. Stancil, Kenly	C. S. Creech, Kenly	4th	2000		5	1	1		5	55	80	
Bethel	R. L. Gay, Smithfield	Luther Stone, Kenly	4th	1000	20		1	3	4		5	9	
Bethesda	M. P. Davis, Four Oaks	E. Smith, Wilson's Mills	2nd	2500	5	9		3		2	104	123	1
Blackman's Grove	M. P. Davis, Four Oaks	P. J. Morgan, Four Oaks	2nd	1500	3	2		2		1	24	56	5
Burnell	J. L. Powers, Bentonville	W. L. Massengil, Four Oaks	1st	1200						5	8	10	2
Calvary	J. L. Powers, Bentonville	T. J. Lee, Dunn	3rd	1500							10	13	1
Canaan	W. D. Stancil, Kenly	T. L. Hudson, Bentonville	1st	600							17	23	1
Carter's Chapel	A. O. Moore, Clayton	J. M. Eastman, Selma R 1	F. T.	1500		4	1	2	1		51	61	
Clayton	B. M. Shacklett, Augier	W. P. Creech, Clayton	1st and 3rd	7500	52	7		6		7	244	315	
Clyde's Chapel	C. H. Cashwell, Wake Forest	C. J. Johnson, Wendell, R L	4th	800		5		5	1	6	90	124	
Corinth	M. P. Davis, Four Oaks	L. T. Davis, Wendell, R 1	1st and 3rd	3000	19			3		1	65	122	
Four Oaks	C. H. Cashwell, Wake Forest	B. B. Creech, Four Oaks	4th	3000	24	7	4	2		1	41	72	
Hale's Chapel	N. D. Blackman, Goldsboro	A. D. Parish, Zebulon	3rd	2000	7		6	1			42	38	
Hephzibah	J. L. Powers, Bentonville	G. A. Braswell, Princeton	3rd	700				2			3	10	
Hood's Grove		G. L. Blackman, Bentonsville R2	4th	4000		4		1			26	30	
Kenly	J. E. Hocutt, Nashville	F. A. White, Kenly	4th	2500	27	12	15	2	1	5	18	24	
Lee's Chapel	N. D. Blackman, Goldsboro	W. I. Green, Zebulon, R. 2	3rd	800		3		3			126	135	2
Live Oak	J. S. Johnson, Kenly	J. M. Richardson, Selma, R 2	3rd	2000	13	2		4					
Micro	J. W. Nobles, Middlesex	S. C. Barton, Micro	2nd	5000	8			6	1	1	32	34	
Middlesex	R. T. Vann, Raleigh	G. J. Johnson, Middlesex	4th	4200	6	1		3		1	34	61	2
Mount Moriah	J. S. A. Edgerton, Buies Creek	Russell Powell, Auburn	1st	2000	13	2		6	1		95	105	1
New Bethel	A. L. Goodrich, Wake Forest	Geo. W. Bryan, Garner	4th	1000	8	3	1	3			56	74	1
Noble's Chapel	W. D. Stancil, Kenly	N. L. Stott, Simms	4th	2000		1	1	6			49	65	
Oliver's Grove		Miss Lena Tyner, Four Oaks	2nd	800				1			5	11	

TABLE II—FINANCIAL

CHURCH	Pastor's Salary	Building and Repairs	Incidentals	S. S. Expenses	The Poor	Minute Fund	Other Objects	75 Million [Undesig'ted]	State and Associational Missions	Home Missions	Foreign Missions	S. S. Missions	Orphanage	Christian Edu.	Ministers Relief	Hospitals	TOTAL
Antioch	386.76		69.82	22.00		5.00	90.00	115.25	1.00			6.00					608.83
Bailey	232.85	22.00	55.13	50.00		5.00		82.34	3.19				16.15				501.53
Baptist Chtter	300.00			30.00		1.35		43.50									429.98
Beaty's Chapel	25.80			29.71													55.01
Benson	1935.70	43.00	467.17	291.62		10.00	410.00	465.03									4682.32
Benson Grove	100.01			10.00		5.00		40.00									155.00
Bethany	55.86	1211.68	15.00	20.00	14.00	10.00	4.25	149.85					15.00				1457.74
Bethesda	400.00		30.85	92.50		2.10	50.00	472.25									1049.75
Blackman's Grove	300.00		1.00	25.86		5.00	3.56	130.90									496.17
Burnell	50.00			16.00		2.50	35.50	28.50									133.50
Bethel																	
Calvary	75.00					2.00	1.75	50.00									128.75
Canaan	41.00					1.50	1.00	56.50			2.55						100.00
Carter's Chapel	105.00			36.00	32.65	1.90	39.60		53.10	52.65	4.50		131.15	20.55	5.00		104.15
Clayton	2708.31		2197.55	489.32		10.00	251.30	3150.00					50.00				8970.18
Coats Chapel	350.00	1146.68	5.40	40.00		2.00		422.00					10.00			5.00	972.00
Corinth	450.00		56.50	40.00				210.70					27.65				506.16
Four Oaks	1000.00			109.15		4.45	250.84	98.76					5.00				2984.77
Hale's Chapel	150.00			20.00		2.00	10.00	11.45									198.45
Hepzipah	93.25		6.50	13.36		2.00	5.00	22.85					2.82				74.10
Hood's Grove	100.00			18.31		2.50	11.00	35.50					12.00				165.18
Kenly	140.00	35.00	210.29	30.25	6.00	5.00	18.31	120.50			2.00			2.00	4.00		463.85
Lee's Chapel	300.00	140.00	15.00	16.01		8.50	32.00	5.00	5.00	5.00	2.00						683.01
Live Oak	20.66		98.10	7.00		6.00											59.26
Micro	250.00	500.00	52.49	75.00	15.00	2.50	3.75	234.40					70.64				883.65
Mount Moriah	625.00	163.59	31.32	157.67	37.00	2.00	175.85	1101.91	5.00				70.64	9.00			1483.97
New Bethel	300.00	12.85	156.36	66.75		5.00	348.08	383.00		2.00			231.51				2274.46
Noble's Chapel	300.00	6.50		89.11		10.00	32.85	62.50									771.46
Oliver's Grove	300.93		131.06	57.81		1.00		5.00	5.00		.50		1.00	.50			596.37
	20.00																35.00

																Total
									5.00	5.00	1.00	5.00	5.00	5.00		
Parrish Memorial	150.00	15.00	.....	15.00	.....	5.00	20 00	15.00	5.00							246.00
Pauline	40.00	35.00	180.00	15.00	15.00	1.00	1.00	7.75								98.75
Pine duel	390.00	200.00	180.00	53.00		10.00	50.00	400.00								1398.00
Pinkney	102.70	2.55		17.93		3.75	9.00	81.36								217.29
Pisgah	500.00	30.00	45.22	80.39		5.00	2.50	378.55								1041.66
Pleasant Grove	50.00			12.00		1 00		13.00	1.00							77.00
Princeton	150.00		12.00	52.53		.5.00	10.00	12.00		10 00			5.00		5.00	256.53
Sardis	250.00	368.68	20.80	38.86		10.00	70.41	135.10								878.75
Selma	2100.00	504.42	274.11	305.41		5.00	78.74	429.20	12.32	14.30		120.00				3848.50
Thanksgiving	185.77		19.61	23.00		5.00	2.28	57.00								297.66
Smithfield	1797.00		258.38	-	5.00	15.00	306.33	1478.91	33.50							3889.07
Shiloh																
Trinity	150.00	64.20		60.00	3.00	5.00	6.80	75.00								363.00
White Oak	500.00			35.00	18.25	5.00	1.00	905.43								864.68
Wilson's Mills	300.00	75.00		50.00		5.00	35.00	90.75					23.25			585.00
	17,630.16	4,566.15	4,380.52	2,538.24	144.90	204.55	392.29	11,976.24	124.11	88.95	47.55	732.17	37.50	19.00	500	44,777.69

TABLE III—SUNDAY SCHOOLS

CHURCH	Superintendent	Post Office	Secretary	Post Office	No. of Schools	Officers and Teachers	Pupils	Total Enrollment	Church members in S. S.	Months Kept Open	Baptisms from Schools	School Expenses	Missions	Orphanage	Other Objects	Total Contributions
Antioch	A. D. O'Neal	Middlesex, R. 3	W. O. Hocutt	Middlesex. R. 3	1	5	105	110	40	12	17	22.00	7.00			29.00
Bailey	Redmon Warren	Bailey	H. Underwood	Bailey	1	9	50	59	30	12		50.00	10.19	16.50		76.69
Baptist Center	Milton Austin	Clayton	Wade Tippett	Clayton	1	10	150	160	100	12	15	30.00				30.00
Beaty's Chapel	J. J. Parrish	Smithfield	E Noye	Smithfield	1	4	40	44	12	12		29.71				29.71
Benson	J. E. Wall	Benson	H. O. Dixon	Benson	1	27	203	280	150	12		174.15	17.42		100.00	291.57
Benson Grove	L. E. Barbour	Benson, R. 1	Curly Harper	Benson, R. 1	1	5	40	45	90	6		10.00				10.00
Bethel	B. B. Batton	Kenly	Carmel Creech	Kenly	1	10	75	85	45	12		20.00			4.25	24.25
Bethesda	J. B. Coats	Wilson's Mills	Earl M. Smith	Wilson's Mills	1	12	150	163	75	12	20	60.00		7.50	15.00	82.50
Blackman's Grove	J. R. Blackman	Four Oaks	P. J. Morgan	Four Oaks	1	8	75	88	45	12	5	29.42				29.42
Burnell	W. L. Massengill	Four Oaks	Miss M. Massengill	Four Oaks	1	7	80	87	29	12	3	16.00		5.50		21.50
Calvary																
Carter's Chapel	Jes Price	Selma R 3	Frank Woodruff	Selma, R 1	1	12	133	145	50	12	21	36.00				36.00
Clayton	W P Creech	Clayton, R 3	Chas. G. Gulley	Clayton	1	23	390	413	313	12		439.82	24.06	131.15		595.03
Clyde's Chapel	J. B. Boyett	Wendell, R 1	Miss Mamie Boykin	Wendell, R. 1	1	4	130	138	100	12	5	40.00				40.00
Corinth	L. T. Davis	Wendell, R. 1	H. V. Andrews	Wendell, R. 1	1	8	150	158	80	12	14	38.00			2.00	40.00
Four Oaks	J. W. Sanders	Four Oaks	Jesse	Four Oaks	1	13	162	175	88	12	19	100.15	11.00	9.15	59.55	179.85
Hale's Chapel	A. D. Parrish	Zebulon	M. H. Price	Zebulon	1	9	82	91	60	12	1	20.00				20.00
Hepzipah	W. G. Creech	Princeton	J. F. Earp	Pine Level	1	7	36	40	7	12		15.00				15.00
Hood's Grove	Y. L. Blackman	Bentonsville, R. 2	Mrs W. H. Kackley	Bentonsville	1	4	50	54	40	8		13.38		2.82		16.18
Kenly	A. J. Broughton	Kenly	W. H. Hackley	Kenly	1	6	31	81	81	12	8	80.25		19.21	28.00	77.46
Live Oak	Joshua Snipes	Middlesex	A. E. Denton	Middlesex	1	4	135	139	75	12	25	16.01				16.01
Micro	J. E. Tatum	Selma, R. 1	W. B. Mis	Selma R 1	1	5	124	129		12		7.00				7.00
Middlesex	D. H. Jones	Micro	E. B. Wall	Micro	1	8	50	58	25	12		75.00				75.00
New Bethel	W. R. Ballentine	Middlesex	J. M. Davis	Middlesex	1	10	124	134	40	12	7	159.67	5.00	70.64		228.81
Oliver's Grove	R. I. Smith	Clayton, R. 3	John Baucom	Raleigh, R. 2	1	12	150	162	105	9	5	90.75			198.06	514.83
	Lewis Boykin	McCullers	Eugene Britt	Garner	1	9	131	138	60	12	8	39.11				39.11
		Simms, N. C.	O. Bullock	Simms	1	10	100	110	60	12	7	37.81				37.81

Church	Pastor	Location	Clerk	Location										
Parrish Memorial	T. M. Olive	Pine del	Thos. Parrish	Selma, R 2	1	5	50	55	40	12	12	15.00			15.00
Pinkney	R. E. Lee	Kenly, R.4	Otis Lee	Kenly	1	6	60	66	15	12	1	17.93			17.93
Pine Level	B. L. Strickland	Pine Level	Miss Sadie Britt	Pine Level	1	10	90	100	50	12	1	53.00	10.06	3.48	66.54
Pauline	Miss Naomi Lee	Four Oaks	Tom Strickland	Four Oaks	1	6	76	82	35	12		15.00			15.00
Pisgah	J. A. Smith	Smithfield, R. 1	Paul E. Whitley	Smithfield, R 1	1	8	105	113	35	12	4	85.00		30.13	3.80 118.93
Pleasant Grove	J. E. Gilbert	Selma, R. 3	Claude Stephens	W. Bw Springs	1		30	34	7	12		12.00			12.00
Princeton	W. I. Pearce	Princeton	J. J. Boyett	Princeton	1	7	114	121	60	12	6	49.95	2.59		52.53
Sardis	W. S. Stephens	Smithfield	Mrs J. B. Gardner	Pine del	1	8	100	108	53	12	21	38.86		70.41	9.27
Selma	W. B. Crumpton	Selma	G. A. Earp	Selma	2	20	425	445	320	12	30	305.41	12.32	120.00	50.00 487.73
Shiloh															
Smithfield	T. S. Ragsdale	Smith field	John Ives	Smithfield	3	21	332	353	250	12	45		171.50	171.50	
Thanksgiving	W. S. Earp. —	Selma, R 1	O. J. Branson	Selma, R 1	1	8	152	160	25	12	4	23.00			5.00 28.00
Trinity	W. P. Lee	Benson, R. 2	Victor Lawham	Benson	1	9	67	76	25	12		60.00			1.80 61.80
White Oaks	A. L. Batton	Clayton, R. 2	W. H. Green	Clayton, R 2	1	7	100	107	85	12	16	35.00			35.00
Wilson's Mills	J. T. Hall	Wilson's Mills	Walter Boyett	Wilson's Mills	1	7	50	57	30	12		50.00			50.00
Selma Branch S.	L. Batton	Selma													
					44	366	4704	5070	2802			3182 676.34	59.63 804.58	504.39 3762.96

TABLE IV—WOMANS MISSIONARY UNION

CHURCH	NAME OF ORGANIZATION	PRESIDENT	POST OFFICE	Number of Members	75 Million Undesignated	Missions	Christian Education	Orphanage	Training School	Other Objects	Total Contributions
Bailey	Woman's Missionary Society	Miss Ruth Bragg	Bailey	15	690.60						690.60
Bailey	Sunbeam Society	Miss Hazel Finch	Bailey	34	15.07						15.07
Benson	W. M. Society	Mrs. J. L. Hall	Benson	25	9.05						9.65
Blackman's Grove	W. M. Society	Mrs. C. C. Wheeler	Four Oaks	25	1276.50	50.00				27.00	1353.50
Clayton	W. M. Society	Mrs. Electa Wood	Clayton	51	219.87						219.87
Clayton	Y. W. M. Society	Mrs. A. O. Moore	Clayton	15	283.51			5.00			288.51
Clayton	G. A. Society	Miss Jessie Gulley	Clayton	35	116.09	2.55					118.64
Clayton	Sunbeam Society	Mrs. W. J. Payne	Clayton	41	139.65						189.65
Clayton	Royal Ambassadors	Mrs. D. J. Thurston	Clayton	15	117.20						117.20
Clyde's	W. M. Society	Mrs. Mamie Batton	Wendell, R 1	30							
Corinth	W. M. Society	Mrs. J. B. O'Neal	Zebulon, R. 1	34	31.75						81.75
Four Oaks	Sunbeam Society	Mrs. J. W. Sanders	Four Oaks	44		116.49	7.00	5.00	10.55	55.64	194.59
Four Oaks	W. M. Society	Mrs. M. P. Davis	Four Oaks	10		31.85			3.00	5.50	40.35
Kenly	W. M. Society	Mrs. J. E. Jones	Kenly	20						70.00	70.00
Middlesex	W. M. Society	Mrs. J. T. Moore	Middlesex	8	137.40				6.50	2.00	145.90
Middlesex	Y. W. M. Society	Mrs. J. J. Ballentine	Middlesex	36	10.00						10.00
Middlesex	Sunbeam Society	Miss Fr...	Middlesex	30	35.80		3.50			.25	39.55
Mt. Moriah	Sunbeam Society	Mrs. J. G. Lane	Auburn	20	10.00						10.00
Noble's Chapel	W. M. Society	Mrs. T. B. Boykin	Simms	8	12.50					37.58	50.08
Pine	W. M. Society	Mrs. B. L. Strickland	Pine Level	35		52.00	10.00	20.00	10.00	8.00	100.00
Pine Level	Sunbeam Society	Mrs. O. B. Johnson	Pine Level	10		3.00	1.00	1.00	.75		5.75
Pisgah	W. M. Society	Mrs. N. D. Johnson	Smithfield, R. 1	40	27.00						27.00
Selma	W. M. Society	Mrs. Geo. D. ...	Selma	35	93.00					14.30	107.39
Selma	Sunbeam Society	Mrs. A. E. ...	Selma			33.50					
Smithfield	W. M. Society	Mrs. W. N. Holt	Smithfield	35	527.41	33.50			58.25	197.08	816.24
Smithfield	Sunbeam Society	Mrs. J. M. Beaty	Smithfield	20	64.11					1.00	65.11
				636	3827.1	289.30	21.50	25.00	89.05	418.35	4671.35

MINUTES

OF THE

TWENTIETH ANNUAL SESSION

OF THE

Johnston County Baptist Association

HELD WITH

NOBLE'S CHAPEL BAPTIST CHURCH

OCTOBER 25 and 26, 1922

The next session will be held with Bethany Baptist Church,
beginning on Wednesday, after the Fourth
Sunday in October, 1923

To Preach Introductory Sermon, Rev. M. P. Davis.
Rev. A. A. Butler, alternate.

RALEIGH
BYNUM PRINTING COMPANY
1922

MINUTES

OF THE

TWENTIETH ANNUAL SESSION

OF THE

Johnston County Baptist Association

HELD WITH

NOBLE'S CHAPEL BAPTIST CHURCH

OCTOBER 25 and 26, 1922

———

The next session will be held with Bethany Baptist Church,
beginning on Wednesday, after the Fourth
Sunday in October, 1923

———

To Preach Introductory Sermon, Rev. M. P. Davis,
Rev. A. A. Butler, alternate.

———

RALEIGH
BYNUM PRINTING COMPANY
1922

OFFICERS

Moderator, R. H. Gower..Clayton
Vice-Moderator, M. P. Davis..Four Oaks
Clerk, R. M. Von Miller..Wilson
Treasurer, J. A. Smith..Smithfield
Auditor, N. L. Stott..Sims

EXECUTIVE COMMITTEE

A. O. Moore, Chairman..Clayton
M. P. Davis..Four Oaks
H. F. Brooks..Smithfield
J. J. Lane..Auburn
H. E. Earp..Selma

DELEGATES AND BOARD MEMBERS

Member of the State Board of Missions—A. O. Moore, Clayton.
Delegate to Southern Baptist Convention—R. M. Von Miller, Wilson.
Delegates to Baptist State Convention—H. F. Brooks, J. F. Poole,
Mrs. C. M. Thomas.

COMMITTEE IN CHARGE OF AND TO MAKE REPORTS ON CONVENTION OBJECTS

Business—Church Government, Church Finance: J. J. Lane
Social Service — Orphanage, Ministerial Relief, Temperance, Hospitals: N. H. Shepherd.
Missions — Associational, State, Home, and Foreign, and Woman's Work: M. P. Davis.
Christian Education— Colleges, Preparatory Schools, Periodicals, Books, and Tracts: R. M. Von Miller.
Teaching and Training--Sunday Schools, B. Y. P. U., and Demonstration: A. A. Butler.

LIST OF MINISTERS

A. A. Butler..Selma, N. C.
E. B. Booker..Smithfield, N. C.
C. H. Cashwell...Wendell, N. C.
F. T. Collins..Smithfield, N. C.
A. N. Corpening..Wake Forest, N. C.
S. A. Edgerton...Buie's Creek, N. C.
R. L. Gay...Smithfield, N. C.
J. E. Hocutt...Nashville, N. C.
A. O. Moore...Clayton, N. C.
J. W. Nobles..Middlesex, N. C.
B. M. Shacklett...Angier, N. C.
N. H. Shepherd...Kenly, N. C.
W. D. Stancil..Kenly, N. C.
R. L. Tate...Benson, N. C.
R. T. Vann, D.D...Raleigh, N. C.
D. E. Vipperman...Pine Top, N. C.
R. M. Von Miller...Wilson, N. C.

ENROLLED DELEGATES

Antioch—R. R. Creech, Mr. and Mrs. E. H. Narron.
Bailey—B. L. Taylor, Mrs. J. W. Privett, J. W. B. Finch.
Beaty's Chapel—E. B. Booker.
Benson--Mrs. R. B. Brady, Mrs. G. W. Goodrich, Velma Finch, D. J.
    Hill, J. B. Smith.
Benson Grove—W. B. Brown. C. P. Stewart, J. C. West.
Bethany—Moses Creech, Mr. and Mrs. C. S. Creech, Jessie B. Creech.
    Stephen Creech.
Bethesda—G. A. Smith.
Blackman's Grove—R. Lee, Hessie Phelps, Nogah Wood, B. Black-
    man, H. Lee, Betta Lee,
Calvary—L. R. Tate, W. D. Tart.
Carter's Chapel—J. R. Atkinson, N. M. Boylin.
Clayton--Mrs. M. Spence, A. O. Moore, Mrs. B. A. Hocutt, J. D. Bar-
    bour, D. J. Yelverton, R. H. Gower, Thelma Yelverton, C. W.
    Pesselor, J. D. Smith, Mrs. L. M. Bass, Mr. and Mrs. J. D. Smith.
Corinth—Christine Oneal, J. B. Oneal, L. T. Davis.
Four Oaks—B. B. Creech, Mrs. B. B. Creech, M. P. Davis, Alton Mas-
    sengill.
Hale's Chapel—C. H. Cashwell.
Hepzibah—L. Creech, J. F. Earp, W. G. Creech.
Kenly—N. H. Shepherd.
Lee's Chapel—J. W. Creech.
Micro--G. Brown, D. H. Jones, C. L. Batten, R. Pitman, J. P. Davis.
Middlesex—Mr. and Mrs. J. W. Nobles.
Mount Moriah—S. Wilder, Veola Pool, R. G. Pool, N. R. Pool, E. D.
    Kelly, Mr. and Mrs. J. F. Pool.

Noble's Chapel—O. Bullock, N. L. Stott, T. B. Boykin.
Parrish Memorial—Carrie Weston, J. D. Creech, J. W. Parrish, J. N. Watson.
Pauline—W. B. Joyner.
Pine Level—N. M. Gurley, Mrs. D. B. Oliver, Mrs. B. L. Strickland, J. F. Watson.
Pinkney—Mrs. B. R. Edgerton, Mrs. F. M. Holland, N. Stone.
Pisgah—R. L. Gay, J. A. Smith.
Selma—A. A. Butler, Mrs. A. A. Butler.
Smithfield—J. D. Dickens, H. F. Brooks, F. T. Collins, D. H. Jones, L. Brown.
Thanksgiving—R. M. Von Miller, Mr. and Mrs. George R. Whitley, Misses Wood.
Trinity—P. H. Lee, J. L. Johnson, A. G. Parker.
White Oak—Mr. and Mrs. I. M. Price, A. L. Batten.

CONSTITUTION

1. The Association shall be known as the Johnston County Baptist Association.

2. Its object shall be to extend the privileges of the Gospel and liberal culture to all the people within its bounds, and, by hearty co-operation with the Baptist State Convention, to help offer these privileges to all mankind in and out of its bounds by the cordial co-operation of all the churches constituting this body.

3. It shall be composed of the pastors in active service in the Association and such delegates as shall be annually elected by the churches connected with it, each church being entitled to three delegates, unless the membership shall exceed fifty, and then an additional delegate for every twenty-five members: *Provided*, no church shall have more than eight delegates.

4. The New Hampshire Declaration of Faith shall be the summary of Divine Truth for determining questions of faith and order in this body, and the churches desiring membership in it must commit themselves to the substance of it, together with the covenant herewith submitted and this Constitution.

5. This Association shall not have power to annul this discipline or exercise authority over any church connected with it, but it may advise with and sever its connection with any church that neglects to preserve Gospel order, or that treats with contempt the objects or advice of the Association.

6. Each church shall send to the annual meetings of the Association a letter (the blanks to be furnished by the Clerk of the Association), carefully filled as per blank suggestions, stating the full work of the church for the year ending with the Sunday previous to the meeting of the Association.

7. The Association shall foster State Missions, Home Missions, Foreign Missions, Christian Education, the Aged Ministers' Relief Board, the Thomasville Orphanage, and the Sunday School Board, and each church shall be requested to contribute to the support of these objects annually.

8. Missions and Education shall have precedence in their claims upon the consideration of this body in its regular sessions.

9. Whenever a church shall fail to be represented by delegates or letter at the annual sessions of the Association, inquiry shall be made for the cause, and efforts shall be made to induce such church to do its duty; and the effort shall be continued till the church is recovered or dropped from the roll.

10. The officers of the Association shall be a Moderator, a Vice-Moderator, a Clerk, a Treasurer, and an Auditor, elected annually by ballot (or in case when only one brother is put in nomination for an office, then the vote may be by acclamation), from among the members, to serve until their successors shall have been elected, and to perform the duties of such offices, namely, the Moderator, in presiding over the meetings, or the Vice-Moderator, in his absence; the Clerk, in recording and preserving minutes and other papers belonging to the body; the Treasurer, in receiving and disbursing funds belonging to or entrusted to the body, according to its will; the Auditor, to examine the Treasurer's books at each meeting of the Association, and report the same before adjournment.

11. The Association shall appoint annually an Executive Committee of five (5) from its members, who shall be entrusted with the prosecution of Missions in the Association and any other work for the interest of the Master's Kingdom which may be referred to them. This committee shall, as far as possible, co-operate with the State Mission Board in supplying the destitution in our territory, and between the meetings of the Association, take such action as may seem to them advisable for the advancement of its interest. The committee shall present to the Association at its annual meeting a report of its proceedings, with the names of the missionaries supported on the field, time of service and details of their work, together with such recommendations as, in the judgment of the committee, the Association should follow in planning its subsequent work.

12. The annual sessions of the Association shall begin on Wednesday after the fourth Lord's Day in October, at such place as may be chosen, and an introductory sermon shall be delivered on the first day of the session. Representatives from ten of the churches constituting the Association shall be a quorum.

13. This Constitution may be amended at any annual session by a two-thirds vote of all the members present.

14. The proceedings of the Woman's Central Committee shall be recorded as a part of the minutes of the Association.

BY-LAWS

1. The daily sessions of the Association shall be opened and closed with prayer.

2. Delegates shall be recognized by letters from their churches designating them as such.

3. The Moderator shall recognize corresponding messengers or the delegates of newly received churches by extending to them his right hand.

4. The report of the Executive Board and the Missionary work of the Association shall take precedence of all other business during the morning session of the second day of the annual session.

5. The Clerk shall record and read the proceedings when called for, superintend the publication and distribution of the minutes, preserve a file of them and have it present at each annual session, and deliver to his successor all papers belonging to the body.

6. Members desiring to speak shall first rise and address the Moderator, shall use the term "brother" in speaking to each other, shall not speak on the same subject more than twice without permission, and shall observe the courtesy that becomes Christians.

7. The roll of members shall be called at least once, and absentees marked.

8. Corresponding messengers and visiting brethren shall be invited to seats, with privilege of speaking, but not voting.

9. A copy of the minutes shall be sent to the Secretary of the State Mission Board, the Secretary of the Southern Baptist Convention, the American Publication Society, 1420 Chestnut Street, Philadelphia; the Sunday School Board of the Southern Baptist Convention, and the Thomasville Orphanage.

10. All questions of order not herein provided shall be decided by Kerfoot's Parliamentary Law.

Proceedings

The Johnston County Baptist Association met in its twentieth session with the Noble's Chapel Baptist Church, October 25-26, 1922.

WEDNESDAY MORNING

At 10:30 a. m., Bro. J. M. Hilliard conducted the devotional exercises, after which the Moderator declared the Johnston County Baptist Association open for the transaction of business, and appointed Brethren T. A. Yelverton and O. Bullock to serve as a Committee on Credentials and Enrollment.

The Clerk then called the roll of the churches. A quorum being present, the body proceeded with the business as per program, the first item being organization. The following officers were elected to serve for the ensuing year: R. H. Gower, Moderator; M. P. Davis, Vice-Moderator; R. M. Von Miller, Clerk; J. A. Smith, Treasurer; N. L. Stott, Auditor.

Under miscellaneous business the following new pastors were recognized and welcomed into the fellowship of the Association by the Moderator: N. H. Shepherd, C. H. Cashwell, A. A. Butler, E. B. Booker, and L. R. Tate.

Rev. J. M. Hilliard was also recognized as a visitor from the Piedmont Association.

After singing "I'm Pressing on the Upward Way," Bro. A. A. Butler led in prayer, after which Bro. A. O. Moore preached the introductory sermon, using for his subject "Modern Heresies." At the close of this timely and most excellent sermon, Bro. R. L. Tate led in prayer.

Under miscellaneous business, Bro. M. P. Davis offered the following resolution, which was adopted:

Be it resolved, That this body set apart a period as a memorial service in memory of our late Bro. J. M. Beaty, and that a committee be appointed to present suitable resolutions in his memory.

On motion, the evening hour, 7:30, was set aside for this service.

The next item on the program was Church Finance. The Moderator recognized Bro. R. M. Von Miller, who presented the

REPORT ON CHURCH FINANCE

In response to the task allotted to me at this hour, to make a report on church finance, I ask your indulgence, as I shall endeavor to present to you what I consider to be a constructive church finance policy, for the use of our churches within the bounds of the Johnston County Baptist Association, in proper form for presentation to our churches.

While incomplete, it will prove suggestive in formulating an official policy, which can be modified from time to time. Of course, no church can use it without modification to suit existing conditions, and including additional features. A church should consider and adopt each recommendation separately:

1. *A Scriptural Standard.*—Whereas the Bible constantly assumes that the Lord has a right to a share of the income of every Christian, to be used for His work; therefore, be it   _

Resolved, That our churches do henceforth rely on scriptural giving on the part of their members, believing that the people, if properly trained in systematic and liberal giving to the Lord; made intelligent concerning the work to be done, and given the advantage of a suitable system efficiently worked. can be relied on as intelligent Christians to furnish the money needed.

2. *Modern, Businesslike Management.*—Whereas, business sense is a talent given of God; and whereas, God instituted a definite system for financing the religious work and worship, and all His universe is governed by system: and whereas, God expects progress in His business as well as our own; therefore, be it

Resolved, That we who no longer ride in stage coaches, or wear homespun, but make use of business sense and modern ways in all places of personal interest, shall give the Lord's business the best of modern business management.

3. *Unified Management Needed.*—Whereas, the financial interests of each church are one; and whereas, the successful financing of the local church conduces to missionary liberality and increase in missionary liberality, leads to better support of the home churches; therefore, be it

Resolved, That we suggest the centralizing under one management the financing in each church; that a finance committee be appointed in each local church, which shall have the exclusive duty to manage the finance of the church, whether for the support of the local church or missions, as directed by the church, making a monthly and an annual report to the church.

4. *Budget.*—Whereas, all the interests of the local church must be liberally financed, since self-preservation is the first law of life, growth, and usefulness; therefore, be it

Resolved, That a liberal budget shall be provided for local needs, to be made up as follows: Before the first of January, each year, the needs for the current year, approximated, shall be presented to the church, and the total sum shall be known as the current expense budget, after approval by the church, shall be fully provided for by pledges, eliminating all special appeals, except in emergency cases.

5. *Pledges and Payments.*—Whereas, pledging and paying on the weekly basis is in accord with Scripture teaching, conduces both to broadening the meaning of the worship of God and to bringing religion into a new and vital connection with the money-making during the preceding week, makes it possible for the subscriber to pledge larger amounts and to pay more easily, and eliminates the worry of officials about lack of funds; therefore, be it

Resolved, That all pledges be made on the weekly basis, allowing each subscriber the privilege of making payment weekly, monthly, or quarterly, as he may prefer, though urging the weekly practice upon every one; and that pledges be secured from every member of the church by personal solicitation; the same method to be applied in financing the benevolent and mission objects fostered by the church in its co-operative work.

Resolved, also, That we look forward to the day when our churches shall contribute to missions and benevolence as much as for the local work, and that we endeavor in the coming year to enlist every member, in conformity with the reinforcement campaign just launched by our Southern Baptist Convention.

Resolved, also, That we suggest to our churches the use of the double-pocketed envelopes, which are of great value for the keeping of the records, and are convenient to the subscriber.

Respectfully submitted,

R. M. VON MILLER, *Committee.*

On motion to adopt, Bro. R. M. Von Miller spoke to the report, after which, by consent of the body, it was decided to carry the discussion of this report over for the night session.

A motion by Bro. M. P. Davis that Wednesday night be chosen for the memorial service in memory of Bro. J. M. Beaty, and also for the further discussion of the finance report, was carried, after which the body adjourned for recess, with prayer by Bro. L. R. Tate.

WEDNESDAY AFTERNOON

Bro. R. L. Gay conducted the devotional exercises.

Under miscellaneous business, Bro. R. L. Gay made a motion that Bro. R. M. Von Miller be requested to present his address on Church Finance to the *Biblical Recorder* for publication. The motion was carried.

The Moderator then appointed the following committees:

To arrange suitable memorial resolution in memory of Bro. J. M. Beaty—Judge H. F. Brooks, Chairman; J. F. Pool, N. M. Gurley.

Committee on Place and Preacher—J. P. Underwood, Chairman; R. R. Creech, and W. B. Joyner.

The Moderator then called for the next item on the program, which was Social Service, and recognized Judge H. F. Brooks, who presented the

REPORT ON SOCIAL SERVICE

Your Committee on Social Service is pleased to report that the Baptist churches of the South, as well as other denominations, have come to the realization of the need of emphasizing social service; for if the Christian people do not direct the pleasures and social functions for the boys and girls, then the agencies of the evil one will do so. And we firmly believe that it is the duty of the churches and the Sunday schools to supervise the amusements for our young people.

This report includes the orphanage, ministerial relief, temperance, and hospitals, and we will discuss them in the order given.

ORPHANAGE

The institutions that are included in this organization are the Orphanage at Thomasville, which is taking care of 426 children, and the Kennedy Home in Lenoir County, which is taking care of 85 children in their homes. On account of the crowded conditions at the Orphanage, and because of the efforts to try to keep the home circle unbroken, the Orphanage has adopted a policy of assisting the mothers in taking care of the fatherless children, and at the same time saving an expense at the Orphanage, as the children can be assisted in their homes for one-third as much as it takes to take care of them in the Orphanage. The annual cost of caring for a child in the Orphanage is $214.02. The daily cost of the 531 children at the Orphanage is $310.65. It might be interesting to know that the

Orphanage produced and consumed in farm products during the year 1921 $8,120.75 in dairy products, $24,714.70 in milk, 63,857 gallons, or $22,347.85. During the year 1921 there were 724 applications for admission received by the Orphanage, and they were able to care for about 63 of that number, leaving 661 which they were unable to take care of just now. There are six officers, twenty teachers, twenty-five matrons, and 14 farmers, dairymen, and carpenters.

MINISTERIAL RELIEF

The power of distributing the funds for ministerial relief is through the Board of Ministerial Relief and Annuities of the Southern Baptist Convention, but the State Board of Missions is to see to the collections of the needy funds, investigate the worthiness of the applicants, and endorse the applications. This fund is supposed to receive $60,000 annually from North Carolina's part of the 75 Million contribution. Dr. William Lunsford, of Dallas, Texas, is Corresponding Secretary of the Ministers' Relief and Annuities. Sixty-one North Carolina beneficiaries are being cared for.

In the 75 Million Campaign, there is part of the contribution set aside for this work. The Permanent Investment fund is placed in the hands of the Baptist Foundation, and the interest from it is used for the Ministers' Relief and Annuity. This is one of the greatest objects of the Convention in our humble judgment because it is written: "A laborer is worthy of his hire," and a Baptist preacher who has devoted his entire life to the gospel of Jesus Christ and the saving of souls, when he is old and unable to work, he and his family should be provided for, and I believe that we cannot accept the judgment at the Bar of God if we fail to take care of these old Soldiers of the Cross. The State and Nation take care of their disabled soldiers, and it is not expecting too much of the church that she take care of her disabled ministers.

TEMPERANCE

The cause of temperance has been slowly but steadily advancing, thank God, and our people have lifted their eyes and looked afar and have caught a world vision. From a few consecrated "dry" men and women we have seen the cause of prohibition, steadily, though slowly, move on into communities, counties, States, the United States, and the three miles beyond her borders, and now by recent order no floating barrooms can land at an American port. When Europe gets sober, she will get rid of a great many of her troubles— including both military and financial. In our Association the law has been reasonably well enforced, also in the State, but until the law is amended so as to make the man who buys the liquor from the blockader or bootlegger guilty of aiding and abetting in the sale of liquor, the business will never be completely broken up. Again the State should provide for a Revenue Department and special revenue officers, similar to the U. S. Revenue Department, whose business it should be to see to the enforcement of the prohibition laws. This Association should go on record as to forming such a Department, and should present the matter to the State Convention for consideration.

The first and only Baptist hospital to be built in North Carolina is now under construction at Winston-Salem. This was made possible through the 75 Million Campaign. And we believe the location to be a wise choice, and we believe many others may be developed later. The people of Winston-Salem raised in one day $140,000.00, to be paid in eighteen months from October, 1920. Thirty-two thousand dollars of this amount was to go for the site of about ten acres on Ardmore Hill.

The State and Southern Baptist Convention added to the Hospital Commission four local members consisting of Gilbert T. Stephenson, A. H. Eller. B. F. Huntley and J. Wilbur Aews. Building was commenced in November, 1920, and it is believed that by the time the State Convention meets in December the first unit of 88 beds—a fire-proof, five-story structure will be completed.

In concluding their report at the State Convention last year the Commission stated: "The whole meaning of this movement is to bring the healing art more definitely under the domination of the Great Healer. We have doctors who feel called to serve Him by their ministry in China. Why may we not through the Christian Hospital, call out the called among the doctors, who with the same spirit will do the same service in North Carolina, what their brethren are doing in the far country."

Respectfully submitted,

F. H. Brooks, *Committee.*

Upon motion to adopt Judge F. H. Brooks, R. M. Von Miller, R. L. Gay, M. P. Davis, J. P. Underwood and J. M. Hilliard spoke to the report. The report was adopted. The next item on the program was Christian Education, Colleges and Preparatory Schools, periodicals, books and tracts. The Moderator recognized Brother A. A. Butler who presented a

REPORT ON CHRISTIAN EDUCATION

North Carolina Baptists have been leaders in distinctively Christian education from the beginning, and are leaders now; and yet we have only made a beginning. Our faith, our numbers, our position in the Kingdom, our material and spiritual equipment, and the unspeakable need, all call for larger things than we have ever yet attempted.

We now own and maintain three colleges—Wake Forest for men, and Meredith and Chowan for women. There were enrolled in these three institutions last year 1,002 students. Together their plants, equipment, and endowment amount to $1,888,603.31. We also own and operate five academies: Boiling Springs, Buies Creek, Dell, Liberty-Piedmont and Wingate. These enrolled last year 1,523 students, and own property worth $316,000.00. The Home Mission Board controls and supports in North Carolina nine mountain schools which enrolled last year 1,900 students, and own property valued at $554,000.00.

In addition to the above, we have in North Carolina one Baptist College for women at Oxford, privately owned, and two privately owned Baptist academies—Pineland for girls, and Mountain Park for boys and girls.

We join with Baptists of the other Southern states in supporting the Southern Baptist Theological Seminary at Louisville, Ky., with 339 students enrolled last session, and owns property valued at $2,130,000.00. This institution has a woman's training school attached, with 166 students enrolled last session. We join also with them in supporting the Southwestern Baptist Theological Seminary at Fort Worth, Texas, with an enrollment of 691 students, men and women, and property valued at $1,454,700.00; also a Bible Institute in New Orleans, La., enrolling 329 students, with property valued at $300,000.00.

We had about 85 ministerial students at Wake Forest last session, and about 35 at Louisville, also four young women preparing for the foreign field at Meredith. Our high schools reported over 100 ministerial students and student volunteers last year. Our State' law now requires everybody to go to school. This means that the churches of the next, and future generations will be composed of educated people, and this amounts to an imperative demand for educated pastors and leaders. An educated people will not long be content with uneducated pastors and church officers. It is a fact that the Lord has nothing but men and women as material out of which to make trustees, presidents, and headmasters of our educational institutions, and so long as this is so, mistakes are going to be made sometimes as to policies and management, but the institutions are still ours, and we can either correct the mistake or remove the management. Let us remember that when our state institutions teach and practice the same things to which we object in our Baptist schools, we are without power to correct or improve them. A failure to properly maintain our own institutions means that we must send our sons and daughters to schools over which we have no control.

Nothing is more certain now than this: Every educational institution in all this land, belonging to Baptists, if it is not already Christian and Baptist in every fibre of its being, is going to be made so, and that the Lord and the Baptists working together, can be trusted to bring it to pass in His own time and way.' Of the hundreds and thousands of young men and women who have gone out from our own Baptist institutions none have been swept away into false doctrines or rationalism, except a limited few who have taken further training in some northern institutions. "By their fruits ye shall know them," applies here as elsewhere. Institutions bringing forth such fruits cannot be vitally bad. For men do not gather grapes of thorns, nor figs of thistles.

A. A. BUTLER,
For Committee.

On motion to adopt, Brethren A. A. Butler, R. M. Von Miller and M. P. Davis spoke to the report, the report was adopted. No further business, the session adjourned until 7:30 p. m., with prayer by Brother J. M. Hilliard.

WEDNESDAY EVENING

Brother L. R. Tate conducted the devotional exercises. The Moderator then called the body to order. The discussion of the Finance report carried over from the morning was continued, Brethren R. L. Gay, M. P. Davis and R. M. Von Miller spoke on the report, the report was adopted. After singing "Can We Say We Are Ready," Dr. E. B. Dillard was recognized, who spoke interestingly on the Thomasville Orphanage.

The rest of the evening was devoted as a memorial service in memory of the late Brother J. M. Beaty. Suitable resolutions are to be written and printed later in the minutes by Judge F. H. Brooks. After the singing of a duet by Mrs. J. H. Grice and the pastor, N. H. Shepherd, the following brethren spoke very feelingly of their reminiscence in relation to the late Brother J. M. Beaty, and paid a high tribute to the memory of this saintly brother; R. M. Von Miller, W. B. Joyner, J. A. Smith, J. F. Pool, M. P. Davis, N. H. Shepherd and Mrs. B. A. Hocutt. After which the body adjourned until Thursday morning with prayer by R. L. Gay.

THURSDAY MORNING

Brother M. P. Davis conducted devotional exercises, after which the Moderator called the body to order. The Clerk read the journal, which was approved as read.

On account of the death of Brother J. M. Beaty, who served as Chairman of the Executive Committee, Brother J. F. Pool presented a brief

REPORT OF THE EXECUTIVE COMMITTEE

We, your committee, wish to report that the following brethren served as missionary pastors in the following fields and received aid from the Board of Missions. Brother N. H. Shepherd served Bethel, Princeton, Bailey and Kenly churches. He reports forty-five baptisms. Benson Grove, Pinkney, Beaty's Chapel, Hepzibah, Live Oak and Olivers Grove were served by Brother E. B. Booker, who reports nine baptisms. Hales Chapel was served by Brother C. H. Cashwell who reports twelve for baptism. Brother A. N. Corpening served at Parrish Memorial. Brother M. P. Davis served at Blackman's Grove, Burnell and Pleasant Grove, reporting eight for baptism. Brother L. R. Tate served Pauline, Hood's Grove, Canaan, 'Calvary and Trinity, reporting fifty-three for baptism. In view of the death of our beloved Brother J. M. Beaty, who was chairman of this Executive Committee we regret that no detail report can be furnished, but sincerely urge upon the churches to continue to support the parsonage fund.

Respectfully submitted,

J. F. POOL,
For Committee.

On motion to adopt, the missionary pastors gave a very encouraging report of their respective fields, the report was adopted after which Brother A. C. Hamby led in prayer for these brethren and the churches they serve. The Moderator then recognized Brother A. O. Moore who presented the

REPORT ON MISSIONS

In a report that is to cover our entire mission activities it will be necessary to give only the outstanding achievements.

FOREIGN MISSIONS

The past year has been a trying and difficult one on the Foreign Mission Board, due to the financial condition that prevailed throughout the South, which reduces the amounts given on our pledges.

Some of the work that was begun had to be`suspended temporarily, such as enlargements of schools, hospitals, compounds and dispensaries. But in spite of this temporary entrenchment, our work on the mission field has been marked by a marvelous growth. For the 'first time in history of our denomination, our mission fields have girdled the globe. At last we have entered the European field, Spain, Jugo-Slavia, Hungary, Roumania, Italy, Russia, Syria, Palestine and Siberia. We have the most extended territory ever occupied by any denomination, and it embraces a population numbering nine hundred million, or more than half of the world's inhabitants.

The only solution to the vexing question of Europe is the gospel. The only power that will tame the unspeakable Turk is Christ, and those open doors we have entered must not be abandoned. The world stands at the cross-roads of its destiny and our Foreign Mission program will be the deciding factor in the way which it takes.

HOME MISSIONS

Home Missions has experienced an unprecedented growth. Never has its departments been more ably manned than at present. The department of evangelism has been most efficient. These men of God have gone up and down the Southland calling the masses to repentance as did John of old, and the answer has been multitudes that have come confessing their sins and accepting Christ as their Saviour and asking for baptism, more than a quarter of a million have been baptized in the past year.

There has been organized 2,276 new Sunday-schools, 759 new churches, 1,409 houses of worship built or repaired, 9,523 volunteers for definite Christian work.

The untarnished ideals that have been preserved throughout the South is due largely to the fires of the gospel kindled by the Home Mission Board, and today the world is looking to us for a gospel that has not changed or lost its positive note, but rings as true as it did on the day of Pentecost.

STATE MISSIONS

While the State Mission Board has been somewhat cramped due to the falling off of our Campaign funds, and this time faces a debt, unless our people pay up their pledges in full by November 30th, which I am hoping we will do, for it has been the history of North Carolina Baptists to stand squarely behind the State Mission work. Let us see that our State Mission Secretaries hands are not tied because we have not discharged our solemn obligation to God.

The Mission Board has kept on the field about 210 missionary pastors, and these men have served 350 churches. The Board has paid on their salaries sums ranging from $5.00 to $175.00 per month.

The monthly pay roll amounts to about $5,500.00. The Board has placed strong men at every educational center in the State, that the gospel might be brought to bear upon the lives of youth in this formative period.

The growth of the Sunday-school department has been wonderful under the leadership of Secretary E. L. Middleton who has been aided by the field secretaries, one in the east and the other in the western part of the State. We have 2,225 Sunday-schools and the past year has witnessed better organizations in these schools which has produced more efficient work in Kingdom building.

The B. Y. P. U. will close the greatest year in its history. We have over 800 unions in the State and they are being organized every day. This department is training the young generation for efficient church service.

The enlistment department has had a staggering task assigned to it, but Brother A. C. Hamby with five assistants is laying a foundation upon which North Carolina Baptists can build in the coming years.

The department is helping in the problem of enlisting 1,800 country churches and helping them to a worthy pastoral support and an adequate benevolent program.

The department of evangelism with a superintendent and three evangelists have had a wonderful year of ingathering and has been almost self-supporting.

The church at the University of North Carolina is well on the way toward completion and Pullen Memorial at the State College has finished its Sunday-school unit. These splendid structures will count tremendously for Baptist influence throughout the State.

The Book Department is filling a long felt need, and the profit that comes from the sale of books goes back into the Mission treasury. Buy your books from them because you are helping our State work as well as getting full value for every dollar you spend.

ASSOCIATIONAL MISSIONS

It is the opinion of your committee that our Associational work is in a desperate plight. In fact, the most disorganized it has been in years. So many of our fields have suffered loss due to pastors moving away, and then the neccessity caused by delay that follows getting another man to fill the vacancy. The oldest man in the Association has been in the Association less than four years. During that time he has seen every church change pastors at least once, and some three or four times. It is impossible to do permanent work with such kaleidoscopic changes. We have suffered a tremendous loss due to the inactive condition of our Executive Committee. The long continued illness of the Chairman, J. M. Beaty, was largely responsible for this. In his death the Association has sustained a loss that will be felt for years to come. He did more for the cause than any man that lived in the Association, and if Baptist history is ever written from an Associational standpoint the story will be largely that of the life of this good man.

What we need most is an Executive Committee that will be sure to function, having supervision of all the Associational work. We have turned over our funds of the Association to the State Treasurer for disbursement, but it is the opinion of your committee that the Executive Committee should look after all the missionary pastors and that they should be employed by this committee and not by the State Board. We believe further that we would be able to keep pastors on the field longer, if each field had a parsonage. Let us push our building fund and see that a home is built for every country pastor in the Association.

Your committee especially recommends that we as an Association see to it that every dollar of our Campaign pledges is paid. Only by doing this will we be worthy of our past history and able to grasp the golden opportunities that are presented to us in this crucial hour to preach the gospel of Christ to all the world.

Respectfully submitted,

A. O. Moore,
Committee.

The Moderator recognized Mrs. C. W. Carter, who presented the

REPORT ON WOMAN'S WORK

There are 46 churches in the Association, and 40 Societies to whom quarterly letters are sent.   Sixteen W. M. S.'s; 5 Y. W. A.'s; 4 G. A.'s; 2 R. A.'s; and 15 Sunbeams. Twenty-eight sent annual reports. Nine more than last year. Two new societies were organized at Wilson's Mills, White Oak, Selma (2), and Benson. Two societies were reorganized. Number of churches without missionary societies, 29. Number of Female members in the churches of our Association, 2,952. Number of members of societies reported in 28 reports, 707. The Superintendent reports 61 Home and Foreign Fields taken. Sixty-six Royal Services taken. One hundred ninety-four Biblical Recorders. There are 36 tithers. Seventeen mission study classes. Superintendent wrote 182 postals and 472 letters. Traveled 132 miles, visited 10 societies. Amount raised by these societies this year, $5,215.60.

Respectfully submitted,

Mrs. C. W. Carter,
Committee.

On motion to adopt these reports on Missions, the following addresses were made by: Brother R. L. Gay on Foreign Missions; Brother M. P. Davis on Home Missions; Brother

A. C. Hamby on the 75 Million Campaign; and Mrs. C. W. Carter on Woman's Work. The reports were adopted. After singing "More Love to Thee," Brother F. T. Collins preached the Missionary sermon, taking for his text: Matt. 28: 18-20, and Acts 1: 8. At the conclusion of the sermon Brother A. C. Hamby led in prayer.

Under miscellaneous business the Moderator announced the following committee to nominate the Executive Committee: R. M. Von Miller, Chairman; N. H. Shepherd and E. B. Booker, after which the body adjourned for recess and dinner, with prayer by Brother J. W. Nobles.

Thursday Afternoon

Brother N. H. Shepherd conducted the devotional exercises.

The Moderator called the meeting to order and called on Brother J. M. Hilliard to lead in prayer.

Under miscellaneous business, the committee on nominating Executive Committee made the following report which was adopted:

We, your committee, nominate the following delegates to serve as the Executive Committee for the ensuing Associational year:

A. O. Moore, Chairman; M. P. Davis; F. H. Brooks; J. J. Lane; H. E. Earp.

Respectfully submitted,

R. M. Von Miller, *Chairman.*

N. H. Shepherd,

E. B. Booker,

Committee.

The committee on nominating delegates to Southern Baptist Convention and State Convention made the following report which was adopted:

We, your committee, nominate Brother R. M. Von Miller to represent this Association at the Southern Baptist Convention, and F. H. Brooks, J. F. Pool and Mrs. C. M. Thomas as delegates to the State Convention.

J. A. Smith,

For the Committee:

Brother A. C. Hamby stated that he would appreciate it
if this Association would appoint a standing Committee on
Enlistment and Stewardship. Upon motion by Brother R. M.
Von Miller, the Moderator was asked to appoint a Committee
to select such a committee and report before the close of the
session of this Association. The Moderator appointed
Brethren M. P. Davis, J. F. Pool and A. A. Butler.

Brother R. M. Von Miller presented the following resolution which was adopted by a rising vote:

"Whereas, the delegates of this Association have enjoyed such
bountiful hospitality, accorded to them by the Noble's Chapel Baptist
Church, *therefore be it resolved,* that we express our sincerest appreciation, to the pastor, the church and community, for the kind
hospitality, bountiful refreshments served on the church grounds,
and every other kindness extended by them to this body."

R. M. VON MILLER,
Committee.

The Moderator then recognized Brother R. L. Gay, who
presented the

REPORT ON SUNDAY SCHOOLS AND B. Y. P. U. WORK

In the report of the Sunday School Secretary, made to the last
meeting of the State Convention, we find this statement: "In the
State Convention Annual of 1895 we find a Sunday-school statistical
table showing 848 Sunday schools, with a membership of 58,954."
The table for the last Convention year shows 2,154 Sunday schools,
with an enrollment of 247,699 members—a gain in twenty-six years
of 1,306 schools and 188,745 members. Far greater, however, has been
the progress in the facilities for better Sunday schools. Our splendid
leadership, literature, and other equipment give promise of far
greater progress in the future than we have ever known. Our periodicals are the best, while our other publications for teacher-training,
together with teacher-training classes, Sunday-school institutes, etc.,
furnish the finest equipment for the production of our greatest need—
trained teachers. In these publications we have also suggestions for
Sunday-school rooms, classrooms, etc. Still, with all the progress
that has been made, we have only fairly begun the great task of
winning and training the multitudes. The North Carolina Sunday
School Association publishes the following figures for this State:
White population (1920 census), 1,783,779; Sunday-school enrollment, 617,502 (34¾ per cent); not enrolled in Sunday school,
1,166,277, or 65⅔ per cent. We have 313,594 church members in

North Carolina Baptist churches, while we have only 247,699 in Sunday school; so that, if all the members of the Sunday schools were members of the churches, we would have 65,896 church members who are not in the Sunday schools. Of course, a large number of the Sunday-school members are not church members; so that, the number of church members who take no part in Sunday-school work is appalling. In the territory embraced in the Johnston County Association—due largely to certain teachings which have for many years influenced people—the number of unsaved people is distressingly large. The principal, if not the only means by which this condition can be remedied is through the young people, and the young people must be won mainly through the Sunday school. If we win the young people, we must have better-equipped schoolrooms and better-trained teachers. There should be evergreen training classes in all our churches, and the churches should prepare comfortable rooms, suitable for the classes.

B. Y. P. U. WORK

The B. Y. P. U. work is a tardy recognition, on the part of some of our churches, of the need of training our young people for service. The old plan—the one still followed by a great number of our churches—was to win the young people to Christ, receive them into the churches, baptize them, and then leave them to their own resources. Some of the young people, through the encouragement of certain individuals, developed into useful members. Some few, through their own initiative, struggled into church activity; but the majority drifted into nominal church members — useless to the church, to the community, and to God. To enlist and to train these young people for service to their churches and for the Kingdom is the task of the B. Y. P. U. Their Bible study courses, their Christian culture courses, their social service work, and their insistence upon church attendance and their encouragement of personal piety entitle them to be classed as the churches' best agency for developing the young Christians who have been won for Christ through the Sunday school and other agencies. The success of some of the B. Y. P. U.'s prove that they can be maintained in the country churches, where they are, perhaps, even more needed than in the towns. At the time of the last State Convention there were in the State 505 Senior and 106 Junior unions, making a total of 611— an increase over the previous year's report of 161, or a fraction over 35 per cent. At present there are 982 organizations.

May we soon have a live B. Y. P. U. and a wide-awake Sunday school in every church in the Johnston County Baptist Association.

Respectfully submitted,

R. L. GAY, *Committee.*

On motion to adopt, Bro. R. L. Gay spoke to the report. The report was adopted.

The Committee on Place and Preacher made the following report, which was adopted:

We, your committee, recommend Bethany Baptist Church for the place of our next meeting, and Bro. M. P. Davis to preach the introductory sermon, and Bro. A. A. Butler the missionary sermon.

J. P. UNDERWOOD,
R. R. CREECH,
W. B. JOYNER,
Committee.

The Committee on Nominating a Standing Committee on Enlistment and Stewardship made the following report, which was adopted:

We, your committee, nominate the following delegates to serve as a Standing Committee on Enlistment and Stewardship: A. A. Butler, for pastors; T. S. Ragsdale, for Sunday schools; William Woodall, for B. Y. P. U.; Mrs. J. J. Lane, for W. M. S.; and C. W. Carter, for laymen. M. P. DAVIS, *For Committee.*

Bro. J. A. Smith presented the following financial report:

TREASURER'S REPORT

1921   ASSOCIATIONAL MISSIONS

Nov.	1.	Received from Building Fund	$ 33.13	
		Balance due from Building Fund	165.97	
		Disbursements:		
Nov.	28.	For expense to R. L. Gay, J. A. Smith	2.50	
Dec.	29.	Loaned to Building Fund	$ 165.97	
			$ 168.47	$ 199.10
		Balance in treasury		30.63

BUILDING FUND

Received from the churches...................................... $ 443.33

Disbursements:

1921			
Nov.	1.	To First National Bank	$ 400.00	
	15.	To J. A. Smith, due from 1920	10.20	
Dec.	21.	To Associational Missions	33.13	
		Total	$ 443.33	$ 443.33
		Balance due Associational Missions		165.97

Received from churches..	$ 184.30
By special collection at Association.........................	8.83

Disbursements:

1921

Nov.	7.	To R. M. Von Miller, salary.........................$	60.00
	15.	To J. A. Smith, due from 1920......................	17.11
Dec.	9.	To R. M. Von Miller, for printing of minutes, and postage.................................	124.00

Total..$	201.11	$ 193.13
Balance due Treasurer J. A. Smith.........................		7.98

Respectfully submitted,

J. A. SMITH, *Treasurer.*

I have examined the Treasurer's books and found them correct.
This October 26, 1922. N. L. STOTT, *Auditor.*

A motion by Bro. M. P. Davis, in connection with the report before the body, was that the balance of Mission Funds be turned over to the Building Fund. This motion was carried. The report of the Treasurer was adopted.

On motion, which was carried, the Clerk was instructed to write to the churches that have not yet contributed to the Minute Fund.

There being no other business before the body, the meeting of the twentieth session of the Johnston County Baptist Association adjourned, with prayer by Bro. A. O. Moore, to meet in 1923 with Bethany Baptist Church, Wednesday after the fourth Sunday.

R. H. GOWER, *Moderator.*

R. M. VON MILLER, *Clerk.*

· Woman's Missionary Union

The Woman's Missionary Union of the Johnston County Baptist Association held its annual session with the W. M. S. of the Baptist Church at Smithfield, N. C., October 12-13, 1922.

THURSDAY NIGHT, OCTOBER 12TH

The session opened by singing a hymn, and special music by the Smithfield choir. Devotional by Rev. D. H. Tuttle, of the M. E. Church. Violin solo by Miss Winona Pool, of Clayton, with Mrs. Charles Gulley at the piano, and vocal solo by Miss Bessie Lee Pool, also of Clayton.

The speaker for the evening, Rev. John Arch McMillan, Alumni Secretary of Wake Forest College, was introduced by Rev. A. O. Moore, pastor of the Clayton Baptist Church. Brother McMillan made a wonderful and most helpful talk, using as his subject "Opportunity." After the sermon, the congregation sang "How Firm a Foundation." Then the Woman's Missionary Processional, which was very impressive, each officer of the Union telling of her particular work.

After announcements and benedictions, we adjourned to meet Friday morning, the 13th.

FRIDAY MORNING, OCTOBER 13TH

The morning session opened with twenty-five societies represented, eleven churches, eighty-six delegates, and fifteen visitors.

In the absence of Mrs. Henry Johnson, Mrs. Paul Brown led the devotional, using for her subject "Faith." Song, "By the Touch of His Hand on Mine," and prayer by Mrs. C. W. Carter. Warm words of welcome from W. M. S. of the Smithfield Baptist Church by Mrs. W. N. Holt; Presbyterian W. M. S., by Mrs. F. H. Brooks; Episcopal W. M. S., by Mrs. F. H. Skinner; Methodist W. M. S., by Mrs. J. J. Broadhurst; and response by Mrs. J. Dwight Barbour, of Clayton.

Recognition of visitors: Miss Pearl Johnson, missionary from Shanghai, China; Miss Mary Cox, of the Wilmington Division of the Eastern Association, were recognized. We also enjoyed a few words from a former Superintendent, Mrs. Carey J. Hunter, of Raleigh.

The minutes of the last meeting were read and approved.

The reports of the societies were very encouraging, and Mrs. Hocutt's report showed a broadening of the work in the county. The amount contributed this year was $5,215.60.

The following ladies made interesting talks on the following subjects: Mrs. E. V. Woodard, Foreign Missions; Mrs. E. R. Youngblood, Home Missions; Mrs. A. O. Moore, Education; Mrs. R. B. Brady, State Missions; Mrs. D. B. Oliver, Social Service; and Standard of Excellence, Miss Mary Cox.

Special music, arranged by Mrs. C. M. Thomas, of the choir of the Clayton Baptist Church.

Mrs. W. N. Jones, of Raleigh, made a most impressive talk on the great work the women are doing, and the reinforcement of the 75 Million Campaign.

Committees were appointed, as follows:

Committee on Time and Place—Mrs. M. A. Peacock, Mrs. H. V. Woodard, Mrs. J. J. Williams.

Nominating Committee—Mrs. N. B. Lewis, Miss Hazel Finch.

Committee on Obituaries—Mrs. J. W. Massey.

Resolutions — Mrs. Swade Barbour, Mrs. George Vick, Miss Veola Pool.

To make a report on Woman's Work at the 1923 Association—Mrs. Howard Gray.

Closing devotional by Mrs. N. B. Lewis, using as subject "Loyalty," reading 2 Tim. 3:14.

The session then adjourned for dinner, which was served in the church, in cafeteria style.

Friday Afternoon

The session opened with singing "O Zion, Haste," and with prayer by Mrs. W. N. Jones. Words of welcome by Miss Bridgette Williams, of Smithfield.

The afternoon session was for the young people, and Mrs. Howard Gray, Junior Superintendent, presided over the meeting. Mrs. Lois Massey Bass gave a beautiful response to Miss Williams warm words of welcome.

The report of Mrs. Gray on the work of the young people in the Association, the needs and how we may meet them, showed a great work she has done.

Miss May Cox, always interesting—her heart is full with interest in the work of the Y. W. A. and the G. A.—spoke very helpfully.

Song by Smithfield Sunbeams, and as we all love the children, we always love to hear them sing. We missed Miss Briggs so much.

The Training School, always interesting, was made more so by a splendid talk by Mrs. Fred Collins, of Smithfield.

We are also interested in our missionaries, but to see them face to face, and have them tell of their work, is an inspiration to all. Miss Pearl Johnson, of Shanghai, China, told of the work being done and the great needs, too, of the missionary work in China.

Song, "I Am Listening," by Mesdames Moore, Carter, Thomas, Bass, and Smith, with Mrs. John Talton at the piano.

The Mission Study demonstration by the Smithfield young people showed the importance of the study of the different books.

There were many who had seals and certificates.

The Time and Place Committee reported an invitation from both Pine Level and Benson. It was decided to meet with the Benson W. M. S. in October, 1923.

The Nominating Committee recommended the re-election of all the officers.

Mrs. Howard Gray offered her resignation, but was asked to reconsider and keep the work.

A rising vote of thanks was given to the *Smithfield Observer, Smithfield Herald,* and *The Clayton News* for advertising the program, etc.

Mrs. A. O. Moore, as President for the Clayton W. M. S., pledged $50 of the $200 it takes to furnish one room at the Baptist Hospital at Winston-Salem, N. C.

Here we paused in memory of those who had passed away since our last meeting—only one, Mrs. C. A. Jenkins, of Clayton. Mrs. Jenkins was one who loved the work, always ready to help in any way.

We cannot forget our good friend, Mr. J. M. Beaty, who died just the week before. His good work will linger with us.

After a most beneficial meeting, we adjourned to meet with Benson W. M. S., October, 1923.

Mrs. B. A. Hocutt, *Superintendent.*

Cleve Barnes, *Secretary.*

APPORTIONMENT FOR ASSOCIATIONAL, BUILDING, AND MINUTE FUND

Name of Churches	Bldg. Fund	Minute Fund
Antioch	$ 15.00	$5.00
Bailey	15.00	5.00
Baptist Center	10.00	5.00
Beaty's Chapel	5.00	2.50
Benson	50.00	10.00
Benson Grove	5.00	2.50
Blackman's Grove	25.00	7.50
Bethel	5.00	2.50
Bethesda	25.00	7.50
Burnell	5.00	2.50
Calvary	10.00	5.00
Canaan	5.00	2.50
Carter's Chapel	25.00	7.50
Clayton	100.00	15.00
Clyde's Chapel	25.00	7.50
Corinth	25.00	7.50
Four Oaks	25.00	7.50
Hale's Chapel	10.00	5.00
Hepzipah	10.00	5.00
Hood's Grove	15.00	5.00
Kenly	15.00	5.00
Lee's Chapel	25.00	10.00
Live Oak	5.00	2.50
Micro	10.00	2.50
Middlesex	10.00	5.00
Mount Moriah	150.00	15.00
New Bethel	50.00	10.00
Noble's Chapel	25.00	7.50
Parrish Memorial	20.00	5.00
Pauline	10.00	2.50
Pine Level	50.00	10.00
Pinkney	5.00	2.50
Pisgah	25.00	7.50
Pleasant Grove	5.00	2.50
Princeton	25.00	5.00
Sardis	25.00	5.00
Selma	50.00	10.00
Shiloh	10.00	5.00
Smithfield	50.00	15.00
Thanksgiving	15.00	5.00
Trinity	10.00	5.00
White Oak	25.00	7.50
Wilson's Mills	15.00	5.00
Total	$1,045.00	$ 257.50

STATISTICAL TABLES

Churches	When Constituted	Pastors and Postoffices	Clerks and Postoffices	Regular Days
		CHURCH DIRECTORY		
Antioch	1859	R. M. Von Miller, Wilson	W. O. Hocutt, Middlesex, R. 3	2
Bailey		N. H. Shepherd. Kenly	J. P. Underwood, Bailey	1
Baptist Center	1871	R. L. Gay, Smithfield	Milton Austin, Clayton	3
Beaty's Chapel	1910	E. B. Booker, Smithfield	Mrs. J. J. Parish, Smithfield	2 & 4
Benson			Julian Godwin, Benson	2 & 4
Bethany		W. D. Stancil, Kenly	C. S. Creech, Kenly	4
Benson Grove	1906	E. B. Booker, Smithfield	L. E. Barbour, Benson, R. 1	2 & 4
Bethel		N. H. Shepherd, Kenly	Luther Stone, Kenly	4
Bethesda		R. L. Gay, Smithfield	E. Smith, Wilson's Mills	4
Blackman's Grove	1892	M. P. Davis, Four Oaks	J. R. Blackman, Four Oaks	2
Burnell	1921	M. P. Davis, Four Oaks	W. S. Massengill, Four Oaks	1 & 2
Calvary	1894	L. R. Tate, Benson	T. J. Lee, Dunn	1
Cannan		L. R. Tate, Benson		
Carter's Chapel		W. D. Stancil, Kenly	Zeb Eatman, Selma, R. 1	1
Clayton		A. O. Moore, Clayton	W. P. Creech, Clayton	F T
Clyde's Chapel		B. M. Shacklett, Angier	C. I. Johnson, Wendell, R. 1	1 & 3
Corinth	1874	C. H. Cashwell, Wendell	L. T. Davis, Wendell	4
Four Oaks	1892	M. P. Davis, Four Oaks	B. B. Creech, Four Oaks	1 & 3
Hale's Chapel	1918	C. H. Cashwell, Wendell	A. D. Parrish, Zebulon, R. 2	4
Hepzipah	1912	E. B. Booker, Smithfield	W. T. Creech, Princeton, R. 1	1
Hood's Grove	1903	L. R. Tate, Benson	Y. L. Blackman, Bentonsville	3
Kenly		N. H. Shepherd, Kenly	F. A. White, Kenly	2
Lee's Chapel	1847	J. E. Hocutt, Nashville	W. I. Greene, Zebulon, R. 2	3
Live Oak	1852	E. B. Booker, Smithfield	J. M. Richardson, Selma, R. 2	1 & 3
Micro	1904	W. D. Stancil, Kenly	S. C. Batten, Micro	2
Middlesex	1906	J. W. Nobles, Middlesex	J. C. Overman, Middlesex	4
Mount Moriah	1830	R. T. Vann, D.D., Raleigh	Russell Powell, Auburn	1
New Bethel	1834	S. A. Edgerton, Buies Creek	Geo. W. Bryan, Garner	4
Noble's Chapel	1900	N. H. Shepherd, Kenly	N. L. Stott, Sims	4
Oliver's Grove	1885	E. B. Booker, Smithfield	J. E. Ryals Four Oaks, R. 4	2 & 4
Parrish Memorial	1900	A. N. Corpening, Wake Forest	J. D. Creech, Selma, R. 2	1
Pauline	1904	L. R. Tate,,Benson	J. R. Massey, Four Oaks, R. 1	2
Pine Level		D. E. Vipperman, Pinetop	F. C. Price, Pine Level	1
Pinkney	1909	E. B. Booker, Smithfield	B. R. Edgerton, Kenly	3
Pisgah	1894	R. L. Gay, Smithfield	R. H. Higgins, Smithfield	1
Pleasant Grove	1920	M. P. Davis, Four Oaks	Claude Stephenson, Willow Springs	4
Princeton	1889	N. H. Shepherd, Kenly	W. I. Pearce, Princeton	3
Sardis	1880	A. A. Butler, Selma	T. G. Strickland, Smithfield	1 & 3
Selma		A. A. Butler, Selma	G. A. Earp, Selma	F T
Shiloh	1865	R. L. Gay, Smithfield	J. W. Williams, Garner	2
Smithfield		F. T. Collins, Smithfield	L. T Rovall, Smithfield	F T
Thanksgiving	1899	R. M. Von Miller, Wilson	Carl Whitley, Selma, R. 1	2
Trinity	1885	L. R. Tate, Benson	J. S. Lawhorn. Benson	4
White Oak	1875	A. O. Moore, Clayton	W. H. Green, Clayton, R. 2	2 & 4
Wilson's Mills			Ernest Price, Wilson's Mills	2
Totals				

					CHURCH MEMBERSHIP					CHURCH HOUSES AND PARSONAGES								
..INS			LOSSES															
	Statements	Restorations	Letters	Exclusions	Deaths	Total Present Members	Revival Meetings Held During Year	Observances of Lord's Supper During Year	Families Receiving State Baptist Paper	When Built	Materials Used	Persons Seated	Number of Rooms	Value of Church House and Grounds	Indebtedness on Property	Insurance Carried	Value of Pastor's Home	Total Value All Church Property
..	--	1	1	9	6	193	yes	4	1	1910	wood	400	3	$ 3000	$----	$----	$----	$ 3000
	--	--	--	--	--	86	yes	4	5	----	wood	300	1	4000				4000
1	--	--	4	--	--	144	yes	4	---	1919	wood	500	3	3000	800			3000
.	--	--	5	--	--	11	yes	4	---	1910	wood	300	1	1500				1500
9	--	--	7	--	--	173	yes	4	---	1916	brick	600	18	25000		10000		35000
4	--	--	--	2	1	143	yes	4	3	1921	wood	800	1	2500	300			2500
6	--	--	2	4	--	67	yes	4	2	1908	wood	350	1	1500				1500
	--	--	--	--	--	14	no	4	1	----	wood	200	1	1000				1000
1	--	--	6	7	2	213	yes	4	---	1914	wood	500	5	5000				5000
8	--	3	1	3	1	90	yes	4	12	1892	wood	300	1	1500				1500
.	--	--	2	--	--	20	yes	4	2	1911	wood	300	1	1200				1200
1	--	--	1	--	--	31	yes	4	---	1894	wood	200	1	2000	450			2000
..	--	--	2	13	1	94	yes	4	---	----	wood	400	1	1500				1500
8	--	--	8	--	3	567	yes	4	65	1920	brick	750	20	75000	25000	30000	10000	85000
2	1	11	14	53	--	187	yes	4	20	1888	wood	400	1	1000				1000
4	--	6	12	15	4	191	yes	4	6	1914	wood	300	2	4000				4000
3	1	1	6	--	--	113	yes	4	16	1918	brick	300	8	20000	2160	5000		20000
3	--	--	3	3	7	78	yes	4	1	1922	wood	350	5	2000	525			2000
	--	--	1	1	--	15	yes	1	2	1918	wood	200	1	1500	100			1500
4	--	--	3	1	1	68	yes	4	---	1904	wood	350	1	1000				1000
2	--	--	3	2	--	35	yes	4	---	----	wood	300	4	4000				4000
	--	2	4	--	1	270	yes	4	6	1882	wood	400	1	2250				2250
	--	--	--	--	--	6	yes	4	1	1892	wood	300	1	1500				1500
1	--	1	2	4	--	64	yes	4	1	1904	wood	500	5	2500	125			2500
6	--	--	1	--	1	100	yes	4	15	1906	wood	250	3	5000		1000	2500	7500
3	--	--	2	1	1	199	yes	4	12	1913	wood	500	5	4200		2000		4200
3	--	--	2	--	1	135	yes	4	20	1834	wood	400	1	5000				5000
	--	--	--	1	2	111	yes	4	5	1901	wood	300	1	1000	50			1000
	--	--	--	--	1	15	yes	4	---	1885	wood	300	1	1000				1000
	--	1	--	9	--	73	yes	4	1	1900	wood	250	1	. 2550				2550
	1	--	1	--	--	65	yes	4	---	1905	wood	200	1	2000				2000
1	--	--	1	2	--	76	yes	4	4	1911	wood	350	4	5000				5000
2	--	--	2	1	1	22	yes	4	2	1912	wood	300	1	1500				1500
1	--	--	6	3	--	71	yes	4	6	1895	wood	200	1	2500			4000	6500
	--	--	--	--	--	10	yes	4	---	----	wood	300	1	500				500
2	1	--	--	--	--	72	yes	4	---	1892	wood	300	1	2000				2000
	--	--	1	1	2	81	yes	4	---	1912	wood	200	1	2500				2500
6	--	--	18	2	1	322	yes	12	---	1907	brick	500	7	25000				25000
	--	--	5	--	1	74	yes	4	---	1921	wood	500	1	3000	450			3000
4	--	--	4	--	1	318	yes	4	---	----	wood	500	11	20000		5000	8000	28000
1	--	--	5	2	1	1?6	yes	4	2	1900	wood	300	1	2750				2750
3	--	--	2	1	1	119	yes	4	2	1916	wood	250	3	3000	125		300	3300
1	--	2	7	--	--	231	yes	4	50	1910	wood	300	2	4000				4000
	--	--	--	--	--	88	yes	4	3	----	wood	300	4	1500				1500
0	4	27	144	140	41	5131	---	---	266	----	----	----	--	243450	30185	53000	24800	

TABLE No. 2—FINANCIAL

CHURCHES	REGULAR TREASURERS AND POSTOFFICES	Pastor's Salary	Other Salaries	Incidentals	Building and Repairs	Ministerial Help	Help for Local Poor	Literature for Sunday School, B.Y.P.U.	Printing and Publicity	Other Objects	Total Local Church Contributions
Antioch	A. D. O'Neal, Middlesex, R. 3	$330 53			3 00	50 00		26 39	5 00	49 50	$414 92
Bailey	J. W. B. Finch, Bailey	300 00	30 00					42 00			421 50
Baptist Center	Milton Austin, Clayton	300 00				30 00		35 50			365 50
Beaty's Chapel	Mrs. J. J. Parrish, Smithfield	16 87				6 06		17 43			40 36
Benson	Mrs. H. O. Dixon, Benson	175 00	120 00	109 70	8 50	215 00		84 95	18 00		731 15
Benson Grove	L. E. Barbour, Benson	97 93			7 50	16 25		12 00			133 68
Bethany	C. S. Creech, Kenly	85 21			1200 00		10 00	49 00	5 00	4 07	1353 28
Bethel	Luther Stone, Kenly, R. F. D.	50 00			7 50			8 00			65 50
Bethesda	L. B. Smith, Wilson's Mills	400 00	30 00	43 80		35 00		27 00		6 00	541 80
Blackman's Grove	Nogah Wood, Four Oaks	300 00			60 50	32 80	15 00	25 13			433 43
Burnell	J. S. Johnson, Four Oaks, No. 4	100 00		16 00		14 80		20 00	13 00		163 80
Carter's Chapel	T. J. Lee, Dunn, R. 2	150 00						15 00			170 00
Clayton	Y. M. Eatman, Selma, R. 1	100 00		16 50				14 00	1 50		132 00
Clyde's Chapel	D. M. Hall, R. 1	3000 00		1212 80	1500 00	231 22		520 00		1902 18	8366 20
Corinth	E. T. Davis, Wendell, R. 1	400 00	86 09	1 00				25 00	3 75		514 84
Four Oaks	D. H. Sanders, Four Oaks	250 15	5 00		10 10	61 61	19 41	30 28	3 00	5 00	385 55
Hale's Chapel	J. H. Parrish, Zebulon, R. 2	1000 00		72 50	862 15	59 00		116 13	8 00	16 30	2134 08
Hepzibah	W. G. Creech, Princeton, R. 1	150 00		1 50		27 30		20 00	4 00	5 00	206 30
Hood's Grove	R. Hayes, Four Oaks	25 00				12 00		12 00			50 50
Kenly	A. J. Broughton, Kenly	100 00				25 50					125 50
Lee's Chapel	L. M. Price, Zebulon, R. 1	225 00	62 00	38 40	66 45		10 00	50 00	5 00	15 00	399 95
Live Oak	J. M. Richardson, Selma, R. 2	300 00		25 00	75 00		20 00	25 00		100 00	597 00
Micro	S. C. Batten, Selma, R. 2	9 69				5 20		10 00			24 89
Middlesex	E. H. ___, Middlesex	104 65		6 25		100 00	20 00	54 55	20 00	52 40	256 60
Mount Moriah	E. S. Poole, Clayton, R. 3	375 00	30 00	221 41		75 00	10 00	25 00		54 25	536 25

Church	Pastor									Total
Mw Bethel	Geo. W. Bryan, Garner	300 00	10 00	5 00	15 00	45 00		40 55	18 45	425 00	859 00
Noble's Chapel	N. L. Stt, Sis	300 00		10 00				38 21			348 21
Oliver's Grove	J. E. Ryals, Four Oaks, R. 4	23 68				6 50		5 00			35 18
Pauline	J. R. ...y, Four Oaks	34 95			84 00			19 64			138 59
Parrish Memorial	J. G. Creech, Selma, R. 2	150 00		20 00				20 00		10 50	200 50
Pine Level	N. M. Gurley, Pine Level	350 00	18 00	30 00		65 00	10 00	45 00	18 00	15 00	568 00
Pinkney	M. B. R. Edgerton, Kenly, R. 1	109 25		3 60				15 19		30 00	261 04
Pipah	W. D. ...n, Smithfield	500 00	12 00	3 75		52 85	19 24	48 00			664 09
Pleasant Grove	Claude Stephenson, Mw Springs	54 00		3 75							57 75
Princeton	Chas. H. Holt, Princeton	161 47		12 00		74 50		30 00			277 97
Sardis	J. R. Oliver, Smithfield, R. 2	250 00						27 51		5 00	282 51
Selma	E. V. Woodard, Selma	2100 00	120 00	50 00	431 90			150 00		35 00	2886 90
Shiloh	J. W. Williams, Garner	250 00			15 30	60 00	31 71	18 00			359 71
Smithfield	F. H. Brooks, Smithfield	2400 00		36 90		325 00		350 00	63 86	96 00	3287 06
Thanksgiving	Carl Mey, Selma	224 82		2 00		18 40		22 42	5 00	15 00	287 64
Trinity	H. C. Lee, Benson	150 00				28 00		20 00			198 00
White Oak	W. H. Greene, Dayton, R. 2	420 00				113 16		40 00			573 16
Wilson's Mills	J. I. Adams, Wilson's Mills	300 00						30 00			330 00
Totals		14523 10	523 09	1970 11	4416 90	1785 15	145 36	2183 88	191 56	2897 20	30840 55

TABLE No. 2—FINANCIAL—Continued

Churches	Special Campaign or Benevolence Treasurers and Postoffices	Regular 75-Million Campaign Funds (Undesignated)	Foreign (D) Missions	Home (D) Missions	State (D) Missions	Associational (D) Missions	Schools and Colleges (D)	Ministerial (D) Education	Orphanage (D)	Hospitals (D)	Ministerial (D) Relief	Foreign (D) Relief	Total 75-Million Campaign Funds	Other Benevolences	Total of all Denominational Contributions
Antioch	A. D. O'Neal, Mex, R. 3	108 50			7 75								116 25	15 00	131 25
Bailey	J. W. B. Finch, Bailey	70 50			1 51				11 13			4 28	87 42		87 42
Baptist Center	Milton Austin, Clayton	44 85							8 43				53 28		53 28
Beaty's	Mrs. J. J. Bush, Smithfield														
Benson	Mrs. H. O. Dixon, Benson	634 95		148 95	203 60								987 50		987 50
Benson Grove	L. E. Barbour, Benson								4 70				4 70		4 70
Bethany	C. S. Creech, Kenly	131 25							25 07				156 32		156 32
Bethel	Luther Stone, Kenly, R. F. D.														
Bethesda	L. B. Smith, Oaks Mills	320 67											320 67		320 67
Blackman's Grove	Nogah Wid, Four Oaks	105 75							12 50				118 25	17 50	135 75
Burnell	J. S. Kenn, Four Oaks, R. 4	30 00							21 75				51 75		51 75
Calvary	T. J. Lee, Dunn, R. 2	100 00											100 00		100 00
Carter's Chapel	Y. M. Eastman, Selma, R. 1	52 00											52 00		52 00
Clayton	D. M. Hall, Clayton	3000 00	202 50						231 15			400 00	3833 65		3833 65
Clyde's Chapel	D. C. Painter, Wendell, R. 1	268 00											268 00		268 00
Corinth	H. V. Andrews, Wendell	71 10											71 10		71 10
Four Oaks	Mrs. J. W. Sanders, Four Oaks	158 28	48 15	37 10	43 10		9 85		44 00			13 00	353 48	28 39	381 87
Hale's Chapel	J. H. Parrish, Zebulon, R. 2	23 00											23 00		23 00
Hepzibah	W. G. Creech, Princeton, R. 1														
Hood's Grove	Roland Hayes, Four	75 00											75 00		75 00
Kenly	A. J. Broughton, Kenly	34 50			9 75								44 25		44 25
Lee's Chapel	C. W. Hinton, Zebulon, R. 1	92 36	25 00	10 00	10 00	10 00	5 00	10 00	10 00				172 36	10 00	182 36
Live Oak	J. M. Richardson, Selma, R. 2			10 00				5 00		5 00	5 00				
Micro	Mrs. C. L. Batten,	155 75							24 29				180 04	12 50	192 54
Middlesex	Mrs. N. B. Lewis, Middlesex	195 45	15 00		34 45				70 00				314 90		314 90
Mt Moriah	J. J. ...ne, Auburn	917 33							300 45				1217 78	165 00	1382 78

TABLE No. 3—SUNDAY SCHOOLS

STATISTICAL SUMMARY

Churches	Superintendents and Postoffices	Secretaries and Postoffices	Officers and Teachers	Total Enrolled	Average Attendance for the Year	Number on Cradle Roll	Total of Beginners, Primaries and Juniors	Total in Home Dept.	Is the School Graded?	Is it Standard A-1?	Teachers Holding Diplomas	Teachers Holding Seals	Number of Organized Classes	Baptisms from School	Contributed to Local Expenses	Contributed to Missions	Total of All Contributions
Antioch	A. D. O'Neal	W. O. Hocutt, Middlesex, R. 3	6	116	70	—	66	—	no	no	—	—	—	3	26 39	7 75	34 14
Bailey	R. E. Finch, Bailey	W. P. Finch, Bailey	9	67	44	—	42	—	yes	—	—	—	4	1	26 73	—	26 73
Baptist Center	E. H. Rogers, Clayton	Wade Tippett, Clayton	8	101	75	—	53	—	yes	—	—	—	5	—	35 00	8 43	43 43
Beaty's Chapel	J. W.	Estella, Smithfield	4	35	—	—	—	—	—	—	—	—	—	1	17 43	—	17 43
Benson	J. E. Wall, Benson	H. O. Dixon, Benson	21	252	144	—	67	—	yes	—	—	—	—	—	211 44	—	211 44
Benson Grove	W. B. Benson, Benson, R. 1	L. E. Barbour, Benson, R. 1	8	75	70	—	42	—	—	—	—	—	4	4	12 00	—	12 00
Bethany	B. B. , Kenly	C. S. , Kenly	10	148	90	—	—	—	—	—	—	—	—	6	49 00	—	49 00
Bethel	Perry Barnes, Kenly, R. 4	Stone, Kenly, R. F. D.	5	100	40	—	25	—	—	—	—	—	4	—	8 00	—	8 00
Bethesda	I. B. , Wilson's Mills	V. S. Smith, Wilson's Mills	12	74	75	6	60	—	yes	—	4	—	—	6	43 80	—	43 80
Blackman's Grove	, Four Oaks	J. R. Blackman, Four Oaks	8	92	50	—	29	—	—	—	—	—	—	3	27 87	—	27 87
Burnell	W. L. Massengill, Four Oaks	Myrtle Massengill, Benson, R. 1	8	70	35	—	52	—	—	—	—	—	5	—	20 00	—	20 00
Calvary	T. J. Lee, , R. 2	R. B. , Dunn, R. 2	8	139	115	18	37	—	yes	yes	1	1	12	1	14 65	2 30	15 00
‍r's Chapel	Zeb. Eatman, Selma, R. 1	J. B. , Selma, R. 3	25	387	245	—	80	—	yes	yes	22	1	10	1	520 00	248 15	768 15
on	W. P. , Clayton	, Clayton	—	—	—	—	174	59	—	—	—	—	4	—	25 00	3 00	28 00
‍le's	I. B. Boyette, , R. 1	Mamie Boykin, Wendell, R. 1	9	141	81	—	92	—	yes	no	5	1	2	16	35 28	—	35 28
Corinth	Lee Hocutt, Zebulon, R. 1	J. R. Poe, Zebulon, R. 1	15	109	55	16	39	—	—	—	—	—	5	4	184 93	23 85	208 78
Four Oaks	I. H. Strickland, Four Oaks	Jessie , Four Oaks	12	177	102	—	72	—	yes	—	5	—	4	8	20 00	—	20 00
Hale's Chapel	A. D. , Zebulon, R. 1	S. V. , Zebulon, R. 2	5	98	60	—	35	—	—	—	—	—	—	—	12 00	—	12 00
Hephzibah	W. G. , , R. 1	J. F. Earp, Pine Level, R. 1	5	55	25	—	33	—	—	—	—	—	1	—	15 00	—	15 00
Hood's Grove	Y. G. Blackman, Bentonsville	Hattie Hood, Bentonsville	6	86	—	—	—	—	—	—	—	—	—	—	50 00	—	50 00
Kenly	A. J. Broughton, Kenly	W. G. Rackley, Kenly	7	45	35	—	—	—	—	—	—	—	1	10	26 70	—	26 70
Lee's Chapel	Joshua Snipes, Middlesex	Bettie G. Bunn, Zebulon, R. 2	3	140	30	—	29	—	—	—	—	—	—	—	10 00	—	10 00
Live Oak	J. M. Richardson, Selma, R. 2	W. B. Morris, Selma, R. 1	7	38	52	25	85	—	yes	—	—	—	2	2	20 00	2 78	210 33
Micro	S. C. Batten, Selma, R. 2	D. H. Jones, Micro	7	87	70	—	42	—	yes	—	—	—	2	4	67 55	142 78	210 33
Mount Moriah	E. S. , Clayton	John Baucom, Raleigh, R. 2	15	170	112	—	57	—	yes	—	—	—	2	—	46 65	390 45	437 10

Church	Clerk	Pastor	C1	C2	C3	C4	C5	C6	C7	C8	C9	C10	C11	C12	C13	C14	C15
New Bethel	R. I. Smith, McCullers	E. C. Britt, Garner	5	157	90	—	76	—	yes	2	2	2	—	8	40 65	—	40 65
Noble's Chapel	L. F. Boykin,	O. ..., Sims, R. 1	10	77	50	—	38	—	—	—	—	—	—	—	38 21	—	38 21
Oliver's Grove		J. E. Ryals, Four Oaks, R. 4	5	18	—	—	—	—	—	—	—	—	—	—	5 00	—	5 00
Parrish Memorial	James Watson, Pine Level	E. L. Pittman, Micro.	10	119	59	—	50	—	yes	—	—	—	—	—	20 00	—	20 00
Pauline	Naomi Lee, Four Oaks, R. 1	Lizzie Edwards, Four Oaks, R. 1	10	89	62	—	38	—	—	—	—	—	—	—	19 64	—	19 64
Pine Level	B. L. Strickland, Pine	Miss ..., Pine	6	81	60	2	58	—	—	1	1	—	—	1	45 00	28 50	73 50
Riley	A. P. Lee, Kenly, R. 1	Seth ..., Fremont, R. 2	8	33	20	—	—	10	—	—	—	—	—	—	14 39	1 00	15 39
Pisgah	John A. Smith, Smithfield	Paul E. Whitley, Smithfield	6	82	60	30	50	—	yes	3	3	—	—	4	48 00	—	48 00
Pleasant Grove	J. E. Gilbert, Benson, R. 2	Claude Stephenson, ... Springs	10	24	—	—	10	—	—	—	—	—	—	—	5 00	—	5 00
Princeton	J. Ira Lee, Princeton	J. J. ..., Princeton, R. 1	3	168	75	—	80	—	—	—	—	—	—	8	54 34	3 45	57 79
Sardis	I. G. ..., Smithfield	A. F. Bizzel, Smithfield, R. 2	8	86	65	20	—	15	yes	1	1	1	—	3	27 51	—	27 51
Selma	... Eason, Selma, R. 2	G. A. Earp, Selma	17	275	175	20	105	28	—	—	—	3	—	4	280 20	64 12	344 32
Shiloh	S. H. ..., Garner	W. F. Honeycutt, Garner	6	93	60	—	44	—	yes	1	1	4	—	1	18 00	—	18 00
Smithfield	L. T. Royall, Smithfield	John Iver, Smithfield	21	283	200	33	128	—	yes	6	6	4	—	9	350 00	—	350 00
Thanksgiving	W. S. Earp, Selma, R. 1	J. O. Narron, Selma, R. 1	6	162	120	—	80	—	yes	—	—	4	—	2	22 42	88	23 30
Rice Oak	O. H. Barefoot, Benson	Verta Lawhorn, Benson	6	60	40	—	32	—	—	2	2	5	—	19	28 50	—	28 50
	A. L. ..., ..., R. 2	W. H. ..., ..., R. 2	10	158	79	—	89	—	yes	—	—	—	—	—	48 00	—	48 00
Wilson's Mills	J. T. Hall, Wilson's Mills	Walter Byett,	7	60	40	—	32	—	—	—	—	3	—	4	30 00	—	30 00
Totals			399	4952	2980	150	2061	112	—	47	6	85	2	134	2635 28	924 66	3559 94

STATISTICAL SUMMARY

Churches	Organizations, Presidents Counselors or Leaders, and Postoffices	Woman's Societies	Y. W. A.'s	G. A.'s	R. A.'s	Sunbeams	Total Woman's Organizations	Total Enrolled in All Organizations	New Organizations (One year old or less)	Pieces of Literature Distributed	Total Mission Study Classes Conducted	Enrolled in All Mission Study Classes	Total Seals Received	Total Articles Furnished Needy	Total Subscribers to Royal Service	Total Contributions to 75-Million Campaign	Total Contributions to Special Benevolences	Grand Total W. M. U. Contributions
Bailey	Mrs. J. W. Privett, Bailey, W. M. S.	1					2	28								$ 40 00	$	$ 40 00
Bailey	Miss Hazel Finch, Bailey, Sunbeam Band					1												
Benson	Mrs. J. L. Hall, Benson, W. M. S.	1					2	69								819 55	60 00	879 55
Benson	Mrs. W. D. Cavenaugh, Benson, Sunbeam Band					1												
Blackman's Grove	Miss Hessy Phelps, Four Oaks, W. M. U.	1					1	20							20	18 75		18 75
Clayton	Mrs. A. O. Moore, ___, W. M. S.	1					6	172		200	6	70	27	100	30	2090 06	330 00	2420 06
Clayton	Mrs. Lois M. Bass, Clayton, Y. W. A.		1															
Clayton	Mrs. J. D. Barbour, ___, Girls A., Sr.			2														
Clayton	Mrs. B. ___ Hocutt, ___, Girls A., Jr.																	
Clayton	Mrs. C. W. ___, ___, R. A.				1													
Clayton	Miss Bessie ___, Clayton, ___ Band					1												
Clyde's Chapel	Mrs. ___ Batten, ___, R. I. W. M. S.	1					1	15	1							105 25		105 25
Corinth	Mrs. J. B. O'Neal, Zebulon, R. I. W. M. S.	1					1		1							31 00		31 00
Four Oaks	Miss Mabel Coffenburger, Four Oaks, W. M. S.	1					3	68	1		1	10	10	109	6	7 25	165 49	172 74
Four Oaks	Mrs. M. P. Davis, Four Oaks, G. A.			1														
Four Oaks	Mrs. S. M. Boyett, Four Oaks, ___ Band					1												
Kenly	Mrs. J. E. Jones, Kenly, W. M. S.	1					2	32								4 75		4 75
Kenly	Mrs. J. A. Hodge, Kenly, Sunbeam Band					1												
Middlesex	Mrs. W. K. Ballentine, Middlesex, W. M. S.	1					3	58		200				100	12		154 05	154 05
Middlesex	Mrs. J. M. Lewis, Middlesex, G. A.			1														
Middlesex	Mrs. N. B. Lewis, Middlesex, Sunbeam Band					1												
Mount Moriah	Mrs. James G. Lane, ___, Sunbeam Band	1				1	1	33										
Noble's Chapel	Mrs. T. B. Boykin, ___, W. M. S.	1					1	26										
Pine Level	Mrs. B. L. Strickland, Pine ___, W. M. S.	1					2	25						10	2	176 75		16 75
Pine Level	Mrs. D. B. Oliver, Pine Level, Sunbeam Band					1												
Princeton	Mrs. T. D. Sasser, Princeton, W. M. S.	1					1	25	1							9 00	305 48	24 48
Selma	Mrs. Geo. D. Vick, Selma, W. M. S.	1					3	70	1							186 89		86 89
Selma	Mrs. N. E. Ward, Selma, R. A.				1													
Selma	Mrs. A. E. McKeather, Selma, Sunbeam Band					1												
Smithfield	Mrs. H. G. Gray, Smithfield, W. M. S.	1	1				4	100	1		2	40				578 09		578 09
Smithfield	Mrs. D. H. Creech, Smithfield, Y. W. A.																	

Churches	Presidents of B. Y. P. U.'s and Postoffices	Senior B.Y.P.U.'s	Seniors Enrolled	Intermediate B.Y.P.U.'s	Intermediates Enrolled	Junior Unions	Juniors Enrolled	Total Unions	Total Enrolled	Members Keeping Up Daily Bible Readings	Unions Taking Study Course Book	Total Systematic Givers in All Unions	Members Volunteering for Ministry or Mission Work	Names and Postoffices	Ministers Ordained This Year	Volunteers for Ministry or Missions	Other Ordained Ministers in the Church
Antioch																	
Bailey	W. P. Finch, Bailey	1	15					1	15					R. L. Hocutt, Zebulon, R. 2			1
Benson	Mildred Parrish, Benson, Senior	1	27											Miss Ruby Hobbs, Benson		1	1
Benson	Gladys Benton, Benson, Intermediate			1	35									Miss Ruth Lawhon, Benson		1	1
Benson	Fleta Martin, Benson, Junior					1	42	3	104					Moses Peacock, Benson		1	1
Benson Grove														C. C. Wheeler, Benson			
Bethany														W. J. Heath, Benson, R. 1	1		
Bethesda														A. R. Creech, Kenly, R. F. D.			
														J. W. Smith, Clayton			1
Blackman's Grove	I. R. Blackman, Four Oaks, Senior	1	22				15	2	37								
Blackman's Grove	Miss Hessie Phelps, Four Oaks, Junior					1											
Corinth	L. T. Davis, Wendell	1	30					1	30								
Four Oaks	Miss Esther Creech, Four Oaks, Senior	1	12				15	2	27								
Four Oaks	Hubert Massengill, Four Oaks, Junior					1											
Hale's Chapel	A. D. Parrish, Zebulon, R. 2	1	15					1	15								
Clayton	Mrs. J. B. Turley, Clayton	1	30					1	30								
Mount Moriah	J. G. Lane, Auburn	1	47					1	47								
Princeton	W. S. King, Princeton	1	21				42	2	63		23	6	2				
Princeton	DeLeon Holt, Princeton					1											
Selma	Mrs. Emma Blackman, Selma, Senior																
Selma	Miss Ida Parker, Selma, Junior																
Smithfield	Miss Bridget Williams, Smithfield, Senior	1	64				20	2	84	20	18	30					
Smithfield	Ida Patrick, Smithfield, Junior					1	20	1	20								
Trinity	O. H. Barefoot, Benson, R. 2	1	20					1	20								
Totals		11	303	1	35	5	134	17	472	20	41	36	2	2	1	3	4

MINUTES

OF THE

TWENTY-FIRST ANNUAL SESSION

OF THE

Johnston County Baptist Association

HELD WITH

BETHANY BAPTIST CHURCH

OCT. 31 to NOV. 1, 1923

•

The next session will be held with the Four Oaks
Baptist Church, beginning on Wednesday after
the fourth Sunday in October, 1924.

To preach Introductory Sermon, Rev. R. S. White
To preach Missionary Sermon, Rev. O. A. Keller

RALEIGH
BYNUM PRINTING COMPANY
1923

MINUTES

TWENTY-FIRST ANNUAL SESSION

OF THE

Johnston County Baptist Association

HELD WITH

BETHANY BAPTIST CHURCH

OCT. 31 to NOV. 1, 1923

———

The next session will be held with the Four Oaks
Baptist Church, beginning on Wednesday after
the fourth Sunday in October, 1924.

———

To preach Introductory Sermon, Rev. R. S. White
To preach Missionary Sermon, Rev. O. A. Keller

———

RALEIGH
BYNUM PRINTING COMPANY
1923

OFFICERS

Moderator, R. H. Gower..Clayton
Vice-Moderator, L. S. Morgan..Smithfield
Clerk, R. M. Von Miller..Wilson
Treasurer, J. A. Smith....................................Four Oaks, R. 4
Auditor, Julian Creech..Kenly, R. 2

EXECUTIVE COMMITTEE

L. S. Morgan, Chairman..Smithfield
Jas. A. Ivey..Four Oaks
J. A. Smith.............................,.............................Four Oaks, R. 4
J. J. Lane, Secretary..Auburn
H. E. Earp...Selma

LIST OF MINISTERS

C. H. Cashwell..Wendell
A. R. Creech..................:.................................Buie's Creek
R. L. Gay..Smithfield
J. E. Hocutt..Nashville
Jas. A. Ivey...........,...Four Oaks
O. A. Keller..Benson
S. N. Lamb..Wake Forest
J. W. Nobles..Middlesex
W. D. Stancil..Kenly
B. M. Shacklett..Angier
L. R. Tate..Benson
R. T. Vann, D.D...Raleigh
D. E. Vipperman..Pine Level
R. M. Von Miller..Wilson
R. C. White..Clayton

DELEGATES TO CONVENTIONS

Delegate to Southern Baptist Convention—Hon. F. H. Brooks.
Delegates to Baptist State Convention—J. J. Lane, R. C. White, and
O. A. Keller.

STANDING COMMITTEES TO MAKE REPORTS ON CONVENTION OBJECTS

Business—Church Government and Finance: To be appointed
later.

Social Service—Orphanage, Ministerial Relief, Temperance and
Hospitals: O. A. Keller.

Missions—Associational, State, Home, Foreign, and Woman's
Work: L. S. Morgan.

Christian Education—Colleges, Preparatory Schools, Periodicals,
Books and Tracts: R. C. White.

Teaching and Training—Sunday Schools, B. Y. P. U. and Demonstration: Jas. A. Ivey.

Enlistment and Stewardship—R. M. Von Miller.

Antioch—B. C. Strickland, R. R. Creech, W. H. Maden, A. D. O'Neal.

Bailey—Mrs. Pearl Stott, J. W. B. Finch, Hazel Finch, Mrs. J. W. Privett, Mr. and Mrs. R. L. Finch.

Benson—O. A. Keller.

Benson Grove—Mr. and Mrs. C. P. Stewart.

Bethany—D. C. Smith, Jesse Edwards, G. N. Wood, N. Stancil, Jesse B. Creech, W. D. Stancil.

Bethel—Mrs. J. R. Bunch, Mrs. J. H. Bell.

Blackman's Grove—Hessie Phelps.

Burnell—T. F. Lassiter, T. H. Lassiter.

Calvary—J. K. Hudson, H. Hudson.

Canaan—A. W. Bizzell, W. B. Hill.

Carter's Chapel—A. R. Creech, A. Richardson, M. Thorne, Zeb Eatman, H. S. Woodruff, R. Atkinson.

Clayton—D. M. Hall, D. J. Thurston, Mrs. J. M. Cox, Mrs. B. A. Hocutt, R. C. White, Cleve Barnes, Argoes Brown, Mrs. Chas. Turley, Mrs. E. H. Steger, D. J. Yelvington, Mrs. H. G. Eason, Mrs. Jesse Ellis.

Clyde's Chapel—Earl Phipps, J. H. Painter, B. N. Hobgood, J. B. Boyette.

Corinth—J. L. Liles, S. F. Price.

Four Oaks—James A. Ivey, Florence Stanley, Mrs. J. W. Sanders, R. A. Bain, C. E. Parrish, Mrs. B. B. Creech.

Hale's Chapel—B. M. Price.

Hepzibah—J. F. Earp.

Kenly—A. J. Broughton, F. A. White, Mrs. J. Watson, Ivey Watson, Mrs. A. B. Williams, N. H. Shepherd.

Lee's Chapel—W. I. Green, J. W. Creech, H. W. Wilder, P. Bunn.

Live Oak—J. M. Richardson.

Micro—J. H. Broadwell, Joe P. Davis, Fred Batten.

Middlesex—J. C. Overman, M. B. Alford.

Mount Moriah—J. J. Lane, S. Wilder, J. F. Pool, Mrs. N. R. Pool.

Oliver's Grove—J. E. Ryals.

Noble's Chapel—G. T. Manning, S. T. Winborn, L. Williams, Mrs. G. M. Boykin, L. A. Boykin, Mrs. J. H. Price.

Parrish Memorial—G. W. Parrish, J. N. Watson, R. F. Batts, Frank Batten, A. J. Price, J. D. Creech, Della Creech.

Pauline—Mrs. Effie Strickland, A. Strickland, J. H. Adams.

Pine Level—Alex Strickland, N. M. Gurley, J. F. Watson, B. Godwin, Mrs. D. B. Oliver, Mrs. W. A. Herring, D. E. Vipperman.

Pinkney—J. S. Lewis, S. T. Davis, J. Davis, Mrs. B. R. Edgerton, A. P. Lee.

Pisgah—A. J. Whitley, J. A. Smith, Mrs. J. A. Smith, Mrs. A. Whitley, R. L. Gay.

2

Princeton—W. I. Pearson, C. H. Holt, W. M. Holt, D. T. Sasser, Jasper Boyett.

Selma—Mr. and Mrs. H. E. Earp, C. C. Liles, N. J. Creech.

Smithfield—F. H. Brooks, J. F. Underhill, S. L. Morgan, Mr. and Mrs. J. D. Dickens.

Thanksgiving—W. S. Earp, Mr. and Mrs. D. T. Bailey, H. P. Earp, Miss M. Lynch, Mr. and Mrs. J. R. Lynch, D. H. Price, R. M. Von Miller.

Trinity—O. H. Barefoot, R. L. Tate, A. J. Parker, H. C. Lee.

White Oak—E. Green.

Wilson's Mills—G. G. Beatty.

CONSTITUTION

1. The Association shall be known as the Johnston County Baptist Association.

2. Its object shall be to extend the privileges of the Gospel and liberal culture to all the people within its bounds, and, by hearty co-operation with the Baptist State Convention, to help offer these privileges to all mankind in and out of its bounds by the cordial co-operation of all the churches constituting this body.

3. It shall be composed of the pastors in active service in the Association and such delegates as shall be annually elected by the churches connected with it, each church being entitled to three delegates, unless the membership shall exceed fifty, and then an additional delegate for every twenty-five members: *Provided*, no church shall have more than eight delegates.

4. The New Hampshire Declaration of Faith shall be the summary of Divine Truth for determining questions of faith and order in this body, and the churches desiring membership in it must commit themselves to the substance of it, together with the covenant herewith submitted and this Constitution.

5. This Association shall not have power to annul this discipline or exercise authority over any church connected with it, but it may advise with and sever its connection with any church that neglects to preserve Gospel order, or that treats with contempt the objects or advice of the Association.

6. Each church shall send to the annual meetings of the Association a letter (the blanks to be furnished by the Clerk of the Association), carefully filled as per blank suggestions, stating the full work of the church for the year ending with the Sunday previous to the meeting of the Association.

7. The Association shall foster State Missions, Home Missions, Foreign Missions, Christian Education, the Aged Ministers' Relief

Board, the Thomasville Orphanage, and the Sunday School Board, and each church shall be requested to contribute to the support of these objects annually.

8. Missions and Education shall have precedence in their claims upon the consideration of this body in its regular sessions.

9. Whenever a church shall fail to be represented by delegates or letter at the annual sessions of the Association, inquiry shall be made for the cause, and efforts shall be made to induce such church to do its duty; and the effort shall be continued till the church is recovered or dropped from the roll.

. 10. The officers of the Association shall be a Moderator, a Vice-Moderator, a Clerk, a Treasurer, and an Auditor, elected annually by ballot (or in case when only one brother is put in nomination for an office, then the vote may be by acclamation), from among the members, to serve until their successors shall have been elected, and to perform the duties of such offices, namely, the Moderator, in presiding over the meetings, or the Vice-Moderator, in his absence; the Clerk, in recording and preserving minutes and other papers belonging to the body; the Treasurer, in receiving and disbursing funds belonging to or entrusted to the body, according to its will; the Auditor, to examine the Treasurer's books at each meeting of the Association, and report the same before adjournment.

11. The Association shall appoint annually an Executive Committee of five (5) from its members, who shall be entrusted with the prosecution of Missions in the Association and any other work for the interest of the Master's Kingdom which may be referred to them. This committee shall, as far as possible, co-operate with the State Mission Board in supplying the destitution in our territory, and, between the meetings of the Association, take such action as may seem to them advisable for the advancement of its interest. The committee shall present to the Association at its annual meeting a report of its proceedings, with the names of the missionaries supported on the field, time of service and details of their work, together with such recommendations as, in the judgment of the committee, the Association should follow in planning its subsequent work.

12. The annual sessions of the Association shall begin on Wednesday after the fourth Lord's Day in October, at such place as may be chosen, and an introductory sermon shall be delivered on the first day of the session. Representatives from ten of the churches constituting the Association shall be a quorum.

13. This Constitution may be amended at any annual session by a two-thirds vote of all the members present.

14. The proceedings of the Woman's Central Committee shall be recorded as a part of the minutes of the Association.

BY-LAWS

1. The daily sessions of the Association shall be opened and closed with prayer.

2. Delegates shall be recognized by letters from their churches designating them as such.

3. The Moderator shall recognize corresponding messengers or the delegates of newly received churches by extending to them his right hand.

4. The report of the Executive Board and the Missionary work of the Association shall take precedence of all other business during the morning session of the second day of the annual session.

5. The Clerk shall record and read the proceedings when called for, superintend the publication and distribution of the minutes, preserve a file of them and have it present at each annual session, and deliver to his successor all papers belonging to the body.

6. Members desiring to speak shall first rise and address the Moderator, shall use the term "brother" in speaking to each other, shall not speak on the same subject more than twice without permission, and shall observe the courtesy that becomes Christians.

7. The roll of members shall be called at least once, and absentees marked.

8. Corresponding messengers and visiting brethren shall be invited to seats, with privilege of speaking, but not voting.

9. A copy of the minutes shall be sent to the Secretary of the State Mission Board, the Secretary of the Southern Baptist Convention, the American Publication Society, 1420 Chestnut Street, Philadelphia; the Sunday School Board of the Southern Baptist Convention, and the Thomasville Orphanage.

10. All questions of order not herein provided shall be decided by Kerfoot's Parliamentary Law.

Proceedings

The Johnston County Baptist Association met in its twenty-first session with the Bethany Baptist Church, October 31 to November 1, 1923.

WEDNESDAY MORNING

After singing "I Am Thine, O Lord," and prayer by Brother R. L. Gay, the Moderator declared the twenty-first session of the Johnston County Baptist Association open for the transaction of business. The Moderator appointed the following brethren as a Committee on Credentials and Enrollment: D. J. Thurston, W. S. Earp, and Julian Creech. The Clerk read the roll of the churches, which revealed a quorum present. The following brethren were recognized: Brother F. B. Hambrick, who represented the Orphanage at Thomasville, and L. S. Morgan, of Smithfield; Jas. A. Ivey, of Four Oaks; R. C. White, of Clayton, and O. A. Keller, of Benson, welcoming them as new pastors in the Association. The election of officers for the ensuing year resulted as follows: R. H. Gower, Moderator; L. S. Morgan, Vice-Moderator; R. M. Von Miller, Clerk; J. A. Smith, Treasurer, and Julian Creech, Auditor.

After singing "I'm Pressing On the Upward Way," Brother Jas. A. Ivey preached the introductory sermon, using for his subject "The Stewardship of the Country Church," and for his text 4th chapter of first Corinthians, 1-8. At the conclusion of this very helpful and appropriate sermon, the body joined in singing "On Christ the Solid Rock I Stand," after which the Moderator recognized Brother J. J. Lane, who presented

REPORT ON CHURCH GOVERNMENT AND FINANCE

In making this report we wish to bear in mind that in matters of church government and finance each church is supreme in its own sphere. However, our success as a body of churches, in co-operating together in the Lord's work, depends largely upon the management of the agencies of the denomination in the State. While recognizing the great good accomplished in the past, we believe our effectiveness as a denomination would be promoted by changing our Constitution so as to provide for the election of an Executive Committee of twenty members to take the place of the State Mission Board and the Board of Education. The manner of the election of men to be left to the Convention, with the understanding that they are to be selected so as to represent all sections of our territory. There should be no ex officio members of the Executive Committee, and the Executive Committee should have general supervision of the work and see that there is full co-operation among the various officers and agencies.

We further recommend that our associational delegates bring this matter to the attention of the Baptist State Convention at its next session.

J. J. LANE, *for Committee.*

On motion to adopt, Brethren J. J. Lane and J. F. Pool spoke to the report. A motion by Brother R. C. White to defer the discussion of this report until after dinner was carried. After prayer by Brother O. A. Keller, the body adjourned for dinner.

WEDNESDAY AFTERNOON

After the devotional exercises, led by Brother N. H. Shepherd, the Moderator recognized Brother Arthur Creech, welcoming him as a new pastor to the Association. The following brethren were appointed as a committee on place and preacher: J. F. Pool, R. R. Creech, and J. D. Dickens. In resuming the discussion of the report on Church Government and Finance, Brother R. C. White offered a motion that this report be referred to a committee for reconsideration, which was carried. The Moderator appointed the following brethren to serve as such a committee: R. C. White, O. A. Keller, and Jas. A. Ivey, after which the chair recognized Brother N. H. Shepherd, who presented the

REPORT ON SOCIAL SERVICE

I doubt the wisdom of the use of the words "Social Service" to include Temperance, Ministerial Relief, Hospitals, and Orphanage. To the average man it does not carry, without explanation, the meaning desired. The good old words, Temperance, Ministerial Relief, Hospitals and Orphanages, are good words. Social service sounds good to only a few.

TEMPERANCE

Your committee would recommend, first, a revival of the old church rule, forbidding the manufacture, sale, or use of intoxicating drinks as a beverage, together with a rigid enforcement of the same. And let the church, led by a courageous preacher, outlaw everything that smells like wine or strong drink for beverage purposes. We would further recommend, second, the teaching that the use of strong drinks is dangerous and sinful of itself, and that it is doubly sinful in that it violates our church rule, and encourages the violation of the law of the State and nation. And third, we would recommend the cultivation of a strong sentiment, showing that the starting point is the danger point, that all who have anything to do with intoxicating drinks, either at social functions, the usual "punch" in the parlor, the barrel of home-made wine, for the family and friends, is equally guilty with the whole class of violators of the law and the rule of the church. The fight against intemperance will be won when we observe church rule and the teachings of the Bible on the subject of intemperance. And we would further recommend that we, as churches and individuals, commend every effort to abolish the liquor traffic and the use of alcoholic drinks as a beverage by every organization, and enactment of laws on the part of our legislators, and that we endeavor to help the cause of prohibition by using our influence in the election of men in favor of prohibition and law enforcement, and assure those who do their duty of our moral support.

MINISTERIAL RELIEF

The Relief and Annuity Board of the Southern Baptist Convention is located at Dallas, Tex.; Dr. W. Lunsford is the corresponding secretary. With this board every Baptist minister in good standing can carry a policy of one or more units. One unit supposed to be worth five hundred dollars annually, after the preacher arrives at the age of 68 years old, or sooner, if he becomes unable to do full ministerial work. And after his death his widow draws an annuity of $300 while she remains a widow, and the children then receive $300 until the youngest reaches majority. This board takes the place of our Relief Board, and is one of our most worthy and needy objects. Your committee would recommend large contributions from churches and individuals, that there may be ample provision for our veterans of the Cross.

HOSPITALS

The North Carolina Baptist Hospital is located in Winston-Salem; Rev. G. T. Lumpkin is the superintendent. It has been open only a few months. Brother Lumpkin will gladly furnish any

one with tracts giving specific information' that will ask. Our
Baptist Hospital is a long-felt want supplied, and it is the last
word our denomination has uttered in a practical, tangible way,
by putting the Gospel into action, being "doers of the Word and
not hearers only."

The building is five stories high, thoroughly equipped, with some
of the best doctors and surgeons in the State. Moreover, a corps
of well-trained, sympathetic Christian nurses are at the patient's
command. The mission of this institution is to supply the means
necessary, by giving to the suffering the best relief and comfort
at the lowest possible cost, and to give treatment gratis to the
indigent.

Orphanage

North Carolina Baptists have two orphanages under one management, known as the Baptist Orphanage at Thomasville and the
Kennedy Home near Kinston. Dr. M. L. Kessler is the general
manager and Rev. T. B. Davis is the superintendent of the Kennedy
Home. Altogether there are 550 children in these homes, at a cost
of $19.85 per child each month, all expenses included. They are
provided with the best school advantages, are taught to work; they
are protected against many encroaching temptations and town al-
lurements, sins and dangers to which most of our children are
subjected at home. In some cases the children are taken as low as
one year old and are kept until they are eighteen. The orphanages
are kept up and supported by the voluntary gifts of the churches,
Sunday schools and friends. We would recommend that our people
remember the orphanages in their will. Several fine gifts have
already been made in this way. We also recommend the erection
of memorial buildings, associational buildings, etc. Earnestly we
recommend that the collection of one Sunday in each month be
designated to the orphanages by each church, and one day's earnings on or near Thanksgiving day by individual members be given
for the support of these needy children every year. No investment
has ever brought finer results. From this Orphanage of ours there
have come forth hundreds of capable men and women, some of the
best mothers, some of the best students in our colleges, universities
and seminaries; some are in the foreign field, and words would
fail us to tell the gladsome story of the results of the benefits of
our own Baptist Orphanage.

And now a word about the plan of using about $15,000 for the
support of indigent, worthy widows to keep the "family circle unbroken." So far this is proving very satisfactory, and this is helping a large number of children that could not be cared for at the
Orphanage.

In conclusion, remember you are always welcome as a visitor at
the Orphanage. Any information you desire will be gladly furnished
you, upon application, by the general manager.

Respectfully submitted,

N. H. SHEPHERD.

On motion to adopt, the following brethren spoke to the report: N. H. Shepherd and F. H. Brooks, Temperance; R. L.
Gay, Ministerial Relief; S. L. Morgan, Hospitals; F. B. Hambrick, Orphanage. The report was adopted.

The Moderator recognized Brother R. M. Von Miller, who
presented the report on Christian Education. This includes
Colleges, Preparatory Schools, Periodicals, Books and Tracts.

CHRISTIAN EDUCATION

It would be difficult to over-estimate the importance of Christian
Education, and equally difficult not to see that it has at present an
exceedingly large place in the thinking of the most thoughtful and
influential people of our nation. We are glad to say that the demand
for Christian Education is very intense and nation-wide. The
expression of the foregoing opinion gathered from all parts of the
United States, the millions that the different denominations are
giving to their schools, the vastly increased, and in many cases the
overflowing attendance upon these schools, justify the assertion
that the reaction in favor of Christian education is one of the outstanding characteristics of post-war thinking, and the Baptists of
the South therefore were in harmony with the best thought of the
time when they created the Education Board, thus elevating education to the dignity of the other special interests fostered by them.

Baptists in the past have emphasized missions and evangelism
but minimized education, with the result that we have in the South
masses of ignorant Baptists, who actually are worth little to the
cause of Christ, but potentially they are worth a great deal. Since
our 75-Million Campaign began, hundreds of thousands have been
added to our churches. Their value, however, to kingdom interests
will depend in a large measure upon their education.

The tendency of our State is to make too large appropriation to
State institutions as over against the deplorable need of our rural
schools, and Baptists should exert their influence to counteract this
tragic mistake. Illiteracy in North Carolina is largely a Baptist
problem because of our numerical superiority. If we would save
our Southland from the awful peril which wrecked the German
nation and made the world the scene of barbarious slaughter, if
we would not fall into the clutches of a soul-destroying rationalistic

movement, with which at the present time our Northern Baptist brethren are grappling in the fight for their very existence, if we are to be the leaven to save our State from a Christless education and build an enduring and world-serving civilization, then let us be 100 per cent loyal to our Baptist Christian Educational Program, for it is a fundamental need in this day of testing.

OUR COLLEGES AND PREPARATORY SCHOOLS

We now own and maintain three colleges—Wake Forest for men, and Meredith and Chowan for women. These three colleges had an enrollment of over 1,000 students. Together their plants, equipment, and endowment amounts to over two million dollars. We also own and operate five academies—Boiling Springs, Buie's Creek, Dell, Liberty-Piedmont, and Wingate. These enrolled last year nearly 2,000 students, and own property worth $316,000. The Home Mission Board controls and supports in North Carolina nine mountain schools with an enrollment of about 2,000 students, and own property valued at $554,000. In addition to this we have in North Carolina privately owned one Baptist college for women at Oxford and two privately owned academies, Pineland for girls and Mountain Park for boys and girls. We also join with Baptists of the other Southern States in supporting the Southern Baptist Theological Seminary at Louisville, Ky.; the Woman's Training School attached to the Southwestern Theological Seminary at Fort Worth, Tex., and the Bible Institute in New Orleans, La. These institutions have an enrollment of about 1,600 students and own property valued at $3,484,700.

May we offer two suggestions here? Let us cultivate the Baptist educational conscience, and in selecting a school for our children consider, in the fear of God, whether you have more right to be disloyal to your own school than you have to be disloyal to your own church. We also suggest that the churches in our Association will give "Christian Education Day" an abiding place in the calendar of special days observed in our Sunday schools.

PERIODICALS, BOOKS AND TRACTS

The increase in number of Baptists in North Carolina has been marvelous, and we have become a great people in many respects— great in the tenacity with which we have held to the teachings of God's Word in the face of misconception and perversion of the truth; great in evangelization, great in that we have produced a literature worthy of our history. Without citing any long list of tracts, books or periodicals, may we urge upon our churches the vital importance of the use of our own State paper, the *Biblical Recorder*. When the history of the mighty achievements of North

Carolina Baptists shall be written, it will be a history inseparably linked with the *Recorder*. The organized life of our denomination in North Carolina is coextensive with the life of the *Recorder*, and the paper was never quite so strong and splendid as today—always at the front of our denominational advance, pointing the way and proclaiming the principles purchased with the heroic sacrifices and heaven-born consecration of the Baptist fathers—our pride and our best friend; always virile, optimistic, aggressive—always better because of the consecration and sterling worth and great ability of our editor, L. Johnson, the princely gentleman, the unselfish friend of every man, the writer and genius—gifted, sane and loyal. Our paper is better than ever before, because of the faith and vision, consecrated common sense and business ability of the business manager, Brother J. S. Farmer.

What does the *Recorder* stand for? It is a great source of denominational unity. It binds us together and makes us one—one of purpose and spirit, one in doctrine and outlook. It is our trumpet of progress, always calling us to better things and higher undertakings for the kingdom. It calls us to the battle in a campaign for the endowment of our colleges and schools, for the enlargement of our Orphanage, and for heroic things in missions.

The *Recorder* is our voice of defense. It stands for the defense of the faith of our fathers. There are grave and subtle errors creeping into the religious life of our people. The South is fast becoming a hotbed of isms and religious sects. Let us strengthen the *Recorder* that it may give voice to our defense in our most holy religion.

The *Recorder* is a great clearing house for denominational affairs. It brings us the news of the kingdom and tells to others, far and wide, how the battle goes with each of us.

The imperative need of the *Recorder* is a larger circulation. We therefore suggest that we commit ourselves to this task, and we urge that the heads of all our Baptist families see to it that the *Recorder* is received and read in the homes, and also *Charity and Children* and *Home and Foreign Fields*, if practicable, and that our own literature is used in our Sunday schools.

Respectfully submitted,

R. M. Von Miller.

On motion to adopt, Brethren R. M. Von Miller, R. C. White, O. A. Keller, and D. E. Deaton spoke to the report. The report was adopted. The Moderator appointed Brethren R. M. Von Miller, J. A. Smith, and L. R. Tate as a committee to nominate the executive committee and delegates to the conventions. After prayer by Brother R. C. White, the body adjourned to meet Thursday morning at 9:30 a. m.

THURSDAY MORNING

After the devotional exercises, conducted by Brother O. A. Keller, the Moderator called the meeting to order. The Clerk read the minutes of the preceding sessions of the previous day, which were approved as read. The Moderator appointed a committee, consisting of Brethren J. F. Pool, J. T. Holt, and J. A. Smith, to draft resolutions in memory of Brother J. M. Beaty, same to be inserted in the minutes. Brethren A. C. Hamby and W. R. Beach were recognized and welcomed to the session, representing the State Board of Missions and the *Biblical Recorder* respectively. After which Brother J. J. Lane presented the

REPORT OF THE EXECUTIVE COMMITTEE

Your committee, after its appointment, selected Smithfield as its regular meeting place, and agreed to meet once a month. It was organized by electing Brother A. O. Moore as chairman and Brother J. J. Lane as secretary. On March 12, 1923, the committee met at Pisgah Church jointly with the pastors and Brother A. C. Hamby, the Enlistment Superintendent of the Board of Missions, with several others present. An outline of a program for grouping the churches into fields, with the idea that each field should build a parsonage and locate a pastor therein was stressed. This list was sent to the church clerks in the Association in order that it might be considered as a suggestion, and we hope that this will result in great good, though the result now may seem meager. The committee agreed to co-operate in the improvement of the parsonage at Kenly, but the undertaking was abandoned for the present owing to a decision of the Kenly church not to build now.

At Mt. Moriah a parsonage has been built and efforts are being made to locate a pastor therein. We call attention to the fact that there are a good many short-time pastorates in our Association, and recommend a careful investigation as to its cause, and that this condition be remedied if possible.

Respectfully submitted,

J. J. LANE, *for Committee.*

Upon motion to adopt, Brother J. J. Lane spoke to the report. The report was adopted. After which Brother O. A. Keller was recognized who presented the

REPORT ON MISSIONS

The mission of Jesus Christ on earth was to seek and to save that which was lost. Our mission is part of that work. The world will never be saved until we realize our place in the kingdom of

Christ. There must be Christian living and Christian giving. Giving during the last four years has increased wonderfully, and yet our giving has not kept pace with our material prosperity. During the last two years our section of the country has been wonderfully blessed. We have had abundant crops; God, it seems, has rebuked the devourer; and yet we are distressingly backward in the payment of our pledges.

STATE MISSIONS

Our State Mission work, which is divided into several different departments, is in a very flourishing condition. Our State Mission Board, with our very efficient secretary, has laid out a State Mission program that will make North Carolina the greatest Baptist commonwealth in the South in five years, if we furnish them the necessary money to carry it out. About 175 missionary pastors have been supported wholly or in part during the last year. The Board has placed strong men at every educational center in the State, that the Gospel might be brought to bear upon the lives of the youth in this formative period. The calls next year upon the State Mission Board will doubtless be larger than ever before. The Department of Evangelism, Rev. Herman T. Stephens, superintendent, with two assistants, has done a blessed work.

HOME MISSIONS

Advances in the home field have been very encouraging. Never has this department been more ably manned than at present. The Department of Evangelism has been most efficient. They have been preaching the pure Gospel of Jesus Christ; and, like John of old, have been calling to repentance, and the answer has been gratifying. During the four years that have passed since the campaign was projected the workers of the Home Mission Board have baptized 173,602 persons, received into the church a total of 277,968 people, enlisted 11,772 young persons in dedicating their lives to the ministry, missionary work and other forms of Christian service, built or improved 1,872 church houses, organized 935 New Baptist churches, and formed 2,898 Baptist Sunday schools. The number of mission schools has increased from 39 to 53, the number of pupils has grown from 5,065 to 7,498, while the number of ministerial students in those schools has grown from 103 to 242.

FOREIGN MISSIONS

Marvelous growth in our Foreign Mission work has been made possible by the campaign. Our Board has been able to enter six new fields, and reports a total of 34,334 baptisms for the campaign period so far, and the number is growing each year. Other gains include 386 churches, 39 houses of worship, 53,666 members, increase in annual contributions of foreign churches of $264,196, 31,292 Sunday school pupils, and 229 missionaries sent out. Yet with all this wonderful growth it must be remembered that our Board has been compelled in the last two years to deny the missionaries more than $2,000,000 in needed equipment, and is now laboring under a crushing debt caused by the nonpayment of our pledges.

ASSOCIATIONAL MISSIONS

Your committee is of the opinion that our associational work is in a rather serious condition. We face the loss of several of our missionary pastors and the possible breaking up of the pastorates. We recommend the appointment of the best executive committee to be found and that the committee meet at least quarterly to consider the needs of our associational work. Your committee especially urges that every dollar of our campaign pledges be paid. To do less will be dishonoring to ourselves and displeasing to God.

O. A. KELLER.

In connection with this report, Mrs. A. B. Hocutt, Superintendent of the Woman's Missionary Union of the Johnston County Baptist Association, presented the

REPORT ON WOMAN'S WORK

While we had our discouragements in our work, we have certainly had much to encourage us. Twenty years ago in 1903, at Selma, as many of us will remember with a thrill and a feeling of thanksgiving, the W. M. U. of Johnston County Baptist Association was organized with three societies. In 1904 there were four societies, contributing $332.74. I will not go into detail, or give figures from year to year, only say the records show a going forward and a falling back, but striking somewhere about the half-way mark. In 1915 we find we had 23 societies contributing $790.10. In 1923 we have 44 societies contributing $5,568.35. I cannot say how many churches we had in 1915, but in 1923 we have 45 churches in our Association with 21 W. M. S., 5 Y. W. A., 5 G. A., 1 R. A., and 12 Sunbeam Societies, making a total of 44 societies to whom quarterly reports are sent. Of these there are 28 who have reported quarterly. These are as follows: W. M. S., Y. W. A., G. A., R. A., and Sunbeam societies at Clayton. W. M. S. reporting regularly: Benson, Canaan, Four Oaks, Kenly, Micro, Middlesex, Pine Level, Mt. Moriah, Pisgah, Selma, and Smithfield. Sunbeams reporting regular: Benson, Middlesex, Micro, Pine Level, and Selma.

Twenty-one societies reported every quarter. Societies reporting personal service are increasing; 18 reported to State officers. Three organized or reorganized. There are 26 churches without any society. There are 2,952 female members in the churches of our Association of which 525 are members of societies; where are the 2,427? Fifty-four *Home and Foreign Field* taken, 66 *Royal Service*, 160 *Biblical Recorder;* 72 tithers against 36 of last year; 14 Mission Study classes; 14 observed special season of prayer for Home, Foreign, and State Missions respectively; 15 have organized personal service work. Standard of Excellence Honor Roll as follows: A-1 societies—W. M. S., Clayton; Y. W. A., Clayton; G. A., Clayton; Sunbeams, Benson, Clayton, and Middlesex. I have written 250 postals and written 400 letters; Mrs. Steger ·69; total, 469. I traveled 150 miles, Mrs. Steger 130; total, 280. I have visited 6 societies. A most successful junior missionary rally was planned and carried out by Mrs. Steger, Junior Superintendent, at Four Oaks during the summer. Twelve W. M. S. contributed $163 for our Hospital at Winston-Salem. ·At our annual meeting in Benson in 1923, 26 societies, 13 churches, and 105 delegates with 28 financial reports showing $5,568.35 contributed, as against 25 societies, 11 churches, 101 delegates with 26 financial reports showing $5,215.60 contributed last year at Smithfield.

One of the most encouraging features of our work this year was the presence of four of our pastors at our annual meeting in Benson, and an urgent invitation is extended to every pastor to attend our meeting in Selma, October, 1924. We beg for your support and co-operation in this our great work.

MRS. B. A. HOCUTT, Supt.

Upon adoption of these reports Brother Keller, in charge of the program at this hour, recognized Mrs. B. A. Hocutt, who spoke very interestingly to her report. In the absence of Brother A. A. Butler, who was to have preached the missionary sermon and presented report on Enlistment and Stewardship, it was unanimously decided to continue discussion of mission report. Brethren A. C. Hamby, Jas. A. Ivey, and O A. Keller spoke on Associational, State, Home, and Foreign Missions. The report on Missions was adopted. The Committee to nominate Executive Committee and Delegates to the Conventions reported as follows:

We, your committee, respectfully nominate for Executive Committee S. L. Morgan, Chairman; Jas. A. Ivey, J. J. Lane, H. E. Earp, and J. A. Smith.

Brother F. H. Brooks as delegate to the Southern Baptist Convention, and Brethren O. A. Keller, R. C. White, and J. J. Lane as delegates to the Baptist Convention.

R. M. VON MILLER,
R. L. TATE,
J. A. SMITH,
Committee.

The report was adopted. After prayer by Brother N. H. Shepherd, the body adjourned for dinner.

THURSDAY AFTERNOON

After the devotional exercises, the Moderator called the meeting to order and recognized Brother R. C. White, who reported on behalf of Committee on Revision of Report of Church Government and Finance. The recommendations of this committee as well as the report on Church Government and Finance were adopted. The Committee on Place and Preacher reported as follows:

We, your committee, suggest Four Oaks as the place for our next session, and Brother R. C. White to preach the introductory sermon and Brother O. A. Keller to preach the missionary sermon.

Respectfully submitted,

J. F. POOL, *for Committee.*

The report was adopted. A motion by Brother Jas. A. Ivey to instruct Clerk to have a map showing location of churches in our Association printed on the back cover of the Minutes was carried. The Moderator then recognized Brother R. C. White, who presented the report on

TEACHING AND TRAINING

The growth of the Sunday schools of the Southern Baptist Convention has been marvelous. Southern Baptists have made wonderful progress in every line of Sunday school activity. Their growth has been visible. We are happy to put teachers' training at the head of the best of agencies that have come to be potent factors in the marvelous growth of our Sunday schools. Southern Baptists have led the world in this most significant movement. Our Normal and Post-Graduate courses for the instruction of teachers and officers and others in our churches, generally, are unmatched by any denominational or interdenominational group. By steadfastly adhering to their own distinctive system of teacher training, Southern Baptists have gained for themselves the most outstanding position along such lines in the entire religious world. There is little doubt in the mind of the writer that this remarkable state of efficiency is due to our teacher-training work. Our churches now abound with bright and happy Christians, who are converted teachers, workers, and soul-winners because of the vision and training received from the books of these courses in the hands of capable and faithful instructors. In order that our Association may accomplish the work which is possible for us to achieve, your committee recommends that the churches give special attention to the training of teachers. Further, that the churches seek to provide adequate classrooms and teaching facilities. We recommend the above, realizing the great necessity of each in reaching the people for the Sunday school and for the church.

B. Y. P. U.

The B. Y. P. U. work, like every other Baptist enterprise in the State, is making great strides. Its growth and development for the past year has been most gratifying. The B. Y. P. U. has not had a better year in its history in this State. Secretary Perry Morgan and his helpers have led valiantly in carrying on a great program and have shown their efficiency by the results achieved. Too much emphasis cannot be given to such a force for good in our churches. The greatest work of the church is in the training of the young people, thus large numbers of training classes have been held in the churches; but greater than these is the work of discovering a large group of young people to themselves and to the churches, the holy task of awakening their youthful dreams for the kingdom of God, the kindling of inspiration, and the calling to consecrated living and sacrifices and service. This is the work of which heaven only can keep record. It is not ours to tabulate and report the fine things which are accomplished. Ours is a more enviable task— the carrying on of such work. Every unenlisted and undeveloped boy and girl in our churches is a silent challenge to our loyalty and faithfulness in enlarging our work and in making a more aggressive campaign for the ensuing year. The Minutes of the last associational year reveal eleven Senior Unions in 45 churches, one Intermediate Union in 45 churches, and five Junior Unions in 45 churches.

The committee recommends that the Association give its hearty support to this great task of training its young church members; that the Association give more thought and place to the B. Y. P. U.; that an evening be given during the Associational Meeting for such demonstration as the Associational B. Y. P. U. officers desire to give.

Respectfully submitted,

RUSSELL C. WHITE, *for Committee.*

Upon motion to adopt, Brethren Jas. A. Ivey and R. C. White spoke to the report. The report was adopted. Brother N. H. Shepherd presented the following resolution:

Resolved, That we, the visitors and messengers to the session of the Johnston County Baptist Association, hereby express our appreciation of the hospitality of the church and community in so abundantly providing for us while meeting with them, and pray God's blessing and guidance for them in the future.

Respectfully submitted,

N. H. SHEPHERD.

The resolution was adopted by a unanimous rising vote of thanks. The Moderator then recognized Brother J. A. Smith, who presented the

TREASURER'S REPORT

BUILDING FUND

Received from churches October 30, 1923.................................$ 403.95
Received from Associational Missions... 30.63

                                                                    $ 434.58

MINUTE FUND

Received from churches October 30, 1923.............................$ 205.19

DISBURSEMENTS

Due to J. A. Smith from 1921...$ 7.98
To R. M. Von Miller for salary and postage.............................   62.45
To R. M. Von Miller for printing and postage.........................   147.90

                                                                    $ 218.33
Due to J. A. Smith, Treasurer, October 30, 1923...................$ 13.14

Respectfully submitted,

J. A. SMITH, *Treasurer.*

I have examined the Treasurer's books and found them correct. November 1, 1923.

JULIAN H. CREECH, *Auditor.*

The report was adopted. Brother R. C. White presented the following resolution:

Resolved, That when a deficit is found to exist in operation of Association, the Treasurer shall make known such deficit to the Executive Committee, and the Executive Committee shall provide for same by appeal to the churches.

Respectfully submitted,

R. C. WHITE.

The resolution was adopted. After which Brother S. L. Morgan presented the following resolution, which was adopted:

Resolved, That each committee appointed to prepare a report on any convention object is hereby requested to see that due notice shall be given to one or more who are to speak to the reports, that thorough preparation shall be made, and addresses given of as great inspirational value as possible.

Respectfully submitted,

S. L. MORGAN.

REPORT OF THE COMMITTEE ON RESOLUTIONS IN MEMORY OF BROTHER J. M. BEATY

Brother J. M. Beaty for many years was one of the most self-sacrificial members of this Association, and whom our Heavenly Father in His wisdom removed from our midst, has so endeared himself during his life to the entire Association that it is a sacred duty to record in the Minutes of our Association a memorial to serve as a token of the esteem in which he was held and an inspiration to those who come after us. Brother Beaty, who has gone to his reward, was an outstanding character in his lifetime as he lived and labored among us. It can be said without hesitation that he was the most consecrated, most ardent promoter of the development of our churches in the Johnston Association, as well as the most sacrificial giver for the Lord's cause within the bounds of our Association. No man knew the churches and the individual member better than he did, and knowing them he knew their needs. No service was too great, no labor too fatiguing, no difficulty so unsurmountable; by day and night his heart was in the work of our Lord's work in Johnston County. It would be a revelation, and it would stagger imagination, could we say in round figures the amount he gave for the work in Johnston County; only God has a record of that. In his life he was so simple, so unassuming, so patient, always hopeful, never tiring; time and again when others lost hope he would encourage to keep on trying. And it can be said with truthfulness that many a church house stands today in Johnston County due largely to the sacrificial gifts of Brother Beaty. Many an underpaid minister had his salary supplemented by this noble man of God. And so his life was indeed beautiful because of his unselfishness. He gave himself unto the Lord first, and therefore all that he had, and all that he was, belonged to the Lord, whom He served so faithfully. But his unceasing toil told on his health and at last, after a long, lingering illness, in which he still continued to show an abiding interest in the work of the Kingdom, and be an inspiration to those who visited him during these long-drawn-out days of sickness, and after he had first made a handsome provision in his will for the good work in our Association, God transplanted him, took him home to his reward he so richly deserves. His life was a perpetual blessing; his works will follow him, and it is for us to follow his noble example of love, service, and sacrifice. Brother Beaty finished his work when he left us, October, 1920. May we continue it until we, like him, shall pass from the scenes of noble activity to the realms of our reward.

Respectfully submitted,

J. F. Pool, *for the Committee.*

The Moderator, Brother R. H. Gower, and Brother S. L. Morgan, after the close of business of the Association, made some very helpful remarks, after which Brother J. J. Lane led the body in a closing prayer. The Moderator then declared the meeting of the twenty-first session of the Johnston County Baptist Association closed, to meet Wednesday after the fourth Sunday in October, 1924, with the Baptist Church at Four Oaks.

R. H. Gower, *Moderator.*

R. M. Von Miller, *Clerk.*

MINUTES

of the

WOMAN'S MISSIONARY SOCIETY

The Woman's Missionary Union of the Johnston County Baptist Association held its annual session with the W. M. S. of the Baptist Church at Benson, N. C., October 25, 1923. The session opened by singing "Come, Women Wide Proclaim." The devotional was led by Mrs. Brady, who read Mark 16:1-10. The Minutes of the last meeting were read and approved; after which warm words of welcome were voiced on behalf of the W. M. S. of the Baptist Church at Benson by Mrs. C. C. Canady, and on behalf of the Methodist W. M. S. by Mrs. W. T. Martin, the Presbyterian W. M. S. by Miss Roberta Bain, to which Mrs. F. Gray, of Smithfield, responded, after which visitors were recognized. Among those present were four pastors of our Association—Rev. R. L. Tate, Rev. Jas. A. Ivey, Rev. O. A. Keller, and Rev. R. C. White; also Dr. T. W. O'Kelley, Mrs. Chas. E. Maddry, Miss Mary Warren, of Raleigh.

The reports of the societies were very encouraging, and Mrs. Hocutt's report was splendid and showed a broadening of the work in the Association and more interest in the work of the societies. Thirty-four reported. The amount contributed this year is $5,568.35.

A brief survey of our missionary work was ably discussed by Miss Veola Pool, of Mt. Moriah. We were happy to have Miss Mildred Parrish to sing for us. Her solo was "The Ninety-first Psalm," by McDairmid. In the absence of Mrs. Thurston, Mrs. Paul Wallace gave the report on Personal Service. This was a splendid report. Mrs Chas. E. Maddry, in her address on Personal Service, brought to us new thoughts as to the meaning of personal service. Are we giving our time to help those who are in need? Stewardship, not of money but of our lives; how are we spending our lives. The "Standard of Excellence," playlet by the Benson M. S., was impressive and taught the lesson of perseverance. Dr. T. W. O'Kelley gave some thoughts on his trip to the Baptist World Alliance, held in Stockholm, Sweden. He told us many interesting things about the different places he visited. He was greatly impressed with the service he attended at Spurgeon's Church in London. Felt perfectly at home with the great throng that had met at Stockholm to do the Master's work. The chair appointed the following committees:

To Nominate—Mrs. Jones, Mrs. Batten, Mrs. Earp.

Time and Place—Mrs. J. M. Beaty, Mrs. Cox, Mrs. M. A. Peacock.

Resolutions—Mrs. D. B. Oliver, Mrs. C. W. Carter, Mrs. Ballance.

Closing devotional by Mrs. C. W. Carter.

The session adjourned for dinner, which was served in the Sunday school rooms.

AFTERNOON—OCTOBER 25TH

After the devotional led by Miss Hazel Finch, who read the 100 Psalm, with Mrs. S. L. Morgan leading in prayer. Greetings on behalf Junior Societies of Benson to the Auxiliaries were presented by Miss Juanita Martin, of Benson; to which Miss Margaret Lee Jones, of Clayton, responded. We were indeed grieved at the absence of our Junior Superintendent, Mrs. E. H. Steger, of Clayton, who was called away on account of the death of her aunt, Mrs. Will Thurston. Her report was read by Mrs. B. A. Hocutt. The W. M. U. Training School, as it is known to us as the "House Beautiful," was very interestingly presented to us by Mrs. George Vick. This subject always interests many, especially those who attended this school. A solo, "Entreat Me Not to Leave Thee," by Mrs. E. M. Hall, was enjoyed by all. The Mission Literature Pageant by Benson young people was impressive and helpful. Mrs. N. H. Shepherd presented Mission Study in a wonderful way. The demonstration by the Benson Sunbeams manifested fine training. Miss Mary Warren, from the Central Office at Raleigh, presented the subject "Victory," based on 1 John 5:4, and gave us a very helpful talk.

The Time and Place Committee reported invitations. both from Bailey and Selma. It was decided that we meet with Selma W. M. S., October, 1924.

The Nominating Committee recommended the re-election of all the officers, with Mrs. S. L. Morgan as Mission Study Superintendent.

The Union gave a rising vote of thanks to the various papers for their services.

We paused to ask God's blessings on the families of those who have lost some one since we met last. Among those are Miss Dorothy Gower, little Doris Hinnant, Mrs. A. Creech, and Mrs. Hobbs of Benson. Miss Grace Barbour read a beautiful tribute in memory of her dear friend, Miss Dorothy Gower. Miss Bessie Lee Pool sang "I've Done My Work."

After silent prayer, we adjourned with prayer by Mrs. S. L. Morgan.

NIGHT SESSION—OCTOBER 25TH

This session opened at 7:30 p. m. Rev. E. M. Hall, of Benson M. E. Church, led the devotional exercises, with prayer by Rev. A. T. Lassiter, of Benson Presbyterian Church. The offering then taken amounted to $5.50 for expense of the meeting. The quartet, "He Will Hold Me Fast," was very beautifully rendered by Benson Baptist Choir.

Rev. O. A. Keller, of Benson, introduced Rev. Russell C. White, of Clayton Baptist Church, who gave us a very inspirational missionary sermon.

Mrs. C. W. Carter reported resolutions of thanks to all who helped to make the meeting of the Union a success. After which we adjourned to meet with the W. M. S. of the Selma Baptist Church, October, 1924.

                    MRS. B. A. HOCUTT, *Superintendent.*
CLEVE BARNES, *Secretary.*

APPORTIONMENTS FOR ASSOCIATIONAL BUILDING AND MINUTE FUND

Name of Churches	Bldg. Fund	Minute Fund
Antioch	$ 15.00	$ 5.00
Bailey	15.00	5.00
Baptist Center	10.00	5.00
Beaty's Chapel	5.00	2.50
Benson	50.00	10.00
Benson Grove	5.00	2.50
Bethany	15.00	5.00
Blackman's Grove	25.00	7.50
Bethel	5.00	2.50
Bethesda	25.00	7.50
Burnell	5.00	2.50
Calvary	10.00	5.00
Canaan	5.00	2.50
Carter's Chapel	25.00	7.50
Clayton	100.00	15.00
Clyde's Chapel	25.00	7.50
Corinth	25.00	7.50
Four Oaks	25.00	7.50
Hale's Chapel	10.00	5.00
Hepzibah	10.00	5.00
Hood's Grove	15.00	5.00
Kenly	15.00	5.00
Lee's Chapel	25.00	10.00
Live Oak	5.00	2.50
Micro	10.00	2.50
Middlesex	10.00	5.00
Mount Moriah	150.00	15.00
New Bethel	50.00	10.00
Noble's Chapel	25.00	7.50
Parrish Memorial	20.00	5.00
Pauline	10.00	2.50
Pine Level	50.00	10.00
Pinkney	5.00	2.50
Pisgah	25.00	7.50
Pleasant Grove	5.00	2.50
Princeton	25.00	5.00
Sardis	25.00	5.00
Selma	50.00	10.00
Shiloh	10.00	5.00
Smithfield	50.00	15.00
Thanksgiving	15.00	5.00
Trinity	10.00	5.00
White Oak	25.00	7.50
Wilson's Mills	15.00	5.00
Total	$1,045.00	$ 257.50

STATISTICAL TABLES

TABLE I—

Church	Pastor and Postoffice	Clerk and Postoffice
Antioch	A. R. Creech, Buie's Creek	W. O. Hocutt, Middlesex, R. 3
Bailey	N. H. Shepherd, Kenly	J. P. Underwood, Bailey
Baptist Center	R. L. Gay, Smithfield	Willie C. Hardee, Clayton
Beaty's Chapel		Mrs. J. J. Parrish, Smithfield
Benson	O. A. Keller, Benson	Julian Godwin, Benson
Bethesda	R. L. Gay, Smithfield	J. E. Smith, Wilson's Mills
Bethany	W. D. Stancil, Kenly, R. 2	Julian H. Creech, Kenly
Bethel	N. H. Shepherd, Kenly	J. R. Bunn, Kenly
Benson Grove	E. B. Booker. Smithfield	L. E. Barber, Benson
Blackman's Grove	Jas. A. Ivey, Four Oaks	J. R. Blackman, Four Oaks
Burnell	Jas. A. Ivey, Four Oaks	W. L. Massingill, Four Oaks
Calvary	L. R. Tate. Benson	T. J. Lee, Dunn
Canaan	L. R. Tate, Censon	T. L. Hudson, Bentonsville
Carter's Chapel	Arthur Creech, Buie's Creek	Zeb. Eatman, Selma, R. 1
Clayton	R. C. White, Clayton	W. P. Creech, Clayton
Clyde's Chapel	B. M. Shacklett, Angier	C. I. Johnson, Wendell, R. 1
Corinth	C. H. Cashwell, Wendell	L. T. Davis, Wendell, R. 1
Four Oaks	Jas. A. Ivey, Four Oaks	B. B. Creech, Four Oaks
Hale's Chapel	C. H. Cashwell, Wendell	A. D. Parrish, Zebulon, R. 2
Hepzibah		W. G. Creech, Princeton
Hood's Grove	L. R. Tate, Benson	Y. L. Blackman, Bentonsville
Kenly	N. H. Shepherd, Kenly	F. A. White, Kenly
Lee's Chapel	J. E. Hocutt, Nashville	W. I. Green, Zebulon, R. 2
Live Oak		J. M. Richardson, Selma, R. 2
Micro	W. D. Stancil, Kenly	S. C. Batten, Micro
Middlesex	J. W. Noble, Middlesex	J. C Overman, Middlesex
Mount Moriah	R. T. Vann, Raleigh	Russell Powell, Auburn
New Bethel	T. Z. Seymoure, Raleigh	Geo. W. Bryan, Garner
Noble's Chapel	N. H. Shepherd, Kenly	N. L. Stott, Sims
Oliver's Grove	E. B. Booker, Smithfield	J. E. Ryals, Four Oaks
Parrish Memorial	D. E. Vipperman, Pine Level	J. D. Creech, Selma, R. 2
Pauline	L. R. Tate, Benson	J. R. Massey, Four Oaks, R. 1
Pine Level	D. E. Vipperman, Pine Level	F. C. Price, Pine Level
Pinkney	N. H. Shepherd, Kenly	Mrs. B. R. Edgerton, Kenly, R. 1
Pisgah	R. L. Gay, Smithfield	R. H. Higgins, Smithfield
Pleasant Grove	B. M. Shacklett, Angier	Claude Stephenson, Willow Springs
Princeton	N. H. Shepherd, Kenly	W. I. Pearce, Princeton
Sardis	A. A. Butler, Selma	T G. Strickland, Smithfield
Selma	A. A. Butler, Selma	Theo. Easom, Selma
Shiloh	R. L. Gay, Smithfield	S. H. Averitt, Garner
Smithfield	S. L. Morgan, Smithfield	L. T. Royall, Smithfield
Thanksgiving	R. M. VonMiller, Wilson	Carl Whitley, Selma, R. 1
Trinity	L. R. Tate, Benson	J. S. Lawhorn, Benson, R. 2
White Oak	C. H. Cashwell, Wendell	W. H. Green, Clayton, R. 2
Wilson's Mills	S. N. Lamb, Wake Forest	Ernest Price, Wilson's Mills
Total		

Treasurer and Postoffice	Time of Preaching	Value of Church Property	Value of Pastor's Home	Gains				Losses			Total Membership
				By Baptism	By Letter	By Statement	By Restoration	By Letter	By Exclusion	By Death	
). Oneal, Middlesex, R. 3	2	$ 3,000	$ ----	5	1			11	2	1	185
/. B. Finch, Bailey	1	4,000		4	3			3			73
ie C. Hardee, Clayton	3	2,500	3,000	2				2			140
. J. J. Parrish, Smithfield	2	1,500									11
. H. O. Dixon, Benson	F. T.	35,000		18	9			6			204
?. Smith, Wilson's Mills	4	3,500		5	1	1		5	26	4	184
an H. Creech, Kenly	4	6,000		22				1	2		162
:. Bunn, Kenly	4	1,000									7
?. Barber, Benson	3	2,000		2	1	1		2	5		50
;ah Wood, Four Oaks	2 & 4	1,500		4	2						97
. Johnson, Four Oaks	1	1,500		1							21
. Lee, Dunn	1	2,000						1			29
,. Hudson, Bentonsville	3	1,000		3	3						40
. Eatman, Selma, R. 1	1	1,500		12	5	3	2	1	12	1	110
M. Hall, Clayton	F. T.	75,000	10,000		9	1		7		7	563
., Boyette, Wendell, R. 1	1	750			7		2	5		2	142
". Davis, Wendell, R. 1	4	4,000						9	13	2	167
H. Sanders, Four Oaks	1 & 3	20,000		3	3			4	1	1	112
(. Parrish, Zebulon, R. 2	4	2,500		4	4	2		1	5		82
?. Creech, Princeton	1	1,500			2						14
ind Hayes, Four Oaks	3	1,000		4	4			3	3		52
. Broughton, Kenly	2 & 4	2,500	1,500	1	5	4					43
(. Price, Zebulon, R. 1	3	2,000		1	4			4		4	255
.. Richardson, Selma, R. 2	3	1,500									6
C. L. Batten, Micro	3	3,000		1	2			2			65
.. Barber, Middlesex	4	2,500	2,500		1			2		1	100
!. Pool, Clayton	1	4,200	3,200	9	2						210
. W. Bryan, Garner	4	5,000		3	2			1	3	2	143
,. Stott, Sims	4	1,000		10		8				3	117
. Ryals, Four Oaks	2 & 4	800									12
. Watson, Selma, R. 2	2	2,500					1	2			25
. Massey, Four Oaks, R. 1	2	2,000		12							78
W. B. Oliver, Pine Level	1	5,000			1			1	1	1	75
B. R. Edgerton, Kenly, R. 1	3	1,500		1	1				1		25
). Johnson, Smithfield	1	3,000	1,000		1			2	2	1	66
ide Stephenson, Willow Springs	- 3	500									10
;. H. Holt, Princeton	3	2,000		1							73
. Stevens, Smithfield	1 & 3	2,500						1	2	2	81
). Easom, Selma	F. T.	25,000	2,500	3	1		1	21	22	2	242
. Williams, McCullers	2	3,000									74
. Brooks, Smithfield	F. T.	20,000	8,000		7			8	3	1	313
Whitley, Selma, R. 1	2	2,750		7	7			2	12	1	135
!. Lee, Benson, R. 2	4	2,000		9	2			2	1	3	118
(. Green, Clayton, R. 2	1	4,000		8	5		1	2	1		242
Adams, Wilson's Mills	2	2,000		2	2			4			78
----		$366,450	$ 31,700	157	97	20	7	115	106	39	5,031

TABLE II—FINANCIAL

				LOCAL						
CHURCHES	Pastor's Salary	Other Salaries	Ministerial Help	Building and Repairs	Incidentals	S.-S. and B.Y.P.U. Expenses	Local Poor	Minute Fund, etc.	Other Objects	Home Total
Antioch	$ 230.00	$	$	$	$ 55.70	$ 25.50	$	$ 5.00	$	$ 314.20
Bailey	300.00	2.50	50.00		35.80	30.00	17.50	5.00	15.00	405.80
Baptist Center	300.00					18.00		5.00		373.00
Bethany	101.00					20.00		1.70		627.70
Benson	933.34	300.00	245.00	500.00	186.15	190.74	5.00	10.00	395.00	2,383.04
Benson Grove	150.00			122.81		40.00		2.50		192.50
Bethel	50.00		75.00	75.00		8.30		2.00		135.30
Beaty's Chapel		36.75								
Bethesda	400.00		13.00		25.00	68.00		7.50	28.00	497.25
Blackman's Grove	300.00		40.00		38.56	26.54		7.50	255.00	429.06
Burnell	119.50		30.00		2.05			2.50		418.59
Calvary	100.00					6.00		2.65		142.65
Canaan	100.00							1.25		137.25
Carter's Chapel	224.95			475.00		84.21	10.00	6.00	2.70	702.86
Clayton	2,125.00	220.00		32,555.00	1,819.74	365.27		10.00		37,095.01
Clyde's Chapel	350.00					33.54		5.30		388.84
Corinth	352.23		50.65		31.40	73.80		3.50		511.58
Four Oaks	1,000.00		160.58	1,527.50	15.50	230.18		7.50	12.46	2,941.26
Hale's Chapel	150.00		46.50	317.00		30.46		2.50		42.95
Hephzibah	17.45		8.00			15.00		2.50		558.92
Hood's Grove	125.00		30.00		10.00	8.00		2.75		175.75
Kenly	225.00	90.00		49.36	53.88	69.72		5.00		492.96
Lee's Chapel	300.00	45.00		124.00	45.00	49.66		10.00	100.00	673.66
Live Oak	37.50				10.00			.50		48.00
Micro	128.46		18.00	225.00		27.59	1.25		26.00	426.30
Middlesex	500.00		54.00	291.00	60.00	128.23		2.00	216.64	1,251.87
Mount Moriah	300.00	30.00	90.00	3,200.00		100.61	21.61	15.00		3,757.22
New Bethel	300.00	400.00	26.00		94.00	45.00		8.00		873.00
Noble's Chapel	300.00		35.00	117.00	62.75	53.69		7.50	71.55	647.49

Oliver's Grove	17.00	9.00	.83	2.00				1.00	5.00	34.83
Parrish Memorial	150.00	12.00		199.38				3.00		364.38
Pauline	100.00		21.05			14.00		2.25		137.30
Pine Level	350.00	18.00	20.00	417.15	162.01	45.73	18.28	5.00		1,036.17
Pinkney	96.00		87.50	300.00	30.00	14.63		2.50		143.13
Pisgah	500.00			300.00		52.93	12.00	10.00		962.43
Pleasant Grove	60.00	12.00	25.00	136.50	37.00			1.50		61.50
Princeton	225.00	65.00	25.00			65.08		5.00		558.58
Sardis	250.00					21.00		5.00		276.00
Selma	1,583.29	120.00	180.00	496.30	201.72	176.56		10.00	10.04	2,777.91
Shiloh	233.35			100.00				5.00	40.00	377.35
Smithfield	2,400.00			150.00	150.00	400.00	100.00	15.00	150.00	3,215.00
Thanksgiving	250.00		25.40		265.21	61.34		5.00		606.95
Trinity	150.00		60.50			46.00		3.50		260.00
White Oak	347.90		98.75			40.00		7.50		494.15
Wilson's Mills	250.00				98.00	12.00	50.00		25.00	435.00
Total	$ 16,481.97	$ 1,348.25	$ 2,915.76	$ 40,930.00	$ 3,487.47	$ 2,704.31	$ 223.64	$ 211.90	$ 1,352.39	$ 69,655.69

TABLE II—FINANCIAL—Continued

Churches	75-Million (Undesignated)	Foreign Missions	Home Missions	State and Associational Missions	Christian Education	Orphanage	Hospitals	Ministerial Relief	Other Benevolences	Denominational Total	Grand Total
	$	$	$	$	$	$	$	$	$	$	$
Antioch	105.00	2.12				11.50			17.50	136.12	450.86
Bailey	58.00		1.50		3.75	20.20			32.00	115.45	521.25
Baptist Center	26.50									26.50	399.50
Bethany	171.22			10.00		20.00				201.22	828.92
Benson	1,250.05			10.00		15.72				1,275.77	3,638.81
Benson Grove			5.00			4.80				9.80	202.30
Bethel	4.85									4.85	140.15
Beaty's Chapel	355.50									355.50	852.75
Bethesda	174.05								2.50	176.55	605.61
Blackman's Grove	40.60					10.00				50.60	469.19
Burnell	38.17									38.17	180.82
Calvary	75.40									75.40	212.65
Canaan	56.75		2.00	2.90		13.04	1.00		12.70	88.39	791.25
Carter's Chapel	2,200.00	257.00				248.12				2,705.12	39,800.13
Clayton	239.00									239.00	627.84
Clyde's Chapel	51.00								5.00	56.00	567.58
Corinth	366.35	32.26	33.90	33.75	11.66	58.71	8.00		25.00	569.63	3,510.89
Four Oaks	45.70									45.70	604.62
Hale's Chapel	8.00			4.00					5.00	17.00	59.95
Hepzibah	23.00									23.00	198.75
Hood's Grove	66.00	3.75	3.00	3.25	1.00	70.24		3.61	65.00	215.85	708.81
Kenly		20.00	10.00	25.00	5.54	15.00		5.00		80.54	754.20
Lee's Chapel						1.00				1.00	49.00
Live Oak											
Micro	243.52					125.00			8.52	377.04	803.34
Middlesex	319.43								22.72	342.15	1,594.02
Mount Moriah	818.56					325.60			30.00	1,174.16	4,931.38
New Bethel	250.00					60.00			12.40	322.40	1,195.40
Noble's Chapel	72.00					28.14				100.14	747.63

	1	2	3	4	5	6	7	8	9	10	Total
Oliver's Grove	2.75	.50	2.00	1.00	.50	2.75	1.00	1.00	1.50	13.00	47.83
Parrish Memorial		5.00	5.00	15.00	5.00	5.00	5.00	5.00	20.00	60.00	424.33
Pauline	10.60			30.00						40.60	177.90
Pine Level	462.61			6.00		10.00			35.00	513.61	1,549.78
Pinkney	42.39					11.34			5.00	58.73	201.86
Pisgah	468.41					56.84			25.00	550.25	1,512.68
Pleasant Grove											61.50
Princeton	34.00	3.85	5.35	5.45	4.30	25.37	2.75	5.05	13.80	65.92	624.50
Sardis	287.51									34.00	310.00
Selma	32.53					75.00				362.51	3,140.42
Shiloh	1,985.84					49.11			20.00	101.64	478.99
Smithfield	61.00					66.91			50.00	2,102.75	5,317.75
Thanksgiving	64.20					9.00				70.00	676.95
Trinity	80.50									64.20	324.20
White Oak										80.50	574.65
Wilson's Mills						60.00				60.00	495.00
Total	$ 10,360.99	$ 324.48	$ 67.75	$ 146.35	$ 31.75	$1,423.39	$ 12.75	$ 19.66	$ 358.64	$ 12,745.76	$ 82,401.45

TABLE III—

Church	Superintendent and Postoffice	Secretary and Postoffice
Antioch	A. D. Oneal, Middlesex, R. 3	W. O. Hocutt, Middlesex, R. 3
Bailey	J. W. B. Finch, Bailey	W. P. Finch, Bailey
Baptist Center	R. B. Ellis, Clayton	Wade Zippett, Clayton
Beaty's Chapel		
Benson	M. T. Britt, Benson	J. C. Morgan, Benson
Benson Grove	W. B. Benson, Benson	L. E. Barber, Benson
Bethany	D. C. Smith, Selma	J. H. Creech, Kenly
Bethel	James Bunn, Kenly	
Bethesda	J. B. Coates, Wilson's Mills	V. S. Smith, Wilson's Mills
Blackman's Grove	Joseph Wood, Four Oaks	Nogah Wood, Four Oaks
Burnell	W. L. Massengill, Four Oaks	C. Johnson, Four Oaks
Calvary		
Canaan		
Clayton	W. P. Creech, Clayton	Chas. S. Gulley, Clayton
Carter's Chapel	Zeb. Eatman, Selma, R. 1	J. R. Atkinson, Selma, R. 2
Clyde's Chapel	B. N. Hobgood, Wendell, R. 1	Mamie Boykin, Wendell, R. 1
Corinth	L. E. Hocutt, Zebulon, R. 1	O. Thomasson, Wendell, R. 1
Hale's Chapel	J. B. Richardson, Zebulon	A. L. Tippett, Zebulon, R. 1
Hepzibah	W. G. Creech, Princeton	J. F. Earp, Pine Level
Four Oaks	J. H. Strickland, Four Oaks	W. Jesse Stanley, Four Oaks
Hood's Grove	D. J. Wood, Jr., Bentonsville	Mrs. J. Hudson, Benson
Kenly	A. J. Broughton, Kenly	W. F. Rackley, Kenly
Lee's Chapel	A. G. Lewis, Middlesex	Bettie G. Bunn, Zebulon
Live Oak	J. M. Richardson, Selma	W. B. Morris, Selma, R. 1
Micro	C. L. Batten, Micro	J. L. Brown, Selma, R. 2
Middlesex	W. K. Ballentine, Middlesex	J. M. Davis, Middlesex
Mount Moriah	J. G Lane, Auburn	J. P. Jones, Clayton, R. 3
New Bethel	R. I. Smith, McCullers	E. Britt, Garner
Noble's Chapel	L. F. Boykin, Sims	O. Bullock, Sims
Oliver's Grove	J. E. Ryals, Four Oaks	Lena Tyner, Four Oaks
Parrish Memorial	J. N. Watson, Selma, R. 2	H. Parrish, Selma, R. 2
Pauline	Mrs. Effie Strickland, Four Oaks	Miss C. B. Massey, Four Oaks
Pine Level	F. C. Price, Pine Level	Miss Pearl Britt, Pine Level
Pinkney	Leslie Davis, Fremont, R. 2	Seth Davis, Fremont, R. 2
Pisgah	J. A. Smith, Four Oaks, R. 4	P. E. Whitley, Smithfield
Princeton	Chas. H. Holt, Princeton	W. M. Holt, Princeton
Pleasant Grove	S. H. Averitt, Garner	W. F. Honecutt, Garner
Sardis	B. L. Strickland, Smithfield	J. W. Oliver, Smithfield, R. 2
Selma	N. J. Creech, Selma	J. N. Wiggs, Selma
Shiloh		
Smithfield	L. T. Royall, Smithfield	John Iver, Smithfield
Thanksgiving	W. S. Earp, Selma, R. 1	J. O. Brannon, Selma, R. 1
Trinity	O. H. Barefoot, Benson, R. 2	Verta Lawhorn, Benson, R. 2
White Oak	A. L. Batten, Clayton, R. 2	W. H. Greene, Clayton, R. 2
Wilson's Mills	J. T. Holt, Wilson's Mills	W. N. Todd, Wilson's Mills
Total		

	ENROLLMENT MAIN SCHOOL							MISCELLANEOUS							
Officers and Teachers	Beginners 3 to 5	Primary 6 to 8	Junior 9 to 12	Intermediate 13 to 16	Senior and Adult 17 and up	Home Department	Total	Cradle Roll	Is School Graded?	Is School Standard?	How Many Normal Diplomas?	Baptisms from School	Contributions for Home Expenses	Contributions for Orphanages, Missions, etc.	Total Contributions
7	20	25	18	12	24	----	106	----	yes	no	----	3	$ 25.50	$ 17.00	$ 42.00
7	20	18	16	10	26	----	97	----	yes	no	----	----	25.00	----	25.00
7	13	10	17	19	31	----	97	----	yes	no	----	----	18.00	9.82	27.82
----	----	----	----	----	----	----	260	21	yes	no	----	18	169.40	----	169.40
7	12	15	15	25	56	----	130	----	yes	no	----	2	40.00	----	40.00
7	----	16	16	----	58	32	129	----	yes	no	----	----	20.00	----	20.00
6	14	----	11	12	21	----	64	----	yes	no	----	----	8.30	----	8.30
10	25	----	12	15	40	----	102	----	yes	no	----	5	40.00	6.00	46.00
12	15	17	8	22	15	----	89	----	yes	no	----	3	58.00	----	58.00
7	10	17	18	20	11	----	83	----	yes	no	----	1	26.54	10.00	36.54
24	30	45	60	45	150	60	414	----	yes	yes	22	----	335.27	133.32	468.59
7	18	26	36	18	55	----	160	----	yes	no	1	4	25.00	14.43	39.43
8	----	56	----	----	58	----	122	----	no	no	----	----	33.54	----	33.54
8	19	18	17	----	65	----	127	----	no	no	----	----	53.35	30.50	83.85
8	10	18	12	10	12	----	70	----	no	no	----	4	12.46	----	12.46
4	15	----	15	10	----	----	44	----	no	no	----	----	15.00	----	15.00
18	15	9	31	25	42	----	140	40	yes	no	8	2	204.15	47.20	251.35
5	6	----	8	----	15	----	34	----	no	no	----	1	8.00	----	8.00
7	10	12	14	----	21	----	64	----	yes	no	----	1	69.72	65.74	135.46
8	----	22	13	22	51	----	116	----	yes	no	----	1	49.66	----	49.66
----	----	----	----	----	----	----	30	----	no	no	----	----	8.00	----	8.00
7	10	10	15	10	45	----	97	15	no	no	----	----	27.59	----	27.59
10	20	14	20	14	27	----	105	----	yes	no	----	----	128.23	155.59	283.82
13	24	----	20	22	105	----	184	----	yes	no	----	9	110.61	316.56	427.17
8	----	48	38	24	58	----	176	----	no	no	----	2	45.00	----	45.00
7	----	8	15	----	15	----	45	----	no	no	----	5	45.69	8.00	53.69
5	3	6	6	8	10	----	38	----	no	no	----	----	3.00	5.00	8.00
5	10	15	10	8	----	----	48	----	no	no	----	----	15.00	5.00	20.00
4	----	10	----	----	11	----	25	----	no	no	----	----	14.00	----	14.00
8	25	31	18	12	18	----	112	----	yes	no	3	----	45.73	56.09	101.82
5	15	10	10	9	15	----	64	----	yes	no	----	1	14.63	6.34	20.97
10	10	9	9	20	20	12	90	25	yes	no	3	----	52.93	31.96	84.89
7	18	16	16	25	34	----	116	----	yes	no	----	1	65.08	----	65.08
4	----	20	30	21	23	----	98	----	yes	no	----	----	24.31	32.53	56.84
9	18	17	----	10	32	----	86	----	yes	no	----	----	20.00	----	20.00
12	20	30	40	56	42	----	200	----	yes	no	----	2	176.56	75.00	251.56
18	25	52	62	16	138	----	311	17	yes	no	1	3	400.00	----	400.00
9	15	20	32	17	81	----	174	----	yes	no	----	3	61.34	9.00	70.34
7	6	10	15	10	12	----	60	----	yes	no	----	5	46.00	----	46.00
10	37	31	21	25	34	----	158	----	yes	no	----	1	40.00	----	40.00
7	16	----	16	----	42	----	81	----	no	no	----	2	10.00	----	10.00
332	524	681	730	572	1,513	104	4,746	118	----	----	38	76	$2,590 59	$1,035.08	$3,625.67

TABLE IV—WOMAN'S MISSIONARY UNION

Church	Name of Organization	President and Postoffice	Number of Members	75-Million (All objects)	Other Benevolences	Total Contributions	Enrolled Mission Study
Bailey	W. M. S.	Mrs. W. J. Privett, Bailey	15	$ 44.00	$ 11.01	$ 55.01	
Bailey	Sunbeam Soc.	Miss Hazel Finch, Bailey	16	5.00	2.00	7.00	
Benson	W. M. S.	Mrs. R B Brady, Benson	30	523.00		523.00	
Benson	Sunbeam Soc.	Mrs. W. V. Cavenaugh, Benson	30	18.00		18.00	
Blackman's Grove	W. M. S.	Miss Hessie Phelps, Four Oaks	15	57.30		57.33	
Clayton	Y. W. A.	Mrs. W. P. ..., Clayton	57	1,671.33	70.00	1,741.33	17
Clayton	G. A.	Mrs. Emmit Steger, Clayton	20	269.58		269.58	
Clayton	R A.	Mrs. B. A. Hocutt, Clayton	21	250.52		250.52	
Clayton	Sunbeam Soc.	Mrs. C W Carter, Clayton	16	185.63		185.63	
Clayton	W. M. S	Mrs. ... Wallace, Clayton	44	100.00		100.00	
Hyde's Chapel	W. M. S	Mamie Batten, Wendell, R. 1	30	150.50		150.50	
Four Oaks	W. M. S.	M W A. Massengill, Four Oaks	20	144.66	162.90	337.56	
Four Oaks	Sunbeam Soc.	Miss Esther ..., Four Oaks	10	3.50		3.50	
Kenly	W. M. S.	Mrs. J E Jones, Kenly	15	25.00	66.75	94.75	
Micro	W. M. S.	Mrs. C. L. Wall, Micro	17	131.35	15.00	146.35	
Middlesex	W. M. S.	Mrs. C. A. Barber, Middlesex	12	8.16	7.72	15.88	
Middlesex	G. A.	Mrs. J. M. Davis, Middlesex	8	24.43		24.43	
Middlesex	Sunbeam Soc.	Mrs. N. B. ..., Middlesex	38	147.55	13.00	160.55	
Mount Moriah	W. M. S	Mrs. J. C. Barrington, ...eigh, R. 2	23	32.16	71.55	103.71	
Noble's	W. M. S	Mrs. G B. Boykin, Sims	19	152.62		152.62	
Pine Level	Sunbeam Soc.	Mrs. B. L. Strickland, Pine Level	6	8.62		8.62	
Pine Level	W. M. S	Mrs. D. B. Oliver, Pine Level	38	46.34	1.00	47.31	
Pisgah	W. M. S.	Mrs. W. D. ...nson, Smithfield	8	65.00	175.10	241.10	
Princeton	W. M. S.	Mrs. G W Howell, Princeton	26	287.50		237.50	
Selma	Sunbeam Soc.	Mrs. Dr. G. D. Vick, Selma	30	13.75	10.00	23.75	
Selma	W. M. S.	Mrs. G. M. Willets, Selma	50	438.00	88.49	526.49	
Smithfield	W. M. S.	Mrs. Paul V. Brown, Smithfield	40				
Smithfield	Y. W. A.	Mrs. D. H. Creech, Smithfield	12	19.50	1.20	20.70	
Smithfield	G. A.	Mrs H. G. Gray, Smithfield	14				
Smithfield	Sunbeam Soc.	Mrs H. P. ..., Smithfield	13				
White Oak	W. M. S.	Mrs. J. J. Williams, Wilson's Mills, R. 2	24	30.00		30.00	
Total			720	$ 4,853.00	$ 609.72	$ 5,551.72	17

TABLE V—BAPTIST YOUNG PEOPLES UNION

CHURCH	PRESIDENTS AND POSTOFFICES	No. Unions	No. Members	A-1 Unions	No. in Study Course	No. of Bible Readers
Bailey	Mrs. J. P. Underwood, Jr., Bailey	1	32			15
Benson	William Woodall, Benson, Senior	1	24			
Benson	Jesse Jones, Benson, Intermediate	1	27			
Benson	Alonzo Parrish, Jr., Benson, Junior	1	35			
Blackman's Grove	W. C. Blackman, Four Oaks	1	25			
Burnell	Miss Eva Johnson, Four Oaks, R. 1	1	31			6
Carter's Chapel	Clifton Richardson, Selma, R. 2	1	33		22	9
Clayton	Alton Hilliard, Clayton, Senior	1	28		21	25
Clayton	Harry Lee Hall, Clayton, Intermediate	1	40		15	20
Clayton	Francis Gulley, Clayton, Junior	1	27			18
Corinth	L. T. Davis, Wendell, R. 1	1	32	yes		
Four Oaks	Miss Mabel Coffenberger, Four Oaks	1	18		12	10
Four Oaks	James Parrish, Four Oaks	1	33		22	9
Mount Moriah	C. Parker Pool, Clayton	1	30		12	15
Smithfield	Miss Ruth Wilson, Smithfield	1	38			23
Trinity	O. H. Barefoot, Benson, R. 2	1	20			
Wilson's Mills	Mrs. E. R. Youngblood, Wilson's Mills	1	20		9	
Total		17	493		113	150

MINUTES

OF THE

TWENTY SECOND ANNUAL SESSION

OF THE

Johnston Baptist Association

HELD WITH

FOUR OAKS BAPTIST CHURCH

October 29th to October 30th, 1924

———

The next session will be held with the Thanksgiving
Baptist Church, beginning Wednesday after the
fourth Sunday in October, 1925

———

To preach Introductory sermon, Rev. C. H. Cashwell
To preach Missionary sermon, Rev. Jas. W. Rose

———

MEDLIN PRINTING CO., SMITHFIELD, N. C.

OFFICERS

Moderator, R. H. Gower	Clayton
Vice-Moderator, S. L. Morgan	Smithfield
Clerk, R. M. Von Miller	Wilson, R. 1
Treasurer, J. A. Smith	Four Oaks, R. 4
Auditor, R. A. Bain	Four Oaks

EXECUTIVE COMMITTEE

S. L. Morgan, Chairman	Smithfield
Jas. A. Ivey	Four Oaks
J. Dwight Barbour	Clayton
H. E. Earp	Selma
A. J. Broughton	Kenly
Mrs. J. M. Beaty	Smithfield
Mrs. B. A. Hocutt	Clayton

LIST OF MINISTERS

G. A. Bain	Dunn
C. H. Cashwell	Selma
J. S. Connell	Dunn
A. R. Creech	Buies Creek
W. T. Evans,	Kenly
R. F. Hall	Raleigh, R 2
Jas. A. Ivey	Four Oaks
O. A. Keller	Benson
S. L. Morgan	Smithfield
S. T. Morris	Buies Creek
S. S. McGregor	Smithfield
J. W. Nobles	Middlesex
S. W. Oldham	Wendell
A. A. Pippin	Wakefield
Jas. W. Rose	Pine Level
W. D. Stancil	Kenly
R. M. Von Miller	Wilson, R. 1
R. C. White	Clayton

DELEGATES TO CONVENTIONS

Delegate to Southern Baptist Convention _____Hon. F. H. Brooks
Delegates to Baptist State Convention—R. C. White, O. A. Keller,
J. F. Pool.

STANDING COMMITTEES TO MAKE REPORTS ON
CONVENTION OBJECTS

The Spiritual State of the Churches .... Jas. W. Rose

Social Service—Orphanage, Ministerial Relief, Temperance, and
Hospitals .... Jas. A. Ivey

Missions—Associational, State, Home, Foreign and Woman's Work
.... R. C. White

Christian Education—Colleges, Preparatory Schools, Periodicals,
Books and Tracts .... S. L. Morgan

Teaching and Training—Sunday Schools and B. Y. P. U............
.... J. S. Connell

Enlistment and Stewardship .... O. A. Keller

ENROLLED DELEGATES

Antioch—D. E. Narron, R. R. Creech, W. H. Madden.

Bailey—J. P. Underwood.

Baptist Center—J. C. Hardee, Mrs. L. C. Barbour, Judson Talton,
D. T. Duncan.

Bethany—B. B. Batten, D. C. Smith, W. D. Stancil, A. R. Creech.

Benson—O. A. Keller, Mrs. S. P. J. Lee, Mrs. B. B. Brady, C. C.
Wheeler, Mr. and Mrs. Alonzo Parrish, J. C. West, Mrs. J. F.
Woodall.

Beulah—K. Moore, L. H. Moore.

Bethesda—Elbert Godwin, C. T. Godwin, Mrs. G. A. Smith, G. A.
Smith, Julia Wallace, W. B. Wallace, Mr. and Mrs. J. B. Coates,
W. E. Godwin.

Blackman's Grove—G. W. Wood, Herbert Lee, Bella Lee, Thelma
Lee.

Burnell—Mr. and Mrs. J. S. Johnson, Mrs. T. H. Lassiter.

Calvary—J. K. Hudson.

Carter's Chapel—R. G. Narron, W. H. Scott, W. M. Boykin, J. R.
Atkinson.

Clayton—Mrs. Martha Spence, D. J. Yelvington, R. C. White, Mr.
and Mrs. J. D. Barbour, Miss B. Ellis, Mrs. Chas. Turley, Mrs.
B. A. Hocutt, Mrs. R. H. Gower, R. H. Gower.

Clyde's Chapel—J. C. Pace.

Four Oaks—R. A. Bain, E. B. Johnson, D. H. Sanders, W. P. Mas-
senglll.

Hepzipah—J. F. Earp.

Kenly—J. M. Woodard, Jr., A. J. Broughton, F. C. White.

Lee's Chapel—J. W. Creech.

Live Oak—J. M. Richardson.

Micro—Ernest Wall, D. H. Jones.

Middlesex—J. W. Nobles.

Mount Moriah—J. H. Honeycut, Mr. and Mrs. Jas. G. Lane, R. A.

Baucom, J. M. Baucom.

New Bethel—Mrs. Herbert Britt, S. T. Morris, W. P. Dowd.

Noble's Chapel—Mrs. G. M. Boykin, Mrs. J. H. Grice.

Oliver's Grove—Mr. and Mrs. J. E. Ryals, Lena Tyner, T. V. Allen, J. A. Tyner.

Parrish Memorial—J. W. Godwin, G. W. Parrish.

Pauline—W. P. Joyner, A. G. Adams.

Pisgah—A. G. Jones, R. L. Gay, Mrs. R. L. Gay, J. A. Smith.

Pine Level—B. Godwin, J. F. Watson, Jas. W. Rose, Alex. Strickland.

Pinkney—Mrs. B. R. Edgerton, Mrs. K. C. Atkinson.

Pleasant Grove—Mr. and Mrs. Claude Stephenson.

Selma—H. E. Earp, E. F. Woodard, C. H. Cashwell.

Shiloh—Kitty Coates, S. H. Averitt, Mr. and Mrs. J. W. Williams.

Smithfield—S. L. Morgan, J. A. Underhill, M. A. Wallace, Mrs. W. N. Holt, Mr. and Mrs. T. S. Ragsdale, F. H. Brooks, Mrs. J. D. Dickens.

Thanksgiving—Meline Lynch, Mr. and Mrs. H. P. Earp, J. R. Lynch, R. M. Von Miller.

Trinity—J. L. Johnson.

Wadkins—J. H. Hales, Curtis Hinton.

White Oak—Mr. and Mrs. D. M. Brannan, Mrs. K. C. Atkinson.

CONSTITUTION

1. The Association shall be known as the Johnston Baptist Association.

2. Its objects shall be to extend the privileges of the Gospel and liberal culture to all the people within its bounds, and, by hearty co-operation with the Baptist State Convention, to help offer these privileges to all mankind in and out of its bounds by the cordial co-operation of all the churches constituting this body.

3. It shall be composed of the pastors in active service in the Association and such delegates as shall be annually elected by the churches connected with it, each church being entitled to three delegates, unless the membership shall exceed fifty, and then an additional delegate for every twenty-five members: Provided, no church shall have more than eight delegates.

4. The New Hampshire Declaration of Faith shall be the summary of Divine Truth for determining questions of faith and order in this body, and the churches desiring membership in it must commit themselves to the substance of it, together with the covenant herewith submitted and this Constitution.

5. This Association shall not have power to annul this discipline or exercise authority over any church connected with it, but it may advise with and sever its connection with any church that neglects

to preserve Gospel order, or that treats with contempt the objects or advice of the Association.

6. Each church shall send to the annual meetings of the Association a letter (the blanks to be furnished by the Clerk of the Association), carefully filled as per blank suggestions, stating the full work of thhe church for the year ending with the Sunday previous to the meeting of the Association.

7. The Association shall foster State Missions, Home Missions, Foreign Missions, Christian Education, the Aged Ministers' Relief Board, the Thomasville Orphanage, and the Sunday School Board, and each church shall be requested to contribute to the support of these objects annually.

8. Missions and Education shall have precedence in their claims upon the consideration of this body in its regular sessions.

9. Whenever a church shall fail to be represented by delegates or letter at the annual sessions of the Association, inquiry shall be made for the cause, and efforts shall be made to induce such church to do its duty; and the effort shall be continued till the church is recovered or dropped from the roll.

10. The officers of the Association shall be a Moderator, a Vice-Moderator, a Clerk, a Treasurer, and an Auditor, elected annually, at the close of the annual session to serve the following year, by ballot (or in case when only one brother is put in nomination for an office, then the vote may be by acclamation), from among the members, to serve until their successors shall have been elected, and to perform the duties of such offices, namely, the Moderator, in presiding over the meetings, or the Vice-Moderator, in his absence; the Clerk, in recording and preserving minutes and other papers belonging to the body; the Treasurer, in receiving and disbursing funds belonging to or entrusted to the body, according to its will; the Auditor, to examine the Treasurer's books at each meeting of the Association, and report the same before adjournment.

11. The Association shall appoint annually an Executive Committee of seven (7)—five brethren and two sisters—from its members, who shall be entrusted with the prosecution of Missions in the Association and any other work for the interest of the Master's Kingdom which may be referred to them. This committee shall, as far as possible, co-operate with the State Mission Board in supplying the destitution in our territory, and, between the meetings of the Association, take such action as may seem to them advisable for the advancement of its interest. The committee shall present to the Association at its annual meeting a report of its proceedings, with the names of the missionaries supported on the field, time of service and details of their work, together with such recommendations as, in the judgment of the committee, the Association should

follow in planning its subsequent work.

12. The annual sessions of the Association shall begin on Wednesday after the fourth Lord's Day in October, at such place as may be chosen, and an introductory sermon shall be delivered on the first day of the session. Representatives from ten of the churches constituting the Association shall be a quorum.

13. This Constitution may be amended at any annual session by a two-thirds vote of all the members present.

14. The proceedings of the Woman's Central Committee shall be recorded as a part of the minutes of the Association.

BY-LAWS

1. The daily sessions of the Association shall be opened and closed with prayer.

2. Delegates shall be recognized by letters from their churches designating them as such.

3. The Moderator shall recognize corresponding messengers or the delegates of newly received churches by extending to them his right hand.

4. The report of the Executive Board and the Missionary work of the Association shall take precedence of all other business during the morning session of the second day of the annual session.

5. The Clerk shall record and read the proceedings when called for, superintend the publication and distribution of the minutes, preserve a file of them and have it present at each annual session, and deliver to his successor all papers belonging to the body.

6. Members desiring to speak shall first rise and address the Moderator, shall use the term "brother" in speaking to each other, shall not speak on the same subject more than twice without permission, and shall observe the courtesy that becomes Christians.

7. The roll of members shall be called at least once, and absentees marked.

8. Corresponding messengers and visiting brethren shall be invited to seats, with privilege of speaking, but not voting.

9. A copy of the minutes shall be sent to the Secretary of the State Mission Board, the Secretary of the Southern Baptist Convention, the American Publication Society, 1420 Chestnut Street, Philadelphia; the Sunday School Board of the Southern Baptist Convention, and the Thomasville Orphanage.

10. All questions of order not herein provided shall be decided by Kerfoot's Parliamentary Law.

Proceedings

The Johnston Baptist Association met in its twenty second session with the Four Oaks Baptist Church, October 29th, to October 30th, 1924.

WEDNESDAY MORNLNG

After singing, "I'm pressing on the Upward Way," and prayer by Bro. R. L. Gay, the Moderator, Bro. R. H. Gower, declared the twenty second session of the Johnston Association open for the transaction of business and appointed Brethren H. E. Earp, N. J. Creech, and H. S. Britt to serve as a Committee on Credentials and Enrollment. The clerk called the roll of the Churches, with a quorum present the Association proceeded and elected the following officers: R. H. Gower, Moderator; S. L. Morgan, Vice-Moderator; R. M. Von Miller, Clerk; J. A. Smith, Treasurer, and R. A. Bain, Auditor. After singing, "There Shall Be Showers of Blessings," Bro. R. C. White delivered the introductory sermon, using as his subject: "The Fundamental Principles of the Kingdom of Jesus Christ." Following the sermon the Moderator recognized Bro. F. B. Hambrick, who represented the Orphanage. The following new pastors were recognized and welcomed into the Association: G. A. Bain, J. S. Connell, Jas. W. Rose, S. T. Morris. The first item on the program being: "The Spiritual State of our Churches," the Moderator called on Bro. S. L. Morgan to preside. Bro. S. L. Morgan read the following paper: .

SPIRITUAL STATE OF OUR CHURCHES

A very frank diagnosis of conditions and tendencies is important. The spiritual state of the home determines the spiritual state of the church and the community. It is not pessimistic to say that home religion among our people in general is at a low ebb. The family altar is in ruins. Only here and there is there a home with Bible reading and prayer in the family circle. Few parents seem to teach the Bible to their children. Very few children or adults in Sunday school report lessons prepared. Our nation grew strong and great on the solid food of God's Word.

The early home was one of piety. Our nation will decay, unless more is made of religion in the home. Tides of worldliness are beating against the home. The frivolities of social life and the rush of business blind even parents to the deeper values in life. A literature of slush and filth, and moving pictures often unclean and debasing, are poisoning the atmosphere our children breathe. Youth unchaperoned and unrestrained by age or reason goes on a joy ride, often in the night hours, playing with virtue and gambling with death. Unless the Christian parent takes the helm, and with desperate seriousness does more to saturate the home atmosphere with vital piety, the result must be disastrous.

We dare not ignore the fact that the church is facing new dangers. The automobile and a fair Sunday may empty our church house. The carnival or the moving picture show may cripple the prayer meeting. In the average church in town the young people scamper away after Sunday school, and ignore the service of worship. It is a painful fact that in town few of the young church members attend the preaching service morning or night. Church loyalty is too often forgotten in loyalty to a class or group in the church. Again, the solution must rest mainly with the home. Parents, seeing the dangerous drift, must take hold, and train a new generation in reverence for God and loyalty to his church.

Our use of money is an important test of our spiritual state, A large proportion of our people give little, many nothing. Most who give, give without principle or system. Our people in general know nothing of sacrifice. They spend much for pleasure and self. Churches have a struggle to introduce systematic giving. To see the historical background is to be charitable and patient. Our people for generations have breathed a Hardshell-Free-Will atmosphere. The Hardshell has said to our people, almost with a sneer, "If God wills, the church can do its work without money." The Free-Will has said, "Halleliuiah! I feel good; don't bother me with talk about money and methods." A deep need of our churches is to meet this cry with the solemn word of God during the years before us, saying, "The silver is mine and the gold is mine, saith the Lord of hosts," adding Paul's demand for method in giving, "Upon the first day of the week, let every one of you lay by him in store as God hath prospered him." Already the idea of stewardship is laying hold of our people, and we can see the dawn of a new day.

Due largely to the chilling atmosphere blown upon us from earlier days, our people are yet below the average in their concern for the salvation of the world. The fires of missions and

8

evangelism burn low. The pastor or layman in our churches whose heart flames with missionary zeal, must in such an atmosphere feel a chill at his heart. He secretly cries, "O Lord, how long are we to be pained by this indifference to the great command to give the gospel to all the world!" In such a situation the primary need is a ministry that feels a Christ-like passion for souls.

But the morning light is breaking. Our older members have seen marvelous progress in the last two decades. The missionary and evangelistic passion burns in an ever increasing number of our people. Stewardship is laying hold of the minds of many in our churches, and systematic and proportionate giving is rapidly becoming the rule. Many able laymen are offering themselves freely in active service. The tides of worldliness are being met intelligently by the churches. The solution is being found partly in making definite provision under church auspices for the social satisfaction of our young people. Persistent work is being done through the B. Y. P. U. and other church agencies in training the young people in loyalty to the church, and in consecrating their time and means to Christian service. Revival fires are beginning to burn brightly, and a great host are being won to Christ year by year. We have but to press forward with faith in God, with an unfaltering purpose to sow the seed, assured that the harvest is not far distant, yea, is already being reaped.

Upon motion to adopt, and in connection with the subject before the body, the following Brethren spoke on the condition of their respective churches: O. A. Keller, Jas. W. Rose, S. T. Morris, W. D. Stancil, R. M. Von Miller, R. C. White, J. W. Nobles, J. A. Ivey, R. L. Gay, J. D. Barbour, and F. H. Brooks. The next item in order was the report of the Executive Committee, the Moderator recognized Bro. S. L. Morgan, Chairman of the Executive Committee, who presented the report of the Executive Committee:

REPORT OF EXECUTIVE COMMITTEE

Your committee began the year in a situation that was almost disheartening. Most of the churches of the association were without pastors, and several of the fields had broken apart, either through internal dissension or through the decision of individual churches to act separately in calling pastors. We are glad to report that, after much effort in cooperation with the State Mission Board and the churches concerned, nearly all the churches have been supplied with pastors, and the situation is encouraging.

At present the State Mission Board is helping churches in the association as follows, to the amount of about $2,200: The Pine Level-Princeton field $700. and the Trinity field about the same amount; Thanksgiving $150, Burnell $150, Bailey $150, Benson's Grove $150, Oliver's Grove $100, and Hale's Chapel $100.

Consistent with the policy of the State Board, help has been withheld from several churches pending their forming a field and locating a pastor in the midst of a group of churches. It seems to your committee an eminently wise policy to give aid, not to the individual church as a rule, but rather to a group of churches forming a field and locating a pastor among them, who will give all his time to them, thus giving promise of permanency to the work and ultmiate self-support. It should be added that a further policy of the State Board is to cooperate with a field in making a minimum salary of $1,500, on the theory that no pastor with a family and the cost of running a car in the country can give his time whole-heartedly to his work, and justify the Board in spending money on him, when the salary is less than this amount.

Your committee begs leave to call attention frankly to a main difficulty in supervising the mission work of the association. It is the unrestrained exercise of the boasted independence of Baptists. Repeatedly some church in a field, displeased with its pastor, or else taking a fancy to another preacher, has acted separately, consulting neither the executive committee nor the other churches in the field, called its own pastor, and left the other churches of the field high and dry. Sometimes a pastor, discouraged or displeased with one of the churches of his field, has simply resigned and left it to struggle alone. Neither course seems to your committee either wise or gracious. If differences between pastor and church cannot be adjusted, the friendly offices of the executive committee might often prevent the disruption of a field. It would seem wise, before either a church or a pastor acts separately in breaking the unity of a field, to refer the difference to the executive committee for possible adjustment. This tendency to independent action ither by churches or pastors seems to your committee the most serious difficulty in the way of maintaining permanent fields, and securing the steady development of the churches. At present several fields, which were formed and held together for a time at the cost of much prayer and effort on the part of the executive committee, are broken apart; while certain of the churches, left alone and embarrassed, are anxiously waiting to learn

10

whether the other churches of the field will return and cooperate in securing a pastor for another year, or whether they must struggle on alone with little hope of securing a permanent pastor. The example of Rev. J. W. Rose in relation to Pinkney church cannot be commended too highly as illustrating the proper course to pursue in such cases. Knowing that Pinkney had belonged to the Kenly field, now without a pastor, he declined overtures from the church to become its pastor until assured that it would please both the executive committee and the State Board for him to serve it until the Kenly field can be re-united, with the clear understanding that he will then release it to return to the Kenly field. Cooperation marks a much higher state of progress than independent action.

The peculiar blight to mission work in our association has been the unbroken succession of short pastorates, often with long intervals when no pastor was on the field. This condition must be remedied before there can be any substantial progress. And it calls for heart-searching among the churches of our association. There must be some deep-seated cause for this inglorious record our churches have won for short pastorates. Your committee grant readily that the blame has sometimes rested largely with the pastor. But it has become clear to your committee that in many of our churches there is such indifference to any large program of missions and evangelism, such a deaf ear to appeals to sacrifice and go forward, as to chill and dishearten a zealous pastor. It is borne in mind that this indifference is due largely to the Hardshell influence handed down from generations of ancestors who were anti-missionary. This fact should make us charitable and patient. Pastors must resolve to remain and endure, to teach and train a new generation, and await the dawn of a new day. And the churches, if the new day is ever to be ushered in, must resolve to show more sympathy and a more generous response to the progressive and zealous pastor. Potentially the people of Johnston are among the finest to be found in the State, and God is pouring into their hands abounding wealth. A few years more ought to make all our mission churches strong and self-sustaining, able to release the State Mission Board, that its funds may go to meet more pressing needs elsewhere. Each mission church should ask less of the Board each year, until it becomes independent at the earliest moment possible.

Churches now receiving aid from the State Board should bear in mind that help is given with a view to helping the churches to become self-sustaining, and that in due time help is to be withdrawn. Already the executive committee has been advised that some churches cannot be given as much as last year. In the words of the Board itself, "The State Mission Board is always overwhelmed with applications for much more than it has to give." It expects each church, either through growth in membership or growth in liberality, to raise more each year than it did the year before. The Board reasonably asks that each church receiving aid shall put on the everymember canvass, as the simplest and most effective means yet found for lining up the entire membership in systematic giving. Your committee believes that the Board in requiring this is doing the best thing possible for the church itself.

A very encouraging feature of our work is the steady progress of the parsonage building movement in the association. Steps are being taken toward the building of a parsonage for the Trinity field. Much of the material has been offered without cost, and Brother Connell, the pastor, is an experienced builder, and offers his services freely, giving promise that a parsonage can be built at a remarkably low figure. A minimum of $300 has been offered from the associational building fund whenever the building is under way. Understanding it came under the scope of the building fund as authorized, a like amount has been granted to the Pisgah church to apply to the erection of more Sunday school rooms.

Your committee recommend that the number on the committee be increased to seven, two or three of the number being women, as a means both of increasing the efficiency of the committee and of more closely aligning the women's organizations with the work of the association as a whole.

S. L. MORGAN
J. A. IVEY
J. J. LANE
J. A. SMITH
H. E. EARP

Upon motion to adopt, Bro. S. L. Morgan spoke to the report, report was adopted. A motion by Bro. O. A. Keller to make some changes in the constitution was carried, and the Moderator appointed Brethren O. A. Keller, S. L. Morgan, and R. C. White, on changes in constitution with instruction to report same to the Association during the present session. The Moderator also appointed Brethren O. A. Keller, J. W. Nobles, and Jas. W. Rose to serve as a Committee on reception of new churches, after which the body adjourned for the dinner with prayer by Bro. J. F. Pool.

Wednesday Afternoon

After the devotional exercises lead by Bro. C. H. Cashwell, the Moderator called the session to order and appointed the following brethren: F. H. Brooks, R. C. White, and R. M. Von Miller, to serve as a committee to nominate the Executive Committee and delegates to the Convention. On behalf of the committee on reception of new Churches, Bro. O. A. Keller made the following report:

"We your committee have examined the organization and covenant of the Wodkins Chapel Baptist Church and found them in order and recommend that this church be received into the fellowship of this Association."

"We further recommend the reception of Beulah Baptist Church into the fellowship of our Association by letter from the South River Association."

Respectfully submitted

O. A. KELLER, for the Com.

The Moderator on behalf of the Association gave the right hand of fellowship to the delegates of these churches. According to the program of the hour Bro. O. A. Keller was recognized who presented the report on:

SOCIAL SERVICE

In presenting our report on Social Service we wish to report first on

Our Orphanage

The Orphanage is the one vital living department fo our denominational work that keeps us in constant touch with the crying needs of our dependent children.

For 39 years this work has been growing until we are now caring for 575 children at Thomasville and the Kennedy Home, and 325 out in the State with their own mothers.

The current fund necessary to maintain the Orphanage is around $175,000.00 per year. The contribution of one Sunday in each month from the Sunday Schools and a great Thanksgiving offering equal to "One Day's Income," has become the main source of supply. The marvelous way in which the Lord has blessed this big home is a loud call for our continued loyalty. The denomination from mountain to sea has been wonderfully strengthened by the

13.

reflex influence of their generous giving to the Orphanage.

The helpless childhood of our state lays upon us the obligation to widen our work and to reach out the hands of help to those who are without a penny, a home or a friend. And there are hundreds of children in North Carolina utterly destitute who are as worthy and as promising as those who are already enjoying the blessing and the protection of the Orphanage. So the task ever widens and we are therefore asking the Sunday Schools and churches of this Association to continue to make larger investments in the Orphanage.

We also recommend that one Sunday's collection in our Sunday Schools be set aside each month for the Orphanage, and that each church will make a Thanksgiving offering equal to One Day's Income for the Orphanage.

Ministerial Relief

We now have 95 beneficiaries—the largest number by a score or more than we have ever had. Twenty five preachers and widows of preachers have been received as beneficiaries since the last meeting of the Convention. This is far more than have ever been received before in any year. The number asking for aid from this fund has been increasing at an unusual rate ever since the launching of the 75 Million Campaign and there will probably be more and more to apply for help for the next number of years. Seven have died during the year. Most of these worthy foundation builders are nearing the great Beyond. There are more "silver threads among the gold" than when we met last year. It is easy to imagine that the Son of Man has arisen already and is standing as in case of Stephen, ready to meet and ready to greet. We must never let suffer while they are in the cities of earth, those whom God the Son will rise to usher into the City Celestial.

This work gets 5 per cent of our contribution. If we meet our pledges, we will have given quite worthily to these saints of God.

The annuity side of the work should be stressed at all times. It offers a great opportunity to the preacher who can spare a few dollars now. A certificate of membership in the Annuity Fund will take care of disability and guarantee a definite income after 68, and in addition makes provision for the dependent ones. The guarantee after January 1924, will be the maximum of $500.

Temperance

Temperance thought has crystalized around the use, or non-use of intoxicating liquor and the word "temperance" is used almost exclusively in connection with strong drink. The objective sought by temperance workers for years has been "Total abstinence by the individual and prohibition by the state." The latter is an accomplished fact and towards the accomplishment of the former wonderful strides have been made. The statement is made with disgusting frequency that "prohibition is a failure." The statement is glaringly false and is a part of the propaganda of the opponents of prohibition, the object of which is to discredit prohibition laws and ultimately if possible, to repeal them. The latter is not even a remote possibility but it must be admitted that there is a deplorable laxness of four classes of men—(a) The indifference of real prohibitionists, who think that their duty ended with the adoption of the laws and to interfere with enforcement would involve a great deal of unpleasantness, and, possibly, expose them to real danger. (b) The selfishness of men who want prohibition, for the other man (the poor working man who spends his wages for drink while neglecting his family), or the drunken rowdy who destroys the peace of the community) but is willing to condone the breach of law in order to have it himself. (c) The longing of the man who will stoop to anything to satisfy his craving for drink, and, (d) the avarise of the man who will sacrifice the character and lives of his fellow men, and, even his own soul for money.

We must not forget the makers and venders of intoxicating liquors are criminals of the lowest order, who destroy the bodies, minds and souls of all whom they influence, and their places of business are cesspools of vice which menace the home, the church, the school and the state.

We as Christians owe it to God and our fellow men to make our communities safe—physically, mentally and morally—for ourselves and our neighbors, especially the young. We should do our utmost to create sentiment which would not tolerate this crime in our community. We should co-operate and organize, if need be, to be more efficient in uprooting this business from the land. We should never cast a vote to elect a drinking man to office. The man who drinks must get it before he can drink t and he cannot get it unless some one makes it and sells it. So the dipling officer is in sympathy with the criminals who make and sell it. Finally, we should ever seek the "All Power" without which we can never succeed in destroying the most strongly entrenched evil that curses the world.

Hospitals

The North Carolina Baptist Hospital is a five story, fire proof brick building, located in the center of a ten acre plot of ground, on a beautiful elevation on the outskirts of Winston-Salem. It has a capacity of 106 beds, or 3500 patients a year. It is equipped with three operation rooms, laboratory, X-Ray and other necessary equipment needed in a modern hospital.

With Christian nurses, a fine medical and surgical staff, a beautiful Christian atmosphere, and with the great physician as chief of staff. Our Hospital can offer the best in efficiency, skill, facilities and service, at the lowest cost and under the ministry of love and prayer.

About 2000 patients, 300 of whom were charity patients, have been treated during the first 15 months of its operation.

Primarily this institution is for the unfortunate poor, to which class they give their best. Pay patients are admitted at a cost less than that of the average private hospital. Rev. G. T. Lumpkins, Winston-Salem, N. C., is the very efficient Superintendent.

Respectfully submitted
O. A. KELLER, for the Com.

Upon adoption of the report, Brethren F. B. Hambrick and S. H. Averitt spoke very interestingly on the Orphanage. Brother Jas. A. Ivey spoke to the report on Ministerial Relief, and Brethren R. L. Gay and F. H. Brooks spoke to the report on Temperance. The report was adopted.

The next item on the program was Christian Education. The Moderator recognized Bro. R. C. White, who presented the report on:

CHRISTIAN EDUCATION, COLLEGES, PREPARATORY SCHOOLS, PERIODICALS, BOOKS AND TRACTS

Christian Education

The life of a nation depends upon its schools. The value of a school depends upon its ideals. The ideals of a school have their highest worth only as they are Christian. It is the duty of the churches to make these ideals dominant in education.

To this end, North Carolina Baptist have inaugurated a broad and systematic educational program. They are undertaking to maintain in this state one college for men, at Wake Forest, and two for women—Meredith, at Raleigh, and Chowan, at Murfreesboro. From last reports Wake Forest enrolled 873, including the Summer School, and among these 873 there are 90 ministerial students and volunteers; the two women colleges enrolled 582, including 26 student volunteers. The combined property value of the three including endowment is $3,453,700.

Mars Hill and Wingate are maintained as Junior Colleges, enrolling last year 738, including 76 ministerial and volunteer students; with a combined value of $261,030.

The three High Schools enrolled 780 in the High School and 389 in the Elementary School, including 82 ministerial students and volunteers. Their property value is $369,065. Also, there are 100 High School students in the Thomasville Orphanage.

In addition to these institutions, the Home Mission Board maintains 7 High Schools, enrolling last year 776 in High School and 284 in Elementary School, including 62 ministerial students and volunteers. Their property value is $437,693.

The total for all Baptist schools in the State are: Students enrolled 4422; ministerial students and student volunteers 336; total property valuation $4,521,488.

South-wide institutions in which we have a part include the Southern Baptist Theological Seminary and W. M. U. Training School, at Louisville, Ky.; the Southwestern Theological Seminary, and Training School for Women, at Fort Worth Texas; and the Baptist Bible Institute, in New Orleans. These institutions in the past year enrolled 1484 pupils, and their property valuation is $2,-277,000. It is for the maintenance of these institutions that our Education Board is laboring.

While the $5,000,000, in round numbers, which we have invested in school property in this State seems a large sum, it is small in comparison with the many millions invested in State schools; and the few thousands which we raise annually for our schools is a trifling sum when compared with the State's annual appropriation to her High Schools, Colleges, and University. In addition to maintaining these institutions themselves, we are helping to support uor 336 young ministerial and missionary students, which are being trained in them; on these we expend about $18,000 a year.

The necessity for maintaining our schools, great as it has been in the past, must increase rather than diminish for the future, for the following reasons:

1st. Because our institutions must be kept in the front rank, along with those of the state in the cultured training that they give, or we cannot hope to keep our Baptist boys and girls in our schools.

2nd. Heretofore, practically nine-tenths of our educated ministers and missionaries have come out of our Baptist institutions; and in the nature of the case, these still must be trained in our schools or nowhere. Moreover, the State is rapidly enlarging and strengthening her educational program, and compelling all her children to be educated. This, of course, means a much more intelligent membership in our churches, and that we must educate a still larger proportion of our ministers and leaders; for an educated membership will demand an educated leadership.

3rd. Because of the tendency of some students of science to at-

17

tack the Bible from the standpoint of science, we must train our God-fearing men and women to meet these scientists on their own ground, and while pursuing knowledge in all realms, to relate all knowledge and all science to God Almighty. In our schools the Bible is revered and taught as the inspired word of God, and the study of it is required by all.

4th. The denominational schools emphasize not only the religious spirit but the denominational principles as well, and thus they help to enlighten and strengthen their students in respect to our distinctive doctrines, and also to enlist them loyally in our Baptist enterprises.

Periodicals, Books, and Tracts

It is needless to say that our Baptist Organ the Biblical Recorder is an important factor in the education of our Baptist people. The great need of the hour is an educated Baptist constituency; that is an informed Baptist host. "Home and Foreign Field," "In Royal Service," "Charity and Children" are indispensable periodicals for the enlightenment of our people, and the education of our people along all the different phases of our denominational work. Realizing that it is much easier to lead a people with a knowledge of the great cause of Christ; that an uninformed people are lax in their carrying on the work of the Kingdom of our Lord, uninterested in our great denominational enterprises; and feeling that our denominational periodicals are the correct medium through which denominational affairs should be transmitted to our people we would urgently beseech the people to read our periodicals.

Our Sunday School Board publishes and sends out thousands of tracts each year, free of charge, which if used in the churches will afford reading matter that will educate and enlighten our people to the extent of hearty co-operation and response to the calls of our denomination.

We therefore suggest that greater use be made of our periodicals, that we commit ourselves to the task of putting our Baptist State papers, at least, in every Baptist home, that we utilize tracts sent out by our Boards for the purpose of having a greater people of zeal, and co-operation, a ready people to support the Cause of our Lord; for an informed people are an active people.

Respectfully submitted,

RUSSELL C. WHITE.

Upon motion to adopt, Bro. R. C. White spoke to the report, the report was adopted. No other business, the body adjourned with prayer by Bro. A. R. Creech.

WEDNESDAY NIGHT

After the devotional exercises lead by Bro. C. C. Wheeler, the session was called to order by Bro. S. L. Morgan the Vice-Moderator. This being the hour for the annual Missionary sermon, Bro. O. A. Keller preached a very helpful sermon, using for his text John 15:16 and Chapt. 20 verse 21. At the conclusion of the sermon Bro. Jas. W. Rose lead in prayer.

The next item on the program was an address by Bro. J. M. Broughton of Raleigh, who spoke on the subject: "Stewardship and the Baptist Task." Every one present enjoyed this most helpful and interesting address. After singing "All Hail the Power of Jesus Name," and prayer by Bro. O. A. Keller, the body adjourned to meet Thursday morning at 10:00 A. M.

THURSDAY MORNING

After the devotional exercises lead by Bro. R. L. Gay, the Moderator recognized the following visitors: Brethren T. W. O'Kelly, J. S. Farmer, and A. C. McCall. Under miscellaneous business, Brother R. C. White presented the following report:

"We your committee nominate the following Brethren and Sisters to serve on the Executive Committee: S. L. Morgan, Chairman, Jas. A. Ivey, J. Dwight Barbour, H. E. Earp, A. J. Broughton, Mrs. J. M. Beaty, and Mrs. B. A. Hocutt.

We further nominate Bro. F. H. Brooks as a delegate to the Southern Baptist Convention, and Brethren J. F. Pool, R. C. White, O. A. Keller, as delegates to the Baptist State Convention.

Respectfully submitted

F. H. BROOKS
R. C. WHITE
R. M. VON MILLER, Com.

A motion by Bro. J. A. Smith, that the amount of $20.00 be paid to the Chairman of the Executive Committee for expense, and that the amount be paid from the Minute Fund, was adopted.

A motion by Bro. Jas. A. Ivey, that a map of the location of the churches in the Association be prepared by a committee and inserted into the Minutes was carried, and the Moderator appointed Brethren O. A. Keller, Jas. A. Ivey, and Sister B. A. Hocutt to serve as such a committee. The next item on the program for the hour was on the subject of Missions. Bro. S. L. Morgan was recognized who presented the report on Missions:

REPORT ON MISSIONS

In the divine plan the one business of every saved soul is to give the gospel to all the world, without distinction of race or nation, color or condition. It is fitting therefore that the report on missions shall cover all the world as a mission field.

Associational Missions

Perhaps the situation in our association is more encouraging than for years before. Nearly all our mission churches are now supplied with efficient pastors. Many report fruitful revivals, with large additions in membership during the year. The spirit of missions and evangelism is spreading among the people. Looking back over a decade or two one sees remarkable progress, and feels a thrill of hope for the future. Let us not forget that our association yet has vast need for missions. One passing through the county on Sunday has noted stores often open as on other days. There is widespread handling and drinking of liquor, and a menacing spirit of lawlessness. Our people need Christ, and without Him our progress in education and wealth will prove a curse. Every church and every Christian should be passionately devoted to giving the gospel to the community round about. It is to be regretted that no new work was undertaken during the year. The executive committee earnestly invite Baptists everywhere to keep them informed as to opportunities to begin new Sunday Schools, conduct revivals, or begin mission work in needy sections of the association.

State Missions

Our own association gives us a vivid picture of the work of State Missions. The State Board is pouring money into our association at the rate of more than $2,000 a year. Nearly half the churches of the association are now being helped by the State Board. Many others in the past received its help. In our association particularly it should seem disloyalty and a disgrace not to give hearty support to State Missions. And, seeing how great is the debt our mission churches already owe to the State Board, these churches ought to do their utmost to go rapidly to self-support, releasing the Board at the earliest moment possible. For the needs elsewhere in North

Carolina are vast and urgent. God is marvelously blessing our State, and it is developing with a rapidity that is staggering. Capital is pouring into North Carolina, vast industries are springing up, and the eyes of the continent are turning toward us. Tides of population are beginning to pour in, and towns and cities are growing with a rapidity that is alarming. And the Christian statesman has long since discovered that the only way to save the city is to save it before it becomes a city. If our State or our civilization is to be saved at all, we must plant the gospel and the church firmly in the village, and dominate its growth into the city. As yet the State Board is able to meet but a fraction of the great need. The Board has in the State 180 missionaries—seven of them in our own association. It employs 3 evangelists, 3 enlistment men, 3 student workers, 4 Sunday school workers, 3 B. Y. P. U. workers, and 3 W. M. U. workers. It has been seriously handicapped by a heavy debt during the present year,, amounting August 1 to $70,000. Unless contributions are greatly increased before the Convention meets in December, the work will be seriously crippled for another year. Encouragement may be held out in the fact that in the 1925 program 20 cents in every dollar will go to State Missions, instead of 13 cents, the amount going to State Missions in the 75 Million Campaign.

Home Missions

For four years Home Missions has been crippled by the great debt on the Board, amounting last May to $363,000 on its running expenses. A drastic cut in its program of work was the only remedy. Last year the Board employed 1,250 missionaries, including 22 evangelists. Its missionaries were distributed as follows: 71 among foreigners, 15 among the Indians, 30 among the Negroes, 36 in Cuba, 3 in Panama, 8 in camp work, and the rest in cooperative work with the various State Mission boards, mainly in cities. Through its missionaries 180,000 were baptized into our Baptist churches. As was said of North Carolina, so it may be said of the South as a whole, that its amazing development is a challenge for aggressive work in missions. Millions in capital is flowing into the South, and vast developments are in progress. The cotton mills of New England are moving to the piedmont section of the Southern states. The South is growing rich faster than any other section of the United States, and with our riches come the destructive forces that have brought ruin to the great empires of the past. Our civilization is being sorely tested. The Home Mission Board has for two generations been the great agency among Southern Baptists for unifying and stabilizing the forces of the kingdom. And yet the receipts of the Board have grown less and less during the last

21

four years. The situation calls loudly for sacrificial giving in payment of the pledges made five years ago.

Foreign Missions

For Southern Baptists last year may be set down among the miracles of missions. During the year our Foreign Board went literally staggering under a vast debt, a debt on which we paid in interest $70,000, and yet this was the most fruitful year in all our history. During the year our foreign missionaries baptized 12,856—more than one-fourth as many as the total number of church members we had on the foreign field five years ago, when the 75-Million Campaign began. During these five years the growth in membership of our churches on the foreign field has been far above 100%. The membership of our churches is now 111,872. Our foreign missionaries now number 544, with 582 ordained native helpers.

The past year also records one of the greatest tragedies in the history of missions. Paralyzed by the great debt, the Board cut appropriations to the bleeding point. Year after year the receipts of the Board became lower and lower. To bring the missionaries home from the distant fields was out of the question. The expense would be enormous, and the consequences disastrous in the extreme. Every dollar not necessary to the existence of the missionaries themselves was cut out of the appropriation for Foreign Missions. Buildings, long needed on the foreign field had been begun on the strength of the pledges made and the receipts of the first year of the Campaign, but these now stand unfinished, often roofless and rotting, on every foreign mission field. With hopes deferred and hearts sick our missionaries wait in tears on the distant firing line, able to do little more than mark time, until our people pay their pledges, and bid them go forward with the work we sent them to do. Meanwhile a great number of our finest young men and women, who have felt called of God to go as missionaries, have been told that they cannot be sent. They are awaiting the word from us to go to distant lands to carry out the imperative command of Christ to give the gospel to the lost heathen nations. And this distressing situation faces us at a time when a revival spirit, perhaps without a parallel in the history of nations, is sweeping through all lands. It is on the tide of this revival spirit, even while we have tied the hands of our distant missionaries, that far more have come into our churches on the foreign field during the last five years than we had in our churches at that time, following 75 years of slow sowing and reaping. This situation is God's trumpet call to our people to awake from their sinful sleep and pour their money into the coffers of the kingdom, that the most distressing

22

situation in all the annals of missions may be relieved.

S. L. MORGAN.

Upon motion to adopt, Mrs. B. A. Hocutt, Superintendent of the W. M. Union of the Johnston Baptist Association presented the report on:

WOMAN'S WORK

In presenting this report I present the facts as presented at the annual meeting of the W. M. U. of the Johnston Baptist Association held at Selma, N. C., October 10th, 1924.

In 1903 the W. M. U. of Johnston Association was organized in Selma, N. C. In that most trying period of 1917, we again met in Selma, and in 1924, the last year of the 75 Million Campaign, we again find ourselves as members of the W. M. U. of Johnston Association, the happy guests of the good people of Selma.

Does it not seem singular and rather auspicious that each time of our coming to Selma is associated with some epoch making year? And what greater epoch in the history of our denomination have we ever faced than the finishing of our great campaign, and the planning for, and the facing our new program for the coming year? This report which I am to give you is a good one in many respects. But I leave it to you to decide if it is one worthy of such a time as we are now facing. At present there are 26 churches in our Association without any Woman's Society of any kind. With 45 churches in the Association our hope would be for a W. M. U. in every church, and our aim would be unworthy of our cause, if it were for less than two-thirds of the churches with a W. M. S. And yet we have only 26 churches in which W. M. S. have been organized, 17 of which are active now, the other 9 are, I hope, living. Y. W. A.'s— 3 active, 2 inactive. G. A.'s—5 active, 2 having disbanded. R. A.'s —4 active, 1 having disbanded. Sunbeams—8 active and 5 inactive.

Total number of societies having been organized at one time or another 56, leaving as you see 19 societies once organized not reporting now. I make a plea here to and for those 19 societies. It is most encouraging to say, and has been to my effort, that 9 churches without societies have reported to me more or less regularlry this year, and just here I pause to thank those who have made these reports and the pastors who have given their interest and support in this and my often repeated requests regarding reporting. These are the churches I think deserve special mention: Canaan, Bethesda and Pinkney reported every quarter. Hales Chapel, Carter's Chapel, Sardis, Lee's Chapel, Baptist Center and

Live Oak, reported one or more quarters. ` Each quarter I have striven to communicate with every church in the Association, by letter, cards, visiting or otherwise, besides writing each pastor every quarter. I have written 500 letters, 250 postals, and travelled 223 miles, also visited 3 societies. Six societies were organized W. M. Society, Calvary, Y. W. A. Middlesex, G. A. Selma, R. A. Smithfield, Selma and Pine Level. Several societies have been re-organized. I have averaged getting 34 reports each quarter. The following societies reported every quarter. W. M. S.'s Smithfield, Clayton, Middlesex, Pine Level, Selma, Blackman's Grove, Princeton, Clyde's Chapel, Four Oaks. Benson, Kenly, Mt. Moriah Y. W. A.—Clayton, Middlesex. G. A.—Selma, Clayton. Middlesex. R. A.—Selma, and Clayton. S. B.—Middlesex, Selma, Smithfield, Clayton, Benson. Number of Annual Reports sent in this year 31. Statistics from these reports are as follows:

Number of members in societies _____866 against 525 of last year
Home and Foreign Fields taken _____ 59 against 54 of last year
No. of Royal Service taken _____102 against 66 of last year
No. Biblical Recorders _____199 against 160 of last year
No. of tithers _____ 78 against 72 of last year
No. of Mission Study Classes _____ 19 against 8 of last year
No. Having organized personal service 19 against 15 of last year

No. observing special services of
prayer for Home Missions _____ 18 against 14 of last year
No. For State Missions _____ 18 against 14 of last year
No. For Foreign Missions _____ 19 against 14 of last year

27 societies reported to State officers all 4 quarters. Mrs. Thurston is chairman of personal service. Mrs. S. L. Morgain is chairman of Mission Study.

Standard of Excellence report: Class A.—W. M. S.'s Selma, Mt. Moriah, Four Oaks, Clayton. G. A.'s Clayton, R. A.'s Clayton. Three more than last year. S. B.'s Clayton. Class B.—W. M. S.'s Middlesex, Smithfield, Benson, Kenly, Pine Level. (Three more than last year.) R. A.—Smithfield. S. B.'s—Smithfield, Middlesex, Benson. Class C.—M. S. Princeton. Class D.—Y. W. A. Clayton. S. B.—Mt. Moriah.

$38.00 left in treasury. (From Hospital Fund, after paying for furrnishing of Wood) sent to Mrs. J. J. Roddeck as authorized and she reported its being used for Victrola for Hospital.

Amounts received past year for expense of the W. M. U. Ass. work as follows: $5.50 from offering taken at meeting in Benson. For Associational Expense Fund from Kenly W. M. S. $2.00, from

Pine Level W. M. S. $2.00, from Smithfield W. M. S. $3.00.
Comparative statement of Annual Meeting,
31 societies represented this year against 26 of last year.
17 churches represented this year against 13 of last year.
200 visitors and delegates this year against 105 of last year.
47 financial reports showing $7,880.37 raised as against 28 reports showing $5,568.35 raised last year.
Amount received from offering taken at Selma this year for expense of meeting and work, $21.40. And thus has been rendered my report and yours for the year which is ours no more. Are we satisfied? I venture to say not one of us are. Will you not stop and think with me, what is needed to make our report for the coming year worthy of our cause, and one we would be proud to proclaim to our State W. M. U., yea, to our Southern Baptist W. M. U., most of all render to our Master? I believe you will after prayerful thought say, what is most needed to carry forward our work acceptably is yielded lives. "Only one life to live," and we are living ours now. Let each of us take our commission and do our part toward the fulfillment of the Gospel in Johnston Association, and then on, to the uttermost parts of the earth.

Respectfully submitted

MRS. B. A. HOCUTT, Supt.

Mrs. J. W. Sanders was then recognized who made an additional report including some recommendations:

The Woman's Work of the churches is an important factor in the life of the Association. The work of the Church reveals the progress of the Kingdom of our Lord. The work of the individuals in the Church will be revealed in the accomplishments of the church. The local Church is the foundation and strength and power in the Kingdom of God, to do the work our Master has commended us to do.

The strength of the church depends upon its membership. A Church is no stronger than the individual's faith in God. A church is certainly no stronger in its work than the individuals are in their knowledge of those things which the Christ would have us do, no stronger then than that which is done after knowledge has been received. The W. M. S. stands for progress in the Kingdom. The W. M. S. stands for better churches, because its aim is to instruct, its aim is to impart the spirit of the Master.

Then the greatest need of our Association is the enlistment, and the development of every woman in all the churches. The dire need of the church, we feel, is the thorough organization of the women.

25

The enlistment of each and every one in the W. M. S. of the church would mean an instructed membership of women, boys and girls. This would mean a greater church, a better Association, the further evangelization of the world.

Realizing the great opportunity in our Association, in the women of the churches we feel that some means should be provided through which a thorough work will be accomplished in the organization of a W. M. S. in each and every church. Further we recognize that such organization when brought into existence must have proper supervision from time to time by one who is thoroughly acquainted with the work. Feeling that is not only important that a W. M. S. being organized in each church, but that such W. M. S. will function, will be maintained.

Therefore, we resolve that because of the importance of the individual enlistment, the need of individual information, because of the necessity of the maintenance and sponsoring of the W. M. S. in the church, In order that the greatest results be derived from the work of the women in the church, we recommend that the churches of the Association employ a trained woman to superintend the work of the Association Woman's Missionary Societies.

We further resolve that this recommendation be submitted to the Executive Committee of our Association and that they ratify this movement in our Association that it become a part of our Associational work to be supported by the Churches in the Association.

Respectfully Submitted

MRS. C. W. CARTER
MRS. J. W. SANDERS
MRS. BALLANCE
MRS. BRADY
MRS. D. B. OLIVER
MRS. N. B. LEWIS
MRS. J. M. BEATY
MRS. G. D. VICK
MRS. J. C. BARRINGTON

At the close of the reading of the report on Woman's Work Bro. F. H. Brooks presented the following resolution, which was adopted:

"Resolved that the resolution presented in the report of the Woman's Work be put into operation, and a leader be selected by the Executive Committee of the Association, as soon as financial arrangements can be perfected by said Committee."

Respectfully submitted
F. H. BROOKS.

Upon motion to adopt the report on Missions and Woman's Work, Dr. T. W. O'Kelley spoke to the report. His address was comprehensive, full of interests and greatly enjoyed. Bro. O. A. Keller was then recognied who spoke on "The Baptist Task for 1925." The Moderator recognized Bro. J. S. Farmer, who spoke in his usual interesting way on the Biblical Recorder. Bro. Jas. A. Ivey introduced Mrs. B. B. Adams, a leader of the local M. E. Church, who paid a beautiful tribute to the memory of sister Laura Creech, for long considered the mother of the Four Oaks Baptist Church. She was followed by Brethren Jas. W. Rose and F. H. Brooks, who spoke very feelingly about the life of this consecrated sister. A motion that Mrs. B. B. Adams be requested to publish her address was carried. A motion by Bro. R. C. White that the Moderator be requested to appoint a Committee on Obituaries was adopted. No other business before the body the session adjourned with prayer by Bro. C. C. Wheeler to meet again 2 P. M.

Thursday Afternoon

After prayer by Bro. A. C. McCall, the Moderator called the session to order and recognized Bro. J. F. Pool who made the following report which was adopted:

"We your Committee on place and preachers recommend that the Association meet next year with the Thanksgiving Church, and that Bro. C. H. Cashwell preach the Introductory and Bro. Jas. W. Rose preach the Missionary sermon."

Respectfully submitted

J. F. POOL, For the Committee.

Bro. S. L. Morgan on behalf of the Committee on change of constitution made the following report which was adopted:

"We your committee recommend that paragraph I in constitution be changed that the Association be known as "The Johnston Baptist Association" instead of "The Johnston County Baptist Association."

We further recommend that under paragraph 11 the number of members of the Executive Committee of 5 be changed to 7, of which 5 shall be male and 2 female members."

Rsepectfully submitted

S. L. MORGAN, For the Com.

Upon motion by Bro. S. L. Morgan a change in the election of officers shall be changed from the present order, and that hereafter all officers of the Association shall be elected at the close of each annual session to serve the following year. The motion was adopted, and the clerk was instructed to insert change in the constitution of the Minutes.

Brother S. L. Morgan presented a report of his revised paper on "The Spiritual Condition in our Churches," the report was adopted and the clerk instructed to insert same into the Minutes.

The next item on the program was Enlistment and Stewardship and Bro. R. M. Von Miller was recognized who presented the report on:

ENLISTMENT AND STEWARDSHIP

Let us contemplate and try to visualize the wonderful forces and field which God has given to Southern Baptists.

The Southern Baptists have greater numbers and greater resources in their rural churches than the whole denomination of the Disciples of Christ, in the whole World! They have two and one-half times greater religious forces if they were properly enlisted and developed, than all the Congregationalist churches in America! They have a half million more church members and greater resources than Northern Presbyterians, and five times as many members and as great resources as Southern Presbyterians have! They have a million more church members than the whole Protestant Episcopal Church in America comprises! Incidentally also the Southern Baptists in their rural churches have the greatest number of members affiliated with any great evangelical denomination in the world today. Beloved is it not high time, therefore, that we discovered the vast and mostly undeveloped possibilities of these unenlisted churches and its members, and bring the whole impact of our denominational life into a greater concerted and constructive effort to arouse, enlist and develop their full powers of service for God and humanity?

It is idle talk about Baptists co-operating in a great denominational program about which they know next to nothing. This brings to us the perplexing phase of the problem our Baptist churches are confronting today.

Most of our people are uninformed, and uninformed, they will not co-operate. A survey relative to enlistment and stewardship calls attention to ten great imperative needs.

(1) Evangelistic Spirit. 38.4% of our Southern rural churches reported no baptisms. 245.% of our rural churches in the South reported slight losses in membership, due to the same great need of the spirit of evangelism.

(2) Consolidation. There are too many weak, little struggling churches, occupying in many instances the same field. 5.615 of our rural churches have less than 50 members. 2000 of them should be merged or consolidated with other Baptist churches.

(3) More Pastors and especially resident pastors. 18.8% of our rural churches in the South are pastorless. And 6000 pastors change fields every year. And only 29% of the pastors live in the same community with their churches.

(4) Trained Leaders and Preachers. Only 20.7% of our rural pastors have a college or Seminary training. And 48.5% have neither college, seminary or any other kind of special training, for their work. Only 20% of the Sunday School teachers taking the South as a whole have any special training for their task.

(5) More Modern Church Houses. 17.8% of our churches in the South worship in School houses. 5.9% worship in Union Church houses. A total of 23.7% therefore are houseless, and as far as making any progress is concerned, are hopeless. About 60% however worship in old time one-room church houses, every one of which needs remodeling, half of which greatly need enlarging, and every one of them which needs better equipment. Fully 90 per cent are without adequate houses of work and worship.

(6) More larger and better Organized Sunday Schools, 22% of our churches in the South are without Sunday Schools of any character. 54% are ungraded and unorganized. 68% of the members are not enrolled in the Sunday Schools, and 80% do not attend regular.

(7) More W. M. U. Organization and Work. At least 62% of our rural churches have no distinct Woman's organization of any character. 86% of our total female membership are wholly unreached, untaught and unorganized along any of the various lines of work carried on by the S. W. U.

(8) More and better young peoples Work. 72% of our rural churches have no organized B. Y. P. U. work of any character, and out of a total of over 800,,000 young people between the ages of 10-30 years of age. 74.4% of them are wholly unreached, unenlisted, unorganized and untrained for the Master's service.

(9) Closer touch with denominational life. While 72% sent messengers to the Association, only 12.5% sent representatives to the State Convention, and 6.3% sent representatives to the Southern

Baptist Convention. And 73.3% held no kind of denominational rally or institute during the past year and were visited by any state convention or Southern Baptist Convention worker. Country pastors and leaders, moreover, though far outnumbering those of the towns and cities, are rarely ever put on our important boards or committees, or called into the councils of the brethren who are shaping the policies of our denomination.

(2) Introduction to Stewardship and training in systematic Benevolence. Our churches for the most part, are almost untaught in the great Bible doctrine of stewardship, and untrained in any form of systematic giving. And if we do not begin this neglected indoctrinating in stewardship and training in systematic benevolence, devoting at least a definite period every year in our churches for this task, carefully selecting the right kind of men and women who engage under the leadership of the pastor in this work, this problem will remain unsolved, and the great host of our Baptist people will remain in the wilderness, where we have been all these years.

We therefore ask you as representatives of the various churches of the Johnston County Baptist Association, to urge upon your individual Churches the need and ask them to begin at once, an intensive campaign of enlistment and stewardship.

Respectfully submitted

R. M. VON MILLER, For the Com.

Upon motion to adopt Bro. R. M. Von Miller called attention to the lateness of the hour and refrained from speaking to the report, the report was adopted. The Moderator recognized Bro. Jas. A. Ivey who presented the report on:

TEACHING AND TRAINING

Too much emphasis cannot be given to the teaching and training agencies of our churches. A properly organized and efficiently functioning Sunday School is a true index to the life and activities of the whole church.

The day has come in the development of B. Y. P. U. work when no intelligent Baptist can ignore the far reaching importance of training the Baptist youth through this organization. The trained leadership of tomorrow is the direct resultant of intensive training of our young people today.

Sunday School

There are now in North Carolina 2,263 churches with a member-

ship of 337,258. There are 2,159 Sunday Schools with a membership of 274,524. Some of these are branch or mission schools. There
are possibly 125 churches that have no Sunday School. Some of
these churches are dead, but 75 to 100 of them ought to have
schools. For four years there has been a fine steady growth in
membership of 60,769. This is a larger gain than during the preceding ten years.

During these four years there has been a real Sunday School revival in the Southern Baptist Convention. Every line of Sunday
School work has taken on new life,, and the outlook was never
more hopeful. The southwide improvement in buildings, organization, teacher training and organized class work is great.

From the rural survey being issued by the Sunday School Board
I give these facts: There are 1,998 churches in the open country
and in villages with a population less than 1000. There are 1,873
Sunday Schools in these churches, but 343 close for the winter. The
enrollment of these Sunday Schools fell short of their church membership by 59,332. There are 155,686 church members in these
churches not in Sunday School. Only 869 of the 1,873 schools claim
to be graded, with 1,004 wholly ungraded. In buildings 433 have
some class rooms, 423 use curtains, and 1,017 meet in one room.

Teacher training is our largest and hardest task. We must go
at this task courageously and earnestly. Fine progress is being
made. To date in North Carolina we have 11,298 Normal Diplomas.
There were issued last year 5,800 awards in our state and over
65,000 in the entire Southern Baptist Convention. The time urges
us to this task. Every Sunday School can and ought to put in training every officer and teacher and many prospective workers.

We give the following facts regarding our own Association:

Out of 45 churches in the Association, 42 have Sunday Schools,
28 of these are graded, only one has reached the first standard,
(Clayton). Five report a Cradle Roll. We do not dare neglect the
babies after this fashion. Six churches report Normal Diplomas,
only 38 in all. Such churches as Smithfield and Benson did not
have any Normal Diplomas in their Annual report of last year.
The annual report of last year did not show as many Normal Diplomas as there were Sunday Schools in the Association.   .

The Committee urgently insists that the following steps toward
growth and development challenge our best efforts for the coming
year, namely: First, That a religious census be taken with a view
to reaching the local constituency.

Second. That no energy and time be spared until each and every
Sunday School has an organization properly graded in classes and
departments.

Third, That our people be brought face to face with the realization that the one room church house is altogether inadequate for maintaining the present day activities in Sunday School and B. Y. P. U. work. Several of our one room churches are building to their one room house. Others would do well to follow their example.

Fourth, In this day of efficiency in Sunday School work no school should be satisfied to get along without trained officers and teachers. Let's give ourselves to this task after an earnest fashion.

In the last place may we adopt for our slogan during the next Associational year, "Save the lost and train the saved."

B. Y. P. U.

In the state there are 14000 B. Y. P. U.'s with an approximate membership of 50,000. More than 40 of these are in our schools and colleges. There are 1100 Baptist churches in North Carolina without any training service. There were in the state last year 281 unions more than the previous year. The work is growing and I think the increase will exceed that this year.

In the Association there were 17 unions reported last year. This year the number has been raised to 30, including 20 Seniors, 3 Intermediates and 7 Junior Unions.

From the statistics given above it is seen that B. Y. P. U. work is making rapid progress in both the state and the Association.

B. Y. P. U.'s are doing for our young people what West Point and Annapolis are doing for our soldiers and sailors—training them to be leaders. We have too many church members who are "The Lord's Hallelujah Chorus but unable to raise a tune, the Lord's Cavalrymen but unable to ride a horse, the Lord's soldiers but unable to carry a gun." This situation can be remedied only through training in the organizations of the church.

The Association is thoroughly organized for intensive work during the coming year. Progress should be made surpassing the accomplishments of any past year. The committee feels that B. Y. P. U. work should b egiven a more prominent place in the thinking of pastors and the work of churches.

Respectfully submitted,

JAMES A. IVEY, for Committee.

Upon motion to adopt, Bro. Ivey presented 7 young people of Four Oaks church who gave a fine demonstration of how a B. Y. P. U. meeting should not be, and how it should be conducted. The report on teaching and training was adopted. After which the Moderator recognized Bro. J. A. Smoth, who pre-

32

sented his report as treasurer of the Association:

Building Fund:

Nov. 1923 Balance in treasury	$	434.58
Received from churches		387.90

Total	$	822.48

Disbursements:

Nov. 29th, 1923 Paid to Pisgah Church for repairs and Sunday School rooms		200.00
Oct. 27th, 1924, Paid to Pisgah Church for repairs and Sunday School rooms		100.00

Total	$	300.00
Balance in treasury	$	522.48

Minute Fund:

Received from churches	$	225.90

Disbursements:

Nov. 5th, 1923, To J. A. Smith, treas., balance due	$13.14	
Nov. 12th, 1923, to R. M. Von Miller, salary and postage	62.52	
Jan. 26th, 1924, to R. M. Von Miller, for printing of Minutes and postage	$147.90	
	$	223.56

Balance in treasury	$	2.34

This is to certify that I have audited the books of the treasurer and found same correct to date. This Oct. 29th, 1924.

R. A. BAIN, Auditor.

Respectfully submitted

J. A. SMIITH, Treasurer.

Report was adopted. Brother R. M. Von Miller presented the following resolution which was adopted.

"Resolved that the Executive Committee be instructed to apportion Building and Minute Funds among the churches and have same inserted in the Minutes."

"And that the Moderator appoint a Committee to make inquiry

33

of churches who fail to contribute to Associational Funds."

The Moderator appointed Brethren S. L. Morgan, J. A. Smith and R. M. Von Miller to serve as such a committee.

The following motion by Bro. R. C. White was adopted:

"I move that it be the duty of the Executive Committee to prepare and have printed and properly distributed the program for the Association, and expense of same to be cared for out of the Minute Fund."

The following motion by Bro. S. L. Morgan was adopted by a rising vote:

"Moved, That we express to the Four Oaks Baptist Church and the people of the Community our hearty appreciation for their very gracious and generous hospitality."

No other business before the body, a motion to adjourn was carried and the Moderator declared the meeting of the twenty-second session of the Johnston Baptist Association adjourned, and called on Bro. O. A. Keller to lead in a closing prayer. This brought one of the best sessions of the Association to a close, to meet next year with the Thanksgiving Baptist Church.

R. H. GOWER, *Moderator.*

R. M. VON MILLER, *Clerk.*

JOHNSTON BAPTIST ASSOCIATION

MINUTES OF THE W. M. U. OF THE JOHNSTON BAPTIST ASSOCIATION, HELD IN SELMA, N. C., OCT. 7TH, 1924.

The annual session of the Woman's Missionary Union of the Johnston Baptist Association was held with the W. M. S. of the Baptist Church at Selma, N. C., October 7th, 1924. The session opened with prayer by the Superintendent Mrs. B. A. Hocutt, followed with the singing of "Onward Christian Soldiers." The devotional was lead by Mrs. M. S. Johnson, who read part of I. Cor. 12, and launched the inspiration for the day with her interesting remarks on "Co-operation. After a prayer that we might hear the Divine Voice and co-operate more devotedly, sincere and appropriate words of welcome were voiced by Mrs. E. V. Woodard of the Selma W. M. S., and Mrs. L. D. Debnam of the Selma M. E. Church, and Mrs. J. M. O'Neal of the Selma Presbyterian Church, to which Mrs. R. B. Brady of Benson responded.

In absence of the Secretary, the Minutes of the last meeting were read by Mrs. J. M. Cox, and approved, after which visitors and visiting pastors were recognized by the Superintendent, amnog whom were Rev. R. C. White, Rev. Jas. A. Ivey, Rev. O. B. Fitzgerald, Dr. John E. White of Anderson, S. C., Mrs. H. M. Finch of Rocky Mount, and Miss Mary Warren, of Raleigh.

The roll was called and the reports were very gratifying, and gave assurance that the growth of the work is steadily increasing. The number of financial reports had increased to 47. The amount contributed for this year was $7,880.37 against $5,568.35 of last year.

Officers reports were given as follows: Mrs. D. J. Thurston gave a splendid personal service report. In absence of the Secretary and Treasurer, Miss Cleve Barnes, this report was included in the annual report by Mrs. B. A. Hocutt. Mrs. R. C. White presented the Circle plan, after which Mrs. C. M. Thomas gave the first number of the special music which she had arranged for the program, "Have Thine Own Way Lord," by members of the choir of the Clayton Baptist Church. "When Number Three Came In On Time" was told in a most interesting manner by Mrs. W. J. Payne. Mrs. H. M. Finch, in her address, made an urgent appeal to women for misions in forceful and inspiring words. Mrs. S. L. Morgan then gave a good report with splendid suggestions for the following year's work. The offering for the expense and the work of the meeting was then taken and amounted to $21.40. After special music, "Open The Gates," arranged by Mrs. Thomas, Mrs. Cary Hunter introduced in her most charming manner the speaker, Dr. John E. White, of Anderson, S. C., formerly of our own county, who gave as his text for his great inspirational sermon, Acts 19:

18. He divided the Southern Baptist History in North Carolina into three great epochs: 1st, The call, or Independence and Freedom, 2nd, Evangelization, or Growth, and third, the Test or Demand from God to prove who we are. The essence of religion is Fidelity. You are of Jesus and Paul according to your Fidelity, is the answer to the text. Press forward in the line of His purpose.

The chair appointed the following committees: To nominate—Mrs. J. M. Beaty, Mrs. J. J. Lane, Mrs. A. D. Ballance. Time and Place—Mrs. Geo. D. Vick, Mrs. D. B. Oliver, Miss Alberta Boyett. Resolutions—Mrs. D. J. Thurston. Closing prayer by Dr. O. B. Fitzgerald, of Selma. The session adjourned for dinner, which was served on the Church Lawn.

Afternoon—Junior Session

Devotional lead by Miss Gladys Wallace, who read Luke 18:16, Mark 16:15, and Isaiah 11:6. The Union sang, "Trust and Obey," after which Miss Josephine Pool lead in prayer. Greetings on behalf of Junior Societies of Selma to the Auxiliaries, were presented by Miss Vera Blackman, to which response was made by Miss Ruth W. Woody, of Smithfield. The report of the Y. W. A.'s showed decided growth and new enthusiasm, one of the most interesting being given by Harry Lee Hall, of Clayton R. A.'s, who presented a map of mission work under their study. Presentation of several volumes of "Ann of Ava" by the Clayton G. A.'s, represented by Ethlyn Turley, to the Jr. societies of the Johnston W. M. U. were gladly received by Mission Study Chairman, Mrs. S. L. Morgan. An interesting description of our first Y. W. A. Camp was given by Miss Josephine Pool of Clayton. A duet by Mrs. R. C. White and Mrs. C. M. Thomas, "Nailed to the Cross," was enjoyed by all. The introduction of the "Sunbonnet Baby", by little Miss Catherine Ellis was most effectively made. A very interesting and helpful talk on "The Calendar of Prayer" was given by Miss Mary Warren, from the Central Office at Raleigh, N. C.

We paused to vote that a telegram of regrets and sympathy be sent to our Secretary, Miss Cleve Barnes, who was absent on account of illness of her sister. Interesting two minute talks on W. M. U. special Funds were made as follows: W. M. U. Training School, Mrs. N. B. Lewis; Margaret Fund, Mrs. A. B. Balance; Bible Fund, Miss Alberta Boyette; The playlet "World's Comrades", by the Selma Young People was impressive, and presented the helpful articles of which this magazine is composed. The talk by Mrs. S. L. Morgan in behalf of the G. A.'s was also inspiring. A suggestion made by Mrs. Morgan that Rev. J. A. Ivey of Four Oaks, be Associational leader of the R. A.5s met with a ready motion and was carried unanimously. A brief and appropriate talk and farewell was made by our former Junior Superintendent, Mrs. E. H. Steger. The Union gave a rising vote of thanks to Mrs. Steger for her services, and good will for her new work in Reidsville, N. C. Recommendations by Mrs. C. W. Carter, Chairman, that a full time Associational Worker among the women be employed were presented and motion carried that Mrs. Carter present same to the Association meeting at Four Oaks. New plans for the Circle work for the churches of the Union were given by the Superintendent. The time and place committee reported that invitation from W. M. S. of Mt. Moriah had been accepted, to meet next October, 1925.

The nomination committee recommended the following officers: Mrs. B. A. Hocutt, Superintendent; Miss Annie R. Southerland, Jr. Superintendent; Miss Cleve Barnes, Secretary and Treasurer; Mrs. D. J. Thurston, Personal Service Chairman; Mrs. S. L. Morgan, Mission Study Chairman; Mrs. R. C. White, Stewardship Chairman; Mr. Jas. A. Ivey, Associational R. A.'s Leader. These officers were unanimously elected.

After singing "Bless be the Tie," we engaged in silent prayer, and adjourned with prayer by Mrs. H. M. Finch.

MRS. B. A. HOCUTT, Superintendent.

MRS. J. M. COX, Acting Secretary.

APPROPRIATIONS FOR ASSOCIATIONAL BUILDING, AND MINUTE AND EXPENSE FUND

NAME OF CHURCHES	Building Fund	Minute and Expense Fund
Antioch	$ 15.00	$ 5.50
Bailey	15.00	5.50
Baptist Center	10.00	5.50
Beaty's Chapel	5.00	2.50
Benson	50.00	12.00
Benson Grove	5.00	3.00
Bethany	15.00	5.50
Bethel	5.00	2.50
Bethesda	25.00	8.00
Blackman's Grove	25.00	8.00
Beulah	5.00	2.50
Calvary	10.00	5.00
Cannan	5.00	3.00
Carter's Chapel	25.00	8.00
Clayton	100.00	17.00
Clyde's Chapel	25.00	7.50
Corinth	25.00	8.00
Four Oaks	25.00	8.50
Hale's Chapel	10.00	5.00
Hepzibah	10.00	2.50
Hood's Grove	15.00	5.00
Kenly	15.00	5.00
Lee's Chapel	25.00	10.00
Live Oak	5.00	2.50
Micro	10.00	3.00
Middlesex	10.00	5.50
Mount Moriah	150.00	15.00
New Bethel	50.00	10.00
Noble's Chapel	25.00	8.50
Parrish Memorial	25.00	5.00
Pauline	10.00	2.50
Pine Level	50.00	10.00
Pinkney	5.00	2.50
Pisgah	25.00	8.00
Pleasant Grove	5.00	2.50
Princeton	25.00	5.50
Sardis	25.00	5.50
Selma	50.00	12.00
Shiloh	10.00	5.00
Smithfield	50.00	15.00

JOHNSTON BAPTIST ASSOCIATION

Thanksgiving	15.00	5.50
Trinity	10.00	5.00
White Oak	25.00	8.00
Wilson's Mills	15.00	5.00
Wadkins Chapel	5.00	2.50
Total	$1,065.00	$289.50

TABLE I—

CHURCH	Pastor and Postoffice	Clerk and Postoffice
Antioch	A. R. Creech, Buies Creek	W. O. Hocutt, Middlesex
Bailey	W. T. Evans, Kenly	J. P. Underwood, Bailey
Baptist Center	R. C. White, Clayton	W. G. Hardee, Clayton, R. 1
Beulah	G. A. Bain, Dunn	G. G. Barefoot, Dunn
Beaty's Chapel		
Benson	O. A. Keller, Benson	Julian Godwin, Benson
Benson Grove	O. A. Keller, Benson	L. E. Barber, Benson
Bethany	W. D. Stancil, Kenly R. 2	A. J. Price, Kenly, R. 2
Bethel	W. T. Evans, Kenly	Mrs. J. R. Bunn, Kenly
Bethesda	R. C. White, Clayton	J. E. Smith, Wilson's Mills
Blackman's Grove	Jas. A. Ivey, Four Oaks	Joseph Wood, Four Oaks
Burnell	Jas. A. Ivey, Four Oaks	W. L. Massengill, Benson 1
a ary	J. S. Connnell, Dunn	Mrs. Maude Smith, Dunn
Calvan		
Carter's Chapel	A. R. Creech, Buies Creek	F. Woodruff, Selma, R. 2
Clayton	R. C. White, Clayton	W. P. Creech, Clayton
Clyde's Chapel	S. W. Oldham, Wendell	C. I. Johnson, Wendell, R 1
Corinth	W. D. Stancil, Kenly R. 2	L. T. Davis, Wendell, R. 1
Four Oaks	Jas. A. Ivey, Four Oaks	B. B. Creech, Four Oaks
Hales' Chapel	A. A. Pippin, Wakefield	A. D. Parrish, Zebulon, R 2
Hepzibah	Jas. W. Rose, Pine Level	W. G. Creech, Princeton
Hood's Grove	J. S. Connell, Dunn	P. L. Hayes, Four Oaks
Kenly	W. T. Evans, Kenly	F. A. White, Kenly
Lee's Chapel	A. A. Pippin, Wakefield	W. I. Green, Zebulon, R 2
Live Oak	R. M. Von Miller, Wilson, R 1	J. M. Richardson, Selma, R 2
Micro	A. R. Creech, Buies Creek	S. C. Batten, Selma, R 2
Middlesex	I. W. Nobles, Middlesex	I. C. Overman, Middlesex
Mount Moriah	R. F. Hall, Raleigh, R 2	Russell Powell, Auburn
New Bethel	S. T. Norris, Buies Creek	Geo. W. Bryan, Garner, R 2
Noble's Chapel	W. T. Evans, Kenly	N. L. Stott, Sims
Oliver's Grove	O. A. Keller, Benson	J. E. Ryals, Four Oaks
Parrish Memorial	Jas. W. Rose, Pine Level	J. D. Creech, Selma, R 2
Pauline		J. R. Massey, Four Oaks
Pine Level	Jas. W. Rose, Pine Level	Mrs. F. C. Price, Pine Level
Pinkney	W. T. Evans, Kenly	Mrs. B. R. Edgerton, Kenly 2
Pisgah	S. S. McGregor, Smithfield	A. J. Whitley, Jr., Smithfield
Princeton	Jas. W. Rose, Pine Level	W. I. Pearce, Princeton
Sardis	Jas. W. Rose, Pine Level	T. G. Strickland, Smithfield
Pleasant Grove		Claude Stephenson, W. Grove
Selma	C. H. Cashwell, Selma	Theo Easom, Sr., Selma
Shiloh	J. S. Connell, Dunn	S. H. Averitt, Garner, R 1
Smithfield	S. L. Morgan, Smithfield	J. H. Wiggs, Smithfield
Thanksgiving	R. M. Von Miller, Wilson, R. 1	J. R. Lynch, Selma, R 1
Trinity	J. S. Connell, Dunn	J. S. Lawhorn, Benson
White Oak	C. H. Cashwell, Selma	W. H. Green, Clayton, R 2
Wilson's Mills	S. N. Lamb, Wake Forest	Ernest Price, Wilson's Mills
Watkins Chapel	W. D. Stancil, Kenly	Lester Hales, Middlesex 3

STATISTICAL

Treasurer and Postoffice	TIME OF PREACHING	VALUE OF CHURCH PROPERTY	VALUE OF PASTOR'S HOME	GAINS				LOSSES			TOTAL MEMBERSHIP
				BY BAPTISM	BY LETTER	BY STATEMENT	BY RESTO-RATION	BY LETTER	BY EXCLUSION	BY DEATH	
A. D. Oneal, Middlesex, R 3	2	$ 3,000		13	1		4	8	1	1	191
J. W. B. Finch, Bailey	1	4,000		5	1			5		1	69
W. C. Hardee, Clayton, R 1	3	2,000		13	2						150
G. G. Barefoot, Dunn	4	1,250		7			1	5	8		63
Mrs. H. O. Dixon, Benson	F. T.	3,500		1	7			11			196
L. E. Barber, Benson	1 & 3	1,000			2						50
A. J. Rice, Kenly, R 2	4	6,000		20		2		2	3		125
Mrs. J. R. Bunn, Kenly	4	1,000									7
L. R. Smith, Wilson's Mills	4	3,500		40	7	1	2	9	4		220
Nogah Wood, Four Oaks	2 & 4	1,500		7				4	1	1	100
J. S. Johnson, Four Oaks, 4	1 & 3	1,500		1							22
Mrs. Maude Smith, Dunn	1	2,000		4	5			2		1	38
Martin Thorn, Selma, R 1	1	3,000		12	4	2		2	1	1	125
D. M. Hall, Clayton	F. T.	75,000	10,000	70	25	2		9			651
J. B. Boyett, Wendell, R 1	3	750		61	4	7	25	16		2	227
Lee Hocutt, Zebulon, R 1	3	4,000		23			4	12	7	2	172
D. H. Sanders, Four Oaks	1 & 3	22,000		6	1		1	7		1	113
J. H. Parrish, Zebulon, R 2	3	3,000			2	4					83
W. G. Creech, Princeton	1	1,500									13
Roland Hayes, Four Oaks	3	1,000						1		1	50
A. J. Broughton, Kenly	2	2,500	1,500	1							44
L. M. Price, Zebulon, R 1	3	2,500		17			3	8		3	277
J. M. Richardson, Selma, R 2	2	1,500									6
Mrs. C. L. Batten, Micro	3	3,000		12	4			4	2	1	71
C. A. Barber, Middlesex	2 & 4	2,500	2,500	21	15					1	135
E. S. Pool, Clayton	1	4,200	3,600	11	9			11	1	1	217
Geo. W. Bryan, Garner, R 2	4	5,000		15	5		1	4		1	155
N. L. Stott, Sims	4	1,000		28				2	2		113
J. E. Ryals, Four Oaks	2	800									12
J. N. Watson, Selma, R 2	4	2,500						2			62
J. R. Massey, Four Oaks	2	2,000		5					3		78
Mrs. D. B. Oliver, Pine Level	1	5,000		1	6		2	1			80
Mrs. B. R. Edgerton, Fremont	3	1,500				1			1		24
W. D. Johnson, Smithfield	1	4,000	3,500	2	2		1	1			70
Chas. H. Holt, Princeton	3	2,000		12	2			1			84
J. R. Oliver, Smithfield, R 2	2	2,500		1				2	5		75
Claude Stephenson, W. Grove	3	500								1	9
Theo. Eason, Selma	F. T.	25,000	3,000	30	17	4	1	16	4	2	322
J. W. Williams, McCullers 1		3,000			1		1	3		1	55
J. H. Creech, Smithfield	F. T.	20,000	8,000	12	32	2		9		2	335
J. R. Lynch, Selma, R 1	2	2,500		10	1		1			1	134
J. H. Lee, Benson	4	2,000		3				3			115
W. H. Green, Clayton, R 2	1	4,000		50	10	3			7	1	299
J. C. Adams, Wilson's Mills	2	1,500		11	7		1	2			90
Lester Hales, Middlesex 3											17
TOTAL		$273,000	$32,100	525	172	28	47	162	50	28	5644

TABLE II—FINANCIAL, CONTINUED

CHURCHES	75 MILLION (UNDESIGNATED)	FOREIGN MISSIONS	HOME MISSIONS	STATE AND ASSOCIATIONAL MISSIONS	CHRISTIAN EDUCATION	ORPHANAGE	HOSPITALS	MINISTERIAL RELIEF	OTHER BENEVOLENCES	DENOMINATIONAL TOTAL	GRAND TOTAL
Antioch	78.48	3.35				18.12	6.20	1.81		107.96	718.99
Bailey	120.00					32.00				152.00	539.04
Baptist Cer	69.52									69.52	404.50
Beaulah	42.85									42.85	171.61
Benson	3,455.96	23.00	10.00	65.00		100.00				3,653.96	6,747.83
Beaty's Chel	8.00									8.00	175.50
Benson Grove											2.00
Bethany											
Bethel											
Bethesda	390.00					9.00				399.00	1,075.18
Blackman's Grove	183.56	6.86				92.25				282.67	908.76
Burnell	45.50					10.85				56.35	205.06
Calvary	74.50			5.00		3.00				82.50	298.73
Canaan											1.50
Carter's aChel	22.95	9.00	9.00			70.16	4.13	3.50	25.40	374	1,177.74
Clayton	3,400.00					286.88	33.67			3,720.55	9,565.60
Clyde's aChel	394.59									359	992.09
Corinth	68.75					7.10		5.00		75.85	428.10
Four Oaks	285.26	30.90	64.97	50.00	3.00	43.20	2.00			509.73	4,306.49
Hales' Chel	19.15									19.15	551.70
Hepzibah	3.00	3.00	2.00	3.00						3.00	56.00
Hood's Grove	6.45	5.00	5.00	6.00	2.00					9.45	121.95
Kenly	46.50			5.00		65.57	2.50		3.50	129.07	561.17
Lee's Chapel						2.50				19.50	227.85
ike Oak											35.50
Micro	337.00								78.68	415.68	607.80

42

Middlesex	202.90						56.66	10.01			274.57	1,392.14
Mt	1,125.20	22.00	17.00	150.00			447.76	10.00			1,771.90	2,250.25
New Bethel	287.00										287.00	755.86
...es Chapel	175.50										188.64	577.47
Oliver's		4.00	2.00	5.50			13.14				13.75	104.02
Parrish Mal		7.86	10.00	24.00	5.00	5.00	2.25	5.00			61.86	326.86
Pauline							5.00					126.90
Pine Level	166.13	38.00	38.00	62.87	5.00	10.00	50.00	20.00	15.00		405.00	1,147.72
Pinkney	38.25			8.00			34.48				84.73	320.53
Pisgah	261.50			100.00			58.50				420.00	2,371.13
Pleasant Grove												
Princeton	9.98						25.37				35.35	368.83
Sardis												177.50
Selma	223.08	60.79	20.65	151.50	9.00		242.06	6.42	3.40		7.90	1,710.86
Shiloh	103.32						49.00				152.32	469.32
Smithfield	2,452.09	50.50	41.50	140.48			2.81	20.00	90.20		4,092.58	8 995.94
Thanksgiving	60.00						7.00	1.45	19.00		87.45	633.81
Trinity							3.00				3.00	237.75
White Oak	43.10										43.10	213.84
Wilson's Mills							1.30				1.30	405.80
Watkins Chapel	25.00										25.00	81.00
Total	14,225.07	264.26	129.15	776.35	24.00	25.31	2,033.96	121.38	1,234.18		18,934.57	56,538.22

TABLE II—FINANCIAL

CHURCHES	PASTOR'S SALARY	OTHER SALARIES	MINISTERIAL HELP	BUILDING AND REPAIRS	INCIDENTALS	S. S. AND B. Y. P. U. EXPENSES	LOCAL POOR	MINUTE FUND, ETC.	OTHER OBJECTS	HOME TOTAL
…th Bailey …er	261.20			220.00	52.50	27.84	12.49	5.00	32.00	611.03
Baptist	300.00			15.00	30.00	37.04		5.00	10.00	387.04
Beaulah	300.00					19.98		5.00		334.98
Benson	75.86	44.00		7.92		6.40		2.50		128.76
Beaty's …el Grove	2.0 0.0	0150.00	241.56		366.95	311.69		15.75		3,093.87
Bethany	150.00		15.00			15.00		2.50		167.50
Bethel								2.00		2.00
Bethesda …ve	500.00	50.00	45.25	39.00	36.00	35.28	7.40	7.50	40.00	676.18
Burnell	480.00		12.00		1.00	49.49		7.50	4.85	626.09
…y	180.00		8.00			24.21		2.50	9.00	148.71
Canaan						24.33		2.50	1.40	216.23
…'s …el								1.50		1.50
…h …el	172.00		45.00	20.00	214.50	138.40	15.60	7.50	450.00	1,063.00
…'s	3,000.00	81.00	665.11	2,188.11	1,598.18	466.76		15.00	100.00	5,845.05
…th	450.00		65.08	34.10		35.00		7.50		597.50
Four …ks	1,000.00		232.00	5.00	7.56	67.43	5.67	2.00		652.25
Hales' …el	204.51		46.32		60.00	241.74		17.76	57.15	3,796.76
Hepzipah	125.60		5.00			19.53				532.55
Hood's Grove	30.00					8.00		5.00		53.00
Kenly …el	100.00					4.55		2.50		112.50
…'s	200			76.05	109.05	55.00	5.00	5.00	15.00	432.10
Live Oak	300.00	10.00	70.00	64.50	35.00	18.85		10.00		208.35
…s …el	4.75							.75		35.50
Mro	100.00			25.00	30.00	71.12		1.00		197.12

44

Church										
Middlesex	750.00		106.00	125.00	40.00	133.57	13.35	3.00		1,117.57
Mt Moriah	300.00		125.00			71.00		15.00		478.38
New Bethel	300.00		70.00	12.00	12.00	68.86		6.00		168.86
Bethel	350.00					31.33		7.50		388.83
Oliver's Grove	75.00		3.00			1102		1.25		90.27
Parrish Memorial	150.00			100.00		250		2.50		265.00
Pauline	125.00			1.90						126.90
Pine Level	350.00	18.00		250.00	18.00	65.68	10.00	5.00	25.00	741.72
Pinkney	96.00			115.00	5.00	14.30	3.00	2.50		235.80
Pisgah	500.00	12.00	66.00	1,287.74		67.89	10.00	7.50		1,951.13
Pleasant Grove										
Princeton	225.00			90.48		18.00				
Sardis	150.00		217.25	847.10	7873	17.50		5.00	5.00	177.50
Selma	1,260.50		27.00			4096	54.00	10.00		3,993.96
Siloh	2,400.00	285.00	350.00	400.05	226.31	25.00	100.00	4.50		317.00
Smithfield	280.00		23.95		0100	350.00		10.00	782.00	4,9936
Thanksgiving	200.00					37.41		5.00		546.36
Trinity	450.91	128.21	152.85	10.75	1.25	25.00	6.00	2.50		234.75
White Oak	210.00	50.00		70.00	40.00	113.00	195.00	7.00	70.02	1,160.74
Will's Mills	54.50				25.00	40.00	2.50	1.50		404.50
Zions Chapel										56.00
Total	$18,895.75	828.21	2,576.37	6,311.70	3,926.03	3,188.66	440.01	229.01	1,601.42	$36,350.94

45

TABLE III

CHURCH	Superintendent and Postoffice	Secretary and Postoffice
Antioch	A. D. Oneal, Middlesex, R. 3	W. O. Hocutt, Middlesex, R 3
Bailey	J. W. B. Finch, Bailey	Dorman Finch, Bailey
Baptist Center	J. C. Hardee, Clayton, R. 1	Wade Tippet, Clayton, R 1
Beaulah	J. M. Lawhorn, Benson	G. G. Barefoot, Dunn
Benson	M. T. Britt, Benson	J. C. Morgan, Benson
Beaty's Chapel		
Benson Grove	L. E. Barber, Benson	L. E. Barber, Benson
Bethany	Carmel Creech, Kenly, R. 2	D. C. Smith, Selma, R 2
Bethel		
Bethesda	J. B. Coates, Wilson's Mills	V. S. Smith, Wilson's Mills
Blackman's Grove	W. H. Lee, Four Oaks	Nogah Wood, Four Oaks
Burnell	W. L. Massengill, Benson, R 1	Calbert Johnson, Four Oaks F
Calvary	G. W. Wagestaff, Dunn	Herbert Lee, Dunn
Canaan		
Carter's Chapel	Z. M. Eatman, Selma, R 1	J. B. Atkinson, Selma, R 2
Clayton	W. P. Creech, Clayton	Chas. G. Gulley, Clayton
Clyde's Chapel	D. C. Painter, Wendell, R 1	D. Martin Wendell, R 1
Corinth	Lee Hocutt, Zebulon, R 1	Ottie Thomasson, Zebulon, R
Hales' Chapel	J. D. Snipes, Zebulon, R 1	A. L. Tippett, Zebulon, R 1
Four Oaks	W. P. Massengill, Four Oaks	Alton Massengill, Four Oaks
Hood's Grove	Y. L. Blackman, Bentonsville	Annie Belle Wood, Bentonsvi
Hepzipah	W. G. Creech, Princeton	J. F. Earp, Pine Level
Kenly	A. J. Broughton, Kenly	J. E. Jones, Kenly
Lee's Chapel	A. G. Lewis, Middlesex	A. D. Driver, Zebulon, R 2
Live Oak		
Micro	C. L. Batten, Micro	J. L. Brown, Selma, R 2
Middlesex	W. K. Ballentine, Middlesex	J. M. Davis, Middlesex
Mount Moriah	C. Parker Pool, Raleigh, R 2	J. P. Jones, Clayton, R 3
New Bethel	R. I. Smith, McCullers, R 1	Eugene B. Britt, Garner, R 1
Nobles Chapel	L. F. Boykin, Sims	O. Bullock, Sims
Oliver's Grove	J. E. Ryals, Four Oaks	Miss Lena Tyner, Four Oaks
Parrish Memorial	J. N. Watson, Selma, R 2	R. I. Batten, Selma, R 2
Pauline	Effie Strickland, Four Oaks	M. Bryant, Four Oaks
Pine Level	Mrs. F. C. Price, Pine Level	Sarah Oliver, Pine Level
Pinkney	A. P. Lee, Freemont, R 2	S. T. Davis, Freemont, R 2
Pisgah	J. A. Smith, Four Oaks, R 4	P. E. Whitley, Smithfield
Princeton	W. M. Holt, Princeton	Henry Holt, Princeton
Pleasant Grove		
Sardis	N. S. Stevens, Smithfield, R 2	Paul Oliver, Smithfield, R 2
Selma	N. J. Creech, Selma	Roy Driver, Selma
Shiloh	S. H. Averitt, Garner, R 1	F. Honeycutt, Garner
Smithfield	W. H. Lassiter, Smithfield	Paul Brown, Smithfield
Thanksgiving	W. S. Earp, Selma, R 1	J. O. Brannan, Selma, R 1
Trinity	O. H. Barefoot, Benson	Verter Lawhorn, Benson
White Oak	J. M. Green, Clayton, R 2	W. H. Green, Clayton
Wilson's Mills	J. T. Holt, Wilson's Mills	Arthur Price, Wilson's Mills
Watkins Chapel		
		Total

46

¹DAY SCHOOLS

	Enrollment Main School							Miscellaneous						
3 TO 5	PRIMARY 6 TO 8	JUNIOR 9 TO 12	INTERMEDIATE 13 TO 16	SENIOR AND ADULT 17 AND UP	HOME DEPARTMENT	TOTAL	CRADLE ROLL	IS SCHOOL GRADED?	IS SCHOOL STANDARD?	HOW MANY NORMAL DIPLOMAS?	BAPTISMS FROM SCHOOL	CONTRIBUTIONS HOME EXPENSES	CONTRIBUTIONS FOR ORPHANAGE, MISSIONS, ETC.	TOTAL CONTRIBUTIONS
16	18	21		18	8	88		Yes	No	0	7	$ 27.84	$ 10.00	$ 37.84
20		14	13	18		72		Yes	No	0		37.04		37.04
26	17		17	40		107		Yes	No	0	9	19.98		19.98
	10	20	15	15		65		Yes	No	0	4	6.40		6.40
47	29	58	23	114		291	24	Yes	No	4		311.69		311.69
	12	15	15	25		63		Yes	No	0		25.00		25.00
33	27	18	10	18		113	6	Yes	No	0				
30		20	20	45		125		Yes	No	0	1	35.28	9.00	44.28
12	18	23	24	16		106		Yes	No	6	2	39.49	6.86	46.35
6	10	20	20	11		65		Yes	No	0	1	24.21	10.82	35.03
8	7	8	15	20		70	32	Yes	No	5	2	24.33		24.33
18	19	29	20	33		133		Yes	No	2	11	118.40	27.13	145.53
75	30	84	93	153	55	514	26	Yes	No	22	60	466.76	241.97	708.73
36	28	17	16	43		150		Yes	No		50	35.00	18.48	53.48
19	8	20	43	28		132		Yes	No		16	44.57	1.34	45.91
	32	27	19	29		119		Yes	No			19.53	1.25	20.78
9	12	25	27	35		140	33	Yes	No	9	5	241.74	35.56	277.30
8	12	10		12		51		Yes	No			4.55		4.55
	10	10	5			27		Yes	No			8.00		8.00
8	9	12		20		54		Yes	No		1	55.00	65.57	120.57
29	20	10	35	30		131		Yes	No		17	18.85	12.50	31.35
15	10	10	10	48		100	20	Yes	No		11	71.12	7.56	78.68
15	16	18	10	24		95		Yes	No		20	133.57	155.64	289.21
19	21	17		94		162		Yes	No		10	71.00	447.67	518.67
32	28	34	25	58		186		Yes	No		14	68.86		68.86
	17	20	15	24		83		Yes	No		15	31.33	13.14	44.47
		18		20		43		Yes	No			11.02		11.02
7	8	7	8	40		76		Yes	No			12.50		12.50
10	10	13	15	20		72		Yes	No			7.00		7.00
15	20	12	18	24	1	98		Yes	No	2	1	106.50	42.50	149.00
7	8	10	18	20		69		Yes	No			14.30	3.99	18.29
10	11	16	15	12	6	79	15	Yes	No	3	1	67.59		67.59
38	31	14	21	38		148		Yes	No		12	39.28		39.28
12		18	8	20		64		Yes	No		1	22.50		22.50
42	42	10	35	263		412	64	Yes	No	4	20	168.96	97.65	266.61
	22	25	15		24	92		Yes	No			25.00	58.77	83.77
	62	33	35	125	36	316	97	Yes	Yes		11	500.00		500.00
	20	20	109	48		204		Yes	No	1	3	37.41	27.45	64.86
12	9	11	7	10		53		Yes	No	10	1	25.00	3.00	28.00
32	40	27	41	70		220		Yes	No		29	113.00		113.00
2	15	12	8	25		68		Yes	No		10		40.00	40.00
38	718	809	843	1706	130	5356	317			68	345	$3,089.60	$1,337.85	$4,427.45

47

TABLE IV.—WOMAN'S MISSIONARY UNION

CHURCH	NAME OF ORGANIZATION	PRESIDENT AND POSTOFFICE	NUMBER OF MEMBERS	75-MILLION (ALL OBJECTS)	OTHER BENEVOLENCES	TOTAL CONTRIBUTIONS	ENROLLED MISSION STUDY
Bailey	W. M. S.	Mrs. D. N. Finch, Bailey	19	8.70		8.70	
Benson	W. M. S.	Mrs. R. B. Brady, Benson	35				
Benson	Sunbeams	Mrs. M. A. Peacock, Benson	30				
Blackman's Grove	W. M. S.	Mrs. Norah Wood, Four Oaks	14	22.00		22.00	
Calvary	W. M. S.	Mrs. Maude Smith, Dunn	10				
Clayton	W. M. S.	Mrs. D. H. McCullers, Clayton	92	2,489.54	31.26	2,520.80	36
Clayton	Y. W. A.	Miss C. B. Simmons, Clayton	30	400.22		400.22	
Clayton	G. A.	Miss F. Wilder, Clayton	21	217.29	115.00	332.29	18
Clayton	R. A.	Mrs. C. W. Carter, Clayton	20	246.32	3.76	250.08	8
Clayton	Sunbeams	Mrs. P. S. Wallace, Clayton	50	130.66	3.10	133.76	16
Clyde's Chapel	W. M. S.	Mrs. Mamie Batten, Wendell, R 1	40	96.25		96.25	
Four Oaks	W. M. S.	Mrs. J. W. Sanders, Four Oaks	22	38.10	109.60	147.70	
Four Oaks	Sunbeams	Mrs. Jas. A. Ivey, Four Oaks	12	8.51	3.61	12.12	
Kenly	W. M. S.	Mrs. J. E. Jones, Kenly	10	46.20	79.87	126.07	
Micro	W. M. S.	Mrs. Frank Batten Selma, R 2	17	117.35		117.35	
Micro	Sunbeams	Mrs. C. L. Batten, Micro	25	7.20		7.20	
Middlesex	W. M. S.	Mrs. C. A. Barber, Middlesex	14	109.75	34.94	144.69	
Middlesex	Y. W. A.	Mrs. J. M. Davis, Middlesex	8	10.01	1.86	11.87	
Middlesex	G. A.	Miss Dewla Lewis, Middlesex	12	12.30	5.11	17.41	
Middlesex	Sunbeams	Mrs. N. B. Lewis, Middlesex	36	22.25	26.73	48.98	
Mount Moriah	W. M. S.	Mrs. J. C. Barrington, Raleigh, R 2	24	406.05	75.83	481.88	
Mount Moriah	Sunbeams	Miss Mildred Hinnant, Clayton, R 3	35	12.00	2.00	14.00	
Nobles Chapel	W. M. S.	Mrs. G. B. Boykin, Sims	12	147.00	40.75	187.75	4
Pine Level	G. A.	Mrs. D. B. Oliver, Pine Level	16	352.00	15.00	367.00	12
Pine Level	R. A.	Mrs. D. B. Oliver, Pine Level	6	2.50		2.50	
Pine Level	Sunbeams	Mrs. Bessie Scherr, Pine Level	9				
Princeton	W. M. S.	Mrs. G. W. Howell, Princeton	8	3.10		3.10	
Selma	G. A.	Mrs. Geo. D. Vick, Selma	23	9.98	89.50	99.48	
Selma	W. M. S.	Mrs. N. G. Blackman, Selma	38	42.25	165.69	207.94	15
Selma	R. A.	Mrs. J. F. Brown, Selma	35				
Selma	Sunbeams	Mrs. G. M. Milletts, Selma	20				
Smithfield	W. M. S.	Mrs. Paul Brown, Smithfield	35	25.87	9.26	35.13	
Smithfield	Y. W. A.	Miss Ila Brady, Smithfield	40	453.35	80.20	533.55	
Smithfield	G. A.	Mrs. H. G. Gray, Smithfield	15	53.75		53.75	
Smithfield	R. A.	Mrs. S. L. Morgan, Smithfield	12	7.00		7.00	
Smithfield		...on, Smithfield	30	45.00		45.00	
			50	22.50		22.50	

MINUTES

OF THE

TWENTY-THIRD ANNUAL SESSION

OF THE

Johnston
Baptist Association

HELD WITH

THANKSGIVING BAPTIST CHURCH

October 28th to 29th, 1925

———B———

The next session will be held with the Baptist Center Baptist
Church beginning Wednesday after the first Sunday
in November, 1926.

———B———

To preach the Introductory sermon, Rev. W. T. Evans
To preach the Missionary sermon, Rev. R. F. Hall

OFFICERS

Moderator, R. H. GOWER _____Clayton
Vice Moderator, C. H. CASHWELL _____Selma
Clerk, S. L. MORGAN _____Smithfield
Treasurer, J. A. SMITH _____Four Oaks, No. 4
Auditor, JUDSON TALTON _____Clayton

EXECUTIVE COMMITTEE

S. L. MORGAN, Chairman, 3 years _____Smithfield
H. E. EARP, 3 years _____Selma
MRS. B. A. HOCUTT, 3 years _____Clayton
JAS. A. IVEY, 2 years _____Four Oaks
J. DWIGHT BARBOUR, 2 years _____Clayton
A. J. BROUGHTON, 1 year _____Kenly
MRS. J. M. BEATY, 1 year _____Smithfield

LIST OF MINISTERS

C. H. CASHWELL _____Selma
A. R. CREECH _____Micro
W. T. EVANS _____Kenly
L. E. GODWIN _____Wake Forest
R. F. HALL _____Raleigh No. 2
JAS. A. IVEY _____Four Oaks
O. A. KELLER _____Benson
S. N. LAMB _____Wake Forest
S. S. McGREGOR _____Smithfield
S. L. MORGAN _____Smithfield
S. T. MORRIS _____Buies Creek
S. W. OLDHAM _____Wendell
A. A. PIPPIN _____Wakefield
P. A. PRIDGEN _____Benson
JAS. W. ROSE _____Pine Level
W. D. STANCIL _____Kenly, No. 2
R. C. WHITE _____Clayton
R. M. VON MILLER _____Wilson, No. 1

DELEGATES TO CONVENTIONS

Delegate to Southern Baptist Convention _____R. C. WHITE
Delegates to Baptist State Convention—C. H. CASHWELL, W. T. EVANS,
    and S. L. MORGAN.

STANDING COMMITTEE TO MAKE REPORTS ON CONVENTION

OBJECTS

Spiritual condition of the churches _____R. C. WHITE

Social service, Temperance, Ministerial Relief, Orphanage, and
    Hospitals _____C. H. CASHWELL

Missions—Associational, State, Home and Foreign _____O. A. KELLER

Christian Education—Colleges, Preparatory Schools, Periodicals,
Books, Tracts _____P. A. PRIDGEN
Teaching and Training—
Sunday Schools _____L. L. LEVINSON
B. Y. P. U. _____JAS. A. IVEY
Enlistment and Stewardship _____J. DWIGHT BARBOUR

ENROLLED DELEGATES

Antioch—Mrs. D. Parrish, R. R. Creech, J. Brannan, Raymond Price, D. Parrish, Mary E. Whitley, Albert Whitley.

Bailey—Mrs. J. E. Bragg, Mrs. E. P. Harper, J. P. Underwood.

Baptist Center—V. Austin, J. Talton, R. B. Ellis, J. C. Hardee.

Benson—O. A. Keller, W. P. Lee, L. L. Levinson, Mr. and Mrs. Alonzo Parrish.

Benson Grove—L. E. Barber, J. B. Harper, J. C. West.

Bethany—Q. N. Watson, C. Creech, B. B. Batten, S. B. Batten, Jesse B. Creech, W. D. Stancil.

Bethesda—J. E. Smith, C. T. Godwin, J. J. Wallace, W. N. Parrish, Mr. and Mrs. L. G. Godwin.

Blackman's Grove—J. R. Blackman.

Burnell—J. S. Johnson.

Canaan—Mrs. S. T. Hudson.

Carter's Chapel—Mrs. W. H. McCall, Mrs. J. R. Atkinson.

Clayton—D. J. Yelverton, Mrs. B. A. Hocutt, R. C. White, Mrs. J. E. Markham, W. P. Creech, Mrs. Martha Spence, Mrs. D. M. Parrish, Mrs. Chas. Turley, Mrs. H. G. Eason, Miss Bessie Ellis, C. M. Carter, C. T. Beddingfield, Mrs. C. L. Barnes, J. Dwight Barbour, and R. H. Gower.

Clyde's Chapel—W. B. Phillips, J. B. Boyette.

Corinth—Mr. and Mrs. T. B. Woodard.

Four Oaks—Jas. A. Ivey.

Hale's Chapel—W. D. Ellis, F. P. Hales, Mrs. F. P. Hales, Mr. and Mrs. W. H. Price, Mr. and Mrs. J. B. Price.

Hepzipah—J. Woodard, J. F. Earp.

Kenly—W. T. Evans, A. J. Broughton, F. A. White.

Lee's Chapel—A. A. Pippin, J. W. Creech, W. I. Green.

Live Oak—J. M. Richardson, Lucilla Edwards.

Micro—A. R. Creech, J. Brown, D. H. Jones, E. Wall.

Middlesex—J. W. Nobles, L. H. Hales.

Mount Moriah—R. F. Hall, F. B. Woodall, Mrs. H. A. Pool, J. F. Pool, A. Bunch, Mrs. E. H. Johnson, J. W. Johnson, R. A. Baucom, W. H. Kelly, J. W. Johnson.

New Bethel—W. T. Johnson, Geo. W. Bryan, Mrs. Geo. W. Bryan.

Noble's Chapel—Mr. and Mrs. O. Bullock, Mr. and Mrs. N. L. Stott, Mrs. J. H. Grice, Tom Manning, Sidney Manning.

Oliver's Grove—J. A. Tyner, Mrs. T. V. Allen.

Parrish Memorial—Bruce Bender, Mrs. A. Bender, Mrs. R. F. Batten, Miss Mamie Parrish, Frank Batten, Cl. Bender, T. H. Parrish.

Pauline—T. H. Adams, T. C. Creech, S. C. Creech.

Pine Level—Jas. W. Rose, N. M. Gurley, C. F. Godwin, B. Godwin, Mrs. N. M. Gurley, J. F. Watson, L. E. Godwin, T. E. Britt.

Pinkney—Mrs. B. R. Edgerton.

Pisgah—S. S. McGregor, Mrs. S. S. McGregor, C. W. Thompson, A. J. Whitley, Robt. Lassiter, Mrs. Robt. Lassiter, W. C. Gregory, J. A. Smith.

Princeton—W. M. Holt, G. W. Harrell.

Sardis—Mrs. N. S. Stevens, N. S. Stevens, Mrs. B. C. Powell.

Selma—Th. Eason, C. H. Cashwell, J. H. Talton, Mrs. N. T. Blackman, Mr. and Mrs. H. E. Earp, A. R. Driver, E. V. Woodard.

Smithfield—S. L. Morgan, Mrs. M. A. Wallace, Mrs. J. M. Beaty.

Thanksgiving—Mr. and Mrs. H. E. Earp, W. S. Earp, David Murphy, J. R. Lynch.

Trinity—O. H. Barefoot, L. J. Johnson, P. A. Pridgen, P. T. Allen, J. B. Godwin.

White Oak—Mrs. D. M. Brannan, Mrs. N. E. Jeffreys, J. S. Barnes, D. Murphy, W. M. Whitley.

Wilson's Mills—G. G. Beaty.
Watkins Chapel—Mrs. Nancy Hales, Curtis Hinton, S. M. Bunn.

CONSTITUTION

1. The Association shall be known as the Johnston Baptist Association.
2. Its object shall be to extend the privileges of the Gospel and liberal culture to all the people within its bounds, and, by hearty co-operation with the Baptist State Convention, to help offer these privileges to all mankind in and out of its bounds by the cordial co-operation of all the churches constituting this body.
3. It shall be composed of the pastors in active service in the Association and such delegates as shall be annually elected by the churches connected with it, each church being entitled to three delegates, unless the membership shall exceed fifty, and then an additional delegate for every twenty-five members: Provided, no church shall have more than eight delegates.
4. The New Hampshire Declaration of Faith shall be the summary of Divine Truth for determining questions of faith and order in this body, and the churches desiring membership in it must commit themselves to the substance of it, together with the covenant herewith submitted and this Constitution.
5. This Association shall not have power to annul this discipline or exercise authority over any church connected with it, but it may advise with and sever its connection with any church that neglects to preserve Gospel order, or that treats with contempt the objects or advice of the Association.
6. Each church shall send to the annual meetings of the Association a letter (the blanks to be furnished by the Clerk of the Association), carefully filled as per blank suggestions, stating the full work of the church for the year ending with the Sunday previous to the meeting of the Association.
7. The Association shall foster State Missions, Home Missions, Foreign Missions, Christian Education, the Aged Ministers' Relief Board, the Thomasville Orphanage, and the Sunday School Board, and each church shall be requested to contribute to the support of these objects annually.
8. Missions and Education shall have precedence in their claims upon the consideration of this body in its regular sessions.
9. Whenever a church shall fail to be represented by delegates or letter at the annual sessions of the Association, inquiry shall be made for the cause,

and efforts shall be made to induce such churche to do its duty; and the effort shall be continued till the church is recovered or dropped from the roll.

10. The officers of the Association shall be a Moderator, a Vice-Moderator, a Clerk, a Treasurer, and an Auditor, elected annually, at the close of the annual session to serve the following year, by ballot (or in case when only one brother is put in nomination for an office, then the vote may be by acclamation), from among the members, to serve until their successors shall have been elected, and to perform the duties of such offices, namely, the Moderator, in presiding over the meetings, or the Vice-Moderator, in his absence; the Clerk, in recording and preserving minutes and other papers belonging to the body; the Treasurer, in receiving and disbursing funds belonging to or entrusted to the body, according to its will; the Auditor, to examine the Treasurer's books at each meeting of the Association, and report the same before adjournment.

11. The Association shall appoint an Executive Committee, composed of seven members—5 Brethren and at least 2 Sisters, whose term of office shall be: 3 for 3 years, 2 for 2 years, 2 for 1 year. In case of death or removal, between sessions of Association, the Moderator may appoint members to fill these vacancies until the meeting of the Association—from its members, who shall be entrusted with the prosecution of Missions in the Association and any other work for the interest of the Master's Kingdom which may be referred to them. This committee shall, as far as possible, co-operate with the State Mission Board in supplying the destitution in our territory, and between the meetings of the Association, take such action as may seem to them advisable for the advancement of its interest. The committee shall present to the Association at its annual meeting a report of its proceedings, with the names of the missionaries supported on the field, time of service and details of their work, together with such recommendations as, in the judgment of the committee, the Association should follow in planning its subsequent work.

12. The annual sessions of the Association shall begin on Wednesday after the first Lord's Day in November, at such place as may be chosen, and an introductory sermon shall be delivered on the first day of the session. Representatives from ten of the churches constituting the Association shall be a quorum.

13. This Constitution may be amended ata any annual session by a two-thirds vote of all the members present.

14. The proceedings of the Woman's Central Committee shall be recorded as a part of the minutes of the Association.

BY-LAWS

1. The daily sessions of the Association shall be opened and closed with prayer.

2. Delegates shall be recognized by letters from their churches designating them as such.

3. The Moderator shall recognize corresponding messengers or the delegates of newly received churches by extending to them his right hand.

4. The report of the Executive Board and the Missionary work of the Association shall take precedence of all other business during the morning session of the second day of the annual session.

5. The Clerk shall record and read the proceedings when called for, superintend the publication and distribution of the minutes, preserve a file of them and have it present at each annual session, and deliver to his successor all papers belonging to the body.

6. Members desiring to speak shall first rise and address the Moderator, shall use the term "brother" in speaking to each other, shall not speak on the same subjject more than twice without permission, and shall observe the courtesy that becomes Christians.

7. The roll of members shall be called at least once, and absentees marked.

8. Corresponding messengers and visiting brethren shall be invited to

seats, with privilege of speaking, but not voting.

9. A copy of the minutes shall be sent to the Secretary of the State Mission Board, the Secretary of the Southern Baptist Convention, the American Publication Society, 1420 Chestnut Street, Philadelphia; the Sunday School Board of the Southern Baptist Convention, and the Thomasville Orphanage.

10. All questions of order not herein provided shall be decided by Kerfoot's Paarliamentary Law.

Proceedings

The Johnston Baptist Association met in its twenty third annual session with the Thanksgiving Baptist Church, October 28th, to October 29th, 1925.

Wednesday Morning

After singning "Revive Us Again," and prayer by Rev. A. C. McCall, the Moderator announced the session of the Association ready for the transaction of business, and appointed Brethren J. F. Pool, M. A. Wallace and W. S. Earp, to act as a committee on credentials and enrollment, after which the clerk was asked to read the roll of the churches. A quorum being present the body proceeded with the program. It was agreed to have the program committee to make its report after the sermon. The Moderator then recognized Rev. C. E. Maddry, D. D., Corresponding Secretary of the Mission Board of the N. C. State Convention, also Brethren A. C. McCall, and A. A. Pippin. After which Rev. C. H. Cashwell preached the introductory sermon, having chosen for his subject: "Baptist fundamentals." After the sermon Bro. A. A. Pippin led in prayer.

The next item on the program presented by Bro. Jas. W. Rose, was:

THE SPIRITUAL STATE OF THE CHURCH

Report on Spiritual State of the Churches.—Your committee on the Spiritual State of the churches do not deem it advisable to go into a report of the statistical and financial growth of the churches as these facts will be shown in the tables of the minutes.

Your committee is rejoiced to report that a large number of our churches have enjoyed a great evangelical wave of soul-saving, which began in the early part of the year. This revival wave was greatly augmented and deepened by the Ham-Ramsay meetings that were held in Smithfield during the entire month of June. These meetings were interdenominational; and were County wide in their influence. Following these meetings, rvivals sprang up throughout the County in most of the evangelical churches. Religious federations were organized and went out to the rural and village churches and greatly aided in the revival work, and have kept the Spiritual fires burning all these months. For months in succession many of our churches have had additions by baptism without any special revival effort.

This Spiritual wave has greatly quickened the Sunday School and B. Y. P. U. work of our churches. And surely the financial support has grown along with the other advancements.

Respectfully submitted,

JAS. W. ROSE, Chairman.

On motion to adopt the following Brethren spoke to the report, each speaking of the condition of their respective churches: P. A. Pridgen, C. H. Cashwell, A. R. Creech, W. T.Evans, Jas. A. Ivey, O. A. Keller, S. L. Morgan, Geo. W. Bryan, S. S. McGregor, J. W. Nobles, J. B. Boyette, A. A. Pippin, B. B. Batten, J. H. Hales, R. M. VonMiller, R. C. White, R. Baucom, L. E. Godwin, G. G. Beaty, and Jas. W. Rose. The report was adopted.

After singing "Praise God from whom all blessings flow" the Moderator recognized and welcomed to our Association brethren: P. A. Pridgen, L. E. Godwin, and W. T. Evans, as new pastors, after which the program committee made its report, this report was adopted. Bro. O. A. Keller then led in prayer and the body adjourned for dinner.

Wednesday Afternoon

Bro. W. T. Evans led the devotional exercises. The Moderator announced the appointment of the following committees. Committee on place and preachers: W. P. Creech, T. B. Woodard, and R. R. Creech. Committee on nominating the Executive Committee, and delegates to the Conventions: R. C. White, T. C. Smith, and Theo. Eason. Committee on resolutions: O. A. Keller, W. T. Evans, P. A. Pridgen. Bro. R. C. White was then recognized who presented the:

REPORT ON MISSIONS

About 2000 years ago Jesus Christ made known to his disciples heaven's plan of the redemption of the world. "Go ye into all the world and preach my Gospel to every creature." We see immediately that the divine plan takes the individual for its basis. Threfore it behooves every reddeemed soul to launch out into the realm of service which the Lord hath appointed.

Our Mission Field is divided into the following groupes: Associational, State, Home and Foreign. Associational Missions is embodied in another repore.

State Missions—The Baptist State Convention was organized at Greenville in 1830. At this first meeting a State Mission Board was elected and correspondence was sent out to raise funds with which to evangelize North Carolina. We have been in this business of Statae Missions for 94 years, and the work was never more vital and constructive than today.

We have 145 missionaries in the employ of the State Mission Board this year and this Board is making it possible for many communities and destitute sections in the State to have the Gospel message. The labors of these missionaries have been wonderfully owned and blessed of the Lord. Together with several associational workers the State Board also employed 4 full-time workers. Together, also, with the associational workers who give half time to the work of the B. Y. P. U., we have 4 full-time workers in the W. M. U. department. We have 4 evangelists to the white people and 1 negro evangelist to our negro people.

It is needless for us to go very far to be convinced of the necessity of a great State Mission program, neither do we have to go out of the bounds of our Association, to find the great results of its work. The State Mission Board expends about $2000 yearly in our Association and if it were not for this substantial aid, nearly half of our churches would seemingly have to close their doors. State Missions shuold appeal to every Johnston County Baptist. We see in our midst the effective work of our State Mission Board. The many accomplishments cannot be recorded here, we therefore only name one: the great Church structure at Chapel Hill which affords an adequate place for worship for the students in our great State University. This is a monument of State Missions.

Home Missions—Eighty years of service by this group of our Mission work since its organization in 1845. Through many vicissitudes and steady and unvarying purpose for the salvation of the lost and the upbuilding of the kingdom in our Southland, the Home Mission Board presents an unbroken history of fidelity and spiritual conquest. It has been for Southern Baptists the one great constructive, cooperative and unifying agency. It has been the foster-mother of our weaker enterprises, the founder and support of thousands of our churches, and the forerunner of most of all our State Conventions and a stimulating factor in their organization and progress. The Board in its report presents a significant comparison as follows:

	Money raised	Miissionaries	Stations	Baptisms	Churches Organized
1845-1903	$ 3,520,000	10,586	39,973	82,742	3,649
1903-1924	$13,731,985	27,468	72,629	642,492	4,524

Since the 75 Million Campaign the Board has made severe and drastic retrenchments, chiefly on account of the falling off of receipts. At the recent annual meeting in June on account of the heavy and burdensome debt, the Board had to still further retrench. Enlargement on the contrary is called for in every direction: (1) In an increaase of forces, (2) in better equipment. The Board has need for at least 50 capable young women and as many men in the field at home and a half-dozen young women for Cuba. The greatest need of the Board just now is a mighty increase in financial receipts to lift the heavy burden of debt and prepare for the recovery of lost ground and to enter new fields that are white unto the harvest. Notwithstanding the retrenchmnts made, the Board presents a year of wonderful results:

With 1,077 missionaries, they report 49,219 weeks of labor; 2,381 churches and stations; 144,087 sermons and addresses; 30077 additions by baptism; 4,896 by-letter; total addition 50,354; 2qp churches constituted; 365 church houses built or improved; 608 Sunday-Schools organized; distributed 12,995 Bibles and Testaments.

The Home Mission field was never so great and urgent as now. To save our own land is a condition of saving the lost in distant lands. Home Missions furnish the great base of supplies for the work at home and afar.

Let's remember the Board and all its work in our prayers and come with greater liberality in our gifts.

Foreign Missions—God has blessed our work abroad. Last year was a triumphant year. The fact that our missionaries baptized 12,134 people into the mission fields is an achievement which should set our hearts aglow with joy.

Where the evangelistic spirit reigns new churches spring up. For instance there have been eighteen new churches organized north of the state of Bahia, Brazil during the year. Not only have new churches been organized but the old ones have developed in every line of activity. Many of the churches have bought or built houses of worship this year. One church in Bahia built a new house, outgrew it, and enlarged it all in one year.

It is encouraging to note that many of the better class of Chinese do not seem to sympathize with Anti-Christian movement and take no part in it. There seems to be no need of discouragement on account of it, but rather reason to feel that it will help and not hinder the spread of the Gospel.

It makes us sad to be forced to turn from such triumphs as these to call attention to the embarrassment our Foreign Board is now experiencing on account of the failure of the churches to support it properly.

The Board faces a debt of $1,250,000. This debt is not a result of extravagance. In fact the Board has been cutting appropriations for the last three years and is now holding back more than 100 volunteers. It has also denied for two years any additional equipment to the missionaries. The debt grew because our Baptist people failed to give adequately. What is the remedy for this present distressing situation? The simple remedy is for the people of our churches to put on the 1925-26 program. Let the churches make an every member canvass and support the great program including all the interests fostered by our Southern Baptist Convention, and our Foreign Mission Board will be cared for along with all the others. The practical and the effective thing to do for the churches is to put on the 1925-26 program NOW. In cooperating with the brethren we will serve and strengthen our foreign mission enterprise.·

Respectfully submitted,

·RUSSELL C. WHITE, Chairman.

Upon motion to adopt Bro. R. C. White made a motion that all report on Mission should be adopted after the address by Dr. Chas. E. Maddry, this motion was carried. After which Bro. S. L. Morgan was recognized who presented the

REPORT ON MISSIONS IN THE JOHNSTON ASSOCIATIONS

The Johnston Association has continued to be one of the great mission fields of the State Mission Board. For the past year appropriations by the Board for work in the Johnston Association were made as follows: Bailey, Kenly and Pinkney $400.00, Burnell $150.00; Calvary, Canaan, Trinity and Hood's Grove $700.00; Hepzipah $100.00; Thanksgiving $125.00; Pisgah, Shiloh, Pauline, Beaty's Chapel and Pleasant Grove $200.00; ·Hale's Chapel $75.00, Benson Grove $100.00, Oliver's Grove $100.00—a total of $2,450.00. Because of the lamented death of pastors J. S. Connell not all the appropriation made to the

Trinity field was used.

Grateful mention is to be made of the fact that last spring under the provision of the will of J. M. Beaty, deceased, $1,416.83 became available for work in the aassociation and is now in the hands of treasurer J. A. Smith. Until otherwise instructed, he will treat it as a part of the building fund. Another smaller amount, as is supposed, will acrue to the association on the sale of certain property.

For the churches over most of our association this year has brought unprecedented revivals, most of them influenced by the Ham-Ramsey revival in Smithfield. Reports from the churches will doubtless show the largest gains in membership in all our history. On some of the fields aided by the Board the growth has been remarkable, noteable the Pisgah field, pastor McGregor reporting approximately 140 baptisms, some of the churches almost doubling their membership. Pauline, which came into this field from the Trinity field, also reports very large additions. It is very gratifying to report that Pisgah, which has the largest gains, makes a large increase in its pastor's salary and will claim his services for two Sunday mornings and every Sunday night services. Pauline also expects to make a large increase, and to release the Board. Another noteable gain for us is the beginning of the parsonage for the Trinity field under the leadership of the new pastor, P. A. Pridgen most of the material having been assembled during the pastorate of Brother Connell.

It seems to your committee that the great task before our churches for the ensuing year, and the more so following a year of unprecedented ingathering, is the work of teaching and training and enlisting the large number of new or inactive members. Since the last session of our body an important step has been taken in this direction, which the executive committee wishes both to announce and explain. At our session a year ago the W. M. U. work among the churches. The recommendation was approved, and the matter was referred to the executive committee with instructions to select such a worker" as soon asa financial arrangements could be perfected by the committee." The committee saw little prospect of securing funds to support such a worker during the year now closing. Meanwhile the Sunday School Board offered through State Secretary Middleton to pay half the salary of a worker in the the field of the Sunday school and B. Y. P. U. At the same time a thoroughly trained and highly commended worker became available, Miss Gladys H. Beck, of Georgia. If they secured her, the committee had to act promptly. They believed the churches would endorse their action if they employed her jointly with the Sunday School Board, to major in the field of Sunday school and B. Y. P. U. work, but with the understanding that a minor part of her time would be given to W. M. U. Two prominent members of the W. M. U., Mrs. Hocutt and Mrs. Beaty, were members of the executive committee, and this arrangement was agreeable to them as a step in the direction of securing an all-time W. M. U. worker, in the absence of funds to support such a worker without the help of the Sunday School Board. Since the field covered by the Sunday School, the B. Y. P. U. and the lower grades of the W. M. U. are so nearly identical, and the more since the W. M. U. had taken the initiative in the matter, it seemed to us certain that the Sunday School Board, at least for the present year, could not object to the worker's giving at least incidental attention to the interests of the W. M. U. To our surprise and embarrassment after we had employed Miss Beck with this understanding, we found that the Sunday School Board would not permit her to give any attention to the W. M. U. work, its policy being to concentrate on one or two lines of work. Our well-meant effort to take care in part of the W. M. U. interests, in accordance with the instructions of the aassociation, has failed. Still we were able to congratulate the association on having, through the generous help of the Sunday School Board, a thoroughly trained and capable worker in a field of vast importance. Since March she has given the Association efficient service. Thus far our part of her salary has been met almost entirely out of a fund of $300.00 left over several years ago in the hands of the treasurer for associational missions when that work was discontinued.

The future of this new department of our work is to be determined by this association. A recent conference of the pastors and superintendents of the several churches of the association, after a full discussion of the new office and work of Miss Beck, voted in favor of asking that this office be made permanent, and that she be employed for the ensuing year, our part of the salary being $50.00 a month and half the expenses. Accordingly your committee recommended that Miss Beck be asked to serve another year, and that each of our churches be requested at once to subscribe its proportionate part of this amount to be paid quarterly. It is recommended further that to this amount be added at least $300.00, one half the salary of a W. M. U. worker in uor association for 6 months, an equal sum having been promised by Dr. Maddry for the State Mission Board for this purpose.

It should be pointed out that the embarrassed condition of our State Mission Board makes it imperative that requests for aid be reduced to the minimum for the ensuing year. The executive committee endorses as reasonable and jjust the policy of the State Mission Board announced to discontinue aid to a church or a field after helping it for so many years, and to reduce the aid given to all churches on a percentage basis year by year. Help is given with a view of self-support, and it is doubtful whether a church that cannot ultimately take care of itself alone or by affiliating with other churches, justifies its existence. Indeed, in this new era of good roads and automobiles, it is open to question whether a number of our churches may not rightly combine, and thus solve the problem of support. The time seems ripe for certain of our churches to give this question serious and prayerful consideration. Respectfully submitted S. L. Morgan, A. J. Broughton, Mrs. B. A. Hocutt, J. A. Ivey, H. E. Earp, J. Dwight Barbour, Mrs. J. M. Beaty. Executive Committee.

Upon motion to adopt this report Mrs. B. A. Hocutt was recognized who presented the report on

WOMAN'S WORK

Annual report as given at annual W. M. U. meeting at Mt. Moriah, October 22, 1925, by Superintendent.

It was with high hopes I began this year's work expecting soon to hvae an all time W. M. U. worker in Association as granted by Association in session at Four Oaks. These hopes were soon blasted, as circumstances did not favor the having of an all-time or even a part-time worker. So instead of bringing you the hopes for a splendid report, from a trained worker, a Junior Superintendent and a Superintendent, it is only the results of the feeble efforts of your Superintendent I can bring. For Miss Annie Ruth Southerland, our Junior Superintendent, had to resign her work before she had scarcely begun, owing to her removal from Association. The greatest need in work has been a closer contact on the part of Superintendent with churches and societies, and it is a source of constant grief to me that it is impossible for me as a homemaker to meet this need. Again and again, have I been invited to visit societies, and churches without societies, only to have to try to go and fail.

The report is as follows, far from complete as I have received only 25 annual reports. 47 churches in Association, 26 W. M. S. have been organized since birth of W. M. U. Some of these are much more alive than others. A number have as signs of life: 5 Y. W. A's; 8 G. A's; 6 R. A's; 14 Sunbeams. 59 in all—dead or alive. 400 letters written; 225 postals written; 2 meetings held; 100 miles traveled; 2 societies visited; 5 societies organized and reorganized; 27 the average number of reports received quarterly. Societies reporting every quarter: Clayton—W. M. S., Y. W. A., G. A., R. A., Sunbeam; Smithfield—W. M. S., Y. W. A., R A., Sunbeam; Selma—W. M. S., Sunbeam; Benson—W. M. S., Sunbeam; Micro—W. M. S., Sunbeam; Middlesex—W. M. S., Sunbeam; Jenkins—Vann W. M. S.; Kenly—W. M. S.; Four Oaks—W. M. S.; Princeton—W. M. S.; Clyde's Chapel—W. M. S. 777 members reported; 43 Home and Foreign Fund tokens; 110 Royal Servcie tokens; 151 Biblical Recorders token; 52 Tithers; 31 Mission Study Classes held; 26 reported organized personal service.

Special Sessions of Prayer, 12; observed Work of Prayer for Home Missions, 13; observed Work of Prayer for State Missions, 14; observed Work of Prayer for Foreign Msisions, 22; reported to State officers each quarter.

Societies reaching Standard of Excellence: Smithfield W. M. S.; Smithfield Sunbeams; Clayton W. M. S.; Clayton Sunbeams; Four Oaks W. M. S.; Selma W. M. S.

Funds received for Associational Expense at meeting in Selma and since as follows: $21.40 offered at Selma; $2.00 Pine Level W. M. S.; $3.00 Benson W. M. S.; $3.50 Kenly W. M. S.; $3.00 Smithfield W. M. S.; $1.00 Four Oaks W. M. S. Total $33.90. Expenditure: $10.00 expense of Speaker for Selma meeting; $15.90 paper, postals, postage and mileage; $7.40 programs and tags; $0.30 telegram to Miss Cleve Barnes; $0.30 note books and pins. Total $33.90.

Comparative statement of Annual Meetings 1924: 31 Societies represented at meeting in Selma; 17 Churches represented at meeting in Selma; 200 Visitors and delegates present; 47 Financial reports showed $7,880.37 raised during year 1925; 25 Societies represented at meeting at Mt. Moriah; 20 Churches represented at meeting at Mt. Moriah; 275 Visitors and delegates present; 25 Financial reports showed $5,221.37 raised during year; Amount received from offering at Mt. Moriah $16.34.

And so endeth another year's work for the Master and the great cause of Missions. These past few days have brought us face to face with another fall season and thus I have been impressed to bring these thoughts to you, some of which are borrowed, but most fitting it seems to me.

The frost has transformed the chlorophyll of the emeral forest foliage into a kaleidoscope of rainbow colors, painting a mute announcement that fall is here. Fall-time, alathough the season of plenty begets a tinge of regret.

Fall-time with the tiller of the soil is harvest time, gathering in the sheaves. The first fruits of spring and summer labors is in order. And so it is with you and I and everyone; in the springtime of youth we plant our ideals, our ambitions, our hopes and desires, then the summer time meridian should depict us working diligently in life's field of endeavor, striving hard to cultivate and mature our "Springtime planting."

Then comes fall-time, the autumnal sun drops slowly but surely over the horizon of Eternity and it is harvest time. What we harvest and how much we harvest depends upon the spring-time sowing and summertime cultivation. Each one of us is a planter, a cultivator and harvestor and if our crop in life is planted right, worked right, and harvested right, we will have a crib full of achievements that do not yield to the market fluctuations of the physical things of life.

Have we planted right, worked right, and harvested right in our homes, our communities, our churches, our societies and our W. M. U's?

Fall-time is passing, springtime is coming, a new year is ours. What will we do with it? What will our harvest be for 1926?

Owing to unforseen circumstances, denying us the privilege of having W. M. U. Worker, as Association in session at Four Oaks granted us, we wish to ask that this still be left open so that if a way opens, we may have this much needed addition towards carrying on work of Johnston Association.

MRS. B. A. HOCUTT, Superintendent.

Upon motion to adopt Dr. Chas. E. Maddry spoke on the "challenge of a World Task." After this informing and inspiring address Bro. Gilbert T. Stephenson spoke on the subject of "Financing God's Business." A motion by Bro. R. C. White to defer adoption of report on Missions until a later hour was carried. After prayer by Bro. R. C. White the body adjourned.

Wednesday Night

After devotional exercises conducted by Bro. Jas. A. Ivey, Bro. Jas. W. Rose preached the missionary sermon. No other business on hand the body adjourned until Thursday morning.

Thursday Morning

Bro. E. N. Gardner, pastor of the Orphanage church conducted the devotional exercises, after which the Moderator called for unfinished business. Under

the report on Missions Bro. R. C. White offered the following motion, "That
the executive committee be requested to present the program for Sunday
School, B. Y. P. U., and W. M. U. worker's to the churches and ascertain the
amount they will contribute to the support of these workers." The motion
was carried. A motion by Bro. Jas. A. Ivey, that the adoption of the reports
on Missions be deferred until the afternoon session was also carried.

The Moderator recognized Bro. R. F. Hall as a new pastor and welcomed
him to the association. Bro. Jas. A. Ivey then presented the

REPORT ON SOCIAL SERVICE

The report on Socieal Service is as follows:

Temperance—We have come to think of temperance as having reference
primarily to the liquor traffic, a traffic which as yet remains to curse and
blight civilization and retard the progress of Christianity. Although at least
a three-fourth majority of American citizens has outlawed strong drink when
used as a beverage there is a large host who manifest utter disregard for the
laws, constantl yengaged either in the manufacture, sale or use of same.

The recent decision of the Courts declaring the person who purchases whiskey to be equally guilty with the person who makes the sale opens up a new
and wide avenue of approach, by which the law can more successfully cope
with the liquor situation. The decision is entirely just and proper.

It is our humble judgment that the saving grace of God has done more to
abolish the liquor traffic in Johnston County within the past twelve months
than has any other force or power.

The secular press, religious publications, and even the ministry have become
too well satisfied with a legal prohibition victory when that is but a fair beginning toward the complete wiping out of the traffic.

Therefore, we recommend, that our ministers preach more often on the resultant evils of strong drink, and that we urge the press both religious and
secular to renew the fight in real earnestness against this evil.

The use of tobacco is one of the most popular evils of our day. Young
boys form the habit of smoking when they are barely large enough to roll a
cigarette. It would at least be timely for the ministry to refrain from the
use of tobacco in any form and thus encourage the laaity to do likewise.

We would call attention to the lack of moral training in th ehome. But few
homes still worship around the family altar. An Associational worker gives
it as her experience that in all the homes she has gone during eight months
only five had had family worship. We do not wonder that so many young people lose respect for the religion of their parents and also for parental authority.

Ministerial Relief—The relief and Annuity Board of the Southern Baptist
Convention, Dr. Wm. Lunseford, Corresponding Secretary, has been working
at the matter of ministerial relief for six years. 1,086 ministers, widows, and
orphans are receiving aid throughout the South from the relief side of the
Board. North Carolina at present has 115 beneficiaries as opposed to 95 a
year ago. They receive on an average less than $140.00 a year per individual.

On the annuity side of the Board's work more than 1400 men and women
are now enrolled as active certificate holders. Thirty-one are drawing annuities at the present. For the past eighteen months the Annuity Department
has been paying the maximum of $500.00 per annum.

In addition to the relief work done, a new plan for granting aid is contem-
plated, known as the "Service Annuity Plan." This plan is to include all servants of the denomination who give all of their time to religious work through
some channel of denominational activities. It provides for thirty-five years
of service under this special plan to approximate one half of the minister's
salary through the period of service. The minimum annuity $500.00 and the
maximum $2,000.00. The widow or orphans to receive one half that of the
minister himself. This plan will be put in operation at an early date.

There is certainly no phase of our program which makes a stronger appeal
for our support. They who have walked life's pathway with diligent tread,

followed where the Spirit of God led, calls to us in the words of another, "To you from failing hands we throw the torch." Does it not behove us to see that the evening of their life is not marred by anxiety and want.

Hospitals—During the past year our Hospitals at Winston-Salem under the superintendency of Mr. G. T. Lumpkin took care of 1600 patients. About 225 of these were charity or part pay. To care for these the Hospital spent around $10,000.00, the rate of $40.00 per patient.

The running expenses of the institution are $6,250.00 per month. The Hospital urges that we send our sick to them. They gladly welcome charity patients with the request that where possible the church or friends sending the sick will meet a part of the expenses.

The institution even in its infancy is noted for its Christian atmosphere, blending sympathy, love, prayer and brotherly kindness with the ministry of the professional. This is one of its greatest assets.

Perhaps the most urgent need for the present is a nurse's home. A class of 34 nurses occupy one floor of the Hospital Building at a cost of $3,000.00. This arrangement is very unsatisfactory since it is inadequate as a home and results in the loss of one whole floor to the Hospital work.

At last the Baptists of North Carolina have followed the example of Jesus in the ministry of healing. May we increase our pace in this direction.

Orphanage—The Thomasville Baptist Orphanage under the leadership of General Manager M. L. Kasler has experienced a very successful year. A total enrollment of 602 with 492 at Thomasville and 110 at Kennedy Home. One hundred nineteen have been received during the year.

The annual cost per child is $284.40 making a total annual cost for the 602 children in the two homes $171,208.80. This only tells the Orphanage story in part.

A phase of the work that is becoming very popular with the management is that of mothers' aid. Their plan is to maintain the home ties where possible by means of aiding the mother through the cooperation of the local church or committee. There is a growing conviction that this plan is more desirable than to disrupt the home and take the children to the Orphanage.

For the time being 386 children with 83 mothers are being helped by Mothers' Aid at a cost of about one-third the amount required for a like number of children at the Orphanage.

The Orphanage bears its own appeal. It is separate and distinct from the 1925 Cooperative Program. It is being financed by once a month offerings from the Sunday Schools and a great Thanksgiving Offering. The Thanksgiving offering is unique in that each person is called on to make as his thank offering the equivalent of one day's labor.

Respectively submitted,

JAMES A. IVEY, Committee.

Upon motion to adopt the report on social service, Bro. E. N. Gardner spoke interestingly on the Orphanage, after which the report on social service was adopted. Bro. S. L. Morgan then presented the

REPORT ON CHRISTIAN EDUCATION

Missions and evangelism and education have been married by God; let not man put them asunder. To separate education from religion is as irrational as to separate the mind from the soul. God is the author of wisdom, and He is not pleased with ignorance. Baptists in the past paid too little attention to education, and consequently they have not had in public affairs the proportion of Baptist leaders due the denomination that exceeds all others in numbers. Lately our people have been greatly aroused to the importance of education, but still we need an awakening. Multitudes in our churches are uneducated and untrained, and such members as a whole block the way of progress for the church.

The outstanding problem of education is to put into it the religious element. For, as has been truly said, "Education without religion is simply veneering rotten wood." Without the religious element education is dangerous. There is no greater heresy than the doctrine that, if people know the

Map of Johnston B

DIVISION NO. 1

Four Oaks
Benson
Olivers Grove
Benson Grove
Pleasant Grove
Blackmans Grove
Hoods Grove
Burnell
Beulah
Calvary
Canaan
Trinity

DIVISION NO.2

Smithfield
Pisgah
Wilsons Mills
Beatys Chapel
Selma
Lizzies Mill
Pine Level
Sardis
Hephzibah
Princeton
Pinkey
Parrish Memorial

DIVISION NO. 3

Middlesex
Bailey
Lees Chapel
Watkins Chapel
Hales Chapel
Antioch
Thanksgiving
Live Oak
Micro
Kenly
Bethel
Bethany
Nobles Chapel
Carters Chapel

DIVISION NO. 4

Clayton
Mt. Moriah
New Bethel
Clydes Chapel
White Oak
Corinth
Bethesda
Baptist Center
Shiloh

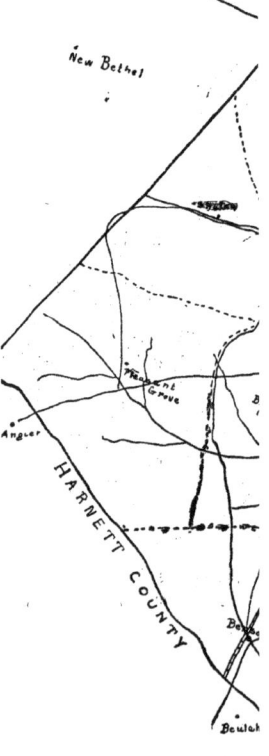

Association

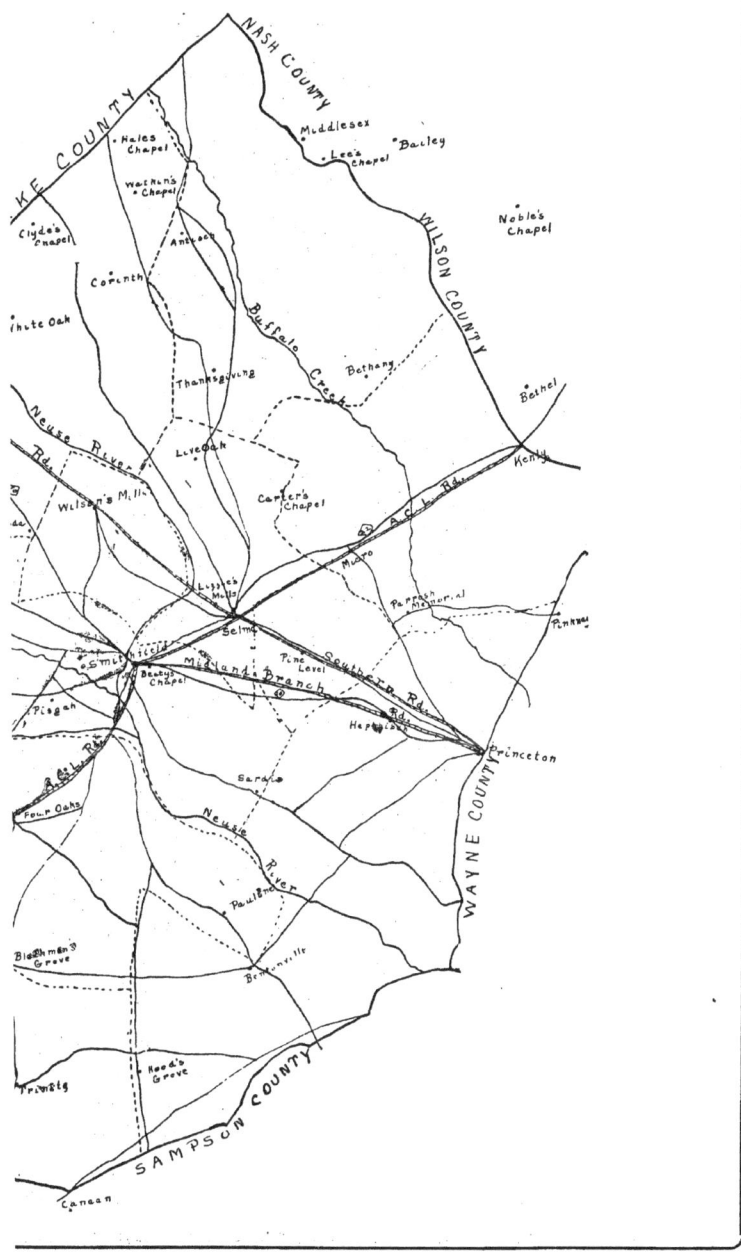

right they will do it; that a people can be made good and great by educating them. Germany once for all refutes the doctrine. The most educated nation on earth, it pulled down on our heads the civilization we had built up. We are not to forget that the tidal wave of lawlessness and crime and immorality that has swept over the earth during the last decade has moved hand in hand with the greatest progress in education the world has ever known. Salvation to individual or society through education is an idle dream. But Christian education is another matter. And that is the subject before us.

To give chief attention to our colleges and preparatory schools and seminaries in discussing Christian education seems to be missing the main point. Unless we put more emphasis on religious education in the home than we are now doing we shall never have an education that is Christian. Christian schools and colleges for our youths can never make up for lack of religious teaching in the home. We need to face seriously the fact that the Sunday school, even if it is made a real school, can do but little toward imparting a Christian education. For at best even the capable teacher in the Sunday school can give only about 20 minutes a week of actual teaching of the lesson. This is to say that our children get only about 20 hours of religious teaching a year in the Sunday school, as against nearly 1,000 hours a year of secular teaching in the day school of nine months, with the Bible and religion left out. This is not to the discredit of the day school. We require that it shall not teach religion. But it is pointing out a serious fact, that our great system of State education is not, and cannot, be "Christian education." This but emphasises the necessity of paying more attention to teaching religion in the home and the Sunday school.

And here we see the necessity of maintaining our system of Christian high schools and colleges. It may be safely said, in spite of all suspicion and insinuation, that all our Baptist schools and colleges continue to require that none but avowed Christians shall be members of their faculties; that all students are required to take a course of Bible study; that opportunities are definitely offered for training in Christian service, and that the school itself strives in a definite way to surround the student with an atmosphere distinctively Christian. If parents fear for the faith of their children in the Christian school, let them remember that the same dangers are present in more pronounced form in the State school. It seems eminently wise for us to place our children in the more pronounced Christian atmosphere of our Baptist schools. It cannot be denied that they come out of our schools more decidedly Christian, and more loyal to the church and its program, than if they had attended other schools.

Within the past year Wake Forest came into possession of the New Bostwick Fund, adding about $1,200,000 to the endowment, which now amounts to about $2,500,000. The Meredith bond issue of $750,000 has been sold, and the splendid new college, now rapidly buliding, will be a new object of pride to every loyal Baptist. Fine development and growth are reported from nearly all our other colleges and academies.

It is earnestly recommended that we rededicate ourselves to the loyal support of all our Baptist schools, and that through the Co-operative Program their minimum needs of $300,000 a year shall be provided in a systematic way. It is also recommended that all our churches shall observe faithfully "Christian Education Day," presenting educationally the cause of Christian Education, and holding up the claims of our Baptist system of schools.

As an integral part of our system of Christian Education too much emphasis cannot be put on religious books and periodicals. A sickening flood of trashy and filthy literature is pouring upon our young people. The home and the church should make more definite and persistent efforts to conteract it through putting wholesome literature in easy reach of all who will read it. Every home ought to regard the Biblical Recorder and the Home and Foreign Fields as indispensable. Every church ought to start its own high-grade library and keep the best books in circulation thrugh the congregation. A multitude of the most valuable tracts are always available from all our boards for the asking, and these can be made a means of the steady education of our people along all the lines of Christian living and activity. Most of all the

iible, as the one text book on Christian education, ought by every means to
e read and taught with unflagging persistence. We seem in grave danger
f forgetting it today amid the rushing flood of other literature.

Upon motion to adopt Bro. S. L. Morgan spoke to the report, the report
ras adopted. In the absence of Bro. O. A. Keller who was to present a report
n enlistment and stewardship, Bro. Walter Gilmore was recognized, who
poke on this subject very interestingly, after which the Moderator recogniz-
d Dr. D. B. Bryan who spoke on Wake Forest College.

A motion by Bro. W. T. Evans to change the first and second line of section
1 of the constitution to read: "The association shall elect an Executive Com-
ittee composed of 7 members—5 brethren and at least two sisters, whose
erm of office shall be: 3 for 3 years, 2 for 2 years and 2 for 1 year. In case
f vacancies by death or removal between session of Association, the Mode-
ator may appoint members to fill these vacancies until the next meeting of
ie Association." The motion was adopted.

A motion by Bro. R. C. White to change time of session in the constitution,
) read: "The annual session of the association shall begin on Wednesday af-
er the first Lord's Day in November." The motion was adopted. After
rayer by Bro. R. F. Hall the body adjourned for dinner.

Thursday Afternoon

Devotional conducted by Bro. W. D. Stancil. Upon motion by Bro. R. M.
on Miller, the Moderator was asked to appoint Bro. W. S. Earp as Auditor,
iis motion was carried. Miss Gladys H. Beck was recognized who spoke in
very interesting manner of her work as S. S. and B. Y. P. U. worker in this
ssociation. In a "Round Table" talk the following Brethren spoke with
reat feeling about the good work of Miss Beck in our Association. W. T.
vans, Jas. W. Rose, R. F. Hall, W. S. Earp, J. A. Smith.

Upon motion of Bro. R. C. White which was carried, the report on Missions
as adopted separate from the report of the Executive Committee. After
hich the report of the Executive Committee was adopted.

Bro. R. F. Hall then presented the

REPORT ON TEACHING AND TRAINING

Three distinct services should be conducted in every Baptist church of to-
iy. One service for preaching the Word of God, aanother for teaching the
ford of God, and still another service for training in Christian service. The
irvice for teaching the Word of God is called the Sunday School, and the
aining service of the church is called the B. Y. P. U. The teaching and
aining services are just as much a function of the church as the preaching
rvice. They are to be directed by the church and guided by the Holy Spirit,
ist as the preaching service. The Holy Spirit should be entreated to guide
id direct in the teaching and training services of the church as well as in
ie preaching service of the church.

Teaching Service—We are just beginning to get away from the obsolete
ea that a Sunday School is a place for young people and children. The lack
! proper business principles applied in Sunday Schools generally was doubt-
ss the reason for this condition.

Statistics contained in the report to the Association in 1924 will be ap-
:oximately correct now, except that there are many more normal diplomas
)w due to the work of Miss Gladys H. Beck, Field Worker, and your com-
ittee desires to commend her work to the Association.

For the purpose of making our Sunday School work throughout the Asso-
ation more effective and uniform an association wide organization has been
rfected, known as the Sunday School Convention of the Johnston Associa-
on, with L. L. Levinson, as president and M. T. Britt as Secretary-Treasurer.
iis was done at the Convention held on July 19, 1925, with the Four Oaks

Baptist Church. Prior to this a Sunday School Institute was held at Benso on March 29.

At this convention matters of interest to all churches in the associatio were discussed and valuable suggestions received by the delegates. The ide is to have one Vice-President from each of the four divisions of the associa tion, each dviision holding a quarterly meeting in charge of its Vice-Presiden during the year. The general Sunday School convention to meet annually.

Your committee hopes that this organization will have the effect of produc ing more effective Sunday School units, of receiving and disseminating va uable information and of solving a great many of the problems which no and will hereafter confront our Sunday Schools.

In spite of all hopeful signs we need to keep before us big things to d For our great state we want to join the other sixty-three associations in doin the following things:

1. Put a Sunday school in every church and run it twelve months in th year.

2. Add 25,000 people to our Sunday school rolls in 1926 and press on unti there are as many in our Sunday schools as in our churches.

3. Earn 3,000 Normal Diplomas and 7,000 Seals for other books studied i our Normal Course.

4. Reach 100 Standard Schools thus having a well balanced program o work in these schools.

5. Start the work of the Daily Vacation Bible School in our midst. Thi new movement is worthy of our best efforts.

6. Never forget our greatest and holiest task of trying to win the lost tc Christ. Thousands of unsaved are in our midst.

We urge all pastors, superintendents, teachers and other workers to secure full and free information from our State Sunday School Secretary, E. L. Mid- dleton, Raleigh, North Carolina.

Training Service—In the Southern Baptist Convention there is a host of weak christians who cannot do anything for the Lord, and the reason is that they have never been trained to do anything for the Lord, and the churches are to blame. We have been eager to preach the Gospel, to make converts, to baptize them, and then to turn them aloose without instructing, training, and developing them in the grace and knowledge of Jesus Christ. We have given the new convert the impression that when he is converted and bpatized, that his obligations cease, not only to the church but to his Lord and Saviour as well. We do our young people a grave injjustice not to begin the day af- ter thier baptism to teach and train them in christian service. The work and function of the B. Y. P. U. is to train the young church members for efficient service in the on-going of God's kingdom in the world.

Annual Report of the Johnston Associational B. Y. P. U.—The Johnston Associational B. Y. P. U. is happy to make its first report to the General As- sociation.

We come to the close of the fiscal year, a year in which every phase of the work surpasses by far the achievements of any past year. The report on B. Y. P. U. in the Associational minutes of last year states that there were at that time (October 30) 20 Senior, 3 Intermediate, and 7 Junior Unions. At present the B. Y. P. U.'s number 46 in all, 24 Seniors, 5 Intermediates, and 17 Juniors. Three Seniors and one Intermediate have disbanded, making a total of 50 Unions having existed during the year, five more B. Y. P. U.'s than we have churches in the Association. Only 14 churches remain to be en- listed in B. Y. P. U. work. At present 17 are without Unions. Three of these have had Unions which are not functioning now. Five churches have three Unions each, namely: Benson, Clayton, Four Oaks, Selma, White Oak. Eight churches have two unions each, namely: Blackman's Grove, Pisgah, Princeton, Thanksgiving, Kenly, Mt. Moriah, New Bethel, Bethesda. This leaves 15 churches with one Union each.

At the time of the state B. Y. P. U. Convention in June, Johnston Associa- tion boasted 34 Unions. Ten of this number were represented at Salisbury, place of the Convention.

Fourteen Unions have attained the A-1 Standard at least one quarter durng the year whereas the best records we can find gives only three A-1 Unions ast year. This is a phenominal increase but only a small beginning of what re feel we shall accomplish through concentrated work.

Through the relentless efforts of the vice-presidents we have been able to :et a report for two consecutive quarters from each Union in the Association.

A three day Associational-wide Training School Convention was held with It. Moriah Church August 26-28. Twenty-four churches were represented.)ver three hundred delegates were registered. Two young women volunteer-d for definite Christian service. Three Study Courses were taught resulting n a total of 85 awards and diplomas: Seniors, 30; Intermediate 23; Juniors, 2.

. The Convention adopted the following aims for the year 1925-26: 20 New Jnions, 24 A-1 Unions, 150 Tithers, Evangelism, 350 Subscriptions to Biblical lecorder.

With a plan in our head, a purpose in our heart, and a prayer on our lips, et us go forward for our Lord, the King.

Respectfully submitted,

R. F. HALL
L. L. LEVINSON
JAS. A. IVEY
Committee.

On motion to adopt the report Brethren L. L. Levinson, R. W. Spillman, as. A. Ivey, and Perry Morgan spoke to the report the report was adopted. A motion by Bro. R. F. Hall that hereafter the Reports on Sunday School nd B. Y. P. U. be made separate, was carried.

Bro. J. A. Smith was recognized who presented the

REPORT OF TREASURER

Suilding Fund:

alance in treasury October 30th, 1924	$ 522.48	
leceived from Churches	$ 683.84	
leceived from J. M. Beaty's Estate, Mch. 2, 1925	$1,416.83	$2,623.15

Disbursements:

ov. 26, 1924 to Parsonage at Trinity field	$ 4.25	
eb. 8, 1925 Olivers Grove	$ 15.00	
Ich. 17, 1925 To Miss Beck	$ 41.67	
Iay 5, 1925 To Miss Beck	$ 142.50	
uly 25, 1925 To Miss Beck	$ 147.50	$ 350.92

alance in the treasury for Building Fund	$2,172.23

linute Fund:

Ictober 30, 1924, balance on hand	$ 2.34	
.eceived from the churches	$ 200.50	$ 202.84

Disbursements:

Iov. 26, 1924 To R. M. Von Miller salary and postage	$ 62.50	
Iec. 6, 1924 To S. L. Morgan for expense	$ 20.00	
eb. 8, 1925 For printing of Minutes, cut for map, postage for distribution	$ 173.25	$ 255.75

alance due treasurer	$ 52.91

Respectfully submitted

J. A. SMITH, Treasurer.

P. S. I find books of treasurer correct.

W. S. Earp, Auditor.

Report of treasurer was adopted. The Committee on time, place and preach-: made the following report:

We your committee recommend the following: "That we meet next year n Wednesday after the first Sunday in November, with the Baptist Center

Church, and that Bro. W. T. Evans preach the Introductory sermon."

W. P. CREECH, for Committe

This report was adopted. The body then elected Bro. R. F. Hall to act a chairman for the Co-operative program in this Association.

Bro. R. C. White offered the following resolution which was adopted by rising vote:

"THat we express to Thanksgiving Baptist Church and the people of th community our hearty appreciation for their bountiful provision for our ever need and comfort during the meeting of the Association."

Report on obituary by Bro. Jas. A. Ivey was adopted.

REPORT ON OBITUARY—REV. J. SEWELL CONNELL—(1871-1925)

On the morning of June 10, 1925, Brother J. S. Connell passed to his ric reward. He left in his parting message many encouraging words that canno be forgotten, also words which were a true index to the great, staunch char acter.

Brother Connell was born in Alabama on the 15th of June, 1871. When young man he entered Howard College and it was at this institution that h did his college work. In 1905 he married Miss Elma Ellard also of Alabama To this union was born one daughter, Cathryn Connell, now eighteen years o age. Brother Connell labored in his own native State until the year 191 when he came to North Carolina. His first pastorate was at Mars Hill, N. C where he served for a year and a half. Then after a brief pastorate wit church near Biltmore, N. C., he moved to Catawba County where he became pastor of the Olivet-Bethel field. For five and a half years he served these churches. His next pastorate was with the First Church at Mooresville. With the people at Mooresville Brother Connell labored for two years. Leaving Mooresville he entered the Southern Baptist Theological Seminary at Louisville. He remained at the seminary for two years. Returning to North Carolina he accepted a call to the Trinity Field churches. This field is composed of Hood's Grove, Canaan, Calvary, Beulah and Trinity. His work on this, his last field, was crowned with great success notwithstanding the fact that he had only served them one year when he was called home.

Brother Connell leaves a loving wife and a daughter, two sisters of Birmingham, Alabama, a mother, a brother now pastor at Denton, N. C., and a host of friends. One year prior to his departure, brother Connell had expressed a desire to be laid to rest at Bethel Church, in Catawba County; consequently on Sunday afternoon July 12, he was laid to rest at this place in the presence of a host of sorrowing friends and relatives, that loved him devotedly.

After years of service in God's great field he came to the "end of the row." Many times aided by the Sword of the Spirit he cut the thorns and brambles out of the row which he was working, but God looking down upon the faithful worker saw best to call him to Heaven. And the call came after over twenty years of working in God's great Harvest Field. He has gone to rest in the midst of the paradise of God for he reached the "end of the row." God called him on to Heaven. Truly he has gone; the seat he occupied one year ago in our association is probably used by another, but still through sweet memories that are ours, we see the noble soul as he was, true, Godly, loving and thoughtful. He lived in the faith and died in the faith.

Many degrees have been conferred upon the noble man, especially so in your committee's presence. God desiring to confer upon Barnabas a degree he gave him this degree: "He was a good man." Now we have herad many degrees conferred upon our dear departed brother, but all over his work—the work which your committee now has—the people are conferring upon Bro. Connell the great degree: "He Was A Good Man."

Respectfully submitted,

P. A. PRIDGEN, for the Committee.

The election of officers resulted in the following: R. H. Gower, Moderator; C. H. Cashwell, Vice Moderator; S. L. Morgan, Clerk; J. A. Smith, Treasurer and Judson Talton, Auditor.

A motion by Bro. R. C. White to give the officers of our Association, who have served during the year just closed, a rising vote of thanks, was carried. No further business before the body the Moderator declared the 23rd session of the Johnston Association closed and called on Dr. W. B. Spillman to lead in the closing prayer. This brought a very largely attended and interesting session to a close, to meet next year with the Baptist Center Baptist Church.

R. H. GOWER, Moderator.

R. M. VON MILLER, Clerk.

Apportionment for Associational building, Minute, and Expense Fund.

Name of Churches	Building Fund	Minute & Expense Fund
Antioch	$ 15.00	$ 5.50
Bailey	15.00	5.50
Baptist Center	10.00	5.50
Beaty's Chapel	5.00	2.50
Benson	50.00	12.00
Benson Grove	5.00	3.00
Bethany	15.00	5.50
Bethel	5.00	2.50
Bethesda	25.00	8.00
Beulah	5.00	2.50
Blackman's Grove	25.00	8.00
Burnell	5.00	2.50
Calvary	10.00	5.00
Canaan	5.00	3.00
Carter's Chapel	25.00	8.00
Clayton	100.00	17.00
Clyde's Chapel	25.00	7.50
Corinth	25.00	8.00
Four Oaks	25.00	8.50
Hale's Chapel	10.00	5.00
Hepzibah	10.00	2.50
Hood's Grove	15.00	5.00
Kenly	15.00	5.00
Lee's Chapel	25.00	10.00
Live Oak	5.00	2.50
Micro	10.00	3.00
Middlesex	10.00	5.50
Mount Moriah	75.00	15.00
New Bethel	50.00	10.00
Noble's Chapel	25.00	8.50
Oliver's Grove	5.00	2.50
Parrish Memorial	25.00	5.00
Pauline	10.00	3.00
Pine Level	50.00	10.00
Pinkney	5.00	2.50
Pisgah	25.00	8.50
Pleasant Grove	5.00	2.50
Princeton	25.00	5.50
Sardis	25.00	5.50
Selma	50.00	12.00
Shiloh	10.00	5.00
Smithfield	50.00	15.00
Thanksgiving	15.00	5.00
Trinity	10.00	5.00
White Oak	25.00	8.00
Wilson's Mills	15.00	5.00
Watkins Chapel	5.00	2.50
Total	$1,070.00	$292.00

The W. M. U. of the Johnston Baptist Association held its annual session with the W. M. S. of Mount Moriah Baptist Church, October 23rd, 1925.

The session opened at 9:45 by singing "Stand Up, Stand Up for Jesus." The devotional exercises were led by Mrs. W. R. Stallings of Mt. Moriah Address of welcome by Mrs. Parker Poole of Mt. Moriah and response by Mrs. Geo. W. Vick of Selma. Minutes of the last meeting were read and approved. Mrs. D. J. Thurston being absent, her report on personal service was read by Mrs. W. F. Weathers. Report on Mission Study was presented by Mrs. Holt of Smithfield. Mrs. B. A. Hocutt presented her report as Superintendent of the Union, which was very encouraging. She mentioned some missionary work which is done by the Fidelis class of the Clayton Baptist Church, consisting of supporting a native Chinese and his wife. Visitors were then recognized, among those present were Mrs. W. N. Jones and Miss Susie Herring of Raleigh, Miss Mary Cox of Magnolia, Mr. and Mrs. A. R. Phillips of Buenos Aires, Argentina. We were happy to have Miss Bessie Poole to sing for us "This Is My Task," accompanied by Mrs. W. McCullers.

Minutes and Money for God by Miss Mary Cox was very helpful to all. Mrs. W. J. Payne reported on W. M. U. periodicals. Message from our State W. M. U. president, Mrs. W. N. Jones, was very inspirational. "Be much in prayer" was the subjject of her address. Mrs. W. McCullers sang "Come Ye Blessed" with Mrs. Gleve Pope at the piano. This was followed by a Violin solo "Ave Maria" by Mr. H. E. Brooks.

The president then appointed the following committees: To nominate officers: Miss Viola Poole, Mrs. Paul Wallace, Mrs. W. N. Holt. Time nad place: Mrs. Brown, Mrs. D. H. McCullers, Mrs. Cannady. Recommendations: Mrs. D. B. Oliver, Mrs. J. M. Beaty, Mrs. Markham. Resolutions: Mrs. Jas. A. Ivey. Watchword Committee: Mrs. Mark Gulley.

The sermon Mr. A. R. Phillips, who labors in Argentina was enjoyed by all. And we who are interested in the work at Buenos Aires were glad to hear from that field. After prayer by Rev. R. F. Hall we adjourned for dinner which was served on the lawn.

The afternoon session was young peoples session. Devotional by Rosa Lee Coats, solo "Room in the Arms of Jesus" by little Miss Mary Williams. Address of welcome by Catherine Williams, response by Esther W. Barbour. Roll call representatives responded with financial report also two minute verbal report on work. Mrs. W. McCullers sang by special request: "On Jordan's Stormy Banks I Stnad," accompanied by Mrs. Gleve Pope. The pageant, "To the Radiant Life" by the G. A.'s of Mount Moriah, showed the way to this life is by the study of God's Word. Mrs. Jas. A. Ivey of Four Oaks, spoke very interestingly on the Louisville Training School, where she took her training. We were disappointed on account of the absence of Mrs. R. C. White, who was t ospeak on the Training School at Fort Worth, Texas. Miss Susie Herring was charming in her talk on "The New Meredith." Miss Margaret Louise Phillips sang: "Jesus wants me for a sunbeam." An address by Mrs. A. R. Phillips on the great needs of the work in Buenos Argentina, emphasizing especially the need of more workers was very interesting. The R. A's of Smithfield through their leader, Mrs. S. L. Morgan offered two resolutions, one, that our organization may be provided with a state leader, the other, that the R. A's and the G. A's camp be held separately and if possible have sectional camps. No vote was taken as the Superintendent thought best to have these resolutions sent to the different societies to act on. The Secretary was instructed to write a note of thanks to Miss Zuleika McCullers for painting the posters used in the demonstration of W. M. U. periodicals. Twenty five financial reports showed $5,441.63.

The attendance at this meeting was very encouraging there being over 200 enrolled. The time and place committee reported an invitation from Pine Level. It was decided that we meet with the Pine Level W. M. S. in October, 1926.

The nominating committee reported the re-election of all the officers wiht Mrs. Jas. A. Ivey as Junior Superintendent. We then paused to ask God's blessing on the families who have lost some one since we met last. Among those are: Mrs. Quint Poole, Mrs. W. A. Barnes, Mrs. Laura Creech. Memorial prayer was offered by Mrs. J. W. Massey. All then joined hands and sang, "Blest be the Tie that Binds," with closing prayer by Mrs. J. M. Beaty. This brought to a close another very interesting annual session of the W. M. U. of Johnston Baptist Association.

MRS. B. A. HOCUTT, Supt.

CLEVE BARNES, Secretary.

TABLE NO. 1—MEMBERSHIP AND CHURCH PROPERTY.

CHURCH	PASTOR AND POSTOFFICE	CLERK AND POSTOFFICE
Antioch	A. R. Creech, Micro	W. O. Hocutt, Middlesex, 3
Bailey	W. T. Evans, Kenly	J. P. Underwood, Bailey
Baptist Center	R. C. White, Clayton	J. N. Bryan, Clayton
Beaty's Chapel	S. S. McGregor, Smithfield	Mrs. J. J. Parrish, Smithfie
Benson	O. A. Keller, Benson	Julian Godwin, Benson
Benson Grove	O. A. Keller, Benson	L. E. Barber, Benson
Bethany	W. D. Stancil, Kenly, 2	A. L. Price, Selma, 2
Bethel		
Bethesda	R. C. White, Clayton	J. E. Smith, Wilson's Mills
Beulah	P. A. Pridgen, Benson	G. G. Barefoot, Dunn, 5
Blackman's Grove	Jas. A. Ivey, Four Oaks	Joseph Wood, Four Oaks, 3
Calvary	P. A. Pridgen, Benson	Mrs. Maude Smith, Dunn
Canaan	P. A. Pridgen, Benson	T. L. Hudson, Bentonsville
Burnell	Jas. A. Ivey, Four Oaks	W. L. Massengill, Four Oal
Carters Chapel	A. R. Creech, Micro	F. Woodruff, Selma, 2
Clayton	R. C. White, Clayton	W. P. Creech, Clayton
Clyde's Chapel	S. W. Oldham, Wendell	J. E. Johnson, Wendell, 1
Corinth	W. D. Stancil, Kenly, 2	L. T. Davis, Wendell, 1
Four Oaks	Jas. A. Ivey, Four Oaks	B. B. Creech, Four Oaks
Hales' Chapel	A. A. Pippin, Wakefield	F. P. Hales, Zebulon, 1
Hepzibah	Jas. W. Rose, Pine Level	W. G. Creech, Princeton
Hood's Grove	P. A. Pridgen, Benson	
Kenly	W. T. Evans, Kenly	F. A. White, Kenly
Lee's Chapel	A. A. Pippin, Wakefield	W. I. Green, Zebulon, 2
Live Oak	L. E. Godwin, Wake Forest	J. M. Richardson, Selma, 2
Micro	A. R. Creech, Micro	S. C. Batten, Micro
Middlesex	J. W. Nobles, Middlesex	J. C. Overman, Middlesex
Mount Moriah	R. F. Hall, Raleigh, 2	Russell Powell, Clayton, 3
New Bethel	S. T. Morris, Buies Creek	Geo. W. Bryan, Garner, 2
Noble's Chapel	W. T. Evans, Kenly	D. L. Flowers, Sims
Oliver's Grove	O. A. Keller, Benson	J. E. Ryals, Four Oaks, 4
Parrish Memorial	Jas. W. Rose, Pine Level	Clarence Pender, Selma, 2
Pauline	S. S. McGregor, Smithfield	J. R. Massey, Four Oaks
Pine Level	Jas. W. Rose, Pine Level	Floyd C. Price, Pine Level
Pinkney	W. T. Evans, Kenly	Mrs. B. R. Edgerton, Fremor
Pisgah	S. S. McGregor, Smithfield	A. J. Whitley, Jr., Smithfiel
Pleasant Grove	S. S. McGregor, Smithfield	Cl. Stephenson, WillowSprin
Princeton	Jas. W. Rose, Pine Level	W. I. Pearce, Princeton
Sardis	Jas. W. Rose, Pine Level	T. G. Strickland, Smithfield
Selma	C. H. Cashwell, Selma	Theo. Eason, Selma
Shiloh	S. S. McGregor, Smithfield	F. T. Holland, McCullers
Thanksgiving	R. M. Von Miller, Wilson, 1	J. R. Lynch, Selma, 1
Trinity	P. A. Pridgen, Benson	J. S. Lawhorn, Benson
White Oak	A. A. Pippin, Wakefield	W. H. Green, Clayton, 2
Wilson's Mills	S. N. Lamb, Wake Forest	H. E. Mitchener, Wilson Mill
Watkins Chapel	W. D. Stancil, Kenly, 2	Lester Hales, Middlesex
Smithfield	S. L. Morgan, Smithfield	J. E. Coats, Smithfield

Baptisms	Letters	Statements	Restorations	Letters	Exclusions	Deaths	Total Present Members	Regular. Days of. Meeting	When Constituted	Revival Meetings Held During Yr.	Families Getting State Paper	Materials Used	Persons Seated	Number of Rooms	Value of Church House and Grounds	Value of Pastor's Home	Total Value all Church Property
2	----	----	----	4	1	1	187	2	1859	1	5	W	400	3	3,000		3,000
3	----	----	----	1	1	1	69	1	1909	1	4	W	300	1	1,500	----	1,500
33	4	----	----	1	1	----	185	3	1871	1	13	W	225	3	2,800	----	2,800
----	----	----	----	1	----	----	6	2-4		1		W	200	1	1,500	----	1,500
6	12	----	----	6	5	----	203	1-3	1887	1	25	br.	500	23	40,000	----	40,000
6	----	----	----	----	----	----	60	2	1908	1	----	W	200	1	1,500	----	1,500
47	----	2	1	7	1	1	166	4	1879	1	30	W	500	1	1,500	----	1,500
----	----	----	----	----	----	----	7			0	1	W	200	1	1,000	----	1,000
27	1	----	4	5	1	1	244	4	1840	1	6	W	500	5	3,500	----	3,500
----	----	----	----	----	----	----	60	2	1895	1	2	W	300	1	1,250	----	1,250
28	1	2	2	9	----	2	121	2-4		1	3	W	300	4	2,500	----	2,500
6	4	----	----	5	1	1	31	1		1	3	W	200	1	2,000	----	2,000
----	3	----	----	1	1	----	45	3	1894	2	7	W	150	1	1,500	----	1,500
----	----	----	----	3	----	----	19	2-4		1	7	W	300	1	1,500	----	1,500
9	1	9	2	4	----	3	140	1	1888	1	6	W	300	4	3,000	----	3,000
16	11	----	----	11	2	9	656	1-3		1	60	br.	1100	22	75,000	10,000	85,000
.1	----	----	7	49	----	2	184	3	1888	1	5	W	300	1	750	----	750
6	2	1	----	3	1	2	175	3	1874	1	4	W	300	2	4,000	----	4,000
27	6	2	----	4	----	----	143	1-3	1891	1	15	br.	350	12	22,000	----	22,000
6	4	----	1	----	1	----	95	3		1	1	W	400	5	3,000	----	3,000
6	1	----	----	----	----	----	20	1	1912	1	4	W	300	1	1,500	----	1,500
5	2	1	----	----	----	----	52	2-4	1907	1	2	W	300	4	2,000	----	2,000
10	2	----	2	9	----	4	242	3	1825	1	6	W	400	1	4,000	----	4,000
9	1	----	4	----	1	----	21	3	1868	1	1	W	300	1	2,500	----	2,500
5	3	----	----	----	2	1	73	3	1904	1	6	W	250	5	3,000	----	3,000
7	4	----	----	3	----	----	129	2-4		1	25	W	300	3	2,500	2,500	5,000
19	11	----	----	12	----	----	235	2-4	1832	1	10	W	400	5	4,200	3,600	7,800
23	3	----	1	4	----	----	180	4	1854	1	5	W	300	1	4,000	----	4,000
6	----	----	----	----	3	1	122	4	1901	1	6	W	300	1	2,000	----	2,000
----	----	----	----	----	----	----	12	2		1	2	W	300	1	1,000	----	1,000
7	----	1	1	6	----	----	65	4		1	5	W	200	1	2,500	----	2,500
35	2	2	4	4	----	1	117	4	1904	2	----	W	350	1	2,000	----	2,000
18	1	4	----	4	----	1	98	1		1	12	W	350	8	5,000	----	5,000
2	----	----	----	----	1	----	24	3	1909	1	4	W	300	1	1,500	----	1,500
62	11	2	2	6	----	----	141	1-3	1894	1	12	W	400	7	4,000	3,500	7,500
5	4	----	----	----	----	----	18	3	1920	2	----	W	300	1	700	----	700
32	2	----	----	1	----	----	113	3	1889	1	5	W	300	2	2,000	----	2,000
9	2	----	----	1	1	----	84	2		1	2	W	300	1	2,500	----	2,500
45	19	11	----	30	6	----	274	1-3		2	20	br.	500	9	26,000	3,000	29,000
27	----	1	2	9	1	1	81	2		1	2	W	300	1	3,500	2,000	5,500
7	----	----	----	3	----	----	138	2	1899	1	5	W	300	1	2,500	----	2,500
1	2	----	----	1	5	1	104	4	1885	1	3	W	250	3	2,500	----	2,500
11	1	1	1	5	5	11	302	1	1875	1	5	W	400	3	4,000	----	4,000
3	1	----	1	2	----	----	87	2	1884	1	2	W	250	4	2,000	----	2,000
5	7	----	----	----	----	----	30	1	1924	1	1	W	300	1	1,000	----	1,000
32	22	1	----	15	----	2	373	1-3		0	25	W	500	11	20,000	8,000	28,000
606	150	40	35	223	47	46	1147				367		170		281,200	32,600	313,800

CHURCH	SUPERINTENDENTS AND POST OFFICES	SECRETARIES AND POST OFFICES
Antioch	A. D. O'Neal, Middlesex 3	W. O. Hocutt, Middlesex 3
Bailey	Geo. B. Brantly, Bailey	D. Finch, Bailey
Baptist Center	J. C. Hardee, Clayton	Wade Tippett, Clayton 1
Beaty's Chapel		
Benson	M. T. Britt, Benson	J. C. Morgan, Benson
Benson Grove	L. E. Barber, Benson 1	L. E. Barber, Benson 1
Bethany	Carmel Creech, Selma 2	F. Creech, Kenly 2
Bethel		
Bethesda	J. B. Coats, Wilson's Mills	V. L. Smith, Wilson's Mills
Beulah	Hattie Peacock, Benson 2	G. G. Barefoot, Dunn 5
Blackman's Grove	W. H. Lee, Four Oaks 2	Miss V. Wood, Four Oaks 3
Burnell	Calhart Johnson, Four Oaks	Josephine Johnson, F. Oaks 4
Calvary	G. W. Wagstaff, Dunn	E. D. Barefoot, Dunn
Canaan		
Carters Chapel	R. G. Narron, Selma 2	J. R. Atkinson, Selma 2
Clayton	J. Dwight Barbour, Clayton	Chas. G. Gulley, Clayton
Clyde's Chapel	D. C. Painter, Wendell 1	N. B. Boyette, Wendell 1
Corinth	Ronald Hocutt, Wendell -	Miss H.Richardson, Zebulon 1
Four Oaks	W. P. Massengill, Four Oaks	Jas. Parrish, Four Oaks
Hales' Chapel	W. E. Bunn, Zebulon 2	W. H. Price, zebulon 1
Hepzibah	W. G. Creech, Princeton	J. F. Earp, Pine Level
Hood's Grove		
Kenly	A. J. Broughton, Kenly	J. E. Jones, Kenly
Lee's Chapel	A. G. Lewis, Middlesex	A. Driver, Zebulon 2
Live Oak	J. M. Richardson, Selma 2	Miss L. Edwards, Selma 1
Micro	S. C. Batten, Micro	J. L. Brown, Selma 2
Middlesex	W. K. Ballentine, Middlesex	J. M. Davis, Middlesex
Mount Moriah	C. Parker Pool, Raleigh 2	J. P. Jones, Clayton 3
New Bethel	R. I. Smith, McCullers	Clifford Wrems, Garner 2
Noble's Chapel	L. F. Boykin, Sims	O. Bullock, Sims
Oliver's Grove		
Parrish Memorial	Clarence Pender, Selma 2	Mamie Parrish, Selma 2
Pauline	Sam Joyner, Four Oaks	S. C. Creech, Four Oaks
Pine Level	N. M. Gurley, Pine Level	W. B. Oliver, Jr., Pine Level
Pinkney	K. C. Atkinson, Fremont 2	Seth Davis, Fremont 2
Pisgah	J. A. Smith, Four Oaks 4	Thos. J. Wright, Smithfield
Pleasant Grove	J. E. Gilbert, Benson 3	Cv. Coats, Willow Springs
Princeton	W. I. Pearce, Princeton	Carlyle Woodard, Princeton
Sardis	N. S. Stevens, Smithfield	B. C. Powell, Smithfield
Selma	N. J. Creech, Selma	W. M. Henry, Selma
Shiloh	J. W. Williams, McCullers	W. F. Honeycutt, Garner
Smithfield	W. H. Lassiter, Smithfield	W. N. Lassiter, Smithfield
Thanksgiving	W. S. Earp, Selma 1	O. J. Brannan, Selma, 1
Trinity	O. H. Barefoot, Benson	Miss C. Cole, Benson 2
White Oak	J. M. Green, Clayton, 2	D. M. Brannan, W'n's Mills 2
Wilson's Mills	J. T. Holt, Wilson's Mills	Arthur Price, Wilson's Mills
Watkins Chapel	J. H. Hales, Middlesex	Roy Hinton, Middlesex

	Sunday School Enrollment									Special Information						
Officers and Teachers	Beginners 3-5 Years	Primaries 6-8 Years	Juniors 9-12 Years	Intermediates 13-16 Years	Seniors and Adults 17 and Up	Cradle Roll Under 3 Years	Home Department	Total Enrollment	Is the School Graded?	Is it Standard A-1?	Teachers holding Normal Diplomas	Baptisms from School	Gifts to Local Church Work	Gifts to Missions, Orphanage, etc.	Are all Departments & Classes Provided for?
5	5	17	17	16	30			85	No	No			21.03	11.87	No
8	22		20	14	24			88	No	No		3	2.23	7.51	No
8		40	20	30	25			123	Yes	No				5.00	No
									Yes	No					No
45	40	42	28	39	77	20	41	332	Yes	No	12				Yes
6		15	12	30	20			80	No	No		6	10.00	10.00	No
12	20	15	38	22	54			161	Yes	No					No
									Yes	No					No
20	35	15	25	25	20			140	No	No		20	15.00	59.22	No
7	5	12	24	9	25			82	Yes	No	2				No
11	14	16	16	12	20			89	Yes	No	3	14		6.30	No
8	10	8	10	8	13			57	No	No					No
									Yes	No					No
									Yes	No					No
11	8	15	33	35	27			129	Yes	No		3		14.07	No
58	35	45	90	80	168	62	51	531	Yes	No	15	10	371.03	165.81	Yes
11	16	10	15	25	76			122	No	No			76.00	31.97	No
8	21	13	32	47	33			154	No	No		3	19.75	1.13	No
16	15	6	28	27	55	34	13	194	Yes	Yes	7	23	190.30	136.43	No
12	27		37	29	32			125	No	No					No
5	12		12	14	12			58	No	No					No
									Yes	No					No
10	15	10	12	24	10	25		106	Yes	No	2	5	24.00	42.24	No
7		20	35	20	30			138	No	No		10			No
7	23	23	20	18	23			104	Yes	No		9			No
10	16	16	20	15	36	14	7	134	Yes	No	1	2	8.30	45.00	No
10	20	21	25	10	35			121	No	No		5	125.19	156.22	No
16	24	16	21	39	95	27		238	Yes	No				237.39	No
11	25	25	20	25	80			186	Yes	No		14			No
7	10	17	21		29			84	No	No	4	2	36.44	7.96	No
									Yes	No					No
7		8	7	6	10			38	No	No		7		15.05	No
8	8	10	12	20	20			88	No	No		35	2.00	20.00	No
10	12	12	18	22	32	9	2	117	No	No	2	9	106.00	75.00	No
5	8	6	8	8	6			41	No	No				24.59	No
21	20	13	59	12	52			177	Yes	No	4	55		113.47	No
5	5	6	5	9	10			40	No	No					No
7									No	No					No
7	16		19	9	17			68	No	No		7			No
22	52	32	24	21	215	71	12	449	No	No	5	25	420.00	232.01	No
6	21		34	24	31			116	No	No		25			No
16		71	42	79	122	40	36	406	Yes	No					Yes
14		42	14	26	48			144	Yes	No	1	6	31.94	6.00	No
6	5	6	5	9				40	No	No	3				No
8		45	45	42	118			258	Yes	Yes	6	10			No
10	6	7	10	8	12	18		71	Yes	No		3	12.00	2.50	No
6	28	19	16		29			98	Yes	No					No
487	599	684	689	908	1790	310	162	5812	Yes	No	69	311	1,471.21	1,426.74	Yes

TABLE NO. 2.—FINANCES

CHURCH	TREASURER AND POSTOFFICE	FOR SUPPORT OF LOCAL CHURCH WORK										FOR SUPPORT OF MISSIONS, EDUCATION AND BENEVOLENCE										
		Pastor's Salary	Other Salaries	Ministerial Help	Building and Repairs	Incidentals	Sunday School and B. Y. P. U. Expenses	Local Poor	Minute Fund Etc.	Other Objects	Home Total	Cooperative Program (Undesignated)	Foreign Missions	Home Missions	State and Associational Missions	Christian Education	Orphanage	Hospitals	Ministerial Relief	Other Benevolences	Denominational Total	GRAND TOTAL
tioch	A. D. O'Neal, Middlesex, 3	270.00		2.00		1.00	21.03	14.67			324.20	14.38		2.43			3.58			5.57	23.90	358.10
isley	J. W. B. Finch, Bailey	350.00	30.00	36.00		25.30	15.50	15.50			501.80	32.25			11.50		34.74				78.49	724.33
ptist Center	J. N. Bryan, Clayton	225.50		132.50	350.00		5.50	15.50			1,155.00	9.00									9.00	1,164.00
aty's Chapel	J. J. Parrish, Smithfield	50.00		3.00	113.00		1.00	12.00			299.00											59.00
nson Grove	Mrs. H. O. Dixon, Benson	2,000.00	240.00	506.00	113.21	80.71	61.98			280.00	3,293.90	311.45		34.25	12.85	150.00				366.51	881.56	4,175.46
	L. E. Barber, Benson	25.00									25.00											25.00
thany	A. J. Price, Selma 2	101.61			15.00		10.00	5.50			132.11	100.00									100.00	232.11
	L. B. Smith, Wilson's Mills	500.00	18.00	111.36	38.00	15.00	38.60	33.00	2.65		756.61	26.75		4.00				3.25			96.75	853.36
ida	G. G. Barefoot, Benson 2	60.00		20.00	431.00		23.77	2.50			105.27	4.00			70.00						81.75	117.52
dah	Noeah Wood, Four Oaks 2	480.00		43.00			33.83	7.50		19.00	580.83	81.75			10.00						81.75	668.58
ckman's Grove	J. S. Johnson, Four Oaks	185.00		16.71	35.00	6.00	23.00	5.00			237.50											237.50
nell	Mrs. Maud Smith, Dunn	155.68									227.67			10.00			3.00				13.00	237.30
lvary	Mrs. A. Hudson, Bentonville		584.00	1.00			54.68	10.31	1.40		644.39	11.70				128.20	16.60			228.36	810.13	8,088.60
yers Chapel	D. M. Hall, Clayton	450.00	254.00	413.66	113.66	629.71	371.04	17.00		216.65	5,120.04	2,000.00	537.50	44.50	67.92	31.60	107.56			228.36	2,968.19	8,088.60
de's Chapel	J. B. Boyette, Wendell 1	3,000.00		65.25	50.00	12.00	70.00	18.54	2.50		633.39	133.98		2.90	33.80	5.27	31.84				164.75	371.32
nth	Lee Hocutt, Zebulon 1	206.65	24.00	80.00	35.00		100.77	14.00	7.50		483.11	50.00		8.00	40.52	7.65	84.81	8.90		13.40	564.72	3,041.85
ur Oaks	W. H. Price, Zebulon 1	1,250.00	72.00	253.84	547.35	20.72		7.50			373.66	40.52					98.13				371.33	3,041.85
les Chapel	J. F. Earp, Pine Level	30.00		17.69	187.45			2.50			58.19	8.00					4.00			54.00	66.19	66.19
d's Grove	A. J. Broughton, Kenly	375.00	15.00	77.35		19.70	40.00	5.00	5.00	168.48	701.03	77.85	7.50	10.75	22.10		43.84	2.00		134.44	835.47	835.47
	L. M. Price, Middlesex 3	300.00	45.00	229.00		25.75	25.00	6.75			680.39			10.55		5.00	10.00	7.35		75.15	144.92	724.33
e Oak	L. M. Richardson, Selma 2	58.89				3.00	32.25				239.32	2.00				1.00	3.75			5.75	5.75	86.14
ro	D. H. Jones, Micro	750.00		9.00		2.00	32.25	6.60		11.00	1,044.36	152.38		2.90	45.00	162.32	30.00	7.87		5.14	244.29	244.81
ddlesex	C. A. Barber, Middlesex	7,500.00		83.17	530.59	33.00	125.19	5.60		40.00	2,541.83	100.00			33.80	167.22	31.84			15.00	714.80	3,255.63
	G. S. Pool, Clayton 3	1,500.00	30.00	70.00		20.00	74.24	17.00		375.00	540.00	75.00			30.00	60.00					675.00	3,255.63
unt Moriah	Geo. W. Barefoot, Garner 2	300.00	12.00		160.00		90.00	6.00		42.00	198.00	25.00					30.00			30.00	30.00	961.68
Bethel	N. L. Stott, Sims	300.00			487.14		38.44	8.00			198.00	30.10					25.00				55.10	200.00
ver's Grove	J. A. Tyner, Four Oaks 4	25.00		38.00		6.00	10.00				191.08	44.35		4.00			9.20				78.55	280.85
lesboro	J. N. Watson, Pine Level	25.00		33.00		35.77	60.42	2.00		134.00	983.25	19.80			25.00		63.99	18.00	21.20	347.89	251.14	1,322.65
rish Memorial	B. R. Creech, Four Oaks	100.00		20.00	278.06	16.68	13.93	5.00	7.50		261.00	20.05		7.00		7.70	24.59			78.59	78.59	251.70
	Mrs. D. E. Oliver, Pine Level	350.00		110.00		31.65	86.00	10.00		11.00	173.11	54.00								15.67	1.67	1,322.65
ne Level	Mrs. B. R. Edgerton, Fremont	750.00	12.00	54.00				25.00			1,273.11	139.00		36.00	75.00					139.00	139.00	1,682.65
ney	W. D. Johnston, Smithfield	225.00		46.65	83.50	20.00	60.00	5.50		20.47	405.15	59.16					42.37	5.00			111.00	56.17
zah	Cl. Stephenson, Wilo Springs	250.00		26.00	6.00	585.86	22.00				293.97	43.87	36.00				43.87				89.16	113.18
asant Grove	Chas. H. Holt, Princeton	1,340.00	143.15	21.00	200.00		173.38	3.25			3,126.31	867.65			75.00	236.00	31.84	73.65	124.27	924.02	924.02	4,050.33
nceton	J. R. Oliver, Selma	2,400.00	223.05	159.56	509.25	260.82	509.64	15.00		118.70	4,113.87	1,757.88	12.50		50.00	236.00	31.84	73.65	124.27	2,277.80	2,277.80	6,391.87
rris	Theo Eason, Selma Cullers 2	280.00	22.86	22.86	150.00	16.17	45.25	5.00		48.75	516.50	80.00			6.00		8.00		5.00	33.50	56.34	575.84
field	D. N. Creech, Smithfield	280.00		6.50		6.50	25.04	2.50		59.00	412.60	60.66			4.50		8.00				100.66	512.82
annserine	J. R. Lynch, Selma 1	180.00		89.90	240.88	40.35	60.42	5.00	2.00	9.16	779.58	29.00			14.93		44.10	11.00		144.42	144.42	924.00
mity	J. T. Lee, Benson	220.73		75.00			12.50	15.00		15.00	463.00	56.78					33.50	1.00	17.52	144.42	332.40	795.40
tte Oak	V. H. Green, Clayton 2	300.00					15.00	16.00			328.00	328.00										113.50
son's Mills	W. A. Price, Wilson's Mills	75.00	18.00					6.00			113.50											113.50
kins Chapel	Curtis Hinton, Middlesex																					
		20,737.52	1,480.06	2,435.94	5,182.99	2,099.60	2,588.42	1,243.45	301.35	2,054.71	31,877.124.14	5,742.81	138.05	118.88	420.95	160.68	1,722.45	253.52	25.02	789.45	19,617.41	46,741.55

TABLE NO. 4—B. Y. P. U. AND W. M. U. WORK

CHURCH	PRESIDENTS OF B. Y. P. U.'S AND POSTOFFICES	THE YOUNG PEOPLE'S WORK											WOMAN'S ORGANIZATIONS OF CHURCHES	PR
		Senior Unions	Interm. Unions	Junior Unions	Total Unions	Seniors Enrolled	Intermediates Enrolled	Juniors Enrolled	Total Enrolled	Number Daily Bible Readers	Unions Taking Study Courses	Total Systematic Givers in Unions		
Bailey	Miss Nell More, Bailey	1			1	8		8	16	16	8	18	Bailey	Miss
Benson	Sr. Sarah Duncan, Benson	1			1	21	23	25	69	15	8	18	Benson	Mrs.
Benson	Int. Margaret Peacock, Benson		1		1					17	8	14	Benson	Mrs.
Benson	Jr. Ethel Benton, Benson			1	1					19	8	8	Blackman's Grove	Mrs.
Bethesda	Sr. T. C. Hines, Wilson's Mills	1			1	33			33				Clayton	Mrs.
Beulah	Sr. Vida McLamb, Benson	1	1		2	22	36	7	22	9	2	9	Clayton	Mrs.
Blackman's Grove	Sr. Herbert Lee, Four Oaks	1			1	29			36	10	7	16	Clayton	Mrs.
Blackman's Grove	Jr. Vinnie Wood, Four Oaks			1	1								Clayton	Mrs.
Bunnell	Sr. Joe Johnson, Four Oaks	1			1	9			9	34	36	32	Clyde's Chapel	Mrs.
Clayton	Sr. M. Houghton, Clayton	1	1	1	3	40	36		40	29	31	27	Four Oaks	Mrs.
Clayton	Int. Levy Wall, Clayton							35	36	31	33		Four Oaks	Mrs.
Clayton	Jr. Mary P. Turley, Clayton								35	9		10	Kenly	Mrs.
Clyde's Chapel	Sr. N. B. Boyette, Wendell 1	1			1	34			34	7	9	10	Micro	Mrs.
Four Oaks	Sr. Mrs. J. H. Strickland, 4 Oaks	1	1		3	10	18	18	46	10	15	9	Micro	Mrs.
Four Oaks	Int. Miss Esther Creech, 4 Oaks							15	15	15	16	5	Middlesex	Mrs.
Four Oaks	Jr. W. Sanders, Four Oaks			1	1			15	15	10		5	Middlesex	Mrs.
Kenly	Jr. Beatrice Hooks, Kenly			1	1		8						Middlesex	Mrs.
Micro	int. Ray Mozingo, Micro	1	1		2	22		24	22	15	22	11	Mount Moriah	Mrs.
Mount Moriah	Jr. Rosalie Coats, Clayton 3			2	2			24	24	16	16	15	Noble's Chapel	Mrs.
Mount Moriah	Jr. Judson Smith, Auburn					24		24	24	10	8	11	Pine Level	Mrs.
New Bethel	Jr. C. Wrenn, Garner	1		1	2								Princeton	Mrs.
New Bethel	Jr. Ruby Brown, Raleigh 2											8	Selma	Mrs.
Pine Level	Sr. W. B. Oliver, Pine Level	1		1	2	17			17	10	13	7	Selma	Mrs.
Pisgah	Sr. A. J. Whitley, Jr., Smithfield	1			1	35		24	59	10	13	4	Selma	Mrs.
Pisgah	Jr. Mrs. Cl. Jones, Smithfield											12	Selma	Mrs.
Princeton	Sr. Miss Alma Pearce, Princeton	1			1	18			18	4	6	10	Smithfield	Mrs.
Selma	Int. Roy Driver, Selma		1		3	32	18		65	5	10	9	Smithfield	Mrs.
Selma	Sr. Roy Driver, Selma	1								6	3	10	Smithfield	Mrs.
Selma	Jr. Mrs. C. H. Cashwell, Selma			1				15		12			Smithfield	Mrs.
Shiloh	Sr. Miss Ellis Hardee, Clayton	1			1	18			18			10	Wilson's Mills	Mrs.
Smithfield	Sr. Miss Ruth Wilson, Smithfield	1	1		2	25	25		25	8	15			Mrs.
Smithfield	Sr. J. R. Lynch, Selma 1			1	1	20			20					Mrs.
Thanksgiving						12			12					
Thanksgiving						40			100	30		30		
Trinity	Sr. Ora Bradly, Benson	1			1					30	25	30		
White Oak	Sr. Delma Murphy, Wilson Mills									35	26	15		
White Oak	Int. Mrs. Rainer, Clayton 2						25	25	18	8	10	25		
White Oak	Jr. Mrs. R. E. Barkham, Wendell			1	1	18			18	10				
Wilson's Mills	Sr. Mrs. E. R. Youngblood, W.M.	1			1									
		21	6	12	39	513	128	230	847	428	328	349		

Lightning Source UK Ltd.
Milton Keynes UK
UKHW041246180119
335297UK00007BA/334/P